RECORD OF PROCEEDINGS

INTERNATIONAL LABOUR
CONFERENCE

NINETY - SECOND SESSION
GENEVA, 2004

RECORD OF PROCEEDINGS

VOLUME I: PLENARY SITTING
DELEGATIONS

INTERNATIONAL LABOUR OFFICE
GENEVA

ISBN 92-2-113048-7
ISSN 0074-6681

First published 2004

The designations employed in ILO publications, which are in conformity with United Nations practice, and the presentation of material therein do not imply the expression of any opinion whatsoever on the part of the International Labour Office concerning the legal status of any country, area or territory or of its authorities, or concerning the delimitation of its frontiers.
The responsibility for opinions expressed in signed articles, studies and other contributions rests solely with their authors, and publication does not constitute an endorsement by the International Labour Office of the opinions expressed in them.
Reference to names of firms and commercial products and processes does not imply their endorsement by the International Labour Office, and any failure to mention a particular firm, commercial product or process is not a sign of disapproval.

ILO publications can be obtained through major booksellers or ILO local offices in many countries, or direct from ILO Publications, International Labour Office, CH-1211 Geneva 22, Switzerland. Catalogues or lists of new publications are available free of charge from the above address.

Formated by TTE
Printed by the International Labour Office Geneva Switzerland

Corrigenda

92nd Session of the International Labour Conference, June 2004

PR No. 10

Page 10/5, first column, seventh paragraph, replace "verything" by "everything". Move the block of text starting with "everything" and ending at the bottom of the column, to the end of the first line, seventh paragraph of the second column.

Page 10/24, second column, sixth paragraph, second line, change "youth" to "health".

PR No. 12

Page 12/28, first column, in the first line of Ms. Christova's speech, replace "delegates" by "President and the Vice-Presidents". In the second column, second paragraph, second line, change "pre-emptive" to "prior". In the third paragraph, last line, change "12" to "13". In the fifth paragraph, 14th line, after the word "revenue", insert "in the pension funds". In the 16th line, replace "protection of" by "guaranteeing". In the sixth paragraph, last line, after the word "exchange" insert "of opinions".

PR No. 14

Page 14/13, second column, eighth paragraph of Mr. Konditi's speech, third line, change "founded" to "funded". At the end of the tenth paragraph insert the word "We". At the beginning of the 11th paragraph delete "Some of us" and run the paragraph on from the

"We" in the line above. In the last paragraph, third line, change "must" to "should" and, in the fourth line, delete the sentence "Therefore, we should like to appeal to the ILO".

Page 14/14, first column, eighth paragraph, fourth line, change "agricultural sectors" to "agricultural subsectors". In the second column, second paragraph, fourth line from the end, delete "and more".

Page 14/27, second column, first line, change "discreet resolution procedures" to "dispute resolution procedures".

Page 14/34, second column (Mr. Apostolov's speech), instead of *"Original Bulgarian"* read *"Original Russian"*. In the second paragraph, second line, replace "has been" by "is". At the end of the fourth paragraph, insert "and trade unions" after "associations". In the fifth paragraph, seventh line, insert "bipartite" before "dialogue". In the sixth paragraph, sixth line, insert "and trade unions" after "associations".

Page 14/35, first column, second paragraph, sixth line, after "today" delete the remainder of the sentence. In the third paragraph, seventh line, replace "all of the rights that we have then ratified" by "all of these rights". In the ninth line, change "unionists" to "unions". In the fourth paragraph, third line, replace "that path, and if you look at the overall picture in Bulgaria" by "that path. If you look at the overall picture in the report".

PR No. 15

Page 15/1, first column, move the heading "Reports of the Chairperson of the Governing Body and of the Director-General: Discussion (cont.)" 12 lines down, to below the statement by the Clerk of the Conference.

Page 15/44, second column, add the following paragraph at the end of Mr. Hristov's speech: "I wish to express my deepest sympathy regarding the suffering of the Libyan children and their relatives and as a doctor I would like to declare that there is no medical worker who would break the Hippocratic oath and who would violate the principle "Primum non nocere" – first of all do not harm."

PR No. 23

Page 23/21, first column, second paragraph of Mr. Alkhulaifi's speech, third line, instead of "30 per cent" read "90 per cent". In the following line, after "Qatar", replace "approves the scale of assessment" by "respects the consensus reached in the Finance Committee on the scale of assessment".

PR No. 27

Page 27/14, first column, third line of Mr. Malevich's speech, replace "in attendance here" by "who have doubts in this regard". In the second column, fourth paragraph, replace the last seven lines by the following text: "in Belarus able to work are not actually able temporarily to exercise their right to work. Finally, Belarus, according to the index of human development ranks 53 thus belonging to the group of highly developed countries and that shows that the socio-economic situation in this country is quite well".

CONTENTS

Detailed contents of the Provisional Records

PR No.	Volume		Page
1	I	*Resolutions: Resolutions submitted in accordance with article 17 of the Standing Orders of the Conference*	1
		Resolution concerning the strengthening of the role of the ILO in supporting workers and employers in Palestine and the other occupied Arab territories as a result of continued Israeli occupation and aggressive practices	1
		Resolution concerning the role of the ILO in efforts to secure global peace, justice and security around the world	3
		Resolution concerning pay equity	5
		Resolution concerning the ILO's efforts to combat poverty	7
		Resolution concerning the social responsibilities of business	9
		Resolution concerning the application of international labour standards to international civil servants	11
		Resolution concerning older workers and employment and social protection	11
		Resolution concerning peace	13
		Resolution concerning gender-equal pay	14
		Resolution concerning poverty	16
		Resolution concerning corporate social responsibility	21
		Resolution concerning democratic values, good governance and transparency in a global economy and their impact on the world of work, competitiveness and sustainable development	26
		Resolution concerning the promotion of gender equality	27
		Resolution concerning the fourth anniversary of the Maternity Protection Convention, 2000 (No. 183)	30
		Resolution concerning the role of the ILO in conflict prevention and resolution	31
		Resolution concerning corporate social responsibility	33
2	I	*Standing Orders questions: Note concerning Standing Orders questions submitted by the Governing Body of the International Labour Office at the 92nd Session of the Conference*	1
		A. Purpose of the proposed interim provisions	1

PR No.	Volume		Page
		B. Practical arrangements	3
		C. Appendix	5
3	I	*Report of the Chairperson of the Governing Body to the Conference for the year 2003-04*	1
4	II	*Reports of the Selection Committee*	1
5	II	*Reports of the Selection Committee: Composition of Committees*	1
6	II	*Reports of the Credentials Committee*	1
7	I	*Follow-up activities by the Office under the Declaration on Fundamental Principles and Rights at Work: Freedom of association and collective bargaining, forced or compulsory labour, discrimination*	1
8	I	*First sitting:*	
		Opening of the session	1
		Speaker: Mr. Chung *(Chairperson of the Governing Body of the International Labour Office)*	
		Election of the President of the Conference	1
		Speakers: Mr. Sawers, Mr. Funes de Rioja, Sir Roy Trotman	
		Presidential address	2
		Election of the Vice-Presidents of the Conference	2
		Nomination of the Officers of the groups	2
		Constitution and composition of Conference committees	3
		Composition of the Selection Committee	3
		Suspension of certain provisions of the Standing Orders of the Conference	3
		Report of the Chairperson of the Governing Body: Submission	4
		Speaker: Mr. Chung	
		Statement by Mr. Somavia, Secretary-General of the Conference	5
		Delegation of authority	8

PR No.	Volume		Page
9	I	*Second (special) sitting:*	

        Address by Heads of State and Government on the Report of the World Commission on the Social Dimension of Globalization, Their Excellencies, Ms. Tarja Halonen, President of the Republic of Finland, Mr. Benjamin Mkapa, President of the United Republic of Tanzania, Mr. Georgi Parvanov, President of the Republic of Bulgaria and Ms. Helen Clark, Prime Minister of New Zealand 1

        Speakers: the President, Ms. Tarja Halonen, Mr. Benjamin Mkapa, Mr. Georgi Parvanov, Ms. Helen Clark, Mr. Funes de Rioja, Sir Roy Trotman, the Secretary-General

| 10 | I | *Third sitting:* | |

        Supplementary presentation by the Director-General of the Report, *A fair globalization – The role of the ILO* 1

        Speakers: the President, the Secretary-General

        Suspension of certain provisions of the Standing Orders of the Conference *(cont.)* 6

        Reports of the Chairperson of the Governing Body and of the Director-General: Discussion 6

        Speakers: Mr. Fahey, Mr. Larcher, Mr. Soodhun, Mr. El Amawy, Mr. Panayiotopoulos, Mr. Maroni, Mr. Dimas, Mr. Berzoini, Mr. Basesgioglu, Mr. Khaleghi, Mr. Tou, Mr. Kjørven, Mr. Al-Hajji, Ms.Dello, Mr. Swain, Mr. Dimovski, Ms. Rosas Pérez, Mr. Perigot, Mr. Halilović, Mr. Ryder, Ms. Dembsher, Mr. Sweeney, Mr. Eremeev, Ms. Knuppert, Mr. Szirmai, Mr. Mangwana, Ms. Muňoz, Mr. Dowla, Mr. Zarb

        Ratification of an international labour Convention by Cuba 26

| 11 | I | *Fourth sitting:* | |

        Reports of the Chairperson of the Governing Body and of the Director-General: Discussion *(cont.)* 1

        Speakers: Mr. Mogami, Mr. Aoun, Ms. Filatov, Mr. Potter, Mr. Lublin, Mr. Majali, Mr. Wang, Mr. Abascal, Mr. De Meireles V. de Castro, Mr. Kim, Mr. Galea, Mr. Nordmann, Mr. Mwakwere, Mr. De, Mr. Thys, Mr. Biltgen, Mr. Trogrlic, Mr. Fong, Mr. Lee, Mr. Guider, Mr. Morales Cartaya, Mr. Papiev, Mr. Iversen, Mr. Hamadeh, Mr. Xu, Mr. Caldera Sanchez-Capitan, Mr. Boti, Mr. Nkili

PR No.	Volume		Page
		Fifth sitting:	
		Reports of the Chairperson of the Governing Body and of the Director-General: Discussion *(cont.)*	24

Speakers: Mr. Negron Tejada, Mr. Gomes Proença, Mr. Mansouri, Mr. Mdladlana, Mr. Andreoli, Mgr.Tomasi, Mr. Monteiro, Ms. Sasso Mazzufferi, Mr. Villavicencio Rios, Mr. Pérez del Castillo Mr. Andres, Mr. Marcotic, Mr. Doz, Mr. Herczog, Mr. Pirler, Mr. Basnet, Mr. Gallardo Flores, Mr. Zinck, Mr. Jiménez Aguilar, Mr. Lloyd, Mr. El Azali, Mr. Bejtaj, Mr. Biyama, Ms. Chao, Mr. Ranjivason, Mr. Stoyan, Mr. Lee, Mr. Farrugia, Mr. Rachman, Mr. Akouété, Mr. Bobrowski, Mr. Silva, Mr. Calixte, Mr. Salimian, Mr. Sukomal Sen, Ms. Romchatthong, Mr. Monaheng, Mr. Echavarría Saldarriaga, Mr. Barrenechea Calderón

12	I	*Sixth sitting:*	
		Reports of the Chairperson of the Governing Body and of the Director-General: Discussion *(cont.)*	1

Speakers: Mr. Athauda, Mr. Al-Khatib, Mr. George, Mr. Silwal, Mr. Chen, Mr. Ng, Mr. Stijepović, Mr. Pond, Ms. Hunt, Mr. Neffati Mr. Dalley, Mr. Kilic, Mr. Aloewie, Mr. Ivala, Mr. Meyer, Mr. Sarbu, Mr. Allam, Mr. Latif, Mr. Winn, Mr. Grönlund, Mr. Taliadoros, Ms. Karagousova, Mr. Pater, Mr. Meriton, Ms. Iglesias, Ms. Gawanas, Mr. Azoz

Seventh sitting:

Reports of the Chairperson of the Governing Body and of the Director-General: Discussion *(cont.)* 22

Speakers: Ms. Bakoko Bakoru, Mr. Fattori Costa, Mr. Luquinda, Ms. Thienthong, Mr. Dinur, Mr. De Geus

Ninth sitting:

Reports of the Chairperson of the Governing Body and of the Director-General: Discussion *(cont.)* 27

Speakers: Mr. Pais Antunes, Mr. Barde, Ms. Christova, Mr. De Payva, Mr. Kaník, Mr. Thapaliya, Mr. Iyanga Djoba Malango, Mr. Wijffels, Mr. Aman, Mr. Gryshchenko, Mr. Vaz de Almeida, Mr. Kearney, Mr. Poddar, Ms. Lucero, Mr. Phengkhammy, Mr. Zharikov, Mr. Kairelis, Mr. Fernández Fajalde, Ms. Mint Bilal Ould Yamar, Mr. Scherbakov, Mr. Saed, Mr. Gaskó, Mr. Petcu, Mr. Nditabiriye, Mr. Tilahun, Mr. Marica

Ratification of international labour Conventions by Belgium and Sweden 44

PR No.	Volume		Page
13	I	*Eighth (special) sitting:*	
		Address by His Excellency Mr. José Luis Rodríguez Zapatero, President of the Government of Spain..	1
		Speakers: the President, the Secretary-General, Mr. José Luis Rodríguez Zapatero	
14	I	*Tenth sitting:*	
		Global Report under the follow-up to the ILO Declaration on Fundamental Principles and Rights at Work: Interactive sitting	1
		Speakers: the President, the Secretary-General, Sir Roy Trotman, Mr. Potter, Mr. Al-Tayer, Mr. De Geus, Mr. Neffati, Mr. El-Amawy, Mr, Sweeney, Mr. Pais Antunes, Mr. Raïs, Mr. Konditi, Mr. Seguin, Mr. Farshori, Ms. Arango de Buitrago, Mr. Shenoy, Ms. Tørsøe, Ms. Engelen-Kefer	
		Eleventh sitting:	
		Global Report under the follow-up to the ILO Declaration on Fundamental Principles and Rights at Work: Interactive sitting *(cont.)*	19
		Speakers: the President, Mr. Potter, Sir Roy Trotman, Mr. Anand, Mr. Buwalda, Ms. Ssenabulya, Mr. Villavicencio Rios, Mr. Echavarría Saldarriaga, Ms. Boegner, Mr. Mwakwere, Mr. Salmenperä, Mr.Aoun, Mr. Ahmed, Mr. Anderson, Mr. Richards, Ms. Bayers, Mr. Shepard, Mr. Atwoli, Mr. Prince, Mr. Dzviti, Ms. D'Hondt, Mr. Rambharat, Mr. Sidorov, Mr. Kettledas, Mr. Gammampila Don, Mr. Apostolov, Mr. Benydin, Ms. Franco, Mr. Derbi, Mr. György, Mr. Mahadevan, Ms. Gencianos, Ms. O'Neill, Ms. Sajida	
15	I	*Twelfth sitting:*	
		Ratification of an international labour Convention by Mauritius.........	1
		Reports of the Chairperson of the Governing Body and of the Director-General: Discussion *(cont.)*..	1
		Speakers: Ms. Marius, Mr. Kozik, Mr. Al Ansari, Mr. Naghiyev, Mr. Barimah, Ms. Ngindinwa, Mr. Tabani, Ms. Sto. Tomas, Mr. Solari Saavedra, Mr. Trogen, Ms. Menkerios, Mr. Tomada, Mr. Ross Leal, Mr. Togari, Mr. Hached, Ms. Sinjela, Mr. Louh, Mr. Valerio, Mr. Martínez Molina, Mr. Okuda, Mr. Djilani, Mr. Mammadov, Mr. Peet, Mr. Paiva, Mr. Van Vuuren, Mr. Palacio Betancourt, Mr. Musenge, Mr. Van Leeuwen	

PR No.	Volume		Page
		Thirteenth sitting:	
		Reports of the Chairperson of the Governing Body and of the Director-General: Discussion *(cont.)*..	23

Speakers: Mr. Al-Rizaiqi, Mr. Vaccari Neto, Ms. Poncini, Mr. Georgetti, Mr. Rampak, Mr. Le, Mr. Ortega Nadal, Mr. Keira, Mr. Techateeravat, Mr. Soriano, Mr. Batbayar, Mr. Kassey, Mr. Kapuya, Mr. Boisson, Mr. Edström, Mr. Halkin, Mr. Kusano, Mr. Guardián Castellón, Ms. Morava, Mr. Mehbaliyev, Mr. Trabelsi, Mr. Magaya, Mr. Vardanyan, Mr. Monges Espínola, Mr. Daer, Mr. Djemam, Mr. Evans, Mr. Shmakov, Mr. Hristov, Mr. Jrad, Ms. Cu, Mr. Al Rabaie, Mr. Ricci Muadi, Mr. Semov, Mr. Shenoy, Ms. Theodorsen

PR No.	Volume		Page
16	II	*Report of the Standing Orders Committee*...	1
17(Rev.)	II	*Second item on the agenda: Programme and budget and other questions*	
		Report of the Finance Committee of Government representatives.......	1
		Resolutions submitted to the Conference	13
		Appendices	17
18	II	*Report of the Resolutions Committee*	1
		Resolution submitted to the Conference:	
		Resolution concerning the promotion of gender equality, pay equity and maternity protection..	26
19	I	*Fourteenth sitting:*	
		Reports of the Chairperson of the Governing Body and of the Director-General: Discussion *(cont.)*...	1

Speakers: Mr. Fernández, Mr. Infante, Mr. Ola, Mr. Maatough, Mr. Say, Mr. Sevene, Ms. Beaumont, Mr. Nuñez Salcedo, Mr. Espinal, Mr. Eastmond, Mr. Nicolescu, Mr. Dahlan, Mr. Briesch, Mr. Hagh-Bayan, Mr. Arnold, Mr. Farshori, Mr. Tongaai, Mr. Al-Kuhlani, Mr. Abdella, Mr. Qarqein, Mr. Abdulhusain, Mr. Tugushi, Mr. Tartaglia, Mr. Wojcik, Mr. Ghandour, Mr. Flores Flores, Mr. Sukhbaatar

Fifteenth sitting:

Reports of the Chairperson of the Governing Body and of the Director-General: Discussion *(cont.)*... 22

PR No.	Volume		Page
		Speakers: Mr. Celi Vegas, Mr. Kara, Mr. Mussanhane, Mr. Alvis Fernández, Ms. Valkonen, Mr. Mancilla Garcia, Mr. Lawal, Mr. Sunmonu, Mr. Alemayehu, Mr. Corries, Mr. Jennings, Mr. Puga Rodríguez, Mr. Ledouble, Mr. Parras Rojas, Mr. Mononga, Mr. Repossi, Mr. M.D. Zafrul, Mr. David, Mr. Sithole, Mr. Yagual, Mr. Pajobo, Mr. Ilolov, Mr. Dave, Mr. Guiseppi, Mr. Djibrine, Mr. Numas	
20	II	*Fourth item on the agenda: Human resources development and training – Revision of the Human Resources Development Recommendation, 1975 (No. 150) (standard setting, second discussion)*	
		Report of the Committee on Human Resources	1
		Proposed Recommendation concerning human resources development: Education, training and lifelong learning	91
20A	II	*Text of the Recommendation concerning human resources development: Education, training and lifelong learning submitted by the Drafting Committee*	1
21	II	*Fifth item on the agenda: Work in the fishing sector – A discussion with a view to the adoption of a comprehensive standard (a Convention supplemented by a Recommendation) (first discussion)*	
		Report of the Committee on the Fishing Sector	1
		Proposed conclusions	81
		Resolution to place on the agenda of the next ordinary session of the Conference an item entitled "Work in the fishing sector"	103
22	II	*Sixth item on the agenda: Migrant workers (general discussion based on an integrated approach)*	
		Report of the Committee on Migrant Workers	1
		Resolution concerning a fair deal for migrant workers in a global economy	55
		Conclusions on a fair deal for migrant workers in a global economy	56
23	I	*Sixteenth sitting:*	
		Reports of the Chairperson of the Governing Body and of the Director-General: Discussion *(concl.)*	1
		Speakers: Mr. Arthur Errázuriz, Mr. Ahmed, Mr. Gutiérrez Madueño, Mr. Gonzáles Gaitán, Mr. Aung, Mr. Cortebeeck, Ms. Muganza, Mr. Barak, Mr. Benydin, Ms. Dejanovic, Mr. Devendra, Mr. Lambert, Mr. Lewis, Mr. Mattar, Mr. Ruggiero, Mr. De Pury, Mr. Walimann, Mr. Parra Gaona, Mr. Goodleigh, Mr. Fostik, Mr. Finlay, Ms. Wintour, Mr. Funes de Rioja, Sir Roy Trotman	

PR No.	Volume		Page

Seventeenth sitting:

Report of the Finance Committee of Government representatives: Submission, discussion and approval 20

Speakers: Mr. Jonzon *(Chairperson and Reporter of the Committee)*, Mr. Alkhulaifi

Resolution concerning the Financial Report and Audited Financial Statements for 2002-03: Adoption.. 21

Resolution concerning the arrears of contributions of Iraq: Adoption 21

Resolution concerning the arrears of contributions of Paraguay: Adoption 21

Resolution concerning the assessment of the contributions of new member States: Adoption.. 21

Resolution concerning the scale of assessments of contribution to the budget for 2005: Adoption.. 21

Resolution concerning the composition of the Administrative Tribunal of the International Labour Organization: Adoption 21

Resolution concerning appointments to the ILO Staff Pension Committee (United Nations Joint Staff Pension Board): Adoption...... 21

Second report of the Selection Committee: Submission, discussion and approval... 21

Speakers: Mr. Hasegawa *(Chairperson and Reporter of the Committee)*, Mr. Noakes, Sir Roy Trotman

Report of the Standing Orders Committee: Submission and approval 22

Speaker: Mr. Oni *(Chairperson and Reporter of the Committee)*

Report of the Resolutions Committee: Submission, discussion and approval 23

Speakers: Ms. Santestevan *(Chairperson and Reporter of the Committee)*, Mr. Botha, Mr. Blondel, Ms. Rahmani, Mr. Sen, Ms. Anderson, Mr. Rampak, Mr. Howard, Mr. Thullen

Resolution concerning the promotion of gender equality, pay and maternity protection: Adoption... 28

| 24 | II | *Third item on the agenda: Information and reports on the application of Conventions and Recommendations* | |

Report of the Committee on the Application of Standards................... 1

PR No.	Volume		Page
25	I	*Reply by the Director-General to the discussion of his Report*	1
26	I	*Eighteenth sitting:*	

Ratification of the Instrument of Amendment of the ILO Constitution by Nigeria 1

Report of the Committee on the Fishing Sector: Submission, discussion and approval 1

Speakers: Mr. Boumbopoulos *(Reporter)*, Ms. Karikari Anang, Mr. Masemola, Mr. Ribeiro Lopes, Mr. Pender, Mr. Potter

Resolution to place on the agenda of the next ordinary session of the Conference an item entitled "Work in the fishing sector": Adoption 7

Record vote on the resolution concerning the arrears of contributions of Iraq 7

Record vote on the resolution concerning the arrears of contribution of Paraguay 7

Final record vote on the withdrawal of 16 Recommendations 7

Nineteenth sitting:

Report of the Committee on Human Resources: Submission, discussion and approval 8

Speakers: Ms. Murty *(Reporter)*, Mr. Renique, Ms. Yacob, Mr. Chetwin, Mr. Tricoche, Ms. Lenoir, Mr. Raman, Ms. Oiz, Mr. Abdulhusain, Ms. Riggs, Mr. Lambert, Mr. Wajda, Ms. Awassi Atsimadja, Ms. Goldberg, Mr. Patil, Mr. Arnold, Mr. Lewis, Mr. Rojvithee

Proposed Recommendation concerning human resources development: Education, training and lifelong learning: Adoption 23

Speakers: Mr. Renique, Ms. Yacob

Second and third reports of the Credentials Committee: Submission and noting 24

Speaker: Mr. Oni *(Chairperson and Reporter)*

Report of the Committee on Migrant Workers: Submission, discussion and approval 25

Speakers: Mr. Kebbon *(Reporter)*, Mr. de Regil, Ms. Burrow, Mr. Dé, Mr. Pender, Mr. Gammampila Don, Ms. Saab, Mr. Manley, Mr. Anderson, Mr. Terán, Mr. Cester Beatobe, Ms. Coke-Lloyd, Ms. Phillips, Ms. Kipulu Katani, Ms. Avendano Denier, Mr. Joubier

PR No.	Volume		Page
		Resolution concerning a fair deal for migrant workers in a global economy: Adoption	38
		Conclusions on a fair deal for migrant workers in a global economy: Adoption	38
		Record vote on the resolution concerning the arrears of contributions of Iraq: Results...	39
		Record vote on the resolution concerning the arrears of contributions of Paraguay: Results..................................	44
		Final record vote relating to the withdrawal of 16 Recommendations: Results...	49
27	I	*Twentieth sitting:*	
		Final record vote on the Recommendation concerning human resources development: Education, training and lifelong learning......................	1

Speakers: Mr. Funes de Rioja, Mr. Pender, Ms. Alvesalo-Roesch, Mr. Shepard, Ms. Arango de Buitrago

Report of the Committee on the Application of Standards: Submission, discussion and approval 3

Speakers: Ms. Robert Lopes *(Reporter)*, Mr. Wisskirchen, Mr. Cortebeeck, Ms. Rial, Mr. Nkhambule, Mr. Mangwana, Mr. Sánchez Oliva, Mr. Cahalane, Mr. Etty, Mr. Steyne, Mr. Fernández, Mr. Sankar Saha, Mr. Sithole, Mr. Dorado Cano, Mr. Malevich, Mr. Ahmed

Closing speeches... 15

Speakers: Mr. Maatough, Mr. Wade, Mr. Attigbe, the Secretary-General, the President

Final record vote on the adoption of the Human Resources Development Recommendation, 2004: Results 21

Discussion in plenary sitting (Volume I)	PR No./Page
Global Report under the follow-up to the ILO Declaration on Fundamental Principles and Rights at Work: Interactive sitting	14/1
Examination of the report of the Finance Committee of Government Representatives...	23/20
Examination of the second report of the Selection Committee	23/21
Examination of the report of the Standing Orders Committee	23/22

Examination of the report of the Resolutions Committee	23/23
Examination of the report of the Committee on the Fishing Sector	26/1
Examination of the report of the Committee on Human Resources	26/8
Examination of the report of the Committee on Migrant Workers	26/25
Examination of the report of the Committee on the Application of Standards	27/3

Governing Body (Volume I) PR No./Page

Report of the Chairperson of the Governing Body to the Conference for the year 2003-04	3/1

Record votes (Volume I) PR No./Page

Resolution concerning the arrears of contributions of Iraq	26/7, 26/39
Resolution concerning the arrears of contributions of Paraguay	26/7, 26/44
Withdrawal of Recommendations Nos. 2, 12, 16, 18, 21, 26, 32, 33, 34, 36, 43, 46, 58, 70, 74 and 96	26/7, 26/49
Recommendation concerning human resources development: Education, training and lifelong learning	27/1, 27/21

Delegations (Volume I)

Committee reports (Volume II) PR No./Page

Selection Committee

First report	4-1/1
Second report	4-2/1
Withdrawal of 16 international labour Recommendations	4-2A/1
Composition of committees	5/1

Credentials Committee

Brief report presented by the Chairperson of the Governing Body	6/1
First report	6/5
Second report	6/11
Third report	6/21

Standing Orders Committee

    Report 16/1
    Appendix: Interim provisions concerning verification of
    credentials, effective from the 93rd Session (June 2005)
    to the 96th Session (June 2007) of the International Labour
    Conference 16/7

Finance Committee of Government Representatives

    Report .... 17(Rev.)/1
    Resolutions submitted to the Conference .... 17(Rev.)/13

Resolutions Committee

    Report 18/1
    Resolution submitted to the Conference 18/26

Committee on Human Resources

    Report 20/1
    Proposed Recommendation concerning human resources
    development: Education, training and lifelong learning 20/91

Committee on the Fishing Sector

    Report 21/1
    Proposed Conclusions 21/81
    Resolution to place on the agenda of the next ordinary session
    of the Conference an item entitled "Work in the fishing sector" ... 21/103

Committee on Migrant Workers

    Report 22/1
    Resolution concerning a fair deal for migrant workers in a
    global economy 22/55
    Conclusions on a fair deal for migrant workers in a
    global economy 22/56

Committee on the Application of Standards

    Part One: General report 24/1
    Part Two: Observations and information concerning
    particular countries .... 24 Part 2/1
    Part Three: Special sitting to examine developments concerning
    the question of the observance by the Government of Myanmar
    of the Forced Labour Convention, 1930 (No. 29) .... 24 Part 3/1

Authentic texts adopted by the Conference (Volume II)   Page

    Withdrawal of Recommendations Nos. 2, 12, 16, 18, 21, 26,
    32, 33, 34, 36, 43, 46, 58, 70, 74 and 96 2
    Retrait de recommandations nos. 2, 12, 16, 18, 21, 26,
    32, 33, 34, 36, 43, 46, 58, 70, 74 and 96 3

    Recommendation concerning human resources development:
    Education, training and lifelong learning 1
    Recommandation concernant la mise en valeur des ressources
    humaines: éducation et formation tout au long de la vie 2

Resolutions adopted by the Conference (Volume II)   Page

I.	Resolution concerning the promotion of gender equality, pay equity and maternity protection	1
II.	Resolution to place on the agenda of the next ordinary session of the Conference an item entitled "Work in the fishing sector	4
III.	Resolution concerning a fair deal for migrant workers in a global economy	4
IV.	Resolution concerning the Financial Report and Audited Financial Statements for 2002-03	12
V.	Resolution concerning the arrears of contributions of Iraq	12
VI.	Resolution concerning the arrears of contributions of Paraguay	12
VII.	Resolution concerning the assessment of the contributions of new member States	13
VIII.	Resolution concerning the scale of assessments of contributions to the budget for 2005	13
IX.	Resolution concerning the composition of the Administrative Tribunal of the International Labour Organization	13
X.	Resolution concerning the appointments to the ILO Staff Pension Committee (United Nations Joint Staff Pension Board)	14

PLENARY SITTING

International Labour Conference

Provisional Record

Ninety-second Session, Geneva, 2004

Resolutions

Resolutions submitted in accordance with article 17 of the Standing Orders of the Conference

Resolution concerning the strengthening of the role of the ILO in supporting workers and employers in Palestine and the other occupied Arab territories as a result of continued Israeli occupation and aggressive practices, submitted by the Government delegations of Bahrain, Djibouti, Jordan and Oman; the following Employers' delegates: Mr. Al-Rabah (Kuwait); Mr. Al-Rabaie (Oman); Mr. Alsaleh (Bahrain); and Mr. Koullou (Morocco); and the following Workers' delegates: Mr. Al-Kuhlani (Yemen) and Mr. Ben Assadallah (Oman) [1]

The General Conference of the International Labour Organization,

Recalling the provisions of the ILO Constitution which states that "universal and lasting peace can be established only if it is based on social justice" and that "conditions of labour exist involving such injustice, hardship and privation to large numbers of people as to produce unrest so great that the peace and harmony of the world are imperilled",

Reaffirming the Declaration of Philadelphia which states that "all human beings, irrespective of race, creed or sex, have the right to pursue both their material well-being and their spiritual development in conditions of freedom and dignity, of economic security and equal opportunity",

Noting the resolution (No. 9) concerning the policy of discrimination, racism and violation of trade union freedoms and rights practised by the Israeli authorities in Palestine and in other occupied Arab territories adopted by the International Labour Conference at its 59th Session in 1974, and the resolution concerning the implications of Israeli settlements in Palestine and other occupied Arab territories in connection with the situation of Arab workers, adopted by the International Labour Conference at its 66th Session in 1980,

Expressing its deep concern regarding the sharp increase in unemployment in Palestine, in the number of persons with special needs, as well as the collapse of the

---

[1] The Employers' delegate Mr. El-Gurashi (Sudan) and the following Workers' delegates: Mr. El-Zlitni (Libyan Arab Jamahiriya); Mr Ghandour (Sudan); and Mr. Jrad (Tunisia), were among the authors of the resolution. At the time of receipt of the resolution, their credentials had not reached the Office or they were not accredited as delegates.

economic and social situation as a result of continued Israeli occupation, economic blockade, collective punishment, the construction of the separation wall, the destruction of infrastructure and homes, the bulldozing of agricultural land and the endangering of the lives of civilians, by displacement, poverty and unemployment;

1. Requests the Government of Israel to carry out an immediate and total withdrawal from the Palestinian territories and other Arab territories occupied since 1967, especially Al-Quds, and to dismantle all the settlements established in these territories as they are an insurmountable obstacle to the fulfilment of a lasting and comprehensive peace according to international resolutions, the implementation of the Road Map, and the establishment of an independent Palestinian State.

2. Calls upon the Members of the ILO to provide material and moral support to the tripartite social partners in Palestine and in the other occupied Arab territories to help eliminate the destructive effect of occupation and military aggression.

3. Calls upon the Government of Israel to remove all obstacles impeding the movement of Palestinian workers including the separation wall that is being constructed at the expense of Palestinian lands, in view of their destructive economic, social and human impact on the Palestinian people.

4. Requests the Governing Body and the Director-General of the ILO to:

(a) increase ILO programmes of support to the production partners in Palestine and in the other occupied Arab territories aimed at developing work opportunities, a reduction in poverty and unemployment and the reconstruction and rehabilitation of productive, social and trade union institutions;

(b) effectively contribute to and assist the Palestinian Fund for Employment and Social Protection, including calling on international organizations and financial institutions to support the Fund financially to enable it to implement its programmes which effectively contribute to providing decent work for Palestinian workers;

(c) call on the Israeli Government and employers to allow the return of those Palestinian workers who were forcibly prevented from going back to work as a result of the economic blockade and military barricades.

5. Requests the Governing Body of the International Labour Office and the Director-General to take the necessary steps for the implementation of this resolution.

Resolution concerning the role of the ILO in efforts to secure global peace, justice and security around the world, submitted by the following Workers' delegates: Mr. Basnet (Nepal); Ms. Brunel (France); Ms. Burrow (Australia); Ms. Byers (Canada); Mr. Edström (Sweden); Ms. Engelen-Kefer (Germany); Mr. Howard (South Africa); Ms. Hunt (United Kingdom); Mr. Katalay Muleli (Democratic Republic of the Congo); Mr. Kusano (Japan); Ms. Lekang (Norway); Mr. Norödahl (Iceland); Mr. Rampak (Malaysia); Mr. Sidorov (Russian Federation); Mr. Stech (Czech Republic); Mr. Svenningsen (Denmark); Ms. Valkonen (Finland); Mr. Wojcik (Poland); Ms. Yacob (Singapore); and Mr. Zellhoefer (United States) [2]

The General Conference of the International Labour Organization,

Recalling the opening words of the ILO Constitution of 1919, that "universal and lasting peace can be established only if it is based upon social justice",

Reaffirming its commitment to achieving a peaceful and secure world in which people from all countries coexist in mutual respect and tolerance,

Deeply concerned about the armed conflicts raging in many countries around the world, which are ruining the lives of millions of women, men and children and producing devastating social and economic consequences,

Recalling that many conflicts have their origins in profound injustice, poverty, inequality, the denial of human rights and democracy, as well as poor governance and corruption,

Convinced that increasing expenditure on efforts to preserve law and order nationally and internationally, without investing in measures to tackle the roots of the conflicts and tensions caused by inequality and lack of opportunities, is a strategy doomed to failure,

Also convinced that the situation of working families depends crucially on ending armed conflicts,

Rejecting unilateralism in world affairs and categorically rejecting all forms of terrorist activity,

Supporting the United Nations as the multilateral framework for peace and security around the world and its role as the principal actor in the maintenance of peace and the peaceful resolution of disputes,

Considering that international cooperation based on principles of solidarity and respect for international law is essential in solving social, economic, juridical and administrative problems,

Recognizing the need to act promptly against the most widespread and abhorrent forms of human rights violations during armed conflict, including sexual assault against women and girls, forced use of child combatants and the displacement of millions of

---

[2] The following Workers' delegates: Mr. Attigbe (Benin); Mr. Oshiomhole (Nigeria); Mr. Petrecca (Argentina); Mr. Sidi Saïd (Algeria); Mr. Tartaglia (Italy); Mr. Trotman (Barbados); Mr. Urbieta (Venezuela) and Mr. Vaccari (Brazil), were among the authors of the resolution. At the time of receipt of the resolution, their credentials had not reached the Office or they were not accredited as delegates.

people within and between countries, which have profound effects on the lives of those concerned, their societies and their economies,

Convinced that adherence to and action in accordance with the international Conventions and Recommendations of the ILO and other international instruments can provide the framework for overcoming obstacles to development, peace and security,

Welcoming the assistance already provided by the ILO and the measures it has taken towards rehabilitation and reconstruction of countries affected by armed conflicts;

1. Appeals to all parties to armed conflicts to take the bold steps necessary to achieve peace, for a rapid end to hostilities, reinforcing and establishing, under the auspices of the United Nations, democratic national governments free from military or any other form of autocratic control.

2. Urges governments to achieve substantial reductions in military expenditures, to increase spending on social programmes and investment in economic development, and calls for new initiatives to regulate and control world production of and trade in arms, and to convert armaments production to peaceful means, accompanied by effective transitional measures with employment promotion as a central objective.

3. Appeals to intergovernmental and non-governmental international organizations, to governments and to member States to reinforce multilateral or bilateral international cooperation in the economic, social and cultural fields.

4. Acknowledges that social, economic and political empowerment of people and their communities is directly linked to peace and to the realization of basic human rights, especially those concerned with freedom to work in conditions of equity, security and human dignity.

5. Requests the Governing Body of the International Labour Office to instruct the Director-General to:

(a) direct the Organization's efforts towards promoting just and sustainable development to improve people's lives;

(b) determine which forms of technical support and assistance the ILO can appropriately provide in rehabilitation and reconstruction programmes;

(c) sustain the unique capacities of workers' and employers' organizations to prevent and resolve conflicts, and provide assistance to unions and employers' organizations which are often targeted in conflict situations;

(d) offer support for the rapid implementation of programmes of activities within the ILO's competencies, covering in particular the following areas: implementation of core labour standards; re-entry into working life and vocational rehabilitation, with specific programmes on equality; labour administration and industrial relations; labour and social security legislation in conformity with ILO standards; and free and independent trade unions and employers' organizations;

(e) work for the full respect of human rights and international law, as the only way to protect those least able to defend themselves.

Resolution concerning pay equity, submitted by the following Workers' delegates: Mr. Ahmed (Pakistan); Mr. Basnet (Nepal); Ms. Brunel (France); Ms. Burrow (Australia); Ms. Byers (Canada); Mr. Edström (Sweden); Ms. Engelen-Kefer (Germany); Mr. Howard (South Africa); Ms. Hunt (United Kingdom); Mr. Katalay Muleli (Democratic Republic of the Congo); Mr. Kusano (Japan); Ms. Lekang (Norway); Mr. Norödahl (Iceland); Mr. Rampak (Malaysia); Mr. Sidorov (Russian Federation); Mr. Stech (Czech Republic); Mr. Svenningsen (Denmark); Ms. Valkonen (Finland); Mr. Wojcik (Poland); Ms. Yacob (Singapore); and Mr. Zellhoefer (United States) [3]

The General Conference of the International Labour Organization,

Recalling that the Equal Remuneration Convention, 1951 (No. 100), and the Discrimination (Employment and Occupation) Convention, 1958 (No. 111), are universally recognized as embodying fundamental workers' rights and part of the ILO Declaration on Fundamental Principles and Rights at Work and its Follow-up of 1998,

Emphasizing that the achievement of pay equity is integral to any successful poverty eradication strategy, and that quality jobs as well as quality public services are fundamental in promoting equal opportunities for all,

Noting that the process of globalization is experienced by many women and men as heightened insecurity and marginalization, and that the global gap between economic growth and social development is also fundamentally a gender gap,

Recognizing the importance and value of existing technical assistance programmes carried out by the International Labour Organization on pay equity issues, as reaffirmed in the Global Report *Time for equality at work* adopted by the International Labour Conference in its 91st Session (2003);

1. Appeals to all governments, employers' and workers' organizations to adopt and implement without delay strategies and measures to achieve pay equity.

2. Appeals to all Governments of ILO member States to:

(a) ratify the Equal Remuneration Convention, 1951 (No. 100), and the Discrimination (Employment and Occupation) Convention, 1958 (No. 111);

(b) introduce legislative changes and affirmative action programmes to detect and eliminate discrimination in the workplace,

(c) compile, publish and disseminate annual statistical indicators on the wage gap based on gender and other factors, including race, ethnicity and disability.

3. Calls upon employers' and workers' organizations to:

(a) negotiate the adoption of employment equity plans;

---

[3] The following Workers' delegates: Mr. Apecides (Colombia); Mr. Attigbe (Benin); Mr. Oshiomhole (Nigeria); Mr. Petrecca (Argentina); Mr. Sidi Saïd (Algeria); Mr. Tartaglia (Italy); Mr. Trotman (Barbados); Mr. Urbieta (Venezuela); and Mr. Vaccari (Brazil), were among the authors of the resolution. At the time of receipt of the resolution, their credentials had not reached the Office or they were not accredited as delegates.

(b) negotiate the introduction of gender-neutral job evaluation schemes;

(c) carry out gender and race audits at the workplace in order to detect and eliminate discrimination.

4. Calls upon workers' organizations to carry out capacity building, training and advocacy programmes on all aspects of pay equity.

5. Invites the Governing Body of the International Labour Organization to request the Director-General to:

(a) design a model method and provide technical assistance to governments wishing to develop statistical indicators on the gender, race and disability wage gap;

(b) intensify the campaign for the universal ratification and implementation of Conventions Nos. 100 and 111 together with the other fundamental Conventions;

(c) continue and strengthen substantively ongoing work to provide capacity building, training and advocacy programmes on all aspects of pay equity for governments, employers' and workers' organizations;

(d) strengthen research work on:

   (i) the impact of a minimum living wage on earnings in order to understand its potential impact on the gender, race and disability wage gap and its impact on workers in the informal economy;

   (ii) the impact of the privatization of public services and the increasing casualization of work on the gender, race and disability wage gap;

   (iii) ways of publishing research results in simple and accessible format for wide distribution.

(e) develop guidelines on how to carry out gender-aware job evaluations and workplace auditing and support the dissemination of good practice in this area through newsletters or web-based resources;

(f) Establish a training programme on gender-aware job evaluations at the Turin Training Centre for governments, and employers' and workers' organizations.

Resolution concerning the ILO's efforts to combat poverty, submitted by the following Workers' delegates: Mr. Basnet (Nepal); Ms. Brunel (France); Ms. Burrow (Australia); Ms. Byers (Canada); Mr. Edström (Sweden); Ms. Engelen-Kefer (Germany); Mr. Howard (South Africa); Ms. Hunt (United Kingdom); Mr. Katalay Muleli (Democratic Republic of the Congo); Mr. Kusano (Japan); Ms. Lekang (Norway); Mr. Norödahl (Iceland); Mr. Rampak (Malaysia); Mr. Sidorov (Russian Federation); Mr. Stech (Czech Republic); Mr. Svenningsen (Denmark); Ms. Valkonen (Finland); Mr. Wojcik (Poland); Ms. Yacob (Singapore); and Mr. Zellhoefer (United States) [4]

The General Conference of the International Labour Organization,

Considering poverty to be a threat to humanity and reaffirming that "Poverty anywhere constitutes a danger to prosperity everywhere" (Declaration of Philadelphia, 1944),

Conscious of the need to address the "ethical vacuum" in which globalization has come about, with unprecedented levels of wealth but also a widening gap in income and wealth both within and between countries,

Aware of the intolerable persistence at the beginning of the third millennium of unacceptable levels of absolute and endemic poverty throughout the world, with half the world population – some 3 billion people, two-thirds of whom are women – living on less than US$2 a day and more than 1 billion people living on $1 a day or less,

Emphasizing that the provision of decent work, with good labour standards and adequate wages, has proven to be the most effective way of achieving poverty reduction,

Stressing the urgent need to speed up concrete actions in order to meet the eight Millennium Development Goals [5] by 2015;

1. Invites governments, in collaboration with trade unions and employers' organizations, to:

(a) focus on human and trade union rights as an integral part of development strategy, in particular through the recognition of ILO core labour standards encompassed by the ILO Declaration of Fundamental Principles and Rights at Work and its Follow-up (1998), i.e. the benefits of growth reaching the poor (collective bargaining), their empowerment being ensured (freedom of association), women and other equity-seeking groups participating fully as active agents in the process of change (non-discriminatory policies), while the new generation and the most vulnerable gain new hope (combating child labour and forced labour);

---

[4] The following Workers' delegates: Mr. Attigbe (Benin); Mr. Oshiomhole (Nigeria); Mr. Petrecca (Argentina); Mr. Sidi Saïd (Algeria); Mr. Tartaglia (Italy); Mr. Trotman (Barbados); Mr. Urbieta (Venezuela); and Mr. Vaccari (Brazil), were among the authors of the resolution. At the time of receipt of the resolution, their credentials had not reached the Office or they were not accredited as delegates.

[5] Eradicate extreme poverty and hunger; achieve universal primary education; promote gender equality and empowerment of women; reduce child mortality; improve maternal health; combat HIV/AIDS, malaria and other diseases; ensure environmental sustainability; and develop a Global Partnership for Development.

(b) recognize the relation between poverty reduction, sustained high economic growth and a redistributive policy framework, since the pattern and sources of growth as well as the manner in which its benefits are distributed are interlinked;

(c) build policies that increase real wages (including minimum wages) and earnings of wage-paid workers and real earnings of the self-employed, respecting the principle of pay equity, as a crucial element in channelling the benefits of growth to the poor;

(d) recognize the need to address the plight of the millions of workers in informal and unprotected employment, and the imperative need to extend social protection and legal rights to those workers;

(e) develop a demand-supply approach which, inter alia, would include (from the demand side) employment intensity of growth, higher productivity sectors, technology, creation of assets for the poor, and (from the supply side) the ability of the poor to integrate into the process of economic growth and access the jobs that are created (e.g. through access to education and health, skills development, labour-market information flow, access to productive assets and finance);

(f) support flexibility and country ownership in such areas as macroeconomic management, determination of price stability, trade policy, public spending levels and sources of taxation, financial sector reforms, capital account management, agricultural policies, privatization policies, social spending;

(g) increase resource flows to developing countries through increased official development assistance, debt relief and other means, through which education, skills, health and other elements of the comprehensive development strategy could be funded;

(h) re-orient and increase coherence among policies of international organizations, using the report of the World Commission on the Social Dimension of Globalization as a platform for action.

2. Invites the Governing Body of the International Labour Office to instruct the Director-General to:

(a) intensify work at national level in order to integrate core labour standards, genuine tripartite involvement and the concept of decent work in national development strategies, including the IMF and World Bank-sponsored Poverty Reduction Strategy Papers (PRSPs), using the ILO Global Employment Agenda as a guiding framework;

(b) develop advisory capacity – both at headquarters and in the field – for the tripartite constituents on the issues referred to above, especially providing autonomous and complementary advice vis-à-vis the Bretton Woods institutions;

(c) upgrade work on social economy initiatives and linkages between decent employment and poverty reduction (for example through the expansion of programmes such as Employment-Intensive Investment and Cooperatives and through the full implementation of the conclusions on the informal economy);

(d) upgrade resources and guidance on how to boost productivity and incomes in the rural economy, a sector where ILO leadership has dramatically declined in the last decade;

(e) address the specific problem of poverty in transition economies, identifying strategies that would prevent a downward spiral in these countries;

(f) tackle the links between poverty and gender discrimination, which contributes both to the feminization of poverty and the perpetuation of poverty from one generation to the next;

(g) consider setting up a special fund for the fight against poverty through ILO-oriented activities, with contributions from each country at a rate of at least 1 per cent of their military expenditure.

Resolution concerning the social responsibilities of business, submitted by the following Workers' delegates:
Mr. Ahmed (Pakistan); Mr. Basnet (Nepal); Ms. Brunel (France); Ms. Burrow (Australia); Ms. Byers (Canada); Mr. Edström (Sweden); Ms. Engelen-Kefer (Germany); Mr. Howard (South Africa); Ms. Hunt (United Kingdom); Mr. Katalay Muleli (Democratic Republic of the Congo); Mr. Kusano (Japan); Ms. Lekang (Norway); Mr. Norödahl (Iceland); Mr. Rampak (Malaysia); Mr. Sidorov (Russian Federation); Mr. Stech (Czech Republic); Mr. Svenningsen (Denmark); Ms. Valkonen (Finland); Mr. Wojcik (Poland); Ms. Yacob (Singapore) and Mr. Yelhoefer (United States) [6]

The General Conference of the International Labour Organization,

Recognizing that a concept of business ethics referred to as corporate social responsibility has attracted interest in the business world and elsewhere, and that this concept is based on the idea that enterprises should be accountable to stakeholders broadly defined as all those affected by the activities of the enterprise,

Acknowledging that this concept underpins efforts by business to identify, measure and report the impact of business activities on stakeholders and that these efforts have spawned a dramatic increase in private voluntary initiatives,

Further recognizing that the growing interest in this concept reflects a growing appreciation of the social responsibilities of business generally that has been brought about by rapid changes in the world economy and in international economic relationships,

Mindful of the ILO's role in identifying and establishing internationally many of the most important and relevant social standards reflecting the interests of society through a process involving governments, employers' and workers' organizations,

Recognizing that the underlying principles for many of these standards are the principles that define what it means for business to be socially responsible,

Affirming that social responsibility of business must include respect for and active advancement of all the fundamental rights at work, and that social responsibility must also reflect the principles and rights embodied in many other standards,

Further recognizing that business responsibility cannot be determined or measured by unilateral initiatives alone, and that relationships with other institutions in society must be taken into account,

---

[6] The following Workers' delegates: Mr. Oshiomhole (Nigeria); Mr. Petrecca (Argentina); Mr. Sidi Saïd (Algeria); Mr. Tartaglia (Italy); Mr. Trotman (Barbados); Mr. Urbieta (Venezuela) and Mr. Vaccari (Brazil), were among the authors of the resolution At the time of receipt of the resolution, their credentials had not reached the Office or they were not accredited as delegates.

Reaffirming the importance and proven effectiveness of collective bargaining and social dialogue for ensuring that business activities have their most positive social impact,

Recalling the consensus reflected in the ILO Tripartite Declaration of Principles concerning Multinational Enterprises and Social Policy on these issues and reaffirming the continuing relevance of this instrument,

Further recalling important intergovernmental definitions of responsible business behaviour such as the OECD Guidelines for Multinational Enterprises and international initiatives such as the United Nations Global Compact, based on established principles of behaviour and on social dialogue;

1. Calls on governments, workers' and employers' organizations, as appropriate, to:

(a) promote concepts of business social responsibility that emphasize the role of social partnership and social dialogue and the importance of good industrial relations;

(b) work together to ensure that all the fundamental rights at work are taken into account and respected in all business relationships;

(c) undertake private voluntary initiatives that recognize the role of government, promote a culture of compliance with law and strengthen representative organizations in society;

(d) ensure that governmentally agreed instruments such as the OECD Guidelines for Multinational Enterprises are properly implemented, including effectively functioning national contact points;

(e) undertake forms of social dialogue at an international level through such means as participation in the United Nations Global Compact and by encouraging framework agreements between multinational companies and international trade union organizations;

2. Calls on the International Labour Organization to:

(a) inform consideration of the social responsibilities of business generally and within the United Nations system by emphasizing the importance of social partnership, social dialogue, good industrial relations and ILO standards;

(b) intensify the promotion of its Tripartite Declaration of Principles concerning Multinational Enterprises and Social Policy and pursue means to give them greater effect, including assisting member States in establishing tripartite forums at national level to do so;

(c) provide advice and information concerning the meaning and observance of international labour standards for the purpose of assisting business in realizing its social responsibilities;

(d) marshal and bring to bear expertise available from employers' and workers' organizations and from governments in order to make private voluntary initiatives addressing the social responsibilities of business more effective in all relevant areas including expertise on how to improve labour inspection techniques and on how to improve the competencies of private workplace auditors;

(e) use its tripartite structure to develop guidance and recommendations including best practice benchmarks that can be applied to voluntary initiatives addressing business social responsibility;

(f) ensure that the ILO continues to play the leading role in the identification, development, interpretation and application of all international labour standards including those relating to the social responsibilities of business;

(g) act as a clearing house for different initiatives, measures and instruments relating to the social responsibility of business.

Resolution concerning the application of international labour standards to international civil servants, submitted by the following Workers' delegate: Mr. Prince (Switzerland)

The General Conference of the International Labour Organization,

Recalling the Constitution of the International Labour Conference,

Recalling Conventions Nos. 87, 98, 135, 144, 151 and 154 and the accompanying Recommendations,

Recalling that in adopting the ILO Declaration on Fundamental Principles and Rights at Work and its Follow-up, all member States of the International Labour Organization have undertaken to respect, to promote and to realize these principles and rights, including freedom of association and the effective recognition of the right to collective bargaining,

Reaffirming that, even if the member States of the International Labour Organization did not include the international organizations among the addressees of the international labour standards, those organizations are still required to adhere to them by virtue of the universal nature of the principles embodied in the Declaration of Philadelphia;

1. Invites all the international organizations to safeguard conditions conducive to social dialogue, in particular respect for the fundamental principles and the right to organize and collective bargaining, an atmosphere of sound labour relations and respect for the role of the social partners.

2. Invites governments to ensure, through their representatives in the international organizations, that this objective is achieved.

Resolution concerning older workers and employment and social protection, submitted by the Government delegations of Canada and the United Kingdom

The General Conference of the International Labour Organization,

Recalling the ILO Declaration on Fundamental Principles and Rights at Work (1998), and the Declaration's specific recognition that the ILO should give particular attention to those with special social needs,

Recalling the ILO's Decent Work Agenda, the ILO's Global Employment Agenda, and the Report of the World Commission on the Social Dimension of Globalization, all of which emphasize the central role of employment and employment creation in combating poverty,

Recalling the commitment of the Copenhagen Declaration on Social Development to promoting the goal of full employment,

Recalling the International Plan of Action on Ageing and the accompanying Political Declaration adopted by the Second World Assembly on Ageing in Madrid 2002,

Recalling the resolutions of the United Nations Commission for Social Development and the United Nations General Assembly on Ageing and the Madrid International Plan of Action on Ageing,

Recognizing the important contributions of employers' and workers' organizations, in partnership with governments, to furthering the participation of older people in the labour market and combating discrimination against them in employment and the workplace,

Welcoming the key message put forward by the ILO to the Second World Assembly on Ageing, that a genuine solution to the challenge of ageing is to be sought by increasing participation in the labour force and thus through the creation of more and better jobs,

Recalling the specific concern articulated in the Madrid Plan of Action in regard to the effects of HIV/AIDS on older caregivers, particularly in Africa and particularly on older women, and welcoming the ILO's commitment to responding effectively to the threat posed by HIV/AIDS to its Decent Work Agenda,

Recalling the specific reference in the Madrid Plan of Action to enhanced international cooperation as being essential to the effective implementation of the Plan;

Calls upon the Director-General of the International Labour Office, in response to the emphasis which the International Plan of Action gives to mainstreaming ageing into global agendas and linking ageing to other frameworks for social and economic development and human rights, to develop a comprehensive strategy to assist ILO constituents in responding to the opportunities and challenges of population ageing. This strategy should, inter alia:

(a) recognize and promote the potential social and economic contributions of older people;

(b) promote employment opportunities for older people through the goal of full employment, by putting employment growth at the heart of economic and social policies;

(c) encourage increased participation of older people in the labour market, including by promoting self-employment initiatives;

(d) remove barriers and disincentives to the employment of older persons, including by tackling discrimination against the employment of older persons, and promote the business benefits of employing older workers;

(e) pay particular attention to older workers in the informal economy, older women in the labour market, older workers with disabilities and older persons from other disadvantaged groups;

(f) help those older people who are disadvantaged in the labour market through lack of skills, including by improving opportunities for access to knowledge, education, training and technology;

(g) improve access to, and promote a culture of, lifelong learning which will enable all workers to update and improve their knowledge and skills;

(h) recognize and promote action to meet the needs of caregivers, both those with caring responsibilities for older persons and older persons with caring responsibilities, giving particular attention to those with caring responsibilities for persons with disabilities and HIV/AIDS;

(i) promote programmes which enable all workers to acquire basic social protection and social security;

(j) promote other appropriate action to combat poverty and disadvantage among older people including through enhanced international cooperation.

Resolution concerning peace [7]

The General Conference of the International Labour Organization,

Evoking the historical fact that the International Labour Organization has its origins in the Peace Conference of 1919,

Recalling that the General Conference of the International Labour Organization in its 26th Session adopted the Declaration of Philadelphia stating the aims and objectives of the International Labour Organization that must inspire the policy of its members,

Conscious that the Declaration of Philadelphia embodies the same principles as the United Nations Universal Declaration of Human Rights,

Emphasizing that international peace and security constitute an essential condition for the enjoyment of workers' rights, above all, the right to life,

Considering the Declaration on the Right of Peoples to Peace, adopted by the General Assembly of the United Nations in 1984,

Recognizing that it is the obligation of all States to solve their international disputes by peaceful means in such a way that neither international peace and security, nor justice, is put in danger,

Insisting that it is incompatible with the principles of the United Nations that States in their international relations should resort to the use or the threat of force against the territorial integrity or political independence of another State in matters that are essentially within their internal jurisdiction,

Reaffirming that all peoples have the right to free self-determination, by virtue of which they establish their political conditions freely and also provide freely for their own economic, social and cultural development,

Mindful of the fact that the Declaration of Philadelphia reiterates what is expressed in the Constitution of the International Labour Organization, namely, that lasting peace can be established only if it is based on social justice,

---

[7] The Workers' delegate from the Syrian Arab Republic, Mr. Shaaban Azzouz, was the author of the resolution. At the time of receipt of the resolution, his credentials had not reached the Office or he was not accredited as a delegate.

Emphasizing that, together with the persistence of the present unjust, immoral, untenable and unequal international order have arisen more serious and immediate dangers that arise from wars and threaten the right to development,

Convinced that without peace, development is not possible, and without development there will be no peace,

Recognizing that what the world needs is to declare global war against underdevelopment, hunger, poverty, illiteracy and prevailing diseases like HIV/AIDS,

Observing the continuing absence of political will to make effective the noble aspiration to pursue disarmament for the sake of development;

Affirms:

(a) that the just right of all peoples to peace must become a reality;

(b) that the decision of the General Assembly of the United Nations in 2000 when the Millennium Declaration was adopted referred to establishing a just and lasting peace all over the world in accordance with the purposes and principles of the United Nations Charter;

(c) that the Charter's rejection of violence to attain political objectives emphasizes that only peaceful political solutions will be able to guarantee a stable and democratic future to all the peoples of the world;

(d) that it is in the interests of the workers and peoples of the world that they, in accordance with the intentions and principles of the United Nations, fully and actively support its role and effectiveness in strengthening international peace, security and justice and promoting the solution of international problems, as well as in the development of relations of friendship and cooperation between States;

(e) that these principles emphasize that what workers and their families need are not armies of soldiers seeding destruction and death but armies of doctors, teachers and engineers to ensure health, education, progress and well-being;

(f) that we must win the support of all peoples for the logical and inescapable demand: "Disarmament for development".

Resolution concerning gender-equal pay, submitted by the following Workers' delegate: Mrs. Thi Hau (Viet Nam)

The General Conference of the International Labour Organization,

Recalling the principle of article 1 of the Universal Declaration of Human Rights, that "all human beings are born free and equal in dignity and rights", including the observance of equality of opportunities and humane treatment that has been one of the ILO's objectives,

Considering that, since the ILO's foundation, the question of the observance of equality of opportunities and treatment has been one of the main goals of this Organization and that the first ILO Constitution indicated that this principle is among those "of particular and urgent importance",

Reaffirming the conclusions, recommendations and policies and the development of gender perspectives, contained in resolutions of the United Nations, the ILO, UNESCO, UNICEF, UNHCR, the UNDP and the World Conferences on Women,

Considering that from the origins of the ILO, the Organization's Constitution has recognized the principle of equal remuneration for work of equal value,

Observing that in the first binding international instruments adopted with the specific objective of promoting equality and eliminating discrimination, namely, the Equal Remuneration Convention, 1951 (No. 100), and its Recommendation (No. 90), it was recognized that equality of remuneration could not be obtained without the elimination of discrimination in all work areas and that other causes of discrimination also had to be eradicated,

Recalling that in 1981, the International Labour Conference adopted the Workers with Family Responsibilities Convention, 1981 (No. 156), and its Recommendation (No. 165);

Affirms:

(a) that the protection of women at work must be an integral part of the efforts to be made for continuous improvements of the conditions of life and work of all employees;

(b) that all countries should be called upon to ensure strict compliance with all the standards that protect equality of wages in all enterprises, especially ILO Conventions Nos. 100 and 156;

(c) that governments, and organizations of employers and workers should be urged once again to adopt measures to eliminate all forms of discrimination at work, to obtain total equality of participation of women in employment through the ratification of the existing Conventions;

(d) that the ILO should be asked to report periodically on the conditions of women workers in each member State and on the prospects of integration of young women workers in the world of employment.

Resolution concerning poverty [8]

The General Conference of the International Labour Organization,

Agreeing with the World Commission on the Social Dimension of Globalization that the present course of globalization must change,

Remembering that during the Trade Union Forum held in the framework of the World Summit for Social Development in Copenhagen, whose main agreements, proclaiming that global action is necessary to fight the sources of the injustice and inequality between nations as well as within them, were adopted nearly ten years ago and are still waiting to be made a reality,

Celebrating the recognition expressed in the Declaration adopted by the Heads of State and Government at the Millennium Summit of the fundamental value of solidarity for international relations in the twenty-first century when affirming that worldwide problems must be approached in such a way that the costs and loads are distributed with justice, according to the fundamental principles of fairness and social justice, and that those who suffer or receive fewer benefits deserve the aid of those who have greater benefits,

Manifesting that the persistence of poverty supposes the negation of the rights consecrated in the Universal Declaration of Human Rights and the consequent international norms in the matter plead for "… a life in dignity, in which all the people have an adequate level of life and access to the essential goods that give practical content to that type of life …",

Observing that the reality of a globalized world, where so many people live in conditions that are degrading and where the gap between the rich and the poor increases, not only between countries but within them, contradicts the humanitarian enthusiasm expressed in the Universal Declaration of Human Rights where "all human beings are born free and equal in dignity and rights",

Understanding that pauperization is inseparable from social polarization, a modern phenomenon that is not just represented by insufficient income to survive, but that also designates, faithfully, the social effects of the present tendency in the evolution of humanity because, in fact, this modernization of poverty has devastating effects in all dimensions of social life,

Realizing that the drama which today involves all of us, employers and workers, is serious beyond the margin of individual beliefs or political militancy, wherever we live, because, in one way or another, poverty will affect all of us,

Stating that:

– nearly 3,000 million people live today on an income of less than US$2 a day;

– more than 1,200 million people live with a per capita income of less than $1 a day, while some developed countries spend $2 a day per head to subsidize the sale of cattle;

---

[8] The Workers' delegate of Sudan, Mr. Ghandour, was the author of the resolution. At the time of receipt of the resolution, his credentials had not reached the Office or he was not accredited as a delegate.

- some 8 million children die every year as a result of poverty;

- some 150 million children under the age of 5 suffer from malnutrition;

- every seven seconds a child under the age of 10 dies as a result of hunger;

- some 840 million people in the world do not have enough to eat;

- some 100 million children live in the streets in conditions of absolute poverty;

- some 30,000 people die daily in the underdeveloped countries because the medicines they need, 90 per cent of which are patented by the pharmaceutical transnationals, are unavailable or are very expensive;

- the underdeveloped countries pay $100 billion annually in commercial tariffs to the developed countries, double the amount of aid that they receive from them;

- the rich countries spend $1 billion daily in agricultural subsidies, and pay the producers of the less economically favoured countries a price that is sometimes barely 1 per cent of the price for which they sell these products;

- some 25 million North Americans have an income equivalent to that of 2 billion of the poor people of the world,

Deploring that there is no agreement to seek out and identify the reasons that generate this poverty, as without evaluation of the causes and without action to eradicate them, it will be impossible to really face them and, therefore, there will be no development,

Recognizing that the current policies of globalization are contrary to the International Development Strategies adopted by the General Assembly of the United Nations 30 years ago and conflict with the well-known United Nations General Assembly Declaration on the Establishment of a New International Economic Order, adopted with a view to eliminating all vestiges of imperialism, colonialism and neo-colonialism,

Appreciating that the present policies of globalization trample and obstruct the application of the action programmes of United Nations summits held in the 1990s, such as the World Summit for Social Development in Copenhagen, the Fourth World Conference on Women in Beijing, and others dedicated to crucial global subjects,

Concerned that instead of having implemented the call of the United Nations for "disarmament for development", the great powers, headed by the American Administration, are rapidly increasing their military budgets, thus increasing tensions even more,

Considering that the economic policies prevailing in the world today are contrary to the designation of this decade as the United Nations Decade for the Eradication of Poverty, as, in spite of all the promises and the potential of new technologies, countries remain in a state of underdevelopment,

Troubled particularly by the fact that most of the developing countries will not fulfil the objectives adopted by the United Nations to overcome the problems associated with poverty by the year 2015,

Affirming that after 60 years of Bretton Woods, millions of human beings and whole nations pay, with their starvation, for the policies applied by those institutions,

Considering that the economic and financial opening-up demanded by these international institutions, far from offering advantages to the Third World, prevent their economic development, dismantle the capacity of States and worsen the inequities to the sole benefit of the large transnational companies and the economy of the rich countries,

Appreciating that the poor countries are forced to liberalize their markets, but that the developed nations reserve for themselves a succulent dose of protectionism in the form of tariff or non-tariff barriers and subsidies to their national producers, mainly for agriculture, and that these policies drain the resources of the underdeveloped countries by two strategic routes: external debt and privatization of their natural resources,

Added to the estimate printed in the report of the World Commission on the Social Dimension of Globalization that the reduction of barriers in the multilateral commercial system is essential so that the so-called in-development countries can have access to the markets of merchandise in which they have a comparative advantage,

Expressing its preoccupation with the increasing trafficking in persons and the migratory movements at national and international level, as verified by ILO experts,

Calling attention to the discrimination in employment and occupation that migrant workers suffer, while being employed in the worst jobs, in conditions of inequality, as a result of not enjoying basic human rights, including the right to organize, which has been verified by ILO experts,

Sharing the proposal of the World Commission on the Social Dimension of Globalization that energetic measures should be taken to avoid fiscal evasion as well as to demand consideration of the existing potential derived from the new sources of financing, assigning funds up until now allocated to military expenses to aid for development,

Understanding the assertion of the World Commission on the Social Dimension of Globalization that if all countries were to reach the objectives agreed to for the financial contributions promised to consolidate and promote development, which in recent years has been smaller than that planned (only 0.23 instead of 0.7 per cent of GNP), during the past 30 years, an additional amount of $2.5 trillion would have been available for development,

Noting the statement by ILO experts that poverty and inequality of income have been growing and that new forms of discrimination have appeared,

Confirming that this process would not be so successful were it not for the role of precarious employment, which also produces insecurity, and the existence of a reserve army of manual labour made docile by the permanent threat of unemployment, which also plays a part in employment contracting,

Concerned by what migrant workers suffer, in addition to discrimination as a result of race, in occupying the worst jobs, in conditions of inequality, owing to their being denied basic human rights such as the right to organize and the right to bargain collectively,

Lamenting that the abysses continue to grow significantly deeper, escalating the breach in labour relations by establishing the absolute reign of flexibility, with recruitment under contracts of specific duration or provisional contracts – for the sake of productivity – breaking the link between competition for a living between workers, through the individualization of wages, which implies establishing individual objectives, individual evaluation interviews, permanent evaluation, individual wage increases or concessions of premiums based on individual competition, and "merit", which constitutes techniques for rational submission that, while imposing concerted efforts in work, contribute to abolishing collective standards and solidarity,

Stating that never before has company language spoken so much of confidence, cooperation, loyalty and company culture at a time when every moment brings the disappearance of all temporary guarantees, as three-quarters of the contracts have a definite termination point, the sector of precarious jobs continues to grow and individual firing is not subject to any kind of restriction,

Emphasizing that, while unemployment and underemployment increase, global monopolies take increasing advantage of the crisis to abrogate the social achievements won by the trade unions and social organizations in terms of building the welfare state, defence of human rights, democracy and trade union rights,

Sounding the alarm that the extension of so-called informal work leaves hundreds of millions of workers without legal or social protection,

Stating that it is impossible – with the type of globalization that we are confronting – to conceive and promote a strategy of development, given the enormous process of concentration of property that prevents equitable access to the benefits achieved by the economies in their process of development,

Considering that we are witnessing an unjust distribution of income not only in each region and in each nation, but also between the regions and the nations, as well as an unjust distribution of income in that of the different economic sectors, which makes it possible for financial capital to seize the greater part of the wealth generated in the world;

Affirms that:

(a) All economic decisions adopted by governments and employers, as well as the Bretton Woods institutions, must have an authentic social dimension, such as that of the Summit for Social Development held in Copenhagen in 1995.

(b) It is necessary to contribute to implementing the agreement of the States at the World Conference on Human Rights in 1993 to cooperate to achieve development and eliminate the obstacles which prevent it.

(c) It should be reaffirmed that all countries, in particular the most developed countries, must take every step to eliminate the growing disparity between the economically developed States and the countries in development, as this is unacceptable and unsustainable and prevents the realization of human rights in the international community.

(d) Specifies that one of the many internationally adopted agreements requiring implementation – *one which must be made a reality* – is the Declaration on the Right to Development, adopted by the General Assembly of the United Nations in resolution 41/128 of 4 December 1986, which states that:

> The right to development is an inalienable human right by virtue of which every human person and all peoples are entitled to participate in, contribute to, and enjoy economic, social, cultural and political development, in which all human rights and fundamental freedoms can be fully realized. The human right to development also implies the full realization of the right of peoples to self-determination, which includes, subject to the relevant provisions of both International Covenants on Human Rights, the exercise of their inalienable right to full sovereignty over all their natural wealth and resources.

(e) The enormous benefits resulting from the process of globalization and economic interdependence should be guaranteed to reach all countries, communities and persons, ensuring that these do not become increasingly out of reach of many countries, in particular the least advanced and the African countries.

(f) It is necessary to promote an increase in the resources assigned to official assistance for development, remembering that the industrialized countries have promised to assign 0.7 per cent of their gross national product to this and that they have assigned only 0.23 per cent, less than one-third, and the United States has provided the least with only 0.11 per cent.

(g) We must exhort all governments to fulfil their promises made at the various summits, and in particular those adopted in 2001 in Durban, to increase to the maximum the benefits of globalization among them by strengthening and bettering international cooperation in order to promote equal opportunities for trade, economic growth and sustainable development, and improved world communication through the use of new technologies; reiterating that it is only through broad and sustainable efforts to create a common future, based on our common humanity in all its diversity, that it will be possible to have equitable and all-inclusive globalization.

(h) The call of the ILO Constitution to fulfil its objectives through efficient action in the national and international fields, which includes favouring the less developed regions, assuring a more equitable commercial trade and promoting improvements in health, education and the well-being of all peoples must be implemented.

(i) Transparent, democratic and fair international institutions that are accountable in all spheres of cooperation must be promoted and consolidated, taking as a fundamental value the solidarity to endorse the principles of equity and of social justice, ensuring that those who suffer, or benefit less, receive help from those who benefit more.

(j) The foreign debt of poor countries must be resolved in a fair and lasting way, as this debt makes it impossible for them to achieve development.

(k) It is necessary to reach an equilibrium – that which the president of the World Bank called for – between the concerns of the rich countries for the "war on terrorism" and the need to assist the economies of the poorest on the planet.

(l) Access by poor countries to new technologies must be made possible rather than knowledge and intellectual property being increasingly privately concentrated.

(m) Means should be found and put into effect to allow the unjust robbery of intelligence – the "brain drain" – to be resolved.

(n) The preservation of the environment must be demanded, preventing the present lords of consumption and wasteful extravagance from continuing to make development unsustainable.

(o) The rights of workers must be improved, respecting the international labour Conventions on the fundamental labour standards, ensuring that the regulation of social rights will continue to be part of the responsibility of the ILO and will not be able to be used for protectionist ends, nor as a mechanism for commercial barriers. The WTO must respect the decisions of the ILO.

(p) The call of the ILO Constitution to maintain the link between social progress and economic growth to guarantee the fundamental principles and rights of labour, which will make it possible to demand equitable participation in the wealth it has helped create and to develop fully its human potential, must be implemented.

(q) We must reaffirm the criterion upheld by the ILO that employment is a vital element in any strategy which attempts to increase the benefits of globalization.

(r) New and additional financial resources must be dedicated to the struggle against poverty and illiteracy, raising the levels of education of the people of the poor countries in order to help tackle the enormous challenge of the increasing growth of populations.

(s) Together with the free circulation of financial capital demanded by big capital, the circulation of people should be guaranteed, based on agreements reflecting the interests of the migrants themselves, and that of the countries of origin and destination.

(t) An international economic order based on equity, sovereign equality, interdependence, common interest and cooperation between all States, whatever their economic and social systems, to correct inequalities and mend present injustices should be urgently established – as the United Nations General Assembly has called for.

(u) It is necessary to promote social development through peaceful coexistence, friendly relations and cooperation between States with different social, economic or political systems.

(v) We must adopt actions that lead to the realization, as laid down in the United Nations Declaration on the Right to Development, of the fact that "the human person is the central subject of development and should be the active participant and beneficiary of the right to development".

Resolution concerning corporate social responsibility [9]

The General Conference of the International Labour Organization,

Noting that the Declaration of Philadelphia states that "the war against want requires to be carried on with unrelenting vigour within each nation, and by continuous and concerted international effort in which the representatives of workers and employers, enjoying equal status with those of governments, join with them in free discussion and democratic decision with a view to the promotion of the common welfare", and that "lasting peace can be established only if it is based upon social justice",

Noting that the ILO Expert Advisers in the introduction to the compilation of annual reports under the follow-up to the ILO Declaration of 1998 consider that "The reality in the world today is that since the Declaration came into operation in 2000, reports indicate that progress has been made in a number of countries […] The other reality is that […] there is growing poverty, inequalities in income, and new forms of discrimination". They go on to say that "Under these global conditions, millions of people are anxious to obtain work, preferably decent work. In this context, we are concerned that current economic situations

---

[9] The Workers' delegate from Peru, Mr. Gorriti, was the author of the resolution. At the time of receipt of the resolution, his credentials had not reached the Office or he was not accredited as a delegate.

and growing insecurity of employment will lead those who have power to flout the fundamental principles and rights at work",

Recognizing that the ILO has stated its conviction that "the advances made by multinational enterprises in organizing their operations beyond the national framework may lead to abuse of concentrations of economic power and to conflicts with national policy objectives and with the interests of workers",

Taking into account the fact that the enormous economic power accumulated in the hands of the more than 63,000 transnational enterprises, which is the result of the labour of the workers they employ, gives them a degree of influence such that they are able to determine the course of the current globalization process, which by virtue of its neo-liberal nature is producing the harmful effects experienced by workers, their families and peoples,

Considering that the United Nations Sub-Commission on the Promotion and Protection of Human Rights has expressed its support for draft norms on the responsibilities of transnational corporations and other business enterprises in view of the enormous importance of the activities of transnational corporations for the effective enjoyment of human, civil, political, economic, social and cultural rights,

Noting that the transnational corporations are a phenomenon of contemporary society of enormous importance which poses specific economic, financial, legal, social and human problems, and that not the least of those problems are their transnational character, their economic and legal versatility, their enormous economic and financial power and their considerable political and social influence, which are also major obstacles to any attempts to exercise legal and social control over them, and that this fact, together with the support given by some of the major powers, has enabled them to create a global network of standards that are contrary to national and international public law, in the form of bilateral treaties protecting foreign investment, regional treaties such as NAFTA and the proposed Free Trade Area of the Americas (FTAA), as well as the WTO,

Aware of the fact that failure to include legal persons and the economic and environmental crimes that come within the competence of the International Criminal Court, has left the transnational enterprises beyond the reach of said international jurisdiction, and that they nevertheless have an international arbitration body at their disposal within the World Bank system, namely, the International Centre for Settlement of Investment Disputes, which is headed by the President of the World Bank and whose basic texts include none that refer to human rights or environmental law, so that when certain States refuse to comply with the "liberalizing" demands of transnational capital embodied by the transnational companies, greater pressure is felt from the international financial bodies to settle any disputes on terms favourable to the transnational enterprises before a tribunal whose partiality in favour of private interests is beyond any doubt,

Taking into account the fact that the ILO's Tripartite Declaration of Principles concerning Multinational Enterprises and Social Policy is an instrument which urges these institutions to act with respect for the societies in which they operate,

Reaffirming that the transnational enterprises are legal persons under private law and, like all physical and legal persons, should respect the law which certainly includes current international standards in the area of human, civil, political, economic, social, cultural and environmental rights,

Observing that in practice it has been found that settlements that to some extent endorse the actions of transnational enterprises have no other result than to "soften" their image, without fundamentally affecting their nature and the objectives for which they were established and operate every day, as shown in an ILO study of some 215 codes of conduct and 12 social labelling programmes relating to labour practices in the light of the internationally recognized fundamental principles and rights, a study which has revealed that these codes were highly selective with regard to inclusion of such principles, so that for example the elimination of child labour figured in less than half the codes; wage levels were specified in fewer that 40 per cent; the elimination of forced labour and the refusal to use products or services from companies that exact forced labour were referred to in only one-quarter of the codes examined; while only 15 per cent of the codes of conduct examined by the ILO include references to freedom of association and the right to collective bargaining – which are fundamental to the development and functioning of trade unions. Furthermore, the study showed that more than a few of these codes sought to put an end to trade union activities in order to eliminate opponents of their exploitative labour policies. At the same time, the study referred to the fact that the content of the codes was often decided in non-transparent and non-participatory processes, in closed meetings of consultative councils or through negotiations between parties that were unequal in terms of information and negotiating strength. The study also concluded that it was not exceptional for a code launched with great publicity in an industrialized country to be unknown, unavailable or not to have been translated at the production or service centres of the transnational in question. In such cases, according to the ILO study, it was common for workers to have no access to the code or to be unable to read it or report infringements without running the risk of disciplinary sanctions,

Noting that the ability of transnationals to be present at various locations simultaneously, or at none, enables them to evade national jurisdictions,

Deploring the fact that security staff of transnationals, their suppliers, subcontractors and concession holders not infrequently act outside the company premises and become a private militia operating also in public areas,

Aware that the transnationals do not assume any responsibility for violations of labour law and environmental protection standards in countries to which they relocate their production, or any liability for any harm or damage they do, and indeed obtain guarantees from the host State of protection against any loss of profits caused by reforms to labour or environmental law, thus creating a major obstacle to progressive reforms in the human rights field,

Recognizing that many of the countries of origin of transnationals maintain that as regards the environment and industrial relations, it is not the transnationals that should be accountable for failure to comply with standards, even though it is the transnationals that cause disasters and exploit workers, but States for failing to assume responsibility for monitoring enforcement of law, which in effect gives transnationals absolute immunity in plundering resources and exploiting workers, as seen in the provisions relating to the proposed FTAA, since if that Agreement comes into effect no country will be able to hold transnationals to account for non-compliance with national standards or contracts, but transnationals will be able to hold countries to account if in their view they do not yield to their demands, a situation that will reduce the power of governments to collect taxes, which will also be affected by the elimination of tariffs and duties required under the FTAA,

Recognizing that efforts have been made to promote awareness of the Tripartite Declaration of Principles concerning Multinational Enterprises and Social Policy, including the work done by the international trade union organizations to promote respect for that Declaration, but that it is clear that there will be more support for this if the ILO seeks new and more practical methods to improve knowledge of the Tripartite Declaration on the basis of critical monitoring of its implementation,

Emphasizing that, for the trade union movement, it is essential to maintain and increase its opposition to anything in the activities of the transnational enterprises that affects the interests of workers and their families;

Affirms that:

(a) it is necessary to oppose more effectively the violations by transnational enterprises of rights won by oppressed workers, in many cases after painful and even bloody struggles over decades, in which cause a decisive contribution will be made by uniting the actions of the international trade union movement so as to force transnational enterprises to respect international standards relating to labour rights;

(b) such is the magnitude of the suffering caused by the activities of the transnational enterprises that there is an urgent need to move on from knowledge of the ILO's Tripartite Declaration to demanding in specific terms the application and observance of its provisions by those who currently disregard it;

(c) efforts have been made by various departments of the ILO to promote knowledge of the Tripartite Declaration but that new methods and practices have not yet been found on the scale required to improve knowledge of the Declaration. A wider knowledge of the Declaration should be promoted, based on critical monitoring of its implementation;

(d) it is important to go beyond simply raising awareness of the Tripartite Declaration. The objective of achieving compliance with the Tripartite Declaration would make it possible to promote the demand formulated in the document on future directions for the work of the Workers' group to channel efforts towards ensuring that transnationals conclude tripartite agreements in which they accept the obligation to indicate, in their annual reports, what they have done to apply the Declaration in practice, what they have done to ensure respect for the principal international labour standards especially Conventions Nos. 87 and 98, what progress they have made in recognition of trade union organizations, and what collective agreements they have concluded and how they are implementing them. This would promote the Declaration by ascertaining to what extent it was respected;

(e) sectoral activities – closer to the locations where things actually happen – should be reviewed to determine what are the activities of the transnationals and how in specific terms it is possible to promote respect for workers' interests, which would entail at the sector level regular reviews of the major disputes involving transnational enterprises, so that it may be determined whether such disputes are the result of failure to apply the Tripartite Declaration. On the basis of the knowledge obtained of developments, it would be possible, in coordination with ACTRAV, to organize sectoral seminars which could identify the situations of concern, which transnationals are involved, which national policies or trade union actions have given rise to them, and how to proceed at the trade union level to remedy these situations;

(f) the efforts should be directed in essence at reaching tripartite agreements in which the transnationals accept the obligation to indicate in their annual reports what they have done to ensure effective application of the Tripartite Declaration, and what they have done to ensure observance of the principal international labour standards of the ILO, especially Conventions Nos. 87 and 98. This would provide information on the extent to which each transnational complies with the Tripartite Declaration, enabling the trade unions to confront it with the facts and demand compliance;

(g) the ILO departments responsible for examining the conduct of the transnational enterprises should regularly review all the available information on the major labour disputes involving such enterprises and systematically determine whether such conflicts are the result of failure to apply the Tripartite Declaration, and inform the Governing Body of the ILO. Such studies could conveniently be complemented by efforts by ILO representatives to monitor the conduct of transnationals at workplaces. It would be advisable for information to be as decentralized as possible, and provided by studies carried out in each country by regional ILO offices in their areas of jurisdiction;

(h) the principle of social responsibility of the transnationals is crucial, in view of the habitual practice of externalizing costs and risks and the consequent assumption of liabilities by providers, subcontractors, concession holders and subsidiaries, while the principal enterprises make extraordinary profits;

(i) "social auditing" institutions should be established to monitor the social effects of economic decisions made by enterprises and governments, and that these institutions should present reports setting out their assessments to national parliaments and other elected bodies. A contribution to these initiatives could be made by the ILO departments responsible for analysing the conduct of transnationals;

(j) efforts must be made to counter the strategy of perpetuating impunity by transnational enterprises;

(k) the transnationals, their suppliers, subcontractors and concession holders and "other business enterprises" (*de jure* or *de facto* subsidiaries) must recognize the principle of the primacy of human rights and the public interest over private economic interests;

(l) the security staff of transnationals, their suppliers, subcontractors and concession holders and "other business enterprises" should not be able to act outside the company for which they work;

(m) support should be given to the suggestion made by the Europe-Third World Centre (CETIM) and the American Association of Jurists (AAJ) to the Commission on Human Rights to set up an open-ended working group, as proposed in resolution 2003/16 of the Sub-Commission on the Promotion and Protection of Human Rights, with a view to improving the draft norms on the responsibilities of transnational corporations, making good obvious omissions and ensuring follow-up;

(n) for the trade union movement it should be essential to maintain and increase its opposition to every aspect of the activities of transnationals which affects the interests of workers, and that its unity of action towards that end should be capable of forcing the transnationals to respect international standards with regard to labour rights;

(o) the United Nations should be called on to contribute effectively to ensuring that transnational companies respect human rights and are penalized for violating them.

Resolution concerning democratic values, good governance and transparency in a global economy and their impact on the world of work, competitiveness and sustainable development, submitted by the following Employers' delegates: Mr. Botha (South Africa); Mr. Eremeev (Russian Federation); Mr. Finlay (Canada); Mr. Huntjens (Netherlands); Mr. Potter (United States) and Mr. Tabani (Pakistan) [10]

The General Conference of the International Labour Organization,

Affirming that democratic values and principles are fundamental to effective governance,

Recognizing that the absence of an effective and responsive regulatory environment, respect of the rule of law and private property rights, fair and independent judicial processes and effective national governance structures that are transparent, free of corruption, democratic and above all genuinely serve the public interest, is a major obstacle to investment and thus deprives countries and their working people of the benefits of globalization, including increased productivity and improved standards of living,

Confirming that there is now a consensus that a system of governance that incorporates democratic values and the principles of the market economy offers the best chance of promoting political, social and economic well-being for all,

Noting that democracy is most vulnerable if it is not seen to improve the lives of people,

Acknowledging that some governments, in spite of their efforts, may lack the capacity in terms of effective administrative, legal, educational, judicial and enforcement systems and may not have the expertise to draft effective implementing legislation as well as the administrative institutions or the human resources necessary to put good governance practices into operation,

Taking into account that the report of the ILO's World Commission on the Social Dimension of Globalization recognized that "globalization starts at home" and that the need for good governance and democracy is the key to providing the environment that will enable globalization to work for all,

Calling upon the governments of member States and, where applicable, employers' and workers' organizations:

– At the institutional level, to advocate the importance of good institutional governance of member States, enterprises, workers' and employers' organizations and non-governmental organizations.

– At the national level, to foster the effective participation of employers' and workers' organizations in national policy formulation and implementation, as these organizations are advocates for participatory, transparent and accountable governance; to promote social dialogue between employers' and workers'

---

[10] The following Employers' delegates: Mr. Ferrer Dufol (Spain) and Mr. Lima Godoy (Brazil), were among the authors of the resolution. At the time of receipt of the resolution, their credentials had not reached the Office or they were not accredited as delegates.

organizations; and to remove any obstacles to the growth of representative organizations of employers and workers.

- At the global level, to advocate the importance of increased effectiveness within the international multilateral system through better coordination and management, noting in particular the importance of good governance throughout all the international organizations of the multilateral system;

Requests the Governing Body of the International Labour Office to instruct the Director-General to:

(a) use the ILO's expertise – in collaboration with other international institutions – to assist countries in formulating appropriate policies that strengthen and improve their governance, in order to draw benefits from globalization and attract investment, promote business growth, and as a consequence create an appropriate environment for enterprises and employment creation;

(b) offer the ILO's education and skill development expertise to assist countries in improving their human resources development policies as well as their knowledge of the democratic values and good governance principles which are essential in order to deliver a better globalization for all;

(c) discuss and find the best way to give effect to this resolution in the context of future Governing Body debates on the report of the World Commission on the Social Dimension of Globalization and its follow-up.

Resolution concerning the promotion of gender equality, submitted by the Government delegations of Denmark, Finland, Iceland, Norway and Sweden

The General Conference of the International Labour Organization,

Recalling the Equal Remuneration Convention, 1951 (No. 100), the Discrimination (Employment and Occupation) Convention, 1958 (No. 111), the Maternity Protection Convention, 2000 (No. 183), the Workers with Family Responsibilities Convention, 1981 (No. 156), and the principles enshrined in other relevant Conventions,

Reaffirming the ILO Declaration on Fundamental Principles and Rights at Work and its Follow-up (1998), and the importance of ratification and implementation of ILO core Conventions covering prohibition of forced and child labour, freedom of association and the right to collective bargaining as well as the principles of non-discrimination and equal remuneration,

Recalling the United Nations Convention on the Elimination of All Forms of Discrimination against Women, in particular its article 11 on elimination of discrimination against women in the labour market,

Recalling the Decent Work Agenda as well as the Global Employment Agenda which aim at promoting productive, inclusive and equitable change so that women's work, as well as men's, is fully acknowledged and rewarded and economic efficiency is balanced with gender equality,

Recalling the United Nations Millennium Goals,

Taking into consideration the Beijing Declaration and the Platform for Action adopted at the Fourth World Conference on Women, and the convening of the 23rd Special

Session of the General Assembly entitled "Women 2000: Gender equality, development and peace in the twenty-first century" (Beijing+5) and the "World Summit for Social Development and beyond: Achieving social development for all in a globalizing world" (Copenhagen+5) and the ILO's contribution in this regard,

Recognizing the ILO's work on the social dimension of globalization and giving full support to the follow-up to the report of the World Commission on the Social Dimension of Globalization,

Considering also the need for the ILO to take stock of global developments in order to update ILO policy and to determine priority areas for the ILO's work in promoting gender equality goals as well as the importance of collection and dissemination of knowledge, research, statistics and best practices in this field,

Recognizing that although progress in this field has taken place, a number of imbalances and gaps continue to exist and call for intensified and continued efforts to dismantle sex segregation and other barriers to gender equality in the labour market,

Concerned that gender gaps in earnings persist despite the fact that many countries have adopted equal pay legislation,

Alarmed that poverty and social exclusion increasingly afflict girls and women, and deeply concerned that in many countries, women workers are disproportionately faced with unemployment, income insecurity and poor working conditions,

Welcoming the ILO's four strategic objectives and recognizing that one of the primary goals of the ILO today is to promote equal opportunities for women and men,

Welcoming also the ILO's efforts to ensure that gender aspects are integrated into all ILO activities and programmes in accordance with the mainstreaming principle as well as the gender-audit which is presently being conducted;

1. Calls upon all governments and social partners to actively commit themselves – in their respective fields of competence:

(a) to eliminate all forms of gender discrimination on the labour market and to promote gender equality between women and men; and to this end:

   (i) develop gender-sensitive national employment policies which guarantee women and men equal access to employment and equal pay, training and career development and which take into consideration the need to eliminate gender segregation on the labour market and to dismantle all barriers which prevent women from obtaining economic autonomy as a result of their labour market participation on an equal footing with men;

   (ii) develop gender-sensitive national policies to stimulate entrepreneurship and business creation at all levels, also in the informal sector, and to ensure that both women and men have access on equal terms to capital, including land, other financial resources, financial services and counselling;

   (iii) eliminate pay differences based on sex;

   (iv) ensure a safe and sound working environment for both women and men;

   (v) promote measures to better reconcile work and family life;

(vi) develop gender-sensitive social security schemes;

(vii) develop a social dialogue which will promote the representation of women at all levels of decision-making in working life;

(viii) ensure that the gender aspect is taken into consideration in labour market regulation whether such regulation takes the form of legislation or collective agreements – making use of the mainstreaming strategy;

(ix) promote the participation of women and men on equal terms in working life as well as in civil life at all levels;

(b) to promote the ratification and implementation of ILO core Conventions and to give special attention to the promotion of the principles enshrined in other relevant ILO Conventions and in this connection:

2. Invites the Governing Body of the International Labour Organization to instruct the Director-General:

(a) to continue, strengthen and accelerate the efforts to achieve the objective of equality between women and men and equal opportunities in working life at all levels, and to this end:

(i) vigorously continue its work with the Action Plan on Gender Equality;

(ii) make use of the mainstreaming strategy in all walks of gender-sensitive policies related to the labour market;

(iii) take fully into account the need for the ILO to continue to actively follow up on the Platform for Action adopted at the United Nations Fourth World Conference on Women and the outcome of the 23rd Special Session of the General Assembly (Beijing+5) as well as the World Summit for Social Development and the outcome of the 24th Special Session of the General Assembly (Copenhagen+5);

(iv) introduce benchmarking and monitoring systems, indicators and mechanisms in all programmes and activities, including standard setting, to promote gender equality and equal opportunities;

(v) promote the collection, processing and dissemination of up-to-date gender-sensitive knowledge, studies and research, including best practices in this field, as well as the production of reliable data and analyses of labour market developments and trends broken down on gender;

(b) to ensure the necessary financial resources by:

(i) allocating sufficient funds within the framework of the regular budget for activities and projects to promote equality between women and men and equal opportunities; and

(ii) identifying appropriate funding for technical cooperation to ensure the maximum effects and impact of gender-sensitive projects and programmes in the member countries;

(c) to report back to the Governing Body on the implementation of this resolution.

Resolution concerning the fourth anniversary of the Maternity Protection Convention, 2000 (No. 183) [11]

The General Conference of the International Labour Organization,

Recalling that this year marks the fourth anniversary of the Maternity Protection Convention, 2000 (No. 183),

Noting the provisions of the Universal Declaration of Human Rights (1948), of the United Nations Convention on the Elimination of All Forms of Discrimination Against Women (1979), the United Nations Convention on the Rights of the Child (1989), the ILO Declaration on Equality of Opportunity and Treatment for Women Workers (1975), the Beijing Declaration and Platform for Action (1995), the ILO Declaration on Fundamental Principles and Rights at Work and its Follow-up (1998) and of the international labour Conventions and Recommendations aimed at ensuring equality of opportunity and treatment for men and women workers, in particular the Workers with Family Responsibilities Convention, 1981 (No. 156),

Recalling article 16 of the Universal Declaration of Human Rights, which clearly stipulates that the family is the natural and fundamental group unit of society and is entitled to protection by society and the State,

Noting with concern that only eight member States have ratified Convention No. 183,

Condemning the numerous violations of rights related to maternity and health protection to which women are subjected in many countries,

Considering that globalization and its corollary, deregulation, are new sources of discrimination and threats to the right to maternity protection,

Concerned about the lack of maternity protection for certain categories of workers, such as women employed in informal activities in export processing zones, women migrant workers, domestic workers, women with disabilities and those belonging to ethnic minorities,

Recognizing the ILO's essential contribution to defending maternity protection,

Convinced of the need to respect maternity protection rights in all situations and forms of employment;

1. Calls on all member States, in consultation with employers' and workers' organizations:

(a) to mark this anniversary by taking urgent steps to ratify the Maternity Protection Convention, 2000 (No. 183), if they have not already done so;

(b) to ensure the effective application of the Convention;

---

[11] The following Workers' delegates: Mr. Cortebeeck (Belgium) and Mr. Allini (Gabon), were the authors of the resolution. At the time of receipt of the resolution, their credentials had not reached the Office or they were not accredited as delegates.

(c) to ensure that maternity protection rights are fully respected in every sector, including export processing zones;

(d) to protect maternity protection rights at every stage in the production and service chain, including subcontractors, as well as during and after restructuring exercises;

(e) to guarantee that all workers enjoy the right to maternity protection, including domestic workers and migrant workers, and in particular those in the informal economy;

(f) to design education programmes for the social partners on the provisions of the Convention.

2. Invites the Governing Body and the Director-General of the International Labour Office:

(a) to launch a campaign for the promotion and ratification of the Convention;

(b) to increase financial and technical support to workers' organizations seeking to strengthen their capacity for the promotion and defence of maternity protection rights;

(c) to increase, if necessary, the financial and human resources allocated to the branch in charge of maternity protection in the International Labour Office;

(d) to step up ILO action in the field of training related to maternity protection.

Resolution concerning the role of the ILO in conflict prevention and resolution [12]

The General Conference of the International Labour Organization,

Noting the principles contained in the Universal Declaration of Human Rights,

Recalling the Declaration of Philadelphia, which provides that all human beings, irrespective of race, creed or sex, have the right to pursue both their material well-being and their spiritual development in conditions of freedom and dignity, of economic security and equal opportunity,

Recalling the Preamble to the ILO Constitution, which states that universal and lasting peace can be established only if it is based upon social justice,

Concerned about the growing incidence of poverty, social exclusion and the decent job deficit and the spread of atypical forms of employment, as well as the attendant threats of insecurity, intolerance, instability and violence,

Recalling that poverty anywhere constitutes a danger to prosperity everywhere, as stated in the Declaration of Philadelphia,

Noting that women, children and workers are the first to suffer from situations of conflict or war,

---

[12] The following Workers' delegates: Mr. Cortebeeck (Belgium) and Mr. Allini (Gabon), were the authors of the resolution. At the time of receipt of the resolution, their credentials had not reached the Office or they were not accredited as delegates.

Noting that conflicts are one of the key factors giving rise to migration movements, very often in inhuman conditions,

Concerned about the medium- and long-term impact of conflicts on the political, social and economic stability of States,

Emphasizing the economic, financial and social difficulties faced by these countries in the peace-building and reconstruction phase, in particular by their bodies responsible for the administration of employment, health, social security and education,

Recalling that war and armed conflict open the way for all kinds of abuse and human rights violations, jeopardizing decent work in every respect, with a detrimental impact on global economic growth, human resources and social security, health care and education systems,

Recognizing that any dispute between States or within a State should be settled through dialogue and consultation in the framework of national or international mechanisms and in accordance with human rights principles;

1. Invites governments of member States, in consultation with employers' and workers' organizations:

(a) to make every effort to ensure that social dialogue and social justice constitute the cornerstone of relations between States and within States;

(b) to use every available means to combat poverty and social exclusion effectively and offset the jobs deficit;

(c) to this end, to ensure greater policy convergence at national, regional and international levels;

(d) to use every peaceful means available through the United Nations and its specialized agencies for the settlement of national and international disputes.

2. Invites the Governing Body and the Director-General of the International Labour Office:

(a) to use every means available to the ILO to contribute to the debate on world peace and conflict prevention;

(b) to strengthen the ILO's InFocus Programme on Crisis Response and Reconstruction;

(c) to increase technical and financial support to countries affected by armed conflict or war under the InFocus Programme on Crisis Response and Reconstruction;

(d) to enhance the promotion of the Decent Work Agenda in all national and international policies, including economic and financial policy, as a key element of conflict prevention and resolution.

Resolution concerning corporate social responsibility [13]

The General Conference of the International Labour Organization,

Reaffirming the importance of the tripartite nature of the ILO, which, among all the international agencies, provides the only framework within which governments and representatives of employers' and workers' organizations may freely and openly confront one another's ideas, compare their experience and promote mechanisms for permanent consultation,

Concerned about the many violations of workers' rights, including fundamental rights, that persist in enterprises, in particular multinational enterprises and their subcontractors,

Recalling that corporate social responsibility, as pointed out by the report of the World Commission on the Social Dimension of Globalization, refers to "the voluntary initiatives enterprises undertake over and above their legal obligations. It is a way by which any enterprise can consider its impact on all relevant stakeholders",

Recalling further that corporate social responsibility "is a complement to, not a substitute for, government regulation or social policy",

Having regard to the pressures on States' social policy and regulation and with respect to the ILO's standards,

Given the proliferation of initiatives based on private standards and private monitoring of such standards, bypassing a system based on legal, contractual and binding agreements and on transparent, independent and impartial monitoring mechanisms,

Concerned to strengthen democracy at work and social dialogue,

Supporting the proposal put forward by the World Commission on the Social Dimension of Globalization which calls on the ILO, with its tripartite composition, to take its unique place for research, dialogue and policy development on the issues related to corporate social responsibility,

Supporting the proposal put forward by the World Commission on the Social Dimension of Globalization to convene a forum to develop a practical agenda around the contribution of business to the social dimension of globalization,

Welcoming the increasing number of "framework agreements" between global union federations and multinational enterprises;

1. Requests the International Labour Office:

(a) to ensure that corporate social responsibility is monitored as widely and as deeply as possible through databases, thematic analyses and comparative evaluations with the ILO's normative system. Without giving preference to one activity or experience over another, the ILO should contribute to analyses and debates, in the light of the criteria provided by the normative system, reports on the application of standards by the

---

[13] The following Workers' delegates: Mr. Cortebeeck (Belgium) and Mr. Allini (Gabon), were the authors of the resolution. At the time of receipt of the resolution, their credentials had not reached the Office or they were not accredited as delegates.

Committee of Experts on the Application of Conventions and Recommendations, and the case law of the Governing Body;

(b) to strengthen discussion and follow-up on this debate with its constituents on this issue:

  (i) by improving supervisory tools and procedures,

  (ii) by supporting sectoral operations, including those involving supply chains;

  (iii) by enhancing its technical assistance towards rehabilitating labour administration services in many countries;

  (iv) by increasing its technical cooperation activities in this area with its constituents, in particular with all the trade union organizations,

  (v) by stepping up its educational activities with the economic and social actors on legislative and contractual modes of regulation, including at the international level;

  (vi) by further developing discussions and, on that basis, defining a policy taking account of developments with regard to international framework agreements;

  (vii) by consulting before taking decisions;

(c) to consider the possibility of the ILO becoming the venue for registration of enterprise or corporate framework agreements and for the establishment of an international labour inspection system.

2. Requests the Governing Body to place the abovementioned points on its agenda.

3. Requests the International Labour Office to play a strategic role in setting up and coordinating the corporate social responsibility forum proposed by the World Commission on the Social Dimension of Globalization, which will follow the ILO's tripartite structure while being open to partnership with other civil society actors.

CONTENTS

Page

Resolutions:

Resolution concerning the strengthening of the role of the ILO in supporting workers and employers in Palestine and the other occupied Arab territories as a result of continued Israeli occupation and aggressive practices 1

Resolution concerning the role of the ILO in efforts to secure global peace, justice and security around the world 3

Resolution concerning pay equity 5

Resolution concerning the ILO's efforts to combat poverty 7

Resolution concerning the social responsibilities of business 9

Resolution concerning the application of international labour standards to international civil servants 11

Resolution concerning older workers and employment and social protection 11

Resolution concerning peace 13

Resolution concerning gender-equal pay 14

Resolution concerning poverty 16

Resolution concerning corporate social responsibility 21

Resolution concerning democratic values, good governance and transparency in a global economy and their impact on the world of work, competitiveness and sustainable development 26

Resolution concerning the promotion of gender equality 27

Resolution concerning the fourth anniversary of the Maternity Protection Convention, 2000 (No. 183) 30

Resolution concerning the role of the ILO in conflict prevention and resolution 31

Resolution concerning corporate social responsibility 33

No. 1 – Friday, 21 May 2004

International Labour Conference

Provisional Record 2

Ninety-second Session, Geneva, 2004

Standing Orders questions

Note concerning standing orders questions submitted by the Governing Body of the International Labour Office at the 92nd Session of the Conference

1. At its 289th Session (March 2004), the Governing Body recommended that the Conference, for a trial period of at least three years, replace the provisions of its Standing Orders concerning the Credentials Committee with the new provisions reproduced in the appendix.[1] These provisions are the result of a process of deliberation requested by the Credentials Committee at the 90th and 91st Sessions of the Conference with a view to improving its work and effectiveness.[2]

A. Purpose of the proposed interim provisions

2. The interim provisions proposed to the Conference are intended to strengthen the control and monitoring functions of the Credentials Committee in order to ensure that constitutional obligations regarding the appointment of Conference delegations are adhered to, on the one hand, and to enable the Committee to examine objections concerning incomplete delegations, on the other. These provisions are also accompanied by a number of practical measures which the Governing Body has asked the Office to adopt.

(a) Strengthening the control and monitoring functions

3. According to the Standing Orders of the Conference, when the Credentials Committee considers that the credentials of a delegate or adviser have not been established in a manner consistent with constitutional obligations, the sole means available to it to ensure that those obligations are met is to propose the invalidation of the credentials in question. This mechanism has certain limitations and drawbacks, both juridical and practical, which have prompted the Governing Body to propose strengthening of the powers of the

---

[1] GB.289/11.

[2] ILO: Third report of the Credentials Committee, International Labour Conference, 90th Session, *Provisional Record* No. 5D; Second report, International Labour Conference, 91st Session, *Provisional Record* No. 5C. As regards examination of the question by the Governing Body, see also the following Governing Body documents: GB.286/LILS/3, GB.286/13/1, GB.288/LILS/4, GB.288/10/1 and GB.289/LILS/1/1.

Conference, through the Credentials Committee, to monitor situations deemed to be not in conformity with article 3 of the Constitution of the ILO.

4. For the purpose of this monitoring, the Governing Body recommended introducing a means of referring objections presented to the Credentials Committee to the Committee on Freedom of Association in cases where what is alleged in the complaint concerns observance of the principles of freedom of association. The Governing Body also recommended that the Conference be authorized to request reports on a year-by-year basis from governments concerned by an objection or complaint.

5. In order to ensure that any recourse to these mechanisms has a sufficiently broad tripartite basis, the procedure proposed by the Governing Body provides that such an initiative should be taken by the Credentials Committee only in cases where there is unanimous agreement for this within the Committee. In addition, any unanimous recommendation by the Credentials Committee must also be approved by a decision of the Conference.

6. As regards specifically the possibility of referring an objection to the Committee on Freedom of Association during the March meeting of the Governing Body,[3] the Governing Body considered that any such referral should in addition be subject to the condition that the case has not already been examined by the Committee on Freedom of Association. That condition has therefore been added to the draft of the proposed new interim provisions reproduced in the appendix.

(b) The mandate of the Credentials Committee as regards incomplete delegations

7. Under the terms of article 3 of the Constitution, at every session of the Conference, each member State is required to appoint a complete tripartite delegation that is representative of the tripartite actors of the country concerned. While the Credentials Committee does, under the terms of the Standing Orders, have the power to examine objections regarding the representativeness of a given delegate or adviser, its mandate does not include examination of the possible reasons in certain cases for the absence of an Employers' or Workers' representative from a particular delegation. This is because its mandate as defined under articles 5 and 26 of the Conference Standing Orders is limited to examination of objections "concerning the appointment of a delegate or adviser" whose name and functions are indicated in the credentials of the member State in question.

8. In order to fill this gap, the Credentials Committee requested that its mandate be worded to include an express reference to complaints based on failure to designate the Employers' or Workers' delegate in a national delegation. This is the purpose of the interim provisions proposed by the Governing Body under article 5, paragraph 2(b) and article 26, paragraph 1(a).

(c) Practical measures

9. In proposing the aforementioned legal provisions, the Governing Body has decided to link them to a series of practical measures which require no changes to the Standing Orders.

---

[3] See 333rd Report of the Committee on Freedom of Association, GB.289/9, Part I, paras. 11-13.

10. The first of these measures is intended to ensure that the Credentials Committee is able to begin its work earlier on in the Conference. It involves bringing forward the date of publication of the list of delegations, from which the deadline for the presentation of objections is calculated. Under the terms of article 26 of the Standing Orders, for an objection to be receivable, it must be lodged within 72 hours of publication of the name and function of the individual to whose nomination objection is taken in the provisional list of delegations published on the opening day of the Conference, or within 48 hours following publication of the delegate's name in the revised or final list appearing on the seventh and penultimate days, respectively, of the Conference. It often happens that objections are received just before the deadline, that is on the first Friday of the Conference or on the second (for practical reasons the Credentials Committee cannot examine objections that appear for the first time in the final list). Given that examination of an objection can begin only after the reply from the government concerned has been received, and that the government has at least two days to prepare its reply, the Committee cannot begin its examination before the beginning of the second or third week of the Conference, depending on whether the objection concerns credentials appearing in the first or second list.

11. In order to allow the Credential Committee more time to examine cases referred to it, the Governing Body at its 289th Session (March 2004) requested that, from the 92nd Session of the Conference onwards, publication of the lists be brought forward by one week. Starting this year, the Office will publish a preliminary official list one week before the opening of the Conference. Given that the delegations will not yet be in Geneva, the Office will see to it that the list is widely distributed through the secretariats of the groups and the permanent missions of member States in Geneva, and also by publishing it online on the ILO web site. The period of 72 hours provided for in article 26 will therefore begin one week before the opening of the session, so that governments cited in objections can be invited immediately to give their response. The Credentials Committee will thus have complete case files at its disposal as soon as it is appointed. A preliminary revised list will be published the day after the opening session of the Conference, a second on the Wednesday of the second week and the final list will as usual be published the day before the Conference closes.

12. The other practical measures approved by the Governing Body are intended to improve the visibility of the Credentials Committee and its means of action. There are two such measures, namely:

   – Publication of a detailed information brochure on the role, functions and practice of the Credentials Committee. This is intended to be sent as an attachment to the invitations to each session of the Conference. It is intended that it should be ready for the invitation to the 93rd Session of the Conference and will include a reference to the interim changes that may be adopted by the Conference during the 2004 session.

   – Development of a data bank containing the reports of the Credentials Committee from previous sessions of the Conference. An initial version containing the reports of the 30 previous sessions of the Conference in English, French and Spanish should be available on the ILO public web site during 2004.

B. Practical arrangements

13. The Governing Body considered that any change should be made on an interim basis so that there would be no need for definitive amendments to the Standing Orders until the amendments had been evaluated and, where appropriate, adjusted. In view of the

disadvantages and constraints associated with the procedure for suspending provisions of the Standing Orders provided for in article 76, the Governing Body considered that the Conference could adopt a number of provisions in the place of existing ones for a predetermined period of three years. At the end of that period, the provisions would lapse automatically unless the Conference took a decision to renew them, it being understood that the Conference could also modify or annul them at any time.

14. If the Conference adopts the proposed provisions on these conditions, they will come into effect from the 93rd Session of the Conference in June 2005 and will remain in force, in the absence of any decision to the contrary by the Conference, until the end of the Conference in June 2007, after which the Governing Body will have to evaluate the system with a view to reporting to the Conference in June 2008.

15. In order to avoid the confusion that might, during that period, arise from the coexistence of two sets of provisions (those in the Standing Orders that are not formally abrogated or suspended, and the interim provisions intended to replace them for a certain period), the annex should be published separately with a view to being published with the Constitution of the ILO and the Standing Orders of the Conference.

Appendix

Interim provisions concerning verification of credentials, effective from the 93rd Session (June 2005) to the 96th Session (June 2007) of the International Labour Conference

INTERNATIONAL LABOUR CONFERENCE
VERIFICATION OF CREDENTIALS

ARTICLE 5

Credentials Committee

1. The Conference shall, on the nomination of the Selection Committee, appoint a Credentials Committee consisting of one Government delegate, one Employers' delegate and one Workers' delegate.

2. The Credentials Committee shall examine, in accordance with the provisions of section B of Part II:

(a) the credentials of persons accredited to the Conference;

(b) any objection relating to the credentials of delegates and their advisers or to failure to deposit credentials of an Employers' or Workers' delegate;

(c) any complaint of non-observance of paragraph 2(a) of article 13 of the Constitution;

(d) the monitoring of any situation with regard to observance of the provisions of article 3 or article 13, paragraph 2(a), of the Constitution about which the Conference has requested a report.

PART II

Standing Orders concerning special subjects

SECTION B

Verification of credentials

ARTICLE 26

Examination of credentials

1. The credentials of delegates and their advisers and of all other accredited members of the delegation of a member State shall be deposited with the International Labour Office at least 15 days before the date fixed for the opening of the session of the Conference.

2. A brief report upon these credentials shall be drawn up by the Chairman of the Governing Body. It shall, with the credentials, be made available for inspection on the day before the opening of the session of the Conference and shall be published on the day of the opening of the session.

3. The Credentials Committee appointed by the Conference in pursuance of article 5 of the Standing Orders of the Conference shall consider the credentials, as well as any appeal, objection, complaint or report concerning them.

ARTICLE 26BIS

Objections

1. An objection in pursuance of article 5, paragraph 2(b), shall not be receivable in the following cases:

(a) if the objection is not lodged with the Secretary-General within 72 hours from 10 a.m. of the date of publication of the official list of delegations on the basis of which the objection to the inclusion or exclusion of the name and function of a person is submitted. If the objection is based on a revised list, the time limit shall be reduced to 48 hours;

(b) if the authors of the objection remain anonymous;

(c) if the author of the objection is serving as adviser to the delegate to whose nomination objection is taken;

(d) if the objection is based upon facts or allegations which the Conference, by a debate and a decision referring to identical facts or allegations, has already discussed and recognized to be irrelevant or devoid of substance.

2. The procedure for the determination of whether an objection is receivable shall be as follows:

(a) the Credentials Committee shall consider in respect of each objection whether on any of the grounds set forth in paragraph 1 the objection is irreceivable;

(b) if the Committee reaches a unanimous conclusion concerning the receivability of the objection, its decision shall be final;

(c) if the Credentials Committee does not reach a unanimous conclusion concerning the receivability of the objection, it shall refer the matter to the Conference which shall, on being furnished with a record of the Committee's discussions and with a report setting forth the opinion of the majority and minority of its members, decide without further discussion whether the objection is receivable.

3. The Credentials Committee shall consider whether every objection deemed to be receivable is well founded and shall as a matter of urgency submit a report thereon to the Conference.

4. If the Credentials Committee or any member thereof submits a report advising that the Conference should refuse to admit any delegate or adviser, the President shall submit this proposal to the Conference for decision, and the Conference, if it deems that the delegate or adviser has not been nominated in conformity with the requirements of the Constitution, may, in accordance with paragraph 9 of article 3 thereof, refuse by two-thirds of the votes cast by the delegates present to admit the delegate or adviser. Delegates who are in favour of refusing to admit the delegate or adviser shall vote "Yes"; delegates who are opposed to refusing to admit the delegate or adviser shall vote "No".

5. Pending final decision of the question of his admission, any delegate or adviser to whose nomination objection has been taken shall have the same rights as other delegates and advisers.

6. If the Credentials Committee considers unanimously that the issues raised by an objection relate to a violation of the principles of freedom of association which has not already been examined by the Governing Body's Committee on Freedom of Association, it may propose referral of the question to that Committee. The Conference shall decide, without discussion, on such proposals for referral.

7. When, in the light of the examination of an objection, the Credentials Committee unanimously considers that it is necessary to monitor the situation, it may propose this to the Conference, which shall decide, without discussion, on the proposal. If it is so decided, the

Government concerned shall report on such questions that the Credentials Committee judges necessary, to the subsequent session of the Conference when it submits the delegation's credentials.

ARTICLE 26TER

Complaints

1. The Credentials Committee may consider complaints that a Member has failed to comply with paragraph 2(a) of article 13 of the Constitution where:

(a) the Member is alleged to have failed to pay the travelling and subsistence expenses of one or more of the delegates that it has nominated in accordance with article 3, paragraph 1, of the Constitution; or

(b) the complaint alleges a serious and manifest imbalance as between the number of Employer or Worker advisers whose expenses have been covered in the delegation concerned and the number of advisers appointed for the Government delegates.

2. A complaint referred to in paragraph 1 shall not be receivable in the following cases:

(a) if the complaint is not lodged with the Secretary-General of the Conference before 10 a.m. on the seventh day following the opening of the Conference and the Committee considers that there is insufficient time to deal with it properly; or

(b) if the complaint is not lodged by an accredited delegate or adviser alleging non-payment of travel and subsistence expenses in the circumstances set out under (a) or (b) of paragraph 1 or by an organization or person acting on his or her behalf.

3. The Credentials Committee shall, in its report, present to the Conference any conclusions that it has unanimously reached on each complaint considered by it.

4. When, in the light of the examination of an objection, the Credentials Committee unanimously considers that it is necessary to monitor the situation, it may propose this to the Conference, which shall decide, without discussion, on the proposal. If it is so decided, the Government concerned shall report on such questions that the Credentials Committee judges necessary, to the subsequent session of the Conference when it submits the delegation's credentials.

ARTICLE 26QUATER

Monitoring

The Credentials Committee also monitors any situation relating to respect by a member State for the provisions of articles 3 or 13(2)(a) of the Constitution with regard to which the Conference has requested the government concerned to report. With this objective, the Committee shall report to the Conference on the evolution of the situation. It may unanimously propose any one of the measures contained in paragraphs 4 to 7 of article 26bis or paragraphs 3 and 4 of article 26ter. The Conference shall decide, without discussion, on such proposals.

CONTENTS

Page

Standing Orders questions

A. Purpose of the proposed interim provisions 1

B. Practical arrangements 3

Appendix 5

International Labour Conference

Provisional Record

Ninety-second Session, Geneva, 2004

Report of the Chairperson of the Governing Body to the Conference for the year 2003-04

This report on the work of the Governing Body is submitted to the Conference in accordance with article 14 of the Standing Orders of the Governing Body. It covers the period since the last general session of the Conference (June 2003), i.e., the Governing Body's 287th (June 2003), 288th (November 2003) and 289th (March 2004) Sessions. It focuses only on the highlights of the Governing Body's year, and does not cover matters that are otherwise before the Conference.

Those seeking more extensive and detailed information on the work of the Governing Body as a whole are referred to the notes at the end of the report. They may also consult the minutes of its 287th, 288th and 289th Sessions (June and November 2003; March 2004) or the documents submitted to its committees and to the Governing Body itself. Other relevant material, as well as the reports and other Governing Body documents mentioned in the text and in the endnotes, are available on the Governing Body Internet site. [1]

I. ILO Declaration on Fundamental Principles and Rights at Work

Compilation of annual reports

In the fifth annual review under the follow-up to the ILO Declaration, the Governing Body engaged in a discussion on the basis of the compilation of reports prepared by the Office [2] and the Introduction of the ILO Declaration Expert-Advisers. [3] The Governing Body acted upon a number of observations made by the Expert-Advisers and engaged in a more in-depth discussion of certain aspects of the reports. In particular, it called upon the Office to develop further the means for countries to assess their progress in moving towards fuller realization of the fundamental principles and rights at work; to expand upon the positive measures taken by the Gulf Cooperation Council (GCC) countries; and to engage further with those countries which have never reported (Afghanistan, Kyrgyzstan, Sierra Leone, Solomon Islands and Somalia) and assist further those that are able to report only irregularly, such as the Lao People's Democratic Republic.

The Governing Body again drew the attention of national and international employers' and workers' organizations to the need for them to provide comments under the Declaration's annual review, and asked them to make special efforts to promote and facilitate the organization of workers and their engagement in collective bargaining, as regards those that tend to be excluded from enjoying the Declaration principles and rights.

These include agricultural workers, workers in export processing zones, migrant workers, domestic workers, workers in the informal economy and some workers in the public sector.

Technical cooperation activities

In November 2003 the Committee on Technical Cooperation examined and approved the *Priorities and action plans for technical cooperation* under the Declaration, which focused on eliminating discrimination in employment and occupation. [4] This action plan, which was submitted by the Office in follow up to the Global Report on non-discrimination in the workplace, *Time for equality at work*, aims to raise the coherence, visibility and impact of the ILO's action and to achieve measurable results between 2004 and 2007, when the next Global Report on the subject is due. The main thrusts of the action plan to eliminate discrimination are: (a) racial/ethnic discrimination at work and development, with attention to its gender dimensions; and (b) equal remuneration between genders and racial/ethnic groups.

Discussion of the Global Report

The Governing Body approved ad hoc arrangements for the discussion of this year's Global Report on 10 June 2004. [5]

II. Child labour

Through the established practice of dual reporting, the Governing Body examined the work of the InFocus Programme on Child Labour (IPEC) during the 2002-03 biennium, and in particular in 2003. In November 2003, the Governing Body received an oral report by the Executive Director for Standards and Fundamental Principles and Rights at Work, as well as an advance copy of IPEC's comprehensive report on action and future priorities regarding child labour. The discussions were continued during the Governing Body's session in March 2004, based on the final IPEC report on its activities undertaken during the biennium.

Follow-up to the June 2002 discussion of the ILO
Global Report: *A future without child labour*

The Action Plan to Abolish Child Labour, discussed and endorsed by the Governing Body in March 2003, was based on IPEC's experience and reflected a shift in strategy. Its main components include a new focus on the worst forms of child labour, the promotion of national initiative and ownership, and the generation of reliable information on child labour, as well as global and broad-based partnerships. Further to this Action Plan, the Governing Body has been kept informed of the activities pursued, in particular by IPEC. The celebration of the *World Day against Child Labour* to commemorate the Conference debate on 12 June 2002 has now become established as an annual campaign event to be organized by the Office and its field structure worldwide, with a selected theme each year, the theme for 2004 being "Child domestic labour".

IPEC action against child labour 2002-03: Progress and future priorities

During the biennium, IPEC continued to intensify its programme to support large-scale, innovative interventions by governments, the social partners and other concerned groups to combat child labour, especially its worst forms, as a matter of urgency. In addition to the target-specific achievements described under the following section, some of the main progress is covered here.

For 2003, IPEC programme expenditure reached US$47.2 million, bringing the total for the biennium to US$88.1 million. This represents an increase of approximately US$31.8 million or 56 per cent over the preceding biennium. The Time-Bound Programme (TBP) approach has been further developed. The concepts, explanations and advice on the many facets of TBPs are elaborated further in the recently published TBP MAP (*Manual for Action Planning*) Kit. During the biennium, IPEC began several networking initiatives as an additional cost-efficient modality to disseminate the message and methodologies. IPEC also continued to reply to the demand from member States for technical assistance in carrying out child labour surveys, and to raise the profile of the fight against child labour through its two major global awareness campaigns: *Red Card to Child Labour* and SCREAM (*Supporting Children's Rights through Education, the Arts and the Media*).

IPEC's research base was also strengthened further to support interventions and to broaden the child labour knowledge base. Research projects carried out during the biennium included those on HIV/AIDS and the special situation of girls in child labour. In early 2004, IPEC published a report entitled: *Investing in every child: An economic study of the costs and benefits of eliminating child labour*, to help reinforce the economic argument against child labour by showing that the benefits of eliminating child labour largely outweigh the costs in the long run.

IPEC's achievements relative to targets for the biennium

Firstly, in terms of ratifications of child labour Conventions, as of 31 December, 2003, out of 177 member States, 147 had ratified Convention No. 182 (34 additional member States during the biennium) and 131 had ratified Convention No. 138 (15 additional member States). While the pace of ratifications is slowing down as universal ratification approaches, these total figures are in line with the expectations, given that actual ratifications for both Conventions during 2000-01 largely exceeded the projections.

Secondly, as regards information and knowledge, during the biennium 28 additional countries undertook national child labour or other types of surveys. In terms of technical cooperation to ILO member States, the IPEC programme continued to expand at a very rapid rate during 2002-03.

Thirdly, in the field of technical cooperation provided to member States in formulating policies and TBPs for the elimination of the worst forms of child labour, additional funding for national TBPs secured during the biennium amounted to US$38 million for 11 countries. This brings the total number of countries that have formulated national TBPs to date to 14. An additional seven countries put in place plans of action to eliminate the worst forms of child labour with IPEC support during the biennium. Several countries were assisted with sectoral programmes of national or regional scope that develop time-bound targets in selected sectors or industries within a more limited time frame.

Fourthly, the beneficiary target for IPEC's programmes for the biennium was set at 1 million children, a goal which was exceeded by more than 10 per cent. Preliminary indications based on the coverage of the different national campaigns and awareness-raising activities linked to projects suggest that an additional 33 million children have been reached. The analysis of the direct beneficiaries of IPEC's projects and programmes shows that more than half of the total have been girls, while seven out of every ten beneficiaries were found in one of the worst forms of child labour. Regionally, 11 per cent were from Africa, 35 per cent from the Americas, 48 per cent from Asia, and 6 per cent from Europe and the Arab States.

The importance of education for eliminating child labour

With IPEC's strategic shift towards enhancing the enabling environment for action against child labour, education policy has begun to receive greater emphasis as well. Convention No. 182 reaffirms the importance of free basic education and recognizes that the long-term solution to child labour will involve universal education. The importance of education for eliminating child labour has been emphasized in IPEC's education strategy in terms of both policy reform and targeted interventions to assist children. IPEC has been working very closely for instance with SECTOR, as well as ACTRAV.

Child labour and the Decent Work Agenda

IPEC's work on child labour is an important facet of the ILO's Decent Work Agenda because child labour perpetuates the vicious cycle of poverty by preventing children from acquiring the skills and education they need for a better future with decent work. IPEC has made systematic efforts to mainstream its work at the country and global levels as well as in relation to the ILO's Decent Work Agenda. To ensure coherence and integration at the country level, IPEC is grouping its field staff into IPEC country teams and is designating IPEC focal points to enhance coordination. In 2004-05 IPEC will also establish IPEC country strategy and country operational objectives within individual countries. These will be closely linked to the ILO country programmes, including the decent work initiatives in the country.

Partnership between IPEC and employers' and workers' organizations

The importance of cooperation with employers' and workers' organizations in the programmes and projects against child labour has been underlined on several occasions during the discussion on child labour in the Governing Body. It has been reiterated that tripartism is essential in IPEC's work as an integral part of the ILO's tripartite work. Further efforts have continued and will be pursued to improve such cooperation. A major investment was made by IPEC to promote and assist global sectoral alliances among employers' and workers' organizations, such as those concerning the cocoa/chocolate industry and the tobacco sector. These cooperative arrangements are in line with the ILO's philosophy of tripartism, and are oriented towards finding constructive and broadly supported solutions with tangible and lasting effects and dividends for all parties concerned.

III. Working Party on the Social Dimension of Globalization

Corporate social responsibility and international labour standards

In November 2003, an "Information note on corporate social responsibility and international labour standards" [6] was placed before the Working Party in order to keep it abreast of developments in this area. The Working Party took note of the information provided and expressed the wish to deal with this issue in the context of the discussion of the final report of the World Commission on the Social Dimension of Globalization in March 2004. The Office was requested to continue to monitor developments and make this information available to ILO constituents through various means.

Policies and social partnerships for good governance

At the same session, the Working Party discussed the topic "Policies and social partnerships for good governance". The paper [7] submitted to the Working Party built on the discussion of a related document in March 2003. It addressed the relevance of social partnership to broader questions of governance in the context of economic and social development, and reviewed some elements identified in the external literature on governance. Although there were many positive illustrative examples, social partnership was still not fully appreciated or universally put into practice. The Working Party recognized that the subject of social partnership, social dialogue and good governance was important, particularly when it came to considering the forthcoming report and recommendations of the World Commission. It noted that the ILO played an important role in identifying and developing the right conditions and policy frameworks for good governance in relation to social, employment and economic policies. It was important to communicate to the development community the ILO's own approach to labour market governance through social partnership.

World Commission on the Social Dimension of Globalization

Statement by Her Excellency Ms. Tarja Halonen, President of Finland and Co-Chair of the World Commission

In November 2003, Ms. Tarja Halonen, President of Finland and Co-Chair of the World Commission on the Social Dimension of Globalization, addressed the Working Party on the ongoing work of the Commission. She congratulated the Working Party on its courage and open-mindedness in setting up an independent World Commission. The work of the Commission was highly relevant, not only to the ILO, but also to the rest of the multilateral system. President Halonen described some of the salient points which the Commission had discussed at length and in depth, and which were important for arriving at balanced conclusions on what to do to strengthen the social dimensions of globalization. The Commission had started from the idea that, in order to be sustainable, globalization must meet the needs of people. The ultimate goal was to help make globalization a resource to promote decent work, reduce poverty and unemployment and foster growth and development. Based on this challenging goal the Commission had developed a vision for change. The main points in this vision were that: the current course of globalization had to change because too few shared its benefits and too many had no voice in its design and no influence over its course; globalization should be a force to increase human freedom and well-being, and bring democracy and development to the communities where people live; and the principles that must guide globalization should also be reflected in national institutions, rules and political systems based on democracy, human rights and the rule of law.

President Halonen also noted that the economic benefits and social costs of globalization were not evenly distributed among countries and social groups. Successful participation in globalization was bound up with national capabilities and policies. For these reasons it could be said that the response to globalization began at home. It was also a good reason to make the nation State a stronger entity. In order to make globalization a positive force for people it was important that the rules governing it be fair, both in creating opportunity and determining outcome. They needed to reflect the diverse situations of peoples and countries.

She emphasized that action to achieve fairer rules also needed more coherent and equitable policies at the international level. This was essential to ensure that the benefits of globalization were more widely distributed and common global goals were realized.

Presentation of the report, A fair globalization: Creating opportunities for all, by His Excellency Mr. Benjamin Mkapa, President of the United Republic of Tanzania and Co-Chair of the World Commission

In March 2004, Mr. Benjamin Mkapa, President of the United Republic of Tanzania and Co-Chair of the World Commission on the Social Dimension of Globalization, addressed the Working Party to present the report of the World Commission, *A fair globalization: Creating opportunities for all*. His opening remarks set the basis for two days of extremely fertile debate on 24 and 25 March 2004. He highlighted the significance of the discussion on the report of the World Commission [8] and said that he looked forward to hearing how the ILO proposed to take forward the agenda set out in the report. He concluded by launching an appeal to Governments, Workers and Employers not to run away from the weaknesses of globalization, but to fight now.

IV. International labour standards

Improvements in ILO standards-related activities

Articles 19, 24 and 26 of the Constitution

As part of the ongoing discussions on the improvement of ILO standards-related activities, in November 2003 the Governing Body considered the question of reinforcing the procedures for submission to the competent authorities of the instruments adopted by the International Labour Conference, for representations and for complaints provided for under articles 19, 24 and 26 of the Constitution. [9] The Governing Body will examine the amendments proposed to improve these procedures at its 291st (November 2004) Session.

Technical assistance and promotion

In November 2003, the Governing Body held a second discussion on technical assistance and the promotion of international labour standards. The Governing Body considered that the comments of the supervisory bodies, the conclusions of the Working Party on Policy regarding the Revision of Standards, as well as the differences in national situations should be taken into account in the development of the tools necessary to support technical assistance and promotional activities, especially the integration of standards into the country programmes, in particular the decent work country programmes. These elements should also be taken into account in the preparation of the programmes and budget and in the joint programming between headquarters and the field structures. Information made available in thematic databases, such as the one concerning occupational safety and health following the first integrated approach, could also be important for planning activities. Standards-related technical assistance and promotional activities need to be discussed with the social partners as well as the governments in the countries concerned and should equally reflect both their wishes and priorities, and the mandate of the Organization.

Practices for the preparation of international labour Conventions

In November 2003, the Governing Body requested the Office to draw up a manual of good drafting practices aimed at facilitating the drafting of instruments submitted for adoption at the Conference. [10] A draft will be examined by a tripartite group of experts and submitted to the Governing Body at its March 2005 session.

Ratification and promotion of ILO fundamental Conventions

The campaign for the ratification of the ILO's core Conventions, initiated in 1995, has continued to stimulate member States to ratify these vital instruments. Since June 2003, there have been 16 ratifications of ILO fundamental Conventions by ten countries. These ratifications have added nine countries to the list of member States having ratified all the ILO's core Conventions.

There are now 103 States that have ratified all eight fundamental labour Conventions, and 30 that have ratified seven of them. The total number of ratifications obtained for these instruments amounts to 1,225, or 87 per cent of the possible 1,408 ratifications (all numbers at 18 May 2004).

General status report on ILO action concerning discrimination in employment

As in previous years, the Governing Body had before it, at its March 2004 session, a general status report on ILO action concerning discrimination in employment. The report contained an overview of the ILO's activities during 2003 promoting these standards and instruments, highlighting selected examples of such activities and their impact.

Freedom of association

The Committee on Freedom of Association received a growing number of complaints concerning trade union rights and collective bargaining, and examined about 200 cases between May 2003 and March 2004. Positive developments were observed during the period under review, such as release of detained trade unionists, registration of trade unions, or reinstatement of trade unionists dismissed by reason of union membership or activities.

Consolidated Convention on maritime labour standards

In March 2004, the Governing Body considered a progress report on the proposed consolidated maritime labour Convention and in particular the outcome of the fourth meeting of the High-level Tripartite Working Group on Maritime Labour Standards (HLTWG). [11] It took note of the agreement that had been reached on certain elements of the structure of the proposed Consolidated Convention and of the compromise reached on the precise status to be given to provisions in the non-mandatory part of the Convention, namely those in Part B of the Code. The fourth meeting of the HLTWG had discussed the content of the five Titles. The Governing Body noted the consensus that had been reached on some of the Titles and aspects that needed further discussion, in particular social protection. The general result of the discussions had been to narrow the areas of potential disagreement and consequently to facilitate the work of the Preparatory Technical Maritime Conference to be held from 13 to 24 September 2004.

The Governing Body also endorsed a resolution adopted by the HLTWG setting out the general lines of an appropriate procedure in order to enable the Preparatory Conference to concentrate on settling points of disagreement and to avoid unjustified discussion of provisions that have matured over years of discussion in the HLTWG and its Subgroup. In addition, it adopted a set of Standing Orders to govern the Preparatory Technical Maritime Conference. Finally, the Governing Body took note of a declaration adopted by the HLTWG concerning the accidental grounding of the M/V *Tasman Spirit* on 27 July 2003 in the port of Karachi, Pakistan, and the detention of the crew members.

The Governing Body has continued to follow progress in the work relating to a Consolidated Convention on maritime labour standards, scheduled for submission to the Conference for adoption in 2005. A draft of this Convention is being prepared by the Office under the direction of the HLTWG.

At the Governing Body's request, the Office submitted to the Governing Body, in March 2003, a progress report prepared with the assistance of the Subgroup of the High-level Group. [12] Particular reference was made in that report to the role that the ILO supervisory system might play in relation to the new Convention. Many members commended the work that had been achieved so far. It was, at the same time, pointed out that the existing maritime labour standards should continue to be promoted, pending the adoption of the new Convention, and to be ratified by member States, as this would facilitate the acceptance of the new instrument.

Constitutional procedures

Observance by the Government of Myanmar of the Forced Labour Convention, 1930 (No. 29)

In November 2003, the Governing Body had before it two reports from the Liaison Officer on developments since June 2003. The Governing Body endorsed the Chairperson's conclusions, in particular regarding the importance he felt should be accorded to the introductory statement made by the representative of Myanmar, from which it appeared that the Myanmar authorities were in agreement that the representatives of the Director-General should undertake, according to the modalities that had been successfully applied previously, a complete review of the situation with the aim of an implementation of the Plan of Action as rapidly as possible. On this basis, the Governing Body agreed to postpone until its March 2004 session the consideration of the proposal to reactivate the measures envisaged under the resolution adopted in June 2000 by the Conference, on the understanding that a complete report on the situation, with appropriate recommendations, would be submitted to it by the Director-General.

The Liaison Officer, Ms. Hông-Trang Perret Nguyen, completed her appointment at the end of November 2003. Mr. Richard Horsey was appointed Liaison Officer *ad interim* from 1 December 2003.

In March 2004, the Governing Body had before it three reports: (i) a report from the Liaison Officer *a.i.* on his activities; (ii) a report of the preliminary phase of an evaluation visit to Yangon under the November 2003 understanding reached by the Governing Body, carried out by Mr. Francis Maupain, Special Adviser to the ILO Director-General together with the Liaison Officer *a.i.*; and (iii) a report on the latest developments in the case of certain persons sentenced to death for high treason, including the observations of the future Facilitator concerning his visit to two of the detained persons. The Governing Body concluded that while positive developments had taken place since November 2003 and the authorities had demonstrated an openness to cooperate, the discovery of a court judgement against certain persons in relation to contacts or exchange of information with the ILO had undermined prospects for future cooperation.

The Governing Body identified three separate concerns which had been expressed. The first concern was that contacts or exchange of information with the ILO could in any way have judicial consequences in Myanmar. In this regard it took note of the assurances given by the Myanmar Ambassador and the Minister for Labour. It also supported the future Facilitator's clear recommendations for action as regards the persons involved. The second concern was that contacts with third parties on matters of concern to the ILO could similarly be punished, thus calling the principle of freedom of association into question. The third concern was whether, in light of the court judgement, the Plan of Action, and more specifically the Facilitator mechanism, could be credibly implemented. The Office was to examine this question more thoroughly in light of the results of the review of the recent cases and any further assurances provided by the Government and report on the results of this examination to the Officers of the Governing Body, which should be found sufficiently convincing before proceeding to the implementation of the Plan of Action.

***Observance by the Government of Belarus of the
Freedom of Association and Protection of the
Right to Organise Convention, 1948 (No. 87),
and the Right to Organise and Collective
Bargaining Convention, 1949 (No. 98)***

In view of the situation set out in the complaint concerning the non-observance by Belarus of the Freedom of Association and Protection of the Right to Organise Convention, 1948 (No. 87), and the Right to Organise and Collective Bargaining Convention, 1949 (No. 98), submitted under article 26 of the Constitution by a number of Worker delegates to the June 2003 session of the International Labour Conference and further to the examination of the case by the Committee on Freedom of Association, the Governing Body decided in November 2003 to engage the procedure provided under article 26, paragraph 4, of the Constitution and, accordingly, to establish a Commission of Inquiry to examine the allegations made in the complaint.

V. Employment and social policy

Implementation of the Global Employment Agenda

The Committee on Employment and Social Policy discussed the implementation of the Global Employment Agenda (GEA) at its November 2003 and March 2004 sessions. The papers before the Committee [13] pointed to the need to make ministries of finance and planning aware of the feasibility of incorporating employment concerns in policy-making; the importance of sound analytical work to underpin the ILO's policy advisory services; the need to ensure the active involvement of the social partners in developing policies and institutions; and the political commitment at all levels to undertake comprehensive employment policy reviews under the GEA framework. The Committee welcomed the examples for implementation at national level, emphasizing the importance of the regional and global dimension of the GEA. It called upon the Office to ensure greater coordination and integration of programmes that supported decent work at country level, such as the GEA, the Decent Work Pilot Programme, and the ILO's work in the context of Poverty Reduction Strategy Papers (PRSPs) and the Youth Employment Network.

Active labour market policies

In March 2003, the Committee on Employment and Social Policy had chosen active labour market policies (ALMPs) as the first core element of the GEA to be reported on in November 2003. The paper that was before the Committee in November 2003 [14] provided an overview of the background, functions and definition of ALMPs, examples of their use in different countries and regions, and an evaluation of their effectiveness. The Committee in principle supported the four main objectives of ALMPs: (1) direct and indirect employment creation; (2) security in change; (3) equity; and (4) poverty reduction, as well as the proposed medium-term work in this field. It also gave guidance and recommendations on the Office's future work, such as, for example, the role of collective bargaining and of minimum wages, the integration of economic and social policies, and the use of ALMPs in developing countries. The paper's emphasis on the diversity of country situations was very much welcomed by the Committee.

HIV/AIDS and the Decent Work Agenda

In November 2003, the Office submitted a report to the Committee on Employment and Social Policy on this issue,[15] in which it also presented the objectives, current activities and future plans of ILO/AIDS. The report included an overview of how the Office contributes to the global response to HIV/AIDS by strengthening the capacity of the constituents to develop and sustain workplace policies and programmes; and how it promotes the Decent Work Agenda. In addition to the specific responsibilities of the ILO/AIDS programme, the Office mainstreams HIV/AIDS-related issues in all its major programmes and activities, and important partnerships have been developed beyond the Organization, principally with UNAIDS and the fellow co-sponsors, but also with the Global Fund to Fight AIDS, Tuberculosis and Malaria and the Global Business Coalition on HIV/AIDS.

During the discussion, the ILO was requested to focus and strengthen its efforts to address the ways the epidemic threatens each of the strategic objectives of the Decent Work Agenda, especially by increasing and monitoring the mainstreaming of the issue throughout the Office. Employers and Workers also drew attention to the increasing collaboration between the two social partners in the framework of the joint statement by the International Organisation of Employers (IOE) and the International Confederation of Free Trade Unions (ICFTU), *Fighting HIV/AIDS together*. The need for trade unions, employers and labour ministries to move from the current focus on prevention to include measures to ensure access to affordable drugs was also underlined.

The Global Social Trust pilot project

In November 2003, the Committee on Employment and Social Policy acknowledged the progress[16] which had been made on the Global Social Trust pilot project: following tripartite negotiations, Luxembourg and Namibia had been identified as the donor and recipient countries, respectively, to test the introduction of a new social security benefit in Namibia for surviving partners and children of those who had died. The benefit would be supported by donations from individuals in Luxembourg channelled through a trust fund administered by the National Social Trust Project of Luxembourg, made up of two trade union-based non-governmental organizations (NGOs). Additional financial support would come from the Government of Luxembourg for the duration of the pilot. The Committee further noted that a reserve project would be carried out in Ghana should negotiations between the Governments of Namibia and Luxembourg fail to reach a satisfactory conclusion. The Governing Body finally noted that the Officers of the Committee had been authorized by the Committee to make nominations at the appropriate time for members of a tripartite advisory board to the project, whose nominations would in turn be approved by the Governing Body and the Director-General.

The Decent Work Pilot Programme

A first report on the implementation of the Decent Work Pilot Programme (DW/PP) was discussed by the Committee on Employment and Social Policy in November 2003,[17] followed by a review of an update on progress in March 2004,[18] covering the implementation of the GEA, the DW/PP and the PRSPs. The Governing Body commended the approach taken by the DW/PP. The programme contributed to raising the profile of decent work in higher-level national policy agendas and demonstrated the benefits of policy integration around social and labour issues. This had strengthened the role of national constituents in policy dialogue. Satisfaction was also expressed with the high degree of national ownership and the active involvement of national constituents. Capacity building of constituents was crucial for impact and sustainability. Attention needed to be paid to potentially overlapping ILO frameworks to ensure coherent national ILO programmes. Further work was also needed to evaluate the outcomes. The Governing Body urged the Office to bring the DW/PP to a successful conclusion and to document the lessons learned. These should contribute to a "tool-kit" for operationalizing decent work in member countries, so that the decent work country programmes to be introduced over the next years as the general mode of ILO cooperation with member countries could build on the experience of the pilot programme.

Promoting decent employment through entrepreneurship

In March 2004, the Committee on Employment and Social Policy reviewed an Office paper [19] on the fifth core element of the GEA, "Promoting decent employment through entrepreneurship". The paper showed the links between this and other core elements of the GEA and indicated what strategy the Office had taken to promote entrepreneurship, including lessons learned. The Committee expressed its support for the suggested future priorities for Office work, which include additional research on effective enterprise development policies, a further refinement of the tools to promote an entrepreneurial culture in line with ILO values, the further development of elements promoting decent work as a productive factor, enhancing the capacity of the social partners to contribute to national and local policy-making, and the further development of strategic alliances. In particular, closer cooperation with the United Nations Development Programme (UNDP) was encouraged, as well as a stronger emphasis on lessons learned.

Productive employment for poverty reduction and development

Productive employment for poverty reduction and development constitutes the tenth core element of the GEA. It was discussed by the Committee on Employment and Social Policy in March 2004. The paper before the Committee [20] gave an overview of the world-wide poverty situation, of the link between growth, productive employment and poverty reduction, and of the Office's strategies and work in this area. This included work on the informal economy, women, labour-based approaches in infrastructure, capacity building through skills development and improved access to finance, and programmes in crisis-affected countries. The Committee supported the approaches presented and the proposals made for future action, including increased efforts to integrate employment into PRSPs and demonstrate the role of employment in achieving the Millennium Development Goals and to address the problem of poverty in transition countries.

Global Campaign on Social Security and Coverage for All

In March 2004, the Committee on Employment and Social Policy discussed a progress report on the Global Campaign on Social Security and Coverage for All. [21] Based on a consensus reached by the International Labour Conference in 2001, the Campaign was officially launched during the International Labour Conference in 2003. The overall objective of the Campaign is to develop awareness and achieve universal access to health care as well as basic income security for all. In countries such as Honduras, Mali and Sri Lanka, the Campaign attempts to achieve this through a process of social dialogue. It also develops new mechanisms to reach the informal economy, in particular through its

Strategies and Tools against Social Exclusion and Poverty Programme (STEP) that has so far involved more than 30 developing countries.

In December 2003, the Tenth African Regional Meeting devoted a special session to launching the Global Campaign in Africa. At the beginning of 2004, national launches took place in Mozambique, Nepal and Senegal. During 2004 the Campaign will develop two regional initiatives. One will focus on Africa and is expected to play an important role in the Extraordinary Summit of Heads of State and Government of the African Union on Employment and Poverty Alleviation. The second – developed in collaboration with the Pan-American Health Organization – will focus on extending health-care coverage in Latin America and the Caribbean.

VI. Multinational enterprises

Promotion of the Tripartite Declaration of Principles concerning Multinational Enterprises and Social Policy

Activities report for 2003

In March 2004, the Subcommittee on Multinational Enterprises discussed a paper entitled "Promotion of the Tripartite Declaration of Principles concerning Multinational Enterprises and Social Policy: Activities report for 2003". [22] It outlined the activities carried out by the Office in 2003 to enhance the awareness of the Tripartite Declaration of Principles concerning Multinational Enterprises and Social Policy (MNE Declaration) such as the Symposium on the MNE Declaration and related multilateral initiatives, participation in a wide range of country-level and international meetings on corporate social responsibility (CSR), publication of working papers and the organization of national seminars in Costa Rica and Uganda. The Multinational Enterprises Programme also continued to mainstream the MNE Declaration in the work of other programmes in the Office through, for example, the joint organization of national seminars with the InFocus Programme on Social Dialogue and ILO field offices.

The Governing Body authorized the Office to invite to the November 2004 sitting of the Subcommittee on Multinational Enterprises, as observers, the international organizations represented at the 2003 symposium. The Governing Body also asked the Office to prepare in future years an annual substantial report reflecting both the workplan endorsed by the Subcommittee and the activities undertaken to promote the MNE Declaration in the previous calendar year and the strategy and activities proposed for the immediate future. The Subcommittee on Multinational Enterprises indicated its interest in being consulted on, and participating in, the outcomes of any CSR-related recommendations and decisions by the Governing Body on the follow-up by the Office on the report of the World Commission on the Social Dimension of Globalization.

Priorities for action in 2004-05

In November 2003, the Subcommittee on Multinational Enterprises reviewed a paper entitled "Promotion of the Tripartite Declaration of Principles concerning Multinational Enterprises and Social Policy: Priorities for action in 2004-05". [23] It outlined the following planned activities: enhance the awareness of the MNE Declaration, including through the organization of subregional tripartite seminars in the ASEAN, SADC and MERCOSUR subregions; mainstream the MNE Declaration in the work of the Office, in particular through closer cooperation with the Sectoral Activities Programme; and enhance relations with other organizations, particularly the United Nations agencies supporting the Global Compact, the European Commission, the Organisation for Economic Co-operation and Development (OECD) and the World Bank group, in order to position the MNE Declaration as a complement to the efforts of these organizations in the area of CSR. The Governing Body requested the Office to take into account the observations by the Subcommittee when implementing the planned activities.

Composition and size of the Subcommittee on Multinational Enterprises

In November 2003, the Subcommittee on Multinational Enterprises examined a paper reviewing its history, to facilitate a discussion on possible changes in its composition and size.[24] Since the Governing Body was considering a reform of its structures, the discussion in the Subcommittee aimed at contributing to but not prejudging the outcome of that more comprehensive discussion. The Subcommittee recommended that the Governing Body, when reviewing its functioning and structure, consider how to achieve a better balance between representatives of home and host countries of multinational enterprises in the Subcommittee.

Eighth Survey on the effect given to the Tripartite Declaration of Principles concerning Multinational Enterprises and Social Policy

In November 2003, the Subcommittee on Multinational Enterprises reviewed a paper entitled "Draft questionnaire for the Eighth Survey on the effect given to the Tripartite Declaration of Principles concerning Multinational Enterprises and Social Policy".[25] The paper had been prepared following consultations with the Bureaux for Employers' and Workers' Activities and with the Officers of the Subcommittee. The Governing Body requested the Office to conduct the Eighth Survey on the effect given to the Tripartite Declaration of Principles concerning Multinational Enterprises and Social Policy on the basis of the report form [26] approved by the Subcommittee.

Developments in other organizations

In March 2004, the Subcommittee on Multinational Enterprises discussed a paper concerning "Developments in other organizations".[27] The paper highlighted developments in the area of CSR in a number of international organizations relating directly or indirectly to multinational enterprises and social policy issues.

VII. Sectoral activities

Sectoral meetings

In November 2003, the Governing Body, through its Committee on Sectoral and Technical Meetings and Related Issues, approved the purpose of the tripartite meetings in the media, cultural and graphics and the transport equipment manufacturing sectors to be held in 2004-05, as well as the type of meeting, the duration, the number of delegations, Governing Body representation and the method of selecting the participants for these meetings and those in the basic metals and forestry and wood sectors, also scheduled for the biennium.[28] The purpose of the latter two was decided in June 2003 as part of the sectoral activities review (see below). In November 2003 and March 2004, the Governing Body took note of the reports of various sectoral and technical meetings and endorsed the recommendations adopted by them.[29] At these sessions, the Governing Body also took note of the reports of various joint bodies co-organized in the framework of the sectoral activities programme and authorized their distribution to member States where relevant.[30]

Review of the Sectoral Activities Programme, 2002-03

In March 2004, the Governing Body took note of a detailed report reviewed by the Committee on Sectoral and Technical Meetings and Related Issues on sectoral activities in 2002-03. It also noted an overview of major trends and issues in all 22 sectors, including information available through the One-Stop Window portal web site.[31]

A new approach to sectoral activities in 2004-05

Following decisions adopted in March 2003 on the nature of some of the activities of the sectoral activities programme for the 2004-05 biennium,[32] the Governing Body approved in June 2003 proposals of the Officers of the Committee on Sectoral and Technical Meetings and Related Issues on additional activities for the biennium which confirmed a shift towards action programmes in several sectors, but also the need to maintain international tripartite sectoral meetings to foster dialogue in other sectors. The approved activities consist of: a tripartite planning meeting to develop and agree on national action programmes in the construction sector; tripartite meetings of experts for the basic metals and forestry and wood sectors; a small tripartite technical meeting for the transport equipment manufacturing sector plus development of a statistical database for the sector's metals sub-sector; and a proposed sectoral approach to HIV/AIDS in the workplace.[33] In November 2003, and again in March 2004, the Governing Body was apprised of progress made in the implementation of the programme for 2004-05, particularly regarding the seven action programmes, based on extensive consultations with governments, as well as with employers' and workers' organizations, including during regional meetings for some sectors, as well as among ILO units worldwide.[34]

Meetings of experts: Purpose, function and lessons learned

Also in March 2004, the Governing Body took note of the review by the Committee on Sectoral and Technical Meetings and Related Issues of a paper on the purpose as well as the function of and lessons learned from meetings of experts organized by the ILO, many of which took place under the sectoral activities programme. The paper and discussion helped to clarify the previous history of meetings of experts and the position of the tripartite constituents on issues in preparation for future meetings.

VIII. Technical cooperation

The ILO Technical Cooperation Programme for 2002-03

In November 2003, the Committee on Technical Cooperation received the latest information [35] on ILO technical cooperation figures and trends in 2002-03. During the biennium, the Office received US$327 million as extra-budgetary funds, i.e. a 13 per cent increase over 2000-01. The Office also improved the delivery of its technical cooperation programme compared to the previous biennium, with an overall delivery rate of nearly 69 per cent. Against this generally positive background, the Committee was alerted to the need to ensure a more balanced distribution of resources among sectors and to redress the declining trend in the share of funds allowed to least developed countries and particularly to Africa. The issue of greater involvement of the ILO's social partners in the design and delivery of technical cooperation and the need to improve evaluation policies and procedures were also repeatedly highlighted. In order to stabilize the flow of development cooperation resources and to enhance the coherence between regular budget and extra-budgetary-funded activities, the Office has promoted programme and partnership agreements with an increasing number of donor agencies. The Office also started negotiating a new framework agreement with the European Union.

In March 2004, the Committee on Technical Cooperation received a special update [36] on the InFocus Programme on Child Labour (IPEC), which was the largest ILO technical cooperation programme in the biennium. The report highlighted the quantitative increase and the accelerated delivery of the programme. From a qualitative point of view, the programme is moving upstream from direct implementation to supporting the development of national policies and institutional capacity; it is placing greater emphasis on effective design, monitoring and evaluation; it is increasingly networking with other relevant international organizations; and it is opening up new areas of cooperation with the social partners. Largely through IPEC's support, ILO Conventions Nos. 138 and 182 have experienced a record pace of ratification in the 2002-03 biennium. The Committee members noted with interest the evolution of the programme, whilst at the same time insisting on the need for greater involvement of employers' and workers' organizations.

Further developments regarding technical cooperation activities in the United Nations system

In November 2003, the Committee on Technical Cooperation was briefed [37] on efforts under way in the United Nations system to rationalize and harmonize procedures for the planning and management of development cooperation among different development agencies, with a view to enhancing the effectiveness of development aid and to relieving developing countries of an excessive administrative burden. The Committee encouraged the Office to continue to network with other bilateral and multilateral partners to ensure that the decent work perspective was fully integrated in their development agenda and that ILO constituents were adequately involved in Poverty Reduction Strategy exercises and other development assistance frameworks. Committee members expressed their wish to be regularly updated on progress made in this respect.

Thematic evaluation: Strengthening institutions, processes, legal frameworks and capacity of tripartite constituents for tripartism and social dialogue

The thematic report [38] presented to the Committee on Technical Cooperation in March 2004 was based on evaluation reports of a number of projects aimed at enhancing the capacity of tripartite constituents and at using social dialogue in substantive policy-making. The report demonstrated the importance of social dialogue as an instrument for policy formulation and delivery, both important components of ILO technical cooperation; and, therefore, the need to ensure that social dialogue is more systematically applied across ILO technical cooperation programmes, through a better appreciation of its added value in addressing a wide range of developmental situations.

The Committee on Technical Cooperation stressed the need to ensure that attention to tripartite social dialogue was not limited to social dialogue activities only, but extended to all ILO technical cooperation programmes by enhancing the social partners' participation in development processes. In particular, Committee members warned about the risks of ILO departments working with other stakeholders at the expense of employers' and workers' organizations. The report also triggered a discussion on the ILO's criteria for undertaking independent evaluation and measuring the impact of its programmes. The Committee also agreed on the need to monitor the social partners' involvement in technical cooperation on a regular basis.

On-the-spot review in Africa

A three-member tripartite team of Governing Body members had undertaken an on-the-spot review of the Kenya component of the project on Strengthening Labour Relations in East Africa (SLAREA) financed by the United States Department of Labor. In March 2004, the Committee on Technical Cooperation deliberated on the report on the review,[39] which highlighted some of the positive findings with regard to strengthening labour administration, reform of labour laws, strengthening employers' and workers' organizations and expansion of their membership. The report pointed out, however, that the resources available were inadequate to address the problem and that the time span for project implementation had been too short for attaining substantial impact. Being of the opinion that capacity-building efforts need to be sustained over a longer period of time, the Committee requested the Office to make all possible efforts to secure donor funding for an extension of the project at least until 2006.

The Committee on Technical Cooperation agreed that the issue of future on-the-spot reviews would be discussed by the Officers of the Committee on Technical Cooperation during the International Labour Conference and that proposals could be made for consideration at the November 2004 session of the Governing Body.

Technical cooperation – Resource allocation mechanism

Since 2001 the Office has been establishing a new modality for the planning and allocation of funds provided by two important ILO donors, the Governments of the Netherlands and the United Kingdom. This new modality – called Technical Cooperation Resource Allocation Mechanism (TC-RAM) – differs from the traditional mechanisms in place with other funding agencies in that, based on common criteria previously agreed with the donor concerned, the Office has the final say on the selection of projects and can therefore ensure greater coherence between ILO technical cooperation activities and the Organization's overall strategic priorities and objectives.

The report submitted to the Committee on Technical Cooperation in March 2004 [40] provided a summary account of the experience with the exercise, particularly on the process that was followed by the Office to plan and allocate funds from the Netherlands and the United Kingdom Department for International Development. The Office considered that TC-RAM allowed for greater rigour and transparency and – through its competitive nature – put a premium on the relevance and quality of project design. The TC-RAM exercise had already been reviewed on two occasions, which had enabled the Office to identify areas for improvement of the mechanism. The Office invited other donors to join the TC-RAM process, which accounted for 15 per cent of all extra-budgetary allocations in the 2002-03 biennium. An independent external evaluation of TC-RAM is scheduled for 2006.

Several Government representatives, including the two donors concerned, expressed satisfaction with the way TC-RAM had operated and with the improvements progressively introduced to enhance its effectiveness. They considered that this type of modality empowered the Office to plan and design its technical cooperation activities in line with its own priorities. However, the employers' and workers' representatives criticized the mechanism on the grounds that it gave insufficient attention to the involvement of the social partners in the different stages of the process. As a result, the projects selected did not reflect the Office policy as defined in the 1999 Conference conclusions concerning the role of the ILO in technical cooperation and the 2002 resolution on tripartism and social dialogue. They proposed different measures to ensure greater participation of the Bureaux for Employers' and Workers' Activities in the planning and selection of future TC-RAM projects and requested an update on steps taken by the Office in that regard.

Special Technical Cooperation Programme for Colombia

In June 2003, the Governing Body examined a progress report [41] on the activities initiated under the Special Technical Cooperation Programme for Colombia. Several members expressed their strong support for the Programme, especially as regards initiatives taken to strengthen social dialogue and promote fundamental principles and rights at work. The Governing Body acknowledged the regret expressed by the Workers' group that insufficient funds had made it impossible to appoint a programme coordinator and, further to the special request formulated by the same group that the attacks and assassinations which continued to be perpetrated against trade union members and their families should be duly denounced so that measures to end them could be engaged, urged the Colombian Government to remedy, as a matter of urgency, the problem of impunity enjoyed by the perpetrators of the acts of violence against trade unionists.

Further to the decision of the Officers of the Governing Body that the progress made by this Programme should be examined by the Committee on Technical Cooperation, in March 2004 an update was presented to this Committee [42] on the evolution of the Programme with an emphasis on the promotion of fundamental labour rights and on labour conflict resolution as the ILO's contribution to addressing the causes of violence in this country. Several members of the Committee expressed appreciation for the ILO's work and suggested an expansion to new areas of intervention such as human security and social protection. At the same time, the Workers' representatives drew the Committee's attention to the continued violations of unions' rights and violence against trade unionists, and urged the Office to ensure that the Special Technical Cooperation Programme took into consideration the recommendations of the Committee on Freedom of Association and work with the Government and social partners in its implementation.

Enhanced Programme of Technical Cooperation for the occupied territories

Despite the prevailing difficult situation in the occupied Arab territories, the ILO made progress in implementing the programme as endorsed by the Governing Body in June 2002. In the 2002-03 biennium, the ILO's financial commitment reached US$1.75 million for both ongoing and new technical cooperation projects for capacity building of the Ministry of Labour and the employers' and workers' organizations, including the establishment of the Palestinian Fund for Employment and Social Protection (the Fund). A proposal was also made to the Government of Saudi Arabia to use its contribution of US$500,000 to build a new vocational training centre in Ramallah in support of the Fund's activities, as requested by the Ministry of Labour.

In addition, a new project aiming at promoting social dialogue, approved last year by the Italian Government for funding of approximately US$1.6 million, will be launched this year by the International Training Centre of the ILO in Turin following a recent mission to discuss with all the stakeholders. Further to the ACTRAV needs assessment mission in 2003, a project on *Assistance to Palestinian Trade Unions* was formulated for both internal and external resource mobilization. To assist Palestinian workers in obtaining work permits through employment services offices of the Ministry to work in Israel, technical and financial support will be provided by the ILO in the biennium to render the legal aid and counselling services with respect to workers' rights.

Significant steps have been undertaken to operationalize the Fund in terms of both setting up the Fund office and launching fund-raising activities. The Board of Directors met for the first time last February to lay the groundwork for the functioning of the Fund administration and the organizational structure based on the operation manuals and guidelines, which will be completed in May. To ensure sustainability and commitment to the Fund, the Palestinian Authority has approved provision of a proper location and some equipment for the Fund office.

The Arab Fund-Raising Committee held a meeting as a side activity during the Arab Labour Organization Conference in February in Damascus. A major resolution adopted by the Conference includes a request to the Arab Committee to take action in addressing all Arab countries and specialized Arab funds to support the Fund programme and to channel the contribution to the Fund's account.

IX. Financial questions

Information Technology Systems Fund

In November 2003, the Governing Body revised the figure of up to US$3 million previously approved for improvements to the headquarters/field telecommunications infrastructure to US$500,000 and approved the use of the unearmarked balance of the Information Technology Systems Fund (US$3.4 million) towards meeting the budgetary shortfall in project IRIS. In March 2004, a paper [43] was submitted for discussion, which provided details of the external review of the project and decisions made as a result. A new governance structure had been decided upon, the implementation date had been moved to

November 2004 for headquarters, with the regions to "go-live" after the system stabilizes, and the cost estimates had been increased to US$40 million, in addition to a US$2.5 million contingency reserve and US$2 million transition cost. Other steps were planned to determine options for technical infrastructure and total production costs. Increased user involvement was also planned.

ILO programme implementation 2002-03

In March 2004, the Governing Body considered the programme implementation report for 2002-03. It welcomed the presentation and format, which emphasized results achieved, successes as well as failures and lessons learned. The Governing Body further encouraged the Office to review the formulation of performance indicators in order to better assess, qualitatively and quantitatively, the impacts of the ILO programme.

Evaluation of InFocus programmes

In November 2003, the Governing Body discussed summary evaluation reports of the *InFocus Programme on Boosting Employment through Small Enterprise Development* and the *InFocus Programme on Crisis Response and Reconstruction*. The Governing Body expressed its appreciation for the objective and frank assessments provided by the reports. It encouraged the Office to present more detailed factual evidence of results achieved, as well as to strengthen the independence of evaluation.

Use of the 2000-01 surplus

In November 2003, the Governing Body received a report on the use of the 2000-01 surplus funds approved by the International Labour Conference in June 2002. Just over 50 per cent of the US$51.3 million surplus had been allocated by 30 September 2003.

Strategic Policy Framework 2006-09

In November 2003, the Governing Body held a preliminary discussion on the Strategic Policy Framework for 2006-09. The Governing Body confirmed the relevance of the Decent Work Agenda and the four strategic objectives. It discussed a number of challenges the ILO would have to address in the forthcoming period, in particular in relation to globalization, poverty reduction in the context of the Millennium Development Goals and decent work in enterprises. The Governing Body also considered institutional capacities, in particular human resources, knowledge development, decentralization, the balance between regular budget and voluntary contributions and the strengthening of programme evaluations.

Technical meetings reserve 2004-05

In November 2003, the Governing Body agreed to hold the following meetings: The Social Dimension of Globalization: From Debate to Action; International Symposium on Trade Unions and Poverty Eradication; Youth Employment: The Way Forward; and three tripartite symposiums on promoting the MNE Declaration in ASEAN, MERCOSUR and SADC countries. In March 2004, the Governing Body deferred consideration of the balance of the technical meetings reserve to a later date.

New premises for the ILO offices in Santiago and Dar es Salaam

Following discussion of the report of the Building Subcommittee in November 2003 and March 2004 by the Programme, Financial and Administrative Committee, the Governing Body agreed to the proposals to build new premises for the ILO offices in Santiago and Dar es Salaam and to accept gifts of land from the Governments of Chile and the United Republic of Tanzania for this purpose. The Governing Body decided that the cost of the buildings in Santiago and Dar es Salaam would be funded from the Building and Accommodation Fund and would be kept within a ceiling of US$1.8 million and US$1.7 million, respectively.

Security and safety of staff and premises

In November 2003, the Director-General addressed the Governing Body on the subject of safety and security of ILO staff and premises. He was requested to submit proposals for dealing with this important issue to the following session and an update on measures being taken was provided in March 2004.

X.   Decision-making bodies of the ILO

International Labour Conference

Proposed improvements in the functioning of the Conference

In November 2003 the Governing Body held a discussion on possible improvements in the functioning of the International Labour Conference. This discussion was based on a document [44] which was prepared after informal consultations with the Government, Employers' and Workers' groups of the Governing Body in September 2003. The discussion continued in the March 2004 session of the Governing Body on the basis of another document [45] which included a progress report as well as specific proposals resulting from further informal consultations with the constituents.

The Governing Body recalled that significant changes in the length, methods and practices of the Conference had been introduced in the past ten years. It was further noted that the Conference by and large was working well, while there was room for further improvement in its functioning and, in general, this could be done within the framework of the existing structures and Standing Orders.

The Governing Body endorsed the need to ensure continued high-level participation in the Conference. It also considered that any measures to enhance the political dimension of the Conference should not be to the detriment of its technical work. Issues that were addressed included possible identification of alternative methodologies for the work of technical committees and possible changes in the format and programme of the plenary, as well as operational issues such as time management and better use of resources.

The Governing Body was informed that the 92nd Session of the Conference would consider the implications for the ILO of the report of the World Commission on the Social Dimension of Globalization. This session of the Conference would therefore have a full and high-level debate on several key topics in the framework of its plenary. The Governing

Body decided to revisit, at its meeting in November 2004, the question of possible reforms to the functioning of the Conference on the basis of the experience acquired in June 2004. In the meantime it authorized the Office to proceed with the implementation of improvements and measures that were enumerated in the document and had been endorsed by a wide consensus in the discussion.

Follow-up to the Seafarers' Identity Documents Convention (Revised), 2003 (No. 185), and to the resolutions adopted at the 91st Session (2003) of the International Labour Conference

Seafarers' Identity Documents Convention (Revised), 2003 (No. 185), and related resolutions

The Seafarers' Identity Documents Convention (Revised), 2003 (No. 185), adopted at the 91st Session of the International Labour Conference, provides for a new seafarers' identity document facilitating the movement of seafarers, but not replacing a passport. It introduces a viable system for meeting contemporary security concerns while maintaining the necessary facilitation of shipping and recognition of the needs of seafarers. The Convention requires each ratifying country to put in place a comprehensive security regime. This would cover not only the production by the national authorities of a modern identity document embodying security features, but also the maintenance of national databases for the document. In addition, the processes and procedures for the production, personalization and issuance of the document, which would include quality control of the entire national system, would be subject to international oversight (Article 5 and Annex III of the Convention).

The International Labour Conference also adopted, at the same time, a resolution concerning the development of the global interoperable biometric. This resolution was discussed at the November 2003 session of the Governing Body, which approved a plan of action to be pursued by the Office for the adoption of the technical specifications for the interoperable biometric template.

In March 2004, the Office submitted to the Governing Body as a matter of urgency a document accompanied by draft technical reports which called for a decision on the selection of the type of fingerprint biometric template, i.e. either "pattern" or "minutiae" based. [46] After considerable discussions, the Governing Body selected the "minutiae-based" method and endorsed the technical report, ILO SID-0002, as embodying the standard for the fingerprint template required under Convention No. 185.

The Governing Body also considered the resolution concerning technical cooperation relating to seafarers' identity documents adopted by the Conference. In keeping with this resolution, based on a document submitted by the Office, in November 2003, the Governing Body requested the Director-General to give due priority, in the use of resources allocated to the Organization's technical cooperation programme, to assisting countries with respect to the technology, expertise and process required. In March 2004, the Governing Body endorsed the need to provide technical assistance to developing countries in particular to enable them to ratify and implement the Convention and the biometric standard adopted.

Resolution concerning occupational
safety and health

In November 2003, the Governing Body examined a report [47] describing the wide range of ongoing activities and the approach being explored by the Office to promote occupational safety and health pursuant to the 2003 Conference resolution. It noted the activities already undertaken by the Office to give effect to the resolution concerning occupational safety and health and approved the follow-up action proposed for the 2004-05 biennium.

The Governing Body also decided to place an item on the agenda of the 93rd Session of the Conference, [48] to develop a new instrument establishing a promotional framework in the area of occupational safety and health pursuant to the 2003 Conference resolution.

The role of the Credentials Committee

In March 2004 the Governing Body concluded its examination of the role of the Credentials Committee, and in particular the strengthening of its means of ensuring tripartism at the International Labour Conference. The Governing Body recommended that the Conference should adopt temporary regulatory provisions for a period of three years, which would enter into force at the 93rd Session of the Conference. The Governing Body also adopted a series of practical measures to improve the efficiency of the Credentials Committee, which will be instigated at the present session of the Conference. [49]

93rd Session (June 2005)

Following a decision in March 2003 to postpone the decision on the items that would complete the agenda of the 93rd Session (June 2005), and taking into account the results of the general discussion on ILO standards-related activities in the area of occupational safety and health held at the 91st Session (June 2003) of the Conference, the Governing Body decided, in November 2003, to include on the agenda of the 93rd Session of the Conference the questions of: (a) a new instrument establishing a promotional framework in the area of occupational safety and health; and (b) promoting youth employment for a general discussion based on an integrated approach. Furthermore, in order to enhance the efficiency of Conference servicing through an intensified form of cooperation with the World Health Organization, the Governing Body agreed in March 2004 [50] to modify its previous decision [51] and to bring forward the opening of the 93rd Session of the Conference by one week. That session of the Conference will now open on Tuesday, 31 May 2005.

95th Session (June 2006)

After a first discussion on the agenda of the 95th Session (June 2006) of the Conference in November 2003, the Governing Body selected seven proposals for more in-depth examination at its forthcoming session. In March 2004, the Governing Body decided that the 95th Session of the Conference should open on Tuesday, 30 May 2006, and that it should be held in Geneva. It further decided that, in addition to the standing items that the Conference would have before it, and the second discussion on the item of a new instrument establishing a promotional framework in the area of occupational safety and health, the following items should be placed on the agenda of the 95th Session of the Conference: (a) the role of the ILO in technical cooperation *(general discussion)*; and (b) the employment relationship *(standard setting, single discussion)*.

ILO Governing Body: Proposed improvements in the functioning

In November 2003, the Governing Body discussed a document [52] on possible improvements in the structure and functioning of the Governing Body. It agreed on the mandate proposed for such a review. This led to a further discussion of various procedures and methods of work of the Governing Body in March 2004 on the basis of another document [53] submitted by the Office. Informal consultations were held on this topic with the Government, Employers' and Workers' groups prior to the November and March sessions. In the discussions that took place the Governing Body endorsed several proposed practices and measures and instructed the Office to implement them accordingly. In particular there was an emphasis on measures to enhance the governance and the policy orientation roles of the Governing Body. It underlined the need to achieve a better balance between the work of the committees and the plenary of the Governing Body and to prevent repetition and overlap.

Measures were discussed to ensure a high-quality debate at the committees by involving the three groups in deciding the agenda of the committees in advance, and by limiting the number of items on the agenda and a better discipline in their discussion. The documents submitted to the Governing Body needed to be more focused and concise, and shorter if possible.

The Governing Body welcomed the increased interaction among its Government, Employers' and Workers' groups. The structure and number of committees were discussed and the Governing Body decided to revisit this issue in order to ensure proper coverage of all the strategic objectives of the Organization. This could be done possibly by adjustments in the mandate of the existing committees. The Governing Body decided to implement measures to improve time management in the work of its plenary and committees. It was also decided to authorize the Office to prepare and present a consolidated compilation of the rules and Standing Orders for the Governing Body and its committees, with a view to their subsequent publication.

Tenth African Regional Meeting
(Addis Ababa, 2-5 December 2003)

The report and conclusions of the Tenth African Regional Meeting [54] were discussed and adopted by the Governing Body in March 2004. The Regional Meeting concluded with a broad set of recommendations on putting employment at the centre of Africa's development strategies and, on the basis of views expressed in the Director-General's thematic report, *Decent work for Africa's development*, agreed on the priorities for action by the ILO to strengthen its role in Africa for the coming two to four years. The Meeting also held a special session on the preparation of the Extraordinary Summit of Heads of State and Government of the African Union on Employment and Poverty Alleviation in Africa to be convened in Burkina Faso in September 2004. His Excellency Blaise Campaoré, President of Burkina Faso, addressed the meeting and stressed that the ILO's contribution to the Summit would highlight the critical correlation between employment and the reduction of poverty in Africa. During this session, it was agreed to activate the ILO's tripartite network to support the 2004 Summit. The participants called on the Organization to highlight examples of successful initiatives generating employment, so that the African leaders attending the Summit can focus on how to replicate and scale-up action on poverty.

The Meeting further adopted two resolutions. The first resolution, on the role of social dialogue in addressing HIV/AIDS in the world of work, appeals to African governments to support the efforts of employers and workers to combat HIV/AIDS by providing an enabling legal and policy framework for workplace action, measures to oppose stigma and discrimination, and the strengthening of national AIDS plans through the inclusion of a strategy for the world of work. The second resolution, on decent work for youth in Africa, calls on the ILO to increase its focus on promoting the employment of young people on the continent. [55]

XI. Relations with other international organizations

During the course of the reporting period, the Governing Body continued to follow closely the issue of ILO relations with other international organizations. This included enhanced ILO involvement in both regular and special events of the United Nations system, further strengthening of ILO collaboration with the Bretton Woods institutions and other economic and financial organizations, as well as with other partner institutions. ILO efforts have been focused on further promoting the Decent Work Agenda within a broad development perspective, and advocating policy coherence. The Governing Body was kept fully informed of major developments within the multilateral system of special relevance to the ILO. This included ILO involvement in the most important international development initiatives, such as the Millennium Development Goals, Poverty Reduction Strategies and the Global Compact, as well as the ongoing United Nations reform process. The Governing Body has confirmed its growing interest in the issue of ILO external relations and partnerships, and has expressed the wish to receive advance information on forthcoming major international events of particular interest to the ILO.

* * *

Notes

[1] http://www.ilo.org/public/english/standards/relm/gb/index.htm

[2] The compilation of annual reports by the International Labour Office, March 2004, can be consulted on the Declaration Programme's public web site: www.ilo.org/declaration

[3] GB.289/4.

[4] GB.288/TC/4.

[5] GB.289/LILS/1/2.

[6] GB.288/WP/SDG/3.

[7] GB.288/WP/SDG/2.

[8] The oral report of the Chairperson of the Working Party, as well as the record of the discussion of the report of the World Commission at the 289th (March 2004) Session of the Governing Body, are appended to this report (appendices I and II).

[9] GB.288/10/1.

[10] op. cit.

[11] GB.289/LILS/5(Rev.).

[12] GB.286/LILS/8.

[13] GB.288/ESP/1(Rev.) and GB.289/ESP/3.

[14] GB.288/ESP/2.

[15] GB.288/ESP/3.

[16] GB.288/ESP/4.

[17] GB.288/ESP/5.

[18] GB.289/ESP/3.

[19] GB.289/ESP/1.

[20] GB.289/ESP/2.

[21] GB.289/ESP/5.

[22] GB.289/MNE/1.

[23] GB.288/MNE/1.

[24] GB.288/MNE/3.

[25] GB.288/MNE/2.

[26] Report form in GB.288/11, appendix.

[27] GB.289/MNE/2.

[28] GB.289/14.

[29] These included: the Joint Meeting on Public Emergency Services: Social Dialogue in a Changing Environment (Geneva, 27-31 January 2003 (GB.288/STM/2/1)); the Tripartite Meeting on the Future of Employment in the Tobacco Sector (Geneva, 24-28 February 2003 (GB.288/STM/2/2)); the Tripartite Meeting on the Employment Effects of Mergers and Acquisitions in Commerce (Geneva, 7-11 April 2003 (GB.288/STM/2/3)); the Tripartite Meeting on Challenges and Opportunities facing Public Utilities (Geneva, 19-23 May 2003 (GB.288/STM/2/4)); the Tripartite Meeting on Best Practices in Work Flexibility Schemes and their Impact on the Quality of Working Life in the Chemical Industries (Geneva, 27-31 October 2003 (GB.289/STM/3/1)); the Tripartite Meeting of Experts on Security, Safety and Health in Ports (Geneva, 8-17 December 2003 (GB.289/STM/3/2)); and the Interregional Tripartite Meeting of Experts on Safety and Health in Ship Breaking for Selected Asian Countries and Turkey (Bangkok, 7-14 October 2003 (GB.289/STM/5)).

[30] These included: the Joint ILO/IMO Working Group on Port Security (Geneva, 9-11 July 2003 (GB.288/STM/4)); the Subcommittee of the Joint Maritime Commission and the Joint Working Group on Wages of Seafarers (Geneva, 5-8 July 2003 (GB.288/STM/5)); the Eighth Session of the Joint ILO/UNESCO Committee of Experts on the Application of the Recommendations concerning Teaching Personnel (CEART (GB.289/STM/4)); the meeting on ship scrapping between the International Labour Office (ILO), the secretariat of the Basel Convention (SBC) and the secretariat of the International Maritime Organization (IMO) (Geneva, 13-14 January 2004 (GB.289/STM/8/1)); and the Fifth Session of the Joint IMO/ILO Ad Hoc Expert Working Group on Liability and Compensation regarding Claims for Death, Personal Injury and Abandonment of Seafarers (London, 12-14 January 2004 (GB.289/STM/8/2)).

[31] GB.289/14, based on GB.289/STM/1.

[32] The activities included: action programmes for 2004-05 in the agriculture, education and textiles, and clothing and footwear sectors, small tripartite planning meetings to be held in 2004 to develop year-long action programmes for the construction, financial and professional services and hotel, catering and tourism sectors to be undertaken in 2005; and an international tripartite meeting for the media, cultural and graphical sector to be held in 2004.

[33] GB.287/7.

[34] GB.289/14.

[35] GB.288/TC/1.

[36] GB.289/TC/4 and GB.289/TC/4/Inf.

[37] GB.288/TC/2.

[38] GB.289/TC/1.

[39] GB.289/TC/2.

[40] GB.289/TC/3.

[41] GB.287/6.

[42] GB.289/TC/5.

[43] GB.289/PFA/3.

[44] GB.288/4/1.

[45] GB.289/3/1.

[46] GB.289/7.

[47] GB.288/3/1.

[48] See section on 93rd Session (June 2005) below.

[49] GB.289/11.

[50] GB.289/2/1.

[51] In March 2003, the Governing Body had decided that the 93rd (June 2003) Session of the Conference should open on Tuesday, 7 June 2005.

[52] GB.288/4/2.

[53] GB.289/3/2(Rev.).

[54] GB.289/5.

[55] The texts of these resolutions as well as the conclusions and report of the Credentials Committee adopted by the Meeting were appended to the report of the Meeting.

Appendix I

Oral report of the Chairperson of the Working Party on the Social Dimension of Globalization at the 289th (March 2004) Session of the Governing Body

Oral report by the Chairperson of the Working Party, Ambassador Eui-Yong Chung of the Republic of Korea

1. This is a succinct summary of the discussion in the Working Party on 24 and 25 March 2004, focusing on the key themes which emerged and the procedural follow-up. A full report of the discussion over the two days will be prepared after the Governing Body and provided to delegates to the International Labour Conference in June 2004.

Presentation of the report of the World Commission on the Social Dimension of Globalization: *A fair globalization: Creating opportunities for all*

2. Mr. Juan Somavia, Director-General of the ILO, welcomed His Excellency Mr. Benjamin Mkapa, President of the United Republic of Tanzania, and co-Chairperson of the World Commission on the Social Dimension of Globalization, to the ILO as the first African Head of State to address the Governing Body and highlighted the significance of the discussion on the report of the Commission. His Excellency President Mkapa presented the report of the World Commission to the Governing Body. He looked forward to hearing how the ILO proposed to take forward the agenda set out in the report. The ILO's Governing Body had shown vision and foresight in establishing the Commission. He was looking to the ILO to fully exploit its mandate and provide leadership in the international system.

3. In his opening statement, the Employer spokesperson said his group appreciated the attention given in the report to the principles and values which should underpin globalization. He stressed the positive contribution of globalization in terms of the expansion of trade, production and freedom. The Worker spokesperson said that his group attached special importance to the recommendations concerning the need for coherence in economic and social policy at the national and international level, to those that addressed the widening gap between rich and poor countries and within countries, and to those that underscored the importance of labour standards and social dialogue. He strongly endorsed the recommendation that all relevant international organizations should assume their responsibility to promote these standards and ensure that their policies and programmes do not impede their realization.

Overall reactions by the Working Party to the work of the Commission

4. There was widespread appreciation for the work of the Commission, and all who spoke welcomed the report and thanked the co-Chairpersons and the Commission for their work. There was praise for the high quality of the report and for its balance, coherence and comprehensiveness. It was a timely contribution to the debate on globalization. The report should be circulated as widely as possible and would "serve us all well in the international community".

5. The report provided a credible basis for achieving a breakthrough in the debates on globalization. The recommendations set out in the report were described as being realistic. The diversity of the Commission, the broad and diverse dialogues that informed its work, and the demonstrated effectiveness of dialogue as an instrument for forging consensus were repeatedly highlighted. Some underlined the way in which the report had sought to separate perceptions from facts.

Values and approach

6. The values which informed the report's orientation were underscored: the emphasis on fairness and inclusiveness, the focus on people and their needs, the importance of fundamental rights, and the importance of dialogue. While globalization had brought many benefits and offered much potential, its benefits could be harnessed for more people. To this end there was a need, as set out in the report, for good governance at the local, national, regional and global levels. Fairer global rules and better policies were also crucial if the benefits of globalization were to be more equitably distributed.

Response to the key recommendations

7. It was encouraging to note the convergence of views on many key instruments that the report recommended for achieving a fair globalization:

   - *Stronger national action.* The governance of globalization began at home with a focus on local and national policies, actions and responsibilities. International efforts could only be successful if they were undertaken in concert with strong commitments at the national level. The importance of a well-functioning market economy on the one hand, and an effective and democratic State to address market failures on the other, was highlighted. Higher sustainable growth and development of domestic entrepreneurship were crucial. Integrated policy frameworks addressing both economic and social aspects of national policy needed to be developed and supported. National and global policy actions were not necessarily sequential but needed to be pursued in parallel. Some noted that sound national responses might require wider policy space in global rules and there was thus a need to pursue national and international reforms simultaneously.

   - *Fair rules.* There was a need to re-examine global rules for trade and finance, and reform of the financial architecture. The negative impact of agricultural subsidies, greater market access for products from developing countries and improved measures for special and differential treatment were all recognized by many as issues requiring urgent attention.

   - *Increased aid.* Priority attention had to be given to raising sufficient resources for development. This included increasing development assistance, action on debt relief and delivery on international commitments made.

   - *Accountability.* Improved national and global governance of globalization required democratic accountability of the actors influencing the process. Reform of the multilateral system, and a stronger and more effective United Nations within it, were highlighted as priorities by many. Regional integration and other regional initiatives needed to be reinforced as possible ways of increasing the benefits of globalization, and the New Partnership for Africa's Development (NEPAD) was cited as an example.

   - *Global production systems.* Within global production systems, voluntary private initiatives and social dialogue with multinational enterprises (MNEs) were emphasized as important means to promote social objectives. Special attention needed to be given to efforts to ensure decent work in export processing zones. More thinking and dialogue were needed on policy frameworks for investment and to promote competition within global markets.

   - *Cross-border movement of people.* It was agreed that more thinking, discussion and dialogue were needed to address the issue of the cross-border movement of people. The limited freedom of movement of people across borders contrasted with freer international movement of other factors of production. A multilateral framework for migration could facilitate greater freedom of movement. However, it was also argued that this was an issue best dealt with on a bilateral basis. Several speakers said they looked forward to the forthcoming discussion on migration at the June 2004 session of the International Labour Conference.

8. *Decent work as a global goal.* There was widespread support for making decent work a global goal. Every effort should be made to advance all four of its components, and attention was drawn to specific proposals in the report:

   - The objective of full *employment* needed to be a priority with special emphasis on women, youth and the informal economy. Poverty alleviation was strongly linked to employment generation. The private sector and enterprise had an important role to play in employment creation. Greater emphasis needed to be given to wealth creation.

- The ILO's capacity to promote *labour standards* in general and fundamental principles and rights at work in particular needed to be strengthened.

- Emphasis was placed on the importance of a *global socio-economic floor*, of social protection and of support for workers displaced by industrial restructuring.

- *Social dialogue* was highlighted as an important tool to bring about more equitable outcomes in the workplace, at the national level and at the international level in the context of global production systems.

9. *Policy coherence.* Globalization could not be cut up into slices. There was broad agreement that greater policy coherence at both the national and global levels was an essential condition for success in achieving the decent work objective. National policy coherence was an essential counterpart to global coherence and the report provided a useful tool for dialogue and policy coherence at the national and international levels. Rather than establish new institutions, the report recommended action and dialogue to improve policy coherence at both the national and international levels. This included proposals for policy coherence initiatives, a globalization policy forum and policy development dialogues. These proposals were interesting and worth exploring, and the Office was encouraged to develop them in more detail. While the ILO should work with other international organizations to promote policy coherence, this should not distract the Organization from its primary mandate and concern with labour and employment.

10. Some issues had not been adequately addressed by the report, and required further work. These included: the role of technology and of the media; the impact of globalization on the environment and on culture, values and traditions; the international security environment; policies in respect of the rural poor and HIV/AIDS; and human resource development and training.

Next steps

11. The recommendations contained in the report now needed to be translated into concrete action. There was a need to get an early start, to determine priorities, develop concrete action plans and begin to implement the recommendations. The International Labour Conference in June 2004 and the Governing Body sessions in June and November 2004 provided occasions to move forward in many areas. The Director-General would undertake discussions with other organizations on relevant follow-up issues and consult with the Officers of the Governing Body to review developments and particular aspects of the follow-up.

12. In his closing remarks, the Director-General thanked the Working Party for the stimulating discussion that had taken place over the two days. It had provided the ILO with important signposts for its future action. The Commission's report placed tripartism at the centre of a fair globalization. He noted that this was a challenge to the ILO to use its methods to contribute to policy coherence at both the national and international levels, and the follow-up was now in the hands of its tripartite structure. In closing, President Mkapa called for a consistent, comprehensive and coherent approach to global issues that touched the lives and prospects of people everywhere. Together, the Commission and the ILO had set in motion a credible process that could truly make globalization more fair and make its benefits and opportunities more accessible to more people in countries.

Geneva, 25 March 2004.

Appendix II

289th Session of the Governing Body of the International Labour Office, Geneva, March 2004

Working Party on the Social Dimension of Globalization
(Wednesday, 24 and Thursday, 25 March 2004)

Record of the discussion of the Report of the World Commission on the Social Dimension of Globalization

Chairperson: Mr. Chung

The Director-General, **Mr. Juan Somavia**, welcomed His Excellency, President Benjamin Mkapa of the United Republic of Tanzania as the first African Head of State to address the Governing Body. His task as Co-Chair of the World Commission on the Social Dimension of Globalization had been a high-risk undertaking, given the difficulty and complexity of the issue. The President did not speak for the United Republic of Tanzania, nor even for Africa, alone. He spoke for the excluded and marginalized everywhere. However, with the Presidential Summit on Employment and Poverty Alleviation to be held in 2004, Africa was leading the world in a new direction, in the clear recognition, at the highest political level, that, without jobs, efforts to reduce poverty could not succeed. This was echoed in the Commission's report, which put its trust in dialogue, reinforced tripartism and established decent work as a global goal.

President Benjamin Mkapa *of the United Republic of Tanzania and Co-Chairperson of the World Commission on the Social Dimension of Globalization* opened his remarks by quoting from a work by the poet Paulin Joachim, which stressed the "unconquerable hope" that guarded men and women from yielding to the "demons of despair". The World Commission on the Social Dimension of Globalization also delivered a message of hope. Its report – *A fair globalization: Creating opportunities for all* – outlined a vision of global unity, justice, equality and shared prosperity. The report would not put an end to the controversy spurred by the debate on globalization, but the fact that the Commission, with its diverse composition and perspectives, could agree on the broad recommendations contained in the document, showed that it was possible to move the debate from acrimony to dialogue, solidarity and cooperation. The broad public consultations conducted under the World Commission were further proof of this possibility. These consultations enabled the Commission to hear the views of, and discuss with, governments and opposition politicians, groups representing the widest possible cross-section of professional bodies, interest groups, non-governmental organizations, trade unions, representatives of religious organizations, businesses, employers, the media, academia, and more. A number of studies on issues requiring in-depth analysis and rigorous examination of options for action were also commissioned, and helped advance the work of the Commission. The result was a report on globalization as seen through the eyes of people who did not agree on everything, but were convinced of the urgent need for corrective action. The potential of globalization for good or for bad was immense; it had many positive aspects, but certain of its elements had to be tamed for the sake of common civility and existence.

The problems related to the social dimension of globalization could be attributed to globalization without accountability. While governments were increasingly held accountable by their citizens, other global actors were not. These actors needed to be held accountable for policies, processes and outcomes. The report stressed that globalization began at home. It was therefore important to create an environment conducive to building local capacity to access the opportunities for self-advancement that globalization presented.

Decisions should not be confused with progress. Many decisions had been taken to speed up the global war on poverty, but few advances had been made. The report urged action on all previous commitments, and two particular fields could be singled out: official development assistance and debt relief. At the Monterey Consensus of March 2002, donors committed to increasing official development assistance by US$16 billion a year by 2006. This increase was only a third of actual requirements if the Millennium Development Goals (MDGs) were to be met, and the 2004 report of the Organisation for Economic Co-operation and Development concluded, while noting a rise of US$6 billion for 2002, that current levels of increase were nowhere near to ensuring that Monterey commitments would be kept. New efforts should be made to mobilize global resources to meet the MDGs.

In respect of debt relief, the report stated that it was vital that the debt problem was solved as soon as possible to enable the countries concerned to face their difficult development challenges with a clean slate. The report urged coherence in development policies within developing countries, but also in the policies of donor countries. Moreover, it was clear that the coherence agenda did not simply apply to economic policies: the importance of development needed to be included in policies of every kind, from the environment to foreign affairs, defence and anti-terrorism. The Commission called for a series of coordinated measures across a broad front to improve governance at both national and international levels. These included fairer rules for international trade, investment, finance and migrations, the promotion of core labour standards and a minimum level of social protection in the global economy. Efforts to promote the ILO Declaration on Fundamental Principles and Rights at Work should also be increased, together with the promotion of decent work in global production systems.

The role of markets, investment and entrepreneurship was critical in creating growth and providing employment. Ways should be found to bring the entrepreneurial energy of the informal economy into the mainstream economy. The private sector had a role to play in building fairer globalization, and governments should engage the private sector to tap into its potential to contribute to development and poverty reduction.

The report represented a common commitment to urgent decisive action. From the diversity of the Commission came the agreement that sustainable globalization had to create opportunities for more people. The report was of particular relevance to developing countries, and especially Africa. If the benefits of globalization were to be expanded, there must be fairer terms for developing country goods in global markets. The rules for foreign direct investment should also be fair, to ensure that investments contributed to meeting development objectives.

There was already a growing momentum for action around the messages of the report and many initiatives had been launched. In the Declaration of Santa Cruz de la Sierra in November 2003, Heads of State and Government in the Americas reaffirmed their conviction that decent work was the most effective means of promoting better living conditions. The Extraordinary Summit on Employment and Poverty Alleviation, involving African Heads of State, would be held in September 2004, with ILO participation. President Halonen of Finland, Co-Chair of the World Commission, would shortly be taking up the issues raised in the report with the European Council in Brussels. The United Nations Development Programme Commission on the Private Sector and Development had, in March 2004, presented its report to the United Nations Secretary-General. The purpose of that Commission was to develop strategic recommendations on how to promote strong indigenous private sectors, and its report was a welcome, concrete contribution to the global strategy for growth, investment and employment. All these initiatives echoed the message of the report of the World Commission in seeking to devise practical measures on how to empower people to overcome poverty and exclusion.

The report was a base on which to build. It was now for the members of the Working Party to provide leadership in the international system to take the work forward. The ten key needs identified by the World Commission in its report were the following: a focus on people; a democratic and effective State; sustainable development; productive and equitable markets; fair rules; globalization with solidarity; greater accountability to people; deeper partnerships; an effective United Nations; and policy coherence for global development.

Mr. D. Funes de Rioja *(Employer Vice-Chairperson of the Governing Body; Employers' delegate, Argentina)*, speaking on behalf of the Employers' group, thanked President Mkapa and President Halonen for their personal commitment, guidance and spirit of dialogue to build up consensus during the Commission debates. He found the report essential and vital and echoed President Mkapa's belief that the diversity, not just that of the members, but also of the problems, must be looked at. The report had the virtue of being produced by a group of persons with diverse backgrounds and diverging experience, from different regions and perceptions, who had come together to identify significant issues and solutions to make the best use of the potential of globalization and to share that fairly in all areas, including the economic, social, cultural and political dimensions. Because of this, the Governing Body and the ILO as a whole, had important material to use as a basis for reflection and developing proposals.

The debate on globalization was essential for the Employers, and the report provided a timely basis for reflection to carry this debate further. The report did not condemn globalization outright, but stressed the values that should guide societies and institutions, in particular highlighting good governance, locally and globally. The Employers' group fully endorsed the statement that universally shared values and principles had to be the basis of the democratic governance of globalization; they recognized the need to create a framework for investment, to integrate the informal economy, promote employment, education and training and develop an appropriate physical and social infrastructure. Respect for human rights, for fundamental rights at work, for contracts and for property, the rule of law and transparency were all necessary elements of a democratic market, associated with the financial, technological and commercial aspects, together with social dialogue. Earlier, confrontational, models of globalization must be put to one side and a cooperative spirit should be developed.

Globalization had contributed to sustainable development. Many countries recognized that it was a positive factor in the elimination of poverty in a model including the correct associated policies on administration, social protection and health and education. The report stressed the importance of foreign direct investment as a key element; such investment could only be made if the correct environment were provided with policies ensuring respect for the law.

The multilateral system should be improved, but not changed radically. The Bretton Woods institutions were undergoing a positive process of reform, but the various agencies, while interacting effectively, should retain their own mandates and act within them.

The report did not place enough emphasis on the positive impact of globalization in terms of trade and production, on the expansion of political and economic freedom, facilitating economic initiative and technological development. Certain countries had successfully achieved a consolidation of their democratic systems with a sustainable market economy. Globalization could not be held responsible for all ills. Unfortunately, poverty did exist in many countries, but it would certainly be reduced by better governance, transparency, good management of public expenses, the creation of employment and the integration of the informal economy. The provision of adequate housing, education and health infrastructure would also improve the situation.

Multinational enterprises were not a barrier to new enterprises. There should be interaction within a network of enterprises, allowing the expansion of local wealth, not simply the expansion of multinational enterprises. However, the contribution of multinationals to economic and technological development was a fact. The Employers, as entrepreneurs, were committed to growth in employment.

Closed capital markets were not better armed to deal with crises. Australia and New Zealand rode through the Asian crisis in their own manner. The group disagreed with the introduction of global rates of taxation, and believed that the provision of tax advantages to enterprises could be valuable. Modern and efficient state mechanisms should be crafted to balance economic and social requirements.

He concluded by saying that the report was relevant for the Employers and that there were many points for action by the ILO, both internally and in terms of external coherence and policy, associated with other international forums.

Sir Roy Trotman *(Worker Vice-Chairperson of the Governing Body; Workers' delegate, Barbados)* congratulated President Mkapa and the other commissioners and noted that the report listed, as the basic principles which should guide globalization, democracy, social equity, respect for human rights and the rule of law. The Workers' group added "free trade unions" to this list. It was appropriate that the report was being discussed within the Governing Body and that the Governing Body should take decisions about the implementation of the recommendations that directly related to the ILO. It had already been agreed that the Director-General would present a report to the International Labour Conference in June focusing on the implications of the World Commission's recommendations for the work of the ILO. The Governing Body would examine a concrete and realistic plan of action, based on the Conference debate, in November.

The recommendations to which the group attached most importance fell into three categories. The first of these were recommendations promoting coherence in economic and social policy at international level, several of which related to the multilateral system. Multilateral organizations should examine their own procedures to ensure coherence of action with respect to universal values and human rights. International organizations should launch policy coherence initiatives to work together in designing complementary policies to achieve fair, inclusive globalization; the first of these should address the question of growth, investment and employment in the global economy. A globalization policy forum should be established by interested international organizations. Decent work for all should be made a global goal and pursued through more coherent policies within the multilateral system. Governments should devote the political will and the resources necessary for the implementation of the recommendations fostering coherence.

The ILO should ensure that the recommendations on coherence were noted within the key international organizations. To this end, the Workers' group approved the recommendation that formal structures for consultation within the international labour movement and the business community be established in the Bretton Woods institutions and the World Trade Organization.

Globalization had led to widening gaps between rich and poor countries, and between the rich and poor within countries. The group strongly supported the recommendation that affirmative action should be taken in favour of less-developed countries, and that the World Trade Organization's special and differential provisions should be strengthened significantly. Relief measures should be designed to increase resource flows to developing countries. The capacity of the ILO to promote respect for core labour standards should be reinforced, an aspect on which the report unfortunately lacked recommendations, and social dialogue should be strengthened to promote decent work, particularly in export processing zones and with multinational corporations. The group would be developing the proposals outlined more fully, as well as further ideas, but, overall, it supported the report and its findings.

*The Worker delegate from France, **Mr. M. Blondel**,* recalled the Director-General's words that the current model of globalization had not succeeded in creating jobs, a condition essential to the elimination of poverty, and that the advantages which devolved from globalization were not being fairly distributed. This statement fully coincided with the opinion of the Governing Body. Consequently, the work of the independent World Commission, although not committing the Governing Body de facto, was clearly of significance. The Workers' group thus approved the analysis and recommendations of the report, in particular since it upheld the general idea of better coordination in respect of international economic policy. It was important to stress that employment should not be considered as a by-product of the economy, but as an objective in its own right.

Greater coordination was needed between the competent international organizations: the World Bank, the International Monetary Fund (IMF), the United Nations Conference on Trade and Development (UNCTAD), the World Trade Organization (WTO) and the ILO. Within nations, certain governments led financial and monetary policies which destroyed all social guarantees. The group therefore approved the recommendation that new methods should be made to promote coherence between economic and social goals in the global economy, in coordination with other organizations of the multilateral system. The necessary international labour standards, the fruit of regular negotiations between governments, employers and workers, were already in place.

The group noted the reiteration in the report of the commitment to devote 0.7 per cent of GDP to official development assistance. This level should be rapidly achieved despite difficulties encountered, for example the pretext of giving priority to national unemployment. It should be recalled that the resources came from taxpayers, and this solidarity should also be expressed in terms of generalized social protection, a goal upheld by the ILO.

The report indicated the responsibility of States and governments in the construction of the required socio-economic dynamic. Clearly this was to be built around democratic choices made by the people. To this extent, the inclusion of international non-governmental organizations (INGOs) in the decision-making process disturbed the democratic procedure. This was not the case of the ILO, which should maintain its tripartite structure and define its action on this basis. It was this that gave international labour standards their universal nature, and made them a force for cohesion. The report noted the consequences when such standards were not applied in export processing zones.

Regarding the future of the report, contacts could be arranged between representatives of the steering bodies of the relevant international organizations in Geneva to help coordinate multilateral action. For this reason, the Workers' group strongly supported the proposal to establish a globalization policy forum, which should be attended by a tripartite ILO delegation.

The representative of the Government of Ecuador, **Mr. R. Izurieta Mora-Bowen**, *Minister of Labour and Human Resources*, speaking on behalf of the Group of Latin American States and the Caribbean (GRULAC), congratulated and thanked the World Commission on the Social Dimension of Globalization. GRULAC expressed its appreciation for the detailed and valuable work done in bringing together information that pinpointed the main injustices of the current process of globalization. He said that the report highlighted the imbalances created by globalization, to the disadvantage of developing countries. To attain a more inclusive globalization, the report was right to suggest that changes should be made in internal national policies. However, GRULAC believed that this should not be considered a prerequisite to international change, which could be conducted at the same time, at a different rhythm. In this context, the group agreed with the suggestion that there was a democratic deficit inherent in the United Nations system and the Bretton Woods institutions.

The report stressed the need to reform the present financial architecture, with a view to achieving greater stability on the markets, and consequently prevent crises such as had recently affected some Latin American States. GRULAC supported the monitoring of current activity to produce more detailed studies on an acceptable apparatus to regulate capital flows.

GRULAC believed it was important to highlight the negative effects on developing countries of the agricultural subsidy policies adopted by the industrialized countries. These were very detrimental to the countries of the region. Decent work should be promoted as a global goal. It constituted an important means of reducing the negative social effect of the current process of globalization and would be very instrumental in achieving MDG objectives. Countries should make firm commitments to official development assistance, such as agreed at the Monterey Summit, and at the same time reduce foreign debt.

Regarding migrant workers, GRULAC believed that there was a need for more coordination between the international organizations dealing with the problem. The 92nd Session of the International Labour Conference would provide an excellent occasion to discuss this question in depth. The report also pointed to the effects of globalization on the media, and as a result on national cultures; this was a theme which should be developed further. With respect to the proposal to establish a globalization policy forum, the follow-up process which had been initiated by the present discussion would surely throw light on this initiative, and clarify its implementation, mandate and composition.

The report concluded that extra-budgetary funds would be required to finance many of the initiatives suggested: GRULAC hoped that this would not lead to additional obligations for the developing countries, nor to a diversion of resources currently allocated elsewhere. GRULAC considered that the report constituted an important consideration on the socio-economic effects on both developing and developed countries of the process of globalization. The Office should keep the Governing Body and constituents informed of all comments and suggestions received regarding the report. GRULAC wished to be associated in future debates and decisions on the follow-up adopted by the ILO.

The representative of the Government of Cameroon, **Mr. R. Nkili**, *Minister of Employment, Labour and Social Welfare*, spoke both for the Government of his country and for Africa. He supported the recommendations in the report on the formulation of coherent policies to ensure better governance of the global community. The ILO should intensify its cooperation with the other organizations of the United Nations system, to give real impact to the findings and conclusions of the report, and to spread more fairly the benefits derived from globalization.

The report called for urgent change, to bring in a new era of global governance, as well as for the conception and implementation of new global architecture which took account of all peoples of the world, through the widening of social dialogue and a constant search for consensus. The

Government of Cameroon believed that the ILO, with its tripartite structure and its approach through social dialogue, was the institution to implement such action. All efforts should be made to put in place a plan instigating fairer global commercial rules, a more humane management of the developing world's debt problem, more support for efforts to eradicate HIV/AIDS, and measures to facilitate the transfer of new technologies. Africa was fully committed to participating in the process, and ready to make its voice heard.

The representative of the Government of India, **Mr. P.D. Shenoy**, *Secretary of Labour*, said his statement was widely supported by the delegates from Indonesia and the Islamic Republic of Iran. He congratulated the World Commission for a well-researched, comprehensive and balanced report. Globalization had the potential to usher in material prosperity and reduce world poverty, but had so far created serious imbalances. The Government of India fully supported the road map presented by the report, prescribing a fair and more inclusive globalization, the involvement of all stakeholders, reinforcement of multilateral systems, complementarity of State and markets, and more equitable sharing of benefits.

The report emphasized the need for good national governance based on democracy, respect for human rights, gender equality and the rule of law, the provision of decent work and opportunities for capacity building, enhancement of economic competitiveness, integration of the informal economy, and a prudent management of the process of integration into the global economy. India, Indonesia and the Islamic Republic of Iran had made diligent efforts in this direction, but with mixed results. The more developed sectors, such as information technology, had benefited; the socially deprived and rural poor had lost. The Government of India had responded by creating additional employment opportunities, training and empowerment. Any support in this endeavour would be welcome, for example with regard to the movement of natural persons. Globalization opened frontiers to investment, trade and technology, but the cross-border movement of people was highly restricted. The WTO framework was limited to the temporary movement of service providers; other international conventions also had limited coverage, and even activities which did not involve the movement of natural persons, such as business process outsourcing, were coming under close scrutiny.

To combat the inequities in the global market, an effective multilateral framework was important. The ILO, which was well equipped to handle such sensitive issues, could well play a coordinating role. The report recommended that the international organizations should work on the design of more balanced and complementary policies for achieving a fair and inclusive globalization. They should also have multi-stakeholder policy development dialogues on issues including building a multilateral framework for the cross-border movement of people, corporate social responsibility, a development framework for foreign direct investment, social protection, capacity building, regional and subregional integration and gender equality. A globalization policy forum should be established as a centre for dialogue, but the primacy of the ILO in resolving contentious labour issues should not be compromised.

The representative of the Government of Ireland, **Ambassador Whelan**, spoke on behalf of the European Union. The EU accession countries, Cyprus, Czech Republic, Estonia, Hungary, Latvia, Lithuania, Malta, Poland, Slovakia and Slovenia, the candidate countries, Bulgaria, Romania, Turkey, and the countries of the stabilization and association process and potential EU candidates, Albania, Bosnia and Herzegovina, Croatia, The former Yugoslav Republic of Macedonia, Serbia and Montenegro also aligned themselves with the statement.

She declared that the fact that 26 eminent individuals had been prepared to serve on the Commission in a personal capacity was testament to the importance of the issue. The European Union wished to compliment and thank them for their work and time, and welcomed the publication of the report which constituted an important contribution to the discussion on globalization. As the report stated, it offered no miraculous or simple solutions but rather delivered balanced, critical but positive messages. The report acknowledged that there were many good aspects to globalization but more could be done at national and global levels to address the social dimension of the phenomenon.

The very existence of the report was a remarkable and comprehensive demonstration of policy coherence, underlining the interrelation between economic, employment and social issues. One of the key themes of the report was coherence in economic and social policies and among existing international organizations. The EU fully supported this, while acknowledging that, given the variety of functions of these organizations, it might present difficulties. Many of the report's recommendations were relevant for EU policies and strategies, both internally and externally. The EU was already active in promoting the social dimension of globalization through economic, employment and social policies. Efforts should be made to improve the participation rate in the labour market, and this meant maintaining an adequate level of social protection, and promoting increased flexibility and security in the workplace. The EU would play an active role in further discussions and follow-up, and looked to the ILO for guidance as to the initiation of the different processes outlined in the report at global level.

She acknowledged President Mkapa's outstanding contribution to the work of the Commission.

The representative of the Government of Brazil, **Mr. R. Berzoini,** *Minister of State for Work and Employment,* thanked the World Commission for its report and said that the document represented the end of one stage and the beginning of a new, more important stage of analysis and action in order to maximize the good results of globalization. He highlighted the Commission's statement on the degree of injustice inherent in the current process of globalization, made on the basis of specific cases. It was clearly the developing countries that were benefiting least from the phenomenon and that action should be taken to ensure a fairer and more inclusive process. The action undertaken by governments, multilateral organizations and civil society should be based on ethical values, as stated in the report. The gap between declarations and practical action, particularly on the part of donor countries, was too wide. The effect of the work of the World Commission should not be restricted simply to the ILO, but should have an impact on national institutions and on the multilateral organizations as well. Good governance was an essential element of national systems and of the multilateral system, which should operate more democratically. Urgent structural changes should be made in the functioning of the United Nations and Bretton Woods institutions, to enhance the participation of all members and increase transparency. The Government of Brazil hoped that the voting system within the United Nations would be altered, to give developing countries a stronger voice. This issue should be present on the agendas of international forums, and the reinforcement of the Economic and Social Council (ECOSOC) was an essential step in this direction.

It was impossible for governments to commit more resources to health and education when labouring under an excessive level of debt. The present terms of international loans at high rates of interest meant that resources devoted to social development were scant. Measures should be introduced to regulate international flows of capital: the recent crisis in Latin America could still be felt and had resulted in increased unemployment in the region. There was a need for fairer international finance and trade regulations, and for reform of the international financial architecture. Under the present system, capital was transferred from the developing countries to the developed. Governments of the industrialized countries should also consider the impact of their policies on the developing world. The effect of the common agricultural policy on the economic and social development of the Latin American region was particularly serious and concrete measures should be taken urgently to redress the situation.

The capacity of the ILO should be reinforced to allow it to coordinate measures in favour of fundamental rights and principles at work. It was, however, necessary to avoid protectionism: the subject of migrant workers, of importance for many Latin American States, called for management through a multilateral framework. The 92nd Session of the Conference would provide an excellent opportunity to discuss this question.

The report urged an increase in donations of development assistance to attain the MDGs. Any increase in contributions would be useless unless accompanied by increased commitment on the part of governments. Decent work should be taken as a goal within the multilateral system, as part of the global agenda, and was not simply a matter of implementing policies. The ILO should take the lead within the United Nations system in coordinating efforts to promote decent work.

To reduce the negative impact of globalization, action was necessary. More in-depth studies and debate were required before decisions were taken on how changes should be implemented. The United Nations system should play a central role in the process, and the Government of Brazil would remain fully involved. The debate today was an initial step in establishing a policy of international dialogue. Regarding the extra-budgetary resources needed for carrying through the recommendations of the report, these should in no way represent an additional burden for developing countries. His Government wished to receive information from the Office on all comments and suggestions received from other international organizations, and from civil society on the report.

The representative of the Government of Romania, **Mr. M. Sarbu**, *Minister Delegate for Relations with the Social Partners*, expressed his Government's thanks to the Co-Chairpersons and said that his country was as aware of the challenges posed by globalization as of the opportunities it presented. The global economy was certain to lead to a global society which would call for a global political project able to give form to the institutions, and fix the rules, of globalization. The European social model might provide an example for the reduction of the economic divide before that divide became a source of international conflict and instability.

To develop and modernize the national economy, the Romanian Government had chosen to take full advantage of the opportunities presented by globalization. At the social level, combating poverty was the first priority. This implied sustained development, economic growth based on efficiency, increased employment, diversification, including rural development, the creation of new social structures and the enlargement of those already in place. Over the past three years, Romania had maintained a growth rate of 5 per cent, coupled with one of the lowest rates of unemployment in Central Europe of between 7 and 8 per cent. Of particular note was the mobility of the Romanian workforce within Europe. In this connection, the Minister paid homage to the victims of the terrorist attacks of 11 March in Madrid. Among the dead had been a number of Romanian workers.

The representative of the Government of Japan, **Mr. S. Hasegawa**, *Assistant Minister for Health, Labour and Welfare*, expressed thanks to the Commissioners under the chairmanship of Presidents Halonen and Mkapa, and appreciated the efforts in grappling with the difficult issue of the social dimension of globalization and for drawing up the comprehensive report. While globalization was a strong source of growth and could bring about improved living standards for all countries, it was important, in the light of the current situation, to address its social dimension. The Government approved the report's approach to viewing globalization through the eyes of people: fair globalization and human-centred development were crucial for creating opportunities for all. Many important issues were raised in the report – the choice of decent work for all as a global goal, the creation of employment, the need for human resources development, for occupational safety and health and social dialogue. Coherence in economic and social policies was crucial to the promotion of decent work, as was good national governance. However, the role of the private sector and of enterprise in employment creation was also significant. More employment opportunities for young people should be created. Ownership by developing countries and partnerships with developed countries and the international organizations were essential. The ILO should strengthen its activities in these fields and disseminate best practices. To share the benefits of globalization as widely as possible, the ILO should provide technical cooperation in human resource development and employment creation, backed up with official development assistance.

Japan, with other countries and international organizations, was reforming its legislation to prevent human trafficking, and to ensure that transgressions were punished.

ILO activities in addressing social and labour issues should be promoted in a more visible manner in the international community. There should therefore be reinforced cooperation between the ILO and other international organizations. The ILO should be the institution responsible for ensuring respect of core labour standards, but these should not be used for protectionist purposes. The ILO should regularly and systematically review the current situation of globalization.

The representative of the Government of Uruguay, **Mr. S. Pérez de Castillo**, *Minister for Labour and Social Security*, approved the report's apt conclusion that the essential elements to achieve international social justice were full employment, social protection, respect for the fundamental rights of workers and social dialogue. Economic growth in itself, however, did not bring fair distribution of wealth. The question was to decide to what extent to intervene in the market. As the dictum went, there should be as much market as possible, and as much intervention as necessary. The market economy provided an instrument for economic growth through individual initiative, but did not ensure fair distribution. Specific steps were called for within the United Nations system, the Bretton Woods institutions and other multilateral bodies. Action in the most developed countries should also be engaged to raise living standards in the developing world. This should involve establishing fair trade rules, rather than providing development aid. We should seek to reduce the dichotomy between the social and the economic. Rather than working in two separate directions, to combat poverty and to stimulate economic progress, the economic dimension should also be put at the service of human beings. Increasing the number of jobs and trying to prevent unemployment were major tools to right the current situation.

Education was also very important, and closely linked to employment. Knowledge, technology and skills were part of the personal wealth of individuals. The global economy could not be held responsible for all ills, however, and action should concentrate on favouring the positive impact, while reducing the negative side. Fair globalization required an international financial architecture which regulated capital flows and protected against external shocks, such as those which had so damaged many Latin American economies. The report noted that, in industrialized countries, agricultural subsidies ran at more than a billion dollars a day, while 70 per cent of the poor in the world lived on less than 1 dollar a day. Technical cooperation should be more effective and should be better managed by international institutions. There should be a joint examination by the ILO, the World Bank, the IMF and the WTO of the social implications of economic, financial and commercial policies.

He congratulated the World Commission, the ILO and the Governing Body for having created a focus for the work on globalization. The report was an extremely useful reflection on a topic of great contemporary concern. The issue fell squarely within the mandate of the ILO, and followed on from the call in the Declaration of Philadelphia to ensure that any international measures were fully compatible with the material well-being and happiness of all human beings.

*The representative of the Government of the United States, **Mr. A. Levine**, Deputy Under Secretary of Labor for International Affairs,* commended the members of the World Commission for their work and supported the central goal of the Commission to bring the many benefits of globalization to all people throughout the world. He took note of the statement made in the report that the most critical reforms to ensure that the benefits of globalization were more fully available could only be initiated at the national and local levels. The report correctly identified that good national governance, democracy, respect for human rights and sound economic institutions were fundamental to development and, without them, no matter how much was spent on technical assistance, nor how great the desire to change global trade, investment and finance rules, development could not take place. Corruption, inefficiency, an absence of law and justice all resulted in a stunting of the opportunities provided by globalization. Enterprise, creativity and the freedom to exercise these were the driving forces of economic growth. The private sector operating in a market economy with sound legal protection remained the most effective generator of wealth, and the United States was pleased to note the recommendations for empowering local communities and strengthening local economic capabilities. However, international efforts directed against poverty, disease, child labour and other social wrongs would only succeed if undertaken in concert with strong commitments at national level. The creation of new institutions, new bureaucracies and new international arrangements was not in itself a formula for ridding the world of poverty.

The report's strong endorsement of the ILO's current activities and policies was welcome and the United States hoped that the ILO would focus on advancing the report's strategic goals and not on areas better suited to other organizations, such as intellectual property rights, competition policy, investment treaties, debt relief and cross-border migration. However, there should be active dialogue between the ILO and its sister international organizations on the social dimension of globalization.

He thanked the Commission for its significant contribution to the discussion of the potential and the challenges of globalization and looked forward to working with the Director-General to translate the report's broad recommendations into discrete steps that the ILO could undertake in its areas of expertise.

*The representative of the Government of Bangladesh, **Ambassador Ali**,* extended heartiest congratulations to the members of the World Commission for a timely, comprehensive and objective report. He deeply appreciated the personal commitment of President Mkapa to the work of the Commission and thanked the Director-General for his initiative in organizing the Commission. He asked what hope globalization offered to developing countries, particularly those with structural constraints. In Bangladesh poverty alleviation was closely linked to sustained growth and employment generation, but the prescriptions for economic growth had frequently been ill-suited to the country's needs. It was interesting to note that success stories came from countries that had chosen their own route, outside conventional advice. The key to growth was to encourage domestic, not foreign, investment by developing domestic entrepreneurship. Economic development required experimentation, local knowledge and local solutions and he was pleased that the report recognized that countries must have the autonomy and freedom in policy formulation that best suited their needs.

Mobility of labour was an issue that should be regulated by clear rules. Two areas required more detailed attention: the impact of globalization on culture, values and traditions, and the impact on cultures, peoples and development prospects, of security issues such as weapons of mass destruction, conventional arms and growing security considerations. Bangladesh considered the proposal for policy coherence initiatives, especially those on investment, growth and employment, to be very important and asked for further information thereon.

The representative of the Government of Malawi, **Mr. B. Khamisa**, *Minister of Labour and Vocational Training*, thanked President Mkapa for his inspiring speech. He highlighted the critical importance of global governance. He noted that globalization had removed territorial barriers around nation States and had brought them closer to each other. However, barriers of a different order, born of a "cold war" mentality, should not be allowed to form: the developing world needed the help of the industrialized countries. There was also a need for an active implementation plan and follow-up to the report's recommendations.

The Employer member from the United States, **Mr. T. Niles**, notwithstanding certain reservations, found much in the report with which he agreed, and wanted to work with the ILO and the Director-General in its implementation. It was essential to define what policy coherence meant and what its limits were. The ILO could not intervene in the policy decisions of another organization or interfere in its work. Organizations should consult each other, but each should be allowed to carry out its mandate without the intervention of other agencies. He welcomed the report's emphasis on governance at the national level, commenting that even if all the recommendations for changes in international trade and financial systems were adopted, many countries would not benefit substantially on account of failures in either governance or corruption, or both. One shortcoming in the report was its tendency to shift responsibility for the implementation of international agreements away from governments to other actors, often corporations. The implementation of international agreements was, and must remain, the responsibility of ratifying governments, as the policies and programmes of international organizations such as the international financial institutions and the WTO must remain their responsibility. Concluding, he recalled that wealth creation was fundamentally the role of business.

The representative of the Government of Germany, **Mr. G. Andres**, *Ministry of Economic Affairs and Labour*, said the report supplied a coherent and balanced picture of globalization, acknowledging its ability to create wealth, but demanding that more should be made of its development opportunities. The Government of Germany was of the opinion that dynamic and growth-oriented policies and markets were required – and that policy coherence at an international level should be fostered. The national level was the starting point for all political answers to globalization. Good governance at the national level, the creation of functioning democratic rules, respect for human rights, social justice, and the creation and enhancement of partnership structures in the world of labour, constituted an indispensable basis for effective and equal participation in the world economy. Germany supported greater regional integration as a key element of effective global economic management and advocated enhanced dialogue between individual world regions, particularly in the areas of growth and employment. To this end, close and constructive cooperation between stakeholders was essential and could be achieved through a greater and more effective exchange of information between international institutions as well as more coherence in political target setting. Better interconnection between international players – such as the ILO, the WTO and the Bretton Woods institutions – would also be an appropriate step.

He thanked the Office and fully supported its role in implementing the report.

The representative of the Government of the Republic of Korea, **Ambassador Choi**, conveyed warmest congratulations to the members of the World Commission on the completion of their mandate and expressed deep appreciation for the work of the Co-Chairs. The report was a groundbreaking achievement and a systematic attempt to analyse the social dimension of one of the most prominent and complex phenomena of the era. He echoed the need for efforts to begin at home. Free, creative and empowered individuals were a country's most important asset in meeting the challenges of globalization. The Republic of Korea concurred with the observations on the need for social protection, creation of decent work and open social dialogue. There was also a necessity for better global governance. The proposals for policy coherence initiatives, policy development dialogues and globalization policy forums went to the heart of global policy coordination and he looked forward to constructive and efficient Office follow-up measures and initiatives to muster support from the broader international community.

The representative of the Government of Venezuela, **Mr. R. Dorado Cano-Manuel**, congratulated President Mkapa, his Co-Chair, and the Commission members for the document. He saw the debate on globalization becoming a discussion of democracy in the world economy. He supported the idea of a humanist economy and said that achieving this required political will and international coherence. It was vital for the State to play a key role as a promoter of public policy to ensure general welfare.

The Worker member from Benin, **Mr. G. Attigbe**, added his congratulations to the members of the Commission and saw the report as a major analysis of the nature and social impact of globalization. He spoke of the continuing impoverishment of Africa and outlined proposals for the future of the continent. The first was to focus attention on the role of the State and the public sector at the national level, as Africa needed democratic States that would utilize the market, world trade and economic policy to meet the development needs of their population and not external demands. The second was world governance and the need for fair rules in international trade and finance. Finally, he stated that the Workers' group keenly awaited the definitive decision on follow-up to the World Commission's recommendations.

Ms. L. Pavan-Woolfe, *European Commission*, welcomed the report as an important contribution towards better addressing globalization, and expressed compliments and thanks to the members of the Commission for their work and commitment. The report delivered balanced, critical but positive messages, contained an interesting analysis and innovative proposals to improve policy coherence, which were worth further investigation. She welcomed the emphasis on operational proposals and effective follow-up. Key issues in her opinion were balanced economic, employment and social policies, better governance, policy coherence, the strengthening of multilateralism, and trade and development. She declared that the report was relevant for European Union policies, competencies and strategies, both internally and externally, where the European Union was already promoting the social dimension of globalization. The European Commission agreed that governance of globalization started at home and that reform of global governance was needed as well as the strengthening of coordination between organizations and stakeholders. The report made important observations on the potential merits of south-south trade and the European Commission was in agreement that complementarities were needed between multilateral commitments in trade and domestic policies and reforms, in order to make growth sustainable. Regarding human rights and core labour standards, the European Commission was of the opinion that the ILO's capacity for promoting their implementation should be reinforced. The management of migration was necessary at the international level and called for multilateral dialogue and initiatives. The objectives of sustained growth and more and better jobs should be at the top of the agenda. Effective and systematic follow-up to the report's recommendations was of vital importance and the European Commission hoped that the ILO would give guidance on the way it intended to initiate the different processes at a global level.

The representative of the Government of Burundi, **Mr. D. Nditabiriye**, *Minister of Labour and Social Security*, thanked President Mkapa and the Commission members for a report of high quality, based on objective analysis, despite the diversity of its authors. The recommendations were powerful and so appropriate that comment was hardly necessary. He remarked that the Commission now had the difficult task of convincing world leaders to join it in bringing about a change in globalization. He urged that the starting point be Africa and African governments. He also proposed that the ILO appoint the Chairperson of the Commission to draw up a report and an action plan on the moral dimension of globalization.

The Employer member from Pakistan, **Mr. A. Tabani**, speaking on behalf of the Employer members from the Asian region, said that the Commission represented diverse views and perspectives and that making recommendations could not have been an easy task. He commended the Co-Chairs, Commissioners and the Director-General for their work. He found the most significant aspect of the report to be its recognition that globalization had generated many significant benefits throughout the world and even more importantly had the potential to lift people out of poverty. In view of this, individual governments needed to face up to their responsibilities and create the conditions to enable globalization to be spread wider. Regarding the importance of governance, he found the idea of national commissions to be worth exploring. He pointed out two specific areas that required more prominence, i.e. policies to address the situation of the rural poor; and special poverty reduction programmes, which, in the past, had often failed to deliver results.

The representative of the Government of Argentina, **Ms. N. Rial**, *Deputy Minister of Labour, Employment and Social Security*, thanked the World Commission for its excellent work. The report was rooted in the unique and moral mandate of the ILO and had started a long-overdue debate. She declared that globalization had not been the ideal tool for achieving decent work and a process based on solidarity was needed. The policy for the consolidation of global governance should place people at its centre, which also meant enhancing the responsibility of civil society. The rules imposed on developing countries needed revision to ease the burden of foreign debt. Investment in infrastructure was perceived as unproductive public expenditure and this had to be reviewed. Finally, core labour standards should be applied to all workers to ensure that globalization offered equality and opportunity.

The representative of the Government of France, **Mr. P. Séguin**, *Former Minister*, hailed the quality of the work accomplished by the World Commission, led by Presidents Mkapa and Halonen. He offered thanks to all, including the Director-General, without whom the Commission would never have got off the ground. It was the ILO that had organized the initiative and this deserved mention. He declared that the report's recommendations were in keeping with France's own thinking on globalization, especially the need to strengthen governance at both national and international levels, as well as regarding an increase in the regular budgets of United Nations organizations, including the ILO. New ideas in the report, such as that of a multilateral framework for cross-border movement, a world forum for migration and a permanent forum on globalization, were, in his opinion, also of interest as they allowed improved coordination of international efforts on decent work and the fight against poverty. He thought it necessary to create a list of priorities of the proposals outlined in the report and to identify both the ILO's responsibilities and those of others. It was vital to reflect on ILO operational action and to study the resources available to the international community to act alongside the ILO. There had to be reflection on the role of not only international institutions but also of civil society organizations. He looked forward to in-depth discussions at the Conference which would provide a mandate for the ILO to carry out follow-up work on the report.

The representative of the Government of Gabon, **Mr. C. Ivala**, *Minister of Labour and Employment*, expressed his gratitude to President Mkapa for having co-chaired the Commission and strongly supported regional integration, which was already a strategic objective of the New Partnership for Africa's Development. He also approved the creation of a forum on globalization.

The Worker member from Mexico, **Ms. H. Andersen**, recalled that Latin America had been brought into turmoil by globalization. Democratic processes, eradication of hunger, universal education and decent work were key in countering the technological and economic trends which had prevailed to date. In America, people aspired to equality in the workplace – especially to allow the predominantly female section of the informal economy to shift to the formal economy. She also sought the application of core labour standards and fair trade rules.

The representative of the Government of the United Kingdom, **Ms. M. Niven**, appreciating the fact that the report did not suggest creating a plethora of new structures, strongly agreed that increasing employment was key to reducing poverty, particularly in developing countries. Work and employment were critical to meeting the needs and aspirations of individuals and families: record increases in unemployment could not be allowed to continue. She welcomed the emphasis on the particular needs of women, youth, indigenous groups, ethnic minorities and, particularly, workers in the informal economy, as well as the ILO's commitment to pursue and intensify its efforts to integrate employment into Poverty Reduction Strategy Papers. Education and training were paramount in an employment-focused agenda for poverty reduction and she was pleased to note the assessment that all countries needed to increase investments in education and training if they were to maximize the benefits of globalization. However, as the report argued, there was a need to look beyond employment creation and embrace the concept of decent work and freely chosen employment that provided a reasonable income and respected labour standards. It was encouraging that over half of the ILO's member States had ratified all eight ILO core labour Conventions. She commended the World Commission for its report and looked forward to a plan for specific action.

The representative of the Government of Lithuania, **Mr. R. Kairelis**, *Ministry of Social Security and Labour*, said the report was comprehensive and would serve as a basis for wider discussions, analysis and follow-up. He stressed that relevant national policy, regional integration and cooperation could promote a more equitable balance of globalization. He looked forward to discussions on regional policy coordination at the follow-up to this debate to be held at the forthcoming session of the Conference.

The representative of the Government of Norway, **Ambassador Johansen**, commented on the fine job carried out by the Commission and remarked that the report not only represented an important contribution to understanding the phenomenon of globalization but also provided interesting ideas on how to achieve fair globalization. The fundamental spirit of the report closely resembled the approach taken by the Government of Norway. The focus on people was one of its strengths. He shared the report's fundamentally positive assessment of globalization, but there was a need to adjust course if the potential of the phenomenon was to be realized. Its placing of decent work at the centre of national and international policy-making, its clear focus on coherence in policy-making, particularly among existing international organizations, were very positive. The increased openness, interdependence and connectivity of a globalized world represented an immense potential for inclusion, greater solidarity and commitment to shared values. A stronger and more effective United Nations was the essential instrument in creating a democratic, legitimate and coherent framework for globalization and the report could be very useful as an input to the ongoing work initiated by the United Nations Secretary-General on how to improve the functioning of the world body. Norway believed that the key challenge was to make existing institutions and mechanisms work more effectively for the common good.

The Employer member from Brazil, **Mr. Lima Godoy**, speaking on behalf of the Employer members of Latin America and the Caribbean, applauded and welcomed the report. The work of the Commission provided a clear call for a fair globalization, which recognized human values and the need to promote welfare by raising prosperity, security and well-being. Competition played a fundamental role in the globalization of the economy; furthermore, each country and each national government bore primary responsibility for ensuring that the fruits of globalization were reaped. On the first point, the Employers agreed that governance on the international level would come about through greater coordination between multilateral organizations. On the second point, governments of developing countries would require outside help both in implementing international trade rules and procedures as well as in the area of migration, in order to put an end to protectionism in agriculture and the creation of barriers by developed countries to products from developing countries. Clear intellectual property rules and foreign investment rules were also required. Poorer countries needed official development assistance and debt relief. The conclusions of the Commission confirmed that the process of globalization fell very short of making the world a better place. To do so, the process needed to be less haphazard, and to be guided by progressive, democratic governance, operating at all levels from local to global.

The representative of the Government of Bulgaria, **Mr. A. Evtimov**, *Ministry of Labour and Social Policy*, expressed gratitude for the comprehensive report and satisfaction for the work done by the Commission. He called for respect of core labour standards to ensure decent work for all. He supported the initiatives within the framework of the relevant international organizations aiming at the development of more balanced policy conducive to fair and more inclusive globalization.

The Government of Bulgaria was eager to host, with ILO assistance, a subregional tripartite conference for south-eastern Europe on the social dimension of globalization, to be held in the latter part of 2004, in Sofia. High-level meetings of this sort, bringing together national ministers of finance, labour and social policy to review policy coherence, preferably with the participation of the social partners, would play a key role in expanding the scope of the positive effects of globalization.

The representative the Government of Nigeria, **Ms. Koripamo-Agary**, *Ministry of Labour*, found the report compelling and balanced, as it addressed the critical social problems related to globalization. She congratulated the Commission and the Director-General for their work in producing a document that was fair, while scrutinizing the critical social problems created by the phenomenon. She reflected that, while globalization had produced some benefits, they were a remote concept to ordinary people in developing countries. The situation in Africa was compounded by the high rates of HIV/AIDS infection and loss of manpower through brain drain.

The Nigerian Government strongly agreed with the statement that there was a serious democratic deficit at the heart of the system of global governance, resulting in developing countries having very limited influence on global negotiations on rules, and on determining the policies of key financial and economic institutions.

It was clear that the success of national development efforts was critically dependent on the emergence of a set of fairer rules as well as a more equitable process of rule formulation. It was imperative for developing countries to be given the necessary policy independence to respond to the challenge of development in the era of globalization. Such independence should be complemented by special treatment in the multilateral trading system as well as by fairer rules in the international financial system and in policies of cross-border movement of people. It was also important to emphasize respect for core labour standards. Proper governance of globalization should be based on a stronger ethical framework and driven by dialogue and universally shared values; her Government had taken note of the recommendations on policy coherence initiatives, policy development dialogues as well as on the establishment of a globalization policy forum.

*The Worker member from Malaysia, **Mr. Z. Rampak***, speaking on behalf of the Workers of the Asia-Pacific region, expressed appreciation for the comprehensive report, and was in agreement with its key recommendations, but wondered how it would be possible to move towards their implementation. It was high time for world leaders to take full account of the social costs of globalization and implement an appropriate plan of action to sustain social stability, particularly in developing countries. The workers called for a globalization that empowered the State to establish a socially inclusive delivery system.

*The representative of the Government of South Africa, **Mr. L. Kettledas**, Deputy Director-General, Ministry of Labour*, commended the Commission for its report and applauded the consultative spirit that had guided the approach. The current path of globalization, as the Commission had identified, must change: its advantages were too distant for too many. To be fair, globalization had to create opportunities for all. Agreeing with most of the report's recommendations, he took heart from the recognition of better global governance as being critical to the reform of the multilateral system – to make it more democratic, transparent, accountable and coherent. The proposals in the report regarding resource mobilization, debt relief and the adoption of more equitable international trade and finance policies were very welcome. A global policy forum would further debate on how globalization could be of benefit to all and serve as a constant reminder that the developing world needed fair, people-centred development and that as partners in this development, the developed world should begin to provide a comprehensive system of assistance that addressed national challenges. It was through processes such as the global policy forum and the implementation of many of the report's recommendations that further impetus could be given to the United Nations Millennium Summit, the Doha Development Round, the Monterrey and the Johannesburg Summits. He supported follow-up action that spread awareness of the report and initiated steps to change the current process of globalization.

***Mr. C. Fortin Cabezas**, Deputy Secretary-General of UNCTAD*, complimented the excellent and comprehensive report, and was pleased to observe that its premise of making globalization into a positive force was also the main thrust of the UNCTAD XI Conference, to be held in June 2004. Technological progress in information and communication processes was inevitable, irreversible and highly welcome, but the national and international policies of globalization were neither inevitable nor irreversible. The report correctly maintained that globalization could and must be improved, to make it a "positive force for all people and countries". The notion that globalization involved minimizing the role of the State should also be rejected. The issue of policy space for national governments had emerged as central and controversial in discussions and preparations for the UNCTAD Conference and was particularly relevant in connection with WTO rules, disciplines and commitments, which had a legally binding character and were enforceable through the WTO dispute settlement process. UNCTAD believed that policy space had three dimensions: agenda setting – bringing new ideas to the negotiation of trade disciplines; implementation – preserving a maximum of national policy space for the application of trade rules and compliance without entailing a flouting of obligations and rules; and interpretation – attempting to favour the preservation of national policy space. In these respects, he found the report's discussion enlightening.

***Mr. J. K. Ingram**, World Bank Special Representative to the United Nations and the World Trade Oorganization*, believed that the report constituted a milestone in comprehensively addressing the issue of the social aspect of globalization and welcomed its presentation. He thanked the members of the Commission for their dedication, wisdom and insights in preparing it. He said the report presented a fair picture of the challenges faced in creating a more inclusive globalization with benefits extending to all members of the global population. He appreciated the recognition that the increasing interconnectedness of trade, finance and production systems had increased global welfare. It was essential for States to pursue sound governance for sustained economic progress and a stronger, not weaker, State was needed, one that facilitated private investment and provided social services. The World Bank fully concurred that the Millennium Development Goals could be effective targets which served to unify both government and donor efforts to create equitable development, and could also be effective in helping to increase financial assistance. On the question of migration, he welcomed the report's support for assuring the appropriate movement of labour, within an agreed international framework that provided respect for human rights of transient and migrant labourers. The World Bank, perceiving this as an emerging issue of critical importance to the development process and to the alleviation of poverty, had created a research group on migration which was working in partnership with the International Organization for Migration (IOM) and closely cooperating with the recently formed Global Commission on Migration, whose Co-Chair was one of the World Bank's managing directors.

The World Bank was in broad agreement with the priority attached by the report to the creation of decent work and employment, and would continue to support the efforts of governments to identify how best to create such employment.

The World Bank also supported the call for a renewed commitment to the multilateral system, which would be effective through greater policy coherence at the global level amongst members of the international donor community. Such policy coherence should begin at the national level to reflect consensus between ministers of labour, industry, finance, social policy and others. Regarding the report's recommendation that a policy coherence forum should be created, the World Bank was giving serious consideration to this proposal, while bearing in mind the forums already in place in the United Nations system.

Mr. A. Di Liscia, *Assistant Director-General, UNIDO*, congratulated the Commission for the report and said that the conclusions of the report matched the central topic of UNIDO's corporate strategy, which focused on the promotion of productivity growth for sustainable industrial development by reinforcing the links between entrepreneurship, technology, productivity enhancement and growth. The report had not only implications for the work of UNIDO, but was becoming a source of inspiration for the concept that UNIDO was developing in relation to the need to enhance coordination of the multilateral system to support better the challenges of globalization and to obtain real and sustainable economic development. An integrated thinking approach was necessary within the United Nations system as well as more multilateral coherence, he concluded.

Mr. J.P. Chauffour, *Senior Economist, International Monetary Fund*, commended the World Commission, saying the report contained much with which the IMF could agree. Better policies at country and global level were required, together with better global governance. The IMF was taking action in this respect. Domestic ownership of the reform agenda was one of the main guiding principles of IMF involvement in low-income countries through the Poverty Reduction Strategy Papers. Successful implementation of country-owned poverty reduction strategy would require a considerable transfer of expertise to build capacity and, to this end, the IMF had been providing more focus on prioritized technical assistance, had improved coordination with other technical assistance providers, and significantly expanded its network of regional training institutes and assistance centres, including in sub-Saharan Africa. For advanced economies to play their part, official development assistance levels needed to rise well above current commitments – if progress was to be made towards meeting the Millennium Development Goals. Regarding better global governance, the IMF was trying to mitigate the negative effects of globalization on the international system in two ways: by ensuring the stability of the international financial system and by helping individual countries take advantage of the financing offered by international capital markets in endeavours to reduce vulnerability to adverse shocks or changes in investor sentiment.

To strengthen the framework for crisis prevention, the IMF was encouraging its members to increase the transparency of their financial and corporate sectors as a way of reducing financial abuse, such as money laundering and fraud, and ensuring a level playing field for all investors. This could also be achieved through the promotion of international standards and codes based on international best practices. The IMF was also stepping up its surveillance of international capital markets and improving its ability to predict and pre-empt crises. To strengthen the framework for crisis resolution, the IMF had been supporting more orderly processes, for example, through a voluntary code of conduct for restructuring debt or the use of collective action clauses in international bond issuance. In the context of the report's call for change in the governance structure of the Bretton Woods institutions, the IMF's Executive Board had agreed to increase staff dealing with over 20 member countries, including those in sub-Saharan Africa.

The representative of the Government of Australia, **Mr. J. Lloyd**, *Department of Employment and Workplace Relations*, thanked the Governing Body for opening the discussion to non-members. Agreeing with the report's assessment of globalization, declared that the Australian Government continued to support the approach taken to trade and labour standards in the 1996 WTO Singapore Ministerial Statement. This supported the ILO as the body competent to set and deal with core labour standards. Any duplication or dilution of this ILO authority to supervise implementation of international labour standards would be a matter of concern. Regarding the proposal that formal consultative structures, similar to those operating within the OECD, be established for the World Bank, the IMF and WTO, with a view to enhancing transparency, accountability and credibility, the Australian Government supported measures to improve the governance arrangements of international financial institutions and encouraged the use of capacity-building measures to improve the quality of representation for developing countries. Australia also supported enhanced voting power of countries that had increased their share in the world economy over the last 50 years. Regarding the report's recommendation on increasing resources available to the ILO for the supervision and monitoring of labour standards, and promoting the follow-up to the Declaration on Fundamental Principles and Rights at Work, he asked member States to bear in mind the recent increases in contributions and large surplus. Consideration should be given, he said, to the scope of the implementation of appropriate recommendations within the existing budget.

He also asked that proposals for a multilateral framework of labour migration be examined carefully. While issues relating to workers' rights and to host countries were important, he was of the opinion that they could be addressed effectively without the need for a migration framework. Another potential issue was the extent to which a multilateral labour migration scheme would recognize the fundamental right of each country to determine who should pass its borders. These issues should be addressed as part of the general discussion on labour migration at the Conference.

The representative of the Government of Belgium, **Mr. M. Jadot**, *Federal Public Service*, said that it was an advantage for the ILO to have such a high-level report at its disposal. It was neither complacent nor did it set the protagonists against each other. He was of the opinion that States should undertake the reforms necessary in a globalization context with the assistance of the international organizations in order to pre-empt the damage done by major crises. Minimal social protection safety nets were needed to attenuate the impact of financial crises and, alongside employment, should be a priority of the social agenda. The call for a platform of international cooperation, made at Copenhagen in 1995, was still as valid as ever, and he was disappointed that the report was unclear in this respect. Belgium believed that the United Nations should carry out this task and organize itself to this end, but did not see the need for a new body to be created, rather a coherent approach to international commitments around the Millennium Development Goals, sustainable development and the Copenhagen development platform. The global stakes should not be reduced to a debate over labour standards and trade, although such a debate was necessary. He wondered if the Governing Body should not be the forum where issues such as growth and public expenditure would be identified as well as a forum for many of the players in globalization.

The representative of the Government of China, **Ambassador Sha**, congratulated the World Commission on the report which had required two years of hard work, and he expressed sincere appreciation to the Co-Chairs. He spoke of China's experience with globalization, saying that the country had adopted an open door policy and put into practice economic and social policies that led to sustainable development, while protecting workers' rights and interests, particularly those of vulnerable groups. China was, however, still faced with a series of challenges associated with unemployment, a widening gap in income, insufficient coverage of social security. The report, he said, presented quite innovative recommendations as to follow-up measures. It was his Government's belief that the ILO should make full use of tripartism in cooperating with member States to eradicate poverty, promote employment, protect the fundamental rights of workers, enhance social protection and social dialogue and realize decent work. Developed countries and international organizations should be encouraged to provide, in real terms, more effective technical assistance to developing countries and raise their capacities to participate in the globalization process and enable them to benefit fairly from the outcome of economic globalization, so as to realize common prosperity and development worldwide.

*The Employer member from Switzerland, **Mr. M. Barde**,* also speaking on behalf of the European group of the International Organisation of Employers, was pleased to note that the report had provided answers to the various criticisms of globalization by accepting the need for a market economy and its link with democracy, the need for good governance at all levels, human rights, gender equality, social equality and the respect for the rule of law. On the role of the State, it was his opinion that there was a need for a strong State in matters of arbitration and redistribution, but a State that was less active in the management of the economy. The United Nations supported the idea of initiatives for policy coherence as well as multiparty dialogue on policy development, the first of which could focus on the coherence of world growth, investment and job creation, and decent work. The year 2005 would see the review of the Millennium Development Goals and Copenhagen's tenth anniversary. He hoped there would be high-level cooperation with the ILO to find specific forms of cooperation.

***Mr. J. Baudot**, Coordinator of the International Forum for Social Development, Department of Economic and Social Affairs, United Nations,* found the report to be accurate and that its recommendations reflected the concerns of the international community. He highlighted three aspects of the report that he found to be of particular importance. Firstly, it gave back its real meaning to the word "social", i.e. the search for individual well-being and the harmonious functioning of society. There was a political and moral dimension to the word "social", that implied processes and institutions that sought freedom and justice. Secondly, the report showed depth of analysis; thirdly, it demonstrated the need for global governance.

*The representative of the Government of the Russian Federation, **Mr. Y. Lyublin**, First Deputy Minister of Labour and Social Development,* expressed gratitude to the members of the Commission and to the Co-Chairs. He said the report gave very specific answers to the problems involved in the process of globalization and was a successful attempt to provide a balanced picture of the way in which globalization was developing and of its consequences, in particular regarding labour-related issues. He highlighted that the report was unique and that it provided an excellent basis for discussions at national level, with involvement of the various political and social forces existing in a country, particularly the social partners. His Government supported the idea of coordinated efforts by international organizations, with the ILO playing a leading role as far as social and labour problems were concerned.

*The representative of the Government of Pakistan, **Ambassador Umer**,* thanked the Commissioners for a landmark study, based on in-depth scholarship, intellectually sound analysis and supported by statistics. As endorsed by leading economists such as Professor Stiglitz, it contributed to a much-awaited shift in the discourse on globalization. He noted that the report constituted a much-awaited shift in the discourse on globalization. Developing countries had long advocated a realistic rather than an idealistic approach to globalization and the report was a step in that direction. The shrinking national policy space and erosion of economic sovereignty in developing countries were crucial issues. A review of global rules, particularly trade rules, to allow greater policy space must be operationalized. It was paradoxical that the protagonists of globalization called for improved national governance, yet the present set of global rules progressively encroached on developing countries' essential policy space. The report's recognition of the responsibility of the international community towards an even and fair distribution of the fruits of globalization, as spelt out in the Millennium Development Goals, and the all-important question of resource mobilization were a welcome development. He expressed the belief that debt swaps for social sector development could significantly contribute to addressing simultaneously the problem of unsustainable debt, on the one hand, and meeting the demands of good governance, on the other. Issues he listed that required more elaborate treatment related to cases of developing countries that achieved robust GDP growth rates but failed to acknowledge and analyse issues of persistent poverty, agricultural subsidies – that adversely affected the mostly agro-based economies of the developing countries, with profound social consequences – as well as corporate social responsibility.

*The representative of the Government of Sudan, **Ambassador El Haj**,* said that the report proved the Director-General right in setting up the Commission. He expressed thanks to the members and the Co-Chairs and thanked the ILO and the Director-General for supporting the work of the Commission. He called for non-discriminatory rules to govern globalization, democracy, free institutions and accompanying social and economic policies, decent work, better copyright and intellectual property rules, open markets, direct investment, open borders for migrant workers, and better international institutions that served developing countries, with increased budgets. Given its importance, he trusted that the report would be translated into Arabic.

A Worker member from Germany, **Ms. U. Engelen-Kefer**, stressed the importance of the report as a global analysis of the financial, economic and social developments in countries with different developmental levels; it also provided useful conclusions and recommendations for action at all levels. She appreciated the report's focus on the human dimension and decent work. Europe itself needed an effective campaign against unemployment. She was in favour of an integrated approach, as isolated treatment of policy areas would not lead to the desired results, and she hoped that the proposals in the report would be taken up constructively with a view to overcoming blockages and achieving forms of cooperation between the ILO, the World Bank, the IMF and the WTO. When dealing with international and national coherence building, tripartism was of the essence because governments, employers and workers were the parties best equipped to deal with the conditions of work and economic and related human issues. A reasonable form of cooperation with NGOs was also required that supplemented these partners' work.

The representative of the Government of the Philippines, **Ambassador Manalo**, spoke of the importance of a global conscience, sensitive to inequities, as vital for enhancing the benefits of globalization. The global goal of full employment and decent work could be achieved by enhancing coordination of macroeconomic policy among countries. Making full employment a goal of macroeconomic policy would guarantee that developing countries, such as the Philippines, were provided with policy space to implement employment-generation activities that directly impacted on higher employment levels without eliciting adverse reactions in international markets. The promotion of decent work in global production systems should form part of economic and social policies. Respect for core labour standards should be at the heart of a broader international agenda for development; affording a minimum level of social protection was a prerequisite of the global economy. Finally, he said, a policy of inclusiveness was a guarantee that the gains from globalization accrued to the benefit of the population.

The representative of the Government of Mexico, **Mr. R. Vasquez**, said the Government of Mexico supported the report, and associated himself with the GRULAC statement and particularly supported the consistency of international action taken by States through commitments such as those made at the Monterrey Summit, which could be an important step forward in increasing official development assistance levels. He noted and supported the importance that the ILO, the United Nations and other organizations attached to the family, social responsibility and solidarity, as well as to the dignity of the individual. He believed that the focus should be not only individuals but also their families, especially in view of the fact that a properly functioning market economy required the promotion of social responsibility and solidarity. He requested an additional reference to the important issue of legal reforms in respect of the informal economy, stressing the need to recognize the existence of the so-called informal economy.

The representative of the Government of New Zealand, **Ms. D. Tse**, congratulated the Commission for a robust and comprehensive report. She remarked that working to achieve greater coherence between economic and social policies, both at the international and national levels, would result in a more holistic approach which was essential for capacity building and sustainable development. These two elements were at the heart of strong States and successful globalization. The proposals in the report specific to the objectives of decent work should be integrated into the work programme of the ILO. New Zealand considered that the ILO could demonstrate leadership by facilitating dialogue between United Nations system organizations and agencies to ascertain their views on the report and to look for ways of working together, within the scope of their respective mandates, to pursue the stated objectives. But she cautioned against any extension of the ILO mandate in following up on the recommendations of the Commission. She looked forward to the development of a clear plan of action at the Conference.

The representative of the Government of Canada, **Ms. C. Bradshaw**, *Minister of Labour and Human Resources*, congratulated the Commission for a very comprehensive report, reflecting the aspirations of all people everywhere for a fair globalization that created opportunities for all. Canada sought efficient multilateral institutions and increased cooperation between countries in the fight against poverty. The Canadian Government had launched an integrated review of its international policy and the report would contribute to efforts to achieve greater policy coherence in this domain. Her Government had invited a member of the World Commission to lead a dialogue on the report with labour, business and other key Canadian stakeholders. She shared the desires of the

World Commission to make globalization a means to expand human well-being and freedom, and to bring democracy and development to local communities. Dialogue was the key to achieving the goals of democracy and development. In the Americas, a historic breakthrough on policy coherence was achieved when the Ministers of Labour of Brazil and Mexico joined Canada in presenting a report on the social dimension of globalization to trade ministers of that hemisphere in autumn 2003. Canada accepted the simple economic principle that those who produced the products and services in the economy should also be able to consume them, which was why growth and employment and respect for fundamental labour standards had to be made the focus of coherent social and economic policies. This all implied national democratic institutions, transparent public governance, the rule of law and fair social and economic institutions as well as investment in health, education, employment, training and skills development.

An Employer member of Burkina Faso, Mr. B. Nacoulma, said that, in setting up the World Commission, the ILO and its Director-General had once again proved their vision and capacity to respond to social needs. He reported that a Pan-African Employers' Confederation study had shown that Africa received only 2 per cent of direct investment and, in an attempt to correct this situation, the Confederation had developed a code of good governance for both governments and company heads in order to combat corruption and promote transparency. African employers were also seeking, through social dialogue, to promote national policy based on decent work, as well as regional integration. He, like other Employers' delegates, argued for a greater role for the Governing Body in the follow-up to the report.

The representative of the Government of Belarus, Ambassador Aleinik, expressed full support for the report and appreciated the work of the Commission. The proposals made were ambitious, courageous and innovative, and fully justified the establishment of the Commission. The nature of globalization needed urgent change, saying that it was a threat to the culture and national identity of small countries and was having a negative impact on the environment. Belarus had already experienced the various consequences of globalization since independence in 1991, given its reliance on the import of raw materials and energy, and had decided on gradual development rather than shock therapy. The results were that Belarus was in 53rd position in the United Nations *Human Development Report* for 2003, out of a total of 175 countries worldwide. Belarus supported basic labour standards and minimum standards of social protection for individuals and families.

The representative of the Government of Indonesia, Mr. E. Situmorang, Ministry of Manpower and Transmigration, welcoming and supporting the report, stated that within a global partnership, the problems of poverty and underdevelopment could be tackled in the fulfilment of the Millennium Development Goals. Concessionary financing, particularly in the form of official development assistance, he said, was imperative. He supported decent work, noting that the Government of Indonesia had developed the National Decent Work Agenda which involved the social partners. In addition, it was of the greatest importance to develop a global framework for an orderly and well-managed migration process. If globalization was to become a force for progress, it was necessary to work at the national and global levels in tandem so that the two could interact and reinforce each other.

The representative of the Government of the Islamic Republic of Iran, Mr. S. Heftadan, Director-General for International Relations, Ministry of Labour and Social Affairs, remarked that if the world was not to slide into further insecurity, terrorism, hatred and conflict, an urgent rethink of globalization was needed. Globalization should be utilized to create balance, sustainable development, political convergence and unity of all nations. He declared that equal rules for unequal players would never secure equal outcomes.

The Worker member from Lebanon, Mr. G. Ghosn, spoke of the negative social impact of globalization in the Arab world, which had not been mentioned in the report. Globalization had had a negative impact in the region, as the region had not sought to maximize its developmental possibilities. The main losers were workers, whose capacity to organize had been reduced. This had led to opposition in certain quarters to free trade and to free movement of capital. The hegemony of transnational corporations over the local markets further impeded local developmental possibilities and concentrated production potential and capacity in the hands of a few. The flagrant contradiction that could be concluded from the impact of globalization could be measured in the pattern of the flow of goods and the restrictive nature, or its restrictive impact, on the migration of manpower. International organizations, he suggested, could be one of the means of assisting change in the Arab world as they could be the channel to overcome resistance and refusal and to improve the rights of workers' and human rights.

Mr. J. Vandermoortele, *Socio-Economic Development Group, UNDP*, applauded the report and said that it shared many concerns addressed in several human development reports, as well as in the UNDP publication entitled *Making global trade work for people*, published in 2003. Common positions were based on five basic premises. The first was that globalization, if it was to be sustained, must have a human face. Second, globalization represented interconnectedness, not only between firms, markets and financial systems, but also between people. Third, globalization led to a continuous shrinking of time and space, as better communications raised aspirations around the world. Fourth, globalization was only as good as the rules, tools and institutions that governed it. Fifth, globalization created many opportunities, but also aggravated insecurities and vulnerabilities. The linkages between human development and decent work were strong and obvious. Their common denominator was human rights. Both were crucial for enlarging human choices. Ultimately, he said, the question to be asked was – what happens to people? The benefits of globalization were not equally distributed and it was often the countries and the people who most needed to gain from globalization that benefited the least.

He commended the ILO for taking the debate on globalization forward in a balanced and professional manner. The World Commission had produced a landmark report. Global governance had to be enhanced if it were to meet the challenges of poverty, trade development and gender equality. Equality and the empowerment of women would be crucial to the success of the Millennium Development Goals.

Mr. G. Malempré, *Representative to the United Nations and Specialized Institutions in Geneva*, UNESCO, spoke of the three world commissions that had been convened by UNESCO in recent years. Experience with these had clearly shown their usefulness in bringing prominent personalities together. However, they only served a purpose if they led to action. There were two areas of concern regarding globalization which were common to UNESCO and the ILO: the need to create an ethical reference framework based on human, civil, political, social and cultural rights, and, on the other hand, a governance of the processes of globalization that would prevent the marginalization and exclusion of a large part of humanity.

Ms. C. Golden, *Division of Social Science Research and Policy, UNESCO*, was pleased to note that many of the report's recommendations were of high relevance to UNESCO, including the Education For All (EFA) fast-track initiative, the Millennium Development Goals and policy coherence initiatives. For UNESCO, such issues included, inter alia, the eradication of poverty and gender inequality, the promotion of education, and the empowerment of women.

Mr. R. Torres, *Directorate for Employment, Labour and Social Affairs, OECD*, associated himself with those speakers who had expressed satisfaction with the report and added that it was an important document, which provided a balanced approach to the issue of globalization in that it made clear that action was needed at both national and international levels. It also formulated a comprehensive set of recommendations aimed at improving the returns from globalization. He saw the implementation of the report's recommendations as a key issue and mentioned three areas where OECD work might be relevant in this respect. First was the issue of efficient redistribution mechanisms, such as social protection systems that compensated for income losses of those affected by trade and investment liberalization; this included core labour standards, which could help create conditions for workers and employers to discuss how to share the gains from trade and investment liberalization; second was wealth creation in sectors that offered new opportunities; and third was the implementation of the report's recommendations. On this last point, he saw solutions in the form of viable tax collection systems, as well as a comprehensive approach to ensure that various reforms did not conflict. Other priorities for a comprehensive approach were the interlinkages between core labour standards and economic development, as well as migration. He was confident that the OECD and the ILO would find common ground for cooperating on these issues.

Mr. M. Cox, *Sustainable Development Department, FAO*, agreed particularly with what had been said by the representative of the World Bank that, for the first time in many years, the international community would be able to address the issues which concerned it through the eyes of ordinary people, not simply from the point of view of an ideological, a particular, or a market-designed instrument. He pointed to hunger as affecting the primary right of all humankind to food. He agreed with the vast majority of the recommendations contained in the report. He recalled that, for the report's recommendations to be achieved, it had to be borne in mind that 66 per cent of the poor lived in rural areas and that their livelihood was inextricably linked to agriculture, which had borne the brunt of the negative aspects of globalization. The initiative launched by the FAO and ILO on rural development was extremely promising and the FAO would be submitting further proposals for cooperation.

Ms. V. Kulaçoglu, *Director, Trade and Environment Division, WTO*, considered the work of the Commission to be valuable and believed that the social dimension of globalization merited serious consideration. She stated that the Doha Development Agenda, launched in 2001, promoted an open, equitable and non-discriminatory multilateral trading system and was undergoing an important phase, with serious attention being paid to agriculture, market access and trade in industrial goods. The Doha Development Agenda could play an important role in contributing to economic growth and generating employment opportunities. It had the capacity to deliver benefits to developing and developed countries alike. However, she said, careful management of trade liberalization and globalization was required at the national and international levels to ensure the inclusiveness of globalization. She welcomed the complementarity of the ILO's work in this respect.

The representative of the Government of Italy, **Mr. G. Tria**, expressed appreciation for the work carried out by the Commission and congratulated and thanked Presidents Halonen and Mkapa and its members, who had made a significant contribution on a key theme for the future of the world – how to make the globalization process beneficial to all countries and all peoples. He believed that governments everywhere had to take up the challenge, committing themselves to promoting discussions and exchange of ideas at both national level and within the international multilateral system, on the analysis and recommendations provided by the report. He said that his Government shared the World Commission's view of the importance of governance of the globalization process and believed that the definition and implementation of coherent national and regional policies for fair globalization had to be conceived within a framework of international rules. But global governance could be effective only if based on fair national institutions that ensured democracy, good governance, respect for human rights, social justice, economic freedom – and last but not least – national autonomy in drawing up policies and strategies for sustainable development. The Italian Government was concerned with the problems of labour immigration and cross-border movement of people, but was strongly committed to implementing policies for the inclusion of immigrant workers in the workforce where they could benefit from occupational safety and health measures and social insurance laws. Italy also shared the report's view on fair rules and policies at the international level and agreed with the proposal for a global forum, which should be examined by the competent agencies, namely the International Organization for Migration, the ILO and the United Nations system. He believed that industrialized countries could not avoid issues such as the access of goods from developing countries that allowed those nations to increase resources to attain the Millennium Development Goals. He was confident that the ILO would now identify the fields on which to focus its action and elaborate appropriate policies and strategies.

The representative of the Government of Kenya, **Ms. D. Ongewe**, *Ministry of Labour*, congratulated the Co-Chairpersons for the landmark report. She said that the core issue for the ILO was to identify the kind of globalization that was desired, then identify its actors and its beneficiaries. Positive measures should include fairer rules for international trade, investment, finance and migration, while all interests, rights and responsibilities were taken into account. Core labour standards and a minimum level of social protection should be seriously promoted and efforts to mobilize international resources for the Millennium Development Goals were also critical. Kenya agreed that fair globalization depended on better national governance and that decent work should be made a global goal. As far as Kenyans were concerned, poorly managed globalization had exacerbated poverty on account of a decline in investment and low wages for unskilled workers.

The representative of the Government of Algeria, **Mr. B. Sedki**, *Minister Plenipotentiary*, congratulated and thanked the Co-Chairpersons and the members of the Commission for the work accomplished, and assured them of Algeria's support for follow-up action and implementation of the report's recommendations. He noted the trend towards trade liberalization, as supported by developed nations; at the same time, there was a trend towards trade based on human, social, political and cultural rights, supported by civil society, NGOs and developing countries. Governments had to settle these economic and social differences within the framework of the ILO.

The representative of the Government of the Dominican Republic, **Mr. M. Guevara**, *Secretary of State for Labour*, thanked and congratulated the Commission for its extraordinary contribution.

He also thanked the Governing Body and the Director-General for providing the vision and direction for the report. He believed that the World Commission had provided an impetus towards fair globalization, and had placed people at the centre of the process. He wished to see the family placed at the centre of the globalization process in a multilateral framework that applied transparent rules to migration. He believed the ILO should promote a globalization policy forum, inviting the IMF, the World Bank, the Inter-American Development Bank and others to the table.

*The Employer member from India, **Mr. Anand***, urged action rather than debate and supported promotion of entrepreneurship initiatives. Entrepreneurship was where the private sector and employers could make the most significant contribution.

The Employer Vice-Chairperson concluded that radical reforms to the multilateral system were not called for; only fine-tuning was required. He noted employment as a fundamental issue and that there was a Global Employment Agenda to which entrepreneurs and employers had attached major importance. Youth employment in particular was a prominent issue that was connected to the elimination of child labour and the promotion of the Declaration on Fundamental Principles and Rights at Work. Social dialogue required a continuation of work within the ILO as a tripartite forum. The issue of migration would have outcomes at the 92nd Session (2004) of the International Labour Conference. With regard to the informal economy, interaction between various institutions and structures was necessary for the implementation of the conclusions of the 2002 session of the Conference. The fight against HIV/AIDS, the development of human resources and corporate responsibility were also areas where the Employers were willing to work actively. On the issue of regional action, he noted that Burkina Faso was to be the focus of the first regional project, and insisted that the process of learning should go from the local level upwards towards the global level. He accepted the challenge of working with other organizations and believed that the Turin Centre had its role to play. Speaking of policy coordination initiatives, he believed that it was urgent to harmonize fundamental information, particularly in the light of the divergence of data and statistics provided by the World Bank, UNDP and the report. He listed policy coherence, regional responses and education as constituting possible topics for discussions on globalization. In order to be able to support activities, initiatives and forums, all possible scenarios should be explored. He proposed that the Director-General, together with the Officers of the Governing Body, be responsible for looking at the alternatives which would contribute at the opportune moment its recommendations on the viability of such measures and their composition and characteristics. He proposed that the Director-General and the Officers of the Governing Body be responsible for investigating various possibilities for an agenda.

The Worker Vice-Chairperson praised the support for policy coherence and inter-institutional cooperation, and noted virtually universal support for core labour standards, which he highlighted as requiring a major promotional effort by the ILO and other international organizations. Effective follow-up activities were now required to ensure that the report became well known at grass roots and that its purpose was understood. He noted the cautious interest from institutions such as the World Bank and the IMF, and believed that the proposals for greater coherence between these institutions and the ILO needed to be followed up. He looked forward to an early start to discussions on the issues of growth, employment and investment. The challenge was to make proposals for follow-up in a way that was complementary to current ILO programmes and did not compromise the Decent Work Agenda or the Global Employment Agenda. He hoped that, following its declaration on helping Africa, the World Bank would assist the Workers' group in its demand for debt forgiveness or, alternatively, for the repayment of a country's debt to be diverted into its own education, health and social welfare programmes. He also expressed interest in the development of the theme of partnership in the UNCTAD XI Conference and was impressed by the number of speakers who urged more partnership, but deplored those interventions which specifically stated that the ILO should not go beyond a certain point in endeavours to achieve fair globalization. He also requested that national governments speak in a single voice before the different international institutions for the sake of coherence. He reminded the meeting that the Singapore Declaration had failed and he did not want the ILO to suffer a similar setback. Concluding, he stressed the importance of pressing ahead speedily with follow-up action. He requested that the Director-General move swiftly to investigate the potential for giving immediate effect to some of the most urgent conclusions on the basis of a full tripartite consultation with the various constituents of the ILO. He trusted that a successful balance between the imperatives of urgency and the requirements of due democratic process would thus be achieved.

The Director-General spoke of the generally positive reaction to the report and the clear direction given by the meeting. His comments at the beginning of the meeting that the discussion was important in helping him shape his report to the Conference had been validated. He was struck by many of the words used to describe the report, such as "landmark", "breakthrough", "milestone", "visionary", but particularly by the word "balanced", especially in view of the fact that the Commission had deliberately been created as a "non-like-minded" group. The report was neither the first nor the last on globalization, but it was the first to use dialogue to search for solutions and common ground. It was the first report that had sought to place dialogue at the service of finding solutions and common ground. This enhanced the ILO approach and philosophy, and demonstrated that dialogue could produce common ground.

The report had been highlighted as both critical and positive. It did not seek to reject globalization, but to manage it, while pointing out that globalization itself was not the problem. It argued that globalization needed to be shaped through adequate management, rules and governance. Although the ideas posited had national political implications, the recommendations had been described as realistic, and not a single speaker had qualified the report as unsuitable. He personally found that the report had integrated the issues such as finance, trade, labour and education, making it a holistic work that required comprehensive solutions. Globalization was an integrated phenomenon that demanded integrated solutions, and global problems required global solutions. The limits of purely national action had already been observed. He also felt that it was a common sense report with sound propositions. However, there were dangers: governments should find ways of discussing the report at government level and not slice it up between ministries; the global vision will thus be protected.

The key message in the report, taken up by many, was that dealing with globalization began at home. The second was the need for fair rules in trade, finance, movement of people, labour standards and technology. The question of international governance was very strongly underlined, as was multilateralism. In addition, efficiency, effectiveness, transparency, accountability, democratic decision-making and, above all, the whole issue of coherence were frequently referred to. Another element in different presentations was that solutions required the convergence of the principal actors.

On the implications for the ILO, the Director-General thought that probably the most important was decent work as a global goal, which should be pursued through coherent policies within the multilateral system. This would respond to a major political demand from countries everywhere and would demonstrate the capacity of the multilateral system to find creative solutions to a critical problem. The message regarding the ILO's strategic objectives was clearly a reinforcement of the Decent Work Agenda and of ongoing activities. At the same time, the report invited the ILO to intensify its relationship with the multilateral system, on the basis, and within the limits, of the ILO mandate, and he found this a very important subject for reflection. The report suggested that the ILO exercise its full mandate. There was a reference in the report to the Philadelphia Declaration, which required the ILO to examine economic and financial policies as they affected its mandate. This was a very important issue that would require careful consideration.

He addressed two specific proposals from the floor, one on policy coherence, the other on the globalization policy forum. The mandates of most international organizations intersected in different ways; it was important to focus on the ILO's areas of strength, to promote its products, knowledge and experience where a qualitative edge was perceived. But the policy coherence initiative had been launched specifically because policy interaction among organizations was so highly developed. He suggested that growth, investment and jobs should receive priority treatment for a global approach.

The key challenge for the ILO was to see how globalization affected the Decent Work Agenda and to identify the ILO's comparative advantages in dealing with the social dimension of globalization. This issue would be part of an entire follow-up process and would affect decent work country programmes, as well as deepen the core mandate. It required the strengthening of the external relations capacity with other international organizations, as with other actors, and development of the knowledge base. His own point of view was that the report boosted and challenged tripartism, especially at the international policy-making level. Social dialogue and tripartism were the foundation of fair globalization and could not be dispensed with. Tripartism would play an important role at national level and also with other organizations. The report clearly advised the ILO to become involved in national policy coherence. Tripartism had to face up to globalization and this would stimulate discussion within the groups. The one recommendation in the report that was aimed at Heads of State and prime ministers was responsibility for national coherence. In the separate group discussions, Governments, Employers and Workers would determine how they perceived this challenge, how they could organize themselves, and how the ILO could support them in their work.

On the issue of follow-up and implementation of the approach and recommendations of the World Commission, the Director-General said that other organizations would also play a role. He recalled that the report, written by an independent Commission, would carry forward into the work of organizations such as the WTO and the IMF. ILO follow-up was in the hands of the Governing Body and he was keen to consult with the Officers of the Governing Body for guidance so that he could gradually enter new territory with a basic framework for action. He saw at least four spaces for short-term follow-up. One was the normal ongoing work of the ILO; many of the aspects of the report would impact directly on existing projects and programmes. The immediate stages ahead were the Chief Executive Board of the United Nations in April 2004, where an agenda item for discussion of the report had been requested; this would provide an opportunity to obtain feedback from heads of agencies. He would also make a presentation to the Economic and Social Council (ECOSOC) in June 2004. Finally, reflection was required on how to bring the issues in the report to the attention of the United Nations General Assembly for discussion within a wider context.

President Mkapa spoke of the hopes the report had raised around the world. The next great challenge would be delivering on those hopes. The real test of the efficacy of the various actions that could be taken was whether their benefits would prove more inclusive. These actions did not need to be taken sequentially. Parallel initiatives could be taken at regional, national and international levels, as long as they were consistent and coherent. The thread that ran through all possible solutions was political will and he pledged to be proactive in preaching the need for political will among fellow Heads of State and Government. He once again stressed policy coherence, beginning at home – in all countries – with a political decision. The proposed improvement in the governance of globalization was a political decision. The policy coherence the Commission wanted had nothing to do with reallocation of duties and mandates among international organizations. The ILO was certainly not being asked to encroach upon the mandates of other organizations. Nations could not demand good democratic and participatory governance in international organizations and yet fail to address such issues nationally. Countries could not demand accountability within global institutions and yet fail to work for accountability within their own national institutions. It had to be remembered that international organizations were nothing but sovereign governments united for a particular purpose. The IMF, the World Bank, the WTO and all others were the sum total of their members, who were governments. The policy incoherence the report pleaded against occurred when a government supported an issue at one forum and undermined what it had agreed to in another forum. If governments agreed at Doha that negotiations should focus on development, the same focus should be echoed in all other different forums where governments met, as well as in national political decisions. In his view, the Doha commitments would have been met on schedule if there had been greater domestic policy coherence among the member countries.

He repeated that the report was never meant to encourage the ILO to go beyond its established and known mandate. It did, however, call for a comprehensive, consistent and coherent approach to global issues that affected the lives and prospects of people everywhere.

The question was where to start and what was the way forward? He echoed the Scottish writer Robert Louis Stevenson, who said: "You cannot run away from a weakness; you must sometimes fight it out or perish. And if that be so, why not now, and where you stand?" Governments, workers and employers must not run away from the weaknesses of globalization. They must fight now where they stood.

The Chairperson announced that a full report of the discussion would be appended to his report to the 92nd Session of the International Labour Conference. He noted that the World Commission's report had struck most speakers as a credible basis for achieving a breakthrough in the quest for fair globalization and that there had been agreement that the values and basic orientations of the report should guide the follow-up process. There should be a focus on people and their needs, values and fundamental rights, as well as on fairness and good governance, from the local level up to the global. This would be a solid foundation for moving ahead with the follow-up process. He was encouraged by the convergence of views on many of the key instruments that the report recommended. The meeting had been of one mind that decent work should be a central global goal and that every effort should be made to advance all four components: employment, fundamental workers' rights, social protection and social dialogue. There had also been broad agreement that greater policy coherence at both national and global level was an essential condition for success in achieving the decent work objective. He indicated that the forthcoming session of the Conference would be an occasion to move forward, as would the Governing Body sessions in June and November 2004. But to maintain momentum, the Director-General would undertake consultations with other international organizations on relevant follow-up issues and remain in contact with the Officers of the Governing Body to review developments and consult on particular aspects of such follow-up action.

CONTENTS

Page

I. ILO Declaration on Fundamental Principles and Rights at Work 1

    Compilation of annual reports 1

    Technical cooperation activities 2

    Discussion of the Global Report 2

II. Child labour 2

    Follow-up to the June 2002 discussion of the ILO Global Report: *A future without child labour* 2

    IPEC action against child labour 2002-03: Progress and future priorities 3

    IPEC's achievements relative to targets for the biennium 3

    The importance of education for eliminating child labour 4

    Child labour and the Decent Work Agenda 4

    Partnership between IPEC and employers' and workers' organizations 4

III. Working Party on the Social Dimension of Globalization 5

    Corporate social responsibility and international labour standards 5

    Policies and social partnerships for good governance 5

    World Commission on the Social Dimension of Globalization 5

        Statement by Her Excellency Ms. Tarja Halonen, President of Finland and Co-Chair of the World Commission 5

        Presentation of the report, *A fair globalization: Creating opportunities for all*, by His Excellency Mr. Benjamin Mkapa, President of the United Republic of Tanzania and Co-Chair of the World Commission 6

IV. International labour standards 6

    Improvements in ILO standards-related activities 6

        Articles 19, 24 and 26 of the Constitution 6

        Technical assistance and promotion 7

    Practices for the preparation of international labour Conventions 7

    Ratification and promotion of ILO fundamental Conventions 7

    General status report on ILO action concerning discrimination in employment 7

    Freedom of association 8

    Consolidated Convention on maritime labour standards 8

    Constitutional procedures 9

        Observance by the Government of Myanmar of the Forced Labour Convention, 1930 (No. 29) 9

        Observance by the Government of Belarus of the Freedom of Association and Protection of the Right to Organise Convention, 1948 (No. 87), and the Right to Organise and Collective Bargaining Convention, 1949 (No. 98) 10

V.	Employment and social policy	10
	Implementation of the Global Employment Agenda	10
	Active labour market policies	10
	HIV/AIDS and the Decent Work Agenda	11
	The Global Social Trust pilot project	11
	The Decent Work Pilot Programme	11
	Promoting decent employment through entrepreneurship	12
	Productive employment for poverty reduction and development	12
	Global Campaign on Social Security and Coverage for All	12
VI.	Multinational enterprises	13
	Promotion of the Tripartite Declaration of Principles concerning Multinational Enterprises and Social Policy	13
	Activities report for 2003	13
	Priorities for action in 2004-05	13
	Composition and size of the Subcommittee on Multinational Enterprises	14
	Eighth Survey on the effect given to the Tripartite Declaration of Principles concerning Multinational Enterprises and Social Policy	14
	Developments in other organizations	14
VII.	Sectoral activities	14
	Sectoral meetings	14
	Review of the Sectoral Activities Programme, 2002-03	15
	A new approach to sectoral activities in 2004-05	15
	Meetings of experts: Purpose, function and lessons learned	15
VIII.	Technical cooperation	16
	The ILO Technical Cooperation Programme for 2002-03	16
	Further developments regarding technical cooperation activities in the United Nations system	16
	Thematic evaluation: Strengthening institutions, processes, legal frameworks and capacity of tripartite constituents for tripartism and social dialogue	17
	On-the-spot review in Africa	17
	Technical cooperation – Resource allocation mechanism	17
	Special Technical Cooperation Programme for Colombia	18
	Enhanced Programme of Technical Cooperation for the occupied territories	19
IX.	Financial questions	19
	Information Technology Systems Fund	19
	ILO programme implementation 2002-03	20
	Evaluation of InFocus programmes	20

		Page
	Use of the 2000-01 surplus	20
	Strategic Policy Framework 2006-09	20
	Technical meetings reserve 2004-05	20
	New premises for the ILO offices in Santiago and Dar es Salaam	21
	Security and safety of staff and premises	21
X.	Decision-making bodies of the ILO	21
	International Labour Conference	21
	Proposed improvements in the functioning of the Conference	21
	Follow-up to the Seafarers' Identity Documents Convention (Revised), 2003 (No. 185), and to the resolutions adopted at the 91st Session (2003) of the International Labour Conference	22
	The role of the Credentials Committee	23
	93rd Session (June 2005)	23
	95th Session (June 2006)	23
	ILO Governing Body: Proposed improvements in the functioning	24
	Tenth African Regional Meeting (Addis Ababa, 2-5 December 2003)	24
XI.	Relations with other international organizations	25

Appendices

I.	Oral report of the Chairperson of the Working Party on the Social Dimension of Globalization at the 289th (March 2004) Session of the Governing Body	29
II.	Record of the discussion of the Report of the World Commission on the Social Dimension of Globalization at the 289th (March 2004) Session of the Governing Body	32

International Labour Conference

Provisional Record 7

Ninety-second Session, Geneva, 2004

Follow-up activities by the Office under the Declaration on Fundamental Principles and Rights at Work: Freedom of association and collective bargaining, forced or compulsory labour, discrimination

1. This note has the purpose of informing delegates at the 92nd Session of the International Labour Conference (Geneva, June 2004) of activities in pursuit of the action plans approved by the Governing Body in November 2000 on freedom of association and the effective recognition of the right to collective bargaining, [1] in November 2001 on forced or compulsory labour, [2] and in November 2003 on discrimination. [3] The action plan approved by the Governing Body in March 2003 on the abolition of child labour [4] is essentially congruent with the most recent orientations concerning the InFocus Programme on Child Labour (IPEC).

2. The note updates *Provisional Record* No. 2 of last year's session of the Conference. Not listed here are the many activities, such as meetings, publications and advisory services projects, handled by the Bureau for Workers' Activities (ACTRAV), the Bureau for Employers' Activities (ACT/EMP) and other headquarters or field units that are concerned with or touch upon freedom of association and collective bargaining, forced or compulsory labour, or discrimination which complement the action plans. They tend to be reflected in the Office's programme implementation reports regularly submitted to the Programme, Financial and Administrative Committee of the Governing Body. [5]

A. Freedom of association and collective bargaining

3. The Global Report *Organizing for social justice*, to be discussed at this year's session of the International Labour Conference, gives a complete picture of the activities implemented since the adoption of the action programme at the November 2000 Governing

---

[1] GB.279/TC/3.

[2] GB.282/TC/5.

[3] GB.288/TC/4.

[4] GB.286/TC/2.

[5] For the last report, see GB.289/PFA/10.

Body session, and thereby updates the information provided during last year's session of the Conference.[6]

B. Forced and compulsory labour

4. The Special Action Programme to Combat Forced Labour (SAP-FL) expanded its activities in Europe, Latin America, Africa and Asia, in selected priority countries. Four major new technical cooperation projects on combating forced labour and trafficking came on-stream during the period. Research and awareness raising on combating forced labour accelerated. Close working relationships were cemented with other international agencies, particularly in the field of combating trafficking (notably with the European Union, the Organization for Security and Co-operation in Europe (OSCE), the Stability Pact for South-Eastern Europe (the Task Force on Trafficking in Human Beings) and the Council of Europe), and in the field of bonded labour with the World Bank. SAP-FL continued as joint coordinator of the Inter-Governmental Organizations' (IGO) Contact Group on Human Trafficking and Migrant Smuggling. It also took the lead in the new internal office trafficking working group, which aims to enhance coordination, collaboration and knowledge sharing between the various ILO units that work on the topic.

Applied research and its dissemination

Misuse of cultural traditions

5. *Niger:* Following an in-depth study of forced labour and slavery in Niger, SAP-FL supported an awareness-raising programme with the Association of Traditional Chiefs of Niger (ACTN). A first regional workshop was held in December 2003, in the Tahoua region, for a group of chiefs and advisers from the surrounding areas. Two further regional and one national workshop will be held in the coming two months. A radio campaign, through community-based radio stations, is about to be launched.

6. *Western Africa:* Studies of forced labour in Burkina Faso, Guinea and Mali were completed and validated at tripartite workshops in the countries concerned. Draft action plans were formulated for consideration by the constituents and donors. A new anti-trafficking programme covering Ghana, Nigeria and Senegal includes a study of the cultural factors that give rise to trafficking and forced labour.

Trafficking and its forced labour outcomes

7. *Eastern and Western Europe:* A research programme covering ten countries of Eastern and Western Europe has generated important insights into forms of coercion and deception of irregular migrant workers throughout the trafficking cycle, in source, transit and destination countries. The results allow more systematic conclusions to be drawn with regard to the profile of victims, economic sectors, forms of exploitation and coercion. Interviews with more than 1,200 migrant workers confirmed the significance of trafficking for labour exploitation, in addition to the already well-established fact of trafficking for sexual exploitation. Whereas most women who are trafficked for sexual exploitation are deceived either by individual intermediaries (friends, neighbours or family) or criminal networks, victims of trafficking for labour exploitation are usually caught in a net of

---

[6] ILO: *Provisional Record* No. 2, *Record of Proceedings*, Vol. I, International Labour Conference, 91st Session, Geneva, 2003.

dependence through "semi-legal" recruitment and employment practices that are very difficult to detect.

8. In the Russian Federation, a major study on the new forms of forced labour was launched in March 2004. A further study examined the particular plight of Tajikistan migrant workers in the Moscow construction industry.

9. *North America:* Preliminary research has been undertaken in the United States, focusing on trafficking for both labour and sexual exploitation from Latin America and Asia, and on best practices associated with the United States Victims of Trafficking and Violence Protection Act of 2000.

Bonded labour

10. *South Asia:* Rapid assessment studies of bonded and related labour arrangements in ten economic sectors in Pakistan were completed, published and launched, in collaboration with the Ministry of Labour, at a national seminar in January 2004. The studies have shed valuable new light on the range of labour arrangements that prevail, and have helped in the design of practical interventions under the Government's National Policy and Plan of Action for the Abolition of Bonded Labour. The Pakistan Federal Bureau of Statistics completed a household sample survey of bonded labour in agriculture and brick kilns, with ILO support. In India and Nepal, studies were conducted on the gender dimensions of bonded labour and on employers' perspectives on bonded labour.

Debt bondage and servitude

11. *Latin America:* The ILO assisted (or currently assists) Governments and social partners in Bolivia, Guatemala, Paraguay and Peru to increase their knowledge base of forced labour through field investigations. Preliminary results indicate the existence of practices similar to those prevalent in Brazil – primarily debt bondage in remote rural areas. Other, more country-specific forms of forced labour, were also detected. In Brazil, an ILO-supported project has worked with national partners to set up a reliable data system to bring together information on cases of forced labour from government departments, agencies and other groups. Research was also undertaken on the pattern and incidence of forced labour, concentrated in illegal logging activities in the Amazon region. The research aims to inform President Lula's action plan against forced labour adopted in March 2003, with the objective of eradicating the problem by the end of 2006.

Awareness raising on forced labour

12. *Eastern Asia:* In China, a study tour on forced labour was organized for selected high-level Chinese officials to France, Germany, Hungary and the Russian Federation. Participants were from the key agencies to be involved in the process of law and policy reform, including China's re-education-through-labour system. The study tour prepared the ground for follow-up activities, including an inter-ministerial workshop on forced labour, held in Beijing in January 2004.

13. In Mongolia, a course on core labour standards was held in June 2003, followed by a national study on law and practical aspects of forced labour. The study identified some new forms of forced labour, as well as certain outstanding problems from the former socialist era. Employers' organizations have since proposed some specific activities for the eradication of forced labour.

14. A series of consultations in Viet Nam paved the way for an inter-ministerial workshop on forced labour in February 2004. Agreement was reached on the establishment of a tripartite inter-ministerial task force on forced labour concerns, as well as on terms of reference for a comprehensive study.

15. Two important events were held in East Asia in September 2003, in which SAP-FL was able to participate and draw attention to the forced labour dimensions of trafficking. The first was the Expert Group Meeting on Prevention of International Trafficking and Promotion of Public Awareness, hosted by the Ministries of Justice and Gender Equality in Seoul, Korea. The second was the ILO Symposium on Combating Trafficking in Human Beings, in Tokyo, Japan.

Advisory services

16. *Madagascar:* An in-depth study of the legal and policy environment and of different manifestations of forced labour in the country was completed and will be discussed and validated soon at a tripartite workshop.

17. *Germany:* Germany recently requested ILO guidance on the concept of forced labour in order to implement Article 3 of the United Nations Convention Against Transnational Organized Crime and the Protocol to Prevent, Suppress and Punish Trafficking in Persons, Especially Women and Children (the Palermo Protocol). In response, SAP-FL developed draft legislative guidelines to assist governments in the ratification and implementation of the Protocol. Support was also offered to the International Union of Food, Agricultural, Hotel, Restaurant, Catering, Tobacco and Allied Workers' Associations (IUF) and the German trade union IG BAU in their effort to draft a human rights charter for migrant workers in agriculture, demanding better protection of migrant workers from exploitation by smugglers or traffickers. A workshop in June 2003 was held to draft the charter and discuss follow-up action.

Programmes and projects

Coercive recruitment, debt bondage and bonded labour

18. *Brazil:* The ILO project continues to support members of the Executive Group for the Abolition of Forced Labour (GERTRAF) and other key partners within and outside government, at federal, state and municipal levels. The project has offered training and other support to the mobile inspection units and law enforcement agencies, and has helped to improve coordination between the various agencies involved in combating forced labour. A national information campaign was launched in October 2003, with the media as important partners. Since early 2002, more than 4,000 workers have been freed by government inspection teams.

19. *South Asia:* As of mid-2003, SAP-FL became a partner in the subregional project initiated by the Social Finance Programme (SFP) in Bangladesh, India (Andhra Pradesh), Nepal and Pakistan. It also continued the joint project with SFP in Tamil Nadu, India. The project has so far focused primarily on the prevention of bonded labour through the provision of a range of services, including financial and non-financial. In its new phase, it will expand the scope of activities. The project seeks to develop a proven "package" of interventions both to reduce the vulnerability of families at risk of falling into bondage and to rehabilitate those released from bondage. These approaches can then be replicated more widely by national partners. Increased emphasis is being placed on strengthening the institutional environment, including the role of District Vigilance Committees at local level and the role

of the social partners in combating bonded labour. The project also engages at the policy level with governments and the social partners across the subregion.

20. *Pakistan:* SAP-FL continued to support implementation of the National Policy and Plan of Action for the Abolition of Bonded Labour and Rehabilitation of Freed Bonded Labourers. The Ministry of Labour hosted an inter-ministerial round table discussion in August to seek wider involvement of other key government agencies in action against bonded labour; a national seminar was held in January 2004 to launch the findings of the rapid assessments, as endorsed by the Bonded Labour Research Forum; an adviser on bonded labour was appointed to work with the Ministry of Labour and manage ILO-sponsored activities on bonded labour, as of late 2003; and the National Committee for the Abolition of Bonded Labour and Rehabilitation of Freed Bonded Labourers held its first meeting in January 2004. An awareness- and consensus-building event was held by the brick-kiln owners' association of Pakistan, resulting in recommendations for follow-up activities. Under the auspices of the subregional project, collaboration continued with the National Rural Support Programme in Sindh Province, involving assistance to freed bonded labourer families living in camps around Hyderabad.

21. *Nepal:* Implementation of the joint Declaration/IPEC project on the sustainable elimination of the *kamaiya* system of bonded labour continued. The project works with the Ministry of Land Reform and Management and other partners to provide an integrated package of support to freed *kamaiyas* living in five districts of western Nepal. The project includes support for income generation through credit and skills training, group organization in the resettlement areas, small-scale infrastructure development, support for unionization of farm workers and campaigning for minimum wage and other labour standards, awareness raising on labour rights, non-formal education and mainstreaming of school-age children, and provision of micro-health insurance. To date, around 650 men and women have received skills training, more than 6,000 children have been mainstreamed into formal schools and 2,800 have been given non-formal instruction. Some 70 per cent of agricultural labourers in the target districts receive at least the minimum wage.

Internal or international trafficking resulting in forced labour situations

22. *South-eastern Asia:* As an outcome of the regional consultation for domestic workers' organizations held in February 2003, a technical cooperation project, Mobilizing Action for the Protection of Domestic Workers from Forced Labour and Trafficking in South-East Asia, has just been launched. It targets Indonesia and the Philippines as source countries, and Hong Kong, China, and Malaysia as transit/destination countries, in an integrated programme of action. Initial preparatory research has been undertaken.

23. *Central Asia:* A new technical cooperation project to combat human trafficking and its forced labour outcomes in Central Asia and the Russian Federation has recently commenced. It focuses on the exploitation of mainly Tajik and Uzbek migrant workers in the Russian construction industry and other sectors. Project components include awareness raising, law and policy reform, capacity building and demonstration projects for prevention and rehabilitation.

24. *South-eastern and western Europe:* SAP-FL, based on its European experience, has developed training tools to enhance the capacity of law enforcement authorities to detect and prosecute abusive recruitment practices and trafficking. Two modules – one for law enforcement agents and another for trainers – are currently being tested. The main target groups are police officers and labour inspectors involved in monitoring private recruitment agencies and anti-trafficking programmes. The training also encourages self-regulation by

private recruitment agencies. Additional work aims to foster cooperation between law enforcement authorities and labour market institutions in European Union Member States, accession countries and third countries.

25. *West Africa:* A new technical cooperation project is under way to combat trafficking in Ghana, Nigeria and Senegal, with Italy as a destination country. The project aims to improve the knowledge base (while there is considerable knowledge on child trafficking, little is known about adult trafficking in the region for labour exploitation), to mainstream forced labour and trafficking concerns into Poverty Reduction Strategy Papers and other important policy frameworks and to implement pilot prevention, protection and rehabilitation schemes, involving all key stakeholders.

C. Discrimination

Employment and occupation

26. In June 2003, the Global Report *Time for equality at work* was discussed at the Conference. Many Conference delegates voiced their concern about the rise in racial and ethnic discrimination stemming from the intensification of cross-border migration, the redefinition of national boundaries in Central and Eastern Europe, which had exposed national minority issues, and the persisting social and economic inequalities in multi-ethnic or multiracial countries. Concern was also expressed in respect of the persistent inequalities in remuneration between men and women worldwide, which were only in part to be ascribed to gender differences in education or work experience. Many speakers highlighted the nexus between discrimination at work and poverty and the failure of anti-poverty strategies to address this link.

27. Between May and December 2003, the InFocus Programme on Promoting the Declaration, in cooperation with the Department of Communication (DCOMM) and many regional and subregional offices, carried out multimedia campaigns and organized round tables and seminars to disseminate the main messages and findings of *Time for equality at work*. In several countries, including Brazil and the Philippines, national compendia, focusing on the national situation and complementing information contained in the Global Report, have been discussed with national governments and social partners and have led to immediate follow-up in Brazil (see paragraph 29).

28. In November 2003, the Governing Body Committee on Technical Cooperation adopted a four-year follow-up action plan regarding the elimination of discrimination in employment and occupation.[7] The action plan aims to help constituents develop their own policies and strategies to address discrimination in the world of work. It focuses on two main themes: racial/ethnic discrimination at work and development, with attention to its gender dimensions, and equal pay for work of equal value between women and men and between mainstream and racial/ethnic minority groups. Strategies promoted by the action plan include strengthening the capacity of governments and social partners to understand the causes and dynamics of discrimination, the need to tackle it and how to eliminate it; generating and disseminating knowledge about which policies and strategies work and which do not and why; and encouraging dialogue and consultation on selected themes – such as racial/ethnic discrimination and pay equity – between ILO constituents, nationally and globally, and between them and members of groups that suffer discrimination. The

---

[7] GB.288/TC/4.

action plan includes a global task force on the elimination of discrimination, to be created within the Office. Its aim will be to improve communication and enhance coordination and synergy between present and future activities in this domain. While this action plan is yet to be adequately funded, some activities – mainly seminars – have been started with limited regular budget funds, as well as funds provided by initial donors.

Addressing racial/ethnic discrimination

29. In Brazil, as part of the preparation of the national compendium to the Global Report, the ILO undertook a study assessing the effectiveness and impact of several regional centres *(núcleos)* that comprise the Ministry of Labour's programme to combat racial, gender and other forms of discrimination in employment and occupation. The ILO and the Ministry of Labour discussed the study's conclusions and recommendations. As a result, a number of changes in the programme's location in the Ministry's structure, its priorities and work methodology have been introduced. Since November 2003, the InFocus Programme on Promoting the Declaration, with the financial support of the Government of the Netherlands, has been implementing a technical cooperation project to assist the Special Secretariat of Policies to Promote Racial Equality, established in March 2003, and the Ministry of Labour in the design and implementation of a national policy to prevent and combat racism in the world of work.

Strengthening the capacity of trade unions to address discrimination at work

30. The InFocus Programme on Promoting the Declaration has provided technical and financial support to a number of trade unions to improve their capacity to tackle different forms of discrimination. These activities included:

(a) the ICFTU Conference on How to Oppose Discrimination in the Labour Market in South-East Europe (Skopje, Macedonia, 3-4 March 2003). The Conference was co-sponsored by ICFTU, ACTRAV, the InFocus Programme on Promoting the Declaration and the Subregional Office for Central and Eastern Europe in Budapest and was attended by trade union leaders, trade union officers and young trade union representatives of ten trade unions from Albania, Bosnia and Herzegovina, Croatia, Romania, Serbia and Montenegro, Slovenia and The former Yugoslav Republic of Macedonia. The Conference highlighted the difficulties that trade unions face in promoting policies geared towards the elimination of discrimination at work, owing to mass redundancies and erosion of social rights and benefits, and the legacy of socialism under which equity and non-discrimination were supposedly underpinning values of the regime. A declaration and a plan of action were adopted confirming the commitment of trade union leadership to respect the principles and rights enshrined in the Declaration on Fundamental Principles and Rights at Work and its Follow-up and identifying capacity building for the elimination of discrimination at work as a priority for both themselves and their membership.

(b) The first Regional Conference of Public Services International (PSI), Racism is a Trade Union Issue: Developing a Public Sector Trade Union Response (Bahia, Brazil, 8-10 October 2003), brought together 70 delegates representing PSI affiliates from 13 countries in the Americas and five countries in Africa. The Conference adopted a statement and an action plan for trade unions to fight racism in the community, the workplace and within trade unions. Proposed actions at the international level include developing regional and international anti-racism networks of public sector trade unions, adopting affirmative action in decision-making structures, implementing training programmes on racial equality for union members and staff and building alliances with community organizations and groups of workers facing multiple forms of discrimination.

(c) A six-month technical assistance project to the women's secretariats of the three trade union confederations of Central America, the Dominican Republic and Panama to strengthen their capacity to advocate and improve women's participation in the labour movement. This joint venture, involving, among others, the Subregional Office for Central America in San José, the InFocus Programme on Promoting the Declaration and ACTRAV, consisted of a series of activities at the country and subregional levels ranging from participatory assessment studies on the patterns and trends of women's participation in trade unions, by economic sector and by country, on gender inequalities in the labour market, and on the main factors and processes hampering women's representation in trade union leadership, their access to skill-enhancing opportunities and their involvement in key negotiations to preparation and validation by national trade union leadership of national action plans.

Addressing various forms of discrimination

31. In April 2004, the InFocus Programme on Promoting the Declaration, in collaboration with the Subregional Office for Central and Eastern Europe in Budapest, launched a project aimed at promoting the development of a national policy of non-discrimination and equality in employment and occupation in Albania, Bosnia and Herzegovina, Bulgaria, Croatia, the territory of Kosovo under interim international civilian administration, the Republic of Moldova, Romania, Serbia and Montenegro and The former Yugoslav Republic of Macedonia. The project, which is financed by the Government of Belgium, is part of a broader project aimed at strengthening social dialogue and tripartism and enhancing national technical expertise in labour law in south-eastern European countries, in the framework of the Stability Pact for South-Eastern Europe.

32. At the request of the Ministry of Labour of Peru, and in cooperation with the Subregional Office for the Andean Countries in Lima, a technical assistance programme was designed, in May 2004, to assist the recently established Intra-Ministerial Committee on Equality of Opportunities in reviewing all the Ministry's policies and programmes with the aim of mainstreaming non-discrimination and equality of opportunities throughout the Ministry's work. This technical assistance also envisages supporting the Ministry of Labour in the preparation of its contribution to the National Plan for Equality of Opportunities between Men and Women (2004-10).

Pay equity

33. In November 2003, the third Pay Equity Discussion Forum, jointly convened by the ILO and PSI, brought together the global union federations and the different departments of the ILO working on gender issues and pay equity in particular. The forum allowed participants: (i) to share updates on work on pay equity by the ILO and the global unions; (ii) to review and make recommendations to the pay equity component of the follow-up action plan on the elimination of discrimination, as endorsed by the Governing Body at its November session; and (iii) to plan strategies to raise the profile of pay equity issues in the global trade unions' agendas.

CONTENTS

Page

Follow-up activities by the Office under the Declaration on Fundamental Principles and Rights at Work: Freedom of association and collective bargaining, forced or compulsory labour, discrimination

A.	Freedom of association and collective bargaining	1
B.	Forced and compulsory labour	2
	Applied research and its dissemination	2
	Misuse of cultural traditions	2
	Trafficking and its forced labour outcomes	2
	Bonded labour	3
	Debt bondage and servitude	3
	Awareness raising on forced labour	3
	Advisory services	4
	Programmes and projects	4
	Coercive recruitment, debt bondage and bonded labour	4
	Internal or international trafficking resulting in forced labour situations	5
C.	Discrimination	6
	Employment and occupation	6
	Addressing racial/ethnic discrimination	7
	Strengthening the capacity of trade unions to address discrimination at work	7
	Addressing various forms of discrimination	8
	Pay equity	8

No. 7 – Wednesday, 2 June 2004

International Labour Conference

Provisional Record 8
Ninety-second Session, Geneva, 2004

First sitting
Tuesday, 1 June 2004, 10.15 a.m.
Presidents: Mr. Chung, Chairperson of the Governing Body of the International Labour Office, and Mr. Ray Guevara

OPENING OF THE SESSION

Mr. CHUNG *(Chairperson of the Governing Body of the International Labour Office)*

I have the greatest pleasure in declaring open the 92nd Session of the International Labour Conference. Our first task is to elect the President of the Conference. I call upon the Chairperson of the Government group, Mr. Lloyd, Deputy-Secretary for Employment and Workplace Relations, Australia, to propose a candidate for the President of the Conference.

ELECTION OF THE PRESIDENT OF THE CONFERENCE

Mr. SAWERS *(Government delegate, Australia)*

It is my honour, on behalf of the Chairperson of the Government group, Mr. Lloyd, Deputy-Secretary for Employment and Workplace Relations, who has been urgently called away for a brief but important meeting, and on behalf of the Government group itself, to propose as candidate for the post of President of the 92nd Session of the International Labour Conference, Mr. Ray Guevara, Secretary of State for Labour of the Dominican Republic. Mr. Ray Guevara has an exemplary legal background and has been a professor of law since 1970. He became Secretary of State for Labour for the Dominican Republic in 2000, having previously acted as consultant to the Secretary of State. Many national bodies have profited from his guidance, particularly in the field of social protection. He has represented his country as Ambassador Extraordinary and Plenipotentiary to France and the United Kingdom. Mr. Ray Guevara, without doubt, possesses all the qualities to guide the complex questions that will come before this session of the Conference.

Mr. CHUNG *(Chairperson of the Governing Body of the International Labour Office)*

I thank the Government group for the nomination of Mr. Ray Guevara of the Dominican Republic as the President of the Conference. I now give the floor to the spokesperson of the Employers' group, Mr. Funes de Rioja, Employers' delegate, Argentina, on behalf of the Employers' group.

Original Spanish: **Mr. FUNES DE RIOJA** *(Employers' delegate, Argentina)*

As spokesperson of the Employers' group at this session of the Conference, I would like to second the nomination made by the Government representative of Australia speaking on behalf of the Government group. May I say that, in the case of Mr. Ray Guevara, this is not mere ritual or formality; it is substantiated by the conviction of the Employers' group, which is familiar with the personal merits of the Minister, his abilities and his dedication to the work of the International Labour Organization.

I have no doubt whatsoever that, given his personal and professional qualities, Mr. Ray Guevara will serve as an excellent President during this crucial year of debate at the Conference. It is therefore with great enthusiasm that the Employers' group seconds the nomination of Mr. Ray Guevara.

Mr. CHUNG *(Chairperson of the Governing Body of the International Labour Office)*

I thank Mr. Funes de Rioja, speaking on behalf of the Employers' group. I now give the floor to Sir Roy Trotman, spokesperson of the Workers' group and Workers' delegate from Barbados.

Mr. TROTMAN *(Workers' delegate, Barbados)*

As spokesperson of the Workers' group, and as my Employer colleague has done, I also wish to second the nomination of Mr. Ray Guevara. Were I to speak as a member of the Barbados delegation, I would have the same pleasure in seconding this nomination. Mr. Ray Guevara, who comes from a neighbouring State, exercises the kind of warmth and the level of understanding and appreciation that is necessary to the work of the International Labour Organization. The Workers' group firmly believes that these qualities are crucial if we are to have the kind of social dialogue that is important. Both Mr. Ray Guevara and his country respect human rights and social dialogue and uphold labour standards to a level which we find tolerable. We hope that his nomination to the presidency of this session of the International Labour Conference will indicate the importance that we all attach to the promotion of decent work throughout the world. We are pleased to serve under him.

Mr. CHUNG *(Chairperson of the Governing Body of the International Labour Office)*

I thank Sir Roy Trotman, speaking on behalf of the Workers' group. The nomination of Mr. Ray Guevara, Secretary of State for Labour of the Dominican Republic, has been duly proposed and seconded. In the absence of other proposals, I declare Mr. Ray Guevara President of the 92nd Session of the International Labour Conference and offer him my warmest congratulations. I invite him to take the President's Chair.

(Mr. Ray Guevara, Secretary of State for Labour of the Dominican Republic, is elected President of the Conference and takes the President's Chair.)

PRESIDENTIAL ADDRESS

Original Spanish: The PRESIDENT

First of all, I would like to thank my colleagues from the Americas group who submitted my candidature to the presidency of this session of the Conference. My thanks also go to all my other colleagues in the Government group and to the delegations representing the Employers and Workers which supported my candidature.

Although the ILO is celebrating its 85th anniversary this year, this is the first time that a government of a country which is both Latin American and Caribbean has had the honour of presiding over the Conference. I consider that your vote in favour of my candidacy is an expression not only of confidence in my country, the Dominican Republic, but also of recognition of the Caribbean region as a whole, to which my country belongs, and with which it has a close and long-standing historic relationship, including – and I have to say this today – its share of suffering.

The people of my country, like our neighbours in Haiti, have just been hit by a natural disaster of unusual violence, even for a country which, like our neighbours in the Caribbean, is accustomed to the extremes of the tropical climate. I would like to ask you to spare a thought for all the lives we have just lost and for all the men, women and children who have survived and who, at this very moment, are struggling to find a reason to go on living after a tragedy which has deprived some of their loved ones, some of their whole family, and others of their home.

The presidency of this session of the Conference by the Dominican Republic is yet another landmark in the recent – but very fruitful – close cooperation between my country and the ILO. Over 20 years ago the ILO helped us to find solutions to problems inherited from a long dictatorship, which still persisted in the agricultural sector and which were contrary to fundamental standards of the ILO. Just over ten years ago the ILO offered us advisory assistance on the drafting of our Labour Code of 1992, and the ILO's proposals enabled the Code to reflect to a great extent not only the fundamental Conventions of this Organization, which have all been ratified by my country, but also the key aspects of the jurisprudence of the Committee of Experts on the Application of Conventions and Recommendations and the Committee on Freedom of Association.

And more recently, thanks to a technical cooperation project supported by the Government of Spain, the ILO has provided exceptional assistance to raise the professional level of our labour administration.

Similarly, I would like to highlight the unique support provided by this Organization for our programmes aimed at eliminating the worst forms of child labour. The ILO's cooperation has been appreciated by successive governments of widely differing political orientations in my country which – I must point out – succeeded one another in full respect of the rules of democracy. The support of the ILO has been so productive that it is my fervent hope that it will continue to cooperate in the same way with the new government that is to take office in a little over two months.

To sum up, the ILO is an institution which the Dominican Republic has learnt first to understand, then to respect, and finally to love, and it is the wish of my country's Government, led by President Hipólito Mejía, that our country's presidency of this session of the Conference be seen as a token of the full measure of our respect for this institution, our affection for it and of our great indebtedness to it.

To conclude, I would like to make one or two remarks upon the agenda of this session of the Conference. Next Monday, when we open our debate in plenary, I will have the opportunity to speak about the contents of some of the topics before the Conference. Today, may I just remind you that we do have a very full and complex agenda, and we must adhere strictly to the rules of debate if everyone is to be able to express their point of view during our deliberations. I do not have to remind you that the freedom of expression of each one of us at this Conference must be accompanied by full respect of the opinions of others, and that personal attacks are not appropriate in this forum. I may be obliged from time to time to remind you of these rules as the discussions move forward, but I sincerely hope that this will not be the case. I count on the cooperation of my Vice-Presidents and I trust that I can count on each of you as well.

I would ask for your understanding if at any time I have to take a difficult decision. The Conference is a joint effort by each and every one of us, and I trust in God that we will all do what is necessary to bring it to a successful conclusion.

ELECTION OF THE VICE-PRESIDENTS OF THE CONFERENCE

Original Spanish: The PRESIDENT

In accordance with Article 25, paragraph 2, of the Standing Orders of the International Labour Conference, we will now elect the Vice-Presidents of the Conference. I now call upon the Clerk of the Conference to read out the nominations made by the groups.

Original French: The CLERK OF THE CONFERENCE

The nomination to the posts of Vice-Presidents of the Conference are as follows:
Government group:
    Mr. Maatough *(Libyan Arab Jamahiriya)*
Employers' group:
    Mr. Wade *(Senegal)*
Workers' group:
    Mr. Attigbe *(Benin).*

Original Spanish: The PRESIDENT

May I take it that the proposals are adopted?

(The proposals are adopted.)

NOMINATION OF THE OFFICERS OF THE GROUPS

Original Spanish: The PRESIDENT

I now call on the Clerk of the Conference to read out the names of the persons who have been elected as Officers of the various groups.

Original French: THE CLERK OF THE CONFERENCE

The groups have chosen their Officers as follows:

Government group:
  Chairperson: Mr. Lloyd *(Australia)*
Employers' group:
  Chairperson: Mr. Funes de Rioja *(Argentina)*
  Vice-Chairpersons: Mr. Suzuki *(Japan)*
                        Mr. Botha *(South Africa)*
                        Mr. Lima Godoy *(Brazil)*
                        Mr. Potter *(United States)*
                        Mr. Barde *(Switzerland)*
  Secretary: Mr. Peñalosa *(International Organisation of Employers)*
Workers' group:
  Chairperson: Mr. Trotman *(Barbados)*
  Vice-Chairpersons: Mr. Ahmed *(Pakistan)*
                        Ms. Anderson *(Mexico)*
                        Mr. Diallo *(Guinea)*
                        Mr. Sidorov *(Russian Federation)*
  Secretary: Mr. Cunniah *(International Confederation of Free Trade Unions)*

The members of the Officers of the Workers' group, apart from the Chairperson and the Vice-Chairpersons are: Ms. Engelen-Kefer *(Germany)*, Ms. Valkonen *(Finland)*, Mr. Nakajima *(Japan)*, Ms. Beaumont *(New Zealand)*, Mr. Saïd *(Algeria)*, Mr. Atwoli *(Kenya)*, Ms. Byers *(Canada)*, Mr. Zellhoefer *(United States)*, and Mr. Attigbe *(Benin)*.

CONSTITUTION AND COMPOSITION OF CONFERENCE COMMITTEES

Original Spanish: The PRESIDENT

The next agenda item concerns the establishment of the various committees that will examine matters put before the Conference. The Conference may wish to establish the following committees: the Committee on the Application of Standards, the Committee on Human Resources, the Committee on the Fishing Sector, the Committee on Migrant Workers, the Resolutions Committee, the Selection Committee, and the Standing Orders Committee.

If there are no objections, may I take it that these proposals are adopted?

(The proposals are adopted.)

COMPOSITION OF THE SELECTION COMMITTEE

Original Spanish: The PRESIDENT

I would now like to ask the Clerk of the Conference to read out the nominations made by the groups for the composition of the Selection Committee.

Original French: The CLERK OF THE CONFERENCE

The appointments for the Selection Committee, in accordance with article 4 of the Standing Orders are as follows:

The 28 Government members are the titular members of the Governing Body of the following countries: Argentina, Bahamas, Brazil, Bulgaria, China, Dominican Republic, Ecuador, France, Gabon, Germany, India, Indonesia, Italy, Japan, Libyan Arab Jamahiriya, Lithuania, Mali, Mexico, Nigeria, Norway, Pakistan, Republic of Korea, Russian Federation, Saudi Arabia, South Africa, Sudan, United Kingdom and United States.

The Deputy Government members are: Bangladesh, Barbados, Belarus, Belgium, Burundi, Cameroon, Canada, El Salvador, Ethiopia, Ghana, Islamic Republic of Iran, Jordan, Kenya, Luxembourg, Malawi, Morocco, New Zealand, Niger, Oman, Philippines, Romania, Singapore, Slovenia, Spain, Turkey, Uruguay, Venezuela and Viet Nam.

The 14 Employer members are: Mr. Barde *(Switzerland)*; Mr. Dahlan *(Saudi Arabia)*; Mr. Funes de Rioja *(Argentina)*; Mr. Jeetun *(Mauritius)*; Mr. Lambert *(United Kingdom)*; Mr. Lima Godoy *(Brazil)*; Mr. M'Kaissi *(Tunisia)*; Mr. Noakes *(Australia)*; Mr. Potter *(United States)*; Ms. Sasso Mazzufferi *(Italy)*; Mr. Suzuki *(Japan)*; Mr. Tabani *(Pakistan)*; Mr. Trogen *(Sweden)* and Mr. Wade *(Senegal)*.

The Deputy Employer members are: Mr. Anand *(India)*; Mr. Arnold *(New Zealand)*; Mr. De Arbeloa *(Venezuela)*; Mr. Eremeev *(Russian Federation)*; Mr. Ferrer Dufol *(Spain)*; Mr. Finlay *(Canada)*; Mr. Hilton Clarke *(Trinidad and Tobago)*; Ms. Horvatić *(Croatia)*; Mr. Konditi *(Kenya)*; Mr. Makeka *(Lesotho)*; Mr. Nacoulma *(Burkina Faso)*; Mr. Nathan *(Malaysia)*; Mr. Oshinowo *(Nigeria)*; and Mr. Ricci *(Guatemala)*.

With regard to the 14 Worker members, the nominations are the same as those of the Officers of the Workers' group which I read out previously.

The Deputy Worker members are: Ms. Burrow *(Australia)*; Mr. Cortebeeck *(Belgium)*; Mr. Mortensen *(Denmark)*; and Ms. Yacob *(Singapore)*.

Original Spanish: The PRESIDENT

If there are no objections, may I take it that the composition of the Selection Committee is adopted by the plenary?

(The proposals are adopted.)

SUSPENSION OF CERTAIN PROVISIONS OF THE STANDING ORDERS OF THE CONFERENCE

Original Spanish: The PRESIDENT

The next agenda item refers to the suspension of certain provisions of the Standing Orders of the Conference to implement recommendations made by the Governing Body at its 289th Session, in March 2004, regarding the discussion of the Global Report that the Director-General presents annually under the follow-up to the ILO Declaration on Fundamental Principles and Rights at Work.

In order to implement these recommendations, the President and the three Vice-Presidents unanimously recommend, in accordance with article 76 of the Standing Orders, that the Conference decide that the discussion of the Global Report should not fall under the limitation concerning the number of statements by each speaker in the plenary, but that, within each Government delegation, interventions be made either by the minister or by the Government delegate and that, to that extent, article 12, paragraph 3, of the Standing Orders should be suspended; and that the Conference decide that the discussion should not be governed by the provisions regarding time limits to speeches and, to that extent, suspend article 14, paragraph 6, of the Standing Orders; and that the Conference decide not to apply, to the extent required, the provisions of article 14, paragraph 2, of the Standing Orders on the sequence with which the floor is given to speakers, in order to facilitate an exchange of views.

If there are no objections, may I take it that these proposals pursuant to article 76 of the Standing Orders will take effect, with the agreement of the Conference, as from its next plenary sitting, which will be held next Monday, 7 June. As I can see no objections, I take it that the proposals are adopted.

(The proposals are adopted.)

The discussion of the Global Report, *Organizing for social justice*, will take place on Thursday, 10 June, during two plenary sessions. There will be no other plenary sessions on that day and there will be no list of speakers established prior to the sitting. On that day, speakers must register to speak once the session has been declared open, making use of the application forms that will be available in the room.

In accordance with the recommendations made by the Governing Body at its 288th Session in November 2003, security provisions have been established this year to control access to the ILO building during the Conference. We ask participants to kindly accept any inconvenience that such security measures may entail and we count on the cooperation of all participants so that the Conference activities may proceed smoothly. We ask you to bring to the attention of the guards or secretariat staff any irregularity which anyone may feel could compromise the security of the buildings or individuals. We also ask all participants to scrupulously respect the health rules that have been established and to bear in mind that we are all responsible for health and security. We urge everyone to wear the conference badge that they received at registration.

May I also bring to the attention of all participants that, under article 13, paragraph 2, of the Standing Orders of the International Labour Conference, the President of the Conference is responsible for maintaining order throughout the proceedings. Again, I thank you for your understanding and for your cooperation.

REPORT OF THE CHAIRPERSON OF THE GOVERNING BODY: SUBMISSION

Original Spanish: The PRESIDENT

I now call upon Mr. Chung, the Chairperson of the Governing Body, to submit the report of the Governing Body, which was published in *Provisional Record* No. 3.

Mr. CHUNG *(Chairperson of the Governing Body of the International Labour Office)*

It is my honour to present to you my report on the work of the Governing Body over the past year. The text of this report is published in *Provisional Record* No. 3 and I shall confine myself here today to brief introductory comments grouped under the Organization's four strategic objectives.

In the field of international labour standards, the Governing Body has continued to follow closely the work of the International Programme on the Elimination of Child Labour (IPEC). As stated in my report, the Programme has made systematic efforts to mainstream its work at country and global levels, and to operate coherently with the ILO's Decent Work Agenda. The programme is the largest ILO technical cooperation programme and it continues to expand at a very rapid rate.

The Governing Body has also paid close attention to the work of the InFocus Programme on Promoting the ILO Declaration on Fundamental Principles and Rights at Work. It followed up on last year's Global Report, *Time for equality at work*, by approving an action plan aiming to raise the coherence, visibility and impact of the Organization's action, and to achieve measurable results in this field between 2004 and 2007.

This year is the fifth annual review under the Programme's follow-up and the Global Report before the Conference is entitled *Organizing for social justice*. The Declaration Expert-Advisers have this year returned to the first of the four categories for annual review: freedom of association and the right to collective bargaining.

The Governing Body, in examining the Expert-Advisers' introduction to the review of annual reports under the follow-up to the Declaration, called on the Office to develop further the means for countries to assess their progress in promoting fundamental principles and rights at work.

The Committee on Freedom of Association which, as you are aware, reports to each of the three Governing Body sessions, has continued its very important work and examined some 200 cases over the review period, noting a certain number of positive developments.

The Governing Body also followed with great interest the progress on the proposed consolidated maritime labour Convention, which is designed to replace almost all maritime labour Conventions adopted since 1920. Work has been going ahead on the proposed Convention in the High-level Tripartite Working Group on Maritime Labour Standards, which held its fourth meeting in January 2004. The discussions of the Working Group have narrowed areas of potential disagreement and I am confident that the meetings will greatly ease the work of the Preparatory Technical Maritime Conference to be held in September. The proposed instrument will come before the 94th (Maritime) Session of the Conference in 2005.

The question of the observance by the Government of Myanmar of the Forced Labour Convention, 1930 (No. 29), has also been intensively followed, and some progress towards an implementation of the tentative Plan of Action has been observed. In March 2004 it was felt that although the Myanmar authorities had demonstrated an openness to cooperate, the discovery of sentences for high treason against certain Myanmar nationals, in which contacts or exchange of information with the ILO appeared to be cited as criminal offences, undermined the prospects of a credible implementation of the Plan of Action, and more specifically, of the Facilitator mechanism. The Office and the Officers of the Governing Body were requested to study available information more closely, before any further decisions on proceeding with the Plan of Action and particularly the function of a Facilitator foreseen by it.

In 2003-04, the Governing Body devoted much attention to improvements in standards-related activities, and in particular to reinforcing the operation of the supervisory bodies of the International Labour Organization. The procedures for submission of instruments adopted by the Conference to the competent authorities, and for filing representations and complaints under articles 19, 24 and 26 of the Constitution were considered, and the Governing

Body will study the proposed amendments to these procedures in November this year. The Office has also undertaken to produce a manual of good drafting practices to improve the drafting of instruments submitted to the Conference, and this is to be reviewed by the Governing Body in March 2005.

Under this heading, I should also mention that the Governing Body, following the complaint submitted at the last Conference under article 26 of the Constitution by a number of Workers' delegates, decided to establish a Commission of Inquiry to examine the allegations of non-observance by Belarus of Conventions Nos. 87 and 98. In the meantime, all other procedures have been suspended.

In the field of employment, the Governing Body's Committee on Employment and Social Policy continued to discuss the implementation of the Global Employment Agenda, advocating greater integration of the various ILO programmes presently operating. The Committee was pleased with the high level of national ownership and national involvement in the Decent Work Pilot Programme. These experiences should constitute a tool-kit for future activities. The Committee discussed the theme of productive employment for poverty reduction, supporting proposals for increased efforts to integrate employment into Poverty Reduction Strategy Papers, and Millennium Development Goals. The Subcommittee on Multinational Enterprises turned its regard inwards, considering possible internal changes to its structure, and outwards, considering priorities to promote awareness of the Tripartite Declaration of Principles concerning Multinational Enterprises and Social Policy.

In respect of social protection, the Committee on Employment and Social Policy noted progress in the Global Campaign on Social Security and Coverage for All, which had been launched for Africa at the Tenth African Regional Meeting, and would likely be taken up at the African Union Extraordinary Summit on Employment and Poverty Alleviation to be held in a few months' time in Burkina Faso.

In June 2003, the Governing Body reviewed progress in activities under the Special Technical Cooperation Programme for Colombia. The Committee on Technical Cooperation received a further report in March this year. The Workers' group strongly denounced the continued assassinations and attacks against trade union members and their families, and the Governing Body called upon the Government of Colombia to take urgent steps to redress the situation of impunity in the country.

The enhanced Programme of Technical Cooperation for the Occupied Arab Territories also received close attention. The Governing Body noted that significant steps had been taken to make the Palestinian Fund for Employment and Social Protection operational, and to launch fund-raising activities.

In respect of social dialogue, a theme that cuts through all ILO activities and on which the organization's tripartite nature is founded, the Governing Body approved proposals to take action in certain specific industrial sectors, while maintaining international tripartite sectoral meetings to foster dialogue in other sectors. It has been well informed, with reports in November 2003 and March 2004 on progress in this important and active area, noting the reports of the sectoral and technical meetings which took place during the period, and endorsing their recommendations and conclusions.

In February this year the World Commission on the Social Dimension of Globalization concluded almost two years of discussions and published its report: *A fair globalization: Creating opportunities for all*. As you are aware, the Director-General has submitted a Report to the Conference entitled: *A fair globalization: The role of the ILO*. The Governing Body Working Party on the Social Dimension of Globalization was able to follow the work of the World Commission through visits by both co-Chairs of the Commission: in November 2003, President Halonen of Finland gave a progress report on the Commission's work. In March 2004, President Mkapa of the United Republic of Tanzania presented a report of the Commission to the Governing Body; President Mkapa was generous enough with his time to remain for two whole days of discussion. A full summary of the debates on these two days is included in Appendix II of my report.

Before concluding, I should like to take this opportunity to thank my two fellow officers, Mr. Funes de Rioja, Employer Vice-Chairperson and Sir Roy Trotman, Worker Vice-Chairperson. Their cooperation and friendship have been invaluable over the past year, and without their support the many tasks undertaken by the Governing Body would have been impossible. I should also like to thank the Director-General and his staff for their constant support. It has been a great honour for me to hold the Chair of the Governing Body of the International Labour Office.

With these introductory remarks, I submit my report to you for your consultation.

STATEMENT BY MR. SOMAVIA, SECRETARY-GENERAL OF THE CONFERENCE

Original Spanish: The PRESIDENT

It is now my honour to give the floor to Mr. Somavia, Director-General of the ILO, so that he may present his Report entitled *ILO Programme implementation 2002-03*, with its Appendix, *Report on the situation of workers of the occupied Arab territories*, and the Global Report, *Organizing for social justice*, which is a part of the follow-up to the ILO Declaration on Fundamental Principles and Rights at Work.

The Report entitled *A fair globalization: The role of the ILO* will be introduced by the Director-General on Monday, 7 June.

Original Spanish: THE SECRETARY GENERAL

Mr. President, I congratulate you on your election. I am really very pleased in as much as we have worked together over many years and in particular in the ILO Governing Body.

(Speaker continues in English.)

Ministers, representatives of workers' and employers' organizations, friends of the ILO from the international community who are here with us, thank you for accompanying us. Welcome to the 92nd Session of the International Labour Conference.

With this Conference, I begin my second mandate. So let me begin by thanking you for your support and for your trust. I am proud of our ILO. I am convinced that tripartism has a global role to play in the year of globalization. You can count on my commitment to forge into the future with the ILO flag flying high, with all my energy and my heart and soul – that is my commitment to you today.

We have come a long way together. Over the last five years, we have worked in a tripartite manner to develop three fundamental and inter-linked concepts: the Decent Work Agenda as a development tool; employment as the main route out of poverty; and achieving a fair globalization as a source of global stability. On this foundation we shall build for the future.

While we have accomplished much together, there is no room for complacency. We have many challenges ahead. But I think that we can be satisfied that these three concepts express in simple terms the perceptions, the needs and the growing political pressures that people everywhere place on their leaders. We are connecting with people when we refine these three areas.

I will synthesize this in the following way: "Give me a fair chance at a decent job". Today that call is a worldwide demand. We are answering that challenge with a full Conference agenda, focused on real issues that address real problems. We will continue our discussion on a new instrument on human resources development that will reflect twenty-first century approaches to lifelong learning, portability of skills and the education and training that are needed for small and medium enterprises. All these are central issues in the emerging knowledge economy.

I am sure the Committee will also take up the challenge of skills development in the informal economy in order to turn its creativity into productive gains and generally address issues of particular importance to the developing countries.

We will have a general discussion on migrant workers in the global economy. A growing number of migrants, as you know well, are crossing borders in search of employment and human security that they may not find at home – eighty-six million workers at the last count and growing. And, taken together with their families, migrants would make up the fifth largest country in the world. This is just to say how key and crucial the issue of migration is for the world today, for the world of globalization and for the mandate of the ILO.

The difficulties in managing migration are having profound political and human consequences, exacerbated by an unbalanced globalization process. This is a timely discussion because the challenges of migration apply to North and South. We need to develop a more cooperative approach that could lead to a plan of action to strengthen the ILO's capacity to assist member States in managing migration based on the values of opportunity, fairness and equality. I want to thank Mr. McKinley who is here with us and will participate in the discussion of this issue.

In the fishing sector, we will focus on developing a new instrument to replace seven existing ILO standards. International trade in fish products is worth US$55 billion, a third of which is exports from developing countries. The sector employs 25 million people, mainly on smaller vessels. It illustrates graphically one of the major issues of globalization because we need to find a way to ensure that the 90 per cent of workers in the small-scale and artisanal part of the industry can compete with those working on the big industrial fishing vessels; and that both can improve their working conditions.

The Committee on the Application of Conventions and Recommendations, the anchor of our system of standards supervision, will review reports on a large number of countries. Large or small, East, West, North and South – the Committee will ensure that all countries have a fair hearing and that the principles we work so hard to formulate are adhered to in practice.

The latest Global Report on freedom of association shows encouraging signs of progress, increased ratifications, more openness as to ILO technical assistance and changes in laws. But it is clearly not enough. We still see too many threats to the life and freedom for those attempting to organize and make their voice heard.

The right to organize of workers and employers and the ensuing social dialogue is one of the most powerful tools for promoting decent work and finding and fighting poverty. We must all do more to make this fundamental right a reality in the lives of people and the institutions of society. The right to organize and social dialogue are the foundations of stability for the future. We are not going to have stable societies when people, sectors and interested parties do not talk to each other; and in order to talk, and to talk well, they need to be organized. That is a rule that is absolutely essential in this first part of the twenty-first century.

We also have the latest Report on the situation of workers in the occupied Arab territories. The findings continue to be disturbing. The image of "collective punishment" is still the defining feature of life in Palestine. The focus of this year's Report is on the dramatic social effects of the economic disruption caused by restrictions, security measures, systematic acts of violence and other impositions on the daily life of Palestinians. For the first time there is a special emphasis on the impact on Palestinian women. It also reflects the insecurities that violence brings to the life of Israelis.

The Report makes a number of practical suggestions in our field of action, including a call to the donor community for resource commitments that permit a real activation of the Palestinian Fund for Employment and Social Protection. We at the ILO pledge to do our part within our mandate to promote dignity and a normal life to the long-suffering people of that troubled region.

We have for consideration our regular financial report. We also have this year's Report on programme implementation, which presents our performance against the objectives set five years ago and outlines how we have tightened up our management systems using results-based targeting methods.

It shows what we can do and all that we are doing in the face of a zero real growth budget and a list of requests that keeps on growing. And we will continue to strengthen our management capacities. In the last five years, we have been successful in mobilizing extra-budgetary funds with a 53 per cent increase in programme implementation. In the same period, our delivery rate has increased by 40 per cent.

We are doing all of this while pursuing a gender mainstreaming policy and implementing an office-wide plan to promote gender equality. But if you permit me, I must add that we are not fulfilling our mission when it comes to gender balance at the International Labour Conference. At the Conference last year, and I hope that this year we will do better, women were represented in about 20 per cent of delegations and constituted 12 per cent of delegates. The situation was similarly skewed in terms of speakers.

During the last Conference, a delegate suggested we should start by implementing a 30 per cent positive action policy for future sessions: I must say that I agree with that idea. Addressing this issue must be a priority. Frankly speaking, we need to see more women in delegations and not hear any more excuses.

Finally, when it comes to the Conference agenda, let me say that I greatly look forward to hearing your views about my Report on the implications for the ILO of the findings of the World Commission on the Social Dimension of Globalization. I am happy to see that the Report has been welcomed, and sometimes highly welcomed, in all regions of the world. It is a Report that is making its own road. The ILO's role in creating a fair globalization that creates opportunities for all is a major challenge for the institution and for tripartism.

Next week we will be honoured by Presidents Halonen and Mkapa who will be here to present the report of the World Commission to the Conference. I am glad that they will be joined by the Prime Minister of New Zealand, Helen Clark, and the President of Bulgaria, Georgi Parvanov, for a Presidential Panel discussion. Prime Minister Rodríguez Zapatero of Spain will also honour us later next week.

This full agenda is an expression of our mission – age-old and yet forward-looking – to connect values and ideals with the demands and concerns of families and communities today.

We move into the future building on the three concepts we have developed: decent work; working out of poverty; and a fair globalization.

The decent work message is resonating around the world. The last reference to it was given to me just a few days ago. At the recent EU-Latin American/Caribbean Summit, the heads of governments of Latin America and Europe reiterated their agreement with the principles of decent work as defined by the ILO. We are thus receiving a constant flow of support for the notion that we have put forward as an institution.

Our challenge today is to deepen our tripartite capacity to make the Decent Work Agenda an operational concept, for it to become a reality in the life of people; and that we need to do together. We need to consolidate and advance results on the ground – and for that decent work country programmes are key. I invite all of you to reach tripartite agreements on the best way to move forward in each one of your countries: the reality in each country specific to you. It is through tripartism within society that you can best evaluate the manner in which the Decent Work Agenda may be implemented within your own reality. So I invite you to utilize tripartism to show its vitality and its strength, giving thought to the concepts and the principles that can be applied within your own context. The ILO will be behind you to service.

The notion of working out of poverty – that employment is a sustainable way out of poverty – is also taking hold. It is our policy contribution to reaching the Millennium Development Goal of reducing poverty by half. And later this year the African Union will convene an Extraordinary Summit of Heads of States and Governments on Employment and Poverty Alleviation in Burkina Faso. The ILO has been singled out to play a leading role in preparation for that Summit in support of the African Union. We are mobilizing to deliver for that Summit – and for its follow-up.

And, of course, the concept of a fair globalization and the report of the World Commission on the Social Dimension of Globalization opens up tremendous new scope for ILO action. I will speak in greater detail when I present my Report next week. But I would say today that the Report defines what I see as four challenges for the ILO: making decent work a global goal; mobilizing tripartism for global action; making the ILO a global player; and all of this makes it necessary for the Organization, the Office included, to become a global team. Global goal, global action, global player, global team.

It is clear that if there is an institution at the forefront of the emerging global community of multiple actors, rooted in a knowledge economy and a network society, an institution that is key to a fair globalization – it is the ILO.

A new opportunity to be meaningful is coming in front of us – and I believe that we should seize this opportunity. But as we address these challenges, where do we draw our strength to forge ahead? What makes us move forward; what are the foundations on which we can address these challenges? I think that, first of all, we continue to be a value-based institution. It is the source of our legitimacy. The ILO has always been about finding its place, its space, its voice to be an advocate for social justice at different moments in history; and these moments have been very varied. We have achieved this through the vehicle of dialogue and consensus-building, and we can be proud of the ILO today and of its history.

This year marks the 85th anniversary of the ILO; the 60th anniversary of the Declaration of Philadelphia and the 35th anniversary of the Nobel Peace Prize. In these last decades, the work of our founders has been carried forward for such leaders as Wilfred Jenks, a firm advocate of the rule of law, tripartism and asserting the moral authority of the ILO in the international system; Francis Blanchard and his expansion of technical cooperation, demonstrating how we could work with and assist countries moving into independence; and Michel Hansenne in the advancement of our cause through the Declaration on Fundamental Principles and Rights at Work – just to mention some of their many achievements.

Each in their own way enriched the gifts that our founders bestowed upon us. The gift of an institution rooted in social justice and borne out of conflict, an institution that gradually emerged as a moral compass for the global system. The gift of a Constitution that gives us a wide economic and social mandate. And the gift of the simple, yet path breaking concept of tripartism, of dialogue, of finding common ground – which this Conference and all of you here today represent.

Taken together, our founders gave us another gift, perhaps the best one of all. They gave us an institution with a mandate to dare and to dream. President Roosevelt, a strong advocate of the ILO, called it a "wild dream". "Who had ever heard of governments getting together to raise the standards of labour on an international plain" he said. "Wilder still was the idea that the people affected – workers and employers – should have a hand in it".

He was right. But what was once seen as "wild", soon became possible, then practical, and I would say today, essential. We are the heirs of that proud inheritance – forged in Versailles, reaffirmed in Philadelphia, rewarded in Oslo, and renewed every day in Geneva and around the world.

When our institution received the Nobel Peace Prize, the Committee said: "There are few organizations that have succeeded to the extent of the ILO in translating into action the fundamental moral idea on which it was based".

Nothing could be more inspiring as we celebrate our past. Nothing could be more empowering as we forge our way into the twenty-first century: decent work, working out of poverty, a fair globalization that creates opportunities for all. To some it may seem like a dream; yes, even a "wild dream". But through our history, our mandate and our record, many dreams have become reality in the halls of the ILO and in the lives of workers, employers and governments these last 85 years.

What others may call wild, we call possible. What others dismiss as a dream, we strive to make real in the lives and the hopes of people. That is our ILO foundation. It is what the ILO family of the past put in our hands to shape the ILO of the future. Let us carry forward these traditions with the humility that acknowledges difficulties and the passion that overcomes them.

Original Spanish: The PRESIDENT

I should like to remind you that the discussion on the report of the Chairperson of the Governing Body, the Report of the Director-General on ILO programme implementation 2002-03 and its Appendix, and the report on a fair globalization and the role of the ILO, will begin on Monday, 7 June, in the afternoon.

At the beginning of this plenary session, the Director-General will make a detailed presentation of his Report, *A fair globalization: The role of the ILO*.

Also on Monday, 7 June, there will be a special event which will bring together a number of Heads of State and Government to comment on the report of the World Commission on the Social Dimension of Globalization.

DELEGATION OF AUTHORITY

Original Spanish: The PRESIDENT

The fact that the next plenary sitting will not be held before 7 June implies that the everyday tasks related to the organization of the Conference will be carried out by the Officers of the Conference, if the Conference wishes to confer on them the necessary powers to do so.

I shall now ask the Clerk of the Conference to read out, for your approval, the delegation of authority.

Original French: The CLERK OF THE CONFERENCE

The General Conference of the International Labour Organization hereby delegates to its President and three Vice-Presidents authority to take any decisions or perform any functions which fall within the competence of the Conference with respect to any matter that needs to be dealt with before the Conference resumes its plenary sittings, unless the Officers consider that the Conference should hold a sitting to discuss such matters.

Decisions taken under this authority will be set out in the *Provisional Record* of the work of the Conference.

This delegation of authority shall take effect at the end of this sitting and shall terminate when the Conference resumes its plenary sittings.

Original Spanish: The PRESIDENT

If there are no objections, I take it that the delegation of authority is accepted.

(The delegation of authority is accepted.)

I now declare closed the first sitting of the 92nd Session of the International Labour Conference.

(The Conference adjourned at 11.30 a.m.)

CONTENTS

Page

First sitting

Opening of the session 1
    Speaker: Mr. Chung *(Chairperson of the Governing Body of the International Labour Office)*

Election of the President of the Conference 1
    Speakers: Mr. Sawers, Mr. Funes de Rioja, Mr. Trotman

Presidential address 2

Election of the Vice-Presidents of the Conference 2

Nomination of the Officers of the groups 2

Constitution and composition of Conference committees 3

Composition of the Selection Committee 3

Suspension of certain provisions of the Standing Orders of the Conference 3

Report of the Chairperson of the Governing Body: Submission 4
    Speaker: Mr. Chung

Statement by Mr. Somavia, Secretary-General of the Conference 5

Delegation of authority 8

No. 8 – Friday, 4 June 2004

International Labour Conference
Provisional Record
Ninety-second Session, Geneva, 2004

9

Second (special) sitting
Monday, 7 June 2004, 10.40 a.m.
President: Mr. Ray Guevara

ADDRESS BY HEADS OF STATE AND GOVERNMENT ON THE REPORT OF THE WORLD COMMISSION ON THE SOCIAL DIMENSION OF GLOBALIZATION

Original Spanish: The PRESIDENT

It is for me an honour to declare open the second sitting of the 92nd Session of the International Labour Conference. Today we have a special session, during which the Conference will have the great honour of welcoming four eminent personalities from the world of politics. I refer to the two co-Chairs of the World Commission on the Social Dimension of Globalization, Her Excellency Ms. Tarja Halonen, President of the Republic of Finland, and His Excellency Mr. Benjamin Mkapa, President of the United Republic of Tanzania. I also refer to His Excellency Mr. Georgi Parvanov, President of the Republic of Bulgaria, and the Right Honourable Helen Clark, Prime Minister of New Zealand.

Ms. Halonen and Mr. Mkapa have, for two years, led the World Commission on the Social Dimension of Globalization, carrying out the arduous task of guiding the very varied group that has been plunged in the study of a very complex and extremely topical issue.

Both presented the report of the World Commission on the Social Dimension of Globalization to the Governing Body of the ILO. We are very appreciative of the fact that they have agreed to present it to the Conference this morning. After the presentation, we shall have the pleasure of listening to the President of the Republic of Bulgaria and to the Prime Minister of New Zealand, who will give us their opinions on the report. We shall also listen to the comments of the representatives of the social partners, Mr. Funes de Rioja, Chairperson of the Employers' group and Employer Vice-Chairperson of the Governing Body, and Sir Roy Trotman, Chairperson of the Workers' group and Worker Vice-Chairperson of the Governing Body.

The fact that we have here four distinguished public figures from four different regions of the world, symbolizes the world interest that globalization has aroused. Its importance is such that it has been dealt with at the highest level and this is why the ILO is very pleased to have here today four of the highest representatives of their respective countries.

The presence in this room of Heads of State and Government is a great honour for the ILO, and at the same time it is a challenge for the Organization to be able to fulfil its responsibilities when the time comes to implement the recommendations that have been made. Before giving the floor to our distinguished speakers, I wish to remind you that Her Excellency Ms. Halonen, President of the Republic of Finland, made available to the World Commission all the experience that she acquired in her country and internationally during a political career devoted to the fight for social justice, equality and the search for solutions which would make it possible to overcome the shortfalls in employment and social protection. She has been an exceptional ambassador for the World Commission on the Social Dimension of Globalization and she was able to develop the necessary team spirit to obtain understanding between the different interest groups. I am very pleased now to give the floor to Her Excellency Ms. Halonen.

Ms. HALONEN *(President of the Republic of Finland)*

It is a great pleasure and privilege for me to speak at the 92nd Session of the International Labour Conference. The ILO and the International Labour Conference are a unique part of the multilateral international system. Worker and Employer representatives participate in international cooperation as equals alongside Government representatives. This is the ILO's special strength, and provides an exceptionally strong justification for the Organization's decisions and activities.

I owe great thanks to the ILO: the International Labour Conference, the Governing Body and Juan Somavia. Thank you for having the courage and foresight to appoint the independent World Commission on the Social Dimension of Globalization. I thank you for inviting me to co-Chair this Commission, together with President Benjamin Mkapa of the United Republic of Tanzania – or, as I have learned to call him during our days in the Commission, dear Ben.

Two years at the head of the World Commission is definitely one of the most important experiences and greatest high points in my professional life. This is an experience that I will never forget. At this point I would like to thank all the members of the Commission for their excellent cooperation, and my special thanks of course to my co-Chair, Benjamin Mkapa.

Our Commission began work in February 2002 and our report, *A fair globalization: Creating opportunities for all*, was published on 24 February 2004. Our work was not always easy. Commissions are often composed of the people who are like-minded, but ours was largely one of "not like-minded" people: 26 people who came from different backgrounds, have different political views, are from different parts of the world and have their own strong opinions. The Commission was nevertheless able to publish a unanimous joint report. This is proof of the new attitude and desire to find common answers to common challenges. Our report is proof of the power of discussion and dialogue.

Each one of us would have written a different report and would have emphasized different things. What is important is that ours is a joint report. Everyone had to make compromises but noone had to abandon basic views.

The Commission also arranged an extensive series of consultations around the world. I had the opportunity to attend regional dialogues in Asia, Africa and Europe, as well as national dialogues in China and in my own country, Finland. These consultations were invaluable in helping us to understand how people experience globalization in different parts of the world.

The World Commission's report has been given a good reception by governments, international organizations and civil society. Work is only getting started, however. We do not intend for the report to be just one more publication. We intend for it to be part of a process that will give globalization a human face. All of us are needed in this work.

The Director-General, Juan Somavia, has prepared an excellent report on our Commission's work for this Conference. His Report outlines the role of the ILO in advancing the World Commission's work. It is of key importance to make decent work a global goal and to promote a policy coherence initiative on growth, investment and employment. Both of these suit the ILO quite well. I hope that this Conference will discuss the Director-General's Report carefully and will give the ILO and its secretariat a clear mandate to promote the recommendations in the World Commission's report.

The recommendations in the World Commission's report cover a much wider field than the ILO's direct scope, however. One section consists of recommendations to nation States and civil society, including business and employers' and labour organizations. Another clear whole is formed by matters that come within the sphere of international organizations. In particular, employment and cross-border movement of people are issues which have received the most attention in public discourse. A new kind of cross-border movement of people is especially important for developing countries. Millions of people move for a shorter or longer time, both from developing countries to industrialized countries and to other developing countries. I am very happy to hear that your activities at this session of the Conference will also address this sector.

With regard to the international system, the main emphasis in promoting the work and recommendations of the World Commission on the Social Dimension of Globalization has been by the United Nations as well as the ILO. In April this year, I attended the Special High-level ECOSOC Meeting with the Bretton Woods Institutions and the WTO in New York. I told the participants about the Commission's work and our report. The reception was positive, in my opinion. The Director-General, Juan Somavia will attend the ECOSOC substantive session at the end of June in New York.

President Mkapa and I have planned to focus on making the report and its recommendations better known this spring and summer. Our goal is for the 59th Session of the United Nations General Assembly to approve a resolution this autumn requesting ECOSOC and other relevant bodies to consider our Commission's report and then report back to the 60th Session.

We are currently identifying a suitable agenda item for Finland and the United Republic of Tanzania to present an operational resolution.

It is also our intention for the Bretton Woods institutions to discuss the World Commission's report in a suitable manner. Work is also under way in this regard. The World Bank and the International Monetary Fund cooperated actively in the preparation of the report. I was asked to come and brief the World Bank's European meeting about the report but unfortunately, owing to a previously agreed official visit, the time was unsuitable for me.

Within the World Trade Organization, there seems to be some hope in sight. European Trade Commissioner, Pascal Lamy has said that the European Union (EU) is, in principle, ready to give up agricultural export subsidies if others are ready to do the same.

At the regional level, the European Commission has prepared a communication on our report. The statement is positive in tone and the European Commission recommends that the EU should carefully discuss the report's recommendations and take them into consideration in the EU's internal and external activities.

President Mkapa has similarly informed his African colleagues of our Commission's report, and I believe that this report is also on the agenda at the African Union Summit in Addis Ababa, Ethiopia, a month from now. But you will hear about this, of course, from my colleague himself.

I also had the opportunity to talk about the World Commission and the follow-up work at the Third summit of Heads of State and Government of the European Union and Latin America and the Caribbean.

Finland and the United Republic of Tanzania, have become friends, as you have noticed. We were already, but now our friendship has become even stronger. We also have a joint project to promote a fairer globalization: the Helsinki process. This process seeks new and empowering solutions to global governance problems. It also offers an arena for open and broad-based discussion among interest groups to come up with practical recommendations that the different actors can implement and promote. Although the Helsinki process is an independent and separate process, its work is also based partly on the results of the World Commission on the Social Dimension of Globalization.

It is also good to talk about national activities. I do not know them all, but I can tell you, for example, that my own country, Finland, is currently preparing a national globalization strategy and I believe that already now, there are other countries which are doing exactly the same. There is a lot of information on issues which are important strengths of a nation State, such as good governance and the fight against corruption. I think that you will have the opportunity to discuss all this during the Conference.

Once again, the ILO showed courage and foresight in appointing the World Commission on the Social Dimension of Globalization. The Commission has published its report but, I repeat, this is only the beginning.

Making globalization more human will take time. I hope that the work of our Commission can be part of this process. Achieving change requires a commitment from all of us here. I trust that the International Labour Conference is ready to do its part to promote change. The Director-General's Report provides a good basis for this work.

I am thankful for the privilege of co-chairing the World Commission on the Social Dimension of Globalization. I am also thankful for the excellent cooperation with governments, employers, workers and the secretariat. Without their support, your support, our Commission could not have succeeded in its work. I do wish you a successful Conference.

Original Spanish: The PRESIDENT

I would now like to call upon His Excellency, Mr. Mkapa, President of the United Republic of Tanzania. Mr. Mkapa has had an outstanding national and international career that started in journalism and which led him to play a role at the highest levels of diplomacy, culminating in the presidency of the Republic, where he is now in his second term.

In the World Commission on the Social Dimension of Globalization he used his gift of communication, constantly encouraging consultations and ensuring that the work was carried out in an atmosphere propitious for consensus. We all recall his brilliant work and his patience during the last session of the Governing Body. I have great pleasure in giving the floor to His Excellency, Mr. Mkapa.

Mr. MKAPA *(President of the United Republic of Tanzania)*

The last time I addressed the International Labour Conference was on 12 June 2001 on the theme of the worst forms of child labour, in itself a manifestation of poverty and the negative aspects of globalization. I am honoured to be back this time with my friend and colleague, co-Chair of the World Commission on the Social Dimension of Globalization, President Ms. T. Halonen of the Republic of Finland.

I thank her for the unstinting energy, contagious enthusiasm, indomitable will and vitalizing humour with which she has led the Commission's work, and for the powerful statements she has just made, which I fully endorse. I join her in presenting to you on behalf of our fellow commissioners, the report of the Commission established by the ILO. I also pay tribute to the Commission secretaries, and the whole secretariat for facilitating so efficiently and honourably the foundation, the construction and the follow-up to the work of the Commission.

The report is appropriately entitled: *A fair globalization: Creating opportunities for all.* For that was the essence of the remit of our mandate: to explore innovative and sustainable ways that would integrate economic, social and environmental objectives for rendering globalization a force for good for all people in all countries. I believe we have discharged this mandate with the utmost diligence and objectivity. I commend the ILO Director-General Juan Somavia for his great initiatives and visions to use this organization's unique experience to move the discussion on globalization beyond a stand-off and confrontation to dialogue and cooperation and to recognizing rights and responsibilities of all nations and peoples in an increasingly integrated and networked world.

The global anti-globalization movement encompasses a disparate group, united in their understanding and experience of the unfairness of globalization, of poverty, of inequitable opportunities and outcomes.

Supporters of globalization on the other hand, tell us that globalization is a good thing for the world. We in the Commission also believe that globalization has great potential for good. Indeed it has already done a lot of good and can do more. All we are saying is that, a new thinking is needed to ensure that the good that comes out of globalization reaches more people. Otherwise it will always be politically unbalanced, materially unsustainable, morally indefensible and, from a security standpoint, graphically catastrophic.

Globalization and the conflicting views on it remind me of an Ethiopian proverb which says: "A cow gave birth to a fire, she wanted to lick it but it burned her, she wanted to leave it but she could not because it was her own child." The world has given birth to the fire of globalization. We see and love its huge potential and want to lick it, but some of us get burned in the process. Yet we cannot leave it either, for it is our own child. Protagonists from both sides of the debate must learn to work together to make sure that we all embrace globalization profitably without getting burned.

The Commission's greatest asset was its diversity in terms of the origins, backgrounds, experiences and interests of its members. Its best practice was to consult widely, viewing globalization through the eyes of the people. Its best outcome was that people from such diverse backgrounds and experiences, on a controversial subject such as globalization, could discuss and come up with the largely agreed report we present to you today.

For Africa, the report is in keeping with the aspirations of the New Partnership for Africa's Development, NEPAD, which warns that: "The poverty and backwardness of Africa stands in stark contrast to the prosperity of the developed world and is a blight on humanity. The continued marginalization of Africa from the globalization process and the social exclusion of the vast majority of its peoples constitute a serious threat to global stability". From the ancient Chinese sage Confucius we learn that, in a country well governed, poverty is something to be ashamed of, and I say that in a world striving to be well governed, poverty must be something to be profoundly ashamed of.

The reforming democratic African governments are increasingly under pressure to provide proof that open market systems can work for all. Sustainability of the reform agenda depends critically on this. With the continued erosion of commodity prices eating into farmer's incomes, it is becoming difficult for African and other developing countries' governments to provide the proof. With the little we are doing towards the repayment of debts, there is even less available for invest in human development. Frankly, and this is my personal view, for the least developed countries no amount of debt can be sustainable. Every cent that goes to service the debts we owe each developed country, directly or through multilateral financial institutions, is a cent less from the resources we so sorely need to work towards the Millennium Development Goals. Debt cancellation for the poorest is in my view the best option. Additionally, developed countries must live up to the commitments of official Development Assistance contained in the Monterrey Consensus.

The report of the Commission argues that globalization must begin at home. If countries are to develop they require sound and stable policy frameworks, they need to espouse market-based policies that are manifestly pro poor and encourage integration in the global economy. They must emphasize economic development with social protection, decent work and good democratic governance at all levels, including the global level. Globalization has many faces but the face that most people protest against is global trade, as currently promulgated and governed by the WTO, and the face of global asymmetry of power, as presented by the G8.

My experience is that even the most virulent opponents of globalization recognize its positive side. What drives them to desperation is the power asymmetry, the lack of voice, the inequalities and the unfairness that seem inbuilt and embedded into the current system of global governance, notably in global trade. We must collectively pursue a global agenda of trade for development of all countries and peoples. The spirit of Doha that makes global development a goal, rather than a by-product of global trade, must not be allowed to die.

I encourage trade unions to continue addressing the political question of how to respond to the unfolding realities of a globalizing world and its impact on work. Globalization is changing the world in ways most of us were not prepared for. Even the concepts of work and the workplace are changing. Inbuilt capacities at all levels for adaptability and flexibility, through appropriate education, skills and knowledge are urgently needed.

The prospects for many developing countries are threatened by inadequate human development, made worse by the spectre of HIV/AIDS that so viciously decimates the workforce, particularly in sub-Saharan Africa. In areas such as these, many countries will require significant assistance from the international community. In Africa, we are looking forward to the Extraordinary Summit on Employment and Poverty Alleviation, scheduled for September 2004 in Ouagadougou, that will establish an important political link in our economic agenda for development and poverty reduction as a way of building up an inclusive global economy. Most developing countries are determined to turn the corner to ensure a brighter future for their people. But to do this, the tripartite constituents must work together in a broader alliance to unleash our full potential, which must also include the immense potential of women. One of the gears in the engine that drives globalization is the multilateral institution system. Each of the system's component organizations has its own mandate and share of operational cover. But in my view, there is a serious deficit of a formal coordinated coalition vision of holistic development between them. For this reason, I wish to underscore the report's recommendation for the establishment of a globalization policy forum between the United Nations and other principal international organizations with a view to evolving a fairer globalization as a sustainable anchor of each social dimension. The report identifies what, in our view, are the necessary tasks ahead if we want to make globalization fairer and, given the diversity of cultures, if we want more people and countries to be included in these processes, opportunities and outcomes. As in other major global undertakings, it needs political will and vision. Blind opponents of globalization are as unhelpful as blind proponents of globalization. If we all open our eyes and become more objective, we will see manifold opportunities to expand the benefits of globalization and reduce its negative consequences. Yes, a better world is possible and is within our collective reach if the leaders of our world summon the courage and the will needed to lead us in that direction.

I wish to end with the same conclusion that the German poet and scientist Goethe reached two centuries ago. He said, and I quote, "I have come to the frightening conclusion that I am the decisive element. It is my personal approach that creates the climate. It is my daily mood that makes the weather. I possess tremendous power to make life miserable or joyous. I can be a tool of torture or an instrument of inspiration. I can humiliate or humour; hurt or heal. In all situations, it is my response that decides whether a crisis is escalated or de-escalated and a person is humanized or dehumanized. If we treat people as they are, we make them worse. If we treat people as they ought to be, we help them become what they are capable of becoming."

I agreed to serve on this Commission because I believe in the human capacity to rise above parochialism, to be worldly wise, to take the correct turn when confronted with difficult choices and to promote and celebrate the vision of a global human family. Globalization presents humanity with among the most far-reaching decisions of our time and, like Goethe, I believe that it is in our power to do what is right. I appeal to all of you in your different capacities to accept and support the Commission's humble endeavour to engender the correct turn at the fork in the road of our headlong march towards globalization, in the interest of the humanity we all share.

Original Spanish: The PRESIDENT

I would now like to introduce His Excellency Mr. Giorgi Parvanov, President of the Republic of Bulgaria and a firm defender of democracy in his country, where the winds of modernization are blowing.

President Parvanov is guiding his Government towards stabilization of the labour market, improvement of social security and harmonization of legislation and the bodies of social dialogue with European models. The ILO welcomes the ratification by Bulgaria of the eight fundamental labour Conventions and the links of cooperation that it has forged with Bulgaria in different areas of activity. I am greatly honoured to give the floor to the President of Bulgaria, President Parvanov.

Original Bulgarian: Mr. PARVANOV *(President of the Republic of Bulgaria)*

It is a great honour for me to be here and to have the opportunity to discuss the social aspects of globalization before such a prestigious and competent audience. For more than ten years, the trends, nature and consequences of globalization have held our attention and provoked heated debate and even controversy at times. Unless this can be overcome, there is a risk that these differences may deepen and lead to a lasting divide between countries and nations, something that would inevitably be to the detriment of global security, trust and development. This is why I wish to commend the ILO and its Director-General, personally on the initiative to address this issue comprehensively for the first time. I would also like to pay tribute to my esteemed colleagues and the co-Chairpersons of the World Commission on the Social Dimension of Globalization – the President of the Republic of Finland, Ms. Tarja Halonen, and the President of the United Republic of Tanzania, Mr. Benjamin Mkapa – and their team. I wish to commend them on the brilliant way they implemented their ideas. The best thing about their report is that it brings together the various views on globalization in a forceful common message that gives us confidence to believe that, through dialogue, we can make the world a better place to live. We all – Heads of State and representatives of governments, trade unions and employers organizations – today have an opportunity and a responsibility to take up this valuable achievement and to implement its message within our governments and our organizations.

Indeed it is hard to find arguments against globalization. The new technologies shorten distances and facilitate communication. The social processes have long since transcended national borders and it is therefore impossible to confine them any longer.

The debate is no longer a question of being for or against globalization but of whether, in its present form, globalization is the best thing for humanity. I fully support the idea that globalization should have a very strong social dimension; it should be based on universal values and should be beneficial for every country, without exception. The report of the World Commission defends this stance in a very convincing fashion. Globalization cannot, and should not, be impeded; globalization should be fairer – and it should have an acceptable social cost. Governments and business should be aware that investment in social policy is a condition for stability. Indeed, we have no right to close our eyes to the fact that extremism, notably terrorism, finds fertile ground in the unresolved social problems of the various regions; we should not see the recourse to military or other force as the only solution to these problems. I would like to assure you that Bulgaria welcomes the specific proposals in this report on improving international cooperation to identify the trends and pace of globalization. Within all the organizations in which we participate, my country will work for active international cooperation to hammer out our positions in shaping world policies and maintaining global political dialogue. Two years ago the ideas in this report may have seemed rather naive; today there may still be people who view these ideas with scepticism, but I believe that the time is near when these ideas will prevail and will dominate world policy. I hasten to endorse fully another of the ideas from this report: I am convinced that regional cooperation is the key to allowing individual countries, especially those with limited resources, to play a more active role in ensuring an equitable distribution of the benefits of globalization. Regional cooperation increases the power of the small, and economically weaker, countries. This is particularly valid for the region of south eastern Europe, which I represent today. Bulgaria has been working for a long time for more active cooperation among the countries of south eastern Europe and has sponsored a number of initiatives to this end. At the internal level, the role of individual States is vital for the achievement of a fairer globalization. Here we face the question of the role of the state and its institutions. A very delicate balance is needed; on the one hand, the withdrawal of the state from direct involvement and interference in the economy, which is only natural, and on the other hand the creation of potent institutions that will ensure that the rules of the game are respected – the rules that apply to everyone, both employers and workers. For countries like Bulgaria, at least, this is how I see things: the state cannot and should not shirk its social obligations and should continue to play an active role in a number of areas of public policy, especially when it comes to creating a stable microeconomic environment or a modern infrastructure, and to reducing unemployment, providing opportunities for decent work, and working to curb poverty. The traditions and future development of my country, and the region it represents, call for a strong civil society and for us to continue to be mindful of social problems.

I am here today as Head of State of a country that has been successful, and which has the ambition of having a stabilizing influence on the whole of south eastern Europe. What is unusual about Bulgaria and the other countries of south eastern Europe is that the emergence of globalization has coincided with the beginning of a very difficult transition towards a market economy and the establishment of democracy and democratic values. It has also coincided with the process of European integration in the region, as a result of which some of the Balkan countries are members of the European Union and others are still on its threshold. We must admit, of course, that despite all our efforts the vast majority of people have paid a very high social price for this policy of reform. Today, when my country has been recognized as a market economy; has an acceptable, fairly low rate of inflation; enjoys political and economic stability; and is in the final phase of its negotiations with the European Union, we realize that we have chosen the right path.

At the same time, I am aware that the process of negotiations with the European Union should not be reduced to a mechanical going through the motions. The important thing is that the countries of south-eastern Europe should be able to create sufficient capacity to adapt and integrate into the European social model. As the Director-General, Mr Somavia, has pointed out on more than one occasion, this European social model is, in turn, going to play a key role in the international organizations' efforts to achieve a fairer process of globalization. I find the proposals made in the report of the World Commission especially useful, notably those aimed at increasing public control of national positions within international organizations in order to improve the transparency of these organizations. I look forward to having these matters discussed later this year in our capital, Sofia, during the tripartite conference for Central and Eastern Europe on the social dimension of globalization, which is to be held under the aegis of the ILO.

I would like to thank the Director-General and his team for accepting this idea with understanding and for supporting it. In closing, may I salute the ILO once again, and particularly Mr. Somavia; the President of the Republic of Finland, Ms. Halonen; and the President of the United Republic of Tanzania, Mr Mkapa. May I congratulate them on this excellent initiative and the well-prepared report, and assure them that Bulgaria will continue to participate in the efforts of the international community to turn globalization into a fairer process that will benefit all countries and peoples.

Original Spanish: The PRESIDENT

I would now like to introduce the Right Honourable Helen Clark, Prime Minister of New Zealand. From the very start of her long political career, during which she has also been Minister of Labour and therefore well known to us here in this house, Prime Minister Clark has been recognized for her unyielding defence of international peace and the fight for disarmament. Over the past five years, under her leadership, the Government of New Zealand has strengthened minimum standards in equity, safety at work and employment opportunities.

The support shown by New Zealand for the concept of decent work has been reflected in different initiatives at the legislative level aimed at encouraging the participation of workers and employers, paid paternity leave, considerable wage increases and equal remuneration. Ms. Clark has championed decent work across the whole of the South-East Asia and the Pacific subregion. I now give the floor to Prime Minister Helen Clark.

Ms. CLARK *(Prime Minister of New Zealand)*

I thank the Director-General of the ILO for his invitation to me to participate in the special sitting of Heads of State and Government this morning.

I begin by commending the Governing Body of the ILO for establishing the World Commission on the Social Dimension of Globalization and by congratulating the members of the Commission on the comprehensive and thought-provoking report which they have produced. I have personally read it with great interest.

The report analyses the process of globalization in the late twentieth century, examines both its potential and its pitfalls, and suggests ways in which nation states, multilateral institutions and non-state actors might work to ensure that globalization creates opportunities for all and not just for the already powerful.

In so doing, the report moves well beyond the slogans so often associated with discussions of globalization. It recognizes that the process of globalization is here to stay, but that significant policy changes are needed at the national and international levels if it is to contribute to fair and just work. The report also identifies major twenty-first century issues like mass migration across borders, for which there are not, at this time, adequate multilateral frameworks.

I speak today as the leader of a social democratic government in a small western country which, 20 years ago, began exposing itself to radical economic change. Indeed, the New Zealand experience fits the report's description of a "Big Bang" approach to liberalization. From the mid-1980s, New Zealand quickly deregulated its economy, stripped away its tariff and import-control barriers and privatized many of its state companies. The economic liberalization of the 1980s was then followed by significant cut-backs in social provision and by labour market deregulation in the 1990s.

While there is no disagreement that the New Zealand economy was in trouble in the early 1980s, the pace and extent of the moves which followed were highly controversial. The changes in New Zealand came without adequate adjustment mechanisms and created a good deal of social distress. Even as the economy began to rebuild in the 1990s, the distributional effects on society were very uneven.

My Government was elected at the end of 1999 on a platform of bringing a better balance to economic and social policy. We set out to strengthen the economy's capacity to grow sustainably, to put employment growth at the top of our priorities, to strengthen social safety nets and to re-regulate where deregulation had gone too far. The path we have taken is consistent with the approach which the World Commission's report sets out for ensuring that the benefits of progress are widely shared.

The New Zealand experience is of international interest, both because New Zealand is in the vanguard of economic liberalization and has taken its to a greater extent than other western countries and also because the New Zealand people then voted for a change of direction in order to reassert traditional values in our country of fairness, opportunity and security.

To date, the results have been encouraging. The New Zealand economy has averaged over 3.5 per cent annual economic growth during the last four and a half years of our term in office and unemployment has dropped sharply. In May five years ago, the unemployment rate stood at 7.2 per cent; in May this year it stood at 4.3 per cent.

Our Government has been redefining and rebuilding the role of the State in an open economy. While twenty-first century governments exercise fewer formal and regulatory powers than in the past, there are still critical and important roles for governments to play, and roles which only governments can play. We have defined those roles as being roles of leadership, partnership, facilitation, brokerage and funding and direct provision where appropriate.

We think that governments have a unique ability to develop strategies and bring a range of actors together to work for common goals. Securing our country's niche in the global economy in a way which builds and sustains higher living standards for all is not a task which can be left to market forces to produce. It requires clear and deliberate strategies both to grow the cake and then to ensure that it is fairly distributed.

The World Commission's report notes that "one of the effects of globalization has been to reduce the space for national macroeconomic policies", but that there are policy instruments which can be used. Our Government has been busy creating those instruments to increase the national space for action.

With a population of only 4 million people, New Zealand has a small domestic market. Its very open economy means that all its sectors must be internationally competitive. The expectations of New Zealanders are that they will and should continue to enjoy first-world living standards. The challenge for us has been to apply new-economy principles across all our industrial sectors so that we position our goods and services more consistently at the top of the market and the value chain.

Our Government has adopted a strategy of growth through innovation which focuses on building a highly skilled workforce, increasing investment in research and development and in the commercialization of innovation, getting new products and services to market more quickly, attracting quality overseas investment in areas which add to New Zealand's capacity and promoting what we call "enabling sectors" which have horizontal benefits across the economy and society; thus government-industry partnership taskforces develop strategies to grow the information and communications technology sector and, through that, to modernize the processes of government, business, education and society. We have organized a taskforce to promote the growth of the biotechnology sector and to see its insights applied across the primary sectors and in food processing and other applied industries. We have been promoting the importance of design in products and markets and we have developed our screen production industry strategies, both because we see this as an outlet for New Zealand talent and also as a vehicle for the promotion of our country as unique and creative and for the spill-over benefits which film has for tourism and other industrial sectors.

As a Government, we have operated on the assumption that there can be no going back on the open economy and that we owe it to our population to secure the very best living standards we can for it. That means working for the kind of economy which can pay high wages and sustain strong public services. We aim to have New Zealand compete on quality, value and innovation, not on low cost and low skills.

As our economy has grown we have been able to invest more in education, in health care and other public services and in infrastructure. We have also had the confidence to improve minimum wages, legislate for an extra week's holiday for workers and implement, for the first time, a statutory right to paid parental leave for new parents. Labour-relations law has been reformed to give more weight to collective bargaining and to enable New Zealand, for the first time, to ratify the Right to Organise and Collective Bargaining Convention, 1949 (No. 98).

This year, having built strong structural budget surpluses, we have been able to target tax credits and cuts to low- and middle-income families with dependent children. It is estimated that the result will be to reduce the number of children living in households below the poverty line by up to 70 per cent.

We have been particularly sensitive to the impact which globalization has on national and cultural identity. That has led us to invest more heavily in the arts, culture and heritage in order to protect, enhance and promote what is unique about us and our country. That includes supporting the maintenance of the indigenous language and culture of Maori, including through a dedicated Maori television service established this year.

We have also acted in two other important areas identified in the World Commission report, on sustainable development and on strengthening local government. We now have a sustainable development plan of action prioritizing transport, water allocation, youth development and sustainable cities.

We have ratified the Kyoto Protocol, accepting our share of the global responsibility to slow down and reverse climate change.

New legislation gives greater powers to local and regional government to respond to the needs of their communities and also for new district health boards with elected members to plan and oversee the delivery of local health services.

At the national level, therefore, we have taken many steps to ensure not only that in the age of globalization New Zealand has a strong and viable economy, but also that the results of that percolate down to, and are reflected in, the quantity and quality of life of all our people.

Of course, we acknowledge the need for action at the international level to address the serious power imbalances there which the World Commission's report identifies.

Globalization has had a very bad reputation in many quarters because it has been held responsible for wiping out jobs and local companies and because global trade and finance rules are seen to disadvantage developing countries in particular. As I have outlined, we have taken steps in our own country to secure our niche in the global economy with innovative products and services which trade for a high value and secure our living standards.

We also work hard with like-minded agricultural exporting nations for better treatment for agriculture in the current WTO Doha Development Round. The recent indication from the European Union that it is prepared to negotiate an end date for the elimination of agricultural export subsidies is very encouraging, although it has made little movement yet on improving agricultural market access.

Last year, at the WTO Ministerial Conference in Cancun, developing country frustration with unfair trade rules boiled over and saw the meeting collapse without achieving any results. That is surely a strong signal to the developed world that the Doha Round cannot succeed unless there are substantial gains for developing countries.

But it is not only the WTO and the international trade rules over which it presides which need change. The Bretton Woods institutions, as the report points out, favour the interests of developed countries and the United Nations Security Council still reflects the international order of 1945. In addition, a lot of power to determine the destiny of the international community lies with more exclusive clubs, whether they be the G7/G8, the OECD, or even the EU. That places a particular responsibility on those clubs to think of the broader responsibility they have, just as the G8 has done in recent years with its new partnership with the African Union for development.

The World Commission report identifies the lack of coherence and the compartmentalization between the multilateral organizations with those in trade, finance, health, social affairs, labour and development often working at cross purposes. This is a phenomenon which nation States also have to deal with as what we call "silo mentalities" can develop in government departments and agencies, which are each charged with their individual missions. In New Zealand we have consciously worked to try to achieve a "whole of government approach" to policy which draws the efforts of diverse agencies together and the same effect would be desirable at the international level.

The central challenge posed by the World Commission is to contemplate reform of global governance in order to ensure that globalization operates according to fair rules and offers opportunities and decent work for all.

Recognizing that governance reforms are not easily achieved, the report initially advocates sustained action based on dialogue. It invites the heads of relevant United Nations bodies, the World Bank, IMF, WTO and ILO to work together on global growth, investment and employment creation in what is termed a policy coherence initiative.

The President of the Republic of Finland's address this morning suggests that there has already been a constructive interest in the World Commission's report from those bodies.

In addition, policy development dialogues are advocated between the multilateral agencies and the non-state actors to work on pathways for more inclusive globalization. The proposal that the WTO or the ILO should take the initiative to establish a globalization policy forum is a useful one which could ensure that platforms are created for sustained dialogue between stakeholders.

This report should be welcomed for injecting a new sense of urgency into the debate about how to channel the forces of globalization in a more consistently positive direction.

At the multilateral level, the running on globalization has been made by the finance and trade institutions within which the power imbalances internationally have been the most marked.

It is now time not only to address the inequalities within those institutions and the rules they set, but also to focus more attention on the social and economic outcomes of their work. As the World Commission report says, trade liberalization, for example, should be seen not as an end in itself, but as a means by which economic growth, full employment and poverty elimination can be achieved.

A fair globalization can distribute new opportunities to those who have been marginalized and disempowered and I share the World Commission's optimism that "the benefits of globalization can be extended to more people and better shared between and within countries, with many more voices having an influence on its course". The alternative of seeing even greater disparities develop within and between nations can only exacerbate international conflict and tension.

The seeds of a more peaceful world lie in addressing the most basic socio-economic issues. That task is well within the ILO's mandate and I wish it well as it seeks to engage other parts of the multilateral system, formal and informal, nation-state-based and civil-society-based, in concerted action to ensure that globalization benefits the many and not the few.

Original Spanish: The PRESIDENT

The venerable Prime Minister, Ms. Clark, has shared with us her successful experience as Head of her Government and her vision of globalization. We are, indeed, most grateful. As you see, we are gender-equal: of the four distinguished public figures honouring us with their presence, two are ladies and two gentlemen. Let us hope this will continue in future.

As you all know, the ILO is a tripartite organization and this makes it unique within the United Nations family. Tripartism is an essential part of the ILO's structure. It is not, however, merely a static part, because there is the ongoing concern to strengthen it and to make it a reality through social dialogue. In pursuance of this principle, it is my pleasure to yield the floor to the representatives of the social partners, starting with Mr. Funes de Rioja, Chairperson of the Employers' group on the Governing Body.

Mr. FUNES DE RIOJA *(Employers' delegate, Argentina)*

It gives me pleasure to convey to this distinguished audience some of my reflections on the report of the World Commission, in whose work I have had the privilege of participating.

I am particularly happy to see the two co-Chairs of the Commission, President Halonen and President Mkapa, under whose expert leadership we were able to arrive collectively at the final report. This difficult task was achieved thanks to their persistence, hard work and let me also add, from time to time, good humour.

Now, let me turn to the report itself. As President Mkapa said, the unique feature of this report is that it is the first time that a commission of individuals with such diverse backgrounds has come together to discuss the issue of globalization and, importantly, has identified that globalization has generated mainly significant benefits and has great productive potential, in terms of economic, political and social development. This is a very commendable achievement.

Business experts would not agree with everything in the report and perhaps, from a business perspective, it would have been written differently. However, on balance, upon the conclusion of the Commission, I am more optimistic for the future and believe that an opportunity now exists to move the debate on to a different, more proactive and engaged level. I believe that this opportunity should be seized.

The report's key message is that a number of countries are not enjoying the benefits of globalization and that globalization has the potential, in terms of economic, political and social development, to lift developing countries from poverty. This is a really important signal to help guide the wide debate on globalization. The consequences of globalization, be they good or bad, are heavily affected by the way the values upon which political and economic options are based and understood, accepted and implemented by all actors in society, be they government actors, businesses, trade unions or responsible citizens. It is a values-based approach to globalization that has the best chance of making globalization work for all.

An extension of this concept is the link that has been developed in the Commission's report between the market economy and democracy. Economic openness is not properly sustainable without democratic institutions and processes to support it. The two – democracy and the market economy – are linked and together they hold the solution to inclusion in the process of globalization. What we must do is address any shortfalls in the democratic market economy model and make that model accessible to all who want to benefit from it. This entails facing up to difficult questions, such as: what makes the model work for some and not for others; and what do the actors need to do to make the model work effectively for the good of all society?

Perhaps the main reason for exclusion from globalization is poor governance and the report focuses strongly on this fact. Certain essential components are needed to create an environment conducive to investment, development and inclusion. For example, productive public expenditure on infrastructure, human development, health, education and skills; open, transparent governance; economic policies that promote economic development and fair rules; the right regulatory environment for entrepreneurship and small and medium-sized enterprise growth; enabling those hundreds of millions who work in the informal economy to be able to migrate and to stay in the formal economy; and helping young people to find opportunities to develop skills and training. These are some of the key issues that are necessary for economic and social development. In this respect, the role of private sector in promoting investment as a way to fight against poverty and exclusion is an important component of the Commission's recommendations.

I strongly believe that if we are to try and capitalize and harness the private sector in development, then the role of the national employers' organization and business is crucial. This is another indication of the important role of business in economic development and job creation. Increasingly this message is receiving greater resonance through out the multilateral system. Most recently, it was emphasized in the report of the United Nations Commission on the Private Sector and Development entitled *Unleashing Entrepreneurship: Making Business Work for the Poor*. This message also needs to be seized.

At the international level, business needs a multilateral system that complements itself and works fluidly in different areas – which may overlap but where competencies remain different. A multilateral system of competing mandates is one that is a recipe for incoherence and breakdown. The existing multilateral system needs to be more effective, better resourced and more responsive, and efforts need to be made to avoid duplication and mismanagement. Therefore, I welcome calls for greater policy coordination across the international system.

One of the many interesting things that has come out of the research studies conducted during the World Commission is that people are not against globalization but have strong views on certain related aspects of globalization. I think that this is an important distinction and should be a starting point in attempts to make changes to the multilateral system. But, in order to be successful, any process of change has to be underpinned by adept leadership at the local, national, regional and global levels. Leadership that seeks to create a value system for its citizens, that can judge when to promote change, adapt policies and, fundamentally, leadership that takes responsibility for its actions.

Let me conclude by saying that perhaps the greatest achievement of this World Commission is the fact that the time for confrontational debates and "discussions of the deaf" is over. The Commission has underlined that, if we want to achieve a globalization that works for everybody, then we need to engage in collective debate, listen to different points of view and explore ways in which we can move forward constructively.

(The speaker continues in Spanish.)

May I conclude in my mother tongue, Spanish.

I, personally and on behalf of the Employers' group, would sincerely like to thank Presidents Mkapa and Halonen. We not only learned a great deal but we appreciated the level of debate in the Commission thanks to their reciprocal attention and respect. I would also like to indicate my group's satisfaction with this opportunity for debate, which brings together so many distinguished government leaders. I would say to the Director-General and his team that we are appreciative, not only of his initiative, but of the secretariat he made available to us as a Commission. This has generated deep debate and much thought amongst the employers. We are ready to participate in this debate with commitment and responsibility, taking into account the important role of ILO, its values and its action in the context of globalization.

Original Spanish: The PRESIDENT

Now for the voice of the Workers: I call on Sir Roy Trotman, Chairperson of the Workers' group on the Governing Body, to take the floor.

Sir Roy TROTMAN *(Workers' delegate, Barbados)*

We in the Workers' group, as delegates to this Conference, wish to welcome and express our appreciation to the Presidents of Finland, the United Republic of Tanzania and Bulgaria and the Prime Minister of New Zealand, for their courage and their support to the work that we in the ILO have sought to do, particularly in putting together this Commission which is before us today.

This wave of globalization is not something that we can wish away by anything that we might seek to do; that is a fact. It is also a fact that globalization has brought with it much suffering, and pain and anguish. But what is also a fact is that this was not, as we understand it, the intention of the framers of this economic order. Nor, indeed, may I say, was it the intention of the organizers and planners of the World Bank or the IMF.

The World Commission's work seeks to put this contradiction into perspective. It seeks to put forward a body of recommendations to reverse the pattern, and, in the Director-General's words, "to make globalization a force for positive change".

Workers across the world and their families awake on a daily basis in fear of what new sacrifices they will be forced to make, and this is as true in the North as it is in the South. Therefore, we must say that the members of the Commission were quite brave in citing greed and global insensitivity, in my interpretation of the document, as part of the cause of current problems. They have challenged all and they have challenged sundry, to appreciate the level of inter-dependence which now characterizes world relationships. They know, as indeed we know, that unless the worst pockets of poverty and deprivation are removed, then there will never be real peace or real global prosperity. Indeed, I need to say at this stage that although I admire my colleague in the social partnership very much, I cannot agree with him when he says that governance is a factor. This is because we in the Caribbean, for example, have in my view the most democratic institutions in the world, and I do not apologize to anybody for saying that. And yet the problem is to be found there, as elsewhere. It would therefore seem to me that there are natural as well as man made disequilibriums which together are causing some of the difficulties we speak of. And this is why we go to express our great appreciation to the Commission for the recommendations that it has made regarding what has to be done. The Workers' group within the International Labour Organization believes that we have gone well beyond the time for reciting what has been, and that we need action and we need it now. This is because, as President Mkapa has said, globalization has great potential to bring real relief to the many, as opposed to the few. So why do we not think of starting then with a clean slate, a completely clean slate. I start by forgiving you for all the debt that any of you may owe me. Let us ask the governments that do have debtors to forgive all the debt.

Let us recognize that there is a need to set common standards for all, and let us further recognize that all must be willing and ready to obey such common standards. Let us give due regard to those countries which have handicaps of one kind or another and to prepare to take affirmative action in bringing them to a level where they may be truly competitive.

Also, let us give international empowerment to the International Labour Organization, because we have to make sure that there is a reputable body which has the integrity to oversee the standards that we talk about and to ensure that we are all kept honest.

I liked it when our speakers said that the report is part of a process to give globalization a human face. I do not believe that any commentary I may make would vary from that position, and that challenge today is a challenge to make the World Commission's report work.

The Workers' group sees it as a great opportunity. We stand ready, and we seek daily to demonstrate that we are ready. Our hope is that there is matching action and matching commitment by everyone. Let us do our part.

Original Spanish: The PRESIDENT

We have heard a presentation of the report of the World Commission by the Commission's co-Chairs. We have heard the comments made by the President of Bulgaria, by the Prime Minister of New Zealand and by the representatives of the social partners.

We shall now hear from the Director-General, in his first session of the International Labour Conference to take place since his re-election. It is my pleasure to call on Mr. Juan Somavia, Director-General of the International Labour Office.

The SECRETARY-GENERAL

I would like to thank the leaders who came here today from across the globe to share their insights and perspectives with the Conference, as well as the representatives of workers' and employers' organizations for your encouraging comments on the ILO and myself. You represent different corners of the world. You face very different economic realities and challenges, and thank you for sharing with us the benefit of your experience and your ideas. Taken together it is a fantastic framework for the activities that we have to develop in the next days, with a rich exchange of views, and I believe that this will clearly influence our own discussions. I want to thank also the Heads of the Employers' and Workers' groups for their comments. Let me also say a special word of thanks to President Halonen and President Mkapa for being here and for their collective leadership in co-chairing the World Commission's report and their absolutely permanent commitment to the success of this endeavour. This Organization is very grateful to them for the fact that they did take the decision to co-Chair. I want to thank them for their courage. I know it was not easy to accept the decision to take on this responsibility. There were political reasons. The task was complex and success was hardly assured. It is not the best invitation that I imagine you have received as politicians! So I want to thank you so much for taking the risk!

The welcome that your report has received around the world is clear evidence of a mission accomplished and, as we have seen this morning, it is stimulating more dialogue, more ideas, more interest. Perhaps there is no better measure of its success. And a fair globalization, as we have heard today, is the foundation of global stability. I think these discussions have advanced that goal. I thank Prime Minister Clark and President Parvanov for sharing their experience. It is very clear, as President Parvanov said, that the implications of globalization, when one is in the process of transition and trying to create not only new political structures, but also new economic structures, are complex, and difficult. But the decision is yours. Prime Minister Clark, you told us that there had been a "Big Bang" application of many of these policies and that suddenly your people were saying, "We don't all seem to be hearing the same thing, and we would like our Government and our system to reflect the fact that not everybody is in on this new situation." I think that both of you have expressed in very clear terms what this report is about. It is about the enormous opportunity we have in front of us if we do not become ideological; is about the incredible instruments that are there, provided we are fair; and it is about the reality that we will not move forward unless we have the capacity for dialogue and the capacity to understand that everybody has a responsibility for ensuring fair globalization. There is no single activity today about which one can say, "That is not my problem." And this has been made very clear by the presentations of our political leaders today. Let me then say that we are talking about change, about leadership. The change that globalization must undergo for its full potential to bloom for everybody requires leadership, and what we have heard this morning is precisely that. We need leaders that are not afraid to lead; leaders who take action; but, as we have heard today, leaders who also have vision. So let me ask you to applaud give them a resounding round of applause for what they have brought to us today.

Original Spanish: The PRESIDENT

It is with great expectation that we await the introduction by the Director-General, this afternoon, of his Report, *A fair globalization: The role of the ILO*. This marks the beginning of a process intended to distil the conclusions of the work carried out over the past biennium by the World Commission. on the Social Dimension of Globalization.

After the introduction, there will be a discussion in plenary of the report of the Chairperson of the Governing Body, as well as of the Reports of the Director-General.

I would like to warmly thank the highly esteemed public figures who have been so generous and so courteous as to take time to be with us this morning. Let us show our appreciation for our distinguished guests who have so honoured us with their presence by applauding them.

(The Conference adjourned at 12.15 p.m.)

CONTENTS

Page

Second (special) sitting

Address by Heads of State and Government on the Report of the World Commission on the Social Dimension of Globalization, Their Excellencies, Ms. Tarja Halonen, President of the Republic of Finland, Mr. Benjamin Mkapa, President of the United Republic of Tanzania, Mr. Georgi Parvanov, President of the Republic of Bulgaria and
Ms. Helen Clark, Prime Minister of New Zealand.. 1

Speakers: The President, Ms. Tarja Halonen, Mr. Benjamin Mkapa, Mr. Georgi Parvanov, Ms. Helen Clark, Mr. Funes de Rioja, Sir Roy Trotman, The Secretary-General

International Labour Conference

Provisional Record 10

Ninety-second Session, Geneva, 2004

Third sitting
Monday, 7 June 2004, 3.15 p.m.
President: Mr. Ray Guevara and Mr. Wade

SUPPLEMENTARY PRESENTATION BY THE DIRECTOR-GENERAL OF THE REPORT, *A FAIR GLOBALIZATION – THE ROLE OF THE ILO*

Original Spanish: The PRESIDENT

I declare the third sitting of the International Labour Conference open. This is the first meeting at which the important reports before the Conference will be debated. As you know, we will be looking at the Report of the Chairperson of the Governing Body on the work carried out by this body since the last session of the Conference and at its two valuable appendices which contain the oral report of the Chairperson of the Working Group on the Social Dimension of Globalization to the Governing Body, as well as the record of the discussion of the Report of the World Commission. We will consider the Director-General's Report on *ILO programme implementation for 2002-03* and we will also be looking at its Appendix, *The situation of workers of the occupied Arab territories*. We will examine the report entitled *A fair globalization – The role of the ILO*, which the Director-General will present to the Conference in greater detail in just a few moments.

The debate on these two reports and on the Director-General's Report will begin after that on Thursday, 10 June, in a special plenary session, when we will be looking at the Global Report, *Organizing for social justice*, which deals with the freedom that offers bread and real recognition of the right to collective bargaining and when we will continue our evaluation which began with the first Global Report which, as you will recall, was entitled *Your voice at work*.

Before I give the floor to the Director-General for his detailed presentation of his Report on the role of the ILO in the quest for fairer globalization, I would like myself to say a few words to you.

Once again, I would like to thank you all for having elected a representative of the Dominican Republic, on the proposal of the Central American and Caribbean group, to preside over the work of this Conference. The Dominican Republic is a small country, often known for its difficulties – and the natural tragedy that my country is experiencing at present is only one of those difficulties. Nevertheless, I believe that it also deserves to be known for its hospitality, its tourism, its baseball players, the catchy rhythm of the merengue as well as for its achievements and its values which I would like to share with you briefly.

The first of these is democracy, which has already demonstrated its maturity in an exemplary way. We Dominicans have organized successive elections, all of them highly transparent, which have permitted genuine political alternation. Democracy is a value which is often taken as a given. Nevertheless, we should realize that democracy is a precious asset, which must be cultivated and protected. We believe that we can only rely on stable and protected democracies when the latter are based on a framework of justice and, above all, of social justice.

Without social justice our democracy is in danger and our peoples may yield to the temptation of authoritarianism or populism, which offer bread without freedom.

The second of our values is the tolerance of our society towards differences. In our country, a very wide variety of political opinions, beliefs and religions, national origins and colours of skin coexist in complete harmony. We are convinced of the right of each and every person to equal treatment and equal opportunities and this is why we have ratified not only all of the core Conventions of the ILO, but also regional and international instruments which refer to basic human rights, including, obviously, the right to equal treatment and non-discrimination. The membership of our tripartite delegation at this session of the International Labour Conference is very eloquent proof of the mutual respect which we all have in the Dominican Republic for one another. I must add with special pride that, for the first time, our governmental delegation is composed of more women than men. I reiterate emphatically, that, in my country, the only thing we do not tolerate is intolerance itself. No discrimination will be found in our laws, in our culture, or in our society.

Our society's third value which, I think, it is important to share with you all, is our faith in the power of social dialogue to identify our problems and to come up with a solution to them, with the participation of all the interested sectors. It is customary to say that in Latin America an effort is made to solve problems by finding a scapegoat rather than a solution. I think that today this idea is part of a catalogue of stereotypes which have little to do with reality. We are convinced that problems need solutions rather than finding someone to blame. Nevertheless, these solutions must be legitimate. And in my view, this legitimacy cannot stem from ideological speeches, or cabinets full of technocrats, or economic adjustment programmes which confuse monetary stability with social stability. Legitimacy is to be found in the democratic institutions of society, first and foremost in the upper and lower houses of parliament and also in social dialogue. My country has set up a Consultative Labour Council and in my former position as a senator of the Republic and today as Minister for Labour, I have promoted the establishment of an Economic and Social Council.

We believe that social institutions are just as important as political institutions and that they are vital for the good governance of society.

In the Dominican Republic, social dialogue and agreement have enabled us to begin to create a new labour culture. We recognize the leading role played by the National Trade Union Council (CNUS) as well as by Dominican employers and their representative bodies. I earnestly beg the ILO to help our subregion to send out a call that will stimulate social dialogue, not only at a national level, but also at the regional and international levels, since we are convinced that when we are faced with global problems, we have to try to find broader frameworks than that of each separate country for discussing solutions. I especially ask the ILO to invite to this discussion, not only the public authorities responsible for social issues – the ministries of labour and social affairs – but also the authorities responsible for economic questions – the ministries of the economy and finances. Just as social concerns must not ignore economic realities, so economic policies must not forget the needs of the people. We say "yes" to the market economy, "no" to the market society.

Within this dialogue, I would like very special attention to be paid to the social and labour issues covered by free-trade agreements. The social dimension must be an ongoing concern in processes of economic integration and not the poor relation of the economy. Free-trade agreements between the United States, Central America and the Dominican Republic are valuable tools for the protection of the working class. If globalization does not have an ethical and social dimension, then I wonder who would be interested in globalization and for what reason. I have very serious doubts that this type of globalization might be of any interest or might offer any hope to our peoples. As for globalization, we are told that there is a need to promote competitive economies, but we ought to remember that a competitive economy is not a goal in itself, but the means to create a competitive society.

I wish to warmly congratulate the Office for the quality and content of the reports submitted at this plenary sitting. Once again, the ILO has done an impeccable job that does credit to its professional competence. Rather than referring specifically to one report, I would prefer to recall some passages of the Preamble to the ILO Constitution written some 85 years ago, but which looks as if it could have been written yesterday. The Constitution reminds us, I quote, that "universal and lasting peace can be established only if is based upon social justice". It also reminds us that "conditions of labour exist involving such injustice, hardship and privation to large numbers of people as to produce unrest so great that the peace and harmony of the world are imperilled", and last but not least, that, "the failure of any nation to adopt humane conditions of labour is an obstacle in the way of other nations which desire to improve the conditions in their own countries".

It seems difficult to explain why, 85 years later, our society, which is becoming more globalized every day, still has not been able to find an answer to the concerns which led to the creation of the ILO back in 1919. The twentieth century has brought big scientific advances and technical discoveries and in recent years an amazing ability to communicate across borders. It has also brought us great possibilities of increasing the wealth that our economies are able to produce. Nevertheless, it has been unable to produce wider distributive justice.

In rich countries the differences between rich and poor have grown in recent years. In poor countries the wealth of a privileged few and the poverty of the great majority have increased as well. The growth of global wealth has been distributed unevenly between the north and the south and very few countries in the south have really been invited to share in the north's feast. And in the small number of countries in the south which are no longer poor this newfound wealth tends to be distributed most unequally.

If this is the case, then, why should we find it surprising that, as the Director-General said when he opened this session of the Conference, migrant workers together with their families represent today a population equal to that of the fifth most populous country in the world? There is no indication that the south to north flows of migrants in search of better standards of living for themselves and for their families will diminish in the coming years. On the contrary, there is every reason to believe that until the factors that push migrants to emigrate disappear, then this migration will only increase. We all know what problems arise as a result of efforts to control migration flows; and we are all deeply concerned about the conditions of exploitation and abuse suffered by so many migrant workers and their families; but we also know that the effective management of migration can be mutually beneficial for both the host countries and the countries of origin. The agreement on migratory flows between Spain and the Dominican Republic is one example of cooperation in this area. We are anxious to know what conclusions will be reached by the Committee on Migrant Workers after its general debate at this session of the Conference.

The Report of the World Commission on the Social Dimension of Globalization reminds us that, unfortunately, the public debate on globalization is at an impasse. Opinions is frozen in the ideological certainties of entrenched positions and fragmented in a variety of special interests. The will for consensus is weak. Key international negotiations are deadlocked and international development commitments go largely unfulfilled.

The least we can say is that the World Commission has reached some alarming conclusions. It is our duty to examine these conclusions with care. I strongly believe that the debate over the next few days will provide us with the opportunity to move towards a future where an organization such as the ILO, strengthened by the social legitimacy that its tripartite structure provides, can enrich the world debate on globalization by adding elements that will not only have an economic content but also the, human and ethical content that is still lacking.

In this context, and with this I will conclude, the opportunities that are offered by the ILO's Decent Work Agenda provide us with a perspective that my Government supports wholeheartedly. The four areas – or four strategic objectives – referred to by the Director-General, Mr. Juan Somavia, in his 1999 statement to the Conference, constitute four pillars on which we are confident that it is possible to build a fairer and more human type of globalization.

Obviously, there cannot be decent work without employment, and employment must be our main concern. Nevertheless, having a job is not, in itself, a guarantee of decent work, and the reports presented by the Director-General to the Conference since its 1999 session demonstrate that there is an alarming shortage of decent work in the world. The issue of employment is at the heart of the concerns of the Council of Ministers of Labour of Central America and the Dominican Republic.

This is why we should be concerned, not only about employment, but also about the quality of employment. In this respect, we must once again reiterate our faith in this standard-setting approach of the ILO. We are aware that the ILO standard-setting system has room for improvement and we are prepared to participate in international dialogue in order to improve both its effectiveness and its credibility. Nevertheless, we are by no means willing to adopt the idea that has occasionally been put forward in some media, namely that ILO standards reflect an organization of labour and the economy pertaining to the twentieth century – a century of industrialization of national borders – and are therefore poorly adapted to the twenty-first century – a century of information and globalization. Nothing can convince us to share this type of reasoning. On the contrary, much of what we see before us leads us to believe that those who call into question the ILO's standards, and state that they belong to the twentieth century rather than to the twenty-first century, are, in fact, only trying to propose solutions that belong to the nineteenth century. I do not need to point out that it was precisely the approach taken in the nineteenth century that gave rise to the injustice and the absurd conflicts that in fact led humankind to consider, in 1919, the need to create organizations such as the International Labour Organization.

In 1969, the year in which the ILO received the Nobel Peace Prize, His Holiness Pope Paul VI stated before this very Conference that this Organization was more than an economic conception and better than a political conception and that rather it was a moral and human conception that inspired the establishment of social justice on a day-to-day basis, freely and by mutual agreement. In sum, His Holiness the Pope said that the Organization was fine-tuning and promoting the moral conscience of humanity. I think that, in the twenty-first century, it is our duty and our responsibility, more than ever before, to be this moral conscience that humankind needs so badly.

I would like, once again to thank you, on behalf of the Government of President Hipólito Mejía, and on behalf of the people of the Dominican Republican – especially those of Jimaní, and on my own behalf, for having elected me. May God bless you all.

Original Spanish: The SECRETARY-GENERAL

Mr President, Ministers and friends, I cannot imagine a better introduction to our debate than the conversation we had this morning with the presidents who were with us – with their words of wisdom, their experience and, of course, with the speech we have just heard from our President.

(The speaker continues in English.)

Today, I want to seek your guidance as we move forward to fulfil the challenge of building a fair globalization that creates opportunities for all. This, I think, is a defining moment for the ILO. The report of the World Commission on the Social Dimension of Globalization offers many rich insights for strategic reflection and practical action. What does it mean for us? How can it help shape our future activities? I have submitted some ideas for your consideration on the role of the ILO in the light of the report and I think that it poses a central leadership challenge for us as an institution and a fundamental test for the relevance of tripartism in this first half of the twenty-first century.

Our task is to deal with globalization through the lens of decent work – entrepreneurship, investment and productivity on one side, and decent jobs and social protection on the other, all bound together by rights, the practice of social dialogue and tripartism. And, by putting fairness and opportunity at centre stage, the World Commission clearly engages our institutional values.

The report is balanced: it is critical, positive and shows commonsense. It is critical in that it clearly states that the benefits are not reaching enough people and the present path is not sustainable. It is positive in that the point is not to stop globalization but to manage and shape it – fair rules, greater expansion of opportunities, benefits that are broadly shared, costs that are effectively minimized. It shows commonsense in that the recommendations are feasible and realistic. Some may be more difficult to implement than others, but they are all doable.

In sum, it proposes a wise governance of globalization in the interests of all, and it says that this can be done. As the members of the World Commission declare, we are convinced that a better world is possible.

The report has been welcomed in all regions of the world. It is not seen as the last report on globalization, atop a pile of many others, but as the first report that is based on real dialogue. It closed the dialogue divide, identified common ground and, through convergence of ideas, opened new avenues for practical solutions. It showed that dialogue is today the only true path to sustainable change.

I want to focus on three messages of the report and four challenges for the ILO. First, start at home. Much policy advice has been given to facilitate global finance, trade and investments, but very little to reinforce local communities and local markets where people live and want to stay, if given the opportunity. There cannot be a successful globalization without a successful localization. Sound local and national policies in a democratic setting are crucial to enhancing the benefits for its people of a country's integration into the global economy, particularly, in support systems for the workers and enterprises, which are most affected by globalization, but we are seeing the limits of national action.

Second, focus on fairness. We know that a fair globalization starts at home, but it does not end at home. Unbalanced patterns in investment, trade and labour markets are prime sources of today's political turbulence. We need fair rules for trade, capital, technology flows, migration and labour standards. Dealing with unstable commodity prices, excessive debt burdens and greater access to markets are all urgently needed. All of this will provide more policy space for developing countries to have real national ownership of development policies, especially the least developed countries.

Third, rethink global governance. Global markets are moving ahead at full speed. Economic and social institutions are lagging far behind. We need to improve the way global institutions perform and talk with each other and to adapt the post-World War architecture to twenty-first century priorities.

I think that it is key, and I see this particularly from the developing countries' point of view, that to reap the full benefits of good national governance we need good global governance. A lot of emphasis has been put on good national governance, but what about good global governance, and the responsibility of those with greater capacity to give global governance so that national governments can perform better in favour of their people? We need good governance – transparent, accountable, democratic, efficient and equitable. If not, power imbalances produce all sorts of conditionalities.

I see four challenges for us as we seek to do our part to create a fair globalization and make our contribution to meeting the Millennium Development Goal of reducing poverty by half: making decent work a global goal, making the ILO a global player, mobilizing tripartism for global action, and making the Organization as a whole a truly global team.

First, making decent work a global goal.

This is the most far-reaching implication of the World Commission's work for us. It stresses the importance of work as a major prism through which people view and interpret globalization and the way it impacts on their lives. By acknowledging that decent work, in its four strategic dimensions, is a widespread democratic demand of women and men everywhere and the best recipe for stability in all societies, the World Commission calls on the ILO to play a leading role in shaping globalization.

For us, meeting the challenge in our own work takes a combination of things. In some cases, it means deepening the effectiveness of existing programmes and mandated activities such as strengthening the labour-standards system, servicing constituents on employment policy issues or promoting gender equality. In others, it means a new way of looking at things; for example, addressing global production systems or building a socio-economic floor for the global economy.

The road to decent work as a global goal is through policy coherence, nationally and internationally, backed by advocacy at all levels. A fair globalization will not come about only through disjointed decisions on trade on one side, finance on the other, or labour, education or health policies conceived and applied independently. It is an integrated phenomenon and it takes integrated solutions. Coherence must grow from the local to the global level. You build coherence through dialogue. The more voices and interests that participate in the formulation of policies, the more balanced and efficient the results will be. I think that this is a major lesson to draw from the work of the World Commission itself.

Many sound national efforts are under way; for example, to implement the Millennium Development Goals and to make poverty reduction strategies more in tune with social and employment priorities. There is increasingly better coordination of international organizations at the country level. But, as the World Commission has said, when it comes to international policy coordination, we need an upgrade. The need for more integrated and balanced policies has never been more urgent as globalization has intensified.

Among other proposals, the report calls on the relevant international organizations to work together on sustainable growth, investment and employment creation through Policy Coherence Initiatives.

The World Commission states that this would respond to a major political demand in all countries and demonstrate the capacity of the multilateral system to find creative solutions to address the uncertainties in the lives of workers, families, enterprises and communities.

The stakes are, of course, high. We all know that if we do not solve the employment challenge global stability is at risk. This is one of the most serious conclusions of the World Commission: 26 consultations worldwide, and everywhere decent work and jobs were at the heart of the way people would like to see globalization respond to their needs.

As the World Commission proposes, if there is to be a successful outcome, the results of the Policy Coherence Initiatives would be submitted to the respective boards or governing bodies of the participating organizations for their consideration. So, this is not about creating new structures or institutions, it is simply about more efficient methods of work.

I have to tell you I keep being asked, worldwide, why these institutions, the Fund, the Bank, the WTO, ILO and the relevant United Nations bodies, cannot work and talk together. People want to know why we cannot work together. I think that this is one of the most important challenges that the multilateral system has laid before us. I am talking about this particular recommendation, and now the whole system has that challenge. I personally believe that if we move forward on this recommendation, with a serious commitment to make it work, we will significantly enhance the credibility of the international organizations.

Second, making the ILO a global player.

There is a hunger today for the type of global problem-solving approaches that the ILO stands for, that all of you represent and have developed together: the notion of dialogue as a vehicle for change, the idea that more voices must be part of the practical solutions.

With the exception of the ILO, the current multilateral system is exclusively intergovernmental, but globalization, as we see every day, is being shaped by many forces other than governments.

We need mechanisms that, like the ILO, move us from an international community of governments towards what the World Commission calls an emerging global community of diverse actors. This means, for example, governments plus business, trade unions, parliaments, local authorities, private international organizations, the international cooperative and consumer and other movements, Porto Alegre and Davos, citizens' organizations and so many others.

We are also the only major international organization with a presence in both worlds. I believe that we are, in many ways, the bridge to the future.

The World Commission suggests this might be the time and place for a globalization policy forum that brings the diverse actors of the emerging global community together. We should help organize this, together with other interested international organizations.

We should not forget that if we want decent work to become a global goal we will not be able to do it alone. We need partnerships to be developed, shared hopes to be expressed, common understandings to be deepened. We cannot be global players unless our team is working at full capacity.

If we believe that the ILO has a key role to play in shaping globalization, then the next step is to shape our own programme to give us the means to do it. In my report, I suggest six major policy areas identified by the Commission where the ILO is well placed to take the agenda forward: national policies to address globalization, decent work in global production systems, global policy coherence for growth, investment and employment, constructing a socio-economic floor, the global economy and the cross-border movement of people, and strengthening the international labour standards systems. I definitely welcome your comments.

Third, mobilizing tripartism for global action.

Tripartism is the key that can open the lock to a fair globalization. Much tripartism has been about securing social peace and productivity, a fundamental role that must expand, but now it also needs to reach out: a tripartism open to the world.

The world needs your voices not only as constituents of the ILO but as vital instruments of a stable global community.

Tripartism has the right to demand a greater voice in national and international policy-making. Its future influence will depend on making that happen.

The challenge in our hands is not simply to react individually to the forces of globalization but to help shape them together in open economies and open societies. We must move ahead with self-assurance, based on the many assets of tripartism.

Look at your potential. You represent the productive forces of the economy. You have the knowledge of what is happening in enterprises and the workplaces around the world. You represent people's issues in the seats of governments dealing with social and labour affairs and, increasingly, economic questions. You constitute one of the biggest global networks representing millions of enterprises and millions of workers, the community of work. You have shown the power of dialogue tested throughout the 85 year history of the ILO.

Yes, you have differences, sometimes strong differences, and you reflect diverse interests, but that is the richness which ensures balance when you decide to move together. Together you can be a powerful lobby for decent work in a fair globalization.

All of this leads to our fourth and final challenge.

The Organization as a whole, the constituents and the Office, must become a truly global team: clear in our strategic choices; efficient in our operations; committed to our values; confident in our message.

Of course, we cannot do verything. The Commission has put a lot on the table. If we try to eat our way through the whole menu we will certainly get indigestion. If we go slowly, when globalization is moving forward by leaps and bounds, we will miss our chance. We must push ahead decisively with measured ambition and aware of the means at our disposal.

Fortunately, our Governing Body has the necessary institutional instruments to forge our response after your discussions: the strategic policy frameworks; the next budget cycles; and the Working Party on the Social Dimension of Globalization.

Let me conclude by saying that, in this 85th anniversary year, our history both inspires us and empowers us. But it is also demanding.

We are the heirs, after all, of those who made it possible for the ILO to receive the Nobel Peace Prize. They show us the way.

Recently the media has shown programmes on D-Day and the closing chapters of the Second World War. This also permits us to have a rich insight into our own history, because it was also sixty years' ago, almost to the day, that ILO delegates gathered in Philadelphia.

I would like you to know that a few days ago we had an anniversary luncheon and we honoured five former ILO officials who served our institution sixty years ago, precisely during the Philadelphia era. They devoted their lives to the values and the cause of our institution. They are veterans in the global fight for social justice. I am pleased to tell you that four of them are here with us today: Angela Butler; Alejandro Flores; Carol Lubin; Mirjam Newman-Staal, and I think that they merit being honoured not only at a luncheon at the Office, but at the whole Conference.

So, as bombs were dropping and soldiers and civilians were dying, our predecessors in Philadelphia were charged with an awesome task to look beyond the boundaries of the day, to help to find the values of peace and to plant the seeds of hope, and they produced one of the most significant social documents of our times. Poverty anywhere constitutes a danger to prosperity everywhere. Labour is not a commodity. All human beings, irrespective of race, creed or sex, have the right to pursue both their material well-being and their spiritual development in conditions of freedom and dignity, of economic security and equal opportunity. The war against want requires to be carried out with unrelenting vigour.

The host in Philadelphia was one of the first female Labour Ministers in the world, Frances Perkins. She welcomed delegates with these words: "the ILO", she said 60 years ago, "is an assembly of those who are charged in the midst of war to lay one of the foundation stones of the great peace – the stone of social justice – on which human hope and human life can be rebuilt". That is our foundation.

But why do I review our history: our birth 85 years ago, the Declaration of Philadelphia, the Nobel Peace Prize? Because institutions that forget their past cannot build a sound future.

In the midst of the opportunities and imbalances of globalization described by the report of the World Commission, we are again challenged to look ahead, to imagine our tomorrow, by building today a fair globalization where decent work is possible for all.

My friends, there are precious moments in history when opportunities come and go. Seizing them requires vision to chart our actions, commitment to face the obstacles and courage to take decisions. We are at such a moment today. Our future is in your hands.

Original Spanish: The PRESIDENT

Thank you very much, Director-General, for those thoughts that you have shared with us this afternoon. They are a summary, a consensus, of the document you provided for us: *A fair globalization – The role of the ILO.*

I think that I speak on behalf of all delegates, ministers and those present here today when I thank you for your participation and for the way in which you deal with all these issues, and for the very pleasant surprise which you have provided us by having these four veterans share with us this afternoon's debate.

I am certain that all the delegates present here are going to keep in mind the content of the contribution made with regard to a fair globalization and the role of the International Labour Organization in creating that globalization.

SUSPENSION OF CERTAIN PROVISIONS OF THE STANDING ORDERS OF THE CONFERENCE *(CONT.)*

Original Spanish: The PRESIDENT

You will recall that at the first plenary sitting last Tuesday the Conference took a number of decisions regarding the suspension of certain clauses of the Standing Orders of the Conference in order to allow for a more lively, interactive discussion on the Global Report on freedom of association and the effective recognition of the right to collective bargaining. Under article 76 of the Standing Orders of the Conference, we are now called upon to confirm the decisions taken last Tuesday. Are there any objections? I see that there are no objections so I take it that the Conference adopts the proposal to suspend the relevant clauses of the Standing Orders.

(The proposals are adopted.)

Before I open the debate, I would like to remind you of the rules that the Vice-Presidents and myself have agreed to apply. A certain degree of discipline is required so that our discussion may flow smoothly. However, I would like to state here and now that, in periods of acute political tension, the International Labour Organization has a twofold responsibility – to uphold the values of human freedom and dignity enshrined in its Constitution, and to circumscribe rather than extend the area of international tension by ensuring the fullest possible degree of continued cooperation in pursuit of the objectives of the ILO.

I would also like to recall here that the debates of the International Labour Conference must not encroach on what is being discussed by the Security Council and the General Assembly of the United Nations in New York, which have responsibility for political decisions under the United Nations Charter. I trust that I can count on each one of you to ensure that our discussions are carried out with both the openness and the dignity that are appropriate to the highest international body in the realm of social and labour-related matters.

Freedom of expression is a vital feature of the International Labour Organization. However, in order to exercise this right in a spirit of mutual respect, it is of utmost importance that all delegates use parliamentary language, respect the accepted procedure, refer only to the items under discussion and avoid raising questions alien to these matters.

Each delegate can exercise the right of reply if he or she feels that there is a need to respond in the event that his or her government has been challenged. In such a case, the request for the right of reply should be submitted to the President of the sitting before that sitting is over. This request should be transmitted to the President through the Clerk and not by asking for the floor at the sitting.

They must not ask for the floor during the session in order to raise a point of order. The President, assisted by the Clerk, will agree with the delegation concerned on a time when the reply will be made.

The reply should refer only to the point under discussion. It should not exceed two minutes, and it should be delivered in correct parliamentary language. I must stress also that in order to avoid endless debate, it has been a practice of the presidents to refuse to allow replies to a reply.

The Standing Orders of the Conference set out that the maximum length of all speeches is five minutes. I would ask all delegates and ministers who are attending the Conference, when they prepare their speeches, to take into account this five-minute time limit so that the President will not be obliged to stop speakers before they have finished their speeches.

As is our customary practice, the speeches made by our special guests are, of course, not subject to this five-minute rule.

I would like to remind you that the list of speakers for the discussion of the Report of the Chairperson of the Governing Body and the Reports of the Director-General will close on Wednesday, 9 June at 6 p.m.

REPORTS OF THE CHAIRPERSON OF THE GOVERNING BODY AND OF THE DIRECTOR-GENERAL: DISCUSSION

Mr. FAHEY *(Minister for Labour Affairs, Ireland)*

It is indeed a great honour for me to address the 92nd Session of the International Labour Conference in my capacity as Minister for Labour Affairs of Ireland as well as the presiding Minister for Employment and Social Affairs of the European Union.

I want to congratulate the President and the Officers of the Conference on their respective appointments and wish them well in their work. I also want to congratulate the Director-General, Mr. Somavia, on his very focused, succinct and indeed provocative speech in which he outlined three messages and four challenges for all of us.

But, firstly, on 1 May 2004, Ireland was privileged to host a Day of Welcomes in Dublin to mark the accession to the European Union of ten new Member States. We look forward to working together in Europe, and within the global structure of the International Labour Organization, to promote the harmonious development of programmes with our partners across the globe. The International Labour Organization, given its unique tripartite nature, belongs to all of us and we share the responsibility of ensuring that it remains vibrant and dynamic as we move into the twenty-first century.

I was both struck and heartened to note the similarity between many of the themes of the Irish Presidency of the European Union and the recommendations contained in the Director-General's Reports which are before us today. Let me explain.

Over the past five months, the Irish Presidency of the European Council has focused on the issues that we believe engender and sustain innovative and high performance workplaces. Innovation, adaptability and most of all people-centred policies have all featured in the Irish Presidency programme.

The overall theme of the Irish Presidency is "Europeans – Working Together". This theme captures the accession of ten new Member States into the European Union on 1 May. This enlargement of the European Union has been a major factor for our

Presidency, both in terms of preparing for the accession and then ensuring the effective integration of the new Member States into the workings of the Union.

Our Presidency theme also captures the need for all stakeholders to work together. Whether at European level, national level, or at individual enterprise level, the Irish Presidency is convinced of the importance of the process of partnership.

If we are to meet the challenges presented by the globalized twenty-first century, our workplaces must be geared towards constant change and innovation. All involved – employers, employees, policymakers and social partners – need to create a shared understanding of what needs to be done, particularly at the level of the workplace. We also need to embrace new ideas and ways of working.

In Ireland, for many years now, we have had a tradition of partnership between trade unions, employers, the Government and NGOs. Involving all the stakeholders in the processes of decision-making has paid dividends in the form of a more stable industrial relations climate and in particular the possibility to get beyond conflict to a shared approach and I want to acknowledge the contribution of the Irish social partners in this respect.

In March this year, the Spring European Council stressed that Member States should give urgent attention to four particular challenges: adaptability; attracting more people into the labour force; improving the quality of employment; and investing in human capital.

The Employment and Social Policy Council that I have been chairing has concentrated on the themes of *Making Work Pay; Adaptability and Change; Investment in Human Capital; and Lifelong Learning* – all culminating in the workplace of the future.

The Spring European Council also emphasized that support and advocacy for change must reach beyond governments. In order to generate this support, the Council called on Member States to build reform partnerships involving the social partners, civil society, and the public authorities, in accordance with national arrangements and traditions. In Ireland, we have already started this process. We have undertaken to strengthen our social partnership process as part of the New Reform Partnership in Europe. Through this mechanism, the Irish Presidency hopes to add renewed dynamism and drive to the process of reaching the Lisbon goals.

It was for this reason, as I stated earlier, that the Irish Presidency priorities mirrored closely the contents of the Director-General's Report and indeed his very fine speech today. Themes such as making work pay, or decent work, to use the ILO's terminology, increasing adaptability of both workers and employers to change, investing in human resources and ensuring reforms through dialogue and better governance are very much to the fore in the Director-General's Report. These two reports constitute documents of major importance in relation to the activities of the ILO and in progressing the debate on the report of the World Commission on the Social Dimension of Globalization.

The report *ILO implementation programme for 2002-03* is an assessment of the work of the Organization as a whole, of the relevance of its strategic objectives and the effectiveness of the means used to attain those goals. The second of the Director-General's Reports, *A fair globalization: The role of the ILO,* is the key issue before us at this session of the Conference.

I wish to acknowledge the contributions of President Halonen of Finland and President Mkapa of the United Republic of Tanzania, who chaired the Commission and who addressed us so eloquently this morning. I want to compliment all 26 members of the Commission for their time, wisdom and work.

It was refreshing to see that such a diverse range of actors represented on the World Commission, who were drawn from a wide spectrum, including governments, civil society, trade unions, as well as multinational companies, were able to reach a common accord in their report. They have, in the words of Giuliano Amato, the former Prime Minister of Italy, shown that debate on globalization can be moved forward from rhetoric and acrimony to dialogue and cooperation.

Just in conclusion, can I say that we have been presented with some challenges by the Director-General this afternoon. He mentioned this morning the need for change and the vital involvement of leadership, which is a prerequisite to that change. I think it is incumbent on all of us, if this 92nd Session of the Conference is to be successful, that we take up the challenge from the Director-General and that we achieve the objectives to which all of us aspire.

Original French: Mr. LARCHER *(Minister Responsible for Labour Relations, Ministry of Employment, Labour and Social Cohesion, France)*

First of all, I would like to congratulate the President on his election to steer the deliberations of this 92nd Session of the International Labour Conference – a session whose agenda is dominated by the theme of the social dimension of globalization. The introductory remarks of Mr. Juan Somavia, illustrates more than ever the loyalty of our Organization to its mandate and its ability to adapt constantly to a changing world.

I would like to thank the Director-General for the excellence of the reports submitted to us, for the wealth of information provided and the diversity of the lines of reflection that have been proposed. But first of all I would like to praise the quality of the Report: *A fair globalization: Creating opportunities for all,* and I would like to thank the World Commission – and in particular its two co-chairpersons – Ms. Halonen and Mr. Mkapa. Globalization brings with it progress, but since we have not been able to place human beings at the centre of process, it has produced some perverse effects which today have to be corrected. This is the precondition that has to be met if we want to build a model of society which should not just be an economic model but which should also remain a social model for all men and women. The report of the World Commission concludes that it is necessary to strengthen governments at all levels and it advocates measures to improve the consistency of policies and to ensure a better balance between the economic, social and developmental aspects. This report, which is going to help us structure better the discussion on globalization in our various countries, has the merit of encompassing all the aspects of globalization by decompartmentalizing them. The result of several years of reflection it is, as the Director-General has correctly stressed, not an outcome but indeed the starting point for a process in which the ILO has a decisive role to play in the implementation of future mechanisms or instruments. In his report, the Director-General examines ways and means of giving an impetus to ensure the convergence of all the other players in the search for a fairer form of globalization. The ILO has the assets and as a result of the elements which support its legitimacy to act in this direction, this legitimacy is doubly supported by the ethical and social basis of the organization and in its original tripartite dimension. The organization is, as part of its mandate, responsible for evaluating the economic policies in the light of their impact on social and labour policies. Making decent work a global objective seems to us to be a concrete implementation of this responsibility and we can only endorse it. As the only tripartite organization in a multilateral system, the ILO brings together real economic players. It is the ILO which brings together men and women at a daily level, who are best able to gauge the effects of the transformations which our world is undergoing. No other body has this expertise or such precise "hands-on" knowledge of today's problems. This gives us an idea of the importance of the role which it has to play today. I am thinking in particular of the idea of a forum on the policies of globalization which follows on immediately from the declaration by the Ministers of Employment of the G8 in Stuttgart in December 2003. According to France, overall regulation of globalization and the improvement of consistency between international organizations requires strengthening in multilateralism and the creation of an Economic and Social Security Council. This idea was in fact expressed in the communication of the European Commission and is one which we support. In this respect I would like to remind you in conclusion of the strong words uttered by the President of the French Republic when speaking on 28 May this year at the Summit between the European Union and the Latin-American and Caribbean countries. He stated that although it was rich in promise, globalization had not found a solution for the exclusion of whole countries and peoples. He went on to say that half of humanity lived on less than $2 a day and nearly 1 billion women, men and children were confronted daily with the fear of starvation at a time when the world had never been as prosperous.

Faced with this situation, I can only share the diagnosis of the report on the social dimension of globalization which the Director-General of the ILO has made public. Social cohesion is indeed a question of global interest. We have to mobilize ourselves so that our actions are always inspired by concern for justice and solidarity. It is in this way that we will ensure cohesion in the world. This then is the position of France on these issues. You can rely on the support of France to ensure that this social dimension of globalization will not simply remain a dead letter, but will enter the daily lives of women and men and be loyal to Albert Thomas' message, "let us build world peace".

Mr. SOODHUN (Minister of Labour, Industrial Relations and Employment, Mauritius)

I wish to congratulate the President on his election to preside over this 92nd Session of the International Labour Conference.

This year's Conference will certainly be remembered for the historic report of the World Commission on the Social Dimension of Globalization. This report comes at an opportune time, when we members of the African Union are in the process of formulating a social policy framework for Africa and are planning to meet with regard to employment and poverty issues at the Summit to be held in September in Burkina Faso.

With this report, the link between poverty and unemployment is now being understood in its proper perspective. While new opportunities have emerged with globalization, there are also numerous threats, in terms of job losses, with increasing delocalization, resulting from the quest for achieving greater competitiveness. It is the most vulnerable people who are losing jobs and dropping back into poverty, which itself is aggravated by problems of AIDS, illiteracy and lack of skills, while fast technological changes increase their insecurity and restrict their employability.

To what extent is the imperative of cost reduction and competitiveness compatible with the labour standards and the dignity of human beings? As a follow-up to the report of the World Commission, the ILO could conduct a study on the positive impact of labour standards and human rights on competitiveness.

In response to the numerous challenges facing it, my own country has restructured the sugar sector and is developing new sectors such as ICT, a seafood hub and a knowledge hub. Interesting incentives exist for investors so as to create an environment that facilitates job creation. At the same time, government spends about 44 per cent of its budget on social expenditure, which includes free education and health services, social security benefits, social housing programmes, special assistance for the education of children from poor families, community development projects and microcredit schemes.

Employment creation is our main priority. Government has set up an equity fund and a textile emergency support scheme as a means of preserving employment in the Export Processing Zone. A redeployment programme has been introduced to assist retrenched workers in finding a new job. Self-employment is being promoted to job-seekers as an alternative and sustainable form of employment.

In order to give a new impetus to the small and medium-sized enterprises sector, the Government has recently set up a ministry for small and medium-sized enterprises, and a hawkers' palace is being built with a view to offering a safe and customer-friendly market to the street operators of the informal sector.

Despite all the economic constraints, the Government of my country has taken great care to adjust the wages of the lowest income groups by granting an annual increase in wages which is higher than the Consumer Price Index (CPI). This year, an increase of 4.5 per cent was granted while the CPI was only 3.9 per cent. The same increase also applies to social benefits.

The Government of Mauritius has, in addition, given special attention to fundamental labour standards and has ratified six ILO Conventions over a period of two years. It is currently examining the ratification of Convention No. 87 and the replacement of the Industrial Relations Act by new legislation, as well as the modernization of the Occupational Safety, Health and Welfare Act and labour legislation. It is our aim to reinforce structures for conciliation and mediation and the practice of collective bargaining, and to strengthen workers' participation in productivity gains.

As a country whose population is based on labour migration, we are very pleased that migrant labour is on the agenda of this session of the Conference. We have been ensuring that the rights to decent wages and decent accommodation of migrant workers are protected. We shall continue to strengthen administrative and legal mechanisms so as to improve the management of migrant labour.

The Government of Mauritius wishes to reiterate its commitment to promoting tripartism and social dialogue, as advocated by the Director-General, as a means of addressing emerging social and economic issues effectively. We wish also to assure the Director-General, Mr. Juan Somavia, that we fully support him in his crusade to make decent work a global objective. This is not a dream, but an objective that we shall attain together guided by the clear vision and strong leadership of the ILO.

Original Arabic: Mr. EL AMAWY *(Minister of Manpower and Emigration, Egypt)*

It is a great honour for me to congratulate the President upon his election to preside over this session of the Conference. I would like to wish him every success.

We have read very attentively the Report of the Director-General, *A fair globalization – The role of the ILO,* and we agree with this Report in that decent work should be the focal point of our work at the international level. The management of globalization itself should be based on collective respect for human rights on the international scene.

The greatest challenge henceforward will be to find a balance between trade liberalization and social progress, particularly as regards the establishment and protection of international standards, and without opting for selective policies – or brandishing certain rights that are sometimes used as weapons to serve certain interests that are far removed from their true objectives.

The achievements of globalization have been unevenly distributed throughout the world, with the African continent benefiting the least. The marginalization of African countries is clearly shown in the small share that they hold of world trade and foreign investment. This situation is exacerbated by the reduction in development aid and the burden of foreign debt, which is limiting the continent's ability to develop.

Developed countries must remove protectionist barriers against exports from developing countries and put an end to subsidies which are harmful to exports from developing countries. Furthermore, dialogue between countries of the North and South must push ahead to establish a fairer system of world trade.

We agree with the idea that achieving democracy is essential, at both the international and national levels. Egypt has undertaken a commitment to the development of a free democracy nationally through policies that take account of the social dimension in our economic structure.

We welcome the report, which deals with issues relating to emigration. Indeed, emigration is an integral part of development and growth, and the rights of migrant workers are one of the essential components of the ILO Declaration. Discrimination based on national citizenship is an important areas, which we must deal with under the follow-up to the ILO Declaration. We therefore urge the Organization to increase its efforts to encourage countries to immediately ratify the Conventions relating to migrant workers and their rights, and to implement the recommendations of the World Commission on the Social Dimensions of Globalization as regards holding a third global forum to establish a global and fair system for migration.

We would agree with the Director-General, who states in his Report, *The situation of workers of the occupied Arab territories,* that the restrictions imposed on the freedom of movement of Palestinians have been aggravated by the construction of the separation Wall which is impeding the economic activity of the country. We agree with the reference made in the Report to the need to lift these restrictions so that the fundamental rights of workers are respected.

Allow me to state the importance of supporting the ILO programme of technical assistance in the occupied Arab territories and the need to increase the amount allocated by the Organization's budget. Similarly, we urge donor countries to finance the funds established for this purpose.

Allow me to say too that all the efforts aimed at guaranteeing workers' rights and providing them with decent work, will be in vain unless we create a climate conducive to peace, security and stability in the Middle East. It is essential that a just and comprehensive solution to the Arab-Israeli conflict be found, through Israeli withdrawal from all the occupied Arab territories, including the occupied Golan, and the establishment of an independent Palestinian State. It is also essential to put an end to the tragic situation in Iraq and to ensure that the rights of the Iraqi people are respected. We would also recall that we reject all practices which are detrimental to the Syrian people and prevent Syrian workers and employers from exercising their rights.

Original French: Mr. PANAYIOTOPOULOS *(Minister of Employment and Social Protection, Greece)*

I should like first of all to express my sincere congratulations to the President of the Conference on his election to this office, as well as to the other officers. I should also like to thank the Director-General, as well as the International Labour Office, for the quality of the reports submitted to us for discussion.

We are meeting here at a time when the world is facing a number of challenges. I should like to commend the initiative of the Director-General, who has so ably organized an objective dialogue on the problems arising as a result of globalization. All of the debates on the immediate future as aimed at seeking a more fair globalization, one that is synonymous with opportunities for all.

The European Union, with its characteristic social model, intends to keep its place in the world by becoming most competitive knowledge society, creating more and better jobs, thus strengthening social cohesion.

We consider that this determination to bring together development, employment and social cohesion is entirely consistent with the studies that have been carried out by the International Labour Office.

Allow me to highlight some of the aspects upon which we should focus our efforts towards more fair globalization.

Two recent reports, that of the World Bank and that of the World Commission on the Social Dimension of Globalization, emphasises the danger inherent in the effects of globalization on cultural diversity in our world. I sincerely believe that such concerns will only be alloyed when globalization succeeds in ensuring that the uniqueness and identities of the world's peoples are protected.

Only if it is based on a sound economy will there be a globalization in which lasting social cohesion is a priority and the social benefits of globalization are equitably shared among all.

I should also like to mention three points which are essential for Greece.

The first is a more effective and more dynamic governance. The idea of a State created in the interests of its citizens implies not only that the economy must be healthy but also that those who govern the country must be attentive to the needs of the social partners and civil society.

Better governance means first of all combating bureaucracy, which constrains and stifles small and medium-sized enterprises and the entrepreneurial spirit. It also means fighting against corruption and improving public finances. And lastly, it means ensuring that the public sector responds more quickly to investors, needs and hence contributes to development.

Better governance means ensuring that everyone has access to the benefits of development.

Secondly, I should like to raise the issue of small and medium-sized enterprises. We are happy to note that the ILO's strategy calls for supporting small and medium-sized enterprises, upon which the creation of more and better jobs depends.

Thirdly, I should like to highlight the importance of establishing a global minimum level of social protection. We are convinced of the soundness of the approach adopted by the ILO, which aims to provide priority coverage of the most vulnerable population groups, such as the elderly. We support the action undertaken by the ILO to develop and disseminate the principle of a minimum level of socio-economic security for the world economy. We are ready to take such initiatives at the national level and in the Balkan region.

Another important issue I should like to address is that of migration. Since this issue is already on the agenda of this session of the Conference, I will merely note that our country, which has experienced a huge wave of immigration in a very short time, urgently needs a policy which is both reliable and respectful of human rights.

The strength and effectiveness of a State are measured in the first instance by its ability to offer assistance and support to its most vulnerable citizens.

By the same token, the development of globalization and in the way in which it is perceived by the peoples of the world will depend on whether it can offer opportunities for everyone where they live and work. It is the task of all of us here today to shoulder this responsibility.

We are determined to do everything in our power to achieve this. Accordingly, I should like once again to thank the Director-General for the initiatives he has taken and to assure him of my support. Allow me to say a few words in my native language and to say ... *(the speaker continues in Greek).*

Mr. MARONI *(Minister of Labour, Italy)*

This year, the International Labour Conference is focusing on globalization. Let me express the support of the Italian Government for this initiative, considering how important good governance of globalization is for its economic and social effects on both industrialized and developing countries. We greatly appreciate the work done by the World Commission on the Social Dimension of Globalization and the Report presented today by Mr. Somavia on the implication for the activities of the ILO. We believe that the analogies and the guidelines for action depicted represent a good basis for designing the organization's next strategic policies.

Italy is aware of the risks that an unfair globalization carries for international situations – improving the conditions of the richest and more developed countries and worsening those of the poorest. To counter these effects, we are committed to promoting a large programme to help the countries lagging behind, particularly in Africa. The first results are encouraging but a more comprehensive strategy needs to be developed. For this reason, the work done by the World Commission should be strongly sustained, especially when focusing its attention on new policies necessary to ensure a fair and equitable globalization. The ILO must act quickly, strengthening the social dimension and the role of the multilateral system. A fair globalization can be obtained only by reinforcing the role of core labour standards and promoting stronger actions to respect them in production systems, firms or export processing zones. Globalization should produce growth and employment and reduce the differences between countries. Decent work should be made a global goal and pursued through coordinated international policies. The Italian Government shares these conclusions, but expresses its concern over the low quality of working regulations in many countries. Lowering labour standards is not a safe policy for promoting growth and jobs. It undermines international competition and can push industrialized countries to adopt defensive strategies and restrict the offshoring of manufacturing and services.

The consequences on international trade could be negative in terms of financial flows and wealth. Therefore, we reaffirm the central role of the ILO for promoting core labour standards and for addressing governments, firms and other parties, in considering social issues in their international cooperation practices. The ILO is the most suitable United Nations agency to develop a multilateral system of cooperation based on integrated and balanced economic, social and environmental policies. We encourage the ILO to continue, together with social partners and in close cooperation with the other international organizations. At the same time, we appreciate that the World Commission envisages the ILO's role as promoter of a multi-stakeholders' forum, a proposal that Italy made some months ago at the G8 conference in Stuttgart. This initiative is aimed at developing a culture of corporate social responsibility. A fair globalization that respects the dignity of each human being can obtain relevant results only if it is accompanied by a stronger social responsibility worldwide. Decent work should be accessible to everybody and core labour standards should be respected by each country, even in the poorest areas of the world. Only under these conditions can globalization substantially improve the wealth of our societies and peoples, increasing the level of social cohesion.

I hope that this Conference can make important steps in this direction and contribute to developing a new era of relations between our countries and peoples.

Mr. DIMAS *(European Commissioner for Employment and Social Affairs, European Union)*

First of all, it is a great pleasure and honour for me to address the 92nd Session of the International Labour Conference.

The overall economic gains from globalization are visible and tangible. However, such gains have not always been evenly distributed among various regions of the world. Therefore, we need to strengthen the social dimension of the current process of globalization, otherwise it may not be sustainable.

I am glad to see that these ideas are developed in the recent report of the World Commission. In reply to this report, and as a first contribution to the ensuing debate, the European Commission has recently published its own communication on the social dimension of globalization.

The European Union is well aware of the advantages and risks of greater economic integration. After all, the European construction has been in itself a process of globalization, of a smaller geographic scale, of course. The elimination of internal frontiers and the creation of a single economic area should be accompanied by policies which promote both economic progress and social cohesion.

The European Union's economic and social model cannot be transposed simply in other parts of the world. But, as the World Commission's report points out, it can be a useful source of inspiration. Indeed, there has always been a strong social dimension in the economic integration of the European Union. In the early years, this took the form of workers' rights, gender equality, and social cohesion through structural funds. But as integration developed, the social dimension expanded to encompass a broader range of objectives. For instance, full employment, higher quality jobs and training, adequate and sustainable social protection, promotion of social dialogue and the struggle against discrimination and social exclusion. The integrated strategy, known as the Lisbon Agenda, serves a most audacious and challenging project: to make the European Union the most dynamic and knowledge-based society and economy in the world by the year 2010 with more and better jobs and increased social cohesion. And it does so by promoting, at the same time, competitiveness, employment, social progress and environmental protection. In its external actions, the European Union objective is to maximize the benefits of globalization for all social groups. The European Union has negotiated agreements with virtually all countries of the world. Most of these agreements contain bilateral or multilateral commitments to achieve social goals. Its open trade commitments can be used to support more socially equitable development. The European Union already secures high levels of access to its markets for developing countries through initiatives such as the "Everything but arms" initiative and the Cotonou Agreement and its generalized system of preferences.

In addition, the European Union is the world's largest donor of development aid, much of which is focused on support for social development. However, much of the responsibility for social development lies with the partner countries themselves. Their domestic policies must respect the rule of law and human rights and ensure transparent and accountable governments. National development strategies should integrate trade and secure a better distribution of its benefits.

Responsibility for social development does not lie only with governments. The private sector too can play a part in the complementary conduit for change. Companies, the wider business community, trade unions and the broader civil society can advocate more social governance.

Finally, globalization presents challenges for all international institutions. The European Commission strongly believes that the World Commission's report should be a part of the agenda of other international forums which have responsibility for financial, economic and trade issues. Achieving all these objectives will require 'joined-up' global governance.

The time has come to turn the results of our debate into a concrete action plan. We all have a duty to contribute to bringing the World Commission's report to life. To do that, we need the full commitment, as the Director-General said previously, of all stakeholders: international organizations, governments, social partners, civil society and the business community. They all need to join forces to promote better global governance and to ensure that even the low-income groups of the poorest countries can enjoy the benefits of globalization.

Original Portuguese: **Mr. BERZOINI** *(Ministry of Labour and Employment, Brazil)*

I should like to congratulate the President on his election. Brazil would like to express its satisfaction with the report from the World Commission on the Social Dimension of Globalization, not simply because of its balanced diagnosis, but, above all, because of its recommendations for initiatives to achieve a fairer, more equitable and inclusive globalization, giving rise to less inequality and suffering.

We would also like to thank the constituents of the ILO and its Director-General for this initiative and for their support of the Commission's work. The diagnosis of the devastating social effects of a globalization process, dominated by the financial market is the first step in getting back on course towards a process which is focused on individuals and the opportunities offered to them.

The World Commission on the Social Dimension of Globalization has tackled key issues for our countries in a balanced and objective manner and has stressed the following points. The process of globalization as it has developed today is extremely unfair, and has exacerbated the inequalities between rich and poor. The way in which it has developed up to the present means that the process of globalization has contributed significantly to the increase in the decent work deficit. An international system of governance must be an essential element in a globalization which has any prospect of bringing about social inclusion and the reduction of inequalities, and this requires greater democratization of multilateral institutions. It is necessary to strengthen and facilitate access for all countries to all multilateral bodies. The problems which affect the most vulnerable, such as hunger, unemployment, child labour, slave labour and forced labour, must be tackled by state policies in partnership with society.

We believe that the creation and promotion of decent work is both the best way of bringing about social inclusion and the most appropriate way of achieving sustainable development, from the point of view of the economy, society and the environment. It is essential to combine macroeconomic policies with employment policies, that is, to work towards economic growth in conjunction with social development and environmental protection. To do so we need to be consistent in our action, both nationally and regionally, to think globally and act locally. This can be done by: integrating economic, social and employment policies, increasing both the efficiency with which the labour force is deployed and its level of professional qualification and skills; linking local and regional development policies with the creation of job opportunities, jobs and income; promoting and strengthening social dialogue at all levels, beginning with the workplace; reforming systems of social security to include the many workers who have been displaced by informal labour; increasing the capacity of labour administrations, particularly in order to eradicate child labour and forced labour, through assistance and horizontal technical cooperation, without creating new structures and with the objective of reducing the decent work deficit; and increasing government action with regard to those groups who are most subject to exclusion from the labour market, particularly young people and workers who are less than 40 years old and have a low level of skill or qualification.

The Brazilian Government is committed to this agenda. At national level, under the leadership of President Lula da Silva, the Government's policies on public investment, credit and industry, are being orientated towards activities with the greatest possible potential to create jobs and income. Within the Americas, we have the Inter-American Conference of Ministers of Labour, MERCOSUR mechanisms such as the Socio-Labour Commission and the Economic and Social Consultative Forum, and direct relations between the Ministers of Labour of Argentina, Brazil, Paraguay, Uruguay, Chile, Peru, Bolivia and shortly, we hope, also Mexico.

I would like, however, to stress that the necessary progress in the process of globalization will have to involve aspects of international trade relations. Notwithstanding internal actions, which each country must undertake responsibly; we need an environment of greater cooperation and less protectionism, within which the integration of markets can be an effective and fair instrument to create the conditions for an increase in decent work and social inclusion.

Original Turkish: Mr. BASESGIOGLU *(Minister for Labour and Social Security, Turkey)*

I congratulate the President and the two Vice-Presidents on their election and wish them every success.

I thank the Director-General, Mr. Juan Somavia, for his Report, *ILO programme implementation 2002-03,* in which the developments in member States regarding the four strategic objectives of the International Labour Organization are indicated in an objective manner. We consider the report, *A fair globalization: Creating opportunities for all,* by the World Commission on the Social Dimension of Globalization, published last February, as a significant study that is in line with efforts to establish a better world order, by truly implementing tripartism and social dialogue, as indicated in the report. I would like to stress that I share the view of the Director-General where he indicates that decent work should be adopted not only as an ILO objective, but also as a global one.

The *Report on the situation of workers in the occupied Arab territories* shows once again the seriousness of the economic, social and humanitarian costs of the chronic conflict accompanying the Middle East question. The Report also underlines the necessity of the ILO's continued interest and support for this issue. In this connection, I am glad to mention that my Government has decided to make a humble contribution to the Palestinian Fund for Employment and Social Protection. Turkey attaches great importance on the implementation of the Road Map, and to reaching a peaceful solution through negotiations as soon as possible.

Globalization, which has emerged as a result of the rapid developments in information and communication technologies in the economic and social fields, has increased international competition and, consequently, working life has become more flexible so as to adapt to changing conditions. In the globalization process enterprises have to adapt themselves to the newly emerging conditions which govern their organizational and production patterns.

With this in mind, our Government launched a series of important reforms and legislative arrangements. The new Labour Act No. 4857, which came into effect in June 2003, is one such reform. The economic, social and political conditions closely related to labour, the problems encountered in actual practice, the need for flexibility, and the need for harmonization with ILO standards and European Union legislation all necessitated radical amendments of the provisions of the old Labour Act, along with changes to the laws on Social Security and on Turkish Employment Services. Our country has ratified a total of 56 ILO Conventions, 16 of which within the last year (including all the fundamental ones).

Promoting employment and combating unemployment constitutes one of the top priorities on the agenda of my Government; therefore, the year 2004 has been declared "The Year of Combating Unemployment".

In this context, the Turkish employers' organizations have been strengthened and modernized with a view to taking the necessary active employment measures in line with the European Employment Strategy. In addition to these general measures regarding improvement of our national economy, a series of active employment programmes and projects have been implemented.

In order to maintain industrial peace, further promote trade union rights and freedom of association in the country, and to enable the full harmonization of national legislation with ILO norms and European Union legislation in this field, a draft law prepared by a board of academics including the amendments deemed to be necessary to the Trade Unions Act and the Collective Agreements, Strike and Lock-out Act, has been submitted to the social partners in order to obtain their respective views.

We believe that social dialogue, based on effective exchange of views, cooperation and consensus between social partners, is one of the fundamental mechanisms of a peaceful industrial relations system. With this in mind, we ratified the Tripartite Consultation (International Labour Standards) Convention, 1976 (No. 144), in 1993. In this context, necessary amendments have been made in the new Labour Act and the Regulations on the Working

Methods and Principles of the Tripartite Consultation Board relating to Labour Life were put into effect.

With the sincere belief that new ideas and reflections to be introduced in this house would help us further to improve our labour legislation and its implementation, I hope that this 92nd Session of the International Labour Conference will yield very successful conclusions.

(Mr. Wade takes the Chair.)

Original Farsi: Mr. KHALEGHI *(Minister of Labour and Social Affairs, Islamic Republic of Iran)*

In the name of God, the Merciful, the Compassionate! I would like, at the outset, to congratulate the President on the occasion of his election.

The report of the World Commission on the Social Dimension of Globalization has, by offering logical and realistic recommendations, opened up a new way for the ILO constituents to ensure that globalization begins at home. This includes: creating more viable macro-level policies to better run their respective countries; promoting democratic institutions; promoting human rights; fostering gender equality; offering social opportunities; incorporating adequate employment and labour provisions into macroeconomic plans; taking more serious steps to protect workers' fundamental rights; bolstering social protection; and promoting tripartism and social dialogue.

Even though all the delegates consider reform of national macro-level policies to be main prerequisite for enjoying the fruits of globalization, many States are extremely concerned over the present crisis in governance of the globalization process. This concern stems from the fact that globalization cannot lead to sustainable development, international security and peace unless it promotes more equitable access to commercial and economic opportunities. The necessary political infrastructures needs to be put in place at the international level, and hurdles and unjust commercial tariffs need to be removed to facilitate access to the global market, especially in regard to commodities such as textiles, clothes and agricultural products, for whose production and supply the developing countries currently enjoy an advantage.

Developing countries are delighted that 0.7 per cent of the industrialized countries' GDP is to be allocated in the form of official development assistance. This will form an effective tool for the fulfilment of the Millennium Development Goals and for the consolidation of North-South relations. The efforts of Norway and other countries in this regard are to be applauded; however, it is regrettable that these commitments have not been fully implemented by all countries. The rational globalization model should offer all countries, especially the developing States, a fairer chance at a national level to prevent political, economic and social reforms from heading towards a stalemate.

Post-September 11, labour force migration is fast developing into a major concern for both countries of origin and destination. It is my hope that the 92nd Session of the International Labour Conference will address the growing concern regarding labour force migration at the global level and encourage the ILO member States, especially those hosting immigrants, to reach an international consensus on sustainable policies to bring an end to illegal migration and boost legal emigration. Migration has undergone a dramatic change over the last decade, so much so that today, a huge number of immigrants are educated people in highly skilled vocations, especially from the developing countries. As a result, devising more open national laws, especially in countries hosting immigrants, and advocating the rights of the immigrant workforce are among the principal issues that should top the ILO's technical cooperation programmes.

To foster globalization, the Islamic Republic of Iran has placed development and tripartism at the top of its socio-economic agenda, deeming it a solid bridge to the link the social partners. In this regard, the Islamic Republic of Iran has chosen dialogue as the most effective means to bring down the walls of distrust among these partners and to promote confidence-building. The fact that numerous workshops, in collaboration with the Geneva-based ILO experts, as well as with the Sub-Regional Office in New Delhi, have been held, both in the past and, particularly during this year, is indicative of the Islamic Republic of Iran's serious commitment to this.

Thanks to the Iranian President's efforts and the Government's firm resolve, the Fourth Economic Development Plan aims at generating employment. Enjoying a 7.4 per cent economic growth rate, the Iranian Government created around 700,000 jobs in 2002-03. The material and spiritual needs of workers are of the utmost importance to the Islamic Republic of Iran and, as such, I am pleased to announce that the Decent Work Agenda has been incorporated into the Fourth Economic, Social and Cultural Development Plan for implementation and that the measure will gradually be extended to the informal sector.

Original French: Mr. TOU *(Minister of Labour, Employment and Youth, Burkina Faso)*

It is an honour and a pleasure to take the floor and, first of all, to congratulate on behalf of my country, Burkina Faso, and on my own behalf, Mr. Ray Guevara and the other Officers of the Conference on their election to preside over our Conference.

Allow me also to congratulate the Director-General of the International Labour Office for his excellent Report, *ILO programme implementation 2002-03*.

Although considerable progress has been made, the Report also reflects the concerns of the international community, including poverty reduction and the issue of employment. The Report comes at a very special time, marked by the setting up of the World Commission on the Social Dimension of Globalization.

The establishment of the Commission has been widely acclaimed and its work has highlighted the numerous needs and challenges facing our Organization and the international community, in particular unemployment, the protection of migrant workers and social protection for all.

On the same subject, I am happy to report that the Commission has enabled our Organization to enhance the clarity and impact of its work. As the Director-General so aptly put it in his Report, *A fair Globalization: The role of the ILO*, by putting fairness at centre stage, the Commission clearly engages the institutional values of the ILO. As a member of the Commission, I am proud of my modest contribution to its work, and entirely satisfied with its main conclusions, in so far as the report takes into account the major concerns of the African peoples for a more equitable globalization bringing opportunities for all.

As regards the other items on the agenda of this session, allow me to make a few remarks.

The Director-General's Report, *ILO programme implementation 2002-03*, bears witness to the substantial progress made in the implementation of the four strategic objectives.

As regards the promotion and application of standards and fundamental principles and rights at work, my country commends the special attention given to child labour. By addressing this problem and contributing to its solution, the usefulness of standards in the development process is confirmed yet again. My country takes a keen interest in following the implementation of cooperation programmes in this field.

The importance of tripartism and social dialogue in the development process cannot be overemphasized; neither can the need to strengthen it by providing it with a sound framework.

Despite the real difficulties hampering its effectiveness, social dialogue is a key component of the design and implementation of economic and social policies in our countries. Promoting social dialogue and tripartite cooperation is a priority for the Government of Burkina Faso.

To this end, my country has set up appropriate machinery taking due account of the concerns put forward by the social partners, in particular through an annual meeting between the Prime Minister and the representative of the country's trade unions; an annual meeting between the Government and the trade unions to hear the workers' grievances; an annual meeting between the Government and the private sector to hear their concerns in the context of promotion of entrepreneurship and business; and involvement of employers and workers in the design of sectoral policies, in particular through promoting the activities of the Consultative Labour Commission.

Allow me to point out that, if social injustice is a danger to humankind, it is high time for us to mobilize against poverty and unemployment, which are its principal manifestations.

Hence the relevance in this context of the Global Employment Agenda approved in 2002, aimed at more and better jobs worldwide.

While the fact remains that poverty is incurred through a multitude of different factors, such as crises and upheavals, the spread of AIDS and poor governance, it must be borne in mind that employment is the key factor in the fight against poverty.

My country, Burkina Faso, is keenly aware of this. At national level, a number of measures have been taken in this respect, in particular, the elaboration of the national employment policy, the national social protection policy and the mobilization of resources to support job creation, vocational training and apprenticeship.

My country has also embraced employment promotion as a key element in poverty alleviation. To this end, our Head of State, His Excellency Blaise Compaoré, has proposed an Extraordinary Summit of Heads of State and Government of the African Union on Employment and Poverty Alleviation in Africa, to be held in Ouagadougou on 8 and 9 September this year. This summit will be preceded by a forum of the social partners and a ministerial meeting on the same subject.

I would like to commend African leaders for their support for this initiative, which will certainly be an important milestone in the determination of Africans to identify and implement themselves the concrete solutions that can free African populations from poverty, unemployment and underemployment. This will certainly be Africa's way out of marginalization.

I would like to convey here all my thanks to the International Labour Office for its constant support in the preparations for the abovementioned meeting.

To conclude, I hope that our deliberations here will give a new impetus to the fight for social justice and lasting peace.

Mr. KJØRVEN (State Secretary, Ministry of Foreign Affairs, Norway)

Fair globalization, creating opportunities for all, is indeed one of the more pressing issues of international affairs at the beginning of this millennium. Fairness and inclusion are not only ends in themselves, but equally important as a means to achieving social stability and sustainable peace.

On behalf of Norway, I would like to thank Presidents Halonen and Mkapa, and all the members of the World Commission, including the Director-General Juan Somavia, for making these points abundantly clear to all of us.

Knowing the Director-General and what he stands for, I was not at all surprised to receive his impressive Report on the role of the ILO in the follow-up of the Commission's Report. Congratulations!

You have given us ample food for thought – on the issue as such, on the role of the ILO, and, not least, on our own roles as member States and ultimate owners of this and all other relevant intergovernmental organizations.

Norway fully agrees that the time has come to make the social dimension and, particularly decent work for all, a global goal. We agree that we must move beyond the current state of affairs, where quality employment is treated as merely an expected outcome of our pursuit of economic targets. Decent Work for All must be made an end in itself, not only in the corridors of the ILO and in labour ministries or trade unions, but throughout economic policies, at both national and international levels.

As recent surveys show: if you ask the poor themselves, access to work, or starting a business on their own are the most important avenues out of poverty. Thus, the relevance of the ILO in today's world is clear as day.

Director-General, we welcome your call for revitalizing the ILO. To Norway, such revitalization should have two dimensions, recalling that you have an integrated economic and social mandate and, not least, recalling your unique tripartite structure.

Firstly, on the action of the ILO: recognizing that respect for core labour standards, in each and every country of the globalized economy, is vital to achieving fair and sustainable development; you should strengthen your efforts in promoting decent work and labour standards at the country level, in close cooperation with member States, workers and employers, and within the framework of the overall UN efforts, thereby contributing actively to achieving the Millennium Development Goals.

A more vital and action-oriented ILO, promoting labour standards, not only implies more technical assistance and improvement in supervision, monitoring and promotional work. It also implies, as you rightly point out in your Report, a more active use of the full normative mandate, including in the reaction to cases of grave and persistent abuse, in accordance with the ILO Constitution's article 33.

We agree that this also calls for increased effort on behalf of member States, workers and employers. We agree that decent work, socio-economic floors and proactive employment policies should be given higher priority – in national poverty-reduction strategies and in international development cooperation.

Let me now turn to the second dimension of a revitalized labour organization, ILO the advocate: we agree, as you also point out in your Report, that the ILO, in staying true to the mandate, has an obligation to interact with other relevant organizations.

We therefore welcome the more proactive role you personally have taken in the follow-up of the Commission's report, advocating this message both in other relevant organizations, such as the United Nations, the World Bank, the IMF and the WTO, as well as in member States. A more integrated approach to socio-economic policies through better coherence is crucial.

We find several of the proposals to promote such policy coherence worth considering. In the first instance, we would welcome constructive reflection around the suggested Policy Coherence Initiative on global growth, investment and employment.

And again, Director-General, as the globalization agenda goes way beyond the ILO, the fruits of your efforts ultimately depend on us, the member States. Coherence starts at home. Norway will therefore actively contribute to bring this agenda forward in all relevant organizations, not least in the United Nations.

Finally, I would like to bring special attention to a cross-cutting issue of the utmost importance – an issue which both you and the Commission in your reports have emphasized as fundamental to combating poverty and achieving a fair globalization. The issue is formalization of the vast, and in many developing countries rapidly increasing, informal economy.

As eloquently explained by one of your fellow members of the Commission, Dr Hernando de Soto, the lack of access to secure property rights deprives hundreds of millions of the world's poorest people from participation in the formal economy, indeed, they fear participation in globalization. This is, in itself, a key barrier to employment creation and to decent work.

This needs our immediate attention and should be addressed at both the country level and at international level, and the ILO should play an important role.

Today, peoples and leaders in developing countries and economies in transition in many parts of the world seem to understand the importance of property rights for economic development far better than most industrialized countries – perhaps because we have forgotten their impact on our own history.

I thank you, Mr. Somavia, for taking on this challenge and inviting everyone present to join in the debate on how best to respond to the call from the poor: "Give us the chance to make a living!" Most poor people are not asking for handouts. They are asking for the opportunity to open a business or to find a decent job. Let us pay attention. This is fundamentally a question of governance, and, as the Director-General pointed out, good governance at both national and global levels must go hand in hand. We must all accept and embrace responsibility. This is the road to fairer globalization.

Original Arabic: Mr. AL-HAJJI (Minister of Social Affairs and Labour, Minister of Electricity and Water Supply, speaking on behalf of the Cooperation Council for the Arab States of the Gulf, Kuwait)

In the name of God, the Merciful, the Compassionate! I want first of all to take the floor on behalf of the countries of the Cooperation Council for the Arab States of the Gulf and I would like to congratulate the President on his election and to convey to Mr. Somavia my appreciation for the way in which he is conducting the work of this Organization. The Director-General has played a major role in directing the work of this Organization with determination and resolve in order to ensure social protection, social justice and equality.

Likewise, I wish to express my appreciation for the technical assistance granted by the Beirut Regional Office.

Our countries have carefully studied the Report presented by the Director-General concerning the situation of Arab workers in Palestine and in other occupied Arab territories and we would all here again like to express our appreciation for the interest shown and the efforts made by the Director-General in this area. We also appreciate the role played by the Commission of Inquiry and the participation of the ILO in the financing and the support of the Palestinian Fund for Employment and Social Protection. We emphasize the importance of continuing the support of that fund.

We are following with concern the deterioration of the situation in the occupied Palestinian territories because of the policy of aggression and destruction adopted by the Government of Israel and also because of the unilateral polices such as the attempts to block the road map and the construction of the separation wall in flagrant violation of international law. The Palestinian cause does not only concern the suffering of a people but is in itself a humanitarian issue which requires the concerted efforts of the international community in order to put an end to the occupation of the Palestinian territories and the Arab territories that have been occupied since 1967, including the Golan Heights and the Lebanese territories, so as to enable the Palestinian people to build its own independent State with its capital in Al-Quds.

With regards to Iraq, we congratulate the Iraqi people on having chosen their President and for having appointed a transitional Government. We hope that full sovereignty will be handed over at the at the end of this month.

I would like to underscore the importance of migration for employment, given that this is extremely important for this session of the Conference. Indeed, it is an important and sensitive issue due to the rapid growth in immigration, the increase in unemployment, the deterioration in living standards and the multiplication of armed conflicts and wars. So far as migrant workers are concerned, we have to say that our countries have a unique composition. We have a very large number of migrant workers in the counties of the Cooperation Council for the Arab States of the Gulf, sometimes reaching 60 to 80 per cent of the total workforce.

In our countries we have the good fortune of being able to provide job opportunities. A large number of people of all nationalities come to our countries, skilled and unskilled labour. They do not intend to stay permanently but to have short-term contracts to work for limited periods of time on development projects in the Cooperation Council countries, which, of course, have very great advantages, both for the countries of origin of migrant workers as well as for host countries.

When speaking of the remarkable Report of the Director-General concerning the Social Dimension of Globalization, that is before us for consideration, we would like to give our support to its content and to the conclusions of the Commission on Social Dimension of Globalization about the need to allow all peoples to benefit from globalization. We must establish a multilateral framework with clear, transparent rules regulating cross border movement of persons so that we can strike a balance between migrant-sending and host countries to achieve more effective cooperation in the regulation of international migration.

In conclusion, I would like to assure you that our countries wish to give their support to all ILO projects which involve strategic goals for justice and progress.

Original Arabic: Ms. DELLO *(Minister of Social Affairs and Labour, Syrian Arab Republic)*

It is my pleasure to extend, on my own behalf and on behalf of the delegation of the Syrian Arab Republic, my heartfelt congratulations to the President of the Conference for the confidence that has been placed in him and to wish him every success in his mission. We hope that the work of the Conference will be crowned with success under his wise leadership, and that it will be able to adopt proposals and recommendations that will contribute to the promotion of decent work, the application of occupational safety and health standards and the creation of employment opportunities for all.

I would like to commend the efforts made by the Director-General of the ILO, the ILO Regional Office for the Arab States in Beirut and the mission which prepared the Report entitled *The Situation of workers in occupied Arab territories*. It is an objective report, which calls things by their name. It reports cases of discrimination between Palestinian and Syrian Arab citizens in the occupied Arab territories, on the one hand, and Israeli settlers who have seized lands and resources, on the other. It also cites the arbitrary imposition of taxes and penalties, adversely affecting citizens' lives.

The ideal solution to redress the economic and humanitarian situation of Arab citizens lies in the eradication of its chief cause, namely the Israeli occupation.

To quote the preface of the Report presented by the Director-General of the ILO, Mr. Juan Somavia, on the situation of Arab workers of the occupied Arab territories, "the situation prevailing in the occupied Arab territories continues to be a source of tension in the region and beyond: this at a time when all available energies and resources need to be harnessed for dialogue to improve the overall political, economic and social conditions in the region".

The Report examines "the impact that the heightened state of tension in the territories has on the daily life and work of Palestinian women and men and their families, and on their institutions". The Report documents in detail the many obstacles Palestinians face in trying to earn a living and support themselves in dignity and independence. It also shows the extraordinary resilience of the human spirit in overcoming the barriers to a normal life to make a space for physical and mental survival".

The expression uttered by one of the Syrian citizens in occupied Syrian Golan gives us in a nutshell the essence of the case. He said, and I quote: "We are strangers in our own house".

Despite the difficulties it is experiencing, the Syrian Arab Republic has improved and modernized working conditions in accordance with the instructions given by President Bashar El-Assad and with the method followed in the process of modernization and improvement, this being done in close cooperation between the Government, the workers and employers in an effort to modernize legislation and labour relations.

The Syrian Arab Republic has managed to honour its commitment to the ILO and respect its Constitution and principles. Syria has ratified the eight core Conventions, the most recent of which were Minimum Age Convention, 1973 (No. 138), and the Worst Forms of Child Labour Convention, 1999 (No. 182). Thus Syria has ratified 48 Conventions in all and several legislative texts have been amended in order to comply with those Conventions.

The Syrian Arab Republic is the cradle of civilization and of humanity and it is duty-bound to denounce all violations of international law, or of the Constitution of this Organization.

This Conference is meeting at a time when the Middle East is experiencing a considerable deterioration in the working conditions and living conditions of its citizens. This situation is characterized by the barbaric practices of the Israeli occupying forces who starve and murder, destroy infrastructure and home and build settlements and this wall which divides the territories. These practices seriously harm workers and employers alike. They constitute a flagrant violation of the Fourth Geneva Convention, of international law and of the Charter of the United Nations. This requires a firm and determined stance by the international community to bring this occupation of the Arab territories to an end.

In conclusion, we reiterate our support for the Palestinian people. We call for support for the Palestinian Fund for Employment and Social Protection so as to reduce poverty and unemployment. Thank you for your attention and I wish you every success in your work.

Mr. SWAIN *(Minister of Labour, New Zealand)*

I would like to congratulate the President on election to preside over this 92nd Session of the International Labour Conference. I would like to congratulate the Director-General on his Report, *ILO programme implementation 2002-03*, and particularly on the assessment of the progress made and the challenges faced by the International Labour Organization in implementing the Decent Work Agenda. I would also like to congratulate the Director-General for sponsoring the World Commission on the Social Dimension of Globalization.

As the recently appointed New Zealand Minister of Labour, I look forward to continuing New Zealand's tradition of active engagement with, and support of, the activities of the ILO.

I would like to share with you a few aspects of New Zealand's progress with implementing the Decent Work Agenda in areas that complement the activities described in the Report and that demonstrate that New Zealand is facing similar organizational challenges.

New Zealand supports the introduction and implementation of strategic budgeting and results-based management into the ILO. The integration of an outcomes approach to government activity is a current challenge being faced by New Zealand.

As the Minister of Labour, I am focused on helping New Zealanders achieve high quality working lives in thriving and inclusive communities. I see very clear linkages between this outcome and the Decent Work Agenda. To achieve this outcome, the Department of Labour's work is broken down into four areas of focus: the workplace, the workforce, work opportunities and international participation. The Department is undergoing a structural change to align itself with these outcomes, much as the ILO has done in respect of the four strategic objectives of decent work. The focus is ensuring that the greatest connections are made within our organization so that we are best placed to provide information, services and support to everyone in the labour market.

Improving workplace relationships and productivity are priority areas for New Zealand, as we see them as key factors in sustaining economic growth. Productivity is not about employees working harder for less pay. It is about businesses operating smarter. New Zealand's focus is on finding business practices that improve timeliness and quality, minimize costs and waste and involve employee participation in innovation and technology. We have set up a Workplace Productivity Working Group to stimulate debate, collect information and help identify priorities for future action. This working group relies heavily on input from our social partners, and we look forward to sharing what we have learned with you in the near future.

The Report notes that one of the strengths of the ILO is its tripartite structure. New Zealand has traditionally had a strong tripartite dynamic. The New Zealand Government is currently looking at ways to encourage tripartite structures. One example is that the Government has recently endorsed a five-year plan of action to implement pay and employment equity in the public service, together with the public health and education sectors. Worker and employer representatives are on the steering group that will oversee and monitor the implementation of this plan.

The debate that occurred today on the report of the World Commission, *A fair globalization: Creating opportunities for all* revealed the diversity of issues faced by individual countries in working to maximize the social benefits arising from globalization. Our Prime Minister, the Right Honourable Helen Clark, has outlined New Zealand's views on the report and the proposals by the World Commission. As our Prime Minister said, the theme of the report is within the existing mandate of the ILO but there is also a need for all relevant organizations to work together to ensure that the benefits of globalization are enjoyed by all.

This is a time of increased demand for the ILO to be involved in international debate, while also maintaining momentum on its core activities. The Director-General's Report rightly acknowledges that competing resources will require prioritization and a reassessment of current activities.

In conclusion, New Zealand supports the Director-General's ongoing efforts to reform the ILO. We believe that the ILO is in a strong position to contribute to the challenges of work in the twenty-first century. New Zealand looks forward to continuing its support for the ILO's programme implementation.

Mr. DIMOVSKI *(Minister of Labour, Family and Social Affairs, Slovenia)*

First of all, I wish to welcome the excellently prepared report of the World Commission on the Social Dimension of Globalization, which includes a series of concrete proposals focused on equalizing opportunities arising from the process itself. I strongly believe that the report will provide an important basis for future action at global, regional and national levels to extend the benefits of globalization to all. In this regard, I would like to associate myself with the statement already presented by the Irish Minister on behalf of the European Union.

We are all aware that although globalization brings numerous benefits, they are not equally distributed among countries and individuals. In order for the advantages of globalization to be experienced by as many people as possible, carefully planned management of the globalization process is needed. This consequently requires coordinated action and broad-based dialogue among the various actors.

In line with this, I wish to mention the significant role of international institutions responsible for shaping and implementing international policies. In contrast to the often-discussed economic dimension of globalization, one could argue that, at the international level, its social consequences have been relatively neglected until recent years. In this respect, the ILO's initiative to establish a World Commission on the Social Dimension of Globalization has not only brought about a necessary counterweight to the prevailing trade-oriented discussions, but will also significantly contribute to more integrated views of economic and social objectives in the future. In addition, the already broad-based internal dialogue enabled by the ILO's unique tripartite structure should be supplemented by enhanced coordination with other institutions. This would enable effective monitoring of the different aspects of globalization.

Despite the fact that international institutions are taking over some of the responsibilities traditionally in the hands of nation States, the latter continue to be the basic and essential facilitators of balanced development. It is important to be aware that, in the case of Slovenia, the State as an aggregate of various political interests, was the decisive factor in ensuring that stable economic growth was also accompanied by the relative equality in society. This argument is very important at a time when we are more and more often confronted with pressures that suggest that globalization requires radical reform of the social state. In most cases, States continue to determine the extent to which policies agreed at the global level are in fact implemented, depending on their commitment to universal values. Slovenia accords great attention to the full implementation of international commitments, including those arising from membership of the ILO.

I would like here to highlight the important role of the ILO as an Organization which sets standards to ensure women and men decent work and successfully promotes their implementation at State level. With its system of monitoring, it also provides one of the means of monitoring respect for the social dimension of the globalization process. Slovenia has ratified all of the eight core ILO Conventions which provide a social grounding for the global economy, and also 65 other Conventions. Their implementation provides a firm basis for the successful path towards accomplishing the four strategic objectives of the Decent Work Agenda.

Together with its endeavours to achieve the aforementioned aims, Slovenia has gained considerable experience during the period of transition to the market economy, which it will gladly share with the countries that could benefit from it. I am thinking in particular of good experiences in the area of social partnership, reform of the pension system, reform of the labour market and measures for reducing poverty and increasing social inclusion. These have already been presented on a number of occasions to countries of south-east Europe, confronted with similar challenges. Slovenia wishes to enhance these activities so that they become an integral part of regional development cooperation policies.

Original Spanish: Ms. ROSAS PÉREZ *(Government delegate, Panama)*

The Republic of Panama wishes to take this opportunity to congratulate the President and Vice-Presidents elected to preside over this 92nd Session of the International Labour Conference, which began its deliberations on 1 June and will conclude on 17 June 2004.

We express our pleasure and satisfaction with the scheduling on the agenda of the Report of the Chairperson of the Governing Body and the Report of the Director-General, Mr. Juan Somavia. We note that the Director-General's Report provides details of programme implementation and activities carried out by the Organization during the financial year 2002-03, together with proposals on long-term planning, information on the steps taken by the Governing Body and the office of the Director-General to give effect to the decisions adopted by the Conference at its previous meetings, and the results achieved.

We also welcome the tabling for due consideration in this forum of the document entitled *A fair globalization – The role of the ILO* also put forward by the Director-General. The Report draws on the conclusions contained in the Report of the World Commission on the Social Dimension of Globalization, which in our view is of crucial importance, given the evident inequalities that result from an inadequate governance of globalization. That governance of globalization in the way it has been implemented in terms of its rules and policies has become disjointed from considerations of social equilibrium, and the rules and polices widen the existing poverty gap with inevitable consequences for our peoples.

In this regard, we agree with the view set out in the proposal by Director-General in the sense that, in order to achieve positive change in the globalization process and in order to achieve fairness, equal opportunities and social justice, we need to pool the determination, efforts and commitment of all social actors, with a view to planning and implementing international policies that promote the incorporation of a social dimension that would generate good governance and that would also favour nations that until now have benefited less from the globalization process.

According to information from the Panama's Ministry of the Economy and Finances, the Republic of Panama is one of the ten most globalized Latin American countries. Nevertheless, because of the inequalities caused by the implementation of a system of governance designed by more economically developed countries with the limited involvement of developing countries, when it comes to negotiating regulations there is a disadvantage: Panama is struggling against the consequences of this subjection and understands that the key to our countries joining the globalization process on equal footing is integration, through the adoption of joint strategies and by strengthening our regional position so that we are able to exercise specific influence on the implementation of new rules and policies for a fairer and more equitable globalization.

This is the direction of and the message contained in the second Panama Declaration which resulted from the special meeting of the Council of Ministers of Labour of Central America and the Dominican Republic, and which was signed in Panama on 20 May 2004. The Declaration proposes that we participate actively as a group in harmony with the different groups that already exist in the Americas, namely the group of the Americas (GRUA) and the group of Latin American and Caribbean Countries (GRULAC), by tabling initiatives that will enable our peoples to adapt successfully to the global economy.

By way of conclusion, my delegation wishes to thank the Organization for the interest it has shown in considering and finding a solution to this issue of great importance for the whole world and more particularly for developing countries. We reiterate our willingness as a country to join forces in this great mission, namely that of achieving a fairer globalization for all.

Original French: Mr. PERIGOT *(representative of the International Organisation of Employers)*

On behalf of the IOE, I would like to congratulate the Director-General on his Report on the implications of the report of the World Commission on the Social Dimension of Globalization for the work of the ILO. Over the last two years I have had the privilege of participating, in a personal capacity, in the work of the Commission and I would like to take the opportunity given to me today to express IOE's position on the way the ILO should react to the recommendations in the Director-General's Report.

The report of the World Commission recognizes the potential benefits of globalization and also recognizes its potential in terms of economic and social development. The conditions needed for this entail giving real and serious consideration to the basic principles and values that must imbue the democratic market economy model. Essentially, this means that all the actors of a society resting on private initiative and a free market must shoulder their responsibility. They must all practise good governance and demonstrate commitment, be they citizens, governments, national institutions or international institutions.

The report recognizes the central role that business creation and growth play in economic development, job creation and hence, poverty alleviation. This is not a lone view. The Director-General was able to ascertain this as a member of a commission established by UNDP, which in its recent report *Unleashing entrepreneurship*, also clearly noted this fact.

(The speaker continues in English.)

The ILO response therefore needs to reinforce the fundamental message and the Director-General's statements in his Report that call for more to be done on employment creation and the creation of the economic conditions that would allow business to succeed have our full support. We have long argued that employment creation should lie at the heart of the work of the ILO. The Employment Sector should reinforce its programmes as part of the ongoing development of the Global Employment Agenda. Similarly, existing focuses on youth employment, the informal economy and skills development provide a ready-made response by the ILO to the recommendations of the World Commission. The World Commission also stressed the fact that the best way to respond to globalization was by first taking action at the local level. Again, the ILO is currently well placed, on account of its presence through a large national and regional network, to focus on the needs of its constituents. Each country is different, each country's needs and priorities are different. The strength of the ILO and its mandate lies in harnessing that national potential through strong social partners. The Director-General also emphasized this and we welcome his idea of paying more attention to strengthening the social partners so as to enhance their capacity to contribute to their national development.

The IOE believes that a major opportunity now exists for employers to intensify their efforts and give more focus to the numerous initiatives companies are taking on corporate social responsibility. The IOE is ready to actively explore areas of collaboration with the ILO in the labour field, including the international forum suggested in the World Commission report.

Over the last few years, the ILO has also provided a unique forum where topical issues related to the social dimension of globalization could be discussed in open and frank exchanges with governments and multilateral actors. The Governing Body's Working Party on the Social Dimension of Globalization should be further encouraged to bring to the attention of the ILO the views and issues that require debate. It is through this forum that the ILO and its constituents can really have an impact on achieving a better understanding among international and multilateral actors of the need for more collaboration and cooperation in meeting challenges of the future. The ability of the ILO to bring various actors together, its unique tripartite structure and its relevant mandate combine within the Working Party to provide an avenue for dialogue which would be difficult to replicate elsewhere.

This discussion here is but one step in a process of working out ideas on how the ILO should respond to issues of relevance to its mandate. The debate will continue in November at the Governing Body where these ideas will be considered alongside others in the melting pot of the Programme, Financial and Administrative Committee. The ILO does not have unlimited resources and is unlikely either to have the luxury of resources sufficient to meet all the aspirations of its three constituents, so it will have to focus, be realistic in its expectations and give greater recognition to the tools and means of action it already has to respond to the issues that will, through social dialogue and consensus, be identified as being the business of the ILO.

The IOE is a network of 138 national employers' organizations in 133 countries, most of them in developing countries. It is the largest network of organizations both large and small representing the private sector, throughout the world. The IOE regards this report and its recommendations as an opportunity and it takes a positive proactive approach. We will strive to involve our members and to promote a debate within our organization on the Report's recommendations and its implications for IOE members at the national, regional and international level. The IOE now intends to engage with other international actors, such as the World Bank, UNDP, OAS, OECD and the development banks in exploring ways to spread the benefits of globalization to all.

We believe that there is, through effective follow-up, a great opportunity to show that the work of the ILO over the last 85 years was relevant and remains relevant to the world and that, by implementing that mandate, ongoing labour and social policy challenges can be addressed by the right actors of the world of work.

Original Bosnian: Mr. HALILOVIĆ *(Minister of Civil Affairs, Bosnia and Herzegovina)*

I have the particular honour and pleasure of attending this 92nd Session of the International Labour Conference and of having a chance to extend regards to this Convention on behalf of the tripartite delegation of Bosnia and Herzegovina, Council of Ministers of Bosnia and Herzegovina and in my personal capacity. In this brief address I would like to congratulate the ILO for its decision to initiate preparation of the report of the World Commission on the Social Dimension of Globalization, to place it on the agenda and to launch a dialogue on issues pertaining to the economic and social objectives of the economy.

The reason for my pleasure in launching the global dialogue on this matter is the fact that globalization affects developing and poor countries in particular and the report seeks to highlight a need for the global processes to lead to enhanced justice and consequent global stability. As you are aware Bosnia and Herzegovina is a country in transition, in addition to being a country that emerged from the war several years ago and, among other things, it still has to cope with structural problems, mass unemployment and poverty. The devastating aftermath of the war is still evident, not only in its physical and economic structure, but also in its rapid accession to global processes. Furthermore, the war affected its most valuable asset, human resources, human potential, the foundation of every society. Therefore, the report's emphasis on the effects of globalization on people's life and work, not least in the context of fairer socio-economic relations, makes the report particularly important for us.

The role of the ILO in shaping just globalization is not only part of its ongoing efforts to contribute to global stability, but also confirms its capacity to identify and react to the challenges of the modern world in a timely manner. I would like to take this opportunity to refer to the constant support the ILO has extended and continues to extend to Bosnia and Herzegovina which has yet to recover fully from the destruction of the war. During the war and in the immediate post-war period, international aid to Bosnia and Herzegovina was targeted primarily towards humanitarian aid and physical reconstruction and now it reflects more of a necessity to support the democratic processes in the country.

Through active partnership between the government and social partners, the ILO has drawn up and implemented the technical cooperation programme. This assistance has continued up until now and I would like to take this opportunity to extend, on behalf of the Council of Ministers of Bosnia and Herzegovina, words of thanks to both the ILO and bilateral donor countries, for their financial support in this regard.

I sincerely hope the assistance will continue, particularly bearing in mind the numerous challenges which Bosnia and Herzegovina is facing now, including those stemming from globalization. We are also fully aware of the delay concerning our fulfilment of some of the obligations in respect to ILO membership, particularly reporting on the implementation of the Conventions we have ratified.

On this occasion I would like to appeal for your understanding, taking into account the complex nature, the structure of Bosnia and Herzegovina and its slowness in forming its new institutions and fostering existing state institutions because the funding of these is a serious obstacle to the effectiveness and the speed with which we have delivered our commitments.

Finally, I wish this session of the International Labour Conference every success in its work.

Mr. RYDER (Representative, International Confederation of Free Trade Unions)

The International Confederation of Free Trade Unions (ICFTU) welcomed the report of the World Commission on the Social Dimension of Globalization, and today we welcome the Report submitted to the Conference by the Director-General. It serves well the purpose for which it was written: to enable the ILO's tripartite constituents to meet the challenge of putting this Organization at the forefront of the struggle for a fair globalization. The Commission and the Director-General have helped to take the globalization debate out of the crossfire of polemics and the halls of academia. They have offered a way to break the policy impasse which has allowed the injustices of the status quo to persist long after its dangers and its dysfunctions have become so flagrantly obvious.

We have before us today not another discourse on globalization, but a set of concrete proposals of the utmost significance. They are realistic; they are practical; they are pertinent to the key policy issues of the day; they deserve our support and our engagement. So the ICFTU's answer to the challenge that the Director-General puts to us is yes; we are ready to play our role in improving the key initiatives he outlines and, more importantly, in making their implementation successful. The ICFTU is preparing for its own World Congress dedicated to the task of organizing and strengthening the capacities of our international movement to meet the challenges of globalization, and we will equally mobilize those capacities behind this agenda for justice in the global economy.

It is a strength of the Report that it recognizes that the values resoundingly proclaimed in the ILO Constitution and 60 years ago in the Declaration of Philadelphia have to be at the heart of any approach to globalization today. They call on us to prosecute the war on want with unrelenting vigour. It is a call that has frankly gone unheeded by the policy orthodoxies of the last quarter century which, with unrelenting monotony, have served up the same mantras that have got us to where we are now. Now, if we choose to act, we can put that right. It is a strength too that the Report argues so strongly that tripartism and social dialogue are essential tools for fashioning a fair globalization. Together these two constitute a tremendous statement of confidence in the objectives and the potential of our Organization. But it is clear equally that the ILO cannot and should not do the job on its own. Its mandate is wider than some have interpreted it as being. For different reasons, large parts of the ILO's mandates have been left untended for too long and that is to the detriment of the ILO and of the international system's work on globalization. Because just as different policy dimensions of globalization intersect, so too do the mandates of different international organizations. That does not have to lead us into a series of institutional frontier wars; instead, as the Report says, it points to the compelling and urgent need for cooperation and coherence between organizations.

So, let us set up the policy coherence initiative on growth, investment and employment. If it works well, then others must follow. Equally we urge the Director-General to act on the Commission's call for the ILO to take the lead in the establishment of the Globalization Policy Forum. We welcome too, the idea of policy development dialogues on foreign direct investment flows, and on corporate social responsibility and the vision of a global framework for migration, which can be advanced by work being done already at this session of the Conference.

The Commission rightly did not shirk its responsibility to call for acceleration of the universal realization of workers' fundamental rights. No issues, no challenge is greater than that of reversing those workings of the global economy which today offer reward for violation of workers' rights, for example, in the world's export processing zones, which do so little to promote their respect. So, the ICFTU welcomes the Commission's call to strengthen the ILO's international labour standards system and stands ready to explore constructively, with the Director-General, the specifics of how it might more effectively capture the essentials of the Decent Work approach.

This is of course at the very centre of the ILO's mandate. The Director-General is right to point to that respecting the rights of the world's workers depends on the commitment of numerous global actors and institutions. Trade unions understand and support the concept of decent work as a package of objectives of which universal respect of fundamental rights is but one. It is a logical, yet innovative step in making decent work a global policy objective to propose, as the Director-General does, that it be given form in a worldwide social economic floor for globalization. And so by placing full employment generation, generating a secure income, and universal access to basic social protection firmly at the centre of our agenda, the Director-General has reminded us of our responsibilities, and today there are global responsibilities to fight together the war on wants and against poverty and exclusion. And as we weigh today the likely results of acting on these challenges, let us ponder also the consequences of inaction. At this time of deep insecurity and conflict in the world, we should recall that social justice remains the surest guarantee of universal and lasting peace. And joining together to fight this war is our best contribution to making sure that we and our children will not fight others.

Original German: Ms. DEMBSHER *(Government delegate, Austria)*

In the wake of the discussion this morning, I would like to focus on the recommendations of the World Commission and the contributions of the ILO to the implementation of those recommendations in so far as they are covered by the ILO mandate.

The World Commission's report is a comprehensive picture of the socio-economic aspects of globalization and the proposals which have already been discussed with regard to strengthening the social dimension.

It goes without saying that Austria is also prepared to support other ways forward which have been proposed to allow decent work to become a goal for all international players. And in this respect, I would like to say a few words with regard to the recommendations of the World Commission.

Effective initiatives for a joined-up political approach are necessary – urgently necessary. Mechanisms must be defined more precisely with regard to how the core principles can become part and parcel of the activities of the Organization. The steps we have already taken in terms of growth, investment and employment are to be welcomed. A more joined-up, coherent approach can be achieved through recourse to and better use of existing structures. New bodies should only be set up in exceptional cases, where they can add some valid input to existing bodies.

A multilateral framework for investment is something that Austria has been calling for some time now. The WTO would indeed be an appropriate forum for such negotiations. At the same time, it is vital that social and ecological principles be taken into account.

With regard to the recommendations in the trade sector, I would like to point out that, in the WTO and at EU level, intensive work is being carried out with regard to solutions to this, in order to achieve the aim of the Doha Round – effective integration of the developing countries into the multilateral trade system. Now is not the time to go into the details of that, but what I will say is that the main and crucial factors here will be what consensus can be achieved to eliminate trade-distorting agricultural subsidies or to improve market access for agricultural and industrial goods. What will also be important is the degree of readiness of the more developed countries to provide improved conditions of market access for the developing countries.

It is vital that measures be taken with regard to respect for the human rights of all labour migrants and to ensure that migration can occur in a legal, well-ordered way and to combat human trafficking, racism and xenophobia are necessary or vital. However, before we generously encourage legal migration, the absorption capacity of the labour market and the implementation of minimum standards when hiring workers should be a priority.

Austria would be prepared to give its constructive support to a multilateral framework for a transnational mobility agreement, a formal mobility of persons which would indeed be comprehensive and balanced and be in the interest of the countries of origin and of reception. Because the low ratification rate of existing international standards is sometimes because of their inappropriate provisions. I could mention, for example, the United Nations Convention on the Protection of Migrants' Rights, which equates illegal labour migrants with legal ones.

The setting up of formal consultation structures, on the OECD model, with the international labour movement and the business community in the WTO, the IMF and the World Bank is something that Austria would basically not oppose, but we do raise the question of the value added of such a consultation procedure. In Austria, the social partners are very closely involved in shaping the position of national government with regard to those organizations anyway. And that seems to us to be a better way forward.

Since the Declaration of Philadelphia, the ILO's mandate has included an analysis function and a warning function with regard to the social consequences of international economic and fiscal measures. To do justice to this part of the ILO mandate, we must strengthen the economic expertise of the staff in the Office. Country audits with regard to the effects of fiscal and trade policy on social development should be carried out regularly by the ILO and appropriate international organizations and the results of those audits must be discussed and negotiated in coordination between all parties.

I have not been speaking only about ILO measures because, of course, an organization cannot rebalance globalization on its own. That is why it is important that governments should stand up for the integration of the aim of decent work and the protection of core labour standards in all international forums.

Mr. SWEENEY *(Workers' adviser and substitute delegate, United States)*

I want to thank the Director-General for his leadership in addressing one of the most difficult questions of our time: how do we bring the benefits of globalization to all people throughout the world? I am honoured to have served on the World Commission and to have had the opportunity to learn from and work with so many distinguished colleagues. A special thanks is owed to the co-chairpersons of the Commission, President Mkapa of the United Republic of Tanzania and President Halonen of Finland. They tackled a mission impossible. They had to focus Commissioners with very different perspectives, analysis and political realities to look at globalization through the eyes of people everywhere. The single most significant conclusion of the report was simply this: that decent work is the cornerstone of creating a fairer globalization. The Director-General urges us at this session of the Conference to take this central conclusion "decent work for all" and help to make it a global goal, not just an ILO goal. This is the right challenge and the right question to put to this 92nd Session. The mandate of the ILO to influence all national and international policies of an economic and financial character with a view to promoting social justice has been reinforced by the recommendations of the Commission.

For what does that mean for our practical work? Let me highlight a few of the specific proposals: at the national level, it means that realizing the rights of workers to form and organize unions. In my own country that would mean that millions of workers would have the opportunity to form unions, to live their lives and have a voice on the job without the intimidation and harassment that is so pervasive in our organizing campaigns. A vibrant labour movement can then work to achieve many of the objectives laid out in the report, including constructing an economic floor to stop the widening income gaps between rich and poor that are evident in all regions; extending social security to the excluded; promoting living wages; reforming minimum wages, income taxes and welfare benefits for low-waged workers. At the global level, it means creating global growth through decent work coordinated through the multilateral system. This means taking on all the obstacles to fair and equitable development; influencing poverty reduction strategies (PRSPs) and the economic framework underlying traditional adjustment, budget and fiscal policy; eliminating labour abuse in the global production systems; and calling for far-reaching activities for the ILO in the export processing zones; improving the quality of employment in small- and medium-sized enterprises, and broadening activities to provide incentives and technical cooperation on all aspects of job quality; supporting the work of this Conference in addressing a new multilateral framework for migration; and, most significantly, we much achieve respect for international labour standards worldwide.

We need to establish global coherence in the multilateral system and to look at macroeconomic financial trade investment and labour market policies through a global policy forum. The ILO should also undertake decent work audits of the World Bank, International Monetary Fund and World Trade Organization, to review the impact of their policies and programmes on core labour standards and employment. There is much to do: we have a mandate and a mission, and the Director-General has asked us to mobilize for change. Now is the time to go out and organize for a world of decent work for all.

Original Russian: Mr. EREMEEV *(Employers' delegate, Russian Federation)*

The Report of the Director-General, *ILO programme implementation 2002-03,* which we have before us, gives us the opportunity to take a critical look at the main results of ILO activity in the last two years, particularly from the point of view of the practical implementation of the Decent Work Programme. We would like to applaud the way the Report is set out: it is very concise but informative, and it sheds light on the state of play with regard to each of the four strategic objectives. Of course, this document is something that we are seeing as if through the prism of pressing concerns which need to be addressed by Russian employers, and also taking into account our experience of cooperation with the ILO.

If asked whether we have made any headway in terms of developing labour relations in The Russia Federation over the last two years, and whether our relationship with the ILO has been useful, we would answer "yes" without any hesitation. For two years now The Russian Federation has been living and working with a new Labour Code, incorporating the provisions of many ILO Conventions. By ratifying Convention No. 182, which bans the worst forms of child labour, The Russian Federation has completed the process of ratifying all eight core Conventions of the ILO. We are still working on the ratification of several other Conventions. We draw on ILO experience in our national programmes for poverty eradication, and in working to modernize our social, pensions and medical programmes, using insurance principles. Hand in hand with the ILO, Russian social partners are working on a series of practical projects, for example, to assess the social consequences of the Russian Federation's accession to the WTO. The fact that there is a good relationship between the Russian Federation and the ILO can be seen from the recent extension of the cooperation programme to 2004-05.

At the same time, in discussing the question of the implementation of the ILO programme for 2002-03, I have to express a certain amount of concern, at least on three counts. Firstly, we object to the complete lack of corresponding assessments in the Report from the social partners; we feel that their opinions should be represented in some form, particularly with regard to the implementation of projects, and that this would enhance the objectiveness of the document and the effectiveness of the work of the ILO itself. Secondly, we feel some of the aims and indicators used in the programmes are too subjective and contrived, thus becoming devoid of any practical meaning in terms of assessing the activity of the ILO; and finally, as was also the case two years ago, we once again regret the lack of attention paid to the opinions of employers in drawing up and implementing ILO operational programmes. On the one hand, some projects are launched which we do not feel bear any relation to priorities, and on the other there is an attempt to finance programmes of great importance to Russian employers on a "leftovers" basis, and we must and will continue to object to this practice.

We would like to express our gratitude to the Director-General, Mr. Somavia, for this very informative Report on the possible ways and means of implementing the recommendations of the World Commission on the Social Dimension of Globalization. The broad programme of ILO activity contained in the Report, seeking to strike a better balance in the process of globalization, deserves serious consideration at meetings of the Governing Body. We are planning to play a very active role there. Here, however, we would like to make two general remarks. First of all, we feel the need to warn against too broad an interpretation of the mandate of our Organization; this is something which is contemplated in some sections of the document. We feel that the ILO should focus its attention primarily on creating effective jobs, through stimulation of and support for enterprise, training for staff and developing human resources. With regard to the need for a better balance in the process of globalization, we feel this task should be achieved through the combined efforts of all the relevant international organizations.

We support the World Commission's report on the primordial importance of improving national methods of governance. In our opinion, the best contribution the ILO can make to fulfilling the World Commission's recommendations is not to broaden the theoretical debate but to provide practical assistance to the tripartite partners in achieving the aim of decent work.

Ms. KNUPPERT *(Workers' adviser and substitute delegate, Denmark)*

On behalf of the Danish Workers' delegation, I am proud to have the opportunity to congratulate you on having been elected President of this year's International Labour Conference.

The main theme for this year's Conference: *A fair globalization: Creating opportunities for all* is so comprehensive and so complex that we cannot cover it by focusing on a few individual issues. Generally speaking, all aspects of the way our societies act must be included in the discussions. Globalization is not an end in itself. Today, it is a precondition for the economic and social development of our society. Fair globalization can provide us all with invaluable benefits in the form of democracy, economic growth and equal opportunities for populations and nations.

Fighting globalization will prevent us from solving the world's most important problems and would create far more losers than winners.

I would like to thank the ILO for taking the initiative of setting up a World Commission on the Social Dimension of Globalization. The composition of this Commission alone contributes to giving the report political weight and promotes the discussion of and interest in the project. The proposal cannot be rejected simply on the grounds that it is yet another expert report. The challenge we all face is to secure the ILO initiative nationally. We need to define our own contribution to a national policy that provides the preconditions for globalization that creates opportunities for all.

My organization supports the initiatives of the ILO in favour of decent work, poverty reduction strategies and the promotion of regional cooperation.

Naturally, globalization is an issue which is also debated in Denmark. In our view, economic growth and low unemployment rates have always been closely linked with the possibilities of having free access to the European and global markets. This fact is hardly ever questioned in Denmark but there are, of course, many suggestions as to how Denmark should react to the effects of globalization. In Denmark, worst-case scenarios, such as millions of jobs will be moved abroad, have been proved wrong. Fears were, up to now, out of proportion. At the moment, Denmark has an unemployment rate of about 5 per cent, which is too high, of course. This contributes to increasing the fear of seeing workplaces moved abroad. The surveys made by the trade union movement show that, from 1993 to 2000, 126,000 new jobs were created in spite of the fact that imports and foreign investments rose considerably. This development primarily hit unskilled workers while there were more jobs for skilled workers and those who were highly educated.

My organization does not dismiss the possibility that outsourcing in workplaces may accelerate. However, we are of the opinion that a lot can be done to avoid any increase in the unemployment rate, but it requires taking conscious priorities.

The present Danish Government has given low priority to training and education and it has introduced user fees for adults and continuing education. The Danish trade union movement wants all young people to get a higher level of education. Those already in the labour market should have better opportunities of getting continuing education. Research and technology should, to a higher extent, support future development in the corporate sector. In Denmark, we traditionally have good cooperation between the social partners. The Danish Confederation of Trade Unions and the Danish Employers' Confederation, the two largest organizations in the Danish labour market, have recently concluded a collective agreement. In this agreement, we agree to jointly prepare a report on the international competitiveness of Danish companies with a view to examining how we can contribute to supporting a stable labour market. The continuous development of an efficient system of cooperation, bargaining and training is to be part of these discussions.

Allow me to mention a very concrete matter which is of importance to the Danish labour markets and relevant in connection with the ILO and globalization. In 1989, the organization I represent lodged a complaint with the ILO regarding the implementation of the Act of the Danish International Receipts Register. The Act discriminates against foreign seafarers without permanent residence in Denmark who work aboard Danish ships. These seafarers cannot be covered by a Danish collective agreement. The ILO Committee of Experts has asked the Danish Government to amend this Act time and time again. However, the Danish Government continues to refuse to bring the Act into conformity with the ILO's fundamental labour standards. I mention this example in order to illustrate that you cannot ignore problems in the international labour market by discriminating against certain workers and by ignoring fundamental rights that have been established by the ILO.

In my view, the ILO, the Heads of State from Finland and Tanzania, the Director-General of the ILO and the staff have provided an important contribution to improving international cooperation.

Mr. SZIRMAI *(Employers' delegate, Hungary)*

On behalf of the Hungarian Employers' delegation, I would like to congratulate the President on his election.

The year 2004 is an important year for Hungarian society. The first of May saw Hungary's accession to a Europe of 25. We Hungarian employers and entrepreneurs are aware of the enormous challenge this accession poses for us. In our ability to meet this challenge, a key element has been the fact that for a decade and a half now, we have been practising labour dispute prevention through a democratic reconciliation of interests and tripartite conflict resolution, with help from the ILO.

In the discussions in the National Council for the Reconciliation of Interests, which are in many cases hard and heated, we often complain about the limited time we have to formulate a professionally sound position reflecting often highly differentiated entrepreneurial interests. In addition, the lack or unreliability of statistical data measuring the performance of the economy is another obstacle to arriving at a carefully considered position.

The Hungary of today is a stable market economy and a stable political democracy. A considerable part of its problems now stems less and less from the legacy of socialism and is familiar to advanced market economies as well. Yet, as employers we disapprove of the lack of resolve of successive governments over the past 15 years to carry out a reform of the transfer systems. Despite a pressing need for fundamental reforms, they continue to be delayed not only in public finances and health care but also in agriculture. The lack of reform perpetuates the need for a strong centralization of revenues and high taxes, which are detrimental to the ability of Hungarian businesses to withstand intensifying global competition. Centralized revenue concentration and redistribution induce tensions and contradictions at the regional level, while entrepreneurs continue to have a limited say in the decisions of institutions and organizations of regional distribution.

High taxation, and especially the high cost of labour, have led to the emergence in Hungary of a significant informal economy with its attendant labour market implications, including illegal employment and atypical forms of employment on the "shady side of the law". We receive a lot of help from the ILO, and in particular from the Budapest-based Central and Eastern European Multidisciplinary and Advisory Team, in managing these issues. Allow me to highlight an exchange of views on the questions of productivity and poverty which took place a few weeks ago in my country. We find that on many issues employers' interests and positions do not differ from the interests of society and the Government's position. On the contrary, in many cases employers tend in fact to be impatient, try to hasten decisions, and find that reforms and the Government move too slowly.

With its accession to the European Union, Hungary has once again become a border fortress (by "once again" I refer to a part of our history a few hundred years ago); therefore the problem of migration, handling the influx of a multitude of people seeking jobs in our country or just transiting through it is, and will be, of particular relevance to us. We have no doubts that the discussion at the 92nd Session of the Conference will be of assistance to us, as will the ILO's European Regional Meeting in Budapest, scheduled for early next year. As a host of the latter, I can assure you on behalf of the Hungarian employers that we will do our utmost for the success and smooth conduct of that European Meeting to make sure that the community of which we are now a full member finds its interests well served by it.

Mr. MANGWANA *(Minister of Public Service, Labour and Social Welfare, Zimbabwe)*

Allow me to commence my address by congratulating the President and his officers on being elected to preside over this session of the International Labour Conference. Their combined wisdom and experience in labour matters are essential to ensuring that the objectives of the Conference are met.

I would also like to congratulate the Director-General of the International Labour Office and his team for producing a Report, *ILO programme implementation 2002-2003*, which chronicles the Organization's activities over the period in a systematic manner. While the Report is informative about what took place, it also suggests in some instances action for the future. It is the forward-looking nature of the Report that interests us most.

The manner in which the activities of the Organization, in the context of the four strategic objectives, the pillars of the Decent Work Agenda, are presented, gives us hope in our collective endeavour to achieve social justice.

In the context of Zimbabwe, we are addressing some of the challenges posed by the Director-General as follows.

Firstly, to promote decent work: the issue of decent work does not arise without reference to the provision of work in the first place. Zimbabwe is a developing nation whose primary resources are its land and its people. Zimbabwe has recently finalized the land redistribution exercise, which has seen a reallocation of land from 4,000 farmers controlling seventy per cent of the most arable land to the black majority. This programme can only enhance decent work in the context of our nation, in which the majority of our people are either unemployed or in the informal sector.

Besides providing the resources for employment generation, we have been reviewing laws to ensure the well-being of workers at the workplace and in retirement. In this regard, we have undertaken the following: Firstly, we have reorganized and revamped occupational health and safety to refocus its activities on core business in order to reduce accidents at the workplace. Secondly, we have increased contributions and benefits in the national social security authority to meaningful levels. Thirdly, we have refocused the national social security authority to invest in policies to favour housing developments in order to provide workers with decent housing.

We are also in the process of introducing a national youth fund under the auspices of national social security to cover the provision of basic health and medical care to our workers.

As regards the role of the ILO, we see the ILO's role in globalization as a bridge between the developed and the developing nations. The structures and processes of the ILO must be sensitive to the expectations of both the rich and the poor. The tendency has been to understand the needs of challenges of the "first world". If this does not change with the times the role of the ILO may be threatened.

We are ready to work with the ILO to forge a partnership to embrace the challenges of globalization.

As regards the mobilization of tripartism, in Zimbabwe we have well institutionalized tripartite forums which can be harnessed to ensure that the local and global challenges of globalization can be met to foster decent work.

Good governance is the enemy of bad globalization. The ILO therefore must strive to build a global team with universally applied rules and sanctions to ensure the success of the decent work programme through proper globalization governance.

I wish to point out that as a member of the African Group of the ILO Zimbabwe welcomes the initiative of the Director-General to engage the African Heads of State and Governments under the auspices of the African Union, on employment and poverty. Unemployment and poverty are the major challenges confronting Africa today, in addition to HIV/AIDS.

We look forward to meeting you in Burkina Faso.

Original Spanish: Ms. MUÑOZ *(Employers' adviser and substitute delegate, Venezuela)*

We are certain that the President's wide experience will ensure that this tripartite event will be successful because it will help confirm the values and objectives that we share, in order to bring about full freedom, genuine democracy, respect for human rights as well as for obligations, responsibilities and rights which are required of members of this Organization within the United Nations system.

It is the first time that I have had the honour of addressing this assembly and I do so as president of FEDECÁMARAS (the Venezuelan Federation of Chambers and Associations of Trade and Production), which is the most representative employers' organization in Venezuela, founded in 1994, sixty years ago.

FEDECÁMARAS has shared and supported the activities of the International Labour Organization in the quest for social justice advocated by the ILO, whose objectives are clearly identified in the statutes governing our organization.

As has been stated time and again by the representatives of FEDECÁMARAS in the ILO and in the Governing Body, I wish to affirm our deepest respect, acceptance and support for everything covered, both directly and indirectly, in the Declaration on Fundamental Principles and Rights at work.

We believe that freedom of association and the right to organize, as well as building democracy with due respect for private property and due respect for both national and international investment are fundamental pillars that we have to require from our governments as a prerequisite to foster development.

It is impossible to think of the existence of a government that calls itself democratic and which portrays itself as such in the international community, when it fails to respect or undermines, overtly or covertly, what is the very raison d'être of the ILO, that is to say, the application of tripartism and fruitful social dialogue with the most representative organizations of workers and employers in an atmosphere of freedom, not only of association, but also of expression.

With regard to globalization, Venezuelan employers agree with IOE and offer our most sincere support for a process of integration.

However, due to the radical opinions which this subject has prompted, I would like to stress that at FEDECÁMARAS, globalization is not a rigid dogma; that is, we understand this process as an integral part of our time, with both positive and negative elements, which each country has to adapt to its own national reality.

At FEDECÁMARAS we are very clear that, in order to capitalize on the advantages of globalization, to minimize its risks and to fulfil its social role, it is indispensable that it is founded on an effective democratic state, supported by the balance of powers, with autonomous institutions, and that the rules be applied transparently and fairly by respecting the abilities and needs of each country.

Likewise, we are convinced that globalization must encompass a concept of solidarity in order to help remedy the unacceptable inequalities between countries, with the aim of eradicating poverty in all its forms through decent work fostered by the ILO, to which each human being has the right to aspire.

We consider that the tripartite deliberations and decisions which brought the ILO to approve unanimously the Declaration on Fundamental Principles and Rights at Work, as well as the culmination of the excellent work of the World Commission on the Social Dimensions of Globalization, which was rightfully appointed by the Director-General, are today, as never before, guiding examples and cornerstones to channel and guide the tripartite components of the ILO in its future action.

This global forum has the full support of Venezuelan private-sector employers, to ensure that in this, the twenty-first century, the gap between rich and poor countries is reduced, for the benefit of all, achieving real growth which allows economic growth in all societies, improving the quality of life for individuals, while preserving the spirit and the cultural values of every nation, all within a framework of democracy, freedom and peace.

I must conclude with a brief mention of my country, Venezuela, by asking for your firm support for the complaint made jointly by the IOE and FEDECÁMARAS to this distinguished Organization, so that it may receive the backing of this Conference.

Venezuelan employers hope that our country can overcome, through growth, and as quickly as possible, the political, social and economic crisis we are currently experiencing.

I hope that you understand the urgent need for support in the areas mentioned.

Mr. DOWLA *(Employers' delegate, Bangladesh)*

I congratulate the President and the Vice-Presidents on their elections at the 92nd Session of the International Labour Conference.

I also congratulate the Director-General on his excellent Report to the Conference. The Report does justice to the task given to the ILO under its 1919 Constitution and the 1944 Declaration of Philadelphia, stating that poverty anywhere constitutes danger to prosperity everywhere. It is correctly stated in the Director-General's Report that work is the principal route out of social injustice and that, to create work, the economy must generate opportunities for investment, entrepreneurship, job creation and sustainable livelihoods.

Since there is a strong correlation between social justice and poverty, South Asia has the misfortune of having the worst scenario of social justice, as the highest number of poor people live there. Despite the improving GDP growth rate, progress in poverty alleviation has been slow in most of the countries. In fact, the number of poor people – that is, those living on less than one dollar per day – has remained roughly unchanged over the last decade. Most of the South Asian countries have taken up major economic reforms to reduce poverty and inequality, but the basic problem is that the poor, being assetless and unskilled, are not able to respond adequately to the new opportunities. Thus, there is a need for empowerment and skills development, but most of the South-Asian countries are handicapped in this regard, due to constraints on resources.

The fact remains that the poorer South Asian countries are finding it difficult to have the requisite access to markets in the developed countries. There are empirical studies on the reasons for this.

The ILO should have major involvement to ensure that, as per the Doha Declaration, the international community provides substantial resources for trade-related technical assistance to needy countries. The ILO and other international development organizations must ensure that these commitments are honoured.

It is a fact that the share of the Least Developed Countries (LDCs) in world trade has not increased as a result of globalization. Studies show that in recent years globalization processes have adversely impacted on poverty and on the LDCs which adopted an open trade regime. Poverty is increasing. It is feared that this trend will continue until such time as the poorer countries are provided with higher levels of development assistance and greater inflow of private capital.

What is particularly alarming for us is the scheduled phasing out of the Multifibre Arrangement (MFA) by January 2005. This will cause serious dislocation in our textile sector, which employs more than 20 million people in our country of which 75 per cent are women. Regional trade also seems to be in jeopardy due to tariff and non-tariff barriers. While improved market access and technical assistance by the developed countries can make important contributions to decent livelihoods, it is important to note that the poorer countries themselves need to undertake appropriate reforms and create a congenial investment climate in their own countries.

Also, LDCs should make greater investment in rural infrastructure so as to increase agricultural productivity, and promote industries in rural areas, where the bulk of their poor people live.

Mr. ZARB *(Workers' adviser and substitute delegate, Malta)*

I want to congratulate the Director-General for his well sounded and fine-tuned Report and for his clear vision of how globalization can be fair and how it can be adjusted to benefit all.

Today, the world is still entrapped in a global recession and a global crisis, which have led to the creation of a lot of imbalances between and within many countries. This will certainly remain a very serious worry in the twenty-first century.

Very often we hear that globalization is more or less solely associated with economics and that it forms the worldwide free-market economy. However, the greatest impact of globalization seems to be on the worker, who is made to shoulder the worst consequences without any hope of reaping the benefits.

Globalization tends to undermine national protection of workers' fundamental rights, which are being weakened in many countries. Such a situation entirely substantiates the Director-General's assessment of globalization.

The General Workers' Union of Malta thus fully agrees with the proposals made in the Director-General's Report and also with the main conclusions of the World Commission on the Social Dimension of Globalization, which stresses the need for well functioning labour markets and appropriate restructuring processes together with wider adjustment policies.

In fact, this year, the General Workers' Union launched its national campaign on the right to work, in order to achieve two objectives. The first is to increase awareness of the rising level of unemployment while at the same time pushing for immediate decisions to be taken to lessen the hardships on the unemployed and to increase our competitiveness and thus create new job opportunities. This campaign is based on the same lines as the ILO is proposing.

We especially emphasize the need for more training to have a more employable labour force which attracts higher value-added industries. This is based on our belief that the solution to more competitiveness is not cheap labour through the worsening of the conditions of work, but to have a better-trained workforce which is then prepared to be employed in high-tech modern industries.

But, to achieve this aim, we need a framework of social dialogue and social justice. Social dialogue is needed, as all social partners must feel that they are stakeholders in this process, and it must be ensured that the approach will be such as to avert unnecessary hardships.

The last remark I want to make is that of social justice. Social justice highlights the need to reinforce rather than dismantle the social security system. This is contrary to the current strategies promoted by most governments, for we have, unfortunately, been witnessing for a long time the implementation of policies to curb the welfare State.

The impact of such policies is to inflict hardship and social injustices on pensioners, workers and their families.

The threat to the welfare State has not only caused hardships to these sectors of society but also insecurity to all strata, which, in turn, has had the effect of creating a downturn in economic activity, which had produced rising unemployment.

As the Director-General's Report stated, good support systems are needed to combat social exclusion, smooth out structural changes and enhance workers' skills and productivity and the competitiveness of enterprises. We believe that this will be the win-win situation.

Original French: The PRESIDENT

Before closing this sitting I would like the Clerk of the Conference to take the floor to make an important announcement.

RATIFICATION OF AN INTERNATIONAL LABOUR CONVENTION BY CUBA

Original French: The CLERK OF THE CONFERENCE

I am pleased to announce to the Conference that on 1 June 2004, Cuba deposited the instrument of ratification of the Maternity Protection Convention, 2000 (No. 183). This Convention will enter into force in that country on 1 June 2005.

Original French: The PRESIDENT

We have reached the end of our sitting for today. I should like particularly to thank all speakers for complying with the allotted time limit on speeches, and I now declare this sitting closed.

(The Conference adjourned at 7.15 p.m.)

CONTENTS

Page

Third sitting

Supplementary presentation by the Director-General of the report, *A fair globalization – The role of the ILO* 1

    Speakers: The President, the Secretary-General

Suspension of certain provisions of the Standing Orders of the Conference *(cont.)* 6

Reports of the Chairperson of the Governing Body and of the Director-General: Discussion 6

    Speakers: Mr. Fahey, Mr. Larcher, Mr. Soodhun, Mr. El Amawy, Mr. Panayiotopoulos, Mr. Maroni, Mr. Dimas, Mr. Berzoini, Mr. Basesgioglu, Mr. Khaleghi, Mr. Tou, Mr. Kjørven, Mr. Al-Hajji, Ms. Dello, Mr. Swain, Mr. Dimovski, Ms. Rosas Pérez, Mr. Perigot, Mr. Halilović, Mr. Ryder, Ms. Dembsher, Mr. Sweeney, Mr. Eremeev, Ms. Knuppert, Mr. Szirmai, Mr. Mangwana, Ms. Muñoz, Mr. Dowla, Mr. Zarb.

Ratification of an international labour Convention by Cuba 26

No. 10 – Tuesday, 8 June 2004

International Labour Conference

Provisional Record 11
Ninety-second Session, Geneva, 2004

Fourth sitting
Tuesday, 8 June 2004, 10.15 a.m.
President: Mr. Ray Guevara, Mr. Attigbe, Mr. Maatough

REPORTS OF THE CHAIRPERSON OF THE GOVERNING BODY AND OF THE DIRECTOR-GENERAL: DISCUSSION (CONT.)

Original Spanish: The PRESIDENT

We shall now resume the discussion of the Reports of the Chairperson of the Governing Body and of the Director-General.

Mr. MOGAMI *(Minister of Labour and Home Affairs, Botswana)*

I would like on behalf of the Botswana delegation and on my own behalf to join those who have already congratulated the President on his election to chair this 92nd Session of the International Labour Conference.

Permit me to preface my remarks by expressing the appreciation of my delegation to the Director-General and the staff of the ILO for the immense effort that has gone into the preparation of the Report, *ILO programme implementation 2002-03*. The Report clearly and comprehensively gives an assessment of the performance of the ILO.

More importantly, the Report merits our serious attention because it provides an opportunity for reflection on the strategic direction of the ILO and the effectiveness of the means for attaining the goals and objectives of the Organization.

Our expectations on the ILO, as its constituents, are very high. The demand for the services of the Organization by member States continues to grow, albeit the dwindling resources at the disposal of the Organization. Consequently, nothing can be more inspiring than the qualitative and quantitative improvement in the implementation of the activities of the ILO brought about by the results-based management approach. The self-evaluation, the debate and lessons generated by the Director-General's Report are undoubtedly critical to the process of further rationalizing the activities of the ILO and enriching the quality of its work.

The subject areas of democracy and human rights, unemployment and poverty, equality, child labour and social protection covered in the Director-General's Report are topical issues for almost all member States, the more so in view of our endeavour to fulfil our obligations arising from the Declaration on Fundamental Principles and Rights at Work and the Decent Work Agenda. However, for a developing country like Botswana, the full realization of the principles we have worked so hard to promote is proving a daunting task without the technical assistance of the ILO.

Botswana has been able to make substantial progress in the promotion of freedom of association, the right to organize and collective bargaining. Amendments to labour laws aimed at incorporating the provisions of ILO Conventions Nos. 87, 98 and 151 have been concluded and implemented with effect from 23 April 2004. The provisions of the Protection of Workers' Claims (Employer's Insolvency) Convention, 1992 (No. 173) have also been incorporated into our labour laws.

With the assistance of the ILO/Swiss Project for Regional Conflict Management and Enterprise-based Competitiveness Development in Southern Africa, improvements have been introduced in the dispute prevention and resolution system with a view to establishing a system that is speedy, more credible, easily accessible and that emphasizes consensus and dispute prevention.

Further work aimed at strengthening labour administration, including inspection systems, is being carried out with the assistance of the United States Department of Labor project on Strengthening Labor Systems in Southern Africa. One of the lessons cited in the Director-General's Report is that it will not be feasible in the long run for the International Labour Office to continue accepting new priorities and increasing existing services whilst maintaining all areas of activity and expertise. Certainly, if these limitations are not addressed, it will make it difficult for the ILO to respond to future challenges.

The increase in the workload of the ILO's supervisory mechanism and the build up of a backlog of reports awaiting review threaten to derail the achievements made on compliance with international labour standards by member States. Consideration must, therefore, be given to strengthening collaboration between the ILO and regional and subregional bodies dealing with employment and labour matters. Such collaboration must include encouraging and assisting these bodies to manage compliance with ILO standards by member States, in the hope that complaints to the ILO pertaining to violations of Conventions would be reduced.

We believe that the continuation of the debate on globalization is welcome. Previous debates on the subject have recognized the potential of globalization to promote decent work and force sustainable development. We agree that the imbalances of globalization are, however, deemed obstacles to the realization of these objectives.

May I conclude by affirming that the ILO has a distinct role to play in mitigating the adverse social effects of the global economy. The establishment of the World Commission on the Social Dimension of Globalization presents an opportunity to carry the debate beyond rhetoric and to seek consensus for action. Indeed, for globalization to be acceptable and sustainable, it must put people first. Its benefits must serve the needs and aspirations of the people.

Original Arabic: Mr. AOUN *(Government delegate, Lebanon)*

This year, the International Labour Conference is examining some crucial issues, issues that lie at the heart of the concerns of those people of the world who are aspiring to a just peace and social justice.

The topics that are addressed in the Reports of the Director-General on the social dimension of globalization, trade union rights and freedoms and the situation of workers in Palestine and in the other occupied Arab territories, as well as all of the other items on the Conference agenda that deal with promoting international labour standards in the fishing sector, migrant workers, human resources development and following up programmes aimed at eliminating the worst forms of child labour.

These are all issues that confirm the International Labour Organizations role as a guide for social partners throughout the world. In addition, they place emphasis on social rights and the importance of those rights and on all of the issues that have to be considered in order to establish global social justice. It is social justice that will act as a cornerstone of sustainable world peace.

The Director-General's Report mentions with seriousness and objectivity the social effects of globalization. This, I believe, is a subject of primary concern for developing countries. These effects are being exacerbated at a time when the institutions and protagonists of globalization are not taking sufficient account of the social dimension of globalization. This is the reason why the harmful effects of globalization are constantly being felt in social terms.

Although economic globalization has brought about considerable progress in numerous regions of the world, in other regions it has led to unemployment, poverty, labour force migration and privatization, which has caused the deterioration of many services and an erosion of the basic rights of workers.

This is why we are saying here that globalization has to go hand in hand with the development of social services and social protection. It is necessary to reinforce the role of the relevant bodies responsible for guaranteeing social services and social rights, in particular the tripartite institutions that are used as a forum for social dialogue and economic development. In other words, the interdependence of social development and economic development is the guarantee of fair globalization and opens the way to globalized social progress.

In the light of globalization, the concept of social justice must transcend the national context so that this justice can become a common objective of all the people of this world. Likewise, the sovereignty of peoples over their territories and over their natural resources and wealth is one of the basic criteria in the implementation of social justice at the global level.

Reducing social and economic disparities among nations must be one of the cornerstones of a fair globalization and will necessarily be a cornerstone of sustainable world peace.

Despite the positive indicators with regard to workers' fundamental rights worldwide, the spread of democracy and the increase in the number of member States that are ratifying the fundamental international labour standards, as indicated in the Director-General's Report, it is still the case that in Palestine, the Syrian Arab Golan and other parts of occupied southern Lebanon there are still workers whose rights are violated. These violations occur as a result of the economic embargo, collective punishment, the destruction of infrastructure and homes, the devastation of farmland, poverty and unemployment.

The Iraqi people are also at the mercy of the American and British occupying forces. This occupation makes a mockery of the fundamental rights of workers in that part of the world and contravenes international law.

I would also like to mention the law on sanctions against Syria which has been adopted by the American Congress and which breaches international law.

Lastly, it is necessary that the ILO should, like all other international organizations, examine the national economic rights of the social partners, and that is why we invite the International Labour Organization to examine the harmful social and economic impact of the occupation in Palestine and Iraq, in addition to the impact of the United States economic sanctions which are imposed on the Syrian people, in breach of the Declaration of Philadelphia, which states that all human beings, irrespective of race, creed or sex, have the right to pursue their material well-being in conditions of economic security.

Finally, human rights are the basis for all legislation. They are an indivisible whole that must be applied as such to all people. Human rights should be ensured in conditions that are propitious to national sovereignty, freedom and stability.

Ms. FILATOV *(Minister of Labour, Finland)*

I would like to thank the Director-General and his staff for the Reports. It is encouraging to note that the Decent Work Agenda seems to be working. The statistics on ratifications of fundamental Conventions are also good news. They contain a message of political will and of hope that is so much needed at times like this, with much turmoil and vicious circles of hatred. The Report also well illustrates what has been achieved in relation to the target set. The overall record is encouraging and it shows that we are on the right track.

The report *A fair globalization: Creating opportunities for all* sets the record straight. From the beginning it has been a delusion to expect that market forces alone would do the trick. The market economy accelerates growth and innovation, but to contribute to the fair and sustainable welfare of people at large, it needs responsible governance at the enterprise level as well as at national and international levels. The architecture of this governance has not been up to the task. The recommendations of the World Commission are straightforward. What is needed now is action.

One of the concerns of the World Commission is the cross-border movement of people and how to manage the migration flows. I would like to underscore the importance of improving the equal treatment and fair conditions of migrant workers and members of their families. We should do our utmost in order to prevent the emergence of a divided labour market in our countries. Safeguarding the full integration of migrant workers and their families into the labour markets and into our societies is also the best way of promoting tolerance and mutual understanding between different ethnic and religious groups.

The report of the World Commission points out that we need to begin at home. In this sense, we all have a task. Good and democratic governance is something that can always be improved. This year's Global Report under the follow-up to the ILO Declaration on Fundamental Principles and Rights at Work amply demonstrates the that problems relating to the exercise of trade union rights are usual even in the most developed countries.

We can see that here again the forces of globalization have been defined as follows: "Through the liberalization of capital flows, deregulation of labour markets and privatization of public services, globalization can undermine the power that workers have traditionally exerted through their essentially national organizations." So these results might have a lot to do with policy choices that we have made earlier, which is to say that for the future we have the same possibility with better choices.

It is evident that trade unions together with employers' organizations are the backbone of this Organization and the tripartism that it represents. It is as important to note that without the voice of the social partners, the idea of good governance in the world of work remains but a dream. As we clean up our own backyards we must not forget the multilateral and international front. As has been said time and again, the question is not about changing the mandate of the ILO. But clearly there is need for consistent and coherent policies to achieve decent employment everywhere.

Fiscal and monetary policies need to be considered together with employment issues. The weaknesses of the governance of globalization should be addressed. This cannot be accomplished without active cooperation between the relevant international organizations. Cooperation needs to be formally structured and a clear-cut agenda for it should be set. In this effort we, once again, need not only the governments but also the social partners.

In the Report of the Director-General on the World Commission's report, the concrete actions needed are further elaborated. I would specifically point out the need for action on Policy Coherence Initiatives for growth, investment and employment and to the idea of a Globalization Policy Forum. Also, there is need to strengthen the ILO's capacity in respect of entrepreneurship, enterprise growth and employment creation as part of a broadly-based Office-wide effort as underlined in the report.

Mr. POTTER *(Employers' delegate, United States)*

On behalf of the United States employers, I would like to offer our congratulations to the President of the Conference on his well-deserved election. The annual session of the International Labour Conference provides an opportunity for us to chart the course of our Organization, not only over the coming year but for several years in the future. Our experience demonstrates that in order to be strategically relevant, every organization must engage in an ongoing process to assess its focus and operating practices for the near and longer term. The Director-General's Report on the role of the ILO in implementing the World Commission's recommendations gives us the chance to do that. Whatever the outcome of this plenary debate, what certainly will be needed is further discussion in the Governing Body before proceeding further.

Having achieved a broad consensus around the ILO's four strategic objectives, nothing should be done that would undermine them and their effective implementation. One can be sure, however, that for the foreseeable future the resources the ILO will have with which to play its important role in the global economy will not be greater than they are today. One has the impression, reading the Director-General's Report, that the issues being addressed are somehow new or more urgent. In fact, from a historical perspective, what we have is old wine in new bottles. The fact of a global economy and the related ethical and social problems addressed in the World Commission's report were as much a reality in 1900, when the share of international trade in the world economy was as high as it is today in 2004. This global reality was the basis on which the ILO was founded in 1919. The International Labour Commission, which was part of the settlement emerging from the Peace Conference in Versailles, was considered necessary because all governments were committed to the establishment of an international organization to solve a broad range of multilateral workplace problems, including establishing a common ethical and social framework, and taking terms and conditions of employment out of the hands of international commerce. The protectionism of the 1920s and the Great Depression that occurred shortly thereafter seriously injured the world trading system. It was not until the fall of the Berlin Wall that world trade began to reach the levels last found in 1914. We should take care not to "throw the baby out with the bath water".

It is astonishing not to see any reference to the 1998 Declaration on Fundamental Principles and Rights at Work in the first section of the Director-General's Report, on making decent work a global goal. The 1998 Declaration is a watershed achievement that, as this year's Global Report, *Organizing for social justice*, demonstrates, is now just beginning to bear fruit. The Declaration represents a political commitment under the ILO Constitution that encompasses the considerations found in this year's Director-General's Report. The Declaration shines as a beacon for preserving and enhancing the ILO's central role in assuring that there is a basic level of human decency below which no nation state should fall in the global economy.

The Director-General's Report places much emphasis on policy coherence. A seat at the table where key decisions are taken is earned by being credible. The ILO should not become a house of economic analysis at the expense of the needs of its constituents and maintenance of its entire mandate. However, as we said in 1999, the ILO needs a credible, world-class macroeconomic research programme that recognizes, among other things, that enterprises are the source of wealth creation and that job creation and a rising standard of living are achievable only if a number of economic, political and legal factors are present. They include: a stable political, legal and social environment; good governance and a consistent struggle against corruption; low inflation; low interest rates; coherent macroeconomic policies; stable exchange rates; and a variety of other factors.

As a fundamental matter, whatever the issue, the ILO should "stick to its knitting". Ultimately, United States business believes that the key to whether the ILO will be seen as relevant in the foreseeable future depends on its success on its core activities. That is: are ILO standards high-impact standards on which there is a broad international consensus for ratification? Is the ILO's supervisory machinery meaningful and effective and able to take prompt action in serious intractable workplace, human rights cases like Myanmar; is the ILO comprehensively and effectively implementing the 1998 Declaration? Are the ILO's technical cooperation activities timely and maintained at a high level? Are the ILO's employment, job-creation, skills and enterprise development and poverty programmes effective? And is the ILO's economic and employment research programme a reliable and credible source of aggregate employment data and trends?

Original Russian: Mr. LUBLIN *(Government delegate, Russian Federation)*

It is my pleasure to note that the discussion of issues related to the social dimension of globalization is taking place today as part of a constructive dialogue. This is most importantly to the credit of the International Labour Organization and its Director-General, Mr. Juan Somavia, as well as the World Commission on the Social Dimension of Globalization.

Globalization affects all areas of human activity and all segments of the population.

As a result of the rapid transition to an open economy and market relations, the Russian Federation fully experiences both the positive and the negative consequences of the process of globalization.

For this reason, we fully share the concern of the world community as regards the costs of this process. We also share its concern as to the weakening of national systems of social protection, the erosion of social solidarity and the highly unequal distribution of benefits and burdens of globalization between different countries and different social groups within the population.

The Government of the Russian Federation and Russian society highly value the activities of the International Labour Organization directed towards endowing the process of globalization with a more humanistic and civilized nature and ensuring its social orientation. As correctly noted by United Nations Secretary-General Kofi Annan in Davos, if we do not make globalization work for all then, in the final analysis, it will work for no one.

We support the idea of establishing more effective control and management of this process on the part of international organizations, national governments and civil society.

The work of the World Commission on the Social Dimension of Globalization in preparing its final report has been successfully completed.

In our view, the report manages to provide full and objective assessments of the basic components of the process of globalization as well as to indicate specific ways to solve the problems arising at national, regional and international levels. We believe that the carefully thought-out recommendations in the report fully meet the requirements of all participants in the process of globalization.

It is extremely important that we create concrete mechanisms for the transition from confrontation between supporters and opponents of globalization to a constructive dialogue between the parties

It is rightly pointed out in this document that the key to solving social labour problems in the era of globalization is effective action at the national level, which is based on international standards and norms, as well as on the decisions of international forums.

I should like to point out, in this context, that the main international guidelines for Russia are the decisions of the Social Summit in Copenhagen (1995), and the ILO Declaration on Fundamental Principles and Rights at Work (1998). Russia also endorses the concept of decent work drawn up by the ILO and the Global Employment Agenda, as well as the Millennium Development Goals determined by the United Nations.

With the help of the ILO and the secretariat of the World Commission, the first national dialogue on the social dimensions of globalization was held in Moscow in 2002. At the end of this month in St. Petersburg, we plan to hold a presentation of the final report of the Commission for Russian Society and Russian social partners.

Russia is preparing for its accession to the World Trade Organization. In this connection, we are devoting much attention to studying the possible consequences of this step for the social and labour fields, including through studies being carried out with the help of the ILO. Preparatory activities have begun in various economic sectors in order to overcome or attenuate the possible negative consequences of this accession.

At the same time, broad consultations are being carried out with various of our national partners in this process, within the framework of dialogue between government structures and non-governmental organizations, as well as with the social partners; this is based on the principles of tripartism.

It was in this context that, in 2003 in St. Petersburg, the first tripartite consultative meeting was held on the economic and social consequences of Russia's accession to the WTO. At this meeting, reports on this issue were discussed by Russian academics and specialists from the ILO, the World Bank and the OECD.

In conclusion, I should like once again to emphasize the importance of a balanced integration of economic and social policies at all levels, and the importance of placing a stress on overcoming the glaring inequalities and poverty in our world, on strengthening levels of social protection and on improving the quality of life for all.

The market is only one component of the economy; no country, nor humanity as a whole, can be subject solely to the interests of the markets, nor base itself solely on market relations. There exist other human values which must determine the direction of development of the world in the twenty-first century.

While we are certainly in favour of uniting the forces of the world community in order to address global issues, at the same time we believe that there can be no one panacea for all ills; no one medicine for all diseases. Each country has its own particular characteristics and has the right to determine its own path of development, taking into account national realities and interests.

We do not want the globalization of the economy and of the information society to lead us to a global cultural standardization, or to the obliteration of the variety of ethnic differences, national languages, customs and traditions of peoples large and small.

Original Arabic: Mr. MAJALI *(Minister of Labour, Jordan)*

First of all I would like to congratulate the President very warmly on his election as President of the 92nd International Labour Conference and to wish him a most successful Conference.

I would also like to take this opportunity to thank the Director-General for his Report entitled *Organizing for social justice*, which deals with fundamental principles aimed at strengthening social justice and the trade union freedoms guaranteed by the Constitution of our Organization, which dates from 1919.

The International Labour Organization, as the most long-standing organization would never have been able to cope with difficult circumstances and the changing international scenario without its lasting values in the field of economic development, which are based on the fair and equitable distribution of the fruits of development and on the consolidation of cooperation and social peace among the social partners.

I am proud to announce that my country has embarked on this path and that we have done so by ratifying international conventions and by strengthening industrial relations, especially in the field of collective bargaining with a view to concluding bipartite collective agreements between the social partners. We should add that trade unions and employers' organizations enjoy the freedom to bargain collectively.

The Report of the Director-General rightly mentions the importance of political will and of effective machinery for applying the basic norms and principles adopted by countries and incorporated in national laws. In Jordan we draw inspiration from this political will, which is based on our national interests and on our social and human experience in order to confirm our commitment to the fundamental rights guaranteed by the Declaration of the International Labour Organization, by the pertinent international instruments and by international custom.

His Majesty the King of Jordan addressed this Conference last year saying, and I quote, "Only by defeating want can we heal the divisions and despair that feed global violence. This requires sustainable socio-economic development, development that enables all people to live in dignity. Such development is an important tool in the battle against extremism." He also added that "our strategy has had one goal – to improve the well-being and opportunities of our citizens." His Majesty the King has given substance to these objectives through an initiative designed to strengthen social dialogue. For example, the Government has established machinery and implemented programmes to promote socio-economic development. Through these reforms and initiatives, we have strengthened social dialogue among our social partners. We have also set up a tripartite national committee which will help us to achieve our objectives.

We note that the Report has objectively and rightly analysed the situation of migrant workers in the global economy. We think that the ILO must continue to play its central role and that the social partners must participate in the various global and regional initiatives whose purpose is to improve the situation of migrant workers.

What the Report on *The situation of workers of the occupied Arab territories* says about the continuing hardship proves that the only way to alleviate the suffering of the Palestinian people is to bring about the establishment of a just and lasting peace, the withdrawal of Israel from the occupied Arab territories in Syria, Palestine and Lebanon and the creation of an independent Palestinian State with its capital in Al-Quds.

In the meantime, we must pursue our efforts to help Palestinian workers whose rights are flouted. As long as the Palestinian problem remains unsolved and the occupation of Iraq, with all its disastrous humanitarian repercussions, continues, there will always be obstacles to development in the region. Consequently there must be a complete withdrawal from the occupied Arab territories and the Palestinian problem must be solved. The occupation of Iraq must be ended so that Iraqis can have territorial integrity and can enjoy their right to self-determination. Only stability, security and a just global peace can bring development and prosperity for all peoples in the region.

Allow me to thank all the Heads of State and Government who yesterday mentioned the report of the Commission on the Social Dimension of Globalization. I would like to emphasize that it is up to the rich countries to shoulder their responsibilities towards the poor countries by helping them to benefit from the positive aspects of globalization which will bring them political, economic and social stability.

We in Jordan are very much aware of the importance of globalization and of the need to take part in it. Nevertheless we acknowledge the impact it can have and we are trying to take advantage of its beneficial social and economic effects while at the same time curbing the harmful effects of a fragile social justice, since that would only increase deprivation, poverty and despair and exacerbate terrorism, thus jeopardizing international peace and solidarity.

Original Chinese: Mr. WANG *(Government delegate, China)*

First of all, please allow me to congratulate the President on his election. I believe that under his leadership the session is certain to be a complete success.

The Director-General's Report reviews the work and activities of the International Labour Organization during the past two years. We have noted with appreciation that, by centring on the four major strategic objectives, with decent work as the main theme, the International Labour Organization has made positive progress in employment promotion, poverty eradication and workers' protection, thus contributing to the achievement of the United Nations Millennium Development Goals.

Thanks to the past two years' hard work, the World Commission on the Social Dimension of Globalization has completed its report. The Chinese delegation congratulates the World Commission on that achievement.

Peace and development remain the overriding theme of our times. However, in the process of globalization, the gap between the rich and the poor is still widening. Some developing countries are running the risk of being marginalized, which has posed a new challenge to social justice and sustainable development.

It is our common task to eradicate poverty. In the face of the challenges and difficulties stemming from globalization, developing countries should formulate feasible strategies for the sustainable development of their economy and society, in the light of their own circumstances.

The peaceful development of developing countries would contribute significantly to peace and development throughout the world. Developed countries should shoulder more responsibilities in regional and global endeavours to secure poverty reduction and development. Our thesis is that all countries, developed or developing, big or small, should benefit from globalization. The way to achieve this goal is through the establishment of a new international political and economic order that is fair and rational.

China has steadfastly pressed ahead with reform and opening-up in all sectors. China has continued to put people first and has focused on the parallel progress of its economy and society, guided by the concept of comprehensive, coordinated and sustainable development. We have scored remarkable achievements in both social and economic spheres. However, we are well aware that China still has a big population. China's economy is underdeveloped, and such development as we have is imbalanced. For a long time to come, one of our major endeavours in the social sphere will be to create productive and decent jobs for millions of Chinese workers.

More recently, the Chinese Government and the International Labour Organization have co-sponsored the China Employment Forum in Beijing, which has produced a basic common understanding. The success of the forum has once again shown that employment promotion has become a top priority in all countries' social development strategies and measure an effective means of implementing the Decent Work Agenda.

China supports the ILO in defining employment promotion and poverty eradication as one of the priority areas of action within the framework of the four strategic objectives. In this connection, the Chinese delegation wishes to make the following suggestions.

First, the International Labour Organization should use its advantageous position to make the eradication of widespread poverty a motor for social progress, through tripartite cooperation in ILO constituencies, in accordance with its mandate. It should encourage the developed countries and international institutions to provide more practical and effective technical assistance to the developing countries, so as to increase the latter's participation in a globalization process, enable them to enjoy the fruits of economic globalization in an equitable manner and hence promote common prosperity and global development. It is important for the ILO to enhance solidarity among developing countries and to help them to maintain stability, increase their capacity for self-development and achieve progress in a manner suited to their own national conditions.

Secondly, the International Labour Organization should make employment promotion its priority and utilize its unique expertise to identify and develop cooperation projects according to the needs of the member States and the challenges facing the labour world, so as to help member States to narrow the wealth gap, realize full productive and decent employment and facilitate common development.

Thirdly, the International Labour Organization should speed up its own reform, improve its work efficiency and respect the principle of promotion. International labour standards are of positive significance for the protection of workers' rights and interests. We believe that, while applying labour standards, it is very important to respect the diverse development levels and institutions of different regions. There should be fewer accusations or sanctions and more assistance and promotive measures. It is time for us to act immediately in a concerted effort to ensure a decent job for everyone and decent globalization.

Original Spanish: Mr. ABASCAL *(Minister of Labour and Social Welfare, Mexico)*

First of all, I would like to congratulate the President upon his election, which is an honour for our Americas region.

Social dialogue, which is a central element of President Vicente Fox's policies, has enabled Mexico to strengthen social cohesion and peace, as well as to make progress in the attainment of major national objectives.

Consequently, the Government of Mexico deems it most important for the ILO to increase its constituents' capabilities, intensify its awareness-raising activities and strengthen the capabilities of national and international institutions in order to extend the benefits of social dialogue to economic and social policies, as suggested in the Director-General's Report.

Mexico also agrees with the statement in the Global Report, *Organizing for social justice*. It states that "the fundamental principle of freedom of association and the right to collective bargaining is a reflection of human dignity."

Those unions called to play a decisive role in globalization are unions committed to the individual, to training in order to increase the productivity and competitiveness of enterprises, which are human productive communities, and to increasing the living standards of workers and their families.

It is extremely important to have a legal framework that establishes and guarantees freedom of association. However, the unwavering commitment of unions to the comprehensive development of individuals through productive work is just as important.

The ILO contributes to improving respect for freedom of association. For this reason the Government of Mexico supports the review of control mechanisms which is currently under way at the ILO. This review will contribute to strengthening their effectiveness.

Another remarkable achievement of the ILO is the importance given to tripartite discussions on migration. International labour migration is important, above all, because of the ethical duty to protect the human dignity of migrants. Growing migration flows require us to address the subject as soon as possible on a realistic basis, with a social vocation and within an appropriate legal framework.

This is a challenge not only for Mexico, as a sending, transit and receiving country of migratory workers, but also for the world as a whole.

Thanks to the ILO's vision, the conclusions reached by the World Commission on the Social Dimension of Globalization offer concrete proposals to the world in order to dignify productive work and gear it towards the effective welfare of individuals and their families.

Such proposals have opened up opportunities for tripartite discussions on how to combine economic and social development of globalization. Thus, the decent work concept has been relaunched and it has permeated in all member states. In Mexico, it has found especially fertile ground given our previous efforts towards a new labour culture. Discussions have dealt with the individual. They have given much deserved attention to the family as the origin and ultimate end of true development, thus introducing an ethical element and a humanist aspect to globalization.

On these premises today, before you all, at the greatest labour forum in the world, I am pleased to inform you that the Government of Mexico, as well as our workers' and employers' delegations, will introduce a proposal to the Governing Body for tripartite discussions towards a new instrument or different type of follow-up measure concerning social and labour rights and duties as regards globalization.

Given the role that the Organization currently plays in search of a globalization that is consistent with human development, such an instrument or measure should be the next step in the efforts promoted by the ILO. As the President of Finland said, the World Commission's report is only the beginning of giving globalization a human face and a human heart.

We are all the authors of globalization and we have the urgent duty to transform it into an effective instrument, in order to achieve a more just, equitable and free world, where the unlimited potential of personal dignity is developed to create solidarity, social justice and common good.

Mexico would like to reiterate its multilateral and humanist commitment to its own people and to the world.

Original Portuguese: Mr. DE MEIRELES V. DE CASTRO *(Employers' delegate, Portugal)*

First of all, on behalf of the Portuguese employers' delegation, I would like to congratulate the President on his appointment to this important post and wish him every success in carrying out his work.

This year, the agenda of the International Labour Conference covers some extremely important issues, such as human resources development and training, a fair deal for migrant workers in the global economy and the Global Report under the follow-up to the ILO Declaration on Fundamental Principles and Rights at Work.

As I do not have much time for my address, I will focus only on two points. The first is corporate social responsibility (CSR), particularly as regards its links with the issue of delocalization. The second, we consider to be an extremely important issue, namely tripartism and social dialogue in the Portuguese-speaking African countries, otherwise known as the PALOPs.

Social corporate responsibility is a very topical and important issue and has recently been the subject of debate at many meetings and round tables at the global and European Union levels. At these meetings, it has become clear that for many years now, a growing number of companies are beginning to develop on a voluntary basis and with commitment, socially responsible practices aimed at establishing fairer and more satisfactory relations with shareholders, workers and the environment.

Given the many economic activities at national and global levels, and the variety of different companies that carry them out, corporate social responsibility practices naturally reflect this great diversity and adapt to the particular conditions of each situation in a dynamic way, because reality is always changing, and new situations and new challenges are constantly arising.

In other words, there is no single CSR approach or model that can be applied across the board to all companies because each CSR policy is a reflection of the philosophy of a given company or business and is linked to developments and a set of procedures that have come to be accepted over the years.

Although the most visible CSR policies are being developed by big companies, there is a knock-on effect which means that numerous smaller companies that work with the bigger ones also start behaving in a socially responsible way.

The growing trend of company delocalization at the global level has brought a new aspect to corporate social responsibility in that this concept was previously confined to fairly limited areas of the world, for instance, the European Union, North America and Japan. The delocalization of big companies and the close relations that those companies develop with many companies in developing countries has meant that the latter spontaneously, or perhaps in response to pressures, have started to be more concerned with certain issues, such as, worker relations, the quality of work, the environment and respect for human rights.

It goes without saying that delocalization has both positive and negative aspects. We hope that, in the area of CSR, the effects will be largely positive.

The second point that I would like to raise in my statement is tripartism and social dialogue in Portuguese-speaking African countries (PALOPs).

Well aware of the advantages that social dialogue brings to economic and social development, particularly in countries such as Angola and Mozambique, that have suffered from lengthy armed conflicts, the Confederation of Portuguese Industry for some time now has been working with the ILO with a view to arranging seminars and other forms of support aimed at promoting social dialogue and consultation in the so-called PALOPs.

The Confederation of Portuguese Industry took part with great interest and satisfaction in the first meeting of employers' organizations of Portuguese-speaking African countries, which was held in Cape Verde, on 30 and 31 March 2004. The meeting had been organized by the ILO and brought together representatives of employers' organizations from the host country, Cape Verde and also Angola, Guinea-Bissau and Sao Tome and Principe.

The meeting produced a number of conclusions. First, the role of employers' and workers' organizations in PALOP countries in dialogue and consultation has not, to date, been very relevant, inter alia because of the lack of technical and financial support; second, the history, people and language common to all the Portuguese-speaking countries are factors that facilitate cooperation, particularly at the business level; third, it is necessary to encourage greater contact between the PALOP countries through transport and communication systems that are modern, reliable and inexpensive; and fourth, it is essential to promote the movement of individuals, goods and capital in the PALOP area.

It is true that, in the future, much will be asked of the employers' organizations in the PALOP countries in terms of social dialogue, and in the context of creating the necessary conditions for business competitiveness in those countries.

The ILO, through its competent services, has an extremely important role to play in terms of technical support, the qualification of human resources, arranging seminars and implementing other, well-targeted measures to promote social dialogue, greater competitiveness and, therefore, wealth and job creation.

We would like to take this opportunity to thank the ILO, and more specifically the Bureau for Employers' Activities for having organized this first meeting, which was very important for the PALOP countries. We certainly hope that it will be followed up with similar meetings in the not too distant futures.

(Mr. Attigbe takes the Chair.)

Mr. KIM *(Government delegate, Republic of Korea)*

I would like to begin by expressing my heartfelt congratulations to Mr. Ray Guevara on being elected President of the 92nd Session of the International Labour Conference. I would also like to congratulate the Director-General, Mr. Juan Somavia, who started his second term in March with overwhelming support from tripartite constituents. Allow me also to express my warm gratitude to the members of the World Commission on the Social Dimension of Globalization for their report.

Today, the rapid process of globalization has faced us with many challenges. Its characteristics – free trade and investment, the spread of technology and information sharing, and fierce global competition – have brought not only sunny spots but also dark shadows, both domestically and internationally. Without a doubt, globalization will eventually lead to increased wealth. However, if current instability persists, increasing social inequality and poverty will begin to undermine the overall growth potential.

Against this backdrop, the report of the World Commission, *A fair globalization: Creating opportunities for all*, is seen to provide appropriate the solutions, as well as recommendations on how member countries should set fair rules on economic and social issues.

Globalization has become so pervasive in our daily lives that we need to summon all our wisdom to achieve humane globalization, fair globalization, by sharing its fruits more broadly and minimizing its negative aspects. To that end, I would like to share some specific recommendations.

First, the social actors, including workers, employers and governments, need to take a keen interest not only in increasing economic efficiency and transparency, but also in overcoming social inequality.

Second, the ILO and its member States should put more effort into enhancing the employability of workers, through human resource development, with the ultimate goal of creating more stable and decent employment on a more flexible labour market.

Third, the ILO needs to strengthen its technical assistance programmes through protecting the vulnerable working class, establishing a social safety net infrastructure, and sharing specific job creation strategies which meet the economic needs of each individual member country.

Last, but not least, I would like to ask donor countries to spare no effort to share their advanced knowledge and techniques on education and training with developing countries, and also to take active measures in increasing official development assistance (ODA).

In this era of ongoing globalization, the Government of the Republic of Korea recognizes job creation and advancement of industrial relations as unavoidable tasks, with the aim of establishing mutually beneficial labour relations through dialogue and cooperation. For this purpose, the tripartite partners concluded the Social Pact for Job Creation in February this year, on the basis of social consensus on the principle that the jobs are the best form of welfare. All the social actors will make efforts to build a balanced society in which employment and growth are equally respected.

The Government of the Republic of Korea is taking steps to adopt legislation based on the Measures to Advance Industrial Relations Laws and Institutions, taking international labour standards into account. While pursuing this legislation, the Government will try its best to elicit consensus among workers, employers and the Government.

Lastly, the Government will do its best to resolve major industrial relations issues through dialogue and compromise in line with the ILO spirit of tripartism.

On the last day of May, a high-level tripartite dialogue took place in my country, presided over by President Roh Moo-Hyun. Just four days later, the tripartite constituents agreed on measures to strengthen the social dialogue system, including the reform of the Korean Tripartite Commission.

I would like to ask the member countries for their support so that these directives for positive changes our Government is now adopting can be successfully implemented.

Mr. GALEA *(Minister of Education, Youth and Employment, Malta)*

This is the first year that Malta is present at this Conference as a member of the European Union.

Before, during and after the long-drawn-out accession negotiations, the Government of Malta insistently declared that it did not regard the European Union as an end in itself. We see it rather as a stepping stone towards global governance in a different form from that towards which the present process of globalization seems to be taking the world.

In other words, we share the perspective implied by the Director-General in his Report on the World Commission on the Social Dimension of Globalization *A fair globalization: The role of the ILO*. On page 14 of the English version of the Report, there is a single brief paragraph devoted to the topic of the ILO's collaboration with the regional communities. Six of these are listed by the Director-General, with the European Union mentioned after the South African Development Community (SADC).

In the present particular circumstances of Malta's accession to the European Union, I feel that it is appropriate for me to devote my short intervention entirely to underlining the special significance which the two core sentences at the heart of the paragraph on the 'regional stepping stone' have for us in Malta. I need hardly remind any of you here that Malta is situated at exactly the point where the three continents of Europe, Africa and Asia meet; and transcultural communication is still today, as it has always been, literally a matter of life and death for us.

The two sentences on page 14 of the Director-General's Report which I have taken it upon myself to underline are the following: "The ILO is also called upon to offer advice on ways in which institutions and policies for decent work could provide a foundation for regional integration processes. A particular focus is the role of mechanisms for dialogue involving the ILO's constituents in contributing to a social dimension of regional integration."

The Director-General considers this task to be "an important new priority for constituents". I wish to underline that there is indeed a novel challenge in this regard, arising from the most recent European developments. Admittedly, the novelty does not lie so much in the rhetoric of the reiterated declarations of the "social dimension" of the European Union, more vigorously formulated than usual, but still poised mostly at the level of abstract principle. Rather, the novelty lies in the draft Constitution, in the envisionment of a new area, referred to as the "immediate environment" of the Union, comprehending consequently the whole of the Mediterranean world as well as the Eastern borderlands, as territory for a "privileged relationship". The most natural meaning of this equivocal phrase is that this territory, even though partly, geographically non-European, is to be treated as a laboratory in which, to quote the Director-General's words once more "institutions and policies for decent work could provide a foundation for regional integration processes": in this instance, for the creation of a new, Euro-Mediterranean entity, as original in nature as the European Union itself.

The major problems that are making our part of the world – the Mediterranean and the Middle East – one of its most disquieting corners, such as illegal migration, destruction of fishery resources, the sense of external exploitation, all cry out for precisely the only possible remedy so succinctly captured in the Director-General's golden phrase: "institutions and policies for decent work" in the region.

It is still not clear how the European Union intends to proceed in pursuit of the objective to which it has dedicated a whole section of its draft Constitution, a section that has revealed an undoubted consensus among all the member States. I am sure, however, that the Director-General is right in highlighting the special importance that is due to "the role of mechanisms for dialogue involving the ILO's constituents".

Indeed, I was prompted to make this intervention because it seemed to me that, almost as if concealed between the lines of the Director-General's Report, here there was a pointer to a region crying out for an initiative that perhaps only the ILO, with its tripartite, constituent experience, could successfully take. Naturally, as I noted at the start, the Director-General in this paragraph clearly had southern Africa most prominently in his mind. It may be, however, that there is now a timely opportunity which may not arise again, to seek to press home the main thrusts in the central paragraph of page 14 of his Report, in a region that is not called by name among the six in his list – that is, the Mediterranean. I wish to assure him, and you all, of the wholehearted support that the Government of Malta, within its very modest means, would give to any extension of these proposals, as indeed to all the other excellent ones in the Report.

Original German: Mr. NORDMANN *(Secretary of State, Directorate of Labour, Federal Department of Economy, Switzerland)*

First of all, I would like to congratulate the President on his election. In my statement, on this year's Report of the Director-General, I will be commenting on his ideas about the implementation of the recommendations of the World Commission on the Social Dimension of Globalization.

The Director-General has taken stock of the strategic fundamental policy framework at the half-way point of the 2002-05 period with remarkable openness. Thus, he lists the successes that have been achieved to date and which have contributed to ensuring that the ILO has gained visibility and influence in recent years. We would like to congratulate the ILO on this success and we would like to encourage it to optimize its unique qualities, its tripartite structure, its efforts in standard-setting and the quality and relevance of its services.

In addition, the Report shows starkly where the ILO has reached the limits of its capacity. We therefore support increased investment in knowledge creation, more efficiency evaluations, more sustained personnel development and use of resources and improved integration of the ILO services and their fundamental policy objectives. Successfully taking up these challenges is a central prerequisite for the achievement of sustainable results in the implementation of the recommendations of the World Commission.

Switzerland has repeatedly said in recent years that it believes that progress in the following areas is crucial to the vision of the ILO's objectives.

The reform of standards: we support your call for a further strengthening of the standard-setting system – as this session of the Conference aims to do in the field of human resources – and a streamlining of ILO procedures. We therefore support your ideas on how the corresponding World Commission recommendations should be implemented.

With regard to your concern for promoting decent work in global production systems, which constitutes a central component of Switzerland's commitment to ILO projects, we support the transfer of knowledge for the sake of transparency and accountability of private initiatives and would again encourage that training courses be devised for the observance of international labour standards at company level. Our Government is constantly being asked for advice in this respect from Swiss companies.

Secondly, the strengthening of the ILO in the context of the social dimension of globalization: in this respect, we welcome your ideas with regard to the home front - strengthening the technical capacities of the social partners; optimization of the skills profile of the International Labour Office, in particular by increasing the number of top notch economists; and increased representation of women. In addition, we support your proposals for an improved impartial profiling of the ILO and for the building of partnerships with institutions and interest groups which share our concerns.

With reference to the multilateral initiative which Switzerland has previously endorsed within the framework of Geneva 2000, we support increased coherence of fundamental policies, particularly in order to better manage the interconnections between sustainable growth, investment and the creation of employment opportunities. We have noted with great interest the idea of a multidisciplinary working group for this area. We think it is meaningful to continue the impetus given by the World Commission's report by having regular exchanges of information and situation reports. It is essential for this that the individual players should work within their specific terms of reference, that they should avoid duplication and that the standardized indicators should be devised.

Mr. Director-General, by setting out your vision of drawing up recommendations for a fairer form of globalization, you have made it possible for the ILO to continue the pioneering role based on its Constitutional mandate and the Decent Work Agenda.

Based on the pointers that you have given in your review of the ILO's activities in 2002-03, and based on the messages and challenges you referred to yesterday in your Conference address, it is now up to us, the member groups, to get into the driving seat together with you and the International Labour Office within the framework of the Programme and Budget for 2006-07 and to examine the strategic fundamental policy framework for 2006-09, in order to continue to do justice to this role.

Switzerland is willing to follow your call to harness the potential of the global tripartite structure. Not because others could do this in our place, but because of the ILO's Constitutional mandate and its comparative advantage, which confers upon it its unique responsibility. You can count on Switzerland's active and reliable support.

Mr. MWAKWERE *(Minister for Labour and Human Resources Development, Kenya)*

On behalf of the Kenyan tripartite delegation, I congratulate the President together with the other Officers, upon his well-deserved election to guide the deliberations of this session of the Conference.

We know that the main theme of our discussion is the ILO's programme implementation for the biennia 2002-03, the report of the World Commission on the Social Dimension of Globalization and the Report entitled *A fair globalization: The role of the ILO*.

It is pleasing to know that the results of the ILO's programme implementation for the biennia 2002-03 clearly show that all four strategic objectives on fundamental principles and rights at work, that is employment creation, social protection for all, social dialogue and tripartism, were realized with varying degrees of success.

The Kenyan delegation congratulates the co-Chairs of the World Commission on the Social Dimension of Globalization, namely His Excellency President Benjamin Mkapa of the United Republic of Tanzania and President Tarja Halonen of Finland for their ground-breaking report entitled *A fair globalization: Creating opportunities for all*.

The report acknowledges that globalization's "potential for good is immense", but that owing to "deep-seated and persistent imbalances in the current workings of the global economy", globalization has, in the eyes in the vast majority of men and women, "not met their simple and legitimate aspirations for decent jobs and a better future for their children".

We recall that this report was presented and debated by the Governing Body on 24 March this year and that, at the request of the Governing Body, the Director-General submitted a Report which identified six areas in which the ILO can make a major contribution towards realizing the specific recommendations of the Commission.

The achievement of fairer and more inclusive globalization focusing on people and their needs will have to depend on better national governance in all countries, developed and developing.

International efforts, including efforts by the ILO, can only succeed if they gain acceptance at the national level. We therefore welcome the Director-General's emphasis on the need to make decent work a national, as well as a global goal; and indeed it must become a local goal.

On the issue of trade, we strongly believe that there is a need to follow up the multilateral trading system and to reduce unfair trade barriers to market access for goods like textiles, garments and cultural products where developing countries have a comparative advantage and very limited access to markets.

It is also clear that, in order for the Millennium Development Goals to be met by the year 2015, especially by developing countries, priority will have to be given to increasing development assistance, urgent action on debt relief and delivery on international commitments made, and so on and so forth.

Kenya also sees a need for new rules on foreign direct investment and competition. In this respect a balanced multilateral framework that takes into account all interest rights and responsibilities and the special needs of developing countries is needed. In order to make globalization inclusive and beneficial to all people, there is a need for follow-up action and dialogue, aimed at improving policy coherence at both national and international levels, and between international organizations.

With regard to the other agenda items, we note that this session of the Conference will hold discussions on the item on migrant workers, based on an integrated approach. Kenya endorses the view that there is a need for follow-up work aimed at building a multilateral framework that provides uniform and transparent rules for the cross-border movement of people and balances the interests of both migrants and countries of origin and destination.

As concerns the revision of the Human Resources Development Recommendation, 1975 (No. 150), Kenya is of the view that this session of the Conference should explore ways of reorienting our various educational and training programmes in order to ensure that the beneficiaries, and particularly the youth, have skills that match the needs of the economy.

The decision to adopt a comprehensive standard in the fishing sector is timely, given the fact that the sector is one of the most hazardous and has the highest fatality rate. Let me take this opportunity to express the Kenyan Government's appreciation of the ILO for the technical assistance given in the review just completed of six core chapters of our country's labour laws, with the aim of ensuring harmony between our domestic legislation and various international labour standards which we have ratified.

I wish to reiterate that the Kenyan Government remains fully committed to the basic provision of decent work for all workers through the promotion of ILO standards. To date, Kenya has ratified and continues to implement 49 ILO Conventions, which include seven out of eight core labour standards.

In conclusion, allow me to further reiterate the plea made here by the late Vice-President of Kenya as he presided over our Conference. The late Honourable Michael Kijana Wamalwa made a plea to provide our unemployed youth with decent work to persuade them not to live a life of violence. For the present Government in Kenya, this is a commitment we have undertaken seriously and intend to fulfil.

Thank you, may this session of the Conference be very fruitful and successful.

Original French: Mr. DE *(Minister of Public Services, Labour, Employment and Professional Organizations, Senegal)*

On behalf of the Senegalese delegation, which it is my honour to lead at this 92nd Session of the International Labour Conference, I should like, first of all, to express my warm congratulations to the President on his election to lead this session of the Conference.

I address my congratulations equally to the other Officers of the Conference.

I remain convinced that under the leadership of the President our work will meet with success.

The Report of the Director-General, *ILO Programme Implementation 2002-03*, with its appendix, *The situation of workers of the occupied Arab territories*, and the Global Report under the follow-up to the ILO Declaration on Fundamental Principles and Rights at Work have inspired me to reflect upon a number of issues that I should like to share with you.

It is my pleasure to note that the ILO has been able to effectively implement many actions and programmes in the Strategic Policy Framework for 2002-05 as defined by the Governing Body.

The Decent Work Agenda, which is an essential theme in the many activities carried out by the Office, has proven its utility and today is enshrined in law in all member States of the ILO and in global fora and bodies where issues of concern to our Organization are debated.

If this is the case, it is because our Organization, through remarkable consensus, has managed to define clear objectives and to set a coherent programme of work, which is the path to follow for our immediate and future actions.

The ILO has carried out activities with real impact in a country such as my own in standards-related activities, in promoting the Declaration on Fundamental Principles and Rights at Work and in initiatives promoting access to sustainable and productive employment, as well as in promoting tripartism and social dialogue and social protection.

During the period under review, advice and consultative services of very high quality have been made available to us, as well as a number of technical cooperation programmes which form part of the framework and the priorities determined by the Senegalese Government and social partners.

The Government of Senegal greatly appreciates the readiness to help and the high quality of assistance on the part of the subregional Office of the ILO in Dakar.

This close collaboration with the Office has allowed my country to make great progress in promoting social dialogue and in beginning reflection on how to improve social protection.

The desire to implement the institutional frameworks and mechanisms for promoting dialogue and permanent consultation has led to a deepening of the implementation of the national charter on social dialogue, upon which foundation Senegal intends to build its model for labour relations.

The National Committee for Social Dialogue, the main body of the charter, works closely with the ILO on priority questions such as extending social protection to all segments of the population. This is a major concern.

In this respect, the Government should like sincerely to thank the ILO for having chosen Dakar as the site for the West African launching of the Global Campaign on Social Security and Coverage for All. This ceremony was held on 14 April and was presided over by the President of the Republic of Senegal.

The ceremony met with great success and allowed us to focus upon the current state of social protection and to determine progress already made in working towards universal health coverage for all.

By pure coincidence, this year's discussion of the Global Report under the follow-up to the ILO Declaration on Fundamental Principles and Rights at Work addresses the right to organize and the effective recognition of the right to collective bargaining. The promotion and the realization of these principles are the main objectives of the Pamodec Senegal project which was launched in April 2003. The discussions and exchanges that will take place on this subject shall receive our full attention.

Senegal is a country of both emigration and of immigration and we will be especially attentive to the reflections carried out on this major issue of the migration of workers, a problem which is posed acutely around the world.

For my part, I should like to take this occasion to thank the delegates at the Conference who have honoured me by electing me Chairperson of the Committee on Migrant Workers.

Another subject of concern for this 92nd Session of the International Labour Conference is that of the social consequences of globalization.

In this respect, we should commend the remarkable results of the work of the World Commission on the Social Dimension of Globalization.

As I emphasized during a national consultation held in Dakar on the same subject, an accent must be placed on good communication policies which allow for the diffusion of the driving principles and the sharing of these principles with other institutions and organizations who are as concerned as we are at the process of globalization.

In conclusion, as Chair of the Committee on the Exercise of the Inalienable Rights of the Palestinian People, Senegal highly values the commendable efforts made by the Office and the measures which are envisioned to improve the fate of Palestinian workers in the occupied territories. Senegal calls upon the international community for the effective implementation of the United Nations resolutions guaranteeing the Palestinian people the right to reside in a safe and recognized territory.

I should like to restate my confidence in the future of our Organization, the pertinence, rightness and topicality of the ideals and values which are an important gage in our constant quest for greater peace, justice and prosperity.

(Mr. Maatough takes the Chair.)

Original French: Mr. THYS *(representative, World Confederation of Labour)*

International news and the daily lives of workers are dominated by violence – violence in the Middle East, violence in Iraq as well, violence in countries such as Colombia, where the lives of trade unionists are constantly threatened and where impunity is almost total. Structural violence, almost all over the world, caused by the imbalances of neo-liberal globalization and reinforced by policies which concentrate the wealth produced by the workers without redistributing it and which show contempt for their established rights and which undermine democracy in a scandalous way.

The International Labour Organization has a fundamental role to play today and this applies more than ever in this context. The Report, *ILO programme implementation 2002-03*, highlights the strengths and weaknesses of the ILO programme. What sets the ILO apart from the other international organizations is its standard-setting function and its tripartite structure.

The World Confederation of Labour shares this point of view. That is why we are insisting that the standards-monitoring system should be strengthened and this has to go hand in hand with an increase in the financial allocation that it receives on a structural basis. The workload of the International Labour Standards department is constantly increasing.

The workers would like more technical assistance, but also, and above all, a standards-setting system which is based on standards that are tailored to the reality of the world and on effective, swift, impartial and independent procedures. Tripartism too is in itself one of the foundations of world governance.

Another pillar of the ILO's plan of action is social protection. Today one person in five does not have adequate social protection. The privatization of this service, combined with the meagre budgets of excessively indebted states, means that we are moving away day by day from integral social protection for everybody and especially for all workers in precarious employment or in the informal economy. It is essential to strengthen this pillar and to do so by listening to and with the participation of all the constituents of the ILO. Taking into consideration the workers in the informal economy, a majority of whom are women, in order to defend the elementary rights within trade union confederations is a priority to which the World Confederation of Labour is devoted. Promoting peace is also a task to which the ILO should pay greater attention. We welcome the Report of the Director-General on *The situation of workers of the occupied Arab territories*, where Israel's policy of targeted assassinations is exacerbating a situation which is already strained and where the hope of a fair, peaceful and negotiated solution for the creation of Palestinian State becomes more distant day by day. The ILO has to devote itself more than ever to the task of creating decent work, which is the best way of combating poverty and it has to do so with all the constituents, particularly with all the trade union organizations of that region. We face two challenges here: rebuilding the domestic market in the occupied Arab territories and reinforcing a strategy of decent work in Israel itself, where the socio-economic situation has deteriorated considerably.

We are at a historic point in time, when the vital forces of society are coming together to affirm that a different world is possible. Finally, the report of the World Commission on the Social Dimension of Globalization has also established milestones for this different world. Ever since it was created in 1920, the World Confederation of Labour has struggled to introduce a social dimension to the policies carried out at all levels. This report urges us directly, as the World Confederation of Labour and as a constituent of the ILO, to guarantee follow up to the recommendations that have already been made. We would like to take action in this direction right away, within and alongside the ILO, and together with other trade union organizations, in order to strengthen a world based on solidarity, a world that is more democratic and more respectful of social justice.

Original French: Mr. BILTGEN *(Minister of Labour and Employment, Luxembourg)*

First of all I would like to congratulate the President warmly on behalf of my Government. The work of the International Labour Conference this year should be a decisive step for the future of our Organization's work. It will certainly also guide future joint efforts towards an inclusive and fair globalization.

The discussion on the conclusions of the World Commission on the Social Dimension of Globalization have shown that there is a new awareness on the part of the stakeholders, as well as a marked shift in attitudes on all sides. I can only express my admiration for the determination shown by the co-Chairs, President Halonen and President Mkapa, as well as the constructive attitude of all of the members of the Commission. It is now up to us to take up the challenge and rise to the occasion.

I would like to focus on a possible – and necessary – follow-up or practical implementation of the conclusions of the World Commission and of the action plan put forward by the Director-General in his Report, *A fair globalization: The role of the ILO* and further developed in his remarkable speech yesterday. My special thanks go to Mr. Somavia.

I would like to offer our Government's support for the implementation of the recommendations of the World Commission, and for the efforts made by Mr. Somavia with a view to refocusing the work of our Organization.

As regards the future of the ILO in the current context, I would like to begin by making a few remarks on two of the three messages and four challenges put forward by the Director-General: making decent work a global goal and making the ILO, with its unique tripartite structure, a true global actor while, in a wider sense, working for an "emerging global community", in the words of the World Commission. My Government is ready to cooperate.

If we are to translate the recommendations of the Commission and the Director-General into reality, in my view, we need to focus on five watchwords.

First, we need to reach consensus on a specific political vision that is aimed at inclusive globalization, which excludes no one. While based on the economic potential of markets, this approach will rest on a framework to ensure that the benefits of globalization are lasting and equitably shared. To this end, the global community needs to have fair rules on trade, investment, finance and migration. It needs to promote fundamental social and labour standards; and efforts need to be made to secure the necessary financial resources for capacity building and achieving the Millennium Development Goals.

Second, this vision needs to be translated into a strategy that is informed by solidarity and coherence. By "strategy" I mean a voluntarist policy approach, and "policy" here means the political will to assume responsibility and take action at all levels: the market alone will not automatically bring about the social equity that should be possible and even normal, given the enormous potential of globalization.

This strategy should reflect independent and mutually reinforcing elements as follows: economic growth arising out of a smoothly operating market and efficient investment; job creation, providing decent work for those who want it; social cohesion at every level, from local to global, starting with poverty eradication; sustainable development in all its aspects and at all levels; and respect for cultural identity in a world that is increasingly interdependent.

The European Union has acquired positive experience in this area. What is needed is a coherent strategy at every level, starting with coherence within each government, from which coherence in international organizations stems. Indeed, coherence at the second level, that of the multilateral system, depends on that of member States, for the organizations of the multinational system are in fact an expression of the sum of all the views of their constituents.

Our strategy must be based on solidarity, because ultimately the aim of all economic activity is the welfare of the greatest number of people. To this end, my country intends in the near future, to devote close to 1 per cent of our GDP to development policy and this is a source of pride and happiness for us.

Third, the implementation of the strategy means that all actors have to be publicly accountable, both internationally and nationally. If necessary, ad hoc fora should be created in addition to traditional institutional supervisory mechanisms.

Fourth, this strategy will only succeed if it is part of a framework guaranteeing better global governance. This means institutionalized governance with a public monitoring system covering the different policy areas affected by globalization; such governance is after all only the logical corollary of accountability of the stakeholders and proper coordination of policies.

Far from being some misconstrued idea of dirigisme, governance is a means of checking whether we are achieving our shared goals.

Fifth and last, the conclusions of the World Commission and the action plan put forward by Mr. Somavia concerning the specific role of the ILO must now be followed up by real and rapid action. My Government will strongly support the setting up of a regular forum on globalization policies, under the auspices of the United Nations, as was rightly proposed by the World Commission. The future largely depends on the comments and suggestions that will be made by our Conference to the Director-General of our Organization, who will play a key role in ensuring that they are implemented at the multilateral level. Beyond the confines of the ILO, all the players in the globalization process are waiting for a clear signal. I trust that we at the ILO will not disappoint them.

Original French: Mr. TROGRLIC (Workers' adviser and substitute delegate, France)

First of all, I would like to congratulate the President upon his election as well as congratulating all the Officers of the Conference.

On behalf of the workers of France, I would like to commend the World Commission on the Social Dimension of Globalization for the work it has carried out. Though many were doubtful of its capacity to progress beyond noting the different effects that globalization has on us or analysing its causes and mechanisms, the Commission can, in fact, be proud of itself on two counts. First, its methods, as has been highlighted by the ILO's Director-General, Mr. Juan Somavia, in his Report on the role of the ILO. The Commission has in fact proven that by allowing dialogue and exchange of views between people with initially very different opinions, a consensus can emerge. Second, it can be proud of the content of the report, over and above the rich, in-depth analysis that has been carried out. The report also contains proposals and advice which are realistic and adapted to the problem of global sustainable development.

I would like to thank the Director-General for his excellent Report on the role of the ILO. It displays the vital quality of being specific in translating broad trends into action; choices into acts. The goal has been set and the pathway is clear: that of a global, integrated and consistent approach, involving not only international decision-makers but also leaders at regional, national and local levels, along with all the elements of an emerging world society: economic players, social partners, organizations of civil society ... . We all have a role to play. We each can contribute something in order to meet the challenge of creating decent work for all and eradicating poverty for a fairer globalization.

But above all, there are two elements which are necessary in order to make effective progress along the path which has been set for us today. First of all, we need the political will to go down that path. At all levels of political responsibility, our leaders must coordinate their efforts to achieve this goal. We need to reform global government so that our policies in different areas can work together in order to provide better results. We need strong and active commitment from the different players involved through open dialogue, a meaningful exchange which, by bringing together conflicting points of view, can enable collective interests to be properly served.

I fully agree with the Report in so far as it supports and builds on the importance of tripartism and the participation of all those directly involved in our economic and social lives, i.e. the social partners. Trade unions have a great deal to bring to the formulation and implementation of development policies and to regulating globalization. In order to move forward, they will have to be able to extend their missions in a new and changing context, to develop and to strengthen their action at national, regional and global level.

The ability of enterprises to invest is particularly important. Their role in job creation is vital. The presence of trade unions in the workplace gives them a particular impetus and unmatchable strength in promoting and creating decent work for all. The social responsibility of enterprise must become part and parcel of the negotiation and social dialogue whose outcome must be agreements which can be implemented in practice in all countries concerned. Trade unions must learn to work together with civil society organizations who are also, in their own way, striving for development and social well-being. They can work with trade unions toward a common goal, lending it more strength and giving it a better chance of succeeding. This would be the best way to halt those people who tend toward the most radical or extreme views, not recognizing the potential for development that globalization can bring to us and the fact that, in spite of everything, it is indeed essential.

As a European, I note that the regional dimension retained in the Commission's report could be used as a springboard for the promotion of decent work. The European Union has demonstrated the usefulness of the regional integration process in accelerating the development of the least developed countries, through economic and social policies. At a time when the European Union is undergoing enlargement, we are confident of its ability to guide the international community to decisions based on respect and to values which the ILO, since its creation and with the signing of the Declaration of Philadelphia, has sought to uphold.

This is why, to conclude, I would ask in particular all European Governments to show an example and be a driving force in taking international action to achieve the global objective of a fairer globalization.

Mr. FONG *(Minister of Human Resources, Malaysia)*

On behalf of the Malaysian delegation I wish to congratulate the President of the 92nd Session of the International Labour Conference on his election. I would also like to congratulate the Employer and Worker Vice-Presidents on their election. We are confident that under their wise and able leadership this Conference will achieve its desired objectives.

The social dimension of globalization has been a topic of discussion for the past few years and it is one of the main concerns of the International Labour Organization. Malaysia welcomes the report of the World Commission on the Social Dimension of Globalization, which constitutes an important contribution to finding better ways of addressing globalization. Malaysia wishes to compliment and thank the co-Chairs, President Mkapa of the United Republic of Tanzania and President Halonen of Finland, and all the members of the Commission for their work, commitment, energy and ideas.

Overall, the report delivers a message that balances criticism and positive findings. The report contains some interesting analyses and proposals, including those on innovative working matters for improving policy coherence. Amongst the key issues highlighted are balanced economic, employment and social policies, better governance, policy coherence and strengthening multilateralism, trade and development.

In his Report on the World Commission on the Social Dimension of Globalization, *A fair globalization: The role of the ILO* the Director-General reminded us of the objective of the founders of the Organization 60 years ago, as set forth in the Declaration of Philadelphia, namely that we must not forget our strong ethical mandate which means that globalization should evolve on the basis of respect for justice and humanity.

To this end, globalization must be planned and planned carefully. The planning must involve everyone from every part of the globe. Government leaders, corporate players and unions bear equal responsibility for tackling globalization. Globalization should not be about business only but it should be about the well-being of everyone. Then and only then will globalization be meaningful to the world at large.

The livelihood of many families throughout the world are under serious threat; social policies must respond to their needs and aspirations. There cannot be successful globalization without successful national policies. As we continue to address the globalization process, we must not lose sight of the fact that the global goal remains decent work. At the same time, while globalization requires international responses, countries should be given the requisite latitude to implement policies based on their needs, circumstances and priorities.

Hence, in order to take account of reality and at the same time to ensure that globalization can work for more people, states must be allowed to determine their policies and priorities for implementing globalization in keeping with their own speed and capacity.

Malaysia, however, remains deeply concerned over the continued exclusion of developing countries from the benefits of globalization and over persistent income and economic gaps between the developed and developing countries, which must be bridged if developing countries are to benefit from the whole globalization process.

The Director-General's Report pointed out that the ILO has a central role to play in bringing about fair globalization, but only if global tripartism can cultivate its considerable potential for mobilizing the global community.

My delegation is pleased with the Report of the Director-General on *ILO programme implementation 2002-03*. In implementing the ILO Decent Work Agenda, Malaysia would like to emphasize that there is a need to create more jobs in order to absorb new entrants into the labour market and to make some inroads into the problem of unemployment. The ILO and other multilateral agencies must play a significant and useful role in supporting the member countries in their efforts. In the present context of liberalization, globalization and a changed economic scenario, the emphasis needs to be on upgrading the skills of the labour force, by providing adequate opportunities for implementing formal and informal vocational training programmes, keeping in mind the demand of the labour market.

In order to achieve this objective, it is vital to maintain an adequate level of social protection, and promote increased flexibility and security in the workplace. Addressing change, promoting adaptability in the labour market and investment in human resources must be priorities for all of us.

We share the deep concern expressed in the Report of the Director-General on *The situation of workers in the occupied Arab territories*, as the situation of workers and their families has worsened. According to the Report, the economic and social circumstances of workers in the occupied territories, human security, rights at work, income, access to employment and social protection are under constant threat. Restrictions on the movement of Palestinian workers resulting from road closures, prolonged security checks and curfews have increased the cost of goods and services and the loss of earnings. This has led to a dramatic decline in consumption, income and employment levels. The removal of these restrictions is a prerequisite for the application of fundamental principles and rights at work. Israel is continuing its demolition of Palestinian houses and civilian properties and its massive confiscation and destruction of Palestinian land. If this situation continues, we can only sadly conclude that the prospects for the well-being of the Palestinian people will continue to remain bleak.

Malaysia welcomes the efforts of the ILO to assist the Palestinian people through its ongoing technical cooperation programmes and capacity-building projects. More effort should be devoted to generating employment and providing social protection. However, the plight of the Palestinian people can be overcome only through a political solution, with the establishment of an independent and sovereign State of Palestine. Malaysia reaffirms its commitment to the peace process in the Middle East, on the basis of full implementation of the Road Map and the Arab Peace Initiative.

Malaysia, as Chairman of the Non-Aligned Movement, welcomes the effort of the ILO to assist the Palestinian people. At the same time, the Non-Aligned Movement calls on the ILO to step up its programme of support to employers and workers in Palestine and other occupied Arab territories, which is aimed at developing work opportunities and eradicating poverty and unemployment.

The Non-Aligned Movement wishes to reiterate its concern over the current methods and procedures for supervising labour standards. We welcome international cooperation as an important contribution to the effective realization of international labour standards and, to this end, we particularly regard the effective review and improvement of the working methods of the Committee on the Application of Standards as vital for the sake of transparency and impartiality.

In this regard, the Non-Aligned Movement supports the draft paper presented to the Committee on the Application of Standards by Cuba on behalf of 18 countries, which provides inputs on ways of improving the working methods of the Committee on the Application of Standards.

The Non-Aligned Movement also urges that the benefits of globalization be shared equitably amongst all countries.

Mr. LEE (Employers' delegate, Republic of Korea)

On behalf of the Korean employers, I would like to extend our sincere congratulations to Mr. Ray Guevara on his election as President of this session of the Conference.

It is encouraging to note that the report of the World Commission on the Social Dimension of Globalization is entitled *A fair globalization: Creating opportunities for all*. Fair globalization does not secure the same results for all, but it does create opportunities for all.

However, the report overemphasizes the negative impact by arguing that the current process of globalization is generating imbalances, both between and within countries. We should not simply assume that globalization alone is the cause of poverty and inequality. Poverty and inequality are affected by a diverse range of factors such as political instability, poor governance, corruption and a poor investment climate.

Over the last decades we have witnessed the emergence of globalization. Now, globalization is a phenomenon which is not likely to disappear because it may cause problems. It is like a force of nature at this point and it is no longer a matter of choice.

The report aptly emphasized the importance of good governance at the national level. The basic ingredient in the effective construction and operation of a democratic market economy model is the accountability and responsibility of all actors at the national level – enterprises, workers and government.

Firstly, we have to recognize the crucial role enterprises play in order to meet the challenges and reap the benefits of the opportunities presented by globalization. The enterprises should become competitive through financial stability and efficient management. Employers should also make bold efforts to attain good corporate governance by implementing transparent management and promoting business ethics, which will help eliminate prevailing anti-business sentiments, win public confidence and maintain cooperative labour-management relations.

Secondly, workers and trades unions must maintain social responsibility to provide remedies for problems identified. It is erroneous to merely attribute social problems to globalization or denounce productivity and competitiveness as exploitation by employers. They should recognize that productivity and competitiveness are directly related to their own best interests. They should implement more globalized practices in order to reap the benefits of globalization with adequate knowledge and skills. They should develop new work ethics that are based on the spirit of "live and let live". Sometimes they must share their unavoidable problems in order to save their jobs and help marginalized workers to enter the labour market.

Thirdly, governments wishing to benefit from globalization need to promote political transparency, economic openness and institutional reform. At the same time, governments should examine obstacles to business growth and competitiveness in order to create an appropriate economic environment to attract investment for business development and employment creation.

The responsibilities should be shared by all those involved. Also, there is a need to strengthen the social dialogue among those involved to reach proper solutions that will lend policies greater legitimacy and promote fair distribution of the benefits of globalization.

The report has many far-reaching recommendations and proposals, many of which are key areas in the work of the ILO. An agenda needs to be devised that is based on bringing the benefits of globalization to all countries that wish to participate in it. This agenda must recognize the crucial role of enterprises for economic and social development in general, and for job generation in particular.

In the Republic of Korea, public debate on policies and ideology, be they conservative or liberal, be they growth or distribution, is now at an impasse. We are doing our utmost to break the current impasse by focusing on the concerns and aspirations of the people – and that is job creation.

It is my firm belief that increased productivity, based on entrepreneurship and new technologies, coupled with the self-adjusting power of the free market economy, will eventually lead to increased wealth and greater sense of well-being for people.

Original Arabic: Mr. GUIDER *(representative, Arab Labour Organization)*

In the name of God, the Merciful, the Compassionate, first of all, I would like to congratulate the President, Mr. Ray Guevara, and my fellow engineer, Mr. Maatough, and the other Vice-Presidents on their election. On behalf of the Arab Labour Organization, I would like to extend my gratitude and respects to Mr. Juan Somavia, Director-General of the International Labour Organization, for his efforts and organized work to increase the ILO's activities in all areas.

In this respect, I wish to praise the fruitful cooperation over the past year between the International Labour Organization and the Arab Labour Organization, thanks to our distinguished brother, Dr. Taleb Rifai, Director of the Regional Office for the Arab States.

The agenda of this session of the Conference contains some very important subjects, one of which is the Report of the Director-General concerning programme implementation and the activities of the Organization. In this regard, and on behalf of the Arab Labour Organization, I wish to express my appreciation for what has been done, and I hope for further beneficial technical cooperation between the tripartite social partner and the ILO in our region.

I would like to highlight the progress made in promoting the ILO Declaration on Fundamental Principles and Rights at Work, in particular the rights to freedom of association and collective bargaining. Similarly, I should also mention the positive steps taken by Qatar and Oman in adopting new legislation on these issues. The report of the World Commission on the Social Dimension of Globalization, working conditions in the fishing sector, migrant workers and human resources training and development are important questions to which answers must be found, to the benefit of the whole of humanity.

It is only right for me to thank the Director-General for the personal interest he has shown in monitoring the situation of Arab workers in Palestine and the other occupied Arab territories, as seen from the preface to this Report and his speech last Tuesday. I would like to point out that the Arab group participating in the present session has several observations in this respect, which it is to submit in writing to the Director-General.

The idea of human rights has become one of the most fundamental issues in contemporary societies based on human conscience since it forms the foundation upon which should be built the system of humanity. It is regarded as a major component that should be used by governments and indeed the economic and social system of any society. These human rights are considered to be important values which should be respected and implemented without any changes, regardless of the nationality, religion, race, origin, and economic and social status of any person.

Based on this, the issue of protecting freedoms and rights has been one of the focuses of the International Labour Organization ever since it was created, and is also one of the Arab Labour Organization's objectives, as enshrined in its Constitution and the Arab Labour Agreement.

Using the agreements and declarations of the past in order to build a greater future does not mean that we should mourn the past; we should rather be aware that these agreements will remain mere words if we do not strive to make them a reality.

Where are these wonderful agreements when it comes to the actions committed by those who say they are protecting the Arab territory of Palestine? Where are these noble principles when it comes to the day-to-day humiliation of our workers in Syrian Golan and southern Lebanon and the economic sanctions imposed on the population there, such as the law on sanctions against Syria, and previously against the Libyan Arab Jamahiriya and Sudan? Where are these great humanitarian values when it comes to the fate of Arabs in Iraq? Where are these humanitarian values and principles when it comes to acts of violence and their consequences for humankind the world over?

You will no doubt share our view that violence breeds violence, and that history shows how the use of force to subdue the will of the people and control them has always ended in failure. Does he who holds power realize that there is a power greater than him, a power which, if called upon, could alone make all the peoples of the world equal?

I will end my speech with a well-known Arab saying which I would like to address to each and every despot: "If your power leads you to commit injustices against others, do not forget that God is more powerful than you."

(Mr. Guevara takes the Chair.)

Original Spanish: Mr. MORALES CARTAYA *(Minister of Labour and Social Security, Cuba)*

I would like to congratulate you on your nomination, President. The ILO has always been a standard-bearer in helping to achieve labour rights, including the aim of full employment and promoting universal social security services, social protection services. However, when we look at what is going on in the world today, and particularly in the countries of the south, I think the very sad conclusion is that the situation is dramatic.

Let me give you some figures to illustrate that. There are 185.9 million jobless. This is the highest figure ever recorded. Two hundred and eleven million children are forced to work, 40 million people are living with AIDS, only 20 per cent of the world population has access to social security, and more than half have no type of social protection available to them. We are seeing a massive increase in the informal economy and in casual employment. Five hundred and fifty million workers get by with one dollar a day. Twelve million children die every year from preventable or curable diseases, 826 million go hungry, and 854 million are illiterate.

Original Spanish: Mr. MORALES CARTAYA *(Minister of Labour and Social Security, Cuba)*

I would like to congratulate the President on his election. The ILO has always been a standard-bearer in helping to achieve labour rights, including the aim of full employment and promoting universal social security and social protection services. However, when we look at what is going on in the world today, and particularly in the countries of the South, I think the very sad conclusion is that the situation is truly dramatic.

Let me give you some figures to illustrate this. There are 185.9 million jobless, the highest figure ever recorded; 211 million children are forced to work; 40 million people are living with AIDS; only 20 per cent of the world population has access to social security, and more than half have no type of social protection available to them; we are seeing a massive increase in the informal economy and in casual employment; 550 million workers get by on one dollar a day; 12 million children die every year from preventable or curable diseases; 826 million go hungry; and 854 million are illiterate.

We have an abundance of commitments, goals and world action programmes with a view to working towards a better world. That better world is, of course, possible, but it is turning into an absolute illusion, given the conditions we are seeing of selfishness and barbarity which are being imposed through neo-liberal globalization and a world order which is subject to the hegemonic domination of a single superpower which has recourse, and I quote, "preventively" to war and coercion which flagrantly violates and tramples on the basic principles and standards of international law and the Charter of the United Nations.

Workers in the occupied Arab territories will only be in a position to truly achieve and enjoy international labour standards and social and labour rights when South Lebanon is totally liberated, when the Golan returns fully to the sovereignty of Syria and when in the West Bank and Gaza we see a Palestinian State which is both free and independent.

The international economic order is immoral, it is unjust and it is unsustainable. It feeds on the sweat and the suffering of the huge majority of workers who are doomed to a wretched existence and, worse still, on the very existence of further millions of people who are not even given the opportunity to be exploited at work.

The unilateral – let us say this clearly – and aggressive actions of the United States, underpinned by their military superiority and, indeed, their self-proclaimed role as world policemen, are an outrage to peace, development, justice and world democracy.

Cuba, whose heroic workers are not afraid to show dissent and are not afraid to stand up and fight this imperial domination which seeks to impose itself on the peoples of the South and large majorities in the North, has a very different reality. It is putting into practice numerous programmes and projects aimed at enhancing equity and social justice, overcoming the restrictions and obstacles imposed on it thorough the longest and most genocidal economic, commercial and financial blockade in history.

In Cuba, all children go to school, they all have the opportunity to study at university and are all entitled to highly specialized medical care, free of charge. No child is forced to work. There are no people left by the wayside in Cuba.

Our main wealth is our human capital which arose from the ashes of the illiteracy inherited by the Cuban Revolution. An expression of our deeply humanist and united values can be seen in the fact that more than 17,000 doctors work in very difficult conditions in 65 countries, many of which are represented in this room. More than 17,000 young people from 110 different countries are able to study in Cuba, free of charge, most of them in higher education.

So what is the crime that has been committed by the Cuban people that can justify the sickening and aggressive behaviour of the United States Government as it applies new and even more brutal measures with the aim of destroying the constitutional order established by the workers and all Cubans.

The only faults committed – and only vis-à-vis the empire – are the defence of our sovereignty, freedom and independence, the building of a fairer and more united society and maintaining the conviction that a better world is possible.

Amongst the new anti-Cuban measures announced by the United States Government we have the allocation of US$59 million to promote and finance a fifth column to support its hostile actions and to involve governments from other countries, non-governmental organizations and international bodies in anti-Cuban campaigns, and even – and I quote – "to work with NGOs and other interested parties to assure that a Cuban independent labour representative, or a labour representative in exile, is able to speak at ILO conferences".

These new measures are doomed to failure. As a member State of the ILO, we have always fulfilled our obligations and will continue to do so. It is imperative, however, to be aware that we are not yet too late to prevent, if we take effective action, the ILO from becoming a hostage to discriminatory practices and political manipulation.

We reiterate Cuba's decision to stand up to, with truth and the necessary serenity, any attempt, be it overt or concealed, to discredit or harm the conquests achieved by its people with heroism, dignity and steadfast resolution.

Original Russian: Mr. PAPIEV *(Government delegate, Ukraine)*

First of all I should like to join in the congratulations and wishes for success addressed to the President of the Conference in connection with his election to this important position.

I should like to thank the Director-General of the ILO, Mr. Juan Somavia, for the informative Report that he has submitted to the current session of the Conference.

The Report of the Director-General on *ILO programme implementation 2002-03* contains, in our view, a comprehensive analysis of the implementation of the programme aims of the ILO, the backbone of which are such strategic objectives as promoting the implementation of fundamental principles and rights at work; ensuring decent work and decent wages; ensuring effective social protection for all; and the strengthening of tripartism and social dialogue. The Report provides detailed information on ILO efforts in these areas and includes useful statistics, in addition to the basic content.

I should like especially to note that, together with the tangible progress made in strengthening and developing the regional activities of the organization, the ILO has begun to pay significantly greater attention to ensuring the effectiveness of its work at country level.

We are convinced that it is the adoption of a comprehensive approach to the development of international cooperation under the aegis of the ILO that will allow us to take fully into account the specificities and requirements of individual countries and of regions.

In our view, the Report of the Director-General, *Organizing for social justice*, deserves particular attention. Through its nature and content it confirms the consistent implementation of ILO activities in implementing the Declaration on Fundamental Principles and Rights at Work. It is also fully in keeping with the recently published conclusions of the World Commission on the Social Dimensions of Globalization.

Democratic states can only develop in an effective and stable manner in conditions of social dialogue, which ensures strong and independent trade unions and employers' organizations.

The conclusions found in the Global Report concur with the position of the Government of Ukraine, which is implementing that position through consistent daily work to reform labour and labour relations legislation.

As a young State, after 13 years of independence, Ukraine has rapidly travelled a path that corresponds to many decades of development in democratic countries. Recent years have shown that the Government of Ukraine acted correctly in its efforts to develop social dialogue and tripartism. This policy is strengthened in the Government's programme of activities, which has been approved by the Parliament of Ukraine. We are convinced that strengthening social dialogue must remain an important component of the efforts to ensure rapid economic growth, and steady increases in wages and in the standard of living.

In our country reforms have been successfully carried out in the area of state social security. Reforms to the pension system have significantly increased pensions for more than 3.5 million pensioners. There are also positive changes taking place in the labour market; all social contributions have been increased and salaries have risen by 23 per cent. Debts are being paid off and the Government is trying, through dialogue and collective bargaining to reach a decision regarding an increase in the minimum wage.

In Ukraine the practice of direct participation of all social partners in formulating social labour legislation, as well as strategic programmes for social and economic cooperation is developing. This practice is enshrined in a general agreement for the next two years. In addition to the Government and employers' organizations, more than 70 Ukrainian trade unions were involved in the signing of that agreement.

The Government supports the recommendations of the Global Report regarding the necessity of broadening the practice of concluding sectoral agreements at the national level.

Ukraine has ratified 57 ILO Conventions, including all of the core Conventions. Last year alone, Conventions Nos. 135 and 159 were ratified. Four further Conventions are being prepared for ratification. Another clear example of our cooperation is the implementation in Ukraine of eight ILO programmes. These programmes touch on various fields, including vocational training for the unemployed, socio-economic protection, the eradication of child labour, the prevention of the trade in women and children and the problem of HIV/AIDS at the workplace.

A new Labour Code has been formulated, which has been examined by ILO experts and adopted by Parliament on its first reading.

In the future, we continue to count on technical and advisory assistance on the part of the ILO for a series of important issues, which will be identified in a new programme of cooperation between Ukraine and the ILO. One of them is the social protection of Ukrainian migrant workers. The Government of Ukraine is taking necessary legal and administrative measures to stem the tide of illegal migration and of trafficking in human beings, but we do not have the necessary support from a number of European countries. In our view, the ILO could play a more active role in promoting ratification of the Migrant Workers (Supplementary Provisions) Convention, 1975 (No. 143).

In conclusion, I should like to wish the Conference every success.

Mr. IVERSEN *(Government delegate, Denmark)*

Let me start by thanking the Director-General and the ILO staff for the excellent and very transparent Report, *ILO programme implementation 2002-03*.

Furthermore, allow me to thank the ILO and the World Commission on the Social Dimension of Globalization for the enormous and valuable contributions to enable us to give responses to the negative effects of globalization.

Employment, indigenous people, gender equality and the fight against child labour are some of the things governments prioritize in their cooperation with the ILO. In this context, the Danish Government is happy to learn from the Report that the ILO has given more emphasis to results-based management and country-based programming.

Denmark is also happy to learn that the Report puts a special focus on the ILO Decent Work Agenda. Denmark is actually one of the pilot countries in the decent work strategy.

The four pillars of decent work – promotion of rights at work, employment, social protection and social dialogue – contain many of the challenges that must be dealt with if we are to obtain more welfare for many more people.

In the WTO context, discussions frequently relate to the question of whether rights for workers in real terms constitute hidden protectionism or are meant sincerely as improvement of workers' conditions, especially in developing countries.

I cannot give you an answer today to this question. I can only share with you that it is our experience that people in Denmark, as well as in other parts of the developed world, focus not only on their personal well-being but also on global ethics. Therefore, we have to find regional and international solutions to common problems and not give in to short-term solutions that only benefit the nearest few. We must look for win-win objectives.

The Decent Work Agenda really gives a sympathetic and tangible approach to the task.

As foreseen in the Report entitled *ILO programme implementation 2002-03*, working with the Decent Work Agenda requires continuous consideration of new ways and means of how to create improvements. Probably there are not many one-size-fits-all solutions. Within the ILO, we must act together in a sensible manner and must be able to adjust to specific situations.

The Report reveals that the ILO has moved towards country-based programming in combination with a revised Strategic Policy Framework, which emphasizes external communications. This is a step that appears to be both intelligent and logical. Achievements of tangible benefits for individuals locally, and the ability to "hit" the media with such news, are really strong tools in the modern world.

Original Arabic: Mr. HAMADEH *(Employers' delegate, Lebanon)*

On behalf of the employers of Lebanon, I would like to thank the ILO for providing me with this opportunity to address the social partners with regard to subjects as varied as economics, development, productivity, social justice, equality, decent work and all the other subjects which are of concern to us here today.

We are delighted to be able to participate in this annual session of the Conference, and are particularly pleased that the ILO has sought to set ambitious objectives for our economic and social actions – objectives that we strive to achieve throughout the year in order to create a productive society.

Universality is a source of energy. Openness brings new perspectives. This is why we cannot but endorse the objectives of the Director-General concerning the social dimension of globalization and decent work. Whatever the differences in our national priorities, these do not detract from the fact that we must labour to create a climate favourable to work for all our workers. The wind of globalization blows over our lands. Globalization is happening whether we know it or not – sometimes even whether we like it or not. This is, in fact, the revolution of the third millennium. The world is constantly changing. There is no country, no society, no enterprise that is sheltered from this revolution. No one can prevent it. It is a revolution with the unstoppable momentum of a runaway train. All those already on board the train will arrive at their destination, while the rest watch helplessly from the platform.

In this era of globalization, enterprises, banks and cartels have been become obsessed with acquisitions and mergers as they try to reap the benefits of globalization and the opportunities it offers. In the future, there will be two types of organization: those at the head of the pack and those at the rear, the conventional ones. The fate of these organizations is in your hands. What do you think is the best alternative? To continue working in a conventional way or to innovate? To preserve the best or to innovate by improving the best? For waiting around with our arms folded is certain death. We must discover the new; we must innovate.

At this point, I must highlight the occupation, oppression and aggression to which our region is victim and which prevents us from attaining our economic, social and development goals. I do not need to remind you that these goals are also the goals of the ILO and of the overwhelming majority of the member States. As I stand on this platform, therefore, I would like to salute my Palestinian brothers, these workers and employers, in the hope that they too, one day, achieve their social rights, their human rights, and all the rights held by all the people who do not live under the yoke of occupation. I also wish to greet my Syrian and Libyan brothers as they try to liberate their national territory. They are free men in their rights, their thinking, their allegiance and their loyalty. I would like to tell them that the values that we strive to defend here, within the ILO, are the values which will triumph and which will defeat oppression, injustice and occupation.

This is why we will continue to demonstrate openness, to work with the Lebanese social partners and the Arab partners on the international stage, under the leadership of the ILO, to put these human values into practice – the values on which this Organization is founded and which are expressed in the Director-General's Report.

In this regard, we feel duty-bound to mention some achievements that we have been able to make in the area of industrial development in Lebanon. The Government of Lebanon has responded to certain demands made by industrial leaders, which are based on serious studies, and which were made in collaboration with the relevant ministers. We have been able to lower the cost of social security coverage and increase the number of beneficiaries. We have succeeded in reducing custom duties on core industrial products. We have also been able to subsidize interest rates to encourage small and medium-sized enterprises to take out investment loans. Last year, we were able to increase exports to 28.6 per cent. We were successful in job creation; we created 20 per cent more jobs which enabled us to offset losses in public funds. This facilitated the creation of more jobs and made it possible to encourage enterprises. Thus, we organized a meeting which we entitled "National Lebanese Industry Day", under the patronage of the President of the Republic. Five prizes were given to the five best-performing enterprises.

Finally, I must reiterate that my association will not cease to work to improve economic performance, which is the means through which productivity and competitiveness can increase. We believe that this must be the basis of all economic and social activity aimed at bringing justice and equality, particularly in the face of competition and of the interests of the large cartels.

Original Chinese: Mr. XU *(Workers' delegate, China)*

First of all, I would like to extend my heart-felt congratulations to the President on his election.

The annual International Labour Conference is a grand gathering for working people across the world. The Report, *ILO programme implementation 2002-03*, delivered by the Director-General, Mr. Somavia, has made a comprehensive summary of the ILO's effective activities for the past two years and of progress made in the four strategic objectives of decent work.

Through fruitful efforts over the past two years, the World Commission on the Social Dimension of Globalization has presented its report to the Conference. The report has had strong repercussions in the international community. Economic globalization is a much talked about subject as it has a bearing on every aspect of life. In fact, economic globalization is an inevitable process in the development of the world economy. The trend of globalization is unstoppable, whether you like it or not.

There are many reasons behind economic globalization, but the main reason is the cross-border flows of capital. The internationalization of capital has promoted the globalization of trade, production, products, markets, labour and technology. The rapid advancement in new and high technologies, especially information technology, has accelerated the process of economic globalization.

Both developed and developing countries have faced pressures and challenges in the context of economic globalization. The unfairness, irrationality and active impact of economic globalization is felt by more and more people; they long for it to be fairer and more rational.

At the same time, there is a growing awareness that the key cause of such a situation is the old international economic and trade order, namely unbalanced global rules, irrational trade policies and abnormal economic operations. Therefore, there is a common aspiration to bring an end to such a malpractice and put in place a new fair and reasonable international economic and trade order.

Historical experience has proved many a time that, without the backing of social progress, economic development cannot be sustained. Economic globalization has varying adverse effects on all working people around the world, particularly the vast number of employees, which is a severe challenge to each and every trade union. The key is how to secure workers' rights, protect their interests and to do practical things for them. Every country has its own success stories and experience in respecting and safeguarding workers' fundamental rights. The Chinese trade unions have set themselves a clear objective: to get workers organized and protect their rights. We maintain that a sound tripartite machinery should be established where governments, workers and employers can have consultations on an equal footing and find solutions to their common concerns. We are also of the opinion that trade unions in various countries should develop cooperation and conduct dialogue, give up confrontation and seek common ground, whilst putting aside differences. Cooperation and dialogue is the world trend; confrontation goes against it and thus has no future. Every trade union should earnestly perform its responsibilities and duties and protect workers' rights and interests. Only in doing so can economic development and social stability be achieved and workers' interests be protected. The Chinese trade unions call on working people all over the world to unite and make joint efforts to safeguard workers' rights and face up to the challenges of economic globalization.

We support the draft resolution of Arab countries regarding Palestine and the other occupied Arab territories and call on the ILO to pay more attention to, and be more concerned with, the issue and facilitate an early realization of peace in the Middle East and in the world for all workers.

Peace and development are the overriding themes of today's world. The Chinese trade unions will, as always, support an enhanced cooperation with trade unions from other countries and with the ILO, to defend peace and oppose war, promote common prosperity and fight poverty. The Chinese trade unions are ready to join hands with other trade unions and press ahead with greater contributions to the course of peace and development.

Original Spanish: Mr. CALDERA SANCHEZ-CAPITAN *(Minister for Labour and Social Affairs, Spain)*

First of all, I would like to start by congratulating Mr. Milton Ray Guevara, Secretary of State for Labour of the Dominican Republic, for his appointment as President of this 92nd Session of the International Labour Conference. The Spanish delegation, of which I am head, will continue to work with you to ensure that the objectives of this session of the Conference are reached.

I would also like to congratulate the Director-General on his Report, *ILO programme implementation 2002-03*, which takes stock of the activities carried out and the aims achieved during that period. We are also reminded that decent work, or working with dignity, as we call it in Spain, is still a universal aspiration. Unfortunately, we are still far from achieving this and cannot therefore rest on our laurels. However, my Government is showing its will to work towards this universal aspiration, which represents the hopes of everyone: productive work in conditions of freedom, equity, safety and human dignity.

Decent work is a concept which encompasses the four strategic objectives of the ILO which relate to employment, fundamental labour rights, social protection and social dialogue. These strategic objectives of the ILO are a global and coherent response to the social problems which afflict all countries, and indeed to the new challenges of globalization, trade liberalization and regional integration.

As we heard yesterday, we want globalization with a human face, which corrects the inequalities that exist worldwide, and where social protection and economic efficiency are compatible.

We agree with the Director-General when he says in his Report that the ILO is effective in and should focus on, according to his words, a normative function and tripartite structure; in other words, drawing up international instruments which should be the subject of major campaigns with a view to their adoption by member States.

To this end, I would like to remind you that Spain has ratified 129 Conventions. Together with standard-setting activities, we would like to underscore another essential objective of the ILO: its work in the field of technical cooperation. The Spanish State contributes positively to the ILO's activities in this area. In addition to financial contributions, we are doing our best to maintain our prominent position as regards extra-budgetary contributions provided through technical cooperation. This can be seen through our active cooperation in the IPEC programme and many other cooperation projects, mainly those being developed in Latin America.

I would like to briefly say something about the guiding principles inspiring the social policy of my country, and which I think are closely linked to the work carried out by this Conference. In the Ministry of Labour, we are giving priority to dialogue and consensus; this is the best way of achieving our work. This is one of the reasons why it is an honour for me to address you within the framework of this unique tripartite body within the United Nations system, where governments, employers and workers are on an equal footing.

My Government feels that this is an essential factor, a vital tool if we are to make progress in the area of labour policies, develop our social safety net and also consolidate many labour policy instruments. We have already taken the first steps and we hope to reach a broad agreement with employers and trade union organizations to achieve competitiveness and stable employment.

As regards training, my Government is banking on the knowledge-based society, in line with the European Union's recommendations related to general guidelines for the economic policies of Member States. This requires major investments in training as a way of ensuring professional qualifications and guaranteeing the employability of the entire active population.

With reference to the quality of work, in Spain, we are trying to create more dignified work with rights, through the following. As regards temporary contracts, which are very common in Spain and represent 30 per cent of overall contracts, the Government wants to reduce the number of these contracts. One of the reasons for this is that in many cases the temporary nature of this work cannot be justified, and it also has negative effects on the quality of the job, access to training and accident rates.

Reducing accident rates is another priority of our Government. We want to make our labour market a safer one for individuals, where decent work is something more than empty words.

Last, but not least, is the issue of immigration. My open recognition of migration is a result of the situation in my country. Millions of Spaniards have gone abroad, and thousands still live abroad, leaving their mark in various places throughout the world.

As the labour minister of a socialist Government, I can only declare myself in favour of strengthening social policies in the twenty-first century. We are going to move in this direction with a new vision of deep respect for individuals, human rights, and workers' rights, and with respect for plurality, different cultures, religions and traditions, whilst continually combating racism, xenophobia, social exclusion, unfair treatment and discrimination based on ethnic or racial origin.

My commitment is also to actively struggle for the integration of immigrants, who form part of our society, to the point of dying amongst us, as we so tragically witnessed, on 11 March, in Madrid.

We want to move forward by promoting a policy of normalizing social relations, of acceptance of all, and of support for logical integration policies inside Spain, and the proper management of flows abroad. Such a policy will actively intervene to combat mafia organizations, provide individuals with training, coordinate needs and formulate, design and implement integration policies targeting people intending to migrate before they leave their country of origin; these policies should, as far as possible, prevent initial cultural shocks and enable and promote appropriate integration into the labour market, whilst helping people to avoid exclusion, the underground economy and marginalization.

We also need policies to monitor and regulate migration. The struggle against illegal immigration is one of our priorities in this area and aims to guarantee a new type of management and appropriate integration, including through legal means.

Lastly, I would like to thank you for having given me the opportunity to address this Conference, and I wish you every success in your work.

Original French: Mr. BOTI *(Minister of Civil Service, Labour, Social Security and Occupational Integration, Central African Republic)*

As I come to the podium to address this assembly I would like, first of all, like those who have preceded me, to extend my heartfelt congratulations to the President of this session of the Conference for his election to this post. It is evidence of his high qualifications as a man aware of the problems faced by the world of work at a time of technological change when poverty and HIV/AIDS control are of grave concern.

I would also like to extend my congratulations to the Vice-Presidents appointed to assist the President in his difficult task over the next 17 days. I would like to take this opportunity as well, on behalf of the President of the Central African Republic, His Excellency, General François Bozize, on behalf of the Vice-President of the Republic, Professor Abel Goumba, that of the Prime Minister, His Excellency Célestin Leroy Gaombalet, on behalf of the delegation accompanying me and on my behalf to congratulate the Director-General of the ILO, Juan Somavia, for his choice of the themes addressed in his Report, and for the quality and the relevance of their content which in fact have taken into account all of the concerns interacting in the world of work and which make the challenges more complex and difficult.

I would also like to thank the whole ILO team and in particular the ILO subregional office for Central Africa which certainly wanted, in November 2003, to help the Central African Republic to carry out the last phase of its labour administration that had been badly shaken by numerous military and political crises in the preceding years.

We listened to the speeches by Their Excellencies Ms. Halonen, the President of Finland and Mr. Benjamin Mkapa from the United Republic of Tanzania who emphasized important points from the report on the social dimension of globalization.

The true value of globalization can only be appreciated if it offers all levels of society in Northern and Southern countries well-being and social justice. This means that we need to have solidarity among all states.

In the ILO's report on the social dimension of globalization and decent work, social dialogue and respect for basic rights of workers are essential for successful globalization.

For less affluent states, success in these areas depends simply on sustained aid and cooperation from our partners.

We have noticed that each day that goes by marks a day of history and this is true for the Central African Republic as well. The Central African Republic is emerging from a situation which contained all types of bad experiences: poor public management, ethnic exclusions, vendettas, our rupture with our social partners and development partners. Impunity was established under the regime of Ange Félix Patasse, thereby opening the door to deeper poverty, to the HIV/AIDS pandemic, to unpaid wages, scholarships and pensions. All of this has become an endemic problem.

General questioning of this predatory authoritarianism has, in fact, led to all kinds of acts of vandalism: plundering, massive destruction of personal estate and units of production. This has left thousands of men and women unemployed, out on the street. Today, the buildings which once housed the labour inspection offices have been plundered and their occupants, the labour inspectors, are now without a place to work.

Since the political events of 15 March 2003 led by General François Bozize, substantial efforts have been made in order to respect the commitments made to our social partners and international organizations in order to give renewed credibility to the Central African Republic which, at one point in time, was managed as though all of its wealth was simply personal fortune.

New authorities in the Central African Republic rapidly understood that the problems with which they were faced were multidimensional and multisectoral and that they needed a solid moral and strategic compass to guide the way.

This is why the process of transition which will end in January 2005 with elections – free and transparent elections – at a presidential, legislative and municipal level is handled by institutions created by consensus with representatives from all parts of the Central African nation. This is why, in order to rebuild, the Government has decided to fight poverty, to reform labour rights, to respect workers' basic rights, to integrate social partners in our decision-making process, to promote social dialogue and to try to address the problem of HIV/AIDS.

The transition Government of the Central African Republic has tried to deal with each of these problems with determination despite the post-conflict situation we are faced with. This is why with respect to standards the Central African Republic is among the countries that have ratified the eight core Conventions and we are trying to enact them into national law. Of the eight Conventions ratified, only Convention No. 182 with regard to the worst forms of child labour has not yet been enacted into law. It will be soon once we have validated the draft Labour Code which has tried to address this issue within its laws.

With regard to social dialogue, 15 March 2003 was a catalyst for us to start again with our labour relations between social partners and public authorities. We have noted in the Government that the text dealing with social dialogue in the Central African Republic itself has become a cause of dysfunction and we have set up a tripartite mechanism working night and day in order to set up a standing national labour council so that we can deal upstream with all of the problems related to working conditions – social protection, and occupational training.

With the transition Government we have organized, along with the PRODIAF-ILO (Promotion of social dialogue in French-speaking Africa) programme and the Central African Monetary Community (CEMAC) a subregional seminar on social dialogue which has led to the creation of two new social dialogue structures at a subregional level: the Central African Workers' Trade Union Organization (OSTAC) and a subregional coordination body for social dialogue.

The Government is monitoring all administrative advice from bodies under the supervision of the Minister for Labour to have representatives from workers and employers. Now this is also the case of the Central African Occupational Training and Employment Agency.

In our programme for fighting HIV/AIDS in the workplace, we are deeply concerned with seropositive rates and one of the measures that the Government has taken is to try to introduce in all ministerial organigrams different cells to deal with the HIV/AIDS problem in the workplace. In order to do so we have national coordination and subcommittees within businesses.

With regard to tripartite consultation and submitting Conventions to our competent authorities, the Government would like to set up a tripartite committee responsible for dealing with ILO standard-setting activities. This committee may be assisted by an ILO expert whose role would be to advise us on how to address different issues. Given that the larger workers' organizations are already well-known in our country, they can freely appoint their representatives to participate in this committee. In the meantime a ratification procedure has begun dealing with Conventions Nos. 120, 122, 131, 132, 144, 150, 155, 158 and 160.

With regard to submitting these Conventions to the competent authorities, and consultations with Employers' and Workers' groups, as well as regular reporting on ratified Conventions, I would like to reassure you here that I will ensure that these procedures are carried out as they should be.

I would like to give due recognition to the Director-General of the ILO for the many types of assistance he has brought to the Central African Republic during this crisis. The Central African Republic history has shown that our development partners must come to our aid for us to survive critical moments. This is why on behalf of our transition Government I would like to appeal urgently to all organizations, especially the traditional partner of our country, the ILO, to assist us at all levels to enable us to rebuild. Long live the ILO, long live international cooperation.

Original French. Mr. NKILI *(Minister of Employment, Labour and Social Welfare, Cameroon)*

As a representative of Cameroon, I would like to express my nation's warm congratulations to the President on his election. The delegation which I lead is certain he will succeed in his efforts in virtue of his past experience. I would like to join with the preceding speakers in expressing to Mr. Juan Somavia, the Director-General of the ILO, the appreciation of the President of the Republic of Cameroon, His Excellency Paul Biya, and that of the Government of Cameroon, for the many actions undertaken in favour of Africa in general, and Cameroon in particular. We join with you in your fight for a fairer globalization. By virtue of its constitution and its tripartite nature, the ILO can and must play a major role in the current stage of globalization, since it brings together the main participants of this globalization.

For the Government of the Republic of Cameroon, a fairer globalization means, first and foremost, fair international trade, in which each country receives a fair price for its labours, leading to a reduction in the social inequalities which have been highlighted in this report.

This also means that greater priority should be accorded to good governance and to appropriate local and community development policies, as well as to the creation of decent work. This creation of jobs is at the centre of the proposals made by the Director-General. He has made decent work a priority objective in order to reduce poverty in our countries. In this respect, Cameroon has long been taking steps to create environment and an institutional framework which are propitious to the development of decent work. Many employment programmes have been set up in order to combat the rise of unemployment. It is with pride that I note the "Employment in Enterprise" programme, which encourages Cameroonian enterprises to recruit young Cameroonians and to restrict unfair dismissal of workers to conserve existing jobs.

With regard to governance, vigorous steps have been taken to eradicate corruption and better manage public affairs. Clearly, Cameroon relies first and foremost on its own capacities. However, we are certain of and value the vital contribution of the ILO Director-General Juan Somavia. The Government of the Republic of Cameroon thus reiterates its support to the Director-General and hopes that the implementation of his proposals will engender greater social justice and shared well-being for all peoples.

(The Conference adjourned at 1.25 p.m.)

Fifth sitting

Tuesday, 8 June 2004, 3.05 p.m.

President: Mr. Guevara

REPORTS OF THE CHAIRPERSON OF THE GOVERNING BODY AND OF THE DIRECTOR-GENERAL: DISCUSSION (CONT.)

Original Spanish: The PRESIDENT

This afternoon, we shall resume with our discussion of the Report of the Chairperson of the Governing Body and of the Director-General.

Original Spanish: Mr. NEGRON TEJADA *(Workers' delegate, Dominican Republic)*

On behalf of all the men and women workers of the Dominican Republic, I would like to extend our heartfelt greetings to the President of the 92nd Session of the International Labour Conference, and to wish it every success.

I would also like to congratulate the Director-General of the ILO, Mr. Juan Somavia, for his judicious choice of subject for his reports this year, including *ILO programme implementation 2002-03*. For those attending this 92nd Session of the International Labour Conference, this remains the most important democratic forum in the world.

Exactly 85 years ago, the International Labour Organization was founded with the objective of ensuring that work has a social dimension and is not just a means of exploiting the poor. The ILO has made a substantial contribution to improving working conditions in my country through its dynamic and proactive participation in amending labour and social security legislation, strengthening tripartite dialogue and the social partners who take part in it, and monitoring fundamental labour rights – just to mention a few of its contributions.

Our country has ratified 35 Conventions, among them the eight instruments underpinning the ILO Declaration on Fundamental Principles and Rights at Work. However, labour rights still continue to be violated.

This also is an appropriate occasion to point to positive developments. Recently, the National Council for Trade Union Unity (CNUS) and the federations of trade unions of workers in the free zones signed a protocol of understanding with the Dominican Association of Free Zones (ADOZONAS) to guarantee productivity and labour dispute settlement in the free zones. We hope this will yield positive results to defuse labour tension in this sector, as well as to reach consensus in meeting the challenges raised by a globalized economy and especially by the phasing out of the Multifibre Arrangement.

It should be a matter of concern to all of us that there has been a dramatic decline in trade union membership and stagnation in collective bargaining in most Latin American countries. It is obvious that we need a higher level of commitment by all the social partners to put a stop to violation of this fundamental right.

Child labour in its worst forms continues to afflict our society, and we have to recognize the huge efforts made to eradicate this scourge by the Dominican Government, through the State Secretariat for Labour, through trade union organizations and employers' associations, and through civil society, with the support and cooperation of the ILO through its InFocus Programme on Child Labour (IPEC). However, the increasing poverty in which most of our people live, in contrast to the figures put forward by the international finance organizations, still has a brutal effect on our country, with the result that thousands of children and teenagers enter the labour market in worse conditions than adults, instead of going to school, preparing themselves for the future, and having fun, as they should at their age.

In its pursuit of economic growth through opening up its economy indiscriminately and facilitating foreign investment, our country has concentrated its growth strategy on the development of free zones, tourism, trade, telecommunications and the financial sector – all of which belong to the services sector, where most of the jobs created show a marked trend towards flexibility, with a shift away from stable employment to part-time and temporary work and subcontracting arrangements, where the link between the worker and the enterprise is increasingly tenuous, wages are poor and working conditions minimal.

Despite economic growth, the labour market is still unable to provide sufficient jobs to keep pace with the increase in the economically active population, which swells the ranks of those working in the informal sector of the economy.

Although equality of opportunity and treatment is guaranteed in legal terms, in practice women continue to work in more precarious and more difficult conditions than men, and segmentation of the labour market is becoming more and more visible.

Recurrent violations of labour rights tend to be the lot of workers who have to go abroad in search of employment, and the phenomenon of migration is becoming increasingly widespread today owing to the differences that exist among countries, and as a result of globalization; hence the importance of this subject being one of the main items for discussion at this session of the Conference.

The Dominican Republic is a receiving country for workers migrating chiefly from Haiti, and in recent years we have seen an increase in workers from Central and South America. At the same time, our own people are emigrating to the United States in very large numbers, while mainly women are migrating to European countries in deplorable conditions, thousands of them trapped in human trafficking networks, often forced into degrading activities.

Most labour standards define work as a social function and we hold that this is still an invariable principle and therefore hope that all the issues discussed at this Conference will be based on this principle, and that labour will not be treated as a commodity for the sake of furthering business interests and desired economic growth.

As the ILO's constituents, we trust that this Organization will continue to work for a more equitable society, in line with the principle that universal and lasting peace can be established only if it is based upon social justice.

Original Portuguese: Mr. GOMES PROENÇA *(Workers' delegate, Portugal)*

On behalf of Portugal's workers I would like to commend the President upon his election.

The Reports of the World Commission and of the Director-General, submitted to this Conference, call upon us to think about the future of globalization and the central role of the ILO. They are documents which are worthy of our full attention and support.

Globalization should be an instrument for positive change, for economic and social development. Thus far it has not been. On the contrary, it has contributed to growing inequalities and poverty, and to an increase in new forms of exploitation. However, a return to the protectionism of the past is not the answer. We need a different kind of globalization, with international regulation of financial markets to combat purely speculative capital movements, as well as fraud and tax evasion, so that economic and social globalization can move forward side by side, giving globalization a human dimension.

The role of the ILO in terms of regulation, through Conventions and Recommendations, should be constantly expanded and updated so as to respond to the changes occurring in the economy and in society and new realities such as increased international migration, technological change, the emergence of new forms of organizing work, and the protection of atypical workers and the informal economy.

The actions of countries and international communities are vital. The European Union should introduce social and environmental clauses into international trade agreements, along with respect for social rights, both individual and collective. We need dialogue in which everyone has a role and a responsibility. National economic growth which is sustained solely by exports and which does not improve the living conditions of the people does not promote development. We have to fight unemployment and promote decent work, with better standards of education and training and more social protection; we should reject job insecurity and the deregulation of the labour market. In this connection public services have a key role to play.

We therefore need to strengthen collective bargaining and tripartite social partnership, and respect the actions of the various organizations of civil society, in particular trade unions. Responsible globalization involves all sections of society. It involves trade union freedom, the right to collective bargaining and compliance with ILO Conventions. We support healthy businesses which create and distribute wealth, which uphold quality of work, which have an ethical dimension, which exhibit corporate responsibility, and which support social dialogue and collective bargaining.

We are striving for a world of peace and security through increased international cooperation for development. Globalization requires discussion of the competitiveness of economies and enterprises and more and better employment. The role of international tripartite dialogue is vital, and the ILO must therefore establish forums on globalization policy. The Report demonstrates our responsibilities and makes it all the more necessary for us to strengthen this Organization.

We would like to conclude by pointing out the fact that the ILO has an increasingly important role to play and that, under the new mandate of the Director-General, Juan Somavia, which we welcome, it will without doubt embrace the challenges of globalization, poverty and decent work with renewed vigour.

Original Arabic: Mr. MANSOURI *(Minister of Employment, Social Affairs and Solidarity, Morocco)*

In the name of God, the Merciful, the Compassionate! It is a pleasure for me to congratulate the President of the Conference, on my own behalf and on behalf of the delegation of the Kingdom of Morocco, on his election to preside over the 92nd Session of the International Labour Conference. I wish him every success in his work.

It is a pleasure for me to extend my heartfelt thanks to the Director-General of the ILO and all his staff for the efforts they have made to prepare this session so that the Conference could be organized in the best possible circumstances.

The Director-General's Report, *ILO programme implementation 2002-03*, gives a detailed account of the ILO's performance under each of the strategic objectives of the Organization relating to promoting and realizing fundamental principles and rights at work, access of men and women to decent work, social protection, and strengthening tripartism and social dialogue.

The Report also mentions important achievements, such as the implementation of action plans and programmes despite the detrimental effects of recent global events.

We support all of the proposals and recommendations put forward by the Director-General in his Report on the World Commission on the Social Dimension of Globalization, *A fair globalization: The role of the ILO*. We also have to thank the Co-chair of the Commission and all its members for the enormous efforts they have made to achieve results aimed at a fair globalization and a safer world, free of political intrigues, conflicts and war, to ensure that decent work becomes the primordial objective of economic policy and to guarantee equal opportunities for all.

The Government of His Majesty King Mohammed VI, may God protect him, attaches particular importance to labour issues and is aware of the need to meet the new challenges posed by changes in the global economy, and of the importance of basing economic and social progress on tripartite cooperation, by making social dialogue among the social partners a key element in addressing all social and economic issues.

The key event which happened in our country last summer, namely the promulgation of the Labour Code, constitutes clear proof of Morocco's determination to embrace the system of tripartite negotiation consistently advocated by the ILO's Conventions and Recommendations.

This Labour Code comes into force today even as I speak from this rostrum, six months after it was published in the *Official Gazette*.

The new elements introduced by the Code can be summarized as follows:
- seeking a balance between employers' interests and workers' fundamental rights;
- promotion of freedom of association and collective bargaining;
- introduction of a certain degree of flexibility in labour relations;
- strengthening of mechanisms for consultation and dialogue between the economic and social partners.

Moroccan labour legislation is thus in conformity with international labour standards, in particular those adopted by the ILO and ratified by my country.

Morocco has also seen another historic achievement, namely the promulgation of the Family Code, which has been commended both nationally and internationally, and constitutes a landmark in the process of civilization and enshrines the principle of equality between men and women.

Morocco has carried out major reforms in the economic and social fields, which can be summarized as follows:
- strengthening democracy through adopting the rule of law and social dialogue as the civilized way to tackle the issues that arise, and involving the social partners in the design of social and economic policy;
- promoting the ILO Declaration on Fundamental Principles and rights at Work, by stressing the protection of the right to organize and to bargain collectively; combating all forms of forced or compulsory labour and child labour and discrimination in respect of employment and occupation;
- promoting social protection and the protection of vulnerable groups;
- ensuring that employment is a government priority and a cornerstone of economic and social policy.

Our cooperative relationship with the ILO has grown remarkably, as evidenced in the organization of workshops on various subjects, for example on the elimination of child labour, the improvement of labour relations, and health and safety at work. We would like to strengthen this cooperation in other areas to which we have given priority and which are aimed at stimulating job creation, improving working conditions and strengthening social protection.

As we speak of human dignity through decent work, we cannot fail to recall the inhuman conditions and the serious situation afflicting the Middle East and the Iraqi and Palestinian peoples.

Faced with this tragic situation and its detrimental effects on the Palestinian workers and the Palestinian economy, more than ever before, we need to give our full support to our brothers, the Palestinian people. We urge the ILO to make every effort to put an end to the inhuman practices perpetrated against the Iraqi workers and employers, and the Iraqi people as a whole.

Before concluding, allow me to thank the Officers of the Conference for their able guidance, in the hope that it will yield positive results.

Mr. MDLADLANA *(Minister of Labour, South Africa)*

The greatest challenge facing the global community is the chasm between the developing and the developed world. The current amoral manifestation of globalization, with the entrenchment of the super-exploitative relationship between the developed North and the developing South, is deepening this chasm.

In its present guise, globalization has seen jobs disappearing, trade talks deadlock and a continuation of financial instability. Clearly, the benefits of globalization are out of reach for far too many people.

It is a situation that is not only ethically unacceptable – as noted in the World Commission on the Social Dimension of Globalization's report – but politically unsustainable.

As the report also notes, globalization is not inherently bad. It can provide us with the tools to challenge, and overcome, the very crisis which it is currently deepening.

There are no simple solutions, but we agree with the call made in the report for a focus on people, the strengthening of the democratic State, the importance of sustainable development, equitable markets and greater accountability.

We also back the notions of fair rules, solidarity, strengthening partnerships and an effective United Nations.

The Director-General has requested the support of member States for the vision presented by the World Commission of a process of globalization with a strong social dimension, based on universally shared values and respect for human rights and individual dignity; a globalization that is fair, inclusive, democratically governed and which provides opportunities with tangible benefits for all countries. I can assure the Director-General of the ILO of our unwavering support.

I wish to commend the ILO for its report on the road travelled in the period 2002-03 in assisting countries to work their way out of global poverty. I concur that decent work is a strategic tool for fighting global poverty and I believe that employment remains a critical socio-economic tool to bringing dignity and prosperity to the poor.

In this regard, the future strategic policy framework should be flexible, and responsive to the challenges and priorities of the time.

Furthermore, resource mobilization, effective country programmes, capacitating social partners and governments, strengthening of Area/MDT offices should take priority in assisting with implementing the Decent Work Agenda at country level. This, in our view, will go a long way in fighting global poverty. The challenge for the ILO is to turn decent work into a tool for maximising the gains of globalization.

I further want to thank the Director-General for availing the services of the ILO to assist my country in building the capacity of the Roads Authority of

Limpopo (South Africa) to recruit and train road construction and rehabilitation contractors. As mentioned on page 34 of the Report, "To date, the Authority has rehabilitated 90 kilometres of roads and created 266,818 workdays. Of the 54 contractors trained, 90 per cent are women. The Authority has retained all women trained in this new field of work for women in the area. The South African Government has acknowledged the success of the project (it was a runner-up in a construction awards competition), and the project approach is now being replicated and expanded as part of the Government's Expanded Public Works Programme."

The President has now launched the Expanded Public Works Programme in the same province, on 18 May 2004. These launches by the President in all provinces of the Republic of South Africa will be completed in September 2004.

Africa remains marginalized, underdeveloped, under resourced, highly indebted and inflicted with diseases; the Report of the Director-General observes the same trend. In this regard, technical cooperation should be stepped up with a view to assisting Africa to deal with the challenges of achieving decent work for all. Secondly, we applaud the ILO for its effort in contributing to NEPAD processes and for its support in the preparations for the forthcoming African Union Extraordinary Summit on Employment and Poverty Alleviation, which will be held in Burkina Faso.

We would be failing if we did not remark on the plight of workers in the occupied Arab territories. Discrimination on grounds of race, gender and religion; mobility restrictions; curfews imposed in the occupied Arab territories are the key stumbling blocks to achieving a just peace in the Middle East. The solution to this crisis lies not in the destruction of homes, in the building of walls, but through social dialogue. Until a resolution to this crisis is achieved, the plight of workers in the occupied Arab territories will never be alleviated.

The celebrations which South Africa is involved in this year, that are taking place in my country, are, in essence, the celebration of a vision of a society free from oppression and exploitation. This is a vision that is not unique to our people, but is, I believe, a global vision.

Original Italian: Mr. ANDREOLI *(Minister of Labour, Cooperation, Tourism, Sport and Post, San Marino)*

First of all, I would like to congratulate the President and the Vice-Presidents on their election. It is with great personal satisfaction that I take this opportunity to speak today at this important forum in which, every year since it joined the ILO in 1983, the Republic of San Marino has participated through its tripartite delegation.

The ILO is the only international organization where employers, workers and governments are represented on an equal footing. For this reason, the ILO plays a unique role in organizing social dialogue in the world and has become an essential player in debates on the international social and economic order. Our Organization can, and must, play a moderating role to soften the negative repercussions on workers and enterprises of the current global economic development.

The role of the ILO has always been paramount, and yet that role has become even more essential recently, thanks to the efforts of the Director-General, Ambassador Juan Somavia, to give new impetus to the ILO's activities by attaching priority to the social dimension of development policies. This priority is crucial if we are to prevent globalization from neglecting and disregarding the most vulnerable groups of the population.

The ILO has thus made a commitment to harmonize its activities with the Millennium Development Goals to the achievement of which we must all contribute, both at national and international levels.

The promotion of fundamental principles and rights at work, through the implementation of the 1998 ILO Declaration, has resulted in an unprecedented increase in recent years in the ratification of labour laws, which is, and remains, of paramount importance. In particular, the enforcement mechanism specifically devised by the Organization for the implementation of rules will have to be strengthened and made more effective in the future, with all the necessary changes and adjustments.

Monitoring, which is a prerogative of the ILO, is equally fundamental. Accession to conventions and ratification of regulations are a first necessary step. However, commitments taken internationally must necessarily be followed by concrete implementation.

Monitoring on a global scale compliance with the fundamental rules of which the ILO is the custodian is all the more necessary in today's world, where workers are under increasing pressure to adjust to new and more urgent market needs, and where fast trade, financial transactions and technological development are liable to place workers of various categories outside the market, with the consequent risk of generating new and more subtle forms of exploitation.

The first Report of the second cycle of Global Reports to be presented by the Director-General to this session entitled *Organizing for social justice* deals with freedom of association and the right to collective bargaining. It is a major contribution to the promotion of decent work, which is one of the Organizations top priorities.

Freedom of association and the right to collective bargaining are essential prerequisites for the proper functioning of social dialogue, which is at the very heart of economic and social development and the democratic development of countries. As indicated in the Report, today's challenge is to find the best way of defending, promoting and implementing these rights, in particular in national and local situations which can differ so vastly, and in a continuously and rapidly changing labour world.

In this context, the Republic of San Marino is strongly convinced of the rights upheld by this Conference. This position is reflected in our labour legislation which has become increasingly significant since the 1960s, and has led to the enactment of several new laws in this field.

The fact that San Marino has been a member of the ILO for more than 20 years and the fact that it has ratified various Conventions has undoubtedly contributed to the further strengthening and promotion of the right to work and other fundamental rights, such as freedom of association and collective bargaining. As I have said, these rights are essential in order to indicate the level of a country's democracy.

Furthermore, in 1974 the Republic of San Marino included those rights in articles 6, 8 and 9 of the Declaration on Citizens' Rights and Fundamental Principles of the San Marino Constitutional Order.

Our Law No. 7 of 1961 on the protection of labour and workers is also extremely important in this context. The Law is fundamental to the right to collective bargaining. I would also like to mention Law No. 23 of 1981 on the protection of union activity.

However, it is generally recognized that the world of work is constantly changing and therefore we need to take continuous measures to adapt to the emerging needs and implement flexible and more adaptable rules, so as to reveal any concealed work in the black economy and so that labour protection can be guaranteed more equally to all those who enter the labour market for the first time. In this respect, San Marino's Parliament has decided to adopt, by the end of July, a set of guidelines on labour market reform.

We need to intervene now to promote an active society and more qualitative work with increased and more modern employment opportunities for all. Those opportunities should be adequate and adaptable to the needs of both workers and companies. It is in this spirit that the attention paid by the ILO to the weakest and disadvantaged categories of workers should be increased, in particular by stepping up technical cooperation activities.

Importance should also be attached to the Organization's ongoing continuous awareness-raising and information campaigns, which must be intensified and continued in the future. By reiterating the great importance of the decisions adopted by the ILO with regard to individual countries, I wish this Conference every success and hope that it carries out fruitful work in the future.

Mgr. TOMASI *(Apostolic Nuncio, The Holy See)*

I join previous speakers in congratulating the President and his colleagues on their election.

The task of building a society which respects the human person and its work gives priority to the human ordering of social relationships over technical progress, necessary as the latter is. Such concern runs through the preparatory documents of this 92nd Session of the International Labour Conference, especially the Report of the Director-General who carefully highlights achievements and shortcomings, as well as the strategic areas of future involvement demanded by the changing conditions of the world's economy.

In his call for a rediscovery of the meaning and value of work, Pope John Paul II has extended an invitation to "address the economic and social imbalances in the world of work by re-establishing the right hierarchy of values, giving priority to the dignity of working men and women and to their freedom, responsibility and participation ... (and) to redress situations of injustice by safeguarding each people's culture and different models of development."

Looking to the future, the projection that by the year 2015 there will be 3 billion people under the age of 25 makes the challenge of employment creation an issue now already. The search for full employment is not only a legitimate preoccupation, but an ethical commitment involving owners and management, financial institutions, the organization of trade and workers. A joint effort has been the approach and the trademark of the ILO through its social dialogue of government, employers' and workers' representatives – a model that pioneered a method of society-building that has proven fruitful. The resulting economic system has a better chance to preserve the priority of work over capital and of the common good over private interest.

Job creation is the main route to personal and national development. The human person becomes the best capital with his/her creativity, knowledge, relationships, spirituality. Working persons enrich society and foster ways of peace. Besides, the promotion of jobs in the poorer countries is also in the interest of the richer ones. If we take the case, for example, of agriculture, the readjustment and elimination of subsidies in developed countries will allow the employment of thousands, the growth of trade, the improvement of the national economy, in countries where agriculture is still the predominant way of life. As a consequence, the quality of life of everyone will benefit, and forced displacement and international migration will no longer be an unavoidable necessity for survival. Besides, as noted in the Director-General's Report, conflicts disrupt the achievements of set goals of development. But at the root of many conflicts is the lack of work and of a minimum earning capacity to escape poverty and live in dignity with one's family.

The interconnectedness of economic variables and actors on the global scene has been underlined in the important conclusions of the World Commission on the Social Dimension of Globalization. The Commission supports the ILO's strategic objectives and these, in turn, serve as a base for decent work. In this way, securing employment, with social protection, with adequate standards and rights at work, in a constructive tripartite social dialogue opened to others and to new forces of civil society, recognizes that work is an expression of each person's dignity and identity, and that it goes far beyond any quantitative measurable economic value.

It seems appropriate to emphasize that by preserving the priority of the person, globalization too becomes fair as it avoids leaving behind vulnerable groups, women and children in particular, migrant workers, seafarers and other categories of workers, and less-developed populations. An important step in this direction has been the rapid entering into force of the Worst Forms of Child Labour Convention, 1999 (No. 182). Allow me to refer again to the social doctrine of the Church as presented by Pope John Paul II: "A society depends on the basic relations that people cultivate with one another in ever widening circles – from the family to other intermediary social groups, to civil society as a whole and to the national community. States in turn have no choice but to enter into relations with one another. The present reality of global interdependence makes it easier to appreciate the common destiny of the entire human family, and makes all thoughtful people increasingly appreciate the virtue of solidarity."

Work that allows people to live a decent lifestyle requires today a concerted commitment to provide workers with sufficient education and training so that they may have the skills needed to confront successfully the information revolution and the increasingly knowledge-based economy. Initiative in this sense will protect them from poverty and social exclusion. Enhancing human capacity applies also to developing countries if they have to play their rightful role in world trade with the production of quality products.

In conclusion, Mr. President, the just participation of all, individuals and States, in the building up of the future must lead to their fair share in the benefits resulting from decent work for all in the human family.

Original Portuguese: Mr. MONTEIRO *(Minister of Labour and Solidarity, Cape Verde)*

I congratulate the President on his election and I commend the Director-General for the very sound Report he has submitted to this assembly. May I, on behalf of the Government of Cape Verde and in my own name, salute this noble assembly and wish it every success. I wish the 92nd Session of the International Labour Conference every success in its work. I am both happy and honoured to be able to represent my country and my Government in this important forum.

Cape Verde, as a member of this important world Organization, has, for as long as it has been an independent nation, done its utmost to comply rigorously with the various ILO Conventions and to scrupulously respect workers' rights, which it feels has contributed to a climate of peace and social cohesion. Over the years, we have learned to listen, to talk and to build consensus. In a manner of speaking, the tripartite structure, which is the special strength of this forum, resembles the historic situation in which Cape Verde finds itself. Indeed, the Government of Cape Verde has established social dialogue and consensus as a priority for its activities on labour matters and is making efforts, in close collaboration with representatives of all sectors of society, with a view to formulating a labour policy more in keeping with the realities and development requirements of our country. We are aware of the concerns of international bodies in terms of the urgent need to establish a new policy and new governance strategies which would ensure a globalization with equal opportunities for all. In this connection, my Government has chosen to develop human resources as the strategic element in its programme for growth and poverty reduction. This line of action presupposes the sharing of responsibilities and the establishment of a robust partnership between the State, the private sector and civil society.

Furthermore, the Government of Cape Verde has developed, as one of the major priorities in its programme, a policy on employment and training, since these are essential elements for growth and competitivity, and we have already adopted a legal framework for vocational training and built a number of centres for that purpose.

With the forthcoming approval of the Labour Code, a document which has already received a valuable formal opinion from the ILO and the social partners, Cape Verde will have a valuable legal instrument which will help to ensure better conditions within the national labour market. This important document draws on ILO Conventions as additional sources to be incorporated into Cape Verde's labour legislation and applied in our country. This endeavour, I believe, makes us worthy of this House in pursuit of social justice. To this end, freedom of association, the right to collective bargaining, the elimination of forced labour, the eradication of child labour, equal pay for equal work and discrimination-free employment are essential principles enshrined in the new Cape Verde Labour Code.

Cape Verde recognizes the important role that the International Labour Organization played in 2002 and 2003 in sensitive areas, as reflected 0in the Report which has just been submitted. I should like to conclude by expressing the wish that this session of the Conference will meet the goals it has set itself.

Original French: Mrs. SASSO MAZZUFFERI *(Employers' delegate, Italy)*

I would like to congratulate the President on his election and I wish him all the best for the successful conduct of this 92nd Session of the International Labour Conference.

For the sake of brevity, I will deal with just three issues: first, making the most of human resources; second, migrant workers; and third, the report of the World Commission on the Social Dimension of Globalization, because these issues are linked by a common thread which I believe runs through all our work.

Human resources are the cornerstone of the performance of any enterprise, and more widely the cornerstone of the evolution of every country. Training, qualification, updating, reskilling and recycling workers throughout their working life are basically the practical expression of a concept which is based on the priority of the development of the individual not just the worker. This is the context within which the work of our World Commission has taken place.

In the same context I would like to turn to the subject of migrant workers, a crucial issue in our society, which will be dealt with through an integrated approach. This is particularly useful, not only because the existing instruments have often not been ratified or applied, but also because, since those instruments were adopted, reality has changed radically.

There is now a growing need felt in developing and in industrialized countries to have a completely changed framework of reference, one which is inspired by a modern, culturally open approach that is designed to enhance employability and the prospects of high-calibre migrant workers.

Technical cooperation has a role to play in this area. The Turin Centre is an ILO instrument that will be called upon to step up its training activity. We must hope that its facilities will be drawn on more and more widely, facilities which are very much appreciated on the international market.

We need to plan coordinated policies among the various institutions and countries concerned, focused on the different types of official migrant workers and effective recognition of their qualifications and protection of them, based on the same laws that protect other workers and that are duly respected by the migrants themselves.

What we need to do is to protect and enhance this precious human resource, which can breathe new life into enterprises and sectors of the economy, and to promote human resources, because that can benefit the country of origin as well as the host country.

These ideas permeate the report of the World Commission on the Social Dimension of Globalization, which advocates "creating opportunities for all", with a realistic and balanced approach. The report has the merit of encouraging coherence in the policies planned within the international organizations and at national level.

We need to stress the "inclusive" nature of globalization with regard to employment, particularly of young people, the fundamental role of private enterprise because of its contribution to wealth and job creation, respect for the fundamental principles and the fundamental labour standards, and tripartism as a way of achieving fairer globalization.

The Italian employers support the report in these respects.

As the report suggests, in a globalized world, contributing to the elimination of poverty in developing countries will have a positive effect on growth in industrialized countries as well.

In this context I would like to underline the role of the Global Compact, which in my country involves a strategy that allows small and medium-sized enterprises and not just Italian ones, to take the initiative. This project seeks to establish links between Italian small and medium-sized enterprises and their counterparts in developing countries that benefit from technical cooperation with Italy.

The Italian employers reiterate their commitment to this strategy, which involves the close cooperation and support of the ILO as the implementing body, and we are convinced that this will yield the expected results.

Original Spanish: Mr. VILLAVICENCIO RIOS *(Government delegate, Peru)*

First of all I would like to join those who have spoken before me in congratulating the President and his distinguished fellow Officers for having been elected to conduct the work of this 92nd Session of the International Labour Conference. I am especially glad to see an outstanding Minister from our region presiding this year.

Secondly, I would like to commend the Organization for the progress made in applying the Decent Work Agenda. Likewise, I would like to congratulate the Organization for its capacity to adapt itself through sincere self-examination, to the new challenges brought by globalization.

Specialization of the Organization's work, in order to meet the strategic objectives in the Decent Work Agenda by establishing fixed objectives, has meant progress can be effectively measured, and these objectives can be reached, often even going beyond the initial targets, with excellent results, both quantitatively and qualitatively speaking. Today's challenge is to maintain this pace of progress and strengthen the Organization's ability to respond to the new demands for services being made by leaders as a result of the increasingly widespread conviction that decent work is, rather than simply an end in itself, the main means of overcoming poverty, a task to which we are all committed.

Thirdly, I am not going to dwell on what we have been doing in Peru, but I would not like to be remiss and not thank the ILO wholeheartedly for their support in preparing the Decent Work Agenda for Peru, which is now being discussed in our National Labour Council, the reports on the state of progress in each of the fundamental principles and rights, enshrined in the 1998 Declaration, and the diagnosis on the administration of labour with a collection of proposals aiming to modernize and strengthen it. In all these fields and in the framework of the process of democratic consolidation which we are now embarked upon, action plans are beginning to bear significant fruit.

In a final reference to my country, I would just like to say that we have come to the end of the ratification process of the fundamental Conventions, including decent work as a key objective in the 14th States National Agreement Policy, signed in July 2002 by representatives of the main political policies and social organizations.

My delegation wishes to make a few brief comments on the need to make decent work a global objective. I would like to draw attention to the far-sightedness of the founders and those who drew up the goals and objectives of the ILO in the Declaration of Philadelphia, with respect to the necessity of working resolutely to combat poverty and extend social justice. The delegation would also like to draw attention to the ILO's role in establishing the right conditions for this, and in assessing and rejecting any policy, either national or international, that does not move towards, or that hinders, this objective.

So, in its very constitutional framework, the foundations are clearly established for the ILO to take on the challenge of fighting for a fair globalization.

On this subject, my delegation agrees with the report of the World Commission on the Social Dimension of Globalization, and with the Report, *A fair globalization: The role of the ILO,* when they state that the main issue now is employment, in so far as: it is the way people make a living; there is a shortage which does not correlate with the levels of prosperity that have been attained; and, it is the main weapon in the fight against poverty.

We would like to stress an idea that probably oversimplifies the problem but nevertheless draws attention to it: national, regional and global policies should centre on creating and maintaining decent work. I am using the plural because the subject of employment calls for an intersectoral and multidisciplinary approach, but I would like to emphasize that economic policy, which must aim to create and maintain productive work which is freely chosen, combining all policies, be they monetary, fiscal, movement of goods, capital or persons, education, or health, among others, to that end.

Obviously, my delegation understands that there are specific tasks and responsibilities in each country or region, as well as on a global level. This is why national efforts must go hand in hand with a strong element of fairness which, on an international level, is mainly expressed in the need to create fair policies for trade, capital, technology flows, unstable prices and to attain better access to markets.

In this way, leaders at all levels should not only manage macroeconomic indicators responsibly, but should see economic progress from the perspective of its social impact, so that they never lose sight of the fact that they are dealing with human lives.

We are, however, not trying to say that we should only speak of social policies as a parallel, as these generally move at a far slower speed than economic policies, but rather that each political decision must have in mind its social impact.

This line of thinking has a main ally in social dialogue, in so far as it is only with the active participation of the life forces of society that we will be able to measure social consequences properly and to generate measures fulfilling our main objective: creating and maintaining decent employment.

The 85 years of the ILO are a great example of this. Of course, the road is not easy or straightforward, but past experience has taught us that we should not blindly accept that the grave consequences of unchecked globalization will lead to crisis as we take old of the reins. Rather, we should take the opportunity to consolidate the leading role of the ILO in building a globalization which is a window of opportunities for all and not a sentence. Enough diagnosis. Specific workplans on all complex challenges of globalization must be drawn up.

Perhaps in this way we will be able to revive the dream of the great Victor Hugo, in that we might finally arrive at a century of achievement and happiness, an opportunity which we have already missed once.

Original Spanish: Mr. PÉREZ DEL CASTILLO *(Minister of Labour and Social Security, Uruguay)*

A brief appraisal of the current situation is enough to determine how much the world has changed as a result of the greater ties that have been created between countries through trade, the expansion of direct foreign investment and the emergence of massive flows of capital across different States. This situation has come about largely because of the progress made in the field of information technology and communication. We are faced with globalization, and with an ever-smaller world which enables us to know each other better and in which the disparities between the material situation of different people are made glaringly obvious.

Talking about international social justice is nothing new. What is new, however, is the current, urgent need to fight for it, given the circumstances that globalization is currently bringing with it. It is possible to map out the path of globalization. To a great extent, the ILO's challenge is to assume leadership of the task.

It is time for us to apply to inter-country relationships the fundamental principles of the ILO that have not yet been attained, in order to achieve international social justice.

Our actions should be guided by a recognition of human dignity. We should also be guided by the recollection that work is not a commodity, and we should reassert the fact that tripartism is a valuable instrument and is a unique asset of the international institutions which can and should be used to achieve a fairer globalization.

Awareness is not enough; and neither is a call to shoulder responsibilities. Specific steps should be taken within the United Nations system and by the Bretton Woods institutions and other multilateral bodies. Specific steps should be taken in the more developed countries to show solidarity in meeting the needs of those nations which as yet have not attained adequate levels to ensure their inhabitants a decent standard of living.

Economic growth is necessarily linked to the generation of quality jobs, although that, in itself, is not enough. Growth, especially in countries with small domestic markets, is closely linked to foreign trade. Hence the importance of rules of fair trade.

Stronger and fairer trade would be a valuable contribution to the social growth of developing countries.

In this sense, I should like to point out a promising recent development: in a recent letter to the members of the World Trade Organization, European Commissioners Pascal Lamy and Franz Fischler indicated that they were ready to remove export subsidies on agricultural products.

This is no mean achievement. It is an announcement whose significance goes beyond trade negotiations. Export subsidies are one of the most unfair ways of supporting agriculture. They have a negative impact on international trade and devastating consequences for the poorest countries, preventing them from developing their own production capacities and exports.

This announcement by the European Union, if acted on, would imply a tremendous stride towards achieving a fair globalization whose benefits could be distributed fairly and where developing countries would have greater opportunities to secure better levels of material prosperity and spiritual well-being.

It might also lead to an improvement of working conditions; in other words, to decent work.

The issue of decent work has already been placed on the multilateral agenda, which is one of the achievements of the International Labour Organization.

Nevertheless, the task does not end there. The ILO should follow up the conclusions that the Director-General will submit to us. We need to put those conclusions into practice. Mere words are not enough. We also need to strengthen ILO action in order to target those activities more appropriately, and coordinate the efforts of different organizations so that they can work better together in the struggle for social cohesion. In our countries, this must begin with an out-and-out fight against poverty.

In this connection, technical cooperation must be more effective and subject to tighter management, which should take on board the new responsibilities arising from globalization.

Other forums, such as the Guadalajara Summit which brought together Heads of State of Europe and Latin America, have also recognized that poverty, exclusion and inequality are an insult to human dignity, weaken democracy and threaten peace.

Hence, an increase in the number of jobs and promoting an environment conducive to the creation of enterprises, from micro undertakings to those requiring huge direct investment, are crucial to combating the scourge of joblessness and poverty.

Likewise, education and vocational training are an absolute necessity and are closely linked to employment. They should be considered in the framework of a global economy based on knowledge and on new technologies The same could be said of information on the labour market and a proper coordination of labour demand and supply.

We are facing concerns that are particularly relevant to the contemporary man and woman. We therefore congratulate the Office for having had the good sense to make these concerns central to our deliberations. We have before us a great challenge: to map out the path of globalization with a view to making it fairer. The ILO should assume in this task an essential leadership role.

Original German: Mr. ANDRES *(Parliamentary Secretary of State, Federal Ministry of Economics and Labour, Germany)*

The German Government welcomes the report of the World Commission on the Social Dimension of Globalization and its conclusions regarding growth and employment policy. In particular, in its call for decent work for all, the report contains a positive concept of how to adjust the existing globalization process as well as a clear acknowledgement of the connection between growth and employment. We are ready to move forward in the way that the World Commission indicates, although intensive discussions will still be needed on certain subjects, such as the call for international coordination of migration policy or the democratization of international organizations.

The German Government particularly welcomes the fact that the report emphasizes the immense potential of globalization. The political activities that are necessary in order to exploit this potential must extend to the national level as much as to the international context. We need a global alliance for employment, which will combat poverty, will promote sustainability and will ensure that markets are kept open and fair. A particularly important conclusion by the World Commission is that the local and national levels should be the starting point for all political responses to globalization. What we need here is a coordinated approach for growth and employment. The role of local social partners is vital in order to provide security during the period of change through social dialogue. What is still missing is close cooperation between the international organizations. So we are in favour of a more intensive dialogue, particularly between the ILO and WTO. We would like to see an active role being played by the ILO in this context. But we, and that means all of us here in this room, must put our own house in order first. We must particularly consider the question of what the people who we are basically working for, really expect from us, when it comes down to it: i.e. workers in precarious employment, the unemployed, and women who in developed and in developing countries bear the sole responsibility for providing for their families. What comes to mind in this context is that what is expected of us back home in our capital cities is answers to simple but essential questions, such as: am I going to be able to keep my job? Will my child get an apprenticeship or training place? Have I got any chance of finding a job after being unemployed? Developing countries might ask other questions, such as: is the first world going to share things fairly with us? Are customs barriers going to be dismantled to give our products a chance? I think we have to respond honestly to these questions, in Geneva and in our capital cities. We – and the ILO knows this very well – means not just the governments, but the triad of governments, unions and employers. If we cannot come up with these answers, legitimacy will sooner or later be called into question. We will not be able to fend off these questions with doom-laden scenarios or a mad dash towards reform. In Germany, for example, we have to give the honest answer: our social security provisions for old age, for ill health, accidents, unemployment or long term care, the way they have been set up for decades, can no longer be sustained over years of economic decline. We need economic growth of at least 2 per cent to give even halfway convincing answers to the questions which I mentioned above. We owe it to the people to tell them this truth.

In conclusion, I do not want to deny that we sometimes manage to come up with answers that are convincing in the long term. Since I am a European, what springs to mind here particularly is the joyous fact that a month ago we were able to welcome into the European Union eight new Member States from Central and Eastern Europe, as well as Malta and Cyprus. Even though this brings with it, in both new and old Member States of the European Union, fears about jobs and social security, the clear message that comes through is that the advantages of enlargement very much outweigh the disadvantages. After more than 60 years, Europe has finally overcome the division of the continent and our children and grandchildren will be able to benefit from what is now being called the peace dividend.

This is for me, and I think for many of you here in this room, a convincing example of the beneficial aspects of globalization. So, we as governments, employers and unions should ensure that such successful examples of globalization should be repeated as often as possible.

Mr. MARKOTIĆ *(Government delegate, Croatia)*

At the outset, I would like to join those congratulating the President on his election to preside over the Conference, and to wish him every success in performing his duties.

Since it became independent in 1990, Croatia has given particular attention to cooperation with the ILO, as a true authority on balanced social development. I would like to take this opportunity to express my gratitude on behalf of the Croatian Government to the ILO, whose experts, through a large number of programmes of technical and expert assistance, have helped to develop and strengthen the legislative and institutional infrastructure in the field of labour, employment and social security, especially in strengthening tripartite relations. All of this occurred in the very difficult conditions of the war and post-war period, followed by reconstruction and strategic decisions on the direction of economic and social development in Croatia.

Croatia's commitment to the fundamental values of the ILO was one of the decisive factors in our country's moving forward in the process of integration, and contributed to a large extent to the positive avis of the European Commission in relation to the process of rapprochement and Croatia's aspiration to full membership of the European Union.

Amongst other things, Croatia has based its development approach on initiatives and activities in major and complex reforms in the field of the labour market, labour relations, social security and social protection, while facing a high rate of registered unemployment and an uncompetitive economy in an environment which does not encourage competitiveness, a large grey economy, an inappropriate social security system and unfavourable demographic trends.

Our aim is to create conditions conducive to full employment in an environment which encourages the generation of new, productive jobs in compliance with decent work standards and to promote social protection for all, especially social security for basic social risks such as old age, sickness, disability, unemployment and poverty.

We have successfully implemented the difficult reform of the pension insurance system and set up a new three-pillar system, of which the first two pillars are mandatory and the third is voluntary. The new pension system is a combination of an institutional solution for inter-generational solidarity, mandatory individual accounts of capitalized savings, and voluntary accounts of capitalized pension savings. The successful pension reform has invigorated and the financial market and promotes its development, stimulating investment and economic growth. These results have encouraged us and opened the way for further reforms in the area of the labour market and labour relations. We have sought to make the labour relations system more flexible to respond to the new circumstances in the world of work, to adjust to the changed structure of our economy and to enable further reforms to be carried out. At the same time, we have created and strengthened a new legislative framework for the elimination of all forms of discrimination and for the protection of the dignity of working women and men, and instituted an equal opportunity policy.

The Croatian Government has begun to apply new programmes to encourage enterprise development, which recognize the special nature of small and medium-sized enterprises, women entrepreneurs and people with special needs. Acceptable and encouraging conditions for access to lines of credit are particularly important for these programmes. We want Croatia to become a truly business-friendly environment and to create a favourable investment climate. At the same time, we have not neglected the area of social security, in which we have taken account of decent work standards. We have noted the importance of recognizing all forms of work, both conventional and unconventional, and concluded that it is important that every form of work, which necessarily contributes to the national economy, can and must be the basis from which social security rights are derived. It is our opinion that social security should, in the changed world of work, be linked to personal status, and not employment status. In this area, we have already adopted legal solutions which have been validated in modest, but indicative practice. We believe that it is realistic to expect a reduction in the share of the grey economy. Trends indicating a decrease in unemployment are also encouraging, although the problem of unemployment remains the special priority of my Government. By the end of June, the Government will have adopted the first National Employment Action Plan drawn up in accordance with the EU guidelines, and with the cooperation of European experts within the EU's programme Community Assistance for Reconstruction, Development and Stabilization (CARDS). By the end of the year, we also expect to have redefined the criteria and indicators of the national poverty line, as the basis for new policies and a new social protection system. The system follows the reform which has been designed as the new responsibility of local government players in partnership with the civil sector, so that social protection measures can be individually adopted and adapted to the real needs of the beneficiaries.

Croatian government programmes backed by national consensus, such as the programme to remove administrative barriers and to promote the investment climate, and the programme of adjusting national legislation to EU legislation, also encourage our efforts to deal with the complex issues of employment and social security. In this effort we rely especially on the national tripartite infrastructure – the Economic and Social Council. My Government believes that social partnership is a vital factor in the creation and implementation of its programme.

It seems that there is no greater challenge than creating balanced social development. It demands constantly new responses to issues, such as poverty, social exclusion, equal opportunities, freedom and the right to participate in the life of the community.

For the sake of the future, it is our duty to draw on our knowledge, energy, solidarity and cooperation to eliminate poverty, social exclusion and all forms of discrimination. It is our duty to provide a world of work with equal opportunities for all. The civilizations of the new millennium do not see their responsibility as being confined to their own national borders, but as extending to global action as well. Therefore, we should work together to provide the conditions for a world strengthened by social cohesion. This Conference, and especially the extremely important, comprehensive and encouraging Report by the Director-General, Mr. Juan Somavia, is an exceptional contribution to the exchange of opinions, experience, and practice of the future global strategy for economic and social development, which will also strengthen our own national capacity to deal with the tests ahead of us.

Original Spanish: Mr. DOZ *(Workers' delegate, Spain)*

On behalf of the Spanish workers' delegation, I congratulate the Director-General on the interesting Report under the follow-up to the ILO Declaration on Fundamental Principles and Rights at Work, which provides us with useful information on some basic aspects of the labour situation around the world.

Notwithstanding the progress made in ratifying the Conventions referred to in the Declaration, in their effective implementation or in the development of social dialogue in some countries, the situation of labour and trade union rights around the world is extremely unsatisfactory. States which, for various reasons, have not ratified Conventions Nos. 87 and 98 make up almost half of the world's population. Other countries which have ratified them do not comply with them and there are many countries where trade union freedom and rights are violated, in the worst cases through persecution, sackings and the murder of trade unionists. This year again, Colombia holds the sad record of having the highest number of trade unionists who have been murdered. We must put an end to this situation.

Despite the ILO's efforts, the objective of decent work for all persons of working age seems still to be a very distant prospect. Unemployment, which is running at a very high level, fluctuates with the economic cycles, but it has proved impossible to reverse the growing trend of precarious and informal work. Three thousand million people in the world are earning less than $2 a day and that means that only a minority of the world's population has access to decent work. In our view, it is only through radical changes in the principles and practices governing politics and the economy in our globalized world, those which shape the neo-liberal model of globalization, that we will we be able to make progress towards the goal of decent work for all. Nor will we be able to achieve this if we cannot build a peaceful, fair and democratic world, where tolerance among cultures and peoples prevails.

The World Commission on the Social Dimension of Globalization has made an excellent contribution towards steering these changes through its report, *A fair globalization: Creating opportunities for all.* Multilateral institutions, governments, business organizations and trade unions must make a joint effort to turn this into a reality, because at the moment it still exists only on paper. The ILO must become the vital nerve centre of this effort.

We are taking a big gamble because the start of the twenty-first century is full of uncertainties, risks and intolerable situations. Some of them have been caused by continuing hunger, abject poverty and extreme inequality in the distribution of wealth and by the failure to implement effective policies to counter these scourges. Other major risks stem from the fomenting of intolerance, racism, violence, war and the violation of human rights by those in various parts of the world who seem determined to make crazy prophecies regarding the clash of civilizations come true.

Since, 11 September 2001 when the people of the United States suffered the brutal attacks on New York and Washington, many peoples around the world have also endured barbarous mass and indiscriminate terrorism. On 11 March last, in Madrid, 192 people died and more than 1,500 were wounded as a result of attacks carried out by a group whose ideology is rooted in religious fundamentalism. The victims were workers and students from 20 different countries. The Spanish trade union movement, as well as the vast majority of the Spanish people, has, for decades, been committed to the social struggle against terrorism which used to be local but which is now also global. Multilateral institutions and governments must work closely together in this global fight. Social organizations from different countries can and must help to deprive terrorists of their culture medium by promoting respect, mutual tolerance and exchanges between different cultures and by fighting poverty and discrimination.

With the same energy as that with which we face up to terrorism we denounce the violation of democratic principles, human rights and international laws, including the Geneva Convention, which are committed under the cloak of combating terrorism and, what is much worse, the use of terrorist acts and their victims as a pretext for declaring wars and occupying countries for other, quite different purposes, thereby causing the death of thousands of innocent people, as has happened in Iraq, or for practising state-sponsored violence against a whole people which has been denied its rights as recognized by the United Nations which is what the current Israeli Government is doing to the Palestinian people.

Many unresolved conflicts, in which war and violence destroy the most elementary human rights, beginning with the right to life, naturally, have an adverse affect on work and on labour and trade union rights. This is what has been happening for too long in Palestine, occupied by Israel, where the labour rights of its population are being seriously violated and this is what is happening in Iraq.

Among the many instance, in which a failure to solve conflicts affects workers and their rights, we should mention the Saharawi workers in the Western Sahara.

Fundamental labour rights cannot be separated from other human rights and democratic principles. It is especially serious when the governments of democratic nations, in the name of security, cause such a serious deterioration in human rights, whereas they should help to extend them throughout the world as a means of helping to end terrorism. It is impossible to build democracy by infringing democratic principles and human rights.

Because of our concern over this situation, we strongly support the thrust towards strengthening, reforming and democratizing multilateral political and economic institutions, as proposed by the World Commission on the Social Dimension of Globalization. We call on the Governing Body of the ILO to establish a specific plan to publicize it and to discuss its contents with governments, other multilateral institutions and social organizations.

Lastly, I would like to say a few words about Spain. Since the Spanish trade union movement is independent, we trust that the political change which has just been democratically decided upon by the Spanish people will signify an improvement in the social dialogue in our country in order to tackle the main problems of the labour market, including high levels of unemployment, temporary and precarious labour contracts, and the situation of about 1 million immigrants who do not have residence permits and who are working in the informal economy in unacceptable conditions. We look forward to the comments and conclusions of the Committee on Migrant Workers of this Conference on this question.

We also trust that the new Spanish Government will change some important aspects of previous foreign policy and will endeavour to strengthen the multilateral institutions of the United Nations system.

In our determination to achieve a "fair globalization" we are staking the future, in a century that has begun on a very sombre note, although the technical resource, and available for a just, democratic and peaceful world and its moral and political foundations, have been clearly identified.

Mr. HERCZOG *(Government delegate, Hungary)*

I congratulate the President, on behalf of the Government of Hungary, on his election as President of this session of the Conference.

The Director-General's Report informs us about the work of a properly managed and efficient organization. The ILO has carried out its tasks for this period successfully, which I put down to strategic budgeting and result-oriented leadership. Naturally, the most important question is how these activities have contributed to the goals of the ILO. In what follows I would like to deal briefly with this question.

The greatest value of the ILO lies in the system of international labour standards and the supervisory system designed to verify compliance. My Government fully appreciates the completion of tasks under Strategic objective No. 1. I find it important that the follow-up to the ILO Declaration has by now yielded results, and that the contradiction between an increase in expenditure arising from more tasks and the zero growth budget did not cause tangible tensions.

An effective employment strategy is a critical component of endeavours for full and productive employment. It was in this spirit that we participated in the collaboration related to the ILO *World Employment Report 2004*. A conference on the draft report held in Budapest last month produced important lessons. Research proved the importance of public employment services and concerted economic and employment policies in minimizing regional disparities. We have seen how productivity growth can contribute to reducing poverty, and what policies should be pursued to avoid a trade-off between productivity and employment. The latter is of particular relevance to us since my Government is determined to increase the employment level substantially by exploiting the GDP and productivity growth experienced in Hungary.

We are satisfied with the ILO's activities in Europe. The ILO has made an important contribution to the Stability Pact for South and Eastern Europe. We greatly appreciate the work of the Budapest-based Subregional Office; we will do our best to provide the necessary conditions for its effective operation. My Government wishes to promote the success of the ILO's policies in Europe by hosting the European Regional Meeting in Budapest in 2005. Although, rather modestly, the Director-General's Report is silent about it, the ILO contributed to the successful enlargement of the European Union, for which I would like to extend my Government's gratitude.

1 May 2004, the day of our accession to the European Union, is a historical date for Hungary. The early 1990s brought our independence and the freedom to choose our own values. The majority of Hungarian society chose European values: democracy and solidarity. By our accession we have become an equal member of a large community, in which at the same time we can preserve our culture and identity.

Hungarian society considers solidarity to be one of the most important values of the EU. This is the reason why we think that the EU has a key role to play in implementing the recommendations of the World Commission on the Social Dimension of Globalization. Our views are confirmed by the policies the EU has been pursuing, as well as by the fact that the EU itself is a key actor in the global space, where, in case of coordinated actions, it has sufficient weight to represent its position.

Related to the debate on the World Commission's report, I attach particular importance to the European Commission's Communication of 18 May. The key sentence of the Communication states that globalization needs to be harnessed in support of the weakest and most vulnerable if it is to be fair and equitable. Of the Commission's recommendations, I stress the importance of ideas urging the improvement of cooperation between multilateral organizations, increased involvement of employers' and workers' organizations, and coordinated action by the EU.

Finally, let me inform the Conference that the Hungarian edition of the International Labour Conventions and Recommendations adopted between 1919 and 2002 was published this spring. We have sent copies of the publication free of charge to employers' and workers' organizations, courts, ministries, members of parliament, as well as major universities. It is with great pleasure that I have the opportunity to hand over a copy of the publication to the library of the ILO. Thank you for your attention.

Mr. PIRLER *(Employers' delegate, Turkey)*

I have great pleasure in extending to you all personally, and on behalf of my delegation of Turkish employers, my best wishes for a very successful session. Also, allow me to congratulate the President on his election to preside over this session of the International Labour Conference.

This year we have a lot of food for thought and discussion. The report, *A fair globalization: Creating opportunities for all,* is a comprehensive study which needs to be discussed at length, and this Conference provides an excellent forum for such a task.

Since one of the Reports of the Director-General is also based on the social dimension of globalization this year, I will take this opportunity to very briefly dwell on this topic and express the Turkish employers' views on various aspects of it.

I am sure that we all agree on such basic values upheld in the Report as the market economy, democracy, the rule of law, respect for the individual and property, human dignity, equality and freedom. We are also satisfied by the recognition that the global market economy has generated many significant benefits and has great productive potential in terms of economic, political and social development.

To cite a relevant example in this connection from our country, Turkey has managed to increase its exports more than 20 times over the last 20 years. Being a global player in today's world is not an easy job, and you have to face many of difficulties and challenges. But, all countries willing to benefit from globalization in terms of increasing welfare and creating decent jobs should be prepared to take risks and initiatives in this direction.

As Turkish employers, we have no difficulty in agreeing with various proposals and recommendations contained in the Report, such as: private capital flows need to be spread more widely; international action on education must be reinforced; better social protection supported by international action and solidarity is needed; international economic policies should promote decent work; and full employment should be a major international goal.

Nevertheless, regarding the recognition of the ILO's core labour standards, we would like to see a distinction made between the ILO member States which have and have not, as yet, ratified them all. Today, there is international consensus that this particular set of core labour standards with universal reach constitutes the minimum rules for labour in the global economy, as was pointed out in the Report.

As employers in a country which has already ratified eight basic ILO Conventions, which are now widely recognized as defining fundamental rights at work, we are forced to make a point in favour of introducing discriminatory measures in international trade against the countries which have not, as yet, adopted them all. On the other hand, in our opinion, the ILO standards should also be revised within the context of the market economy. It is necessary to bring into the ILO system the flexible working methods and new working patterns which form the basis of the economic and social model of our time.

Another concrete development which was highlighted by globalization is social dialogue. During recent years, we have taken important steps towards integrating social dialogue into the legal system and economic and social structure of our country. Within this process, such important legal texts as the Labour Law, the Trades Unions Act, collective agreements, the Strike and Lock-out Act and social security laws are being reviewed and renewed, which means that a new social reform package is coming into being, with the collaboration of the social partners. I would like to take this opportunity to thank our Minister of Labour, His Excellency Murat Başesgioğlu, who directs these developments, as well as the distinguished representatives of our labour union confederations.

This year, Turkey, as a candidate country, expects a firm date to be given by the European Council to be held in December, for the start of entry negotiations to the European Union. As Turkish employers, we believe that this gesture will not only constitute a significant and concrete indication of international solidarity, which is embodied in globalization, but it will also strengthen the tendencies towards democratization, secularism and modernity in our region. By fixing a date for accession negotiations to be started with Turkey, the European Union will also comply with the rules of equal treatment and non-discrimination of the ILO.

Mr. BASNET (Workers' delegate, Nepal)

It is my pleasure to address this session of the Conference. The International Labour Conference holds special meaning for the workers of the world. Much has changed since we met here last year. Discourses on globalization are no longer confined to economy, science and technology; they also include war, terrorism, poverty and social exclusion. We, the workers of Nepal, are saddened by the fact that the world has become much more intolerant and conservative. Workers all around the world are concerned by this change of environment.

Globalization has created an uneven world because of structural inequality and the absence of a level playing field. It is a fact that, despite initial optimism, globalization has created more poverty than ever before. We, the workers of Nepal, like others in the developing world, are facing the hardened attitude of employers and governments at home and an unfriendly environment at the global level.

As in the past nine years, workers in Nepal are facing the growing violence of Maoist insurgents and, at the same time, an even harsher response from the State and Government, which has caused the suspension of the fundamental rights of all people. Violence and terror has badly hampered the prospects of the economy. It is further complicated by the attitude and behaviour of the State and political society, which are very conservative. Every day workers are sacked, factories and plants are being closed. As I speak before you, my Assistant General-Secretary and 20 trade union friends are still in Maoist hands; they were kidnapped last week as I left Nepal for the International Labour Conference.

We, as a responsible democratic trade union, want to solve the problem. We do not want to be seen as the problem. Protecting jobs and ensuring minimum fundamental rights of workers and people is our first concern. We are committed to peaceful solutions and we firmly believe in tripartism. In this regard, we want the Government of Nepal to respect our rights to organize peacefully and to show its commitment by signing the Freedom of Association and Protection of the Right to Organise Convention, 1948 (No. 87) immediately. Recognizing workers' rights and dignity in social dialogue among the social partners is the only way to solve the problem.

Lastly, I want to thank the ILO, the ICFTU and other international organizations for their help to the workers of Nepal.

Original Spanish: Mr. GALLARDO FLORES (Minister of Labour and Social Welfare, Guatemala)

First, I should like to congratulate the President of the Conference on his election and successful running of the Conference.

We warmly welcome the positive results of the application of the strategic activities of the ILO in connection with the programme on decent work.

Guatemala, like other member States of this Organization, is an example of the vital importance of these programmes, which are implemented in a context of poverty and particularly exclusion from the opportunities provided by economic and social development.

Almost ten years after signing a peace agreement, the process of strengthening the state of law reveals a clear and inescapable horizon towards which our work is directed, with the aim of achieving proper respect for social justice, which is the only way to ensure universal peace.

Currently, and within this context, Guatemala has begun to participate actively in the consolidation of international trade bodies, for which reason it is of vital importance that this take place with respect for the dignity of work for all persons. This is a prerequisite if we are to achieve, with social harmony, the growth and economic development that every citizen of Guatemala wishes to achieve.

The decision of the ILO Governing Body to programme its activities by country will mean it is possible for the activities of the ILO to be directed on a more appropriate historical and social basis, thus ensuring a better use of specialized knowledge, taking into account the specific situation of Guatemala, which is the greatest asset that our country can bring to the international community. This may be the main challenge to achieving the effect that we hope the ILO will have with regard to decent work.

The perspective of a fairer globalization, of introducing a different way of globalizing the economy, is something that is reflected in Guatemalan society through its specific historical situation, which is highlighted by the need to drive change through the ideological and traditional paradigms that still exist in our society and that favour confrontation, which is the enemy of social dialogue.

Another important liberalization that the ILO has implemented is the need to integrate ILO policies to achieve a better response to the needs of the constituents. Guatemala has seen a huge range of well-intentioned initiatives that tackle different aspects of the problem and that, all in all, respond to the main objectives of the various national and international bodies, which all seem to agree with one another.

It is only through pulling together and pooling our efforts that we will achieve concrete results that demonstrate progress with these action programmes and avoid the institutional weakening of the Guatemalan Government and the social partners themselves, workers and employers, that comes out of the various isolated projects and programmes or the creation of new priorities that lead only to dispersal of efforts.

We agree with the ILO that the international system of standards that govern labour is a positive aspect, as are the different control mechanisms for the application of international standards. These are true opportunities for dialogue and cooperation where Guatemala has an opportunity to demonstrate to ILO member States its firm commitment to apply international labour standards in good faith and in the belief that an integrated world, through common rules and regulations, is necessary to consolidate peace and universal harmony.

However, merely applying international labour standards is not enough to combat poverty around the world, and particularly in Guatemala. To achieve that end, it is necessary for Guatemala: (a) to continue with the programmes that strengthen state institutions, such as the labour inspectorate and, particularly, the jurisdictional bodies that administer and dispense justice; (b) to strengthen social dialogue essentially to promote a new awareness of the basis of, and premise for, economic development and to strengthen the existing awareness of decent work; and (c) to continue the actions that address the four pillars of decent work; the creation of employment and the training and provision of skills for human resources.

The decision of the Guatemalan Government to fulfil, with all seriousness, the objectives to be met with regard to the goals of our common policies reflects the strong commitment of Guatemala to achieve greater respect for decent work, to become a paradigm of economic and social development within the framework of a fairer and more human form of globalization.

Mr. ZINCK *(Government delegate, Fiji)*

It is a great honour for me to address this 92nd Session of the International Labour Conference. Like other distinguished delegates who have spoken before me, I congratulate the President, on behalf of the Fiji delegation, on his election to the high office of President for this session of the Conference.

I am happy to assure you of the cooperation and support of the Fiji delegation in completing the tasks which face all of us here at the Conference.

My country, Fiji, sees the two Conventions, the Freedom of Association and Protection of the Right to Organise Convention, 1948 (No. 87), and Right to Organise and Collective Bargaining Convention, 1949 (No. 98), as the primary focus on relationships between government and the two social partners as promoted by our Constitution.

When these fundamental rights are observed other equitable issues will automatically fall in place. I am talking about discrimination in the workplace which is a problem whenever labour is involved.

We have ratified both Conventions and are now amending our laws and practice through the Industrial Relations Bill which we will table in Parliament in September this year after consultations with the social partners.

The Industrial Relations Bill promotes effective operation of the principle of good faith in all aspects of individual and collective relationships between employers, workers and unions by codifying relevant case law, clarifying the nature of the duty and providing penalties for certain breaches of duty.

Our Industrial Relations Bill protects against discrimination in the workplace, in particular, sexual harassment. It is our response to the process of globalization and the winds and waves of change that are associated with it.

We in Fiji are very conscious of the effect of globalization, especially the linking of economic and social activities of nations through the advancement of technology.

The Government of Fiji welcomes the first discussion on the work in the fishing sector as it will give us an insight into how the rest of the member States are dealing with the issue and it applauds the decision of the Governing Body to revise the seven existing ILO standards concerning fishing.

A significant number of our workers are engaged in the fishing industry, in particular, foreign seagoing fishing companies from the Republic of Korea and Japan. To this end, my country supports the rationale of the revision, which is to consolidate the standards for seafarers into a comprehensive new standard that will take into account differences in fishing operations, employment arrangements, methods of remuneration and address other critical issues such as health and safety.

My country welcomes the general discussion based on an integrated approach on migrant workers. Although small in size, a large number of our people are affected each year as they enter new borders for the purpose of acquiring jobs that are not available locally and which fetch them huge payments.

Our workers migrate to countries like Australia, New Zealand, Canada and the United States. Recently our workers have also been employed by international security firms to work in Iraq. A large number of he local workforce has joined the British Army in the last five years and are deployed by the British Army wherever they are engaged.

Accordingly, our Government supports the concept of a new multilateral framework on migrant workers which must be based on preserving and extending the concept of equal treatment and equal opportunity.

The Government of Fiji thanks the Governing Body for calling for the revision of the Human Resources Development Recommendation, 1975 (No. 150). Through ILO assistance we have, through the Integrated Human Resources Development Programme, developed our database to identify much needed skills and their utilization. The programme is now being run by the Ministry of Youth and is successful in training and placing first time employment seekers and those willing to undergo retraining for the purpose of being gainfully employed.

We have always been committed to our responsibility as an ILO member State and this year we have achieved a milestone as all reports on the application of ratified Conventions were submitted on time and we will continue and strive to improve our reporting obligations.

Let us pursue the past we have mapped out for ourselves. Let the ILO and the international community provide us with guidance so that at the end of the day every person in Fiji will enjoy a higher level of social justice.

Finally, I should like to thank you for your attention and hope that the 92nd Session of the Conference is crowned with success.

Original Spanish: Mr. JIMÉNEZ AGUILAR *(Employers' technical adviser and substitute delegate, Spain)*

First of all I should like to congratulate the President and Vice-Presidents on their election to preside over this session of the International Labour Conference.

The Spanish employers' organizations have always participated actively in the work of this Organization because we believe in its valuable contribution to economic and social development.

We aspire to an ILO that is solid in its tripartite structure, open to cooperation with other United Nations agencies and international financial organizations, attentive to events in our societies and focussed on certain basic objectives.

Themes such as employment, the promotion of the business spirit, the strengthening of tripartism and social dialogue, and the updating of international labour standards and social protection should constitute the daily bread and butter of the ILO's work.

In this regard the World Commission's report on the social dimension of globalization, along with the

Report of the Director-General, provide food for thought and some extremely interesting proposals.

Globalization has revealed a key potential for improving economic and social well-being for our peoples. However, the international situation and the tensions and social inequalities that persist in some parts of the world, very often cast a shadow over the unquestionable achievements of globalization.

For our part we can say that we come to the Conference this year with the satisfaction of having taken major steps towards improving the social environment in which Spanish enterprises must operate. In recent years average Spanish economic growth has topped that of Spain's neighbouring countries and at the same time it has become one of the most open economies in the world, converging increasingly with its European partners.

Social dialogue has been a determining factor in these achievements. More specifically, the trade union and employers' organizations in Spain have been sharing assessments and measures in order to preserve our achievements in terms of increasing employment against a backdrop of economic slowdown.

Therefore for the third consecutive year we have signed an agreement to modernize and promote collective bargaining. This agreement, which is of great importance for the negotiators at different levels, contains joint guidelines linked to aspects such as working time, wage structure and systems for classifying workers.

Equally, in addition to the bilateral agreements signed with the trade union organizations, we have played an active part in designing employment and training policies through a number of different initiatives which the authorities have tabled in the last few months.

Progress in these various fields is leading to change in the nature of work and employment standards. The relationship of conflict which governed most labour relations in the past is now being replaced by one of cooperation in which new attitudes prevail.

Lastly, I should like to reiterate my trust in the important role that the ILO can play and I should also like to encourage it to reaffirm its principles on the basis of the tripartism on which it was founded and which renders its activities so meaningful.

Mr. LLOYD (Government delegate, Australia)

I welcome the opportunity to comment on the several reports prepared for consideration by this plenary session. The Director-General's Report on programme implementation is a useful record of the Organization's achievements over the past two years. I am pleased to note that there has been significant progress in the implementation of results-based management in the Office. We would encourage the Director-General to continue his efforts in this area. This is an area to which Australia attaches a high priority.

The Director-General's Report, *A fair globalization: The role of the ILO*, is an important paper. The results of our discussion on the reports of the World Commission and the Director-General will guide the Governing Body in considering their implications for the ILO and the Organization's priorities for many years to come.

A crucial issue for the Governing Body will be the provision of resources for implementing initiatives arising from these reports. The World Commission's report recommends increasing the resources available to the ILO.

The Australian Government supports the appropriate resourcing of the Office and its programmes for the purposes suggested by the World Commission. In this regard, members should bear in mind the recent increases in most member States' contributions and proposals for further adjustments. Also, the recent large surplus which was retained by the Office is relevant.

In my address to the Governing Body on the report of the World Commission in March, I referred to the Australian Government's support for the ILO as the competent body to set and deal with core labour standards. The Australian Government's view is that any dilution of the ILO's authority to supervise the implementation of international labour standards would be a matter of concern. The Director-General commented in his Report *A fair globalization:Tthe role of the ILO* that there is no need to "provoke competition with existing institutions over our respective areas of competence". These comments are encouraging.

The Director-General has also made reference to the World Commission's proposal for a multilateral framework for labour migration. Such proposals need to be examined very carefully. Issues relating to workers' rights in host countries can be addressed effectively without the need for a migration framework. In many cases a bilateral approach is the more effective way of resolving these issues.

Another critical issue is the recognition of the fundamental right of each country to determine who should pass its borders. This is particularly so in these times of heightened security concerns. It is to be hoped that the outcome of the general discussion on labour migration will provide appropriate guidance on the implications of a multilateral framework for labour migration.

The Director-General has also addressed the need to strengthen the international labour standards system. He is to be congratulated on the progress he has made since coming into office in reforming the process for development, adoption and revision of international labour standards. However, we need to keep the reform process going if we are to modernize the Labour Code.

The next step towards making the ILO vision a reality should be to review the basis on which standard-setting items are selected for the Conference agenda. Agenda items should be selected in accordance with several principles.

First, sufficient attention should be given to reviewing existing standards rather than creating new standards.

Second, in reviewing existing standards, priority should be given to rationalising existing instruments. Finally, proposals for the ILC agenda items should have wide support in the Governing Body before they are adopted.

The report of the World Commission and those of the Director-General have important implications for the work of the ILO in the years ahead.

In November, the Governing Body will have to give careful consideration to how the adoption of the reports' recommendations would influence the priorities and the direction of the Organization. One thing is sure: globalization has already achieved higher living standards and more jobs for many people throughout the world, and has the potential to achieve much more.

We must be mindful to take a constructive approach. A response involving rigid regulation would fail. A measured response that advances economic growth, facilitates labour market flexibility, encourages innovation and promotes job growth is essential.

We are challenged to work together to ensure that the benefits that flow from globalization can be shared by all members of society in every country. The ILO has an important role to play in advancing this agenda.

Original Arabic: Mr. EL AZALI *(Workers' delegate, Egypt)*

In the name of God, the Compassionate, the Merciful! Allow me first of all to extend to you the greetings of the workers of Egypt and of the president and members of the governing body of the Federation of Egyptian Trade Unions. It is an honour for me to take the floor before this illustrious assembly of leaders, figures responsible for employment and workers from so many different regions and countries. This is a meeting that takes place on a yearly basis within this venerable organization.

This year we are commemorating the 85th anniversary of the Organization. During these 85 years, the Organization has relentlessly pursued its noble and humanitarian goals. This meeting rekindles people's hope, our hope in this Organization so that we can build together a world that renders life in our countries and on our planet more humane and fairer, and creates a greater degree of solidarity.

Therefore, we very much support the Director-General's words when he says that we should focus at this stage on the work of the Organization, the principles relating to decent work and the objective of using employment as a way out of poverty. We should also focus on fair globalization as a means of achieving international stability.

There is no doubt that the Organization cannot, on its own, accomplish this task. We need to pool national efforts as part of sincere, effective and sustained international cooperation that is supported by the donors, but with the condition that this be done on an equal footing, that the organization does not become dulled, and that the principle of tripartism should not be eclipsed in our discussions, the drawing up of objectives, the drafting of policies, monitoring and assessments. There should be no concession or abandonment of the mandate of this Organization which is to defend social objectives and international labour standards.

There is no doubt that we are currently experiencing a turbulent economic situation and unfair international relations. We have witnessed violence, oppression, intolerance, attempts to impose hegemony and phenomena that arouse our concern, lead to instability, exacerbate poverty and the debt of developing countries, and lead to inequality in terms of development. As a result of this, there is an ever-widening gap between North and South, and there is an increasing lack of trust between the two. Such upheavals and imbalances do not serve either of the two parties. It is an open secret for this august assembly that the Arab region, unfortunately, suffers from the lion's share of all these harmful phenomena. Such problems hamper development.

I could particularly mention the occupation of Palestine, Iraq, and the collective punishment of Libyan and Sudanese workers, something which is now affecting the people of the Syrian Arab Republic.

The Report of the Director-General, *The situation of workers of the occupied Arab territories,* and his statement during the opening ceremony clearly highlight the deterioration of the living standards of workers and the Palestine people. Therefore, we need to give a wake-up call to the international community in order to deal with these inhumane acts of aggression.

We appreciate the importance given by the Organization to providing these people with assistance and its intervention regarding donors. However, we do not believe that this position absolves the Organization or its Members from their responsibilities as regards what is happening in the region, or allows them to close their eyes to the ongoing occupation. The Organization and its Members must adopt a strong position so as to demand the end of the occupation, which is the very cause of this catastrophic situation, as part of the protection of the objectives and values upon which the Organization is based.

Therefore, it is regrettable that at a time when our Conference is discussing the report, *Towards a fair deal for migrant workers in the global economy,* that no reference has been made to undesirable immigration which is dictated by political choices and results in native people being torn away from their work and their livelihood, turning them into displaced refugees, as is occurring in Palestine. With regard to this report, since we are a country which exports labour, we affirm the necessity of ensuring compliance with the Conventions and international treaties in force. Migrant workers must be granted protection and care because they are a vulnerable and marginalized group and yet they contribute enormously to the development and the economy of their countries of origin as well as their countries of destination. We need to look at migrant workers in a new way in order to mirror an equitable globalization.

Thus, we need to see them as a bridge between cultures and civilizations, in an equitable and non-discriminatory context.

Thank you very much for your attention and I wish every success to this session of the Conference, and hope that you will achieve positive, specific results in the interests of working people.

Mr. BEJTAJ *(Minister of Labour and Social Affairs, Albania)*

It is a pleasure for me to participate in the work of the 92nd Session of the International Labour Conference. On behalf of the Albanian Government, I would like to congratulate the President, Mr. Ray Guevara, on his election to preside over this session of the Conference.

I would also like to take this opportunity to congratulate Mr. Juan Somavia for his work and achievements as Director-General of the International Labour Office. I am convinced that he will add to these achievements in the future.

Focusing the attention of this session of the Conference on protection of the freedoms and rights of migrant workers and on their economic and social integration bears witness to the ILO's awareness of this issue and its efforts to ensure the application and improvement of international standards on migrant workers. This is occurring in the context of an increasingly open society with increasingly permeable borders, where the prevailing tendencies are integration and globalization.

I would like to commend the attention given to migration as an issue that is taking on global dimensions and which needs to be managed in full respect of the principles and fundamental rights of every human being, irrespective of origin, nationality, race, cultural views or political convictions. This is another reason prompting the Albanian Government's concern to enhance cooperation with the ILO, not only in recognizing these principles, but also in discharging the obligations deriving from them.

I would like to take this opportunity to give a brief account of the Albanian Government's efforts to address the phenomenon of migration in Albania. Migration has been, and still is, a major and complex problem affecting post-communist Albania. From being a totally isolated country up to 1990, Albania experienced the highest migration flows in Europe. The opening of its borders and freedom of movement brought with them a great desire by Albanians to migrate to seek employment and a better life in western Europe. The restructuring of the economy, a lengthy transition period and numerous economic and social problems triggered an increase in internal and foreign migration of Albanians.

With a population of more than 3 million inhabitants, Albania currently has 20 per cent of its population abroad, most migrants having gone to Greece and Italy, while the remainder have migrated to the other EU countries, the United States and Canada. By its very nature, the global phenomenon of migration poses problems in all aspects of social, economic and political life. The negative aspect of this phenomenon in the receiving countries consists in violation of the civil, economic and political rights of Albanian immigrants, as well as in the lack of opportunity and ability to integrate. The Albanian Government estimates that legal migration brings with it a positive attitude on the part of the individual and society, not only in the countries of origin, but in the receiving countries as well.

The policy of the Albanian State, in compliance with EU migration policies, is not aimed at stimulating Albanian migration abroad, but is concerned with creating proper conditions for them to work and live inside the country. To this end, our policies are geared to stable economic and social development. The intention is that in the medium term, the incidence of poverty should be reduced to 20 per cent, while in the long term (by the year 2015), poverty should be reduced to 13 per cent. Extreme poverty has to be eliminated through economic development, reduction of unemployment, minimizing the informal economy and fiscal evasion, improving the quality of employment services and vocational training, promotion of business and creation of new jobs, and increasing the number of contributors to the social insurance schemes.

One of the main objectives of the Albanian Government is to bring the legislation into conformity with international standards. I would like to mention here the ratification by Albania of the European Social Charter (Revised), as an essential instrument in the field of economic and social rights. In this context, we plan to ratify the ILO's Migration for Employment Convention (Revised), 1949 (No. 97), and Merchant Shipping (Minimum Standards) Convention, 1976 (No. 147), in the field of migration. In the meantime, we are in the process of examining other documents of the United Nations and the European Union in this field. We consider it an achievement to have promulgated the Act respecting the migration of Albanian citizens for employment and to have drafted a Bill on foreigners, which is being reviewed and will be approved in the near future.

The Albanian Government, in cooperation with the EU Mission and the International Organization for Migration (IOM) in Tirana, is currently working on the elaboration, within the year 2004, of a National Strategy on Migration, which aims to improve the free movement of citizens, to support and protect migrant's rights, and to create an enabling environment for their integration and reintegration. The realization of these objectives is inconceivable without the active participation of the social partners. Promotion of the development of social dialogue is an important objective in securing stable social peace.

As a Member of the ILO, an organization with an international reputation, and on behalf of the Albanian Government, I would like to voice the desire of Albanian migrants that the contribution of international organizations to respect for migrants rights be in conformity with accepted standards, and increase in step with the excellent relations at the political level between Albania, Italy and Greece.

To conclude, on behalf of the Albanian Government, I would like to convey once again my heartfelt congratulations and to wish the Conference every success in its work.

Mr. BIYAMA *(Minister for Labour and Industrial Relations, Papua New Guinea)*

On behalf of my delegation, the Government of Papua New Guinea and its people, I extend our very sincere and warm tropical greetings to the 92nd Session of the International Labour Conference.

I convey my Government's acknowledgement and support for the reports submitted to the 92nd Session by the Director-General and by the Chairperson of the Governing Body. Our attendance and participation at this 92nd Session of the International Labour Conference reaffirms our commitment and support for the role that the ILO plays in promoting and developing all aspects of human rights.

We acknowledge the report of the World Commission on the Social Dimension of Globalization, and agree that if globalization is to be a positive force for change, then we must be given the opportunity to benefit from the global economy.

We are well aware that successful participation in globalization is dependent upon our national capabilities and policies.

In pursuing the Decent Work Agenda for sustainable growth and development, the Government of Papua New Guinea has adopted the following broad economic policies: good governance; an export-driven economy; efficient service delivery; poverty alleviation through rural development; and development of human resources.

It is hoped that through these broad economic policies Papua New Guinea will improve its economy and so minimize poverty in all sectors, particularly in rural areas.

In addressing the issues of poverty alleviation and the promotion of decent work, the Government of Papua New Guinea, through the Department of Labour and Industrial Relations, has conducted several forums to address these very important issues.

Decent work, within the framework of Papua New Guinea, focus on four strategic objectives, namely: the promotion of rights at work; employment creation; social protection; and social dialogue.

In 2002, Papua New Guinea took part in a forum organized by the ILO in Fiji, which addressed some of these issues, particularly on Decent Work and child labour in the Asia-Pacific region. Furthermore, in 2003, we participated in the Tripartite Regional Meeting on Youth Employment in Asia and the Pacific in Bangkok. Some of the issues highlighted in this meeting were a national action plan, based on a thorough analysis of deficiencies and priorities backed up by a high level of commitment.

Papua New Guinea, with the assistance of the ILO, has commenced work to address these policy issues and some of them are now at an advanced stage.

Reforms to Labour Law include overhaul of the industrial relations system; development of occupational health and safety policy with relevant legislation; development and implementation of a National Skills Development Authority; new work permit systems; and development of an employment policy and significant revision of our Employment Act.

The employers and workers, as major economic actors, together with the Government, have made profound statements about the state of the economy and jointly have set about removing impediments, which deter foreign investment and hence employment creation in Papua New Guinea. However, much more work remains to be done and the process of policy development needs to be transparent with the full involvement of interested parties, especially the employers' and workers' organizations.

The total population of Papua New Guinea is approximately 5.1 million with over 85 per cent living in rural areas. At a growth rate of 2.7 per cent per annum, the population will have doubled in 35 years. The population is also very young, with 42 per cent under the age of 15 years. This population growth is placing enormous pressure on the economy as well as on the social fabric of Papua New Guinea society and the provision of essential services.

It is projected that between 1990 and 2020 the economically active population will have doubled from 1.5 million to 3.2 million: approximately 1.7 million people will be added to the labour force over this period, assuming that current participation rates remain stable, and that mortality and fertility decline as projected. Thus, the annual net addition to the labour force will increase from 46,000 during the 1995-2000 period to 66,000 during the 2010-15 period. This projection may be low given the results of the 2000 census; nevertheless a major problem of labour absorption lies head for Papua New Guinea.

We appreciate the Director-General's introductory remarks on the *ILO programme and implementation 2002-03* which states that the implementation side has moved towards country-based programmes, developed over 2002-03 to take effect over 2004-05.

We also hope that the establishment of the World Commission on the Social Dimension of Globalization will influence the role of the ILO towards having a much wider and more direct impact on developing countries such as Papua New Guinea. We look forward to the use of available resources on the key objectives and programme priorities highlighted in the Director-General's Report, to support the reforms we have undertaken.

Finally, Papua New Guinea is committed and stands united with other member States that have ratified the eight fundamental Conventions as the standards in ensuring a fair and democratic working environment whereby the benefits of globalization may be realized.

Ms. CHAO *(Secretary of Labor, United States)*

Let me join previous speakers in congratulating Milton Ray Guevara, Minister of Labour of the Dominican Republic, on his election as President of this session of the Conference. Minister Guevara and the United States Department of Labor have worked together on many projects over the years.

I would like to note that the Report of the Director-General on the World Commission on the Social Dimension of Globalization raises many important issues about the increasing interdependence of global economies. I have had very productive discussions with the Director-General about a number of concerns that we had with some of the Report's recommendations and conclusions. Nevertheless, I commend him for his commitment to improving the lives of workers around the world.

The United States' perspective on the issue of globalization has been summed up by our President, George W. Bush. In his remarks on global development on 12 March 2002, he stated that, "We cannot leave behind half of humanity as we seek a better future for ourselves. We cannot accept permanent poverty in a world of progress. There are no second-class citizens in the human race."

The World Commission correctly concluded that efforts to achieve lasting benefits for the world's workers must begin at home, in each sovereign nation. Good national governance, democracy, respect for fundamental human rights and sound economic policies are the essential building blocks of sustainable development and brighter futures for workers and their families.

When these building blocks are in place, international cooperation can contribute to economic development and the alleviation of poverty. Here, the Director-General's decent work initiative has made just such a contribution.

But the creation of new international institutions, new international bureaucracies and new international instruments is not in itself a formula to achieve decent work and poverty reduction. Individual Governments must and can step up to the responsibilities to address the root causes of these conditions in their own nations and within the framework of their own cultures.

I saw this for myself when I visited West Africa in December of last year to launch United States-backed child labour projects in the Congo, Benin and Ghana. In each of these countries, the United States and the ILO are working together with local governments to rescue, rehabilitate and reintegrate children who have been trafficked or conscripted into militias. As recent ILO analysis has shown, exploitative child labour does not alleviate poverty; it contributes to it.

Since 1995, the United States, through the Department of Labor alone, has provided more than US$285 million to combat the worst forms of child labour in these and some 60 other countries around the globe. This year, we will provide an additional

US$120 million to provide exploited children with an opportunity to attend school and to help their families generate alternative forms of income.

During my December trip to West Africa, I also launched a project to address HIV/AIDS in the workplace, which is another tragedy devastating workers today. I am proud that the United States, under the leadership of President George W. Bush, has launched an unprecedented US$15 billion effort to turn the tide against HIV/AIDS in the most afflicted nations of Africa and the Caribbean.

Consistent with the ideas expressed in the Report of the World Commission, the United States is also promoting adherence to international labour standards through bilateral free trade agreements. In the past two years, we have negotiated free trade agreements with more than ten countries. Negotiations are under way or about to begin with another nine. In these agreements, we affirm with our trading partners our shared commitment to establishing and enforcing core labour standards. Furthermore, we are implementing these agreements with technical assistance that helps our partners build the capacity of their labour ministries to develop effective laws and to enforce them as well.

In the area of capacity building, I also commend the work of the ILO in providing technical assistance to workers' and employers' organizations and to the Ministry of Labour in the West Bank and Gaza. We encourage the ILO to continue and expand these efforts.

Through projects such as these, the United States is helping governments meet their responsibilities to adhere to core labour standards and build brighter futures for workers and their families.

In closing, I look forward to continuing to work with the Director-General and the ILO to help the most vulnerable and to strengthen our cooperative efforts to achieve economic opportunity and prosperity around the globe.

Original French. Mr. RANJIVASON *(Minister of Public Services, Labour and Social Legislation, Madagascar)*

On behalf of the delegation of Madagascar which I am heading, I would like to congratulate the President of the 92nd Session of the International Labour Conference and the Officers of the Conference on their election and I would like to congratulate Mr. Juan Somavia, on the faultless organization of this session and for having the brilliant idea of inviting the Co-Chairs of the World Commission on the Social Dimension of Globalization.

I would like to express the joy we feel seeing this august gathering of personalities who have come from all parts of the world to make their modest contribution to the fight against poverty and the promotion of social justice in the context of a tripartite partnership.

The Report of the Director-General enables the members which are present here to appreciate the true value of the efforts made by the international community. It is in keeping with the realities experienced by all the member States of the Organization and the problems that have arisen. Madagascar sees this report from the viewpoint of a country that is emerging from a major political crisis which has had a considerable impact on labour and employment, but whose end enables us to look to the future more optimistically, more serenely and with greater clarity of vision.

My country, Madagascar, is striving to achieve more social justice by adopting a tool, the Strategy for the Reduction of Poverty (DSRP), which aims to reduce poverty by 50 per cent within ten years. This document, which was drafted in an exercise in participatory methodology in 2003, naturally covers employment, but it does so implicitly. It will do so more explicitly in the forthcoming version of the document, which is currently forming the subject of a second round of national consultations. The same is true of the struggle to end child labour in Madagascar.

Madagascar is therefore paying great heed to the actions envisaged by the International Labour Office concerning the ILO Declaration on Fundamental Principles and Rights at Work and the follow-up thereto. In this respect, we have initiated schemes with the active support of the ILO, with a view to implementing the various cooperation programmes that have been agreed upon:

– For first of all, the elimination of forced or compulsory labour. The national stocktaking has been completed and its findings will soon be confirmed by a national tripartite workshop. It must be accompanied by a national implementation plan, after which the ratification of the Abolition of Forced Labour Convention, 1957 (No. 105), will be feasible;

– For the fight against child labour, especially its worst forms Regional consultations and a national strategic planning workshop, to draw up the national programme and set deadlines, have been held with the support of IPEC/ILO. A national workshop to conform their findings is scheduled in the very near future. The updated cooperation memorandum has been signed at this session.

– For the programme to strengthen, social dialogue in French-speaking Africa. A national tripartite workshop on this subject produced a national action plan which has already been submitted for approval to the National Labour Council. The updated stocktaking is in the pipeline. The National Labour Institute will be mainly in charge of this programme.

– For employment as a means of securing decent work. The framework for a national employment policy has been drafted. It has received Cabinet approval and will be forwarded to both chambers of Parliament. Madagascar thus has a national vision of job creation and the fight against poverty. We are actively preparing for our participation in the African Summit for Employment and Poverty Alleviation, which is to be held in September 2004 in Ougadougou.

Without further ado, we have started to implement the first labour instrument, to wit the Madagascan Employment and In-service Business Training Observatory (OMEF). This observatory will set up the databases on employment and will identify at regional level, the trades and sectors promising employment, with a view to offering the requisite vocational training for micro-, small- and medium-sized enterprises through a financing system that has yet to established.

The programme to extend social protection to self-employed workers in rural areas and in the informal sector is well under way and forms part of the fight against poverty. At the same time, the strengthening of the current system in the formal sector is continuing. All this is being done through a participatory mechanism involving a public-private partnership in which our rural communes are associated.

The Director-General's Report constitutes, in the opinion of my delegation, a genuine framework for action to promote a fair globalization, especially for developing countries such as Madagascar. May its message be heard and understood by all decision-makers everywhere and by all national and international partners. We are appealing above all to the international community.

In conclusion, we hope that the synergies, which have prevailed up to now between governments and the International Labour Organization, through its regional representatives and its specialized departments, may continue and go from strength to strength. The ILO is 85 years old. This is both a long and a short time, because many problems are still awaiting solutions, but as we say in Madagascar: "Gentle rains make for big rivers." May all be plain sailing for the ILO.

Original Russian: Mr. STOYAN *(Workers' delegate, Ukraine)*

Let me first of all congratulate the President on his election to this esteemed office and wish him every success in conducting the work of this Session of the Conference. We believe the experience gained in implementing the ILO programmes will provide a sound basis for the achievement of long-term goals and the definition of future activities. I should like to emphasize that this experience is equally important for the social partners of ILO member States, including Ukraine, which has embarked on the path of market reform.

I have, on more than one occasion, had to speak from this very podium of the significant problems in the area of labour organization and wages which rose as a result of poor governance on the part of past governments. With the advent of the coalition Government of Viktor Yanukovych, Ukraine has managed to accelerate economic growth. Most importantly, real wages have grown at twice the pace of GDP. Economic growth has allowed the social partners to aim at the creation of specific measures for the gradual improvement of living standards of workers, as stipulated in the General Agreement for 2004-05. The agreement first of all lays down annual wage increases of no less than 25 per cent. The reference point for this figure is a proposal from the trade unions supported by the President of Ukraine to double average wages in coming years. Secondly, the Government and employers agreed with the trade unions on gradually bringing minimum wages up to the minimum subsistence figure. A corresponding draft law provides for this measure to be implemented in 2007.

What is more, the Government and trade unions have addressed the issue of payment of wage arrears, which had grown in recent years in the manufacturing sector. It should be noted that in the public sector, all wage arrears have been paid. The International Labour Organization played an important role in this process. The Government reported four times to the ILO on this issue. However, the problem of the payment of arrears of wages is not yet fully solved. More than US$320 million of arrears remain unpaid, one-third of this being owed to coalminers.

On the initiative and with the participation of trade unions, the Government has developed a draft law in which priority is to be accorded to payment of wages in the event of employers' being declared bankrupt. According to the draft Labour Code of Ukraine, which was adopted by the Supreme Soviet on its first reading, wages must be paid as a first priority. What is more, the (...) provides for the ratification by Ukraine of ILO Convention No. 173 and the protection of workers' claims in the event of insolvency of employers.

The trade unions support the position of the Government of Ukraine, which has been set out at this rostrum in the hope of obtaining technical assistance from the International Labour Organization. The situation on the labour market remains strained. The level of unemployment, according to ILO parameters, is approximately 9 per cent of the active population, and the official level of persons registered unemployed is 3.8 per cent. Today, for every vacancy there are seven applicants. What is more, 5 million Ukrainians are forced to work outside the borders of Ukraine. In this connection, despite the inclusion in the new Labour Code of Ukraine of the core ILO principles, the trade unions have unfortunately had to fight to avoid erosions of their rights. In conclusion, I trust that the discussion of the Report by the Director-General at this present session will not only encourage increased attention to the needs of workers around the world but also serve to increase their social protection.

Original Korean: Mr. LEE *(Workers' delegate, Republic of Korea)*

I would like to express my deep solidarity with all the participants from all over the world who have come to this session of this important Conference to share the fundamental goal of improving working life for all workers. At this moment in the Republic of Korea, the workers' struggle against this neo-liberal globalization is continuing, as hospital workers and metal workers are about to go on strike. Although I am physically far away from them, in order to address you, my heart and mind are with them. On behalf of the KCTU (Korean Confederation of Trade Unions) members, I would like first to congratulate the ILO for its efforts concerning the Report on the Social Dimensions of Globalization. I recall that, until recently, globalization was perceived as an uncontrollable current which is often embodied by the dismal protest that there is no alternative. Any serious resistance to globalization was condemned as archaic or irresponsible. But, in the wake of the IMF restructuring process, we Korean workers have painfully witnessed how destructive blind globalization is. Therefore, we welcome the ILO report which recognizes the suffering of workers all over the world and the need for fair globalization.

The principles in the report are important and helpful. But what matters more is to take a small, but nonetheless precious, concrete step towards this goal. I would therefore call for the ILO to proceed with concrete actions toward fair globalization, which I believe will better, if not perfectly, address the anxiety, concerns and needs of workers.

The importance of the migration issue, which is taken up at this year's session of the Conference, cannot be underestimated. In the Republic of Korea there are about 400,000 migrant workers and they are desperate to attain basic labour rights so that they can be recognized properly as workers. The KCTU has been actively involved in struggles to organize and attain basic labour rights for migrant workers. It is our sincere hope that the general discussion on migration at this Conference will serve as turning point for the full protection of migrant workers' rights around the world.

The ILO has played a big role in resolving labour issues in the Republic of Korea. However, the number of international standards that the Korean Government has ratified is far behind the international average, and many key Conventions, such as freedom of association and forced labour have yet to be ratified. In addition, many domestic laws have not been revised to address the objectives of those Conventions that have already been ratified. The Korean Government has yet to honour its promise given when it officially joined the ILO in 1996 that it would revise domestic laws according to the international standards and has failed to improve on the five core grounds regarding basic labour rights which the OECD selected as a subject for its monitoring process.

As I mentioned earlier, hospital workers in the Republic of Korea are currently preparing for strike action which can be considered as illegal under the current regulations concerning essential public services. Unless these regulations are revised, their struggle would be suppressed and numerous arrests will ensue. This is exactly what happened in the Republic of Korea last year. The Korean Professors' Union and the Korean Government Employees Union are also faced with oppression and key KGEU leaders are now in jail simply because they expressed their political views before the general elections last April. The Korean Government has made countless promises in the past and recently presented the industrial relations reform plan. However, progress has been surprisingly slow and some of them have never materialized. The new administration led by President Roh has already arrested 213 workers since his inauguration in February 2004. The KCTU has filed about 2,400 requests at the Ministry of Justice to secure pardons or restoration of rights for workers. I believe that this is evidence of the Government's aggressive attitude to workers.

Along with this, conditions for Korean workers have continued to deteriorate in the context of neo-liberal globalization. Around 4 million people are now either unemployed or trapped in credit insolvency, while over 50 per cent of workers have no other option but to take contingent or temporary work and experience low wages and job insecurity.

Even more serious is the fact that because employers have begun to use provisional seizures and damage claims as new means to oppress trade union activities and struggles, the association of basic labour rights is being severely restricted. As a result, this has led to dozens of workers resisting through self-immolation. Neo-liberal globalization is threatening to destroy the achievements that trade union movements have gained through their struggle. We are indeed facing an immense challenge. The only hope of addressing this unprecedented challenge is undoubtedly workers' solidarity around the world. In doing so, it is very important to make sure that the monitoring and supervisory capabilities of the ILO are strengthened so that international standards are respected and workers' rights are expanded in each country.

In the general elections in April in the Republic of Korea we were able to see the possibility of progressive politics being established in the Republic of Korea as ten members of the National Assembly were elected from the Democratic Labour Party.

Once again, I send my warm greetings of solidarity and the KCTU shall continue to fight for the rights of workers in the Republic of Korea and in other parts of the world as well.

Mr. FARRUGIA *(Employers' delegate, Malta)*

On behalf of the Maltese employers' delegation for this Conference, I congratulate the Director-General on his Report, which provides an overview of the progress made by the ILO in the implementation of the Decent Work Agenda. The principle of decent work becomes more pronounced with increased globalization, and one can understand the need to work towards ensuring a better distribution of the benefits of globalization to make the world a better place. As the Report rightly states, globalization has to be judged by what it delivers, by its impact on the social and economic fabric of different regions in the world.

Malta is a small nation that has always survived on trade long before the term globalization was used. Our society has always been subject to influence by external forces that have left an impact on our economy and cultural identity. However, Maltese employers are aware of the increasing volatility of international markets, resulting from faster mobility of resources, which can increase a sense of uncertainty and serve as a threat to investment, employment and the general standard of living of our employees. Malta is passing through a phase of rapid restructuring to keep up with these global developments. On 1 May this year we became part of an enlarged European Union, and the implementation of European Union standards and regulations in themselves offer a commitment by social partners to live up to the ideals of the Decent Work Agenda. The run-up to European Union membership has entailed an improvement in working conditions for Maltese employees through an overhaul of our labour legislation, the introduction of occupational health and safety regulations, together with other conditions of employment that have harmonized Maltese standards with those of the European Union.

Maltese employers have supported these measures not simply because they are a necessary condition of European Union membership, but also because they run parallel with the ILO's objective of providing decent work to a larger section of the labour force. However, there also exist areas of concern regarding the extent to which Malta can generate sufficient jobs to ensure that these benefits are shared by all society. The social partners cannot afford to lose sight of economic realities if the current standard of living is to be sustained and improved. Among these harsh realities one cannot overlook lack of foreign direct investment in recent years; the extent of the fiscal deficit – running at more than 9 per cent of GDP in 2003; and an unsustainable welfare system that crying out for reform.

Employers have been insisting that the only way to overcome these problems is through the creation of productive employment. For employers, the term "productive employment" implies the creation of jobs that generate wealth through their productivity. Unfortunately, our economy is burdened with too many artificial jobs, notably in the public sector, that only serve to disguise unemployment and drain resources that can be reallocated to better uses.

We are appealing to the other social partners to come to terms with the economic situation in order to focus our collective efforts on setting a strategic direction for the country, to keep it on a competitive path in order to sustain and improve the quality of life of its citizens. This is the time to put tripartism to the test, by being humble enough to accept that contemporary issues cannot be approached by seeking sectoral interests.

Government will stand a better chance of improving the state of its finances or implementing the necessary welfare reforms if it has the support of unions and employers. Costs of labour have to be pegged to productivity in order to safeguard competitiveness. Employers stress that only by generating productive employment can the country move forward. This can be achieved by upgrading the skills of the labour force and the technological capabilities of our industry, and by promoting innovation. One negative aspect of globalization that is adversely affecting our economy is that many of our companies are competing with others operating from countries that do not have the same standards of decent work.

Maltese employers are actively supporting any initiatives that might lead to the formulation of a social pact. This will be an exercise in maturity, and will surely contribute to Malta's ability to face the challenges of globalization. The main objective of the social pact will be that of generating productive employment, which is very much in line with the vision of the ILO's Decent Work Agenda.

In Malta, the infrastructure for constructive social dialogue exists in the form of the Malta Council for Economic and Social Development. This is the opportune time for this tripartite forum to enhance its role from one that is predominantly based on exchange of views and consultation between social partners, to a more proactive one where negotiations can take place to set the course for the country's economic and social future. Given the rapid pace at which the international scenario is changing, this may not be a matter of choice.

The ILO's focus on the creation of employment as a central route out of poverty is one which Maltese employers strongly endorse. This is why, at national level, we call for the ongoing development of the appropriate environment for job creation, through the promotion of an entrepreneurial culture. This should be the commitment of all social partners.

Mr. RACHMAN *(Employers' delegate, Indonesia)*

Allow me, on behalf of APINDO, the Employers' Association of Indonesia, to congratulate the President on his election to chair this 92nd Session of the International Labour Conference. I would also like to express our appreciation of the excellent work of his supporting team.

The message contained in the Director-General's Report, namely that fair globalization, job creation as a means of reducing poverty and promoting development through decent work are the foundations of global stability, is something that the Indonesian employer and business community must take as a positive challenge.

Since 2003, many things have happened in Indonesia. A new Labour Law was approved on 25 March 2003 (otherwise known as Act No. 13/2003). Furthermore a new Law on Industrial Relations Dispute Settlement was approved on 14 January 2004 and will enter into force on 15 January 2005.

We are currently getting ready to train ad hoc judges to represent employers in the industrial relations courts.

It is also worth mentioning that our Association, APINDO, played an important role in the process of formulating the new national Labour Law and its implementation guidelines.

Furthermore, our national legislative elections were held on 5 April 2004. Subsequently Indonesia will hold its first ever direct presidential elections on 5 July 2004. We hope that all of these new developments and their resulting stability, predictability and democracy, will help to create an even more attractive environment for investment in Indonesia.

We recognize the need to continue education and capacity-building efforts in order to develop many aspects of our human resources. In the field of human resources capacity building, we have received assistance from the ILO Office in Jakarta. Together we have developed several joint programmes, such as training on negotiation skills, collective labour agreements, industrial relations, HIV/AIDS, small and medium-sized enterprises and women entrepreneurs, the training of trainers, and many others.

In the past, a senior ILO specialist on employer activities was based in Jakarta, but since the person left, the position has been left open. We hope that another senior ILO officer will be assigned to assist the Employers' group in Jakarta. We believe that the appointment of such an officer will further strengthen the existing good cooperation between Indonesian employers and the ILO.

We would also like to take this opportunity to inform you that our Association's members do not use child labour. Nevertheless, it is still a fact, as in so many developing countries, that children help their parents in the informal sector. For instance, children work in their families' small kiosks or home industries.

In order to discuss industrial relations issues, we recently set up a joint secretariat known as FKKBN (the National Bipartite Communication and Consultation Forum) where a bipartite group, composed of unions and employers, meets on a monthly basis or whenever necessary. Together we discuss industrial relations issues and seek out solutions to problems. We also discuss the implications of the new Labour Law.

One of the challenges we are facing is the fact that the number of labour unions has increased dramatically. At present, we have around 87 labour unions at the national level, compared to just one in 1997, and thousands more at the plant or company level. In several cases, such a situation has a negative impact on business in general and on entrepreneurship in particular, especially with respect to the efficiency of running a business.

Another challenge is that we are facing an annual increase in the minimum wage. Every year, we have to negotiate to determine the minimum wage, and this takes a lot of time and effort. The result is that many employers have found it hard to maintain the competitiveness of their businesses and many prospective workers remain unemployed. We hope that, in the future, the minimum wage will be discussed and negotiated only among the bipartite parties at the plant level.

Finally, in facing these challenges and problems, we hope to make tripartite group communication even better in the years to come, with a view to addressing issues in a manner that is more effective and satisfactory to all parties concerned.

Original French: Mr. AKOUETE *(representative, Democratic Organization of African Workers' Trade Union)*

On behalf of the Democratic Organization of African Workers' Trade Union, I would like first and foremost to thank the Director-General of the ILO for the various Reports submitted to this session of the Conference. The discussion of these Reports is particularly interesting this year because it takes place in the context of the publication of the Report of the World Commission on the Social Dimension of Globalization, of wars in various regions of the world and in Africa, and of the precarious and volatile situation in Palestine.

The conclusions of the World Commission have not disappointed us, insofar as for once, we have a document which points out both the failings and the advantages of globalization. The Report of the World Commission reveals to the world what we African workers have been saying all along, that globalization only benefits a minority, who continue to get richer while the others get poorer.

The Commission has made many recommendations but we shall focus on those concerning relations between the ILO, the international financial institutions and other organizations within the multilateral system.

As Africans, this point is one of the most important for us, and we could not tackle this discussion without stressing the harmful, indelible consequences of a compartmentalized approach on African workers, particularly through programmes for structural adjustment without a human face, which have decimated all social services because they have been drawn up without any real knowledge of the needs of populations and workers. We must therefore make sure that the international financial institutions, the other organizations in the multinational system of the United Nations and the ILO are not isolated from one another, so that there can be more effective resolution of global problems.

That is why we agree with the idea of "integrated thinking" as defined by the Director-General of the ILO. This "integrated thinking" we hope, could involve the ILO in those global economic decisions which affect the social dimension, to allow it to achieve its commendable objectives.

Also, even though we agree to a certain extent with the content of the report of the World Commission, we have some questions about its follow-up, and whether it will actually have an effect on everyone. The whole value of this document lies, in fact, in how the recommendations will be applied by the various parties.

The revision of the standards and the strengthening of the standard-setting activities of the ILO are very important issues for the African workers. For my organization, the revision of standards and the strengthening of the standard-setting system to adapt them to the requirements of the day must be done without allowing them to lose their substance. Standards must serve as a spearhead for all the actions and activities of the ILO.

Now is a good time to call to mind that universal ratification in itself would not ensure effective viability of the standards, they must be effectively applied in our various countries.

This year is still marked by the war in Iraq, the situation in Palestine and violence in various places around the world. Violence, reprisals and *ex talionis* are part of day-to-day life for these populations, with countless deaths of men, women and children. Workers in the countries afflicted by these conflicts pay a heavy price.

This must be the place where we again call to mind the fact that these conflicts, although they may appear remote geographically, have insidious consequences for all of us and, if we are not careful, whole regions may be affected.

The situation of workers in these regions is most precarious and their fundamental rights are being violated. Poverty sets in and any chance of a durable solution, a sustainable solution, is compromised by renewed violence.

As African workers, we must remind you that negotiation and consensus, both domestically and, within the framework of the United Nations, internationally, must be used to resolve these conflicts. A huge effort is required, and we have confidence that the willing on both sides will step up. In view of the 60th anniversary of D-Day at which the enemies of yesterday joined hands to achieve sustainable peace, we have confidence that this can be achieved.

To conclude, we must bear in mind the Declaration of Philadelphia which says that, "poverty anywhere constitutes a danger to prosperity everywhere". Eradicating it is therefore a means of achieving social peace.

Mr. BOBROWSKI *(Employers' delegate, Poland)*

Since distances are no longer difficult to cover, today's world seems to be so small. One can easily travel between the continents, and we are no longer surprised that everything seems to be just the same as it is at home. The globalization process, accompanied and supported by the integration of markets and the reduction of trade barriers, is not to be stopped, and it should not be stopped. What we have to consider now, what we have to emphasize, is the social dimension of this process. Human beings should always be treated as the object, not as the subject, of those changes. Politicians should always keep in mind that market integration should never be the goal in itself. It should lead to the improvement of efficiency, economic growth and, what is more important, the welfare of societies.

On 1 May, Poland and nine other countries of Central and Eastern Europe joined the European Union. I am extremely happy that our generation, after so many years of constant battles for freedom and independence, has arrived at this historical moment.

It is now the responsibility of Polish employers and Polish employees to make the most of this enlargement, and social dialogue will be the prerequisite for success.

Poland's last recession was used for the restructuring of its state-owned companies. The restructuring brought with it certain costs – mainly social. Restructuring meant reduction of employment. It was necessary, however, to prepare Poland for favourable economic development, and I believe that this difficult decision has given rise to an environment that offers opportunity, growth and prosperity.

In 1981, the Tripartite Commission on Social Dialogue was established. Since then, we have learned to talk to each other. We have understood that only strong employee and employer organizations will result in the achievement of our common goals –

that is, economic growth accompanied by social peace and well-being.

To continue the progress, it is necessary for governments to form new partnerships with business and to mobilize the support various social groups. Indeed, our social partners play a crucial part in discussing changes and negotiating new procedures. I would like to applaud the Polish example – in adopting the changes regarding the flexibility of the labour market introduced after 2002, employers and the Government consulted with the social partners.

Today, more than ever, we are aware that employment growth and the reduction of unemployment are essential from a political, as well as a social, point of view, and not only in Poland. Older members of the European Union face the same challenge. The problem, however, does not only lie in the amount of new jobs that Europe can create in the short term, but also how Europe can raise its economic potential, transforming it into sustainable employment and productivity growth in the medium and longer term. In other words, Europe needs more people working, and working more productively.

One of the conditions for creating a friendly environment for business and creating more jobs, however, is the introduction of more flexible regulations in the labour market. But while policies can no longer remain solely protective of the social security of workers, employers must consult with their social partners: the trade unions and the government.

Perhaps the Polish experience can become a model for other countries. Recently, a broad set of initiatives was undertaken regarding the labour market. The main aim of the legislative initiatives, approved by the members of Parliament (at least by most of them), was the lowering of labour costs and the introduction of more flexible labour relations.

Here are some of the changes already introduced: reduction in the costs of compensation for a period of illness by decreasing the period of sickness benefit paid by the employer; allowance for reduction of the costs tied to remuneration for overtime work; reduction of the right to paid days off to search for new employment, solely in the case when the employment contract is terminated by the employer; reduction of the cases which oblige the employer to pay the employee cash compensation due to unused vacation days.

The regulations regarding the flexibility of labour relations may be of special interest to you. These are as follows: introduction of the possibility to sign a temporary employment contract for the purpose of replacing an absent employee; more freedom for employers in managing working time; removing the obligation to consult with a trade union on the intention to terminate an employment contract.

The most difficult situation is linked to bureaucratic requirements. The Government and Parliament have come up with a few solutions, such as relieving part of the employers from the duty to set the annual plan of vacations. Yet, this is still too little.

The Polish economy is developing, but the 5 per cent economic, growth, which makes us almost a European tiger, still has no impact on the reduction of the extremely high unemployment rate. We do believe that soon both employers and employees will notice the boom. We need time and we need patience; but, in a society that who was told to wait and to look forward to a better future for so many years, there is not much patience left.

In my country there is still much to do. We need to fight corruption, we need to fight the withdrawal of the average citizen from the public life. The Confederation of Polish Employers aims to change this state of affairs. I know that our country has great potential. I know that together we can achieve much more, especially as we are looking in the same direction. This is the year 2010, the year when, in accordance with the Lisbon Agenda, Europe is to become the most competitive economy in the world. Together we can achieve it!

Original Portuguese: Mr. SILVA *(Workers' delegate, Cape Verde)*

First and foremost, I would like to congratulate the President of this 92nd Session of the International Labour Conference on his election and I would also like to wish him every success in piloting the work of this Conference.

We also congratulate the Director-General for the excellent Report that he has submitted to the Conference, which tackles some extremely important subjects, such as globalization, emigration, freedom of association and collective bargaining.

Today, Cape Verde has a GNP of about US$1,330 per capita. Its human development index, estimated in 2003, is 0.727, which puts it in third place in Africa. Its average annual growth rate is 7.5 per cent, while average annual inflation is 2 per cent.

These indicators which have already made it doubtful whether Cape Verde should remain in the group of least developed countries and are catapulting it towards the MDCs, do not, however, disguise the truth, nor allow us to forget the real situation of the country which is, indeed, one of extreme vulnerability.

Poverty, for instance, which is a structural phenomenon, is all too visible. The last survey of spending and family income, conducted in 2002 by the INE indicates that 37 per cent of the population is poor and 20 per cent is very poor. Unemployment, according to data from the Observatory of Migration and Employment, referring to the first quarter of 2003, was around 16.7 per cent. But know the position at the moment is quite different and this percentage is much higher.

We must therefore analyse these socio-economic indicators with caution, particularly as the country continues to be heavily dependent on the outside world, particularly on official development aid and the remittances of its emigrants.

When talking about emigration, one of the subjects to be discussed at this Conference, it must be pointed out that Cape Verde is a country of emigration par excellence.

We estimate that there is a diaspora of about 600,000 Cape Verdeans, in other words more people than actually residing in the country.

But Cape Verde has recently become a country of immigration. There are many immigrants in our country, most of whom come from the African continent, particularly from ECOWAS countries.

The Government, which has declared 2004 the Year of the Emigrant, will have to take action to ensure not only that Cape Verdean emigrants become better integrated in the host country as a means of defending their rights but also that immigrant workers who are in Cape Verde fully become integrated.

The follow-up to the ILO Declaration on Fundamental Principles and Rights at Work particularly stresses freedom of association and the effective recognition of the right to collective bargaining by member States.

On this subject we must say that Cape Verde has already ratified 12 international conventions, seven of which are among the fundamental Conventions of the ILO. The only one which has yet to be ratified is the Minimum Age Convention, 1973 (No. 138). We would urge our Government to ratify Convention No. 138 forthwith.

As far as freedom of association is concerned, admittedly there has been a fairly positive trend in the country since 2001 following a change in government. Strikes and demonstrations by our workers take place today quite normally, without the violations which we denounced on many occasions from this very podium.

As far as collective bargaining is concerned, apart from some agreements covering specific firms, it may be said that now there is just one single collective bargaining agreement in the sector of private security firms which has been violated on numerous occasions by the companies which signed it.

From our point of view this situation is due to various factors, ranging from lack of a tradition of collective bargaining in the country to a poor awareness on the part of the state bodies responsible for promoting collective bargaining.

We recognize the positive aspects of globalization but we must recognize that there are also negative aspects.

In Cape Verde, and in the framework of the globalization process, there are various reform projects under way, namely the initial draft of the Labour Code and the draft reform of the Social Security Code. With regard to these two draft legislative texts our trade union confederation submitted its views at the appropriate time and with the support of the ILO, and is currently waiting for these texts to be analysed in the context of social consultations.

As far as the initial draft of the Labour Code is concerned, our trade union confederation welcomes the fact that the Government has immediately proposed putting limits on fixed-term contracts which, under current legislation, are without limits and can be established for a worker's entire working life.

We cannot say the same thing with regard to compensation on collective lay-offs without just cause, a matter on which we totally disagree with the Government's proposal.

We must stress the fact that the initial draft of the Labour Code submitted by the Government omits an important aspect which is the fixing of a national minimum wage, although our trade union confederation made a proposal in this respect.

Concerning the social security reform, we think it should go beyond a few individual changes to the legislation currently in force and also encompassing the revision of the basic laws on social protection in order to allow, among other things, the trade unions to participate in the management of the National Social Security Institute.

The reduction of the age of retirement, notably in certain sectors of activity in which wear and tear is particularly great, or the possibility for insured workers to draw their pensions before reaching retirement age, are aspects which are not contained in the Government's proposals but that we feel should have been included.

Original French: Mr. CALIXTE *(Minister of Social Affairs, Haiti)*

At the beginning of my address, I would like to sincerely congratulate the President of the Conference on behalf of the Government of the Republic of Haiti and on behalf of the tripartite delegation which I head, on his election.

It would be remiss of me not to compliment the Director-General on the relevance of his Report and on the choice of the topic for this session the Conference which demonstrates once again the concerns of the International Labour Organization. The aim is, indeed, to place human beings at the centre of the debate in order to determine, after in-depth reflection, the best way of adjusting the challenges of globalization to harmonious development of the interests of the various social partners – States, employers and trade unions.

With these goals in mind, the objectives of the new Government of Haiti, which, more than ever, is grappling with the fight against social inequalities and the deterioration in income of the poorest people, are aligned with the objectives of this Conference, with a view to ushering in an age of social justice. The task is proving to be difficult, given the specific conditions which currently prevail in Haiti. The country has to be rebuilt.

I remain convinced that, nobody is unaware that, following the recent political and social crises which have shaken the country, more than 50,000 direct jobs have been destroyed during the ransacking of the industrial estates, the ports and most of the country. This severe bleeding of our labour force has caused the loss of nearly 200,000 jobs in the informal sector. Unfortunately, these thousands of unemployed people are not covered by any insurance and cannot call on any temporary support while waiting to be reclassified. This situation is a matter of grave concern to the Ministry of Social Affairs and Labour, which I have the honour to head.

We salute the Haitian employers, present at this, the 92nd Session of the International Labour Conference. We greatly appreciate their courage and determination to assist the new Government in creating thousands of jobs despite the losses that they have suffered.

I ask you to support these Haitian entrepreneurs in their bid to modernize and revitalize their businesses.

I would like the International Labour Office to assist Haitian trade unionists in their efforts to organize. In view, therefore, of the urgency of quickly redressing the current situation, it is important that Haiti should be able to count on the support and understanding of the international community in the context of an extensive job-creation programme, as well as with regard to the updating of its labour legislation in order to adopt it to the new requirements of a fast-changing world.

I would like to take advantage of this rostrum to call for the solidarity of all sister nations to assist Haiti along the road to regeneration and progress.

I greatly appreciate the efforts of the International Labour Office, which this year is accentuating its progress towards "a fair globalization" and I hope that the results of this Conference will be of benefit to the entire world.

Mr. SALIMIAN (Workers' delegate, Islamic Republic of Iran)

First of all I would like to join the previous speakers in congratulating the President on his election to preside over this session of the Conference. I wish him every success in his task and hope that the Conference will pave the way and lay the necessary groundwork for securing decent work for all.

Globalization has been a source of anxiety for men and women at all levels and ages, in both North and South, between countries and within them, among workers, within families and throughout enterprises. Worldwide, many are convinced that the rights of capital are better protected than the rights of workers.

In fact, our problems began when our Government started showing an inclination towards globalization. This resulted in flotation of the base of the monetary system of our country and a tremendous decrease in the purchasing power of the lower class, especially the workers. Ultimately, the results of these programmes will provoke upheavals in the countries concerned.

In relation to our country's labour report, the legislation concerning the exemption of carpet weaving units from labour and social security laws was promulgated in 2002. This legislation is in contradiction with Chapter 20 and Section 9 of Chapter 3 of the Constitution of the Islamic Republic of Iran. We submitted a complaint to the ILO in this connection, and the matter is under consideration in the competent department.

Last year, Parliament approved the comprehensive social security system under which the Ministry of Welfare and Social Security would be formed. It intends to merge 28 different organizations and foundations, including the Social Security Organization (SSO), currently providing social services.

The labour community is of the opinion that the SSO, with more than 6 million titular members, provides services to more than 26 million people. With the approval of this Bill, the property accumulated by the labour community over half a century under the SSO would be at the disposal of the Government.

The labour community suffered another blow last year when, under section 94 of the Trade Association System Act, social security inspectors were prevented from entering small workshops except at the request of the workers. This Bill has made the workers in this sector more vulnerable, depriving them of social security benefits.

Thousands of workers participated in this year's May Day demonstrations held in Tehran. The main theme of the May Day was the Fourth Development Plan, contract labour and privatization. Although the Development Plan refers to strengthening tripartism, decent work and freedom of association, subsection (d) of section 83 and subsection 5 of section 158 amount to annihilation of workers' rights. In a resolution, the workers also demanded legislation for the right to strike.

In the past few years, seeking real wages has been one of our challenges vis-à-vis the Government. Taking 1980 wages as the base index, real wages have decreased from 100 to 61. Similarly, the index of the average wage has decreased to 41 in the same period. On the other hand, the productivity index has increased from 100 to 275 in the same period. During the minimum wage negotiations, the workers' organization, after extensive negotiation, reached an agreement with the Ministry of Labour and succeeded in compensating this gap in the purchasing power of the workers. The Supreme Labour Council, a tripartite body, agreed to compensate this gap over the next four years in the minimum wage, starting from this year.

The temporary labour contract has played havoc with workers' lives. In a study conducted in 1,000 large industrial establishments, 43.8 per cent of the workers are employed under the contract labour system. Experts are of the opinion that if this pattern continues, after three years 90 per cent of the workers will be working in contract labour. Before the end of the sixth term of Parliament, a Bill was presented to Parliament to amend note 2 of section 7 of the Labour Law, which would have safeguarded the rights of temporary labour contract workers working in permanent jobs. The Bill, which was put forward by the labour activists from the Workers' House, was unfortunately defeated by a narrow margin.

The labour community, especially the temporary labour contract workers, suffered a devastating blow when, upon a complaint by the Social Security Organization, the General Councils of the Administrative Court of Justice issued a ruling that temporary labour contract workers are not entitled to receive unemployment benefit. This will result in further deterioration of the already deplorable conditions of contract labourers.

The entry of the coalition forces and the occupation of Iraq by the United States, the United Kingdom and their allies has resulted in vagrancy, unemployment, loss of job security and delays in the payment of wages. It is not clear why the ILO is not taking a definite stand. We express our deepest concern regarding the undue occupation of Iraq. In Palestine, the aggravation of operations and the destruction of workers' houses, especially in Rafah city, are considered as an inhuman act perpetrated against the workers and they condemn it.

Long live labour solidarity and unity against globalization!

Mr. SUKOMAL SEN (representative, Trade Unions International of Public and Allied Employees)

At the outset, I congratulate the President on his election and express my gratitude for this opportunity to address the 92nd Session of the International Labour Conference, which is taking place at a time when the world is going through an unprecedentedly difficult phase. Never before have the jobs of workers and employees been so jeopardized and the workers been rendered so completely insecure in respect of their jobs, their economic benefits, social security and trade union rights.

We have raised this point repeatedly in the forum of the ILO. Hopefully, this year's Director-General's Report on the World Commission on Globalization has to a great extent vindicated our point.

The 92nd Session of the ILC is also taking place against the background of the gross violation of international law and the United Nations Charter. As seen the United States and British invasion of Iraq, in wanton defiance of world public opinion and the international opposition of the world trade union movement, and in the most inhuman and immoral acts of torture committed by the invading forces against the prisoners of war in Iraq, which is causing deep revulsion in civilized society in all countries.

The World Bank and IMF-dictated neo-liberal economy, after about one and half decades of implementation, has proved to be decidedly anti-worker. Trade Unions International is concerned primarily with the public service and allied employees, who in either developing countries or in developed countries, have become direct victims of this neo-liberal economic regime.

Public sector industries, including the financial sector, are being closed down or privatized and employees are hit hard. Privatization and even closure of direct government departments and functions are also taking place in various countries. Infrastructure services like telecoms, postal and railway services are being privatized. Casualization of staff, introduction of a contract system of employment instead of a regular system, an increase in home-based workers and the steady reduction of regular and permanent employment in the public and allied service are the order of the day in all developing and developed countries.

Social security, pension benefits and other financial gains are now being reversed, putting the working class in grave insecurity. Hundreds of thousands of workers are losing their jobs, and unemployment has assumed formidable dimensions and poverty increased, which the reports of the ILO itself confirm.

Hopefully, this year's Director-General's Report confirms our contention that for many people the benefits of globalization are today a mirage. The World Commission on the Social Dimension of Globalization has vindicated our stance against globalization when it says in its report that, "worldwide, many are convinced that the rights of capital are better protected than the rights of workers."

The ILO reports paint a dismal employment picture, estimating that global unemployment hit a record of 185 million last year, or 6.2 per cent of the world's workforce. This figure includes only those in the formal economy. Unemployment is highest among younger workers, the ILO reports. The Director-General's Report rightly mentions that global unemployment continues to grow and that the informal economy is growing.

Thus, all our concerns about ongoing globalization have been substantiated by the World Commission and by the Director-General's Report on it. The World Commission has vouched for a fair globalization and the Director-General's Report has also vouched for a fair globalization for decent work. We are sorry that we are unable to understand this point. Looking at the bitter experience of current globalization, we are unable to make out how globalization, which has for the last 15 to 16 years benefited only the profit craze of the big and multinational capitalist companies, mercilessly to the cost of labour, can be converted to a fair globalization leading to realization of decent work.

The Director-General's Report has also rightly mentioned the necessity of proper respect for international labour standards and fundamental principles of rights at work; the Report has mentioned its absence in certain countries. Trades Union International has also complained to the ILO about the flagrant violation of international labour standards in India, as evidenced particularly by the case of the government employees' strike in June 2003 in the State of Tamil Nadu.

Trades Union International recognizes the important role played by the ILO at the present time and desires further strengthening of its role in the formulation and implementation of international labour standards despite financial, political and other forms of pressure by the dominant economic powers and neo-liberal forces who seek to impose their economic and military hegemony.

Finally, on behalf of the Trade Unions International of Public and Allied Employees, representing 20 million public employees of different countries, we strongly feel that there should be more consensus-based and non-discriminatory functioning and decision-making of the ILO with the involvement of all segments of the trade union movement, so that the ILO, through its Governing Body and the Bureau of Workers' Activities (ACTRAV), are able to properly deal with the fast developing situation that the world is witnessing today.

Mr. ROMCHATTHONG (Employers' delegate, Thailand)

Let me first congratulate the President for having the honour to preside over this gathering and I wish to convey to the President, and to all of you, the good wishes of the employers of Thailand.

First, allow me to say that in the world of employment, some have already dropped by the wayside. This is a harsh reminder of what we need to tackle, with the help of all here. We need to ensure good labour practices at the same time as we ensure the flow of business.

As globalization makes our world smaller and breaks down borders, the existence of interdependency among the global communities – a result of the three key advances which include communication, information technology and transportation – together with the rise of the free trade areas, means that employers' organizations are confronting tougher challenges and demands to keep up with globalization in the fast-changing business environment. On the dark side, globalization simultaneously intensifies the magnitude and the spread of drugs, crime, terrorism, disease, uncontrolled migration and unfair labour practices. Globalization is a threat to the unprepared. Failure to prepare will mean that tripartism and similar matters are under threat.

Tripartite efforts are called for to establish a surveillance system in the business world to enforce labour standards at all levels; for instance, with regard to migrant workers, minimum wages, social security, and occupational safety and health need to be enforced at each business unit or compound, regardless of the workforce origin.

Employers' organizations fully support the ILO initiative to strengthen labour market information systems. We are fully aware of the need for well-designed methods and mechanisms to provide reliable and up-to-date information regarding the new facet of labour indicators, which lead on to the development initiatives of decent work.

To realize the goal, employers' organizations need to address the following issues:

First, emerging needs for globalization education for governments, employers and workers. It is necessary that those involved in global trade remain up-to-date and in tune with the new restrictions and benefits that globalization has ushered in. We must ensure that governments provide services and infrastructure to facilitate effective global business interaction, including reallocation and re-skilling of the workforce for new work demands.

Second, increased mobility of production and flexible human resources. Increased mobility of production demands more flexible labour management. If influxes of migrant workers are not controlled, their greater numbers may be inundated and lead to their being voluntarily exploited.

Third, comparable practices, increasing powers of negotiation and codes of business ethics. Manufacturing employers must handle labour disputes effectively. It will be costly to delay settlements as customers will soon learn of the disputes through the network of trade unions and NGOs.

Much has been said about migrant and forced labour. Let us not overlook the need to promote equal employment for people with disabilities and opportunities for women's employment. Regional employers will always join hands with the social partners and the ILO to ensure that equal employment and labour standards exist in each national context.

What then is the contribution that we require from the ILO? We need support to provide up-to-date skills to our workers. We need capacity-building for employers' and workers' organizations, so that they can be self-sufficient in terms of providing the services that are required by their constituents.

In conclusion, along with increasing productivity and profitability, employment does not exist to harvest from but rather to invest in the world of work and the human capital pool of the nation.

We express our sincere appreciation to the ILO for this productive meeting and we look forward to continuing to work together to develop decent work that will benefit each and everyone of us.

Mr. MONAHENG *(Employers' adviser and substitute delegate, Lesotho)*

Let me from the outset add to the congratulations extended to you by those who spoke before me. We pledge ourselves to work with you to make this 92nd Session of the International Labour Conference another success story in the history of this Organization.

The world of work is evolving very rapidly to catch up with the changes that are taking place due to many factors including the now famous globalization. Unfortunately, the social dimension of globalization has not been matched by an increase in jobs, particularly in the small developing countries. It is our firm belief that job creation is at the core of poverty alleviation and this is the position which has been emphasized and re-emphasized by the Employers' group within the Governing Body and at previous sessions of the International Labour Conference. It is also gratifying to note that this same issue has been given prominence in the World Commission Report.

We have a huge unemployment problem in my country which has aggravated an already serious poverty problem. Effort at attracting foreign direct investment by the Government has not yielded enough jobs, nor has it had an impact on the poverty problems of my country. We are gratified to note though that there is an emerging consensus in this house that job creation is at the heart of poverty alleviation. We are however not so sure that the ILO is focusing enough on promotion of employment and job creation as a sure way of tackling poverty. We are consequently looking forward to the September 2004 African Regional Meeting of the ILO in Burkina Faso that will deal with employment and job creation. As employers we do support the principles of decent work championed by the ILO, but to us it is of utmost importance that we secure jobs before we go into the qualities of such jobs. Associated with this is an area where the ILO seems to have reneged in its responsibility, namely the environment or atmosphere within member countries that enables the private sector as engineers of growth to develop the economy and to create much needed jobs. We would like to see the ILO take a more active interest in this area and encourage governments to reduce unnecessary bureaucratic hurdles which make it more difficult, if not impossible, to do business and create jobs in our respective countries.

In conclusion, let me to express our concern and worry at what we perceive as a reduction in technical cooperation or assistance to developing countries. We urge the ILO and the more developed countries to consider this matter very seriously and to assist the employers' organizations and workers' organizations to enhance their capacities to meaningfully contribute towards the aforementioned creation of favourable environment, which can lead to the creation of more jobs and, consequently, poverty alleviation. What is sad and unfortunate is that, without technical assistance or cooperation particularly to the two social partners, it is unlikely that the least developed of the developing countries will be at a more advanced development stage in the foreseeable future. In other words, we would like to see this particular area restored to being part of the technical cooperation priorities of the International Labour Office. The ILO should move to the centre of the consideration of economic conditions in our respective countries that are essential for the promotion and creation of jobs and employment.

Original Spanish: Mr. ECHAVARRÍA SALDARRIAGA *(Employers' adviser and substitute delegate, Colombia)*

Like other delegates, I would like to congratulate the President upon his election to preside over this session of the Conference. Similarly, I am pleased to inform you that Mr. Rafael Albuquerque, a current member of the ILO Committee of Experts on the Application of Conventions and Recommendations, has recently been elected Vice-President of his country.

The Report, *A fair globalization: The role of the ILO,* provides an excellent opportunity to promote employment and to benefit from the advantages provided by the internationalization of our economy. This requires a constructive attitude from various social actors. The challenge lies in creating a system that generates economic, political and social change in order to improve the living standards of humanity in general. The ILO undoubtedly has an important role to play in this regard. Without ignoring the labour problems that exist in the world, I believe that this Organization should, in all of its future documents, present the different aspects of work as a challenge to be met rather than as a complaint about of the lack of due attention on the part of States.

If times are changing, then the way the ILO works should also be changing. Today, more than ever, before the ILO has the opportunity to focus its efforts on assisting different branches of the public sector and social partners in dialogues that lead to improving employment and labour relations. In this role, the traditional standard-setting role of the ILO ceases to be at the forefront of activities, as it has been up until now.

In the report of the World Commission on the Social Dimension of Globalization, a number of activities are proposed which go beyond the labour-related mandate carried out by this Organization within the United Nations system. This report should be examined carefully by the Governing Body because it raises issues that are not relevant to this Organization. For example, the ideas set out with regard to global production systems, largely relating to multinational enterprises, industrial free zones and supply chains, have never been discussed at length in the ILO and do not enjoy the support of the Employers' group. Nevertheless, I should like to highlight two basic issues that are developed in the report and that the ILO should emphasize at all times. These are the advantages of democracy and the market economy as factors that encourage stable investment and new jobs, which no doubt contribute in turn to economic and social benefits.

On the other hand, I would like to make special mention of the technical cooperation programme which is being implemented in Colombia. The assistance of the ILO has contributed to improving standards of living and social dialogue in Colombia, as illustrated by statistics on violence reduction in all sectors of society, and particularly among trade union and human rights leaders and activists.

Furthermore, the Regional Office in Lima has lent its ongoing support to efforts to organize numerous seminars for Government, employers' and workers' groups, not only within each of those groups but also for their joint participation.

I would like to draw particular attention to the seminars arranged by the Office of the Vice-President of the Republic in seven regions of the country, which focused on the promotion and protection of the human rights of workers. Three seminars were held on promoting social dialogue and productivity and four were held on promoting alternative methods of labour dispute resolution.

Furthermore, the National Association of Colombian Industrialists (ANDI) has been implementing a relatively successful workplan within the cooperation programme, aimed at the eradication of child labour in the northern part of the Department of Cauca. This plan has met with some success.

Contrary to what some believe, since last year, there have been some political steps towards greater openness to democracy in our country. This has been demonstrated in several ways: for instance people went to the polls to vote in a referendum organized by the Government. The results were not in the Government's favour, despite the fact that the Government enjoys high levels of popularity according to opinion polls. This openness to democracy was also demonstrated in the election of governors and mayors from popular sectors, and the election of trade unionists to two of the most important public offices in Colombia. We have also seen many different expressions of national opinion in the votes for the departmental assemblies and municipal councils. Nowadays, there is clearly a much greater respect for diversity of opinion and vision with regard to state management in Colombia.

All of these facts, and many more that time constraints will not allow me to mention, lead to an environment of building trust which has been driven by Colombians themselves and, finally, to increased production of goods and services. This has, in turn, generated greater employment. Indicators have shown high economic growth and wealth generation. All of this enables us to build trust between businesses so that we can again invest.

The business sector has committed to the development of the country and has supported structural and institutional reform required by Colombian society, despite the fact that these reforms include problems with tax breaks and increased income tax rates which go beyond levels elsewhere in Latin America. The employers have contributed ideas and economic resources to help achieve peace, improvements in education, child health and labour capacity beyond the relevant legal requirements.

We are pleased to be able to communicate to you that at the last annual ordinary assembly of the members of the ANDI they were able to propose resolutions supporting the Global Compact and decent work and the world responsibility of businesses, the last of these themes highlighting the voluntary use of the methodology of the ILO for social balance.

The ILO can be proud of its positive contribution to well-being in Colombia. The encouraging, but not sufficient, results that I have just mentioned show that we are on the right path towards promoting links between donors and the cooperation programme so that we continue, through the process of technical assistance, to obtain results that urge the armed and illegal players to become aware of the fact that Colombian society is looking for a political solution to the conflict through social dialogue.

Original Spanish: Mr. BARRENECHEA CALDERÓN
(Employers' delegate, Peru)

On behalf of the National Confederation of Private Employers' Institutions (CONFIEP), I would like to congratulate the President and his Vice-Presidents on their election to lead the work of this Conference, and to congratulate the Director-General on his second term of office and for his important Report, *ILO programme implementation 2002-03*, as well as for his Report on the implications for the ILO of the conclusions drawn by the World Commission on the Social Dimension of Globalization *(A fair globalization: The role of the ILO)*. The employers of Peru affiliated to the CONFIEP welcome the ILO's appeal for an improvement of policy coherence throughout the international system. In this respect, we feel that the Governing Body Working Party on the Social Dimension of Globalization has proved to be a useful forum for dialogue between the ILO and the multilateral system.

We also consider that any response by the ILO should endeavour to highlight the advantages of democracy and the market economy. It should note that in its report, the World Commission recognized that globalization has yielded notable benefits and, what is even more important, has enormous productive potential in terms of economic, political and social development. We should also recognize the responsibility borne by all the social actors when it comes to contributing to enhancing this potential.

Our delegation feels that a fair and creative globalization should generate more opportunities than threats, and that shared responsibility will enable us to ensure that those benefits reach more people, especially those who are less well off. To this end, we must prioritize certain issues which call for support from international organizations such as the ILO.

These issues include the following: creating a national and international environment conducive to better and greater economic integration; promoting and developing a national environment which fosters job creation, and in particular, promotes an entrepreneurial spirit and the development of small and medium-sized enterprises in the formal sector, whilst providing the informal sector with the means of moving into the formal economy; developing government structures which are transparent, free from corruption, democratic and above all, which truly serve the public interest; improving the dissemination of democratic values and the principles of good governance; and mobilizing the private sector for poverty alleviation. The poorest regions of my country are in fact those where there is only an embryonic business sector, or none at all. This is why we need to provide these regions with the means to encourage investment, both by local people and by foreign investors, and the creation of enterprises, which in turn will generate employment and incomes for the benefit of the local populations, whose hopes will be rekindled. We need to recognize the key role that can be played by employers' organizations in the public interest, when it comes to creating an enabling environment for job generation and national economic development.

These and other related tasks need to be tackled as soon as possible and will not be easy, as it requires a constant effort and positive action. We trust that the Organization will stand by us and assist us in meeting these commitments, with its widely recognized moral authority based on the values and principles it has preserved throughout the first 85 years of its existence, and which it is now passionately reaffirming.

Before concluding, I would like to congratulate the ILO on behalf of CONFIEP on the construction of its new Regional Office for the Americas in Lima. Among its many functions, this new office can help us monitor our progress in social dialogue and consensus building, as well as ensuring respect for the consensus reached, so as to create decent and productive jobs to overcome poverty through work.

(The Conference adjourned at 7.15 p.m.)

CONTENTS

Page

Fourth sitting

Reports of the Chairperson of the Governing Body and of the Director-General:
Discussion *(cont.)* 1

Speakers: Mr. Mogami, Mr. Aoun, Ms. Filatov, Mr. Potter, Mr. Lublin, Mr. Majali, Mr.Wang, Mr. Abascal, Mr. De Meireles V. de Castro, Mr. Kim, Mr. Galea, Mr. Nordmann, Mr. Mwakwere, Mr. De, Mr. Thys, Mr. Biltgen, Mr. Trogrlic, Mr. Fong, Mr. Lee, Mr. Guider, Mr. Morales Cartaya, Mr. Papiev, Mr. Iversen, Mr. Hamadeh, Mr. Xu, Mr. Caldera Sanchez-Capitan, Mr. Boti, Mr. Nkili

Fifth sitting

Reports of the Chairperson of the Governing Body and of the Director-General:
Discussion *(cont.)* 24

Speakers: Mr. Negron Tejada, Mr. Gomes Proença, Mr. Mansouri, Mr. Mdladlana Mr. Andreoli, Mgr. Tomasi, Mr. Monteiro, Ms. Sasso Mazzufferi, Villavicencio Rios, Mr. Pérez del Castillo, Mr. Andres, Mr. Markotic, Mr. Doz, Mr. Herczog, Mr. Pirler, Mr. Basnet, Mr. Gallardo Flores, Mr. Zinck Mr. Jiménez Aguilar, Mr. Lloyd, Mr. El Azali, Mr. Bejtaj, Mr. Biyama, Mrs. Chao, Mr. Ranjivason, Mr. Stoyan, Mr. Lee, Mr. Farrugia, Mr. Rachman, Mr. Akouété, Mr. Bobrowski, Mr. Silva, Mr. Calixte, Mr. Salimian, Mr. Sukomal Sen, Mrs. Romchatthong, Mr. Monaheng, Mr. Echavarría Saldarriaga, Mr. Barrenechea Calderón.

No. 11 – Wednesday, 9 June 2004

Sixth sitting

Wednesday, 9 June 2004, 10.05 a.m.
Presidents: Mr. Maatough, Mr. Attigbe

REPORTS OF THE CHAIRPERSON OF THE GOVERNING BODY AND OF THE DIRECTOR-GENERAL: DISCUSSION (*CONT.*)

The PRESIDENT

We shall now resume the discussion of the Reports of the Chairperson of the Governing Body and of the Director-General.

Mr. ATHAUDA (*Minister of Labour Relations and Foreign Employment, Sri Lanka*)

On behalf of the Government and delegation of Sri Lanka, let me offer my warmest congratulations to the President and the Vice-Presidents of this Conference on their election.

I also wish to take this opportunity to congratulate the World Commission on the Social Dimension of Globalization and the Director-General for their Reports which take decent work objectives beyond ILO to a global level.

We all have to accept the fact that globalization is inevitable and that it can be a powerful force for positive change. We fully agree with the observations of the Director-General that the Commission's report presents a new way forward for globalization by looking at the existing realities critically and recognizing the positive aspects of its enormous potential, based on a realistic approach to the common aspirations of men and women. It is interesting to note that the key elements in the national agenda proposed by the Commission, that is to say identifying the need to focus on people, good governance, improving the capabilities of the state and integration between social, economic and environmental policies.

Sri Lanka has implemented many policies within the framework of the Decent Work Agenda. The newly elected Government of Sri Lanka, under the leadership of Her Excellency, President Kumaratunga, is fully committed to a decent work plan of action, which will become a policy document ensuring social and economic progress.

The decent work plans of action will outline the key deficits and set out action plans to remedy them. The Reports of the Commission and the Director-General will certainly be immensely helpful.

My Government is committed to creating the required environment for the private sector to operate and expand, thus providing additional employment opportunities. The Government will ensure that the unemployed, especially youth, are trained according to market demand and the necessary changes will be effected to ensure that the supply conforms to demand.

Poverty is the major challenge facing all of South Asia. During the past few years there is a trend of declining absolute poverty in Sri Lanka, yet income inequality has increased. Recent political trends in the region have clearly shown that growth-centred policies alone may not be sufficient and policies that promote fair distribution may be needed as well to ensure social legitimacy and peace.

Migration for employment is a global phenomenon and an estimated 86 million people are economically active the world over. In Sri Lanka, some one-seventh of the labour force has migrated for employment abroad. Sri Lanka welcomes the proposal to improve policies relating to migration for employment and wishes to urge the receiving countries to strengthen policies ensuring welfare, protection and equity relating to migrant workers, in recognition of the vast contributions made to their economies.

Sri Lanka has already ratified all eight ILO core Conventions and is currently working closely with the ILO in filling existing gaps. We are fully aware of the need to strengthen social dialogue. There is a need to strengthen trade union leadership and promote trade union organization in the unorganized sectors. There is a need to change the mindsets of business to look beyond compliance issues as a means to increase competitiveness. While we endorse the role of the ILO as identified in the chapter on mobilizing action for change in the Director-General's Report, we commend the proposal to rely on the tripartite structures, values and traditions and to actively engage the tripartite actors as the driving force in the process.

In conclusion, I wish to place on record my sincere gratitude for the assistance, guidance and co-operation extended to Sri Lanka by the ILO and in particular I would like to thank the ILO office in Colombo and the Country Director for their commitment.

Original Arabic: Mr. AL-KHATIB (*Government representative, Palestine*)

In the name of God, the Merciful, the Compassionate! Allow me at the outset, on my own behalf and on behalf of my delegation, to extend our congratulations to the President and the Officers of the Conference on their election and to wish them every success.

We have examined with interest the Report of the Director-General, *A fair globalization: The role of the ILO*, and we share his conclusion that this phenomenon is a source of both suffering and hope for humanity at the current stage.

The problem lies in the fact that there are some who seek to exploit the wealth derived from globalization in order to extend their political, cultural and economic hegemony.

As indicated in the Report, we have seen a decline in efforts to seek a balance between the growth of wealth and its distribution with a concomitant increase in poverty and destabilization. There is a proven relationship between poverty exclusion on the one hand and extremism on the other. The ILO is called upon to play a lead role on the other side of the fence, namely, with those seeking to use the tools and potential of globalization to bridge the economic and social gaps between the two worlds.

While you are debating the subject of globalization, the lifting of borders and deregulation, the Palestinian people struggling for freedom is living in a state of siege. The territories are subjected to closures and a separation wall is being built. The Palestinian people is suffering from an unjust war, aimed at destroying its economy and starving it, in order to impose political solutions denying its natural and inalienable rights endorsed by the international community: the right to freedom and dignity and to establish their own independent State within the 1967 borders, with Al-Quds as its capital and guaranteeing the right of return of refugees in accordance with the United Nations resolutions.

The Report of the Director-General, *The situation of workers of the occupied Arab territories*, quite rightly emphasizes the suffering of the Palestinian people in general, and the workers in particular. This is due to the measures and actions taken directly and arbitrarily by the Israeli occupation forces, including restrictions on movement, systematic closures of certain territories, confiscation of land, demolition of houses, the construction of the wall and repeated murders. The Israeli occupation forces impose restrictions, collective punishments that are contrary to international law. Those measures are directly responsible for the exacerbation of the situation and the increase in unemployment in Palestine. As a result, unemployment rates range between one-third and one-half of the economically active population. Consequently, two-thirds of the Palestinian population are living in poverty.

Nonetheless, the Palestinian people is determined to continue to resist the occupation forces regardless of the cost and sacrifice required. We stand ready to negotiate a lasting and just peace based on international legality. The occupation of not only Palestinian but also Syrian and Lebanese lands must come to an end.

The Palestinian people is of course ready and willing to make its contribution to putting an end of this occupation, which feeds the cycle of violence.

We are looking forward to your economic support through your contributions to the Palestinian Fund for Employment and Social Protection, in order to fight unemployment and poverty in our country. Thank you for all your efforts to support Palestinian working men and women, as well as employers' associations. May peace and God's mercy be upon you.

Mr. GEORGE *(Government delegate, Trinidad and Tobago)*

It is an honour to address this august body and I thank you most sincerely for the opportunity.

Permit me, on behalf of the delegation of the Republic of Trinidad and Tobago, to say how proud we are to have Mr. Ray Guevara, our Caribbean brother from the Dominican Republic, elected as President of the Conference. Let me offer our congratulations to him and to the Vice-Presidents for their elections to the esteemed positions they hold and for the impeccable manner in which they have been conducting the affairs of the Conference during these plenary sittings. We would also like to congratulate the Director-General on a job that not only is well done but that has surpassed our expectations.

Let me present this august body with some relevant information about Trinidad and Tobago. First, the Government of Trinidad and Tobago remains committed to the Decent Work Agenda that the Director-General so vigorously promotes. This year's Global Report *Organizing for social justice* could not have been more timely, as Trinidad and Tobago, together with other CARICOM member countries, has embarked on an economic integration process, namely the Caribbean single market and economy, involving, in the first instance, the free movement of labour that would change the character of our economies in the future. In this environment, we accept the view that it is important to have an infrastructure of social, economic and legal institutions that promote growth with equity and assist in the resolution of conflicts. We firmly believe that the ILO, through the Decent Work Agenda, is contributing to the building of such an infrastructure, connecting our growth strategies with strategies for improving the quality of people's lives.

Second, the Trinidad and Tobago Government continues to acknowledge labour not as a commodity, but as people, and we have ratified the Conventions Nos. 87, 98 and 144.

In keeping with our focus on people, one of our more significant achievements this year has been the passage of the new Occupational Safety and Health Act No. 1 of 2004. The Act seeks, inter alia, to widen the scope of employers and workers covered by the legislation by including in its coverage workers and workplaces other than factories as in the previous legislation. The legislation clearly identifies rights, obligations, responsibilities and duties of all stakeholders and enforcement mechanisms that encourage compliance.

The Act also stipulates the establishment of a joint trade union employee and employer safety and health committee in every workplace to review health and safety measures in the workplace, as well as to investigate matters considered to be unsafe or a risk to health at the establishment. The Act makes special provisions for pregnant employees and young persons.

Third, I wish to emphasize the commitment of the Government of Trinidad and Tobago to the prevention and elimination of the worst forms of child labour. Our Government acknowledges that childhood is a period of life which should be concentrated on education and the development of the child rather than on work; that child labour often jeopardizes children's possibilities of becoming productive adults; that child labour is not inevitable and that progress towards its reduction and even its elimination is possible when the political will to fight it exists.

In this regard, we are working very closely with the ILO subregional office for the Caribbean in

Port-of-Spain to eradicate the worst forms of child labour existing in our country, and we are in the process of establishing a National Committee for the Prevention and Elimination of Child Labour in Trinidad and Tobago.

Fourth, I am pleased to indicate that Trinidad and Tobago has developed a five-year national HIV/AIDS strategic plan, covering the periods January 2004 to December 2008. The plan provides a comprehensive and decisive response to the pandemic and encourages an "all hands on deck" policy with people working together in a coordinated fashion.

At this juncture, I must express our deepest appreciation for the excellent support and assistance provided to us by the ILO subregional office in improving our responses to HIV/AIDS, in strengthening labour administration systems, labour management relations and development of a labour market information system. Our thanks go to Ms. Grace Strachan, Director of the ILO subregional office for the Caribbean, and her team.

Finally, Mr. President, we wish to conclude by conveying our appreciation for this segment of the Conference. It is through these contributions that we are afforded the opportunity to highlight what we are doing in the important areas and that are the focus of this Conference.

Mr. SILWAL *(Government delegate, Nepal)*

First of all, I would like to congratulate the President and the other Officers on their election. I am fully confident that under the President's able and dynamic leadership, the 92nd Session of the International Labour Conference will be a successful event.

May I begin by expressing our appreciation to the co-Chairs of the World Commission for presenting a seminal document on the social dimension of globalization. The Commission deserves our sincere appreciation for the most incisive and comprehensive analysis it conducted into the impact of globalization. We all agree, as emphasized in the report, that globalization should have a human face. As the report has opened new horizons, the issues contained therein need to be highlighted and pursued further to create an equitable, progressive and open world order. We are eagerly looking forward to the endorsement by the United Nations General Assembly of the report, as submitted by the co-Chairs of the Commission on 7 June 2004. We are also looking forward to its vigorous follow up by all, in order to translate the vision into reality.

Let me also express my appreciation to the Director-General for his valuable Report entitled *Organizing for social justice*. As a member of the ILO, His Majesty's Government of Nepal is committed to the progressive implementation of the intent and goals of international labour standards. In spite of the many challenges faced by my country in the field of economic development, His Majesty's Government, with the help of all its partners, has remained committed to the promotion of labour standards and productive employment to reduce poverty. In fact, the Poverty Reduction Strategy Paper (PRSP), which is our tenth plan, has set poverty alleviation and employment generation as its overarching goals.

The achievements made so far have encouraged us to do more. This is the second year of PRSP implementation and the economic fundamentals remain sound, despite the difficult security situation faced by the country over the past few years. The situation of insurgency in the country has adversely affected the process of development through national strikes, extortions and the disruption of economic activities. However, we are committed to pursuing the fundamental goals of promoting economic growth, employment and labour standards and eradicating poverty in the country, because we believe that these goals are interrelated and constitute a firm basis for sustainable development.

Many developing countries are struggling to come to terms with various issues, including the enforcement of labour standards in the informal sector. An overwhelming informal sector coupled with a very limited inspection capacity has created an enforcement deficit. Not only is the scope of the system limited, but there is also a need to enhance the capability of relevant institutions and personnel. In this context, we think that the ILO can play a role in sharing the best practices around the world and in developing more appropriate promotional frameworks and methodologies. It can also play a role in implementing education and training programmes at various levels.

The elimination of child labour in general and the worst forms of child labour in particular poses another significant challenge to us all. Nepal has been implementing a Time-bound Programme for the Eradication of the Worst forms of Child Labour for the last few years. However, in the absence of adequate alternative economic opportunities and social protection measures, it faces obstacles in sustaining the achievements made so far and in achieving its objectives within the given time frame.

Education and income-generating activities, including the services of micro-lending institutions, are to be expanded to deal with the child labour issue. The ILO can help us to make such mechanisms viable in the country.

Similarly, with the increasing trend towards globalization, the number of migrant workers is increasing day by day. However, the enforcement of labour standards for the protection of these workers is far from satisfactory. Excessive transaction costs, the lack of relevant skills, the growing trend towards the feminization of migrant workers and the lack of an enforcement and monitoring mechanism have made migrant workers extremely vulnerable. We are confident that the deliberation on these issues will lead to concrete outcomes. Therefore, there is need for an effective international mechanism to protect and promote the rights of migrant workers, for the benefit of all.

The ILO's new campaign to promote a universal social security system needs to be examined further in view of the financial resources and institutional technical capacities required for the implementation of such a system.

We have benefited enormously from several programmes that have already been implemented or are in the process of being implemented with the support of the ILO, for instance the ILO-IPEC Time-bound Programme for the Eradication of the Worst Forms of Child Labour, including bonded child labour, and the Decent Work Agenda.

The ILO has been instrumental in initiating and promoting the process of social dialogue as a means to promote democratic and consensual policy-making and legislative reforms in the country. All social partners are united in reaffirming the conviction that, by working together in close cooperation, it will be possible to ensure respect for fundamental principles and rights at work.

The PRESIDENT

One delegation has asked to exercise its right to reply, namely the Israeli delegation wants to reply to the intervention made by Mr. Al-Khatib, Minister of Labour from Palestine, and to the speech made on Monday by the Minister of Social Affairs and Labour of the Syrian Arab Republic.

I would like to remind you that the reply must be limited to, and specific to, the matter in question, and should in no case provide a basis for a new speech. Delegates applying to exercise the right of reply must also abide by parliamentary language and not indulge in violent and insulting attacks. I shall therefore give the Israeli delegation three minutes to exercise the right to reply at the end of the morning sitting.

Original Chinese: Mr. CHEN (Employers' delegate, China)

At the outset please allow me to express our heartfelt congratulations to the President and the two Vice-Presidents on their election.

At present, the international situation is undergoing profound changes, with the world multipolarization and economic globalization developing in a tortuous way. Nevertheless, it remains the common aspiration of all the people of the world, and the theme of our times, to pursue peace and development. The world economy has begun to recover after years of sluggish growth. Through reform and opening up, China has pioneered a road to peace and development suited to its own national situation, with an annual economic growth of 9.4 per cent for the past 25 years, and historic transformation from basic subsistence to a well-off livelihood for the 1.3 billion people. At the same time the economic development of China has provided huge opportunities for development in Asia and throughout the world. At the moment, China is in a stage of fast economic growth, which brings about the most favourable conditions for business and industrial development. It is also the biggest potential market in the world. In recent years, many multinationals have come to invest and develop in China. Going to China to share the benefits of reform and of opening up has become a trend in the world. That is because to invest in China means to invest for the future.

In the course of our modernization drive, in our efforts to be human-centred and achieve sustainable economic, social and environmental development, and in our endeavours to contribute to world economic development, we are also facing many contradictions and problems which need to be resolved urgently. China is a country with a large population, weak foundation, low productivity and imbalances in its development. In particular, China is under grave employment pressure, greater than that in any other countries. Workers made redundant in the course of economic restructuring and enterprise reform, and new entrants to the labour market amount to 24 million, and we need 24 million new jobs every year. We are happy that the ILO and the Chinese Government jointly sponsored the China Employment Forum in Beijing in April 2004 which adopted the Beijing Common Understanding.

The Common Understanding reaffirmed that employment is a fundamental right for all workers, and fully acknowledged the tremendous efforts and great achievements made by China in promoting employment and re-employment, and in poverty alleviation, and emphasized the role of economic growth in expanding employment. The Common Understanding proposed policy suggestions such as promoting the development of small enterprises creating an enabling environment for entrepreneurship, strengthening tripartite social dialogue, upgrading the knowledge and skills of the labour force and reforming the social security system. These play a positive role in helping various countries to better solve the employment problem.

While globalization has provided developing countries with invaluable new opportunities for making use of international capital and markets, it has also impacted negatively on them in various ways. We appreciate the ILO's efforts over the years in this respect and the suggestions put forward by the report of the World Commission on the Social Dimension of Globalization, to the effect that the global economic rules should encompass equitable trade, financial and investment rules. We hope that the ILO will make continuous and ever greater efforts to steer globalization in the direction of justice, equality and benefits for all, and to establish a fair and reasonable international economic order.

The China Enterprise Confederation has made tremendous efforts to encourage enterprises to undertake reform development and to fulfil their social responsibilities. We will, as always, further strengthen our exchanges and cooperation with the ILO and employers' organizations in other countries in our joint efforts for world prosperity and development, and for the realization of the objectives of poverty eradication, full employment and decent work for all.

Mr. NG (Acting Minister for Manpower, Singapore)

On behalf of the Singapore delegation, let me extend our heartiest congratulations to the President on his election to preside over the 92nd Session of the International Labour Conference.

Compared to last year, we meet under better circumstances. Global growth is around 4 per cent. Asia is expected to grow by about 6.8 per cent this year.

Singapore is doing better, too. The forecast for Singapore's economic growth this year is between 5.5 and 7.5 per cent. This has improved employment opportunities and eased unemployment.

Despite better growth, however, globalization and its attendant changes continue to have an impact on all our workers worldwide. Singapore has identified workforce development and upgrading as one of our main strategies to meet this challenge and help Singaporeans remain employable. Hence, my Government set up a dedicated agency, the Singapore Workforce Development Agency, in September last year, to champion our efforts to address current skills gaps and future skills requirements of workers in key growth industries.

The Singapore delegation is therefore pleased that the ILO has placed human resources development and training high on the agenda of this year's session of the International Labour Conference.

Beyond skills upgrading, a national tripartite taskforce comprising key representatives of employers, trade unions and the Government also made recommendations to implement a wage system that was more flexible and responsive to volatile business cycles. A comprehensive programme is being implemented and facilitated by the tripartite partners to help companies adopt a performance-based wage system.

With a resident population of about 3.4 million workers, Singapore needs to augment its population with foreign manpower to meet the labour demands of its industries to achieve sustainable growth.

Recognizing the importance of the well-being of foreign manpower in Singapore, my Ministry formed the Foreign Manpower Management Division last year to specifically attend to the needs of foreign workers. I am confident that we will be able to holistically enhance our framework and provide the best possible environment for foreign workers living and working in Singapore.

In this regard, I am pleased to inform the Conference that, in November last year, my Ministry, together with the ILO, jointly organized the Focus Seminar on Women Migrant Workers. Not only did this enable various government agencies and trade unions to have a constructive discussion on migrant worker issues, but we were also privileged to share Singapore's experience and efforts in managing foreign manpower and womanpower with the ILO's representatives.

The ILO continues to be pivotal in the improvement of working conditions worldwide. Its tripartite approach ensures that all social partners have an equal voice in the shaping of policies, and hence safeguards the interests of all stakeholders.

The Singapore delegation looks forward to a fruitful discussion on the various issues on the agenda. We are confident that, under the able leadership of the President, the 92nd Session of the International Labour Conference will be highly rewarding.

Original Montenegrin: Mr. STIJEPOVIĆ *(Minister of Labour and Social Welfare of the Republic of Montenegro, Serbia and Montenegro)*

It is an honour to have the opportunity to take the floor as the Minister of Labour and Social Welfare of the Republic of Montenegro at the 92nd Session of the International Labour Conference, this time representing not only the State of Montenegro but the State of Serbia as well.

I wish to salute the initiative of the Director-General of the ILO in setting in motion such an important project as the assessment of the social dimension of the process of globalization.

We have followed with great interest the presentations of the co-Chairs of the World Commission, Ms. Halonen and Mr. Mkapa, which confirmed our belief that the process of globalization must be based on universal values and include the social dimension to the benefit of all.

I also wish to support the speech by Mr. Parvanov, President of Bulgaria, especially in relation to regional cooperation in south-eastern Europe, which is a precondition for the full integration of this region into the European area.

Now, please allow me to inform you briefly about the progress achieved in Serbia and Montenegro in relation to social policy.

A new policy concept in this area, as defined by the Constitutional Charter of the State Union, is specified in the action plan that has been prepared by the Governments and adopted by the assemblies of Serbia and Montenegro. To this end, we have provided particular regulation for the issue of free movement of people, services and capital, specifically working on the need to harmonize the rights of the employed in both Republics with the standards defined by international regulations. This aspect of our regulations has been settled to mutual satisfaction and operates in practice without any problems or hindrances.

Montenegro is currently implementing recently adopted laws in the area of labour and social legislation – laws on strike action, on pension and disability insurance, on employment of immigrant workers and on other matters – and we are about to adopt a new law on protection at work and on social and child protection.

In the preparation of these laws, we have developed significant cooperation with the social partners in Montenegro. I am very pleased to say that, during last year and the beginning of this, after a long period of time, we have managed to renew and strengthen cooperation with the International Labour Organization. Cooperation between our Government, trade unions and employers' associations and the ILO will be even more fruitful and comprehensive in the future.

You are probably aware of how painful the transition process is for certain social groups. For that reason, I wish to emphasize that in Montenegro we have managed to reach a general social consensus on the importance of accelerated reform of our society and on the methods that should be employed. These reforms, envisaged by the economic reform agenda of the Government of Montenegro, actually form an agenda for wide-ranging reform, not limited to the economy and business.

I wish to emphasize that we have secured participation of the social partners, not only in the preparatory and decision-making process with regard to basic rights related to economic and social development, but also concerning the implementation of these documents. I am convinced that social dialogue, as the necessary prerequisite for the creation and implementation of the economic policy with its social dimension, is of the utmost importance in the transitional circumstances in which Montenegro finds itself today. For that precise reason, we have put a lot of effort into the development of social dialogue and good tripartite relations in order to reach the social consensus necessary for the successful implementation of urgent reforms in Montenegro.

The situation is similar in Serbia. They are working on a new labour law, a law on peaceful resolution of labour disputes and a law on the Social and Economic Council, and they are also reforming the pension and disability insurance system.

In this way, Serbia will harmonize policy in this area with EU standards, define the rights of the employed in a new manner and improve the collective bargaining process, just as we have done in Montenegro.

I am convinced that tripartism and social dialogue can guarantee the maintenance and further development of the fundamental principles of social justice that reflect the spirit of the ILO. I assure you that Serbia and Montenegro are committed to strengthening such a spirit and implementing these principles.

Finally, I would like to draw your attention to the overall complexity and sensitivity of these new relations within the State Union of Serbia and Montenegro and to thank you for expressing a full understanding of this phenomenon, respecting the fact that these issues are in the exclusive competence of the member States.

I expect that other international organizations will also show the same understanding for the new political and economic relations in the union of Serbia and Montenegro that you have shown from the very beginning.

Mr. POND *(Parliamentary Undersecretary, Department for Work and Pensions, United Kingdom)*

Having spent most of my early career working for an anti-poverty NGO, I have long admired the work of the ILO, but this is the first time that I have had the opportunity to attend a session of the International Labour Conference.

I was very pleased to host the United Kingdom reception to mark the launch of the World Commission's report in London in February.

It is important that we do not lose the impetus which the World Commission's work has created, focusing on the issue of globalization through the lens of employment.

As ILO constituents, we all have a responsibility to breathe life into the report and ensure that its recommendations lead to practical action which will bring about real change.

A key challenge is to engage relevant international institutions in the debate on how stronger coherence in regard to their policy areas could contribute to the goal of a fairer globalization. I note that the Director-General has already personally engaged with colleagues across a range of international institutions in light of the proposed "Policy Coherence Initiative" on growth, investment and employment.

The need to bring greater coherence to economic and social initiatives presents a similar challenge. I am pleased that future "decent work" country programmes will build upon the ILO's experience in promoting policy integration and that the ILO continues to promote employment as an essential component in Poverty Reduction Strategy Papers.

The recent China Employment Forum clearly demonstrated the extent to which there is now an international convergence of views on the policy approach to employment, despite big differences in the scale of the problem, as we have just heard, and widespread support for active labour market intervention delivered through a modern employment service.

The Director-General's Report highlights the role of multinational enterprises in promoting international labour standards through voluntary codes of practice.

My Government will shortly be publishing a White Paper on trade and investment which includes an examination of the relationship between globalization and employment. It recognizes the importance of ensuring that globalization leads to more and better jobs for all, and firmly acknowledges the valuable role that corporate social responsibility can play in promoting labour standards.

There is much scope for the ILO to expand its expertise in this area. I welcome the Director-General's proposals for the ILO to build upon its current knowledge base, particularly in the area of multinational enterprises, in order to further its understanding of the functioning of global production systems and the ways in which voluntary initiatives of companies contribute to decent work.

The World Commission proposes a forum to engage international employers' and workers' organizations on the subject of corporate social responsibility and related matters. I look forward to discussions on the preliminary agenda for such a dialogue. It will be important that the ILO makes full use of existing expertise in this area while, at the same time, ensuring that it does not duplicate existing work. It is essential that the ILO brings a fresh and unique perspective to the debate.

Finally, I agree that it would be helpful to explore further the idea of a socio-economic floor to the global economy. The main components of the concept, fundamental rights at work, combating exclusion in the labour market and social protection policies, are already high on the ILO's agenda.

As the Director-General makes clear, his response provides an initial reaction to the Governing Body's first discussion of the World Commission report. We are very much at the start of the process of taking forward action.

Also in February this year, the Prime Minister of the United Kingdom, Tony Blair, launched a Commission for Africa. Many of the issues and problems identified by the World Commission are writ large in Africa.

We are extremely pleased that President Mkapa of the United Republic of Tanzania has agreed to serve on the Commission for Africa, looking in particular at the issues of employment, education, skills and labour. As one of the co-Chairs of the World Commission on the Social Dimension of Globalization, we are sure that his work with the World Commission will help the Commission for Africa to focus on specific action for decent work, growth and prosperity in Africa.

Ms. HUNT *(Workers' delegate, United Kingdom)*

The plenary is asked to consider many issues in this one debate so I shall refer only to some key Trades Union Congress (TUC) priorities.

I am the first woman United Kingdom trade union delegate to address this Conference. In that role it is incumbent on me to say that there are still far too few women here. We have raised repeatedly a truth reflected in the Global Report. Freedom of association is most commonly denied in the feminized sectors of the global economy, in export processing zones, in agriculture, in domestic and other informal work and in the public services. We in the trade union movement know that we must reach out to women workers and increase the representation of women trade unionists at the International Labour Conference. Governments that allow only one worker to attend the Conference do not help us in that. Equally, governments and employers must also accept their obligations to remove the barriers to women's organization in free trade unions. This is equally true for migrant workers. Convention No. 87 is a human rights Convention because it proclaims the rights of all workers without distinction.

This is linked to our support for a tripartite, standards-based ILO. We work well with friendly NGOs in Britain and elsewhere, but non-representative organizations should have, we believe, no role in ILO governance.

The TUC welcomes the World Commission report, though we believe it would have been even more comprehensive had it examined more closely how denial of workers' rights in China is central to the current nature of globalization. My general council has discussed our role in the British follow-up and we strongly endorse the call for greater global coherence in support of fundamental rights and decent work. A lead ILO role in the follow-up is essential and we call on all governments to ensure coherence in their own policies in all international institutions.

In that spirit, we renew our call for more coherent ILO work on corporate social responsibility (CSR). We believe that there are only two ways to defend working people. Through good law, properly enforced, and through workers' self-organization in free trade unions. CSR is good if it promotes the former and opens up space for the latter. It is bad when it supports bad law or promotes alternative paternalistic models of industrial relations. The ILO must make good the lost ground in the CSR debate and all parties, including companies, must surely recognize the benefits of an ILO role in ensuring greater coherence and competency to replace the prevailing anarchy of commercial social auditing.

There is no special sitting this year so let me turn, on behalf of the TUC, to the situation of the Palestinian workers. We have condemned, and we continue to condemn, the violence on both Palestinian and Israeli citizens. In November, our PGFTU and Histadrut colleagues welcomed a TUC delegation to the West Bank and Israel. In the West Bank we saw an economy in shreds.

We strongly support the Palestinian Fund for Employment and Social Protection and call on all donor governments to contribute. Peace-building requires decent work, but the restrictions on free movement of labour and goods, even within the occupied Arab territories, deter investment and prevent the Palestinian Authority from developing labour market policies to deliver decent work.

Let me turn finally to another TUC priority. Three TUC delegations will visit Colombia this year. Arbitrary detentions, outlawing of strikes and militarization of the workplaces there have all increased.

The ILO's constituents' failure to agree an appropriate ILO response is harming Colombia and undermining the ILO's authority. We believe that it cannot be right that only authoritarian regimes that reject the current globalization model are subject to stronger supervisory measures. They deserve criticism when they violate ratified Conventions but others should not escape similar measures just because they have a market economy. If this atmosphere re-enters the ILO it will not survive long. The TUC wants it to survive as a beacon of freedom, tripartism, decent work and impartial supervision of international labour standards.

Original Arabic: Mr. NEFFATI *(Minister of Social Affairs and Solidarity, Tunisia)*

In the name of God, the Merciful, the Compassionate! I have the pleasure of most warmly congratulating Mr. Ray Guevara, Minister of Labour from the Dominican Republic, the Vice-President Mr. Maatough and indeed all the Officers of the Conference and of wishing them every success in their duties.

The inclusion of migrant workers on the agenda of this session reflects a growing interest in migration in a changing world. Migration is seen as a multidimensional civilizing influence because it brings civilizations and cultures closer together.

As globalization allows the free movement of capital and goods, it must not exclude the free movement of workers. This is one of the inconsistencies which must be overcome if migration is to become an effective mechanism for global development and solidarity benefiting all the peoples of the world.

I would like to play tribute to the Director-General's proposal that an international forum on migration for employment should be established. As Tunisia is convinced of the close link between migration and development, it has supported regional and international initiatives to manage migration and strengthen consultation and coordination in this sphere at the bilateral and multilateral levels. Hence we were the first to convene a conference for Western Mediterranean countries (the 5 + 5 Conference) in December 2003. A substantial proportion of its deliberations were devoted to the joint management of migration, since this topic had formed the subject of the first regional ministerial conference that had been held in Tunisia.

It is a secret to no one that in order to achieve sustainable development, closer attention must be paid to the gathering pace of change throughout the world. The adoption of a new international instrument on human resource development will certainly inspire member countries to formulate policies and establish appropriate mechanisms and programmes in this field. Tunisia has banked on human resource development and has accordingly introduced reforms so as to adapt its educational system to the new demands made by advances in information and communications technology. It has also introduced education for all in an effort to make culture accessible to everyone through modern information and communications technologies. The fact that Tunisia was chosen to host the second phase of the World Summit on the Information Society in 2005 is an acknowledgement of its efforts and of the progress it has achieved in this sphere. We hope that this summit will help to find ways of reducing the digital divide and consolidating development efforts.

The Global Report on freedom of association and collective bargaining highlights progress in securing respect for the fundamental rights at work set forth in the 1998 Declaration, a progress which has been reflected in the large number of ratifications by member States of the Conventions in question and in their commitment to apply the principles contained therein, as well as in the efficacy of the follow-up mechanism.

As for the Report on the social dimension of globalization, we have examined all the main recommendations in this Report which formed the centrepiece of the special sitting at which emphasis was placed on the means of making globalization more humane and more just by anchoring it in respect for human rights and human dignity and by ensuring equal opportunities for all peoples without discrimination.

The size of the challenges highlighted by the report means that the international community will have to resort to cooperation and partnership in order to achieve well-being and security for all.

The situation of the Arab workers in Palestine and the other occupied Arab territories as outlined in the annual Report from the Director-General is still a cause for concern because the Report shows the extent of the suffering borne by various sections of the Palestine people, a situation that is contrary to the most elementary human rights recognized in international charters and labour standards.

We expect the ILO to play a bigger role in this regard through stronger support for the Palestinian Fund for Employment and Social Protection, in the form of the requisite financial resources.

Tunisia, as His Excellency, President Zine El Abidine Ben Ali, stressed in his opening address to the 16th Session of the Arab Summit in Tunis, reaffirms its attachment to international dignity and peace as a strategic choice and calls on the United Nations and other influential international bodies to give renewed impetus to the Road Map and to seek a just and lasting solution to the Arab-Israeli conflict.

Mr. DALLEY (Minister of Labour and Social Security, Jamaica)

I would like to begin by extending, on behalf of the Jamaican delegation, congratulations to the President on his election to preside at this 92nd Session of the International Labour Conference.

Our congratulations also go to the Director-General for his excellent Report on the progress made in implementing the Decent Work Agenda *(ILO programme implementation 2002-03)*. I would also like to convey a very special greeting from the Prime Minister of Jamaica, the most Honourable P. J. Patterson, who has asked me to convey to the Director-General his special greetings and best wishes for his continued leadership and guidance in advancing the work of the ILO. As a token of our appreciation I would like to extend publicly, today, an invitation to the Director-General to visit the Caribbean to gain a first-hand appreciation of our work in the region.

Both the President of Finland and the President of the United Republic of Tanzania must be commended for their brilliant work as co-Chairs of the World Commission on the Social Dimension of Globalization. Their report, *A fair globalization: Creating opportunities for all*, speaks to the urgency of formulating a new governance structure that defines globalization in human terms and provides opportunities and tangible benefits for all the citizens of the world. The report embraces the cardinal principles of humanity – equity, rights, democracy and social justice. Jamaica stands fully in support of these conclusions.

As we contemplate the ILO's role in shaping a fair and equitable globalization for all, the strategic objectives evident in the Director-General's Report become even more instructive. The promotion of standards and the fundamental principles and rights at work, the securing of decent work for men and women, enhancing the coverage of social protection for all, and strengthening tripartism and social dialogue will remain a myth if we ignore the essential theme of President Thabo Mbeki's address to the 91st Session of the International Labour Conference last year. He spoke of the cruel reality of the debt burden on the South, through social adjustment programmes which "caused further deterioration in the living conditions of the most fragile classes of the population" and resulted in "the financial transfers from South to North", which has hampered the development of the South.

The ILO is therefore challenged now more than ever before to ensure that globalization does not manifestly worsen the situation and wreak havoc on the world's poor, but offers hope for a better and improved life for two-thirds of the world's population.

There is a common theme that links the cause of mankind through time, and that is the search for economic improvement to their lives. Globalization, perhaps more than any other phenomenon throughout the sweep of history, has the most profound and far-reaching implications for our social, economic, political and cultural ways of life. As a social system, it cannot ignore the cultural uniqueness and diversities that shape the world. As an economic system, its failure to address the growing disparities in wealth and entrenched poverty in parts of the world will give rise to social malaise and exclusion, with the attendant consequences of social upheavals. This is why Jamaica fully endorses the placing of development at the heart of the Doha agenda and joined its colleagues of the South in directing the Fifth WTO Ministerial Conference in Cancún away from the "Singapore issues" and along the path of sustainable development. We must therefore pursue an agenda of issues that seeks to achieve development and improved living standards for the peoples of the world.

While we struggle to ensure that the global rules and policies on trade provide for equal opportunities for developing countries to gain market access and foster the process of growth and development, and while we fully endorse the need for labour market reform to facilitate the process for competitiveness and increased productivity, we must also ensure that the basic rights of workers to freedom of association and the right to bargain collectively remain fundamentally secured. At the same time, we must equally ensure that the social protection agenda is vigorously pursued. In this regard, Jamaica is proud to state that last August we ratified the ILO's Worst Forms of Child Labour Convention, 1999 (No. 182), and have been actively pursuing a programme of action, with the assistance of the InFocus Programme on Child Labour (IPEC) and the ILO subregional office for the Caribbean, to eliminate child labour in our country.

Our efforts continue to be underpinned by our commitment to the principles of tripartism and social dialogue, the result of which has been an historic signing recently of a Memorandum of Understanding in the public sector between two of our social partners, the Government and the trade union movement, represented by its umbrella organization, the Jamaica Confederation of Trade Unions.

In conclusion, both the reports on fair globalization and that of the Director-General give credence to our work and the important issues we are content to grapple with in the hope of securing long and lasting benefits for the world's poor. We must now enter this period of discussion with a renewed spirit and awareness that the fate of humankind rests upon the work we do, the cause we defend and the challenges we are prepared to relentlessly pursue in order to achieve social justice, equality and development for all of us.

Original Turkish: Mr. KILIC (Workers' delegate, Turkey)

I extend to you all my deepest regards of friendship and solidarity on behalf of the working people in Turkey. I congratulate the President on his election and the Director-General for his successful work.

On behalf of the working people in Turkey, I condemn the inhumanity and torture practised on the Iraqi people and the violence towards the Palestinian people which are currently taking place in this, the twenty-first century. I invite the international community to take immediate action.

The strategic objectives underlined in the Director-General's Report are fully supported by Turkish workers. I should like to congratulate him for his efforts to bring forth the concept of decent work as a global target and also for his struggle to eliminate poverty and unemployment, the worst consequences of globalization.

A considerable portion of the world's population is either unemployed or in search of an additional income to help their families to survive. The increase in national income does not make any sense unless it provides productive employment for more people. I should like to take this opportunity to congratulate the Governing Body's Committee on Employment and Social Policy for their studies on productive employment for poverty reduction and I should like to remind the Government and the Employers' delegations that this concept is their common responsibility.

It is not possible to sustain and secure social peace in the world without a structure offering fair income distribution, otherwise social chaos is inevitable. Income distribution has evolved into an unfair and unstable structure, decreasing the living standards of the workers, especially through the globalization process. Urgent policies must be put into place and urgent measures must be taken.

Without any doubt, the first step is to put an end to the implementation of economic policies imposed by the international finance institutions, such as the IMF and the World Bank which is having a profound effect on the world in the process of globalization. In particular, privatization practices in our country which have no meaning other than unemployment must be addressed.

The concepts discussed in the chapter of the Director-General's Report focusing on issues of organization and trade union rights and freedoms are of the utmost importance, especially for Turkish workers. The labour movement in our country is facing a period of difficulty with regard to organization. Throughout the last decade, membership figures of trade unions seriously decreased due to the economic crisis, privatization practices and the current economic model. Difficulties are being encountered as a result of laws and the abuse of regulations.

The Job Security Act, which is something the workers have wanted to achieve for many years and which was finally put in force last year, was restricted, resulting in 3.5 million workers being excluded from the coverage of job security.

Unfair postponements of strikes by the Council of Ministers, were overruled by decisions of our independent courts. Our legal struggle to fully exercise our right to strike, our right to collective bargaining and our right to end the postponement of strikes will continue.

The concept of "social dialogue", specifically emphasized in the Director-General's Report is also a priority in my country. The tripartite negotiations between the Government, workers and employers are continuing in order to improve our Labour Act and overcome the deficits in legislation to bring it into line with modern times.

Following the latest amendments to our Constitution the international Conventions have gained value in our internal legislative system. Our chief expectation is to make sure that civil servants benefit from the rights provided for in the Freedom of Association and Protection of the Right to Organise Convention, 1948 (No. 87), and the Right to Organise and Collective Bargaining Convention, 1949 (No. 98). Furthermore, necessary measures must be taken to harmonize the existing regulations with the ILO Conventions ratified by Turkey.

Governments must initiate more active measures regarding social protection policies. Much more effort is needed to overcome the difficulties encountered in the field of occupational health and safety resulting from the globalization process implemented for the benefit of transnational capital. Furthermore, governments must improve the social protection measures regarding women workers, child labour and the disabled.

The ILO should improve the universal labour standards and the social model, as globalization is increasing its dominance over labour and capital. In addition to this, globalization has a negative impact on developing countries while creating a positive impact on industrialized countries.

The Turkish Republic and the Turkish community of northern Cyprus has undertaken all its responsibilities towards integrating with the world. Following this positive step, the States of the world and the international community must endeavour to lift the political and economic embargo from northern Cyprus.

Turkish workers call upon the representatives participating in the Conference to take action in this regard.

Turkish workers support human rights, peace in the world and peace in our country. We have deep concerns about the situation in the Middle East. War and terrorism are the biggest enemies of human rights and democracy. Furthermore, they are the biggest enemies of workers' rights and freedoms. Turkish workers desire a peaceful world without any wars. We hope that this Conference will serve to promote world peace and social welfare.

Mr. ALOEWIE (Government delegate, Indonesia)

On behalf of the Indonesian Delegation, I congratulate the President on his election as President of the 92nd Session of the International Labour Conference, as well as the three Vice-Presidents. I am confident that, under his able leadership, the Conference will produce fruitful results.

I should like also to extend my delegation's appreciation for the Director-General's Report, as well as for the report of the Chairman of the Governing Body.

We commend the Director-General's Report on the World Commission on the Social Dimension of Globalization, which outlines how the ILO could play a key role in promoting its decent work programme as part of a global agenda.

Let me begin by sharing with you our views concerning the implementation of the ILO programme.

The document has clearly mapped out the course of action taken by the Organization for that biennium, based on its four strategic objectives which aim to attain of decent work for all. Moreover, the actions undertaken have been directed at efficiently addressing the needs and interests of the tripartite constituents. Nevertheless, we would like to reiterate that the ILO should focus on a holistic approach with respect to the assistance it provides to governments and their social partners.

With reference to the first objective, which is to promote the protection of workers, the Government of Indonesia continues to upgrade its legislation on labour issues. At the beginning of this year, the Government passed an act on the labour dispute settlement, which is the latest legislation forming part of the labour law reform package, launched by the Government in 1998.

Accordingly, in order to implement these labour laws, Indonesia has also ratified the ILO Labour Inspection Convention, 1947 (No. 81). These various measures should strengthen labour protection in Indonesia and lead to more harmonious industrial relations by giving workers the social protection they need. The industrial actors themselves should establish harmonious industrial relations.

The Government consistently makes serious efforts to assist them by establishing an effective bipartite forum.

Since Indonesia still faces an employment problem, the Government has been doing everything in its power to increase employment opportunities. This policy is in line with our mandate as stated in the Constitution whereby every citizen has the right to decent work.

We are aware that an informal economy is an unavoidable fact in the process of national development. Consequently, our national development programmes are directed towards strengthening the informal sector by improving relevant regulations.

I should like to touch on one of the issues in our agenda for this year's session of the International Labour Conference, namely that of migrant workers. This topic is of particular importance to us and my Government appreciates its inclusion in the agenda. We therefore welcome the opportunity to discuss migrant worker issues as part of the agenda. The worldwide dimension of the problem indicates that this issue should be dealt with internationally and it naturally points to the ILO as the Organization best placed to address it and seek relevant solutions.

My Government recognizes that measures should be put in place to protect Indonesian migrant workers. Some measures are in fact already underway, notably with the formulation of draft legislation on the placement and protection of Indonesian migrant workers.

My delegation would like to make a brief comment on the Director-General's Report on globalization which includes some of the arguments contained in the Report of the World Commission on the Social Dimension of Globalization. Indonesia supports globalization as the basis for economic growth. However, globalization should not be disassociated from its social dimension and the fulfilment of public interest which calls for the achievement of the Decent Work Agenda.

The Government of Indonesia is gratified by the assistance and cooperation afforded to us by the ILO in our efforts to implement the four strategic objectives in the country.

Before closing, I should like to add that the Government of Indonesia remains concerned by the workers' situation in the occupied Arab territories. We believe that it is important that the ILO continues to provide its assistance and to give the highest priority to addressing this issue.

Finally, I would like to stress that our success depends on the willingness to work hand in hand in addressing our differences in a spirit of understanding and dialogue.

Original French: Mr. IVALA *(Minister for Labour and Employment, Gabon)*

First and foremost, on behalf of my delegation and on my own behalf, I should like to echo the congratulations expressed by the previous speakers to the President on his election to guide our Conference.

I should also like to congratulate Mr. Juan Somavia for the quality of the reports tabled for our study, without omitting of course the World Commission on the Social Dimension of Globalization for an excellent report entitled *A fair globalization: Creating opportunities for all.*

I should like to submit a number of comments on this subject.

When the World Commission tabled its report in March, His Excellency President Benjamin Mkapa said, and I quote: "the problems related to the social dimension of globalization can be attributed to globalization without accountability. While more and more governments are held accountable by their citizens, fewer and fewer global actors are held accountable by anybody".

We share the key elements identified by the Commission, which show the path that we should follow. I will just quote briefly from that: "globalization with solidarity, policy coherence for global development, fair rules", those are some of the key elements.

However, we should not confuse decisions with progress. The process of globalization, as it is currently happening, is unfair. That is why we should act consistently, both nationally and internationally, to address this.

At national level, good governance, the promotion and respect for fundamental human rights, the strengthening of tripartism and the promotion of social dialogue are all important. It is our collective responsibility to put together national strategies on globalization.

This strategy, in our view, should contain a certain number of elements. At the national level, the Government of Gabon believes that decent and productive employment is one of the essential ways of combating poverty and exclusion and it is in that framework that the President of the Republic, His Excellency El Hadj Omar Bongo Ondimba, has declared 2004 and 2005 full employment years.

In addition, the Government is translating this high-level political determination into a daily reality. Specific actions have been taken. One of these is the Poverty Reduction Strategy Paper (PRSP), which is currently in its final stages. This Paper naturally makes employment a priority in our poverty reduction campaign.

Provincial forums on employment are currently being held in order to determine the employment market better. We believe that we should stifle unemployment, particularly youth unemployment, which has been rising. We advocate, with this in mind, labour-intensive employment.

In order to relaunch our economy, it is essential to create a peaceful social environment. In this connection, a three-year truce between the social partners has been signed. That truce is designed to create a favourable climate for economic recovery, which I mentioned earlier.

One of the manifestations of this truce is the fact that, for the first time, the trade union confederations have launched a single manifesto on the occasion of Labour Day.

We welcome the fact that migration has been put on the agenda of our Conference. As a host country, Gabon, which has a great deal of immigrant labour, believes that labour mobility should be set within a clear regulatory framework.

We approve the process that should lead to the adoption of an action plan designed to strengthen the ILO's ability to assist member countries to manage migration, based on the constant values that guide us here, that is, non-discrimination and equity.

Mr. MEYER *(Government adviser and substitute delegate, Canada)*

May I first take this opportunity to congratulate the President and other Officers of the Conference on their election.

In his Report to the Conference on the follow-up to the report of the World Commission on the Social Dimension of Globalization, the Director-General challenged us to take a hard look at the role of the ILO today and in the future.

His Report is frank in its self-assessment. It says, and I quote: "We can be criticized as inward looking, preoccupied with procedure, relatively slow in response, and having a style of expression that deters all but the most enthusiastic from discovering our ideas." This Report also says: "The Organization and its activities are not well known even within the international networks of employers' and workers' organizations." And yet this somewhat forgotten, often ignored and largely ritualized Organization is being challenged by the World Commission to find a new voice and to make itself heard over the din of a very noisy global marketplace, which in many parts of the world is also torn apart by violence.

The message we are to give the world is both old and new. The old message is found in the Constitution of the ILO: that lasting peace must be based on social justice, that the failure of any nation to adopt humane conditions of labour is an obstacle in the way of other nations, that labour is not a commodity. The Director-General's Report very appropriately begins by quoting these famous dictums of the ILO.

The new message is about governance, both within nations and among nations, and about coherence: integrating the social and the economic – merging the Decent Work Agenda of the ILO with the economic growth agendas of the Bretton Woods institutions.

Before embarking on such a challenging mission, it is worthwhile to take stock of our assets. The main assets of the ILO, pointed out in the Director-General's Report, are also both old and new. First is tripartism itself – the original genius of the ILO founders was to bring the key economic players to the same table.

Second is the governance structure of the ILO, which somehow manages to work despite the complexity of 177 nations. Third is the global consensus on the central ideals and goals of the ILO, most recently expressed in the 1998 ILO Declaration on Fundamental Principles and Rights at Work.

Finally, we should count as a major asset the clear strategic objectives of the ILO's Decent Work Agenda. But, if we are being critical of ourselves, then we must question whether these assets are enough. The ILO, after all, has not just arrived on the scene. It has been actively engaged with many of the issues raised for decades. What have been the results of this activity on a global scale? Einstein is often quoted as saying that the definition of madness is to repeat the same actions while expecting different results. Are we satisfied with the results which the activities of the ILO have been producing? What needs to change if we want to expect different results and call ourselves sane at the same time?

These are strategic questions which are posed by the Director-General in his Report, and to address them he calls for a detailed examination of the strategic directions of the Organization this coming November in the Governing Body.

Canada believes that ILO activities should directly contribute to the creation of decent work in a global economy by fostering the effective use of human capital and respect for workers' rights. In this context, we call on the ILO to focus on supporting activities: to reflect in legislation and effectively implement fundamental principles and rights; to build effective labour administrations that can develop and implement sound labour policies and legislation oriented to the contemporary economy; to establish and strengthen institutions of social dialogue; to obtain and disseminate the best possible information on preventing occupational injuries and disease; to promote training and skills upgrading for workers who want to enhance productive potential; and to ensure that workers have the economic security they need to pursue their own personal development and that of their families.

The Governing Body will need to be clear about the results it wants to achieve and about the selection of a limited set of strategic targets it wants to aim at. It will need to maximize the leverage of the ILO's most strategic assets and make sure it does not deviate from the ILO's most fundamental objectives. Only by being highly focused can our Organization expect to play a leadership role in today's fast-changing world.

Original French: Mr. SARBU *(Minister Responsible for Relations with the Social Partners, Romania)*

On behalf of the Romanian Government, I should first of all like to congratulate the two distinguished co-Chairs of the World Commission on the Social Dimension of Globalization, Her Excellency, Ms. Tarja Halonen, President of Finland, and His Excellency, Mr. Benjamin Mkapa, President of the United Republic of Tanzania, for their valuable contribution to the work of the Commission.

We are truly living in an era of globalization. Together, we are climbing a new rung in the ladder of history, at a time when humanity, no doubt, has the necessary maturity to recognize the incredible opportunities open to it and to be aware of the risks it faces. Every individual in human society stands to benefit from globalization and risks falling victim to it.

A worker who cannot find work is an infinitely more tragic character than any Hamlet or Oedipus, said John Morley about one of the profoundly dramatic and unfortunately very common realities of society today.

This type of reality, in other words the social dimension of globalization, cannot be ignored. The effects of globalization on every individual and the improvements brought about by establishing fairer rules in international trade, finance, investment and migration must be our main concern.

A global problem requires a global solution and the International Labour Organization, through its founding values and the way it implements those values, plays a vital role in the evolution of the dynamic concept of globalization, all the while respecting "justice and humanity". Decent work, security, development based on education and social justice: Romania has been and will be a staunch supporter of these ideals!

On 1 January 2007, we will be joining the European Union. This represents an important economic, political and social step forward for our country in terms of improving the living standards of our citizens. But, this open society towards which we are moving raises other challenges. In the globalized world, migration has become a central problem. In 2001, in order to meet the need for information and advice on migrant workers in Romania, we set up a specialized agency known as the Office for Labour Force Migration. Its main goal is to protect the rights of Romanian workers' abroad and to promote the integration of those who come to work in our country.

All of the efforts made to date by the Romanian Government to regulate the movement of the workforce and to ensure that migrant workers achieve a dignified status require, in the future, the support of our European partners, particularly in terms of negotiating and concluding more bilateral agreements that provide a legal framework for regulating labour force migration.

I would like to reiterate at this point in time the open position of Romania towards forming such partnerships to this end. Experience has shown that these agreements and Conventions are extremely efficient instruments in the fight against clandestine migration and the illegal trafficking for workers.

At the same time, we are committed to continuing to strengthen our partnerships within Romania with our trade unions and Employers' groups.

Aware of the important role played by civil society in our economy, the effects of which are sometimes painful, the Romanian Government has made institutionalized dialogue a permanent instrument for consultation and for the promotion of social cohesion, further harmonizing our government policies on social, educational, scientific and cultural issues in order to ensure genuine economic growth, based on sustainable development.

This shared responsibility is perceived today in Romania as more than just an abstract theory or a simple instrument for social peace. It is more of an attitude in the way we approach realities than a cultural backdrop for cooperation.

The social consultation process brought about through partnership agreements initiated, negotiated and, I might even say, concluded in a positive way by this Government, has been renewed in 2004.

The 2004 Social Stability Pact reflects the efforts of social partners and the Government to find the best and most responsible ways of improving our social protection system, increasing income levels and standards of living, improving our use of human resources and guaranteeing equal opportunities for all.

These objectives are ambitious and our efforts are commensurate to them. In the light of the forthcoming accession of Romania to the European Union, we currently find ourselves at the heart of the globalization process. This historic accession process will not only provide great opportunities for Romania, but also great challenges. In this context, I would like to make a promise on behalf of the Romanian Government: when Romania is ready to adopt the spirit of competitiveness and meet the demands of the European Union, it will continue to remain loyal to, and pursue its commitments to respect, the principles of solidarity and social justice sought by the ILO.

Original Arabic: Mr. ALLAM *(Employers' delegate, Egypt)*

On behalf of the Federation of Egyptian Industries, I would like to congratulate the President on his election to chair the 92nd Session of the International Labour Conference. On my own behalf and on behalf of the Federation of Egyptian Industries, I would like to congratulate the Director-General on his Report, *Organizing for social justice*. The federation that I represent agrees with the content of this Report, which was already the subject of the ILO Declaration on Fundamental Principles and Rights at Work. These principles and the rights resulting from them are of particular interest as they are important factors in all economic, social and political activities.

The Federation of Egyptian Industries believes in the principle of freedom of association and the right to collective bargaining as part of an expression of human dignity, because these allow employers and workers to come together and work jointly, not only to defend their economic interests, but also to guarantee civil liberties, such as the right to life and security, protection against all forms of discrimination, intervention and harassment – and all of this is an integral part of democracy.

It has been proven that respect for freedom of association and the right to collective bargaining plays an important role in a country's healthy economic development. This can only have positive effects on economic growth because it guarantees a fairer distribution of the results of that growth and the promotion of productivity, sound management of adjustment measures and social peace, and this within the framework of a globalized economy that guarantees freedom of association and the right to collective bargaining, which allows us to reconcile social objectives with the needs of the market economy.

The Federation of Egyptian Industries is concerned that, despite a generally positive trend with regard to the spread of democracy and the high-level of ratification of the ILO's fundamental international labour standards and the increase in market transparency on a global basis, there are still major problems. There are still infringements of the rights of employers and workers, for example, murders, acts of violence and arrests, as can be seen in Palestine and in the occupied Arab territories. People who seek to organize themselves and defend their fundamental rights collectively are losing their lives and their freedom.

The Federation of Egyptian Industries notes that the informal economy has still not been really explored. Employers and workers should be able to benefit from the right to organize in the informal economy. It is obvious that representative structures need to be anticipated in this sector, independent of the workers' and employers' organizations in place.

In this respect, the Federation of Egyptian Industries calls on employers' organizations with direct links with the informal sector, through subcontracting or other forms of commercial arrangements that have their roots in the informal economy, to play an important part in promoting respect for fundamental rights without hindering the spirit of initiative and the development of this sector.

As far as migrant workers are concerned, the Federation of Egyptian Industries thanks the secretariat for including this item on the agenda of the Conference. We feel that the Arab region is well acquainted with this problem because we both import and export migrant labour, and so we have to find frameworks and structures that will allow us to defend the interests of these migrant workers. These workers must organize within existing unions, rather than set up new ones, to ensure that they are not excluded from the system of collective bargaining.

Original Arabic: Mr. LATIF *(Government delegate, Iraq)*

In the Name of God, the Merciful, the Compassionate! It is a pleasure for me to convey to you the greetings of my Government which is preparing to take back full national sovereignty from the Coalition Provisional Authority at the end of this month. Now that resolution No. 1546 has been unanimously adopted, I extend my thanks and appreciation to the international community and to the international coalition forces which helped to put an end to the nightmare that was one of the cruellest dictatorial regimes in recent history and which gave the Iraqi people back its dignity.

I would also like to express my regard for the ILO, its Director-General, Mr. Juan Somavia; the Director of the ILO Regional Office for the Arab States, Dr. Rifai; and the chief of the ILO Task Force for Iraq, Dr. Qaryouti, for their sincere efforts, their perseverance and their valuable assistance to us in various fields. A coordination office has been opened in Baghdad in cooperation with our Ministry and the ILO Regional Office in Beirut, which has made it possible to strengthen cooperation and to facilitate the implementation of the draft agreement between the two parties. Training courses have been organized with the assistance of the ILO, and have been able to develop a draft Labour Code, which can be considered as an excellent model for the region, and which incorporated all the international standards, Conventions and Recommendations and especially the eight core labour Conventions.

Turning now to the Report of the Director-General, *ILO programme implementation 2002-03*, despite our absence from the 91st Session and the very difficult circumstances that my country was in, our contacts with the ILO have been uninterrupted. We therefore have to commend the Director-General for the effort put into preparing the Report and for the importance of its substance, especially the Organization's strategies. However, the Report does not include statistics, nor does it refer to states which do not respect international standards or which have adopted them but continually violate them. The Report also does not indicate the poverty level of each member State or the plans developed to improve the situation. Given that our Organization has reached the venerable age of 85, we wish to recall, as the Director-General emphasized, that its programmes and modus operandi must be reviewed.

It is also necessary to develop new ways of achieving the Organization's objectives. It is time to find a new mechanism for bringing pressure to bear on member States, as is the case with the Human Rights Commission, for example. The Report uses terminology that needs to be clearly defined. For example, we need a clear definition of what is meant by decent work or suitable work.

As to the Report *A Fair Globalization: The role of the ILO*, we all agree that globalization is not entirely beneficial and that some aspects are harmful. Those countries which do not recognize its benefits are putting in place adequate social and economic programmes, but those with corrupt administrations or under dictatorships are the first to suffer from the disadvantages of globalization. We therefore have to benefit from the experience of other countries and to demand from the developed countries measures such as opening up markets and putting an end to protectionist policies and subsidies in certain sectors, particularly agriculture.

The international community has concerned itself with the situation in Iraq and is trying to help us. Meetings with donor countries are held one after another not just out of solidarity but because the whole world knows how important Iraq's capacity is in all domains, and particularly with regard to security, peace and the fight against terrorism in the region, as well as the development of the tools necessary for building a real democracy.

Iraq needs your support and this support can take two forms: to bring pressure to bear on the social partners in order to write off Iraq's debts, because those debts were not used for the development of Iraq but were used to buy weapons and to drag the country into destructive wars that claimed many lives and destroyed the economy and the infrastructure. Why should the Iraqi people pay back debts that only served to bring devastation? The other form of assistance must be contributions to the reconstruction of Iraq and the rejection of using the security situation as a pretext for delaying the reconstruction process. On the contrary, the process of implementing contracts should be speeded up. Otherwise, as the Iraqi Minister of Construction and Housing has said, Iraq will be forced to cancel the contracts signed with companies that are delaying their implementation. Once sovereignty is returned to the Iraqi Government and the situation is stabilized, foreign investors will pour into the country in their thousands. Especially since insecurity is not unique to Iraq, but prevails in several countries in the region and in the world, in Asia, Africa, and even in the United States. Terrorism is a multinational and cross-border phenomenon. It is a phenomenon unrestricted by any constraints or values, much less by moral or human values. We must not fold before it, but must find answers to social problems, most importantly unemployment. It is also important to address the political and international aspect of terrorism and this means finding a fair solution to the Palestinian question that guarantees Palestinians the right to establish their own independent state and to live at long last with dignity.

The new Iraqi society also hopes to be able to enjoy its fundamental rights. The young democracy in Iraq has given Iraqis the right to form trade unions and employers' organizations, political parties and civil society organizations as well as the freedom of the press, freedom of expression and the freedom to hold demonstrations. The Iraqi Ministry of Labour and Social Affairs has accomplished important tasks in a relatively short time; 28 buildings near the Ministry have been renovated and the civil servants began working there in March 2003. Retired workers, of whom there are more than 18,000 have been given emergency payments and we have also paid subsidies to poor families. We have also renovated orphanages and homes for disabled people and for the elderly; we opened two centres which receive abandoned children and a reception centre for abused women. UNICEF has undertaken the renovation of 24 other buildings. The Ministry has created a department responsible for child labour and staff will be trained to tackle this problem and coordinate their work with the relevant international organizations and NGOs. We have prohibited forced labour, paid or unpaid, because the former dictatorship made use of forced labour under the pretext of "national work", despite having signed the ILO Abolition of Forced Labour Convention, 1957 (No. 105), in 1959.

In conclusion, I wish our Organization every success in the hunt for solutions to social problems and I hope that, through dialogue, democracy, peace, security and prosperity will be able to reign in the world. The Iraqis will not waiver in their march towards progress and terrorists will not prevent us from building a model society in the fields of human rights and democracy, nor from guaranteeing all the social partners their fundamental rights.

(Mr. Attigbe takes the Chair.)

Mr. WINN (Minister of Labour, Myanmar)

First and foremost on behalf of the Myanmar delegation, I would like to congratulate the President on his unanimous election to preside over the work of this august assembly. I am confident that under his able guidance and leadership the Conference will be successful.

At the outset, I would like to take the opportunity to commend the Reports of the Chairperson of the Governing Body and of the Director-General of the International Labour Office. The Reports allow us to reflect on successes and to further build upon them. At the same time, they remind us that we should pay greater attention to areas where the Organization has been less successful. An important item of concern to an increasing number of countries in the international community is this year's agenda item on migrant workers. Just as globalization has brought about movement of capital and goods and the opening of global markets, it has also affected the international migration of workers. The process has raised concerns regarding the protection of migrant workers. In ASEAN we are taking measures to resolve the problems connected with migrant workers within the region. I would like to inform this distinguished assembly that Myanmar has signed a Memorandum of Understanding with Thailand to address the issue of cross-border workers from the two countries. We have already accepted over 13,000 returning migrant workers in Myanmar. We have also established a reception camp at the border area to facilitate the return of Myanmar migrant workers. All these endeavours are being undertaken at our own cost.

We hope that a general discussion of the problem of migrant workers using the integrated approach will serve to provide us with new, appropriate and comprehensive responses to labour migration. I would like to add that other technical items on the agenda are also of importance for the promotion of standard-setting activities and we are of the view that a proposal concerning the withdrawal of obsolete recommendations is appropriate and timely.

It is opportune for me to briefly review our efforts to eradicate forced labour in my country, in close cooperation with the ILO. I would like to recall that, since May 1999, appropriate legislative changes have been made concerning the Village and Town Act to prohibit forced labour practices. Moreover, relevant administrative and executive measures have also been put in place with a view to enforcing the legislative measures. Above all, an agreement reached in March 2002 has led to the appointment of a liaison officer, which has further helped promote cooperation between Myanmar and the ILO.

With regard to the concluding remarks of the 288th Session of the Governing Body concerning the implementation of the Joint Plan of Action, to which we have agreed and which we initialled in May 2003, we already announced our genuine political will and commitment to implement the plan in cooperation with the ILO during the evaluation visit to Myanmar of Mr. Francis Maupain, Special Adviser to the ILO Director-General in March 2004. Despite our commitment, it has not yet been possible to implement the Joint Plan of Action because some quarters are linking its implementation with extraneous issues. We are of the view that it should be considered objectively, solely in the light of the merits of the elements contained in the plan, on which the two sides have worked so hard to agree on.

At this point I would like to refer to the case of the two convicts who appeared before the 289th Session of the Governing Body. I would like to reiterate that their being sentenced to death was not related in any way to their contact with the ILO. I would like to reassure you that contact with the ILO is by no means considered a criminal offence in our country. The death penalty was passed on the two people because of their contact with an illegal organization formed by dissidents in exile to engage in subversive activities against the Government.

Myanmar's judicial system is independent and free from outside interference. I would like to inform you that the case has been reviewed by the Supreme Court which has revised and commuted the death sentences handed down by the District Court to three years' imprisonment. This is an obvious response by Myanmar to the concerns expressed by the 289th Session of the Governing Body. Moreover, the two convicts still have the right to enter a second appeal to the Supreme Court.

Myanmar is at the moment passing through a most important phase in its modern history. The National Convention adjourned in 1996 was reconvened on 17 May 2004, with nearly 100 per cent participation of representatives from all strata of Myanmar's society. The reconvening of the National Convention to draft a new State Constitution is the first step in the seven-step Road Map proclaimed by our Prime Minister.

At the plenary meeting of the National Convention held on 20 May 2004, the National Convention Convening Work Committee clarified the basic principles on social and management sectors for consideration by the delegates with a view to their subsequent inclusion in the State Constitution. The delegates will deliberate these matters and put forward suggestions thereon. It is therefore expected that the new constitution will reflect necessary provisions which are in keeping with the ILO Conventions ratified by Myanmar, including Convention No. 87.

In conclusion, I would like to state that we are taking all the necessary steps to eradicate forced labour in Myanmar in cooperation with the ILO. We will continue this process in goodwill and good faith until forced labour is totally eradicated in my country. We fervently hope that, in this endeavour, we will receive the understanding, cooperation and support from all concerned.

Mr. GRÖNLUND *(State Secretary, Ministry of Industry, Employment and Communications, Sweden)*

May I begin by congratulating the President and all the other Officers of the Conference on their election.

I have decided to confine my reflections to three issues which, to my Government, are of fundamental importance in any international context. They are not restricted to our dealings with the ILO only.

The first is the subject matter of this year's Global Report, *Organizing for social justice*, namely freedom of association and the right to collective bargaining, the principles of which are laid down in the Freedom of Association and Protection of the Right to Organise Convention, 1948 (No. 87), and the Right to Organise and Collective Bargaining Convention, 1949 (No. 98).

The right to freely create organizations to advance and to defend both individual and collective interests are enabling rights. They are prerequisites for a decent society. It is therefore a matter of deep concern that, in the year 2004, half of the world's workers are still not protected by the provisions of those core Conventions. These women and men can be found on all continents, in the developed and developing world alike, and even among permanent Members of the Governing Body of the International Labour Office.

We find them in export processing zones, with examples of deliberate exclusion of basic workers' rights in order to improve competitive status and to attract foreign direct investment. We consider this an extremely grave issue and a contradiction, as research within the Organisation for Economic Cooperation and Development (OECD), for example, demonstrates that respect for the core Conventions plays an important part in sound economic development.

I would therefore like to repeat what Sweden has voiced for many years in the ILO, namely that core labour standards is an issue for the wider international agenda. The ILO should take action to coordinate measures under the principle that all relevant international organizations should assume their role in the promotion of the ILO Declaration on Fundamental Principles and Rights at Work and its Follow-up. Development must not be achieved at the expense of the working people.

I do hope that the key result of this Conference will be a strong tripartite message to Governments everywhere to ensure that the principles and rights enshrined in the ILO Declaration of 1998 will be fully respected and that all the core Conventions will be ratified and applied. The suggestions for technical assistance to that end have our full support.

The second issue to which I want to draw your attention is employment. Employment is of crucial importance in meeting the needs and aspirations of women and men all over the world, in fostering development, in eradicating poverty and in managing the demographic revolution.

We welcome the growing insight that full employment and decent work for all should be made a global goal. The overriding priority for the ILO, in cooperation with other international organizations, should be the promotion of full employment and decent work globally.

The World Bank has launched a research agenda to ensure that employment promotion policies become an integral part of equitable growth and poverty reduction programmes. We would strongly welcome similar enhanced efforts in the ILO and, of course, international cooperation on those issues. We look forward to, and make a plea for, a reinforcement of the ILO's work on employment and the Global Employment Agenda.

It goes without saying that my final remarks will refer to the thoughts of the World Commission on the Social Dimension of Globalization and the resulting report to our Conference. Allow me to start by congratulating the World Commission and its entire secretariat for its work and final report, *A fair Globalization: Creating opportunities for all*.

The ideas and conclusions themselves are not altogether new; what is new is the comprehensive approach. We find the analyses excellent and most of the proposals are relevant and establish a common ground for a global discussion. Several important issues, however, are dealt with in rather general terms, and they require further thinking in order to identify the value added and reach the final extended and consolidated shape for consensus decisions.

We embrace wholeheartedly the framework which states that the governance of globalization must be based on universally shared values and respect for human rights and core labour standards. We emphatically support the quest for democracy and good governance, social equity and equality between women and men and certainly also, the need for coherence and the focus on national action. These aspects are all fundamental building blocks of development. To be honest, I do think that, in one way or another, we all have our homework to do.

The ILO should immediately take forward the rights-based challenges and the vast and complex global employment issues. And together we – Governments, Workers and Employers – need to continue analysing the various proposals and to seek partners for cooperative strategic action in order to assume our collective responsibility in making globalization fair and inclusive.

As we can see here today, a lively tripartite discussion is already under way, and I am convinced that, once again, we will be able to verify that there is no stronger tool for promoting sustainable changes than constructive dialogue.

Mr. TALIADOROS *(Minister of Labour and Social Insurance, Cyprus)*

I am delighted to have the honour of addressing this august gathering on behalf of the Government of the Republic of Cyprus.

Let me begin by saying that it was an excellent idea to place the work of the World Commission on the Social Dimension of Globalization on the agenda of this session of the International Labour

Conference. Let me also thank and congratulate the Director-General of the ILO for sharing, in a frank and open manner, his reflections on the report of the Commission and, in particular, its implications for the ILO.

We share the vision of the World Commission for a process of globalization with a strong social dimension based on universally shared values and respect for human rights and individual dignity.

The ILO, with its strong ethical mandate, its tripartite character and its near-universal membership can, and should, make a significant contribution to achieving the goal of a more equitable globalization, taking into account the Commission's assessment that the problems identified "are not due to globalization as such but to deficiencies in its governance".

The Director-General's Report emphasizes the major challenge highlighted by the Commission to bring scattered initiatives together into integrated national strategies for poverty reduction and decent work and to "promote a coherent integration of economic and social policies which focus on the well-being and quality of life of people".

Social policies in Cyprus have always aimed at achieving social justice, social solidarity and social cohesion in a free and democratic economic system. In response to challenges brought about by demographic and socio-economic changes, as well as our accession to the European Union and globalization, we are modernizing our social policy agenda which underlines the interdependence between economic, social and employment policies. We are fully aware of the need to find the right mix of policies to promote growth and competitiveness and, at the same time, guarantee social protection and solidarity.

In the fight against poverty and social exclusion, we combine the promotion of access to employment with the investment in human resources through the promotion of specific measures, with the support of the European Social Fund, which aim to: enhance and modernize public employment services; strengthen activities to adapt skills to labour market needs; promote equal opportunities for access to the labour market for all, and especially those threatened with social exclusion; promote women's access to the labour market; utilize new technologies within the framework of lifelong learning; and improve and reinforce secondary and technical-vocational education and training.

In connection with the recommendations of the Commission on constructing a "socio-economic floor", Cyprus has taken a number of robust and affordable measures, which I would like to share with you.

The whole working population is covered by a comprehensive state social insurance system. In addition, a system for those outside the labour market guarantees universal coverage for old-age pensions.

Social assistance ensures a socially acceptable minimum standard of living for everyone and special protection for persons who are more vulnerable to social exclusion.

Decent work is a key goal safeguarded by a comprehensive legal framework which ensures minimum standards.

Community initiative and response to social needs are encouraged through the grant-in-aid scheme which provides advice and support to non-governmental organizations for the development of needed social services and programmes at the local level.

Finally, social dialogue is well developed, and the involvement of the social partners in the formulation and monitoring of policies has become a deep-rooted institution.

Participation in the European Union's employment and social inclusion strategies has contributed to making policy-making even more transparent, to increasing political accountability, to enhancing the effectiveness of national policies, which are required to be based on specific and quantified objectives and targets and to reinforce a culture of evaluation.

On the basis of our national experience, we can only fully endorse the emphasis placed by both the Commission and the Director-General of the ILO on the crucial importance of "starting at home".

We also fully endorse the recommendation to move towards policy coherence among the international organizations. The first step could be the implementation of the Commission's proposal for dialogue and consultations in a globalization policy forum on the social dimension of globalization involving all stakeholders.

Without wishing to make a political statement, as this forum is not a political one, the reference made to the Cyprus issue by the Workers' delegate of Turkey obliges me to point out that the so-called embargos against Turkish Cypriots to which he referred are consequences emanating from United Nations Security Council resolutions and European Court judgements.

The Government of the Republic of Cyprus has taken a package of measures in favour of Turkish Cypriots, who are by no means discriminated against in any respect. The Government is the first to support the economic development of Turkish Cypriots with the ultimate aim of facilitating the unification of our country.

Original Russian: Mrs. KARAGOUSOVA *(Minister of Labour and Social Protection of Population, Kazakhstan)*

Allow me, on behalf of the Government of the Republic of Kazakhstan, to extend greetings to this session of the Conference and express my gratitude to the ILO for the opportunity it has given me to speak.

I share the general opinion of participants of this forum regarding the topicality and significance of the Global Report submitted by the Director-General of the ILO, Mr. Juan Somavia.

As we have heard, the processes of globalization particularly with regard to social issues are causing concern and the disruption of the balance which had previously existed, to a greater or lesser degree, at national level.

The Republic of Kazakhstan is an active participant in the integration processes which are under way and is feeling the full force of the many and varied ramifications of globalization.

We are actively working to improve our social security mechanism so that, as far as possible, we can soften the consequences of globalization for workers, protect our national labour market in a context of active migration, overcome excessive disparities in living standards and work towards the eradication of poverty. Kazakhstan appreciates that poverty is a potential breeding ground for terrorism and organized crime. It has a significant wealth of experience that has allowed it to achieve economic growth while at the same time establishing an effective mechanism of social security. In this work, as mentioned in the Report, we are trying to rely primarily on tripartism and looking for effective compromises which will allow us to comply with fundamental labour rights and freedoms and to ensure the protection of health and safety at work while, at the same time, not damaging the investment climate or curbing the pace of economic growth in our country, which has been quite considerable in the last few years.

The Report and the proposed action plan offer a considerable variety of ways for developing social dialogue, and will allow us to find answers to many of the problems which are facing us now.

The Republic of Kazakhstan was one of the first CIS countries to create a multi-tiered system of collective bargaining in labour relations. In 1995, for the first time, our President, Mr. Nazarbayev, made it compulsory for representatives of the government, unions and employers at all levels to conclude on an annual general agreement. This was the first such regulation in the CIS.

In 1999, Kazakhstan ratified all the fundamental Conventions of the ILO, including the Freedom of Association and Protection of the Right to Organise Convention, 1948 (No. 87) and, in the year 2000, we adopted a law on social partnership in the Republic of Kazakhstan which forms the basis for tripartism.

We have also taken constructive steps to implement the principle of freedom of association within a system of collective bargaining.

As a result, social dialogue now includes all types of negotiations and consultations and exchanges of information between representatives of the Government, the Workers and the Employers.

Priority areas for negotiation are issues of labour relations, unemployment rates, poverty, wages, security, safety and health at work, social security and so on. Within the last decade, we have therefore been able to ensure relative social stability and consensus.

There has been a considerable drop in the number of industrial disputes and conflicts. In the three years between 1999 and 2001, we saw the number of protest campaigns drop by four-fifths.

Kazakhstan is committed to compliance with the implementation of international standards and attaches great importance to cooperation with the ILO and strengthening that cooperation.

We have adopted a new labour code in Kazakhstan, in close cooperation with the ILO, and this will allow us to improve the nature of our labour relations.

We support the ILO decision to include Kazakhstan in the list of countries which will be implementing the provisions of the ILO Declaration on Fundamental Principles and Rights at Work and its Follow-up, and we are also working on a memorandum for cooperation with the ILO for next three years. We believe that the social partnership mechanism should be extended to the international level to serve as a basis for ensuring social justice in globalization.

The fight against poverty and illegal migration should also be a major aspect of work on globalization. Poverty is an international problem, of course, because the active integration processes confronting the world today mean that, even if poverty has been eradicated in the richer countries, it can still be exported there again through migration flows, be they legal or illegal. As the Report rightly points out, poverty is always going to be a problem for the whole world and we need to tackle that to achieve stability and peaceful growth.

We support the main thrust of the Report and we hope that more attention will be given to social security, since, as we have heard, the market economy itself cannot be relied upon to uphold the basic principles of social justice.

It is extremely important to pool the efforts of all countries, bearing in mind the solidarity needed, the responsibility that all bear for the consequences of globalization, and the need to ensure that it should be fairer and more humane.

Mr. PATER *(Minister of Social Policy, Poland)*

With great satisfaction we have read the Director-General's Report on the work of the Organization for 2002-03. It testifies to the significance of the Organization's achievement resulting from its unrelenting everyday toil.

The Director-General's summary gives me the opportunity to also look back on Poland's achievements, with the ILO's cooperation, over the last 15 years.

The Organization was one of the key actors that helped Poland create the structures for social dialogue and helped it lay the foundations for national legislation on collective labour relations. In close cooperation with the ILO, we, the Government, together with the social partners, learnt the lesson of active partnership which have resulted in our ambitious social reforms.

The ILO also helped us establish modern labour market structures which did not exist at the beginning of our economic and social transformation. Now that we are striving to modernize both our labour market and social inclusion policies, we are also tapping into the Organization's extensive expertise.

Hardly a month has passed since our new membership of the European Union. In its programmes of technical assistance, the ILO was very helpful in making our EU membership a reality.

The Director-General's Report also makes us look towards the future – to the challenges ahead of us and our Organization. They now centre around the phenomenon of globalization to which we are trying to find adequate responses, both at national and international levels. While making sure that globalization produces the greatest good for many, we have to ensure that decent employment is a realistic opportunity for our citizens, that social exclusion is prevented or reduced, and that we move from a welfare State to a welfare and workfare society.

These are the objectives of our Organization which can be found in its key programmes. We support them. We see in the International Labour Organization, with its tripartism, great potential for forging the necessary social consensus to achieve those objectives.

We have been very impressed by the work of the World Commission on the Social Dimension of Globalization. The Director-General's Report, *A fair globalization: The role of the ILO*, gives due credit to the World Commission's work and invites this session of the Conference to discuss those very topical issues.

We have gone a long way toward embracing globalization and focusing on how to ensure the fairness of the opportunities it offers. By reducing the physical distance between people, globalization was perceived as expanding the social divide between them. Now, we know that an expanding social gap is not inevitable. If properly managed, the opportunities of globalization will, by far, exceed any incidental dangers.

Good governance is a prerequisite to good management at national and international levels. We believe that every human being has the right to be well governed. I might add that Poland was among the pioneers who introduced that concept back in 1998 in the context of the United Nations Human Rights Commission. We were, therefore, very pleased to see the issue of good governance well-appreciated in the World Commission's report. Indeed, much can be said about improving governance of the global economy. But we have to do our fair share at home, too.

Good governance, built on democracy, social equity, the rule of law and human rights, ensures the high quality of national and local policies and institutions which must be in place if we want globalization to benefit all of our societies.

We should continue to work very hard to improve standards of good governance in our country. We know that we have progressed substantially in that direction over the last 15 years, not least because we have used the expertise of this Organization. We have been impressed by the ILO's support for coherent national policies ensuring the best possible benefits from globalization for all. We also look favourably on the new interesting initiatives in this regard suggested in the Commission's report. We will be following the discussion in this body on globalization very closely.

Mr. MERITON *(Minister for Social Affairs and Employment, Seychelles)*

I would like to extend my appreciation and support to the Director-General, Mr. Juan Somavia, for his well thought-out Report which illustrates the activities undertaken by the ILO in the implementation of the Decent Work Agenda over the last biennium. I indeed treasure the amount of energy mobilized to compile such a thought-provoking document, giving us an insight of the deep-rooted and ever-growing, age-old problems of this world.

The Report invites us to reflect on the pains of the 190 million jobless people and what they have to go through each day in order to survive. These people depend on our support and commitment to enjoy a decent livelihood. We, the ILO constituents, are responsible for charting the course of action to tackle the world's poverty and I entirely agree with the Director-General that the principle route out of poverty is work, and to this end the economy must generate opportunities for investment, entrepreneurship, job creation and sustainable livelihoods.

It is abundantly clear that the problem is not at all a short term one, as had been predicted by the proponents of globalization who said that free market trade policies would bring major benefits to developing countries and would eventually be one of the essential elements to eradicate poverty. The developing countries have yet to see this happen.

Meanwhile, history has proven otherwise. Instead of seeing a brighter future, the poor are becoming poorer whilst the rich are becoming richer, simply because the rules of the game favour the rich and are biased against the poorest.

It is time for developing countries to muster their resources and define strategies to forge ahead in this new global setting. It is also time for developing countries to be given the opportunity to trade and work their way out of hunger, unemployment and, eventually, out of poverty. Indeed, globalization cannot be left to set its own course. It must be managed fairly and equitably with set development goals. If sustainable development is to be achieved it needs to be regarded as a process. An improvement in the quality of life depends on radical social transformation.

The complexities of our contemporary world require both new policy initiatives and a radical paradigm shift in the political arena. The best policies need to be complemented by genuine political will, commitment and linkages in relation to job creation and poverty alleviation. It is only in this way that we will be able to correct the decent work deficit, rampant across the world. Able-bodied men and women are struggling to get not only a decent job, but any job. The world situation prevents them making their contribution to society. What a waste of our potential human resources.

At this juncture I wish to commend the Presidents of United Republic of Tanzania and Finland, who co-chaired the work of the World Commission on the Social Dimension of Globalization, which produced the document charting the way forward to give a human face to globalization. In the same vein, I salute the courage and commitment of the African Heads of State and Government in agreeing to convene the Extraordinary Summit on Employment and Poverty Alleviation in Africa later this year. The Summit, the first of its kind, will attempt to find a viable framework for combating unemployment and poverty on the continent. It is high time that Africa takes control of its own destiny. I am convinced that such an initiative on the part of the African Heads of State will lead to concrete action that will pay dividends.

Allow me to share with you the experience of my small country, the Seychelles, in this area. We have met the targets of most of the eight Millennium Development Goals. Investment in human development has been an essential element of all our policies and national development plans since independence. Access to free education and health services, to safe drinking water and sanitation, active policies to promote full, productive and freely chosen employment for all, have contributed to poverty alleviation and social integration.

This has been achieved through our progressive human-centred development approach. However, this has come at a cost and the challenge that we, as a small island developing State, face today is to sustain development and the high standard of living of our people.

It is in this context that our new President, Mr. James Michel, pledged his commitment to the principles of social dialogue, tripartism and partnership in the process of nation-building for the benefit of all.

The success of the Seychelles did not come by chance or accident. It took vision and genuine political will to achieve a feat that, with committed leadership, the right policies and a concerted effort from all stakeholders, many developing countries can also achieve.

In conclusion, I would like to call on all of us, together, to think globally, taking cognizance of specific local realities and to act accordingly to bring about change. The way forward is through a development that is well managed and will reconcile economic development and social justice, thereby ensuring human dignity, peace and prosperity for all our nations.

Original Spanish: Mrs. IGLESIAS *(Minister of Labour, Venezuela)*

On behalf of the people and the Government of the Bolivarian Republic of Venezuela, may I extend to all here fraternal greetings, and specifically also to the President, whom we would like to congratulate on his election.

I would like to highlight that the programme objectives which the Director-General of the ILO, Mr. Juan Somavia, has set out in his Report, are consistent with the objectives set out in the Constitution of the Bolivarian Republic of Venezuela. This guides our government action in areas such as promoting fundamental rights at work, creating opportunities for men and women to have access to decent work and income, guaranteeing effectiveness of social protection for all and strengthening social dialogue.

The growing preoccupation with the social and economic effects of globalization require closer supervision of compliance with standards. It also requires a certain amount of creativity in order to move toward constructing a state which can guarantee social justice and which enshrines genuine democracy, the kind which can guarantee peoples' participation in designing government policies that truly meet their expectations and needs in all areas, especially in economic and social areas.

Our Constitution, adopted through referendum, set in motion a process aimed at deepening and broadening the rights of workers, doing so by providing decent, dignified and productive work and social protection for all of our population, all of this based on meaningful social dialogue as an instrument for democracy.

The impact of globalization has left the Venezuelan people with an enormous social deficit. The immense wealth generated by oil and administered over the past century did not guarantee people's access to a decent and dignified standard of living. On the contrary, a high percentage of the population still lives in poverty. These people have historically been excluded from our health and education systems, and from the possibility of earning a decent living through decent work. This is why we have adopted the slogan "to overcome poverty we must empower the poor".

If this situation does not change, if this debt to our people is not cancelled, if we do not see justice done, we will not be able to achieve social peace and stability. We will not be able to govern our country. We will not be able to guarantee sustainable and productive development.

This is why our Government believes that its fundamental mission is to ensure that everyone in Venezuela can enjoy the right to health, education, social protection and employment. What we are trying to do is include those who have been left behind without leaving anyone behind.

In order to achieve this, we have set up a programme with the specific objectives to provide primary health care and services to the poorest neighbourhoods in our country. Up until now, 12 million Venezuelans have benefited from this programme. We are trying to teach the illiterate to read and write. More than 1.2 million people learned to read and write in only ten months. We are trying to provide occupational training to a million people out of work and organize them into cooperatives so that they can develop a prosperous and social economy.

All of this is based on meaningful social dialogue in order to build a deep, real and participative democracy, dialogue which directly involves the social partners, workers and employers alike.

In Venezuela, we are convinced that the entire world should move beyond dialogue between the elite, dialogue which reflects less and less the needs of the people. We cannot restrict social dialogue, nor rights nor freedom of association, to conversations at the top while the people, those directly affected by these rights, are left outside closed doors. What we need to do is have social dialogue, rights and freedom of association, which we talk about year after year, take place where the majority wait, outside those closed doors.

We have seen that when we go beyond the confines of the inner circles of the political elite, social dialogue becomes a powerful instrument to protect and generate employment and guarantee respect for rights at work. We have also noted that, when everyone participates, we in fact strengthen our social organizations, both workers and employers, and we legitimize our public institutions.

The high rates of participation of the people in mastering their own destiny is that which has enabled our democratic institutions to withstand crisis situations, among which examples I could cite the *coup d'état*, sabotage of our petroleum industry and lockouts by employers – we have moved beyond all those crises. At this point in time, bodies such as the Economic Commission for Latin America and the Caribbean (ECLAC) indicate that Venezuela is one of the countries with the greatest economic growth rates, at 10.3 per cent. But the most significant point is that we have been able to do this without recourse to any neo-liberal recipe. In other words, we have been able to make substantive improvements in our economy, without reining in our social, political or trade union rights. On the contrary these have increased. This is why we restate our confidence that dialogue is the way to overcome difficulties and to strengthen democracy, giving it real meaning and putting it in the hands of the people so that it can become an economic and social democracy, a real democracy.

Finally, we recommit our people and our Government to fight for justice and truth, to defend the sovereignty of all nations and the self-determination of all peoples, to fight for peace in a world which we want to be multicultural, multi-ethnic, multipolar, capable of eradicating poverty and turning it into a thing of the past, something which we were able to overcome.

Mrs. GAWANAS *(representative, African Union)*

Allow me first and foremost to express my appreciation to the African Union for having given me this opportunity to address this gathering. I want, in particular, to thank the ILO Director-General for having extended an invitation to the African Union. I also bring you greetings from His Excellency Professor Alpha Oumar Konaré, the Chairperson of the Commission of the African Union.

This Conference is important for governments, for trade unions and for employers' organizations as it constitutes a platform for dialogue on the many challenges we face, especially in the area of labour and employment, but also importantly in driving forward the social agenda.

As we are gathered here, the challenges of globalization continue to impact negatively on our people, and the African Union welcomes the report of the World Commission on the Social Dimension of Globalization which has the goal of a fairer and equitable globalization.

More than ever before, unemployment, poverty, disease and hunger continue to afflict the majority of the population, especially in the African continent. We may certainly note that Africa is indeed a rich continent, but it is already being said that Africa could be one of those continents that might not be able to reach the Millennium Development Goals.

There is an imbalance in the distribution of economic resources which is undermining social justice and equality. In most societies there is a growing divide between the so-called formal and informal economy, and this divide means that people living and working in the so-called informal economy are the ones who are excluded, are the ones who are deprived of their rights and benefits, and therefore, in its efforts to address these problems, the African Union is advocating social and economic integration among African countries. In its programmes, the Commission will address the twin problems of poverty and social exclusion in order to achieve sustainable social development, guided by the value that the human being must always be at the centre of any development efforts.

It is also in this regard that an Extraordinary Summit of Heads of State and Government of the African Union on Employment and Poverty Alleviation in Africa is being organized by the Commission of the African Union in Burkina Faso in September 2004.

The previous speaker alluded to the fact that it is time for Africa to determine its destination. I want to say that that time has arrived with the formation of the African Union, which has embarked on mapping for itself and for the continent a vision and a mission for the twenty-first century, together with a four-year strategic programme which will help us to lead the way to an integrated, united, peaceful and prosperous Africa. The integrated approach will include the programmes of the African regional economic communities, as well as the New Partnership for Africa's Development (NEPAD) as a socio-economic programme. In implementing this new vision, the Commission of the African Union will indeed have to work with and be guided by its international partners, social partners, and civil society organizations. The African Union has also put in place two major key institutions, the Peace and Security Council and the Pan-African Parliament. While the Peace and Security Council is expected to strengthen the capacity of the African Union for conflict management, prevention and resolution, the Pan-African Parliament is a crucial step towards enabling Africa to take control of its own political future.

An important issue which is being deliberated at this session of the Conference is that of migrant workers. Labour migration is a current and historical reality in Africa, impacting directly on economies and societies. However, internal and external migration, driven by various factors including poverty, civil strife and conflicts, has been inevitable. Africa has been deprived of its most valuable assets, its qualified professionals. Africa should therefore struggle to reverse the brain drain if it is to keep pace with development and motivate qualified Africans to remain in the service of their countries. In this regard, the African Union Commission has drawn up a draft policy framework on migration in Africa to assist the sector's management of migration.

The impact of HIV/AIDS on all economic and social sectors, particularly the productive labour force, cannot be overemphasized. It affects mostly young people and women, who constitute the majority of the population of Africa. If the strain continues we will lose almost half of our most active labour force in the next decade, to the detriment of the sustainable socio-economic development of our continent.

The Commission of the African Union has therefore taken on board the issue of HIV/AIDS in the workplace in its programmes and will work in close collaboration with the ILO on that issue. Africa's leadership is also determined to promote access to life saving anti-retroviral drugs and prevention methods. In taking a holistic and integrated approach to achieving sustainable development, the African continent cannot ignore its human and social dimensions, but must ensure that people are at the centre of and are the object of development. In many countries, the crisis in the social sector remains severe and social issues are often neglected, thus threatening the very livelihood of the population.

In concluding, I would like to reiterate that Africa's development challenges cannot be met unless African countries work in effective partnerships, first and foremost with one another, with the international community, with social partners and civil society organizations, to create productive jobs and effective social protection strategies, to address the negative impact of globalization, poverty and HIV/AIDS on African individuals, families and communities, and to meet the social needs and benefits of the people, especially the poor and the vulnerable. This will only be possible if our political leaders manifest and sustain a strong commitment, and receive the support they need from the various stakeholders. This is vital, because, if we allow the development gap between Africa and other continents to continue to widen, achievement of global socio-economic development will remain a dream, especially for the African continent.

Original Arabic: Mr. AZOZ *(Workers' delegate, Syrian Arab Republic)*

I would like to congratulate the President of the Conference on his election to steer the deliberations of the current session; I hope that the discussions of this session will live up to the level of challenges facing the world of labour and workers.

This session of the International Labour Conference is an essential turning point, particularly for workers, because their conditions of work are a clear indication of the injustice and deprivation being inflicted on increasing numbers of people and which are generating indignation, thus endangering international security and peace, as well as social harmony.

We believe that the Report prepared by the Director-General of the Organization paves the way for constructive dialogue, aiming to provide decent work for all and help the most vulnerable and oppressed so that the international Organization can fulfil its mission.

The Global Report under the follow-up to the ILO Declaration on Fundamental Principles and Rights at Work relating to the Right to Organise and Collective Bargaining Convention, 1949 (No. 98), is an appropriate step towards guaranteeing workers' rights to organize and collective bargaining. This is a fundamental right which is key in enabling the working class to deal with the negative consequences of globalization.

The Syrian Arab Republic has ratified this Convention and the other fundamental Conventions of the ILO.

Today, 25 independent trade unions are part of the Syrian Trade Union Confederation which was set up in 1938. We are contributing to the widespread continuing efforts in our country, to develop, modernize, and reform the economy and the civil service begun by President Bashar al Assad and a number of important reforms have been introduced.

A number of laws have been enacted recently aiming to increase workers' wages by 20 per cent and develop the social security system.

Amendments to the labour law and other legislation regarding working conditions will be introduced shortly. We are ceaselessly working to achieve a system of social partnership based on dialogue. We are also making efforts towards balanced sustainable development. However, the Syrian Arab Republic and the Arab region face occupation and embargo. Sanctions are imposed on the Syrian Arab Republic through the so-called Syrian Accountability Act which negatively affects our country's development efforts. Any threat to peace in this region is a threat to peace around the world, as indicated in the Declaration of Philadelphia.

These punitive sanctions and measures have harmed our country. This has also been the case for Cuba.

The Arab region is still suffering a dangerous and explosive situation due to the continued Israeli occupation of Arab territories in Palestine, the Golan and south Lebanon, not to mention the US-British occupation of Iraq and the grave practices of the occupation forces in violation of international Conventions and laws.

The workers and people of Palestine whose lands are occupied are still subjected to the most abject practices of oppression, suppression and persecution including physical liquidation which is sanctions through the so-called Serious Accountability Act approved by the American Congress have affected negatively the development efforts because the need to defend our homeland depletes a great deal of our capabilities and resources.

This hinders and puts a brake on the efforts of national development and the attainment of further economic progress and hinders the solution of the problems of unemployment and backwardness. The Declaration of Philadelphia confirms that any threat to peace in the region is a threat to peace in the world at large.

The unjust sanctions and punishment has harmed workers in my country, Libya, Sudan, Cuba and led to impeding the implementation of the development plans in those countries.

The Arab region is still experiencing an explosive situation due to the continued occupation of Palestine, the Golan and southern Lebanon, not to mention the United States and British occupation of Iraq, which is in violation of international Conventions and laws.

The workers and the people of Palestine, whose lands are occupied, are still subject to the worst forms of oppression, discrimination and persecution, including physical liquidation which is one of the most brutal forms of terrorism.

These acts of oppression and persecution are accompanied by an expansion in settlement and land confiscation by the occupying forces with the moral and material support of the Americans.

It is paradoxical in this case that, because of the double standards, that are being applied, these victims of aggression and occupation are being turned into aggressors in order to justify the crimes perpetrated by the occupying forces in the name of legitimate self-defence.

We hope that the high-level mission will have the power to assess the situation during its next visit to the region. The high-level mission has already highlighted in its report the fact that Arab workers and other citizens in the occupied Palestinian territories and the Syrian Golan have been living in tragic conditions. They have been exposed to grave violations of their rights and freedoms by the occupiers.

The workers and people of Iraq are also suffering a tragic situation as a result of the current occupation and as a result of the abuse and the crimes being perpetrated against them. The international media have reported on the abuse of Iraqi prisoners by the United States armed forces who claim to have intervened in Iraq to defend democracy.

This oppression has also led to the assassination of high-level Iraqis, the destruction of infrastructure and the denial of freedom. This has led to greater instability and insecurity and could have disastrous consequences with an increase in unemployment and the adoption of decisions prohibiting Iraqi national companies from contributing to the reconstruction of the country.

We hope that he current session of the International Labour Conference will discuss the issues of migrant workers, the development of human resources and other topics on the Conference agenda. We hope that new Conventions will be adopted, that will meet the expectations of workers and peoples at large.

(The Conference adjourned at 1.15 p.m.)

Seventh sitting

Wednesday, 9 June 2004, 3 p.m.

President: Mr. Maatough

REPORTS OF THE CHAIRPERSON OF THE GOVERNING BODY AND OF THE DIRECTOR-GENERAL: DISCUSSION (CONT.)

The PRESIDENT

We shall now resume all discussions of the Reports of the Chairperson of the Governing Body and of the Director-General.

Ms. BAKOKO BAKORU *(Minister of Gender, Labour and Social Development, Uganda)*

I join my colleagues in congratulating the President upon his well-deserved election to the presidency of this Conference. I also congratulate the other Officers. I am confident that with their vast experience they will steer this Conference to a fruitful conclusion.

The world today is faced with complex challenges: the impact of globalization, the foreign debt burden, poverty, HIV/AIDS and migration. I wish to express my appreciation for the efforts of the Director-General, who has been particularly alert and has carried out a comprehensive survey and analysis of the situation of the workers. He has correctly identified and prioritized the current important issues, proposed action plans and placed them on the agenda for this meeting. I support the proposals in the Director-General's Report, *A fair globalization: The role of the ILO*.

At the global level, the pursuit of social justice is the primary goal for which the ILO was created. The objective was to ensure better living and working conditions throughout the world, to secure work in conditions of freedom, equality, security and human dignity. At the national level, this is my responsibility.

In this regard, I reaffirm Uganda's commitment to the respect and promotion of ILO fundamental principles and rights at work. These principles are embodied in the national Constitution and legislation governing the trade unions and industrial relations. Uganda has ratified the ILO Conventions relevant to organizing for social justice, the Right to Organize and Collective Bargaining Convention, 1949 (No. 98), and the Collective Bargaining Convention, 1981 (No. 154). The Freedom of Association and Protection of the Right to Organize Convention, 1948 (No. 87), is being considered for ratification.

Africa remains the continent with the least favourable conditions. Africa has the lowest investment rate, lowest productivity, heaviest debt burden, highest prevalence of HIV/AIDS, highest incidence of unemployment and highest poverty levels. I want to emphasize two of these, HIV/AIDS and job creation, in relation to organizing for social justice.

Uganda is one of the countries which was first hit very hard by the HIV/AIDS epidemic. Twenty years down the road, the country has moved from being the epicentre of the epidemic to a success story, despite limited resources, thanks to political commitment, destigmatization, an open policy on the disease, a multisectoral approach and the "ABC" – abstinence, behaviour change and a condomized policy. We have received support from many friends. Let me express our appreciation to the ILO for its continued financial and technical support. We especially welcome our inclusion in the ILO Programme on HIV/AIDS and the World of Work. Our special thanks go to the Italian Government for funding the national project on the prevention and mitigation of HIV/AIDS in the world of work. The epidemic still poses a big challenge, but Ugandans have the resolve to fight on.

A combination of migration and HIV/AIDS is devastating. These two factors are competing to drain Africa's already meagre supply of skilled workers. Migrant workers tend to leave their spouses behind to look after the children and elderly, and while at their destination, they seek entertainment from commercial sex workers who often approach them to make some money. Indeed, this is an area that warrants exposure and interest.

There is a need for HIV/AIDS and migration to be tackled together and to increase the scale of responses. We need to deliberately target the mobile and migrant populations, with a focus on preventing the spread of HIV/AIDS through migration. I suggest that governments strengthen their wage policy and, through collective bargaining, improve migration and the working conditions of migrant workers to enable them to keep their families where they work. It is fundamental that we eliminate the separation of spouses.

I therefore call upon the Director-General to increase his concern and efforts to focus on the relationship between HIV/AIDS and migration throughout the world.

Poverty and unemployment are a hindrance to social justice. We welcome the Director-General's Report and objectives for the next four years, as stated in his Global Report, *Organizing for social justice*. We are in total agreement with universal ratification of Conventions Nos. 87 and 98. The ILO should focus on working closely with the member States to assist them in overcoming the obstacles to ratification.

In order to reduce poverty and unemployment, my Government has reviewed the Poverty Eradication Action Programme (PEAP) with a focus on poverty and unemployment.

Finally, I want to emphasize that poverty and unemployment are more severe in Africa than anywhere else in the world. This is because policies designed to increase employment, as part of economic growth, now have to be implemented in the context of globalization, which does not favour Africa.

Let me emphasize that freedom of association and working conditions cannot be discussed in isolation from the surrounding economic climate and other factors, such as population growth, that have an impact on it. When jobs are few the competition is so stiff that people are prepared to sacrifice good working conditions just to be employed; a bad job is better than having no food on the table.

The defence of rights at work involves the obligation to create jobs, otherwise there would be nothing to defend; we cannot discuss one without the other.

The creation of jobs at home is directly restricted by the denial of access to the world's lucrative markets. While the worker in Africa is subject to full free market principles at home, his or her products have no access to the world's lucrative markets; access is denied through tariffs, quotas and subsidies. The world market does not favour Africa.

Finally, developing countries should get their rightful share of these markets. This is fundamental to working conditions and the corresponding freedoms. I therefore call upon the Director-General to engage all relevant world institutions and not to rest before inequalities in the world markets are totally removed. Poverty anywhere is a danger to prosperity everywhere.

Original Portuguese: Mr. FATTORI COSTA *(Employers' delegate, Brazil)*

May I begin by congratulating Mr. Guevara on his election as President of the 92nd Session of the International Labour Conference, which recognizes the efforts that he has made, and his experience in matters which must be examined and acted on if we are to ensure a harmonious relationship between capital and labour. I would like also to praise the confederations of industry and commerce of my country for preparing an excellent document to guide our delegation during this session of the Conference.

Over the last few years, technological progress and the resulting globalization have completely changed how we decide what to produce, where to produce it and at what cost, taking account of the markets to be targeted. This process used to take a long time a lot of preparation, but today, with the amount of statistical data available to us and the facilities provided by electronic systems, the task can be carried out much more accurately and in much less time. Just as important for this change has been progress in the areas of communications and telecommunications; at the touch of a button we can send and receive messages which used to take weeks, or even months, to get to their destination. Similarly, a telephone call from home or office puts us within reach of people almost anywhere in the world, allowing us to exchange ideas and make decisions in a fraction of the time it used to take. Just as extraordinary is progress in the transport of people and products. Nowadays we can move people and products from one side of the world to the other in less than 24 hours. High–capacity ships mean we can much more easily transport large cargoes of low added value, such as commodities, between ports throughout the world.

Ports and airports are now equipped for the rapid movement of enormous volumes of cargo in shorter and shorter periods of time. So that these gains in productivity are not lost in red tape, which would be justifiable in a less–pressured environment, governments and companies are making efforts to eliminate paperwork and rubber stamps except for the absolute minimum necessary to control these operations.

The facilities of communication and transport have radically changed decision-making in business. Companies grow and prosper or fail as a result of their operations. As long as operations in a particular city or country yield good returns, the natural choice is to continue production there, where the potential for profit is greater. And whenever a company transfers production to developing countries, the number of unemployed people in the country of origin increases. This explains why a large number of countries have seen their GDP and per capita income rise very quickly, while elsewhere economies are stagnating or even shrinking.

To reverse this trend, which is becoming more and more serious as businesses become less able to compete in the market and unemployment increases, cosmetic measures will not be sufficient. Labour legislation has always covered new rights, the cost of which cannot be transferred, but which, in many cases, make it unviable to create and maintain jobs because of the bureaucratic burden entailed. What has been ever more difficult is to weigh up the risks of hiring staff, and the higher the risk the greater the difficulty of generating new jobs.

In my country there is a clear dichotomy between technological progress, labour legislation, tax legislation and the ability of small and medium-sized enterprises to comply with such legislation. This legislation was necessary and useful in its time but no longer responds to current needs and should be updated if we wish to maintain existing jobs and create new ones.

Our President, Luiz Inacio Lula da Silva, has very courageously reached an understanding with the financial organizations, contrary to the confrontational stance which many people expected him to take. The results show that he has acted well. We hope to see the same courage in relation to labour and taxation matters in our country.

Original Portuguese: Mr. LUQUINDA *(Deputy-Minister of Public Administration, Employment and Social Security, Angola)*

May I begin by congratulating the President on his election to manage the work of this 92nd Session of the International Labour Conference.

The Republic of Angola is experiencing one of the most important moments of its history. Peace has brought back hope to the country and has created the basis for a new era for our children. Angola is thus in a position to push forward the process of national reconstruction so as to respond to the requirements of economic and social development and to meet short and medium-term challenges, one of which is to reduce levels of unemployment.

Report III (Part 1B) *Promotion of employment: Policies, skills, enterprises,* which has been submitted for our consideration, gives guidelines for formulating and implementing policies for job creation, and also suggests measures for alleviating poverty. These guidelines are expressed as general measures, and I believe that some of them are already being applied in a number of member countries, whereas others require special skills for implementation, and here we hope for commitment and assistance from the International Labour Office.

The Republic of Angola is no exception to the general rule and is therefore developing a series of programmes to rehabilitate economic and social infrastructure destroyed during the war and to establish others. We are also improving procedures to ensure private investment with a view to creating jobs and reducing poverty levels. In its Medium-Term Programme for Stabilization and Economic Recovery, the Government of Angola has set out conditions as an incentive to speed up the process of creating new economic activity and strengthen relations between the Government and enterprise with transparency, rapidity and efficacy. Their purpose is to significantly reduce the legal requirements for setting up companies in the country.

Very recently, a draft bill was brought before Parliament to provide for a "first job" law and a strategy for its implementation. This bill is aimed particularly at citizens of between 14 and 30 years of age, and will allow responsibilities to be shared with other areas and sectors, with the emphasis being placed upon the integration of young people into the world of work.

The social partners have been asked to give their opinion upon this, along with public and private universities, NGOs and a number of professional bodies. These measures will be complemented by other measures in general employment policy, for example, widening the educational basis by constructing vocational training centres throughout the country. Vocational training, together with job creation will allow many of my fellow citizens to be integrated into the labour market, and consequently will create within them better hopes for the future and enhance the exercise of their citizens' rights.

The HIV/AIDS epidemic has now become a world crisis. It is one of the worst challenges ever posed to development and social progress. My Government is concerned by its spread to the workplace. We have already approved legislation to regulate forms, methods, behaviour and the protection offered to workers. The measures contained in this legislation are based upon respect for basic human rights, ethical standards for health, the adoption of practices and attitudes of solidarity, and respect for those individuals who have been infected, and these measures must be observed in vocational training centres and all other workplaces. The Government of Angola is bending its energies towards promoting local programmes which will hold back the devastating effects of this pandemic in our country.

The Republic of Angola endorses the decisions taken with regard to working conditions in the fishing industry with a view to adopting standards which will bring together a range of instruments and allow for a more orderly implementation of legislation.

I would like, finally, to express the wish that the results of the work of this session of the Conference will match the expectations of us all and that, in each of our countries, we will take the necessary efforts to reduce the evil which is such a massive challenge for humanity: unemployment.

Mrs. THIENTHONG *(Minister of Labour, Thailand)*

Let me first of all congratulate the President on his election to preside over this year's session of the Conference.

I support the Report of the Director-General, *A fair globalization: The Role of the ILO,* which recommends that decent work become a global goal to make a full contribution to the building of a social dimension of globalization. As part of this Organization, the Thai Government has committed itself to putting the spirit of decent work into practice, and we have made tangible progress.

As regards labour standards, a ministerial declaration on maximum wage fixing was issued in April which observes the ratified Maximum Weight Convention, 1967 (No. 127), in a complete manner.

To implement the ratified Worst Forms of Child Labour Convention, 1999 (No. 182), we have formulated a national plan of action to direct and monitor the elimination of the worst forms of child labour in Thailand.

Moreover, our ratification of the Minimum Age Convention, 1973 (No. 138), was officially registered last month.

Trafficking and migration-related issues are also of great concern to us. These issues can be best addressed not by a single government, but through engagement and cooperation with other governments. We have signed bilateral memoranda of understanding with neighbouring countries (Lao People's Democratic Republic, Cambodia and Myanmar) in order to regulate the flow of migrants as well as reducing the number of people at risk from trafficking.

The Thai Government has been promoting employment through national poverty reduction strategies by focusing on the development of the grass-roots economy and community business. The schemes call for, at the grass-roots level and in urban areas throughout the country, the creation of micro as well as small and medium enterprises.

We wholeheartedly intend to provide social protection for all, particularly workers engaged in the informal economy. A ministerial declaration on the protection of homeworkers was issued this April. In addition, the Thai Government has decided to launch a historic unemployment insurance scheme, to take effect on 1 July this year.

More importantly, broad participation and close cooperation of all stakeholders, with mutual understanding and a true spirit of dialogue, are key factors to making our efforts successful. A lot more work remains to be done, but I am sure that we will get there in the end.

I wish to take this opportunity, on behalf of the Government of Thailand, to express our heartfelt thanks to the ILO for its continued supporting role, contributing to our efforts to ensure a fairer globalization for all.

Mr. DINUR *(Government delegate, Israel)*

I would like to congratulate the President of this session of the Conference and his deputies on their election and to thank them for their exceptional leadership of this session of the Conference, which has already resulted in many constructive and fruitful discussions and meetings. I would like also to take this opportunity to congratulate the Secretary-General, Mr Somavia, on the excellent preparatory work for this session of the Conference.

The State of Israel has great respect for the values of social justice, equality and prevention of exploitation which are expressed in the international labour standards formulated by the ILO.

These values, which have been with our people for thousands of years as part of our biblical heritage, are today included in our national laws and regulations.

The changes set in motion by globalization pose great challenges to these important social values. These changes can only be met by efforts on the part of all the social partners to focus on providing decent work and opportunities for all peoples and countries.

Another important subject dealt with in this session of the Conference is the development of human resources through the promotion of vocational training. The State of Israel lacks natural resources and therefore regards human resources as the principal and most important resource. As a result, in our country, education and vocational training are promoted as the sources feeding those human resources, while highly trained and motivated manpower is seen as an engine which has driven the national economy.

Two fields which in the past functioned separately, the Ministry of Industry and Trade and the Ministry of Labour, were recently merged by our Government into one unit.

In the field of industry our task is to develop and promote business and trade while in the field of labour our concern is for promotion of human resources, social protection and increased employment.

It cannot be denied that my country is currently experiencing a difficult economic period in which the employment rate is a relatively high 11 per cent of the potential workforce.

In order to jumpstart the economy, our Government is promoting a policy which includes, among other things, increasing investment in labour intensive industries as well as aiding small businesses, lowering taxes on work income and increasing competitiveness in the economy.

At the same time, Israel also faces the challenge of protecting the rights of temporary migrant workers, including those in irregular situations.

Strict measures have been implemented against employers of undocumented foreign workers as well as against manpower companies which violate the relevant labour laws.

I would like to emphasize that Israel attaches great importance to the struggle to eliminate the worst forms of child labour. The Government of Israel has stated its commitment to the principles set out in Convention No. 182 and is now completing the final technical procedures for its ratification.

Although it is our wish that this session of the Conference be free of political statements and arguments, we have, unfortunately, witnessed such confrontations throughout this session of the Conference by representatives from certain countries. We would like to emphasize that the State of Israel extends her hand in peace. It is clear that true peace will lead the whole region to great achievements and to economic and social prosperity.

I would like, once again, to thank this Organization for its wonderful work preparing this session of the Conference and to express our deep desire that it should be a vehicle for promoting the fundamental values and policies of the ILO.

Mr. DE GEUS *(Minister for Social Affairs and Employment, Netherlands)*

This year's Global Report describes the worldwide developments concerning observance of trade union rights and, as a former trade unionist, it is a subject near and dear to my heart. Energetic and vigorous union work is of vital importance, as we all know.

Take, for instance, the textile industry, the world's greatest source of employment, but also a sector in which job insecurity is on the rise.

The increasing demand for flexibility results in fewer permanent jobs, more part-time positions, more subcontracting of work, more flexible contracts, a constant expansion of the informal economy, more work from home and also more forced labour. In short, less or no job security, less or no social protection and bad to appalling working conditions.

The fundamental labour standards laid down in the ILO Declaration on Fundamental Principles and Rights at Work are more important than ever. Observance of trade union rights is vital.

The Netherlands is an active member of the ILO and a strong advocate of the fundamental labour standards. The Declaration and its follow-up are of enormous importance when it comes to freedom of association and negotiation for the abolition of forced labour and child labour, for equal treatment and pay.

The World Commission's report creates a new momentum for the fundamental labour standards, which, even though they are endorsed worldwide, are still ignored in many places.

Other issues the report of the World Commission raises are labour migration and decent work.

Globalization leads to labour migration. One of the major questions in the coming years will be how we are going to deal with migration, and I am pleased to see this important issue on this year's agenda. This enables us to discuss fundamental and strategic issues regarding this matter. The movement of labour worldwide will become a fact in the future. Together, we have to discuss how we can improve the conditions for migrant workers, as well as the opportunities migration provides for employers, for the sending countries as well as the receiving countries.

The Decent Work Agenda can serve as the basis for promoting more and better jobs for all. The Decent Work Agenda should be a key instrument in the fight against poverty in the world.

To ensure this, the ILO will have to take a more vigorous stance within the United Nations system. The World Commission's report is crystal clear about that. More effective international cooperation and better communication between international organizations is essential. Let us focus, not only on what the ILO could be, but also on what the ILO should be – a strong international player with a clear mission: the improvement of human rights concerning social issues and a guardian and an advocate for compliance with the fundamental labour standards.

In my view, the fact that the agreements reached at the United Nations Millennium Summit make no reference whatsoever to decent work for all is an omission, because there is no doubt that decent employment is the most sustainable and effective way of eradicating poverty. The ILO will have to state this message loud and clear during the review of the United Nations Millennium Summit and the evaluation of the Social Summit.

The ILO also has an active role to play in the world.

(The Conference adjourned at 3.50 p.m.)

Ninth sitting

Wednesday, 9 June 2004, 4.45 p.m.

President: Mr. Wade

REPORTS OF THE CHAIRPERSON OF THE GOVERNING BODY AND OF THE DIRECTOR-GENERAL: DISCUSSION *(CONT.)*

Original French: The PRESIDENT

We shall now resume our discussion of the Reports of the Chairperson of the Governing Body of and the Director-General.

Original Portuguese: Mr. PAIS ANTUNES *(Secretary of State for Labour, Portugal)*

On behalf of the Portuguese Government, allow me to congratulate the President and Vice-Presidents of the Conference, on their election at this 92nd Session. I wish them every success in conducting the work of this assembly. Their work is essential to the success of the Conference, and in the light of their record I am sure that this session will produce excellent results.

The Reports of the Director-General and the Chairperson of the Governing Body submitted to this session of the Conference bear witness to the wide-ranging activities of the bodies of the ILO in recent years.

On behalf of the Portuguese Government I would like to congratulate the Director-General and his staff for their excellent work to defend better working conditions and uphold the rule of law.

Throughout this session of the Conference we have heard a number of important contributions on the subject of the social dimensions of globalization. Clearly, globalization raises new problems, with sweeping effects throughout the world.

Faced with these problems that are common to all of us, it is all the more important to be able to rely in our search for solutions on an organization with the scope and prestige of the ILO so as to better uphold multilateralism in the world.

Allow me to point out that the Government of Portugal fully supports the Director-General when he says that the ILO should focus its activities in its areas of expertise – standard setting and supervision of their application. The creation of the World Commission on the Social Dimension of Globalization is convincing proof of this. It has been said that global good governance has to be based on human rights; the defence of democratic values is the major challenge of the twenty-first century.

I am thinking in particular of the defence of decent work, of workers' and employers' rights and duties, the defence of more and better investment in training, the defence of working conditions, job creation and preservation, the defence of children, the unrelenting fight against child labour and constant support for the family.

The ILO is certainly the ideal organization to define and defend the universal values that should underpin what we call globalization. There is clearly an international consensus on the ILO's prestige and competence to adopt labour standards and supervise their application. This is why, on behalf of the Government of Portugal, I would like of remind you that we rely on the ILO, our champion in the fight for these values, including such traditional but no less important issues as freedom of association and the right to collective bargaining.

Globalization raises challenges both new and not so new, but we need to find new ways of meeting them. All our States, and employers' and workers' representatives must, with help from the ILO, work together in a concerted effort to defend unrelentingly the values of human life and dignity.

I pay tribute to tripartism, an approach that affords undeniable advantages in the search for solutions, as evidenced by the ILO itself, and Portugal has always upheld this approach. We need to continue to ratify ILO Conventions, whose relevance and importance are undeniable. But this is not enough: in today's globalized world we need to secure their application in practice. This must always be a core objective of the ILO.

To conclude, on behalf of my country's Government I would like to recall that, in the future as in the past, you may always rely on us to defend unrelentingly the values of freedom and human rights.

Original French: Mr. BARDE *(Employers' delegate, Switzerland)*

The Swiss employers have read with interest the report, *A fair globalization: Creating opportunities for all*. This work was carried out by 26 independent eminent persons, and will be followed up by the Governing Body, with the support of the social partners. As such, this report does not constitute ILO policy, and its recommendations were not unanimously accepted by its signatories. Despite that, many of the ideas which it contains deserve to be explored with the other institutions involved and with due respect for the competencies of each and every one of them. We would hope that the Office will make proposals to the Governing Body on the responses to be made to the various issues raised in this report.

As employers, we believe in the need, both nationally and internationally, for conditions that are conducive to both economic growth and, consequently, job creation. These conditions would particularly involve full participatory democracy, transparency, an independent legal system and respect for the ILO's Declaration on Fundamental Principles and Rights at Work. In a nutshell, they would involve the constant quest for good governance, which is as necessary for ordinary citizens as it is for business and workers.

Switzerland's employers are deeply attached to these principles. We also attach importance to developing entrepreneurial spirit and small and medium-sized enterprises, which are the backbone of the economy. These are as important as any rhetorical eloquence.

Free trade and economic integration should also be encouraged, while respecting the identity and specificities of the various parties involved. If anybody doubts the need for free trade and economic integration, they should look at the negative effects of protectionism which, while protecting monopolies, forms a constitutional obstacle to creativity, innovation and open access to markets.

As the old saying goes, globalization means "thinking globally, acting locally". This means shouldering one's responsibilities in respect of economic and social issues, and employers are, of course, ready to do that, on the understanding that it is primarily up to States to set the rules which stem from their own legislation or in accordance with their international commitments. We need to be crystal clear on this point so as to avoid any ambiguity, which will only disrupt the climate and distort relations between the world of politics and the economy.

We live in a world and at a time where image plays an increasingly important role. We should use this to promote our own ideas, but we should also be careful to ensure that this situation does not lead to misinterpretations. As employers, we do not want to make promises which cannot be kept. We prefer to take a specific and realistic approach because that is the best way of, slowly but surely, building the future.

Mrs. CHRISTOVA *(Minister of Labour and Social Policy, Bulgaria)*

Allow me to start by wishing the delegates successful and fruitful work in the course of this session of the Conference in their highly responsible positions. First of all, I would like to avail myself of the opportunity to voice my satisfaction with the comprehensive Report dedicated to such important issues. The topic of the Report and the conclusions drawn explicitly highlight the central role of the ILO in the common process of laying down conditions for establishing a fair globalization. This central role was also noted by our esteemed guest, His Excellency the President of the Spanish Government, in his in-depth comments on globalization policy governance.

The expected long period of adjustment of national economies and institutions to problems on a global scale is a matter of deep concern to the Bulgarian Government. One measure undertaken as a response to this concern is the new social policy model adopted in Bulgaria. The new approach laid down in this model requires coordination between different policies – economic, financial and social.

The integrated approach is grounded on strategically important relations between economic, financial and social institutions. This approach is of the highest importance when solutions are sought and complex political decisions are to be taken.

In this connection, allow me to state that the Bulgarian new social policy model is a kind of pre-emptive response to the recommendation made in the Report of the Director-General. This recommendation provides for comprehensive, high-level integration in solving diverse economic and social problems on a national scale in the context of a fair globalization.

Of special importance is the conclusion drawn in the Report that, in the course of globalization, the concept of ensuring decent work should become a global goal. Active labour market policies play a key role in laying down the socio-economic framework for the global economy. In this respect, a national action plan on employment for 2004 was adopted in Bulgaria at the beginning of this year. Through employment-providing programmes, it is envisaged that around 112,000 people will gain employment within the current year. Access to legal employment and to social and health insurance is granted, with preference being given to employers who provide jobs for vulnerable population groups. Furthermore, we have fully reformed the social assistance system, which will continue to be guided by the core objectives of improving the targeting and efficiency of the social payments. As a result of all these measures, the unemployment rate, for the first time during the transition, has decreased from 18 per cent in 2001 to 12 per cent (based on April 2004 data).

Human resources development in Bulgaria needs to increase the employability and quality of the workforce. It should be relevant to the demands of the labour market. In this respect, we have launched a broad-scale national survey to identify the specific needs of different enterprises. Depending on its findings, the national vocational education and training system will be adapted to suit these needs. Through ensuring decent work and reliable sources of income, fair and equal opportunities will be provided for everyone.

An important prerequisite for achievement of a fair globalization is the implementation of the principles of social dialogue. The social partners in Bulgaria take part in drafting and carrying out the different components of integrated economic, financial and social policy. In this respect, measures were introduced at the beginning of last year, with the active participation of trade unions and employers' organizations, for compulsory registration of employment contracts. Minimum social insurance thresholds were also introduced by sector and occupation. As a result, over 306,000 employment contracts moved out of the grey economy. The increased revenue amounts to about €240 million. These measures have become an important tool for combating the informal economy and means of protection of workers' basic right to social protection.

Let me assure you now that we consider that the idea of regular organization of globalization policy forums on a tripartite basis would be an excellent ground for comprehensive exchange between all participants.

Thus, cooperation between the ILO member States will be intensified as we travel toward a fair globalization, including on regional and subregional levels.

Mr. DE PAYVA *(Workers' adviser and substitute delegate, Singapore)*

The Singapore National Trades Union Congress delegation joins other delegates to congratulate the President on being elected to preside over the 92nd Session of the International Labour Conference.

The discussion on migrant workers is timely. Some 175 million people are residing outside their country of birth or nationality. Each year millions of men and women leave their homes and cross national borders in search of decent work and better opportunities for themselves and their families. Migration has emerged as an important issue of our times with far-reaching implications on our workers and societies.

While international migration can be a positive experience, far too many migrant workers suffer from poor working and living conditions. Migrant workers face the grim reality of being among the world's most vulnerable and exploited people. Their rights as workers are often undermined, especially when they are in irregular situations. Some suffer severe abuse and violence in forced labour and trafficking situations.

The challenge confronting the global community is to make migration work for all and direct it in a way that serves the economic well-being and social justice of workers. Trade unions around the world share the same mission in protecting all workers, both migrants and locals, from workplace discrimination, exploitation, abuse and violence.

The Singapore National Trades Union Congress is concerned about the welfare of all workers. The labour movement has always recognized and accepted the need for migrant workers to supplement and complement our limited human resources and appreciates their contribution to Singapore's development and growth. In fact, a local study has found that every one per cent increase in migrant workers with work permits would support 2.6 per cent more local skilled workers and 1.4 per cent more local unskilled workers in Singapore.

At the Singapore National Trades Union Congress Ordinary Delegates Conference in October 1998, the labour movement called on the Government to strengthen efforts to stamp out the problem of unscrupulous employers who use non-documented workers. Over the years, the tripartite social partners have increased efforts to protect the interests of migrant workers in Singapore.

There are strict regulations, policies and statutory protection in Singapore to ensure the health, safety, accommodation and remuneration of migrant workers and there are stiff penalties to punish errant employers.

Migrant workers can join trade unions in Singapore. They form about 17.5 per cent of union membership with the majority in shipbuilding, construction, manufacturing and the hotel sectors. In certain house unions, the migrant workers' membership can be as high as 70 per cent. Migrant workers enjoy the same union protection, services and benefits as local members. In some cases unions have negotiated lower subscription fees subsidised by management.

Migrant workers in Singapore also enjoy the opportunity to upgrade their skills and improve their career prospects. Many acquire new skills and formal certification of competency in a trade.

In May 2002 a scheme to accredit foreign domestic workers agencies by the Consumers Association of Singapore, a non-profit organization founded by the Singapore National Trades Union Congress in 1971, was launched. Under this scheme it is compulsory for all employment agencies managing foreign domestic workers to be accredited from June 2004 before their licences can be renewed. These agencies would have to show that they have acceptable, fair-trading practices, counselling/mediation system and other good practices provided under the accreditation to safeguard the interests of foreign domestic workers.

The Singapore National Trades Union Congress Migrant Workers Forum is actively pursuing various means and initiatives to further improve policies and programmes aiming to protect the interests and well-being of migrant workers in Singapore. We are calling on the government and employers to ensure the welfare and rights of migrant workers in Singapore and will continue to work together with them for this purpose.

The issues on the agenda of the International Labour Conference address the challenges we are facing today. We look forward to the second round of discussions on human resources training and development with our Workers' delegate, Mrs Haimah Yacob, spokesperson for the Workers' group.

Our economies today are driven by knowledge and new technologies. There is an urgent need to help every individual have at least the basic knowledge and skills to adapt to change and benefit from globalization.

As the presence of delegations representing workers, government and employers attending the International Labour Conference each year attests, we recognize and accept our shared responsibility to work together to achieve sustainable development and decent work for all.

The challenge is to make real and measurable progress. Our workers and their families will experience a better life, not from what we say about what needs to be done, but from what we are able to do together.

Mr. KANÍK *(Minister of Labour, Social Affairs and Family, Slovakia)*

Allow me to open my address by congratulating the President on his election to preside over the 92nd Session of the Conference of the International Labour Organization and wishing him and the elected Vice-Presidents a successful session of the Conference.

The Slovak Republic, together with nine other States, joined the European Union on 1 May 2004, accomplishing, thus, one of the most important milestones in our history.

Our common goals, the goals of the International Labour Organization and of the EU countries cause us to make an effort to help to create preconditions to develop employment, reduce unemployment and to have decent work, as defined also in the strategic pillars of the ILO.

The advanced economies of the EU and OECD countries, and equally the Slovak economy, fight three elementary problems that create a barrier in overcoming persistent imbalances in the labour market: in particular, the insufficient capacity of economic entities to create productive jobs, limited motivation to become formally employed and distortions and rigidity in the labour market.

In Slovakia, we see these three problems as a major challenge, as principally limiting factors that have, over a long period, inhibited the development of our labour market and, in particular, caused a more significant decrease of the unemployment rates.

For that reason we submitted and adopted in Parliament a principal change in the pension security system last year that is a prerequisite for a reduction in the rate of contributions. Since 1 January 2004, the contribution has been reduced by more than 3 per cent and this trend will continue in the next year.

The second problem, limited motivation to become formally employed, was connected mainly with the demotivating character of social benefits. Minimum difference between the possible social income and the income from regular employment results in a preference for passive reception of social benefits.

We changed the entire social system, introduced activity allowances, made the instruments of the active labour market more transparent and obtainable, all in compliance with the principle of making work pay. With the participation of self-government authorities, civil associations, charities and churches we have scaled up the system of public works. These public works strengthen local partnerships and create a sense of community, solidarity and integrity.

The third problem – rigidity and distortions in the labour market – was caused mainly by inappropriate legislation. That was why we substantially amended the Labour Code. It was an uneasy political struggle accompanied by difficult negotiations with social partners. I, thus, especially appreciate the fact that we have adopted this extremely important law by a consensus of all tripartite social partners.

Also, thanks to the abovementioned changes, unemployment in Slovakia dropped and the trend of decreasing unemployment continues. The new social policy has become a significant incentive for growth in foreign investments and creation of new jobs in Slovakia. Last year, employment grew by almost 2 per cent which is a good indicator of sound development in the labour market.

We are facing serious challenges. Integration within Europe and also worldwide globalization processes places great demands on industrial relations and on labour markets of member countries. I believe that the best path is one of openness and flexibility that respects entrepreneurial spirit, invention and free initiative of the individual. This path, however, also takes into account the need to support, protect and assist those who need it most.

I wish all of you and the participants of the 92nd Session of the International Labour Conference many stimulating ideas, constructive discussions and courage, so vital in adopting tough but necessary solutions.

Mr. THAPALIYA *(Employers' delegate, Nepal)*

It is with great pleasure that I would like to extend hearty greetings to the President and all the delegates at the 92nd Session of the Conference of the ILO on behalf of the Employers' Council of the Federation of the Nepalese Chambers of Commerce and Industry and the employers of Nepal.

At the same time, on behalf of the employers of Nepal, I take the pleasure of extending my heartiest congratulations to the President and Vice-Presidents on their election to preside over the 92nd Session of the Conference.

I would like to extend my sincere appreciation to the Director-General for his comprehensive Report on the role of the ILO in helping build better working relations in the world. The issue of "organizing for social justice" requires a climate of firm commitment on the part of the employers and the workers to the survival and growth of their respective organizations and the economy as a whole.

We, in Nepal, are continuing dialogue with our social partners. But we have felt that excessive and abusive exercise at rights and freedoms at times causes social instability, hampering investment and the process of growth, thus prevent the rising tide of unemployed workers from exercising their right to work.

I think the migrant workforce is a global phenomenon, in the sense that a developed economy needs more labourers with different skills, while the underdeveloped economies have an abundance of workers with a lower skills level. People move from one level of development to another level where there are opportunities. Employers are accused of carrying out bad practices in their employment of migrant workers, and it is said that, in the most simple terms, it is the employers who gain. This is not always true.

Within given parameters, all of us employers would like to give a fair deal to migrant employees. The problem here, and one with most of us employers have faced, is that migrant workers would like to have the best of both worlds and that raises a conflict situation between the employers and the migrant employees, which the employers being blamed as the exploiters.

On the other hand there can arise conflict situations. between the employers and society in general for the employers' hosting of the "herds of unwanted guests". Thus, the protection of migrant workers should be considered through a more holistic approach, with a socio-political and economic consideration, rather than just on emotional issues.

The traditional welfare-based philosophy may not work in the changing context of globalization, requiring workers to be retrained regularly in order to enhance their employability within a broad, flexible employment mechanism. For this, the concept of human resource development has to be redefined, both philosophically and with regards to its value deliverance.

I am sure all of my colleagues here are very well aware of the present conflict in Nepalese society. The biggest impact in such a situation comes in the economic sector and employers are always the first line to face it. The employers of the developing countries are, in a way, shouldering a burden by training people for their counterparts in the developed countries. Though society gets foreign exchange earnings, the burden on the employers is relatively high due to the training and retraining of employees and the quality and competencies lost because of that. Thus, in a conflict-ridden society, as we have experienced, uncompetitiveness may come not from the internal weakness of the management but as a result of external conflict itself.

I think that, in a society like ours, the ILO should explore the possibility, of perhaps increasing its role in human resources development.

We, the social partners, and the Government of Nepal are serious about programmes such as elimination of child labour, the Programme on Decent Work, competitiveness and productivity, which is the main concern of the ILO.

The Nepalese employers continue to dialogue with the Government and several international agencies in order to build suitable mechanisms for the necessary assistance to the conflict-affected enterprises. At present, the framework of social safety requirements must be broadened and supplemented or complemented by the conflict safety requirement of the employers.

At FNCCI we are very appreciative of the Director-General and the support we have received from the ILO over the years, and we look forward to increased fruitful cooperation. We need the good wishes and cooperation of all our friends to emerge from the situation that we are in.

Original Spanish: MR. IYANGA DJOBA MALANGO *(Deputy-Minister, Ministry for Labour and Social Security, Equatorial Guinea)*

I would like to begin by conveying the warmest greetings of peace and solidarity on behalf of the nation of Equatorial Guinea and its President, Head of State, and Founding President of the Democratic Party of Equatorial Guinea, His Excellency Obiang Nguema Mbasogo. Greetings to all men and women throughout the world and particularly the nationalities represented in this Conference, as we are committed to finding solutions to improve the world of work and to rise to the great challenges that are faced by citizens throughout the modern world. Their fate does not depend only upon domestic policies in their respective countries of origin, but also upon decisions that frequently are taken far beyond their own borders.

As we enter into the discussion on the Report of the Chairperson of the Governing Body and the Report of the Director-General, may I begin, personally and on behalf of the delegation that accompanies me, by associating myself with previous speakers in expressing our sincere congratulations to the President for having been unanimously elected to preside over this 92nd Session of the International Labour Conference. We are certain that, under his guidance, wisdom and energy, the work of this session will be hailed a success. These congratulations are extended also to the Vice-Presidents and to the Officers of the Conference.

We have read with care the Director-General's Report, devoted this year to an analytical assessment of the activities of the Organization in the biennium 2002-03. Equally carefully, we have read the other documents that are before this session of the Conference. We must pay tribute to the Director-General and to his colleagues for the quality of the documentation and for the effort that has been made by the International Labour Office to fulfil the strategic objectives of the Organization and the various declarations on the principles of the Organization and the core rights in the workplace. We also pay tribute to the ILO for implementing the mandates received from the Governing Body and the directors of the ILO during the period under consideration.

For reasons of protocol, and because of limited time, I shall refer only to certain aspects of this debate which we would like to highlight. Equatorial Guinea is a State that is committed to universality and solidarity. Not only are we doing all we can to fulfil our commitments as a Member of the International Labour Organization, but we are also involved at the international level, as evidenced by the payment of our financial contributions and above all by the fact that we have ratified all of the Core conventions of this Organization. We are also represented at almost all of the organizations of the United Nations System and at the interregional, regional and subregional organizations in our immediate environment.

In this sense, and following the path traced out by the Director-General when he presented the programme assessment for the biennium under consideration, we can say that, in terms of labour standards and basic rights and principles in the workplace, we have ratified all of the instruments on fundamental rights at work i.e. those on freedom of association, forced labour, gender equality, abolition of forced labour and child labour, discrimination in its various forms, etc., and we are promoting compliance with the obligations enshrined in these international instruments and in other constitutional provisions. With the support of the International Labour Office, we are bringing our legislation and our practices into line with the provisions of these international instruments, with a view to meeting our international commitments to decent work.

With respect to employment, the Government has created a climate that is conducive to capital investment, both national and foreign. This climate entails the adoption of standards that promote investment and create an environment of peace, political stability and concord, which will be attractive to the investor and will protect his investments. We invite any businessman of good faith to conduct his business in Equatorial Guinea, where he will be received with open arms. I must make an appeal and denounce the negative attitude of those who claim to be businessmen but who wish to perpetrate terrorist acts and wish to destabilize the country. I refer, for example, to the attack of 6 March 2004, which was led by a group of mercenaries of various nationalities. Thank God, and thanks to the cooperation of the countries that are the friends of Equatorial Guinea and the efforts of our own security forces to loyally carry out their duties, timely action was taken to prevent this attack from causing a blood bath in the peaceful country that is Equatorial Guinea.

Consequently, I say to this Organization that, convinced of the need to promote lasting peace, at the global level based on social justice and with a single tripartite structure for the whole of the United Nations system comprising representatives of workers, employers and governments, we condemn these acts, which contribute neither to the economic growth needed to promote employment nor to social peace and nor to the security of the people, as recognized by this Organization and all of the organizations of the United Nations system.

We have selected the path of the ILO and we are committed to moving forward. However, our work is not all that straightforward because, as you know, we are a developing country with a major shortage of the human resources that are needed to manage our own development. Nevertheless, we are considered to be a medium-income country because of the presence of oil. The oil industry has inherited an infrastructure that is in a very poor state or inexistent in certain cases.

I would like to conclude by wishing every success to this 92nd Session of the Conference in the hope that its conclusions will lead to a better and more human world with greater solidarity. The delegation of Equatorial Guinea will do everything it can to support the objectives of this Conference.

Original French: Mr. WIJFFELS (representative, International Association of Economic and Social Councils and Similar Institutions)

My speech is not aimed at making comments on the excellent Report of the Director-General. However, I would just like to note that his observations and recommendations are completely in line with our own thinking and our intention to fully commit ourselves to the political process we entered into with the ILO on 27 May 2004 when, upon the invitation of the Director-General, we held the annual General Assembly of the International Association of Economic and Social Councils and Similar Institutions here at the ILO headquarters.

Our concerns are the same as yours. Your ambitions are the same as ours. You have the privilege of bringing together on a tripartite basis the representatives of governments, employers and workers. We are lucky enough during our councils, held on a national basis, to bring together the social partners and various people responsible for civil society. The advice we give to governments is the result of patiently listening to others, conducting joint analyses and seeking compromises, or rather the most acceptable approach for the greatest number of participants at our councils; this advice also gives the social partners the challenge of basing their activities on the common good, without exclusivity and without a monopolistic form of thinking. We think that we are a representative component of organized civilian society.

Because of this characteristic and this responsibility, in 1999 we decided to attempt to develop internationally what we know how to do on a national basis, namely to promote and practice social dialogue.

As we stand today, we represent 50 institutions from all continents; from the Economic and Social Council of China to, most recently, that of Brazil; from the Korean Tripartite Commission to the National Economic and Social Council of Algeria. We have decided to work together in the international association, which has asked me to come here and address you today.

Working together means listening to the priorities of all, from the North and South, on issues of common interest. It means seeking a common way of analysing the situation, and trying to establish a common line of action for major subjects specified by the United Nations.

The year 2004 is witnessing the beginning of cooperation between the ILO and economic and social councils and similar institutions throughout the world. As regards all the difficult subjects that we must deal with, such as globalization, migration flows, child labour, and the economic and social promotion of women, our councils, to help with the initial stages of your work, can communicate the results of our work, and following your decisions we can do our utmost to ensure their effective implementation.

In conclusion, I came here, on behalf of our international association, to say that, in this context, we are entirely at the disposal of the ILO.

Mr. AMAN (Minister of Labour and Employment, Bangladesh)

We warmly congratulate the President and other officers of the Conference on their election. We are confident that under their avid leadership the Conference will be a success. I assure you of our full support and cooperation.

We thank the Director-General for his Report, ILO Programme implementation 2002-03, which provides a comprehensive and focused report of the progress made during that period. We have followed with admiration his efforts to bring labour and employment issues to the forefront of the global agenda. The Director-General deserves our sincere appreciation. We are confident that during his second term as well, he will guide the Organization with his usual dedication and commitment in addressing the challenges to labour issues.

The ILO has improved its ability to focus available resources on key objectives and programme priorities. Technical cooperation and technical assistance are the primary means for the attainment of ILO objectives. It is important that these activities be strengthened in our countries. We ask the membership of the ILO to make sufficient resources available to meet these needs.

I would like to extend our sincere appreciation to the World Commission on the Social Dimension of Globalization for its timely, comprehensive and objective report. The Director-General of the ILO also deserves our special thanks for his efforts in setting up the Commission, selecting its members and for facilitating their task.

While the latent potential of globalization may be immense, as noted in the Report, its benefits are not shared equitably. This is particularly true for disadvantaged countries, such as least developed countries. We believe coordinated efforts are required to bring about fairer rules for international trade, investment and finance. It is imperative that the interests of the least developed countries, the weakest link in the chain of development, be protected through provision of special and differential treatment. We fully endorse the launching of Policy Coherence Initiatives, as recommended in the Commission's Report.

For Bangladesh, poverty alleviation is dependent on sustained growth and employment generation. This requires both national and international efforts. Decent work should be made an element of the global agenda. May I at this stage, refer to the ILO's Decent Work Pilot Programme in Bangladesh. I would like to thank the Director-General for inclusion of my country in the project. Given the large-scale unemployment and high level of poverty in the country, the ILO's Decent Work Agenda is of special significance for Bangladesh. I am happy to note that the ILO is working closely with my Government in implementing this Programme.

The issue of movement and natural persons is of particular importance for a labour–sending country like Bangladesh. We believe labour, an important factor of production, should have the mobility that other factors of production enjoy, but with clear rules and regulations. The services sector is emerging as one of the most important sectors within our economy, and internationally as well. The greatest potential benefits to both originating and destination countries lies in the movement of natural persons as service providers. We are happy that the ILO has placed due importance on this issue. We believe that there is a clear need for a multilateral framework which would provide uniform and transparent rules for the cross-border movement of service providers.

In close cooperation with the ILO, and with support from our development partners, we have achieved considerable success in eliminating child labour from many industries. Our experience in eliminating child labour from the garments sector is now considered as a model. The Government of Bangladesh, under the dynamic leadership of Prime Minister Begum Khaleda Zia, is committed to eliminating the worst forms of child labour. Under her direction, innovative schemes and alternative solutions such as special financial incentives to encourage increased enrolment and stop children dropping out of school on economic grounds.

In conclusion, our lack of resources has prevented us from taking many other measures, such as social safety nets. We hope that, with progress and economic growth, we will achieve our desired goals.

Original Russian: Mr. GRYSHCHENKO *(Employers' delegate, Ukraine)*

It is a great honour for me to address this Conference on behalf of the Ukrainian employers, and to express my gratitude to the President of the Conference, to Mr. Juan Somavia and to the organizers of the Conference for the excellent working conditions and the atmosphere of constructive dialogue which undoubtedly will help us reach a positive result.

In examining the issues on our agenda, I note the importance of the analysis of the level of implementation of the ILO Declaration on Fundamental Principles and Rights at Work. We believe that, for the effective application of the provisions of the Freedom of Association and Protection of the Right to Organise Convention, 1948 (No. 87), we must set priorities which will allow us, within the framework of the activities of the ILO, to further develop the right of organization of workers and employers.

Most important for us is the task of creating a united, strong and representative employers' group at national, regional and sectoral levels. This is a very difficult task, because, just 12 years ago, there was only one employer in Ukraine — the State. The word "employer" did not exist in the vocabularies of official or political figures.

Ukraine shares the concern of the world community with regard to the spread of AIDS. We are grateful to the International Labour Organization for its constructive work in Ukraine to minimize the consequences of the AIDS epidemic. Ukrainian employers are interested in ensuring equal rights for workers. This is reflected in the Labour Code that is currently being drawn up. We are also interested in defeating any further development of this disease.

In order to arrive at a solution to the problems facing us, we require a rational compromise on the part of the social partners. We are deeply convinced that the most important thing is the process of social dialogue. This means the search for a balance of interests which will foster economic and social progress.

We note the extreme effectiveness of the measures which are being undertaken in Ukraine under the aegis of the ILO. We are and will remain grateful for the technical assistance and corresponding consultations of ILO experts as regards the application of Conventions and Recommendations of the ILO in the Ukraine and in studying employment issues in the development of the labour markets, in fighting poverty, and in stemming the trade of and trafficking in human beings.

In this context, the employers have high hopes from new programmes of cooperation between the ILO, and the Government and the social partners. One such programme was initiated during a recent meeting with the Confederation of Swiss Employers.

The last year has been extremely important for us and included a special event – the accession of the Federation of Employers of Ukraine into the International Organisation of Employers. This gives us the possibility to take direct part in drawing up international standards in the area of labour relations and opens up great possibilities for our development.

An array of issues are of interest to us today. The most important of these include the accession of Ukraine to the World Trade Organization, the fact that the borders of the European Union now reach to Ukraine, Ukraine's integration in the world economy and participation in the international distribution of labour, implementation of international legal regulations, standards and certifications.

However, the process of globalization is a nuanced one. We understand very well that the integration of Ukraine into the world economy means that not only will markets be open to us, but that we will simultaneously need to take a series of measures in order to protect domestic production.

The end of the twentieth century was known for the fall of the Berlin Wall as a symbol of the Iron Curtain that had closed society, and now the world has become a more open place. After a number of years of crises, the Ukrainian economy has undergone a resurgence. Ukraine has the same area as France and is genuinely interested in the possibilities offered by European integration – all the more so because we realize that the geographical centre of Europe is, in fact, in Ukraine.

But we note certain trends resulting from the approach of the EU borders that are a cause for concern in our country. Are not the many instances of discriminatory action on the part of various European institutions with respect to Ukraine signs of the introduction of a new iron curtain by the European Union which could close the great Ukrainian people out of the European family?

This is of great concern to employers. The discriminatory conditions for accession to the World Trade Organization, as well as other elements which I shall not mention, hinder Ukraine's economic development and cause continuing poverty and the growth of unemployment.

We call upon the International Labour Organization to begin a separate examination of the issues, which should focus on these processes and try to attenuate the economic consequences for neighbouring countries of the European Union. We also call upon the international community to study how to better distribute employment opportunities, labour resources, flows of labour migration and the well-being of nations as a whole.

Original Portuguese: Mr. VAZ DE ALMEIDA *(Minister for Labour, Employment and Solidarity, Sao Tome and Principe)*

It is a great pleasure and honour for me to add my voice to that of the distinguished delegates and illustrious guests present at this assembly and convey, on my own behalf and on behalf of my delegation, my congratulations to the President on his election to chair the 92nd Session of the International Labour Conference. My congratulations reflect the growing political will of my Government to increase the strength of its existing relations with the ILO.

I should like to take advantage of this unique opportunity to offer a few thoughts, however brief they may be, about the brilliant presentation given by the Director-General. The subjects dealt with include various labour matters and are extremely significant because they list questions which arise at international level on present and future problems concerning the well-being of the member States of the ILO.

This year we have had the opportunity to think about topics such as freedom of association, trade union organization and the effective recognition of the right to collective bargaining. Notwithstanding the numerous difficulties facing Sao Tome and Principe, we still devote particular attention to the matters raised in this first-class Report presented by the Director-General of the ILO.

With this in mind, and in order to take account of the clauses in laws 4, 5 and 6/92, on strikes, trade unions and regulations for individual labour conditions respectively, which are in force in our country, the Government of Sao Tome and Principe ratified the Freedom of Association and the Protection of the Right to Organise Convention, 1948 (No. 87), and the Right to Organise and Collective Bargaining Convention, 1949 (No. 98), in June 1992. As far as freedoms and rights are concerned, our Government, in article 35 of Law 1/2003 on constitutional review, enshrined the right to freedom of association, whereby citizens have the right, without any prior authorization, to establish associations as long as this does not contravene the law of the land or call into question the Constitution or national independence.

At the 91st Session of the International Labour Conference, we took the opportunity to announce publicly our commitment to the ratification of several further Conventions which have been adapted in our own legislation. Today, at the 92nd Session, we are proud, although it has cost us a huge effort because of the lack of sufficient staff in the first instance, to inform this body that the Government has succeeded in completing some of the internal procedures imposed by the Constitution of the ILO in order to ratify ten Conventions: the Abolition of Forced Labour Convention, 1957 (No. 105), the Maternity Protection Convention, 2000 (No. 183), the Safety and Health in Agriculture Convention, 2001 (No. 184), the Collective Bargaining Convention, 1981 (No. 154), the Labour Relations (Public Service) Convention, 1978 (No. 151), the Workers' Representatives Convention, 1971 (No. 135), the Minimum Age Convention, 1973 (No. 138), the Forced Labour Convention, 1930 (No. 29), the Worst Forms of Child Labour Convention, 1999 (No. 182), and the Occupational Safety and Health Convention, 1981 (No. 155). We realize that, to meet all our obligations as a Member of the ILO, we still have a very long way to go, and we are fully aware that our labour regime still has many failings. In order to counteract this, we have drawn up a general bill on labour which will be submitted for discussion by all the institutions concerned and subsequently for approval to the national Parliament. We also plan to revise our laws on trade unions and on strikes.

It is a pleasure to inform this august body of certain measures which could be considered as having been successful with respect to institutionalized social consultation in our country. The cooperation between the various parties involved has been remarkable and noteworthy. All economic and social matters and issues connected with the life of workers in Sao Tome and Principe have been discussed in order to seek consensual decisions. Collective bargaining is still a very new practice for us and we have not seen much success so far because of the lack of diversity in our companies.

All the actions mentioned above, in addition to the tripartite composition of Sao Tome and Principe, are clear signs of our respect for tripartism as instituted by the ILO.

To conclude, I would like once again to call for the technical cooperation of the ILO in order to improve the effectiveness of work at ministerial level and to express a vote of confidence in the quality of the work which remains to be done. We await impatiently the conclusions of this meeting which all delegations will pass on to their respective governments.

Mr. KEARNEY *(Representative, International Textile, Garment and Leather Workers' Federation)*

The ILO deems decent work essential for sustainable development, poverty reduction and the preservation of human rights in a globalizing interdependent world. Decent work is more than a dream for millions employed in the textile, clothing and footwear industries; an unachievable dream in the face of falling wages, deteriorating working conditions and growing exploitation.

Unsustainable development – today the textile, clothing and footwear industries are in turmoil. Millions of jobs are on the move as nations race to undercut each other by ignoring the implementation of labour standards in the quest for a share of world markets. Bangladesh is set to lose more than half of its 1.8 million government jobs because of trade liberalization at the end of this year. Bangladesh's Government has not raised the minimum wage since 1994, does not enforce its labour legislation and has not permitted trade unions in its export processing zones. But rather than protecting the country's industrial base, the absence of decent work is underminded and makes development unsustainable.

Poverty reduction – nearly every nation in Central America is heavily dependant on the garment industry for manufacturing employment. The workers in the sector say that their communities are now worse off than before industrialization. Interestingly, malnutrition among women garment workers is greater than among any other group in the region.

Preservation of human rights – in reality, freedom of association, a key human right, does not exist in many nations. Take Sri Lanka Workers at Workwear Lanka are workers who have been threatened, abused and fired for attempting to form a trade union. Take Uganda. In spite of a 100 per cent membership in a number of factories, unions have been denied recognition for more than ten years. The consequences are dire. At Apparel Tri-star (Uganda) Ltd. workers are virtual prisoners, denied permission to leave the work site, pressured to work when sick, physically beaten by supervisors, fired when they become pregnant and subjected to sexual harassment. Female workers are having to share toilets and even their dormitory beds with their male counterparts.

Take Haiti. This week workers at the Ouanaminthe Free-Trade Zone are on strike because of inhuman treatment, including violence, intimidation, harassment, forced stripping of women union leaders, beatings, kidnappings and non-payment of wages. Nearly all these cases involve export processing zone enterprises and the national governments concerned are either too inefficient, too incompetent or too uncaring to enforce international labour standards or even their own, usually inadequate, national labour legislation. Often governments connive with the exploiters. Such governments' in action not only hurts their own workers and communities, but in a globalized interdependent world impacts on workers everywhere.

Take Indonesia whose Government has taken steps to enact and implement up-to-date labour legislation.

Now, both foreign and domestic investors say they are no longer optimistic about maintaining or creating jobs, because they are being undercut by numerous other Asian nations where labour legislation is weaker and largely unenforced.

Why does a brand name like Nike have to develop an infrastructure for the application of international labour standards through its supply chain? Nike should not have to do the job of the Government of the People's Republic of China. And The Gap should not have to substitute for the inadequacies of the Government of El Salvador on labour issues. If governments were doing their job, voluntary initiatives to avoid sweatshop labour would not be needed.

When governments commit to decent work, the impact is dramatic. Until last year, there was not a single trade union with a contract in any of Guatemala's 350 garment factories. But following The Government's intervention in two problem companies – Choi Shin and Cimatextiles – it took only six weeks to secure trade union recognition, resolve the problems that existed at that time and conclude a good modern contract. Clearly, determined government action can deliver decent work.

The ILO campaigns for decent work will only succeed if it has buy-in from member States. The ILO urgently needs to embark on a new campaign which might be titled "Governments, wake up". Such a campaign would aim to compel governments everywhere to ratify the core Conventions of the ILO, enact and implement the necessary supporting legislation and generally promote decent work.

Governments which fail to respond cannot be permitted to undermine the efforts of their neighbours. The ILO will need to move from persuasion to sanction if it is to enforce sustainable development, secure poverty reduction and preserve human rights worldwide.

In a globalized interdependent world, enforceable global rule and labour standards are essential. And the international community must ensure that individual governments promote and enforce decent work or otherwise forfeit their country's access to world markets. That might finally make every government wake up to the current criminal neglect of workers' rights in sectors like textiles, clothing and footwear, in so many parts of the world. Then, decent work could cease to be merely a dream and become a reality.

Mr. PODDAR (Employers' delegate, India)

I congratulate the President on his election to preside over this session of the Conference, which is going to be historic for debating the Report of the World Commission on the Social Dimension of Globalization and assessing its impact. We have tremendous faith in his wisdom to steer the debate to a meaningful conclusion.

I would also like to compliment the architects of the Report, who very painstakingly mirrored the face of ongoing globalization in a bold manner.

There is candid acknowledgement that the rules of globalization are unfair and support only a few industrialized nations. This is an endorsement of the stand taken by us at the WTO and other forums. Trade of manufactured goods is liberalized, whereas agriculture remains protected. Similarly capital and technology can travel freely across the globe but the movement of labour is restricted. This hampers development of those economies for whom agriculture and skilled workforce are the only comparative advantages.

Global trade has expanded faster than global GDP over the last two decades, yet, it is not uniform. The share of the low-income countries in global exports is only 3.4 per cent whereas the high-income countries accounted for 75.2 per cent. Even the FDI inflow into the 12 developing countries during the 1990s has been in the order of 74.7 per cent, while the rest of the 176 countries had to be content with a meagre share of 25.3 per cent.

It is heartening to see that globalization has lifted 200 million people from the depths of poverty in East Asia, yet nearly 550 million people are living below that line on less than US1$ a day and nearly 1,100 million people are living in absolute poverty, globally. Globalization has failed to change their lives. Global unemployment has also increased to 186 million by 2003 with higher incidents of unemployment in Asia and sub-Saharan Africa. These indicators pose a challenge to the process of globalization, which has to provide a socio-economic floor and a human face to the global economy, as we are reminded of by the Declaration of Philadelphia that "poverty anywhere is a threat to prosperity everywhere". This is the time, globalization needs to be given a new face.

I was very happy to hear Mr. Somavia, on the opening day of this session of the Conference. I entirely agree with him that there cannot be globalization without localization. We need a good national government to deliver, but we also need a transparent and efficient global government to provide a bridge to the future.

Economic development has to have a social face. This is finely ingrained in our value systems. I am tempted to quote Pt. Jawahar Lal Nehru, the first Prime Minister of India, when he addressed the Fourth ILO Asian Regional Conference in 1957, and I quote, "In India, we are very much concerned with increasing our production, because unless we produce wealth we shall not have any means for the betterment of man. But in the production of wealth, we can never forget the social or the human aspect of the process; even if we should forget, conditions will remind us, because the people are politically conscious and will not put up with many things that they might have put up with in the past."

How true his vision was can be seen in the recent elections in India – the present Government won the election on the agenda "Globalization with human face".

To maintain the human dimension and attend to the negative fallouts of globalization, particularly in the developing and underdeveloped countries, strong backup support of skill development, employment generation and poverty alleviation programmes are critically important, and the ILO's role in this is significant.

The cross-border movement of people has seen a spurt during post globalization, since globalization has failed to generate jobs where most of the people live. It is therefore necessary to build national and international policies, regulating cross-border migration which can serve as a force for growth, development and well-regulated globalization with equal opportunity.

Globalization has spurred business process outsourcing to achieve, inter-alia, efficiency, and attempts to stop BPO or restrict immigration of skills through legislative measure would further distort the process of globalization. What we need is to fine-tune the process to make it more participative and not to be selective. I am sure the debate would resolve these contradictions to smoothen the process of globalization for the future.

Before closing, I thank the ILO for the Global Report, which is excellent, but falls short of recommendations and does not indicate clearly where to go from here. I think the debate will draw a road map and concrete conclusions will emerge for its implementation.

Ms. LUCERO *(representative, Brotherhood of Asian Trade Unionists)*

It is indeed a distinct honour and a rare opportunity to address this august body of the 92nd Session of the International Labour Conference that you have kindly accorded to us in the Brotherhood of Asian Trade Unions, (BATU) the regional organization in Asia of the World Confederation of Labour, for which we sincerely thank you.

On behalf of the Brotherhood of Asian Trade Unions, I extend our fraternal felicitations to everyone, and assurance of our full cooperation in the daunting task of jointly reviewing and evaluating our past endeavours, and hopefully learning from these experiences to be able to plan and plot our joint and concerted actions in future toward a better world of work for all.

The first Report of the second cycle of the Global Report, presented by the honourable Director-General under the follow-up to the ILO Declaration on Fundamental Principles and Rights at Work entitled *Organizing for social justice* is an exemplary work in the field of research and analysis, an exposition of competence and objectivity, and a reliable reference and guide material for all social partners in our quest for a more just and humane society.

In close cooperation with, and active participation of, the responsible men and women of the ILO Office in the Asian region, and their technical expertise, my organization, enjoying consultative status with the ILO, has conducted several consultative and strategic conferences with its key leaders and militants in the region during the immediate past year. In two of its recent meetings, in Jakarta and Kuala Lumpur, top national leaders from Indonesia, Malaysia, the Philippines, Thailand, Cambodia, Pakistan, Bangladesh, Sri Lanka, India, Hong Kong (China), Taiwan and South Korea, have come together to engender further awareness and common understanding of the fundamental rights at work, providing a venue for systematic information, education and communication, and strategic actions for an organized and coherent region-wide response to cross-cutting issues concerning the Declaration and the Decent Work Agenda.

We are glad to share with you that the multilateral dialogue among social partners has been successfully employed in these activities, and the results are more than the widespread understanding and trust among them, that further led to sincere commitments to best respect and make use of these principles and rights for a total and sustainable socio-economic and political development for all.

Pursuant to the popular decisions of these evaluation and monitoring meetings, several projects and activities were designed and implemented to follow up implementation and ratification of ILO Conventions, through the BATU norm and socio-economic development programmes in collaboration with our partners.

Advocacy on current issues affecting the Declaration and calls for action are regularly published in our newsletter, *Vision and Milestone,* circulated to all its affiliates and partners on such issues as the assassinations of our trades union leaders in Cambodia and India, as well specific repressive working conditions and violations of the right to freedom of association of workers in the various countries in the region. The cause of migrants, the labour situation in multinational enterprises and expert processing zones, and the precarious working conditions of those in the informal economy, have always been among the issues on the immediate agenda and have been the focus of concerns. We have endeavoured to document and objectively analyse the sad plight under the present realities that has engulfed our workers, especially the women, which is more kindly characterized as bereft of social safety nets in our globalizing, neo-liberal world economy, as well as the consequent decline of membership in trade unions. The BATU delegates are one in expressing our solidarity with you in the task of building on the progress that has so far been achieved in the promotion of freedom of association and rights to collective bargaining in a changing global context. We endorse the recommended objectives of the ILO for the next four years on universal ratification of the ILO Conventions Nos. 87 and 98, updated action plan, building up the institutional framework and strengthening advisory and advocacy activities.

Original Lao: Mr. PHENGKHAMMY *(Minister of Labour and Social Affairs, Lao People's Democratic Republic)*

On behalf of the delegation of the Lao People's Democratic Republic, allow me to express our honour in participating in the 92nd Session of the International Labour Conference in 2004.

I would also like to extend sincere congratulations to the President and the Officers for their election. I am convinced that under their capable and experienced guidance, this Conference will successfully achieve its objectives.

The recent spread of avian influenza and severe acute respiratory syndrome (SARS) negatively affected socio-economic development and impacted on the livelihood and health of the population in the region, as well as in our country. To address this crisis, our Government applied certain procedures and measures in coordination with other countries in the region, and endeavoured jointly with the World Health Organization and other international organizations to restrict and bring remedies to the situation. These diseases have now been eradicated from our country.

To further work towards the general goals set out by our Government within a timeframe of 5 years (2001-05), emphasis is being placed on the implementation of major programmes, such as the poverty eradication programme, the shifting cultivation stabilization programme, and the opium production eradication programme, among others. The successful realization of these programmes requires financial and human resources. Therefore, labour skills and vocational development, especially in the case of former shifting farmers and opium producers, are of primary importance for our country. Nevertheless, the Government's judicious policy and support from friendly countries and international organizations have allowed us to progressively advance our endeavours. Among these, the International Labour Organization has provided support and assistance in many projects relating to training, seminars, prevention of exploitation, trade in women and children, and others.

In the current process of globalization, science and technology have developed rapidly, thus allowing countries to introduce modern progress for national development more rapidly. However, this also represents a challenge for us and, more particularly, for developing and least developed countries. This globalization process calls for enhanced mutual consultations, cooperation and assistance. The Lao People's Democratic Republic will continue to apply its policy of cooperation with the ASEAN countries, neighbouring countries, friendly countries around the world, international organizations, governmental organizations and non-governmental organizations, to acquire the necessary funds and experience for the qualitative development of Lao labour, and for further national socio-economic development to enable the country's gradual integration with ASEAN countries, and the region, and lift the Lao People's Democratic Republic and its people from the ranks of least developed countries and out of from poverty, by 2020.

I am convinced that, with the ILO's extensive experience in extending assistance to its member countries around the world, further and wide assistance will be provided, more particularly to its developing member countries, with increasingly successful results.

Mr. ZHARIKOV (representative, World Federation of Trade Unions)

The World Federation of Trade Unions welcomes the fact that the current session of the International Labour Conference focuses attention on programme implementation, the social dimension of globalization, rights at work, as well as the situation of workers in the occupied Arab territories.

Despite the solemnly declared intentions and programmes of action, adopted at the Copenhagen and the Millennium Summits and the efforts of the ILO, the social and economic situation in the world is not improving, but worsening. According to ILO statistics, unemployment in 2003 was the highest ever registered and poverty is spreading and deepening. Up to 80 per cent or more of employees in most member States do not have the possibility to establish trade unions and to negotiate collectively.

Conventions Nos. 87 and 98 are not observed by a number of employers and Governments. The gross violation of trade union rights in many countries continues. A large majority of the giant transnational corporations prevent their employees from exercising the right to freedom of association, and in many cases, trade unions established by employees are not recognized.

In the name of globalization, liberalization and privatization, strategies are imposed to wipe out almost everything that has been gained by trade unions in the last century. The IMF, World Bank and WTO continue to promote policies that amount to neocolonialism.

While occupation and genocide in Palestine, in the occupied territories of the Syrian Golan and in the south of Lebanon continue, causing brutal violations of human and trade union rights and freedoms, which is the focus of the Report of the Director-General to this Conference, another Arab State, Iraq, is being occupied in violation of international law. The occupying forces are suppressing the rights of workers and people, and are even resorting to torture.

Defying the opinion of the overwhelming majority of United Nations member States, there has been an increase in the cruel, unilateral sanctions that are being used against Cuba and Syria.

What is wrong with this world? The increasing mass actions of people and trade unions throughout the world in recent years provide a clear answer. People no longer demand only declarations, but real solutions to the mounting problems. They no longer believe mere promises and declarations. They resolutely condemn unilateralism.

We support the main directions of ILO activities, especially the decent work for all campaign and the measures to follow up the Declaration on Fundamental Principles and Rights at Work.

As was stressed at the World Trade Union Forum, recently held in Mumbai, India, trade unions are keen to build a trade union coalition to protect the rights and interests of working people, and to contribute towards a greater consensus within the ILO on major issues. Progress in this direction depends also on the elimination of the double standards that are applied in certain cases, and on attempts to utilize the ILO for political aims, which has nothing to do with its mandate and nature. It is also essential that the ILO adopt a sharper, stronger position towards the policies of neo-liberal globalization and the results of such globalization it should also extend its influence on the economic institutions in the direction suggested by the World Commission on Social Dimension of Globalization.

We suggest that the ILO compile a trade union development index assessing the extent of implementation of core Conventions in order to carry out a precise assessment of the non-implementation of these Conventions. The ILO should urge employers and, in particular, transnational corporations to assess in their annual reports the extent of fulfilment of ILO Conventions by their affiliate enterprises in different countries.

We also reiterate our view that it is necessary for all those concerned to make efforts to ensure that real social dialogue in the ILO will include all trends at the international and regional levels, reflecting the principles and practices that are in vogue in all United Nations agencies, to ensure that all regions and interests are adequately represented.

It is also essential that the Bureau for Workers' Activities (ACTRAV) develop fair cooperation with all trends in the trade union movement, especially with regard to of projects and courses for workers' education.

It is also necessary to ensure that the ILO committees are protected from efforts by certain countries to impose sanctions on countries that do not reflect the policies of neo-liberal globalization.

Before concluding my speech, I should like to say that all we need today is to unite our efforts to change the negative course of global development. This is not just a matter of argument, but a matter of interest to us all, and we have to fight for that.

Mr. KAIRELIS *(Government delegate, Lithuania)*

First of all, I would like to congratulate the President on his election and on his successful Chairmanship of this session of the Conference.

Lithuania welcomed the Strategic Policy Framework and budgeting set out four years ago, which identified four priority objectives for the ILO and the strategies required to achieve them. It is of great satisfaction to note, as we can see from the Reports of the Director-General and the Chairman of the Governing Body, that this was the right direction to choose – the Strategic Policy Framework has become the essential tool in the good governance of the Organization and the result-based management of the Office. Results for the reporting period show impressive achievements in its implementation.

The campaign for ratification of the eight core labour Conventions had produced the desired result – the ratification rate increased significantly. In this context, I am pleased to note that Lithuania is among those 103 countries that have ratified all the fundamental labour Conventions.

However, the increased number of ratifications is not an accurate reflection of the situation. Unfortunately, the standards supervisory system continues to identify violations in some regions of the world, and the ILO must pay more attention to these facts.

We endorse the efforts of the Governing Body concerning the development of the more effective tools that are needed to support standards-related technical assistance and promotional activities, and we share the opinion that they have to be discussed with the social partners and the governments of the countries concerned.

Concerning the adoption of new labour standards, we appreciate the first attempts to consolidate various standards in the same area. We are following with great interest the progress being made on the proposed consolidated maritime Convention and we are looking forward to the results of the High-level Tripartite Working Group on Maritime Labour Standards.

A special concern of the Lithuanian Government is employment and job creation. It is clear that, without employment, neither decent work nor prosperity can be achieved, nor living standards improved. Therefore we welcome the fact that the ILO created the Global Employment Agenda at the end of 2001, as a tool to integrate efforts to promote productive and decent employment in each country. It was very useful for the development of our national policy, leading to a significant decrease in unemployment.

We welcome also the shift in the ILO's policy towards social protection issues, especially a partnership with other institutions and organizations and the development of practical tools. We think that building a network of partner institutions and a knowledge base will further serve the implementation of strategies on social protection.

In supporting the ILO's all strategic objectives, Lithuania is committed to promoting and strengthening social dialogue and tripartism. A well functioning social partnership is a necessary precondition for successful realization of socially balanced solutions. We are convinced that the ILO, as a unique tripartite organization, will advocate to its constituents further strengthening of the social partnership.

In setting up an independent World Commission in 2002, the ILO showed its understanding of the great importance of the social dimension of globalization for the international community.

The report of the Commission has a wide response and no doubt will serve as a basis for broader discussion on the issue.

I am pleased to inform you that the Lithuanian Government, with the support of the ILO, in May this year held the Regional Tripartite Meeting with the participation of the Nordic and Baltic countries and as the honoured guest of the Meeting, of the Director-General, Mr. Somavia.

The participants of the Meeting shared their views on regional aspects and challenges of the social dimension of globalization, focusing on possible action to be taken nationally and internationally in pursuit of greater benefits of globalization. National governance of the processes is essential within each country, but joint international efforts and cooperation between institutions capable of influencing globalization processes, are also urgently needed.

We are looking forward to the ILO giving further guidance on the way to initiate further steps indicated in the Report.

As a member of the Governing Body of the ILO, Lithuania shares the opinion that the Governing Body has successfully fulfilled its tasks during the last year and invites it to further identify clear priorities, going forward.

Let me conclude by offering our best wishes to the Director-General, the Governing Body and the Office for further success in running the Organization, and in being flexible enough to respond to the challenges of the fast-changing working world.

Original Spanish: Mr. FERNÁNDEZ FAJALDE *(Minister of Labour, Bolivia)*

I would like to begin by extending our greetings to the 92nd Session of the International Labour Conference. We recognize the major importance of this event, because, throughout history, the most sensitive issues for the human being have been those related to labour, social rights, equal distribution of wealth and the quest for social justice.

In this connection, the dynamics of social trends, especially in Latin America, are now tending to change the features of injustice that occurred as a consequence of a distorted vision of a globalized world and the application of an economic model that, based on an orthodox and rigid perception of a market economy, have only led to the pauperization of major social sectors, increased unemployment, greater job precariousness, the abandoning of the protective nature of the right to work and, consequently, to a heightening of poverty levels.

In these circumstances, which have been seen so dramatically in my country, and despite the deep-rooted social conflict that we are currently grappling with, the Government of President Carlos D. Mesa Gisbert has decided to promote as a government policy far-reaching efforts to ensure that dialogue and agreement are the most appropriate mechanism for resolving the multi-faceted problems that exist in Bolivia today.

Accordingly, the Minister of Labour of Bolivia has proposed to give priority, as a fundamental part of his mandate, to the creation of a National Council for Labour Relations, tripartite in structure, stable in operation and permanent in the exercise of its responsibilities.

This objective, which is being fostered with the basic support of specialists and advisers of the ILO, is designed to become a valid mechanism for the strengthening of social dialogue in Bolivia.

We are convinced that it will only be possible to reverse the deterioration of conditions of employment and the exacerbation of poverty if substantial changes are made to relations between State and society. Therefore, it is important to establish a forum for institutionalized understanding between workers, employers and the State.

In parallel to this, another of our priorities is to do all we can to eradicate the worst forms of child labour, because besides being a consequence of the acute impoverishment of the most vulnerable sectors of Bolivian society, it is a phenomenon that, because of its dimensions, damages the deepest feelings of solidarity. Therefore, every State must guarantee its children unlimited access to education. This must be a central objective in order to prevent thousands of children in Bolivia's case, about 800,000 – from entering the labour market at a tender age.

Reversing this social trend is an obligation of the State and of society. Therefore, in Bolivia, we have been promoting the eradication of child labour through the inter-institutional commission and sub-commissions that are responsible for the progressive eradication of this form of labour in regions where sugar is cane harvested and in the western mining zone.

These objectives are being supported by efforts at various levels of Government to generate decent and permanent employment. The lack of such employment in the past has been a crucial factor in heightening the social crisis.

Incentives to micro and small enterprises in the form of systematic economic benefits from the State are designed to ensure that important segments of our society, in addition to finding a source of employment, can also harness their own creativity and express that creativity through the organization of productive units.

We are simultaneously developing plans to promote the national handicraft industry, as handicrafts are such a rich expression of our cultural heritage and an important source of employment. For the development of micro and small enterprises and handicraft labour units, in connection with training programmes, the State has made a proposal to create better conditions of credit and to create markets to guarantee that these productive activities do not run the risk of seeing their prospects frustrated.

On the basis of these efforts by the Ministry of Labour to tackle the most urgent problems in Bolivia, and despite the difficulties that we are facing today in the light of the obvious social conflict, which is a situation that we hope will be improved against the backdrop of democracy and tolerance, we urge the support and assessment mechanisms of the ILO to continue to lend us their support in the achievement of our institutional and governmental objectives, because, basically, we need a new scenario to solve our social problem. This scenario must be based on democratic dialogue, integral globalization, consensus-building and consultation. This is a new way of making progress in this new millennium in terms of labour relations, under the auspices of tripartism.

Original Arabic: Mrs. MINT BILAL OULD YAMAR *(Minister of Public Services and Employment, Mauritania)*

In the name of God, the Merciful, the Compassionate! It is indeed a great honour for me and the Democratic Republic of Mauritania to congratulate the President and the Officers of the Conference on their election to preside over the 92nd Session of the International Labour Conference, and I wish them every success.

I would like to congratulate the Director-General of the ILO and I welcome the efforts that he has made in order to produce this excellent Report.

The workers are at the heart of the concerns of the President of our Republic and it is during his mandate that we have laid the foundations for sustainable development, to encompass all dimensions of development: political, social, cultural and economic. Desirous of achieving these objectives, the Government is ensuring the monitoring and application of this ambitious development plan that is part of a global strategy to combat poverty, associated with a far-reaching campaign to disseminate knowledge in order to improve living standards. All that has been achieved in a short period of time has enabled us to improve the living standards of our citizens and of our workers.

For these reasons, employment and the struggle against illiteracy, poverty, disease and unemployment are at the heart of our Government's policies.

In the struggle against illiteracy, for example, a large-scale campaign has been launched which encompasses both the private and public sectors. The aim is to improve workers' living standards and to increase their productivity.

Desirous of improving the situation of workers, the President of the Republic has decided to raise wages by 28 per cent. This increase has followed a series of wage increases that we have carried out in previous years. Furthermore, in the near future we are going to ratify a special regulation for labour inspectors in order to guarantee their neutrality. The aim is to apply the provisions of the Labour Inspection Convention, 1947 (No. 81), ratified by Mauritania.

In the framework of efforts made to combat poverty, through the intermediary of the Commission on Human Rights, our country has embarked on the struggle against poverty through the integration and financing of numerous projects aimed at containing poverty in certain targeted areas.

The improvement of labour legislation ranks high on our Government's list of priorities. Our country has recently adopted a new Labour Code following the ratification of all the relevant core Conventions.

As far as freedom of association is concerned, we are trying to ensure trade unions a favourable environment which allows them to exercise their rights in a pluralist democracy with greater freedom.

Lastly, as far as human resources are concerned, we have launched programmes whose priority objective is to strengthen existing training structures, to make vocational training more widely available and to improve its quality. We are determined to achieve this objective.

We would also like to stress the need to improve the situation of workers in the occupied Arab territories.

There will be many obstacles and stumbling blocks along the way, but we are determined to achieve our objectives. We are determined to win this battle in order to ensure a better future.

Mr. SCHERBAKOV *(representative, General Confederation of Trade Unions)*

Let me first of all warmly congratulate the President on his election to this important position and wish him every success in leading this session of the Conference.

Today we are discussing the results of the work of the ILO in the past biennium. This period was complex and filled with events through which the ILO had to fulfil the strategic objectives that it had set itself. Familiarity with the Director-General's Report demonstrates that, on the whole, the ILO managed to deal with an enormous volume of work. We highly value the consistency and perseverance with which the ILO has put into practice the Decent Work Agenda, which, as noted in the Report, can truly be considered "a concept that has relevance for the new millennium."

The General Confederation of Trade Unions fully agrees with the main guidelines and objectives of the ILO's work as highlighted in the programme against poverty. For CIS countries, where 29-49 per cent of the population live below the poverty level, this programme takes on a special significance.

We consider it fitting that one of the most important areas of the ILO's work is the development and improvement of standard-setting activity and strengthening of monitoring of the implementation of international labour standards, as well as the systematic implementation of the provisions of the Declaration on Fundamental Principles and Rights at Work.

The increasing number of ratifications testifies to an understanding on the part of the international community of the significance of ILO social and labour standards. As an unstinting supporter of ILO campaigns for the ratification of key ILO standards, the GCTU actively promotes their success in the territory of the Commonwealth of Independent States. In fact, an overwhelming majority of CIS countries has already ratified practically all of the core Conventions. But we must not stop here. We must ensure their implementation and provide special assistance to those trade unions and workers in regions undergoing transition.

However, ratification of international labour standards is not an end in itself. We must ensure strict compliance, and such compliance must be reflected in legislation and in actual policies. This is, first and foremost, related to the issues of the protection of the rights and interests of trade unions.

It is extremely important that the Director-General address the issue of social dialogue as a necessary factor in social and labour relations. Everyone agrees that for such success, strong, independent social partners are required. We believe that the ILO could pay even greater attention to the issue of strengthening the positions of the social partners in the CIS countries. Naturally, most important to us is the presence of independent and representative trade unions. However, we should not forget about responsible employers' organizations, without whom we could hardly hope for a successful social dialogue. The GCTU, for its part, is ready to help the ILO Subregional office for Eastern Europe and Central Asia in Moscow with this work.

We agree that the annual presentation at the International Labour Conference of reports on the application of ILO Conventions and Recommendations provides us with a tremendous amount of additional and useful information, which allows us to create a large database. We believe that it would be a good idea for there to be discussions following the reports leading to concrete conclusions or recommendations. This would greatly help in the monitoring activities of the ILO.

In conclusion, let me say that we highly value the initiative taken by the Governing Body of the ILO in creating the World Commission on the Social Dimension of Globalization. This competent body can undoubtedly make a significant contribution to the successful implementation of the Decent Work Agenda.

The informative report of the Commission is, without doubt, valuable to trade unions and deserving of careful study. We count on the continuation and further development of ILO's activities.

Mr. SAED *(Workers' representative, Palestine)*

I would like to congratulate the President on his election to preside over this Conference.

I come from a country that is small in terms of surface area, but big in terms of its human and religious significance and heritage. Our country is the focus of attention of millions of peace-loving individuals.

And yet, peace is still a distant prospect, with the Sharon Government in power, a Government whose agenda is reduced to a hit list, the construction of settlements, the annexation of land and the means of imposing cruel and savage measures against the Palestinian people.

Since September 2000, this Government has declared an unrelenting terrorist war that has inflicted human and material losses on the Palestinian people, with Palestinian workers and their families the hardest hit.

Thousands of children, workers, women and leaders have lost their lives or been injured or arrested.

The Palestinian economy is in a disastrous state. The Israeli Government has occupied many Palestinian towns, villages and camps in the West Bank and Gaza Strip. It has destroyed water and electricity supply networks, houses, factories and farmland. The most recent of these operations was the attack on Rafah on 18 May 2004. A total of 220,000 Palestinians formerly employed in Israeli enterprises have lost their jobs. The same number who once worked in the Palestinian territories are now unemployed. According to United Nations statistics, over 2 million Palestinians are affected by unemployment and poverty, representing an unemployment rate of over 70 per cent of the population.

The workers lost over $1.3 billion over this period. What is worse, the Sharon Government has built a segregationist separation wall on Palestinian land, seizing more land and turning Palestinian towns into huge ghettos.

We therefore urge the international community to study the Palestinians' basic human needs in order to generate decent jobs for workers and reinvigorate the Palestinian economy, which has been devastated by the occupation.

We call on all international bodies and all governments to support the Palestinian Fund for Employment and Social Protection set up by the ILO, to which we extend our gratitude, in view of the gravity of the situation, so that we can reduce unemployment, alleviate poverty and attain our goals. I do not think the assistance required will cost more than the price of a few tanks and F-16s, which only sow death and destruction.

The Palestine General Federation of Trade Unions, thanks to your support and encouragement, was the first to launch an appeal for dialogue with all the parties to the conflict in the Middle East. This is why we have adhered to every peace initiative from the Madrid accords to the Road Map. It is obvious, however, that the Israeli Government does not want peace; on the contrary, it is constantly torpedoing peace, by flouting international law and denigrating all the human values on which the international community is based. And that is the democracy of Israel, whose airplanes are bombing our people and whose tanks kill women and children who go out in the streets to demonstrate against the crimes of the occupying forces.

Today, we cherish the hope of obtaining your support in putting an end to the inhuman practices of the Israeli Government and make a stand for right and justice by putting a stop to the bloodshed and massacres that are swelling the ranks of the innocent dead. Our people are the victim of the most heinous crimes known to the modern world.

We hope that this tragedy will end one day so that our workers and their children and grandchildren can live in two independent States that will coexist side by side in peace, in accordance with Resolutions Nos. 187, 191, 242 and 338, adopted by the international community.

Original Hungarian: Mr. GASKÓ *(Workers' delegate, Hungary)*

First, I would like to congratulate the President on his election, and to wish you success for this session of the Conference.

It is a pleasure and a privilege to take part in the 92nd Session of the International Labour Conference and to represent the Hungarian trade unions and the Hungarian workers at this session of this prestigious Conference.

We consider the Report by the Director General to be very valuable as it mentions innumerable issues that are still of particular importance for Hungarian workers. One such issue is the accomplishment of the ILO's most important basic principles and I would like to touch upon that subject.

While Hungary has ratified the ILO Right to Organise and Collective Bargaining Convention, 1949 (No. 98), I must, however, say that Hungarian legislation and judicial practice more recently has resulted in the fact that protection of union officials is currently not fully achieved in Hungary. That is the case even though the laws of Hungary, the Constitution and the Labour Code in force ensure operation of trade unions and protection of trade union officials. The relevant provisions of ILO Convention No. 98 have been adopted in the Labour Code. On the basis of the current legislation, the employer is obliged to cooperate with the existing unions, and elected trade union officials are entitled to protection under labour law. Protection under labour law means that the consent of the higher-level union is required if an official is to be laid off by ordinary dismissal. Extraordinary dismissal requires the higher-level trade union body to be notified, and it is entitled to reject the dismissal at its discretion.

While formerly employers used to dismiss officials without the prior consent of the higher-level trade union body, that practice has now changed. Today, the management goes to the courts to uphold its economic interests in order to compensate for the lack of the legal declaration which is required for the dismissal and has been refused by the higher-level trade union body.

Unfortunately, the courts normally supply these declarations as, in their opinion, the arguments of the employer outweigh the importance of ensuring trade union rights.

As the result of that practice, the protection of trade union officials is not enforced, most of the lawsuits ending with the dismissal of the senior union officials.

The union official is suspended from work for the time of the lawsuit, which weakens the union during a legal dispute which may easily drag on for years. This situation does not support keeping up a working day-to-day relationship with members and is an obstacle to the work of the union.

Because of this detrimental practice, protection of the unions' interests is rather limited in Hungary, due to the current legislation.

That is not the only way some companies have hindered the operation of unions. It is difficult to enforce the laws intended to guarantee the conditions of operation of unions and for mandatory cooperation.

I believe that Hungarian legislators should consider whether current legal regulation on the protection of trade union officials really achieves its goal. In our opinion, it does not, because the laws that should be serving the purpose of protecting trade union officials do not, in reality, deliver what they promise. We therefore suggest that they be reconsidered with a view to strengthening the protection of the interests of union officials.

I hope that the ILO's consistent efforts and wise decisions will help to resolve that problem and in that hope, let me thank you for your kind attention.

Original French: Mr. PETCU *(Workers' delegate, Romania)*

At the beginning of my statement I would like to congratulate the President of the Conference very warmly on his election to this important post and I would like to express, on behalf of all Romanian workers, the conviction that this session of the Conference will be a success under his Presidency.

I am also very honoured to convey the congratulations of Romanian workers to the Director-General for the excellent Report before the Conference.

I would like to describe to you some of the concerns of Romanian workers, some of the problems they are faced with and some of their aspirations for the future.

The Labour Code, which was adopted by the Parliament of Romania in December 2002, came into force on 1 March 2003. This Code expresses the deepest form of tripartism and reflects the clear choice of all the social partners in Romania to progress in practical stages towards the values laid down in the Conventions and Recommendations of the International Labour Organization, in the directives of the European Union and in the good practice of modern democratic societies.

Although the Romanian Labour Code does promote such values, it has been and continues to be the target of destructive attacks which, unfortunately, are launched by some multinational companies which also operate in our country, and these companies in turn are associated with countries that have exemplary democratic systems. The Foreign Investors Council in Romania is leading this assault.

Working hours, workers' right to be protected against any abuses committed by their employer, the right to in-service vocational training and the right to the presumption of innocence are values which are being challenged by foreign investors, who are constantly putting pressure on the Government of Romania in order to prevent the ratification of the relevant sections of the Labour Code. The trade union confederations of Romania are opposed to these destructive procedures, as they informed international forums including the International Labour Organization, at the beginning of this year. We would like to take this opportunity to thank all the bodies of the ILO who have supported us in order to devise, defend and promote the Labour Code.

In our country, the right to collective action is guaranteed in the Constitution and in law. Unfortunately, the mechanisms laid down in the law on labour disputes and certain ambiguities which are still present in this law mean that exercising the right to strike is a lengthy and expensive exercise, rendering this law practically meaningless.

Once again we urge the Government of Romania to take all the necessary measures to speed up the amendment of this law in order to harmonize it with the provisions of the Freedom of Association and Protection of the Right to Organise Convention, 1948 (No. 87) and with the Revised European Social Charter. The trade unions of Romania are ready to perform their constructive role as partners in this area as well. In the Romanian private sector and in the private sector where the employer is foreign, workers' rights to freedom of association are limited. There are not many situations in which one finds trade union members or organizations in these enterprises and often workers are intimidated if they express the desire to join trade unions. One finds similar situations in all sectors, but especially in the private banking system, insurance companies, and also in commerce.

Consequently, we would like to express our surprise, at the very least, that in the structure of the Romanian police, a sector which has been demilitarized for at least one year, not even a nucleus of a trade union has appeared. Romanian workers have proved that they represent an active constituency within the general United Nations system and the ILO system and they realize that they have to fulfil all the obligations which result from this. Romanian workers are also involved in a national effort to approach European standards in order to join the European Union according to the timetable which has been drawn up, in other words in 2007.

You can rely on us in all aspects of support and promotion of the ILO's values in the fight for sustainable development and in combating poverty through work and in the fight for a peaceful world.

Original French: Mr. NDITABIRIYE *(Minister of Labour and Public Service, Burundi)*

I would like to start by extending my congratulations to Mr. Milton Ray Guevara on his election as President of the 92nd Session of the International Labour Conference. I have no doubt that under his leadership the work of this session will be entirely successful.

In this speech I shall confine myself to a few thoughts on the report of the World Commission on the Social Dimension of Globalization, which was presented by Their Excellencies Mr. Mkapa, President of the United Republic of Tanzania and Mrs. Halonen, President of Finland.

When this report was presented to the Governing Body of the ILO in March 2004, I had the honour of addressing Mr. Mkapa, and pointing out to him that for him it was the start of another major task, the huge responsibility of convincing his peers and the leaders of this world to make a personal, sincere and durable commitment to bringing about effective change to the face of globalization. In fact, as the report clearly points out, globalization must be seen through the eyes of the men and women who judge it on its ability to provide them with opportunities for decent work and to meet essential needs, such as food, water, health, education, housing, as well as a viable environment for present and future generations.

It is felicitous today to note the commitment of President Mkapa and President Halonen to mobilizing the international community to ensure that it abides by and implements the conclusions and recommendations of this report.

I am certain that the international community will follow the conclusions and recommendations of this report, as they are so very relevant. The main question is whether they will actually promote their implementation.

Permit me to ask you all whether you really believe in this or whether you are just pretending to believe, in order to appease your consciences? I am not asking you to reply, but I would like you to try to put yourself in the place of the populations and countries which have been victims of globalization, to try and analyse their perception of certain values, such as solidarity, equality, human rights and human dignity, which are the common foundations of the aspirations of all humankind, on which the governance of globalization must be based.

For numerous workers in poor countries, the analysis is very simple and can be summed up in just a few thoughts that a poor worker might address to a rich worker: apply good governance to repay the debts that are stifling you thanks to the generosity of the rich countries. In case you haven't realised, this is what solidarity between poor countries and rich countries is. As far as equality is concerned, everyone gets what he or she deserves: prosperity for the rich, hardship for the poor.

If you are hungry and, moreover, there are too many diseases such as AIDS, malaria and tuberculosis, etc., you are perfectly at liberty to die in the name of respect for human rights. All that anyone is asking you to do is to die with dignity. You may be suffering from a lack of national skills: Well you must invest in education and skills, and to help you with this noble but expensive task, we will organize a brain drain and we will hire a charter plane to repatriate the illegal illiterate people.

You may find these statements somewhat shocking, but tell me how can man with a capital "M" accept that huge fortunes exist alongside total misery? How, in these conditions, can Man clear it with his conscience when he goes into churches, temples, synagogues and mosques to tell God that he loves Him and he loves his fellow men?

To my mind the face of globalization will not change if there is not some fundamental change in man. That, as I see it, is the moral dimension of globalization. Let us nonetheless remain optimistic.

Mr. TILAHUN: *(Employers' delegate, Ethiopia)*

It is a great honour for me to address this 92nd Session of the International Labour Conference, on behalf of the Ethiopian Employers' Federation I wish to convey my congratulations to the President on his election.

On the issue of labour standards, the speed of economic, social and political transformation in Africa, which affects the lives of millions of our people, continues to be slow, and thus still requires the continued effort and attention of Africans and their supporters. Business has to flourish, people have to be employed and earning for us to talk about an improvement in labour standards. One area of focus: capacity building of employers' institutions, would enable them to enhance their skills in the area of their ability to transform the economy, and to undertake effective social dialogue with their strong social partners, including government.

Implementation of the ILO Declaration on Fundamental Principles and Rights at Work is part of the ILO Decent Work Agenda, which we committed ourselves to last year at this august Conference. But for us to provide decent work and implement the ILO Declaration in a sustainable manner, as employers we first need to be engaged in a sustainable economy that can withstand the impacts of globalization and free competition on an uneven playing field. As also pointed out last year, employers need the support of their social partners to maintain check and balance in the economy so they can freely compete globally. The support of the ILO on entrepreneurship development access – to the world economic market – and management skill upgrading programmes are some that my delegation wishes to underline in the context of effective economic management in developing countries, including my own country, Ethiopia.

Having realized this underlying fact, the Ethiopian Employers' Federation places considerable significance on maintaining international labour standards, as only labour makes a difference. The ILO Conventions and Recommendations have been the guiding principles at all stages of our programme when dealing with labour issues with social partners. One of the notable measures taken in Ethiopia is the issuance of a new Labour Proclamation No. (377/2003) which governs employment relations and establishes an effective labour administration system. The revision of the labour law is a major step towards ensuring harmonious industrial relations by providing mechanisms for resolving labour disputes and for the provision of minimum labour standards.

The lack of social protection is one of the core problems and affects over 90 per cent of our population. Except in the civil service and few private businesses, the majority of employers do not have social protection schemes for their workers. The lack of social protection is unfortunately an integral part of our poverty. In this regard, though re-established very recently, our Federation is taking radical reform measures in line with the government development strategy, and has channelled its resources and energy into development activities with a view to achieving rapid economic growth and alleviating poverty.

Another equally important matter indicated in the Report of the Director-General is strengthening tripartism and dialogue. Social dialogue has been and will continue to be the most indispensable instrument in the progress of human civilization. In this regard, it is worth mentioning that the Tenth African Regional Meeting, that was held in Ethiopia only last year, has helped a lot in promoting a smooth relationship between the social partners. We believe that the continuation of such Regional Meetings is a good platform from which to engage effective social dialogue.

Another important item placed on the agenda of this session of the Conference is the creation of decent employment opportunities for our people. This will remain a big challenge for the social partners in the developing world. Investors will need an attractive business environment and incentives to invest, and thereby for business to flourish, which is crucial for job creation and decent working conditions.

It is high time for all of us to join hands and work together on the winning formula to implement the strategies in the Report, the vision set by the ILO. I would like to express my Federation's firm commitment to advocating and implementing the strategies indicated in the Report. Let me once again thank the ILO for providing our Federation, with both technical and non-technical assistance and once again highlight the need for the ILO to continue supporting our Federation to enable us to discharge our responsibilities.

Mr. MARICA *(Minister of Labour, Technological Development and Environment, Suriname)*

Let me start by congratulating the President upon his election to preside over this session of the Conference, and by thanking him for giving me the opportunity to address him and the other distinguished delegates at this session of the International Labour Conference.

Once again, as ILO members States, we are presented with a Report of the Director-General that gives us satisfaction in what the ILO has achieved so far. We are confident that the ILO will ultimately succeed in achieving the four strategic objectives set out by the Director-General.

As the Minister of Labour, Technological Development and Environment of Suriname, it gives me great pleasure to announce that Suriname is committed to implementing the strategic objectives in its national policy.

In this light, the ratification of three ILO instruments was just recently approved by Parliament, including the Worst Forms of Child Labour Convention, 1999 (No. 182), which is one of the core labour standards concerning child labour.

The other two instruments approved for ratification are the Private Employment Agencies Convention, 1997 (No. 181) and the instrument for the amendment of the ILO Constitution.

In compliance with the strategic objective to strengthen tripartism and social dialogue, Suriname ratified the Tripartite Consultation (International Labour Standards) Convention, 1976 (No. 144). In general, principles regarding tripartism are very widely acknowledged and deeply respected in Surinamese society. Preparatory actions of the Ministry of Labour, Technological Development and Environment have been successfully finalized by the establishment of tripartite consultation.

The Act proclaiming the long-awaited constitutional tripartite Social and Economic Council was recently adopted in Suriname. This Council will provide a forum enabling the three social partners to jointly advise the Government on the highest level on broad economic and social policy matters, and gain consensus on such matters, which can lead to national agreements between the three social partners.

In our efforts to create equal opportunities for men and women, to secure decent employment and enhance productivity, the Government of Suriname has joined the Programme for the Promotion of Management-Labour Cooperation executed by the ILO Subregional Office for the Caribbean. In this regard, a successful workshop on productivity enhancement was conducted in April this year in Suriname in which all social partners participated. The recommendations that came out of this meeting are high on the agenda of the Government.

Looking at the agenda for this year's session of the International Labour Conference, I noticed that attention is given to migrant workers. Suriname is confronted with many challenges in terms of managing the flow of migrants. Suriname, as a sending, transit and receiving country, is faced with the full spectrum of regular, irregular, skilled and unskilled migrant workers. I am pleased with this general discussion and I am looking forward to the development of a plan of action which will enable us to deal with this issue.

On behalf of the Government of Suriname, I once again renew our commitment to the principles of decent work proclaimed by the ILO, and the promotion of fundamental principles and rights at work.

But allow me to state that although serious efforts are being made by the ILO and the international community to create decent work and eliminate poverty, these efforts will be worthless if the so-called benefits of globalization are not equally distributed. As you know, developing nations do not experience or enjoy those benefits. I therefore make use of this august assembly to call upon all nations that are in a position to positively influence this process to do so, since having equal benefits is the only sustainable way to resolve today's economic problems.

RATIFICATION OF INTERNATIONAL LABOUR CONVENTIONS BY BELGIUM AND SWEDEN

Original French: The CLERK OF THE CONFERENCE

I am pleased to announce to the Conference that on 9 June 2004, Belgium deposited the ratification instrument of the Prevention of Major Industrial Accidents Convention, 1993 (No. 174), and Sweden deposited the ratification instrument for the Safety and Health in Agriculture Convention, 2001 (No. 184).

(The sitting adjourned at 7.30 p.m.)

CONTENTS

Page

Sixth sitting

Reports of the Chairperson of the Governing Body and of the Director-General: Discussion *(cont.)* 1

 Speakers: M. Athauda, Mr. Al-Khatib, Mr. George, Mr. Silwal, Mr. Chen, Mr. Ng, Mr. Stijepović, Mr. Pond, Ms. Hunt, Mr. Neffati, Mr. Dalley, Mr. Kilic, Mr. Aloewie, Mr. Ivala, Mr. Meyer, Mr. Sarbu, Mr. Allam, Mr. Latif, Mr. Winn, Mr. Grönlund, Mr. Taliadoros, Mrs. Karagousova, Mr. Pater, Mr. Meriton, Mrs. Iglesias, Mrs. Gawanas, Mr. Azoz.

Seventh sitting

Reports of the Chairperson of the Governing Body and of the Director-General: Discussion *(cont.)* 22

 Speakers: Ms. Bakoko Bakoru, Mr. Fattori Costa, Mr. Luquinda, Mrs. Thienthong, Mr. Dinur, Mr. De Geus.

Ninth sitting

Reports of the Chairperson of the Governing Body and of the Director-General: Discussion *(cont.)* 27

 Speakers: Mr. Pais Antunes, Mr. Barde, Mrs. Christova, Mr. De Payva, Mr. Kaník, Mr. Thapaliya, Mr. Iyanga Djoba Malango, Mr. Wijffels, Mr. Aman, Mr. Gryshchenko, Mr. Vaz de Almeida, Mr. Kearney, Mr. Poddar, Ms. Lucero, Mr. Phengkhammy, Mr. Zharikov, Mr. Kairelis, Mr. Fernández Fajalde, Mrs. Mint Bilal Ould Yamar, Mr. Scherbakov, Mr. Saed, Mr. Gaskó, Mr. Petcu, Mr. Nditabiriye, Mr. Tilahun, Mr. Marica.

Ratification of international labour Conventions by Belgium and Sweden 44

No. 12 – Thursday, 10 June 2004

International Labour Conference

Provisional Record 13

Ninety-second Session, Geneva, 2004

Eighth (special) sitting
Wednesday, 9 June 2004, 3.45 p.m.
President: Mr. Ray Guevara

ADDRESS BY HIS EXCELLENCY MR. JOSÉ LUIS
RODRÍGUEZ ZAPATERO, PRESIDENT OF THE
GOVERNMENT OF SPAIN

Original Spanish: The PRESIDENT

It is a great honour for me to declare open this Eighth (Special) Sitting of the International Labour Conference and to welcome, on behalf of the Conference, His Excellency Mr. José Luis Rodríguez Zapatero, President of the Government of Spain.

I shall now give the floor to the Secretary-General, Mr. Somavia, to welcome our distinguished guest.

Original Spanish: The SECRETARY-GENERAL

Your Excellency José Luis Rodríguez Zapatero, President of the Conference, dear friends, the International Labour Organization is being paid a great honour this afternoon in being visited by a true gentleman, a gentleman who has based a political career on the respect of the values of others and on dialogue. He has accomplished this with great strength, a strength that lies in his deep belief in humanist values.

Mr. President, you have said, with pride, that you represent a generation of Spaniards who have grown up and been educated in freedom, for whom democracy is their mother tongue. The entire world recognizes that collective strength which has guided the difficult but natural transition of Spain from dictatorship to democracy. Here in the ILO we are extremely proud of having been able to accompany you in those difficult times when democracy was suppressed for your people.

In 1969, an ILO Study Group went to Spain to look at the application of labour legislation in the light of the principles of our Constitution. I would like to believe that this visit was useful and encouraged the emerging labour movement to organize and prepare for the day when it would be able to assume its responsibilities – once democracy has returned to the country.

We are very honoured to welcome at this august tripartite assembly a political leader who represents modernity but also the history and democratic values of a great European nation open to the world – which is Spain today.

The Spanish model, this complex mechanism of social dialogue and agreements that has brought about an equilibrium in social and economic policy, is a source of learning and inspiration for those of us here in the ILO. We are the international expression of tripartism and therefore I feel I must pay a tribute to those government leaders, leaders of business and trade union leaders who were able to build a consensus at a time when history made that so urgently necessary.

Spanish history has shown that it is possible to become a fully fledged member of the world economy and open up markets, while remaining concerned about social development and social issues. And this concern about social matters is – and always will be – a major task for us all.

Mr. President, in your statement when you assumed office, you recalled the values that had been handed down to you by your grandfather, and you reiterated that improving the social conditions of the most deprived groups in society would be one of the main priorities of your Government. It is for all these reasons that your address to us here today will be of such importance to all of us at a time when the ILO is dealing with issues relating to the social dimension of globalization.

At the ILO, we are trying to lay down the foundations for what we hope will be a worldwide consensus on how to achieve a fairer globalization which will offer opportunities to and provide decent work for all. This is the task facing us now and which will face us in the future; it represents a major challenge for world leadership at all levels – governments, international organizations, enterprises, trade unions, political parties, and society as a whole. The major challenge before us is to reconcile all these diverse interests in such a way as to build a shared and dignified future for all.

The ILO would like to support you in whatever you try to do at a national level, but we would also urge you devote your energy – which has also earned international respect – to the cause of a fairer globalization. I know this is an issue which is dear to your heart. You have shown that throughout your life, you have pursued dialogue with sincerity; you have sought to find solutions to problems with realism and you have upheld the values of dignity, decency and social justice at all times.

You have eight male ministers in your Government, eight female ministers – and that is a clear illustration of the fact that your words are not just words but based on action as well.

I, myself, am a Latin American, and that being so, I cannot but reiterate the major contribution which Spain, once freed of authoritarianism, made to the restoration of democracy in my region of the world. Many of us have experienced the dark night of dictatorship before we returned to democracy but during that dictatorial period we were able to look to Spain as a source of hope and we received a great deal of support from our friends there in our fight to return democracy to our own countries.

We are very honoured that you are here this afternoon. We recognize in you one of the leaders of Europe, a Europe which is determined to move further down the road to globalization while protecting the social dimension, which is at the core of its existence; but also a Europe that does not forget that there are other parts of the world less fortunate, which require Europe's solidarity and support to move forward.

We are honoured to be the first international organization in the United Nations system that you have visited. Thank you for being with us today.

Original Spanish: His Excellency Mr. José Luis Rodríguez Zapatero *(President of the Government of Spain)*

I would like to extend my congratulations to Mr. Ray Guevara, Secretary of State for Labour of the Dominican Republic, on his appointment to preside over the work of this 92nd Session of the International Labour Conference.

I would also like to thank Mr. Somavia for his kind words. I greet him today and I express my admiration for the way in which he is carrying out his office of Director-General of the International Labour Office.

This is the first time that, as President of the Government of Spain, I have taken the floor before an assembly belonging to the United Nations system.

I do so with a special feeling of emotion, only a few metres away from the Salle du Conseil, the symbol of the former League of Nations, where, donated to the Organization by Spain in 1937 and despite the war that was laying waste to my country at the time, are the maxims of Francisco de Vitoria and the frescos of by José María Sert, which were chosen to proclaim the supreme values of peace, justice, respect for international law and the defence of human dignity.

Coming here to talk about labour in a multilateral international organization provides me with an opportunity to express my political concerns in the light of the social effects of globalization, and, more generally, to talk about international governance. Discussing this in a United Nations body involves supporting a multilateral political vision of international relations over the temptations and the realities of unilateralism. The United Nations system opens the path to the institutionalization of international society in a way that goes beyond mere issues of power. And, in today's world, it is crucial that we reform and foster United Nations' activities and models of multilateral cooperation at the global level.

A global cosmopolitan view of international order inevitably involves seeing sovereignty as legitimate authority based on the respect of human rights and democratic values.

The alternative to unilateralism and to neo-liberalism entails a more complex vision of global politics and the development of the world economy. Specifically, social advances should be made in parallel to the application, at the international level of the traditional principles of social democracy and by consolidating progress in international multilateral cooperation.

Accepting the role of the ILO in this new world that we live in means accepting the objective of a social dimension in international relations. This is the overriding objective of the twenty-first century. In the twentieth century, we achieved great advances in the area of human rights and we went on to consolidate and extend political and civil rights to peoples throughout the world. It is now time for the twenty-first century to be the century of social rights. It is social rights that provide the basis of a necessary balance to economic development: for development, for the liberalization of markets, for economic cooperation and for an ever-broader opening-up of world economies. For reform to be effective it has to take place in the framework of a global structure of sustainable development, and the most sustainable form of development is that which encompasses social rights and the defence of human dignity.

This Organization has a dual role to play. On the one hand, it sets international standards. On the other hand, it is also a forum for tripartite consultations among governments, trade unions and employers' organizations against the global backdrop of the international economy. This makes the ILO a key institution to provide the necessary social dimension to the global economy and international trade. Its experience over many years in international standards-related activities means that the International Labour Organization has a body of Conventions that establish frameworks of fundamental principles and rights, which are enshrined in the 1998 ILO Declaration on Fundamental Principles and Rights at Work, and this serves as a guarantee of that fundamental role.

The principles concerning the Fundamental rights: freedom of association, the elimination of forced labour, the abolition of child labour and the elimination of discrimination are crucial for a State to be able to participate in the international economy on the basis of social and economic conditions based on compliance with universally recognized principles.

For a European country such as Spain, and from a Government such as my own, which wishes, above all, to foster a strong European political plan as one that recognizes dialogue, union, peace and social cohesion, I would like to remind you all that the Council of the European Union has used the criteria of compliance with ILO social standards as a fundamental tool in evaluating whether or not it opens up to certain markets.

Europe understands that it is not only useful, but absolutely crucial, to apply social standards to globalization, and this shows just how important the ILO is. Striking a balance between market liberalization and the application of minimum social standards and development assistance is obviously not an easy task, but it is one that is necessary and that should be tackled without delay. Market liberalization that does not take the social effects of these processes into account would be as negative as establishing a new form of protectionism under the guise of social rights.

We cannot take an approach that seeks to raise artificially the social costs of developing countries, even under the politically correct cover of combating social dumping.

Labour relations systems need to be based on freedom of association and collective bargaining. We need systems where social costs are in proportion to the economic situation of the country but also take into account the decisions of the social partners expressed through free negotiation.

The ILO is celebrating its 85th anniversary and, throughout this period, it has never set aside its two principal characteristics: to act as an instrument for world peace, and to do so through the fight for social justice.

In the past 85 years, the world has, however, changed. Our Organization has become universal in character and has left behind it the ideological divisions of the Cold War. But today we are faced with equally major challenges, particularly those that are linked to globalization and the liberalization of trade and universal respect of for human rights and the development of less developed countries.

Social values and aspirations, relations between citizens and States, and also relationships between various countries and regional blocks, are subject to conditions today that simply did not exist when this Organization was born and as it developed.

In the economic context, there have been radical changes in the multilateral situation and conditions. New technologies and scientific progress are now driving the world's economy. They have condensed time and space, they have revolutionized trade and they have cast doubt upon certain social achievements. Furthermore, governments and public authorities have been obliged to revise their role.

The globalization of trade, although full of development possibilities, paradoxically today takes us back to the position we were in 85 years ago, in that it confronts us with new forms of what long ago used to be termed "the social question".

Poverty is gaining ground and this must be repealed; it mainly affects women in all regions of the world.

The disgraceful exploitation of child workers is, unfortunately, a topical issue (especially in certain regions of our planet) which should trigger a collective revolt against such a contemptible practice. The dominant themes of the last decade have been sustainable development and, in particular, environmental protection.

Despite all these changes, the ILO has lucidly, determinedly faced up to this trend in the United Nations system and it is consolidating new methods for optimizing the role of international tripartism in the gradual restoration of rights at work. At this point, I would like to make special mention of two outstanding initiatives: the ILO Declaration of Fundamental Principles and Rights at Work and, the launching of a far-reaching international debate on the social dimension of globalization.

I think that the political points I touched upon a few minutes ago dovetail perfectly with the decision taken in 2001 by the ILO's Governing Body to establish a Commission on the Social Dimension of Globalization. This Commission's report and the debate which began on its conclusions a couple of days ago, on 7 June, in this Conference inspire us with hope that we can count on having some standards whereby we can further defend our position.

I believe that the report of the World Commission provides us with some very useful ideas on how to develop a strategy.

First, it is important to build a social dimension of globalization by strengthening systems of good governance and this task will be the LEITMOTIF of international discussions over the next few years.

My thoughts on the globalization of the economy and its social impact are predicated on the belief that "decent work" must become a major global objective and not just a goal of the International Labour Organization

I also believe that the ILO could heed the call of the Commission to improve participation in and the accountability of the multilateral system by mobilizing tripartite partners all over the world, thereby ensuring that we contribute fully to building a social dimension of globalization.

We want, we advocate, a process of globalization which does have a social dimension based on shared universal values and respect for human rights and human dignity, a fair globalization, an inclusive globalization which is governed democratically and provides opportunities and tangible benefits for all countries and all persons throughout the world.

Attention has often been focused on solely endeavouring to ensure that markets operate effectively, but very little attention has been paid to what globalization means for individuals, families, local communities or identities, or to the possibilities and risks it poses to attaining greater gender equality in the world. It is, however, necessary to remember that the potential benefits from the current process of globalization are enormous. It can promote open societies and economies. It offers more opportunities, freer trade in goods and wider exchanges of ideas, knowledge, culture and persons and it reflects humanity's aspiration to work together in order to build a fairer world.

This form of globalization not only presupposes international flows of capital assets and funds, although these are the factors which move fastest, frequently without control, social accountability or democratic governance; it also presupposes international flows of the labour factor. This is where immigration comes into play. Immigration, like other elements of globalizations, implies challenges and opportunities. There is no doubt that if we are to derive greater benefit from these opportunities and mitigate their possible costs, migratory movements will have to be channelled and managed according to the receptive capacity and the needs of the labour market at a given time in the county of destination, so that migrants are offered decent working conditions complying with the international labour standards.

Immigration should be seen as an opportunity for host countries, which an efficient, go-ahead government must turn into growth and progress.

I would like now to turn my thoughts, to three aspects of globalization: international financial flows, transnational business activities and the development of information and communication technologies.

The increasing power of transnational enterprises, international financial flows and the revolution in information and communication technologies have certainly created unprecedented development opportunities, but they have not yet reached many regions of the world. Many regions watch from the sidelines as others benefit from the changes taking place.

It has been calculated that the goods and services produced throughout the world over the last 100 years, and principally in the last 50 years, are more than humanity has produced since the beginning of history. Our potential is enormous but a comparison of realities today yields some shocking findings:

some countries are immensely rich while others are virtually beggars. One-sixth of the world's population lives in abject poverty, not even knowing whether they will have anything to eat the next day. Many people earn scarcely a dollar a day, yet there are countries whose per capita income is US$30,000, or US$82 a day.

I do not think that the needs of free enterprise force us to choose between economic efficiency and social justice. No such dilemma exists. There are many examples of policies that manage to combine both, but, without a shadow of doubt, the area of education speaks volumes here. An education system that includes the teaching of languages and new technologies and promotes equal opportunities at the same time as it enhances competitiveness and the potential for growth, results in a fairer, more productive society.

Our challenge, and this is something we are fully aware of in Europe, is not to defend a model that may require changes. We need to find effective answers and we need to adapt labour legislation, institutions, social dialogue practices and collective bargaining to the demands of an economic competitiveness in which innovation and knowledge reign supreme.

I am firmly convinced that the answer to such a complex challenge calls for a dedicated effort in social dialogue on a tripartite basis. This requires a certain amount of daring and a willingness to compromise. Without this willingness for dialogue, which is at the heart of this Organization, and without an interaction of responsibilities between the institutional protagonists in political and social life, without this awareness that the collective good and the notion of public service must prevail over individual interests and strategies, I believe that we will significantly reduce the probability of being able to contribute to building truly cohesive societies.

We must also not forget that new players are playing an increasingly important role on the international scene – the International Monetary Fund (IMF) and the World Trade Organization (WTO) in particular. The ILO, with its tripartite tradition, its vast experience and its ability to understand day-to-day reality must take upon itself the role of the pioneer and, in particular, it must develop new ideas and redefine its role within the international community.

Intergovernmental cooperation needs to take place in common accord with the new players in the world economy in various sectors, particularly with the WTO, the Bretton Woods institutions and the whole United Nations family.

As regards the WTO, there is a certain synergy between the objectives of the multilateral trade system and those of the ILO. The opening up of trade has been a powerful means of economic growth and prosperity. The improvement of living standards throughout the world constitutes an important contribution to social progress.

Liberalization does lead to job creation, and all in all, generates advantages for the population at large. However, there are also negative effects for many directly involved stakeholders. It is therefore up to the State and international organizations to help these individuals with specific measures. The World Employment Report 1998 showed that those countries that are most open to international trade also have highly developed models of social redistribution.

But we cannot just leave it to the States to act individually. We should also globalize out response – the social response to globalization. We need to ensure effective cooperation between the WTO and the ILO. This rapprochement should enable us to develop an open discussion on the common ground between trade and international labour standards: new rules, extended rights, social guarantees – in short, dignity for workers all over the world

Furthermore, we require instruments which enable us better to use our knowledge. The ILO Declaration on Fundamental Principles and Rights at Work and its Follow-up is one of these, because it promotes this activity.

Our ultimate objective is to assure each country that respect for fundamental social standards is a comparative advantage that testifies that the national economy is working effectively and that constitutes a decisive step to combining economic policy with social policy.

The international community must respond more effectively to these questions than it did during the Great Depression. It can do with the considerable skills of the international organizations and the growing moral authority of organizations such as the ILO, which is in a position to provide the right answer to our question

Spain's relationship with the ILO is a long one. Of the past, I would like to recall the contribution of the ILO and the International Confederation of Free Trade Unions in restoring the freedom of association that was suppressed by the Franco Government. A decisive part in re-establishing the freedom of association that the dictatorship crushed was played by a person who is well known in the Organization: Francisco Largo Caballero, the Minister of Labour of the Second Republic, whom I would like to honour today.

Of the present, I would like to recall our commitment to the Organization, expressed by the ratification of and compliance with Conventions and by the development of the many forms of cooperation that I propose to broaden and extend.

The future of the ILO and its role in a new world order that fosters the social dimension of globalization, social rights in the twenty-first century, as I have already stated at length today, is a key aspect of my political vision of international affairs. I would Therefore like, once again, to express my thanks to this noble institution for giving me the opportunity to contribute to this vital discussion.

I would like to devote my last word to expressing my solidarity and to ask for your support. As you all know, the terrorist attacks in Madrid on 11 March resulted in a tragic loss of human lives. Recently, the Spanish Government decided to express its recognition to the victims as workers, because we feel that they were all united by the fact that, in one way or another, they were working for society. It is for all of these victims of terrorism whose working lives were cut short that I crave the recognition and solidarity of the participants in this session of the International Labour Conference. Recognition and solidarity, I would extend to all those who are suffering from the effects of violence, poverty and war, especially the citizens of Iraq. Recognition and solidarity must go hand in hand with a commitment from all of us, from all delegations, from all government representatives, from all employers' and workers' organizations, a commitment to the principles of freedom and equality among all human beings, a commitment to end war and terrorism, a commitment to human dignity and the safeguarding of life and limb.

I am saying this at the International Labour Organization, an institution, whose purpose it is, as part of the United Nations system, to send out a clarion call for the strengthening of a universal vision of human civilization.

Because an institution like this which knows no borders between different languages, cultures or peoples, an organization united around one of the most precious rights which gives dignity to the human being, in other words work, represents a call to overcome differences. May dialogue which undoubtedly is a working tool of this organization be the main source of inspiration for a new world order. Dialogue emanates from reason and reason is always based on ethical principles and values of fellowship. Where reason and dialogue reign, where a forum is built, rights will always be improved, the lot of the most humble will be improved and there will always be a readiness to acknowledge that improvements can obviously always be made to the history of humanity, given our experiences in the twentieth century and the great suffering of so many people.

In the former building of the International Labour Organization which today is the headquarters of the World Trade Organization there used to be an inscription which said "He who wants peace, paves the way to justice." And I believe that this is the best rule for the ILO and for all of us to follow and the best way to express our collective commitment.

I represent a government and a country which is committed to defending the rights and dignity of workers throughout the world. I represent a government and a country which has as its overriding objective to bring peace and solidarity to the world. I represent a government and a country which believes in the United Nations, which believes in the ILO, which will do its utmost and which will display its ability to believe in utopia in order to strengthen the United Nations, a shared view of the world and workers' rights in all four corners of the world, since we are convinced that by doing so we will leave a legacy of great dignity on earth and of far-reaching improvements in the twenty-first century.

Original Spanish: The PRESIDENT

I thank the President of Spain, Mr. Rodríguez Zapatero for that address which was permeated by a desire for peace and social justice. We know that he has a very, very heavy agenda and an extremely tight schedule and that he has only been able to spare one or two hours to come to Geneva and to address this Conference.

On behalf of all the delegates here at this 92nd Session of the International Labour Conference and on my own behalf, I would like to take this opportunity to express our very deep gratitude, not only for your splendid address, but also for the effort which you made in order to find the time to come and address this Conference and honour us with your presence. I am certain that I am expressing the feeling of all the delegates attending this Conference when I say that we believe that the effort you made to come here this afternoon is an eloquent illustration of the commitment of Spain as a country and of yourself, as the President, to the ideals of the International Labour Organization.

As a Dominican and as a Latin American, I am particularly proud that we have been able to have you as a guest this afternoon and that I was here as President of this Conference.

Spain is not only the mother country of the Spanish-speaking countries of Latin America; it is also an example of tolerance; an example of democracy; an example of solidarity, of virtue and of dignity. And every country of the Spanish-speaking Latin America has it as a model. It will, I hope now, be our voice in the European Union to thank you for your generosity in sparing the time to come here. Thank you for your address, many, many thanks and could I ask all delegates once again to applaud our distinguished guest before he leaves.

(The Conference adjourned at 4.30 p.m.)

CONTENTS

Page

Eighth (special) sitting

Address by His Excellency Mr. José Luis Rodríguez Zapatero, President of the Government of Spain 1

Speakers: the President, the Secretary-General, Mr. José Luis Rodríguez Zapatero

International Labour Conference

Provisional Record   14
Ninety-second Session, Geneva, 2004

Tenth sitting
Thursday, 10 June 2004, 10.15 a.m.
President: Mr. Ray Guevara, Mr. Maatough

GLOBAL REPORT UNDER THE FOLLOW-UP TO THE ILO DECLARATION ON FUNDAMENTAL PRINCIPLES AND RIGHTS AT WORK: INTERACTIVE SITTING

Original Spanish: The PRESIDENT

It is my great pleasure to open this sitting of the International Labour Conference which is dedicated to the discussion of the Global Report submitted under the follow-up to the ILO Declaration on Fundamental Principles and Rights at Work. This Report is the first of the second four-year cycle of Global Reports submitted to the Conference. As you know, it is entitled *Organizing for social justice*, and it deals with freedom of association and the right to organize, and the effective recognition of the right to collective bargaining.

The Report gives an assessment of trends in this respect as observed over the last four years; in other words, since the first Global Report on these fundamental rights, entitled *Your voice at work*, was published in 2000.

The amount of information we have available to us today is quite considerable. You can find it in Report I(B) and also in *Provisional Record* No. 7, which deals with the various types of follow-up activity undertaken by the ILO in respect of this Declaration.

We would like today's discussion to be lively and interactive. It is for that reason that we have moved into this room because it is a more appropriate setting for a lively and dynamic exchange of ideas and information. Similarly, it is for that reason that the participants will be sitting in groups – the Government group, the Employers' group and the Workers' group – as if this were a committee meeting in plenary.

The discussion will be organized in the following way. To begin with, the Secretary-General will introduce the Global Report. I shall then give the floor to the spokespersons of the Employers' and Workers' groups, who will be followed by the representatives of the regional groups. After that, the floor will be available to those speakers who wish to put forward their views.

The SECRETARY-GENERAL

Organizing for social justice is the second Global Report focusing on freedom of association and the effective recognition of the right to collective bargaining under the follow-up to the ILO Declaration on Fundamental Principles and Rights at Work. It is already having a positive reception in plenary speeches. Here, we need to deepen its analysis.

Four years ago, our first Global Report, *Your voice at work*, signalled our determination to achieve universal respect for these fundamental human rights at work and identify the priorities for an ILO programme of promotional activities.

Let me recall that the Declaration itself placed on the Office the responsibility for preparing a dynamic global picture relating to each category of fundamental principles and rights in a four-year cycle. So, this is our first second Global Report.

I want to make six points about where the Report says we are and where we need to go to make the fundamental right of freedom of association and the effective recognition of the right to collective bargaining real in the lives of people and the institutions of society.

First, there is a wider acceptance of the importance of these fundamental rights.

In fact, ratifications have increased and if we continue at the present pace, we will reach the goal of universal ratification of Conventions Nos. 87 and 98 by the year 2015. I believe that we should not wait that long, but it would be fitting indeed if in the target year for the Millennium Development Goals of poverty reduction, we could say that all countries in the world had bound themselves to respect fundamental principles and rights at work. And this is particularly true for very large and important countries – developed and developing – who have not yet done so. In these past four years, we have implemented some fact-finding promotional programmes with interested countries that stem directly from our review of the Global Report at the 2000 session of the International Labour Conference.

Second, our work is changing.

Our supervisory system is being used by more and more organizations struggling to overcome obstacles of varying types and severity that inhibit the exercise of their rights. I see this as an indicator of a healthy acceptance of the ILO's process for identifying and resolving problems. More often than not, the process leads to a constructive dialogue about how to change a law or improve the administrative system or deal with the particular problem. And its effectiveness lies in the perception by everybody that it operates frankly but also fairly.

Our new joint challenge is to create a legal, administrative, social and political environment where joining and taking an active role in the union or employers' organization is regarded as normal. And I think that this is a very important point: it is a normal activity. To simply decide that you have to put obstacles whatever they are for somebody, employer or worker, who wants to organize is going against something that should be seen as normal. We must defend this basic philosophy in all facets of life and in all circumstances. It is an act of civic choice. Who has the right to restrict that choice if we are advocating democracies? So, this is a very fundamental element. It is normal; it is an individual choice and that choice should not be restricted.

I think that, if we look at it that way, this will have a far-reaching impact. After all, the most effective labour laws are deeply embedded in society and are obeyed, not just because courts will penalize abuses, but because they are assimilated into the reflexes of governments, employers and workers and their representation structures.

The underlying notion of freedom of association and collective bargaining is that negotiation among most participants of equal weight, rather than litigation, is the quickest, most cost-effective and just way of solving problems and creating opportunities for progress.

Third, despite the advances, a number of groups of workers face enormous challenges in organizing in nearly all countries.

Most of these workers are low paid, have little or no security of employment or income, sometimes work in hazardous conditions and face discriminatory practices of various types. Large numbers of these workers are women and work in agriculture.

The approach we adopted at the 2002 session of the International Labour Conference provides a strong platform for action for informal economy workers and small businesses. Established unions and business associations are best placed to offer them support and help in getting organized.

Many of you are already doing that and I commend you for it. Those groups who have most difficulty asserting their rights should be a focus of our next phase of follow-up activities,

Fourth, technical cooperation is key.

The Declaration has given us an important framework that we can use to deliver technical cooperation and support to constituents. The action plan that followed the first Global Report on freedom of association and effective recognition of the right to collective bargaining listed some 50 countries that had asked for technical assistance. In the four years since then, the Office has worked with many of them on the policy priorities that they have chosen.

The substantial flow of technical assistance finance has made it possible to launch a number of sizeable projects, operating in countries in every region. I wish to thank all those governments that have contributed, and urge them and others to continue to help us develop our promotional work. The support of some very important countries has been key in being able to put many of these projects together.

Fifth, capacity building is vital.

The laws in many countries make exceptions that undermine the right of freedom of association and collective bargaining for all. We see it in the informal economy, in export processing zones and elsewhere.

Tackling these loopholes is a painstaking business and we must move faster. I think we can do so because in many cases the blockage is not an absence of political will, but simply the capacity of overstretched government services to draw up the legislative reforms and establish the necessary implementation structures. But what needs to be tackled head-on, and once and for all, is the nefarious idea that a worker in an export processing zone has fewer rights than other workers in the same country. I truly believe that it is an incredible concept that a worker in an export processing zone has fewer rights than another worker in the same country.

This has been a preposterous policy conditionality imposed on developing countries. Fortunately, not all have followed it.

Employers' and workers' organizations need to strengthen their capacity to organize and reach out, particularly in the informal sector. It is also key that they develop the expertise needed to negotiate effectively with each other and with national authorities.

Sixth, and finally, globalization poses new challenges. The Report shows that collective bargaining remains widespread and is constantly adapting to the changing contours of the global market.

What is noteworthy is that countries with relatively strong institutions for social protection and bargaining are better able to manage the volatility of an increasingly interdependent world economy, invest more in skill development and, in general, have less income inequality.

The lesson seems to be: organize well, train your negotiators, decide on the bargaining arrangements that best suit you, be ready to adapt and rebalance them if circumstances change and, most of all, keep talking.

The aim is to raise productivity and competitiveness, together with income and protection, in ways that are accepted as fair and effective. The rights enable this, but they do not guarantee it. That is down to the skill, capacities and experience of the negotiators. But when power imbalances are too big, the law must guarantee equity in the relationship.

We are seeing increasing requests for advice on how to shape bargaining structures and techniques, especially dispute settlement mechanisms, appropriate to the increasingly strong competitive pressures of our times.

This is what, in the Report, we term a rights-based approach to dynamic labour markets. The only way to meet this demand will be to develop better ways to share the experience of our constituents from all over the world so that each country can draw on our collective knowledge as they adapt their own systems.

To conclude, the goal of shaping a fair globalization depends, in a large measure, on strong employers' and workers' organizations founded on respect for freedom of association, organizing for social justice.

Over the past four years, it has become increasingly apparent that, to promote freedom of association as a human right at work, we need to understand its intimate connection with the enlargement of democracy, the efficiency of market-oriented development and social justice.

The Declaration describes the fundamental Conventions as providing enabling rights. When workers and employers are free to join and form organizations of their own choices, they are also free to fight forced labour, to combat child labour and to stand firm against discrimination. The right to organize tackles poverty and injustice at its very roots.

Organizing for social justice takes an important step forward in integrating our thinking on rights with our work on other strategic priorities.

The Report calls on us to work closely to overcome existing obstacles to ratifying and applying the relevant Conventions.

It calls on us to support organization and bargaining for vulnerable groups of workers.

It calls for stronger research and data to build a better understanding of how these principles can help build labour markets that promote rights, economic development, poverty reduction and investment.

It is also important to deepen the knowledge base, advisory services, technical cooperation, awareness raising and our advocacy capacities.

Your interventions today will guide the Office as it puts together an action plan for the Governing Body to consider in November.

Let me conclude by saying that, as Director-General, I am always vigilant on individual cases of trade unionists, particularly trade union leaders, who are put in jail or otherwise persecuted for trying to organize workers and carry out their legitimate trade union activities.

I have also intervened in many cases involving employers.

To all of you I say: keep me informed, I am there for you. Sometimes an opportune call on my part, a public statement or a discreet intervention, the activation of our local offices or other avenues can help afford protection at the right time.

Original Spanish: The PRESIDENT

Before we start the discussion, I would like to remind you of something. You should have been given a piece of paper when you came into the room, on which are listed some points for discussion; the purpose of this is to ensure that this discussion is useful for the Conference and the Office. We must not lose sight of the fact that the discussion of the Global Report at the Conference is a way of providing information and exchanging ideas that will guide the plan of action on the principle of freedom of association and the effective recognition of the right to collective bargaining for the next four years. This is due to be submitted to the meeting of the Governing Body in November.

In Chapter 5 of the Report it has been suggested that knowledge and advocacy of the principle and the right be strengthened and that the services provided to the constituents in this regard be improved.

We think that the Conference might feel it appropriate to consider some of the issues that have been listed on the piece of paper that I just mentioned. For those who do not have it, I will read it out quickly.

(1) Do you agree with the overall conclusion that although there are serious problems, there are some clear improvements in the application of this principle and right? As regards freedom of association? As regards the effective recognition of the right to collective bargaining?

(2) What are the prospects for promoting collective bargaining at different levels, and expanding the bargaining agenda, so as to cover subjects such as equality, competitiveness, productivity, innovation, work organization, training and new forms of employment?

(3) Do you agree with the idea of focusing further work on the sectors and groups identified (those in agriculture, in the public sector, in export-processing zones, migrant and domestic workers, and in the informal economy)? Which would be your priority areas?

(4) What kind of research and data collection should be given priority, that would be useful for governments, employers' and workers' organizations in giving better effect to this principle and right?

(5) With particular reference to Chapter 4 on technical cooperation, how do you think that these activities should best be followed up?

(6) What should be the key items for a Plan of Action for the next four years, to be submitted to the Governing Body in November 2004?

With that, I think we are ready to open the discussion.

Sir Roy TROTMAN *(Workers' delegate, Barbados, speaking on behalf of the Workers' group)*

Today we commence round two of our Global Report under the follow-up to the ILO Declaration on Fundamental Principles and Rights at Work, and we would wish, at the very commencement of the exercise, to thank the Director-General and his staff for the extensive work that they have done in preparing these Reports for us over the last five reporting sessions.

This is by no means an easy task. We are very conscious of the fact that there are still some problems associated with how the Reports are put together and how we treat them, and we firmly believe that we should look for ways to enhance the method by which we can get individual countries, individual groups of employers and individual groups of workers to submit reports, and to make for a more stimulating exercise that properly addresses the issues.

As things stand, I believe that the Governing Body may need to be asked as a result of this discussion to look more fully, in November or some subsequent time, at ways and means by which we can make the work that is being done tighter, stronger and more effective.

That does not mean, however, that the work done by the staff and contributors is not very effective, and we should thank all those who have contributed.

I think we would wish to give special thanks to the Director-General for the very clear comments he made this morning. We would also wish to refer to some of them, and I am sure that my colleagues will do so too. But let me first refer to the second point which he made, namely the point that freedom of association, organizing, should be seen as a normal exercise that does not require the approval of anyone. We think that this is basic and fundamental. As we said, we shall come back to this point in a minute or two.

Another very important matter – featured in the fifth point he mentioned– is that capacity building is vital and that we have to tackle the hindrances which, from time to time, interfere with efforts to promote freedom of association, especially those brought on by what we may term ideological positions – an ideological position, for example, that says that a person who works in an export processing zone is a second-class citizen and not entitled to the same rights and privileges as those who work elsewhere; or one that says that people who work in government services are second-class citizens, who are not entitled to the same freedom of association as others.

So, I think that we have been set a remarkable stage for what I hope will be a very frank discussion. From our point of view, we need to state unequivocally that freedom of association is a fundamental human right. It is a basic entitlement that should be expected and respected without reference to a country's size or its wealth.

All too frequently we have heard – and those of us who have been coming to this Organization, especially during the Conference, from time to time, will be aware of this – excuses being made regarding the failure of countries to respect freedom of association and indeed the right to bargain collectively. We hear excuses being made on the grounds that countries are poor, or that they do not possess the correct level of expertise – and we are saying, as the Director-General himself said, that this right is basic; it is fundamental; it is as correct and proper as the right to life. Of course, there are some places where the right to life is not as obvious as you or I might think. Therefore, we would have to indicate that this is a fundamental right alongside any other rights, and we hope that, at the end of this exercise, everyone here will be looking for ways and means through which we could help to empower the International Labour Organization to be better positioned to influence governments across the world as regards how to achieve the goal mentioned by the Director-General: that all countries will be respecting the right to organize by the year 2015.

For those who are first-timers to the Conference or who are first-timers to these exercises, we need to reflect a little on the need for this debate and why it has been made an interactive debate. Organizations, we believe, and especially an organization like the International Labour Organization, must stand for something; they must believe in something, and that something must be the *raison d'être* that makes us come here and interact one with another, year after year. In the International Labour Organization, we stand for fundamental principles and rights at work, so much so that we have agreed – Governments and the social partners – that, even when countries have themselves not ratified the underlying Conventions, they must still respect fundamental rights and principles at work.

We are of the view, furthermore, that people who do not believe in those fundamental principles and rights at work have joined the International Labour Organization for the wrong reasons. They need to review what exactly it is that makes them recognize the value of this Organization, and if they think that the Organization has value, we believe that they must come back to these fundamental principles and rights at work which are, in fact, the very lifeblood of the Organization.

We want them, at the same time, to understand and recognize as we do that organizations can only move forward effectively if they judge their current position in relation to their point of departure and in relation to where they expect their destination to be.

In short, we are hopeful that those governments that are Members of the ILO have agreed with us that universal social justice underpins the Organization and that they are in a position to see where they are along the continuum from no justice to universal justice. If that is where we are going, we are of the view that we shall be doing the correct thing in having interactive sessions such as this one.

We have said before that we appreciate the field work conducted by the ILO teams so far and, in that regard, we want to indicate further that we recognize its fundamental nature. We have spoken of this, and, we do not want to judge the work that has been done regarding freedom of association only in terms of the number of ratifications. Nor must we view this in terms of the luxury available to selective economies, or the number of loans and investments that people have been able to get.

Unfortunately, there are countries where trade union freedom is being sacrificed for short-term competitive advantages. The Director-General has spoken about this before and we have recognized that the Report itself speaks very clearly about some countries which advertise their economic environments as being union-free environments; in other words, as environments where workers are not free to exercise the normal, natural freedom that the Director-General spoke of.

If we were referring to one or two cases we might excuse them as being an aberration, but the reality is that there are far too many countries that believe they have to behave in this way if they are going to benefit from investment opportunities, either from businesses or, indeed, from established international institutions.

We believe that this debate, if it does nothing more, must confront this issue and show it up for the erroneous way in which it presents the very important factor of human life and human freedom.

We would like to say, that the Report speaks of evidence and that, given the evidence, we have to be careful in our conclusions. I would suggest that not only must our side, the labour side, be very careful about what conclusions we draw, but we must not really look at how many more countries have ratified the Conventions. Instead, we have to look at what further indicators may be able to help us to determine whether there is indeed an improvement to our accurate assessment.

We ask the President, and we ask every man and every woman here to define our true understanding of the real assessment that we can make of the progress that has been made over the last five years.

We think that the true assessment lies in the level of compliance in legislation compared to the degree of compliance in practice.

In essence, what we are saying is that even if we can see evidence of an increased number of countries where the Freedom of Association and Protection of the Right to Organise Convention, 1948 (No. 87) has been ratified, and we are pleased and satisfied that more countries have ratified it, it is not enough for a country to ratify the Convention to satisfy peer countries here at the International Labour Conference. They might have ratified another Convention, but in fact, they might be doing nothing about it when it comes to day-to-day practice.

The Convention has to be transposed into the law of that country and then we have to see evidence that the Government, as the main employer and the employers within that community, are actually observing the practice needed for compliance with the law.

If we do that, we would have to ask ourselves why we have the problems that the International Confederation of Free Trade Unions (ICFTU) has been pointing out from time to time: the ICFTU Survey 2003 reported that 213 trade unionists had been killed around the world in 2002, because they had wanted to exercise their normal and natural right to organize. In 2003, the figure was 129.

In 2002, in addition to the 213 people killed, 1,000 people were the victims of violence when exercising their normal freedom of association; 2,562 people were arrested and detained for exercising their normal entitlement to associate freely and to join organizations or trade unions.

Something has to be wrong – not with the statistics, because we believe the statistics to be correct – but something has to be wrong with the communities that are engaged in such an arrangement that leads to such statistics.

We have to be able, in having this debate, to get to grips with that issue and to be able to put forward some ideas that will help.

The Report entitled *Organizing for social justice* shows us that Colombia is still a problem. I do not take these countries out of the air, I take them out of the Report: we have the Republic of Moldova; Zimbabwe; and Belarus. We have Bangladesh, another country that should be mentioned, which speaks about having welfare committees rather than independent trade unions where workers do not have to ask permission from the employer or the Government in order to exercise the normal behaviour of anyone: animals do not go around asking permission to associate, they just group normally. We are supposed to be a higher breed of animal; what is so different about our breed of animal that we have to ask permission to do what comes naturally to everybody else – to associate freely?

We are of course pleased with the Report. We are pleased with the increased numbers, and we should be. We are sobered by the reality that 50 per cent of workers across the world are still being denied their freedom to associate freely, because of the failure of five major world powers to ratify Conventions Nos. 87 and 98.

These are world leaders which we admire very much indeed, and we believe that they could make us admire them even more if they were to ratify these Conventions. I am not saying that no worker is free to exercise any degree of association, but I am saying that if we belong to an organization that is built and structured on the fundamental freedom to associate, then these countries which are so powerful and so influential should lead the way for the rest of the world by ratifying those Conventions themselves.

This contradiction is thrown in our faces daily when we speak to smaller, less influential countries and I believe that the Director-General and his staff are faced with the same problem every time they are called upon to speak to another country. I have – and I am just a small fry – been called upon by many governments and many trade unionists as well to look at the practice in some other countries and have realized the contradiction which comes from such countries being in the vanguard of those telling other countries how to associate or how to respect fundamental practices and laws. And so I say that today we have to face up to reality, and the reality is that there is "many a slip twixt the cup and the lip", and the "lip" is saying one thing but the reality on the ground is fundamentally different from the "lip-service" that is being paid.

The Report is going to be made public and then the world will clearly see that justifications being used to suppress workers' fundamental rights are based on a false assumption. The Report speaks at some length about the economic arguments for ratification of Convention No. 87, and the ILO quotes not only its own studies, but also those carried out by the OECD and the World Bank, to show that the negative correlation between core labour rights and economic success has not so far been backed by empirical evidence.

The Report reassures us that strong respect for the fundamental right of freedom of association is a key condition for well-functioning, sustainable, innovative and adaptable labour markets. However, it is important to recognize that, although the Report might say that, we have to go back to what the Director-General said at the very outset about the position that we are starting from: i.e. that we should not be acting because the OECD or the World Bank have spoken up for the economic benefits or for the correlation or non-correlation between freedom of association and the economic benefits to a country, but because it is the fundamental right of all workers everywhere.

We want to come back to what the Director-General said about the position of the export processing zones. We identify workers in the export processing zones as being particularly vulnerable. We also have to mention workers in agriculture who are also particularly at risk in the exercise of their freedom of association. Above all, we have to realize the importance of both of these two areas.

Agriculture, because every country has an agricultural base and in every area we can think of efforts that have been made to reduce the standards which would apply to agricultural workers.

When it comes to export processing zones, we have to look to the statistics: there were 500 zones in 1996; 850 zones in 2,000; and now in 2004 there are 3,000 export processing zones. Some of these zones are expressly set down as areas where there must be no workers' right to organize, not only are those workers denied the freedom to organize, but we have practical examples of situations where they go to prison when they are going to work in these places, because the conditions can only be properly described as prison camps. Those conditions include all kinds of abuses, of indecent work – coming from countries which support, develop and promote the Decent Work Agenda. There must be a contradiction in this somewhere. Workers who exercise their freedom to organize in those zones are, in many instances, black-listed and face retribution, including sometimes, physical threats. We believe that this is a problem that has some very serious implications for us, and we hope that we will not want to be so diplomatic as to avoid facing the reality of the problem.

We are very conscious of the fact that not all reports of abuses are able to reach the International Labour Office. We are very much aware that some people do not report violations, sometimes because of fear, sometimes because they say "what is the point, when reporting the problem does not mean anything except that we expose ourselves to further possibility of bad treatment, because nobody cares".

The International Labour Organization, in the estimation of the Workers' group, cares. We believe that the International Labour Organization has demonstrated that it cares and we believe that this debate gives us the opportunity to show, to an even greater extent, the level of our care and of our concern.

The Report properly addresses here the key challenge of organizing the unorganized and, once again, this was referred to in the introduction. There is a place for the informal sector in this discussion, and our preparation and our arrangements must include some structures to deal with that so that they can be given a place in the work that we have to do in order to give them the protection required. They need our protection so that they can enjoy the right to be heard and so that they can perhaps win the right to influence in their individual, domestic environments and, indeed, further afield.

As well as addressing the unorganized, the Report must address the obstacles to workers' rights that exist today in 2004. I have referred to this before: we must be able to tackle the contradictions in having people say to us, "do as I say, not as I do". This is something that we must get to grips with; we must try to deal with the efforts that are made to hinder the freedom which must exist for organization to be possible. The Report mentions greater universal ratification by all governments, but it must urge greater ratification. It must talk about the social commitment by all employers to freedom of association and to commit themselves to respecting that normal behaviour. It must talk about the total organizing effort that all trade unions must make, and say that they must be given the capacity to do so through the assistance of their governments and, indeed, of the International Labour Organization.

The Report makes reference to the global unions' efforts to organize and it does mention consumer awareness and pressure brought by the international community as factors contributing to the improvement of the situation. So, there has been some good news.

The first collective agreements have been signed in Guatemala in the export processing zone; workers in Honduras and Sri Lanka have won union recognition; and Bangladesh, we understand, is committed to reviewing the policies that we referred to earlier. But in the meantime, there are more than 50 million workers in export processing zones, many of whom are denied the right to organize and to bargain collectively. There are some 435 million workers in the public sector, more than half the world's population is in agriculture, over 80 million migrant workers all are working in the informal sector: the right to organize, the right to negotiate decent working conditions through collective bargaining, must not be considered a luxury. We need each of the ILO constituents to pull its weight in strengthening these rights, because we understand that they are fundamental rights of everyone.

During this debate, my colleagues in the Workers' group are going to be making some observations as well, and I hope that you will entertain them as they provide a contribution to strengthening the right to organize and to bargain collectively. We believe that ILO technical assistance is needed, to a very great extent, to help our primary objective of organizing the unorganized and we believe that this second Report, though an improvement on what we have had so far, must be recognized as a work in progress. We must not sit on our laurels, on the part of governments or employers or the workers, or of the Office, but we all must put our noses to the grindstone to make sure that the objective set by the Director-General of 2015 being the absolute deadline for full realization of freedom of association, is not only met, but is met well before that date.

Mr. POTTER *(Employers' delegate, United States, speaking on behalf of the Employers' group)*

First, I would like to commend the Office for having relocated this meeting. It is obvious to us all that here we are on a level playing field, and that this is a meeting room where we can have a conversation, can all look each other in the eye and have a discussion. I already feel differently about this meeting than I did about the four previous meetings, just because of the environment that we have here.

We very much appreciate the fact that the Director-General is here today. We especially appreciate his statement. It is clear to us that he was speaking from the heart, and by doing so, was claiming ownership of an important instrument in the ILO, namely, the Declaration on Fundamental Principles and Rights at Work, and we very much appreciate that.

We want the Director-General and the members of the Declaration team to know that any criticisms we may have of the Report or the direction of the Declaration should be taken in the spirit in which they are given, because we are seeking to ensure that the Declaration achieves its full potential in accordance with the principles of this Organization.

Mr. Trotman's statement, I believe, is a good starting point. He emphasized first the importance of this interactive discussion and demanded that Governments meet their commitments under the Declaration. For this reason, we should look slightly differently at the question of ratification. We think that, what at the end of the day is most important in terms of the Declaration, is the full implementation and achievement of the fundamental principles. Yes, ratification can be important, but ratification is often a symbolic gesture rather than a real gesture. What we are looking for here is the achievement and realization of the first principle of the Declaration, namely freedom of association and the effective recognition of the right to collective bargaining.

This year's Global Report, which, as Mr. Trotman said, represents the beginning of the second cycle of the Global Report follow-up, is a substantial and welcome improvement over the first Global Report on the first principle that we discussed in 2000. This Global Report is well-written, readable and non-legalistic. For this, the Office is to be commended and congratulated.

I think it is important for us all to bear in mind the objectives of the Declaration. In paragraph 2 of the Declaration, the International Labour Conference declares that all Members have an obligation to respect, to promote and to realize, in accordance with the Constitution of the Organization, the principles concerning the fundamental rights which are the subject of the eight fundamental ILO Conventions on human rights in the workplace.

This Global Report addresses the first principle, namely freedom of association and the effective recognition of the right to collective bargaining, which is based on Conventions Nos. 87 and 98. The governmental commitment encompasses the scope of these two Conventions without the detailed legal obligations of the two Conventions unless, of course, the Member has ratified one or both of the Conventions. It is clear that Members have no obligations with regard to specific provisions of Conventions that they have not ratified. The Declaration is not wider in scope than the fundamental Conventions themselves.

Under the first principle, the Declaration seeks to promote a policy environment that promotes freedom of association and the effective recognition of collective bargaining. If that policy environment exists, then the organizational results are up to the workers' and employers' organizations.

Although we understand that the Global Report is intended to provide a dynamic global picture of the principle under consideration, as last year, employers continue to be concerned about the wide-ranging nature of the first-three sections of this Report. These sections address and do a good job of discussing global trends, but do so without making any distinction between the policies that are specifically addressed under the Conventions. For example, while we have no problem with the section on framework agreements, we think that undue emphasis is given to those agreements because, in terms of our view of the Declaration, we are concerned first and foremost with the fundamental policy failures in achieving the principle in question.

As we said in the debate on the 2000 Global Report, we need to determine in an organized way the underlying policies encompassed by this first principle. For example, Mr. Trotman identified a policy that we could agree to, as it is a fundamental principle, in other words the right to life. Clearly, that is the kind of fundamental matter that we are concerned about.

In his opening statement, the Director-General provided a basis for a conversation on the essential matters that are of the utmost concern under the Declaration and its first principle.

In the 2000 discussion, we suggested two or three other possible policies that flow from this first principle, namely the right of employers and workers to establish and join organizations of their own choosing, the right to manage internal affairs without interference from public authorities and the right to be free from acts of interference from employer or worker organizations.

Great care should be taken to keep in mind the constitutional and legal basis for the principles and rights encompassed in the Declaration.

In the context of this Global Report, in our view, the fact that this has not been done gives the Report a somewhat unfocused quality. For example, and I understand the editorial reason for doing this, the Report continually uses the shorthand versions of the Declaration's first principle. This, I think, could create some confusion as to what the principle actually encompasses. This confusion could have been solved at the very beginning by a simple footnote to say that, for purposes of the Report, we will use a shorter version, but it should be understood that, when we use this version, it means the entirety of principle No. 1.

The second point for discussion, I think, illustrates this additionally for us. The second point for discussion, related to collective bargaining, illustrates this lack of focus. In the Declaration we are looking at how, when and where the ILO technical cooperation can address fundamental serious policy failures. We think this question is not focused enough on what the policy failure is relating to collective bargaining but rather, it is looking at what I would consider to be leading ethical issues.

First and foremost we are trying to get at the fundamental problems. I think eventually, hopefully, in our lifetimes, we will be able, in a concrete way, to address leading questions relating to collective bargaining.

Part of the purpose of the Global Report follow-up is intended to serve as a basis for assessing the effectiveness of the assistance provided by the ILO. Chapter 4 sets out the technical assistance programme addressing the first principle. However, we are given no information about when these programmes started, at what stage they are, how effective they were – at least in the short term – plus specific lessons that have been learned beyond the general notions contained in the Report, what follow-on activities are needed and how many programmes may be in the pipeline. These were valuable pieces of information that would have put us in a better position, frankly, to provide some advice and guidance to the ILO for future action plans.

As far as we can see, this Report does not offer a basis for a comprehensive assessment, something the Governing Body's Committee on Technical Co-operation asked for and expected in November 2000, as part of the second Global Report on this principle. We did not see that. This is particularly troubling in view of the acknowledgement in paragraph 382 that "data from ILO technical cooperation should be better extracted and exploited in terms of problem analysis, evaluation of impact on target groups and in drawing policy lessons from the changes effected at the country level through these projects".

Several of my Employer colleagues will intervene this morning and this afternoon and give their views on the value of the ILO Declaration programmes. Another purpose of the follow-up is to determine technical cooperation and action plan priorities. We think the emphasis that has been placed, and is placed, on ratifications on the Freedom of Association and Protection of the Right to Organise Convention, 1948 (No. 87), and Right to Organise and Collective Bargaining Convention, 1949 (No. 98), is the wrong priority. We think for the first round it may have been a correct priority, but I think that at this stage, ratification, or lack of ratification, in and of itself says nothing, says nothing about implementation, the first principle in practice. The priority, in our view, for the foreseeable future should be on implementation by all countries, regardless of whether they have ratified the fundamental Conventions.

Overall there is very little concrete information in this Report on which to determine priorities. It is astonishing to read, in paragraph 379, that the ILO does not have "an up-to-date picture of the legislative situation regarding freedom of association and the effective recognition of collective bargaining".

Surely a global serious policy failure or gap analysis under the first principle can be conducted to identify needs. The fact that the Report acknowledges the challenges in identifying true needs does not inspire confidence that Declaration programmes will be targeted and focused over the next four years, rather than being random and scatter-shot in responding simply to demand. Rather than a passive demand-based system of technical cooperation, attention should be given to a proactive rapid response strategy for serious immediate need situations.

As we begin this second round under the Global Report follow-up, we have entered a new phase. For the most part, in the first four years, governments in their presentations on the special day of the Conference paid homage to the value of the Declaration and their commitment to it. As the Expert-Advisers said in paragraph 9 of this year's Review of annual reports under the follow-up to the ILO Declaration and I quote in full "The Declaration speaks about respecting, promoting and realizing fundamental principles and rights at work. It is worth reflecting upon these concepts. Respect is about the political will to achieve the principles, not mere lip-service. Promotion is advocacy, backed by action and programmes toward positive change. Realization means achieving improvement in the daily lives of individual women and men, their families, workplaces and communities. Thus, the promotional aspect of the Declaration is about change, and it is about evaluating progress, in both legislation and practice. All this work requires a continuous effort in awareness raising. Promotion is about initiating progress from a given starting point – no matter how low that initial point might be – towards full realization of the Declaration principles and rights."

The Employers agree with the Expert-Advisers and consequently we are going to be looking to governments today to say something more than swearing allegiance to the Declaration and platitudes. The constitutional commitment under the Declaration requires member States to tell what they are doing to respect, promote and realize this first principle. Now is the time for countries to step forward and ask for technical assistance and tell us what they are doing to achieve and realize this principle. This will facilitate an interactive discussion that is essential to targeting and prioritizing the Declaration's success.

Original Arabic: Mr. AL TAYER *(Minister of Labour and Social Affairs, United Arab Emirates, speaking on behalf of the Gulf Cooperation Council)*

In the name of God, the Merciful, the Compassionate! It is a great pleasure for me to pay tribute to this distinguished Conference on behalf of the Ministers for Social Affairs of the Gulf Cooperation Council, whose members include the United Arab Emirates, the Kingdom of Bahrain, Kingdom of Saudi Arabia, the Sultanate of Oman, the State of Qatar, the Sultanate of Kuwait and Yemen.

At this special sitting, devoted to the discussion of the Global Report under the follow-up to the ILO Declaration on Fundamental Principles and Rights at Work, we are discussing the Declaration whose purpose is to establish social justice.

It is my duty to express my thanks to the Director-General for his excellent Report entitled *Organizing for social justice,* which deals with the first principle of the Declaration, namely freedom of association and collective bargaining.

We would like to express our support for the contents of this Report, for views, objectives and coherent guidelines on how to tackle this important issue.

We fully agree with the Director-General's opinion regarding the possibility for societies to apply this Declaration in order to consolidate democracy and boost industrial growth. We have embarked on a process of implementing several of the principles contained in this Declaration. We also agree with the Director-General about the challenge that lies ahead. In this connection we have made a successful start in recent years on some aspects of the follow-up to the Declaration. We will continue to strive to apply it better.

An objective reading of development in our countries in the last few years points to successes and indicates that steps have been taken to intensify our commitment and to increase worker representation by insisting on the right of association in accordance with the spirit of the Declaration.

In 2002, we adopted trade union legislation, the General Confederation of the Workers of Bahrain was established and we participated in various trade union movements at the local and international levels.

The Kingdom of Saudi Arabia has also taken steps to implement the Council of Ministers' decisions regarding the creation of workers' committees and some of these committees have actually started to operate. For the first time, the leading officials of these two workers' committees are attending the Conference. Furthermore, a bill which has been submitted to the Shura Council in the Kingdom of Saudi Arabia takes into account labour standards and the need to coordinate activities with the ILO.

The new Labour Code adopted in Oman contains a specific chapter regarding the right to collective bargaining and the setting up of workers' committees in keeping with the provisions of international Conventions and in order to promote social dialogue.

Last May, the Sultanate of Oman adopted two ministerial decrees regarding the rules and the composition of workers' committees in enterprises, as well as the rules and regulations governing the operation of worker representation. They give workers the right to choose their own representatives in workers' committees. These committees provide a framework for organized worker representation within each firm so that they can defend their rights and interests in all matters relating to their protection at local, regional, international and Arab meetings and conferences.

The United Arab Emirates have drawn up a draft law which authorizes the creation of labour institutions. The law is currently in its final phase of adoption.

The State of Kuwait, within the framework of the follow-up, has taken a vital step by adopting Law No. 11 of 2003, which allows civil servants and workers in the oil sectors to organize on an equal footing with workers in the private sector.

The Republic of Yemen has also strengthened freedom of association by establishing a legislative structure in accordance with international instruments. It passed labour legislation and held elections for the General Confederation of Worker Unions at the beginning of this year.

As part of measures to modernize the State, the Emir has adopted the permanent Constitution of the State of Qatar as a further step towards the creation of a state of institutions in Qatar.

A new labour law which was passed in May 2004 contains a chapter on collective bargaining and gives workers the possibility to set up their own works committees to defend their rights and represent them in all matters regarding labour affairs.

The new legislation further provides workers with the right to create general industrial committees. These general committees are members of the General Confederation of Workers of Qatar. This legislation also provides for the right to strike and the right of employers and workers to bargain collectively and negotiate collective agreements. It also establishes equal rights to work, employment, training and to equality between working men and women. In order to promote the Declaration and respect for international labour standards, the State of Oman has gradually ratified most of the basic ILO Conventions over the last few months.

The Committee of Experts, in its report this year, has commended the State for the steps it has taken. It has also welcomed the measures adopted by the Gulf Cooperation Council. In this connection, we would like to reaffirm our determination to pursue dialogue and constructive cooperation between the social partners. These efforts have recently culminated in the organization of joint meetings and symposia, which are a reflection of the cooperative approach to collective bargaining in GCC countries. The latest meeting was held last April in Qatar and took the form of a regional workshop on the ILO Declaration on Fundamental Principles and Rights at Work. It brought together representatives of the social partners from the GCC countries and was supported by the ILO.

It goes without saying that to talk about the right of association constitutes progress in the implementation of workers' rights. The growing number of ratifications of international conventions will acquire its full significance only when we assess the reforms and innovative measures adopted by the GCC countries. These seek mainly to build the capacities of workers and social institutions and to ensure their effective participation in decision-making and the implementation of reforms. We are thus endeavouring to strengthen the role of civil society institutions on the basis of inalienable Islamic principles calling for consultation, peace and equality. This is what the Global Report refers to when it suggests that the authorities of these countries are aware of the implications of establishing mechanisms for the election of persons to head organizations representing the world of work.

We wish here to reaffirm that political will must be backed by effective steps allowing workers to create their own representative institutions. All dynamic societies trying to achieve progress aspire to dialogue and the strengthening of its mechanisms, a dialogue based on an acceptance of the diversity of experiences in a world where attempts to impose a single culture could dehumanize globalization by seeking to standardize all aspects of daily life.

Today humanity is trying to replace confrontation with dialogue and to accept diversity and multi-representation in order to create a peaceful, stable and just society where future generations will be able to build a better future.

Mr. DE GEUS *(Minister of Social Affairs and Employment, the Netherlands)*

Today, 10 June 2004, is a very important date because we are celebrating two world events today. The first is the election of a new enlarged European Parliament; the second is the discussion, here in Geneva, on the second Report, that deals with freedom of association and the right of collective bargaining under the follow-up to the ILO Declaration on Fundamental Principles and Rights at Work. I am happy to be able to take part in both of these world events; if I have to leave early, it is to cast my vote for the new European Parliament.

I am pleased to be taking part in this discussion and I would like to raise five points. I will speak about The Hague, about the "gap", about actions, about allied forces and about the ILO.

So firstly The Hague. The Declaration and its follow-up is of great importance to the Netherlands. Unfortunately during the last two years, the number of people attending the discussion on the Report has decreased. To express our concern, in November last year we organized an informal seminar in The Hague, the city of peace. This seminar was attended by around 60 participants from all over the world, representing the constituents of the ILO. All present expressed their commitment to the Declaration and its follow-up and I hope that the spirit and the energy we saw during that seminar will be with us today and will stay with us in the ILO as we carry out its difficult tasks.

Now about the "gap". I have read the Report with great interest and have to conclude that the overall picture remains troublesome. The last four years have shown continued progress in the ratification of the two Conventions which is definitely a step in the right direction. But, at the same time, we see that the implementation of the Conventions is clearly lagging behind. The Netherlands wants the Global Report to remain a strong instrument in the follow-up to the Declaration on Fundamental Principles and Rights at Work by providing us with a dynamic picture of global development and by leading the way to setting priorities for the next four-year period. There is no doubt that universal ratification of the Conventions concerned remains a priority. This, however, is not enough when universal ratification goes hand in hand with a gross violation of union rights. So the central question is: How can we mobilize the political will to decrease the gap between ratification and implementation? I listened very carefully to the Workers and Employers and I am glad to conclude that this question is a common concern.

So after The Hague and the "gap", I will now move on to talk about actions. Your draft points of conclusion for discussion are very helpful and I will comment a little bit on that. The five actions I take from the points of discussion are the following:

The first action is monitoring: how to monitor social and economic results and how to monitor both in a way which will show the social results that go hand-in-hand with economic growth and prosperity?

The second action is "spreading the good news": how to communicate, invest in communication and let the people of the world know?

The third action is "focusing": you have already raised the question of how to focus not only on sectors but also on regions. I think it is very important, not only from a rational and intellectual point of view, but also from a political point of view, if possible, to focus on the requests of parties in a particular sector or region. So, focus if possible on requests.

The fourth action is cooperation: cooperate with institutions like the World Bank and the IMF. I will come to that. It is very important to cooperate in the international field.

The last action, and I listened very carefully to my friend Mr. Trotman who was also present in The Hague and I listened to him today very carefully. I picked up one thing, and that is an important action as to how to protect individuals involved in processes such as taking a role as a spokesperson. We have to protect those people who make themselves vulnerable to any harm.

After actions, I come to the allied forces. First of all I must mention the report of the World Commission on the Social Dimension of Globalization. I will explain to you how this can be an allied force. But first, I have to say that the long name of this report puzzles me. How can we speak about this report in a simple way? The World Commission on the Social Dimension of Globalization is a bit of a mouthful. Its acronym, WCSDG, is unpronounceable. I tried to make a useful sentence that reminds us of the content of this report; its initials, WCSDG, can also be the initials of the following sentence that expresses the meaning of this report "Worldwide Commitment to Social Rights Deliver Growth". I think this is, in essence, what this report is about. If it is not for social purposes, then it is for economic purposes. We have to follow the lines of this report. It could be a valuable asset when dealing with our questions.

The report not only reconfirms the importance of promoting, respecting and realizing labour standards worldwide. It also urges for more coherence in social, economic and financial agendas. This means that international organizations should cooperate in a more effective way and governments should speak with the same voice in the different organizations in which they are active. The position that governments take on this report could be an important allied force.

By saying this, I underline that it is surprise that for instance the G8 countries are talking about a report like this. It is not only about social justice, it is also about economic growth. Speaking about allied forces, we must not forget the solidarity of workers worldwide. It is not only governments and employers, but also workers and trade unions worldwide who can show solidarity with their colleagues in countries like Colombia, as will be discussed today by the Dutch Christian National Federation of Trade Unions (CNU) in The Hague. So maybe this is the third important world event taking place today. So, expressions of solidarity worldwide are also a very important allied forces.

My last point relates to the ILO. The ILO's role as guardian and promoter of labour standards is crucial and indisputable. We call on the ILO to make its important work more feasible within the international community, especially since a growing body of evidence indicates that respecting union rights and other core labour standards contributes to improving economic performance. This year we are commemorating the ILO's 85th anniversary. A lot has been accomplished by this unique Organization which is close to our hearts. But, as is shown by this Global Reports, many more challenges lie ahead.

The Netherlands is committed to supporting the ILO in facing and overcoming these challenges. We look forward to an inspiring discussion.

(Mr. Maatough takes the Chair.)

Mr. POTTER *(Employers' delegate, United States, speaking on behalf of the Employers' group)*

Just briefly, as a participant in the conference held in The Hague last November, I want to especially commend the Netherlands for hosting that conference. Among many positive things that happened at that meeting which was the first conversation of the Employers' group assessing what had happened during the last four years. The fact that this meeting is being held today is clearly a result of that meeting, due in part, as we have seen today, to the good humour of the Minister, but also to excellent piano-playing skills. I also want to commend the statement by the representative of the United Arab Emirates, because I believe that the substance of his statement goes to the heart of what the Declaration commitment is all about. He talks specifically about the things they are doing to achieve this, so we thank you.

Sir Roy TROTMAN *(Workers' delegate, Barbados, speaking on behalf of the Workers' group)*

It is not my intention to intervene in the discussion, but, like Mr. Potter, I think it is necessary to do so at this stage. He touched on the comment from the representative of United Arab Emirates and I would like to come back to that more fully later to say that they are moving in the right direction, but we want to hear about trade unions and not about works' councils. But, really, I wanted to speak about the position of the Honourable Minister De Geus. Now, I agree with Mr. Potter regarding his piano-playing, and I also wish to make the point that he forced me to sing when my voice was not quite ready for it, but I am now ready to cut a record so if he will accompany me with his playing I am ready to make my first record for 2004.

We would like to thank the Dutch very much for hosting the exercise and preparing us for today's work. They were very generous host, but beyond that we had a splendid occasion where governments, employers and workers, looked very seriously at the question of the work of the follow-up and the principles that underpin it, and I think the Dutch should be congratulated for their contribution.

Original Arabic: Mr. NEFFATI *(Minister of Social Affairs and Solidarity, Tunisia)*

First of all, I would like to thank the Director-General for the efforts he has made concerning the 2004 Global Report under the follow-up to the ILO Declaration on Fundamental Principles and Rights at Work. I am delighted to be able to take part in this discussion, because Tunisia attaches paramount importance to the question of social justice. Social justice cannot exist without development. It is therefore necessary to respect the basic principles of work and this is an essential prerequisite to strengthening competitiveness.

Collective bargaining makes it possible for the workers to fight for their rights and means fair relations between the different partners. Freedom of association and collective bargaining play a decisive role in economic and social development and contribute the development of relations between the various partners, making the achievement of goals possible. They therefore establish the balance which is necessary in the marketplace.

Trade unions play a fundamental role in strengthening the rights of workers. They also make it possible to establish labour standards, particularly against the backdrop of the changes taking place in the world. Workshops and meetings should be organized in order to allow people to take part in discussions that promote the interests of the various partners and monitor respect for their rights.

Tunisia considers human rights to be fundamental rights. We are making considerable efforts to establish these rights because we consider them to be essential and indivisible. Economic and social development is one of the rights of employers and workers. This is why we are preparing and implementing plans aimed at particular aspects of development and why we are taking steps to implement action plans relating to labour. The right to collective bargaining is considered in Tunisia to be a part of our freedom of association and trade unionists' rights. We need to acknowledge the rights of trade unions to collective bargaining at the national and global levels. I believe that the ILO should play a decisive role in assisting countries to apply these principles.

Original Arabic: Mr. EL AMAWY *(Minister of Manpower and Emigration, Egypt)*

Allow me at the outset to express my pleasure in attending this important assembly, since freedom of association and collective bargaining constitute an essential pillar of fundamental human rights, and an integral part of the democratic process, as well as the means of linking social objectives and economic growth.

The Report states that there are about 80 million economically active persons working in countries other than their own, most of whom are employed in jobs at the lowest level. I fully agree with the Report when it points to the need for these workers to be involved in efforts aimed at the effective recognition of their right to collective bargaining and the right of their representatives to participate on equal footing with others in negotiating collective agreements.

The Report confirms the importance of ensuring respect for labour standards within every community. We fully support this principle, since it embodies both the spirit and the letter of the ILO Declaration on Fundamental Principles and Rights at Work, as mentioned in the Report. It is essential to point out that the follow-up to the Declaration provides for a phased process.

It should be borne in mind that industrial relations systems vary from one region to another. Egypt respects the principles of human rights and is committed to the implementation of labour standards. On this basis it has adopted machinery for tripartite consultation to deal with labour disputes, and to draft or amend labour legislation, so as to accommodate the interests of all the parties.

This meeting today to discuss the Global Report, constitutes a step forward in our efforts to strengthen freedom of association and the effective recognition of the right to collective bargaining, and we fully support the recommendations and proposals included therein. I entirely agree with the view that while numerous problems remain, there is no doubt that these problems and difficulties are accompanied by improvements in the field of collective bargaining, which contribute to the solution of these problems. There is a need to strengthen collective bargaining on an equal footing, and we will certainly have an invaluable exchange of views that will help strengthen dialogue.

I believe it is essential to emphasize workers' rights in the informal sector and the agricultural sector, and the latter should be given top priority. Technical cooperation is also an area in which we need to set up the necessary machinery to carry out studies and surveys, and prepare statistics, in particular with regard to migrant workers.

Concerning the Report of the Director-General entitled *The situation of workers of the occupied Arab territories*, in the light of Israeli practices in the occupied Arab territories, consisting of closing down many trade unions and professional institutions, which are being attacked by military personnel, confiscating their documents, and arresting and expelling trade unionists and restricting their freedom of movement, as the Director-General mentioned at the beginning of the meeting, the ILO, as part of its basic responsibilities, must guarantee the exercise of trade union rights and freedoms of the workers in the occupied Arab territories.

In conclusion, I should like to express my gratitude to the Director-General for his Report, and I sincerely hope that in coming sessions we will be able to note improvements with regard to the practices I have just mentioned. I should like to commend our distinguished brother from the United Arab Emirates for his statement, in which he referred to the marked improvements achieved by the member States of the Gulf Cooperation Council in regard to respect for these fundamental rights and principles.

Mr. SWEENEY *(Workers' adviser and substitute delegate, United States)*

The Director-General's Report, *Organizing for social justice*, provides a snapshot of the state of union organizations around the world, as Sir Leroy Trotman has outlined for the Workers' delegates.

The Report highlights a number of positive developments that have emerged over the last four years; the beginning of labour law reform in the Gulf State region, the promotion of freedom of association as an essential component of the global strategy to combat poverty and new forms of employer/worker cooperation.

Unfortunately, despite the Report's forward-looking perspective, the relative number of workers belonging to unions has declined since we last visited this subject four years ago. The trend line is going in the wrong direction, and this is the case in both developing and developed countries, and for workers from virtually every geographic region around the world.

In the United States, over 42 million workers say they would join unions if they had the opportunity, but the truth is that significant categories of workers in our country do not even have the right to organize under the law, including millions of agricultural, domestic and supervisory employees. Millions of other workers who are eligible for union membership cannot freely join or form unions because of intimidation, harassment and termination tactics of employers.

At least one in every four workers directly involved in an organizing campaign in the United States it the victim of an anti-union firing or termination. Even if workers manage to prevail in their struggle to win union representation in the face of overwhelming employer reprisals, they still fail to win collective bargaining agreements in over one-third of the cases owing to bad-faith bargaining tactics and the power of employers to permanently replace economic strikers in the United States continues to fundamentally violate the effective exercise of freedom of association.

In the public sector, employees of our Federal Government and in many states are denied their fundamental rights to bargain over essential terms of employment as well as being denied the right to strike. Moreover, the current administration in the

United States has denied union representation rights to 170,000 homeland security workers, including 60,000 airport screeners, based on the pretext that their rights to self-organization are not compatible with national security.

The Director-General's Report informs us that only 18 member States of the ILO have failed to ratify the Freedom of Association and Protection of the Right to Organise Convention, 1948 (No. 87), or Right to Organise and Collective Bargaining Convention, 1949 (No. 98). The United States is one of these 18 countries. The reality is that our labour laws at the federal and state levels are not in compliance with the provisions of these core human rights Conventions, dimming the prospects for ratification any time soon.

The United States Government acknowledged deficiencies in its 2000 report to the ILO on freedom of association and the right to bargain collectively when it conceded that there are gaps in our labour laws that are inadequate in ensuring that these rights are protected.

For all of these reasons, the United States labour movement, the human rights community and scores of congressional representatives are urging the passage of the Employee Free Choice Act that will bring labour laws more into compliance with ILO standards.

The proposed Act, which now has 200 co-sponsors in the House of Representatives and 31 in the Senate, provides for union recognition upon verification of majority support, first-contact mediation and arbitration and stronger employer penalties for anti-union tactics. Even after this Law is enacted, there will still be areas in our labour law that are in conflict with the principles and rights associated with freedom of association and the right to bargain collectively. The 2000 United States Government report to the ILO held out the possibility of ILO technical assistance to help identify these areas and develop recommendations to address them. It is time for the United States Government to officially request such ILO assistance.

In addition, our Government should implement the recommendations of the Committee on Freedom of Association concerning the Hoffman case to provide legal protections for immigrant workers' freedom of association.

The Director-General begins his Report by emphasizing that the real debate cannot and should not be on whether to respect freedom of association and the right to bargain collectively, but on how best to respect and make use of them. Given the precarious nature of work in today's global economy and the growing need for workers to have voice and representation under such circumstances, it is now time for the ILO to go beyond discussion, as good as today's has been.

In very concrete and practical terms, we need to hold governments and employers to their pledge to protect and promote these core labour standards.

Original Portuguese: Mr. PAIS ANTUNES *(Secretary of State for Labour, Portugal)*

First of all, I would like to congratulate the Director-General for the excellent Report that he has submitted to us on freedom of association and the right to collective bargaining, as part of the follow-up to the ILO Declaration on Fundamental Principles and Rights at Work. When, four years ago, the first report on freedom of association and the right to collective bargaining was discussed, the Portuguese delegation spoke on behalf of the European Union and suggested that successive reports should present a more dynamic and global image, and should give an account of the situation in various regions with regard to these fundamental rights.

It is with great gratification that we take note of the substantial improvement in this presentation, that is, information on the situation of freedom of association and the right to collective bargaining in general. However, we regret to have to note that a lot remains to be done in order for these fundamental rights to be effectively acknowledged and complied with in all member States. About half the workers and employers throughout the world are not yet covered by the fundamental Conventions concerning freedom of association and the right to organize, and the right to collective bargaining. With regard to certain member States that have not, as yet, ratified these Conventions, we have very little information.

It is worrying to note that various regions in the world continue to perpetrate persecution and discrimination against trade unionists because of their trade union activities. Apart from these very serious breaches of trade union rights, there is a considerable number of situations in which there is no effective acknowledgement of the right to collective bargaining.

It is particularly relevant to consider the analysis made in the Report of the situation of certain workers who experience the greatest difficulties in having their trade union rights respected and complied with. I refer in particular to workers in the public sector, agriculture and export processing zones as well as to migrant workers, domestic workers and workers in the informal economy, who in many areas of the world continue to face enormous difficulties with regard to trade union rights.

Allow me to make particular reference to the most vulnerable groups of workers. In the last few decades, export processing zones have developed enormously. However, the legislation that is applied in some of these processing zones does not guarantee trade union rights for workers. On other occasions, although the legislation formally guarantees such rights, there are many practical obstacles to their implementation and to their recognition.

We know that the absence of trade union rights can lead to or encourage investment in the export processing zones, but these situations, which could be described as social "dumping", are unacceptable because they not only jeopardize workers in the export processing zones, but also affect employment in those countries that do respect fundamental labour rights. These situations are clearly rejected in the Declaration, which emphasizes, very justifiably so, that labour standards cannot serve the purposes of protectionist interests.

I am referring also to the very worrying situation of migrant workers with regard to trade union rights. Migrant workers have fundamental rights. Migrant workers who are in an irregular situation also have fundamental rights. In other words, even though their situation may not be regularized, even if they have to leave the country, these migrant workers in an irregular situation should, insofar as they do work, have their fundamental rights recognized and should be able to enjoy them like any other worker.

The position that has been adopted by the Committee on Freedom of Association within the Governing Body of the ILO is most appropriate and should be disseminated accordingly. A globalized world cannot tolerate a situation in which workers continue to live without trade union rights.

The Report that has been drafted within the framework of the ILO's Declaration essentially intends to serve as a basis in order to assess the technical assistance provided by the Organization and to determine future priority with regard to cooperation. From this standpoint, the Portuguese Government supports the proposals put forward by the Director-General, namely that, in cooperation with governments, trade unions and employers' associations, our efforts should be concentrated in four basic areas:

First, the ratification of the fundamental Conventions on freedom of association and collective bargaining; second, providing support to the most vulnerable groups of workers; third, the development of the legislative framework and the public institutions that regulate the labour market; and last, providing consultation services and activities to raise awareness in society as a whole for the purpose of promoting fundamental rights at work.

Original French: Mr. RAïS *(Spokesperson for the Minister of Labour, Algeria)*

Since the Minister of Labour of Algeria is absent I would just say one or two words on his behalf, if I may.

Freedom of association and collective bargaining have now become standard practice in many countries.

Credit for this is, to a great extent, due to this Organization because it has fought so hard to ensure that social dialogue and collective bargaining and freedom of association have become a tangible reality.

We believe that what we have to do in the future is to ensure follow-up on the application of the relevant ILO Conventions and Recommendations.

We also need to assess, analyse and measure the progress that has been achieved in respect of what are, after all, very important matters in the world of work.

We need to aim at perfection and, where perfection is impossible, at least at improvement, so as to spread respect for the right to collective bargaining and freedom of association around the world.

Any approach aimed at achieving this should be developed in a spirit of cooperation between the Organization and its various member States.

Our future work, in our opinion, should be focused particularly on the informal economy and on migrant workers because these two issues seem to us to be matters of priority. They are certainly matters of priority for my country because we are in the process of switching to a market economy and, as a consequence, we have seen an increase in the size of our informal economy.

Technical cooperation by the ILO is extremely important and we would like to see it strengthened in comparison with what it has been in the past.

We would also like to see it contribute to creating the economic and social development strategies in those countries that are in the process of implementing the fundamental rights that direct the labour market.

Technical support and the expertise of the ILO are a sine qua non if we are to bring about social justice and achieve the social progress which so many of our countries, particularly my own, are striving to achieve.

Mr. KONDITI *(Employers' delegate, Kenya)*

Thank you for giving me the opportunity to comment on a few points during the discussion of the Global Report.

I have three or four points that I would like to mention here.

One is human resources development in terms of training. We would like to thank the ILO for giving us an opportunity, or at least two opportunities, to train two of our officers at the International Training Centre of the ILO in Turin during the year 2003.

One of the training courses was on gender equality, poverty eradication and employment promotion. These are very important issues now. The other course was on the role of employers' organizations in combating child labour.

We appreciate these courses and the other courses offered by the Centre. Therefore, we appeal to the ILO to keep us, the Federation of Kenya Employers and other employers in mind, for training opportunities that may be offered by the Centre in the future.

The other issue I should like to mention is law reform, that is labour law reform, not just ordinary law reform.

Kenya is already moving towards the full realization of the fundamental principles and rights at work.

Under the ILO project on Strengthening Labour Relations in East Africa, which is commonly known as SLAREA and which was founded by the United States Department of Labor, the Government appointed a tripartite task force to review our labour laws which we consider today to be quite problematic in some areas.

The task force, which was established back in 2001, completed its work and submitted a report together with draft bills on every piece of legislation that it would like to be implemented.

This was done on 28th April this year.

Some of us would also like to express our gratitude and appreciation to the United States Department of Labor and ILO for this assistance.

We have already started to see the positive effects of the activities carried out as part of this project, particularly in the management of our labour relations. The Government and the social partners are now making earnest efforts, not only to promote tripartism, but also to resolve labour disputes voluntarily at the parties' own levels (and I am referring to the two parties – employers and workers). When they fail, they go to the Government for mediation. As a measure of that success, last year 2,323 labour disputes were reported to the Minister for Labour and only 142 were referred to the Industrial Court for Arbitration. This, to us, is a success. In other words, it is clear that the parties – the workers' and the employers' organizations, or the employers themselves – are making an effort to resolve their labour disputes.

The bills are proposing changes that are very crucial in our labour relations. We consider these bills to be at a very critical stage and they must be translated into operative labour laws. Therefore, we should like to appeal to the ILO. We know that the United States has already indicated to the ILO that it has no further funds to complete this process of translating Recommendations into laws, and so we are appealing to the ILO to see if they can help Kenya to implement these proposals.

It is estimated that in Kenya, about 57 per cent of the population is living below the poverty line. If we can get these laws implemented, we would be able to strengthen our tripartite efforts in the fight against child labour and in the fight against HIV/AIDS in the workplace and promote productivity for the creation of more employment opportunities and reduce our poverty level.

My federation has been running a child labour project under the IPEC programme and we are also running projects on HIV/AIDS in the workplace and on the development of small and medium-sized enterprises with the assistance of the UNDP.

We should like to appeal to the ILO to see how it can strengthen our activities in these areas.

The other area that I would like to mention here is corporate social responsibility. Social dialogue, through the collective bargaining process, is fairly well-developed in Kenya (or if I may use the word, "relatively" well-developed). The parties generally know their rights and obligations, as well as the procedures to be followed when disputes do arise. Our collective bargaining process does not involve non-governmental organizations (NGOs), which are organizations formed primarily to promote social welfare, development, charity, research and the mobilization of resources.

However, of late, employers have been faced with an increasing number of NGOs claiming to be promoting the principles of corporate social responsibility. They use a variety of codes of conduct or codes of practice which they want to impose on employers, particularly those engaged in export activities.

Some of these codes make reference to the international labour standards of the ILO and these NGOs have used them to engineer illegal strikes, particularly in the flower industry and in the garment sector of the export processing zones. They have gone beyond, in our own judgement, their mandate and their activities, and, as a matter of fact, have disrupted our industries and are harmful to our industrial relations system.

We have taken corporate social responsibility as a voluntary initiative, which we have seen to be good for business. We have started to promote it, at least in agricultural sectors such as coffee and sisal, in collaboration with the United Kingdom's Department for International Development.

However, our position on whether NGOs should be involved in industrial relations is very clear. We do not want them to be involved and would not like them to be encouraged to be involved in industrial relations through the use of corporate social responsibility. It has been established that they do not want industries to promote or create employment for the majority of our Kenyan population, and particularly for the young workers. We would like them to observe the rules that govern tripartism in Kenya.

We appeal to the ILO, through the Governing Body, to study the use of corporate social responsibility and its impact on business and to formulate some recommendations that would be appropriate for the promotion of corporate social responsibility as a voluntary initiative.

Freedom of association and freedom to bargain collectively implies that we have employment growth. In Kenya, we would like some assistance creating employment. As we know, job creation cannot be left to the Government alone. However, the private sector cannot be an engine of economic growth given the high costs of doing business.

Now, we may observe here that there is a tendency today, at least in that part of the world where I come from, to shift social costs to employers. This escalates the cost of doing business, particularly in my country. Therefore, I would like to call upon the ILO to come up with a guide that would assist both the Government and the social partners through a tripartite system to look at fundamental issues such as productivity or the promotion of productivity and the cost of doing business at the enterprise level, because I think that is where things make sense, with a view to creating more employment and more opportunities and with a view to maintaining a high level of employment. Redundancy and retrenchment would be last resort options.

Original French: Mr. SEGUIN *(Government delegate, France)*

First, let me say how much freedom of association and the right to collective bargaining are, for us, a core issue in the whole ongoing discussion on the social dimension of globalization. We believe these rights to be an essential component of good governance and, indeed, that was reiterated in the report of the World Commission on the Social Dimension of Globalization. These rights also enshrine the rights and responsibilities of the various parties involved in the real economy and they also enable us to reconcile the laws of the market and social objectives. We believe, therefore, that it should be a priority for our Organization to ensure that throughout the multilateral system we have proper recognition for the idea that social dialogue is an essential element of, and a determining factor in, good governance.

Second, and I believe very importantly, these rights are the foundation of all fundamental and social rights recognized by the ILO. In everything we do to promote recognition of these rights we are going to come up against our limits very quickly unless we use the lever of the social dialogue process in every country. The social components of structural adjustment plans and the strategic poverty reduction frameworks will be confronted by a purely financial logic if active involvement by the social partners is not integrated into the process.

Third, the exercise of these fundamental rights is the best way of responding to the problem of harmonizing the social conditions in which competition takes place. The 1998 ILO Declaration on Fundamental Principles and Rights at Work emphasizes, quite rightly, that fundamental principles and rights at work cannot be used as tools for carrying out disguised protectionism. Recognition of the right to collective bargaining does not in any way undermine the competitive advantage which countries with lower labour costs or a less developed social protection system have. But it does create, in the long term, the conditions for a gradual reduction in the disparities between countries and this as a result of tripartite dialogue and the active involvement of the social partners.

Now let me turn to the interesting issues raised in Chapter 3 of the Director-General's Report which relate to social dialogue at the global level. If, as the Report recalls, it would be premature to consider any true worldwide collective agreements – collective labour agreements regulating on a global scale issues of working conditions and wages – it is interesting to note the signing of at least 27 international framework agreements, often based on the Declaration. These agreements, signed with major multinational companies or in very highly integrated sectors of the world economy, try particularly to specify conditions of adaptation to changing markets, guarantee the right to trade union representation, collective bargaining and joint mechanisms, among other things. I think we need to watch this developing situation closely and support and encourage it.

Finally, I would like to close by paying a warm tribute to the Committee on Freedom of Association. In a situation worldwide that is still precarious in many parts of the world this Committee has brought about improvements in the legislation of a number of countries. It has managed to bring an end to many of the abuses perpetrated against workers and employers and their representatives. It is a useful tool for improving social governance worldwide with its basis in the ILO. I believe it should be consolidated in the context in which globalization also means the globalization of opinion.

I would like to congratulate the Director-General and his team on the quality of this Report. France supports the objectives laid out therein and will do all it can to support the work the Office and the Turin Centre does to contribute to their realization.

Mr. FARSHORI *(Government delegate, Pakistan)*

Thank you very much for giving me the opportunity to comment on the Global Report. The Report discussed core issues including the right of association and collective bargaining which are extremely important in the wake of globalization. The overall picture depicted in the Report is encouraging but it identified certain areas in labour relationships at a tripartite level which need to be addressed. An overall assessment was made and challenges were identified in the context of the global economy. There is a need to promote fundamental rights, to advocate knowledge and to target uncovered and disorganized sectors of the economy.

We fully agree that without involving the most important stakeholder in the economic development, the workers, more visible improvement can be made in the industrial and economic development of the country. However, we are of the view that freedom of association and collective bargaining should be organized responsibly and regulated in accordance with the provisions of law. The important principle of understanding between employers and workers should be to enhance productivity and to share the fruits of productivity fairly.

The interests of workers and employers need to be harmonized. The impact of freedom of association and collective bargaining depends strongly on the context and on the environment in which they occur.

We agree with the observation that there is a need to build a dynamic labour market which is represented by three stakeholders – the workers, the employers and the government. However, we feel that this dynamic market should be able to perceive the social consequences of moving investment from the existing to the new production system.

The concept of the introduction of decent work to reduce poverty is not only new but the approach is also innovative. We fully agree that workers' interests will be protected if we prepare and implement decent work to reduce poverty. This is also part of the Poverty Reduction Strategy Paper which Pakistan is committed to implement. We are committed to prepare such a programme and implement it after getting a consensus at a tripartite level.

I would like to draw your attention to the issue of the ratification of Conventions. The response to ratify Conventions needs improvement, a lot more is required. The non-ratification of Conventions affects the dynamics of the labour market and creates a distortion in the competitiveness of comparable economies.

The international labour agencies need to be more assertive with respect to the ratification of Conventions, especially those relating to social security and workers' welfare.

The Report highlights the group of workers facing obstacles in organizations like public sector employees, agricultural workers, workers within export processing zones, migrant workers and domestic workers. It also highlights the challenges of the informal economy. These issues are important and need to be addressed in a gradual manner with a destined road map.

I would also like to draw your attention to the need for comprehensive data relating to employers and workers to be available.

This is essential for organizing bargaining in the context of the global economy. Such details are either not available, or if information is available, is rather sketchy. The data will help in the exchange of information between employers and also among workers.

The level of unions and their performance can also be judged both at the enterprise level as well as at the sectoral level. With the success and failure of bargaining, labour productivity increases and a declining train of growth can well be realized in the global context.

The empirical research will provide an opportunity to arrive at a genuine core relationship between the development of bargaining institutions and productivity and, consequently, economic growth. At the same time, capacity building of the Government, as well as that of employers and workers, is necessary to ensure freedom of association and collective bargaining. This includes qualitative improvement when imparting knowledge to all the three stakeholders. Labour law reforms, improvement in dispute prevention and certain mechanism for information and awareness raising are to be attended to as a priority and any help given by the ILO is most important.

The importance of collective bargaining to determine wages and social benefit is the most transparent and effective method available in the fiscal market economy. In Pakistan a bilateral council of employers and workers has been established with the sole objective being to start partnerships for peace, productivity and prosperity. This has provided a forum to overcome the tense relationship between the workers and employers and to arrive at a consensus on major issues which require the support and approval of the Government. There are efforts to increase the membership of this association so that it increases and at some stage of time it can be transformed into an organized, legislative, duly-approved body providing important support and help to the Government.

To conclude I congratulate the ILO for preparing the Global Report under the follow-up to the ILO

Declaration on Fundamental Principles and Rights at Work.

Original Spanish: Mrs. ARANGO DE BUITRAGO *(Government adviser and substitute delegate, Colombia)*

We welcome the Global Report under the follow-up to the ILO Declaration on Fundamental Principles and Rights at Work: a Declaration that was adopted by this house in 1998.

As regards my country, we have been making significant efforts to promote the Declaration. In March 2003, the first national forum took place on this issue, where workers' and employers' organizations came together with the Government, represented by the Vice-President of the Republic, and we had the opportunity to discuss a document prepared by the subregional office for the Andean countries at the request of the Government.

The ILO, through the Director of the subregional office, presented the main issues relating to the Declaration and its impact on strengthening freedom of association. At this forum, the Government made the commitment before the ILO and the social partners to hold regional seminars on a tripartite basis, to promote and disseminate the Declaration throughout the country.

It should be mentioned that this is part of the Government's strategy to promote, also at the regional and local level, the policy of respect for human rights, so that regional and local authorities, their social partners and communities themselves make commitments in this area and thereby create a national and local culture of respect of rights, which obviously include fundamental labour rights.

To date, we have carried out eight regional seminars, with seven more planned for this year. We hope to conclude this project by holding a second national forum, which will include the recommendations and conclusions of the regional forums.

Such activities would not be possible without the support of the ILO special technical cooperation programme for Colombia. Unfortunately, within a few months the resources of this programme will have run out. Therefore, it is necessary that the constituents who expressed their concern for the strengthening of freedom of association in Colombia, as well as the ILO, make the necessary effort to ensure the continuity of and increase the technical cooperation which the ILO has been providing in Colombia.

We would like to make some comments on certain statements made in the Report relating to Colombia.

The Government notes with concern two statements made in Box 2.1 on page 25 that we would like to clarify. First, its said that a minority of the murders of trade unionists are "committed by armed opposition groups". Illegal groups of outlaws who attack the civilian population are not, and cannot be considered to be, opposition. They are terrorist groups funded by the drugs trade and are recognised as such by countries and groupings of countries.

Furthermore, and with regard to the status of the opposition in my country, I would like to quote the Vice-President of the Republic, from a speech he made recently: "This policy, of democratic security has also provided guarantees for parties of the opposition, for those who oppose the Government, and for social partners. Much remains to be done to overcome intolerance in our society and improve our political traditions. However, it is clear that democracy in Colombia is constantly getting stronger, becoming more pluralistic, broader and more inclusive. Violence is the greatest obstacle to further democratisation in Colombia. There is no justification or support for violence in Colombia. We Colombian people do not understand how groups that have no limits and are afraid of engaging in political dialogue can be justified as armed opposition. Acaso Lucho and Agelino Garzon, Sergio Fajardo, Antonio Navarro, Gustavo Petro, Wilson Borja and the many others who currently occupy public positions, are they not opposition?"

In addition to the above and in a tripartite spirit, which prevails in the ILO, our Government hopes that in future it will be informed and consulted on such statements before they are actually published, as well as on the statistics on human rights violations against trade unionists and union leaders, so that statistics are taken from the various State research organizations and that union sources are also used when drafting the Global Report under discussion.

Second, the previously mentioned Box 2.1 concludes by stating that the fate of the programme depends among other factors, on the "future conditions in the country and its prospects for finding peaceful solutions".

Our Government would like to understand this statement, not as a recommendation on how to formulate its policies on how to overcome the terrorist threat in its country, because this falls in its exclusive remit, but as a determining factor for the cooperation programme; such statements can only be acceptable by adopting this interpretation.

We are sure that it is crucial to overcome the situation of violence associated with drugs-related terrorism in the country which affects, amongst others, trade unionists and leaders, and other sectors of the population, such as judges, journalists, public prosecutors, medical officers, etc.

Indiscriminate violence against the civil population prompted Colombians to choose by an overwhelming majority the policy proposed by the then candidate Alvaro Uribe by electing him to be the President.

The popularity of the President today, after nearly two years in Government, is at 75 per cent mainly because of the results of that policy.

Today, we Colombians feel safer and more hopeful than ever before in the future of our nation.

I would like to say that in 2003, 40,000 public employees were not dismissed, as stated in the Report. We have previously explained the programme for restructuring the public authorities, and we have stated that this programme involves not filling vacant posts and the retirement of staff who will receive a pension.

In other words, after four years of Government, 40,000 people have ceased to work for the public authorities. Obviously, a number of those who left their jobs, did so as a result of restructuring.

However, I would also like to underline that included in the restructuring programme is the social protection programme which prevents mothers who are also the head of the family, disabled persons and those in line for early retirement from being affected by the restructuring programme; 14,120 individuals have benefited from this. We have also adopted measures for free training to enable former public employees to access other employment opportunities. These measures includes services such as advice, occupational guidance, retraining and cover issues such as labour intervention and self-employment.

In conclusion, I would like again to reaffirm my Government's determination to promote the Declaration of Fundamental Principles and Rights at Work. Therefore, and as we stated within the Committee on the Application of Standards, we will be closely following the provisions adopted relating to the strengthening of the ILO special technical cooperation programme for Colombia.

Mr. SHENOY *(Government delegate, India)*

At the outset, let me convey our appreciation to the ILO for bringing out such a comprehensive document entitled *Organizing for social justice* on freedom of association and collective bargaining.

Collective bargaining is a rational democratic exercise wherein the accredited representatives of workers and management to discuss, negotiate and bargain on an equal footing with regard to all bargainable issues pertaining to all bargainable employees. Hence, collective bargaining is a method which should be available to the workers in all spheres.

We, in India, believe that it should also be available to agricultural and rural workers. That is why we have ratified the Right of Association (Agriculture) Convention, 1921 (No. 11), and the Rural Workers' Organisations Convention, 1975 (No. 141).

The Report rightly recognizes that it is very difficult to ensure collective bargaining in the absence of proper organizations of agricultural workers, migrant workers, domestic workers, workers in export processing zones and, especially, workers in the informal economy.

The world over, the number of workers in unions is falling. The first step forward should be to shore up membership of unions and the second is to ensure that union members are spread throughout the aforementioned sectors, especially in the informal economy. Only then, when we have a unionized workforce, will it be feasible and possible to increase the spread of the collective bargaining exercise. Globalization has resulted in increased competitiveness, casualization and contractualization, which increases productivity requirements. So apart from wages and the various elements of bargaining, productive bargaining will become a very important thing in the years to come.

Effective dispute settlement machinery is essential for ensuring industrial peace and harmony. Collective bargaining, conciliation and arbitration are very important. Only if these three machineries fail should one then resort to adjudication as a last resort. We, in our country, have some difficulties especially because the organized workforce is only 8 per cent; 92 per cent work in the informal economy.

International efforts have been made to improve the ratification record. The ratification record is very high numerically but, considering the percentage of population of the workforce across the globe covered by this ratification record, it is not very high.

We have special difficulties in ratifying Conventions Nos. 87 and 98 because of certain technical issues.

Our government employees enjoy a lot of rights. Some of them perform sovereign functions. They have their own staff council, joint consultative machinery and administrative tribunals. They have the highest level of job security which is enshrined in the Constitution of India itself.

We feel that our convictions and commitment to the principles of these core Conventions are evident in our political tradition, free society, free press and very strong and independent judiciary. Our Constitution guarantees freedom of association, freedom of organization, freedom of expression and all other forms of freedom that constitute a guarantee of the rights against exploitation and discrimination.

These rights are guaranteed under the Constitution as fundamental rights and therefore, there are guarantees against arbitrariness on the part of the executive and the legislator.

In conclusion, I would like to reaffirm my country's commitment to the principles of freedom of association and collective bargaining and our conviction to implement the spirit of these principles in the workplace in India.

Ms. TORSØE *(State Secretary, Ministry of Labour and Government Administration, Norway)*

Norway welcomes the Director-General's Report, *Organizing for social justice*. As the title of the Report indicates, social dialogue between democratic governments and workers' and employers' organizations is perhaps the most important precondition for achieving social justice.

In my opinion, it is no coincidence that so many of the richest countries in the world have long recognized freedom of association and the right to collective bargaining while so many countries, where people have been denied these fundamental rights, remain among the poorest.

Freedom of association is not only about social justice. The Report tells us that in some member States, serious threats to workers and employers seeking to organize, including killings, detention and violence, still persist.

The Report shows us that the ILO is moving toward universal ratification of the Freedom of Association and the Right to Organise Convention, 1948 (No. 87), and the Right to Organise and Collective Bargaining Convention, 1949 (No. 98). The fact is, however, that about half of the world's workers and employers do not enjoy protection under Conventions Nos. 87 and 98, given that some of the largest countries, in terms of size and population, have not ratified these Conventions.

Some groups are facing particular difficulties in exercising their fundamental rights. Those working in agriculture and in export processing zones, migrant and domestic workers and those in the informal sector are facing a difficult situation even in countries that have already ratified these Conventions.

There is growing evidence that fundamental principles and rights at work have played an important part in improving economic development and productivity, management of enterprises and the functioning of the labour market.

In 2000, OECD found that countries which strengthen the observance of core labour standards can increase economic efficiency by raising the skill levels of the workforce and by creating an environment that encourages productivity, growth and innovation. In advocating the work of the ILO, it is therefore important to give real-life examples of employers and workers exercising their rights and achieving results. Information should be gathered on specific cases of good practice in collective bargaining and dialogue that others will wish to imitate.

The ILO should also work closely on a tripartite basis with non-ratifying countries to seek the means to overcome obstacles to ratification. Labour legislation is the foundation of respect for freedom of association and the recognition of the right to collective bargaining. The ILO has a long experience in assisting member States with labour law reform. It is of the utmost important that the Organizations should have enough capacity in this field to be able to meet requests for assistance from member States.

The report of the World Commission on the Social Dimension of Globalization was discussed recently. The report demonstrates very clearly that we have a long way to go to give everybody a fair share of the benefits of globalization. We believe that one important step on that path is the development of good tripartite institutions and cooperation at national level.

In conclusion, Norway strongly supports a new updated plan of action in this area and we believe that the Director-General's Report, *Organizing for social justice,* includes a large number of proposals that will have a sound basis for the plan of action. As pointed out in the Report, however, sustainable change depends on the commitment of governments and social partners in each country and their ability to achieve a strong joint ownership of agreed courses of action. The aim must be the use of these fundamental rights as a foundation for democratic development.

Original German: Mrs. ENGELEN-KEFER *(Workers' representative, Germany)*

I think that the ILO has started along the right path by concerning itself more with the implementation of workers' fundamental rights. The right to freedom of association and collective bargaining, which occupies a key position is simply not possible to implement other labour rights and there can be no sustainable economic and social development. Globalization has rendered the work of the unions more difficult and more complicated. Unions need effective protection of their freedom and their ability to act. In the Report and in the contributions to the debate that we have heard today, we have heard very clearly that multiple violations of freedom of association are still taking place today, probably just as many as in the past.

I would like to raise one issue that is fundamental for us. For us, we believe that speed is of the essence in ensuring that these rights are implemented in order to avoid discrimination against union activities. When cases come up in the Committee on Freedom of Association, we often see that the process is dragged out over five or seven years. Suffice it to say that when delays of that length take place, they severely constrain the right of freedom of association. We are also seeing new forms of discrimination in the implementation of freedom of association, and we have already heard today that many countries are preventing foreigners from obtaining union membership or there are model contracts which offer employers the opportunity to exclude certain workers from the application of wage agreements, and this is particularly true for large groups of workers in the public services, including in developed countries. Convention No. 98 provides for the right to collective bargaining. This does not mean the same as collective begging, but neither does it mean pay negotiations imposed by the Government.

I believe that the Report of the Director-General has been extremely insightful on this point, with regard to Bulgaria, Romania and Moldova, and there we have to make it clear that, according to Convention No. 98, freedom of association encompasses freedom and equality, equality on both sides, bargaining on an equal footing. That brings me to a very important point – the right to strike, which is a part of freedom of association. There are those who cast doubt upon this, who say that the right to strike is not explicitly mentioned in Convention No. 98. That is true, but not because the right to strike was not intended to be included in Convention No. 98 but rather because the detailed definition of the elements of freedom of association was left to the application of law. The legal precedents in the case law of the ILO have shown that the right to strike is an inalienable part of freedom of association. I think that we need to cooperate with member States in order to fully implement these two crucial Conventions of the ILO in various ways. Firstly, we require the support of member States in ensuring full implementation and inclusion of these workers' rights in all international organizations. We also need the member States to ensure that freedom of association underpins their bilateral activities and we also need individual governments to ensure the implementation of these fundamental labour rights on the domestic front.

(The Conference adjourned at 1.15 p.m.)

Eleventh sitting

Thursday, 10 June 2004, 3.15 p.m.

President: Mr. Attigbe, Mr. Ray Guevara

GLOBAL REPORT UNDER THE FOLLOW-UP TO THE ILO DECLARATION ON FUNDAMENTAL PRINCIPLES AND RIGHTS AT WORK: INTERACTIVE SITTING *(CONT.)*

Original French: The PRESIDENT (Mr. ATTIGBE)

We shall now resume our discussion of the Global Report; *Organizing for social justice.*

Mr. POTTER *(Employers' delegate, United States, speaking on behalf of the Workers' group)*

I thought I would just make a short statement about how I think we are doing.

First, I think the Governments overall have been much more concrete, in terms of telling us what they are doing, in terms of meeting their commitments under the Declaration, and that is to be commended. I counted four governments who basically talked in general terms, which is really not constructive.

There was one Government intervention that got into matters that are actually covered and addressed in other supervisory machinery in the ILO. We do not intend to look at the countries' situations in a case environment; it is more appropriate to have those discussions elsewhere and not here, to avoid the question of double scrutiny.

Sir Roy TROTMAN *(Workers' delegate, Barbados, speaking on behalf of the Workers' group)*

I support what Mr. Potter is saying, but I wish to suggest that it would be useful if those of you who have prepared texts could revise them and include in them something that would guide the Governing Body, and especially the Working Party that helps the Governing Body, in determining how we could improve in this area of the work of the ILO. So, what we are looking for, really, are suggestions and not merely recitals of what is being done domestically.

Mr. ANAND *(Employer' adviser, India)*

We have been discussing this Report since the morning, and the Office has raised certain points for discussion. We need an answer, but I would like to address this house on the last point. What should be the key item for the plan of action for the next four years to be submitted to the Governing Body in November 2004?

The document itself, *Organizing for social justice,* elegantly presents some exhaustively argued thought-provoking theses; yet if I look at the totality of the Report, it is obvious to me that we should be concerned about the validity of priorities for the future, as reflected in paragraph 394.

When I saw the Report several weeks ago, I started to have some doubts about the introductory chapter, paragraph 3, itself. I may be in a minority, but despite the position emphatically defended by my friends opposite, I am indeed worried about the fact that the Freedom of Association and Protection of the Right to Organise Convention, 1948 (No. 87), and the Right to Organise and Collective Bargaining Convention, 1949 (No. 98), are stressed as positive factors making for sound economic development in paragraph 3. While I admit that both Conventions are essential for democratic freedom and human dignity they do not suffice to serve the end of sustainable social justice. These Conventions are only a means to an end and, not the end in itself. Sound economic development on its own also spurs social justice, which is the end purpose, if we look at the text of the Declaration as a whole. In a number of the countries included in table 3.5 and Annex 2, economic development has taken place, notably in the United States, India and many others, notwithstanding the non-ratification of the aforementioned Conventions. Therefore, I submit that the converse is also true. Economic growth itself leads to development laying the foundations of social justice. In my view, there is scope for reconsidering the priorities in technical cooperation, which is the key purpose of this four-yearly review. We have the annual review of the four components, but we are concerned overall as to the future of technical cooperation. The ILO has a research institute. I think in fairness that it should undertake a cost-benefit analysis of the annual inputs and outputs of resources invested in this task during the half-century since these two Conventions were adopted. This is an objective way of examining what is, admittedly a minority argument, but it deserves to be examined.

I submit that Part I seeks to promote the ILO Constitution – if you look at the Declaration text, Part I seeks to promote the ILO Constitution buttressed by the Declaration of Philadelphia with its dictum which is again repeated by the Director-General, "poverty anywhere is a threat to prosperity everywhere". Despite the large-scale investment of financial and human resources to promote the ratification of these two Conventions, poverty still persists in substantial areas of the world. Four billion persons are still in the lowest level of the pyramid of world income, i.e. below US$1,500 a year.

Part III of the Declaration in the Annex states the purpose and modalities of this four-yearly review, namely to serve as a basis for assessing the effectiveness of assistance provided and for determining priority through action taken for technical cooperation. Under Part IV, subparagraph (2), of the Annex, this Conference is now required to assess whether it has adequately fulfilled the overall purpose articulated in Part I, in other words, to promote the ILO Constitution and Declaration of Philadelphia with the dictum "poverty anywhere is a threat to prosperity everywhere".

The poverty eradication obligations assumed by the ILO, because of their political, social and economic repercussions, have now been also assumed by the United Nations system as a whole. The report of the United Nations Commission on the Private Sector and Development entitled *Unleashing entrepreneurship: Making business work for the poor* again appeals to the conscience of the business world to serve the masses and the poor. In my personal opinion, the business world consists not only of employers, but also of trade union leaders. The forthcoming World Bank Development Report (2005) will probably focus on the same issue of people and the masses and their economic betterment. Entrepreneurship is now the new flavour in the mouth of the entire multilateral system, but as far as human infrastructure and an appropriate work culture for the future are concerned, the priorities set out in paragraph 394, which is very weakly and obliquely worded, are not on any roadmap in this report. This reflects a lackadaisical attitude, as if the world and mankind were static. These priorities outlined in the document will not promote the integrated aims and objectives of the Declaration.

I finally submit that skill development, entrepreneurship, constructive work culture, mainstreaming of informal economics, job upgrading in the agriculture and manufacturing sectors, advocacy and services through the employment sector and sponsored pilot projects in the underdeveloped world need to be put at that top of the list of challenges and priorities, while basic, further and retraining programmes run by the Turin International Training Centre are also a necessity.

Speaking for the 4 billion people who are in the lowest level of the pyramid described in the report on unleashing entrepreneurship, I request the Director-General and this house to initiate action with vision and courage, without giving way to doubts, and to make history for the ILO in the twenty-first century through proper prioritization. The social partners are with you. Unless this review gives top priority to all the activities in the enterprise and employment sector, the review will be of little consolation to future generations, much less so to the youth of tomorrow.

I am sorry I have taken so much time, from your point of view, but I wanted to make my argument because – even though I may be in the minority – there is room for rethinking the priorities made out in paragraph 394.

Mr. BUWALDA *(Government delegate, New Zealand)*

I would like to congratulate the ILO for this Global Report *Organizing for social justice*. Four years after discussing the first Global Report entitled *Your voice at work* it is heartening to read in this year's Report that we are seeing a generally positive trend in freedom of association and collective bargaining throughout the world.

We also note, however, that this is offset by serious problems that remain in this area. The New Zealand Government commends the ILO for the active role it has taken over the past four years in ensuring that the principles of association and collective bargaining are promoted to its constituents.

We also appreciate the important point made in paragraph 275 of the Report that, while technical cooperation can demonstrate positive outcomes and help build the capacity of a small number of actors, sustainable change depends on the commitment of governments and their social partners in each country. In other words, organizing for social justice is a process of partnership, not one of imposing change from the top. My Government strongly supports this principle.

New Zealand is profiled in the Report as a country where renewed commitment to collective bargaining through the Employment Relations Act is part of the promotion of productive employment relationships.

My Government is strongly committed to ensuring that collective bargaining is protected through our laws, which in turn remain responsive to changing requirements in society.

The Government recently introduced the Employment Relations Law Reform Bill which builds on the foundations laid by the Employment Relations Act four years ago.

This new Bill aims to strengthen the Act in order to better achieve its key objectives of promoting good faith, collective bargaining and the effective resolution of employment relationship problems. The Bill provides disincentives for undermining and avoiding collective bargaining and it provides more effective ways of resolving employment relationship problems.

The Global Report signals a renewed commitment by the ILO to focus its support on those sectors where workers face particular difficulties in organizing. New Zealand supports this strategy, however, we would not like to see the ILO restrict itself only to the six sectors defined in the Report.

Over the last year New Zealand has signalled its commitment to good faith and collective bargaining internationally by ratifying ILO Right to Organise and Collective Bargaining Convention, 1949 (No. 98). We have also sought to work with the ILO and the south-east Asia-Pacific subregion to promote freedom of association and collective bargaining as an aspect of decent work and last year hosted a subregional tripartite forum on decent work that promoted dialogue between social partners across the region.

We applaud the ILO South-East Asia and Pacific Office for its commitment to support governments and social partners as they develop tripartite plans of action to achieve decent work and we look forward to the presentation of these plans at the next Asia-Pacific Regional Meeting.

We would recommend decent work action plans to other ILO member States as a useful tool to achieve decent work and to ensure the continuous dynamic relationships of government, employer and worker organizations and labour law, policy and practice.

Looking ahead, the New Zealand Government agrees that there is much to be done internationally to ensure freedom of association and collective bargaining are accessible to all workers and to stop, as a priority, the murder of trade unionists.

We think that the ratification of Conventions Nos. 87 and 98 are only part of a process where the actual goal is to implement the right to freedom of association and collective bargaining in each state.

As the Report notes in paragraph 5, in some instances countries have ratified ILO Freedom of Association and Protection of the Right to Organise Convention, 1948 (No. 87), and Right to Organise and Collective Bargaining Convention, 1949 (No. 98), and then gone no further to comply. Indeed, the Report notes that in some cases situations have become more precarious.

Therefore, the goal of future ILO action should be to support implementation of the principles outlined in the Declaration and obligations under the fundamental Conventions approaching ratification as part of this process, rather than the end result.

In conclusion, we look forward to working in partnership with the ILO and its constituents to ensure that all people in the world of work have the right to freedom of association and collective bargaining.

Ms. SSENABULYA *(Employers' delegate, Uganda)*

I am privileged in having the opportunity to share the experience of Ugandan employers on the Global Report, *Organizing for social justice*, under the follow-up to the ILO Declaration on Fundamental Principles and Rights at Work.

May I at the outset congratulate the Director-General and his team for their commendable work, as evidenced in the Report we are discussing today.

Technical support is very important in the promotion of the principles enshrined in the Declaration and has borne some fruit in Uganda. My federation was honoured to benefit from this technical support through the ILO project on Strengthening Labour Relations in East Africa which has been going on since 2001. We are grateful to the ILO and the United States Government for their support. Through that technical support, the federation has become more visible and better equipped to render services to its members. Many of our member organizations were also strengthened to improve employment relations at enterprise level. The results have been remarkable. There has been a realization by many employers of the need to associate and, as a result, quite a number have become members of the federation. There has equally been an appreciation by our members, employers, of the need for them to have a voice at the local level and, to this effect, six employers' district committees have been formed.

A strong secretariat with better facilities to effectively and efficiently support members was able to help the Uganda Private Securities Association to conclude a collective agreement with the Amalgamated Transport and General Workers' Union, covering 15,000 workers. It has taken a number of years for these two to complete the agreement but with the assistance of our organization they were able to do that in two months. Similarly, the Uganda Tea Association and the National Union of Agricultural Workers were also given professional support by the federation and were able to conclude a collective agreement within a short time covering 30,000 workers.

It is quite important to note that there are a number of innovative ways in which the Office can promote the principles outlined in the Declaration, besides the use of law. As a federation, three years ago we started a competition for employers which is based on recognizing those organizations that have the best human resource management practices and who comply with the law. This exercise has been appreciated with a lot of enthusiasm, with many employers participating and quite a number taking their own initiative to improve working conditions at their places of work.

There are a number of lessons to learn from this. One of them is that employers who are doing well need to be recognized, rather than always putting the stress on injustices and condemning employers as exploiters. Another lesson which we have learnt through this exercise is the use of the mass media to publicize the principles contained in the Declaration, and to educate the general public, workers and employers. We encourage the Office to take a leaf out of East Africa's book so that more publicity is given to these principles using the mass media.

There are a number of challenges which we have been confronting. One of the biggest challenges is that the majority of the employers employ between one and 20 workers and most of these still lie outside the ambit of the federation, meaning that both the employers and the workers they are employing are not benefiting from the principles in the Declaration. We therefore appeal to the ILO to extend more support to see how these employers and workers who are not yet on board can be brought on board. I also equally call upon the Office to intensify its programmes on mass media which can go a long way to educating a very large number of people.

Original Spanish: Mr. VILLAVICENCIO RIOS *(Government delegate, Peru)*

I would like to begin this short statement by highlighting the importance of the Report which we have before us. It covers many of the core issues surrounding the complex right to freedom of association and the effective recognition of the right to collective bargaining. There is a three-way split, as far as the Declaration is concerned, between the rights encompassed within the broad concept of trade union rights, according to the monitoring mechanisms of the ILO. It seems to me that it is important to mention this, because this way, we will be able to approach each of these issues with the appropriate logic and coherence.

I would like to take advantage of the time available to me to raise one of the subjects which does not appear to have been addressed in the Report that we have before us, namely that of the protection of freedom of association.

All of us in the world of labour relations know perfectly well that the protection of basic rights does not entail only negative aspects, in other words, removing the obstacles which exist in States, but it also has a positive dimension that affects the obligations of all those involved in exercising these rights, so that these rights can really become effective.

In the case of labour rights and in particular freedom of association, this issue is becoming all the more necessary because everyone knows that, without a set of normative and procedural mechanisms to protect freedom of association, then this right is simply devoid of all value. It is widely recognized that the effective protection of the freedom of association is a prerequisite for the real enjoyment of this right. In this sense, I have noted the absence in the Report of even a regional analysis of the various mechanisms that are being implemented in countries so that these rights can become a tangible reality and are no longer merely the words used in the

ILO Conventions, in universal declarations and in the covenants that at one point we believed were part of the legal heritage of humankind.

In this context, I should like to suggest that, in the action plan that is to be implemented over the next four years, before we proceed any further with our deliberations on and appraisals of freedom of association, it would be a good idea to evaluate all of the mechanisms, not just the normative ones or the ones that provide terms and guarantees, but also the procedural mechanisms using thorough and appropriate procedures that will enable us to evaluate the true extent to which this right is being enjoyed in various environments and in different countries.

We consider it important therefore that any action plan should include elements that allow for specific reference to be made to what is taking place in reality. This goes way beyond what is contained in the Freedom of Association and Protection of the Right to Organise Convention, 1948 (No. 87), the Right to Organise and Collective Bargaining Convention, 1949 (No. 98), the Workers' Representatives Convention, 1971 (No. 135), the Labour Relations (Public Service) Convention, 1978 (No. 151), and the Collective Bargaining Convention, 1981 (No. 154), and involves understanding what governments are really doing.

It is necessary, therefore, that the Report itself should not just be an analysis of what governments are doing but also of the practices of employers. We know that, of Conventions Nos. 87 and 98, the former is more directed towards the obligations of States and the latter is aimed more at the obligations of employers. Both are a package, if you like. They are both absolutely essential for the right to freedom of association, which is why the action plan must cover all of these elements. We need to have an idea of how not only States but also employers' organizations are implementing their international commitments. In order to achieve this, the jurisprudence of the control mechanisms, particularly that of the Committee on Freedom of Association, is extremely valuable in the sense that much has already been done to develop this issue. I think it should be used directly in conducting these analyses.

Original Spanish: Mr. ECHAVARRIA SALDARRIAGA *(Employer' adviser and substitute delegate, Colombia)*

This is a very good opportunity for employers in Colombia to present the positive steps taken to develop our country in the area of civil liberties.

Colombia is currently going through a period of internal armed conflict, making the development of basic rights difficult in many ways. However, the ILO can be extremely satisfied with the technical cooperation programme in our country, because obvious results have been achieved. I will report very briefly on this.

First of all, a number of social dialogue meetings have been held, as an alternative solution to labour conflicts, to protect union leaders, and to defend the human rights of workers; many meetings have been held all around the country where employers and workers have been working with the Government.

Action has also been taken regarding child labour, particularly recently, with the training of judges and public prosecutors who are called upon to investigate and meet with the perpetrators of these crimes against all sectors of society, particularly against workers. This programme which, as the Government said this morning, is using up our resources and therefore requires considerable support from the international community.

There are both political and economic indicators. In regard to the political, there is better governance in the country at the moment. The institutions have been strengthened through more open democracy. Two representatives of the Colombian trade union movement have recently been elected into very important public posts in the country. Similarly, there has been greater state presence throughout Colombia. The police and the army are present throughout the country, which is the least a State should do in order to be able to ensure the security of its citizens. There have also been a number of elements which have reduced violence, not just against union members but against the whole population. This has generated a considerable degree of confidence throughout the country.

Also on the subject of politics, I would like to say that there has been a process to reintegrate illegal armed groups. Negotiations are taking place with the United Self-Defence Forces of Colombia who have also attacked Colombian institutions. Recently, the possibility has arisen of the Mexican Government assisting in negotiations with the National Liberation Army, the second largest guerrilla group in the country. It should be noted the United States, the European Union and the Japanese Government have declared both the self-defence groups and the guerrilla groups in Colombia to be terrorist movements. The international community, in general, rejects this, as do the majority of Colombians.

Structural reforms are being implemented by the State to develop public expenditure, one of the big problems which we have. It is still 2.8 per cent of GDP. Employers have recently made new tax contributions to help the State. Income tax rose by 10 percentage points to the current level of 38.5 per cent. Wealth tax has been introduced at 6 per cent to contribute to secure democracy and State presence throughout the country.

These indicators, have generated confidence amongst Colombian employers and thus investment; both national and foreign, has increased over the last year by 30 per cent. Our own investigators have revealed that over the last quarter, production has grown by 8.7 per cent and sales by 7 per cent. In other words, we have prospects of growth of around 5 per cent for this year. It was 4 per cent last year and in previous years did not even reach 1.5 per cent. So this increasing economic growth has provided the opportunity to create 1.2 million additional jobs in the country, which is a positive contribution to economic and social advancement.

I think that this brief report allows me to say that the ILO should be extremely proud of its Cooperation Programme which has given positive results and consequently should be strengthened. It is in this way that we will be able to solve the domestic conflict in Colombia. The results are not perfect but they are on the right track.

To conclude, I would just like to mention that behind all this, the international community is responsible because drug trafficking, our main problem, is a source of finance for all types of illegal armed groups. Therefore, the international community should help us to stamp out this problem, which is a problem for humanity as a whole and not just for Colombians.

Original German: Ms. BOEGNER *(Workers' adviser and substitute delegate, Austria)*

On behalf of the Austrian Workers' delegation, and particularly the Austrian Trade Union Federation, and our President, I would like to express our thanks to Director-General Juan Somavia and his staff for the commitment they have demonstrated. Through the initiative of the creation of the World Commission for the Social Dimension of Globalization as well as the production of the Global Report under the follow-up to the ILO Declaration on Fundamental Principles and Rights at Work, they have taken up the tremendous challenge that the process of globalization presents to industrial relations and to the social systems and all societies, both in North and South.

I would like to make three comments as regards the Global Report. First of all, even though there have been improvements in certain areas, we still see, in many countries, major restrictions as regards freedom of association.

The Global Report quite rightly draws attention to the fact that people continue to lose their lives and their freedom for attempting to organize and defend collectively their fundamental rights.

For example, we see that in Colombia trade union members and activists in the social movement are murdered by death squads, and there is hardly any improvement to be seen according to the information we have from trade unionists.

Then we look at the situation in Myanmar where vast numbers of civilian members of the population are taken and used for forced labour.

And in Belarus we see that the right to organize has been practically reduced to zero. That is just to mention one or two examples.

As Austrian trade unionists and workers, we would like to give our support to the efforts of the ILO to ensure the full application of Conventions that have been signed, especially those relating to freedom of association, forced labour and equal rights, through discussions with those in positions of responsibility and through fact-finding missions as well as through public criticism.

We also think that it is perfectly legitimate for the International Labour Organization to call upon the international community as a whole to take steps against those States that violate continually human rights and trade union rights on a very broad scale.

The example of South Africa, whose democracy is ten years old this year, shows how effective such a focused commitment on behalf of the ILO can be.

In many cases – and the Report also refers to this – we see increasing restrictions imposed on the right to organize, resulting from the pressures of globalization. We see governments turn away from social dialogue in order to impose economic and social policies demanded by multinational enterprises, international financial institutions, and anti-social political advisers.

In respect of this, we see that the Global Report quite rightly draws attention to the fact that a functioning social dialogue, a practical one, linked to high social and employment standards, represents an important element for ensuring sustainable development. Governments which are interested in long-term social development are therefore well advised to counter unfavourable world economic conditions with a national consensus in the area of economic and social policy issues.

And thirdly, with regard to the challenge of globalization, we believe it is essential that the International Labour Organization, as steward of the fundamental global and social rights reflected in a number of different Conventions, should both be strengthened institutionally and politically and this, of course, affects both the question of standard-setting activities which must not be abandoned and also that of monitoring adopted standards.

The International Labour Organization must also be strengthened in relation to the international financial and economic institutions. There are major challenges facing the trade unions and, in general, organizations of the socially weaker groups in the population. We see particularly that organizations of women and in the agricultural sector need to create a stronger social dimension. We do not want to see a world order where the framework for social development is dictated by the unfettered demands of the free market – that is to say, the profit interests of multinational enterprises from the countries of the North. On the contrary, we strive for a society where absolute respect for human and trade union rights is taken as a first principle and where the activities and structures of the economic world are subordinated to justice and solidarity. These priorities, which are essential for sustainable development, must therefore be taken into consideration in the trade negotiations and financial agreements which are presently being negotiated in the context of other international organizations. Here we believe that we have the necessary basis for the implementation of an action plan on freedom of association and collective bargaining.

Mr. MWAKWERE *(Minister for Labour and Human Resource Development, Kenya)*

I thank the President most sincerely for giving me the floor on behalf of the Kenya Government.

We welcome the discussions on this year's Global Report entitled *Organizing for social justice*, as part of the follow-up to the ILO Declaration on Fundamental Principles and Rights at Work.

The Kenyan delegation notes that while significant progress has been made in the acceptance of the principles of freedom of association and the right to collective bargaining, the Report acknowledges that serious problems remain. It further indicates that violations of the freedom of association rights of both employers and workers persist in different forms, including murder, violence, detention and refusal to allow organizations the legal right to exist and function.

The Report further indicates that about half of the world's workers and employers still do not enjoy protection under the Freedom of Association and Protection of the Right to Organise Convention, 1948 (No. 87), and the Right to Organise and Collective Bargaining Convention, 1949 (No. 98).

It singles out groups of workers who still face serious obstacles in achieving freedom of association and effective recognition of the right to organize. Such vulnerable groups include public sector workers, agricultural workers, workers in the export processing zones, migrant workers, domestic workers and informal sector workers, the majority of whom are women.

It is in this respect that the Kenyan Government agrees that "if freedom of association is not respected and promoted, there can be no collective bargaining or social dialogue" and hence the theme for our discussion – *Organizing for social justice*.

At this juncture, please allow me to take this opportunity to reaffirm that in Kenya today, the principle of freedom of association and the effective recognition of the right to collective bargaining is fully recognized and promoted by the Government. The unfortunate incident mentioned in paragraph 88 of the Report concerning the illegal arrests of the Chairperson of the Federation of Kenyan Employers, is an incident the like of which the present Government will never allow to occur.

The Kenyan Government's declared policy has always been to encourage the formation of strong, independent and financially viable employers', as well as workers' organizations. The Government of Kenya is satisfied that both the Federation of Kenyan Employers and the Central Organization of Trade Unions are well organized and competent enough to enter into responsible and conclusive collective bargaining on terms and conditions of employment.

My delegation is pleased to note that the present Global Report acknowledges that the Kenyan Government has allowed the establishment of a union for civil servants to cater for the interests of public sector workers in general. Allow me to reiterate that Kenya firmly believes that respect for freedom of association and the recognition of the right to collective bargaining has a very crucial role to play in achieving the ILO' Decent Work Agenda for all in a globalizing world economy.

The Kenyan Government is therefore committed to the provision of decent work for all workers through the promotion of the ILO's labour standards. In this respect, Kenya has so far ratified and fully implemented a total of 49 ILO Conventions, which include seven out of the eight internationally recognized core labour standards.

Please allow me to express the Kenyan Government's appreciation to the ILO for the technical assistance extended in the recently completed review of six core chapters of our labour laws, with the aim of ensuring harmony between our domestic legislation and the various international labour Conventions that we have already ratified. These new laws will soon become operational and will fully address, among other issues, freedom of association for all workers, including export processing zone workers, casual employment, enhanced maternity protection, equality of treatment between genders, sexual harassment, and a strengthened National Labour Court.

In order to enhance freedom of association and to realize the goal of organizing for social justice, the Kenyan delegation firmly believes that the following challenges will need to be addressed:

One – the universal ratification and implementation of Conventions (Nos. 87 and 98) by all ILO member States.

Two – the facilitation of the enjoyment of freedom by various vulnerable groups, such as public sector workers, agriculture workers, export processing zone workers, migrant workers and informal sector workers.

Three – the need for the ILO to allocate sufficient regular budget resources for the effective implementation of the various freedom of association projects under the Declaration.

Four – the need for the ILO to deepen its knowledge base, as well as to strengthen its advisory, advocacy and awareness activities aimed at promoting the two fundamental Conventions on freedom of association.

Finally, Kenya endorses the view that respect for these fundamental principles and rights at work is good for business, for labour, for governments and for civil society, both domestically and internationally.

Mr. SALMENPERÄ *(Government delegate, Finland)*

In response to the Employer Vice-President's plea on the performance of individual countries as regards the right to organize and the right to collective bargaining, I must say, against the dictates of modesty, that Finland is doing rather well. The rate of trade union membership is among the highest in the world, and so is the coverage of collective bargaining. The same applies to our rating of in terms of competitiveness.

This is not to say that there is no room for improvement. Coming back to my original text, let me start by congratulating the Director-General and his staff for a Report that once again, in an expert manner, sheds light on the application of one of the core labour rights.

If we were to rank core labour rights in order of importance, we would have – or at least should have – come up with the one now under discussion in the first place. The right to organize clearly forms the groundwork on which the fair distribution of prosperity created by work and decent work is built. It is therefore also the key to management of globalization along equitable lines. It is easy to understand then that fair globalization has a long way to go, as the Report points out that half of the world's workers still are not covered by the protection afforded by ratification of the core Conventions – the Freedom of Association and Protection of the Right to Organise Convention, 1948 (No. 87), and the Right to Organise and Collective Bargaining Convention, 1949 (No. 98).

Although developments in this respect seem to be encouraging, the overall situation is still a cause for deep concern. The Report also amply demonstrates how practical implementation of the right to organize and to bargain collectively enhances productivity and competitiveness, rather than posing a threat in that regard. As we are speaking of fundamental rights, this cannot of course be used as a real argument for the promotion of these rights which, as basic human rights, do not need such secondary justifications. It is merely intended to point out that fears in this regard are unfounded and should not be seen as obstacles to policies that promote the advancement of these basic rights.

The Report gives us ample guidance on the need for future work to promote the fundamental labour rights related to freedom of association and collective bargaining. My Government broadly supports the findings and recommendations of the Report in this regard.

We would specifically stress the need to study how the principle of freedom of association could be promoted in the technical cooperation projects of other multilateral agencies, as is suggested in paragraph 383. As to the question of data collection, my Government recognizes the difficulties. However, it would be important to improve and update worldwide data on the coverage of collective bargaining, as this information would indicate the status and measure success in the practical implementation of freedom of association.

Original Arabic: Mr. AOUN *(Government delegate, Lebanon)*

First of all, on behalf of the Committee on Freedom of Association of the Arab Labour Organization, and on behalf of the Government delegation of Lebanon, I would like to thank the Director-General of the ILO for the Global Report which has been submitted to us, *Organizing for social justice*, a report which gives us a general idea of the situation as regards freedom of association throughout the world.

We believe that the concept of freedom of association flows from the whole concepts of democracy and human rights, which underscore the need to guarantee freedom of expression and freedom of association. We would also like to emphasize that the promotion of these rights and of economic, social, cultural and democratic rights, requires the promotion of freedom of expression and freedom of association, because the future of humanity depends on democratic progress.

Freedom of association has to be adapted to the higher interests of the State and so we have to modernize the State in the interests of its citizens.

As regards references to a number of Arab countries in the Report, more particularly as regards freedom of association in these countries and the process of democratization, we would like to note what was indicated in the Report and we would like to add that the political will of the majority of Arab States is moving towards a greater degree of democracy and freedom of association. I think we should pay homage to the International Confederation of Arab Trade Unions, which has played a primary role in the Arab Labour Organization, both with regard to the political follow-up in relation to the relevant Arab governments and as a result of pressure exercised in the context of complaints which have been filed.

What we can say is that there is an increased awareness of the importance of freedom of association and that this will become increasingly important. However, it should also be emphasized that wars and conflicts in the Arab world, particularly the occupation by Israel of the Arab territories, have hampered the process of economic and social development and delayed the development of democracy in our countries.

As regards technical cooperation, we would like to suggest that the ILO intensify its training activities in the field of standards. We have had some experience in this area in connection with the Turin Centre, because the standards activity is more concerned than the political world by the promotion of freedom of association and related principles. Judges preside over labour courts and are concerned in relation to the settlement of certain industrial disputes. The governments consult judges before adopting a decree or an administrative decision relating to freedom of association or collective bargaining.

Administrative judges look closely at the international Conventions and Recommendations before they are ratified and, consequently, it would be appropriate to strengthen the role of the ILO as regards the training of judges in various countries.

In conclusion, I would like to underscore the fact that freedom of association is guaranteed in my country by the Constitution and legislation and we very much hope that it will be developed further.

Mr. AHMED *(Workers' delegate, Pakistan)*

On behalf of the Workers' delegation of Pakistan, one of the developing countries on the Asian continent, we share the feeling of deep appreciation for the Report published by the Director-General: *Organizing for social justice*.

We also endorse the remarks made by our distinguished spokesperson, brother Trotman, and also my other colleague, highlighting the various problems which are being faced by the workers in exercising the fundamental rights of freedom of association and collective bargaining.

We believe that these rights are universal in nature and applicable to all counties – north, south, east and west – and to all workers. We also appreciate the support expressed by the various representatives of governments and employers for respect of these rights and to see some positive development in this regard in the Middle East and Gulf countries, and we hope that legislation will be brought into conformity with the principles concerning the fundamental rights.

The Report highlights that some of the major industrial States have not ratified the fundamental Conventions and we would rightly expect those States to ratify the fundamental Conventions to demonstrate their political will and commitment to these basic principles.

The Report showed that there were 142 ratifications of Freedom of Association and Protection of the Right to Organise Convention, 1948 (No. 87), and 154 ratifications of the Right to Organise and Collective Bargaining Convention, 1949 (No. 98). But there is a great gap between ratification and implementation. We see every year the report of the Committee on the Application of Standards. It indicates the situation in almost all those countries that have ratified the Convention. There is a big gap between ratification and implementation both in terms of legislation and in terms of the difficulties encountered by the workers in exercising these rights – victimization, cases of murder and persistent harassment and arrests. This Committee is the only Conference committee able to tackle these countries that fall short in their implementation measures. We rightly expect the countries that have ratified the Convention to be guided by the Report and to try to bring their legislation into conformity with their international obligations, arising as a result of their ratification of the Convention, to enable workers to exercise these rights.

I must also point out, coming from a developing country, the Report rightly highlights that whereas 1.33 billion people were engaged in agriculture worldwide in 2001, the number dependent on the sector was nearly 2.58 billion, or 42 percent of the world's population. About 70 percent of the world's child labour occurs in farming. These countries need not only to be able to organize to regulate their problems and to improve their social and economic life, but also to call on international involvement because they are the poorest of the poor.

Similarly, in the globalization of the economy, we see workers in export processing zones denied those rights. This needs to be rectified, as it was in the formal sector. In Asia, 65 per cent of workers in non-agricultural employment are in the informal sector. Workers in export processing zones total 33 million, with 30 million in China alone. There are over 80 million persons today working in countries other than their own. Source countries and host countries need to work together to find solutions to the problem of this category of workers, and to create relevant policies to do so.

We would also appreciate that the tripartism system, at the international level should be strengthened at the national level through the participation of workers' and employers' organizations and governments.

In Pakistan, we have ratified six of the seven core Conventions, but the legislation that was promulgated in 2002 is still retrogressive and denies some of the basic principles of these Conventions. We have submitted a compliant to the Committee on Freedom of Association, Case No. 2299, wherein the Government was requested to amend the legislation. We are pressing the Government to amend the legislation and we ask, through this forum, that the Government fulfil their obligation to comply with the Committee's recommendations.

May I also point out that deregulation and restructuring have posed a great problem and that workers are losing their jobs. In this context, we would expect that ILO and ACTRAV to be more active in their objective to improve social dialogue in the frame work of InFocus programme, in order to enhance employment, social protection, international living standards and the capacity-building of the social partners, which would lead to improvements in acquiring skills and knowledge of workers and promote social justice through decent work.

We certainly support the measures taken and the action plan, as laid down in the Report, in particular in the area education.

Lastly, I must admit that the concept of decent work can only be achieved through both national and international action and democracy as an example of developing knowledge and the transfer of knowledge, research and technology. Decent work should be a global goal and an objective of the multilateral system. The major political objective of all countries and multilateral organizations should be to find a tentative solution to this critical problem. We fully support the remarks which have been highlighted in the Report on the globalization of the economy and the need for a social dimension in globalization.

Mr. ANDERSON *(Employers' adviser and substitute delegate, Australia)*

In entering this debate, I acknowledge the presence of the trade union delegates from around the world sitting opposite, some of whom operate, as we have heard, in environments where there is denial of some of the freedoms that we in countries like Australia take for granted.

This debate gives the Australian employers an opportunity not only to welcome the release of the Global Report, but also to reaffirm our support for the ILO Declaration on Fundamental Principles and Rights at Work adopted in 1998. The Global Report is both challenging and, in part, contentious. That is the way it should be. There are a number of findings in the Global Report of particular interest to Australian employers. The finding that there is a generally positive trend and yet that problems still remain. Further, the finding that there is a need to establish for each country the optimal mix between what is negotiated centrally and what is more appropriate for bargaining at a local level. Further, the finding that there are deficiencies in data and information about the coverage of trade unions and employer organizations at a global level, and further, the finding – and I think this is a very important finding – that there are considerable differences across countries, and even within countries, in relation to the adoption of collective bargaining and the way in which the Declaration is implemented.

Australian employers have a long tradition of recognition of the right to both freedom of association and collective bargaining, and there are well-established mechanisms for the enforcement of those rights. In relation to collective bargaining, there has been a very high growth of collective agreements, particularly over the past 14 years, in Australia, in both the public and private sector, and yet there is a need to derive more enterprise outcomes.

I have two points for clarification, though. There is a need for collective bargaining, if it is to succeed, to be subject to the attitudes of the parties and participants. Collective bargaining is dependent on those attitudes. Further, collective bargaining in itself is not a panacea. It would be wrong to take an exclusive or an unreal view of collective bargaining and whether it is appropriate in all circumstances. The key to the Declaration is the right to recognize in an effective way the right to collective bargaining and, therefore, where collective bargaining does fail – and it sometimes does fail – there need to be alternative structures within the concept of freedom of association to ensure that basic rights are exercised.

In relation to freedom of association, the Report quite rightly points out that freedom of association has historically been linked with freedom of expression, freedom of the media, freedom of assembly and universal suffrage. I would add that there is a further freedom that is critical: the freedom to contract, for without the freedom to contract there is no real freedom to associate. That is perhaps a debate for another day.

We have in Australia a very active trade union structure and a very active structure of employer organizations. I note that the Report does refer to deficiencies in data, and perhaps I could assist our discussion by making reference to some data that has recently emerged from research conducted in Australia as a result of a survey of workers by the Australian body that is responsible for the protection and promotion of freedom of association. That recent research indicated that 92 per cent of employee respondents agreed that union membership was left up to the individual to determine and that only 3 per cent of union members felt they had been threatened by their current employer in their earlier periods of employment in order to force them to join or remain a member of a union. Only 1 per cent of employees reported that they had been threatened by their current employer when they started work to prevent them from joining or making them resign from a union. Overall, 83 per cent of employees agreed that the union membership decision was respected by their employer, and a similar proportion of respondents agreed with the statement that the choice to be in a union is respected by the union in the workplace. I think that these conclusions are very consistent with the theme of the Report. They are trends in the right direction, although in some areas there are still problems that remain.

The challenges before us can, I think, be summarized in these terms: it is critical that we maintain a positive trend. It is equally important that our governments and those of us who are participants in our jurisdictions seek to remedy the problem areas where they exist.

Further – and I think this is a matter which both this Organization and its stakeholders can take on board – there is a need to make both freedom of association and collective bargaining adaptable to local circumstances and economic realities. If we can achieve these improved outcomes, then the rights of employees will be protected and employers will see value in a collective organization of employees, we will achieve outcomes consistent with economic outcomes and, after all is said and done – and plenty has been said on this today – the combination of economic and social outcomes is what the underlying purpose of these declarations is about.

Mr. RICHARDS *(Government delegate, United Kingdom)*

First of all, the United Kingdom would like to welcome the Global Report, as a lot of hard work has gone into producing it and we thank the Office and indeed all those who have contributed. As all of us know, the fundamental rights of freedom of association and collective bargaining have been enshrined in the ILO Constitution since 1919.

It is important that these fundamental principles should continue to remain a focus of international attention. With regard to the ILO's objectives, the universal ratification and of course implementation of the Freedom of Association and the Right to Organise Convention, 1948 (No. 87), and the Right to Organise and Collective Bargaining Convention, 1949 (No. 98), is commendable and has the full support of the United Kingdom. The United Kingdom is a signatory to both Conventions. Indeed, the United Kingdom was among the first ILO member States to ratify them over 50 years ago.

Today, I want to speak very briefly about recent developments in the United Kingdom in relation to the aims of the Conventions. Over the last four years or so, in the United Kingdom, there have been a number of important developments concerning trade union legislation many of which derive from the Employment Relations Act of 1999. In July 2002, the Government fulfilled the commitment to review this Act. It worked with stakeholders, unions, employers and others in a full-scale review. The Government's conclusion shows that the Act is generally working well with no major changes needed, only some adjustments. Consequently, the Government is now taking forward the review's findings in an employment relations bill which is currently before Parliament. This bill will build upon the successes of the 1999 Act in a number of ways. For example, trade union membership rights will be enhanced, as the bill ensures that union members have clear rights to use their union services and cannot be bribed to relinquish this essential union right. Trade unions would also have more scope to expel or exclude racist activists within their ranks.

The ILO Global Report refers to the relationship between freedom of association and the settlement of labour conflicts. The United Kingdom Government also considers this to be very important. That is why it has created the right for individuals to be accompanied by a union official at disciplinary and grievance hearings. The new bill will enable that official to play their full role at such hearings. This right takes on a new importance, as from this October, when new regulations and discreet resolution procedures take effect in the United Kingdom.

Trade unions play a vital role in the partnership agenda. The United Kingdom Government wants trade unions to embrace new ways of working and to modernize. That is why it has introduced a new measure in the new bill to provide targeted funding to help unions to modernize their operations, adapt to the changing labour market and meet the increasing needs of their diverse membership. In this way, the Government will provide direct funding to trade unions to support innovative projects that may not otherwise take place. The new bill will also promote partnership in the workplace, and will include the power to make regulations to introduce information and consultation in the workplace by implementing the European Directive on Information and Consultation.

The Global Report rightly emphasizes the importance of tripartism for the role of social partners. All of the measures I have described in relation to the United Kingdom have been brought about through extensive consultation, both formal and informal, with unions, employers and other interested parties. This is in line with the Government's commitment to work inclusively in partnership with all interested parties.

Looking briefly at the Report more broadly, we welcome the focus on workers in the informal economy and the importance of seeking to extend the capacity of such workers to organize. Given that most poor people work in the informal economy, this is clearly a key issue, and of course a challenge. As the Report acknowledges, this might sometimes involve developing different tools for organizing and building new and different forms of partnerships.

Ms. BYERS *(Workers' delegate, Canada)*

There are probably no issues closer to a trade unionist's soul, sense of being and sense of balance than freedom of association, organizing and collective bargaining. In a sense they are head, our hands and our heart. The issues we continue to struggle with are the best ways to organize to provide decent jobs to give economic and social security to workers, and the best ways to organize to achieve social justice for workers, their families and ultimately their communities. We know that there is an advantage belonging to a union both economically and socially. The labour movement organizes to improve and expand workers' rights, to get better wages and working conditions and to improve the quality of life for working families and their communities.

In my country there is not one single workplace right which was just given to workers. We had had to organize to achieve every step forward for our members. And we have to organize and to fight everyday to maintain our rights. We know that if we achieve rights for our own members, we also have a social responsibility to work for those rights to be extended to the unorganized as well. Our responsibility for social justice does not stop at the door of the workplaces of unionized workers. We truly believe acts of social unionism. The Global Report *Organizing for social justice* states that "the biggest challenge in the area of freedom of association and collective bargaining involves extending these rights to more people, especially those in the informal economy or working in sectors less likely to be reached by the ILO's traditional constituents". Organizing for social justice has become increasingly more complex and more difficult. In the discussion of the raw economics of globalization, the discussion of the social dimensions of globalization is often left out. We cannot let this happen – or workers will continue to lose their rights to organize and to bargain. We believe that each time one group of workers loses ground, we all lose ground with them.

If we are truly going to deal with globalization, our country needs to develop, with the social partners, long-term economic policies that help create decent jobs – jobs which have security in the community, which are full time and which have benefits which provide a sense of dignity to workers, both in their employment and in their retirement years. Without these long-term economic policies, more people will be forced into jobs in the informal economy, jobs will be precarious, wages will be low, benefits will be non-existent, communities will suffer and workers will have their rights to freedom of association and collective bargaining diminished, if not removed altogether.

No country can build a healthy economy when workers' rights are attacked. Young workers, workers of colour, aboriginal workers and workers with disabilities are making some very clear demands. They see the union advantage and they believe that it must be extended to many, many more workers, especially workers from their groups. They would join unions if legislation truly supported freedom of association and the right of workers to bargain. It is amazing that in Canada, although we have the right to organize in the Charter of Rights and Freedoms in our Constitution, it is the only right we have to exercise in secret and with the fear of reprisals. There are many challenges. In the Canadian context we looked at both the private and the public sectors. Both of these sectors need to be healthy in order to create and to continue to provide stable jobs that offer dignity, equality and respect to workers.

In the private sector we see three major areas to challenge us in extending full rights of freedom to association and collective bargaining to workers – those are the agricultural industry, the service and hospitality industry and the manufacturing industry.

Canada produces a lot of the world's food, yet workers in the agricultural industry often have the least rights to join unions and to conclude collective agreements. When we try to organize, employers and governments force us to the courts. In fact, in Ontario, we took it all the way to the Supreme Court. We followed the rules and we were still told by government that agricultural workers did not have the right to bargain. We won the right in the Supreme Court and they changed the law. The story is repeated in agricultural workplaces across our country. Workers who are employed in factory farms have few rights and less workplace protection. In our country we need to know how to balance the needs of migrant workers from outside the country with the needs of workers who migrate within our country. Our country was first developed by immigrants. We continue that partnership, but our economic policies must ensure that we are achieving a balance between the infusion of skills of new Canadians with the development of skills of first Canadians.

The statistical work of the ILO is very important as we struggle with these issues at home. While we research the position of Canadian workers, we need to know how we compare globally – what the global trends are and skills migration. How will we ensure that the rights of freedom of association and collective bargaining are extended at home and around the globe? We look forward to working with the ILO, to ensure that the goals stated in the Global Report are extended to all workers and that everyone has the right to dignity, equality and justice in the workplace.

Mr. SHEPARD *(Government adviser and substitute delegate, United States)*

The protection of workers' rights is a fundamental American value and an essential component of the American democratic system. The principles of workers' rights are enshrined in US law, practice and policies. Over 200 years ago, our Constitution established "the right of the people peaceably to assemble". In 1935 our National Labor Relations Act guaranteed workers the right to join unions without fear of reprisal and created the National Labor Relations Board to enforce this right. The act states, unambiguously, that employees shall have the right to self-organization, to form, join or assist labour organizations, to bargain collectively through representatives of their own choosing, and to engage in other concerted activities for the purpose of collective bargaining, or other mutual aid and protection.

Our strong commitment to workers' rights is reflected in our ongoing support of the ILO's technical assistance programme to implement the principles of the Declaration on Fundamental Principles and Rights at Work. The Declaration recognizes the obligation of the ILO to assist its members and commits the ILO to offering technical assistance and advisory services, to promote and realize core labour standards, including the mobilization of external resources and support.

Since the year 2000 the United States' Department of Labor has contributed over $60 million to the ILO for technical assistance and support of the Declaration, and has worked closely with the ILO to help countries throughout the world realize the principles and rights necessary for development, democracy and social justice. The Declaration principles are also integral components of our trade agreements. Strong labour policies are at the core of new US free-trade agreements, and good labour standards are a high priority in our negotiations with other countries. In all of the free trade agreements we have recently negotiated, and are presently negotiating, we have asked our trading partners to affirm our mutual obligation as ILO members to work to ensure that the principles of the Declaration are fully protected in domestic labour laws.

I thank the Director-General and his staff for a valuable and informative Report. It is important that the ILO continue to produce a Global Report on the state of workers' rights, and it is important that we continue to revisit this subject, both here at the ILO and in our own countries.

Mr. ATWOLI *(Workers' delegate, Kenya)*

Thank you very much for granting me this opportunity to join my colleagues who have spoken before me on this very important, crucial, Global Report by the ILO.

On behalf of Kenyan workers, my colleagues on the continent, I acknowledge this Global Report as articulate, informative and appropriate to all of us who are involved in social practice, as practitioners.

I must also thank the Director-General and his entire team for having produced very wonderful work. All areas of our concern are covered in this Report. I shall not feel comfortable if I do not mention the articulate manner in which our Workers' group spokesperson, brother Roy, did make the case that touched every area and every aspect of the social justice application.

But let me deal with an area related to the eight core fundamental Conventions. It is noted that out of 177 member States of the ILO quite a number of these States have not yet ratified all the fundamental core Conventions, particularly the most critical one, the ILO Freedom of Association and Protection of the Right to Organise Convention, 1948 (No. 87).

This calls for a high-level campaign to be undertaken so that all member States of the ILO can ratify all the core Conventions. In addition, a follow-up on the implementation of these Conventions is needed, and this should involve making sure that domestication of these Conventions is carried out, because most of our countries have a tendency to promise the whole world that they have, or they will, ratify these ILO Conventions, and yet, when it comes to domestication of the same, they do not do it.

Education and training through capacity-building programmes, for all the tripartite partners is crucial and mandatory for the smooth existence of industrial harmony. Training should focus on development of skills for collective bargaining and dispute resolution. This will enable both employers' and workers' organizations to maintain industrial peace, which is a factor in any given development, and this also promotes productivity and possible economic growth of any given country.

There is a need for the fundamental Conventions to be applicable to the informal sector, public service, domestic, agriculture, and the export processing zones. I must thank our colleagues in the United States, through the American Centre for the International Labor Solidarity. They have assisted us in Kenya in recruiting and organizing more than 18,000 workers in export processing zones to join the trade union. This, I believe, will ensure that the terms and conditions of employment of workers in these sectors will be taken care of through their respective trade union organizations.

The ILO should, therefore, ensure that suitable programmes are put in place to assist workers in these sectors to be organized to join their respective trade unions, and those errant employers also to join the federations of the organizations in their respective countries. This, I believe, can be done through the existing trade unions and employers' organizations in their respective countries.

In the process of collective bargaining with the employers, workers normally find themselves in an awkward situation, due to non-availability of data on the economic performance of the enterprise. Therefore, as long as we have this problem it will be very difficult for us to operate on an equal footing. I therefore appeal to the ILO to focus on ways and means of assisting workers' organizations to get said information that will reveal, or will help them to reach a proper amicable agreement, and this should be in areas related to the productivity of an enterprise, since production is the purpose of all.

In addition, all social partners should be directly involved in the constriction of cost of living indices; this will ensure that the compiled cost of living indices are accurate and portray the true picture of the rise in the cost of living, and any other inflation-related data. It will also ensure that all the necessary factors like food, shelter, clothing, education, etc. are included in the basket of goods for compilation of that particular data.

I am aware that my friends, the employers, might not agree with this proposal but we need to create a level playing-field and transparent ground for all social partners.

In a nutshell, I will try and put suggestions for the way forward. In my own view, the following should be given priority in the plan of action for the coming four years.

Firstly, an intensified ratification campaign for the eight core ILO fundamental Conventions; secondly, extension of coverage of the eight core Conventions to agriculture, more so in the cut flower sector in Kenya, where employers do not conform to any given law, and exploitation is the order of the day. I am also happy to be the General Secretary of the Kenyan Agriculture and Plantation Workers' Union. This should also be extended to informal domestic public services and other vulnerable groups that require cover. Also, lastly, the establishment of institutional frameworks for the tripartite partners and tripartism should be strengthened as it is a pillar of industrial peace worldwide. And none of the collaborating partners, for example, civil society or NGOs, tamper with this most respected tripartism arrangement.

As we do not want to create confusion in every area of our practice, I believe that by doing this productivity, economic growth and development will be enhanced.

Original French: Mr. PRINCE *(Workers' delegate, Switzerland)*

Allow me to begin by expressing the deep gratitude that is felt by men and women workers here in Switzerland for the pertinent, effective and topical nature of the Report on the social dimension of globalization.

We endorse the extremely positive assessment of and the support that has been expressed by the Conference for the role being played by our Director-General. We know that he is resolute in his efforts to promote the effective implementation of international labour standards throughout the world.

I would like to draw the Director-General's attention to two points that we consider to be particularly important in the light of the plan of action for the next four years.

First, in paragraph 2 of the excellent Report, *Organizing for social justice*, we read that the fundamental principle of freedom of association and the right to collective bargaining is a reflection of human dignity. We also read that, as an integral part of democracy, freedom of association and the right to collective bargaining are key to realizing the other fundamental rights set out in the ILO Declaration.

Nonetheless, if you then look at the information contained in paragraph 209 of the same Report, you have to note that the scope of collective bargaining is extremely limited in some industrialized countries, due to an insufficient coverage of collective labour agreements. Sad to say, this is the case for Switzerland and also for Canada, Japan and the United States.

We would therefore ask whether the Director-General, on behalf of the ILO, could attempt to con-

convince the Governments of these rich, developed and democratic countries to make use of technical assistance provided by the ILO to promote the Right to Organise and Collective Bargaining Convention, 1949 (No. 98), in particular because Article 4 of that Convention stipulates that appropriate measures should, if necessary, be taken to encourage voluntary negotiations in order to resolve questions relating to employment conditions. This could be done whether or not the countries in question have ratified Convention No. 98.

Our second point relates to the fact that the member States of the ILO are the direct beneficiaries of international labour standards and of the technical assistance provided by the ILO. It would appear on that the international organizations benefit neither from these standards nor from that assistance. With that in mind, we would like to congratulate the Director-General for having introduced and for supporting collective bargaining within the ILO. We are very grateful to him for what he has done as, indeed, are all those working in this area. The practice that is being followed by the ILO should now be taken up by the leaders of other international organizations. Unfortunately, that is far from being the case today. Furthermore, we would say that all of those who exercise authority in the name of the Director-General should also engage in the art of negotiating in good faith. Collective bargaining has to be cultivated, strengthened and expanded within the ILO itself so that, quite transparently, it can be used when dealing with all issues of interest to any of the stakeholders present, in order to promote the greater good of the Organization and of those who work within it.

We would therefore urge the Director-General of the ILO, on behalf of the Organization that he heads, to raise awareness among the other international organizations, beginning with those that are part of the United Nations system, of the crucial importance for the organization themselves and those who work within them of implementing the ILO Declaration on Fundamental Principles and Rights at Work.

In order to illustrate the importance of this issue, allow me to point out that the members of a staff union within the United Nations Organization here in Geneva were prevented under risk of penalty from joining the Swiss Federation of Trade Unions, which is a democratic organization that is held in great esteem and that is affiliated to the International Confederation of Free Trade Unions. We consider this to be an unacceptable breach of the right to freedom of association.

We have no doubt whatsoever that the Director-General will be kind enough to heed our concerns, which relate to the promotion of decent work throughout the world, including in some developed countries with regard to Convention No. 98, and also within the international organizations which should not follow the example set by export free zones.

Mr. DZVITI (*Government adviser, Zimbabwe, speaking on behalf of* Mr. MANGWANA, *Minister of Public Service, Labour and Social Welfare*)

I am making this statement on behalf of my Minister as he became committed to other urgent duties.

The Zimbabwe Government would like to join previous delegates in congratulating the Director-General on his task of producing an informative Global Report. The Global Report provides us with the basis for comparing our own situation with what obtains in other countries in relation to how Conventions Nos. 87 and 98 on freedom of association and collective bargaining are being given effect both in law and in practice. Such a comparison is necessary, for there are merits in knowing how other societies organize in order to improve one's own system.

In Zimbabwe freedom of association is enshrined in both our country's Constitution and the Labour Act; in addition, Zimbabwe has ratified Conventions Nos. 87 and 98 and we are currently perfecting the Labour Act with the assistance of an ILO project, for which we are thankful.

If I heard correctly this morning, the Workers' spokesperson cited Zimbabwe as one country where workers were being killed for their belief in freedom of association. I must state that we do not know of any one person in Zimbabwe who was killed for union activities.

The subject of freedom of association in the world of work, particularly as it relates to the wider political discourse, is a cause of concern to many developing economies and those in transition.

The Global Report which we are considering acknowledges the position arrived at by the Committee on Freedom of Association of the Governing Body of the ILO in 1996 to the effect that governments should not attempt to transform trade unions into instruments for the pursuance of political aims.

(The speaker is interrupted.)

Sir ROY TROTMAN (*Workers' delegate, Barbados, speaking on behalf of the Workers' group*)

I am asking for the floor on a point of order.

In all proper parliamentary systems we are advised that we should not mislead the house. The person speaking for Zimbabwe is misleading this house.

If I wanted to say that Zimbabwe had killed people I would have said so. I never said that. I never mentioned any country where people were killed. I referred to a number of people who were killed but I never associated them with a country, and I referred to Zimbabwe and said that Zimbabwe is listed as a country where there are problems.

I would ask that that be struck from the record and I would not mind receiving a decent apology from the member.

Mr. DZVITI (*Government adviser, Zimbabwe, speaking on behalf of Mr. MANGWANA, Minister of Public Service, Labour and Social Welfare*)

I indicated that "if I heard him correctly", and, as he explained, I believe I heard him incorrectly and I wish to apologise for that and withdraw that particular part of my speech. Neither should the trade unions promote essentially political interests.

As I was saying, neither should trade unions promote essentially political interests.

It is our belief that some governments, particularly in the developed world, are interfering in political arrangements in developing countries through sponsoring the politically motivated activities of trade unions in these developing countries, with a view to effecting so-called regime changes. This kind of interference by these governments militates against the pursuance of meaningful tripartite social dialogue in the developing countries concerned.

A trade union centre with a political agenda to remove the sitting government while being backstopped by a foreign government cannot be seen to be engaging government and organized business to resolve national socio-economic problems.

In the case of Zimbabwe, trade union leaders who are also high-ranking members of opposition political parties are preoccupied with furthering the political agenda of removing the sitting government.

These trade union leaders aspire to form a government, hence they pay lip service to tripartite social dialogue. The promotion of essential ...

(The speaker is interrupted.)

Mr. POTTER *(Employers' delegate, United States, speaking on behalf of the Employers' group)*

We have a place to discuss these kinds of things and I believe that is going to occur on Saturday morning in the Committee on the Application of Standards. The scope of the speaker's discussion is beyond anything that is intended in this Global Report.

Mr. DZVITI *(Employers' adviser, Zimbabwe)*

I understand that, in fact, there will be discussions on other issues in Zimbabwe; it is only on the list for discussions, but as this issue of globalization is on the agenda I thought perhaps I should express the feelings of Zimbabwe.

In conclusion, let me say the Decent Work Agenda cannot be pursued in abject poverty. In this regard it becomes desirable for trade union organizations, employers and governments to work together.

It is on this basis that Zimbabwe supports the conclusions reflected in the Global Report. The Global Report says that the ILO needs to examine more closely the means by which the principles and rights of freedom of association and collective bargaining can be used to build an institutional framework for the labour market that promotes sustainable social and economic development, especially the reduction of poverty.

Original French: Ms. D'HONDT *(Government delegate, Belgium)*

Belgium greatly appreciates the possibility of replying to the pertinent questions raised about the thrust of the ILO's work in the future.

As to the first question Belgium wishes to be more cautious than the general conclusion, because the Report highlights more what progress has been made with the ratification and implementation of the two Conventions, although it does at the same time refer to the considerable difficulties which the Committee on the Application of Standards still has to deal with.

With regard to the promotion of collective bargain, this is a subject in which my country is very interested in, from the point of view of technical cooperation. We have effective negotiation systems, both on a centralized basis, within companies and on a sectoral basis, as each level is more suited to handling certain questions than others. The ILO should find examples in support of this argument and develop it in the next Report by comparing modes that perform efficiently. Competitiveness and innovation can depend on agreements at various levels. The question of salaries and wages could be added to the list of subjects.

Thirdly we accept the idea of concentrating forthcoming deliberations on the sectors and groups identified in the Report, but this should not be at the expense of the overall view which is needed in the follow-up to 1998 Declaration on Fundamental Principles and Rights at Work. We suggest that priority should go to the informal economy and the export processing zones.

Question 4 could be discussed in greater depth by the Governing Body after this debate. In order to put forward convincing augments on these topics the ILO should establish correlations, for example, between salaries, competitively, collective bargaining, innovation and job creation, or between collective bargaining, equality of wages and salaries, efforts to boost productivity, wage trends, the number of strikes and competitively.

Fifth, on technical cooperation I would just confine my remarks to urging the Offices of the Conference to encourage ratification of the standards which we are discussing, so that they bear fruit; to take action on the idea that the Director-General proposed at the end of his statement, namely that the Officers of the Conference should intervene in emergencies, at the request of the parties concerned, and to request the ILO Centre in Turin to develop appropriate training courses. In conclusion, I would like to suggest some major themes for the next action plan: strengthen the balance between the right of association and the needs of representative organizations so as to ensure the success of collective bargaining, the context of works councils and multinational corporations, collective bargaining and the social accountability of companies with regard to new challenges, freedom of association for the most vulnerable groups in the informal economy and, in conclusion, freedom of association and the rights of women in the workplace.

Mr. RAMBHARAT *(Employers' adviser, Trinidad and Tobago)*

I wish to acknowledge my regional neighbour, Sir Roy Trotman, and my Trinidad and Tobago labour representative, Mr. Robert Guiseppe.

In relation to the Global Report, I wish to comment on collective bargaining and the global economy, and have five points to make to this plenary.

The first point is that, in my view, over the next four years, the fundamental principles and rights at work may not be viewed in isolation, but must be seen within the context of globalization, enterprise development and the efforts to create a new global economy.

This global economy may present opportunities for many countries, but more likely it threatens the existence of work itself. Therefore, any discussion on rights at work must, by necessity, involve a discussion on the availability of work. You will recall that the Director-General has said that in the face of globalization, the livelihoods of many families throughout the world are under serious threat.

The second point is that the Employers' Consultative Association of Trinidad and Tobago can offer a model for collective bargaining in the global economy, based on the recent experience gained in the restructuring of Trinidad and Tobago's state-owned sugar industry, which had to be reorganized to meet the challenges of the global economy and of a world without quotas and preferential prices for sugar. In 2000, an international study found that Trinidad and Tobago was one of the most inefficient producers of sugar, and this threatened the livelihoods of 20 per cent of the population, whose social and economic lives were in some way linked to sugar. This group includes many mature women and young fathers.

The third point is that true social dialogue between the partners in a framework provided by a consent order of the industrial court of Trinidad and Tobago have enabled the sugar industry to focus on the creation of a policy framework which will replace lost jobs and provide opportunities for secure incomes, cover training and retraining for decent work and will also provide pensions and social support for those who are unable to provide for themselves through employment.

The fourth point is that the agreed framework between these social partners, the trade unions and the Government, entrusts the third partner, the employers' group, with the responsibility for designing and implementing critical policy components, in particular those relating to training and retraining, job placement and social support activities. This approach is consistent with one of the themes of the ILO Declaration on Fundamental Principles and Rights at Work, that is that incomes from work must be adequate to meet the essential needs of families, and that this is central to socio-economic security.

This quest for consensus and consent in Trinidad and Tobago will allow stakeholders to focus their energies on these real issues without the distractions of conflict and division.

The fifth and final point, is that this Trinidad and Tobago model for collective bargaining in the global economy embraces two important elements that are mentioned in the Director-General's Report, *A fair globalization: The role of the ILO*. The first element is that social partners have created a job-placement programme in which the employers' group has ensured that there is a link between the training and retraining opportunities offered by, and paid for by, the Government, and the integrated national activities to promote employment and income-earning opportunities.

The second element is a social outreach programme, called *People on the move*, which has positioned as part of an imperative for decent work in local development.

Our employers' group is satisfied with the response of the social partners in Trinidad and Tobago, which brought about the development of local capacity and strengthened the local social framework.

Regarding the future role of the ILO, we feel that the ILO can provide support to its Members to allow them to access information on the social impact of international, economic, financial and trade policies, on the availability of decent, sustainable and secure work. For example, the ILO, in cooperation with other multinational agencies, may wish to undertake an assessment of the impact of the restructuring of Trinidad and Tobago's sugar industry and support us in the way forward. We therefore agree with the idea of focusing the ILO's work on the sectors identified in your draft discussion document.

Secondly, in response to globalization and the creation of a global economy, the ILO may wish to support the concept of collective bargaining in furtherance of enterprise development at the local level. This will serve as a means of developing the Decent Work Agenda, securing sustainable incomes, knowledge and capacity-building, and as a local response to globalization and a global economy.

Original Russian: Mr. SIDOROV *(Workers' adviser and substitute delegate, Russian Federation)*

I do not know if I am right in saying this, but I am not going to begin by praising the Report or its authors. The Report, after all, is a piece of work and any work should be done well. The main thing is that the Declaration itself, as well as its follow-up that has been in operation for a few years now, is clearly a mechanism that has been effective in promoting freedom of association and collective bargaining.

Now, all the countries of the former Soviet Union, including the Russian Federation, have ratified Convention No. 87 and, with the exception of two, they have also ratified Convention No. 98. In other words, things are not so bad. However, in practice, things are not quite as good as they look on paper.

If you look at what happened just before this 92nd Session of the International Labour Conference, in Moscow we held another conference at which we discussed the question of observance of trade union rights and freedoms within the territory of the former Soviet Union. The message that emerged from that conference in Moscow was that violations of Conventions Nos. 87 and 98 do exist in all countries in that region. In fact, they are so numerous that an examination of those violations could actually take up a special sitting of the International Labour Conference. That being the case, we have many grievances and many complaints submitted by trade unions to the Committee on Freedom of Association, and they bear witness to the wide variety of problems that exist. They show that, both in terms of legislation and in terms of practice, there are problems and the governments and employers are not particularly scrupulous about respecting their obligations vis-à-vis trade unions or vis-à-vis society as a whole.

Further, when you look at the instances of violations of trade union rights, you see that there are, in fact, deliberate violations of those rights and that such violations are increasing every year.

I could list all of these violations, but I am not going to take up your time; I would just ask you to read the report of the Committee on Freedom of Association, and you will see that in its recommendations, referring to guarantees of constitutional and other rights, it says certain things should be done by the state bodies responsible for ensuring the application of legislation. You will also see what it recommends be done by the ILO in order to assist governments in fulfilling their obligations.

The basic idea underlying all this is social justice, involving the tripartite constituents but, clearly, the way that that idea is understood is not the same on all sides.

In our region we are particularly concerned about the fact that in many countries, countries that have declared themselves to be constitutional States, the governments themselves do not abide by their own laws and they do not hesitate to violate the rights of trade unions and their members. I have in mind, for example, interference in the internal affairs of trade unions, attempts to impose the will of the government on trade unions, cronyism, favouritism of different types and sometimes simply a failure to recognize what has to be done in order to comply with the laws that guarantee freedom of association and the right to collective bargaining.

Obviously, governments are not willing to shoulder their own responsibilities, then what are we to expect from employers? I refer to both national employers in those countries and foreign employers operating in our region. It has to be recognized that many foreign companies operating in our region are unwilling to implement the kind of good governance policies in our region that they implement in their own countries. It seems to me that the ILO Declaration on Fundamental Principles and Rights at Work should not just be a statement of pious intent. It should actually be an international mechanism that can be used to resolve the problems that exist and to ensure that fundamental rights are guaranteed. Otherwise, there can be no stability in industrial relations, nor can there be any achievement of social justice and, indeed, there can be no hope of just development for individual countries or for humankind as a whole.

Mr. KETTLEDAS *(Government delegate, South Africa)*

The Minister of Labour of South Africa is unable to attend this sitting. The South African Government delegation wishes to commend the Director-General for an excellent and incisive Report.

The South African Bill of Rights enshrines as fundamental both the right to associate freely and the right to collective bargaining. In the South African labour market these fundamental rights find legislative effect in the Labour Relations Act of 1995 and subsequent amendments. The aim of the South African labour market regime is to ensure that workers and employers can freely and fairly exercise their rights in a manner that ensures stability and that the injustices of the past are rectified. As such, in our tenth year of democracy, we cannot but fully agree with and support the Report on the fundamental principle that all workers and employers have the right to freely form and join organizations to promote and defend their interests without interference from one another or the State.

Our legislative interventions have ensured that the process of registration of either employer or worker organizations has been simplified and brought in line with ILO standards, but our legislative environment also protects workers and employers from bogus unions and organizations by setting very basic minimum standards that such organizations have to adhere to. These provisions were scrutinized against the principle of freedom of association. It was felt that any union or employers' organization that operates within the boundaries of the Constitution, will not be negatively affected or be subjected to the relevant provisions of the Act or the guidelines. The legislation also promotes the establishment of strong trade unions and ensures that full collective bargaining rights are enjoyed where there are representative trade unions.

The South African Government delegation fully agrees with and supports the statement that "freedom of association and the effective recognition of the right to collective bargaining are the foundation for a process in which workers and employers make claims upon each other and resolve them through a process of negotiation leading to collective agreements that are mutually beneficial". The approach of our Government is founded on the belief that the employer and employee parties in an industry, trade or service, are able, through negotiation, to deal with matters of mutual interest best themselves. It would be easier for parties to maintain labour peace in an environment created by them. The State's function is to provide the legislative machinery for the interaction of employers and employees in a neutral framework which balances the power relationship.

The great strength of this approach is that it is conducive to better regulation of matters which affect a whole industry or service and it is able to set minimum standards and conditions which can be operative throughout a sector. But we also understand, within such a context, employer/worker relations can break down to such a degree that dispute resolution mechanisms need to be utilized.

The dispute resolution process in South African law includes making the dispute resolution system more accessible to workers and possibly to limit exploitation by employers. The system also places a premium on conciliation and dialogue.

As noted in the Report, the challenges facing domestic workers and farm workers, in terms of exercising their right to organize, remain considerable. Workers in both these sectors are particularly vulnerable because of the subjective and objective conditions that prevent them from organizing. While the Government has taken all steps possible to ensure that conducive conditions are created for collective organization, we are also of the view that the benefits that emerge from collective bargaining cannot be denied to workers from these and other vulnerable sectors.

Through a process that incorporates social dialogue, we have put in place sectoral determinations that set minimum wages and minimum standards of work for those sectors. I must add that the Government also takes responsibility for ensuring that those standards are met. We will use the examples that are highlighted in the Report as a model in order to strive for ideal solutions to our problems and try to improve in those areas that do not meet expectations.

In conclusion, we welcome the Report and express our commitment to continue with the implementation of fair employment principles. Our support of the principles enshrined in this Declaration should not be doubted and we will continue with the process to ensure an environment of freedom of association common to all which creates opportunities for all.

Mr. GAMMAMPILA DON *(Government delegate, Sri Lanka)*

At the outset, let me offer my congratulations to the President and the three Vice-Presidents on their election. Let me also congratulate the ILO for presenting the first Report of the second cycle of Global Reports under the follow-up to the ILO Declaration on Fundamental Principles and Rights at Work, entitled *Organizing for social justice*, at this special plenary session.

The first Global Report under the follow-up to the ILO Declaration on Fundamental Principles and Rights at Work, entitled *Your voice at work*, brought out a number of issues and a wealth of practical experiences. The Global Report this year, *Organizing for social justice*, continues the assessment of current trends.

We recognize the potential of freedom of association and collective bargaining in sound economic development. Where people have a participatory voice in their work and in the conditions of their work, productivity improves. If workers feel a sense of personal efficacy, sharing in the decisions that affect their lives, they are far more likely to share the enterprise- and national-level goals of increased productivity and competitiveness. Industrial peace, itself a boost to productivity, is also much more surely maintained when all concerned have a voice and feel part of the process.

Sri Lanka has ratified all eight ILO core Conventions including the Freedom of Association and Protection of the Right to Organise Convention, 1948 (No. 87), and the Right to Organise and Collective Bargaining Convention, 1949 (No. 98). However, a few legal hurdles and practical obstacles still remain to giving full effect to the provisions of Conventions Nos. 87 and 98.

Most of the legal deficits pertain to workers in the public sector. Apart from the legal restrictions relating to the Federation of Public Sector Trade Unions, the ILO Committee of Experts on the Application of Conventions and Recommendations has observed restrictions on the freedom of association of prison workers and judges. Sri Lanka is working closely with the ILO in addressing these remaining deficits.

During the past few years, Sri Lanka has made a headway in promoting freedom of association and collective bargaining in the investment promotion zones. The number of trade unions operating in the investment promotion zones has increased.

Some of the trade unions have successfully negotiated collective agreements. Some of the unions that do not have the required membership for the recognition of collective bargaining have been able to achieve the recognition needed to represent the grievances of individual members.

Apart from the argument based on rights, there is also an underlying economic argument for ensuring labour rights, including freedom of association, since some trade quotas and granting of generalized systems of preferences (GSP) are dependent upon a well-ensured implementation of the Convention and a clear commitment from the Government to adhere to its obligations. This has led to the increased awareness of freedom of association and effective recognition of the right to collective bargaining by the business community.

The GSP granted to Sri Lanka by the European Union for its labour relations practices this year, 2004, is an indication of the progress made in this area. The greatest challenge before us is promoting freedom of association and collective bargaining in small enterprises and in the informal economy, where the majority of the workforce is active.

We recognize the diversity of work arrangements, employment relations and the needs and problems of the workforce in the informal economy. We fully agree with the findings of the Global Report that "the traditions and tools of organizing in the informal economy may not be the same as in the organized part of the economy". However, the existing informal organizations that operate within the informal economy exemplify the potential for organization.

Freedom of association is a prerequisite for social dialogue. We believe in the need for the promotion of social dialogue in order to deal with the core problem of an industrial relations climate that is weak and confrontational overall. We believe in strong tripartite social partners and the introduction of democratic procedures.

For this purpose, the trade union organizations and the employer organizations have to be strengthened. There is also need to strengthen the overall credibility of the national tripartite mechanisms, such as the National Labour Advisory Council. The ILO is assisting and guiding us in all these endeavours.

I am very hopeful that the proposed national decent work action plan for Sri Lanka will address most of the challenges in the implementation of the principles of freedom of association and the right to collective bargaining.

Original Bulgarian: Mr. APOSTOLOV *(Government delegate, Bulgaria)*

Allow me to begin by saying how grateful we are to have this meeting and how much we would like to commend the Report that we have before us, the Global Report under the follow-up to the ILO Declaration on Fundamental Principles and Rights at Work. We think it is of extremely high quality.

Bulgaria has been a Member of the ILO since 1920 and it has been a member also of the Governing Body. Bulgaria has ratified all of the core Conventions of the ILO and, that being so, we cannot stand idly by when we are discussing the issues that are referred to in the introductory part of this Report.

We would therefore like to express our concern about the serious problems that exist with reference to violations of freedom of association and we recognize that this is a problem that affects both trade unions and employers' associations in several countries that are in fact members of the ILO. We therefore believe that we should endorse the statement made in the first part of this Global Report, that is to say that free associations of employers and workers and the collective bargaining and other mechanisms of dialogue that they establish are foundations for a democratic development path.

We believe, in the light of our experience in Bulgaria, that standard setting is extremely important, and that means we must have clearly defined criteria. We also consider that the criteria that have been developed by the ILO are of great use in that respect. We in Bulgaria have been able to make use of these criteria in setting standards at national levels ourselves, and they have also been reflected in the work of our employers' associations.

We also regret the fact that, as yet, we do not have sufficient development of collective agreements in our country involving the participation of trade unions and employers' associations, and this is a situation which applies to many countries in Central and Eastern Europe. We therefore recognize that there is a need for us to enhance the way in which dialogue, involving all the social partners, takes place in those countries, and we think that such dialogue is of crucial importance for further progress.

Further, we believe that we must emphasize the fact that the positive results achieved, in accordance with the mechanisms for follow-up to the ILO Declaration, have also been very commendable, and in Bulgaria, for instance, we have been able to involve employers' associations and make them more aware of what is really involved in collective bargaining and collective negotiations. That being so, they are now able to play a greater part in discussion with the social partners and to recognize issues that are of common concern to both employers and trade unions.

We would therefore like to agree with the view expressed throughout this Report, to the effect that collective bargaining has an extremely important part to play in achieving an effective balance between the interests of workers and employers, and this is particularly important in the context of globalization.

We therefore feel that it is important to recognize the crucial importance of collective bargaining in resolving the problems that are arising today, particularly problems of increasing poverty. This is vital if we are to protect those who live in poverty today, and the number of those living in poverty is ever increasing. We recognize that the ILO goal of decent work for all is one that must be achieved if we are to eradicate poverty.

We would therefore like once again to reassert our support for the three-step approach towards achieving that goal. Certainly, what we in Bulgaria tend to do is, first, to ratify international labour standards, second, to create an appropriate legal and administrative framework to allow us genuinely to implement all of the rights that we have then ratified, and third, to continue with capacity building, both for trade unionists and for employers' associations.

I am now very happy to be able to tell you, as I move towards my conclusion, that in Bulgaria we have already gone a long way down that path, and if you look at the overall picture in Bulgaria, then you see that we can be optimistic, despite all the problems that we face. We are able to look to the future with optimism, and we believe that we have been able to draft a lot of extremely good legislation that will guarantee rights, and that is fully in line with ILO standards.

Lastly, I would like once again to underscore the fact that all members of the ILO encountering problems in this area must make use of the experience of the ILO, and it is extremely useful if they can obtain technical assistance which is properly targeted and focused at their needs, that is to say, the needs they have to enhance rights at work for all.

Mr. BENYDIN (Workers' delegate, Mauritius)

I would like in the first instance to associate myself with previous speakers in commending the clarity and quality of the contents of the Global Report under the follow-up to the Declaration on Fundamental Principles and Rights at Work.

"Organizing for social justice" is indeed what we in the trade union movement are cherishing every day, because, over and above our responsibilities of defending and promoting the inalienable rights of workers in the workplace, we are also strongly committed to leading the struggle against the negative aspects of the neo-liberal system and to ensure that social justice, human values and, above all, the dignity of workers should prevail in all circumstances. In this respect, we are convinced that the bedrock of human dignity can be best safeguarded with the fundamental principle of freedom of association, an intrinsic human right, the right to organize, the elimination of all forms of forced or bonded labour, non-discrimination at work and the elimination of child labour.

The ILO has played an instrumental role and we consider that it should continue to be the social pillar of the new world order and a new governance to ensure progress. We also believe that collective bargaining on paper alone is not sufficient. I think that collective bargaining must go hand in hand with the right to strike because, in certain countries where we have collective bargaining, we do not necessarily have the right to strike. So, we want to have the right to strike so that, when we deal with employers or with a government, we can make significant progress in negotiations. We say that we do not only want to bark but must also have the possibility of biting at times. So I think that collective bargaining is very important. Particularly, we see that with new technology and working methods, and factors like outsourcing, deregulation, flexibility, etc., we in the trade union movement are anxious about the tendency to discourage workers from joining trade unions, particularly in view of the precarious nature of the new forms of employment.

We appreciate the fact that the ILO is continuing with its noble campaign to promote decent work involving a living wage to allow workers to meet the basic needs of their families. Indeed, the Declaration on Fundamental Principles and Rights at Work, adopted in 1998, reminds member States of their obligation to respect, to promote and to apply ratified Conventions, particularly the eight core Conventions which reflect the essential characteristics of good industrial relations, good governance and industrial democracy.

By "social dialogue" we mean meaningful and constructive dialogue, and this, together with the consolidation of tripartism is the essential component to obtain results in our struggle for better salaries, better conditions of work, social peace and also poverty elimination. But of course, these two factors require that there should be the necessary and appropriate forum and legal framework in all member States, so that we can have meaningful dialogue and the social partners can join hands together to better the situation of workers and the population in general.

We are the trade unionists. Remember that the world is now a global village and that men and women workers are at the centre of all developments, be it on the social, economic or political field. Neither can we remain indifferent to the plight of migrant workers in a world where mobility has become a reality. In this regard, we want to make the voice of the migrant heard wherever it is present. We have a duty to set up specialized units within our union structure to enforce respect for their rights. To this end, we rely also on the technical support and cooperation of the ILO. We would like, through these means, to ensure that equal treatment and equal opportunities are given to migrant workers on the same basis as native workers.

We would like to commend this Report and we hope that none of us are insensitive to the plight of workers in the export processing zones, where we know that some do not even enjoy the basic rights to join trade unions. Even in countries where this is allowed, we know that it is not easy because now the tendency in export processing zones is towards cheap labour, and I think that we should also fight for a living wage. In this respect, we consider that Conventions Nos. 87 and 98 are very important for us, and we rely on the cooperation of everybody, particularly the ILO, so that we can live in a better world and a better society.

Original Spanish: Ms. FRANCO (Government adviser and substitute delegate, Mexico)

I would like, on behalf of Mexico, to express our thanks for having been invited to take part in this interactive session and to refer briefly to the Global Report.

As regards the efforts and achievements of the Mexican Government in the promotion of the principle of freedom of association and collective bargaining, I would like to share with you our suggestions for the ILO's further work in this direction.

The focus has been primarily on the positive developments which have taken place since the adoption of the Declaration as a result of ILO technical cooperation programmes. The Report also refers to certain sectors where problems persist with regard to freedom of association and observance of trade union rights. To it's credit, the report also cites research carried out by other international organizations. Recalling that the follow-up to the ILO Declaration on Fundamental Principles and Rights at Work is promotional in nature, the Government of Mexico commends the Director-General for the constructive approach taken in his Report with regard to freedom of association and collective bargaining.

Mexico is mentioned in the Report as a country that has not ratified the Right to Organise and Collective Bargaining Convention, 1949 (No. 98), but has sent a report under the follow-up to the Declaration as regards non-ratified Conventions stating that the Mexican Constitution recognizes this right. The Government of Mexico would like to point out that, while recalling the promotional nature of the Declaration, it has promoted discussions between the social partners on the possibility of ratifying Convention No. 98. It has also acted as facilitator in discussions between the social partners on the subject of labour reform.

As regards the growth of the informal economy in Mexico, steps have been taken to ease the transition towards formality, not only through labour law reform, such as the above – mentioned amendments to the Federal Labour Act based on consensus with the social partners, but also through administrative and fiscal measures.

The Report says that the Committee on Freedom of Association has examined a case involving a United States Supreme Court ruling according to which undocumented workers are not entitled to back pay after having been dismissed illegally for trade union activities, over turning the findings on the National Labor Relations Brand (NLRB). The Committee on Freedom of Association concluded that the denial of back pay ordered by the NLRB left workers without adequate protection against anti-union discrimination. The Government of Mexico concedes that the decision of the Supreme Court is within the remit of the legislative branch.

In a landmark agreement, the Mexican Secretary for Labour and Social Welfare and the United States Department of Labor signed a Joint Declaration in 2002 recognising that the labour rights of migrant workers are independent of their migrant status. This principle has since been recognized in a number of other international instruments, such as an opinion issued by the ILO in November 2002 as regards to the scope of international provisions on labour rights with regard to migrant workers. An advisory opinion issued in 2003 by the Inter-American Court of Human Rights referred to the legal status and rights of undocumented migrants. In April 2004 the United Nations Commission on Human Rights adopted resolutions on the human rights of migrant workers and on the International Convention on the Protection of the Rights of all Migrant Workers and their Families. As regards to the points for discussion, the Government of Mexico agrees with the focus on the sectors which have been identified, in particular agriculture, and suggests disseminating information to ensure that it is accessible to those who need to exercise their rights of freedom of association and collective bargaining.

Original Arabic: Mr. DERBI *(Government delegate, Libyan Arab Jamahiriya)*

I would like to congratulate the President on his appointment to chair this meeting at which we are discussing an extremely important Report. Specifically, this is a report which deals with a subject which is very important to all of us, and that is freedom of association, the right to organize and social justice. I would like to thank the ILO for having prepared this Global Report, a report which has been produced as part of the Declaration on Fundamental Principles and Rights at Work and its Follow-up. The efforts that the Office has made in order to prepare this document deserve our heartfelt thanks.

The Libyan Arab Jamahiriya has ratified all the Conventions which are linked with this Declaration. Legislation in the Libyan Arab Jamahiriya covers the content of these Conventions. Freedom of association and the right to bargain collectively are principles enshrined in the labour law of 1 May 1970. This labour law governs the founding of trade unions, whatever form they may take and without any restrictions. We have also passed a law devoted to the trade union movement, quite separate from the original labour law of 1970. The law on trade unions lays down the ways in which trade unions may be established, in conformity with Conventions Nos. 87 and 98, thus resulting from decisions taken by the International Labour Conference.

We are convinced that trade union organizations play a vital role in society and in development. This is particularly true at the present time when we are facing globalization and technological revolution. Trade unions and the freedom to establish trade unions and to bargain collectively will have an essential role in the promotion of civil society, if we wish to make sure that our society develops, makes progress, manages to overcome poverty and establishes social justice. The greatest importance in these cases must be given to trade unions and the trade union movement.

We also have the Green Book, a book which gave Libyans the right to establish trade unions. Under article 6 of the Green Book, Libyans have every right to establish a trade union. We have another law, a law to enhance personal freedom, which also covers the establishment of trade unions. We believe that these laws together guarantee citizens the right to form trade unions.

We support the conclusions of the Report.

Mr. GYÖRGY *(Workers' adviser, Hungary)*

I thank and congratulate all those who worked on and contributed to this excellent Report; it is a report which is unambiguous, realistic and yet which looks to the future in a practical way, by mapping out the work to be done.

Today we heard numerous explanations of the substance and the title of this Report. Out in the real world many would say it is semantics. However, this morning I still assumed that those of us who have gathered here to discuss the Report came in the understanding that we are all committed and dedicated to putting to good use the ideals enshrined in the core labour standards, of incorporating essential elements for social justice into everyday practice.

I need to comment on a widespread misunderstanding or misinterpretation, namely, as has also been expressed earlier this morning in this hall, that the right to collective bargaining is a trade union right. I challenge that statement. Collective bargaining and social dialogue is the right of all protagonists, workers and players, trade unions and business. Even more so it is an opportunity, and for some of us it is an obligation towards this society.

Recognizing each other as real actors and not only taking each other as subjects, but also seeking the mutually beneficial in the world of labour, brings us further in creating the conditions for economic and social success. At this point, let me thank the Dutch Government delegate for sharing his hesitation about the name of the Commission and the way he formulated worldwide commitment to social rights delivers growth. This is an understanding which, when put into practice, can take us to social globalization.

Let me also express disappointment over contributions to this debate which clearly demonstrate the further existence of high-level rhetoric – statements which have nothing to do with the cruel reality of the every day violations of human and workers' rights. Lip service must be replaced with application of these internationally recognized standards.

Coming from a region – Central and Eastern Europe – where over the past decade we have been experiencing radical transformation of the economic, political and social systems and of society itself, we know what a range of open and covert violations of workers' and trade union rights exist. Economic transition, privatization, foreign direct investment and greed for profit, coupled with decreasing union density and loss of union strength, have made the vulnerable even more exposed. Although most of our countries are by now becoming new Member States of the European Union and as such have had to take on the social *acquis communautaire* of the Economic Union, which generally recognizes trade union and workers' rights, the application of those rights in everyday practice is less than perfect. You just have to listen to the presentations of Workers' delegates from that region in the plenary hall over the last few days. I would cite some examples: some employers have suspended wages of trade union leaders; some act to make collective agreements null and void; some demand that new employees pledge not to join trade unions in order to get the job. There are cases of unfair dismissal for union activism; harassment of trade union leaders; foreign investors' anti-union practice; setting up of "yellow" unions. These are just some examples of rights violations, without mentioning the specific details and countries where they happened.

I would strongly recommend that anyone wishing to see the details should consult the ICFTU's annual survey of violations of trade union rights, just published yesterday. In countries where legal systems are under development or being fine-tuned, where legal systems are fragile, court proceedings extremely slow and lengthy, labour inspections ineffective, and fines for the violators are ridiculously low, genuine efforts are needed from the State to give effect to the democratically chosen rules. The implementation of law strengthens democracy and people's commitment.

Concerning social partnership, the tool of collective bargaining must be reinforced too. In the transition countries, as we are often called, bargaining at the workplace level is more of a tradition and more attention is paid to it than to bargaining at the national tripartite level. However, there is an increasing need for sectoral institutions and to begin with real work at the sectoral dialogue level. In economies where only a minority of the workforce is covered by collective agreements, concluded almost exclusively at the workplaces, sectoral bargaining is the way to go.

In Hungary, there are over 900,000 enterprises registered for 3.6 million labourers, and the collective agreements coverage is less than 45 per cent. Our endeavours presently have resulted in the setting up of 19 sectoral committees, with significant support from the European Union and the ILO. Accordingly, reinforcing workers' and employers' organizations, and empowering them at that level is a priority. The legal framework and the creation of functioning structures must be accompanied by motivating the social partners to cooperate in a meaningful way and work as real partners. In their work towards these goals, our region's social partners have been very well served and assisted by the ILO. The tasks ahead of us include capacity building and recognizing the use of dialogue, bargaining and partnership, and this Report gives ample arguments and ideas as to how to do that.

This is where we also express our hope that the Seventh European Regional Meeting in Budapest next February will move forward the ideas summed up in this present Report.

Mr. MAHADEVAN *(Workers' adviser, India)*

We really appreciate the Global Report which is analytical, informative and enlightening. We, of course, join others in congratulating the Director-General for this excellent Report. The Report reflects our view that in many countries there has been a growth in joblessness. There has been a jobless, senseless, fruitless, ruthless, futureless growth in many countries. And this is due to the privatization of profits and nationalization of losses. There has been an exit policy without a proposed entry policy. Unfortunately, direct foreign investments and loans are attached to labour law reforms, and curtail the right to organize and the right to strike. In fact, many of the proposed labour reforms aimed at promoting competition in our country's fishing sector do away with the so-called restrictive provisions that are, in fact, beneficial to workers. In fact, we believe that the right to collective bargaining includes the right to strike.

There are certain deficiencies in the enjoyment of this right which have led us to go to the Supreme Court of India. There has been a huge increase in the informal sector in recent years. We have been demanding a comprehensive law for the labour force groups who carry out 65 per cent of unorganized labour. However, there has been no two-way communication; all communication is one way. So agriculture labour laws will have to apply.

I would like to commend the ILO, which has got a role to play in the informal economy. There is a need for laws to regulate the informal economy.

The ILO should conduct research into existing laws. Data will have to be collected with regard to the informal economy in various countries, as well as with regard to social justice and social protection. We do not agree with the argument that there is no alternative. Everybody feels that there is no alternative but maybe there is one. In fact, the Director-General himself was present in Mumbai when we organized the World Social Forum. Alternatives were found and discussed. It is possible to make another world. In fact, in India, we have problems with two types of migrant labour. We receive migrant labour from various nearby countries who may come as refugees, etc. They are permanently present. In addition, we have been sending migrant labour to other places on a "permanently temporary" basis. I do not know how we can solve this problem because "permanently temporary" migrant workers do not have any rights in either country. Of course, on a lighter note, I can seriously say that migrant persons can even become prime minister in our country. That is the situation. Anyway, in India, we have the largest democracy.

As for the ILO's role, I would like to conclude by saying that, following the recent elections, India has introduced the "common minimum programme". We have made various suggestions to the Government. We have called for labour and land reforms, and for all of the important ILO Conventions to be ratified. The original labour law proposal that would involve the curtailment of rights must be withdrawn. There can be no such labour legislation.

We have held an assembly of trade unions in which both of the country's trade unions participated. As a result of this assembly, a charter of workers' rights was developed. This has become part of the new Government's economic policy. In short, we would like profit for the people and not profit over the people. That should be the law. I think that this Report indicates that position. So finally, I would like to once again congratulate the Director-General for his Report on the follow-up process. Particularly with regard to the ILO, I would like to stress that some research must be carried out into the informal sector, in particular with regard to the legislation governing that sector. Data should be provided, on which we can base our future actions.

Ms. GENCIANOS (representative, Migrants Rights International)

It is with honour that I am addressing this plenary committee on behalf of Migrants Rights International, which is an international federation of migrant workers' unions and associations, church-based groups, legal organizations and non-governmental organizations promoting the human rights of migrants.

This year's discussion of the Global Report, under the follow-up to the ILO Declaration on Fundamental Principles and Rights and Work, focusing on freedom of association and collective bargaining, is but a timely and urgent response to the reality that migrant workers all over the world are faced with. The Report speaks of "the fundamental principle of freedom of association and the right to collective bargaining as a reflection of human dignity. It guarantees the ability of workers and employers to join and act together to defend not only their economic interests but also civil liberties such as the right to life, security, integrity and personal and collective freedom. It guarantees protection against discrimination, interference and harassment".

These same rights which are promoted through freedom of association and collective bargaining, are basic human and labour rights that should be guaranteed to every worker without discrimination of any kind. Unfortunately, however, in the case of migrant workers, the realities they face are different. Migrant workers are generally deprived of this right to freedom of association and collective bargaining, thereby contributing to their vulnerability as workers in a state of which they are not nationals. This issue has been clearly identified in the Global Report, confirming migrant workers as one of the groups often denied the right to organize, either in law or in practice. The Report also mentions domestic workers, including women migrant domestic workers and agricultural workers, as belonging to this category of workers facing barriers to freedom of association and collective bargaining. Moreover, the situation of irregular or undocumented migrant workers, and their exclusion in society, is of particular concern.

Migrants Rights International strongly believes that ensuring migrant workers' right to freedom of association is a fundamental step towards the realization of their basic human and labour rights. Through organization and representation, migrant workers are able to bring out their concerns, identify violations, access channels for grievances and redress, and promote better protection. This right is guaranteed under the Freedom of Association and Protection of the Right to Organise Convention, 1948 (No. 87), and the Right to Organise and Collective Bargaining Convention, 1949 (No. 98). Complementing these ILO Conventions is the United Nations' International Convention on the Protection of the Rights of All Migrant Workers and Members of Their Families, which provides for the right of migrant workers and members of their families, including those who are undocumented, or in an irregular situation, to freely join and participate in the activities of trade unions and other associations.

Furthermore, we also note in the Global Report some of the identified best practices among trade unions in extending membership and representation to migrant workers, including those in irregular situations. This is an encouraging reflection of the strong commitment by trade unions to fighting racism and racial discrimination at work. We hope that this best practice could be widely promoted and implemented.

Therefore, in view of today's discussion, we call on this tripartite body, the States and the social partners, to give serious consideration to the findings in and recommendations of the Global Report, in particular to the right of migrant workers to representation, organization and unionizing, and to work together to remove these restrictions, in both policy and practice, towards the achievement of this right.

Original French: Ms. O'Neill: *(representative, World Organization Against Torture)*

As regards this year's excellent Global Report, *Organizing for social justice,* which deals mainly with the application of the Freedom of Association and Protection of the Right to Organise Convention, 1948 (No. 87), and the Right to Organise and Collective Bargaining Convention, 1949 (No. 98), the

World Organization against Torture would like to raise certain crucial issues before this Conference concerning certain cases that have come before us.

Above all, the World Organization Against Torture is a network of 266 non-governmental, national or international organizations, that provide the international secretariat with information and request it to intervene particularly through urgent appeals made in response to violations of the most essential human rights, such as those that threaten the moral or physical well-being of individuals, or even their lives.

As is stressed by the Global Report, some progress has been made, but a great deal remains to be done on the road towards freedom of association and collective bargaining throughout the world. There is however one country, Colombia, where being a trade union leader is, of course, theoretically recognized in legislation but, in point of fact, these leaders are assassinated by hired killers or paramilitaries, who are not brought to justice.

As to the Government, it states that murders are on the decrease; we all rejoice for each life saved. The number of murders decreased in relation to 2002; however, in 2004 they are on the increase in relation to 2003. The number of urgent appeals we have received prove this. In other words, even the intolerable argument that the situation of trade unionists in Colombia is supposedly better because less of them were murdered this year than last year is already invalid. The problem, however, is not a question of the figures. For as long as even one death threat is issued and carried out, and while those issuing the threats, the murderers and those who provide the financing are not brought to justice, how can the defenders of workers' rights flourish in this country?

As regards the promises made by the Government to disarm the paramilitaries, these are nothing but a smokescreen. The facts speak for themselves. All the observers who have gone to Colombia and their numerous reports have shown that there is fundamental complicity between the paramilitaries and the army. The killing of a few paramilitaries are used as a cover, and the daily reality has shown this to be true.

(The speaker was interrupted.)

Mr. Potter *(Employers' delegate, United States, speaking on behalf of the Employers' group)*

I probably let this go on too long. There is another place in the house where we discuss these kinds of facts. This is not really relevant. This is just a case against one country. This is not a global appreciation and I think it is inappropriate. The Government is not even in the room. So I would ask the speaker to focus more generally on the issues for which her organization has competence.

Ms. O'Neill *(representative, World Organization Against Torture)*

It would be desirable for this Conference to think about certain coincidences, for example, the fact that some of the victims of murder attempts belong to trade unions such as the Single Confederation of Workers of Colombia (CUT) and the Workers' Trade Union (USO). The most vicious conflicts have lined the trade unions up against the state enterprises in liquidation such as Telecom and Ecopetrol.

Ms. SAJIDA *(representative, Migrants Forum in Asia)*

This intervention is being made on behalf of the Migrant Forum in Asia, a network of over 200 migrant workers' associations and trade unions, and migrant support groups based in 22 Asian countries. The Global Report *Organizing for social justice* highlights the growing socio-economic role of the domestic workers' sector in the current labour market.

Moreover, as decided in footnote No. 57 in the Report, "It is symptomatic that all of the Global Reports dealing with the four categories of fundamental rights have singled out domestic workers as one of the groups of workers which are significantly affected by a rights deficit." With this in mind, and in consideration of a multilateral framework on the management of migration from a rights-based perspective, it is imperative that the ILO works effectively to bring domestic work out of the twilight zone it currently occupies within market and non-market relations.

We note with deep concern that, in many countries, domestic work has yet to be recognized as work. The implication of this includes non-coverage of domestic work and the national labour legislation, human and labour rights violation and, most importantly, denial of the fundamental right to organize and collective bargaining.

The Report rightly emphasized that "the organization of domestic workers is a key tool in combating the violations of all the fundamental principles and rights at work, including in respect of freedom from forced labour and non-discrimination". Furthermore, the Report draws attention to the fact that "in sectors where workers are well unionized and labour standards on working hours, health and safety, wages and employment contracts are not only set but also enforced"; there is virtually no demand for forced and traffic labour.

The challenge the Report puts before us today is to recognize that "organizing domestic workers requires innovative strategies and approaches". We are happy to note the Report's citation of examples where migrant and domestic workers have successfully organized themselves such as the Indonesian Migrant Workers' Union in Hong Kong, China, established in 1999 at the first grassroots-based union of Indonesian migrant women domestic workers.

As Hong Kong labour legislation provides migrant women domestic workers with equal treatment, including the right to unionize, the Indonesian migrant workers in Hong Kong enjoy the structural conditions necessary for their self-organization and representation.

Union women members not only engage in policy dialogue with the Hong Kong Government but they have been invited by the Indonesian parliament to debate on the formulation of national migration legislation. They have been therefore recognized as partners in policy formulation.

We reiterate the Report's statement that "the fundamental principles of freedom of association and the right to collective bargaining is a reflection of human dignity". While recognizing their positive social and economic contribution to society, we urge the ILO and its social partners to promote the following measures and principles consistent with the ILO and UN standards to ensure that migrant women domestic workers are provided with decent living and working conditions.

(Mr. Ray Guevara takes the Chair.)

Mr. POTTER *(Employers' delegate, United States, speaking on behalf of the Employers' group)*

The Global Report is the public face of the Declaration on a broad scale. The Global Report is essentially based on a principle-by-principle approach where it all comes together. It is a global view of all countries and trends, regardless of whether the countries have ratified the fundamental Conventions or not.

Today we had, if I counted correctly, 47 speakers – 25 were Governments. I believe that those are lower numbers than any preceding year. If my numbers are correct, there are approximately 165 countries registered at the Conference, which means that approximately 15 per cent of the Governments who have made a commitment to the Declaration actually spoke here today. Obviously, this is disappointing. It seems to us that there might be some value if the Office were to look at this year's participation rate and who participated compared to prior years, to see if there is some trend or some conclusions that might be drawn from this.

I would suggest that the Office should look at it from a variety of angles and perhaps there may be a need for a further discussion of this in the Governing Body.

Certainly, the participation of governments is voluntary, but we would ask the question, how is the overall reality of the Members' commitment to the Declaration to be evaluated if we do not have broad-based participation in this Global Report debate?

Part of the purpose of the Global Report followup is to serve as a basis for assessing the effectiveness of the assistance provided by the ILO and for determining priorities for future action. We did have some indications on both scores here today but I think that the Office has quite a challenge in front of it, if it is going to come up with a comprehensive assessment and determination of priorities in line with the request made by the Governing Body's Committee on Technical Cooperation in November 2000.

To end on a somewhat positive note, I would say that, while we still have some great distance to go, even with the lower participation rate, fundamentally, this was a better interactive discussion than we have had in the past. It is still the case, though, that several Governments did not give us any really concrete information as to how they are seeking to promote and realize their commitments under the Declaration.

We suggest that some thought be given to putting something at the very beginning of future Global Reports that would give some indication of the kinds of information that Governments might consider providing and that would be of use. We do not have any particular items to suggest today but we do think that, if there was some prominent box of some sort, that that might well stimulate Governments to provide useful information that would help to further the achievements of the goals in the Global Report and the Declaration.

Sir Roy TROTMAN *(Workers' delegate, Barbados, speaking on behalf of the Workers' group)*

We wish to thank those of you who have stuck with this debate through the many hours we have been here. Of course, we commiserate with you, Mr. President, and with your colleagues, with those on the platform and with the staff as well as with the interpreters and the technicians who have had to put up with us.

Our debate today did not answer all of our questions, but it represents an effort to do different things as well as an effort to do all things differently. We salute Mr. Potter and the other lead speakers that we have had but, like him, we are of the view that we did not get the benefit of as many Governments as we should have liked to have. I would wish to say, though, that our group was impressed to see the number of Governments from the Arab States which took the time out and came to express their views regarding where they would like to see this matter go and, if you were to remove them, then the ratio would become all the worse for us to look at, and it might be good for us to be able to look at last year versus this year to see who is coming and to try to find out where there is a correlation between the subject that is discussed and the governments that attend. I believe that the result might be very interesting for us in terms of what, really, we can believe is the seriousness of our involvement in the work of the Organization.

Of course, I am not here to judge. I read a book, I still read it, that says I should judge not lest I also be judged. But at the same time, I think that we can analyse things for ourselves and arrive at certain answers from time to time.

We would wish to say that there are, as the Director-General said, still far too many obstacles to organizing and that there is, from our position, a need for the Committee on Technical Cooperation to be called into action and to be used significantly more for promotion because we believe that if the technical cooperation and the funding which goes with it were able to use that facility, it might be better able to promote these core Conventions in a much more meaningful manner.

We think we should make a comment or two regarding some of the things which we heard today before we finally wrap up.

We heard the position given by the chief spokesperson for the Gulf States, who came from the United Arab Emirates, and we would wish to say that we would want to compliment the region for the reported work which we have. We think it's a welcome step that they have given to us in their report but we hope that they would not consider it to be an end in itself, nor that they would consider that we have reached the end of the line.

For example, we have heard about workers' committees and, naturally, they are quite obviously trying to move in the direction of experiencing freedom of association and the right to bargain collectively, but I think that more steps need to be taken to promote that freedom of association and to promote the right to collective bargaining and to make sure that they are not merely incorporated in laws and regulations but rather in practice for implementation. Furthermore, this should be a right not only for nationals, but nationals have to recognize that migrants also need to be able to benefit from this and that there should be some universality in the application of the Freedom of Association and Protection of the Right to Organise Convention, 1948 (No. 87), and the Right to Organise and Collective Bargaining Convention, 1949 (No. 98).

We are hoping that not merely these countries but that all countries would recognize the need for democratic participation and for accountability and transparency in the way that they approach the questions of Conventions Nos. 87 and 98.

We say the need for transparency, because every government that has spoken has talked in very glowing terms about the way governments across the whole world promote, advocate and implement all of the issues that relate to Conventions Nos. 87 and 98. Yet, employers are complaining about the absence of free associations of workers' organizations almost as much as workers are complaining about the particular absence of free associations of employers' organizations. So, there must be some transparency gap.

What there has to be, is a more meaningful dialogue between themselves and ourselves and I would think that it is something that has to be explored between now and November, when there is the interactive session and the consultation. And I would like to believe that we would be able to call "a spade a spade" and that the diplomacy within the house would not make us want to call it by some other name which makes it less identifiable in the circumstances.

Machinery has to be explored here to assist in speeding up the ratification of Convention No. 87 and in having have the consequential legislation which is necessary.

We heard from our own side, Sister Ursula Engelen Kefer, making the very strong point that sometimes the barriers which are put in position are barriers which prevent speedy resolution of those matters. We are of the view as, I am sure, is the Chairperson, that justice delayed is justice denied. If you deliberately delay an individual's efforts to pursue freedom of association, which we have all accepted today – perhaps because the Director-General said that it is a very natural expectation – if we deny that, then we are denying justice. I do not think that anymore, be they governments, employers or workers, should be in the business of denying people a fundamental and a basic right.

Machinery also has to be set in place to train and to support capacity building, so that we can satisfy the responsibility of all three of the partners – the government and the social partners – under Convention No. 98.

It is not enough for us to be satisfied that there is freedom to associate without understanding that Convention No. 87, without Convention No. 98, is a denial of the fundamental right of the worker. If we look at the indices towards the back of the report, we will see that there are not large numbers, but there is too large a number of countries which have ratified Convention No. 87, but have failed to ratify Convention No. 98.

This is a contradiction in terms because if you have one, you have to set in place the training, the support and the capacity building that are necessary to make sure that the logical progression from association to speaking for yourself takes place. Any government that denies this, any employer that denies it, any workers' organization that denies it, is a wrong association, or a true association doing something that is wrong.

We think that under this particular umbrella, regions can do a lot for their members and for each other. They can assist themselves by visiting those areas where there are good examples to be followed. You heard Trinidad and Tobago speak about how well they are doing, we had the splendid example given by New Zealand; we had an example given by the Australian Employers' delegate. Within our regions we ought to be able to find examples which we can follow; it does not always need to be the ILO itself that has to do it. We can learn not merely by reading books, but by visiting, and I believe that the host countries might be willing to accommodate us in those areas.

There must also be machinery to speed the process from organizing to recognition and from recognition to collective bargaining. This process has to be speeded up and the ILO has to be able to help us, but individual governments have got to be able to have their labour departments and labour administration departments help as well.

There are two things further that I wish to say. The Australian Employers' delegate said that when one looks at the summary of reports, one finds that there is in fact no problem with organizing because only small numbers of people claim interference.

Well, before he said it I had anticipated it and had told the President that there are large numbers of people who refuse to report because they say that when they report, nobody does anything about it. It is like the people in some countries who refuse to look for work any more whose argument is – "I have been looking for work for five or six years and I get the same answer all the time, so, why should I look for work any more?" They become what the economists call "voluntarily idle". I am not too sure what it means: when you are looking for work and you cannot find it, you stop; I do not think that you are voluntarily idle, you are frustrated. But, I think that it is part of the position which I would like to put forward: the paucity of reporting does not mean that there are no problems.

We in the labour movement have far too many examples of extreme harassment and denial; we do not want the beauty of the room and the ambiance that Mr. Potter spoke about to lull us into a sense of complacency.

Finally, I would like to refer to what the Employers' adviser, Mr. Anand, said when he spoke of a "minority plea". But if he held a minority position, he did not verbalize it, because when he speaks about Convention No. 87, then goes on to speak about poverty anywhere constituting a danger to prosperity everywhere, he is in fact representing all of what we understand Convention No. 87 to be leading towards. We believe that Conventions Nos. 87 and 98 are crucial for obtaining the tools to create wealth for everyone, so that we can share wealth among all. We do not want Mr. Anand to leave the room and retire feeling that he stands alone. We want him to know that we all stand together: we want the world to create more wealth, but for the world to share that wealth. In the words of my Indian colleague, we must not have a situation where there is wealth taken by the few and there is poverty shared by the whole nation.

We have enjoyed participating in this discussion. However, we think that there is more work to be done and we hope that this will be done at some time in September or October.

Original Spanish: The PRESIDENT (Mr. RAY GUEVARA)

The time has come to conclude our work on the discussion of the Global Report. It is my great pleasure to be able to confirm that our objective, that is, to obtain information and ideas for developing a plan of action through an interactive discussion has been very successful.

More than 60 speakers have unanimously highlighted the importance of thought and action with regard to freedom of association and the effective recognition of collective bargaining as a key means of ensuring social justice – an objective that is called for in the Constitution of our Organization. These principles underlie a state of law and it is, therefore, essential to ensure their application. While much still remains to be done in order to ensure the full application of these rights, there has, nonetheless, been a great deal of progress towards making the need for economic development compatible with the need to guarantee social rights.

The new productive sectors and the most vulnerable groups have been unequivocally identified as the subject of future work. Export processing zones, agriculture, the domestic sector and the public sector are the areas where we need to redouble our efforts and where the failure to apply these principles is most notable.

Collective bargaining and social dialogue have today been reconfirmed as being the highest example of the right to organize and freedom of association. They must therefore be adapted to the needs of economic progress and social reality, along with the traditional but no less important issues of equality, productivity and the application of new technologies.

The efforts that have been identified by Governments, Employers and Workers are considerable, but our task is not yet finished. International solidarity, as the necessary framework for attaining social justice, is indispensable and it is for that reason that the wealthiest countries should, in addition to fully respecting their commitments under the Declaration and support those who request their cooperation in order to ensure that rights and experiences can be shared, and make the principles we have been discussing today a reality.

We need to work for social justice, as has been recognized.

It is only with strong commitment from everyone and a firm belief in our purpose that we will be able to achieve this.

I would like to thank Mr. Tapiola, Mr. Damen, Mr. Attigbe, and all of the technicians who have assisted us, the interpreters as well as all the staff members who have given us their generous and enthusiastic support today. I would also like to congratulate those of you who are in the room and those who have already left the room, for your firm commitment, your involvement and dedication. You are heroes of decent work.

(The Conference adjourned at 6.45 p.m.)

CONTENTS

Page

Tenth sitting

Global Report under the follow-up to the ILO Declaration on Fundamental Principles and Rights at Work: Interactive sitting 1

Speakers: The President, the Secretary-General, Sir Roy Trotman, Mr. Potter, Mr. Al-Tayer, Mr. De Geus, Mr. Neffati, Mr. El-Amawy, Mr. Sweeney, Mr. Pais Antunes, Mr. Raïs, Mr. Konditi, Mr. Seguin, Mr. Farshori, Ms. Arango de Buitrago, Mr. Shenoy, Ms. Torsøe, Ms. Engelen-Kefer.

Eleventh sitting

Global Report under the follow-up to the ILO Declaration on Fundamental Principles and Rights at Work: Interactive sitting *(cont.)* 19

Speakers: The President, Mr. Potter, Sir Roy Trotman, Mr. Anand, Mr. Buwalda, Ms. Ssenabulya, Mr. Villavicencio Rios, Mr. Echevarría Saldarriaga, Ms. Boegner, Mr. Mwakwere, Mr. Salmenperä, Mr. Aoun, Mr. Ahmed, Mr. Anderson, Mr. Richards, Ms. Byers, Mr. Shepard, Mr. Atwoli, Mr. Prince, Mr. Dzviti, Ms. D'Hondt, Mr. Rambharat, Mr. Sidorov, Mr. Kettledas, Mr. Gammampila Don, Mr. Apostolov, Mr. Benydin, Ms. Franco, Mr. Derbi, Mr. György, Mr. Mahadevan, Ms. Gencianos, Ms. O'Neill, Ms. Sajida.

No. 14 – Friday, 11 June 2004

International Labour Conference

Provisional Record 15
Ninety-second Session, Geneva, 2004

Twelfth sitting
Friday, 11 June 2004, 10.00 a.m.
President: Mr. Ray Guevara, Mr. Maatough

REPORTS OF THE CHAIRPERSON OF THE GOVERNING BODY AND OF THE DIRECTOR-GENERAL: DISCUSSION *(CONT.)*

Original Spanish: The PRESIDENT *(Mr. Ray GUEVARA)*

I give the floor to the Clerk of the Conference for an announcement.

RATIFICATION OF AN INTERNATIONAL LABOUR CONVENTION BY MAURITIUS

Original French: The CLERK OF THE CONFERENCE

It is a pleasure for me to announce to the Conference that on 9 June 2004, Mauritius deposited the ratification instrument of the Vocational Rehabilitation and Employment (Disabled Persons) Convention, 1983 (No. 159), a Convention which was adopted by the Conference in 1983.

Original Spanish: The PRESIDENT

Before resuming our discussion, I would like to give a brief summary of the discussion of the Global Report which took place yesterday. In fact, we devoted two entire plenary sessions to the discussion of the Report.

Yesterday, Thursday, 10 June 2004, the International Labour Conference held two plenary sittings in which it examined the Global Report under the Follow-up to the ILO Declaration on Fundamental Principles and Rights at Work. The aim of these sittings was to stimulate an interactive debate that would enable an exchange of information and ideas to be used in the development of an action plan. More than 60 speakers took the floor to stress unanimously the crucial importance of the principles of trade union freedoms, freedom of association and the actual recognition of collective bargaining to guarantee social justice. Those principles are the foundations of a state governed by the rule of law.

While there is still a long way to go to ensure full application of these rights, delegations provided information on progress achieved and recognized the need to accompany economic growth with the guarantee of social rights; indeed, they all agreed this was fundamental.

Export processing zones, agriculture, domestic workers, migrants and those who work in the public sector are all sectors and groups where we really need to redouble our efforts. Because it is precisely in those areas where there are the greatest deficiencies when it comes to the application of these principles.

Collective bargaining and social dialogue have been confirmed as embodying the ultimate expression of trade union freedom and the right of association. They must therefore be adjusted to the latest developments in economic progress and social reality and address not only the usual issues but also equality, productivity and the use of new technologies.

All the efforts and measures taken by governments, workers and employers are remarkable but it is quite clear that much still remains to be done. To complete the process, there needs to be a framework of international solidarity in order to achieve the social justice to which we all aspired.

In addition to respecting the commitments under the Declaration, it is clear that the wealthier countries should support those who ask for their cooperation to disseminate rights and experiences that will allow them to apply these principles of freedom of association and collective bargaining. This is my summary of the discussions that we held yesterday on the Global Report.

We shall now resume all discussions of the Reports of the Chairperson of the Governing Body and the Director-General.

Original Spanish: Mr. MARIUS *(representative, Latin American Central of Workers)*

I would like to join in congratulating the President of the 92nd Session of the International Labour Conference, not only because it behoves me to do so, but also with much affection and we wish him every success.

The Latin American Central of Workers, which is 50 years old and which is getting ready to hold its 12th Congress in Brazilia, would like to reiterate its thoughts on the role, standard–setting process, and mission of the ILO from the perspective of Latin American workers.

First we must note, as did the Latin American Commission for the Rights And Freedoms of Workers and the Peoples in its 12th Annual Report that in our region, living and working conditions are steadily deteriorating. There is a marked continuous increase in precarious employment and structural employment, unfair distribution of wealth, a constant weakening of the welfare and social security systems and generalized, systematic violations of the rights and freedoms enshrined in our national constitutions, international agreements, and in ILO agreements.

Latin America, because of its heritage of biological diversity and natural resources, should certainly not be called the poorest continent, but the antisocial wheeling-dealing of economic and political forces and the big multinational companies make it the most unfair continent on the planet, where the gap between the opulent lifestyle of a rich minority and the poverty, misery and desperation of the vast majority of our peoples is widening with everyday that passes. For this reason, the Director-General's Report seeks well thought out alternatives.

Secondly, this civilization faces the United Nations' system with a huge challenge. I am talking about the task of universal coverage, but in this situation the ILO must play a decisive role. That is what workers around the world are demanding. The World Commission on the Social Dimension of Globalization is not just an important initiative; despite certain gaps and some rather general statements, it has made an interesting contribution. We in Latin America believe that the only way to consolidate democracy with social justice is to provide an alternative development model, quite different from the single track and exclusive mind set that is being foisted upon us.

The ILO must carry much more weight within the multilateral system, essentially in the financial, economic and trade bodies, whose policies and decisions are still making millions of people in our continent poorer.

The ILO cannot allow its role to be reduced to simply being a place for protesting or letting off steam about poverty, misery and social exclusion; on the contrary, it should with greater institutional fortitude adopt a global strategic agenda, so that on the basis of its reading of history it can participate in the fora where every day the new world power structures take the big decisions.

We visualize an instrument which, with the help of the world of work, helps to overcome the anachronistic incoherence, which makes social considerations of secondary importance and where individuals and peoples are at the mercy of financial geopolitics and the new functioning of open markets commanded by the interests of minority sectors.

Thirdly, this remodelling of the ILO involves a management analysis which would call into question the effectiveness of our regulatory and legislative system, analyse irregularities, check on coherence and compare actual results with those of other bodies within the United Nations system. I am not talking about the content of norms, but of their application and development and of the tripartite follow-up to Conventions.

We are talking about, asymmetry or inequality of conditions when faced with a boss who sacks a trade union leader thereby violating The Freedom of Association and Protection of the Right to Organise Convention, 1948 (No. 87), and it is the worker who ends up paying the price for all the time that passes until the national courts go into action or an appeal is heard by international legal bodies.

On the other hand as far as our standard-setting activities are concerned, the text of the Governing Body contains some concerns, some wake–up calls, and makes some suggestions and recommendations to governments, while the World Trade Organization applies drastic sanctions to any States that violate trade agreements.

Just three days ago, Rigoberto Dueñas from Guatemala, completed the first year of a prison sentence imposed on him because he denounced corruption at the Guatemala Social Security Institute. The authorities refuse to release him. Since 1992, no more than 15 trade union leaders have been murdered, but no investigation have been carried out and no one has been punished. In Cuba, nine leaders of a trade union were sentenced to 20-25 years in prison for the "crime" of belonging to our Latin American Central of Workers. In Colombia there is clearly a policy of conditioning violence and repression against the trade union movement, and more than 100 trade union leaders were murdered in 2003. This is an extremely grave situation, the Committee on the Application of Standards has not been able to agree on even one observation and conciliation mission to Colombia.

The ILO needs our full commitment in order to move forward, a global strategic agenda enabling it to consolidate its historic role and to fund more forceful answers to the problems of our civilization. The international social drama demands that we break traditional moulds and make the voice of this institution heard in multilateral bodies. The Latin American Central of Workers is prepared to give its support to meeting this challenge, as this is what Latin America workers are demanding.

Original Russian: Mr. KOZIK *(Workers' delegate, Belarus)*

The Workers' delegation of Belarus has attentively studied the Reports presented for examination at this session, and we have noted that these Reports fairly reflect the important role of the ILO in defending and implementing fundamental principles and rights at work.

Yes, much work has been done in order to fulfil the strategic objectives defined in the ILO programme. We share the view of the Director-General and of his proposals which are contained in the report of the World Commission on the Social Dimension of Globalization, that it is absolutely necessary to concentrate the efforts of the ILO on the social aspects of globalization.

It is absolutely necessary for us to make the process of globalization – one which is fair, democratic and manageable and one which opens equal opportunities for all countries and peoples. It is opportune that the Commission has prepared this report in a timely manner, when we still have the chance to match the processes of economic globalization with the development of political and social institutions which, as correctly noted in the report, are local, national or, preferably regional in nature.

The ILO must continue to provide analysis of the processes of globalization and to formulate codes of behaviour both for governments and workers' organizations. At the same time, I should like to focus on an important element.

Today, the international workers' movement has no united international centre. Certainly, the trade union movement is united in various conferences and federations which are extremely important and play a positive role but, at the same time, each such enterprise follows its own goals, and the information coming from these enterprises is sometimes distorted.

I believe that a group of workers could usefully examine this issue. As a first step, a decision could be taken by these international associations to be open to membership for all without any exclusion. Faced with the rapid development of globalization, workers risk remaining without a clear centre. This idea is partially reflected in one of the reports presented here which notes a positive trend in the trade union struggle to increase their numbers, their links with other trade unions, and their size at the national and international levels.

It is difficult not to agree with this. It is, in fact, a necessary condition for dialogue and equality between the social partners and for giving them the opportunities they require. In fact, only strong trade unions with highly developed structures and financial independence can truly maintain and represent the interest of workers in carrying out negotiations with social partners.

At the same time, we support the ILO initiative and the necessity of carrying out a comprehensive approach to the implementation of programmes based on strategic objectives and having one goal – decent work.

The goal-oriented nature of these programmes and consensus achieved by their effective implementation allows us to study all aspects in order to achieve the best results. The Federation of Trade Unions of Belarus continues to be in favour with the strict compliance of international standards as this will guarantee their implementation in the world of work.

The Republic of Belarus has ratified all of the core ILO Conventions. However, we do have some remaining problems. There is a small amount of unemployment – 3 per cent – and wage levels remain insufficient for workers. We are required to stand up for social guarantees of workers and must regularly remind the Government and employers that only a socially healthy society can achieve economic progress.

Nevertheless, in the last two years, there have been a number of positive steps made in Belarus. We can already talk about fully-fledged social dialogue on a tripartite basis. The ILO has provided technical assistance to the development of tripartite cooperation in Belarus. We consider it absolutely necessary that the ILO resume implementation of its technical assistance programmes in Belarus with the participation of the largest trade union centres.

I would like to take this opportunity to thank you all for the wonderful Reports that you have presented for our examination at this session.

Original Arabic: Mr. AL ANSARI *(Employers' delegate, Qatar)*

In the name of God, the Merciful, the Compassionate! We would like to congratulate the President on his election to preside over the 92nd Session of the International Labour Conference, and to wish him every success.

It is an honour for me to have the opportunity to take part in this annual Conference held by the ILO, which this year, is examining subjects which are of particular interest to the constituents – Governments, Employers and Workers. The Conference is the *raison d'être* of this Organization and its chief importance lies in the subjects for discussion which, in turn, give rise to recommendations and decisions that enable us to strengthen the relationship between the social partners.

It is an honour for me to express my appreciation and thanks to the International Labour Organization, which has constantly strengthened complementary relations between governments, employers and workers.

I would also like to take this opportunity to express my conviction that the human factor is at the heart of our work. The human factor accounts for 60 per cent of production and it is this conviction which should prompt us to create an enabling environment conducive to strengthening workers' productivity and innovative ability.

Qatar is complying with its international commitments and provides workers, be they nationals or residents, with an enabling environment conducive to work, through its legislation, governing relations between employers and workers, and coordination between employers and the Ministry of Civil Service Affairs and Housing. In the framework of labour administration, this Ministry ensures that decent housing and medical services are provided to all workers without any discrimination.

In addition, an Emiri Decree approving a new Labour Code has recently been promulgated, affording workers new rights and advantages. Thus, workers now enjoy rights which are guaranteed by the legislation, with compliance being supervised by the difference organizations and trade unions. The new Labour Code regulates dialogue between employers and workers by means of negotiations, collective agreements and joint committees, thus strengthening the relationship between the two parties. All of this furthers the improvement of working conditions and the development of the national economy.

As we speak of workers' rights and an improvement in working conditions, we cannot close our eyes to the situation in Palestine and in the occupied Arab territories, and the measures taken by the Israeli occupation authorities. We therefore urge you to help Palestinian workers and employers in Palestine and in the occupied Arab territories.

Original Russian: Mr. NAGHIYEV *(Minister of Labour and Social Protection of Population, Azerbaijan)*

Allow me first of all to express my appreciation for the Report that has been presented and the issues discussed at this forum, which once again confirm that the ILO's activities are characterized not just by its sphere of competence but also, and most importantly, by the clear ideal of ensuring social justice around the world.

The Director-General's Report once again demonstrates that the gravity of the current socio-economic situation of the world forces us to search for new approaches and take new decisions with the aim of realizing the fundamental principles and rights at work.

Since the 91st Session of the International Labour Conference, institutional reforms in Azerbaijan have progressed even further, and there is now better recognition that social issues must be an integral part of the transformation process. This is reflected in a number of decrees issued by the President of Azerbaijan as well as in the Government programmes adopted with the aim of reducing poverty and increasing the socio-economic development of the regions. This has allowed us to further strengthen observance of human rights in the area of work and social organization, and to develop social progress in our country.

International institutions such as the United Nations, the ILO, the World Bank, the International Monetary Fund and others are taking an ever greater role in resolving social problems in the Azerbaijani Republic. This cooperation provides a mechanism for us to join forces and take an integrated approach to the development of social policies in our country.

I would like to take this opportunity to express particular thanks to the ILO for having provided us with the necessary consultations, as well as for carrying out seminars to prepare our national employment strategy and to develop systems for safe and secure work and to eliminate the worst forms of child labour, as well as to develop the role of the social partners in formulating employment policy. Azerbaijan is one of the ten countries championing the development of a network of youth employment and has begun working, with the support of the ILO, on an action plan for youth employment, which will become an integral part of a national action plan for implementation of employment strategy.

We, in Azerbaijan, are actively carrying out legislative reform and are paying close attention to international standards. It should be emphasized that Azerbaijan has ratified 55 ILO Conventions, including all those concerning social dialogue and all eight core Conventions.

At the same time, it should be noted that violence and the occupation by Armenia of more than 20 per cent of Azerbaijani territory and the presence of a large number of refugees and displaced persons, as well as the problems of a transitional period, make it more difficult to apply Conventions. It is also obvious that globalization significantly influences our capacity to implement our own socio-economic policies.

The main aims of the Conference arising out of the Report presented are to overcome existing tensions in the development of social dialogue and to ensure the realization of fundamental rights and principles at work. No country can successfully carry out its economic and social policies without developing tripartism. The development and democratization of social labour relations in our country presupposes the active partnership of all the social partners: the State, the trade unions and the employers. The entry into force on 1 July 1999 of the new Labour Code of the Republic of Azerbaijan was an important step in that direction.

Since 2001, social dialogue at the national level has been carried out on a tripartite basis when concluding general collective agreements. Experience shows that Azerbaijan is moving slowly towards further democratization of labour relations; each of the participants in collective labour relations is becoming increasingly aware of the need for cooperation in resolving social labour issues.

Given the results achieved in the context of the development of further cooperation between Azerbaijan and the ILO, we believe that it would be useful to implement joint projects at the national level to develop social dialogue in the following areas:

First, the establishment of the ILO Decent Work Agenda in the Azerbaijani Republic has focused significant attention on creating healthy and safe working conditions, employment protection, the establishment of a national system of management in accordance with international standards and the enhancement of national pay mechanisms in the state sector.

Secondly, the implementation, following the ratification by the Azerbaijani Republic of Worst Forms of Child Labour Convention, 1999 (No. 182), of the International Programme on the Elimination of Child Labour and the organization in that connection of a programme for the monitoring of child labour and the preparation of a national plan of action.

Thirdly, in the framework of the joint initiative by the ILO, the United Nations and the World Bank to create a network for youth employment, and the organization in Azerbaijan of a we have a national centre for the promotion of youth employment, which will help the young people of our country to find employment, and will make it a priority to help refugees, internally displaced persons, women and other vulnerable groups.

I believe that the consensus that we have achieved in this forum regarding future action will allow us to achieve even greater results in developing social justice.

Mr. BARIMAH (Minister of Manpower Development and Employment, Ghana)

The Report of the Director-General, *ILO programme implementation 2002-03,* and the report of the World Commission on the Social Dimension of Globalization reflect this Organization's determination to use its huge potential and influence to effectively tackle the multifaceted problems facing the world of work through its international standards-related activities.

In that regard, Ghana, as a coastal state, is satisfied that the first discussion on the fishing sector at this Conference is aimed at revising the seven standards on fishing. This should lead to effective measures to promote, among other things, health and safety standards for the benefit of the industry, its employees and consumers.

In the same vein, we are extremely happy with the inclusion of migrant workers on this year's agenda. Migration has become an issue of huge international importance. Hence, it is being discussed in various international forums to ensure that the phenomenon benefits all countries involved, as well as the migrant workers and members of their families.

Ghana received close to US$1 billion in 2003 in remittances that came into the country from Ghanaian migrants. However, it is also true that Ghana's health delivery system has been seriously devastated by migration of skilled health workers, mainly to Europe and America. This clearly shows the need for properly managed migration to ensure a win-win situation for all countries as well as for the migrants themselves.

The migration issue is part of the globalization process. Indeed, there cannot be free movement of goods, services and capital without a corresponding free movement of peoples in a globalized world. The Ghana delegation therefore endorses the World Commission's concerns that the extent and intensity of globalization has not resulted in net gains for all countries. Every effort must, therefore, be made to reverse the negative impact of globalization on the economies of developing countries, which have been losers in this process. We do hope that the recommendations of the World Commission could be translated into concrete programmes and comprehensive action to enhance the standard of living of all workers through relevant standard setting under ILO Conventions.

Ghana is grateful to the ILO and supporting donors for the various capacity-building interventions from which the country has benefited in the past. These include global employment and the Decent Work Agenda, ILO/IPEC projects and the new Child Labour Unit of the Labour Department of Ghana, which is working effectively to combat child labour and the worst forms of child exploitation. I am happy to inform you that victims of child labour and trafficking are being liberated and reunited with their families and being given opportunities for education. Funds are also being provided to their parents to invest in alternative means of livelihood.

To meet international standards on fundamental principles and rights at work, Ghana has now enacted a new labour act. It is the Government's determination to apply the act diligently. The act has been drafted in collaboration with the ILO, to meet the developmental objectives of the country and enhance conditions of employment for Ghanaian workers and attract further investment for more employment opportunities. We hope for further support in operationalizing, the new labour commission created under the act and in sensitizing the social partners on its operation provisions. Similarly, the ILO was involved in our joint programme called Skills Training and Employment Placement (STEP), which aims at poverty reduction through the provision of skills training for self-employment in the different communities in the country.

The Government of Ghana and its social partners, are grateful to the ILO for other interventions, which include the guarantee of social security and protection for workers, worker-friendly policies on HIV/AIDS in places of work, employment-intensive investments, enterprise development and social dialogue. These activities have contributed immensely to the spirit of tripartite cooperation and industrial harmony in Ghana.

Finally, Ghana pledges its determination to continue to cooperate with the Organization to formulate appropriate social policies that will ensure equity and improved living standards for our people.

Ms. NGINDINWA *(Deputy Minister of Labour, Namibia)*

It is my distinct honour and privilege to address this 92nd Session of the International Labour Conference on behalf of the Government and people of Namibia.

I want to thank the Director-General, the Chairperson of the Governing Body and the International Labour Office for the comprehensive reports and documents that have been made available to us for committee discussions and policy debates. In particular, I should like to focus my attention on the Report of the World Commission on the Social Dimension of Globalization entitled *A fair globalization: Creating opportunities for all*, and the Report of the Director-General entitled *A fair globalization: The role of the ILO*.

I would also like to congratulate the ILO for having shown the courage and foresight to establish the World Commission and for drawing the membership of this Commission from both developed and developing countries, in order to ensure a balanced representation.

The Commission investigated the impact of globalization on our workers, employers, Governments and societies as a whole, but, even more importantly, the Commission proposed that concerted efforts should be made to manage and drive globalization, not just for the benefit of a few, but ultimately change it for the benefit of countries, societies and people that up to now have been marginalized in the process.

Globalization is not an end in itself, but rather a process, phenomenon or institution. It affects us all, whether employed or unemployed, young or old, rich or poor. Globalization is here to stay and the only choice we have is to decide whether we want to change in order to be part of the institutional mechanisms that manage the process. That is why I am particularly pleased and, at the same time, excited to see the role that the ILO has started to play and intends to playing in shifting the focus of globalization from the privileged few to a wider people-centred focus.

My delegation, therefore, supports the views of the World Commission when it calls for: a focus on people and respect for their rights and cultural identity, decent work and empowerment of their communities; a democratic and effective State to manage integration into the global economy; sustainable development and environmental protection; productive and equitable markets to promote opportunity and enterprise; fair rules for the global economy, to offer equitable opportunities and access for all countries while recognizing the diversity in national capacities and developmental needs; globalization with solidarity to overcome inequality within and between countries and to contribute to the elimination of poverty; greater accountability by public and private actors for the policies they pursue and the actions they take; and an effective United Nations system to create a democratic, legitimate and coherent framework for globalization. These are, to say the very least, far-reaching and all-encompassing objectives that we should aspire to.

It is clear that Governments, employers and workers have to commit themselves to achieving a fairer globalization process.

While acknowledging this, we will inevitably look to the ILO to lead the way. I am happy to note in the Report of the Director-General that the ILO seems more than willing to rise to the challenges laid down for it in the proposals contained in the Report of the World Commission. I would like to assure the Director-General of our support during the process of the ILO implementation of the recommendations in the report. The ILO represents an enormous and unique constituency base and it should consequently use this to its advantage when engaging other international institutions to address the social dimensions of globalization and work towards an equitable and fair social development.

There are two specific issues from the report of the World Commission that I would like to raise.

The first one is empowering people at the local and community levels. It is a well-known fact that, in developing countries in particular, there are large informal economies that are continuously growing and where most of the workforce is employed. The reasons for the expansion of the informal economy are not clear, but its growth might partly be a by-product of globalization. This sector still lacks the recognition and support that the formal economy is receiving. Most workers in this sector do not enjoy any form of social protection, and hence are plagued by low levels of productivity, while being confined to restricted markets. Governments, employers, workers and the ILO, therefore, have a role to play in positively addressing the abovementioned factors in this expanding sector of the economy.

The second issue is the cross-border movement of people. The report recognizes that the migration of workers is a phenomenon that is increasing and that this can, in part be attributed to increasing globalization.

The World Commission proposes that a multilateral framework should be developed to govern international migration and that a global forum be established for a regular exchange of views on the issue.

The proposed new multilateral framework has, as one of its objectives, to facilitate mutually beneficial ways of increasing migration opportunities. I, however, think that more emphasis should be placed on the Recommendations that promote measures to eliminate trafficking and the abuse of vulnerable groups such as women and children; to make the process predictable and legal; and to ensure full protection for the rights of migrant workers and facilitate their local integration, pursuant to the Decent Work Agenda of the ILO.

It is my belief that, when we look at the recognition of rights of workers and their dependants, we should, at the same time, look at the other side of the coin.

The one central message that is expressed in both the Report of the World Commission and the Director-General's Report, is one of consultative communication. Namibia has used its substantial resources to build and establish institutions for the management of our people in the economic, social and labour spheres.

Mr. TABANI *(Employers' delegate, Pakistan)*

In the name of God, the most Beneficent, the most Merciful! I bring you greetings from the Employers of Pakistan who join me in congratulating the President and the Vice-Presidents on their unanimous election. With their experience and wisdom, we are confident they will guide this session of the Conference to a successful conclusion.

The Report of the Director-General is very comprehensive and gives a detailed account of the work done by the ILO for the promotion of decent work. The ILO assistance to workers in the occupied territories of Palestine is also commendable.

The ILO Area Office in Pakistan has been instrumental in getting the subject of employment included in the Pakistani Government's Poverty Reduction Programme. It has also recently completed a national tripartite consultation process on the decent work programme for Pakistan.

The World Commission, consisting of intellectuals and experts, represented a variety of diverse views and perspectives. Arriving at a final set of conclusions and recommendations could not have been an easy task, and I want to commend the two co-Chairs, President Mkapa and President Halonen, all of the members of the Commission, the Director-General and indeed the secretariat for their achievements.

The report is wide-ranging in its recommendations and proposals. In many respects, not all is new in this report – many of the ideas have been debated previously. But this report has a certain credibility since it has been filtered through a wide range of actors and been the subject of extensive dialogues. Perhaps its most significant aspect is the recognition by such diverse individuals and groups that in spite of perceptions to the contrary, that globalization has generated many significant benefits throughout the world and more importantly has the potential to lift people out of poverty. This is a new and commendable conclusion.

The report has done well to try to separate facts from perceptions. The focus of our discussions should now be on the ILO's specific role within the follow-up to this report. It is clear that the ILO is currently well-positioned to give effect to many of the recommendations.

The ILO is a unique organization that has operated in a unique way for over 85 years. I do not think that anyone wants to change this uniqueness, its comparative advantage, or its place and role within the international institutions. Therefore, any recommendations of the report should complement existing activities and should not change the direction of the ILO and its current activities.

The report gives some focus to the current multilateral system, and offers recommendations in this regard. Importantly, while realizing that the multilateral trading system should substantially reduce unfair barriers to market access of goods in which developing countries have comparative advantage, the report places an emphasis on responsibility and the fact that globalization starts at home. Individual governments need to face up to their responsibilities and create the conditions to be able to benefit from globalization.

One of the main recommendations in the report is the call for greater policy coherence and coordination amongst international organizations. Employers welcome the call for greater policy coordination across the international system and see the ILO's role in such policy coordination while operating within its traditional mandate and through the Governing Body.

All institutions would need to engage in such a process in an even-handed manner, cognizant of each others' mandates and responsibilities. Employers want to see the current work of the ILO reinforced and supported without competition with other institutions, for instance, in the sphere of macroeconomic policies.

The ILO is focusing on the promotion of employment as a central route to eliminate poverty. This is a very positive development and one that employers support. Job creation is at the heart of poverty alleviation. Employers would like to see greater policy coherence as regards the role of the private sector in terms of poverty alleviation. A major partner in this respect could be the UNDP and the recent report produced by the Commission on the Private Sector and Development, *Unleashing entrepreneurship: Making business work for the poor,* should be utilized.

The road map given to us by the Director-General in the four challenges are worth repeating here: first, making decent work a global goal; second, making the ILO a global player; third, mobilizing tripartism for global action; fourth, global action with the ILO, with the Organization as a whole becoming a global team along with its constituents – the employers and workers.

To conclude, let me say that if properly implemented, with a strong focus on utilizing social dialogue and tripartism, this report and some of its recommendations could help deliver many more people from poverty. That is something we all want.

Ms. STO. TOMAS *(Secretary, Department of Labor and Employment, Philippines)*

There are two subjects in this year's discussion that are of interest to us in the developing world, the Philippines included. I am talking about globalization and migration.

In a sense, migration and globalization are two sides of the same coin. While one may not cause the other, they go back to the same primal instinct.

They go back to the time when we were all one world. In the beginning there was only one world. While we may have been separated by oceans and mountains, we were not separate countries or states – we were just one world.

There were differences of course, some of us were bigger, some of us were faster, some of us were better off and because of these differences we decided to trade. That was how we found out how the other half lives. Somewhere in the world somebody wanted fabric in exchange for spice, or somebody wanted gold in exchange for goods or guns or pottery or people. Somebody's surplus was somebody else's shortage. Later on this would be called comparative advantage; more benevolently, this would be called complementation.

Out of this wealth of transactions would come rules. Progress after all requires rules in order to bring about civility, and civility would require fairness.

This is how our institutions evolved and this is why we are here today in this 92nd Session of the International Labour Conference, to ensure that even if there are those among us who are bigger, fairer and faster, rules and civility would prevail. That comparative advantage would not be used to gain undue advantage.

Globalization seeks the unhampered movement of goods, capital and services. The logic is that, where this flow is allowed to take its natural course, all of us would benefit. For is not globalization the tide that would raise all boats? Well, not always. Not when the rules do not promote civility and fairness. Globalization has of late taken a human face. In the last 20 years we have seen an unprecedented movement of people. In fact this movement has grown faster than the global birth rate. People move towards perceived better opportunities, or away from war, persecution or poverty. Helped by faster and improved communications, people come by air, sea and land in search of a better world than the one which they were born into. People migrate.

I realize that the world is held together by laws and rules. These imposed regimes for reasonable conduct and appropriate behaviour assure us that not only the fleetest or the mightiest will survive. What nature and genetics did not allow us, the goodness of man will hopefully alleviate through the norms that he creates.

This morning I will not bore you with statistics. You know them, I know them. They are the realities of our everyday existence as ministers, workers and employers.

I will only tell you that on 23 April 2004, we signed an agreement with the Republic of Korea that proposes to hire Filipinos under terms and conditions similar to their Korean counterparts. Last year during the SARS crisis, Singapore took care of our workers in the same way they took care of their own. In Israel and Saudi Arabia when our people are caught in the crossfire of conflicts they do not understand, they are given the care and attention previously reserved only for their own nationals. We have not acquired rights that come from citizenship. These countries, among others, have taken responsibility for the strangers in their midst. They all give us reason to hope and the world is richer and better for it.

I look at this all today and tell myself there is probably not one country in this room that does not host at least one of my countrymen. We have our own diaspora, and I do not propose to engage today in a negotiation for the rights that they may hopefully enjoy in your territory. Right now, my framework is not right-based, it is based on responsibility.

We have a responsibility for the people who leave our shores, even when they leave irregularly we take responsibility for them and we will take them back if it becomes necessary. We shall ensure that they are healthy, skilled and properly oriented. That is our responsibility to them, and even when they are not any of this, we take responsibility for them too. We hope that for the short time that they may be with you in your countries, you will take responsibility for them as well.

They are not apples, coal, wheat or oil. They may not represent insurance services or banks. They may not be what is contemplated under this wonderful concept called globalization, which I call one world. They are human beings and they are our shared responsibility. Whilst we ask them to take responsibility for their personal decisions, the countries of origin and destination who profit from their brain and brawn share in that responsibility as well. The international community which provides the rules that preserve civility are equally responsible for them. We are all responsible for the strangers among us, we are after all brothers and sisters at heart.

We congratulate the President and his Vice-Presidents on their well-deserved election during this session of the Conference. We congratulate the ILO for giving us these background materials that document so well the conditions of migrants and the need for globalization that is fair. Through your leadership, Mr. President, we are optimistic that we will eventually deserve the one world that is our right and everybody's collective responsibility.

Original Spanish: Mr. SOLARI SAAVEDRA *(Minister of Labour and Social Welfare, Chile)*

First of all I would like to express my warmest greetings to all delegates attending the assembly, and to congratulate my friend, Mr. Ray Guevara, on his election.

This meeting is taking place at a particularly challenging time for humanity – a time when the ability of international organizations to promote peace and cooperation is once more being put to the test. For Latin American democracies, this new-world stage requires us to work harder for peace, rights and non-discrimination. This means further challenges for the labour world, the economy, employment and social security.

As the only tripartite world organization, the ILO can contribute a great deal to the search for understanding. The 85 years since the Organization was founded, and in particular the 35 years since it was awarded the Nobel Peace Prize, prove its ability to muster the will and to reconcile different positions to work towards concordance and equality of opportunity for all.

This year we are discussing the report on globalization, which is yet another ILO contribution to a fairer, more cohesive world and a better future for the world's inhabitants. As the Director-General said in his inaugural speech to the Conference, fairer globalization is essential if we are to achieve world stability. Pushing for a new type of globalization is a challenge for our countries and for the ILO.

We must promote labour policies which guarantee, in accordance with the conditions in each country, individual and collective regulations ensuring that the fundamental rights of workers – as established by the ILO, and which are an integral part of the new concept of decent work developed internationally in recent years are complied with.

It is this new concept that has led my country to negotiate bilateral trade agreements, allowing us to increase economic links with our main business partners and to open up new opportunities for enterprise and employment for our citizens.

In the free trade agreements that we have signed with Canada, the United States, and particularly the European Union, the contracting countries are committed to ensuring the full respect of internationally recognized labour rights, which can not be diminished under the pretext of improving their commercial position. In the same way, in the regional courts we have always promoted the inclusion of labour and social issues, particularly those regarding compliance with the law and promotion of basic standards to ensure labour rights.

We have adopted this approach because we want a free trade process without protection and with a stronger and stronger social dimension, based on the shared universal values outlined by the ILO. Incorporating the social dimension of labour into trade agreements ensures that there will be a form of globalization which is more inclusive, governed more democratically and which provides people with more opportunities and tangible benefits.

Inextricably linked to globalization, this year the Conference has discussed the situation of migrant workers and the need to provide social protection for those who, in order to improve their pay and quality of life, leave their native lands in search of work in another country. Naturally, labour mobility across borders increases with commercial expansion, higher investment, the reduction of transport costs, the widening of the wage gap between developing and developed countries, and the segmentation of the labour markets. For Chile, this is an ever-increasing reality; immigration has increased almost sixfold in the last 15 years. Our domestic policies need to be strengthened to ensure that foreign workers have the same labour rights as nationals of our countries, whatever their legal status in Chile. In the same way, it is becoming essential to create innovative ways of ensuring the social protection of these people, so that their contribution to the country does not involve any loss of social security cover should they want to return to their country of origin. Therefore, as part of our international social security agreement policy, we are entering a new phase, allowing workers to transfer their social security contributions if they return home. We are implementing this with Peru, the country of origin for one of the largest immigrant communities in Chile. I urge this Conference to look very carefully at the subject of social security cover for workers when studying migration and the need to better safeguard migrant workers.

Finally, I would like to mention briefly some of the work that we have been doing in Chile on labour and social issues; in particular regarding training and human resources development, something that has also been debated in this session. We have worked determinedly to increase the level of education and skills of our workers because this is the only way that they can get higher quality, and better remunerated employment and for the country to become more competitive, which is necessary for it to complete successfully on a global level.

These are some of the steps we have taken in the last year, which enable us to look to the future with more confidence.

I am certain that, once again, everybody's contribution to this Conference will translate into conclusions and action which will lead to visible improvements in the world of work.

Mr. TROGEN *(Employers' adviser and substitute delegate, Sweden)*

I make these comments not only on behalf of myself, as Swedish Employers' delegate, but also on behalf of the Employers of the other Nordic countries – Denmark, Finland, Iceland and Norway.

The ILO has a unique and important role to play in the further discussions of the challenges that the global society has to meet in the world of work.

The Nordic employers see the recommendations of the World Commission on the Social Dimension of Globalization as an opportunity for the ILO, an opportunity to raise its visibility and also its relevance within the multilateral system. Herewith, countries that are currently excluded from globalization can also benefit. The Nordic employers strongly believe that the ILO has a very important niche within the multilateral system and that its unique structure is its comparative advantage. At the same time, we underline that the recommendations of the World Commission are not the policy of the ILO, nor is the report addressed solely to the ILO. It is the responsibility of the Conference and the Governing Body to draw those parts from the recommendations they find relevant to the mandate of the ILO and then propose how the ILO should respond.

It is very important that the ILO constituents are involved as the follow up goes forward. Any engagement by the ILO within civil society must also be transparent and based on a clear understanding between the Governing Body and the Office.

Thus, our message is: stick to the mandate and to the ILO's current strategic strengths and objectives and cooperate, but do not interfere with the mandates of other multilateral agencies. We would not support turning the ILO into a house of macroeconomic analysis and operations at the expense of the needs of its constituents and the focus on the world of work.

The World Commission's report gives prominence to the creation of employment and calls for greater policy coherence on this within the multilateral system. We support this focus because this is where the ILO's real advantage lies. The Global Employment Agenda developed by the ILO and the poverty reduction strategy process are the means to engage with the United Nations. We are looking forward to working with the Director-General on this key area of employment as he has, in the house, the real actors and specialists in the world of work. It is in this area that the ILO can make the best contribution to what is called "a fair globalization".

The report also reinforces our call for the ILO to engage in a follow up to the ILO Conference discussion on the informal economy. It also underlines the need for promoting youth employment activities and activities related to small and medium-sized enterprises, which we have equally been calling for. The UNDP report entitled *Unleashing entrepreneurship: Making business work for the poor* is a good example of how the ILO could work with another sister United Nations agency.

Regarding national policies to address globalization, the Nordic employers support the need to focus on good governance, the rule of law, recognition of domestic property rights and fighting corruption, among other issues. Without good governance at the domestic level, business cannot play its proper role and contribute to economic and social development.

We consider that the ILO should address national weaknesses, more through social dialogue and less through standard-setting, with the recognition of the differences that exist as to economic and social development. This also reinforces the employers' support for ongoing reforms of the ILO standards-related activities system to ensure that it is able to address the realities of the modern world of work.

To conclude, the further process going forward needs to protect that which the ILO does well, amend or stop things which are not working well and carefully consider what issues should be on the agenda of the ILO. Working life is changing and it is different in many countries. Those changes and their implications need to be discussed. The discussion must fully engage constituents and continue to focus on issues where the ILO can be the most effective – and that is in the world of work.

Ms. MENKERIOS *(Minister of Labour and Human Welfare, Eritrea)*

First, I would like to take this opportunity to congratulate Mr. Juan Somavia, the Director-General of the ILO, for his comprehensive Report on *ILO programme implementation and activities for 2002-03* and the Global Report: *Organizing for social justice*, which deals with the implementation of the Decent Work Agenda.

The Director-General's Report provides a basis for shaping the future strategy of the Organization in terms of addressing key problems. It articulates that the plight of workers and their families is part of the organization's overall long-term strategy.

The Government of Eritrea is committed to the implementation of the seven core human rights Conventions which it has ratified. It is in the process of ratifying the Worst Forms of Child Labour Convention, 1999 (No. 182).

Tripartite consultations and social dialogue are the guiding principles that have led to the sound labour relations that currently exist between the social partners in Eritrea. Protection of women, young people and persons with disability is explicitly provided for in our labour law. On social protection and human welfare, the Government is working to guarantee and provide essential socio-economic services and to meet the basic requirements of every citizen.

Our top priority is to ensure food security for all, which entails the complete eradication and conquest of hunger, poverty and dependence on food handouts. In order to achieve this, different concerned ministries are working together to set up programmes. In the undertaking of all of these tasks, labour is a decisive element. Necessary training is required to increase productivity and to ensure comprehensive economic emancipation in all sectors.

Fighting against unemployment by improving knowledge and skills, maintaining social protection, promoting occupational health and safety, and the application of productive employment are Eritrea's greatest challenges. The Government has placed these issues at the top of its development agenda. A primary tool for realizing these priorities is active labour market policies that are designed on the basis of up-to-date labour market information, which is not available in our case. To this end, the Government has taken steps to carry out the country's first comprehensive labour force survey to use as benchmark information. The results of the survey are expected to answer basic labour market questions. The data from the survey will be used for designing and revising labour policies for setting employment targets and for monitoring and evaluating the development plan and the comprehensive employment plan.

The Government of Eritrea, with its own limited capacity, is determined to increase the productive capacity of its people through increased access to quality education, training and health services. It recognizes that quality education and good health will not only enable the population to participate in the economy to their fullest potential, but will also enrich their social, cultural and political life. Thus, a steadfast commitment to develop our human resources is the hallmark of our development planning. It is also recognized that it is a major challenge for a new nation like Eritrea to develop trained human resources on its own. Therefore, there is a need to support the design, funding and implementation of modern education and training policies to attain development and economic growth.

To minimize occupational accidents and the spread of diseases and HIV/AIDS at work, we have launched an information, education and communication programme to create deep-rooted awareness among both social partners. To safeguard safety and health in the workplace, efforts are being made by the Government to train inspectors and to familiarize them with occupational safety and health equipment.

Furthermore, a national health and safety regulation has been drafted in consultation with the social partners, concerned ministries and institutions and has been forwarded to our Minister of Justice for approval. To improve overall conditions of work and to protect the rights of seafarers, including the fishing sector, a new law has been drafted and is under discussion. To make provision for the maintenance of workers in their old age and for disability and survivors' benefits, a national pension scheme has been in force since January 2004.

Peace is pertinent to development and to the implementation of the Decent Work Agenda. The Government of Eritrea is working hard to resolve its problems peacefully, yet the international community has a duty and a responsibility to pressurize the Government of Ethiopia to enforce implementation of the Boundary Commission's ruling.

In conclusion, let me take this opportunity to request the ILO advisory mission on labour force surveys to render its technical support to conduct the intended labour force survey and develop Eritrea's human capacity through training at different levels and in all labour-related areas.

Original Spanish: Mr. TOMADA *(Minister of Labour, Employment and Social Security, Argentina)*

I would like to congratulate the President, as a representative of our region, on his appointment to preside over the 92nd Session of the International Labour Conference and I thank the Director-

General for his Report. His analysis of the report of the Commission on the Social Dimension of Globalization is especially helpful when he observes that we are called on to "promote a coherent integration of economic and social policies which focus on the well-being and quality of life of people". We agree with this. The social dimension is not just an optional-extra, based on whether or not the economy is doing well, but an essential condition for a new growth model.

Our country has been recovering from the most serious political, economic and social crisis in its history and we have begun a new phase which is driven by social, institutional, fiscal and international responsibility. More than half of our population were living in unacceptable levels of poverty which had never been seen before. The Government's priority has been to concentrate on the most needy, creating employment and revitalizing the national economy. But growth alone is not enough for us. Argentina has decided to grow through employment. Currently, every growth point in our national product creates twice as many jobs as it did ten years ago. Over the last few years, Argentina has been able to create more than a million genuine new jobs and I would like to take this opportunity, speaking from this podium, to thank the ILO and all donor countries who have contributed to specific programmes in that regard.

Secondly, institutional responsibility involves improving legal certainty and trust in the legal system, giving priority to fighting corruption and impunity, at the same time as creating an improved atmosphere to promote direct national and foreign investment. Among other national policies in this context, President Kirchner has taken steps to reform the system of appointment of judges.

Thirdly, the Government has adopted a position based on fiscal responsibility because there have been macroeconomic policies that have been unwise and poorly managed, and this led to an increase in public debt which lit the touch paper of our economic collapse.

Finally, Argentina has assumed its international responsibility by giving priority to regional solidarity and by fully complying with its international commitments. Our country will meet its financial commitments by seeking solutions which provide economic, institutional and social sustainability. In order to pay its bills, Argentina needs to grow. So to achieve this growth, we are making great efforts to promote job creation, since employment is a vehicle for economic and social growth. This represents a turn around compared to the policies which have dominated our national scene for the last 30 years.

Unemployment, underemployment and uncontrolled growth of the informal economy are the main problems in our country. The Decent Work Agenda proposed by the Director-General is a constant source of inspiration for government action. Policies of the past based on more flexibility, deregulation and stripping workers of protection, failed spectacularly and triggered the decline of the employment structure in countries in the region. To regularize the situation we need and will continue to need a great deal of creativity, effort, courage and, above all, tough political decisions.

Employment for Argentine and foreign workers is not a by-product, as far as our Government is concerned, of economic decisions that happen to be right. Economic decisions will only be right if they create jobs, quality jobs and productive jobs. This links up with our belief, born of experience, that not just any type of growth creates employment and social integration. Growth with employment goes hand-in-hand with fair distribution of wealth. For the first time in more than ten years, the minimum wage has increased. The Government now respects international labour Conventions as ratified promotes collective bargaining, and is sanctioning a balanced draft labour law which enjoys unprecedented levels of social and parliamentary support. We are trying to develop not only our domestic markets but also exports and the public-sector work. A vocational training bill is going to be put to Parliament. These basic policies designed for growth are as important as promoting investment. I would go further and say that they are a prerequisite for long-term, sustainable, integrated development.

We believe that, by achieving a fair society which is directed towards economic development, which respects human rights, which has industrial and technological policies stimulating all types of productivity and with responsible and representative participation by workers and employers providing better distribution of results, we will create the user-friendly environment which investors demand. The other option that of reducing labour costs, deregulation and dismantling the State, is something that we have tried in the past and the consequences are the social debt that we still owe our citizens today. We are not promoting a State which sweeps away the free operation of the social partners. What we support is a State which guarantees solidarity in the general interest.

In summary, democratic stability implies that economic growth is guaranteed in order to eradicate poverty and that there is full respect for social and labour rights. Argentina, wants to build labour-based societies and we know that we have the support of the ILO and the tripartite structure in this regard. In tune with the ILO message, which calls for more consistency between economic and socio-labour policies, we support the idea of building a society based on labour as a prerequisite for fostering the basic social cohesion on which open and pluralist democracies are funded. We promote the same principles in building a social dimension in our regional body, MERCOSUR, through the joint efforts of our Ministries of Labour, Economy, Planning and Education. We have recovered our dignity as Argentines; now, let us extend that dignity to labour and productivity.

Original Spanish: Mr. ROSS LEAL *(Workers' adviser and substitute delegate, Cuba)*

To promote decent work so that employment can lead us out of poverty and to achieve what he terms a fair globalization – this is what we have been called on to do by the Director-General.

Spiralling unemployment, which is even affecting the developed countries, is one of the most serious problems facing this Organization. Almost 1 billion individuals of working age do not have stable jobs. The neo-liberal nature of a globalization process managed by the major world powers has led to greater poverty, chronic unemployment and social exclusion for the peoples of the world. We need to fight to make radical changes in the current economic, political and financial order, which only serves the interests of those who control financial institutions and international trade bodies such as the International Monetary Fund, the World Bank and the World Trade Organization.

Only 50 years from now the world's population will reach 10 billion, and if we fail to find solutions to these and other problems, how will our children and grandchildren live just in four or five decades' time?

Hunger is still a scourge for millions of people. HIV/AIDS is spreading at an inconceivable rate, and many peoples in Africa are now threatened with extinction. The political will is lacking to address this serious problem. Four years ago, Cuba informed the United Nations of its willingness to contribute 5,000 medical staff for a programme to control and treat HIV/AIDS, if rich countries were to contribute the necessary funding for medicines and infrastructure. We have not received a single reply to that offer, and now we put the G8, who are going to discuss Africa's problems, on notice that they need to address this problem with deeds rather than words.

As regards Cuba, you are certainly aware of the new programme put in place by the greatest superpower in history to bring down our Government, as announced by its President on 6 May. This is a further attempt to kill off our people through hunger and disease, through a programme that strengthens the criminal blockade which has been imposed for more than 40 years and applies new and cruel measures to strangle our economy, while bringing enormous pressure to bear on governments and businesses around the world to prevent them from investing in or trading with Cuba.

It is also aimed at discrediting Cuba vis à vis world public opinion, so as to justify an attack on our country. We all know very well how these justifications are produced. The war in Iraq is a good example. We express our solidarity with the Iraqi people and all those who are suffering war, occupation and genocide, such as the Palestinian people and the African and Arab peoples. In total disregard for the organizations of the United Nations and the international community in general. For example, there has been an attempt to use the ILO and, trade union organizations acting with the stated goal of destroying the Cuban Revolution. They devote millions of dollars to creating virtual trade unions in Cuba labour centres and with the support of their Interests Section in Havana, whom they serve as mercenaries. We hope that Governments and workers' and employers' organizations will never join this imperial plan that is attempting to destroy such a generous endeavour in social justice.

We are grateful for the many messages of solidarity we have received from the ILO and trade union organizations in order to share the noble aspiration of building a world of peace, solidarity and justice.

In the words of José Martí, the apostle of Cuban independence, night's darkest hour is just before the dawn. We will win every battle, until victory is ours.

Original Japanese: Mr. TOGARI *(Vice-Minister for Policy Coordination, Ministry of Health, Labour and Welfare, Japan)*

It is my honour to address the 92nd Session of the International Labour Conference on behalf of the Japanese Government.

First of all, I would like to give my full support to the ILO's basic policy of "decent work for all", and I would like to pay my sincere respects to the efforts made to achieve this goal by the ILO, Workers, Employers and its member States.

Japan appreciates the ILO's activities over the last two years, described in *ILO programme implementation 2002-03,* specifically its strategically implemented programmes based on the ILO's four objectives for decent work. At the same time, in view of the massive demands on the ILO, and Japan's severe financial situation, I would like to invite the ILO secretariat to implement its activities more efficiently and to make further efforts to reduce personnel costs.

One of the most significant agenda items of the current session will be the discussion of the final report of the World Commission on the Social Dimension of Globalization and the Director-General's Report entitled *A fair globalization: The role of the ILO.*

I highly appreciate the efforts of the World Commission in addressing the difficult issue of the social dimension of globalization. I share the view of the report that "We seek a more inclusive process which is fair and brings benefit and real opportunities to more people." I believe approaching the issue of globalization through the eyes of the people, and proceeding with fair, human-centred developments, is of vital importance in the world of today.

In this regard, the strategy in the opening of the Director-General's Report "Making decent work a global goal", is crucial. In the past, the effects of globalization have been measured by such economic values as efficiency and high added value. On the contrary, this strategy reveals decent work as a concrete goal from the human perspective, and values integration between economic policy and social policy.

Two points need to be taken into account in carrying this strategy forward. First, individual autonomy, based on the situation in each country, should be respected. Second, also important is the economic and social role that the private sector and enterprises are playing, and will play.

Japan is willing to conduct positive activities in cooperation with the ILO. We would like to contribute, in particular, to the fields of employment creation, human resources development, occupational safety and health and social dialogue. We attach great importance to, and continue to support, Asia and the Pacific region. We wish to contribute to achieving decent work in this region, where people have been most affected by the rapid wave of globalization.

As part of our contribution, we are planning to hold an international symposium in December 2004, with the ILO's participation, on youth employment and human resources development that is increasingly gaining international attention. We would like to discuss new initiatives and policies at the symposium so that young people can open the way to a bright and hopeful future in an environment that is changing due to globalization. We hope high-ranking participants from Asian countries will attend.

Concerning Japan's civil service reform, the Japanese Government recognizes that it is important, in the first place, to have earnest negotiations and consultations between the Government and the parties concerned. Meetings at various levels between the Government side and the labour side were promoted after the International Labour Conference last year. On 13 May 2004, the relevant ministers started to meet with labour representatives concerning the civil service reform. I would like to invite the ILO to look patiently at the development of dialogue between the Government and labour sides.

Globalization will progress in every corner of the world. International institutions like the ILO will have a greater role to play in this globalization context. Japan expects a lot from the ILO's role, and is willing to take an active part in the ILO's activities in collaboration with the member countries, workers and employers.

(Mr. Maatough takes the Chair.)

Original Arabic: Mr. HACHED *(Vice-Secretary-General, League of Arab States)*

In the name of God, the Merciful, the Compassionate! I would like to congratulate Mr. Ray Guevara on his election as President of the Conference. I would also like to congratulate the Officers of the Conference. It is an honour for me to speak from this rostrum on behalf of the League of Arab States, and to transmit the greetings of the Secretary-General of the Arab League, who wishes the Conference every success. I have already had the great honour of addressing the International Labour Conference back in 1985.

The League of Arab States appreciates the constant cooperation between the International Labour Organization and the League. We also greatly appreciate the role performed by governments, employers' organizations and trade unions, which is aimed at strengthening ILO activity. This 92nd Session of the International Labour Conference is of particular importance. Indeed, it addresses issues that are complex, topical and form part of the mandate of the International Labour Office, which is to constantly improve the situation of workers and citizens in general. These values are embodied in the Declaration of Philadelphia, according to which poverty anywhere constitutes a danger to prosperity everywhere. We would like to focus on the situation of workers in the occupied Arab territories. We have read carefully the report on this subject. One has only to read it carefully in order to detect that the real problem is not an economic one, but expansionist aims that are destroying trees, houses and Arab lands. The Israeli authorities continue to build this wall, which is paralysing the free movement of Palestinians. You have been witnesses to the recent actions of the Israeli authorities in the camps in Rafah. This is a flagrant violation of international and humanitarian law, and the international community must firmly condemn these acts. It is necessary to contain the evil at its root: we have to end the Israeli occupation. The only way to remedy the drama besetting the Palestinians is to put an end to the Israeli occupation of their land.

It is also necessary to mention Iraq at this point. The situation in Iraq is serious. There cannot be a return to economic prosperity for all workers and employers unless power is transferred to the Iraqis. This transfer of power will guarantee stability and security in this country, which is dear to us all, and which must embark on reconstruction.

The situation of migrant workers is a subject which has been addressed by this Session of the International Labour Conference, and it is necessary to find solutions to improve the lot of migrant workers. We have noted attentively, the report on migrant workers and their role in the global economy, and we endorse the statement of the Secretary-General that migration should be at the heart of our discussions.

Migration gives people the opportunity to meet one another, to get to know one another better, and to enhance solidarity among all human beings. We have also paid particular attention to Arab migrants. In this regard, we have set up a committee, which is presided over by an eminent Arab public figure and which looks at the economic and social situation of migrants.

It is necessary for the ILO to achieve its objectives in this area. We have attentively read the report of the World Commission on the Social Dimension of Globalization and we endorse its recommendations. Globalization has to be fair, inclusive and based on democracy and equal opportunity.

The Arab Summit at Tunis decided to put in place an Arab strategy to combat poverty, based on the studies provided by the Council of Arab Ministers of Social Affairs. We must improve the lot of all poor people. In this respect, we are trying to coordinate our efforts with all the interested parties. It is necessary for the whole world to be able to benefit from justice, fraternity, solidarity and equality in order to ensure a better future for everybody.

Ms. SINJELA *(Government adviser and substitute delegate, Zambia)*

On behalf of the Minister of Labour and Social Security, who could not be with us today, on behalf of the Zambian delegation, and indeed, on my own behalf, I wish to convey to the President our warm and hearty congratulations on his unanimous and deserving election to preside over the deliberations at this session of this important Conference. The Zambian delegation wishes to commend most sincerely the Director-General for his detailed and illuminating Report on the activities undertaken by the International Labour Organization during the period under review, 2002-03.

I must place on record my country's appreciation for the progress made with regard to implementing the Decent Work Agenda. We note with satisfaction that the ILO's Strategic Policy Framework for 2002-05, which was set out in November 2000, is on the right course and is bearing fruit.

It is gratifying to note that the Report highlights that encouraging and satisfactory progress has been made with regard to strategic objectives against performance targets established in the Programme and Budget for 2002-03.

My Government is impressed with the practical efforts that the ILO is making to bring about full implementation of the programme outlined in the Director-General's Report.

Zambia admires and steadfastly supports the promotion and practical implementation of the strategic objectives set out in the Director-General's Report. The ratification by my Government of all the ILO core Conventions dealing with fundamental human rights and its review of labour laws are a clear endorsement of our serious commitment to the implementation of the Decent Work Agenda.

Let me assure this great Conference of my Government's enthusiastic determination to fight social injustice in all forms, particularly in respect of youth and women in the world of work.

To this end, the Zambian Government has formulated a national gender policy which is being used as an effective tool to address gender imbalance and to create equal opportunities for all in the field of employment and other spheres of life. Freedom of association is enshrined in the Republican Constitution and also in industrial labour relations acts.

The people of Zambia are very grateful indeed to the ILO for the material and technical support rendered through the Area Office in Lusaka. This support has facilitated the successful implementation of various programmes and projects undertaken in the country.

Currently, Zambia is a recipient of financial and technical support in the fight against the elimination of the worst forms of child labour, strengthening labour administration through capacity building of relevant institutions and business promotion and development.

I wish to solicit the ILO's further support in future programmes and projects. The fight against HIV/AIDS, which is a threat to labour – a very important factor for economic development – has been intensified in the country as a whole, and at the workplace in particular, and the ILO is doing a commendable job in supporting the crusade. The Government's NGOs and civil society, through the National AIDS Council, are painstakingly working in concert to put efforts in place to deal effectively with this scourge in communities.

This year's debate is, for us, greatly appreciated and we are pleased to actively participate in the deliberations. I wish, on behalf of my delegation, to assure the Director-General of Zambia's continued cooperation and support in the execution of his duties.

Original Arabic: Mr. LOUH *(Minister of Labour and Social Security, Algeria)*

As my time is limited, I will concentrate on only a few of the ideas I planned to speak about. However, my text has been distributed in all three languages.

On behalf of the Algerian delegation and on my own behalf, allow me, at the outset, to congratulate the President on his appointment to preside over this session of the Conference. We would also like to thank the Director-General for the quality of the Report that has been submitted to us.

Very few countries have seen a trade unionist become a minister of labour. I myself was once a trade unionist.

The ILO is proceeding with a timely consideration of the major issues of our time and of the strategies to be adopted. My country wishes to contribute to this reflection. Globalization is indeed a fact, but the counter-current to it is also a reality. These two trends are concomitant and often contradictory, but constantly interactive. The positive reflection on development may be able to reconcile these two trends without any dilemma or confrontation. Development is human, and development activities are carried out at work.

It is worth recognizing that a State whose institutions function democratically in consultation with social partners will, in actual fact, stand as the most secure guarantor for national solidarity, social justice, health and public security. Indeed, we must adapt our responses to the requirements of globalization to national realities, as otherwise they will be rejected by the very people who are experiencing the problems to which globalization claims to offer solutions.

I draw your attention to the reaction of those who defend local cultures, environment and human rights in general. Existing imbalances have in fact been widened here. The Global Report calls for a harmonization of programmes and a concerted effort by the United Nations institutions.

In my country, the political condition of democracy for social justice has been fulfilled. All the observers, experts or not, Algerians or foreigners, trade unionists, employers, workers and all the social partners, have recognized that the recent elections took place transparently and in accordance with international laws.

Algeria has considered the implementation of the recommendations of the World Commission, notably the recommendation that all actors and in particular all States, should be held accountable.

The five-year programme that has just been adopted by the Algerian Government provides for the continuation of the legal reform process by completing the revision of legislative provisions in order to bring them into line with contemporary requirements and international standards.

Both the missions and organizations of the State are also in the process of being reformed. Furthermore, human resources in the field of justice are being improved. The qualification and status of Government employees has been improved.

The 1998 Declaration on Fundamental Principles and Rights at Work and its Follow-up will continue to receive all the attention it needs for its effective implementation.

My country is strongly attached to the principle of collective bargaining, which is considered to be the most appropriate way of regulating labour relations. The fundamental rights enshrined in the ILO Conventions are reflected in the Algerian Constitution and in national legislation. Since 1990, Algeria has made substantial progress in the field of freedom of association and collective bargaining.

Algerian legislation becomes involved only in order to set out the rules of democratic functioning and ensure representatives and transparency in trade unions and internal inspection of bodies belonging to them.

The fisheries sector is extremely important for us. It is a part of the restructuring which is being undertaken to encourage investment, particularly through the support of economic operators and young people.

The issue of the situation of migrant workers has great importance in today's world and there is a great tendency towards globalization. Migrant workers, who were once a source of wealth and work in our world, have today become a source of difficulty and economic and social problems; problems that are often linked to employment restrictions and an increase of unemployment in the host countries.

This situation frequently exposes them to discriminatory treatment that is contrary to the principles of our Organization. The ILO should focus on the current debate on a global strategy and an adaptation and revision of ILO instruments, which would entail notable modifications and changes, provide appropriate protection to migrant workers and their families and develop new mechanisms for international solidarity between host and emigration countries.

Among the many situations in which workers find themselves that are of concern to the ILO, there is one that should be firmly and unreservedly condemned. Migrant Palestinian workers in the occupied Arab territories are prevented from moving freely for work. They are prevented from doing as they wish with what they have earned. The result is extreme poverty and the destruction of their quality of life.

The consequences of this situation are utterly, utterly deplorable.

The Director-General has, quite rightly, said that "we at the ILO have a duty to do what we can to contribute to a peace settlement".

Mr. VALERIO (Workers' delegate, Philippines)

The world moves forward, yet things seem to remain the same.

The economies of the world prosper, yet the situation of workers and their families for most of the world remains stagnant, at best.

The Conference presents another opportunity for the ILO and its tripartite constituents to strengthen actions for the improvement of work and the lives of working people around the world.

We will consider what has been done and what needs to be done in certain things, all in the name of improving living and working standards and eradicating, or minimizing, poverty. The ILO, with its tripartite structure, demonstrates to the world at large the value of involving all sectors in the attainment of social justice and equity.

The Global Report under the Follow-up to the Declaration on Fundamental Principles and Rights at Work shows that a startling group of the world's workers remain unprotected by the Freedom of Association and Protection of the Right to Organise Convention, 1948 (No. 87), and the Right to Organise and Collective Bargaining Convention, 1949 (No. 98). These core Conventions have not been ratified by many, including some large countries. Without this appreciation and without commitment to these Conventions, governments and employers in many countries violate the Conventions with impunity. Others have ratified these Conventions, but have not given much effect to ratification, through implementation.

Continued threats to workers seeking to organize workers' organizations, including killings, detention and violence, persist. Our mother organization, the ICFTU, has time and again called the attention of the world to the most dangerous places for workers exercising these rights, including Colombia.

In other countries, violations are not as prevalent, but are, nevertheless, deadly. We deplore the recent killings of labour leaders in certain countries. Trade unionism has become the most dangerous profession in the world.

In the Philippines, we have not seen as many killings as before, but they are there. Threats, intimidation, harassment and alternative arrangements continue. We have made many strides in labour law and practice over the years, especially with the administration of President Gloria Macapagal-Arroyo. But more needs to be done. Many employers, multinational or otherwise, inside or outside the export-processing zones and industrial parks, may set up active and repressive measures against organizing unions in their enterprises.

The application of the principles of the Conventions remains a daunting challenge for workers, employers and governments.

The leading role of the ILO in promoting decent work for all has impressed on us that decent work has to become a global goal. Decent work is the basic demand of all working people. And we encourage more meaningful joint work with governments and employers for the implementation of decent work at various levels, including international, national, industry, community and enterprise levels.

The work of the tripartite partners in the Philippines in this respect is going in the right direction. A Decent Work Agenda, while not perfect, has been promulgated, but serious implementation needs to be accelerated. This has to be done to secure the moral high ground against those who would seek to further destabilize the economy and society while exploiting parliamentary processes for their hidden agenda.

Decent work is necessary for globalization to be fair. There are a number of interesting recommendations in the report of the World Commission on the Social Dimension of Globalization. These should be quickly translated into practical action. It is only right that the ILO should take a leading role in globalization. The ILO's strength in its structure would facilitate the mainstreaming of fairness in the governance of the global economy and in moderating or alleviating the negative effects of globalization.

The second discussion and a new Recommendation on human resources development and training should focus on new approaches to lifelong learning.

The world, and the employment world, and therefore employment requirements have changed. Millions of jobs have disappeared or been replaced by others. In most cases, those who have lost their jobs have not found comparable decent work.

Provisions for the development and implementation of education and training policies, frameworks for the recognition and certification of skills, should reflect skills, employability and active citizenship.

Original Spanish: Mr. MARTÍNEZ MOLINA (Workers' delegate, Chile)

I bring you warmest wishes from the workers of Chile.

The Director-General has invited us to consider the social dimension of globalization. More specifically, the issue here is how to put a human face on a world order which has until now only had an economic dimension. In fact, globalization, as it exists today, lacks ethical values, because one group ends up with the whole of the cake that we have all baked together. In future, the ILO needs to be part of any debate on major policies designed to put in place a new order which is beneficial to everyone and which involves a fair distribution.

Most countries have signed the ILO Conventions, particularly the Freedom of Association and Protection of the Right to Organise Convention, 1948 (No. 87), and the Right to Organise and Collective Bargaining Convention, 1949 (No. 98). Many of these countries have incorporated these agreements into their national legislation, but that is not enough to guarantee that they are applied. In Chile, the reality is that there is a great shortfall, both in trade union rights and collective bargaining. The implicit wish of the new entrepreneurial class in the service economy is to break-up trade union organizations and deny us our fundamental rights to collective bargaining.

In Latin America there is a low level of unionisation of workers, particularly in Chile, and this is connected with the high level of persecution of trade union organizations by employers. It is also to do with the fragility of States in their ability to monitor and apply legislation which is theoretically in force. Since collective bargaining is a mechanism which leads to the distribution of wealth in countries such as Chile, which has seen sustained economic growth for three decades, we do not have genuine collective bargaining. While, theoretically, 3.6 million workers could take part in collective bargaining, in reality only 160,000 do so and the quality of collective bargaining is also affected by domestic legislation, which establishes negotiating groups in parallel to trade unions, and this flies in the face of the most basic trade union practices. There is also a restriction in the legislation which makes it possible to replace workers and remove them during strike action.

Officials working for the judiciary are excluded from collective bargaining, as are those working for the National Congress, workers in public sector companies and, indeed, in private sector companies where the State is involved.

The Labour Relations (Public Service) Convention, 1978 (No. 151), which Chile ratified over three years ago, still does not apply to public sector workers in the State administration. In the case of workers in municipal authorities, there is an attempt to bring in legislation which would undermine their rights to collective bargaining, obliging them to conduct decentralized negotiations in each of the more than 300 different municipalities.

Chile has seen sustained growth over the last three decades. However, it is one of the countries with the worst distribution of wealth. We are the second largest exporter of salmon in the world, we produce copper, wine and fruit and these products are available in many markets around the world, in many countries, but it is in these particular areas of production that trade union and collective bargaining rights are most seriously undermined. This is also true in the major commercial chains, almost all multinational, where workers' rights and the concept of decent work, as envisaged by the ILO, are undermined and violated. Investigations and monitoring processes that have taken place in these sectors have shown that just one branch of a chain of stores had 152 different contracts for the workers who work there and many of those employed in the store did not even know who their employer was.

The time has come to act with responsibility and to make sure that globalization leads to a better life for all. Otherwise, in the future, we will only be bemoaning the erosion of democracy because democracy means rights and not just choice.

Peace for our peoples is based on social justice and decent work. If we want peace we must be prepared for justice.

Mr. OKUDA *(Employers' delegate, Japan)*

Economic globalization presents us with a host of issues. The report of the World Commission has shed valuable light on the importance of the social dimension. Most notably, it has reaffirmed the importance of meaningful employment to people everywhere. I would like to take this opportunity to express my heartfelt appreciation to the members of the Commission.

The focus now shifts to translating the proposals and recommendations of the Commission's report into action. In this spirit, the Director-General has made several proactive and ambitious suggestions.

An especially noteworthy suggestion pertains to stepping up efforts to promote enterprise growth and job creation. We have learned that the interface with corporate activity is crucially important in sharing the benefits of globalization.

In dealing with labour issues, the ILO has so far concentrated on the ways in which work is provided. The time has come for the ILO to promote better understanding of corporate activity, which is the source of work.

The activity of companies large and small is a matter of creating added value, of creating wealth. Employees and other company stakeholders participate in creating wealth. They share in that wealth through wages earned, through dividend pay-outs, through tax payments, and in other ways.

Multinational companies further contribute to the local economies through human resources development, through technology transfers, through the cultivation of supporting industries, and in other ways. For companies to create more wealth and generate more jobs, they need to deploy resources optimally. They need to undertake suitable research and development and capital spending from a long-term perspective.

Fostering decent work depends on focusing attention on this process of creating wealth and supporting companies in their activities, and that should be an important part of the future role of the ILO.

Last December, leaders of employers' associations in the Asia-Pacific region came together under the auspices of the ILO. We debated a full range of global issues. Globalization highlights the weaknesses of nations and of companies. But we agreed that the challenge of overcoming those weaknesses is a golden opportunity for positive change.

We also agreed that companies are an integral part of society, that the central responsibility of business is to perform well, to be the primary source of prosperity and of well-being, and that, in addition to this, they need to fulfil their social and environmental responsibilities.

Of course, corporate social responsibility is for all companies, regardless of geographical scope. Small companies are especially close to their host communities and are important actors in fulfilling social responsibility.

Based on this understanding, the Confederation of Asia-Pacific Employers (CAPE) aims to be a platform for shaping a business-friendly environment and for promoting a sound balance in economic growth and social progress.

We at Nippon Keidanren are also encouraging our member companies to step up their voluntary initiative on corporate social responsibility by providing a renewed Charter of Corporate Behaviour as guiding principles to link the growth of business to social development.

Fulfilling social responsibility means fulfilling the expectations of consumers, shareholders, employees, customers and partners, and the community at large. Therefore our approach to social responsibility needs to evolve in accordance with the values of our stakeholders.

Sounder globalization depends on the development of social values and sensitivities of members of society, and the ILO can contribute greatly in shaping these values and this awareness.

In corporate management, optimizing resource allocation is a core issue. Companies need to identify their strengths and allocate resources to reinforcing those strengths on a priority basis.

The Director-General has suggested promising activities for the ILO to undertake. Although every suggestion defines an activity of importance, in the spirit of optimal resource allocation, and in the light of meeting current needs, I suggest concentrating on priority issues, such as supporting governments in strengthening their capabilities to promote job creation, encouraging business development, and fostering human resources.

This is a pivotal time in the progress of globalization. I count on the Governing Body to consider the options thoroughly and to make a careful choice.

Original Arabic: Mr. DJILANI *(Employers' delegate, Tunisia)*

In the Name of God, the Merciful, the Compassionate! On behalf of the Tunisian employers, I would like to express to the President my greatest esteem and my congratulations on his election; we wish him every success. I would also like to congratulate Mr. Juan Somavia and thank him for the Report which he has produced and which we are considering at this 92nd Session of the Conference.

The promotion of human resources is a key issue. It is important to focus attention on human resources because this makes all companies more competitive. The success of a company is very closely related to the capacity of its human resources to adapt to requirements, to adapt to the technological revolution that we are experiencing.

For years, Tunisia has been making great efforts in this direction. That is why our President, Mr. Ben Ali, has made employment a core priority. We, as employers, are aware of the enormity of this challenge, and that is why we are trying, in collaboration with the dominant forces in our country, to take up this challenge in order to ensure the stability and progress of our country. Maintaining employment and creating new jobs will enable us to strengthen the competitiveness of our human resources, which will have to adapt to change. We therefore have to concentrate on training, on highly qualified workforce, which will enable us to strengthen the complementarity between education on the one hand, and vocational training schemes on the other. It is essential to strengthen this link, indeed it is vital. That is why today we have to join forces and redouble our efforts to change peoples' mindsets in order to convince each and every person that vocational training is of primary importance, and is not just a stopgap for people who have left school early.

What is more, attracting foreign investment, as developing countries are particularly keen to do, depends on a competent and highly qualified workforce. That is why many industrialized countries have focused their attention on human resources in order to attract investment.

In Tunisia we have put in place a national programme, which is enabling us to improve and promote the industrial sector. We, as employers, are trying to draw attention to the importance of this programme. We are also striving to put in place, with the competent authorities, a national vocational training system. This system tries to match supply and demand in terms of vocational training. This system is a guarantee of technical and educational quality. We are also endeavouring to increase sandwich training courses, and to foster partnership between companies and higher education institutions, in accordance with demand.

In order to promote human resources, it is also necessary to strengthen information technology, and I hope that the World Summit on the Information Society, the second phase of which Tunisia will have the honour of hosting in November 2005, will enable us to reduce the digital divide. I also hope that this will be an opportunity for developing countries to start to take advantage of these tremendous technological advances. As for the number of managerial staff in companies, this is an essential issue. We are trying to increase the employability of new graduates through adequate training programmes.

I would like to draw your attention to the Palestinian cause and to the rights that Palestinian workers and citizens have under international law. I therefore urge the international community to give priority to dialogue and negotiation in this respect.

Lastly, I would like to reiterate my gratitude to the ILO, which has worked constantly to strengthen dialogue among the three social partners in order to tackle the issues before us, for the benefit of all.

Mr. MAMMADOV *(Employers' delegate, Azerbaijan)*

On behalf of the Azerbaijan Employers' delegation, I express my gratitude to the organizers of the 92nd Session who have made it possible for us to participate in this Conference, and I wish success to the session.

The Azerbaijan Employers' delegation to the International Labour Conference would like also to convey its warm greetings and best wishes to all delegations.

The Azerbaijan employers have read with keen interest, the Director-General's Global Report on freedom of association and effective recognition of the right to collective bargaining which provides an opportunity to get a better understanding of the importance of freedom of association and collective bargaining and is the basic right in the world of work and the most important element of economic and political process.

This Report has provided the analysis of legal and practical obstacles and progress in achieving freedom of association and effective recognition of the right to collective bargaining. The employers of Azerbaijan recognize the positive effort of collective bargaining on economic development promoting productivity, adjustment measures and industrial peace and enabling the conditions for efficient functioning of social dialogue.

The Constitution of the Republic of Azerbaijan provides the right of association and ensures the freedom of activity for all associations. The Labour Code stipulates collective bargaining at the level of the enterprise, institute or organization, sector and region and signing of a general collective agreement. Following the labour policy, the current tripartite general collective agreement has been concluded for the years of 2001-03 and signed for the years of 2003-05. The general collective agreement harbours a set of issues as implementation of economic policy in the country, the development of the non-oil sector, labour payment, increase of income or population and improvement of living standards.

In the reporting period, the Azerbaijan Employers' Confederation joined a number of ILO projects on women's enterprise development and gender equality, social dialogue and employment, including the employment of youth and women, the elimination of the worst forms of child labour, tripartite declaration on principles concerning multinational enterprises and social policy. Besides the above-mentioned activity, the employers face particular difficulties.

Firstly, one of the problems impeding their signing of collective agreements is their loss of 300,000 workplaces and the emergence of one million refugees and internally displaced persons as a result of Armenian occupation of 20 per cent of Azerbaijan territory.

Secondly, since 2001, a general collective agreement has been signed at a national level but no collective agreements are being signed at sectoral and regional levels.

Multinational enterprises operating in Azerbaijan do not always have standards for industrial relations and do not affiliate with employers' organizations and allow employees' committees to establish themselves in the enterprises. The draft law on employers' associations has been discussed in the Parliament of Azerbaijan but not approved yet.

Then, it is high time to establish a national, social council to take responsibility to regulate their collective bargaining in labour and economic disputes amongst social partners and develop social dialogue in Azerbaijan.

With the purpose of enhancing the role of employers in poverty reduction processes, economic roles and industrial relations, I would like to submit to the ILO suggestions from the Azerbaijan Employers Confederation, which I represent here.

Firstly, technical assistance through all ILO projects for strengthening the capacity of employers and other social partners to promote and realize freedom of association and the right to collective bargaining: awareness raising and training.

Secondly, seminars for the employers organizations of Azerbaijan, and other countries for the regional framework of employers and training for employers. Seminars on the implementation of the ILO Tripartite Declaration of Principles concerning Multinational Enterprises and Social Policy in the field of collective bargaining and freedom of association and study of the experience of such companies in their home countries, and its application in Azerbaijan.

To conclude, I want to stress again the importance of collective negotiations in economic, social and political processes and that the role of employers should be enhanced in this regard.

Mr. PEET *(Minister of Labour and Immigration, Bahamas)*

First, I wish to congratulate the President and the Vice- Presidents on their election, and to pledge our support as we work together to successfully complete the agenda.

Allow me, on behalf of all CARICOM member States, to express our heartfelt sympathy to this body and the entire African family on the passing of the late Honourable Michael Christopher Wamalwa, Vice-President and Minister of Labour of Kenya and Chairman of the 91st Session of the International Labour Conference. He was indeed a "gentle warrior" who championed the cause of the tripartite social partners; he will be truly missed.

I am indeed honoured to have the opportunity to address this august body on behalf of the Government and people of the Commonwealth of the Bahamas.

We in the Bahamas applaud the progressive work of the International Labour Organization and pledge our unwavering commitment to work with you as one cohesive unit to improve the world of work, as we together advance our tripartite labour agenda.

I take this opportunity first to thank the ILO for its assistance with the most comprehensive occupational health and safety audit that was carried out at our ship repair facility on the Island of Grand Bahama, with the assistance of technical experts and the quick action of Mrs. Grace Strachan of the Caribbean Office and Mrs. Cleo Doumbia-Henry of the Geneva Office.

I am happy to report that we have already begun to put the recommendations in motion, and the workers of our ship repair facility are now able to work in a safer and more secure environment.

I should also wish to congratulate the ILO on the occasion of its 85th anniversary and the 35th anniversary of receiving the Nobel Peace Prize, as it continues to illuminate the path towards decent work, poverty elimination and global stability.

I should like to commend the work of the World Commission on the Social Dimension of Globalization which culminated in the most inspiring and comprehensive report. I am sure that the implementation of the recommendations made will go a long way in assisting governments, workers and employers to respond to the needs of their respective constituents as we collectively seek to address the issues and concerns associated with the unprecedented changes already affecting our lives and the lives of our families and societies.

The Bahamas, like our global economy, has undergone, and is presently undergoing, a metamorphosis that is being fuelled by the flexibility and competitiveness of integrating labour markets, increased competition, global political and social changes, and advances in information technology. As a result, the world of work as we know it today is rapidly changing.

The Government of the Bahamas has renewed its commitment to provide employment opportunities not only for Bahamians, but also for those who legally reside within our borders. In our effort to do so, we in the Bahamas, under the dynamic leadership of our Prime Minister, the Right Honourable Perry G. Christie, have established partnerships with a number of foreign investors since May of last year to provide meaningful employment opportunities for approximately 3,000 Bahamians. An additional 3,000 Bahamians are expected to be employed at Kerzner International Resort on Paradise Island, Bahamas, following the completion of its US$1 billion Phase III development. These are exciting times for our country and its people as we endeavour to make available an opportunity to secure decent work for all who are eligible to work throughout the Bahamas.

Secondly, in keeping with the sworn duty of the Government of the Bahamas to provide job security for all its workers, we have gone to great lengths to ensure that workers' fundamental rights and privileges are protected by law and best practices in our efforts to reduce poverty and promote social and economic justice. We have accepted, and are committed to fulfilling the principles of, the Declaration of Nuevo Leon which seek to advance the labour agenda in our region and, by extension, the global community.

This commitment includes, but is not limited to, ensuring that a safe and healthy work environment exists for our people. In light of the increasing number of issues and incidents regarding occupational safety and health, the Government of the Bahamas has embarked upon an intense training programme for labour inspectors. They, along with others, will be our ears, eyes, hands and feet, all in an effort to reduce violations of health and safety rules, regulations and procedures in the workplace.

In keeping with the ILO Labour Administration Convention, 1978 (No. 150), and its accompanying Recommendation No. 158, we also expect in the immediate future to secure the services of occupational safety and health experts to assist us in the reduction of incidents that threaten the well-being of workers.

Furthermore, the Government is committed to amending the Health and Safety Act with a view to making it a more effective mechanism to better meet the health and safety needs of our people. An occupational health and safety workshop is planned for September of this year for all social partners.

The labour-friendly Government of the Bahamas realizes the vital role that employers, workers and trade unions play in sustaining a safe and secure work environment, as well as a safe, secure and democratic society. Education and training also play a significant role in this regard. Collectively, we will take action to deal with this issue.

My Government, within months, will launch an intensive training programme for workers throughout the Bahamas and in this vein, we will use the College of the Bahamas to do so. I am further pleased to report that many of our employers have "bought into" this programme.

I am also happy to report that my Government's consensus-based approach to industrial relations and my proactive stand as Minister of Labour have resulted in the successful negotiation and execution of 28 industrial agreements over a period of 24 months. Such willingness by employers and unionists to agree augurs well for the future.

Finally, the Government of the Bahamas has, along with our social partners, in addition to the aforementioned, spearheaded the first in a series of labour/management workshops with a view to securing and analysing the protocols and national agreements of two of our sister Caribbean countries, namely Barbados and Jamaica.

In closing, let me reaffirm my Government's commitment to working with and assisting the International Labour Organization in our collective resolve to promote decent work for all, while addressing the social ills that have the potential to adversely affect this and other labour-related goals. This is truly the way forward. Let us therefore, as a distinguished body, do all we can to improve the lot of all who work and invest in our respective countries.

Mr. PAIVA *(representative, International Organization for Migration)*

The International Organization for Migration (IOM) wishes to express its appreciation and support to the ILO for focusing on the situation of migrant workers this year.

The broad issue of migration is now increasingly being addressed at national, regional and international levels. Migration for work is an important part of this equation. More and more, it is recognized that migration is a natural, essential and potentially beneficial phenomenon for migrants and societies alike. The challenge is to manage it properly so that all involved may reap its benefits.

While states retain the right and responsibility to determine which non-nationals may enter and under what conditions, it is now clear that migration requires collaborative approaches to manage it effectively. Moreover, most States are no longer simply countries of origin, transit or destination, but rather a combination of all three. These evolving trends open up new possibilities not only for greater understanding and cooperation between States, but also for strengthened partnerships among all the key migration stakeholders.

Today, migration is a cornerstone of the global economy. Out of the approximately 175 million migrants worldwide, nearly half, some 86 million persons, are economically active workers. But the economic implications of migration are far broader than even these figures suggest. In 2003, migrants sent home some US$90 billion in official remittances. When United Nations official transfers are included, the total is likely to be double that amount. These financial resources, as well as the skills and other invaluable human capital brought back by returning migrants, are potentially crucial support for the development of countries of origin. But much more needs to be done to understand the critical links between migration and development. In early 2005, in collaboration with the World Bank, IOM will be organizing a two-day workshop on just this topic as part of its ongoing international dialogue on migration.

That policy dialogue, launched in 2001, brings together more than 130 States and partner organizations who participate in the IOM Council. Its objective is to foster better understanding and cooperation in the management of the full range of migration issues. It does so by identifying and sharing effective practices. IOM strongly believes that open dialogue, in an inclusive non-negotiating environment, can build greater understanding and confidence amongst the various stakeholders. This, in turn, can stimulate the identification of creative win-win approaches to migration challenges. In the past year, this has meant focusing on themes such as migration data management and trade and migration with the active participation of partner organizations like the ILO contributing their specialized knowledge.

An important cross-cutting element in all of these migration discussions has been the protection of migrants' rights, including those of migrant workers. The ILO's input has been especially valuable. IOM also works in collaboration with the ILO and other partners in the Steering Committee for the Ratification of the International Convention on the Protection of the Rights of All Migrant Workers and Members of Their Families. More broadly, IOM is strengthening its activities in the field of international migration law as part of comprehensive management systems.

Our work at the migration policy level is accompanied by operational programmes carried out in over 150 country missions worldwide. These are designed to provide practical support and assistance to governments and migrants. Programmes cover the entire migration spectrum including emergencies and post-conflict situations, trafficking, voluntary returns, technical cooperation and labour migration. In the increasingly important labour migration field, activities have grown rapidly in response to the requests of governments. They focus on capacity building, orderly migration, integration of migrants and enhancing the development impact of labour migration.

A safe, orderly, humane and fair system for the movement of people worldwide is a vision that we share with other stakeholders at the national, regional and global levels. Ensuring a fair deal for migrant workers, as called for by the ILO, is an important component of this and one which IOM supports. In a similar vein, the Berne Initiative, a Swiss-sponsored consultative inter-governmental process, is working throughout this year to develop a comprehensive, non-binding policy framework for the international management of migration. IOM serves as the secretariat of the Berne Initiative and counts on the continued support and contribution of the ILO and other members of the steering group in their areas of expertise.

We have followed with interest the discussions in the Committee on Migrant Workers on how best to achieve progress toward a fair deal for migrant workers. We particularly welcome the special contribution that the ILO, through its expertise, in the protection of migrant workers' rights and the promotion of standards for labour migration, can continue to make to the effect of broader management of international migration. We look forward to strengthening our institutional partnership, including as fellow members of the Geneva Migration Group, in the interest of making sure that international migration can indeed be of benefit to all.

Mr. VAN VUUREN *(Employers' adviser and substitute delegate, South Africa)*

It is indeed a great honour for me once again to address this most august body. On behalf of the South African employers, I would like to congratulate the President on his election.

This is the first year that South African employers are participating in the Conference as representatives of Business Unity South Africa. As the name implies, this new federation of employers and business organizations has unified employers and business people in a new broad-based and unified organization.

Once again, we have an opportunity to reflect on the comprehensive and well-presented Reports of the Director-General. In doing so, I will focus on only a few pertinent points.

This year, we are celebrating ten years of peaceful democracy in South Africa. This is indeed a significant landmark and can surely stand as evidence to the world of the successful application of social dialogue. As employers, we are fully committed to the principles of social dialogue, as promoted by the ILO and enshrined in its Constitution, and we urge social partners throughout the world to embrace these principles in resolving conflict. It is sad to regularly attend a conference of this nature and to hear many countries express a commitment to using established and accepted dialogue principles, to resolve their conflict, only to return the following year to find that this was merely words without action.

In particular, I wish to refer to the Report, *The situation of workers of the occupied Arab territories*. Having been part of the process in South Africa, where we moved from an apartheid era to a democracy, we can now appreciate and attest to the importance of the application of social dialogue involving all social partners.

The ILO has been instrumental in the establishment of the Palestinian Fund for Employment and Social Protection. This Fund focuses on three core programmes: community infrastructure development, enterprise development and human resources development. In this regard, we urge that employers be closely associated with the design and implementation of these programmes, as it is through entrepreneurship and enterprise development that the issues of unemployment and poverty can start to be addressed.

There is also a need to focus on the education and skill building of young people, so as to prevent deterioration in capacity in the territories. Besides entrenching the principles of democracy in our Constitution, including social dialogue, the biggest challenge that faces South Africa is the education of its people. Should we get this right, then we will have gone a long way in addressing many of our other challenges such as poverty alleviation.

Notwithstanding all the elements contained in the Report, the most important factor that will act as a catalyst for resolving the conflict is the need to recognize the importance of social dialogue as a tool to assist in resolving the pressing issues in the territories.

South African employers are keenly aware from their own experience of the fundamental importance of international labour standards and their role in the promotion and maintenance of democracy. ILO standards have provided the basis of South African labour legislation and inspired the labour rights reflected in our Constitution. However, the implementation and the supervision of standards requires coherent structures through which serious breaches can be identified and dealt with in an expeditious and efficient manner. We support the recent review of standards and their supervision and we support the ongoing assessment of the roles and working methods of the various committees that make up the supervisory machinery.

It is disconcerting to note that many failures in society are currently being attributed to globalization. Indeed, globalization can lead to certain challenges and hardship, but at the same time, it must be said that globalization also can lead to positive outcomes. Giving effect to some of the recommendations of the report on globalization will help raise the relevance of the mandate of the ILO by applying its unique role to promote the creation of an environment that will enable more countries to benefit therefrom.

The ILO is increasingly focusing on the promotion of employment as a central route from poverty. This is strongly supported, as job creation is at the heart of poverty alleviation. Employers would, however, like to see greater policy coherence with regard to the role of the private sector in terms of poverty alleviation.

When considering *A fair globalization: Creating opportunities for all*, the ILO needs to consider particular factors pertaining to developing economies; ours is one in case. This will encourage the principle of self-empowerment and create an enabling climate that will attract direct foreign investment. This would include, inter alia, focusing on: (1) developing appropriate national environments for job creation, entrepreneurship and SME development, in particular, and in both the formal and informal economies; (2) creating an enabling environment at national and international levels for increased economic integration; and (3) building governance structures that are transparent, free of corruption, democratic and, above all, that genuinely serve the public interest.

Business Unity South Africa will pursue these goals both in a national context and in cooperation with our colleagues in the Southern African Development Community and the African Union.

Original Spanish: Mr. PALACIO BETANCOURT *(Minister of Social Protection, Colombia)*

On behalf of the Colombian Government and on my own behalf, I should like to congratulate the President on his election to preside the 92nd Session of the International Labour Conference. I would like to say that he has shown a great deal of skill in steering the assembly and that is a good sign for all participants. His approach ensures that major conclusions will emerge from this meeting for the development of the ILO and, in general, for all workers around the world.

The Director-General has put to us for consideration a Report outlining the outcome of ILO programme implementation in 2002-03. What is striking is that this Report does not just set out activities undertaken, but also lists some aspects that in its view should be improved if we are to ensure that the Organization works more effectively for all its Members.

Colombia, without any doubt, has received a great deal of help from the ILO. We recognize, and indeed we have experienced, some of the difficulties mentioned in the Reports. But at the same time, and I should stress this, Colombia, and more particularly the Colombian people, have enjoyed the cooperation of the ILO through the special technical cooperation programme. We note with satisfaction the various references made by the Director-General in the Report to progress made in Colombia. However, the success of the programmes and the progress made is not just due to the readiness of the ILO to participate, but also to the magnanimity and generosity of the employers and the trade union movement of Colombia throughout the term of office of this Government. Both sectors have made themselves available, have acted intelligently and have participated fully and this has been vital in order to progress and develop through the technical cooperation programme. You have all made an important and a determined contribution to help our country make progress. Joint work with the social partners, the figures and the overall results demonstrate this, and I think we can say unequivocally that we are now on the right track and the outline of a better future for our children is beginning to take shape.

However, Colombia does have difficulties and we have recognized this fact on many occasions. We, the people of Colombia, believe strongly in our country and it is our conviction that with the work we are doing and with the support various organizations are giving us, our country will make great strides forward. It is not yet time to cry victory, and certainly not to lower our guard. On the contrary, we need to redouble our efforts, increase social dialogue, eliminate child labour, create decent employment and thus produce a stronger democracy and greater well-being for all of us in Colombia.

Colombia, as I have told the Director-General, shares the motivation of the Organization to address the subject of migrant workers. A globalized economy requires the whole world to move forward on this issue. My country has many thousands of migrants working outside its borders. They represent a reality that exists and their vulnerability means that organizations like this one need to pay them special attention.

In the same vein, while on the subject of globalization, I also wish to say that we need to recognize and appreciate the efforts made by the Director-General to promote and realize the World Commission on the Social Dimension of Globalization. The results obtained and the fact that the matter has been put on the agenda for national and international discussion is a huge step forward.

Another subject which is part of the ILO's objectives is the concept of equal social protection for all. In this field, the Colombian Government believes that important progress has been made. It is time that there have been difficulties, but the Colombian Government is pulling out all the stops to create a system of social protection in which both formal and informal sector workers are taken into account.

It is a system in which we are not just considering pensioners and the retired, we are also bearing in mind that in Colombia about 80 per cent of those over the age of 65 have no pension entitlements whatsoever. It is not just those in the formal sector who needs training; in fact there are many working in the informal sector and many of the unemployed who need a system of protection to help them become more competitive and take up various employment opportunities. The challenge of creating this social protection system is part of an ongoing objective of our Government.

I could speak at length and share many experiences with you of efforts made and results obtained despite the huge difficulties that arise in our country each day. However, today I just want to make one point clear, and that is our firm conviction that Colombia is working as hard as it can to overcome these difficulties. Evidence of this is the ongoing work of the Government, the maturity and professionalism of the employers and the trade union movement and the way they deal with their differences, and the support of the majority of public opinion. The result has been tripartite work and joint efforts within a framework of social dialogue and détente.

Allow me now to express warmest wishes to Carlos Rodríguez, Apecibes Alvis and Julio Roberto Gómez, as well as our sincere gratitude, because despite the real difficulties they faced in doing their work in Colombia, they demonstrated professionalism and determination to strengthen and support the social development of our country. To them and to the Colombian delegation, I want to say thank you for being there with us and let us remember that the commitment that we have to bear in mind most of all is the commitment to our children, even more so than that to our citizens and the international community. They deserve and need a better future. Our generation has not seen a single day of peace in Colombia and I sincerely hope that our children will not have to say the same thing. It is only our coordinated and efficiently implemented work that will allow us, despite any differences, to be able to pass on a better country than Colombia is at present.

Mr. MUSENGE *(representative, International Social Security Association)*

On behalf of the International Social Security Association (ISSA), it is a great honour for me to address the 92nd Session of the International Labour Conference.

In previous years, ISSA representatives have taken this opportunity to speak with you about the need to ensure strength in our social security systems and to bring you up to date on the work of the ISSA. This year, I will follow a similar path, but with an increased emphasis on the outcomes of a major ISSA project, called "the Initiative".

I focus on this important ISSA project, because its outcomes support the conclusions contained in the final report of the World Commission on the Social Dimension of Globalization. They also reflect the paramount importance of working towards making decent work a global goal, as outlined by the Director-General of the ILO in his Report on the World Commission – a Report for which I congratulate the Director-General and which I fully endorse.

As you are aware, the objective of the ISSA is to cooperate, at the regional and international levels, in the promotion and development of social security throughout the world, in order to advance the social and economic conditions of the population on the basis of social justice.

In order to meet these objectives, the ISSA will continue to serve its members in their quest to improve the technical and administrative functions of social security programmes. However, the ISSA believes that it should also strengthen its capacity to contribute to broader global policy debates, by defending social security programming and by promoting the economic benefits achieved through social programmes.

These moves have been fuelled largely by the outcomes of the ISSA Initiative – a public outreach programme whose activities have provided the foundation for ISSA policy work in the next triennium and beyond and that will come to a close at our General Assembly meeting in Beijing this September.

The ISSA Initiative began in 1999, after a decade of debate about the costs and financing of social security – a debate that had been dominated by the assumption that trade-offs were necessary between economic and social development. The ISSA was concerned that the debate was not based on facts and that the broader benefits of social security were being ignored.

At the same time, it appeared that social security coverage, in terms of both absolute numbers and adequacy, was shrinking. There were concerns about people's rights to social security and whether these rights were being respected, particularly by privately managed schemes. There were also questions about the public's sense of security, as there appeared to be no direct link between the level of social security in a country and the public's confidence in it.

The ISSA Initiative evolved into a nearly five-year conversation on the meaning of the word "security" in social security. Now that the Initiative is completed, what has been learned?

First, social and economic development occur hand in hand. As countries expand their social security coverage, they are likely to experience positive economic impacts.

Second, sustainable economic development is not possible without sustainable social development. Equally, sustainable social development requires sustainable economic development.

Third, Governments must develop integrated strategies to achieve both social and economic development; for example, the implementation of well-designed health insurance schemes will ensure a healthy and therefore productive workforce.

As I mentioned at the outset, in some countries, social security protection, both in terms of coverage and adequacy of benefits, has actually decreased in recent years. The decreases have been due to several factors. Prominent among them have been economic shifts, often related to globalization, that have seen large numbers of persons move from the formal sector to the informal sector. This shift not only leaves a large number of people potentially without any coverage at all, it also provides a difficult starting point for any Government seeking to increase social protection through contributions or general tax revenues.

It must be borne in mind that decisions to increase social protection are often not easy to make. Many countries are coping with limited resources. Globalization has not achieved the desired goals that we had anticipated – it has not provided for a more equitable distribution of global resources, and it has not created much-needed jobs in those regions of the world struggling with severe poverty.

As a means to address these growing concerns, I welcome the final report of the World Commission on the Social Dimension of Globalization, which challenges nations, and the international community, in the context of social protection to undertake to create a minimum level of protection for all. I applaud this move; moreover, I must congratulate the Director-General of the ILO for his recent move to ensure that in the coming years, the ILO will continue to work with nations and international agencies to support the creation and expansion of social protection.

As many of you know, the ISSA has a long and cherished tradition with the ILO. And to this day, we continue to seek the shared objective of social security for all. Together, this partnership will continue to work with governments, multilateral organizations, and social partners to enhance the social protection of all populations.

Delegates, it is up to us, all of us, to decide what kind of a social security system we want and need; this is not an issue for governments alone, or social security administrators alone, or the social partners alone. Our social security systems lie at the heart of the kind of society we want to have, and our values as a people. The social security system also lies at the heart of our social and economic development as a country and in the world. None of us can afford to sit back and let others determine what our level of social security should be, or can be; we all owe it to the other members of society, and to our children and families, to take an active part in the debate on the future of social security.

As I conclude, this debate will continue. As ministers, social security administrators and social partners gather in Beijing in September for the ISSA General Assembly, I want to encourage you, ladies and gentleman, to take active part in this evolving debate.

Mr. VAN LEEUWEN *(representative, Education International)*

Education International welcomes the debate on "a fair globalization". Globalization is a reality, but for many millions of men, women and children, it has come to mean exploitation and injustice.

It is our fundamental belief that one of the keys to global progress is quality education for all; and this is one of the Millennium Development Goals that must be achieved. I want to stress the importance of education of women and girls, and of the ILO's work to stop child labour and let exploited children go to school. There is a great consensus on the importance of education across all of the ILO's constituency – governments, employers and workers – which is reflected in the important work at this session to revise the Human Resources Development Recommendation, 1975 (No. 150).

I have three words of warning, however. First, there is the question of who pays. There is a consensus that governments must bear the prime responsibility for general education, but governments – and employers – must also recognize the long-term benefits of investment in higher education, vocational training and lifelong learning. The current trend to shift costs to individuals is short-sighted, counter-productive and inequitable.

Second, the related trend towards privatization and commercialization of higher and vocational education and training will aggravate inequities and social injustice. Education is a growing market, but if governments fail to live up to their responsibilities, education will not be an instrument for global progress, but rather just the opposite – an instrument of deepening inequity and greater social division.

Third, education is one key, but it is not the only one. Education cannot solve all the problems of society; education helps creates conditions for progress when other conditions, including sound economic policy and fair labour laws, are in place.

We expect the ILO to address seriously the conditions of employees in education. Our Education International represents 26 million of them in 156 countries, and the number is growing.

The report of the Joint ILO/UNESCO Committee of Experts on the Application of the Recommendations concerning Teaching Personnel (CEART) is responsible for monitoring the Recommendation could not be clearer. Over three decades conditions of teachers have diminished to the point that a major crisis is now upon us. As older teachers retire, they are not being replaced by young people, and the industrialized countries are trying desperately to recruit qualified people from the developing countries, at a time when those countries need to increase their teaching forces to achieve education for all.

We welcome and support the new ILO sectoral programme dealing with this problem. The crisis can only be confronted successfully by a joint effort. Education International and its national affiliates are ready to join with governments and the wider community, including parents and business, to find effective, workable solutions, but if governments try to go it alone or to confront education unions, all I can say is that, this will be a recipe for serious social unrest.

As the CEART report before you says, "social dialogue in education remains extremely fragile [...] Without full involvement of teachers and their organizations [...] education systems cannot hope to achieve quality education for all".

In general, social dialogue at the ILO must mean *tripartite* cooperation and negotiations among the three main economic and social actors of society – governments, employers and the workforce. We have a lot of experience of working with other actors of civil society, especially NGOs committed to social justice, but neither we nor our partners in the global trade union movement believe that the ILO should confuse that cooperation with tripartism.

In the same vein, I want to make the case for renewed vigilance to maintain and strengthen the ILO's role in defence of standards. A fair globalization requires a stronger, not a diluted or weakened, ILO role in defence of fundamental standards. Take our cases before the Committee on Freedom of Association on Colombia and on Ethiopia: in Colombia our members are among the most affected by the ongoing murders. We call on the Government to respond to the ILO's recommendations. The killing, the impunity, cannot be allowed to go on.

Time does not permit me to address the issue of migration and its impact on education, or our work on HIV/AIDS.

To conclude, education unions are among the most organized in each national society. We are ready to play our role towards global progress, but there should be no illusion about the need for public resources and the need to strengthen the rules of the global community. Only respect for those standards will make "fair globalization" more than just a slogan.

(The Conference adjourned at 1.15 p.m.)

Thirteenth sitting

Friday, 11 June 2004, 3.15 p.m.

President: Mr. Attigbe

REPORTS OF THE CHAIRPERSON OF THE GOVERNING BODY AND OF THE DIRECTOR-GENERAL: DISCUSSION *(CONT.)*

Original French: The PRESIDENT (Mr. ATTIGBE)

We shall now resume our discussions of the Reports of the Chairperson of the Governing Body and of the Director-General.

Original Arabic: Mr. AL-RIZAIQI *(Workers' adviser, Oman)*

In the name of God, the Merciful, the Compassionate! May peace, God's mercy and blessing be upon you.

It is indeed my pleasure to congratulate the President and the Vice-Presidents on their election to the presidency of this Conference. Their vast experience, wisdom and deep knowledge will undoubtedly help us achieve our goals and the desired results, results that will positively affect our endeavours to achieve the noble mission of this Organization.

It is my honour and privilege to address this august body on behalf of the representative committees in the private sector in the Sultanate of Oman. These committees have been set up as intersectoral bodies under the new Labour Code of Oman, promulgated by Decree No. 35/2003, a Decree that is in total harmony with international and Arab labour standards and conforms to the ILO Declaration on Fundamental Principles and Rights at Work adopted in 1998.

We, the workers of Oman, are proud of these representative committees, which are the result of the commitment of our Sultan, Qabus, may God protect him, protecting workers and respecting their rights as enshrined in international labour law.

These committees act on behalf of workers in all matters relating to them in such a manner that they enjoy stability in their workplace. They help to enforce international labour standards and strengthen dialogue and cooperation between employers and workers which positively affects productivity and allows all stakeholders to participate in social dialogue, furthering the development effort in its humanitarian, economic and social aspects.

This Conference meets at a time when our world faces considerable challenges, in particular the information and communications revolution, and the accelerated pace of developments in production technology. Our agenda is replete with important issues which reflect the leading role of the ILO, based on its experience and accumulated expertise.

The aim is to impart social justice in the process of economic growth and to give development a human face so as to allow a balanced relationship between social partners, and ensure our countries a sustainable development leading to growth and progress.

The Report of the Director-General under the Follow-up to the Declaration on Fundamental Principles and Rights at Work, entitled *Organizing for social justice*, stresses the importance of freedom of association and the right to collective bargaining, as the basis for democratic development and a contributing factor in reducing poverty and ensuring decent work. It makes it incumbent upon us all to strengthen institutional systems in order to build a society which is fair, free and productive.

The development of human resources is one of the main pillars of global development, and, the cornerstone of its sustainability. The situation of Arab workers in Palestine, in Iraq and the other occupied Arab territories behoves the social partners participating in this session of the Conference to offer them every assistance to allow this Organization to implement its plan of action to build their capacities and create job opportunities for all those who suffer under the yoke of occupation, its arbitrary practices and its ceaseless violations of their fundamental rights to work and to freedom.

It is my sincere wish that this session of the Conference be successful. May peace and God's mercy and blessing be upon you.

Original Portuguese: Mr. VACCARI NETO *(Workers' delegate, Brazil)*

This session of the Conference will surely go down in history of the ILO for the importance it has given to the debate on globalization. Globalization has been characterized by a growing deficit of decent jobs and increasing social exclusion. The people who have suffered most from this are the workers of all countries, particularly those in the developing countries.

This Organization has a relevant role in the process of globalization if governments and social actors here undertake the leading role in dealing with the challenges we face. Since the ILO was established, the international labour standards it formulates have formed the framework for social dialogue. This is the great contribution that its tripartite structure has made in the international arena since its foundation.

The report of the World Commission on the Social Dimension of Globalization has indicated the social exclusion and the growing loss of legitimacy of the process of globalization. The ILO must play a proactive role here, and I would like to suggest a few examples.

First of all, the ILO must be a firm defender of the tripartite system. This must begin "at home", by ensuring tripartism in the debates on the report of the World Commission through the Governing Body, as an effective tripartite action of this body in conjunction with the staff of the International Labour Office.

The second fundamental aspect which must be observed is for the ILO to have a proactive role in the regional process of integration. The European Union and MERCOSUR are examples of regional integration processes which have established tripartite institutional mechanisms to monitor and promote the rights of workers.

The role of the ILO must be to stimulate the setting up of regional mechanisms to apply international labour standards which are formulated by the ILO, particularly the eight core Conventions which are the basis of the Declaration of 1998, in the search for a fairer and more equitable system of international governance.

The third aspect which I would like to highlight is foreign trade. The Director-General has already pointed out, in his Report in 2001, that the Declaration of 1998, which followed the Singapore Ministerial Conference, symbolizes the effort to strengthen the central role which this Organization must play in the global debate on labour and the social consequences of globalization. It is therefore unavoidable that we will have to face the issue of the relationship between labour and international trade.

The need to guarantee compliance with the fundamental labour standards in international trade leads us to consider the international instruments we have available to us for this purpose. One of the natural routes to follow is to strengthen our internal control bodies. These bodies share the tripartite structure, thereby ensuring that efforts will be made to establish socially acceptable relations through dialogue. This is the great advantage, from the point of view of a fair globalization, that the ILO has compared with the WTO. To forget the relevance and importance of this system would be to weaken the ILO itself.

The fourth fundamental point to be borne in mind by the ILO is that we are never going to achieve international governance of the globalization process which can create fairer societies if we have international economic relations determined by international trade and based on standards which do not guarantee domestic markets in industrialized countries which are open to agricultural and industrial products from developing countries. How, then, are we going to establish a virtuous cycle to create decent jobs without a guarantee of international trade with fair and equitable rules? This is something else we must confront in discussing globalization.

These issues are fundamental to the ILO's proactive role on the international stage in the follow-up to the Report of the World Commission.

Ms. PONCINI *(representative, International Federation of University Women)*

On behalf of the organization that I represent, the International Federation of University Women (IFUW), and as president of the Geneva-based NGO Committee on the Status of Women of the Conference of Non-Governmental Organizations, I warmly congratulate the President and the Vice-Presidents on their election.

We congratulate and thank the Director-General, Mr. Juan Somavia, for his foresight, dedication and perseverance to push the envelope of gender equality as a fundamental concept for the new social order and economic justice.

We also congratulate the ILO for its initiative to create the World Commission on the Social Dimension of Globalization, an independent body which focuses on people and gender equality as essential elements in the process of globalization. Indeed, fair globalization cannot be attained if we neglect over half of the population – women of all ages.

Women are entering the labour market and are estimated to have reached over 50 per cent of workers in certain countries; also they tend to remain active beyond retirement age, often as care-givers. Women are also living longer than men, and this ageing population will increasingly be in developing countries. Girls continue to be deprived of education, in favour of boys, and, consequently, of their right to develop as the future generation of citizens with decent work. Women from the majority of the informal sector, whose contribution to value added is not included in national accounts, and lacks recognition and protection under formal and legal regulatory frameworks. The spread of HIV/AIDS is affecting more women than men, with up to 58 per cent of those infected in sub-Saharan Africa being women. Poverty is increasingly feminized, as is migration. Human trafficking, particularly of women, has become widespread and is estimated by the International Organization of Migration to affect some 700,000 to 2 million women and children per year. The digital divide of information technology is also feminized.

We are convinced that no amount of social dialogue would have positive effects on globalization unless the root causes of inequalities are addressed. In many societies, women do not enjoy the same opportunities as men. While progress has been achieved in opening doors to education and health protection, political and economic opportunities remain limited.

In this context, one of the fundamental problems is the present socio-economic order and cultural norms, as well as political ideological platforms predominantly based on the male paradigm. Men are still considered the main breadwinners, even in double-income households, which implies that they have priority access to better-paying jobs, market and financial resources, training and upgrading, and also to new information and communications technologies. Men continue to hold economic power because of their rights to credit (women receive less than 10 per cent), to land (women own only 2 per cent worldwide), to property and to inheritance, which many women, notably in developing countries, do not have because of a patriarchal society. Patriarchy also dominates the customs, traditions and religions of almost all countries, which creates gender imbalances and maintains the subordinate reproductive role of women; it also leads to violence against them.

To shift the paradigm, a systematic gender-impact assessment and analysis are essential processes for removing policy biases.

Another method would be through gender budgeting, which would examine the differential impact of macroeconomic policy on women and men, notably through its effect on employment and the provisions of public services. However, the most effective approach is to have a systematic gender balance, especially in decision- and policy-making processes and bodies to increase the cross-fertilization of ideas with a gender lens.

IFUW's theme and resolutions for its Triennial Conference in Perth, Australia, from 4 to 10 August this year, coincidentally is on "Humanizing globalization: Empowering women." Our resolutions include advocating women in decision-making positions in world financial institutions; women occupy only two out of 24 seats on the Board of the IMF; no woman occupies a seat on the Board of the World Bank, and only 5.5 per cent of the governors are women; at the WTO, only 12 among 159 experts are women.

In this regard, I wish to remind this august body, once again, that article 3, paragraph 2, second sentence, of the ILO Constitution is a discriminatory clause against women and I quote: "When questions specially affecting women are to be considered by the Conference, one at least of the advisers should be a woman." This means placing a limit on the presence of women at the Conference. Considering that the ILO has now institutionalised gender equality in its programme and budget, we urge that this clause of the Constitution be amended accordingly.

Mr. GEORGETTI *(Workers' adviser, Canada)*

On behalf of the Canadian Labour Congress and Canadian working women and men, I want to begin by welcoming the important work provided in the report of the ILO's World Commission on the Social Dimension of Globalization. It presents a balanced and candid account of the current state of globalization and highlights both its hopeful potential and its severe shortcomings. I also want to commend the Report of the Director-General to this Conference. We must take up the challenges that the Director-General puts to all of us. But how can we talk about the fundamental principles and rights at work? How can we seriously implement the ILO's Decent Work Agenda when the results of globalization to date, for the vast majority, has made life more difficult and made us poorer?

Today, working women and men in Canada are forced to fight and go out on strike to protect what we have already achieved over decades of collective bargaining. A few weeks ago the Government of my home province, British Columbia, stripped collective bargaining rights and job security from collective agreements between them and their own citizens and cut the wages of the lowest paid by 15 per cent. Across Canada, from British Columbia to Quebec, Newfoundland and Labrador, working people, in particular those who work in the public sector, are being asked to carry the burden, while these governments deliberately disregard our fundamental rights. In our private sector, we are regularly being forced to deal with an ultimatum to make major concessions on wages, pensions and working conditions, or face plant closure due to globalization.

At the same time, though, in Canada, the 1 per cent of Canadians making more than $170,000 a year, now receive 14 per cent of all before-tax income, compared to the 9 per cent they earned just ten years earlier. This means that the rest of Canadians, the other 99 per cent of us, now have a 5 per cent smaller share of all income than we did at the beginning of the last decade.

One in four Canadian workers makes less than $10 per hour. A salary of less than $18,000 a year merely keeps a single person working full time for a whole year below our poverty line. These low-wage jobs are the main reason why too many young working and single-parent families, mostly led by women, can barely make ends meet, let alone contribute to the growth of our domestic economy.

Let us look at some of the results of globalization. Since 1960, the revenue of the richest nations was 37 times larger than that of the poorest. It is now 74 times larger. The situation has reached such extremes that the assets of the three wealthiest persons in the world amount to the GDP of the 48 poorest countries combined. No less than 11 million children under the age of five perish every year from preventable causes, including 500,000 who die from a lack of vitamin A – that is a glass of apple juice a day.

Economic and industrial policies towards development have become subordinated to free trade agreements, resulting in a loss of decent jobs everywhere. That is why we maintain that human development, not trade, must be the centre of international economic agreements.

Another important consequence of these agreements and institutions is that they limit the scope for consensus decision-making by the social partners in shaping countries' economic futures.

The fact that billions of the world's citizens still do not have access to decent work and pay is indeed a human tragedy. It also represents a huge economic waste and the failed promise of the global economic order. We agree, therefore, fully with the suggestion of the Commission that the persistent and growing income gap within and between countries puts the prevailing economic order at political risk.

It is important to look at income growth for poor people and poor countries as opening up opportunities for greater prosperity for all. Economic growth should not be viewed as a competitive game in which the gains for some result in losses for others.

The Commission's strong message that the benefits of globalization must be broadly based cannot, in our view, be stated too strongly, but it does not supplant the real test, which are the results.

Based on the tangible results experienced by the vast majority of the world's citizens, both in the developed and developing world, is it any wonder that we resist, protest, and even fight against the expansion of this selective, elitist and selfish agenda called globalization?

Until the mid-1980s, the citizens of my country shared the benefits and wealth generated by expanding trade. Sadly, the last 20 years have made them at best cynical and more often than not hostile to the suggestions of further trade expansion. This has given trade a bad name and it should not be that way.

The Director General's Report offers some clear opportunities for governments and for us to begin to develop the coherence required within the international system which will help deliver a fair globalization for all.

The ILO is uniquely placed to lead and deliver tangible results if the political will is here. We are ready!

Mr. RAMPAK *(Workers' delegate, Malaysia)*

Let me begin by congratulating the President and Vice-Presidents on being elected to chair this session.

We are gathered here amidst a myriad of new and rapidly changing circumstances on the social, economic and political fronts. Despite active democratic processes, we still hear about the suppression of civil rights, violent interrogations and torture of prisoners by occupying military forces, and a more than overwhelming set of human rights abuses, including workers' rights such as freedom of association and freedom of speech. The gross human rights violations in Iraq and Palestine have shown no signs of abating since last year's session. Many innocent civilians have been killed and grievously injured, and their houses have been demolished by the aggressors. The people are living in constant fear, and are expecting the United Nations to intervene and bring about sustainable peace in the region. The much-touted road map in Palestine, that we deliberated last year, when I was also one of the speakers, now seems to lead nowhere. It is, at best, a set of unfulfilled promises. What we actually see in the affected region is an increase in child labour and further exploitation of those who are already socially marginalized. On behalf of the Workers' group, I will continue to speak on this issue until the State of Palestine has been recognized and is formed by the people of Palestine through democratic processes.

The Director-General in his Report, *ILO programme implementation 2002-03*, has stated that "our commitment as an Organization to decent work as a unifying concept has responded to a widely felt concern, and is helping us to have a greater impact on the global agenda".

Never in the annals of the world of work has decent work ever been more relevant to the global agenda than it is today, in the midst of the political, social and economic uncertainties that the world is confronted with. The Report, while re-emphasizing the importance of rights-based social development strategies, also calls for the implementation of the Decent Work Agenda on the basis of results-based management.

The Workers' group strongly believes that the eventual success of results-based management is largely reliant on the development of tripartite key performance indicators in ILO member States, and this objective can be effectively achieved by all ILO member States ratifying and implementing the ILO Tripartite Consultation (International Labour Standards) Convention, 1976 (No. 144).

The rapid globalization of trade and services has exacted a heavy toll on job security everywhere in the world and on job predictability, equitable remuneration and trade union rights. Contrary to the impressive statements made by government leaders during ministerial meetings and summits, workers have witnessed, with growing frustration and disappointment, that the jobs reportedly created by globalization are lost, often due to stock market crashes, even before these leaders have left their speech podiums. Such is the speed at which globalization has hurt social stability and eroded public confidence in the ability of the State to sustain political harmony in a highly volatile world of work.

The Report of the World Commission on the Social Dimension of Globalization calls for the institutionalization of the globalization process and it has focused on people, establishing democratic and effective States, ensuring sustainable development, operating productive and equitable markets, promoting globalization based on solidarity, ensuring greater accountability to the people, forging deeper partnerships and bringing about an effective United Nations. The Workers' group fully supports these strategic objectives, to be dovetailed with the ILO's Decent Work Agenda, which includes employment creation, core labour standards, social protection and social dialogue. They should become a global mission statement for sustainable development and be adopted by the tripartite dialogue partnership without fear, favour, hesitation, let or hindrance.

In conclusion, in a rapidly globalizing world of work, the way forward is through equitable gain-sharing between the tripartite dialogue partners and certainly not through military aggression and oppression of human rights. We call upon nation States to spend less on military hardware and to channel more funds into rights-based development. We want a globalization with a human face, and not a globalization which places material profit above humanity. As stated in the Director-General's Report, it is only through global peace that we can attain sustainable development, in which job creation, core labour standards, social protection and social dialogue are the key constituents. Let us replace the bombs and bullets with more bread and books.

Mr. LE *(Deputy Minister of Labour, Invalids and Social Affairs, Viet Nam)*

Four years have elapsed, and this year the International Labour Conference is witnessing the advent of the second Global Report on freedom of association and collective bargaining under the Follow-up to the ILO Declaration on Fundamental Principles and Rights at Work. We are happy to share with the Conference the results and plans that the Government of Viet Nam, jointly with social partners, has achieved in pursuit of the goals enshrined in the Declaration.

In the first place, from the legal perspective, amending and supplementing the Labour Code of Viet Nam in 2002 has enhanced self-determination with regard to the rights and responsibilities of the two parties to industrial relations through collective bargaining and social dialogue applicable to all types of businesses. The Government only exercises its state administration and engages in social dialogue at national and local levels. The draft Decree on tripartite consultation has been submitted to the Government for approval. At present, the governmental agencies concerned are working with the social partners in considering the ratification of the Tripartite Consultation (International Labour Standards) Convention, 1976 (No. 144).

Together with the social partners, the state labour administration agencies are encouraging and assisting enterprises in promoting social dialogue and entering into collective labour agreements, which are on the increase. At present, a project on industrial relations is being implemented in 70 enterprises in seven target provinces by the social partners in Viet Nam, with technical support from the ILO. It is our hope that this project will introduce models of social dialogue that work well in the Vietnamese context and could be replicated in other localities and enterprises.

Regarding other principles of the Declaration, we are pleased to inform you that Viet Nam is actively collaborating with the ILO to expedite a National Plan of Action on Eliminating Child Labour, with six action programmes implemented in partnership with the Vietnamese agencies and organizations concerned. As regards forced labour, we have established a National Task Force comprising 21 specialists representing agencies of the legislative, executive and judiciary branches, employers' and workers' associations, and ILO specialists who have embarked on studying, assessing and comparing the existing national legislation of Viet Nam with the Forced Labour Convention, 1930 (No. 29), and the Abolition of Forced Labour Convention, 1957 (No. 105). It is planned that the Task Force will deliver a report to the competent authorities concerned with considering the possibility of ratifying Conventions Nos. 29 and 105 by early 2005.

We appreciate the report of the World Commission on the Social Dimension of Globalization. We advocate the position that the international community should make a concerted effort to make globalization work for all, and should never accept factors that deepen and widen gaps in opportunity, income, and living standards. By reaching consensus with the social partners, the Government of Viet Nam has brought to the fore the elimination of hunger and poverty reduction, assigning it the highest priority in the Comprehensive Poverty Reduction and Growth Strategy (CPRGS). In addition, the Government has turned its attention to the poorest of the poor in remote, far-flung areas where ethnic minorities live, with appropriate and supportive policies aimed at narrowing the gaps in income and standards of living among different groups and localities.

We appreciate the choice of issues to be discussed at this session of the Conference, including human resource development, the fishing sector and migrant workers. Regarding the latter, Vietnamese nationals are now working in over 40 countries and territories. We therefore accord special attention to this issue and would like to see solid international cooperation in protecting migrant workers.

Over the past few years, the Government of Viet Nam, along with its social partners, has been endeavouring to attain the goals enshrined in the Decent Work Agenda through stepping up the amendment of labour legislation; drafting the insurance law, which pursues broader coverage and introduces more schemes; establishing the Bureau of Occupational Safety to further improve occupational safety and health; maintaining and enhancing the quality of programmes and activities pertaining to the National Week on Occupational Health and Safety, and eliminating Fire and Explosions; and dealing with retrenchments resulting from the restructuring of state-owned enterprises.

On behalf of the Government delegation of Viet Nam, I would like to avail myself of this opportunity to express our gratitude to the ILO for its support and assistance to Viet Nam over the past years, and I do hope that this will be strengthened in the years to come. In the future, we will prioritize policies on labour market development including establishing labour market information systems, training and retraining the labour force so as to meet market demands, further strengthening labour legislation for promoting social dialogue, and improving occupational health and safety.

Original Spanish: Mr. ORTEGA NADAL *(Employers' delegate, Dominican Republic)*

The Employers' delegation of the Dominican Republic is proud to be able to congratulate the President of this 92nd Session of the International Labour Conference, our fellow Dominican, Mr. Ray Guevara, on his election. We wish him every success. We also welcome the Report of the Director-General, which is a valuable account of *ILO programme implementation 2002-03*.

Let me also take this opportunity to greet all the delegations present, whose contributions here every year give a sense of direction to this unique Organization within the United Nations system.

I cannot begin discussing the Director-General's Reports without expressing our scepticism regarding the Dominican Republic's inclusion on the list of countries invited to appear before the Committee on the Application of Standards, especially considering the comments made by the Workers' representative, Sir Roy Trotman, supporting the candidature of our Labour Minster as a President of this session of the Conference. This suggests that there could be a hidden agenda here and, being new to these things, this leads us to question how these lists are drawn up and who is responsible.

In the Director-General's Report we noted that despite limited financial resources, the ILO has made a great deal of progress in implementing its Decent Work Agenda and its four fundamental pillars, through the InFocus programmes and the interdisciplinary activities of the International Training Centre in Turin, the International Institute for Labour Studies and other similar institutions, and through the implementation of the work of the World Commission on the Social Dimension of Globalization. In a world where globalization is marching ahead at great speed, the ILO's regulatory work is becoming more important in the multilateral system and its responsibility is even greater because its tripartite structure gives its views and its contribution to the Organization's objectives greater legitimacy.

In the case of the Dominican Republic, we ratified the eight fundamental labour Conventions some years ago and ILO supervisory bodies are monitoring their application, this because our country has been questioned regarding their fulfilment. I am happy to report that we have, of course, been exonerated by the Standards Committee as we are carrying out projects in our country aiming to improve not only our labour legislation but also our judicial practice in these areas.

We are taking steps to implement the Worst Forms of Child Labour Convention, 1999 (No. 182), through the IPEC Programme; we have a tripartite HIV/AIDS prevention programme, which we presented to the ILO last December and is still awaiting implementation due to a lack of funds; we are also still trying to put in place a social security system which is financially viable in the long term and which covers occupational health and safety and social security adequately and simultaneously.

Furthermore, within the framework of technical cooperation with the ILO, the employers' sector has carried out a series of projects which have not been successful because of internal difficulties, but which are in the process of being relaunched as a strategic plan has been drawn up and approved, our organization has been restructured, and modifications to our statutes have come into force.

This restructuring has included the implementation of various projects from different bodies, which have already led to two successful conferences on occupational hazards, and which in Phase 1 includes groups of seminars on different areas related to preventing occupational hazards, and occupational health, and in phase 2 includes prevention programmes through our partner institutions, which will strengthen our organizational and economic structure.

The events of 11 September 2001 and the ensuing wars have had an adverse effect on our country which, along with the unprecedented oil price increase and a badly handled national financial crisis, has led to economic growth being cancelled out, unemployment going up again, inflation reaching very worrying levels, and the purchasing power of our currency and that of workers and the general population being reduced to less than 50 per cent in one year. This has led us to suggest to the newly elected authorities that the issue of pay is not an isolated problem, it is part of a macroeconomic formula that should restore dynamism to our economy, and then the competitiveness and high levels of economic growth we experienced a few years ago. This should be achieved through a social pact in which we commit to pulling the country out of its current problems.

We believe that now is the time for social partners to propose the approval of an Economic and Social Council. This is something that the Employers' Confederation of the Dominican Republic (Copardom) has worked very hard on implementing; it is well known to all parties and it will consolidate tripartite dialogue and facilitate governability at a time when our country needs it most.

All this should be seen against the backdrop of a joint decision-making process on free trade treaties, not just in the framework of the free trade area of the Americas, but also through bilateral agreements with the United States and other countries in the region. Negotiations are also under way for a partnership agreement with ACP and EU countries in the framework of the Cotonou Agreement, which will require a greater creativity if our country to improve its productivity and competitiveness.

We believe that an important job that the ILO could do is to approach the other multilateral agencies to make sure that funds are given as a priority to those who need them most so that poverty can be reduced by creating decent work, while at the same time preserving world peace and respect for human rights.

We trust that the ILO, through its high profile and through its contribution to human progress, will fulfil its role as a vehicle for social peace at times when inter-agency coordination is needed between multilateral institutions, particularly those in Bretton Woods and the World Economic Forum.

As far as we the constituents of the ILO are concerned, we must drive forward the necessary changes in our home countries and, along with the ILO and other agencies in the multilateral system, we should help the Decent Work Agenda become a reality and thus strengthen world peace and the respect for human rights, which are essential if our democratic systems are to be consolidated and disseminate a better life for all the inhabitants of this planet.

Original French: Mr. KEIRA *(Minister of Employment and Civil Service, Guinea)*

I would like, first of all, to take this opportunity to congratulate the President and the Vice-Presidents for their election to preside over the work of this session our Conference. Your personal qualities, together with the long experience you have in this matter, are a true guarantee for us to have the best results.

My delegation has noted with great interest the ideas shown in the different documents, particularly the Report of the Director-General which is dedicated to the activities of the International Labour Office for the period of 2002-03.

Before going on to the Report of the Director-General, I would like to express some views regarding technical issues which are on the agenda of this session of the Conference and which correspond to the current concerns.

Human resources and training were a subject of the first discussion at the 91st Session of our Conference. On this occasion, my country presented its comments on action regarding standards. In actual fact, during this year's sessions, texts have been adopted to guarantee qualitative and quantitative development of vocational training and life-long learning for our workers, without which there is no progress or development.

With regard to the working conditions in the fishing sector, in respect of action on standards the Republic of Guinea, which is a coastal country and has many rivers, appreciates the fact that this has been put on the agenda.

Artisanal or industrial fishing has an important role in Guinean economy because it represents the livelihood for many families. It is for this reason that we are pleased with the adoption of a standard which will enable us to improve the working and living conditions of our workers in this vital sector of our national economy.

The Report of the Director-General is dedicated to the implementation of the programme of the International Labour Office in 2002-03. It is a reaction to the commitment undertaken by the Office to report each year to the Governing Body on the activities carried out by our Organization. It is in this way that the Report of the Director-General is an assessment of all the work of our Organization: the importance of the strategic objectives and the efficiency of the means used to attain our objectives. It is an opportunity for our Organization to concentrate on the good and the less good results so as to take the correct decisions with regard to future strategies and means to be used to implement them.

The Report of the Director-General refers to the activities carried out within the framework of the four main objectives, that is to say standards, fundamental principles and rights at work, employment, social protection, social dialogue and intersectoral activities.

A glance at the regions shows the amount spent per region. We see that my continent, Africa, is the region that has most benefited with the sum of about US$89,402,373. This is the moment for us to express our very sincere thanks to the International Labour Office for this particular attention given to Africa.

The Reports by the Chairperson of the Governing Body and the Director-General of the ILO are an important contribution for the qualification of the working methods of our organization to carry out the permanent or periodic missions which are allocated to us. The activities carried out in 2002-03 show that we have a dynamic presence, but my delegation endorses the comments made by the Governing Body of the ILO about this programme during its session in March 2003 and invites the Director-General to take this into consideration for future strategy.

My delegation is also very pleased with the fact that the Director-General has dealt with the situation of workers in the Arab-occupied territories. We have taken note of all the issues at stake during the mission and while the Report was being prepared.

The pertinent standards of international law, in particular, that of the 4th Geneva Convention of 1949 and The Hague Convention in 1907 have been the source of inspiration for the representatives of the Director-General of the ILO.

We would like to congratulate the International Labour Office for the quality of the Report submitted for discussion and my delegation would like to support the conclusions and recommendations of this Report.

To conclude, I have great hope because the reflections made on these important Reports will surely contribute to the expansion of future activities for the well-being of our populations in our respective countries.

Original Thai: Mr. TECHATEERAVAT *(Workers' delegate, Thailand)*

Once again, I am here to reflect on the overall situation in my country.

In the past, we needed a stabilized government, which was considered essential for the political stability of the democratic regime. We hoped that it would help resolve the problems in our country and lead to sustained and transparent development, with equal participation of people from all sectors. Unfortunately, at present various projects which have been introduced by the Government have not yet provided concrete assistance to the poor and disadvantaged people.

We believe that in the pursuit of our national goal, human development is a key factor which needs to be carried out in all aspects: the economy, society, politics and culture. In the development process, people in all sectors should have equal rights and participate equally, since people from all walks of life are of equal importance for the country in moving towards secured and transparent progress. Unbalanced development might lead to many and varied problems. Nevertheless, governments of developing countries often focus only on the economic aspect. Moreover, in the context of liberalization which has been promoted by the superpowers, the Government has lost its power to protect people at the grassroots level. It has rarely acknowledged how difficult it is for people in poor communities to survive. As a result of a rather monopolized market and complicated capital management, the income gap of people in the country has grown significantly.

We believe that the Government should change its attitude towards workers. Business groups must improve their behaviour with regard to wages and the search for the highest profit gains. Otherwise, government policies in different areas will never attain their goal if more and more workers are still receiving increases in minimum wages of only 1 baht, while the Government has declared that the country has passed through the period of economic crisis and can export to the tune of millions of baht.

Today, human rights have been repeatedly violated, including trade union rights – a fundamental right of workers – and there has been no progress on the disappearance of Mr. Thanong Pho-arn, the leader of the labour confederation.

The fight against privatization is still going on, increasingly violently. The people increasingly support the fight against privatization, especially that of electricity and water supplies, which are public utilities. We believe that privatization could lead to the destabilization of workers' lives. In this regard, the increase in public service fares and costs has become a burden to poor people. Most of them are workers. The deficits resulting from privatization are evident, as can be seen from the change of certain state enterprises into public companies. Consequently, the workers of these companies will be legally exploited and will not have protection on the right to organize trade unions, which are considered as severe violations of fundamental rights.

As regards the issues of health, safety and the environment these are not of serious concern to the Government. Occupational injuries, death and disabilities still occur. We are still waiting for the establishment of an occupational safety, health and environment institute. Furthermore, nothing has been done to help improve the situation of insured persons under section 39 of the Social Security Act.

Lastly, no matter how the globalization issue is defined, investment conditions and forms of employment in the industrial sector have resulted in changes in employers' strategies towards competition and production. The use of subcontracting has become widespread. Workers are discriminated against to such an extent that they have lost their rights and benefits with regard to wages, welfare, opportunity and access to training and development, promotion and career progress, termination of employment and retirement, as well as the right to be members of trade unions. At the same time, production has shifted to households which have now become part of the informal economy. Production has also been relocated to regions with lower wages.

The abovementioned are examples of nine demands submitted to the Thai Government on Labour Day.

However, we believe in fundamental human rights in terms of freedom of association and collective bargaining. Without these rights we cannot achieve sustained progress and lasting peace in our global society. We therefore request once again that Government ratify ILO Conventions Nos. 87 and 98 and strictly observe their obligations.

Mr. SORIANO *(Employers' delegate, Philippines)*

On behalf of the Philippine employers, I would like to congratulate the President on his election and also to thank the Director-General for his comprehensive and lucid Report, *ILO programme implementation 2002-03*. We find the Report meaningful and instructive, as it analyses with precision the progress of the ILO's Strategic Policy Framework for 2002-05, whose driving force is the implementation and sustenance of the Decent Work Agenda.

It will be recalled that the Strategic Policy Framework was laid down by the Governing Body in November 2000 to put into practice the Decent

Work Agenda in order to achieve the strategic objectives within the four-year period covered.

This Report marks the mid-point of this process and is most welcome, particularly to my country, which is one of the many developing member States – which make up 80 per cent of the world's population – for the significant and practical, comparative lessons it gives us. As pointed out in the Report, its most important aspect is that it "allows the Organization to reflect on what has been most successful and least successful" in the programme implementation of the strategic objectives, "and to use that learning in decisions about future strategic directions and the means used to achieve them".

We venture to say that our country's commitment to decent work is not only total, strengthened as it is by tripartite involvement, but also necessary in the context of our country's decent work deficits. Thus, the Decent Work Agenda serves as a unifying concept to underpin our country's democratically based, market-oriented development strategy by aiming to balance growth with equity. Nevertheless, as the Report forcefully implies, the principles as strategies of decent work have never been intended to be applied in a one-size-fits-all way but should be adaptable to the specific economic and social context of each individual country. Implementing a national action plan for decent work remains a daunting challenge in our country, where over 40 per cent of the population lives on less than US$1 a day and where chronic unemployment and underemployment are endemic, fuelled, as it were, by an unmitigated population growth rate of 2.36 per cent per annum, which, in turn, wipes out the effects of our moderate economic growth.

In view of the magnitude of the challenge and the scarcity of resources, the tasks necessary for the reduction of the decent work deficit must be ranked in order of urgency. The most serious deficit is unemployment and the inability of the economy to create enough jobs for a burgeoning labour force. It goes without saying that lack of work is the handmaiden of poverty that can cause societies to fall apart and nations to flounder, amidst the promises of globalization and technological advances. Inasmuch as work is central to people's lives, it is also at the heart of politics. These are the issues on which people vote and elections are won or lost. Moreover, it is axiomatic that where there is no work there are no workers' rights. Indeed, it is chronic unemployment that is the root of all these deficits and which is the major – and very costly – factor for the rising incidence of poverty, which afflicts 40 per cent of the population.

At the National Employment Summit held in March 2001, the President of the Philippines placed employment at the top of the Decent Work Agenda. Accordingly, the Philippines' Medium-Term Development Plan 2001-05 includes a separate chapter on promoting full, decent and productive employment, which was formulated through multipartite consultations led by trade unions and my organization, the Employers' Confederation of the Philippines.

To sustain the momentum in addressing decent work deficits, the social partners, with the support of the ILO, launched a national action plan for decent work in May 2002. At the same time, the social partners brought about the establishment of a decent work national tripartite advisory committee to implement and monitor the action plan on a continuous basis. Currently, the national action plan for decent work does not include methods and tools for measuring impact. The ILO's assistance has been requested to convene a tripartite workshop with the purpose of including a section on impact monitoring and reporting in the action plan.

The respective contributions of Government, the employers within the Employers' Confederation of the Philippines (ECOP), and the workers within their respective trade unions in reducing the decent work deficit are too many to enumerate here. But what I can objectively state is that the collective actions of the social partners are transforming the strategies of the national action plan for decent work into a growing reality for the benefit of the entire nation. The mere fact that the social partners, particularly workers and employers, who used to be traditional adversaries, have found a common cause in promoting and implementing the decent work action plan with synergistic effects is a triumph for social dialogue in itself.

Finally, I am pleased to say that as an active partner in the implementation of the National Action Plan for decent work, my organization, the Employers' Confederation of the Philippines, on behalf of the Philippine employers, has spared no effort and resources in addressing the country's major decent work deficit, primarily through mobilizing employers and the business community to expand opportunities as well as access to decent work. We shall endeavour to expand the outreach of our services and representation, not only to enterprises in the formal sector, but also to those in the informal economy, while at the same time leading the advocacy for the protection of workers' rights through corporate social responsibility. We hope that the success of ECOP in these endeavours, however modest, can serve as attestation to the intrinsic validity of the strategic objectives of decent work amidst relentless globalization and geo-political volatilities.

Mr. BATBAYAR *(Minister of Social Welfare and Labour, Mongolia)*

On behalf of the Government of Mongolia, I warmly congratulate the President on his election to preside over the 92nd Session of the International Labour Conference. I am confident that, under his leadership, the International Labour Conference will fulfil its mandate successfully. I would like to associate myself with previous speakers in their appreciation of the Reports of the Chairperson of the Governing Body and of the Director-General presented to this Conference. These Reports highlight the most challenging issues associated with the social dimensions of globalization. The World Commission has prepared a major report in which it presents a wide range of views, encompassing global, regional and national perspectives. The collaborative way in which this report has been prepared – through numerous consultations to hear the views of national governments, workers and employers, as well as international businesses and labour and civil societies – is an example of an inclusive, mutually respectful and interactive decision-making process among member States. I am pleased to note that these Reports call for action based on dialogue and promote this as a foundation for a genuine global community.

I would also like to draw the attention of the delegates to the importance of the current discussion on international migration issues by the Conference. In this globalized world, it is difficult to divide countries categorically into the sources and destinations of labour migrants. Instead, countries with different levels of social and economic development should strive to find a common language in the good governance of labour migration.

Mongolia continues its far-reaching social and economic reforms as it transforms into a democracy and a market economy. The country is experiencing both the positive and negative effects of globalization. Like other ILO member States, we are concerned by the fact that weakened national systems of social protection are one of the effects of globalization. Mongolia has ratified six fundamental ILO Conventions. Currently, the Government of Mongolia is preparing to ratify the Conventions on forced labour.

The Government of Mongolia is conducting a policy to strengthen tripartism in our country. In November 2003, the Cabinet adopted a social security sector development programme that should become a plan for the development of the country's social sector up to the year 2015. This programme was designed on the basis of regular consultations between the Government, trade unions and employers. This strategy paper provides for the further development of tripartite relations in the country, on the basis of a specific setting.

For the successful advancement of social dialogue in our country, the constituents have started a joint project to strengthen tripartism in Mongolia. This project is supported too by the ILO as part of its efforts to implement the relevant ILO instruments.

The Government of Mongolia, together with other social partners, is working towards the adoption of a national decent work agenda.

Mongolia's social partners have agreed that decent work, socio-economic flaws and proactive employment policies should be given high priority in the national poverty reduction strategies and in international development cooperation.

I would like to express my appreciation to the ILO for its continued support in strengthening social dialogue and in the development of the national decent work agenda.

Mongolia fully agrees that the time has come to make the social dimension, and particularly decent work for all, a global objective.

Original French: Mr. KASSEY *(Minister of the Public Services and Labour, Niger)*

At the outset, may I convey to the President and the other Officers of the Conference the warmest congratulations of the tripartite delegation of Niger upon their brilliant election. At the same time, I would like to congratulate the Director-General of the ILO on the very pertinent report before us, which has the advantage of dealing with a subject the importance of which is known to everyone – globalization and its effects upon the lives of thousands of people. There is no need to demonstrate that globalization is a reality nowadays, but it will offer advantages only if it is of benefit to the whole of humanity.

In this connection I must congratulate the ILO for its very laudable initiative of setting up a World Commission on the Social Dimensions of Globalization, whose pertinent conclusions offer hope for a better, more just world for all those who feel excluded.

I am personally convinced that if globalization is to be truly beneficial for all, it must make humanity central to its objectives and employ strategies that can trigger an improvement in the living conditions of the inhabitants of our planet.

The expert knowledge of the ILO and the values embodied in the Organization certainly make it a unique and appropriate framework for securing a just, fair globalization generating opportunities for all.

Another equally important role which falls to the ILO in this process is that of ensuring the coherence of moves by all the organizations and institutions working for economic and social progress in the world. I am convinced that the ILO must be able to fulfil this mission because of its tripartite structure – employers, workers and governments, provided the latter are aware of their importance and devote themselves to this task with the necessary energy. Such a commitment on the part of the ILO and its constituents is undoubtedly a guarantee of fair globalization based on an approach reconciling economic imperatives and social concern visualized in the Director-General's Report.

Niger, which has ratified eight fundamental Conventions and which endorses the goals of the ILO, is right behind the Organization's strategic objectives. In this regard I would like to mention, among other aspects of our agenda, a programme to combat poverty, a programme within which we are moving towards the definition of a national policy of employment creating enough high quality jobs, for all men and women of our country. This also means strengthening institutional capacity in the health sector in order to ensure better health coverage and facilitate access to care.

I cannot fail to mention the room for manoeuvre the social partners have just given themselves, by denouncing the interoccupational collective agreement, to adapt this instrument which is 34 years old, to conditions today by embarking on negotiations to establish new working conditions.

I will conclude by pointing out that there is now hope regarding the achievement of "a fair globalization", as a result of the pertinent studies made within this Organization and the determination of the ILO and its Director-General to win the battle of creating opportunities for all. It is up to all three constituents to put these findings into practice.

Mr. KAPUYA *(Minister for Labour, Youth Development and Sports, United Republic of Tanzania)*

I would like to start by congratulating the President and Officers of the Conference on their election, and the Governing Body for establishing a Commission to examine the social dimension of globalization in 2002. My assignment has been made easier by the fact that the two co-Chairs of the World Commission on the Social Dimension of Globalization, His Excellency Mr. Benjamin Mkapa, President of the United Republic of Tanzania, and Her Excellency Ms. Tarja Halonen, President of Finland, had an opportunity to present their reports to this august assembly on 7 June 2004. The Commission has ably established a case for balancing the needs of economic efficiency with those of social efficiency, without which balance there cannot be sustainable development.

I would like also to congratulate the Director-General of the ILO, Mr. Juan Somavia, for his summary of the Report to this Conference, in which he he has succinctly indicated its relevance and challenges to the ILO and its constituents. The summary, which the Director-General has carefully entitled *A fair globalization: The role of the ILO*, makes it easier for us to debate the issues, including those on the agenda of this year's session of the Conference, and to come up with implementable programmes of action.

I commend the two co-Chairs and the members of the Commission for a job well done. I am confident that their candid report will define the ILO's agenda for a long time to come.

The Commission's report clearly states that for their recommendations to be implementable, strategies should start at the national level, including the issues of proper policy formulation, institutional reform, good governance, etc., to mention only a few. In trying to realize this, my country has embarked on a process of implementing the Decent Work Agenda by initially reviewing existing policies and regulatory and institutional frameworks, and putting in place those which would enable economic growth and employment creation, while ensuring observance of labour standards and guaranteeing income security.

In this regard, the Government of the United Republic of Tanzania has managed, with the financial support of the Danish International Development Agency (DANIDA) and technical support from the ILO, to complete the first phase of reform, leading to the enactment of two laws, the Employment and Labour Relations Act 2004 and the Labour Institutions Act 2004. These laws, I am glad to report, have incorporated requirements under the ILO's eight core Conventions ratified by my country, which, I hasten to add, is a necessary step in implementing the Decent Work Agenda.

The second phase of the reform, which covers employment creation, skills development, social security, workers' compensation and occupational health and safety, has commenced. In order to successfully carry out this task, we request technical and financial support from the ILO and other development partners.

The Government of the United Republic of Tanzania has been reviewing the Poverty Reduction Strategy with the objective, among others, of putting more emphasis on issues that have a direct impact on the eradication of poverty. Under this review, the linkage between employment and poverty reduction has been reaffirmed, leading to mainstreaming employment creation as a key factor, and not merely a cross-cutting issue, in policies of different sector ministries.

We reaffirm that social dialogue at national and international level is an essential tool in the process of achieving a fair globalization. Admittedly, though, our country, like many others, especially in sub-Saharan Africa, faces a social dialogue deficit challenge, particularly in three areas.

Firstly, our tripartite constituencies still lack adequate capacity to understand, articulate and effectively dialogue on socio-economic impacts of finance, trade and investment policies, both at national and international levels.

Secondly, there is inadequate depth and width of our tripartite and other representative institutions; they need empowering and capacity building to make them indeed a representative voice of society.

Thirdly, we observe sheer resistance from some – though not many – employers to giving room for fertile dialogue to take place.

For this reason, we acknowledge the assistance given by the ILO project on strengthening Labour Relations in East Africa (SLAREA) in this endeavour and would plead for continued assistance from the ILO and our other development partners as we strive towards the idea of achieving a fair globalization for our people.

At the centre of our country's employment creation endeavour is the critical challenge of education, training, multiskilling and lifelong learning to enable our country's human resources to be competitive and keep pace with the demands of a globalizing market.

Further, we face yet another challenge related to the issue of free movement of labour, an inevitable corollary of globalization, on which the Commission's report recommends a systematic approach which aims to extend and revitalize existing multilateral commitments on issues such as the rights and protection of migrant workers and trafficking, especially of women; to develop common approaches to major policy issues through dialogue between countries of origin and destination; and to build a global framework for an orderly and managed process in the common interest.

It is hoped that the recommendations contained in the Commission's report will go a long way towards managing the problems and guaranteeing of decent work for migrant workers.

Lastly, I would like to call upon member States and the social partners to debate the recommendations of the report and formulate implementable strategies to enable us to reap the benefits of globalization

---
Original French: Mr. BOISSON *(Employer' delegate, France)*

The work of the World Commission on the Social Dimension of Globalization carried out by eminent persons who came from all walks of life, but who have an acute sense of dialogue and are remarkably good listeners, has helped to move the debate on globalization away from ideological confrontation and polemic. This is its first and biggest merit.

Employers appreciate the fact that the Report underlines the need to develop entrepreneurship because this is the basis of both wealth creation and job creation. The irreplaceable role of the market economy has been affirmed, but the criticism of its dysfunctions and of its limitation has been severe.

I would like to select two points that I think essential, and which have been highlighted in the Director-General's clear and incisive Report entitled *A fair globalization: The Role of the ILO*

First of all, action must be taken as much at the local level as at the global level. Secondly, the international labour standards system has to be strongly themed.

With regard to the first point, it is clear that the mechanisms of world governance are defective. There is no doubt in anyone's mind that the multilateral system has to be reformed. That requires two things: first of all, we need political will at the highest level. So far as France is concerned, we can be reasonably optimistic: when Mr. Somavia was received less than a month ago – in tripartite forum, actually – by President Chirac, the President said that he agreed fully with the analysis and with most of the recommendations of the World Commission.

This was confirmed before this house last Monday by Mr. Larcher, the French Minister Responsible for Labour Relations.

Then I think we have to establish closer partnership relations between the United Nations system and the Bretton Woods institutions. Each must remain within its own mandate and strengthen its core activities. This means that the economic institutions must take greater account of the social dimension, and we have a responsibility to make sure that they do so. But it also means that the ILO has to pay more attention to the constraints of the competition-based economy and competitiveness of companies.

With regard to the emphasis placed by the Commission on the need to act at the local and national level – this is just a matter of commonsense and being realistic. The traditional technical cooperation activity of the ILO has acquired a new dimension with the follow-up to the 1998 Declaration, a declaration that has led to more account being taken of the specific features of each country.

The social dimension does not mean, as is often believed, the social consequences of globalization; it also means that social conditions for adaptation to the major changes brought about by the international division of labour. By way of an example, an effective training system is one of those conditions.

Now I wish to emphasize the importance of the chapter on strengthening the international labour standards system. As spokesperson for the Employer members to the Committee on Legal Issues and International Labour Standards, I am particularly interested in this.

The Director-General has taken up the recommendation of the World Commission to integrate the strengthening of labour standards into the international development programme. That brings us really to the heart of our mandate. Our authority remains unchallenged as regards the preparation, adaptation and promotion of labour standards.

With the 1998 Declaration, which was welcomed by the World Commission as a valuable governance tool, we have taken a decisive step towards the economically and socially balanced development.

The integrated approach that makes it possible to build action plans that contain more than just legal components is innovatory. In this respect, we should note that the Declaration concern only one of our four strategic objectives, and that the integrated approach is constructed separately for each sphere of activity.

Therefore, I think that the time has come to think about dovetailing the four strategic objectives into one method that would enable us to apply them in an interdependent and simultaneous way. Isn't it this idea that is sketched out when the Director-General talks about the adoption of framework instruments to strengthen the standards dimension of decent work? I think that it would be useful for the Office to go into this issue so that we could discuss it at the next Governing Body in November, perhaps after informal tripartite consultations to shed more light on the subject.

In conclusion, the main obstacle on the road to a fair globalization lies in the great inequality of countries in the face of this phenomenon. A standard-setting policy that makes it possible to establish objectives, to offer assistance and cooperation, to measure the progress made and to assess the effectiveness of policies, especially those designed to combat exclusion from the labour market: this, to my mind, is the significant contribution that the ILO should make towards making globalization a real opportunity for all.

Mr. EDSTRÖM *(Workers' delegate, Sweden)*

The Swedish trade unions believe that among the most important aspects of the social dimension of globalization is the proposal to establish a Global Policy Forum among all the relevant international organizations to secure, with a coherent policy, a fairer globalization focused on social justice and that, to this end, these international organizations respect and actively promote international core labour standards.

Nevertheless, the Kenyan Government reminds us that all up-to-date labour standards should be promoted by member States.

Only governments can ensure that the World Commission's report is being discussed in forums like WTO and the international financial institutions. We, nevertheless, would request the Director-General to report back to the ILO constituents on the results obtained at any such forthcoming discussions – including on the proposal that the social partners should be given a formal consultative status at these institutions and on the recognition of the ILO by these organizations, showing that they understand and respect tripartism.

In the Director-General's Report, *A fair globalization: The role of the ILO*, the export processing zones are mentioned. In our view, this rapidly growing phenomenon – approximately 3,000 zones in 116 countries with 50 million workers (mainly young women) and characterized by excessive concessions to multinational enterprises (MNEs) in order to compete for foreign direct investments – constitutes a serious failure of the world trading system. When governments feel compelled to abstain from much needed tax revenues or allow foreign companies to trample on their workers' fundamental trade union rights in their own territories, then something is indeed wrong.

Why do governments from developed and developing countries not come together and agree upon minimum requirements for international investors?

The ILO's Decent Work Agenda is, of course, a national reference point. Leading developing countries have made a proposal in the WTO context concerning investments and the responsibilities of MNEs and their countries of origin. This was an excellent proposal, except for one aspect: it did not include any requirement to respect the principles of freedom of association. Could we assume that all governments in future will see to it that their own workers are able to exercise their fundamental human rights at work? In the end, no one is better off if unfair and inhuman competition is allowed to exist.

We in the Swedish trade unions give our full support to the proposed international framework for migration. But perhaps we also need to discuss once again the statement made in the Declaration of Philadelphia that labour is not a commodity.

In Sweden, our collective agreements ensure the same wages and working conditions for workers who are not members of our unions. Our aim is, of course, to ensure a minimum wage for everyone. Our hundreds of thousands of local trade union representatives check that no one is exploited – not migrant workers, not young workers or other vulnerable groups. This vital role that trade unions can play to prevent discrimination should be fully recognized.

The Workers' group has tried unsuccessfully to have gender equality matters put on the agenda of the Conference. Fortunately, the Conference itself shouldered its responsibility. The resolution on pay equity shows that gender-based discrimination is not tolerable and, of course, does not make economic sense.

The real challenge for the ruling male-dominated societies all around the world is to ensure that the Equal Remuneration Convention, 1951 (No. 100), becomes a reality in practice.

The Director-General's *Report on the situation of workers in the occupied Arab territories* is most welcome. The extreme hardship suffered by Palestinian workers and their families has so far regrettably not evoked a strong international response. Violent acts of terror have cost the lives of innocent people, mainly in Palestine, but also in Israel.

The ILO cannot solve this political conflict, but, as we can see, the main burden is put on working people in Palestine who now face 60 per cent unemployment.

The ILO Constitution declares that, "whereas universal and lasting peace can be established only if it is based upon social justice," and this is indeed true both for Palestine and Israel.

Measures need to be taken urgently. As necessary part of a political solution, it is our view that the illegal settlements, as well as the building of a wall in Palestinian territory, are unacceptable and should be dismantled.

Original Spanish: Mr. HALKIN *(Employers' delegate, Mexico)*

First of all, on behalf of the employers of Mexico, I congratulate the President on his election to preside over the important work of the 92nd Session of the International Labour Conference. This is an honour and a distinction for our region.

The Director-General has set out a number of points in the Report which are worthy of comment as regards my country. Equally, the work of this session of the conference yields important conclusions for Mexico.

There is no doubt that the work of the ILO around the world has taken on a new dynamism. There is a focus now on day-to-day problems while solutions proposed are more specific and practical in nature. The process of overhauling standards has made us look at national and international standard setting to see whether it is viable and in tune with today's changing world. Globalization has now begun to enter every possible field: labour, trade, finance, information and communications. All this forces us to open up different multinational and regional forums and, at the same time, in every country, the social partners must arrive at the necessary agreements so that our countries can integrate properly into this new environment.

In the case of Mexico I must mention and express gratitude for the important activity carried out by the Regional Office of the ILO in our country. Economic issues go hand in hand with social issues and regulation. Technical assistance ranges from labour reform and social security measures to the eradication of child labour. This openness favours the structural change which Mexico urgently needs. Our country has many free trade agreements, and that means we have to undertake the changes that are required in order to be able to cope with the flow of trade which has begun.

Before this body, with its special and very useful tripartite structure, I would like to appeal to all workers, legislators, entrepreneurs and governors in Mexico and ask them to forget their individual or partisan interests and to complete the process of structural change which we need.

We do not have any time to lose; labour reform, energy reform, fiscal reform and social security reform cannot wait. New generations demand a change which will create more jobs and more opportunities.

We have to modernize our human resources. Migration should be regularized. The fisheries industry should be liberalized and should not be bogged down with non-trade barriers. This is a job that needs to be done quickly because, increasingly, there are more restrictions coming about which prevent us creating jobs.

It is also important to recognize progress in democracy, and I think it is worthwhile, in this important international forum, to recognize the freedom of expression which we now enjoy in Mexico, as well as the rules on transparency that bind us and which apply to employers, workers and the Government equally.

In these areas we call on all countries with which we have signed international trade agreements to fulfil all national and international commitments and to be clear that we are doing this to create the right sort of world for future generations, but also for ourselves, for our own generation.

I believe that, as countries, we should not sign international treaties and adopt agreements we do not plan to fulfil, such as non-tariff barriers which take the form of health regulations or internal security measures which actually cause irreparable damage to jobs, investment and particularly investment security and strategic alliances between countries and regions, affecting employment and specific training for particular activities. We wish to make a very strong appeal here today that everyone should realize the great damage that can be done by such actions.

I should like now to refer to two current issues that we in Mexico have to deal with in particular, and they are Mexican migration and the informal employment sector, both of great interest at both national and international levels.

Mexicans are migrating at ever-increasing rates and this is, as we all know, because of the lack of employment opportunities, which as a Government and as employers we have not been able to reduce or alleviate. We are addressing this issue, but although some positive steps are being taken, other measures are not working. On the positive side, the income from either official or informal workers abroad is about 15 billion pesos per year. However, at the other end of the scale, we are losing valuable human resources and the possibility of creating official jobs, along with the skills and talents which are going abroad.

The other very important issue I wish to mention is that of the informal employment sector. This is something else which has very serious social consequences, because, by saying "illegal" instead of informal, it becomes clear that those who are working in this sector do not receive social benefits of any kind. This creates a completely parallel sector which does not pay tax or make any other contribution to society, yet requires a great deal from the Government. These governmental obligations end up being funded by workers and employers in the formal sector.

These are the two major issues that should be a priority on our agenda and the Government, employers and workers in the official sector should create a united front which will try to generate social responsibility.

It has been an honour to be able to speak to this prestigious meeting and set out our vision for the future and tripartite participation between Government, employers and workers in Mexico.

Mr. KUSANO *(Workers' delegate, Japan)*

This year is a memorable year for the ILO: its 85th anniversary, the 60th anniversary of the Declaration of Philadelphia and the 35th anniversary of the Nobel Peace Prize. With various and serious problems in the world of work incurred by increasing globalization, it is exactly now when the ILO is examined on its raison d'être and role once again.

We regard some issues raised by the Organization recently as those by which the ILO fulfils its current tasks, including such issues as migration, which is of this year's Conference agenda items, poverty eradication, which was emphasized in last year's Director-General's Report and the realization of decent work, which has been a central theme of ILO activities for some years.

We should like to reaffirm that the proper function of the ILO's tripartite structure was, and is, the base upon which the Organization has built its very existence and acquired its reputation and trust from the international community.

The report of the World Commission on the Social Dimension of Globalization clearly identifies the serious widening disparities and social insecurity between and within countries, which is brought about by too much hasty globalization.

In Japan as well, employment, wages and working conditions have been gravely affected by the extreme deregulation policy of the Government and the management restructuring pursued by some employers disguising the "reinforcement of international competitiveness". One typical example is the explosive increase in atypical workers, including part-time, fixed-term and dispatched workers. These workers, who occupy around 30 per cent of the total workforce, are facing serious problems, such as employment insecurity and unreasonable discrimination in wages, working conditions and social security. Their situation is also having a damaging effect on the employment and working conditions of regular workers, and has a severe negative impact on the whole life of working people.

Our attention should be on the serious situation of women. Gender equality is, therefore, the fundamental viewpoint that should be rooted commonly in all the issues.

Overcoming the negative consequences of globalization is a task of urgency for the ILO. It is imperative, therefore, to implement the recommendations of the World Commission concretely and steadily. It is a pity, however, despite favourable appreciation in general, that very few indications have been expressed to secure the funds necessary for implementation. Neither has the importance of social dialogue based on labour relations yet obtained enough recognition.

The ILO is required to reinforce its management based on the tripartite structure in order to fulfil its leading role in collaboration with other international organizations. And, we are fully convinced that the principle of freedom of association should be properly established and function as a basis of tripartism. I quote: "without freedom of association, the concept of tripartism would be meaningless".

Having said that, I would like to refer briefly to the issues of fundamental trade union rights for public service employees in Japan. The Committee on Freedom of Association twice issued reports stating that the current situation on this issue is not in accordance with the principles incorporated in Conventions Nos. 87 and 98, and that drastic reform is necessary, including legislative revision. I would like to express our sincere gratitude and respect to be representing JTUC-RENGO. In response to these recommendations, a table for consultation is now set up with three ministers concerned and also three representatives of trade unions, including myself. I would like to conclude my intervention by requesting you to watch attentively our efforts to establish a new democratic public service system compatible with ILO Conventions.

Original Spanish: Mr. GURDIÁN CASTELLÓN *(Minister of Labour, Nicaragua)*

At the 82nd Session of the Conference in 1995, Nicaragua was honoured to preside over this distinguished international gathering. The election of Milton Ray Guevara, the Minister of Labour of the Dominican Republic, as President of this session of the Conference is extremely significant for my country and I extend my sincere congratulations to my colleague and friend.

International organizations such as the ILO are forums that encourage the search for and formulation of procedures that are mutually beneficial in terms of cooperation and technical assistance. In this context, it is important to mention the strategy designed by the Office under which targeted programmes are used to improve coherence and integration of its activities but above all to improve the sustainability of many of the cooperation projects in our countries in the field of child labour, occupational health and safety dialogue. This is reflected in the Report of the Director-General.

From its very creation, the ILO has been developing a system of international labour standards of true historic value. The standard-setting function of the ILO has been the cornerstone of our activities, and is reflected in the many national legislation of many of our countries in the social and labour fields, and contributes to the improvement of labour standards in all of them.

I recall that, in 1998, a decisive step was taken towards sustainable social progress with the Declaration on Fundamental Principles and Rights at Work and its Follow-up. This indeed was the political, solemn and renewed commitment of the ILO and its Members to respect and promote the fundamental principles and to make them a reality.

Thus, the Report of the World Commission after two arduous years of work confirms that employment is a precondition for the development of social justice and reiterates the need to articulate social and economic policy around employment. In this respect, in the last few years we have been working on the application of poverty reduction strategies which will allow us to create a significant number of jobs. Emphasis is placed on rural development which is gradually bringing us closer to a fair and equitable growth in which: we recognize that the human factor is the most valuable resource and that it is human welfare that we are working towards; we are meeting our goals in terms of the eradication of child labour and are currently endeavouring to identify hidden forms of dangerous work, which is a permanent challenge that we are rising to with enthusiasm and determination and in consonance with human dignity; public investment is directed to the poorest strata of society, through job creation in vulnerable sectors; and emphasis is placed on strategic alliances between the Government and society, aimed at development and democratization based on governance and shared responsibility.

The Government of Nicaragua, led by President Enrique Bolaños, strengthen the private sector and to promote foreign investment. We also intend to provide employers and workers with access to effective dispute settlement mechanisms, within the framework of respect for labour rights, and to promote the exercise of these rights.

The need to create more and better jobs must be our fundamental goal at all times. It is a goal that is supported by the ILO and is crucial for the development of our people and for the welfare of those who are vulnerable.

Original Russian: Mrs. MORAVA *(Minister of Labour and Social Protection, Belarus)*

The past few years of the activities of the ILO are characterized by the seeking of new mechanisms which should enhance the work of the Organization in the various areas of technical cooperation in favour of its participants. Changes have been introduced to the organizational work of the secretariat in Geneva and in the regional offices and a way forward has been achieved to help bring national standards into line with international labour standards. In this regard I would like to mention the practice introduced last year of examining more topical issues at the Conference, which allowed the focus to be placed on more burning issues. This gave a fresh impetus to the activities of the ILO.

Last year, we discussed questions of occupational safety and health. Following these discussions a decision was taken to prepare a new framework Convention in this regard. At the current session we are looking at problems of labour migration. In today's world, the regulating of migratory movements is one of the priority elements in the policies of many ILO member States. However, various relevant ILO instruments have not been widely ratified or implemented. ILO standards are important; they must be implemented. We must develop a unified approach to this issue, and the ILO has already prepared a certain number of draft standards in this connection.

In spite of the different social and economic positions of the member States of the ILO, all of them need technical cooperation from the Organization. One of these forms of technical cooperation is the decent work country programmes, which help to implement the various ILO resolutions and programmes at the national level.

I believe that for the countries which are not involved in the direct implementation of global programmes or In-Focus programmes, and this includes my country, a national programme is the most effective way of collaboration. It provides for an ongoing exchange with the Organization on the basis of the ILO's four strategic objectives.

According to the report of the World Commission on the Social Dimension of Globalization, one of the principal elements of an effective social policy is a responsible government that is fully aware of its social and economic responsibilities and that boosts development, provides social protection and promotes gender equality and access to work for all.

In our country, we fully share this point of view. One of the aims of our Government's social policy is to promote the stable development of the economy and an equally stable social security system.

The Republic of Belarus is doing everything within its power to maintain the level of social protection it has enjoyed up until now. We have been able to maintain unemployment at less than 3 per cent which is acceptable. We have witnessed a constant growth of pensions and wages. We have practically resolved all of the problems of wage indebtedness that have characterized our region.

Our country is currently ranked fifty-third in the human development index of 175 countries in the world and is, therefore, in the group of highly developed nations. We must bear in mind, however, that social and economic processes in our Republic are influenced by the Chernobyl catastrophe.

After 17 years, our Republic is still having to spend tremendous sums of money to counteract the effects of this catastrophe. A significant part of our budget is still earmarked for Chernobyl programmes. In total, we would need the equivalent of 32 annual budgets at the 1985 level to pay for this catastrophe. The ILO should not shy away from this problem. It should devote particular attention to our needs in this area. The aftermath of Chernobyl has a negative influence upon the efforts of the State to create better working conditions and raise the level of social protection.

We are grateful to the Organization for all the help it has given us over the past years, in particular with regard to the reforms of the heath care and pension systems. However, we are forced to point out that over the past three years we have been unable to sign the final agreements on a technical cooperation programme.

In this new millennium, the International Labour Organization has witnessed the emergence of a new issue, namely that of decent work for all. This is of global importance. It raises the prestige of the ILO in the world, but at the same time it increases the Organization's responsibility as a key player in the fight for a fair globalization. It is therefore necessary to guarantee a high level of social protection as well as social peace.

(Mr. Maatough takes the Chair.)

Original Azeri: Mr. MEHBALIYEV *(Workers' delegate, Azerbaijan)*

Globalization and the emergence of the single market have led to more intense competition and an increasing concentration of wealth and resources, which ultimately has a marked impact on wage levels and working conditions. In today's information society, with its two-tier labour market and prevailing demographic trends, the industrialized countries are facing an increasing demand for cheap labour, which they are unable to meet out of the national labour force.

At the same time a number of States, especially in the developing world, are facing economic and social problems, unemployment and poverty, resulting in the relentless growth of migration, including labour migration. Migrants make up a substantial proportion of the population and labour force and play an important part in the economy of the developed countries and countries of origin.

And yet, migration policies in many countries are beginning to shift the focus to the importance of national security, relegating problems of labour market regulation and the priorities of fundamental human and labour rights to the background. Therefore, the issue of labour migration is taking on increasing importance for the trade unions.

As a socially and politically stable country with a developing economy, Azerbaijan is pursuing integration in intergovernmental and international economic, political and social systems. Beginning in 1988, with the Armenian aggression against Azerbaijan and after the collapse of the USSR, Azerbaijan found itself in the midst of extremely difficult mass displacement and relocation processes, which urgently called for a solution to migration problems. Hence our interest in designing measures for the successful and productive integration of migrant workers in society, the protection of migrants and their families, and observance of their labour rights.

Despite the dynamic growth of certain sectors of the economy since the mid-1990s and macroeconomic stability achieved through social and economic reforms, migration flows from our country abroad continue, and illegal labour migration has become a common occurrence. It is these people who are hardest hit by difficulties arising out of the undefined status of labour migrants, disparities in labour legislation, lack of regulation in regard to social insurance and social security, working in a legal vacuum and in total dependence on the arbitrary will of employers when it comes to working conditions and remuneration, being in a de facto illegal situation.

The main labour migration flows in the Republic can be described as follows. The main countries of destination are the Russian Federation, Ukraine, Turkey, the United Arab Emirates and Germany.

According to statistics from the Russian Federation, about 2.4 million citizens of Azerbaijan live in the territory of the Russian Federation alone. According to some estimates, in the period 1998-2000 tens of thousands of Azerbaijanis migrated to Turkey and Western Europe as illegal migrant workers. Most migrants abroad are employed in individual businesses, commerce and catering sectors while in the Russian Federation 35 per cent of Azerbaijani migrants work in construction, 12 per cent in industry, 15 per cent in agriculture and 25 per cent in services and other vital sectors.

The majority of highly qualified specialists from the Republic migrate to Turkey, the United States and European countries.

At the same time, according to the statistics, there are about 2,000 foreigners working in joint ventures in Azerbaijan. Overall, an estimated 25,000-30,000 foreigners work in Azerbaijan.

In addition, with its open-door policy, Azerbaijan is often used by transit migrants. According to a survey carried out by the Baku office of the International Organization for Migration (IOM) carried out from May to September 2003, most of these are from the Near East, south Asia and CIS countries.

Most of the legal migrants were Russian citizens from Chechnya and most of the illegal migrants were from Afghanistan, Iraq and the Islamic Republic of Iran.

As can be seen, our Republic is deeply involved in labour migration processes, hence the need to step up efforts to improve control and management both at the national and at the international level.

Clearly, further development of globalization will bring with it quite a few new aspects of this problem. This is especially true of the European Union, given the imminent accession of several East European countries. At the same time, in view of former ties as well as emerging new processes and relations among the post-Soviet States, certain specific factors will continue to have an influence. And we attach importance to regulating these processes both at the European level and with our main migration partners.

Accordingly, expressing its solidarity with the position of the EU trade union movement and the CIS trade unions, while at the same time taking into account the positive role of labour migration in ensuring employment, raising the standard of living of the population and developing the Azerbaijan economy, we advocate the following approaches to maximize the benefits of migration and minimize the problems it entails: creating the necessary conditions for the civilized use of legal migrant labour, integrating migrants into the world of work and the economy of the receiving country; combating the exploitation of illegal migrants and denial of their rights; and legalizing migrants so that social and labour laws are fully applied to them.

Given the common interest of States on the migration issue, and based on the priorities of national interests, it is necessary to improve and to continue the practice of concluding intergovernmental agreements. Guided by the standards of international law, we need to take measures to harmonize and unify laws on labour migration and the use of foreign labour. It is important to enlist the participation and coordinated action of all the social partners, including employers' organizations and trade unions. Their representative bodies must take an active part in setting out the policy principles and procedures and also in their implementation. Observance of the civil and labour rights of migrant workers by employers can be promoted through cooperation among trade union organizations and a concerted stance by the trade union movement, as well as bilateral agreements between trade union centres. It is necessary to establish monitoring systems and a common information base on migration.

Original Arabic: Mr. TRABELSI *(Workers' adviser and substitute delegate, Tunisia)*

On behalf of Tunisian workers, the Secretary-General of the General Union of Tunisian Workers, and the members of the Executive Bureau, we would like to congratulate the President on his election to the presidency of this session of the Conference. We hope that it will constitute a major step forward towards the tripartite strengthening of the role of this Organization at a time when the gulf in society is widening and international relations are characterized by hegemony and domination.

I would like to take this opportunity to thank the Director-General for the excellent Reports that have been submitted to us. Our union much appreciates the content of these reports, which are very thorough and realistic and which contain proposals which would allow us to strengthen the standard-setting system and the capacities of the social partners to promote decent work and social dimension of globalization so as to avoid marginalization and help those whose rights are denied and violated.

In this context, I should also like to express my appreciation for the activities of the Organization over the period 2002-03 and for its Decent Work Agenda. The results of this work are contained in the Report of the Director-General who encourages, all trade unionists to participate in the dialogue in order to strengthen labour standards, respect for workers' rights and respect for their dignity. That is what we seek to do in Tunisia and we are willing to do this within the framework of a new round of collective bargaining, which has been scheduled for 2005, with a view to drawing up a new three-year agreement. This will be the sixth agreement of this kind since 1990 which is aimed at improving wages, working conditions, laws and the protection of trade union rights.

I would like to take this opportunity, on behalf of the General Union of Tunisian workers to thank the Director-General for his Report on *The situation of workers of the occupied Arab territories*. According to the Report, this situation is steadily worsening and deteriorating and we would have liked this Report to stress the fact that the occupation is the reason for this deterioration. The history of humanity has shown that any occupation is accompanied by war, falling standards of living, collective punishment and the violation of human rights. That is what is happening today in Iraq and in Palestine, where the situation strengthens our conviction that a fair and lasting peace resting on international legitimacy is the only genuine solution to the tragedy being experienced by workers in Palestine, in the Chebaa farms area and in the Golan.

We must have the courage to recognize that this much desired peace can be achieved only if the occupation of Iraq is terminated, if Israel ends its occupation of all the occupied Arab territories and if a Palestinian State is set up with its capital in Al-Quds.

I should like to thank the Governing Body for deciding to discuss the situation of migrant workers who are suffering from racism and xenophobia in many regions of the world, where attempts are made to blame them for economic crises and unemployment. This situation has become worse for Arab and Muslim immigrants since 11 September 2001. They have been subject to acts of vengeance, discrimination and racism, ever since the media and a number of politicians and intellectuals have broadcast or made speeches which have equated Muslims and Arabs with terrorists.

The ILO has an exceedingly important role to play with regard to the situation of migrants. In fact it is a vital role. It must strive to strengthen international labour standards so as to ensure that migrant workers and their families are protected and have equality with the workers of the host country. It must devise mechanisms to promote their genuine integration in society. The role of workers is becoming increasingly important as an element of cultural dialogue and a meeting of peoples in a world where, once again, certain quarters are making much of what, they call the clash of civilizations, cultures and religions.

We therefore support the proposal made by the Arab Labour Organization that an observatory should be set up for Arab and Mediterranean migration. We hope that the ILO will offer its technical and financial support to this project, because it could become a means of constantly monitoring migratory movements in the region, measuring the various consequences and observing the situation of migrant workers.

I wish you every success.

Mr. MAGAYA *(Minister of Labour and Administrative Reform, Sudan)*

It is a pleasure to extend our congratulations to the President on his election to preside over the 92nd Session of the International Labour Conference. No doubt his vast experience will enable us to have a successful Conference.

The Report of the Director-General entitled *ILO programme implementation 2002-03* is highly appreciated. The achievements of the ILO in the previous biennium are recognizable, though what remains to be done is enormous to help developing countries in general and African countries in particular to create employment and alleviate poverty. We think that the ILO could further assist the African countries in the following areas: undertake the development of an accurate information system with special emphasis on labour market information to assist in the drawing up of constructive employment policies and also help in drawing up effective policies for income and employment distribution; assist in the transfer of technology and increase the capacity in areas of vocational training to pave the way for a solid industrial base depending on the available natural resources; assist in building basic infrastructure; and further assist African countries in their efforts against AIDS and other endemic diseases.

I would like to stress the recommendation of the Tenth African Regional Meeting which called for the ILO to establish an InFocus Programme on HIV/AIDS at the workplace in order to have adequate interventions and activities in this area.

The Sudan is now maintaining a very good relationship with the ILO which resulted in different forms of assistance to the social partners. This assistance covers various areas:

– capacity building, which includes the organization of workshops on human resources development and conducting studies to establish new vocational training centres and the rehabilitation of existing training centres. Participation in training courses organized by the International Training Centre of the ILO, Turin, and in drawing up the PRSP in collaboration with the Ministry of Finance. On the same issue of poverty, the ILO conducted a workshop on employment and poverty which will definitely serve in the preparation of the African Union Extraordinary Summit on Employment and Poverty Alleviation in Africa which is planned to take place in Burkina Faso this year; and

– the Sudan ratified the Conventions on child labour – the Minimum Age Convention, 1973 (No. 138), and the Worst Forms of Child Labour Convention, 1999 (No. 182), and the Government started working on them to meet its obligations. We are planning training courses and workshops for our staff to enable them to meet the requirements of the Conventions. We expect the ILO, both at the level of headquarters and in the region, to assist the various parties in the Sudan in this area. Contact has already started with the Cairo Office. I take this opportunity to extend our thanks and gratitude to the ILO staff in Cairo and at the Turin Centre who have greatly supported us.

As for the report of the World Commission on the Social Dimension of Globalization, it is worth mentioning that the report is balanced and acceptable. The most important aspect of globalization is that it should have a human face, as stated in the report.

Having said that, I would like to shed light on some recent developments in the Sudan. To put an end to the protracted civil war in the southern part of the Sudan that destroyed the social infrastructure and caused misery to the population by refuge and displacement, and even hampered economic and social development in the whole country, a peace agreement has been reached between the Government and the warring factions. The agreement guaranteed basic human rights and fundamental freedoms, such as the right to equal treatment irrespective of gender, race, colour, religion or origin; the right to freedom of thought and consciousness, freedom of association and assembly, freedom of movement, freedom of the press, immunity against arbitrary arrest, detention and torture; freedom of religious worship and preaching. The agreement resolved all the issues of the conflict which include power sharing, wealth distribution, security arrangements and the contested areas. It is worth mentioning that all those agreements are based on the Machakos Framework Agreement concluded early last year. There will be a transitional period of six years after which a referendum is to be conducted for the southern Sudan on self-determination.

I take this opportunity to commend the efforts of all IGAD countries and other parties who exerted efforts to assist the Sudan to reach a fair peace deal. Our sincere thanks go to the Government of Kenya, which hosted and took care of the tedious negotiations. Our thanks also go to the United States, the United Kingdom, Norway and Italy which played a crucial role in the peace process. We also thank all the countries and organizations which supported the peace process in the Sudan.

We call upon the international community to support the efforts of the Government of Sudan, particularly those relating to the rehabilitation and reconstruction of southern Sudan, as well as the areas affected by the war in the Sudan. In this connection, we attach special importance to the donor countries' meeting in Oslo which is to mobilize resources to help the Sudan. The ILO is also invited to play a leading role through technical assistance.

To conclude, I would like to say a few word about the situation of Arab workers in Palestine, which is deteriorating harshly. Houses are destroyed, the people are subjected to aggressive practices as a result of the Israeli occupation, including collective punishment and the destruction of civil and productive infrastructure. The result is the loss of innocent lives, destruction and an increase in unemployment. The Sudan denounces all this and asks the international community to take firm action to restore the rights of the people of Palestine and of other occupied Arab lands.

Original Armenian: Mr. VARDANYAN *(Minister of Social Security and Employment, Armenia)*

On behalf of the Armenian delegation, allow me to commend the Director-General for his idea of creating a World Commission On The Social Dimension Of Globalization and the Report, *A fair globalization: Creating opportunities for all.*

Globalization is a complicated phenomenon which has become a leading force for change in today's world and has given rise to new challenges and dangers. The last two years have had particular significance in this respect: the Ministerial Conference of the WTO at Doha culminated in the signing of a global agreement, while, even before that, the ILO had adopted it Declaration on Fundamental Principles and Rights at Work, which has become a vital instrument in strengthening decent work.

Armenia fully supports the Decent Work Programme and the policy of stabilized mobilization and implementation of social agreements as a strategic instrument for the prevention and reduction of poverty, stimulating a process of integration in this broadening world.

Armenia supports the main recommendation in *A fair globalization: Creating opportunities for all.* We feel that the programme of decent work is a strategic means for solving the problems of employment, intensive, constant and equitable social development and quality governance in a globalizing economy. Defending the rights of workers to work, personal safety and representation in dialogue should not be done for its own sake, but rather to promote the improvement of opportunities for the poor strata of our society. Armenia has a programme for overcoming poverty, developed by 50 independent experts alongside representatives of the trade unions and the Union of Employers. In August 2003 this programme was approved by our Parliament.

We are now developing legislative measures directed at reforming our social recommendations. These are the Labour Code and the draft laws "On a State Labour Inspectorate", and "On the Minimum Wage", which are based on ILO Conventions. There adoption is helping us to resolve the issues of labour rights for the citizens of Armenia. We hope that the ILO will participate in the establishment of a legal framework in this field. The development of national legislation and the process of creating a new, genuine environment for labour relations and of creating the conditions for the development of forms of economic relations that are new for our country – these are leading us gradually towards being able to ratify ILO Conventions. Our approach is pragmatic, and it is based on the real conditions of fulfilling the Conventions.

Moreover, with these new labour relations, it is a priority to have real, strong partnerships with active structures that are relevant to the new situations. We intend to draw on the enormous experience of the ILO in these reforms. Over the past few days, we have been able to find mutual understanding in this regard, ensuring a base for further cooperation.

Armenia is represented in many world organizations: WTO, IMF - of which it is member – and the World Bank. At the same time, our cooperation with the ILO is an important element in involving the international community in the process of the successful implementation of our internal reform. We find it necessary to have constant consultation with our chief partners, the employers and trade unions, in order to evaluate situations as well as possible, and to help the most vulnerable segments of the population. This will allow us to make the best decisions to attenuate the social consequences of our reforms.

Original Spanish: Mr. MONGES ESPÍNOLA (Minister of Justice and Labour, Paraguay)

I congratulate the Director-General on the Report before the 92nd Session of the International Labour Conference where two fundamental issues are addressed: how to progress towards a fair and inclusive form of globalization which generates opportunities for all; and the role of the ILO to that end. With its critical but positive message, it proposes a vision of change that has to be brought about so that the benefits of globalization can reach more people, thereby stimulating the social dimension of the processes of integration in keeping with the ILO Declaration on Fundamental Principles and Rights at Work. Today, the challenges in terms of human resources, labour legislation, workers' migration and social security are at the heart of the agenda of all countries and multilateral bodies.

In the Republic of Paraguay, the extremely democratic Government of Dr. Nicanor Duarte Frutos, which bases itself upon the rule of law, respect for human rights and social justice, recognizes that social labour policies are major factors for economic growth and it is bent on bringing about development with social inclusion, which is centred on satisfying people's needs for work.

Just about a year ago, we were experiencing one of the most serious crises of our history which, as you know, had an impact on the labour market, which is still exhibiting high rates of unemployment and job insecurity. We are, however, smoothing the path towards a new phase. Although economic and social indicators have improved, we still have a long road ahead of us to overcome complex structural problems.

To lend impetus to the internal labour market, we are carrying out a plan of public works and housing with clear rules and effective measures to combat corruption and we are building a more effective and more honest institutional system to serve the interests of the people. Regionally, we, the Ministers of Labour of MERCOSUR, have made ourselves responsible for adopting an employment policy with a common design based on the fundamental principles and rights at work.

As the Director-General's Report proposes, we are starting at home and in this connection, I am happy to mention some progress towards compliance with fundamental labour rights, especially with regard to combating child labour whose "World Day" is being commemorated tomorrow, 12 June.

In Paraguay, 265,000 children work. To reverse this alarming trend, the Government has ratified the Minimum Age Convention, 1973 (No. 138), and the Worst Forms of Child Labour Convention, 1999 (No. 182) and it has recently adopted a national plan aimed at progressively eradicating child labour and improving the working conditions of young people. Presidential Decree No. 2616 of 31 May links this plan to social labour policies for children and young people. In the same context, through resolution No. 3631 of 7 June 2004, the Ministry of Education and Culture of Paraguay included 12 June the "World Day Against Child Labour" in the school calendar.

Over a five-year period, we intend to develop a database on the characteristics of child labour, to carry out awareness campaigns and develop state policies to upgrade institutions and create an appropriate framework of standards. In addition, we will endeavour to improve employment and labour possibilities. We have set ourselves the goal of improving the human capital of the country through education, training and the certification of labour skills. It is our job, to give Paraguayan workers the knowledge and skills they need to improve their employability.

We believe that we are making headway towards the legitimate aspirations of progress and social justice demanded by society. With the cooperation of the ILO, we are sure that we will achieve our goals within the framework of a fruitful participatory dialogue with employers' and workers' organizations and civil society.

Original Spanish: Mr. DAER *(Workers' delegate, Argentina)*

On behalf of the workers of Argentina, I would like to congratulate the President on his appointment and the excellent work he has done at the helm of the Conference. I agree with the Report tabled by the Director-General, *A fair globalization: The Role of the ILO*, in that this is going to be one of the key issues on the international agenda in the next decade. Reaching this objective is our joint responsibility as social partners.

The unionized workers of Argentina accept this challenge because we are aware that we have a fundamental role to play in constructing a more equitable society, in terms of distribution of wealth and opportunities for all.

Not only do we share the need to work towards a fair globalization, but we also share the ideas of the Director-General on how to move forward through strengthening dialogue and tripartism. We believe in social, tripartite and institutionalized dialogue, not just as a way of preserving and ensuring social peace but also as a key factor in national development and a fundamental driving force for economic and social policies which could end exclusion and poverty.

In my country, the responsibility of the social partners and tripartite dialogue was a major factor in overcoming the most serious times of our crisis and to avoiding further irreparable damage to society. We deplore the fact that this tripartite dialogue at the highest level is still not being implemented sufficiently or durably today, although we are optimistic that this may be achieved in the coming months.

Argentina has seen the darkest side of globalization, probably more than many other countries in the world. While the main concern of successive governments was to ensure the functioning of markets, unionized workers issued a unanimous warning about the increasing social inequalities which were being consolidated, at the same time as we denounced the spectacular increase in unemployment and exclusion.

External investors were not innocent. They were aware of the economic policies being applied in our country, and leaders and beneficiaries were aware of the social consequences which stood out starkly against the debt which was artificially bolstered to the exclusive benefit of financial institutions.

The alarming decapitalization of industry and other productive sectors, along with the transfer of genuine resources towards foreign financial centres, were constant features which were presented as an essential part of the economic model. Our multilateral creditors were essential to this process and were jointly responsible for the irrational debt process which triggered the final collapse. That is why we strongly support the negotiation which our Government is currently undertaking with foreign creditors. This negotiation is crucial for the future of our nation, and our economic and social development depend on it. Therefore, we fully support, with total responsibility, the position of the Argentine Government.

In the toughest days of the crisis, when we seemed to have no social or political structure at all, and the representiveness of the ruling class was being seriously questioned, the social partners took the risk and shouldered the responsibility of tripartite dialogue to overcome the crisis. This House, the ILO, was witness to our concerns and needs, showing determined support and providing social dialogue which made it possible for us to offset some of the worst effects of the crisis.

We put on the table the need to redistribute wealth amongst workers and the retired, to increase social cover for the unemployed, and to have a health and food policy which would answer the basic needs of the entire population. We also shared in the launching of an ambitious and effective plan to provide social assistance for the most needy.

Today, when hope is once again reborn and society is again rallying behind a national development project, we demand a continued institutionalized process of democratic and tripartite social dialogue to guarantee decent work and a new redistribution of wealth. There can be no proper political democracy without social dialogue.

We share the objective of achieving a more inclusive and fair society; we shoulder our responsibilities and we insist on a debate on State policy. All the Government's efforts should be focused on generating decent work, with fair salaries and an equitable distribution of wealth. The trade unions have a great deal to contribute to the construction of a model based on solidarity and progress and we are ready to do this. Let us overcome our obstacles through joint action.

The construction of a fairer globalization is possible; we can also have a fairer nation. The responsibility of all of us is to find the right way forward towards those goals.

Original Arabic: Mr. DJEMAM *(representative, International Confederation of Arab Trade Unions)*

First of all, let me congratulate the President on his election and wish him every success in conducting the work of this Conference. I would also like to thank the Director-General and his colleagues for the work that they have done preparing the reports, which address essential issues for workers and the world of work.

On behalf of the International Confederation of Arab Trade Unions, let me assure you that we will lend our indefatigable support to the activities carried out by the ILO as an active partner in decision-making to serve the interests of peoples. We will also support the organization in its efforts to recognize the fundamental principles and rights at work so that we can build a better future. We agree with the Director-General in his Report on the globalization that is characteristic of our time, and specifically with the idea that the social dimension of this globalization is necessary to ensure economic peace for all peoples and to put an end to the unfair economic competition that is so harmful to many workers and makes them even more vulnerable to unemployment and poverty particularly in the countries of the third world. We support this trend to create an international forum on globalization and its harmful effects, so that we can face up to the difficulties that arise as a result of this globalization of poverty and economic disorder both at the national and international levels. We hope that this will form the basis of some very serious efforts to build a sound economic and social platform which will enable us to put an end to the marginalization of the countries of the south and guarantee decent work.

As far as migrant workers are concerned, we would stress the importance of adopting an international strategy to bring about justice and to put an end to the suffering that has been going on for too long. In this respect, we would also emphasize the need to solve the problems of migrant workers in Arab countries and to help them to achieve better living conditions. This must be done with the cooperation of all parties concerned, taking into account the interests of both the workers and those living in the host country. I feel compelled to refer to the report on the situation of workers in Palestine and other occupied Arab territories in that respect such as the Syrian Golan and the Sheba Farms in Lebanon. This report refers to the suffering of the workers and the people of Palestine who are under Israeli military occupation and who are subject to the policy of collective punishment, the establishment of military blockades, the construction of this wall of apartheid, and the restrictions that are preventing workers from moving around freely, considered to be one of the essential characteristics of the method used by the Israeli occupying forces against Arab workers, and this has led to an increase in unemployment which has now reached something like 69 per cent, and to a dreadful deterioration in their living conditions.

However, the Report did not mention the following points: Decision No. 9 taken in 1974 concerning discrimination, the violation of trade union rights and freedoms in Palestine, in the Syrian Golan and the farms of Sheba in Lebanon, occupied by Israel, which represents the essential reference text for the mission, and which was not mentioned.

The Israeli occupying authorities have not acted in accordance with international legitimacy. The Report does not mention this flagrant violation, without mentioning the expressions and terms that are not recognized by the Union Nations. The workers are described as being "a community" or sometimes as being simply inhabitants, which is ignoring their Arab identity as true citizens and owners of the land. The Report also ignores the legal status of the Arab city, Al Quds.

We therefore launch an appeal to the Governing Body and the Director-General of the ILO to ensure that all the necessary measures are taken in the framework of the possibilities and principles of the ILO to strengthen the ability of these Arab workers to handle the harmful effects of the occupation, which is totally in contradiction with all forms of human rights.

This will only be possible if the Israeli occupying forces withdraw from all the occupied Arab territories and a Palestinian State is created with Al-Quds as its capital.

As far as the prospects of peace, development and democracy are concerned in our region, we consider as negative the position adopted by the American Administration, which has taken the side of the Israeli occupying authorities by adopting the "Syrian Accountability Act" as it is called. How can a State pass such judgment on another and ask it to be accountable? This would mean that that State considers itself as being the Security Council, the United Nations and the world policeman.

This arrogant approach cannot serve the interests of peace in the region. Everyone knows what is happening in Iraq; we have all seen the human, social and economic tragedies that are going on daily as a result of the occupation there. The international community must mobilize seriously to put an end to this occupation so that the people of Iraq will be able to exercise their right of sovereignty, and freely use their own resources in their own interests, so that they can safeguard their territorial integrity and their national unity.

I would like to indicate the serious steps that have been taken in the area of trade union rights and freedoms in Bahrain and Qatar owing to the creation of national workers' federations, and also in Saudi Arabia and Oman. We welcome these steps and we are ready to collaborate in this area. This also applies to the United Arab Emirates.

I take this opportunity to congratulate the Sudanese people on the signing of the peace agreements between the north and the south of the country, this will allow the whole country to move forward as one and to put an end to the war.

In conclusion, I would like to thank the ILO and the Regional Office for the Arab States in Beirut, which collaborates with us, to serve the objectives of this Organization and its noble mission, and we reaffirm our support for the Organization.

Mr. EVANS *(representative, Trade Union Advisory Committee to the Organisation for Economic Cooperation and Development)*

I am glad to have the opportunity to address the Conference on behalf of the Trade Union Advisory Committee (TUAC) to the OECD. The OECD is a governmental organization grouping industrialized countries, but through the TUAC, and in cooperation with our global union partners, working people have a chance to get their voice heard in those governmental debates.

I would like to focus my remarks on the Director-General's crucially important Report on the follow-up to the Report of the World Commission on the Social Dimension of Globalization. The World Commission report has correctly pointed to the failure to manage globalization so that it serves human needs. It rightly claims that "Key international negotiations are deadlocked, and the international development commitments go largely unfulfilled".

This rings true for many workers who see globalization used as a concept to justify delocalization, reductions in wages and benefits and violations of the ILO's fundamental rights at work. It rings true for the populations in developing countries because, four years into the new millennium, the world is further from achieving the United Nations millennium development goals on poverty reduction than it was when they were agreed.

As the report shows, one billion people in developing countries remain in extreme poverty, and three billion – half the world's population – live on less than two dollars a day.

The World Commission Report is also important because the political fractures and tragedy evident in the Iraq crisis must not be allowed to undermine the multilateral system and what is already inadequate economic and social coordination, as well as basic respect for human rights.

The failure of the Sea Island G8, which ended last night, to even treat the social agenda, although not surprising, is disturbing and must be a warning to all. Similarly, we have important and unfulfilled promises on the table from Monterey and Johannesburg that are in danger of being forgotten.

As the World Commission report shows by its emphasis on coherence, the task is a wider one than convincing ourselves and labour ministers. We have to convince the finance, economics and trade ministers that meeting the challenge of achieving fair globalization is crucial to the very survival of both our societies and our economies.

The report follow-up must be a call to urgent action. I will refer just to one proposal that needs to be followed up – the call for a policy-coherence initiative on growth, trade and employment. Key elements should be as follows.

Firstly, as called for in last year's Director General's Report, we need to double income growth per head from 1 to 2 per cent a year and make sure that this growth generates jobs. The industrialized countries have to take a lead here and re-balance the world economy through coordinated growth and pro-poor policies.

Secondly, we have to make sure that resources are available to fund development. Here, new ideas touched on in the Report need serious consideration, and then to be acted on.

Thirdly, we have to strengthen institutions in the labour market that represent and protect the poor and vulnerable. To start with, that means trade unions and giving the poor the basic rights to organize and bargain collectively.

A coherence initiative is one reason why increased cooperation between the OECD and the ILO is essential. It is an objective that we in TUAC have promoted incessantly at the OECD.

Working with our Global Union partners, TUAC has sought to make the ILO Declaration of Fundamental Principles and Rights at Work a system-wide standard also in the OECD and in the international financial institutions. It is now included in the OECD Development Assistance Committee's Guidelines on Poverty Reduction; in the OECD Guidelines for Multinational Enterprises; and through the OECD's work on trade and labour standards and sustainable development, it is still in the WTO debate.

We have also insisted that all OECD members who are also Members of the ILO have to respect all of the features and, notably, core labour rights. It is for this reason that the TUAC continues to insist that countries, such as the Republic of Korea, which have freedom of association violations, condemned by the ILO, reform their labour legislation to bring it into line with ILO principles. We expect the new government in Korea to act rapidly and live up to their international commitments.

The World Commission Report reinforces the crucial link between poverty reduction and decent work, including respect for human rights at work, the key elements of the ILO's fundamental mandate

– this is now more relevant than ever, given the evident failings of the current model of globalization. We do not have much time to make its recommendations work.

Original Russian: Mr. SHMAKOV *(Workers' delegate, Russian Federation)*

First of all, let me note that the Report presented to us for examination at this 92nd Session of the International Labour Conference gives a full and detailed picture of what the Organization and its Members have accomplished in the last two years.

These last two years have been marked by fairly fruitful cooperation between the ILO and the Russian Federation within the framework of cooperation programmes, which in our view have been, although not entirely, relatively successfully implemented. In these two years, we have begun the first stage of an investigation of the potential social consequences of the Russian Federation joining the World Trade Organization. The results of this investigation did not receive the same reaction from all the social partners. However, the trade unions were more satisfied than the Government and employers' organizations with the conclusions and recommendations of this study. The trade unions were satisfied with the cooperation with the ILO in implementing projects in the area of labour migration, as well as of the monitoring of trade union rights in the Russian Federation.

The Russian trade unions express their complete and full support to ILO activities regarding programmes on decent work the fight against poverty, the elimination of the worst forms of child labour and other forms of forced labour, and attaining gender equality in the workplace, as well as programmes promoting strict observance of trade union rights and freedoms in developing systems of collective bargaining and negotiation.

Unfortunately, in the Russian Federation, as in many other countries of the world, progress in these areas is far from satisfactory. In recent years, the gap between rich and poor countries has become wider. The same could be said of the gap between the rich and poor citizens in almost all the countries of the world. As far as the Russian Federation is concerned, despite the Government's statements about the steady rise in the prosperity of the population, today about 20 per cent of the Russian population receives monetary income below the minimum subsistence level – and yet many of these people work. At the same time, wage arrears are on the rise again. In April, wage arrears amounted to 26 billion roubles, which is around US$1 billion. Approximately 5 million Russian workers do not receive their pay on time. What is more, illegal actions by some unscrupulous employers have forced workers to resort to rather extreme forms of protest, such as the mass hunger strikes that were recently carried out over several days at a Siberian mine.

Under these conditions, the Russian Government continues to try to decrease social benefits. Unemployment insurance has already been abolished, and limitations have been placed on the payment of maternity and sickness benefits. Draft laws are being considered which cause serious concern to Russian trade unions – draft laws on the substitution of pensioner benefits with monetary compensation, and on liberal housing and pension reforms etc. What is more, to please the employers, the Government is suggesting deleting the provisions on a minimum wage, from the Labour Code. When those provisions guarantee workers this important concession in Labour relations.

Still on the subject of trade unions and civil rights, the introduction of new tax rules is equivalent to direct interference in the internal affairs of trade unions and, in fact, creates unlawful strict administrative controls over their activities and puts pressure on them. An imperfect and prejudicial judicial system does not provide much hope of a fair solution to many cases of violations of workers' rights.

At the same time, the Russian Tripartite Commission was only able to resume its activities, after more then four months suspension, as a result of the efforts made by trade unions.

These facts lead us to conclude that there is a new attack being made against trade union rights, but trade unions will not take this lying down, because the Russian Government's deafness to the calls of millions of workers has moved the trade unions to action. Yesterday, on the initiative of the Federation of Independent Trade Unions of Russia, a protest was held across the country involving almost all trade unions. Protesting against the antisocial policies of the Government, the trade unions picketed the buildings of the national and local bodies of executive and legislative power across the country. We will continue to work to overturn these unjust laws. The trade unions will not lose hope that social partnership will allow us to overcome these difficulties, and we are sure that the cooperation between the ILO and the Russian Federation will help considerable in this.

The contents of a recently signed protocol in the development of this cooperation for the coming two years inspired us with great hope.

Original Russian: Mr. HRISTOV *(Workers' delegate, Bulgaria)*

Allow me, on behalf of Bulgarian workers, first of all to congratulate the President and Officers on their election to these important positions, and to express my certainty that the decisions that will be made by the 92nd Session of the International Labour Conference will make an important contribution to increasing opportunities for decent work and pay for workers the globalized world over. Allow me also to congratulate the Director -General, Mr. Juan Somavia, and say that through dialogue we can make the world a better place, and with a unified political and institutional approach we can make globalization a more just and human phenomenon.

In Bulgaria in recent years, there has been a continuing trend towards macroeconomic stability. The statistics show this in terms of real growth of 4.3 per cent in the GDP, a controlled and relatively low inflation rate of 2.4 per cent, a zero budget deficit compared to a projected deficit of 0.7 per cent of GDP, and a fall in unemployment to 13.2 per cent.

We are also seeing some troubling tendencies. The main problem in the Bulgarian economy is a growing deficit in the current account of the balance of payments. This is due to a deteriorating balance of trade – the negative foreign trade balance has reached –13.1 per cent of GDP. We, as trade unions, are also very concerned by the high levels of accumulated business debts, which have reached 122 per cent of GDP. Faced with the threat of bankruptcy, we were forced to stand our ground and, to a certain extent, we can take credit for the adoption, in April this year, of an Act guaranteeing workers earnings in the event of insolvency of the employer.

This Act is also a significant step forward on our path to the European Union, and is in conformity with Part I, Article 25 of the revised European Social Charter and the Protection of Workers' Claims (Employers Insolvency) Convention, 1992 (No. 173).

One of the main challenges ahead is to reach the level of income required of the new accession countries.

Despite a continued increase in the real wage over the last three years (2.8 per cent per year) widespread poverty is still a major problem in Bulgaria. It is a matter of particular concern that a significant proportion of these poor people are working poor.

Representative employers' and workers' organizations at the national level have offered their support to the Government for the introduction of registration of individual employment contracts and minimum thresholds for purposes of social security, according to economic activity and broken down into nine categories of workers, as of the beginning of 2003.

The positive impact of these measures is evidenced by the additional 250 million euros paid into social security funds; over 280,000 workers have made the transition from the grey economy into the formal economy.

Despite the success achieved in certain areas, for the third year running social dialogue is foundering in bureaucracy and ineffectiveness.

At the national level, tripartite collaboration takes the form primarily of consultations, i.e. the Government providing information on its intentions and then implementing them – often without debate and without taking the social partners' views into account.

Despite the fact that we now have 63 industry and branch collective agreements, bipartite dialogue still has a long way to go, especially in terms of its most essential aspect – the setting of a working wage and updating it according to the formula "inflation + labour productivity".

At the same time, to date the Minister of Labour and Social Policy has not availed himself of his right under the Labour Code to extend the coverage of branch and industry agreements or parts of them, at least in cases where positive progress has been achieved.

For the third year running, owing to disagreement by certain employers' organizations, we have not signed a national agreement, which would have provided a framework and basic parameters for concluding collective agreements.

Meanwhile, the Government is attempting to restrict other rights – the right to hold peaceful assemblies, rallies and demonstrations which are also a means of defending labour and trade union rights.

An example of a good decision in our country has been the adoption of the status of refugee, which gives migrants full rights to be integrated in the labour market, together with all the concomitant protections. To enhance their employability, a vocational training centre has been established in the State Agency for Refugees.

In conclusion, I would like to draw your attention to the flagrant and dramatic way in which not only labour rights, but human rights are being flouted in a member State in North Africa, in the case of five nurses and one Palestinian doctor. They were sentenced to death solely on the basis of an extracted confession under duress, totally disregarding the expert conclusions of eminent scientists in the field of one of today's worst problems – AIDS.

As trade unionists, we cannot, and we do not have the right, to remain indifferent to the fate of these working people who are from our own country.

We are convinced of their innocence and, in our efforts to obtain their acquittal and a verdict of not guilty, we have already received the support of our brothers and sisters in the worldwide trade union movement, for which we are deeply grateful.

From this eminent rostrum, I would like to call on all governments, employers' organizations and representatives of civil society organizations to do their part, whether through their institutions or informally, to obtain a review of the death sentence passed on these six medical workers and demand full guarantees of a fair legal process, in full observance of fundamental human rights, dignity and international legal standards.

Original Arabic: Mr. JRAD *(representative, Union of Workers of the Arab Maghreb)*

On behalf of the trade unions which are members of the Union of Workers of the Arab Maghreb it is an honour to congratulate the President. I hope that the deliberations of this session of the International Labour Conference will be crowned with success. I also take this opportunity to congratulate the Director-General, Mr. Juan Somavia, on his excellent Report on the situation of migrant workers. He did not simply analyse migratory movements in the era of globalization, but also stressed the importance of social dialogue, between the North and the South in order to find solutions to migration issues in conformity with the international Conventions guaranteeing the rights of migrant workers.

Today, migration has become a world dilemma, particularly since certain international actors have tried to sow hatred among peoples after the events of 11 September and the war in Iraq. It is this feeling of hatred between the population of host countries and immigrants which has prepared the ground for political dogmas that spread the theory of the clash of civilizations and that produce reactions leading to cultural isolation.

I would also like to grasp this opportunity of saluting on behalf of all the trade unions from the Maghreb countries, all the peace-loving forces in the world who brave the campaigns which tarnish the image of the Arab and Muslim world and the Maghrebian community in Europe, who reject this equation of immigration and terrorism and who remain attached to the principle, of freedom and tolerance in the face of racism and fanaticism. We appreciate the initiatives taken by the ILO to protect migrant workers' rights and we call on the Organization to support the efforts of trade unions to set up a Euro-Mediterranean observatory on migration.

The efforts made by the ILO to strengthen the tripartite dialogue which is the best guarantee of a better balance between economic growth and progress are essential and praiseworthy. Nevertheless, there are still many obstacles to development, such as rising unemployment levels, greater job insecurity and the widening gulf between north and south.

While we approve of the report of the World Commission on the Social Dimension of Globalization, we invite the ILO to redouble its efforts to help the social partners, especially those in the Maghreb and in other Arab countries to arrive at a tripartite agreement through social dialogue and closer collaboration between the International Labour Organization and regional trade union organizations.

Fighting injustice in all forms and encouraging dialogue between civilizations and cultures are the main focuses around which peace may be achieved. Regional conflicts must be resolved in keeping with international law. The suffering endured today by the Palestinian people and the Palestinian workers who are weighed down by the yoke of Israeli occupation is very serious and is evidenced by the economic blockade and the building of the separation wall, the destruction of infrastructure and homes, the murdering of civilians and the assassination of political leaders. We must set up more support programmes to assist and aid the productive forces in Palestine to rebuild the infrastructure of Palestinian society which has been destroyed by the Israeli army.

Our Union strongly condemns terrorism and appeals to all parties to denounce the state-sponsored terrorism perpetrated by the occupying forces and to work for the establishment of an independent Palestinian Sate and withdrawal from the occupied territories in the Syrian Arab Republic and the Lebanon.

The situation in Iraq represents a major challenge for the future of the country, particularly in the face of the war crimes committed against civilians and the scandal of the torture of Iraqi prisoners which have shocked the world. This occupation needs to be brought to an end as soon as possible and Iraqi workers must be helped to establish an independent trade union movement and to regain their national sovereignty.

The role of the ILO is essential in strengthening the credibility of the United Nations and providing assistance to those countries affected by the occupation. The ILO can also contribute to building international relations based on justice, peace and solidarity between peoples.

Original Vietnamese: Ms. CU *(Workers' delegate, Viet Nam)*

First, on behalf of the workers and trades unions of Viet Nam, we wish to convey our congratulations to the President and wish the 92nd Session of the International Labour Conference every success.

The Vietnamese workers and trade unions highly value the Director General's Report, *ILO programme implementation 2002-03,* and the report of the Chairperson of the Governing Body. We share with you the evaluations and recommendations made by the report of the World Commission on the Social Dimension of Globalization. We also share the views in the Report entitled *A fair globalization: The role of the ILO,* presented by the Director-General at this session of the Conference. Globalization creates a lot of opportunities but it also poses challenges for the poor and less developed countries. It requires the world community, in which the ILO plays a key role, to make every effort to make globalization a drive for development, to bring about benefits and opportunities for all. Globalization should be linked to the Decent Work Agenda and the Declaration on Fundamental Principles and Rights at Work.

The workers and trade unions of Viet Nam highly value the efforts and successes made by the ILO. We have all recognized, in recent years, that the ILO has further focused on issues of great concern to the world trade unions and workers in general, and the Vietnamese trade unions and workers in particular.

In Viet Nam, the Viet Nam General Confederation of Labour (VGCL), currently uniting more than 4 million members from all economic sectors, has been recognized by the national Constitution and by laws and regulations, and is going to celebrate the 75th anniversary of its foundation.

The VGCL actively participated in the formulation of the legal system, including the trade union and labour laws and regulations, the social insurance law, the salary reform, the law on unemployment, the national programme on vocational training and the active labour market, poverty alleviation, fighting against discrimination, child labour and promoting sound industrial relations. In practice, the right to trade union membership and the right to collective bargaining has been further enforced and executed. Over the past five years, from 1998 to 2003, the VGCL has formed 10,400 primary trade unions with over 850,000 members in the private sector. Much attention has been paid to collective negotiation and collective agreements. The ratio of collective agreement coverage currently reaches 80 per cent in the state sector, over 30 per cent in the foreign investment sector and over 15 per cent in the domestic private sector.

It is our great pleasure to note that the cooperation relationship between the ILO and Viet Nam in general, and the trade unions of Viet Nam in particular, is achieving positive outcomes. The ILO sent its representative to attend the 9th National Congress of the Vietnamese Trade Unions last October. The National Congress has set forth the overall objectives of the Vietnamese trade unions for the next five years. These are to build a strong working class, to participate in the management of the State and society, to defend and take care of the lawful and legitimate rights and interests of the workers and public servants, to develop membership and set up trade unions in every economic sector to achieve the target of recruiting one million more members in the period from 2004 to 2008, to upgrade the competencies and skills of the trade union activists, to renovate the content and methods of activity of the trade unions aimed at building strong trade unions and to expand and promote international cooperation.

In recent years, the ILO has coordinated with the VGCL to conduct important activities, such as formulating a national commitment on implementation of the Decent Work Agenda, training trade unionists on collective bargaining and combating child labour.

Last April, the VGCL hosted the Asia-Europe Trade Union Forum with the participation of various trade union representatives from the two continents and the ILO representative, with a view to promoting the social pillar within the Asia-Europe cooperation framework and further revitalizing the cooperation between the two continents, for the sake of the workers.

In past years, the workers and trade unions of Viet Nam have received constant support and assistance from the ILO and friendly trade union organizations the world over. We would like to take this opportunity to express our sincere thanks for this valuable and effective support and assistance and our hope to receive further support from the ILO and from other friendly trade union organizations.

Original Arabic: Mr. AL RABAIE *(Employers' delegate, Oman)*

In the name of God, the Merciful the Compassionate! It is an honour for me to address you on behalf of the employers of the private sector in the Sultanate of Oman. It is also an honour to congratulate the President on his election to preside over this session of the Conference. We are convinced that his experience and wisdom will enable him to ensure success for this Conference so that we may achieve our objectives.

I would also like to express my thanks and appreciation to the Director-General, Mr. Juan Somavia, and to the Governing Body for the programmes that they have proposed for their activities to strengthen and guarantee protection and social justice and to improve social dialogue between the social partners.

We would like to welcome the support provided to my country by the Organization in the framework of bilateral cooperation and to pay tribute to the Regional Office in Beirut for its efforts and technical support.

The Sultanate of Oman carries out consultations and coordination with the social partners to develop labour and economic legislation that is in conformity with the relevant international conventions and protocols.

In this respect, we have promulgated a new Labour Code, No. 25/2003, which contains a title on the establishment of tripartite committees in private sector enterprises. These laws are aimed at strengthening social dialogue between the social partners and realizing social justice in our country, as well as achieving a balance between the social partners.

The situation of Arab workers in Palestine and the other occupied Arab territories prompts us to mention the efforts made by the Director-General, which we duly appreciate and commend. It is essential to continue to help the employers and workers in Palestine through the Palestinian Fund for Employment and Social Protection and to do everything necessary to provide them with technical assistance.

We also hope that stability will return to Iraq, so that the social partners can play their part in building prosperity in the country and creating job opportunities so that the Iraqi people can enjoy well-being and peace.

Conflict and war in the Middle East have swelled the ranks of the unemployed and fomented instability. Individual earnings have dropped and the number of people below the poverty line who are unable to meet their most basic needs has increased. The time has come to find appropriate ways to ensure that these workers can live in decency and dignity. But it is also essential to find a solution to the Palestinian-Israeli conflict through withdrawal from the Palestinian territories and the creation of an independent Palestinian State.

The issue of the social dimension of globalization and the Director-General's Report on the subject bear witness to the importance of the role of the ILO in furthering the cause of social justice. We are convinced that the Organization will be able to design policies and a strategic framework that will enable employers and workers to reap the benefits of globalization through dialogue between all the social partners.

To conclude, I would like to thank the President for all his efforts and to express the hope that peace, security and prosperity will prevail in the world, for the common good.

Original Spanish: Mr. RICCI MUADI *(Employers' delegate, Guatemala)*

I would like to commend the initiative taken by the Director-General to discuss an issue which deserves our full attention: looking at globalization in the light of a universal aspiration, that of justice. In order to do so, we have to begin by ridding the issue of ideological positions and placing it within its proper context, which is as one more step in an ongoing quest for progress and civilization. To do this, we are also going to have to focus on the fact that the effects of change bring with them instability and, unavoidably, resistance from those who feel threatened by such changes.

From my point of view, the main concerns felt within the world of work arise from the loss of jobs or the lack of job creation. This is a justified and legitimate concern although its causes go beyond the phenomenon of globalization; its roots go deep into a history of errors of all shapes and forms being committed in many countries –especially the least developed countries – such as corruption, populism, poor public administration, weak institutions, a lack of national strategies, ideological wars, etc.

The problem is a serious one and goes beyond the expertise of our Organization. Nevertheless, our Organization can, and should, play a central role in the specific area of quality job creation. We must concentrate all of our efforts in achieving this goal, and this is where the ILO should make its presence felt at the global level.

Other activities, including standard-setting activities, will no longer have meaning if there are no formal jobs for which such activities can be developed and to which standards can be applied.

I would propose that our resources be concentrated on programmes for creating jobs, without forgetting that it is vital to create an appropriate environment in all countries and region to facilitate private capital investment, which is the only way to create decent jobs in a sustainable way. For this reason it is essential to support the institutions and governance of countries. In this struggle partners from both within and outside of the United Nations system need to come forward whose objective is the strengthening of democratic institutions, economic and social development and poverty eradication.

All activities conducted by this Organization and other international institutions must take into account the differences in the current stages in development in each and every country. This is a reality which, very often, for reasons of self-interest, is ignored by those who feel that practices they themselves once carried out are now unacceptable. Instead of trying to justify these practices, we should be changing them in step with the levels of development in different countries.

At the same time, within the international organizations recognition must be given to a principle that is widely accepted in the business world, that of specialization. This means that although all international organizations must work in the same direction, each one should have its expertise, whilst complementing each other in trying to achieve common goals, the main one being poverty eradication.

In this struggle against poverty, the role of the ILO is fundamental since it is responsible for finding concrete solutions to foster the creation of better and more jobs. Lastly, there is a worrying fact that cannot have gone unnoticed by this assembly owing to its serious implications for the credibility of the supervisory mechanism of the ILO. I am referring to the selection of countries whose cases are examined by the committee on the Application of Standards. For years we have been pointing out an imbalance, which is tilted against Latin America, and more specifically Central America. As we have said, this could be due to interests which do not correspond to the purposes or objectives of this house.

Unfortunately, this year we have seen these attitudes confirmed. It is unacceptable that from a subregion of seven countries, four of those countries are under examination, when there are no technical reasons to justify this. As has already been said by a spokesperson of one of the groups represented in this room, there are criteria which have more to do with trade agreements than labour standards. This is unacceptable.

We cannot allow our supervisory mechanisms to be manipulated in this way; this will only lead to the loss of their credibility.

Original French: Mr. SEMOV *(Employers' adviser and substitute delegate, Bulgaria)*

Over the past year, Bulgarian employers have continued to participate dynamically in the tripartite partnership, as well as in bipartite social dialogue, in the interests of the harmonious development of economic relations in the Republic of Bulgaria.

This joint effort on the part of the social partners has permitted the attainment of many true successes. The tripartite working group has formulated the most recent modifications of the Labour Code specifically to implement European Directives in Bulgarian labour legislation. The tripartite group also elaborated a draft law on salary guarantees in the event of bankruptcy in enterprises. This text has been adopted by the Parliament and the signing of the agreement on tripartite cooperation to improve working conditions in enterprises crowned the entry into force, on 27 December 2003, of the occupational health and safety act.

Currently, there are 63 labour agreements operating at the sectoral and branch levels and the scope of collective agreements within sectors of activity in our economy and in enterprises is around is 38 per cent in total. 29 bipartite agreements were signed in 43 sectors and branches of the economy in 2003; in 2004, the number of bipartite agreements concluded was 44 in 50 sectors and branches. Nevertheless, we regret that this year the national tripartite agreement on the content of sectoral and branch collective agreements has yet to be signed.

The effective beginning of this year's activities of the Economic and Social Council of Bulgaria was a great success for the social partners in particular, and civil society in general. This national body, which was constituted in 2001, includes representatives of employers, trade unions and civil society, in all their diversity.

New tripartite negotiations on issues relating to social and economic activities in Bulgaria began last month.

Unfortunately, however, there are clauses which were negotiated between representative organizations of the employers, on the one hand, and of the workers, on the other, which have yet to be implemented. This is the case particularly for the unfulfilled commitments regarding the progressive redistribution of social charges between employers and employees, which continue to weigh more heavily on the former. The employers currently cover 75 per cent of such charges.

The Bulgarian employers should like to pay tribute to the efforts of the Parliament and the Bulgarian Government in signing the Seafarers' Annual Leave with Pay Convention, 1976 (No. 146), the Recruitment and Placement of Seafarers Convention, 1996 (No. 179), the Repatriation of Seafarers Convention (Revised), 1987 (No. 166), and the Seafarers' Welfare Convention, 1987 (No. 163). However, we would wish for a better understanding as regards the need to ratify the Private Employment Agencies Convention, 1997 (No. 181), as well as strong mobilization in favour of applying the Private Employment Agencies Recommendation, 1997 (No. 188), Part III, regarding cooperation between the public employment service and private employment agencies.

As regards the recommendation presented in the report of the World Commission on the Social Dimension of Globalization on strengthening subregional and regional cooperation as a key instrument in developing a system for managing globalization, the Bulgarian employers support the proposal of holding, at the end of 2004, in Sofia, a subregional tripartite conference for south-eastern Europe on the social dimensions of globalization, with the participation of the ILO Director-General.

The Bulgarian employers also share the view that the Human Resources Development Recommendation, 1975 (No. 150) is no longer in keeping with the times. Thus, the Bulgarian employers in the tripartite delegation will support the proposal of the International Labour Conference regarding the directing of a new Recommendation to replace the Human Resources Development Recommendation, 1975 (No. 150), which was adopted in 1975.

In conclusion, we should like to express our hope that the work of the 92nd Session of the International Labour Conference will contribute to promoting greater respect of the ILO by governments and the social partners, not only fostering support for the ILO as an important promoter of international labour standards, but also as a guarantor of their application. The ratification of international labour Conventions is necessary, but it is also necessary for us to ensure the monitoring of such application on the national level.

Finally, allow me to draw the attention of all democratic countries here present to the very sad fact of the unfair detention, for five years now, of five Bulgarian doctors in the Libyan Arab Jamahiriya.

Despite their innocence, which has been proven categorically by the world's most renowned specialists, these five Bulgarians have just been condemned to death.

We demand justice for these innocent Bulgarians in the Libyan Arab Jamahiriya.

Mr. SHENOY *(Government delegate, India)*

I join the other distinguished speakers to congratulate the President on his unanimous election as the President of the 92nd Session of the International Labour Conference, which is taking place in Geneva. I would also like to take this opportunity to place on record the appreciation of the Government of India for the very comprehensive and informative

Report of the Director-General of the ILO, Mr. Juan Somavia, *ILO Programme implementation 2002-03*.

My delegation compliments the ILO for the improvements achieved under the different ILO strategic objectives vis-à-vis the Decent Work Agenda. It is our considered view that, in order to attain decent work, every potential worker should be given the opportunity to work in a reasonably safe place and it is only after this that measures conforming to other decent working conditions would be possible.

Mahatma Gandhi said that for the hungry man, God can come only in the form of food. We, therefore, are always in favour of according the highest priority to the employment sector. We feel that the success of the other strategic objectives is contingent upon this employment sector alone. We suggest that massive efforts should be made in the employment sector to generate employment, and impart training to unskilled workers. The ILO's approach to employment intensive investment should continue.

We also feel that socio-economic activities like child labour should be tackled with all the seriousness they deserve. However, they are only symptoms of a greater malady, which requires a concerted effort by all social partners and the ILO.

I am happy to inform this august body that in 250 districts of India, we are implementing national child labour projects at the cost of US$135 million. In addition to that, we are contributing US$20 million, along with the United States' contribution of US$20 million for the Indus Project in 20 districts of India.

The success of the ILO's campaign for ratification of the ILO core or fundamental Conventions is laudable. However, we feel that there is a need for better cooperation with the national governments with a view to identifying obstacles in the process of ratification.

I refer to the Freedom of Association and Protection of the Right to Organise Convention, 1948 (No 87), and the Right to Organise and Collective Bargaining Convention, 1949 (No. 98). There are some technical reasons why some of the largest democracies and some of the countries which have a large worker population could not ratify these Conventions. Perhaps we can have a protocol to introduce flexibilities into these Conventions so that they become ratifiable. India is fully committed to the principles enshrined in the ILO core or fundamental Conventions. The right to equality is a fundamental right under the Constitution of India. The various provisions contained in the core Conventions are being implemented in the country for the benefit of our workers through national laws and development programmes. We, however, ratify an ILO Convention only when our national laws and practices are fully brought into conformity with the provisions of the Conventions in question.

Ms. THEODORSEN *(Workers' adviser and substitute delegate, Norway)*

As a representative of the workers of Norway, I congratulate the President and the Director-General on the reports presented, as well as on all the other good work of the ILO this last year. The excellent work performed by the World Commission on the Social Dimension of Globalization, and the report presented, have really given the ILO a new dimension on the world stage and the workers of Norway look forward to seeing the follow-up of the recommendations.

Among all the good work done, the Norwegian trade union movement is especially satisfied that the ILO has also this year shown its great concern for workers in the occupied Arab territories by publishing the special Report about the economic and social situation in the region. It is extremely important that the ILO continues to keep a high profile in this work by both documenting and assessing the situation the workers and their families are living under, as well as giving political and moral support and financial assistance. The Report documents how poverty and unemployment continue to grip Palestinian communities to the extent that people are able to survive only with large-scale external assistance. There will never be peace and prosperity in the region without the end of the occupation. Only then will Palestinian workers be secured a decent job and live in peace in their independent Palestinian State beside the State of Israel.

I also appreciate the emphasis put on the gender dimension in the Report. Palestinian women are facing enormous obstacles and challenges. They have to try to keep their families together in an abnormal life situation. At the same time, they are marginalized on the labour market. It is my hope that the ILO will continue to present this type of objective information as well as promoting dialogue between Palestinian and Israeli workers. Financial assistance to Palestinian workers and their families must be given the highest priority. I hope there will be a special session next year on this issue. There are too many unsolved burning questions. The ILO has an important role to play in this process.

Coming back to the question of gender in general, I want to emphasize the importance of getting better representation of women at all levels in the ILO. It is very disappointing to see that neither the workers nor the employers gives this question the attention it deserves. The representation of women at this year's session of the Conference is not much better than it was last year. Only 15.5 per cent of the delegates are women. The Norwegian trade union movement really appreciates the Director-General's concrete approach to the question by suggesting a 30 per cent positive action policy for future sessions. I can promise him our support.

Both Norway and Sweden now have women as trade union presidents. The impact on gender-related questions can be easily observed. There is more focus on questions of equal pay for work of equal value than before. More attention is given to issues concerning part-time and low-paid work, women-related health and safety measures, pension consequences, etc. We really do look forward to cooperating with the Director-General on this issue.

Among other challenges, it is more important than ever before to be aware of, and let the work in the ILO, be guided by the special characteristics of the ILO and its core function. The practice of tripartism must not be diminished. The social partners are an inalienable part of the ILO. Their contribution in all of the ILO's work must not be underestimated. Social dialogue is a core activity and must be an integrated part of all of the ILO's work in whichever sector it is.

The same can be said about the standard-setting activities. There is unanimous support in our country for the promotion of labour standards, not just labour standards in the core Conventions, but for labour standards in most of the existing Conventions. There must be even more emphasis put on this work in the future. We need to see new standards and we need to see more ratification campaigns on passed Conventions, whether it be on migration or maternity protection or other burning issues.

The normative mandate of the ILO must always be the guiding tool in all the activities of the Organization.

(The Conference adjourned at 7 p.m.)

CONTENTS

Page

Twelfth sitting

Ratification of an international labour Convention by Mauritius 1

Reports of the Chairperson of the Governing Body and of the Director-General:
Discussion *(cont.)* 1

Speakers: Mr. Marius, M. Kozik, Mr. Al Ansari, Mr. Naghiyev, Mr. Barimah,
Ms. Ngindinwa, Mr. Tabani, Ms. Sto. Tomas, Mr. Solari Saavedra, Mr. Trogen,
Ms. Menkerios, Mr. Tomada, Mr. Ross Leal, Mr. Togari, Mr. Hached, Mrs. Sinjela,
Mr. Louh, Mr. Valerio, Mr. Martínez Molina, Mr. Okuda, Mr. Djilani, Mr. Mammadov,
Mr. Peet, Mr. Paiva, Mr. Van Vuuren, Mr. Palacio Betancourt, Mr. Musenge,
Mr. Van Leeuwen.

Reports of the Chairperson of the Governing Body and of the Director-General:
Discussion *(cont.)* 23

Speakers: Mr. Al-Rizaiqi, Mr. Vaccari Neto, Ms. Poncini, Mr. Georgetti, Mr. Rampak,
Mr. Le, Mr. Ortega Nadal, Mr. Keira, Mr. Techateeravat, Mr. Soriano, Mr. Batbayar
Mr. Kassey, Mr. Kapuya, Mr. Boisson, Mr. Edström, Mr. Halkin, Mr. Kusano,
Mr. Gurdián Castellón, Ms. Morava, Mr. Mehbaliyev, Mr. Trabelsi, Mr. Magaya,
Mr. Vardanyan, Mr. Monges Espínola, Mr. Daer, Mr. Djemam, Mr. Evans,
Mr. Shmakov, Mr. Hristov, Mr. Jrad, Ms. Cu, Mr. Al Rabaie, Mr. Ricci Muadi,
Mr. Semov, Mr. Shenoy, Ms. Theodorsen.

No. 15 – Monday, 14 June 2004

International Labour Conference

Provisional Record 19

Ninety-second Session, Geneva, 2004

Fourteenth sitting
Monday 14 June 2004, 10.00 a.m.
Presidents: Mr. Ray Guevara, Mr. Wade

REPORTS OF THE CHAIRPERSON OF THE GOVERNING BODY AND OF THE DIRECTOR-GENERAL: DISCUSSION (*CONT.*)

Original Spanish: The PRESIDENT *(Mr. Ray GUEVARA)*

We shall now resume our discussion of two Reports of the Chairperson of the Governing Body and of the Director-General.

Original Spanish: Mr. FERNÁNDEZ *(Workers' delegate, Uruguay)*

The Uruguayan Workers' delegation would like to congratulate the President on his election.

We agree with what the Director-General's Report says regarding the fact that the benefits of globalization do not reach enough people and that it is not a question of stopping globalization, but rather of managing and structuring it with fair standards.

Humanity has always dreamt of a world that can use its technological progress, as well as its progress in the areas of information and communication, to grant everyone access to better living conditions and human development. However, up to now, globalization has resulted in the exact opposite of this. In Latin America, retrograde trends caused by inequality in the way wealth has been distributed, have resulted in an ever more obvious trend of the wealth being enjoyed by the few, while the majority of men and women on our continent do not have access to adequate living conditions and personal development, leading them to poverty and marginalization.

The Director-General points out that very little has been done to strengthen local communities and markets where people live, and where, given the opportunity, they would like to stay.

Uruguay is a very clear example of this trend. In the last few years, emigration of qualified young workers, who could not find appropriate jobs in their own country, has had negative effects not only on the country, which is losing its most highly-trained citizens, but also on families who are affected by the loss of their members, and by the impact on society which creates the potential for problems in the future.

Decent work as a global objective can be attained if there is coherent national and international policy promoted at all levels. This can be achieved only through dialogue. The social partners and society as a whole have the right to demand that their voices be heard when national and international policies are being developed; whether or not the objective is achieved will depend on their participation.

As workers, we play an important role in this. Through social dialogue and particularly through collective bargaining, our job is to build this society. Collective bargaining is an essential and irreplaceable tool in building solid, democratic societies in which these values can become reality. However, in many countries – including Uruguay – this does not happen.

The International Labour Conventions Nos. 81, 87, 98, 151 and 154 have been ratified by Uruguay. They promote collective bargaining in both the public and private sector, they protect workers who exercise their rights; and they commit governments to fulfil actively the obligations set out in these standards.

However, reality is very far from that. We are watching with concern the breakdown in mutually agreed procedures for reaching agreement between workers and employers on working conditions. There are currently no negotiations. Some companies go unpunished when they fire groups of workers for trying to form a trade union. The Government stays out of such situations, even seeming to agree with this behaviour. The same applies to civil servants who cannot negotiate their working conditions. The Government itself does not negotiate in some cases while in others it concludes agreements only to break them later.

It is not acceptable that international labour Conventions like the ones I have mentioned are ratified, when, faced with concrete situations, the Government then fails to take on any commitment to ensure compliance with them in real life.

Uruguayan workers have always demanded compliance with Convention No. 131. This would lead, through negotiations, to a minimum wage. However, the Government refuses to comply with this Convention, although it has committed itself to do so in this Organization.

The ILO has launched a major campaign to eradicate child labour and this has received all our support. But if the Government does not promote appropriate conditions for access to education and food for children, as well as fair wages and decent working conditions for their parents, it will be difficult to achieve success.

We would like to conclude by drawing attention to a number of aspects we regard as fundamental.

Social dialogue is an essential means of consolidating democratic states and thus ensuring better and fairer development for its citizens, but that will not be possible without strong trade unions which can act and develop freely, and which can participate in genuine collective bargaining. The ILO has an essential role to play in making this possible, not only by providing technical assistance in creating and consolidating the right conditions, but also in detecting and monitoring non-compliance by governments. As the Director-General says in his Report, if we do not put our own houses in order, if we do not comply with the provisions that we have already agreed on, decent work and a just society will be no more than a pipe dream and will never become reality, and indeed, will continue to deteriorate the social situation. Let us hope that ways can be found of correcting this situation, for the good of everyone.

Original Spanish: Mr. INFANTE *(Workers' delegate, Venezuela)*

I should like first of all to congratulate the President on his election to preside over this session of the International Labour Conference. I represent here, for the first time, the workers of Venezuela at this, at this, the greatest participated body of the ILO; the only body at which we, the workers, can voice our opinions, thanks to the rotation agreement of delegates which we, the workers' organizations of our beloved Latin-American country, Venezuela, have also signed for the first time.

Allow me to say that my organization, which belongs to the Latin American Central of Workers (CLAT) and the World Confederation of Labour (WCL), is totally independent from all other national institutions, be they government, entrepreneur or social institutions, and is truly committed to the needs and aspirations of workers.

For this reason, we share the concerns expressed in the Reports of the Chairperson of the Governing Body and of the Director-General of the ILO concerning the application of the Conventions ratified by Governments in 1998. Furthermore, I wish to make it quite clear that in Venezuela many of these fundamental ILO Conventions are still being violated by governmental bodies and by the private sector.

The increase in unemployment, the growing loss of purchasing power of the workers and the worsening of the collective bargaining situation are all things that can only be overcome by the necessary consolidation of democracy, which is the aspiration of all workers and the general public.

It would be wrong to state that these are new problems; as it would be to say that we are in the process of overcoming them. What is even worse is the fact that we live in a country that has an enormous natural wealth which should create better working conditions, and more humane and decent working conditions for all workers.

We should not forget that the Report of the Director-General clearly states that, work is the one and only solution to the problem of social injustice. Thus, the economy must be able to create investment opportunities, entrepreneurial spirit, jobs and a sustainable standard of living.

Lastly, representing Venezuelan workers, I should like to take this opportunity to express our rejection and condemnation of the shameful and barbarous practices of the Government of Burma, where workers are subjected to the wickedness of forced labour, and sacred human rights are violated. I should also like to express our criticism and rejection of the terrible way in which trade union leaders are dealt with in our sister country, Columbia; they are being physically eliminated. This is the way in which these social warriors, who defend the sacred right to organize, are being silenced.

Mr. OLA *(Minister of Labour, India)*

At the outset, let me record my sincere appreciation to the Director-General of the ILO for the detailed and far-sighted Report entitled *A fair globalization: The role of the ILO*. The Report seeks to make globalization a positive power for all peoples through a fair share of existing resources. I am pleased that in this context the World Commission has quoted Mahatma Gandhi, the Father of our Nation, and I quote "There is enough for everybody's need but there cannot be enough for everybody's greed."

While globalization has created exceptional opportunities, it has also created social disparities and individual insecurities. We agree with the ILO that markets without rules for free and equal access would lead to further division within and between the countries. The greatest challenge before all of us is how to guide growth in the global economy and to ensure the development of society at large with a human face.

In order to achieve the global goal of decent work, we have to ensure the systematic global governance based on democracy, social equity and effective participation of all social partners. In India, we have special programmes for workers in the organized as well as the unorganized sectors.

We feel that suggestions in the Report about agreement between multinational companies and a global employment forum will be impractical at the national level. We therefore strongly feel that all issues relating to labour and decent work should be addressed within the existing ILO framework only.

In India, we are still grappling with the issues concerning unemployment and poverty alleviation. We are sensitive to the needs of our people and are committed to providing them with fair opportunities and decent work. However, at this stage of development, we are not in a position to support the concept of a common socio-economic base standard across the globe but we are agreeable to such a concept for all communities within the country.

On cross-border movement, we support the recommendations of the Report for an effective multilateral framework for international migration.

I conclude with a quotation of Pt. Jawaharlal Nehru, the first Prime Minister of independent India: "[Our] ambition ... has been to wipe every tear from every eye. That may be beyond us, but as long as there are tears and sufferings, so long our work will not be over."

Original Arabic: Mr. MAATOUGH *(Secretary, General's People's Committee of Labour Force, Training and Employment, Libyan Arab Jamahiriya)*

I would like to congratulate the President of the Conference on the confidence placed in him, and I hope that it would be possible to achieve all the objectives of the Conference. I would like also to thank the Director-General and the different departments of the ILO for their efforts to ensure that the Organization will achieve the best possible results and meet the aspirations of everybody.

The Director-General's Report is very important in that it emphasizes the importance of decent work at a time when the international system affects all countries. The liberalization of trade and the quest for improved quality have consequences for workers and are resulting in difficulties at the social level, foremost of which is the increased cost of social services such as education and health care, as well as loss of employment for large numbers of people.

The ILO has tried to correct this kind of imbalance by holding conferences and seminars. We would like to emphasize the importance of workers getting a fair share of their production. The Libyan Arab Jamahiriya has contributed to this, and has implemented effective employment policies and enacted a number of laws stressing the importance of social dialogue, ending forced labour, combating the worst forms of child labour, and providing education for all citizens. We are now trying to develop strategies to maximize our national resources.

The Libyan Arab Jamahiriya has tried to provide decent work for women workers by establishing small and medium-sized enterprises and by supporting workers' efforts so as to enable them to enjoy the conditions envisaged for them. It has also cooperated with other countries in Africa to achieve these objectives.

The Libyan Arab Jamahiriya has adopted a policy aimed at achieving equality for men and women, in particular in the areas of employment and education. The number of female workers has increased at all levels of education, notably pre-university and higher education.

Participation by women in the labour force has reached something like 29 per cent, and many women are completing higher education and holding down important posts.

Many NGOs and other associations are led by women, who are very active in all areas.

The situation in the occupied Arab territories is completely contrary to the aspirations of peoples to international law and to international labour standards.

The occupying forces are destroying houses and productive units. They are killing women and children, while the international community is unable to end or condemn these practices.

The International Labour Organization is trying to do something, but has no influence over the occupying forces. On this occasion, we appeal to the Organization to take the practical steps that are needed to establish the rights of all the Palestinian people.

Our country is extremely concerned with the events in Iraq. There is no justification for what is currently happening there. Serious violations of international law are being perpetrated and we believe that the first step to work achieving stability in Iraq is to accelerate the process of handing over power to the people of Iraq within the framework of international law so that they can use their oil resources in accordance with their own interests.

I would like to conclude by thanking you very much for listening. I wish this session of this Conference every success.

Mr. SAY *(Under Secretary of State, Ministry of Social Affairs, Labour, Vocational Training and Youth Rehabilitation, Cambodia)*

On behalf of the Ministry of Social Affairs, Labour, Vocational Training and Youth Rehabilitation in the Kingdom of Cambodia, I would like to thank the Director-General of the International Labour Office very much for inviting the Cambodian delegation to participate in this very important 92nd International Session of the Labour Conference today and the Chairman of the general session of the Conference for allowing me to represent the Cambodian delegation to make some remarks on progress in the field of labour in the Kingdom of Cambodia.

I would like to take this opportunity to inform this session of the Conference about progress in the field of labour, especially the implementation of the provisions of the Labour Law concerning the fundamental principles and rights at work of the Kingdom of Cambodia as follows:

– the Labour Law enacted in 1997 has been enforced by publishing and disseminating
the books of law, conducting training courses under the provisions of the law and virtual guidance on the provisions of the law according to each case which has occurred;

– issuance of ministerial orders to support implementation of the law has played a very important role in protecting the rights and benefits of both parties involved in industrial relations between employers and workers. Most of the ministerial order drafts have been consulted in the Labour Advisory Committee prior to being issued by the MOSALVY;

– the Arbitration Council was established in 2002, started working from May 2003 onwards and has contributed actively in labour disputes settlement;

– the permanent monitoring of the implementation of labour law provisions and regulations has maintained industrial relations harmonization between all parties, employers and workers. From early 2001 and 2002, with ILO technical assistance, two projects have been implemented with the purpose of improving working conditions in Cambodia's textile and apparel sector in order to eliminate discrimination in employment, improve the fundamental principles and rights at work and strengthen the labour disputes resolution. The first is in the Garment Sector Working Conditions Improvement Project and secondly, the Labour Dispute Resolution Project;

– *the Synthesis Report on the Working Conditions Situation in Cambodia's Garment Sector*, based on the findings of independent monitoring, indicates clearly that there is no evidence proving forced labour, discrimination and child labour in this sector;

– the improvement of the effectiveness of human resources development has been implemented and enhanced by upgrading the trainers, building the criteria of the training centres up to standard, formulating skill standards according to the skills of the training courses and the conducting skill testing and certification.

Human resources training is entering a new stage and not only to increase the number of courses or schools or centres. It is important to take into account the qualifications of the schools or training centres and curriculum according to the actual needs of the markets.

I also would like to take this opportunity to inform this session of the Conference that the law on social security schemes for persons defined by the provisions of the Labour Law has been enacted by the National Assembly of the Kingdom of Cambodia and promulgated on 25 September 2002.

The social security schemes defined by this Law are: a pension scheme to provide old-age benefit, invalidity benefit and survivor's benefit; occupational risk to provide employment injury benefit and occupational disease benefit; other possibilities shall be subsequently determined by subdecree based on the actual situation of the national economy.

Last, but not least, I would like to extend my deepest thanks to the ILO that has provided us with efficient and timely technical assistance. I wish this session of the Conference success.

Original Portuguese: **Mr. SEVENE** *(Minister of Labour, Mozambique)*

On behalf of the Government of Mozambique, myself and my delegation, I would like to salute all participants in this 92nd Session and I also congratulate the Chairperson and other members of the panel for their election to guide us through this session of the Conference. I send special greeting to the Director-General, Mr. Juan Somavia, for his commitment and endeavours towards reducing unemployment and poverty alleviation, actions that became clearly evident in his excellent Report.

Mozambique longs for a new world based on justice, peace and social harmony and is committed to this noble task aimed at creating conditions to allow people to enjoy a better life by providing them with fair and decent work.

We are deeply delighted to find these aspects in the Report of the Director-General, which is a starting point, during this session, for engaging in debates related to the social aspects of development policies. We also have attentively analysed the report of the World Commission on the Social Dimension of Globalization and we are pleased to congratulate the respective members, the Presidents of Finland and the United Republic of Tanzania, for their clarity in addressing this issue. We therefore think that the recommendations made in the report meet our views on globalization. We believe that globalization should, above all, be a link between peoples.

In the domain of employment, we would hope that more jobs are created and that better working conditions and improved social protection become the results of this system. We join the appeal that has been made to, without exception, engage firmly in building a better world for all our people.

Mozambique has suffered from a series of natural disasters which have ravaged the country, reducing the positive impact of the sterling activities that we have developed to provide our citizens with subsistence means, and my country is going through a very difficult moment as it grapples with the worldwide HIV/AIDS pandemic. The ILO gives us viable strategic mechanisms aimed at preventing and eradicating this worldwide scourge in the labour sector, whose harmful effects are much more felt in countries with a high rate of poverty.

The Report of the Director-General likewise refers to the respect and attention that must be paid to the rights of children and women, and on that basis I am pleased to inform you that my country has already ratified the eight fundamental Conventions of the ILO.

Mozambique believes firmly that policies oriented towards the capitalization of small and medium-sized enterprises may, within a short space of time, alleviate the pain and suffering that our countries endure. We also give emphasis to vocational training for our workers.

Earlier this year my country hosted the launch of the ILO Global Campaign on Social Security and Coverage for All for the African Portuguese-speaking countries. It is our belief that the right to social security is a fundamental right for all human beings without which it would not be easy to achieve the various Millennium Development Goals set in our countries.

In my country we are presently drafting new social security legislation that will also cover workers in the informal economy and independent workers.

Last May, we started amending the existing Labour Law with a view to bringing it closer to the present social and economic realities. I am sure that, with our total commitment and with the wise leadership of the Director-General, we can, together, bring to this world a true and just social dimension, free from absolute poverty – indeed with more employment and prosperity.

Ms. BEAUMONT *(Workers' delegate, New Zealand)*

I would like to congratulate the President on his election to the presidency of this Conference. I would like to congratulate the Director-General on his Report, *ILO programme implementation 2002-03,* and also for sponsoring the World Commission on the Social Dimension of Globalization. I bring you warm greetings from the New Zealand Council of Trade Unions to all delegates. We are the largest democratic organization in our country.

As a key part of my speech is about the role of unions in building a strong voice for working people and our families and communities, I must note with concern that the voice of women is limited at this Conference. The representation of women in delegations is unacceptably low, and women make up a very small percentage of the speakers in these plenary sessions. It is incumbent on all of us to rectify this situation. This includes trade unions.

The New Zealand Council of Trade Unions is part of a global union movement, which is under significant challenge in an increasingly globalized labour market. This context poses a number of challenges to the union movement: the challenge to build union strength; the challenge to fight for fair trade; the challenge of dealing with globalized companies; the challenge to be relevant to a changing and increasingly diverse workforce; and the challenge to ensure fair global labour standards. Put in these terms, this can seem quite daunting.

In New Zealand we are facing the task of rebuilding a union movement that was severely weakened in the 1990s. We faced a number of challenges; harsh legislation, economic deregulation and privatization, high unemployment and benefit cuts, to name a few.

We survived, but the union movement in 1999, when we had a change of Government, was a very different one to the one that had existed in 1991. We were significantly smaller. Our union density went from 56 per cent of wage and salary-earners in 1989 to 21 per cent in 1999. We no longer had national awards setting out legal minimums, but thousands of collective contracts, primarily at the enterprise level, a legislative minimum wage which had not increased for many years and a majority of workers on individual contracts.

Wages and conditions declined in many areas of the economy as a result. In addition, we saw the wholesale selling of our assets and the reduction of spending on the social wage. The gap between rich and poor grew significantly.

The Council of Trade Unions has focused on improving union organization, campaigning for legislative change and creating opportunities for union engagement as a social partner in a broad range of social and economic issues in our country. Since 1999, the Council of Trade Unions has successfully advocated many improvements in health and safety; paid parental leave; holidays; employment law; minimum wages; support for low income families; and early childhood education funding.

I would like to comment in particular on the promotion of collective bargaining. This is in the context of the objective to promote and realize standards and fundamental principles and rights at work. We will keep pushing for ratification of the ILO Freedom of Association and Protection of the Right to Organise Convention, 1948 (No. 87), but I am pleased to note that the New Zealand Government has now ratified the Right to Organise and Collective Bargaining Convention, 1949 (No. 98).

This is of particular significance to unions in New Zealand given our experience in the 1990s. We fortunately now have a law that promotes collective bargaining as a primary objective. Currently that law is being strengthened.

Collective bargaining is of vital importance to workers as a mechanism to balance the bargaining strengths of employers and workers. Analysis has shown in many countries that collective bargaining delivers better results for workers, not only in wages and conditions, but also better equity results, better health and safety results and better productivity.

In the context of a globalized world, it will be increasingly important for workers to develop collective instruments that stretch across national borders. Such framework agreements will assist with corporate responsiveness and the internationalization of fundamental workers' rights.

What unions are seeking is not a grudging acceptance by employers of collective bargaining, but active promotion alongside unions and governments.

Such promotion is entirely consistent with broader objectives concerning decent work and income, enhancing social protection and strengthening tripartism and social dialogue.

Although we have relatively low unemployment in New Zealand compared to our performance over the last two decades, we have a dysfunctional labour market. Labour and skill shortages are not feeding through to wage increases, in part because of the absence of really effective instruments to promote collective bargaining. This is a key focus for our current review of employment law.

As unionists, we have an active programme that includes improving our own effectiveness as unions, promoting fair employment laws, as well as social and employment protection provision for all workers and a programme of engagement on key social and economic issues, including industry training, economic development, growth and productivity and quality public services.

For unions there are boundaries as well as linkages between these areas of activity. For instance, whilst we seek fair employment laws, we do not ask the Government to deliver terms and conditions of work that should arise out of collective bargaining. But we do argue that where workers are organized into unions and bargain collectively, then they are well placed to engage in wider tripartite dialogue on a wide range of crucial social and economic issues.

We have a vision of union members who do not only actively participate in the union at the workplace and industry level, but get really involved through the union and central organization in concrete proposals and dialogues with the Government and the wider community. There are good signs that this is happening, but we have a long way to go. The key objectives and fundamental principles of the ILO, including the specific aspects highlighted by the Director-General in his Report, *ILO Programme implementation 2002-03*, are of great assistance to us in achieving our goals.

Original Spanish: Mr. NÚÑEZ SALCEDO *(Government delegate, Dominican Republic)*

The Government of the Dominican Republic would like to congratulate the President of the 92nd Session of the International Labour Conference, Dr. Milton Ray Guevara, on his election as President of this Conference and wishes him every success in carrying out the task entrusted to him by members. At the same time, we should like to commend the Director-General for his wise choice of topic for his Report on for the years 2002-03, which surpasses the expectations of countries in terms of the importance it attaches to the role of international cooperation in their development and to the status of implementation of the Decent Work Agenda, which is the cornerstone of protection for the rights and duties of workers in this globalized world.

Undoubtedly, the Office and the Governing Body have done an exceptional job in designing programmes to provide guidance to constituents, such as the World Commission on the Social Dimension of Globalization. The World Commission seeks a process of globalization with a social dimension based on universal values and respect for human rights and individual dignity, in other words, one that is fair, inclusive, democratically governed and provides opportunities and benefits for all countries and people, regardless of their class and where they live.

In the Dominican Republic, the ILO has done some excellent and fundamental work in all areas, but particularly in the sphere of international cooperation. Furthermore, the elimination of child labour is one of the priorities of the Government of the Dominican Republic and one of the most important areas of the Secretary of State for Labour's work.

We are continuously struggling to eliminate this scourge and, thanks to God, we have achieved significant results. To date, we have removed over 2,000 boys, girls and adolescents from the coffee plantations; 1,255 from the tomato-picking sector; and over 600 in the Municipality of Constanza who were working in the fields and applying pesticides. These are children who no longer have to work. With the agreement of their families they can now go to school because, of course, work makes children grow up too fast. Childhood is the time to study, and not to work.

As part of the Programme for the Elimination of Commercial Sexual Exploitation, 37 girls, boys and adolescents in the Municipality of Boca Chica in the Province of Santo Domingo are currently being assessed so that they can go to school and we are working with their families to raise awareness and to give these children other alternatives so that they will no longer be victims of commercial sexual exploitation. We have recently launched another similar programme in the Municipality of Sosúa in the Province of Puerto Plato. We have also launched a programme to eradicate child domestic labour in the Province of Santiago, and to date, about 50 minors have been removed from work.

Thus, in the Dominican Republic we are fighting against child labour with the political will and support that His Excellency, the President of the Republic, Hipólita Mejía, has always given us. This programme has been made possible, thanks to the ILO through its IPEC programme and the generous support of the United States Department of Labor. We should like to thank them for their support.

The Secretary of State for Labour is currently developing a youth and work programme for labour training and modernization, with the financial support of the Inter-American Development Bank, which is also supervising the programme, which aims to place 37,500 young people on the labour market.

We have formulated and implemented a programme to help young people obtain their first job. As a result, over 2,000 young people who had dropped out from school have graduated and today, over 60 per cent of these children have a job because of these retraining programmes. We must of course thank the ILO subregional office in San José, Costa Rica for the support it has provided to various programmes that we have implemented in the name of our Ministry and the social partners.

I must point out that the protection of workers in the Dominican Republic is guaranteed through Law No. 87-01 establishing the Dominican Social Security System which protects workers, and their families in terms of health, protects them from risks at work and guarantees them a dignified retirement after having come to the end of their long working lives, through the establishment of pension funds.

The Welfare System and the Workers' Insurance Scheme are now being implemented. The Family Health Insurance Scheme will soon be introduced, which will guarantee comprehensive physical and mental care for Dominican workers and legal residents. This health insurance scheme will benefit 3.3 million people.

Lastly, I should like to mention the important social dialogue between the social partners in the Dominican Republic. We have a true culture of dialogue in my country which helps to prevent labour conflicts in businesses. We firmly believe that the new world order must be based on social justice and the elimination of the barriers of poverty.

Original Spanish: Mr. ESPINAL *(Minister of Labour and Social Welfare, El Salvador)*

First, may I congratulate the President of this 92nd Session of the International Labour Conference on his election, which is an honour to the region of the Americas and, in particular, to the member States of the Council of Ministers of Labour of Central America, Panama and the Dominican Republic. I am very proud to take part in this Conference on behalf of the Government of El Salvador and to represent its President, Elias Antonio Saca. I would like to take this opportunity to convey his warmest greetings to Mr. Juan Somavia the Director-General of the International Labour Organization and to all the delegations taking part in this forum and to the special guests who are increasing its prestige through their presence.

On 1 June, a new constitutional Government took office in my country. It emanated from the will of the Salvadorian people, as expressed through an election. It is giving priority to doing everything it can for all Salvadorians in keeping with a government plan entitled "safe country" which focuses closely on the human being and on respect of human rights and fundamental freedoms, the creation of opportunities for all, consultation and social dialogue, the rule of law and good governance, providing the appropriate physical and social infrastructures and education and training in order to ensure citizens' safety in the widest meaning of the term.

In El Salvador, the world economic debate is again causing us to consider a formula which gives priority to social aspects without abandoning economic stability and sustainable growth. It is quite clear that economic development cannot be maintained without human development. In countries such as ours, it is more important than ever to stress the social aspect because we have learned with difficulty and to our cost that the social aspect is not a complement to anything, but the basis of everything. In order to give priority to the social agenda, our new Government will immediately set about establishing a social welfare network in order to offer the requisite encouragement to all those who are economically challenged or socially marginalized so that they can join productive life and the formal economy.

Increasing employment opportunities and decent work is therefore our main national challenge. Consequently, President Saca, on the very day he took office, called on the social partners to speed up the signature of a pact for employment, in a quest for constant progress and economic and social development, which will depend to a great extent on employment and improved labour relations and, as the Director-General of the ILO says in his Report, *ILO programme implementation 2002-03,* on a real social dialogue within a tripartite framework, in order to help the social actors to achieve better understanding resting on the full exercise of workers' nationally and internationally recognized rights.

To this end, the partnership between the public and private sectors should jointly meet training needs and step up guidance, counselling and capacity building in order to boost productivity and efficiency. As we have said, in this context, matters of gender will be of singular importance and social dialogue will facilitate concerted action between the social partners and government representatives, the improvement of institutions' technical capacity and the promotion of fundamental rights, principles and norms at work as well as more opportunities for decent work for both men and women thereby ensuring that there is adequate social protection leading to better living conditions and thereby demonstrating a legitimate interest in the implementation of the policies and practical recommendations of the International Labour Office in the various areas of labour law.

I take this opportunity to express my country's full support to the central themes of Mr. Juan Somavia's Report, especially the Report, *ILO programme implementation 2002-03,* which reports on progress made in the implementation of the Decent

Work Agenda and which has allowed the Organization to reflect on what it does well and what it does less well in order to use this information to guide future decisions on strategies and means for achieving its main objectives.

The objective of applying the Decent Work Agenda has four interlinked stages: mapping the concept, promoting the integration and coherence of the concept within the ILO, the building of decent work into policy on the world economy and decent work in practice at the national level.

The body of the Report talks about the progress made towards each of these four and considers the goals established in the Programme and Budget for 2002-03. It notes that the aspiration to decent work has become a unifying concept and that it forms part of a policy on a globalized economy. It refers to the Governing Body's decision to set up the World Commission on the Social Dimension of Globalization.

It is clear that the main achievements in the 2003-04 biennium have included the greater importance that is now attached to promoting and complying with fundamental rights, principles and norms at work with special attention going to child labour. As a result, the ILO has greatly widened world awareness of the importance of international labour standards for the process of development. This is proof that this prestigious Organization has continued to enhance the worldwide significance of international labour standards as a legal mechanism by promoting further ratification and implementation of Conventions and by supporting their implementation in practice, backed by a system of effective up-to-date monitoring.

According to this Report, this has had an immediate impact on the number of ratifications of ILO Conventions, which is already high, which means that the ILO's activities in this domain have been successful. It must not be forgotten that the promotion of the Declaration on Fundamental Principles and Rights at Work and the campaign to do away with child labour have aroused great interest all round. Similarly, it should be remembered that much progress has been made towards the inclusion of the Decent Work Agenda in national poverty reduction strategies.

The ILO is likewise making substantial headway towards the objective of implementing the Decent Work Agenda within four years. That shows that this has become a vital element in an interdependent, globalizing world. As the Director-General said in his Report, this has given rise to a greater demand for the expertise of the ILO in the fields of social dialogue and the norms, policies and practices, which are of real importance for workers.

The importance of decent work in the new millennium cannot be denied. We also need training and capacity building for the human resources who have been plunged into a globalizing world. Nor can we deny that the ILO's strength lies to a great extent in the power of its social actors and the lasting nature of its social dialogue mechanisms, which lead to greater participation in the basic process of formulating policies that always recognize human dignity, the latter being the alpha and omega of government action to attain justice, legal security and the common weal.

Mr. EASTMOND *(Minister of Labour and Social Security, Barbados)*

Let me first extend my heartiest congratulations to my Caribbean colleague from the Dominican Republic on his assumption of the presidency.

Let me also thank the Director-General for a very balanced Report on ILO programme implementation which identifies the strengths and challenges of the Organization and provides indicators for evaluating its performance.

The Report addresses the strengthening of the contribution of the Turin Centre for the ILO's capacity building, learning and knowledge-management strategy. My Government thanks those agencies which facilitated training for Barbados and member State of the Caribbean Community (CARICOM) at the Turin Centre.

However, the cost of participation limits the benefits to CARICOM, and we are seeking a strategic alliance between the Centre and the training institutions in our region. The proposal is currently with the Director of the ILO Caribbean Office, and we sincerely hope that it receives the support of the Governing Body and the Board of the Turin Centre.

My Government commends the Director-General and the Governing Body for their foresight, and the World Commission for its thorough and comprehensive report, *A fair globalization: Creating opportunities for all*. It is a blueprint for formulating strategic solutions to the challenges of globalization, which will benefit both the successful multinational corporations and unskilled workers in the poorest countries.

We agree that the problems associated with globalization can be attributed to deficiencies in its governance and that national commitment is critical. To quote our Prime Minister, Owen Arthur: "We cannot leave people-focused development to the serendipity of market forces. Rather than retreat, this State must forge new smart partnerships with the private sector and with the institutions of civil society."

Developing countries, however, cannot realistically embrace globalization without market access for their products and increased funding for basic infrastructure, health and education projects. Trade, technology, international capital flows, intellectual property rights and market access must therefore be inextricably linked to issues such as poverty reduction, gender equality, social security and workers' rights.

My Government welcomes the ILO's commitment to the promotion of decent work. Employees cannot realize their full potential while working in unhealthy conditions with remuneration that is insufficient to satisfy their most basic needs. Decent work can enhance productivity, competitiveness and efficiency, and improve employees' job satisfaction and commitment.

At the tripartite level, all countries, like Barbados and other CARICOM States, must adopt the ILO's core labour standards – freedom of association and the right to collective bargaining, the abolition of forced labour and non-discrimination in respect of employment and occupation. We must also be committed to the enhancement and the development of social protection systems which guarantee basic living standards for all workers.

The Barbados Government agrees that international organizations such as the United Nations, the

WTO, the World Bank and the IMF must assist nations in achieving a fair globalization. We support the call for increased accountability for their decisions and the consequences of their policies; also for greater involvement of developing countries in policy- and decision-making and for social dialogue to be reflected in international policy.

Cooperation, understanding and the political will of rich and poor nations can ensure that globalization is not a utopian goal steeped in economic and political rhetoric. Sceptics must not gain credence from the unfortunate impasses of Seattle and Cancún.

Countries will eventually fall into two categories: those which embrace change and the victims of change. The ILO, with its unique tripartite structure, is now better positioned to support the establishment of a "global smart partnership" and the implementation of strategies which can maximize opportunities for all.

Mr. NICOLESCU *(Employers' adviser and substitute delegate, Romania)*

I am a member of the Romanian delegation and on behalf of Mr. Costache, the Romanian Employers' delegate, I would like to present our intervention to the International Labour Conference.

Firstly, allow me to extend our delegation's warmest congratulations to the President on his appointment, together with our highest appreciation to Mr. Juan Somavia, Director-General of the ILO and Secretary-General of the Conference, and his staff for the excellent conduct of this 92nd Session of the International Labour Conference. Our thanks go also to the representatives of the State and Canton of Geneva for hosting so generously one of the most complex and unique of international events, our Conference.

With your permission, I will briefly outline the major objectives and achievements of the Romanian employers' associations, all in line with the European and worldwide tendencies in the matter.

As you may be aware, Romania has recently become a full member of NATO and is firmly engaged in the process of European integration, aiming at becoming a full member by January 2007. We are convinced that we, the Employers, have a significant role to play in the achievement of this objective.

From this perspective, I wish to underline that our work is rendered difficult by a continuous polarization of the decision-makers' interest in the trade union movement, a fact which is to be seen also in the various reports and resolutions presented in the framework of this Conference.

Allow me to reiterate a well-known saying: "There may be employers without trade unions, but there may not be trade unions without employers."

All the actions of the Romanian employers are, and will continue to be, oriented towards:
- develop and enabling a business environment;
- respecting the property rights;
- developing a transparent, responsible and continuous social dialogue;
- eliminating corruption; and
- achieving the independence of justice by granting continuous support to the enforcement of laws.

Without sustained efforts to achieve these objectives, it is difficult to eliminate barriers preventing the development of investments, thus depriving the entire society of the benefits of an increase in work productivity and living standards, and of the further development of society, in particular in the context of the globalization era.

Progress in the employers' movement consists in our recent decision to amalgamate all employers' associations and create the Romanian Employers' Union (REU), the aim of which is to align itself, as quickly as possible, with the integration and globalization tendencies that characterize our societies today.

The work instruments of the Union will consist of:
- the active participation of local and central associations of employers in shaping and implementing national policies for harmonization with the provisions of the *acquis communautaire*;
- the promotion of social dialogue with the governmental structures, trade unions and representatives of civil society;
- the creation and implementation of public/private partnerships, including at the community level;
- the creation of a business-friendly environment through the development of training and counselling capacities; and
- public dissemination of employers' success stories.

All these instruments are also helpful for the unification of the employers' associations, thus eliminating all obstacles preventing the equal and fair representation, and the development, of the Romanian Employers' Union.

We wish to confirm that, at the national level, we are in a situation favourable to consensus in which a system of government, incorporating the democratic values and principles of the market economy, offers the opportunity to promote economic and social welfare.

This context has opened the way to tripartite negotiation in order to achieve:
- pay equity;
- poverty reduction, restructuring and accountability of economic reform;
- implementation of international labour norms and standards;
- real social protection of workers and pensioners; and
- encouragement of investors through adequate fiscal policies (reducing fiscality, eliminating tax on reinvested profit and others).

In light of the above, the delegation of the Romanian employers is seeking active support from the international organizations in order to implement a system of binding standards as an instrument of efficiency.

We express our strong wish to share the experience and expertise of the ILO and of other relevant international organizations in the implementation of approved recommendations in order to find and shape the most adequate solutions to benefit from the advantages of globalization and gradually eliminate its negative effects, in particular in countries with economies in transition, such as Romania.

Original Arabic: Mr. DAHLAN *(Employers' delegate, Saudi Arabia)*

In the Name of God, the Merciful, the Compassionate! The impressive amount of documentation submitted to this session of the Conference, as well as the richness and diversity of the subjects raised during the discussion in plenary and in the various committees, bear witness to the scope of the efforts made by the Office in order to ensure that the ILO can assume its rightful place within the multilateral system, with a view to defending its principles, its objectives and its values, and protecting and promoting social justice at the national and international levels. I would therefore like to commend these constant efforts which are reflected in the work of the Governing Body.

Careful consideration of the documents before us this session shows the extent of the challenges and difficulties encountered by the social partners throughout the world.

The Report, *ILO programme implementation 2002-03* bears eloquent witness to what is being done by our Organization at this very difficult time in history. On behalf of the employers in western Asia, and more particularly on behalf of Saudi Arabia, we would like once more to commend the efforts of the ILO's Regional Office for the Arab States in Beirut. At the same time, we would like these efforts to be stepped up in order to keep pace with the transformations that the region is undergoing today.

I would like to draw attention to the fact that the use of Arabic as a language of research and discussion remains at a modest level which falls below the legitimate aspirations of the Arab group to participate more effectively in the work of the ILO. Moreover, Arab representation in the ILO has been reduced despite the professional competence of the Arab world that can be brought to bear at the international level.

The technical cooperation programme should be extended in our region, both in terms of quality and quantity, in order to have a sustained effect and meet the real needs of the social partners.

I would also like to commend the Report entitled *Towards a fair deal for migrant workers in the global economy*. As Employers of the member States of the Gulf Cooperation Council, we would like to see foreign workers benefiting from all the rights specified by ILO Conventions. The considerable increase in the number of migrant workers is an evidence of the positive environment provided to these workers, whose contribution to reconstruction is appreciated alongside that of nationals. This situation reflects a positive image of cooperation among peoples in order to bring about economic and social stability both in the countries of origin and the receiving countries.

As a member of the Governing Body we have followed with keen interest and appreciation the work done by the World Commission on the Social Dimension of Globalization. We would like to congratulate the Commission on its exhaustive report, which has been discussed at this session of the Conference. We endorse the Commissions proposals and recommendations, as well as its vision of the future. We eagerly await the Director-General's proposals as a follow up to the recommendations made by the World Commission, in particular for the status of our tripartite Organization based on dialogue to be enshrined as the body charged with interacting with international agencies, in particular, the IMF and the World Bank, in order to defend the social and humanitarian dimensions of globalization to protect the people and to strengthen cooperation in the global economy. With that in mind, we would support the idea of holding a seminar on the social dimension of globalization so that this key issue continues to be given priority at the international level.

I would like at this point to pay tribute to the efforts of the mission sent by the Director-General to Palestine and the occupied Arab territories this year, whose report is yet another international document condemning Israeli practices and policies in the region. There is no need for me to add to what the mission has said in its report on its findings on site. These Israeli policies have resulted in the destruction of infrastructure and an increase in poverty and in youth unemployment. Our Palestinian fellow employers suffer huge losses on a daily basis owing to the discriminatory practices of the Israelis. The list is very long, it has already been mentioned by others attending this Conference and I do not wish to give a detailed account of all these practices which are seen on our television screens and clearly show the sufferings inflicted on the people and affecting every social category.

My country suffers as others do from the effects of terrorism targeted against innocent people, and in my country we are committed to the security of our partners at work, whether they are our fellow citizens or foreign workers. We defend their rights laid down in international agreements and those concluded with enterprises.

I would like to take this opportunity, in this international assembly, to address an urgent appeal to the United Nations for observance of international law, i.e. non-interference in the internal affairs of other states.

To conclude, I would like to express my heartfelt thanks to the President and all the Chairpersons of the Committees of this Conference for their unstinting efforts.

Original French: Mr. BRIESCH *(representative, European Economic and Social Committee)*

I am delighted to have this opportunity of addressing this session of the International Labour Conference. In particular, I would like to express my thanks to the Director-General, Mr. Juan Somavia. I would like to thank him for inviting me once again to speak here, and thus to make a contribution to the discussion by describing the viewpoint of the European Economic and Social Committee.

The European Economic and Social Committee considers itself a natural ally of the ILO; it has always followed the Organization's work with great interest. I am convinced that cooperation between our two bodies could be even more steadfast, more fruitful and more efficient than it is at present if, in some way or another, we gave it more of a structural framework – exactly how that would be done remains to be determined.

Allow me to take advantage of this opportunity just to say a little about the social dimension of globalization; this, I know, is the subject of your discussion here, and it is also very close to the heart of the concerns of the members of the EESC.

We can only welcome the initiative taken by the ILO and by its Director-General in drawing up the report, *A fair globalization: Creating opportunities for all*. This report, which results from collective effort and intense dialogue involving representatives of the lifeblood on all the societies in our planet, finally gives us a solid and consensual basis for policies to be developed in order to fill in the gaps that had been left by globalization, in terms of its social dimension.

I have read, with a great interest, the Director-General's Report on the role of the ILO in the implementation of recommendations arrived at by the World Commission, and I intend to ask the EESC to draft an opinion on the social dimension of globalization.

The communication by the European Commission on 18 May, which asked how exactly European Union policies could contribute to extending this discussion, indeed calls us to do precisely that; in doing this the EESC will, of course, be able to refer to an information report adopted in May 2001 on the topic, *Coping with globalization: The only option for the most vulnerable*. In that report we pointed out that one of the main weaknesses in the globalization process is the fact that it is seen more as a threat to social rights than as an opportunity of possibility to kick-start economic growth and to improve well-being.

It is, indeed, difficult to explain why we have precise rules on trade, or on capital flows, at a time when we have no similar standard for social issues. In our report, we stressed the necessity, in order to develop the social dimension of the globalization process, to enhance the international institution that is most closely concerned by this issue – namely the ILO – and to establish cooperation between the ILO and other international bodies; basically I am thinking of the WTO. The purpose, then, is to make a contribution to the parallel development of rights for workers and liberalization of trade. It is also necessary to promote ratification and implementation of ILO Conventions.

In order to guarantee respect for fundamental social standards in commercial exchange, it would appear more effective to apply a system based on encouragement, based on incentives, a system intended to promote trade with countries that are trying to protect and develop fundamental social rights. We have, indeed, seen some regional integration forums that have taken this kind of approach through charters for social rights. The Cotenou Agreement between the EU and the 78 members of the African, Caribbean and Pacific group of States stipulates explicitly that the "parties reaffirm their commitment to the internationally recognized core labour standards, as defined by the relevant International Labour Organization (ILO) Conventions – they agree to enhance cooperation in this area – and they agree that labour standards should not be used for protectionist purposes." The EU should continue to include similar text in agreements to be reached in the future and that is certainly something that we believe to be of great importance.

It is clear that globalization offers humankind, as a whole, major prospects for development, with the proviso that we can succeed in enhancing the instruments that will allow us to manage this process, which, in turn, will guarantee that it is beneficial to all, and that the inequalities that have been generated thus far are corrected. With that in mind, the EESC is in favour of introducing greater democracy to international society by enhancing existing international bodies and also by facilitating the participation of developing countries in the decision-making processes of those bodies, as well as by making those bodies more externally transparent; this would also involve consultation mechanisms in which civil society can participate.

As you can see, we are very much on the same wavelength as the World Commission and the ILO in all that we are saying; this confirms the relevance of the EU's economic and social model in meeting the challenges that we all face.

In conclusion, we are making considerable effort in seeking to contribute to the promotion of participatory democracy throughout the world by, wherever possible, seeking to establish a culture of dialogue, and structures for dialogue, between representatives of organized civil society and the political authorities.

I am convinced that by taking this approach and working in this way we can create opportunities for all, and can thereby develop the social dimension of globalization.

(Mr. Wade takes the Chair.)

Mr. HAGH-BAYAN *(Employers' adviser, Islamic Republic of Iran)*

In the name of God, the Merciful, the Compassionate! First of all I would like to congratulate the President on being appointed to preside over the 92nd Session.

I would like to bring to your attention certain aspects of globalization and its social impact on societies. Globalization is a social process through which geographical boundaries that influence sociocultural relationships are gradually diminished and the people become increasingly aware of the disappearance of these boundaries. The concept of globalization, from an ideological perspective, is somehow misleading because, as with the earlier concept of modernization, globalization is justifying the idea that the development and expansion of western culture and capitalist society is the outcome of forces that are not under human control, and thus acts towards the changing of the world.

Globalization is a direct result of European culture which was disseminated through immigration, colonization and imitation of other parts of the world. Globalization is also potentially accompanied by the growth of capitalism, but this does not mean that the whole world should become western or capitalist; it means that each social system should be measured, organized and coordinated according to western capitalism, and should realize its actual situation with reference to western economic and cultural criteria.

The social impact of globalization cannot be studied without considering its economic impact; and globalization can impact on nations in various ways. One positive effect of globalization for many nations is that it allows them to achieve higher levels of economic growth. Economic growth would be followed by a higher standard of living for the population, a growth in GDP, increased government revenues, increasing imports and exports, greater labour flexibility and an increase in non-standard forms of employment.

It is difficult to isolate specific impacts of globalization from other processes which, at the beginning, occurred at the same time – processes like macroeconomic changes, the end of apartheid, the creation of democratic institutions and the adoption of new labour relationships. These processes are interactive and influence each other in a cyclical chain.

Globalization also impacts on the quality of life of the world's people; the poor appear to be getting poorer. When countries open themselves up to international competition, governments must think in terms of economic rationalist principles.

They may reduce spending in essential areas such as health, welfare and education, thus reducing the quality of life for their nation. In addition, countries with minimal government regulations often attract large transnational companies. This can result in the exploitation of workers and the environment in countries where the quality of life may already be low. From a cultural and sociological perspective, globalization has many negative impacts. National and local cultures are influenced by imported cultural products, and nations must be aware of this danger and be on their guard against such phenomena.

The concept of government is being replaced by the concept of government-nation. Governments are thus not as powerful as in the past, and the responsibility of protecting a nation's cultural heritage, way of life and history falls on the nation, not on the government.

The outcome of such a process is the development of a global culture in which geographical, social, ethnic and national boundaries are virtually abolished, and individuals are the most important factors on which concentration must be focused.

It is not an option for us to choose globalization or reject it. Globalization is a historical process that has happened and will continue.

It is the responsibility of each of us, the people of the world, to care about this, and to consider how to deal with it, how to benefit from its advantages and how to prevent its undesirable effects.

Mr. ARNOLD (Employers' delegate, New Zealand)

The report of the World Commission on the Social Dimension of Globalization is timely. Whilst from a business point of view we do not necessarily agree with everything in the report, it does provide significant scope for ongoing debate as part of the ILO programme and budget discussion in November.

The report identifies the importance of creating the right policy environment conducive to growth and development, which we support.

We agree with the Commission in its report where it proposes a number of policy coherence initiatives to address the view that social progress cannot be achieved solely by social policy, that developments in economy, finance, trade, technology, investment, the environment and other related areas are also important. The ILO's mandate already provides input into such coherence initiatives.

The need for a values-based approach that reflects the free market economy and such concepts as individual responsibility, freedom of choice, competition, reward and recognition, responsibility, respect for the law, respect for the individual and property, transparency, integrity, equality, freedom, intellectual honesty and full respect for the rules of the game is commendable and essential.

In the short time available I wish to focus on some of the new directions that the Director-General's Report identifies.

Firstly, not everything in the World Commission report is directed at the ILO and so not all is relevant to the ILO.

What a country does should be driven at the national level and should not be a matter for international institutions to direct or even try to control. In this regard, the ILO should position itself to respond to the constituents' needs in regard to the responses they identify.

Matters of national dialogue, structure and labour and social policy can be informed by the debate in the ILO, but the response to be sustainable must come from the national level.

Secondly, the ILO needs to be open to new realities in the workplace, rather than putting reform and new forms of work within the context of existing ILO responses. New times call for new responses.

If the ILO standards system is to remain relevant in the future, it needs to be modernized to address and respond to the needs of the modern world of work.

Thirdly, rather than trying to establish the agenda for change to local development, the ILO should help strengthen the social partners' capabilities in the art of dialogue at the national level. There is no one-size-fits-all response. There is no one model to promote.

A challenge we face in the New Zealand context relates to changes in the balance between labour and social policy and other policy demands necessary to sustain economic growth. The balance needs to recognize that the burdens necessary in a society need to be shared equitably and, from the New Zealand experience, I would caution others to take care that, in creating that balance, the needs of the business community are neither forgotten nor just seen as broad shoulders to bear the cost and delivery of political promises.

In conclusion, if New Zealand business is going to be in a position to contribute to the Director-General's vision, we must have a regulatory framework that is balanced, with a business-friendly emphasis, which encourages growth, innovation and entrepreneurship and celebrates business success because, through that business success, the social dividend can be paid. Without that growth, social development cannot be assured.

Mr. FARSHORI (Government delegate, Pakistan)

Let me congratulate the President on his election at this 92nd Session of the International Labour Conference. His vast experience and deep knowledge about labour-related issues have added to the richness of the proceedings of the Conference.

Facts of life are bitter. The developing countries are facing multidimensional problems in the economic as well as the social sector. Unemployment is increasing. A large number of people are living below the poverty line, and the income gap between the industrialized and developing countries is on the increase. A large number of countries have been marginalized and live in perpetual fear of becoming a failed state.

These deep-seated and persistent imbalances in the current working of the global economic order call for an urgent rethink of the policies and institutions of global governance. We must understand and recognize the crucial issue of the shrinking of policy space and erosion of economic sovereignty of the developing countries. It is indeed paradoxical that the protagonists of globalization call for improvement in national governance, yet the present set of global rules progressively encroach on their essential policy space.

In this scenario, the ILO's initiative to constitute the World Commission on the Social Dimension of Globalization was highly commendable. The Commission, which was co-chaired by President Halonen of Finland and President Mkapa of the United Republic of Tanzania, produced a landmark document which has provided guiding principles for handling the issue of globalization.

We agree with the finding of the report that fair globalization will create opportunities for all. However, this requires integration of national and regional policies in a coherent manner, in a global framework with basic respect for justice, fair play and human values. Sixty years ago the Declaration of Philadelphia mandated that "poverty anywhere constitutes a danger to prosperity everywhere". We must address the issue of poverty.

We wholeheartedly support the recommendation of the Commission to make decent work a global goal. The emphasis on poverty alleviation, employment generation, social protection and social dialogue are steps in the right direction. However, greater efforts are required by the ILO to translate the guidelines into a workable action plan.

We believe that the enforcement of fair trade rules and improvement of financial architecture alone will not resolve the issue of poverty and underdevelopment of developing countries. There is an urgent need for making an international commitment to substantial debt relief and increased flow of resources. In this regard, the ILO should act as the lead agency at the multilateral level under the auspices of the United Nations.

Our Government is fully committed to fulfilling its international obligations to enforce labour standards in line with the Conventions ratified by us. We have ratified seven out of eight fundamental Conventions. We are rationalizing the existing labour laws in conformity with our national aspirations and in line with ratified Conventions.

Now, let me touch upon the issue of Palestinian workers in territories under Israeli occupation. The Director-General's Report, *The situation of workers in the occupied Arab territories,* makes grim reading, with unemployment touching an average of 35 per cent, leading to the strangulation of the economy. The Report documents many obstacles that face Palestinians trying to earn a living with dignity: restriction on the movements of Palestinian workers and of the goods and services they produce are pervasive. The Report also mentions the plight of Palestinians living in Gaza, where 83.5 per cent of the population is living below the poverty line. The problems have been further compounded by the construction of the so-called security wall, which has only served to separate children from schools, farmers from the land and workers from their work.

In the presence of such conditions, we share the assessment of the Director-General that "security in one country cannot be built on creating insecurity in another". Only a complete and unconditional withdrawal of Israeli forces from all occupied territories could lead to a lasting peace in the region, resulting in the improvement of the living and working conditions of people living under occupation.

I thank you once again for providing me with an opportunity to explain the viewpoint of my Government.

Mr. TONGAAI *(Minister of Labour and Human Resource Management, Kiribati)*

Let me congratulate the President and the Vice-Presidents on the unanimous elections they have secured in obtaining their respective offices. Given the high level of professionalism and experience they have brought to their respective positions, this session of the Conference is now approaching the end of its final week successfully.

Of equal importance, let me take this opportunity, as well, to express our gratitude to the Director-General, Mr. Juan Somavia, for providing an enabling environment for member States to explore, to the maximum, ways and means of countering the undesirable fallouts of globalization and to identify options for a way forward for all. This has been vividly illustrated in the agenda items of the Conference and the various reports that included labour migration, the fishing sector, human resource development and the report of the World Commission on the Social Dimension of Globalization. All such reports, which have been tabled in the Conference for the deliberations of delegates, are of particular importance and concern to Kiribati.

The Decent Work Agenda is the convergence of the many fabrics the World Commission on the Social Dimension of Globalization has been called to address. For its part, Kiribati is therefore committed to developing a decent work national plan of action that includes identification of holistic deficits of the four strategic objectives of decent work, developing a plan of action and the promotion of the decent work principles at all levels of the social partners before it could be adopted for implementation. Labour legislation is one of the areas that has significant shortfalls as far as decent work is concerned. The ILO, through the Multidisciplinary Advisory Team for South-East Asia and the Pacific, in Manila, and the ILO Office for Fiji, Papua New Guinea, Solomon Islands, Kiribati and other South Pacific islands, in Suva has provided various technical assistance to align our labour laws with international labour standards and to address the broader aspects of decent work. My gratitude goes to the Manila and Suva Offices for their constant support in the past and I look forward to their continuing support in the future.

A series of promotional workshops on decent work and labour law changes has been carried out in Kiribati to convince the stakeholders of the relevance and importance of decent work, hence the need to change our laws.

For the first time, the principles of decent work and the role of trade unions in our national development are now reflected in the 2004-07 Kiribati national development strategies. In addition, my own Ministry, for its part, has set its own mission to "improve the quality of life of all I-Kiribati through equitable access to decent work and active social dialogue". In pursuing this mission, the operational plan of my Ministry details the activities it will engage in for the next four years, which are oriented to the Decent Work Agenda.

These are some of the major tasks Kiribati needs to do, for its part, within the ambit of the World Commission on the Social Dimension of Globalization. This is the beginning of a long-term process of responding to a call by the World Commission to work nationally to develop a coherent and consistent policy that provides an environment conducive to reaping the benefits of globalization by all our citizens.

Before concluding, please allow me to say briefly that although the report of the World Commission on the Social Dimension of Globalization is comprehensive and provides options for a way forward for all member States, the scope of consultation did not include the Pacific region with its cultural, social, economic and political diversity that is capable of offering the World Commission a unique beauty of its own and that could be of equal interest to the work of the Commission as well.

Original Arabic: Mr. AL-KUHLANI *(Workers' delegate, Yemen)*

In the name of God, the Merciful, the Compassionate! Let me first of all, on behalf on the Workers' delegation of Yemen, congratulate the President on his election to this important position as President of this 92nd Session of the Conference, which is marked by the economic and political upheavals facing our world. We expect from the Conference decisive resolutions that will define the key factors in peace, stability, and peace in our world, and consolidate the labour principles and standards based on equality, justice and human rights.

I should also pay tribute to the Director-General, Mr. Juan Somavia, for all his efforts in preparing these excellent Reports dedicated to globalization, trade union rights, freedom of association and collective bargaining. These Reports address very important issues, such as the unfair effects of globalization – poverty, unemployment and uncontrolled migration. These issues are to be studied as a priority by our session of Conference. They are very grave matters, as we see clearly today that migration is increasing and work under indecent conditions is becoming widespread. These phenomena have very serious repercussions, especially for developing countries, including my own, Yemen.

We have made great progress in Yemen as regards workers' rights, and we have ratified 29 Conventions, including the fundamental Conventions, which are of great importance in the context of a reform and modernization campaign which is ongoing in Yemen and aims, above all, to develop civil society, ensure the participation of local communities in decision-making processes, and facilitate the integration of women in the word of work and in political and social activity. We reaffirm here that dialogue based on partnership, and not just the outward form of dialogue, is desired by all societies that wish to strengthen such mechanisms.

We commend the countries of the Gulf Cooperation Council for the work they have done in the areas of labour legislation, trade union rights and freedom of association. This is very positive, and will help us to initiate dialogue between the social partners in the member countries of the Gulf Cooperation Council and in other countries.

Globalization is tending to produce a global monoculture, and this poses a threat to human civilization. This situation would make it impossible to realize the aspiration of the world's peoples. The challenge facing us is to promote dialogue over conflict, to accept diversity and differences and to invest in pluralism in order to work successfully towards a more stable and peaceful world. But in order to do this, the ILO must play a strategic role in economic development, especially of the developing countries, in order to combat poverty, unemployment, and uncontrolled migration and to reinforce the capacities of trade unions and social partners in taking up the challenges. We therefore support the recommendations and solutions advocated in the Director-General's Report.

We are extremely concerned by the situation in the occupied Arab territories, which are constantly aggravated by Israeli policies and by the erection of the racist separation wall. We are also concerned by the failure of all attempts at dialogue, especially of the Road Map, and on the flouting of international standards and laws. The international community must redouble its efforts to end the occupation of Palestinian territories, and to allow the Palestinian people to establish an independent State with the holy city of Al-Quds as its capital. The international community must also work to end the occupation of Golan and South Lebanon. In Iraq, only an end to occupation and a return of sovereignty to Iraqis will bring peace and stability. The policy of containment applied against Iran, and sanctions against Syria, can only increase instability in the region.

In conclusion, I assure you of our determination to work towards the success of current and future projects of the ILO in the framework of its strategic objectives, so that justice, equality, progress, trade union rights and fundamental rights at work can become a reality for all.

Mr. ABDELLA *(Minister of Labour and Social Affairs, Ethiopia)*

Allow me, to begin by congratulating the President and the Officers of the Conference upon their election to preside over this Session of the International Labour Conference and to assure them of the Ethiopian delegation's full cooperation in discharging their important responsibilities. I would like to thank the Director-General for his Report to the Conference. The Report will guide our debate and enable us to reassess the ILO's past achievements and look forward to the future challenges ahead.

The challenging international situation has a direct bearing on the outcome of all our countries' plans and strategies. For a weak economy like ours in Africa, freeing itself from the multi-dimensional problems besetting it is by no means an easy task. However, with the changing times, there is now a growing realization that assisting Africa's development is more of an issue of partnership for a common good and less of a purely humanitarian action meant only in Africa's favour. In fact, the United Nations Millennium Development Goals (MDGs) of September 2000 can be seen as a sign of recognition of such an understanding taking root. In the Millenium Declaration, member States of the United Nations made a most passionate commitment to addressing the crippling poverty and increasing misery that grip many areas of the world. Although the primary responsibility for our development rests with us, the developing nations cannot achieve such a huge task set forth in the MDGs alone. We strongly need the support of the rest of the world.

It would be appropriate for me to mention the ILO's contribution to African countries in their all-out effort towards poverty alleviation. The Organization's commitment was further expressed during the Tenth African Regional Meeting of the ILO held at the end of last year in our capital, Addis Ababa. I should like to note here that this meeting provided an effective forum to discuss the challenges ahead for Africa and to draw up concrete guidelines on the major subject of decent work for Africa's development, including economic growth, employment creation and poverty eradication through dialogue. I also wish to take this opportunity to express my country's gratitude to the ILO for giving us the opportunity to host this important meeting, which will be remembered as a memorable landmark in the enhancement of the social and economic progress of

Africa. I must commend, the ILO's subregional office for East Africa and the East Africa Multidisciplinary Advisory Team (EAMAT) in Addis Ababa for their active role in and constant support of our work. Their assistance has been invaluable to my country and we look forward to their continued support in the future.

My country always attaches considerable importance to the work of the ILO. More especially, I would like to emphasize the ILO's constructive and consistent approach to attaining the declared objectives of providing workers with decent and productive work. In order to uphold and implement fundamental principles and rights at work, Ethiopia has now ratified all the fundamental ILO Conventions. Furthermore, I am happy to announce that following extensive tripartite dialogue conducted over several months, the Government of Ethiopia enacted a new Labour Law in February this year with a view to harmonizing the labour conditions in the country with international labour standards. To this end, the new Labour Law permits trade union diversity and prohibits administrative dissolution of trade unions, and the ban on strikes is limited to enterprises that provide essential services to the public.

Turning to the other agenda items before the Conference, my delegation appreciates the reports submitted for our consideration. The issues are all timely and pertinent to the work of our Organization. In particular, the report that focused on the real issues has clearly indicated the tools that should be used to provide solutions to the real problems. These are the Decent Work Agenda as an instrument for development, employment as the main route out of poverty, and achieving a fair globalization as a means to secure global stability. The Global Report, which focuses on freedom of association and effective recognition of the right to collective bargaining, is of primary importance since it provides a global picture and widens our outlook relating to the implementation of these basic human rights.

In closing, I wish the ILO, the Director-General and his staff, and the Conference every success in their important work.

Original Farsi: Mr. QARQEIN *(Minister of Labour and Social Affairs, Afghanistan)*

The Report of the Director-General covers progress in attaining these goals, commenting specifically on the promotion and realization of standards and fundamentals principles and rights at work; the creation of greater opportunities for men and women to secure decent employment and income; measure to enhance the coverage and effectiveness of social protection for all; and the strengthening of tripartism and social dialogue. Let me take this opportunity to assure you of Afghanistan's sincere commitment to working towards achieving the objectives in these areas of common interest.

I would like to take this opportunity to express my gratitude and appreciation for the constructive assistance provided by friendly countries to help fulfil the requests of the Afghan nation and to those who gave their support to Afghanistan.

During the past difficult year, the transitional Islamic Government and the people of Afghanistan have experienced the effectiveness of the ILO through its activities in Afghanistan. We are presently receiving direct support in the areas of the review of the Labour Code and the Organization of the Ministry of Labour and Social Affairs. Practical assistance is ongoing with the National Emergency Employment Programme. New employment centres are being established. Business development projects have commenced as well as microfinance training. We are receiving assistance on ways to support the disabled. We are getting support from ILO on ways to encourage women into the workforce and to help them establish enterprises. In the skills development area we are obtaining support to establish a range of non-formal vocational training centres. Employer and worker representative bodies have received assistance as part of the plan to promote tripartism. My country is committed to making these programmes work and we are extremely grateful for this practical support.

At the same time, I would like to draw the attention of the Director-General to the continuing requirements of my country and people.

The recent civil wars had their effects where social order was threatened by dictatorship and conflicts. Since the Bonn Conference, and later the Tokyo Donors Conference, we have experienced a hard but constructive time.

We have seen the establishment of the Interim government, the reconstruction of dispersed organs of Government, the successful holding of the emergency Loya Jirga Grand Council, the establishment of a transitional Government, the appointment of a constitution commission, the commencement of the Consolidation of Peace (DDR) programme, the continued rehabilitation of the country and the provision of the chance to all to select their president. Even though we have managed to prepare a new constitution and continue to try to implement it so that our people can enjoy the benefits of democracy, social justice, freedom and basic rights, we need a solid, effective and active administration in the country to make it work effectively.

To achieve this goal, a separate commission of administrative reforms has been established by the Government and this commission is responsible for specifying priorities and bringing about needed reforms in government administration.

This project is important for two reasons: to build the capacity for attracting foreign aid and to successfully implement this aid; and to match international developments and achieve international standards in our society.

This project is strongly in need of the international community's support.

Afghanistan has been a member of the ILO since 1934 and over many years my country has worked diligently to establish and maintain the ILO goals of creating opportunities for employment, industrial relations, social security, effective use of manpower, vocational training, advancement of working capabilities, etc. But during the recent decades of war and disaster, we have not been always able to maintain these standards. We also have suffered a brain drain, losing many of our most talented and skilled people. We have also lost much of our physical capacity. To restore these we need the continuing attention of supporting communities.

The fundamental goal of the Government of Afghanistan is to provide employment opportunities for people in all areas, according to Islamic regulations and in accordance with the statement of the United Nations Commission on Human Rights, free from any sort of discrimination, having the right to work, and freedom in their choice of occupation.

Within a few months, we will see the election and establishment of a new Government in Afghanistan. This will be a historical event for our country and also a significant event in the international community because it is only through the establishment of an elected lawful government in Afghanistan that we will remove the frustration of terrorism and such problems as the export of poppies, drugs and insecurity. This will give our people hope for a bright future.

Before going to a free democratic election we have the programme of disarmament, demobilization and reintegration on our hands. This will help remove the pressure from any side opposed to a democratic and justified election.

Before the civil wars, the important sectors of our economy were largely agriculture and livestock production. Today, as a result of the civil wars, these sectors need rebuilding and construction and to do so require investment, particularly from private investors. We will facilitate investment in Afghanistan to achieve economic development and so provide employment opportunities for our people. A further effect of war in our country was the destruction of economic records and economic foundations and networks, either public or private. Their reconstruction is impossible for the Government to achieve on its own.

At the Tokyo and Berlin conferences, as well as the recent regional conference of the European Union's Humanitarian Aid Office held in Kabul and in other trips of official representatives from Afghanistan we have endeavoured to attract foreign investors to invest in Afghanistan to establish industries and to promote business in our country. But, as you all know, Afghanistan has had to begin from scratch. We therefore have a long way to go before we reach the stage of self-sufficiency and self-dependency. To help us reach that goal, we are hopeful that the international community will continue to provide humanitarian, technical and economical assistance.

We acknowledge that whatever we have done so far in our country after the establishment of the Interim Government, it is because of the support of the international community. Achievements such as the preparation of a new constitution, freedom of speech, women and children's rights, development of the domestic economy, and free and democratic elections are all noteworthy, but they are not sufficient. There remains much to be done.

I appreciate the assistance of the Director-General and the assistance of all other members in helping us to solve these problems. The people and the Government of Afghanistan remain hopeful for further cooperation and assistance from your side as our country endeavours to enter into new social, political, economical and cultural life.

Original Arabic: Mr. ABDULHUSAIN *(Workers' delegate, Bahrain)*

In the name of God, the Merciful, the Compassionate!

I would like to congratulate the President of the Conference on his election and wish him every success.

I am also pleased to be able to transmit to you the compliments of the workers of Bahrain and of the new General Federation for Bahrain Workers' Trade Unions, which was established between 12 and 14 January this year. The Bahraini trade union movement is entering a new phase in its history. The workers' dream, which dates back seven decades; has been realized: Workers now have free, independent and unified unions within the Federation, following the adoption by His Majesty the King, of the Trade Union Act on 31 September 2002.

Allow me also to congratulate the Director-General of the Organization, Mr. Juan Somavia, for his the excellent work in preparing for this session of the Conference and the Reports which he and his team have prepared, which reflect the desire to improve the working conditions for the workers in the face of modernization.

I think that these Reports constitute a method of work and guidelines for workers because of the detailed in-depth information that they contain about the reality of work and workers in the world. The Report, *Organizing for social justice,* is a very important tool because it sheds light on key issues, such as trade union rights and collective bargaining, which can serve as a basis for the development of democracy. We cannot talk about democracy while trade union rights and freedom of association are restricted and when collective bargaining between the social partners is at a standstill. The dialogue serves as a basis for development, strengthening it and allowing more balanced development. Moreover, it serves to solve existing and potential problems which makes it possible to create good conditions for reducing poverty and encouraging the creation of decent jobs.

There are challenges which must be taking up. The world is turning more and more towards globalization while the periphery is facing marginalization which leads to economic crises, an increase in domestic and foreign debt and the inability of various countries to pay back their debts. This leads also to increased unemployment and threatens social stability in the countries of the South.

Today, globalization cannot serve as a model because of its very brutal nature. The economic powers monopolize the infrastructure of the world economy with no regard for poor countries which need support and major projects that would allow them to rescue their economies in a way that is compatible with the world we want to live in. We have to realize social justice and fight against poverty, disease and unemployment. There are conditions and requirements which must be met for a fair globalization. The social dimension is a key factor in this. The Report of the Director-General on the World Commission on Social Dimension of Globalization is very important, because it determines an approach that allows us to deal with this crisis and to correct the present imbalance through decent work, whilst finding ways of drawing up national policies, which try to put and end to this brutal globalization. The Report also raised the issues of economic growth, investment, employment and rallying forces in order to establish effective social partnerships capable of achieving decent work.

The intensification of globalization has created more privatization without studying the negative effects that has workers laid off without social guarantees or compensation, which will certainly lead to an increase in unemployment and will have negative impact on social stability.

We read with interest the Report of the Director-General on *The situation of workers of the occupied Arab territories,* and I would like to emphasize here that the occupation is terrorism. A just and lasting peace in Palestine cannot be achieved without an end to the occupation of Palestine and the Syrian Golan, and unless the Palestinian people is granted the right to decide its own future and to establish its own independent State with Al-Quds as its capital. It is also important to end the American/British occupation of Iraq so that the Iraqi people can establish their own independent State and establish a legal and sovereign government on its territory.

We would also like to emphasize the rights of all workers in the State and private sector to establish trade unions in my country, Bahrain, in accordance with the reform directives of His Majesty the King, with the National Charter and with the Trade Unions Act. We also respect the international Conventions and we hope that through social dialogue we will be able to ensure respect for all the basic principles of the International Labour Organization, particularly those relating to freedom of association and collective bargaining, through the ratification of the Freedom of Association and Protection of the Right to Organise Convention, 1948 (No. 87), and the Right to Organise and Collective Bargaining Convention, 1949 (No. 98).

On the other hand, I would like to point to the steps which have been taken in the area of trade union rights and freedom of association in countries of the Gulf Cooperation Council. I am also certain that these steps will be followed by others which aim to guarantee the fundamental rights and principles at work laid down in the Declaration of Philadelphia.

In conclusion, I would like to wish the Conference every success and I reiterate my thanks to the Director-General and to the President and his team, as well as to everybody working in the wings in all areas of the Organization in order to facilitate our work.

Mr. TUGUSHI *(Workers' delegate, Georgia)*

The years following Georgia's regaining independence were marked by a drastic fall in living standards, the collapse of the system of social guarantees and growth of unemployment. A lot of Georgian citizens left the country because of civil war and political instability. The situation in the country became further aggravated by 300,000 refugees from Abkhazia and Samachablo, which is also known as South Osetia.

As a result of widespread corruption, the country's economy fell into deep stagnation. The falsification of the parliamentary election in 2003 by the Government was the last straw that provoked the well-known "Rose Revolution", which was followed by the President's resignation. At present, the new Government faces a lot of complex problems and challenges that need to be resolved.

In conditions of high levels of unemployment and poverty, the trade union movement of Georgia has been doing its utmost to promote effective social dialogue. The ILO's support and promotion of social dialogue in Georgia should be particularly emphasized. Successful collaboration between the Georgian Trade Unions Amalgamation (GTUA) and the ILO Moscow Office in the project, designed to establish productive cooperation with the parties of social dialogue partners, has been very helpful. In this context, the ILO's assistance in strengthening the trade unions' role in the Poverty Reduction Strategy Paper (PRSP) process is of particular importance. We greatly appreciate ILO assistance in providing expertise for the draft Labour Code, which was carried out at our request.

The GTUA, as an organization affiliated to the International Confederation of Free Trade Unions, systematically participates in the implementation of the projects meant to popularize the ILO Declaration on Fundamental Principles and Rights at Work. Despite the GTUA's activity, the question of social dialogue has not become a real priority in the political life of Georgia. Against the post-revolutionary background, the Government tries to deal with social problems without consulting the social partners.

Last year was marked by gross violations of trade union rights on the part of the old Government. Particular attention should be drawn to the event which took place in one of the regions of the country not long before the parliamentary elections of 2003, when the governor of the region, following intimidation and harassment of the local trade union leaders, forced the primary trade unions of the GTUA affiliated organizations to join a so-called regional trade union, established by his order. The GTUA considered this a gross intervention into trade union activity violating fundamental rights guaranteed by the ILO Conventions.

For several years now, labour inspectors in Georgia have been denied entry to any enterprise or organization in order to carry out monitoring of the workplace and the labour situation unless they have permission from a court of law. Despite the GTUA's repeated attempts to convince both the executive and legislative powers that such a decision is unlawful, the above-mentioned rule still remains in force.

The GTUA hopes that now, when the promotion of democracy is declared as a top priority by the new Government, all the barriers to effective cooperation for the establishment of social justice will be removed, especially since the GTUA openly supported the "Rose Revolution", by expressing an uncompromising position with regard to corruption and the rigging of elections.

Hopes are also raised by the steps made into the social sphere, particularly the trends related to increasing pensions and salaries for civil servants, as well as the uncompromising struggle against corruption and contraband.

In addition to the positive impulses, the GTUA considers it necessary to draw attention to the Government's ignorance of labour rights, which is becoming more and more frequent. The point is that civil servants, at all levels and without exception, are being asked by the newly appointed officials to leave their jobs of their own free will, which is a gross violation of the labour rights guaranteed by the international and national legislation. The GTUA considers such actions to be, at best, attempts by the Government to avoid its social responsibilities and, at worst, an expression of violence at the workplace.

With the entry of foreign investment into Georgia, the number of actual violations of labour and trade union rights is increasing. The provisions of Georgian legislation as well as of international Conventions are periodically violated by the company that is involved in the construction of the Baku-Tbilisi-Jeihan oil and gas pipeline in Georgia.

The violation of trade union rights are common by Georgian employers too, and trade unions are involved in daily struggles against such occurrences.

In this connection, I would like to express the hope that social justice and genuine social partnership will become the rule in Georgia.

Original French: Mr. TARTAGLIA *(Workers' delegate, Italy)*

On behalf of the Italian Workers' delegation, I should like to express my congratulation to the President on his election, as well as congratulate the Director-General, Mr. Juan Somavia, on his election to his second term.

I would like to begin my comments by recalling an event held in Florence last month. More than 120 young boys and girls from all countries of the world participated in the first World Congress of Children against Child Labour organized by the Global March Against Child Labour, the NGO Helping Hands and the three Italian trade union confederation CGIL, CISL and UIL. In the final declaration, which the children drafted themselves, it states that before we begin to discuss child labour we must emphasize that children's rights can only be recognized in a situation of peace. Peace is the most fundamental human right and we must ask ourselves why not has everyone the opportunity to enjoy such a fundamental right. Were they to live in peace, each child would have the possibility of seeing their rights recognized and also of being able to improve the world for themselves and for future generations.

Children have thus reminded us of the priority of having a commitment towards peace in a world in which war and terrorism continue to develop rather than being definitively banished from the face of our planet. The Italian Constitution, and I quote: "repudiates war as an instrument for resolving international controversies" and we, the Italian workers, are committed, together with workers' organizations around the world, to translate this principle into reality. This is why a large number of worker delegates have submitted a resolution concerning peace and social justice, two terms that are closely linked.

In Florence, the young people asked very simple questions of the representatives of international institutions present: why are we spending so much money on arms and investing so little in education in order to free children from child labour and finally give decent work to their parents?

The IPEC report, *Investing in Every Child,* suggests that an annual investment over 20 years of just a small percentage of all world military spending would be sufficient in order to eliminate child labour and to confer on all children the right that they deserve to education. It is thus our desire that, out of this report of the World Day Against Child Labour, the efforts of the ILO and all international institutions, arise precise plans for debt servicing and military spending be converted into investment in the future of children. Of all inequalities in globalization today, child labour is surely the most unacceptable. But it is not the only one. The ILO has therefore done well to promote the World Commission on the Social Dimension of Globalization, the conclusions of which are, by and large, agreed with and we strongly support follow-through on it.

I should like to emphasize some points regarding the commitment to a more fair globalization. We must engineer wide-ranging change in the action of many international institutions: first and foremost, in the World Bank, the IMF and the WTO. We must introduce more democracy and transparency in their decision-making processes. These institutions have almost always laid down, in developing countries and countries in transition, economic policies which have sacrificed to free markets, and above all free financial markets, investment in social services, health, education, housing and the rights of workers.

We support ILO action to ensure that all fundamental labour standards and the concept of decent work is made a priority in all of the decisions and policies which other international institutions will make with regard to developing countries and between developing countries and the developed countries. Developed countries must act responsibly towards their populations and the entire world and implement the recommendations of the World Summit on Sustainable Development and the Kyoto Protocol to protect the environment and to direct, in a real and targeted way, 0.7 per cent for development aid to the poorest countries.

The instruments elaborated by the OECD and the ILO Tripartite Declaration of Principles concerning Multinational Enterprises and Social Policy must become instruments that are accepted and recognized by all parties in economic intervention on the part of business in each country. Productive and economic activities must always be based on the respect of labour rights and on all human rights. This framework is the one that will best allow us to work towards the objects laid out in the Report, *Organizing for Social Justice.* In this area, we believe, once again, that it is primarily governments which must create favourable conditions for the full enjoyment of freedom of association and collective bargaining rights. We are convinced that there exists a positive link between these rights, decent work, employment and economic growth. The Report underlines the need to increase efforts in involving governments of important countries which have yet to ratify the Conventions on freedom of association and on collective bargaining. Such efforts will be even more effective if all international actors in multilateral relations and governments in bilateral relations exert pressure aimed at respect of all the rights of workers in these countries.

By the same token as the Report also highlights, enterprises, which seem to give a lot of attention to what is called the social responsibility of the enterprise, should be more coherent. The proliferation of unilateral initiatives on the adoption of codes of conduct or other rules of behaviour, on the part of enterprises, seem more to meet the requirements of their marketing than those of any real acceptance of social and environmental rights. We must state clearly that there is no social responsibility if the enterprise refuses, in the area of codes as in all areas, to negotiate with the free and representative trade union organizations. The true path leading to social responsibility on the part of businesses is negotiations with trade unions and the application, worldwide of fundamental labour rights and decent work. Social responsibility must be an additional element based on the foundation constituted by ILO standards, and not a substitution of these.

We must also call on all governments to be consistent and coherent always as regards tripartism. The trade union confederations in Italy have often had to remind the Italian Government of this. The Italian Government tends to forget that the social partners must be involved in all projects and initiatives. Tripartism is not like donning one's Sunday best; it is something which must be enforced every day.

We hope that, through the coherence of its constituents, the ILO will be able to truly play an important role in contributing to peace and fighting inequality, building a just and fair globalization, affirming everywhere workers' rights and decent work.

Mr. WOJCIK *(Workers' delegate, Poland)*

On behalf of the Polish Workers' delegation and on my behalf, I would like to congratulate the President and all the Vice-Presidents on their election to chair this august body, the 92nd Session of the International Labour Conference. I would like to extend my congratulations also to the Director-General for his Report: A *fair globalization: The role of the ILO*. Similarly, as in previous years, the Report is of the highest quality. It is an instant and concrete reaction to the report of the World Commission on the Social Dimension of Globalization.

"Labour is not a commodity." Sixty years ago, the International Labour Conference confirmed this fundamental truth in the Declaration Philadelphia. This truth must be remembered constantly by everybody. I believe that 'considerable part of contemporary economic and employment problems is provoked by the incorrect implementation of this idea in practice or by lack of its implementation at all.

We appreciate very much the trend in ratification of eight fundamental Conventions. According to the Global Report under the Follow-up to the ILO Declaration on Fundamental Principles and Rights at Work 2004, results seem to be very promising. The number of ratifications has increased significantly since the Declaration has been adopted.

By the year 1998, 69 per cent of the ILO Members had ratified the Freedom of Association and Protection of the Right to Organise Convention, 1948 (No. 87), and five years later, 80 per cent of them had already done it. Respective figures for the other core Conventions are as follows: 79 per cent and 87 per cent for the Right to Organise and Collective Bargaining Convention, 1949 (No. 98); 85 per cent and 92 per cent for Forced Labour Convention, 1930 (No. 29); 76 per cent and 91 per cent for Abolition of Forced Labour Convention, 1957 (No. 105); 39 per cent and 71 per cent for Minimum Age Convention, 1973 (No. 138); 0 per cent and 83 per cent for Worst Forms of Child Labour Convention, 1999 (No. 182); 77 per cent and 91 per cent for Equal Remuneration Convention, 1951 (No. 100); and 75 per cent and 90 per cent for Discrimination (Employment and Occupation) Convention, 1958 (No. 111).

Recalculation of the same ratifications in terms of percentage of population of the respective ILO member States shows quite a different, unpalatable picture. Today, some 54 per cent of the world population cannot be assured of freedom of association, 51 per cent of freedom of collective bargaining. Some one-third of the world population still have no legal guarantee against forced labour, child labour and discrimination at the workplace. This is the real picture of labour conditions in the world. With this view, I am entirely convinced that liberalization of trade cannot lead to better prosperity, equitable economy and fair distribution of goods in the world. Without globalization of at least core labour standards, without globalization of the solidarity, a fair globalization will remain only a beautiful, unrealistic idea.

Non-payment of wages and salaries due has become a problem in Poland in the latest years. Employees are very often deprived of their wages or payment of their wages has been significantly delayed.

However, Poland has ratified the Protection of Wages Convention, 1949 (No. 95), yet more and more cases of non-observance of its provisions have been recorded. In 2003, in the State Labour Inspection (SLI) of the Katowice District, in 38 per cent of enterprises investigated undue payment of wages were recorded and in 32 per cent of enterprises wages were not paid on time. In the other district (Lubuskie) the State Labour Inspection issued at the same time 313 orders concerning non-payment of wages for 6,149 employees.

These unacceptable practices are very widely exercised in the whole country and what is more one can observe a serious lack of effective sanctions in such cases. As was stated by the Polish Workers' delegate in the course of the Committee on the Application of Standards of this session of the International Labour Conference, two-year-old cases are daily practice as regards workers' complaints for non-payment of wages, while at this time the workers concerned are usually deprived both of work and remuneration. This is only an example.

I am deeply regretful that my compatriots from the Government, as well as from the Employers did not mention even one word concerning labour standards in their speeches to this session of the Conference. This is of special importance because they underlined the necessity of good governance and flexibility of labour relations.

I would like to express my strong conviction that good governance cannot exist without the observance of labour standards and the flexibility of labour relations is in clear opposition to labour standards.

Original Arabic: Mr. GHANDOUR *(Workers' delegate, Sudan)*

In the name of God, the Merciful, the Compassionate! Speaking personally and on behalf of the General Confederation of Sudanese Workers, I would like to congratulate the President on the trust the Conference has placed in him to guide our deliberations and arrive at decisions consonant with the aspirations of the social partners that make up our Organization.

The ILO endorses all action that is likely to promote the achievement of the aspirations of the social partners, that is to say decent work and a decent life for all. Despite achievements in the context of the Declaration on Fundamental Principles and Rights at Work, the adverse influences of the economic programmes that dominate today's world jeopardize all these achievements, because the international economic institutions, multinational companies and international decision-taking centres today pursue policies that merely increase poverty, hunger and illness, particularly in the third world. Today while the rich are getting richer, we can see the number of poor rising because international labour standards are being less strictly applied and because of the structural adjustment policies and smaller monetary flows that have to be accepted by some countries. Nor must we forget the exorbitant interest rates that are being charged on debts that have brought no benefits for the people of these countries. Unless urgent measures are taken to establish economic and social justice, we will all be threatened for poverty of any kind threatens prosperity anywhere.

The General Confederation of Sudanese Workers is in favour of the theme of migrant workers which has been chosen as a topic for discussion at this Conference. The world today has become a global village owing to advances in transport and communications. We also know that international trade agreements will make borders disappear and will increase workers' mobility. We hope that we will arrive at constructive recommendations which preserve the fundamental rights and dignity of workers.

In Sudan, thank God we are engaging in a fruitful tripartite dialogue which has enabled us to achieve much for workers since the last session of the International Labour Conference. In the legislative field, for example, a great deal has been achieved for the Government and the employers' federation have agreed to amend our Labour Code. We have also amended two pieces of legislation on pensions and social security with a view to offering additional benefits to those who are approaching the statutory retirement age after a long period out of work. Since April this year, Sudanese workers have received a 66 per cent rise in the minimum wage, the biggest per wage increase in the history of Sudan.

As far as trade unions are concerned, Khartoum hosted the Eighth Conference of African Trade Unions last January. It was attended by the Deputy Director-General of the ILO, the Director of the Bureau for Workers' Activities at the ILO, a number of his staff and the Chairperson of the Workers' group. The opening of the Conference was attended by three African Heads of State and a number of ministers of labour and social affairs. The Federation of East African workers brings together 13 national federations in East Africa which all work for peace and stability in this strategic area of the world.

The Sudan has recently signed a peace agreement putting an end to the longest civil war that Africa has ever known, a war that even predated Sudanese independence in 1956. The signature of this agreement in Naivasha in Kenya was directly brokered by the Kenyan Government and by countries partners to the Intergovernmental Authority on Development.

The General Confederation of Sudanese Workers played a role in these negotiations. These began more than ten years ago and resulted, after direct contacts and nine months of negotiations, in the signing of a peace agreement. We reaffirm that peace will have a beneficial effect on economic, political and social development. We call on the international community to help us to rebuild what the war destroyed and to improve the skill of trade union leader in the region.

We must not forget the other peoples who are suffering from war. Indeed, the Palestinian people regularly suffer from murder, the destruction of homes, the devastation of land and the uprooting of trees, under a policy of collective sanctions and state-sponsored terrorism. Let us not forget the Separation Wall, which is in itself an act of racism. The international community and the ILO must put an end to this human disaster. Nor should we forget the people and workers of Iraq who, every day, are being murdered and subjected to forms of torture that make the blood of any free human being run cold. We should also remember the Syrian Golan and the Chebaa farms area in Lebanon. Syria is being subjected to unprecedented blackmail in the guise of the act on sanctions again Syria, which was recently adopted by American Congress, whereas Syria is still suffering from injustice and occupation.

We are also thinking of Cuba and Afghanistan.

In conclusion, the world today calls for a review of the prevailing standards of justice, for the injustice which is now widespread in various regions is at the root of the catastrophes from which the world is suffering. If we do not react very soon, I fear that we will be unable to avert an imminent disaster.

Original Spanish: Mr. FLORES FLORES *(representative, Trade Unions International of Workers of Energy, Metal, Chemical, Oil and Allied Industries)*

As the secretary-general of the Trade Unions International of Workers of Energy, Metal, Chemical, Oil and Allied Industries, belonging to the World Trade Union Federation, I bring you my fraternal greetings. It is usual in fora such as this, in tripartite meetings and now within the framework of the Mexican Government to hear that work is not a commodity. This sort of statement is made around the world at meetings that presuppose and promote economic development. Furthermore, current governments, who are immersed in globalization, are called on to promote human development. However, the realities in the workplace show us that bosses, governments and the economic policies applied by both are such that they do exactly the opposite of what is preached. The precise measurement of productivity is obtained as the primary indicator of work and production, and never of the commitment of the owner or manager of the company, and never of the performance of investments or the responsibility to innovate or assess directives. Any adjustment in profits are linked to the workers or the costs of collective agreements. Dismissal on grounds of cost is usually used to increase productivity. Work is, of course, a commodity.

Recently, retirement schemes have been thought of only from the point of view of expenditure and liabilities. Sometimes, it is even said that slow economic growth and the current forms of retirement are responsible for hampering and even for causing the bankruptcy of some businesses and even public institutions.

New ways of benefiting have been created, such as domestic pension savings schemes on the basis of the model adopted in Chile where new financial companies use the current contributions of workers for the purpose of investing them. These savings funds are now generating funds to pay for the future retirement of workers. In other words, work is a commodity, it is an income that must be made to work.

Governments are proposing that legislation be amended in order to increase workers' contributions, to increase the age of retirement and to set up financing mechanisms so that the worker has more responsibility towards his or her own retirement. In the last two decades, widespread privatizations have been called for as the most appropriate way to release the federal budgets of governments, to make our economies more competitive and, of course, to change the collective labour agreements that are considered to be too rigid and too obsolete, but most of all are considered by governments to be perks and very costly. In other words, of course, work is a commodity.

The living conditions of our people are socially polarizing our existence. In the present model, the ever-shrinking number of rich people have a growing amount of wealth and more and more poor people are increasingly destitute. This situation of growing social polarization leads many workers in rural areas and the cities to look for more solvent economies or to work on the streets. In both cases, present governments, who are incredibly cynical, include them in the GDP, either because of the money sent back by the migrant workers to their families or because this takes care of their own fundamental needs. Remittances and informal work are becoming decent work, but above all in terms of accounting. So work, of course, is a commodity.

We resolutely, firmly and clearly oppose this vision of the world of work. We oppose and resist privatization that subjects people and national sovereignty to the wishes of the multinational companies, where the thirst for profit controls the development of new public service entities.

In Latin American countries the workers are against the speculative management of these savings funds for retirement, where minimal importance is given to the quality of life of pensioners and retired persons. In Argentina and Chile and even in the United States, we saw clearly that the privatization of electricity increases costs, reduces the capacity to respond to demand, reduces government control over energy and reduces the quality of services. Of course, conditions of work were amended beforehand, as were collective agreements, many jobs were lost and salaries reached a very low level. Therefore, there is growing social and worker resistance in our countries against all these. We therefore call for the existing economic model to be halted and amended. Neo-liberalism globalization is producing destitution and social exclusion and is subjecting national sovereignties to the utilitarian interests of multinational companies. This is our proposal, our declaration to this International Labour Conference. Only work, public education, social justice, in health, the sovereignty of our people, and the strengthening of internal markets against indiscriminate liberalization, higher salaries and the curbing of financial speculation, will allow independent growth and social development. Only this way will be have truly decent work. Constant progress must be based on freedom of expression and association without any restrictions. Social inequality causes poverty in the world. We will fight against it, until it is stamped out completely. This is our objective as trade unionists and our declaration as workers. No more should we condone a policy of exclusion or development without us. Another political model is possible, another economy may be born where the people will be the basis and the focus of development. Let us distribute economic wealth and socialize power in order to achieve social development and to ensure that workers' rights and justice are paramount in the world. We want no more, but no less. Long live the class struggle! Long live the workers of the world!

Mr. SUKHBAATAR *(Workers' delegate, Mongolia)*

First of all, I would like to congratulate, on behalf of the Workers of Mongolia, the President and the Vice-Presidents on their election to preside at this 92nd Session of the International Labour Conference.

Let me also express our appreciation to the Director-General for his Report, *ILO Programme implementation 2002-03*, and particularly on the assessment of the progress made and the challenges faced by the ILO in implementing the Decent Work Agenda.

I wish to welcome the report of the World Commission on the Social Dimension of Globalization which includes a series of concrete proposals.

The policy recommendations made by the World Commission to promote "a fair globalization" are positive and realistic. I fully support making decent work a global goal. The report calls, at the global level, for a greater presence for the ILO in a multilateral system, in line with its constitutional mandate "to examine and consider all the international economic and financial policies and measures". At a national level, this entails reinforcement of the ILO's current efforts to promote decent work and the four strategic objectives. The tripartite constituents of Mongolia have developed the national action plan on decent work in line with the ILO's strategic objectives.

The World Commission's report emphasizes the value of tripartism and the role it can play in making decent work a global goal. We fully agree with the statement in the Director-General's Report, *A fair Globalization: The role of the ILO* that "the ILO's success in surviving for 85 years is a testament to tripartism's ability to continuously reflect the changing world of work". We therefore strongly support the further strengthening of tripartism at international and national levels.

The tripartite machinery introduced a decade ago in Mongolia is working well. The National Conference on Tripartism and Social Dialogue in Mongolia, held last year in cooperation with the ILO, has summarized the success of challenges facing tripartism and social dialogue in our country. The Conference has endorsed a plan of action for further strengthening this machinery. We are happy to note how the ILO has involved Mongolia in the follow up to the resolution, adopted in 2000 at the International Labour Conference, on tripartism and social dialogue.

We fully support the report of the World Commission which raises some of the ways in which the ILO is currently attempting to influence national policies, including through involvement in poverty reduction strategies. By effective involvement in a Poverty Reduction Strategy Paper, the ILO must have the opportunity and the capability to influence the macroeconomic debates and decisions that determine whether resources are available for social policy and poverty reduction at national level.

We are pleased that migrant labour is one of the issues on the agenda of this session of the Conference. Concerning migration, Mongolia is both a sending and receiving country. Our delegation supports the concept of a new multilateral framework on migration, but such a framework must be prefaced on preserving and extending the concept of "equal treatment" and "equal opportunity" which are contained in the existing ILO Conventions on migration.

The strengthening of the international labour standards system is becoming more important in the era of globalization. We consider that each State has made every effort for ratification and proper implementation of the core international labour standards. The social partners in Mongolia are currently examining the ratification of the Forced Labour Convention, 1930 (No 29)m and the Abolition of Forced Labour Convention, 1957 (No 105), and in spite of some differences among our constituents, we believe Mongolia will be included soon in the list of countries which have ratified all of the international core labour standards.

In recent years, Mongolia, as a transition economy, has seen the majority of new jobs and the income opportunities emerge in the informal economy. We are happy to note the ILO project on informal economy initiatives with their focus on strengthening the voice and representation of workers in the informal economy and ensuring the rights of freedom of association and collective bargaining.

In conclusion, I would like to express our sincere gratitude for the assistance and cooperation extended to Mongolian trade unions by the ILO and its Bureau for Workers' Activities.

I wish every success to this 92nd Session of the International Labour Conference.

(The Conference adjourned at 1.00 p.m.)

Fifteenth sitting

Monday, 14 June 2004, 3 p.m.
Presidents: Mr. Wade, Mr. Attigbe

REPORTS OF THE CHAIRPERSON OF THE GOVERNING BODY AND OF THE DIRECTOR-GENERAL: DISCUSSION (CONT.)

Original French: THE PRESIDENT

We shall now resume our discussion of the report of the Chairperson of the Governing Body and of the Director-General.

Original Spanish: Mr. CELI VEGAS *(representative, Exchange and Cooperation Centre for Latin America)*

It is a great honour for me to address this august assembly and, on behalf of the Exchange and Cooperation Centre for Latin America, to congratulate Mr. Ray Guevara on his outstanding work as President of this Conference.

The Global Report of the Director-General, *Organizing for social justice*, recognizes the efforts of the ILO to promote freedom of association and the right to collective bargaining. Most of the populations of developing countries do not necessarily enjoy these freedoms, and their conditions are tending to deteriorate. To the structural problems of the world, linked to the inequitable distribution of wealth, must be added the effects of economic globalization. For the workers, this means mass unemployment and instability; for enterprises, increasing relocation mergers in all sectors; and for governments, lack of the efficiency needed to establish a re-distributive regulatory framework governing the economic players.

Economic globalization has also brought with it political globalization. The leaders of the developing counties are challenging the decisions of the industrialized countries concerning their vision of a future world. Multilateralism has become one of the major mechanisms to be strengthened and extended in the different sectors, with the involvement of all the economic factors. It is worth mentioning the recognition of civil society by the international community. In addition, parallel sessions and specific proposals have accompanied recent international meetings such as the World Summit on Sustainable Development, the International Conference on Financing for Development of UNCTAD, the Doha and Cancún Ministerial Conferences of the WTO, and the EU Latin America and the Caribbean Summits held in Rio de Janeiro, Madrid and Guadalajara.

The Global Report of the Director-General examines the framework agreements concluded between transnational corporations and trade unions over the last 20 years. It is worth mentioning the agreement signed in 2001 between Chiquita Brands International, the International Union of Food, Agricultural Hotel, Restaurant, Catering, Tobacco and Allied Workers' Associations (IUF) and the Latin American Coordinating Committee of Banana Workers' Unions (COLSIBA). Under the agreement, suppliers are required to provide evidence that they respect national legislation and fundamental labour rights, including the right to freedom of association and collective bargaining. We believe that dialogue between companies and trade unions furthers the application of the standards adopted by the ILO since it was established in 1919, with the aim of achieving a balance on the labour market. We also believe that the technical cooperation programmes implemented by the ILO in sectors which are not regulated by governments owing to a lack of legislative provisions or the fragility of state institutions is a vital means of securing application of minimum standards for respect of these workers' dignity.

We realize that these advances are an important step forward, but in Latin America the economic recession and the fragility of political structures have contributed to the proliferation of the informal economy. Informal workers and enterprises are on the increase, in the absence of regulatory machinery put in place by the State. This situation is conducive to exploitation of the most vulnerable sectors of the population.

The lack of resources prompts governments to focus their policies – where such exist – on the major urban centres, leaving marginalized urban and rural areas to the dominant forces in a market economy, speculators and mafia networks. The rights to food, education and formal employment are thus denied to large segments of the population in Latin America.

Organized civil society can play an important role in filling the gap left by governments. The basic framework is democracy, which exists in most countries, as well as the economic agreements increasingly being concluded between European and Latin American countries. NGOs, with their projects in remote areas, their experience in international networks and their contacts and knowledge of the local population, are well placed to play a major role in local and regional development in Latin America. This will require an extension of programmes and projects, with the involvement of enterprises, governments and international organizations.

Mr. KARA *(Workers' delegate, Israel)*

I wish to congratulate the President and his deputies on their election to preside over this 92nd Session of the International Labour Conference and the Director-General and his staff for the Report submitted to this session of the Conference.

Like others, I would like to focus on the role of the ILO in implementing the recommendations of the World Commission on the Social Dimension of Globalization and to welcome the Report submitted to this session of the Conference by the Director-General, which deals with one of the most difficult questions, how the ILO's tripartite constituents can bring the benefit of globalization to all people throughout the world. We think that the ILO can meet the challenge and could be at the forefront of the struggle for a fair globalization.

We have in front of us proposals of the utmost significance. These proposals deserve our support and we are following the ICFTU policy in this regard. It is clear to us that tripartism and social dialogue can be efficient tools to achieve a fair globalization.

My organization, Histadrut, the general federation of trade unions in Israel, strongly supports the initiatives of the ILO which deal with decent work and poverty reduction strategies. In the meantime, we are pleased that the Commission gives the ILO a key role in implementing its mandate to influence national and international policies, promoting social justice and poverty reduction.

We wish to refer to some of the points made by the Director-General. We can see that the ILO has started doing more for the implementation of workers' fundamental rights, the right to freedom of association and collective bargaining, but there are still restrictions in many countries.

We want strong backing from the Director-General to take steps to ensure workers' rights everywhere and to do more for the application of the core ILO Conventions that have been signed. We think that programmes must be introduced in order to guide the constituents in this regard. Consequently, with this, we would like all these decisions to be implemented by concrete steps.

The issue of migrant workers' rights is on the agenda of Histadrut, the general federation of labour in Israel, which I have the honour to represent. We started a debate on a new regulation to ensure migrant workers' rights. This goes along with the Global Report under the Follow-up to the ILO Declaration on Fundamental Principles and Rights at Work focusing on freedom of association.

In my country, the migrant workers are 10 per cent of the workforce. They work in construction, agriculture and domestic work. We are making the necessary efforts to protect them, but we need the support of the ILO to do more to achieve and maintain their rights.

As the representative of the workers of Israel, we are concerned about the violence in our region, which affects both sides (Israelis and Palestinians). We support the immediate return to the dialogue for peace. Only in this way will it be possible to ensure employment and economic recuperation and growth.

Histadrut was, and still is, seeking ways to build constructive dialogue with Palestinian workers in order to enhance cooperation and progress. It is important to comment on this issue, the fundamental role of the ILO's technical cooperation. We are looking forward to the next session of the conference with the wish that this will become tangible and peace will be a reality.

Original Portuguese: Mr. MUSSANHANE *(Employers' delegate, Mozambique)*

On behalf of the Confederation of Economic Associations of Mozambique, I extend greetings to all participants in this session. I also congratulate the President, on his election and the Director-General of the ILO on the Reports he has presented to us and on his defence of decent work and social justice.

Labour legislation in my country needs to be amended so as to bring it into line with the market economy which we have today in Mozambique. It is our wish that the interests of the social partners be reflected in the forthcoming labour law which is currently being revised, and we feel that it is important to respect the following principle: free initiative; the decisive role of the private sector in modern development; constantly increasing productivity; quality of products and services; competitiveness in enterprise; decent work; fair remuneration; a tax system which encourages the growth of enterprises; and the transfer of the knowledge needed for business.

We feel that social dialogue is a fundamental instrument for relations between government, employers and workers, and the law should reflect the interests of them all. I would like to recognize the work that the social partners have carried out, as a result of a very positive and encouraging partnership.

Small and medium-sized enterprises (SMEs) represent most of the industrial sector in Mozambique. We must therefore maximize their potential and amend our legislation so that it differentiates properly between SMEs and large enterprises. At the present time, SMEs are being dealt with as if they were large enterprises and this obviously gives rise to problems. Attempting to transfer the informal economy into a formal economy without a proper understanding of the concept of SMEs leads to confusion and uncertainty over their true function in the national economy. We wish the ILO to play an ever more active role in dealing with these problems. We therefore call on the ILO to intensify its noble actions of assisting our countries to find ways of establishing and maintaining relations with other international bodies, and also of cooperating with us in formulating labour policies and defining strategies on SMEs based on technical matters and professionalism, never on linguistic and cultural factors.

Original Spanish: Mr. ALVIS FERNÁNDEZ *(Workers' delegate, Colombia)*

Allow me, on behalf of the workers of Colombia and their national trade unions, the CUT, CTC and CGTD, to express our congratulations to the President for having been elected to lead the 92nd Session of the International Labour Conference.

The Director-General, in his Report, urges us to reflect upon the working conditions of migrant workers, upon fairness and the importance of decent work as part of the social dimension against the backdrop of inequality and poverty in a globalized world.

This forum of the international community is unique for workers in terms of giving them an opportunity to establish criteria and express their grievances with respect to social policy, human rights and trade union rights when these are infringed upon. Hence, it is important to speak out here about the situation in Colombia in the hope of finding redress to our grievances through the observance of the fundamental standards and use of the supervisory bodies of the ILO, going beyond mere technical cooperation.

Despite widespread poverty, unemployment, underemployment and the displacement of farmers from agricultural areas to cities as a result of the armed conflict, the Government and Parliament are enacting laws in the area of labour legislation, tax legislation, social security and legal reforms which are regressive and reduce the income of workers; they levy the same taxes on the rich as on the poor, thereby increasing the level of poverty, which has already reached 58 per cent of the Colombian population of 44 million people.

Colombian trade unions are still suffering from the tragic situation of violence. The fact that there are fewer murders of trade unionists does not mean that crimes have ceased. In the past 12 months, 108 trade unionists were murdered. The breach of human rights has taken other forms, for example, harassments, forced movements, threats, mass detentions and unlawful entries have all increased. This is a stark contrast to the shocking impunity for these crimes which reaches 98 per cent. So, trade union activity in Colombia is still a high-risk activity and will continue to be so as long as such is impunity continues.

Against this background, a policy is emerging that could be considered a policy of the State which is aimed against the trade unions. This can be seen in the low profile given to the handling of the rights and conflicts that affect workers and trade unions. Other examples of this policy are the fact that the Ministry of Labour and Social Security has been done away with; the failure to implement the Labour Inspection Convention, 1947 (No. 81), thereby contravening the standards of social dialogue; the new forms of recruitment through cooperatives and enterprises which prevent workers from joining trade unions; restrictions on collective bargaining both in the public and private sectors, in clear violation of the Labour Relations (Public Service) Convention, 1978 (No. 151); state-imposed decisions on conflicts, such as the Workers' Trade Union (USO) case. We also see that in 2003 only 49,200 of the 4 million workers in the formal sector benefited from the process of collective bargaining.

The state policy of modernization led to the break-up of the TELECOM trade union, and throughout the communications industry the presence of trade unions in the sectors of social security, health care and in the National Service for Training (SENA) among others, was reduced.

The unions and social sectors lack guarantees that ensure the right to social protest, which will be restricted even further by the establishment of the Anti-terrorist Statute.

Recently, on 18 May, in the city of Cartagena, and in other cities of Colombia, worker rallies were brutally disbanded. They were protesting against the negotiation of the Free Trade Agreement between Colombia and the United States.

Allow me to state that the recent strike of petroleum workers in Colombia requires the same treatment by the ILO as that given to the cases in Costa Rica and Venezuela.

Ms. VALKONEN (Workers' delegate, Finland)

The World Commission's report is of exceptional significance. The implementation of the World Commission's recommendations requires strong political will and extensive commitment. The ILO has a particularly important role in strengthening the social dimension of globalization and the ILO should actively promote the establishment of the globalization policy forum.

The Report of the Director-General is an excellent outline of the ILO's activities. The basic structures of the ILO are in good condition and the mandate is up to date. Decision-making is democratic and transparent. As many speakers have already noted, the strength of the ILO is its tripartism. It is this that makes the ILO unique. The ILO's status must be consolidated further and all the constituents – governments, employers and trade unions alike – must become more committed to the ILO's activities.

The World Commission's report underlines strongly that tripartism and social dialogue are essential for promoting social justice. Global tripartism should be strengthened but, in order for the tripartite system to be effective globally, it must also be effective at the national level. In this respect, we still have a lot of work to do.

The Global Report under the Follow-up to the Declaration on Fundamental Principles and Rights at Work, *Organizing for social justice*, has also been discussed at this session of the Conference.

The Report states that, as to trade union rights, some progress has been made, but serious problems still remain. Freedom of association is continuously violated in many parts of the world, as we just heard.

Free and strong trade unions are a necessary prerequisite in implementing social justice. There are still countries where workers lack the right to organize. The right to organize and to conclude collective agreements are basic human rights. All the ILO member States should ratify and implement the Freedom of Association and Protection of the Right to Organise Convention, 1948 (No. 87), and the Right to Organise and Collective Bargaining Convention, 1949 (No. 98). The strengthening of the international standards system is also discussed in the Director-General's Report. The review carried out by the Governing Body has resulted in the identification of 71 Conventions and 73 Recommendations as fully up to date. Now we need measures to promote ratification and implementation of the ILO Conventions. Effective technical cooperation is, of course, most important.

In Finland we have a solid tradition of tripartite cooperation. I would like to stress that the Finnish welfare society has been built based on tripartite cooperation. Free and powerful trade unions have played a significant role here. In Finland, the Government has launched an extensive preparation for a national globalization strategy. Also, the social partners participate in this process. The sectoral dialogue of the employers' organizations and trade unions on the future of each sector is an important part of this process. It is not yet possible to discuss the results here, but I do believe that this process will, at its best, improve further the cooperation of the social partners and tripartite cooperation in Finland.

Original Spanish: Mr. MANCILLA GARCÍA *(Workers' delegate, Guatemala)*

It is a great honour for me, on behalf of the workers' sector of Guatemala, to congratulate Director-General Somavia on the Report that he has submitted to us, and we hope that it will be addressed in a tripartite way, as the Director-General mentioned.

The topic of decent work and the fight against poverty should be addressed in an urgent way, because the vast majority of the population in my country, Guatemala, struggles between poverty and dire poverty. People often rely on jobs without any guarantees and salaries that do not make it possible to satisfy the minimum basic needs, because the salaries are not consistent with the real cost of the average basket of staple goods. As a result of this, there are thousands of children who work in order to shore up the income of their families, robbing themselves of the right to study, to obtain training and to prepare themselves for the future. Thus, they will become adults who will not be able to provide qualified labour in a globalized world.

Globalization is now a reality: it causes hunger, poverty, pain and death to thousands of inhabitants of Guatemala and to a considerable share of mankind. Globalization in practice does not have a human face. It has the face of the market, of poverty, of exclusion. In order to turn this situation around, we need the provisions of social organization and transparent mechanisms at the international level; thus, we should support the ILO, as a unique tripartite organization, in order to ensure the observance and application of international standards, ensuring they are beneficial to everyone and not just to a minority.

The right to freedom of association and collective bargaining is another fundamental key point for the workers of Guatemala. However, despite the fact that Guatemala is a signatory to the Freedom of Association and Protection of the Right to Organise Convention, 1948 (No. 87), and the Right to Organise and Collective Bargaining Convention, 1949 (No. 98), of the ILO and other fundamental Conventions, the dismembering of trade unions has continued and the establishment of new trade unions, both in the public and the private sectors is being prevented. An example of this is that, before the signature of the peace agreements, the percentage of labour union affiliation nationally was 5 per cent, and currently it is about 2.5 per cent of the active population.

As a result of this persecution of trade unions, 38 workers have been jailed, including Rigoberto Dueñas Morales, who has been accused of embezzling millions from social security, despite the fact that we have demonstrated many times that he is completely innocent of the charges of which he is accused, including embezzlement, fraud and others. And, despite the fact that these charges do not carry a prison sentence, he has been in prison since 8 June 2003.

Victoriano Zacarias has also been detained in prison since 25 February 2004, as have another 30 drivers of heavy trucks. They were put in prison because they supported the resistance of workers belonging to the Trade Union of Heavy Transport Drivers against measure adopted by the Municipality of Guatemala City to restrict traffic of heavy vehicles in eight of the main streets of the capital. This made it necessary for the drivers to find other routes to drive their trucks and to work night hours, putting their physical well-being, their safety and their lives in danger, given the high level of crime in the country and the fact that they are often the victims of attacks. These colleagues are now in jail and accused of terrorism.

The people of Guatemala are at a crucial moment. We have a recently elected Government, and, during the week of 17-20 May 2003, it had to justify its activities to a direct contacts mission from the ILO on the anti-union activities that have been carried out for many years in the country, and that, given the violations of freedom of association and collective bargaining, there are thousands of workers in the rural, *maquila* and *public* sectors, with greater emphasis on the municipal sector, that have been affected and are still awaiting anxiously for their cases to be resolved and to be reinstated in their posts. This particularly in light of the fact that it is now eight years since they were dismissed for establishing or belonging to a union. There are also cases of many families who hope that the murders of their family members who were trade unionists will be resolved.

We hope that the current Government complies with and respects the international Conventions on freedom of association, collective bargaining and minimum wages, ratified by Guatemala, and the Declaration on Fundamental Principles and Rights at Work, and that it also complies with what it has stated with regard to its desire to settle existing labour conflicts. Finally, we hope that the visit of the ILO direct contacts mission will produce the hoped-for results that will benefit the workers of Guatemala.

Mr. LAWAL *(Minister of Labour, Nigeria)*

The Nigerian delegation congratulates the President and all the other Officers of the Conference on their election to steer the affairs of the 92nd Session of the International Labour Conference. I also thank the Director-General of the International Labour Office for his excellent Report: *ILO programme implementation 2002-03.*

We are pleased to have this opportunity for an exchange of views on the excellent report of the World Commission on the Social Dimension of Globalization.

There is no doubt that the ongoing process of globalization has tremendous benefits. However, I should like to point out that such advantages appear distant to billions of ordinary people in many developing countries of the world. We are therefore happy to note that the report of the World Commission has placed the necessary emphasis on localization, fairer rules and better governance in the process of globalization.

In Nigeria, we acknowledge that a great deal ought to be done at the national level to meet the challenges of development in our contemporary world. It is on this premise that the Government of Olusegun Obasanjo has articulated and introduced an economic blueprint known as the National Economic Empowerment and Development Strategy, otherwise called NEEDS. The strategy seeks to reposition the economy by achieving a GDP growth rate of 7 per cent and by creating 7 million new jobs by 2007. The provision of decent work is one of the cardinal objectives of these Nigerian strategies, which is in consonance with the call by the Director-General of the ILO for decent work to be made a global objective.

I wish to observe that domestic initiatives in this direction will amount to nothing, no matter how laudable they may be, in the absence of a fairer process of globalization. It has therefore become imperative to overcome the existing democratic deficit in global governance by increasing the voice and participation of developing countries in decision-making and rule-setting at the international level.

The Nigerian delegation concurs with the World Commission that the application of the principles of globalization should be based on a strong ethical framework and universally shared values.

The Report of the Director-General: *ILO programme implementation 2002-03* provides useful information on the progress made in implementing the four strategic objectives our Organization. In particular, I note that, in this Report, the Director-General has indicated that the process of reviewing ILO standards might reveal the need for new instruments that will help to bring about a more rational framework linking existing Conventions and Recommendations. Indeed, this goes to the heart of policy coherence which will promote greater efficiency in the work of the ILO and contribute to the normative dimension of decent work. More needs to be done as our Organization celebrates its 85th anniversary. We look forward to laying the foundations for its future in terms of providing a solid framework for strengthening the ILO's normative mission. We would welcome further elaboration on this point by the Director-General.

In conclusion, Nigeria appreciates that the ILO has come a long way in the realization of its global mandate. It is, however, important to note that a lot more ground still has to be covered by this Organization. It is therefore my sincere wish that the outcome of our deliberations here and in the various committees of this Organization will help bring us closer to achieving the four challenges that the Director-General outlined in his introductory remarks.

Mr. SUNMONU *(representative, Organization of African Trade Union Unity)*

I would like, on behalf of the Organization of African Trade Union Unity to congratulate the President and the Director-General for their excellent reader-friendly reports. We are happy to note that the Governing Body cooperates with the Director-General and the International Labour Office in executing the programmes of the ILO and in raising its profile within the United Nations family.

The visionary set-up by the ILO, of the World Commission on the Social Dimension of Globalization, whose excellent report has been jointly presented to this session of the Conference by President Mkapa of the United Republic of Tanzania and President Halonen of Finland, will rank as one of the best contributions the ILO has made to the socio-economic development of peoples and countries. We extend our profound gratitude to the two eminent co-chairpersons and the distinguished members of the World Commission for a job that has been very well done.

The report of the World Commission could not have chosen a better title than *A fair globalization: Creating opportunities for all*, which fully captures the essence of the entire report. The Organization of African Trade Union Unity and all the workers of Africa fully support the report and endorse its implementation at local, national, regional and international levels. Tripartite and stakeholders committees for implementation of the report should be set up at all the abovementioned four levels to ensure effective implementation of the report. In our view, the report should also form the basis of the design of a new development paradigm which, in essence, should be people-centred and which should replace the present neo-liberal paradigm that was based on the Washington Consensus. My suggestion is based on the reported admission by Mr. James Wolfensohn, President of the World Bank, at the Shanghai Conference on Poverty which the Bank organized last month that the Washington Consensus, with its emphasis on open markets, fiscal stringency and privatization has been long dead.

Our organization also endorses the Director-General's Report on the suggestions for the role the ILO has to play in the search for fairer globalization. In order for the ILO to play a leading role, as envisaged, the Governing Body has to substantially increase the budget for our unique organization. The three partners of the ILO should rise to the challenge of fairer globalization that creates opportunities for all.

Coming from Africa it makes me happy that the African Union's Heads of State and Government will convene an Extraordinary Summit in Ouagadougou, Burkina Faso, from 8 to 9 September 2004 on Employment and Poverty Alleviation in Africa. I am happy to inform this session of this august conference that African workers and employers will effectively participate in the Social Partners Forum which will take place in Ouagadougou from 3 to 4 September 2004 and deliberate on the theme of decent work: a new development strategy for Africa. The conclusions of the Social Partners Forum will be submitted to the Extraordinary Summit of the African Union as a contribution to the Summit.

I take this opportunity to express our appreciation to the ILO, its African Regional Office and the Bureaux for Workers' and Employers' Activities (ACTRAV and ACT/EMP) for their support for the effective participation of African workers and employers at the Ouagadougou Extraordinary Summit of the African Union.

We also thank the Commission of the African Union, as well as the host nation, Burkina Faso, for their kind assistance.

The OATUU believes that there is no better way to poverty reduction and eradication than through decent well-paid jobs. In this regard, it is in collaboration with the ILO designing effective African trade union and countries' participation in decent job creation.

On the Global Report, on the ILO Declaration on Fundamental Principles and Rights at Work and its Follow-up, I congratulate the Office for the well-prepared Report. Progress has been made in the application of the principle of freedom of association and the recognition of the right to collective bargaining. A great number of workers in the cultural sector, export processing zones and in the informal economy are still denied their rights to form and join unions and bargain collectively. In some countries, civil servants are still denied their fundamental rights to form and join unions. We should all work hard to protect the rights of the affected workers. We therefore call for increased workshops and seminars for workers and trade union leaders by experts from the standards sector, to assist in fighting violations of ILO Conventions.

On human resources development and training, we appeal to all the delegates to this session of the Conference to vote for the adoption of the Recommendation concerning human resources development and training. We should all play our part in working for the early ratification and implementation of the Recommendation by ILO member countries.

I thank the Director-General for his Report on the situation of workers of the occupied Arab territories. The Report paints a sombre picture of what Israeli occupation does to the lives of Palestinian workers and people, particularly to women and children. The OATUU at its Eighth Ordinary Congress in Khartoum, Sudan, in January this year, adopted a unanimous resolution of support and solidarity with the Palestinian workers and people in their struggle against Israeli occupation. African workers and trade unions support the creation of the State of Palestine alongside that of Israel, with Jerusalem as capital.

We call on Israel to withdraw from all occupied Arab territories, in conformity with UN Security Council resolutions. The ILO should increase its financial and technical cooperation programmes to the Palestinian workers and people.

Mr. ALEMAYEHU *(Workers' delegate, Ethiopia)*

On behalf of the Confederation of Ethiopian Trade Unions and for myself, I would like to congratulate the President and the two Vice-Presidents for their election to preside over this session of the august International Labour Conference. I would also like to express my appreciation for the Reports of the Chairperson of the ILO Governing Body and of the Director-General.

The report which was prepared by the World Commission on the Social Dimension of Globalization entitled: *"A fair globalization: Creating opportunities for all"* takes a holistic approach to a complex issue. Therefore, I support the report, because decent work is the most important component necessary to create a fair globalization.

Decent work can be achieved in open economies and open societies if we pursue strategic objectives such as employment rights, social protection and dialogue. Decent work is a development approach based on the realities on the ground, because it is first and foremost a listening agenda. Workers need access to basic social protection and employment because poverty and employment are inextricably linked. The principal manner of linking them is a sound national development policy that puts sustainable growth at the heart of national objectives.

Democratic stability and good governance are essential to economic growth and social development. Employers' and workers' organizations are critically important for more effective policies, particularly to combat poverty. Social dialogue and strong tripartite institutions and practices can ensure greater coherence between economic and social policies. The capacity of social partners to engage in dialogue is critical for enhancing productive employment opportunities, extending social protection and focusing on poverty reduction. Workers need comprehensive training and education programmes to be productive and enable them to contribute to the development of their country.

Employers' organizations and the government have to respond rapidly to the changing needs of their workers. In order for them to be able to do so, they need supportive, transparent and accountable partners for effective social dialogue at the national level. The challenge is to create an environment based on democratic principles that encourages and guarantees respect of human rights, including fundamental freedoms and rights at work. International labour standards should be respected and should be part of the national labour laws.

In this regard, the Confederation of Ethiopian Trade Unions has made great efforts to bring about the amendment of the previous labour legislation of our country. In doing so, the part played by the social partners and the support of the ILO needs to be mentioned and appreciated. In spite of the fact that the new Labour Law was adopted around the end of the year 2003, we have found it to contain certain provisions that are not in line with the interest of workers. We therefore submitted our requests to the Government for revision.

A very important issue that I would like to address is HIV/AIDS. For us it is a priority because our members are dying of this pandemic. To tackle this pandemic, our Confederation conducts many workplace interventions such as awareness creation, care and support programmes, but the magnitude of the problem is increasing. In this regard, I appreciate the support that we have been given by the ILO, but we need more support to carry out additional activities to challenge the problem and to protect workers.

In conclusion, I would like to stress that the ILO should further strengthen its support to African countries, especially those efforts that are targeted at the alleviation of poverty and unemployment; strengthening social dialogue and capacity-building should be seriously backed up. Strengthening of trade unions and their efforts to secure the livelihoods of workers should be given the necessary support. Our Confederation has already established good grounds for effective work cooperation with the ILO subregional office in Addis Ababa and I thank the Office for its unreserved support. Hopefully, we shall better strengthen our cooperation for better results.

Original Spanish: Mr. CORRIES *(representative, World Confederation of Teachers)*

First of all, may I congratulate the President on behalf of the World Confederation of Teachers (WCT) which is affiliated to the World Confederation of Labour, for his election to preside over this assembly. The WCT welcomes the decision of the Director-General to dedicate his Report to decent work. In the reports prepared by the World Confederation of Teachers and presented to the Joint ILO/UNESCO Committee of Experts on the Application of the Recommendations concerning Teaching Personnel (CEART), we once again, as we did in 2001, emphasize the generalized deterioration of the working conditions of teachers during the last decades. This deterioration should be considered within a context of fragile social dialogue which, as indicated in the recent report by the Committee, only leads to the further deterioration of the situation. Social dialogue, carried out between all of the partners involved, is indeed a dynamic force towards change and progress.

We must not lose sight of the fact that the major live forces of education are teachers who are motivated, qualified and dedicated on a daily basis to the service of young people and society. One of the crucial questions in the field of education today is the shortage of teachers. A dearth, on the one hand, because within the framework of the knowledge-based society and the Dakar objectives, more and more young people have access to education, for which we can only be grateful. All we need now is to take the necessary steps so that all young people may have access to quality education provided by qualified teachers. We cannot fail to mention all the groups of young people that cannot exercise their basic right to education, inter alia, the children of immigrants, children from regions in conflict, the children of socially and economically marginalized populations, and also girls who, despite the Dakar objectives, continue to be excluded from education to a much greater extent. Ensuring the right to education for all young people is the best way to combat child labour.

Ensuring quality education for all young people is a responsibility that we all share. It is a responsibility that requires important investments in terms of teacher training, both initial and ongoing. Investments also need to be made in the working conditions of teachers, in ensuring proper salaries and in creating a stimulating pedagogical environment. In other words, if we really want quality education for all, we have to put the students and teachers at the centre of the debate and invest in that which is essential for education, namely teachers. Teachers are not a "human resource"; we are not a means of production; we are not an added value for acquiring knowledge, know-how and know-how-to-be; we are not tools of economic production. We are men and women who very much take to heart our mission to train young people and support them in their education as individuals and responsible citizens.

Thus, we congratulate and thank the ILO for the efforts deployed and for the results already achieved in ensuring decent work, as described in the Director-General's Report, especially in the light of the budgetary restrictions imposed by the zero growth. We share the views of the Director-General and of the ILO concerning the priority to be afforded to action within countries. But, in the knowledge-based society, we want to achieve significant progress in the medium- and long-terms in the field of decent work and with initiatives to endow globalization with a human face. And thus, it is absolutely necessary to implement in full the Recommendations concerning the status of teachers.

Here, there is, of course, the collective responsibility of the ILO but also the individual responsibility of each member State of the ILO. Would it still be decent today to ask teachers to be more professional and to have more expertise, to pay more attention to the quality of education, to be more open to the world, to show more commitment in local communities, more, more, more, but to deny them a decent salary? In many developing and transition countries, the salary received by a teacher is far below the minimum wage.

On 5 October 2006, we will be celebrating the 40th anniversary of the adoption of the Recommendation concerning the status of teachers. Would it not be the ideal opportunity for the ILO to launch a campaign for decent work for teachers and for all teaching personnel? In the WCT, it is clear that if we seriously want to campaign against the shortage of teachers, we must create decent working conditions and at the very least respect the international standards approved by the ILO.

Mr. JENNINGS *(representative, Union Network International)*

UNI is a global union federation committed to union organizing. One thousand affiliated unions are recruiting in over 150 nations. Each year, hundreds of thousands are joining unions in the services sector, both full time and part time as well as a growing number of freelance workers. UNI globalizes union organizing with campaigns for young people, for women, for professionals and in companies from Hollywood and the media sector, through telecoms, graphics, finance, commerce, post, IT business services and social insurance to cleaning and security.

A global labour market with global companies and global outsourcing requires global union recruitment initiatives. We targeted a thousand call centres in 30 nations in Asia, Africa, America and Europe. The results, more members and new agreements. Tomorrow, UNI Telecom will sign with telecom employers a European agreement on labour standards in call centres, including the right to organize. Proof that you can bring labour standards to a new economy.

Offshore outsourcing must not become a race to the bottom. The new UNI offshore charter deals with the migration of people and jobs. We do not accept, that, as one minister said, the entrepreneurial spirit is sufficient to deal with this. It needs active labour-market policies. UNI's affiliates have given collective agreements a global dimension, dealing with outsourcing at home and too often the rights deficit abroad. Globalization agreements has been entered with Barclays, HSBC, Lloyds TSB and British Telecom. We have an agreement with Barclays for the continent of Africa. Global companies should globalize their relations with global union federations like UNI.

We have welcomed the World Commission's report on the social dimension of globalization, as we have welcomed the Global Report *Organizing for social justice* and the Director-General's Report, *A fair globalization: The role of the ILO*. They each recognize that with global production systems, global agreements are a way forward, while exploiting rights-free export processing zones is a step backwards. The ILO Declaration and the OECD guidelines on multinationals have political and moral but not legal force. So companies can wriggle free from compliance.

As the Reports point out, we welcome the strengthening of the ILO knowledge-base – but it is not enough. We accept your offer to support the development of institutions that strengthens the dialogue to achieve decent work – but this is not enough. A pity that President Bush was not listening. For the first time in the history of G8 Summit, he refused a dialogue with the global union movement last week. We can only assume that he does not care about what is on the mind of working people around the world.

We welcome the ILO's commitment to monitor global agreements and provide advice and assistance – but it is not enough. We ask the Director-General to rapidly convene a tripartite policy forum on corporate social responsibility and global framework agreements. We must ensure that global labour standards apply to companies, that there is a mechanism to hold them to account. On 24 June, the Global Compact Summit will take place in New York and we will have the list before us of about 1,500 companies that have signed up. The Compact needs more integrity, a system of checks, a system of accountability. After all the corporate corruption and lies of recent years, we need mechanisms to build trust within which we have confidence.

Companies do not always do what they say or write in their annual reports. Look at Group 4 Falck. They claim to recognize unions everywhere, but their subsidiary Wackenhut does the opposite in the United States. Group 4 Falck should accept the right to organize everywhere.

The ILO can put backbone into the Global Compact by monitoring compliance in dealing with disputes, but for companies in UNI sectors, we say that when you sign the Global Compact, you should enter negotiations with us for a framework agreement.

We will expose the union busters. Let us reject Wal-Mart in the process of Wal-Martization, a company for whom decent work, union recognition and collective bargaining are dirty words in the United States. Wal-Mart has announced a corporate face-lift. Perhaps liposuction would be better; that way we could suck out all of their anti-union policies. Wal-Mart is taking advantage from the shocking finding that half of the world's workers remain unprotected by ILO Conventions Nos. 87 and 98.

In conclusion, we look forward to the ILO insisting on compliance with labour standards throughout the multilateral system, from the IMF and World Bank to the WTO, that the ILO will campaign for all governments to apply core labour standards by 2015 at the very latest.

Wal-Mart and Zimbabwe make curious bedfellows. We salute the courage of Zimbabwean union members' Leaders arrested. Workers summarily dismissed or locked out in banks, posts and telecoms. Shame on the regime that so hammers working people. Our message is that you will not succeed, you will not crush the desire of ordinary working people for change. As we say, shame on the repressive measures in Myanmar, China, Colombia, Nepal and the Russian Federation.

Working people face fire and rain. Last year 129 union leaders and members were murdered. May they rest in peace.

We shall not rest, we shall walk through the storm in our fight for rights to be respected, for corporate abuses of the working people to end and for decent work for working people everywhere, and we look forward to working with the ILO in the implementation of the World Commission's recommendations.

Original Spanish: Mr. PUGA RODRÍGUEZ *(Workers' delegate, Panama)*

The topic of unemployment and the need to create decent jobs is one of the top priorities of the democratic governance agenda of my country. However, it is also true that the work of trade union organizations encounters serious obstacles, given that successive governments as a maker of policy have refused to accept the fact that both Conventions Nos. 87 and 98 do not exclude, for the purposes of freedom of association and collective bargaining, any segment of the labour force. On this point we would like to speak out, as we have done on other occasions, about the fact that freedom of association in our country is subject to all kinds of restrictions and interference, with respect to certain groups such as bank employees, public sector employees, as well as workers in the free economic zone of Colon. In fact, with regard to freedom of association, our domestic legislation does not make any distinctions either.

Furthermore, free and voluntary bargaining as enshrined in Convention No. 98 has also met with obstacles. The labour authorities of our country use all kinds of regulatory loopholes when they examine union lists of demands, and use various formalities to delay or put off the collective bargaining processes. Indeed, they even conclude arrangements with non-unionized workers and disregard the existing unions. This is not in keeping with the spirit of our law, which is consistent with ILO Convention No. 98.

We would also like to mention the situation of public sector workers who are denied their rights to freedom of association and collective bargaining. What is even more serious is the fact that they lack effective procedures for collective bargaining, and, as if that were not enough, they are discriminated against because, although forming part of the Panamanian workforce, they still do not have a minimum wage scale, as successive governments have still not complied with section 198 of the Administrative Careers of Law, No. 9, of 20 June 1994, according to which a general law on salaries should have been adopted.

We would not like to leave this podium without also referring to a topic which is of great concern to all sectors of Panamanian society, and specifically for all workers. For several weeks now the Government of Panama has been involved in a process of fast-track negotiations for a free trade agreement with the United States, with the aim of finalizing it by next September. Workers have not been invited to participate, even as an afterthought. Now we know, from the example of other countries, that this participation would not necessarily be negative. It is thus more a matter of principle that this treaty should reflect the various social clauses, especially those relating to internationally recognized labour rights as set out in the ILO Declaration on the Fundamental Principles and Rights at Work and its Follow-up of 1998, specifically paragraph 5. This means that these treaties must not lead to the weakening or reduction of the fundamental principles and rights recognized by the ILO – including the right of freedom of association, the right to strike, the right to collective bargaining on a minimum wage, working hours and safety and health, as well as having clearly established procedural guarantees. We therefore urge the ILO to play an active role in demanding strict compliance by all countries with the commitments agreed in Conventions ratified by them.

We would like to thank the this Conference for allowing us to make our case and speak out against the violations of trade union and human rights by the Government, and to reiterate the complaint and that the Panamanian workers submitted in 2003.

Original French: Mr. LEDOUBLE *(representative, International Christian Union of Business Executives)*

UNIAPAC, the International Christian Union of Business Executives, would like to express here its appreciation for the work done by the ILO on *A fair globalization: Creating opportunities for all*, not just for the contents of the World Commission's report, but also for having involved the World

Trade Organization, the World Bank and the International Monetary Fund in it's preparation. In our opinion, this sort of cooperation needs to be strengthened to make sure that everyone feels truly concerned by this global challenge.

We share many of the views expressed in this Report. First of all, about the current state of globalization, which is neither satisfactory nor sustainable because of the inequalities, and consequently the injustices to which it gives rise. In our view, any economic order that does not respect human dignity, which restricts the responsibility or freedom of action of human beings, is unfair, even if it generates enormous wealth, and even if that wealth is fairly distributed. We also share the values set out in the report; in particular, the need for us to be at the service of those people who have the greatest need, and the importance of doing this through dialogue. Lastly, we share the conviction that we can do an awful lot better.

All this is directly linked to our current theme for reflection which concerns corporate social responsibility. We are particularly concerned with the social responsibility of Christian businesses with particular attention to our responsibility towards the poor.

UNIAPAC is a federation made up of 26 national associations of executives, business leaders and employers throughout the world, but predominantly from Europe and Latin America. The members of UNIAPAC are therefore right at the heart of the decisions being taken in the business world.

Our activities focus on reflection and raising the awareness of business leaders, particularly during seminars and summer courses; the next one will take place in Lisbon and will focus on the following topic: "Business ethics, a personal challenge for leaders". In 2005, the summer course will take place in Rome, and we are planning to hold the 2006 summer course in Geneva, which will give us an opportunity for further contact with the ILO.

In March, we organized a seminar in Rome, with the Pontifical Council for "Justice and Peace", which was attended by more than 70 world business leaders from large and medium-sized companies, who discussed the general theme of the corporate social responsibility of business leaders in the context of globalization. Work concentrated on the objectives for business and profit, on the fight against corruption, the social responsibility of business leaders in combating poverty, the personal development of the workforce in the face of the financial pressures which businesses are under, as well as on the cultural impact of marketing and advertising policies.

This gives me an opportunity to recall that the raison d'être of business and of profit is not in the acquisition of profit in itself, but in the existence of a community of persons who are trying to meet their own basic needs whilst being at the service of the whole of society

Our aim is thus to support the ILO's endeavours to establish a fairer world, but by taking a complementary approach: the ILO acts by framing regulations, for example on respect for freedom of association, which allows workers to take collective action and influence their own development; UNIAPAC's challenge is to bring about a change in the attitudes of business leaders to ensure that the freedoms afforded by economic activity and legislation are used to the full in the service of human development.

Our two approaches are complementary. They reaffirm the benefits of the partnerships between UNIAPAC and the ILO and give me the opportunity to thank the ILO for promoting dialogue with civil society and for having given us the opportunity to share our thoughts with this plenary session.

Original Spanish: Mr. PARRAS ROJAS *(Employers' delegate, Cuba)*

First of all, allow me to congratulate the President on his election to preside over this 92nd Session of the International Labour Conference.

I agree with previous speakers in recognizing the importance of addressing the subject of globalization, taking an approach based on justice and the creation of opportunities for all.

The scale of the problems facing humanity in the third millennium compels us to address the problem with a sense of urgency and a practical approach, manifested in the will to implement specific plans of action which could solve the major problems identified.

Although there has been progress in the fields of social protection, decent work, and the promotion of and compliance with standards and fundamental principles and rights at work, we are concerned that this is only a small part of the overall problems which exist and which are growing day by day. None of these objectives can be fully achieved without economic growth, particularly in the countries of the South, where problems are accumulating to an alarming extent.

I would like to make the following comments on this point. The liberalization of trade, far from decreasing trade imbalances between developed and developing countries, has increased them. It opens up markets to manufactured products while protecting agricultural products or introducing non-tariff barriers.

The liberalization of financial markets has given rise to speculation, capital flight and the growth of the external debt burden of developing countries at an alarming rate, jeopardizing the social stability of many countries.

There are considerable imbalances between North and South in terms of access to knowledge and technology, and to this we must add the harmful practice of encouraging the brain drain and continuing restrictions on transfer of technology.

These are three examples of ways in which the process of globalization is taking place and which, among other things, prevent many employers in the developing countries from maintaining the necessary growth rates to allow an increase in decent and productive employment.

Cuban employers, whom I represent, are now in the process of enhancing entrepreneurship and promoting more flexible and competitive enterprises to keep pace with the constant changes on the market, by introducing quality management systems and developing training and skills upgrading for their workers in line with the needs of enterprises.

In addition to these challenges, which are to be expected in a globalized world, the employers of Cuba also have to face the effects of the measures applied by the Government of the United States to intensify the economic blockade, which places obstacles in the way of international trade and hampers the efficient performance of Cuban entrepreneurs.

A contribution of the ILO, together with the other agencies of the United Nations system, would be to take a decisive stance against the adoption of such unilateral measures by one State against any other with the aim of attaining political objectives and with the sole effect of increasing the suffering of the people.

Mr. MONONGA *(Government delegate, Malawi)*

May I begin by congratulating the President and Vice-Presidents on their successful elections. We all have confidence in your skills and abilities to make this session of the Conference successful and memorable, bearing in mind that we are also having a triple celebration – the ILO is now 85 years young; the Declaration of Philadelphia is now 60 years and still fresh; and our Organization has, for 35 years, now been a proud holder of the much-respected Nobel Peace Prize. It is therefore with great pleasure that Malawi feels greatly honoured to be part of the family of ILO member countries participating in this auspicious Conference.

The Malawi delegation has read the Reports of the Chairperson of the Governing Body and of the Director-General of the ILO, and we are satisfied that the institution is indeed moving successfully towards its niche area of social peace and justice through its rights-based normative approach in this globalizing world.

As we can all recall, it was very, very difficult to envisage the relevance of the ILO at the end of the twentieth century because it was not clear as to what role an institution based on the mission of norms could play after the Cold War, and when the world was coming close together as a global village driven by openness, liberalization and deregulation. Honestly speaking, a number of people were not sure about the future of the standard-setting role of the ILO in this new millennium, and some of us were worried about the future status of this value-based institution.

The Malawi delegation is, however, very grateful to learn from the excellent Reports put at the disposal of this Conference that, contrary to the fears some of us had had, the ILO has become even stronger now than it was at the end of the last century. Malawi is extremely proud to be a Member of the ILO today because the ILO has delivered, and continues to deliver, quality products and services in Malawi.

We are aware that, at the centre of the ILO Decent Work Agenda, is a child labour free world. Malawi, with the help of the ILO, is doing all it can to fight the evils of child labour. Today, the majority of Malawians are aware that child labour is a serious sin and a crime against the future generations of our country.

With ILO assistance, Malawi has been able to conduct a national child labour survey and we have just completed the survey report which we shall be launching very soon. The ILO has also helped us to train our labour inspectors, employers and trade unions on the issues of decent work, particularly on the Declaration on Fundamental Principles and Rights at Work, through the ILO/SLASA, Strengthening Labour Administration in Southern Africa project, which has now been transformed into International Labour Standards in Southern Africa (ILO/ILSA). It is our sincere hope that the ILO/ILSA project will complete all the activities started by ILO/SLASA including, of course, the purchase of equipment and motorcycles for the labour inspectors.

Since Malawi is the spokesperson for the African group in the Technical Cooperation Committee of the Governing Body, let me end by requesting the ILO and the donor community to kindly ensure that Africa becomes one of the major recipients of ILO technical cooperation assistance.

We note that, apart from the Arab world, Africa was the recipient of the least technical cooperation assistance from the ILO during the 2002-03 biennium, according to Appendix II of the Report of the Director-General on *ILO programme implementation 2002-03*. With the current levels of poverty in Africa, it is only moral and imperative for the ILO to devote more technical cooperation activities to the African continent.

Mr. REPOSSI *(representative, Association of Volunteers for International Service)*

First of all, I would like to thank you for allowing me to speak on behalf of AVSI, a non-profit-making international development NGO and to share some thoughts on the topic of human resources development and training, including insights which have emerged from our years of working with people, especially youth, in more than 30 countries in the world.

We at AVSI appreciate the focus on human resource development, understood as education, training and lifelong learning and valued as a fundamental motor of development at all levels. It should also be noted that we are in complete agreement with the recommendation's holistic approach to this issue, which recognizes that the need for education and training exists alongside the need for economic, social and labour market policies and programmes. One of the most challenging dimensions contained in the proposed Recommendation is the need to encourage individuals to pursue their own development, further their education and take responsibility for their lives.

Please let me set forth three suggestions for human resource development in keeping with the goals of the ILO in the present Conference.

Firstly, policies and programmes can deliver only when one fundamental factor is properly taken care of, that is the person. The person and his or her full human growth are the keys to lasting and fruitful development. Each person can contribute to the common good by building on the very first resource everyone is equipped with, the desire for happiness and the need for love and, being loved, the yearning for good and the need to share it with others.

It is from this basis that we can speak of the right to education and training. All partners in development must work with a positive attitude towards reality and a desire for common good.

The Recommendation emphasizes strategies of lifelong learning, and rightly so, since the limitations of formal education as a means of facilitating the transition into the labour force are clear. In addition, the Recommendation specifically advocates promoting access to education and training for people with special needs, notably youth.

Youth are the source of economic growth and social change and need to be seen as primary agents of such change. Their asset is their self, their desire for truth, for happiness and for meaning, which needs to be awakened and discovered, sustained through education and in companionship. The lack of meaning keeps them far away, or even unwilling to accept a job or an opportunity.

Relating with youth at this level is fundamental, if any job training or entrepreneurship course is to take root. We need to be committed to youth, so that they can perceive work as a way to express and build their own capacity and assets and thereby make an invaluable and long-lasting contribution to society and the nation.

At a more practical level, I would like to stress the value of collaboration with, and among, government agencies and local institutions, mainly the service-providing non-profit-making organizations, in order to strengthen capacity and to address the population's needs for education to work and services that facilitate employment matching and creation. Let us also point out the need for any national policy to be effective and sustainable. It has to draw on the lessons and findings that civil society, youth groups and social entrepreneurship have gained from their day-to-day experience and involvement in the field, seek to establish a conducive environment which facilitates and supports the efforts of the groups involved in youth education, in education to work and in the accompaniment of young people in their jobs and careers, develop action-oriented strategies in order to actually meet the needs of youth at the most ordinary grass-roots level and promote consultation, forums, seminars etc., where the actors of the various initiatives in job creation and employment, particularly those in innovative initiatives, could come together, share their methods, constraints, challenges and results with the goal of contributing to the adaption and refinement of national policies and programmes.

Mr. MD. ZAFRUL *(Workers' delegate, Bangladesh)*

First of all I wish to congratulate the President, the Vice-Presidents and other officials on their respective elections and sincerely wish that this session of the Conference, under their able leadership, moves towards a productive conclusion.

I also wish to extend my thanks to the Chairperson of the Governing Body, the World Commission and the Director-General of the ILO for their very useful, timely works, as reflected in the Reports. My thanks to all members of the secretariat for their efforts organizing and running such a big event.

While we are discussing the social dimension of globalization and other related issues in this Conference hall, please allow me to recall what millions of our fellow workers, women and men, back home in my country and other places think about globalization.

I am sure many of you here are quite familiar, even better informed about the situation.

To tell you the truth, in the eyes of millions of them, globalization is a monster. Why? Because globalization has upset the whole system, values and culture of the lives of common people. With the march of globalization and its inevitable companion, the market forces, many of the industries have been closed down on grounds of financial non-viability resulting in thousands and thousands of workers losing their jobs.

More and more industries will be closed and more jobs will be lost. Poverty, income inequality, insecurity, all those are taking place openly in front of their eyes without anyone listening to their voices because of the process of globalization.

As a least developing country, what are our main concerns? We have a population of 130 million, 39 per cent of them living under the poverty level earning less than $1 a day, 20 million unemployed young people are looking for jobs in a barren labour market and every year, there are more and more. Owing to a better agricultural harvest though, the GDP is showing a slight upward trend, but the industries sector is constantly declining. Owing to the opening of the economy without due preparation, taking advantage of the unfair situation, more experienced outside companies and big multinational companies are taking over and local industries are forced to close down.

Globalization in its present form instead of industrialization, job creation and economic growth, is creating conditions of de-industrialization, increased unemployment, a widening gap between the rich and the poor and creating insecurity and social instability. External pressure is also there to withdraw subsidies from the only contributing agriculture sector. The Millennium Development Goal of reducing poverty thus remains a dream that will never be fulfilled.

Here, I wish to mention another dimension of globalization as seen by our common people.

The common people's idea of creating opportunities from globalization can be seen from the following example.

As a consequence of globalization, owing to a policy shift, unregulated market access has taken place in social sectors like health and education. As reform measures, downsizing, and budget cuts are affecting the ability of the community hospitals and the education institutes to provide health and education at affordable prices to the common people, a few affluent beneficiaries of the globalization process are sending their children for better education at very great expense, at home and abroad, using Medicare for themselves and their families in world-class hospitals wheresoever, at costs unimaginable to the common people, thus creating another imbalance in terms of capacity, future skills and adjustment for the whole future generation.

This is an example of the process of globalization creating advantages for the rich few and far-reaching disadvantages for the majority of the common people.

Some time ago, 30,000 workers in one industry in Bangladesh lost their jobs all in one go when the mill was closed. There was no social security, no safety net. This is a big one, but there are many others. I just wish to remind you that under whatever circumstances or whatever pretext a worker loses his job, typically, as the only breadwinner of the family, it is often not very plain and easy for him to lose his job, to go home in the evening and have to tell his family "look, I have no job and no income today to support you". It is not easy and simple for those who have not been in such a situation to understand what it is like. I am not sure how many will be able to visualize the expressions of those scared faces, the amount of despair, grief and uncertainty.

From my, yet, incomplete study of the Reports – the Reports of the Chairperson of the Governing Body, the World Commission Report on Globalization, the Director-General's Report and, most particularly, from listening to the speech of the Director-General on 7 June, introducing and summarizing his report: *A fair globalization: The role of the ILO*, I have developed a feeling that the people behind this, the authors of these Reports, the co-chairs and other members of the World Commission, the Director-General and the Governing Body of the ILO, did not fail to read the language on those scared faces, whether in Bangladesh or in any other part of the world. To this session of the Conference, on behalf of those toiling workers whom I represent, this is my simple comment on those Reports.

In the interest of the majority of the world population, the ILO has to continue its endeavours to shape globalization in its fairest form, creating opportunities for all, establishing decent work, social protection and fundamental rights. The messages and the goals for the ILO have been set. The duty for all of us after this session of the Conference will be to carry the mandate forward. For our own good and for a better future world the workers of Bangladesh will try to play their correct role.

Mr. DAVID *(Workers' delegate, Indonesia)*

First of all, allow me to congratulate the President and the Vice-Presidents on their election at the 92nd Session of the International Labour Conference. I also congratulate the Director-General on his second mandate, and on his excellent Report to the Conference. Concerning the report entitled *A fair globalization: Creating opportunities for all*, prepared by the World Commission on the Social Dimension of Globalization, I would like to take this opportunity to dwell very briefly upon this topic and to express the Indonesian workers' views on various aspects.

As you will have heard, the Indonesian Government has ratified a total of 15 ILO Conventions to date, including the eight core Conventions on fundamental human rights, i.e. Conventions Nos. 29 and 87 and many others.

As regards these Conventions, certain labour laws have recently been approved, such as Law No. 21 of 2000 on trade unions, Law No. 13 of 2003 concerning manpower, Law No. 2 of 2004 which is a new law on industrial labour dispute settlement, and a law concerning labour inspection in regard to ILO Convention No. 81.

These ratifications must be followed by the next important step, which is to publicize the content of these Conventions among the partners concerned, especially the trade unions, in Indonesia to ensure that all workers are fully apprised of their rights at work and of the provisions of the Conventions, as well as of the various national laws and regulations which relate to them. This is a crucial task which must be undertaken not only at the government level, but also at the level of the social partners.

To this end, we would like to call upon the ILO to provide assistance and, if possible, to finance this campaign in order to increase national awareness regarding the fundamental principle of workers' rights. We would be more than happy to prepare and to submit our detailed proposals in this matter for your review and, hopefully, your approval.

Another important issue is the supervision of ratified Conventions, which needs to be taken into account in order to ensure the proper implementation of the Conventions in Indonesia. In this regard, I would like to recommend the following points.

Firstly, empowerment of the Indonesian trade unions should be ensured through short seminars and/or discussions designed to give a clear understanding of the Conventions and of the role they should play.

Secondly, the trade unions should be able to participate, along with the Government, in the supervision of the implementation process.

In line with these two points, we should like to prepare a training package for the national trade unions and would welcome any financial assistance in order to be able to carry out this project. This project is more relevant than ever in today's globalized world, since the majority of Indonesian workers are under-educated and, consequently, have limited skills to enable them to compete with incoming workers from all over the world.

On the topic of job opportunity, up to now we have been facing a multidimensional crisis which has hit Indonesia since 1997. The uncertainty of the political environment has had tremendous consequences on the economy, leading to the demise of many companies and the loss of thousands of jobs. We are facing a high supply of jobseekers. Employment opportunities are very limited and the workforce also faces obstacles, as most of them are low-skilled.

In ensuring the decent work of those employed informally, Indonesia has set out a policy to protect and develop the informal sector. It is also introducing the concept of community economic development, which focuses on the role of small and medium-sized businesses and cooperatives.

To overcome the situation mentioned above concerning Conventions, we need to keep in mind when drawing up Conventions, that they should not be counter-productive at a later stage, by over-emphasizing the protection of workers who are in employment, but we should also take into account all those who are unemployed or entering the job market.

Finally, allow me to express my appreciation to the International Confederation of Free Trade Unions (ICFTU) for their comment concerning the Conventions, especially Convention No. 29; we realize that these are the mechanisms regarding the preparation of documents in the Committee on the Application of Standards.

We also appeal to our colleagues from the European trade unions, to assist the trade unions in Indonesia in the framework of their new strategy of the technical assistance, in what is called the "informal economy".

To conclude my statement to all the participants, since the opening of this session of the Conference, we are all of us now in the spirit of "a fair globalization".

Mr. SITHOLE *(Workers' delegate, Swaziland)*

As this is my first time to come to the podium to speak in this session of the Conference, please consider all protocols observed.

It is my singular honour, on behalf of my organization and some members of the broad-based workers' organizations and civil society in Swaziland, to address this august assembly under the auspices of the ILO, whose mandate is to promote and advocate economic and social justice, respect for the rule of law and civil liberties for all working people.

We are heartened that the ILO in its 1970 session of the Conference adopted a resolution that reads as follows: "The rights conferred upon workers' and employers' organizations must be based on respect for those civil liberties which have been enunciated in particular in the Universal Declaration of Human Rights and in the International Covenant on Civil and Political Rights and that the absence of these civil liberties removes all meaning from the concept of trade union rights."

The Committee on Freedom of Association has also expressed the view that "a system of democracy is fundamental for the free exercise of trade union rights".

The democracy-loving people of Swaziland have, over time, been heartened each time their Government has ratified one of the ILO Conventions or other human rights-related treaties from the United Nations, the Commonwealth or the Organization of African Unity, now the African Union.

Swaziland is a voluntary Member of the following international organizations whose various treaties and declarations advocate respect for human rights, democracy, the rule of law and social justice: the ILO, of which Swaziland has ratified all the core Conventions; the United Nations; the Commonwealth, membership of which means that Swaziland is bound by the Harare Declaration; and the African Union.

Unfortunately, Swaziland is on a list of countries known to be the best ratifiers of international treaties and declarations, and yet it is one of the worst violators of all the voluntarily ratified human rights-related covenants.

Over time, during the apartheid era, Swaziland was dubbed an "the island of peace in a sea of turmoil". This "peace" was enforced silence, mistaken for peace, and managed in accordance with the draconian 1973 Decree before Mozambique, Namibia, Zimbabwe and South Africa were liberated. And the truth now is that Swaziland is an "island of dictatorship in a sea of democracies".

These assertions are supported by a number of realities that have been systematically sustained by the draconian 1973 State of Emergency Decree. Swaziland remains the only undemocratic country in the sub-Saharan region; the only country ruled by decree in the region; the only country where fundamental freedoms were nullified following the Decree of 1973; the only country where political parties have been banned since 1973; the only country where all dialogue initiatives proposed by stakeholders, other than the Government, are undermined in favour of government-imposed talk shows, in which the Government dictates the agenda and only hand-picked individuals are supposed to participate in the dialogue but organizations are not invited and not recognized; the only country where Court of Appeal judges have resigned en masse owing to the blatant refusal of the Executive to implement its decisions; the only country where the Executive can interfere with the Legislature; the only country where all arms of governance are vested in the office of the King; the only country in the region where peaceful protest actions are brutally dispersed and trade union leaders sometimes denied freedom of movement during lawful protest actions; the only country where the Government, on 28 November 2002, openly pronounced that certain decisions of the Courts will not be observed by the Government (to the nation's amazement, these decisions included decisions that allow citizens a right to return to their place of birth after having been maliciously evicted by the authorities); the only country where bail money is accepted but the authorities refuse to release the suspect.

Whilst the Government has ratified and enacted all the core labour standards in legislation, in practice the situation is diametrically the opposite. Freedom of association is deliberately undermined by the armed forces during peaceful protest activities. The Government systemically denies trade union recognition in the textiles industry.

The right to free collective bargaining is subject to total government interference, both within the private sector, in parastatal bodies and within the civil service.

The Minister of Finance announced in his budget speech that there would be no negotiations this year, and no wage increase, but there will be retrenchments of 1,000 people, without any negotiation with the legitimate organizations.

The Government has ratified the forced labour Conventions, but forced labour is legalized by the Swazi Administration Order of 1998 which was used in maliciously evicting two village chiefs and over 200 of their subjects, who are now refugees in South Africa. It is unfortunate that whilst the Court declared this Order unlawful, the State still vehemently applies it in its entirety, which is yet another proof of its total disregard for the rule of law.

The Law in question has reduced the Swazi citizen to the level of squatters or farm dwellers in their own country, and leaves them with no right to land.

The workers and other progressive forces demanded the Constitution-writing process, but when it was eventually put into operation in response to both internal and international pressure, Decree No. 2 was put in place. Under this Constitution, all powers are vested in the King, and the King appoints the Prime Minister, the Cabinet, the judges and the principal Secretaries. This draft includes derogating clauses.

In these short comments, on behalf of the suffering, bonded and oppressed masses of Swaziland, we appeal to this democracy, peace and social justice-loving international organization, and other organizations of which Swaziland is a member, to apply all forms of pressure to force the Government to address the concerns of its people and allow the people of Swaziland to enjoy their God-given basic fundamental human rights, democracy and dignity.

Original Spanish: Mr. YAGUAL *(Workers' delegate, Ecuador)*

I bring greetings from the Ecuadorian workers and congratulations to the President on his appointment to chair this session of the International Labour Conference, along with congratulations to the Director-General

The economic crisis resulting from the economic strategies imposed by the IMF and the World Bank has become the actual plan of many governments across the world, and Ecuador is no exception. We must also recognize the role played by the traditional economic classes who have taken advantage of these strategies, leading to a deterioration in working conditions, low wages and the limitation of labour and union rights, affecting the quality of life of 80 per cent of the population.

In Ecuador we have not yet recovered from the crisis which resulted from the looting of Ecuadorians' savings by unscrupulous bankers in 1999. This led to hundreds of people secretly leaving the country each week in search of work and a better future for their families, risking their lives crammed into boats heading to the United States, or flying to Europe on tickets bought months in advance. This desperate action is all part of an international trafficking network, which does not get a mention in the international press. It is not newsworthy because our migrants do not have a political impact or cause any scandal, but it does have an impact on employers in the countries to which they go and work as semi-slaves. It means that these countries can improve their GDP, accumulating money by paying poverty wages and failing to recognize basic human rights, particularly those contained in the Abolition of Forced Labour Convention, 1957 (No. 105), which seeks to eliminate forced labour. Migrants have to accept forced labour, otherwise they will be deported and have to return to a life of poverty and crime in Ecuador.

This phenomenon is not unique to Ecuador; it is faced by all countries of the region and other continents where living and working conditions are deteriorating daily.

This total lack of respect for working conditions enjoyed by "legal" workers and the imposition of awful working conditions as a result of the trafficker, along with the abuse which occurs when people want to send money back to their families in their countries of origin, cannot continue in secret. All this must be eradicated.

The work of our compatriots should be considered as capital coming into our countries to finance important work. It should have the same guarantees as other capital, because this is the way in which Ecuador and other countries in the region invest in countries where there is an ageing population which cannot carry out certain jobs in the production or service sectors. This investment should have the same rights, conditions and guarantees required of us for capital investment. In other words, we demand compliance with international conventions, in this case the Conventions of the ILO.

Without wishing to sound repetitive, we invest in Europe and the United States with our labour. Ecuador has done this for a whole generation. Every family has a mother, a father, a son or a close relative working as a migrant. But the cost is enormous: children are abandoned, homes destroyed and people are discriminated against, treated as criminals, and deported at the first opportunity.

The difference between the two investments is as follows: people with money move it around electronically, demanding guarantees, imposing conditions and even deciding which civil servant should run the economy; when they feel like it, they take it out of the country, leaving gaping holes in our economies. Now, with the other type of investment, people risk their lives in boats, and families are indebted to the traffickers. People have to work as slaves and are often deported. They are not important because they come from "the third world". This discrimination and exploitation must be stopped.

As President of the Confederation of Workers of Ecuador, which is a member of the World Confederation of Labour, representing Ecuadorian workers here at this session of the ILC, I suggest that this type of labour should be condemned and those countries encouraging such exploitation should be sanctioned in the same way as drug traffickers are sanctioned. Countries which do not comply with ILO Conventions should be sanctioned. These sanctions should be coercive in nature in order to ensure that workers' rights are respected.

Therefore, as a resolution, this session of the Conference should require that all integration processes which are being negotiated or are already in place should ensure the free movement of labour. Workers are an investment made by our families and the Ecuadorian State should not build barriers, but should knock down these walls of shame.

At the present time, my country, Ecuador is facing a very acute social and political crisis and we must again call for a change of direction in the work of the Government. The Government of the former colonel, Mr. Gutierrez Borbua, has broken its election promises and betrayed the people of Ecuador.

Bad government has broken faith with workers, violating articles 16, 18, 23, 35, 55, 57, 142, 143, 245, 247 and 249 of the Constitution of the Republic of Ecuador, freedom of association and the right to collective bargaining, as enshrined in the Freedom of Association and Protection of the Right to Organise Convention, 1948 (No. 87), and the Right to Organise and Collective Bargaining Convention, 1949 (No. 98), of the ILO. These violations have become law, as a bill entitled "Organic law on the civil service and administration and on the unification and approval of remuneration in the public sector". In reality, this will lead to the dismissal of 30,000 workers in the public sector over the next few years, in accordance with agreements reached between the Government of Ecuador and the IMF.

Workers' federations have presented a complaint to the Constitutional Court on the grounds that this law is not constitutional, and we have submitted a similar complaint to the ILO; we hope that there will be a ruling in our favour.

Long before this law came into force, the Government had violated all the constitutional and labour rights of workers, particularly working together with the management of the state-owned firm PETROECUADOR, in respect of which we have also complained to the ILO.

Attacks on the right to freedom of association, as enshrined in Convention No. 87, have become common practice in Ecuador, as evidenced by the dismissal of 400 workers at the Central Bank of Ecuador, including some members of the management. We have again complained to the ILO. The dismissal of 400 workers from the country's electricity companies has been announced. This is the real situation for workers in the public sector.

Imagine then what the situation is in the tertiary sector, where people do not have the right to organize, have no stability, and suffer from low wages despite the fact that Ecuadorian legislation provides for these workers to receive equal pay for equal work, which means they are effectively working in a state of semi-slavery.

In Ecuador there is open child labour in sectors such as flower-growing, mining and particularly banana cultivation. We would therefore ask that the bodies which the ILO has created to eradicate child labour should be given some decision-making power, and that the inspectors, observers and overseers of child labour should not be dependent either on the Ministry of Labour or on NGOs.

These are the very serious and pressing situations which the organized trade union movement in Ecuador faces, and therefore I ask this 92nd Session of the International Labour Conference to call upon the Government of my country not to violate or refuse to recognize the standards which have been established and recognized through the ILO Conventions, and which have been ratified by Ecuador itself. It is the duty of the participants here present to give the workers of the world a fair deal.

Mr. PAJOBO (Workers' delegate, Uganda)

I wish to congratulate the President and the Officers of the Conference on their election to high office at this Conference.

Let me pose one question. What has been happening in the world during the first few years of the twenty-first century? Security of employment has declined, the share of wages relative to profits has fallen, inequalities between the poor and the rich, women and men, the developed and the developing countries, are widening. The international economic institutions, namely the World Bank and the International Monetary Fund, dominate the developing countries.

While poverty is worsening among the majority of people, wealth is concentrated among a few in a way never before seen in the world. Working people in most of the world are getting a bad deal.

Furthermore, there is a growing democracy deficit. At the national level, national policy options are constrained by global markets. Greater competition exists among governments than among enterprises. Democratic governance barely exists. While global governance and binding rules are beginning to emerge, they are for the purpose of protecting rights in the interest of capital, rather than the rights of labour. The phenomenon of globalization has removed decision-making from individuals and placed it in the hands of the management of global enterprises such as Microsoft, Nokia, etc., and of global institutions such as the World Bank and IMF. As a result of this, millions of subcontracted workers, who are producing brand products for these companies and institutions, who do not employ them, cannot obtain a hearing with them.

We, as workers and a growing number of governments and firms, recognize that business as usual is not good enough. We know that, although unregulated globalization is working for some people and some governments, it is not working for the majority of the people. We also know that unregulated global financial markets have enabled the spread of networks that feed terrorism. There has to be a way to regulate globalization. There has to be a framework for global governance to increase the regulation of globalization.

Markets do not clean themselves up, they do not automatically produce justice, they do not automatically require the respect of human rights. In other words, the world has been on autopilot. This is not satisfactory.

History shows that the trade union movement can help to fill the moral vacuum created by market forces. Trade unions are instruments of the will of workers and become their lever to move the world and to change the distribution of wealth and power inside countries and beyond, through their weapon of collective bargaining. Trade unions have the capacity to transform society. This is why all tyrants, public or private, fear freedom of association. Trade unions are also one of the very few actors capable of transcending the divisions that are polarizing our lives today and they are therefore the building blocks of a better world.

The National Organization of Trade Unions of Uganda reaffirms its conviction that respect for trade unions is essential for social and economic development with social justice. Our goal is to win support for a world that is free from poverty and unemployment, free from discrimination and injustice, free from terrorism in all its forms, free from the threat of war and oppression. We want a world full of democracy and respect for human rights. We want a world where enterprises, large and small, respect the rights of their workers and of the unions and societies in which they operate.

For trade unions, the ILO Report, *Organizing for social justice,* is indeed timely. Perhaps it is worth recalling that this positive development originated in a campaign by the trade union movement aimed at focusing attention worldwide on organizing workers in the informal sector.

It is vital that the fundamental rights of workers, set out in ILO standards, be respected everywhere in the world. While the Report recognizes that the data on membership of employers' and workers' organizations are largely incomplete and outdated, we wish to assure you that the National Organization of Trade Unions of Uganda will strive to provide all data pertaining to membership as requested by the ILO.

We appreciate and welcome the work done by the ILO in Uganda, particularly the Workers' Education Project which has been implemented, the ILO Action Plan on Gender Equality and Mainstreaming Project and the ILO's ongoing SLAREA Project.

The Director-General's Report, *Organizing for social justice,* offers a way of developing further the ideals of collective bargaining and social dialogue. It is our hope that our members will put to proper use the Report that has been submitted to them.

Mr. ILOLOV (Government delegate, Tajikistan)

On behalf of the Tajikistan tripartite delegation, I congratulate the President and the other Officers upon their election.

I would like to thank the Director-General, Mr. Juan Somavia, and the ILO team for the excellent choice of the topics for the Report.

The Report of the Director-General entitled: *A fair globalization: The role of the ILO* and the Global Report under the Follow-up to the ILO Declaration on Fundamental Principles and Rights at Work have inspired me to reflect on a number of issues that I should like to share with you.

Labour migration is a global phenomenon in the contemporary world. It is a consequence of economic integration, on the one hand, and non-uniformity of development, on the other. Practically, all countries of the world are affected in some degree by labour migration, either as receiving, sending or transit countries.

In the last decade in Tajikistan, the processes of the transitional period became a catalyst for external labour migration. Tajikistan was affected by powerful migration flows which changed the shape of the country, and had a significant impact on its social, economic and political situation. The crucial factor that caused the mass migration flows was a civil war that started in 1992-93 and continued until 1997, during which time there was a period of political instability. Labour migration abroad had a decisive influence on the system of life-support for the overwhelming majority of families in Tajikistan. Both the negative and the positive consequences of such migration are becoming clear. Researchers observe that more than 7 per cent of the economically active population leave the country every year.

More than 90 per cent of them go to the Russian Federation.

Life is difficult for the Tajik people living in foreign countries. These migrants agree to carry out any kind of work, simply to avoid deportation. Only 15 per cent work legally. The majority of migrants who are in an illegal situation are employed in private sector enterprises or carry out some form of domestic labour. Private employers are not interested in registering migrant workers. Therefore, migrant workers are excluded from social insurance and medical services and receive the lowest possible wages. In some cases, employers refuse to pay illegal migrants at all, so that they become victims of various structures, including criminal structures created by their compatriots.

Many unsolved problems still exist with regard to the state policy on the regulation of the migration processes. First of all, the infrastructure of the migrants service is weak in terms of informative and legislative support. We have not yet developed a system to provide support prior to migration or to provide professional education and micro-credit to migrants.

In general, activities to create an effective system to regulate migration policy can be implemented successfully only through the formation of structured and balanced systems of government regulation. Those systems must take into account international experience. In this respect, the Government of Tajikistan is interested in the ratification of ILO Conventions Nos. 97 and 143 on migrant workers.

We believe that the globalization process, particularly with regard to labour migration, must be based on universal values and include a social dimension in all countries of the world.

Mr. DAVE *(Workers' delegate, India)*

In the 85th year of the ILO, I find the comprehensive Report of the Director-General to be an introspective internal review of its effectiveness during the last two years. The Report, *A fair globalization: The role of the ILO*, spells out, in detail, the implications of the recommendations made by the World Commission on the Social Dimension of Globalization, which, in offering its comments on making decent work a global goal, has rightly recognized the basic fact that a worker in a particular industry is a consumer of all other industries, including the industry in which she or he works. However, it is elaborately diagnostic.

There is a group which vehemently advocates globalization as a remedy to all problems of growth, employment, equity and industrial peace. But an equally strong opinion is gathering momentum that reform, as a key to salvation, is not the right approach. Any attempt to advocate a particular course of action inevitably involves value judgements that can easily conflict with the ethics of scholarly objectivity and political neutrality, requiring a more than usual dose of intellectual discipline. Experience alone is the final arbitrator.

Globalization, which should be treated as a means for building a better society based on democracy, growth and equity, is being set in motion as an end in itself. Differences among nations, with respect to the level of development, are undoubtedly one of the world's paramount problems. The "development gap" between rich and poor countries is increasing despite the assured intention of most rich nations and international agencies to assist in the creation of a more equal world. For the poor, the question of catching up with the rich does not arise, as their rates of progress (in the narrow economic sense of per capita GNP/GDP growth) are less than those of developed countries. While for others, the time required to close the gap is measured in centuries rather than decades.

Today, the needs of the masses are eclipsed by the greed of an affluent minority. This necessitates a re-examination of the entire gamut of the reform process. The close interrelationship between economic and social elements precludes any purely economic or purely social development. Therefore, a broad multidisciplinary perspective is essential for monitoring social progress.

To respond adequately to the problems of the modern world, the focus must be firmly rooted in human life. The limitations of any academic approach must be recognized, however relevant it may appear to the questions of human welfare. The so-called quantitative approach of review has tended to produce a mechanistic geography somewhat removed from reality.

International labour standards as a straightjacket method cannot be imagined by many developing countries, including my country, India, which, in spite of being the largest technical manpower supplier to several sophisticated systems across the globe, continues to have agriculture as the source of livelihood for nearly 450 million people.

Collective bargaining, at all levels, if pursued to promote self-interest by losing focus on larger social commitments, either by workers or employers, is but a naked trial of strength where ultimately the strong though wrong could have their victory over the weak but right. According to Harold Laski, should the employers and workers of any industry so conspire, they can harm the larger interests of people.

My Indian habit of thought refuses to acknowledge that we are in a world of limited resources. Mother Nature has resources in plenty for all of us, for all years to come, provided we shun the attitude of exploiting her and master the art of milking her. We should look again and begin our course for a fair globalization, starting with nature.

Indians, for several thousand years now, have recognized the right to happiness for all, which is judiciously institutionalized through a duty-based framework (instead of a rights-based approach) called Dharma, where joint family systems were established to inculcate the concept of globalization through a "winner shares with all" instead of a "winner takes all" approach. Even the United Nations Charter glaringly misses out the right to happiness.

Whichever way we look at the present form of globalization, the diagnosis is clear: the problem lies in the prescription. Who, when, why and how is the subtle point of debate. I urge all of you to remember that the right question is more important than the right answer to the wrong questions.

This is indeed a weighty, yet welcome, leadership challenge of vision to identify the circumstances and the courage to take decisions. We have had a very late start though, losing two decades in the bargain. Nevertheless, the Director-General has read the conclusion clear and loud. The current path of globalization must change, as the rules are unfair, the results unbalanced, and the course unsustainable. Yet the potential is there; change is possible.

There is some kind of solution to the broader problem of people learning to live together in a cooperative spirit of mutual assistance, instead of in aggressive competition. The key issue, therefore, is not globalization itself, but the rules and governance system under which it operates.

The Commission, by reminding us of the constitutional mandate of the ILO in detail and seeking its greater presence in the multilateral system, is in fact emphasizing the need for a global round table of all interests involved in, and implicated by, global governance mechanisms.

Until, and unless, there is a true commitment by the rich countries to help the mass of people in the underdeveloped world, instead of pursuing their narrow economic self-interest, the existing inequalities may get worse. Such a commitment itself requires a true change in the conduct of world affairs.

This is definitely a defining moment, provided we decide to act.

Mr. GUISEPPI (Workers' delegate, Trinidad and Tobago)

My special congratulations to the President on his appointment. We in the Caribbean are delighted by his elevation to such an honourable position.

On behalf of the National Trade Union Centre of Trinidad and Tobago (NATUC) and the Caribbean Congress of Labour (CCL) with its 17 affiliates, consisting of nations of the Caribbean, South and Central America, I bring comradely greetings to the President, our Director-General, the Vice-Presidents and secretaries and those who sit on this supreme forum of the 92nd Session of the International Labour Conference in 2004.

The working people of the Caribbean send warmest blessings to all our brothers and sisters who are here representing 179 countries on this globe.

The Director-General's Report continues to demonstrate the vision, understanding and total commitment that he, his colleagues and staff possess, as we continue our quest towards equity, fairness, social justice and happiness in this uncertain era of globalization.

The workers of the Caribbean do accept and will support the ILO's programmes and policies, because we believe that they will help in achieving peace and equality.

The record of the ILO over 85 years has given that assurance and its success and accomplishments have been recorded. But that does not mask the reality that there exist rogue elements that seek to undermine our goals of making the world a fair one within which globalization will present a human face.

These negative forces are even more determined than ever before on building empires of exorbitant materialistic wealth and capital through the sacrifices and sufferings of millions of workers and children. That is why the labour movement in the Caribbean insists that all governments must ratify and implement the Worst Forms of Child Labour Convention, 1999 (No. 182).

The Director-General's Report has not lost sight of this as it reinforces its promotion of decent work and the four strategic objectives. We are convinced that this is done in order to neutralize the capacity of those who still believe that the exploitation and domination of the many by the few is part of nature's plan. The brutal relics of the past still survive and fashion the behaviour of this class, wherever they exist – be it in government or elsewhere.

Working people still have their fears and suspicions, not entirely with the global system, but with those who have manipulated it in order to retain complete control. Their overpowering and uncontrolled desires for amassing wealth at all costs have led some on senseless searches for weapons of mass destruction, or may we say a distraction and/or deception.

It is the same mindset that led those to state for over 500 years that the indigenous people of the New World and African slaves were less than human – the working people of the Caribbean, our history carved and scarred by much misbeliefs and malpractices, have survived.

Today, survival is no longer a major objective but our efforts are now directed at bringing wealth and prosperity for the vast majority who have been denied such for hundreds of years, being victims of mass genocide, discrimination and racial hatred.

Its effect is still present in our societies today, where poverty, unemployment, crime and inequality persist through the grossly unfair distribution of wealth and growth.

These social ills will be eliminated if our governments adopt and institutionalize the ILO agenda, which has to play a major role in defining our governments' – both national and regional – political, economic and social policies and programmes. The labour movement will insist on that course to be taken by our governments.

The removal of poverty, unemployment and the elevation of the dignity of workers are the principles we must adopt if we are to realize and achieve peace, order and real democracy in this era of so-called globalization.

Labour is the only living, human factor that makes any product possible. In today's world, our essentiality can no longer be hidden from us.

I quote Dr. Madsen Pirie, President of the Adam Smith Institute: "Wealth is no longer created on the basis of fixed capital, but increasingly on the talents and abilities of individuals. Talent and skills are the new precious metals, which denote wealth in the modern world. They have to be encouraged, developed, attracted and retrained. Companies and countries which do this successfully can survive and prosper; the others cannot."

Original French: Mr. DJIBRINE (Workers' delegate, Chad)

Allow me first of all to congratulate the President and the Officers of the Conference on their election to guide us in our work, and to wish the Conference every success.

After the bitter experience of structural adjustment programmes which were imposed upon our nations by the International Monetary Fund and the World Bank, the ILO Director-General's Report entitled *A fair globalization: The role of the ILO*, which is in fact a constructive and objective analysis the Report of the World Commission on the Social Dimension of Globalization, in my humble opinion opens up avenues for reflection on more favourable prospects for economic and social development and, most importantly, describes the possibilities for a more just and equitable distribution of the resources generated by such development. Indeed, the Report emphasizes the hopes and aspirations of ordinary people who, after all, make up the overwhelming majority of the population of our planet.

While I share the pertinent conclusions drawn in the Report of the Director-General and in the report of the World Commission, I would also point out some important aspects which are specific to Africa: the role of the social partners, social dialogue and strategic alliances with civil society organizations.

Beginning with the social partners, and on the understanding that there can be no economic development without an extensive job creation programme, just as you cannot reduce poverty without giving decent work to all those who have no work, I believe that it is crucial that social partners be involved in the framing, implementation and evaluation of all economic and social development programmes at all levels, that is, national, subregional, continental and global. The involvement of the social partners can only be effective if the latter are well-organized, representative and capable of doing more than just making speeches and putting motions, i.e. exerting leverage through their actions on the ground.

Here, I would say that the collective agreements and protocols of agreement negotiated and concluded in recent years in many countries are an encouraging sign, provided the parties abide by their commitments.

Beyond the national level, we have, as you probably know, subregional and regional organizations as well: the Central African Economic and Monetary Community (CAEMC), the West African Economic and Monetary Union (WAEMU), the Community of Sahelo-Saharan States (CEN-SAD), and of course the African Union.

While we appreciate the work done by the regional trade union organizations such as the Organization of African Trade Union Unity (OATUU), the ICFTU African Regional Organization (AFRO), the Democratic Organization of African Workers' Trade Unions (DOAWTU) and in terms of awareness-raising and lobbying vis-à-vis the African Union and the New Partnership for Africa's Development (NEPAD), I think it is important to revitalize the subregional trade union organizations under the CAEMC, the CEN-SAD and the WAEMU. Given that the subregional economic and monetary communities state that their main goal is the development of human and natural resources for the common good of their peoples, it is entirely appropriate for the social partners to be involved.

As far as my part of the world is concerned, I would like to mention the establishment of the Central African Employers' Union (UNIPACE) in 2001 and that of the Central African Workers' Trade Union Organization (OSTAC) in October 2003. I would also like to welcome and pay tribute to the decision taken by Heads of State and Government to set up a tripartite structure within CAEMC. It would be remiss of me not to seize this opportunity to pay tribute to the ILO, which played a key role in this positive development, both through its Regional Programme for the Promotion of Social Dialogue in French-speaking Africa (PRODIAF) and through the work of its subregional office. This work by the ILO has made a substantial contribution to revitalizing and consolidating social dialogue both at national level and within the CAEMC.

Moving on to CEN-SAD now, on 3 September 1998, the workers' organizations in the member States set up the Sahelo-Saharan Nations Trade Union Association of African Workers (USTAESS).

Since then, the number of members has doubled and it will certainly increase further, since the number of member States has now reached 22, so that about 45 per cent of the African population is now represented within this trade union organization.

I am certain that this organization's role in economic and social development will increase in the years to come because of the pragmatic policy of integration promoted by the member States, in particular by the Libyan Arab Jamahiriya, already manifested in the fact that in several member States, financial, trade and industrial companies have already been set up, thus offering ample employment to their workers.

At its last ordinary congress held in April 2004 in Tunis, the USTAESS adopted important recommendations and resolutions calling for involvement of the trade unions of member countries in all the programmes and activities of CEN-SAD.

We are of course eager to request the assistance of the ILO and all other sources of goodwill to support the activities of these subregional and regional organizations.

Before I conclude, allow me to mention my last point, namely strategic alliances with civil society organizations. Whilst agreeing with them in principle, especially since in my country we have already successfully initiated a number of joint actions with human rights associations and the liaison committee for women's associations, I urge you to be very vigilant when it comes to these strategic alliances, because in many African countries there are so-called civil society associations which are set up simply as a front and which have no credibility and are not representative. Consequently, if one is not careful one might find oneself in the midst of a hornets' nest and this would undermine one of the fundamental principles of the ILO, namely tripartism.

In conclusion, I would say that Africa has tremendous and varied potential. But unfortunately, today this has benefited only multinational companies and a tiny minority of local rulers. The absence of political will, the eagerness to defend personal interests, and poor governance combined with mismanagement, corruption and debt, not to mention HIV/AIDS, as well as every form of conflict, often created and perpetuated to serve political ends are the main factors that have led to underdevelopment and the inequitable distribution of wealth. This is a measure of the huge challenges that face us and force the world to examine its conscience.

However, if, with the aid of the ILO and that of the international labour movement we can manage to strengthen the capabilities of the social partners in general and of workers' and employers' organizations in particular, I am certain that Africa will be able to take advantage of all the benefits of globalization – benefits which its peoples have a right to expect.

Original French: Mr. NUMAS *(Workers' delegate, Haiti)*

On behalf of the workers of Haiti, allow me, first of all, to join in congratulations already expressed, congratulating the President on his election to the presidency of this 92nd Session of the International Labour Conference. His election was an important event for Latin America and the Caribbean and, in particular, it was an important event in the context of our need for development and the well-being of the citizens of our island.

The agenda for this session, focusing as it does on the social dimension of globalization, and the introductory statement made by Mr. Juan Somavia, the Director-General of the ILO, show more clearly than ever that the Organization remains true to its tripartite vocation, and that it is able to adapt to changing circumstances. I would like to thank the Director-General for the excellent Report submitted to us, containing a wealth of information, and also for the many themes offered for exploration.

The Organization has grown tremendously in recent years, but must rise to a number of challenges. It is said that globalization has the potential to deliver progress, but, up to this point, governments have failed to make the individual the focus of the process, for globalization has adverse effects, which we must now correct. This is the precondition which is required if we are to build a just society which is not just an economic model, but which is also a social model, at the service of everyone.

To take up these huge challenges, the ILO needs to reinforce its structures by establishing an ongoing social dialogue which is absolutely frank. Freedom of association and the right to organize must be seen as the fundamental right of all human beings, and let there be no doubt about it – it is a fundamental right that workers ought to be able to take for granted; everyone must be entitled to exercise this right regardless of the size or wealth of their country.

Many of us attend this Conference regularly, and those of us who do so will have heard many countries present excuses for not being able to ensure freedom of association or the right to collective bargaining because they are poor, or because they do not have the necessary expertise to comply with these standards. I affirm what the Director-General himself said –this is a fundamental right, just as fundamental as the right to life.

Let me take this opportunity to launch an urgent appeal to governments who use this pretext, to make quantum leaps forward and to live up to these requirements. My native country, Haiti, also has to wake up and get into gear. Of course, we appreciate that the nation has just lived through an experience that has ravaged its infrastructure, but now we have to move forward. The democratic transition government – and we welcome its involvement in the affairs of Haiti – must live up to the requirements of the ILO the largest tripartite family in the world.

Past abuses have inflicted damage on our country; we now ask the ILO to provide technical assistance to the new Government of Haiti, to revive the social battle within the context of the tripartite dialogue. Job creation requires respect for the law; strengthening of state institution and political stability. Creating decent jobs is an urgent necessity in Haiti for the country to be able to combat unemployment and poverty. We welcome and encourage any initiative which will help to create large numbers of jobs; initiatives from the private sector in Haiti, and also from business people in Haiti, to promote the well-being of citizens whilst respecting the principles and rights of workers.

Despite everything, the trade union organizations in Haiti have grown. They appreciate the importance of social dialogue and the current need to protect the social provisions that have been achieved thus far.

We therefore ask the ILO's Bureau for Workers' Activities, the Inter-American Regional Organization of Workers (ORIT), the Haitian Confederation of Workers' Trade Unions (CSL), and the International Confederation of Free Trade Unions (ICFTU) to support all the Haitian trade union confederations in the struggle going on in Haiti to promote genuine and effective tripartism. The Haitian trade union world, through the Haitian Trade Union Sector (SSH), the Haitian Trade Union Coordination (CSH), and the Haitian Trade Union Movement (MSH), thank the ICFTU and ORIT for their fact-finding mission to Haiti in February, which aimed to help free fellow free trade unionists who had been imprisoned under the regime of ousted President Lavalas. Thank you, thank you for your efforts. We take note of your advice, and your work with the Haitian trade union movement will not have been in vain.

We continue to pursue tripartite activities within the framework of the ILO project HAI99MO1USA to improve working conditions in the Haitian assembly sector, even though that project has been closed. Despite everything, the evaluation task force described the beginnings of social dialogue between the Haitian State, the Haitian Industries Association (ADIH) and the SSH, as an unexpected positive spin-off of the ILO project, whilst recognizing the status of advisory committee of the project (CCP) as the only working instrument for social dialogue in the country dealing with labour issues. The evaluation task force recommended among other things that this project be extended with the aim of making this committee permanent, giving it autonomy and independence and the resources to strengthen and expand tripartite social dialogue in the country. We are still waiting for the ILO to add to and strengthen these abilities with a view to other activities in the future.

In conclusion, two years after the Independence, the first black republic in the world must be guided by certain principles and must reject the old traditional practices which generate only division and despair. In the international context in which we live, we have to put an end to these struggles once and for all. We need a globalization with a human face that will allow each individual to enjoy decent living and working conditions. This is the responsibility of everyone – of international organizations, governments, employers and workers. These rights are thus the embodiment and the guarantee of freedom and are crucial for the realization of other fundamental rights to allow humankind to live with dignity.

(The Conference adjourned at 6 p.m.)

CONTENTS

Page

Fourteenth sitting

Reports of the Chairperson of the Governing Body and of the Director-General:
Discussion *(cont.)* 1

Speakers: Mr. Fernández, Mr. Infante, Mr. Ola, Mr. Maatough, Mr. Say, Mr. Sevene, Ms. Beaumont, Mr. Nuñez Salcedo, Mr. Espinal, Mr. Eastmond, Mr. Nicolescu, Mr. Dahlan, Mr. Briesch, Mr. Hagh-Bayan, Mr. Arnold, Mr. Farshori, Mr. Tongaai, Mr. Al-Kuhlani, Mr. Abdella, Mr. Qarqein, Mr. Abdulhusain, Mr. Tugushi, Mr. Tartaglia, Mr. Wojcik, Mr. Ghandour, Mr. Flores Flores, Mr. Sukhbaatar.

Fifteenth sitting

Reports of the Chairperson of the Governing Body and of the Director-General:
Discussion *(cont.)* 22

Speakers: Mr. Celi Vegas, Mr. Kara, Mr. Mussanhane, Mr. Alvis Fernández, Ms. Valkonen, Mr. Mancilla García, Mr. Lawal, Mr. Sunmonu, Mr. Alemayehu, Mr. Corries, Mr. Jennings, Mr. Puga Rodríguez, Mr. Ledouble, Mr. Parras Rojas, Mr. Mononga, Mr. Repossi, Mr. MD. Zafrul, Mr. David, Mr. Sithole, Mr. Yagual, Mr. Pajobo, Mr. Ilolov, Mr. Dave, Mr. Guiseppi, Mr. Djibrine, Mr. Numas.

No. 19 – Tuesday, 15 June 2004

International Labour Conference

Provisional Record

Ninety-second Session, Geneva, 2004

23

Sixteenth sitting

Tuesday 15 June 2004, 10.15 a.m.

President: Mr. Ray Guevara, Mr. Attigbe

REPORTS OF THE CHAIRPERSON OF THE GOVERNING BODY AND OF THE DIRECTOR-GENERAL: DISCUSSION (CONCL.)

Original Spanish: THE PRESIDENT (Mr. GUEVARA)

We shall now resume our discussion of the Reports of the Chairperson of the Governing body and of the Director-General.

Original Spanish: Mr. ARTHUR ERRÁZURIZ (Employers' delegate, Chile)

I should like to begin by congratulating the President on his appointment to chair this assembly.

The International Labour Conference has been, and we hope it will continue to be, the best international forum for the exchange of ideas and experience with regard to the labour issues of concern to all of the parties involved.

It also provides the appropriate framework for the preparation of legal standards with a view to creating jobs and also with a view to ensuring fair, modern and humane relationships in the world of labour.

We are here to highlight the importance that should be given to setting standards largely with a view to boosting job creation thereby creating the best tool for defeating poverty which is, and continues to be, a most relevant subject for the majority of countries and of course for this Organization.

It is essential for us to pool our efforts to guarantee equal opportunities in access to employment, through the creation of new standards which will promote recruitment, combat unemployment and furthermore recognize and regulate the new forms of recruitment that have arisen in recent times as a result of the specialization of work, and which have created a new source of work for thousands of workers.

In this regard, it is particularly important to concentrate efforts on implementing standards that promote the recruitment of young people and women, who are sectors of the working population that require ongoing and serious encouragement so that they can become a stable labour force, rather than an unstable and precarious one, as is the case in many countries.

Labour standards, by their very nature, put all companies on an equal footing. However, the fact of the matter is that no two companies are the same. This ought to lead us to a conclusion on the pressing need to create flexible legal frameworks that would allow employers and workers collectively to adapt the said standards to the specific reality of their enterprises.

In Chile, business organizations are trying to find ways to reach an understanding with workers' organizations. We should like to renew our appeal to those organizations, asking them to work together to modernize our labour systems, which is all the more necessary today given that our country has recently entered into free trade agreements with the United States, with the European community and with the Republic of Korea.

We are the only country in America to have achieved such progress, but we are aware that such progress brings with it an obligation to be more efficient and productive. These commitments will be of benefit to all only if we can reach the necessary agreements that will allow us to work in harmony and understanding with no obstacle to the analysis and application of new standards and concepts derived from globalization.

Likewise, we should like to appeal to our Government to renew its efforts to ensure that the social actors in the field of labour benefit from fair and impartial monitoring, which has not always been the case in recent times. All of this should help us to generate more and better jobs which is one of the permanent objectives of the ILO. These jobs should be found without any form of discrimination and should offer fair wages in accordance with the company's current situation. We should also like to highlight the pressing need to implement mechanisms that promote training, which is the most efficient and fastest way of ensuring the personal and professional development of workers. It is through training and by developing trust between workers and employers, in a climate of impartiality and authority, that will allow us to move forward and to achieve our goals.

Our country is proud to have created, at the beginning of the 1980s, a welfare system that has served as a model for many countries in Latin America and Eastern Europe. It is based on the investment of savings and the private management of those savings. This system is flexible, transparent and has demonstrated its effectiveness. It gives the participating workers the freedom to choose who manages their funds and the freedom to choose the type of pension and the way in which they invest their money. These systems have proved to be very successful, both in terms of the capacity of these pensions to offer much higher rates of return than the salary increases that were used to calculate pensions under the pay-as-you-go system, and in terms of contributing to the savings and investment processes in our countries.

In Chile, the funds accumulated by workers have reached a figure of very similar to the gross domestic product.

Last October, the International Federation of Pension Fund Administrators, which I preside over, met in Geneva with ILO specialists in social security matters with a view to demonstrating the results which have been achieved in a system that now has 26 associated countries.

I would like to repeat once again, in conclusion, that Chilean business circles are always ready to cooperate in the implementation of the international standards of this Organization. We believe that, if the ILO had an extremely important function in the past, it is now even more important today, because economies no longer have borders. It does not seem fair that certain countries enjoy unfair comparative advantages over others because of unfair labour systems. Exploiting workers can not be turned into an advantage.

I conclude by congratulating the Director-General of the ILO for his comprehensive Report which addresses issues and concepts that, without a doubt, will help us to achieve the objectives that I have referred to.

Mr. AHMED (Workers' delegate, Pakistan)

On behalf of the Workers' delegation of Pakistan, I offer sincere congratulations to the President on his well-deserved election to preside over this historic session of Conference, as well as to the Vice-Presidents.

We also take this opportunity to convey our fraternal greetings and good wishes from the Workers of Pakistan to all the distinguished delegates.

Globalization of the economy and the deregulation of public services in many developing countries pose a serious challenge to the labour force through the shrinking of their employment opportunities and the failure to achieve the objective of developing decent work.

The trade union organizations in Pakistan are united in their aim of establishing one national platform to impress upon policy-makers and employers the need to devise national policies which will ensure meaningful education and training and productive and voluntary employment for all our young people, and defend and promote core workers' rights. We therefore urge the Government of Pakistan to fulfil its obligations under the ratified ILO core Conventions and restore fundamental trade union rights in all sectors, including the railways, P.I.A., KESK, E.P.Z. and others, and to amend the Industrial Relations Ordinance 2002, the Banking Companies Ordinance, section 27(b), the Civil Service Tribunal Act, section 2/A, and the Ordinance relating to the special presidential powers of removal from service, 2000.

The Government undertook to amend these laws at the Governing Body session held in March 2004 during the examination of Case No. 2229.

We are pleased to inform you that the workers' organizations have been endeavouring, with ACTRAV, to develop and promote the programme of poverty reduction and the decent work concept, and expects and urges the ILO to increase its technical assistance to Pakistan for capacity building of the social partners, particularly in workers' organizations, to cope with the challenges posed by the globalization of the economy and free trade and deregulation and to safeguard and promote the interests of the workers.

On this occasion, we wish to commend the report of the World Commission on the Social Dimension of Globalization, which is headed by the Heads of the States of Finland and the United Republic of Tanzania. The report in question is accompanied by the Report of the Director-General entitled *A fair globalization: The role of the ILO*. We strongly support its recommendations, and also commend the work of the ILO under the dedicated leadership of Mr. Juan Somavia, the Director-General of the ILO and his team. The positive outcome of economic globalization cannot be achieved by most developing countries unless they are provided with a level playing field through the development of technology, provision of adequate resources, access to the markets of developed countries and debt relief. The Director-General of the ILO has himself acknowledged that ratio of the incomes of the richest and the poorest countries, which was 50 to 1 in 1960, is more than 120 to 1 today. According to some estimates, the richest 1 per cent of the world's people receive as much as the bottom 51 per cent. There are more than 1.3 billion people living below the poverty line, with an income of less than US$1 day. More than 2.3 billion people are either unemployed or underemployed and lack any form of social security.

The other day, the Secretary-General of the United Nations, Mr. Kofi Annan, when addressing UNCTAD Conference, said that the world today is a more unequal place than it was 40 years ago. The ILO is rightly expected to play a leading role with other international agencies, such as the IMF, the World Bank and the WTO, to safeguard the social dimension of globalization and to defend and promote the rights of the masses, since experience has demonstrated that IMF and World Bank policies imposed upon the developing countries have resulted in rising unemployment and mass poverty, not its reduction. The free flow of capital should be accompanied by controlled international labour migration.

We also strongly support the resolution concerning the strengthening of the role of the ILO in supporting workers and employers in Palestine and the other occupied Arab territories which could not be discussed owing to the lack of time.

We welcome the Report of the Director-General on the situation of Arab workers of the occupied Arab territories, which has highlighted the continuous economic and social suffering and the denial of basic trade union rights under foreign occupation. We call upon the ILO and the international community to extend all possible help to free workers in those territories from foreign occupation in accordance with United Nations resolutions, and we will extend our full support to poverty alleviation measures and efforts to raise employment and enhance respect for their fundamental workers' rights.

We can convey the deep appreciation of the work done by ACTRAV, and appeal to the Director-General to involve ACTRAV in all the ILO InFocus programmes with a view to raising the capacity of workers' organizations in the fields of employment, international labour standards, social protection and social dialogue. We commend the work done by the ILO Asian Pacific Regional Office and urge the

ILO to consider providing more resources for the country programme to make the ILO more visible.

We would like to express our highest admiration for the contribution of the international Workers' group, led by Brother Roy Trotman's team and Brother Dan Cunniah, secretary of the group. I wish to thank the group for honouring my country by electing me as its Vice-Chairperson.

We hope that the deliberations of this historic session of the Conference under the President's leadership will pave the way for the promotion of social justice, peace, human dignity and a better quality of life for the masses all over the world.

Original Spanish: Mr. GUTIÉRREZ MADUEÑO *(Workers' delegate, Peru)*

Allow me to convey to the President and to the international community of the ILO, the respectful greetings of the Peruvian Workers and, at the same time, urge the International Labour Organization to devote itself with renewed vigour to its mission to protect and promote the rights and working conditions of the workers of the world.

In this regard, we would like to express our support for the focal points raised by the Director-General of the International Labour Organization in his Report submitted to the 92nd Session of the International Labour Conference on the promotion and the application of standards, fundamental principles and rights at work and the creation of decent work.

On the other hand, we wish to inform you that in Peru, despite the efforts made to promote the labour rights of workers, these are not being reflected by the democratic Government, which, far from taking measures along these lines, is trying to make industrial relations even more flexible to the detriment of workers' rights, supposedly to attract investors.

It is our obligation to inform this international forum that there has been no legislative progress enabling us to reverse the violations experienced by workers during the dictatorial and authoritarian decade of Fujimori. The main problem lies in the fact that the Government does not have a clear-cut and consistent labour policy, and is not taking the necessary decisions to solve the problems of the workers, who today are expecting to have their labour rights restored.

Many regional conflicts extend throughout the country. The difficulties of the political system in creating a list of complaints which can be listened to and acted on by the State, as well as the inability of the Government to present real alternatives to social requirements, threatens the fragile democracy which exists in Peru.

The Government already, seriously discredited, is becoming more and more unsustainable. However, it persists with its failed economic and social policy which the people reject, listening more to the dictates of the IMF than the requests of the Peruvian people. Thus, whilst constantly maintaining the privileges of multinationals and the payment of foreign debts, they are not finding a solution to the demands of workers, agricultural producers, the regions or the excluded people of Peru. This is the root of the contradiction between the relative economic growth which the country is experiencing, and falling real wages, increasing poverty and unemployment, and a deterioration in the basic services of education, health, nutrition, etc. Consequently, we are faced with an economic policy which only benefits a few, whilst it excludes the majority and denies them the benefits of economic growth, prompting them with good reason to rise up against this system of inequity.

But this is not all. Representative democracy is also in crisis, and the political institutionality, which Fujimori established in his spurious 1993 Constitution and which the current Government has not been able to derogate, is, in fact, creating even more retrograde reforms such as those which eliminate the rights acquired and freeze the pensions of the unemployed and retirees.

The Congress of the Republic, the judicial authority and the parties are also involved in the crisis of the political system which our country is experiencing. Therefore, we, the workers, are requesting, inter alia, a new Constitution laying the foundations for a new Republic.

Finally, the country is facing a serious moral crisis which affects the whole body of society, imperilling its own viability. Those involved in the Fujimori mafia continue operating in their own political interests while the controlling classes are seeking to prevent any kind of sanction against those who are responsible. The country will not tolerate the application, as always, of a "clean-slate" policy.

The current Government, far from embodying the moral will of the country, is involved in acts of corruption, nepotism and extravagant spending, even influencing some of its members to maintain relationships and agreements with the mafia supporters of Fujimori.

In a nutshell, we are not just faced with a political crisis as some people maintain, but also an economic and moral crisis, the solution to which will necessarily involve dealing with these factors.

We request, from the international community, the necessary support so that violations in our country of those human rights which the ILO rightly views as fundamental can cease.

Original Spanish: Mr. GONZÁLEZ GAITÁN *(Workers' delegate, Nicaragua)*

May I first express our satisfaction before the Workers of this Conference. We are sure that under the President's leadership we will achieve the desired results.

Next, I wish to convey to the distinguished delegates at this meeting, the fraternal greetings of Nicaraguan workers, particularly their trade union leaders, who are united in the daily fight to defend the rights won by the workers of my country.

This Conference, as can be seen from the Report submitted by the Director-General of the ILO, is taking place against a backdrop of dramatic situations where the neo-liberal policies and structural adjustments imposed by the international financial bodies are constantly threatening to turn the standards protecting workers' fundamental rights throughout the world into mere declarations. Perhaps never before have the daily realities experienced by millions of human beings contrasted so radically with the declaration made by the formal democracies of our countries with respect to the historical rights won through the basic Conventions of the ILO.

We can say, today, that violation of the freedom of association, the loss of rights acquired through collective bargaining, the resurgence of labour repression in free zones, job insecurity in the civil and public services. The oppression and abuse of immigrant workers, the pitiless exploitation of child labour and violence against rural trade unions are still a daily reality for the workers of the world. In this context, appeals for social dialogue and tripartite approaches to labour problems are window-dressing to disguise real state policies upholding employers' interests policies which, on the one hand, welcome any formal initiatives but, on the other hand, show total lack of respect for workers' fundamental labour rights and go as far as penalizing the social action of the workers by wrongly accusing them of crimes.

The Report of the Director-General is full of examples which paint a very sorry picture of respect for the fundamental rights of the workers throughout the world, where millions of human beings are subjected to conditions of extreme poverty and misery and even worse, to the generalized threat of an immoral war imposed by the military and economic powers of the world.

The victims of this situation, who include the workers of my country, make great sacrifices due to the conditions imposed by the international financial bodies with the complicity of the Government of Nicaragua which should act on behalf of its people and its nation, whereas it actually represents interests that have absolutely nothing to do with our needs. The signing of the free trade agreement between the Governments of Central America and the United States, with all the risks and disadvantages that it entails for our economies and for our labour and social rights, is clear proof and an example of this submissive attitude on the part of the Nicaraguan authorities.

Today, Nicaraguan workers are tormented by the deep-seated institutionalized corruption of recent governments, by massive unemployment of over 50 per cent, trade union repression in the free zones, above all, against women workers, constant job insecurity in the civil and public services, the fragile nature of collective agreements because of pressure and the dilemma of how to face up to blackmail and the need for great flexibility in order to provide a more propitious climate for foreign investments that curb labour rights, by the indiscriminate privatization of the basic services that used to be state-run by budgetary cuts in the field of health and education and by a weakening of the minimum wages established in a pact between the Government and employers, thus violating the ILO Minimum Wage Fixing Convention, 1970 (No. 131), and lastly by the economic and moral harm caused by current government policy now which awards mega salaries to public officials, headed by the President of the Republic and mega pensions and other economic perks which are a public affront given the extreme poverty and misery against which the Nicaraguan people are struggling. This is what neo-liberalism has done to my country into and the pact between the international financial bodies and the Government is responsible for it.

In conclusion, from this world podium of labour, on behalf of Nicaraguan Workers, we denounce this situation and demand a real and speedy restitution of the fundamental rights, recognized by the ILO and to this end, we request that this honourable Organization do more to follow up and monitor these rights.

Together with all the workers of the world, we reaffirm our confidence in a better future and our firm will to continue fighting for peace, decent jobs and employment with stronger trade unions united in the quest for fairer societies.

Mr. AUNG (Employers' delegate, Myanmar)

First of all, I would like to join the previous speakers in congratulating the President on his unanimous election as President of the 92nd Session of the International Labour Conference.

Globalization has brought about many changes, such as the promotion of open societies, open economies and free exchange of goods, ideas and knowledge. However, the economic problems of the world, especially those of the developing countries, are far from resolved. The simple and legitimate aspiration of the vast majority to have better job opportunities is still far from realization.

My delegation is of the view that in order to solve these problems, employment creation should be one of the first economic priorities, for without employment the goals of a decent living standard and social and economic development will remain ever illusive.

We are greatly concerned to learn that global unemployment has exceeded 185 million people, which is considered to be the highest unemployment figure ever recorded. Unemployment problems have given rise to international migration. Good domestic employment policies, on the other hand, can help resolve the problem of migration. We welcome the initiative taken by the Director-General to discuss the pressing question of migrant workers at this year's International Labour Conference.

In Myanmar, due to a change from a centralized economy to a market-oriented economy, the private sector has grown with increasing momentum, though somewhat stifled by the sanctions imposed on us.

The Union of Myanmar Federation of Chambers of Commerce and Industry (UMFCCI), which I have the honour to represent, is fully in favour of promoting employment growth. In Myanmar, many industrial zones have been established for the development and modernization of the country and due to the emergence of new industries, many job opportunities have been created.

We have also ventured into the human resources development sector. The establishment of an information and communication technology park has enhanced knowledge and skills and enabled entrepreneurs to make progress in gaining access to emerging technological resources.

We are also promoting opportunities for women to obtain decent and productive work. The Myanmar Women's Entrepreneur Association last year hosted the Tenth Global Conference of Women Entrepreneurs in Yangon, at which women's entrepreneurs' organizations from the region actively participated.

Being a developing country, special focus is given to the growth of small and medium-sized enterprises, and we look forward to working closely with similar enterprises from countries within the region to better respond to the contemporary challenges of globalization.

Since successful enterprises are at the heart of the creation of employment and improvement of living standards, employers' organizations are crucial, and sustainable enterprises can contribute to economic and social development. As the representative of the Employers' group in Myanmar, we are supportive of the ILO Global Employment Agenda for it not only aims at reversing mounting unemployment and poverty, but also promoting trade, technology and entrepreneurship.

In Myanmar the historic National Convention has been reconvened since 17 May 2004 to draft a new domestic State Constitution. This is the first step of the seven-step road map announced by the Prime Minister in August 2003. Important and far-reaching developments are taking place at the National Convention. At the meeting of the National Convention on 20 May 2004 basic principles concerning the duties of employers and employees and labour organizations were laid down for discussion so that these principles can be incorporated into the new draft Constitution.

We are hopeful that the necessary provisions to promote the welfare and the rights of employers and employees will be duly reflected in the new State Constitution.

Original French: Mr. CORTEBEECK *(Workers' delegate, Belgium)*

I would like to use this opportunity both to welcome and to offer comments on the report, *A fair globalization: Creating opportunities for all*, by the World Commission on the Social Dimension of Globalization.

We welcome this report because it is full, exhaustive, critical and well-balanced. It recognizes several ways in which globalization is dysfunctional and concentrates on the social challenges it presents. It is the fruit of the reflections of 26 people from very different backgrounds. That is a positive thing in itself. It stresses the need to harmonize the policies we implement at various different levels, be it national, continental or international, and it takes up the proposal of the World Confederation of Labour, among others, to set up an economic and social security council within the United Nations. It points the finger at the tariff and agricultural policies of rich countries and it pleads for more public development aid. It also recommends a more effective voting system to better represent developing countries.

But the main thing is its central theme, the need to tackle the social consequences of globalization, a subject which can never be stressed too often. We would have liked this report to go even further on certain points such as with regard to the debts of poor countries where the report suggests a restructuring rather than cancellation. Then on trade, the report wishes to get rid of unfair barriers to access to markets, but it does not criticize the WTO's decision-making system. Again, on trade, the report does not provide for a formal structure for negotiations between the ILO and the WTO to deal with the relationship between trade and the fundamental standards to be applied in the world of work. In the same way, there is no provision for any formal structure for dialogue between the Bretton Woods institutions and the WTO, on the one hand, and the trade union movement and other forces in civil society, on the other.

But, at this stage, the challenge is not so much to do with analysis of the report. The challenge is to follow up the initiatives it proposes, for instance, assessing the impact of international policies, establishing an international instrument to guarantee harmonization of these policies and, within the United Nations system, setting up an economic and social security council, establishing a world forum for migration and broadening social dialogue to free trade zones and worldwide systems of production.

Globally speaking, the international community should strive for decent work, full employment and better working conditions. Today, we do have international monitoring of countries to see that they conform to international macroeconomic and financial standards. While these indicators are being monitored all the time there are macro-social indicators, like employment rates, salary levels and income disparities, which are to all intents and purposes ignored.

If we target employment and unemployment rates more closely, that will force us have an employment policy, and if we provide for assessments of the social impacts of policies, that will force us into providing measures to limit these negative impacts. That is what a fairer globalization is about.

Ms. MUGANZA *(Government delegate, Rwanda)*

It is an honour and a pleasure, on behalf of the Rwandan delegation, to join the previous speakers in congratulating the President and the Vice-Presidents upon their election to the leadership of the present session of the Conference.

My congratulations also go to the ILO, and in particular, the Director-General, Mr. Juan Somavia for the high-quality Report presented.

The Government of Rwanda supports the ILO's action throughout the world and particularly in Africa, where its activities during the recent years have focused on poverty reduction, the prevention of HIV/AIDS in the workplace, reconstruction after crisis, social dialogue and socio-economic policies, and regional integration.

In this context, the Government of Rwanda would like the ILO's intervention to increase because Africa remains the poorest and the most marginalized continent. Particular attention should be given to countries that are getting out of conflict, with viable plans to reduce poverty through decent work and good governance.

Poverty breeds insecurity, which infringes upon the creation of a conducive environment and employment. Poverty favours the spread of pandemics such as HIV/AIDS which is very threatening to development.

To fight against poverty, Rwanda has developed national poverty reduction strategies and a development vision towards the year 2020.

Rwanda aims at increasing production in agriculture, human resources and institutional capacity, promotion of gender equity, intensive public works, decentralization, good governance and macroeconomic stability.

The current pattern of globalization does not prevent the increase of unemployment and poverty in developing countries. For those countries it seems unfair because it does not allow them access to the developed countries' markets within favourable conditions.

Moreover, new enterprises cannot compete with the big transnational enterprises or subsidized agricultural products on their own markets. In this context, the globalization process does not give the weakest countries a chance to create jobs.

In this regard, I praise the ILO's initiative of establishing the World Commission on the Social Dimension of Globalization. The current discussion on the future of globalization, as reflected in the

Commission's report, entails better perspectives for it to be open and favourable to all, especially the poorer nations.

The discussion on the Global Report under the Follow-up to the ILO Declaration on Fundamental Principles and Rights at Work provides an opportunity to emphasize that both the Rwandan Constitution and the Labour Code enshrine freedom of association and collective bargaining.

My country reaffirms its commitment to implementing the ILO fundamental principles; a commitment made to our people in the national principles of good governance and promotion of human rights.

Human resources are a key element of the agenda at this session of the Conference, and I would like to underscore that the Government of Rwanda knows that all citizens are the fundamental resources of the country and rank first in our 20-year development vision.

In this regard, access to education, training and career development is one of the paths foreseen to reinforce the implementation capacity of our human resources.

Concerning international migration, which is still an uncontrollable phenomenon, particularly in developing countries without data and control of irregular migration, has a considerable dimension and poses serious difficulties in the country of origin as well as in the host countries.

Finally, we hope that the discussions on this issue will result in innovative solutions to the migration of labour force which will increase global productivity and put an end to exploitation.

In conclusion, I am confident that our Conference will contribute to the construction of a world of freedom, solidarity, unity and peace.

Mr. BARAK *(Employers' adviser and substitute delegate, Israel)*

Allow me, even at this late stage, to take this opportunity to congratulate the President and Vice-Presidents on their election to preside over this session of the International Labour Conference and on their excellent leadership in the difficult task of conducting the deliberations of this Conference.

Since the social aspects of globalization is the main theme of this session of the Conference, may I open my statement by congratulating the Director-General on his Report, *A fair globalization: The role of the ILO*, on the implications for the ILO of the report of the World Commission on the Social Dimension of Globalization.

While, from the viewpoint of Employers, we may have some reservations about some features in the report of the World Commission, I think that there is a general understanding that, since globalization has an important role in economic development and therefore in the consideration of employment, it also opens new major opportunities for social development. This is an area in which the ILO, together with its constituents and through its local and regional network, can and should intensify its efforts.

For this task, the ILO should harness its tripartite structure, which provides it with unique capabilities emerging from the potential strength of the social partners that are the backbone of the Organization.

The year 2004 could be a turning point for the Israeli economy. At the end of 2003, the number of employees in industry remained stable for the first time in three years and an increase in industrial production of 2.7 per cent was registered. Furthermore, emerging background conditions seem to support that direction, among them the expected acceleration in global trade, especially in the high-tech areas, alongside positive local factors such as direct and indirect tax reductions, together with a possible increase in wages during 2004, which may result in an increase in private consumption, while public consumption is expected to remain unchanged.

In view of these predictions for the expected growth of the Israeli economy, we as Employers are concerned about the unsettled present situation of labour relations in Israel. The last few years have manifested the outburst of strikes in the public sector which have adversely affected the private sector, especially as regards shipping and transportation of goods and products.

In these circumstances, the Government saw fit to introduce a bill amending the settlement of labour disputes act in order to regulate in a more coherent way, the rules of behaviour governing labour disputes in the public sector, especially concerning essential public services, such as transportation, ports and shipping, health services, state administration, municipal administration, etc.

The main changes to the existing legislation proposed by the Government are: first, to lengthen the cooling-off period of 15 days before declaring a strike to 30 days in the public sector, during which time mediation steps could be taken to settle the dispute; secondly, the strike will be considered legal only if a majority of the workers involved in the strike had agreed to it by a vote in a secret ballot.

The ideas behind these proposals exist in many industrialized countries and although trade unions in Israel object to these proposals, we think that they may be considered as a fair basis for labour dispute management, especially when essential public services are involved.

Another topic that currently occupies the labour relations actors in Israel is the nomination by the Minister of Justice of a distinguished committee, headed by a former judge of the Israeli Supreme Court, to examine the status of the labour courts system in Israel in relation to the general judicial system. Some people think that the labour courts should be integrated within the overall judicial system of Israel, but our position is that the labour courts should retain their present status as a unique judicial system separate from their overall court system of Israel, thus retaining the special status within the Israeli labour relations arena, while some procedural changes may be considered to increase the efficiency and capacity of the courts.

A few speakers, during the debate, decided to deal with the current conflict in the Middle East, especially with the Palestinian issue. In this regard, I would like to make a few remarks.

I would like to quote from the Report of the Director-General on *The situation of workers of the occupied Arab territories*: "a higher degree of conflict leads to a lower level of economic activity, which in turn translates into a higher rate of unemployment." Had the Palestinian leadership not embarked on a three-and-a-half year campaign of violence, both parties would not have faced the current difficulties – economic activity would have increased and Palestinian and Israeli unemployment would have been checked.

For example, the Palestinians have done their utmost by terrorist attacks to disrupt the work in the joint industrial area of Erez, which is the expression of hope for economic cooperation and joint ownership between Israelis and Palestinians. The same has happened in the Karni passage where goods are transported.

In conclusion, I would like to quote again from the Director-General's, Report: "A solution can only be found as part of negotiations and dialogue."

Mr. BENYDIN *(Workers' delegate, Mauritius)*

Permit me, in the first instance, to congratulate the President and the Officers of the Conference on their election to conduct the deliberations of this present session. With the growing pace of globalization and the accelerated changes in technology and new work methods, the challenges posed to trade unions and workers are no doubt increasing. In addition to our fundamental functions and roles of protecting and defending the inalienable rights of workers, trade unions have to act as a watchdog and a countervailing force struggling against the adverse effects of globalization and to direct it in the mainstreams of social justice and human values which provide for dignity of workers and decent work. And, above all, to pay due respects to our essential needs such as food, health, education, housing and a safe environment.

We would like also to promote good governance, which encourages more workers' participation and which ensures accountability, transparency and the rule of law. Globalization in all its forms should also address the pressing problems of unemployment, underemployment and the marginalization of vulnerable groups and, in particularly, poverty. Globalization should in no way be allowed to continue as it is now, that is increasing assets for the rich and the powerful at the expense of the least developed and developing countries. It is regrettable to note that neo-liberal policies within the context of the globalized economy are having more and more adverse impacts on workers' rights and society in general, particularly on the implementation of policies involving privatization of essential services such as telecommunications, water, electricity and transport. Other factors, such as outsourcing, contracting out, deregulation and flexibility are also causes of discontent and deep concern to the workers and trade unions; the more so in the various cases where labour standards and labour legislation are not complied with.

It is comforting to witness the campaign launched by the ILO a number of years ago now, in favour of the dignity of workers and decent jobs involving a living wage to allow workers to meet the basic needs of their families. Indeed the ILO Declaration on Fundamental Principles and Rights at Work and its Follow-up, adopted in 1998, expresses in unequivocal terms that all member States have an obligation "to respect, to promote and to realize workers' rights ... the principles concerning the fundamental rights which are the subject of those Conventions namely: freedom of association and the effective recognition of the right to collective bargaining, the elimination of all forms of forced or compulsory labour, the effective abolition of child labour, and the elimination of discrimination in respect of employment and occupation".

In Mauritius, following repeated representations made by the trade union organizations, we are now patiently looking forward to the ratification of the Freedom of Association and Protection of the Right to Organise Convention, 1948 (No. 87). It should also be stressed that the Mauritian Government has undertaken to come forward with new legislation to replace the existing IRA in force since 1973, which has always been a source of major discontent and rejection by the trade unions. All the trade union federations in Mauritius have joined hands to propose a common document in this endeavour so that we can have, in the near future, a new legal framework for industrial relations which is in harmony with the principles of democratic labour legislation. With the new legislation, the trade union movement hopes that constraints and obstacles on the right to strike will be removed and that collective bargaining will be reshaped and redefined. The workers in Mauritius are also expecting major changes with respect of the mechanism for the settling of industrial disputes without undue delay, and the consolidation of tripartism and promotion of social dialogue.

Social security and protection are considered by the United Nations as a social right and it is regrettable that only a small percentage of workers are enjoying the benefit thereof. It is therefore imperative that private companies and enterprises should develop corporate social responsibility, including effective and real social dialogue with trade unions, and have policies which underpin social benefits to improve workers' status, welfare and well-being. Also of great concern to us is the persistence of socio-economic insecurity and especially the exposure of workers to poor conditions of occupational health and safety. Social policies should be adopted by enterprises to address the issue of HIV/AIDS, which is increasing poverty and fuelling a secondary pandemic of orphans, thus transforming our present society into a less secure one. We therefore require urgently policies geared at consolidating regulations in favour of occupational health and safety at work.

As representatives of trade union organizations whose policies are deeply anchored with workers' rights, we cannot also remain indifferent to the plight and difficulties of foreign workers in the export processing zone. We are disturbed to a great extent that discrimination and exploitation in most countries where migrant workers are affected are on the increase, particularly factors concerning underpayment, poor working conditions, caused mostly by the non-application of the Migration for Employment Convention (Revised), 1949 (No. 97), and the Migrant Workers (Supplementary Provisions) Convention, 1975 (No. 143). We strongly consider that one of the most effective ways to combat exploitation of migrant workers is to allow them to exercise their right to trade union membership in conjugation with the prescriptions of Conventions Nos. 87 and 98 of the ILO. Migrant workers should also have the rights to payment of insurance, pensions and the right to family reunification.

In Mauritius, the trade union movement is not remaining inactive and indifferent to the difficulties and problems of migrant workers. We are looking forward, with the support and technical assistance of the ILO, to setting up specialized units within our trade union's structure with a view to better defend the rights of migrant workers and ensure their protection at all times and in all circumstances.

Finally, I surely wish that the deliberations and conclusions of this session of the Conference will contribute further to improving living standards

Ms. DEJANOVIĆ (Workers' adviser and substitute delegate, Croatia)

It is a great honour for me to be the spokesperson of the Croatian workers at this distinguished gathering. Being one of the few female speakers, I extend my appreciation to ILO's contribution to gender mainstreaming worldwide.

The ILO stands for social justice, decent work and humane globalization. And yet, core labour standards are violated far too often by far too many. Denial of freedom of association, denial of the right to organize in order to protect fundamental labour rights and dignity of workers, remain highly problematic. Organizing migrant workers and workers in the informal economy remains a major challenge.

I wish to thank the Director-General for focusing the world's attention on the social dimension of globalization.

More than ever before, there are contradictory views on how globalization affects the national economies of small countries like Croatia and the daily lives of its workers.

Fourteen years of transition marked by poorly and unsystematically managed privatization and restructuring have generated negative feelings towards globalization and its potential to create employment and wealth.

In view of Croatia's strategic goal to join the European Union, a high-level tripartite consensus between social partners and government is required to support policies for developing and upgrading our national capabilities to use globalization the best we can.

Sustained creation of more and progressively better employment can only be achieved in the context of high and stable economic growth. The Croatian Government's financial arrangements with the IMF and the World Bank do not always support those goals, which makes our task tremendously difficult. International financial institutions deal primarily with issues of fiscal discipline, international liquidity of the State and structural adjustment, not taking into account national priorities such as real growth and the creation of quality employment.

In reference to the report of the World Commission, we support by all means the idea of coordinated debates on different aspects of globalization. We wish our voice to be heard at those international forums.

For small countries like Croatia, policy dialogue and focus group forums are good platforms for discussing the issue of coping with global production and investment structures, not being restricted to negative scenarios.

There is a need to review national policies in areas like human resources development, providing better access to education and skills to empower people to benefit from globalization employment patterns. We need an active labour market policy and an integrated social policy to assist people who cannot cope with open market forces.

The message that "social progress cannot be achieved by social policies" is in many aspects a central message of the report and a challenge for the unions. What should be recognized at this unique moment in time is that topics of coherence between trade, investment, financial and social policies are becoming trade union topics. Trade unions are legitimate to deal with those issues.

Finally, we welcome the ILO's mission to make globalization more of a "win-win" game and a less severe environment for the fulfilment of the United Nations Millennium Development Goals.

In our attempt to influence national policy choices, to minimize the damage and to maximize the benefits for the workers, we would appreciate as much help as possible from the ILO and generally from the redesigned Bretton Woods architecture.

In order to achieve the goal of fair globalization and decent work for all, the ILO mandate should be further encouraged, supported and strengthened.

(Mr. Attigbe takes the Chair.)

Mr. DEVENDRA (Workers' delegate, Sri Lanka)

Please allow me at the outset to congratulate the President on his election and wish him every success in guiding the work of this Conference to fruitful conclusions at this session. I also wish to take this opportunity to congratulate the two Vice-Presidents of the Conference on their election.

This year, the Conference is due to discuss three items which are of special interest to our country and its workers. The subject of work in the fishing sector is of special concern to us: Sri Lanka being an island, fishing is the livelihood of the vast majority of people living in coastal areas. We have nearly 200,000 workers working abroad, and remittances from these migrant workers constitute the largest foreign exchange earner for our country. Both these sectors are unorganized and are not covered by the labour laws of the country, which make workers in these sectors very vulnerable to dangers and insecurity associated with their employment. Therefore, our Workers' delegation will be actively participating in the work of the Committee on the fishing sector and the Committee on migrant workers.

Permit me to place before this assembly the current phase of events in my country, which have a direct bearing on the democratic freedoms and living standards of our people. As is well known, my country is beset with problems arising from the rebellion in the north and east of the country. The previous Government, which left office in April this year, signed a cease-fire agreement with the Tamil militants, and this agreement continues to be in force to date under the new Government which has pledged to continue with the peace process facilitated by the Royal Norwegian Government. The slow pace of progress in negotiations has placed a strain on all those who yearn for a negotiated political settlement to the ethnic problems of my country.

Sri Lanka, as you know, depends much on its exports, and the garment industry occupies a central place in its export-oriented economic activity. Governments of many developing countries are becoming concerned by the uncertainty of their garment industries surviving beyond 2005, when the quota system will come to an end. As a country that has ratified all eight core Conventions of the ILO, Sri Lanka is fortunate to the extent that the European Union, after due inquiry, has granted an additional duty reduction on the present Generalized System of Preferences (GSP). We take pride in the fact that our country has become the first to succeed in obtaining concessions from the European Union on labour compliance.

Whilst our labour laws are generally in consort with internationally accepted human rights and labour rights norms, they have come under attack in the recent past owing to the pressures of international financial institutions and local businesses to make the labour market flexible, supposedly to create an environment conducive to employment creation. Trade unions have found themselves at variance with this policy as it seeks to promote exploitation of workers and insecurity of their employment. The present Freedom Alliance Government has pledged itself to bringing necessary relief to workers in this regard.

I take this opportunity to make special mention of the work performed by the ILO's Regional Offices on labour-related issues. The ILO Colombo Office, led by its dynamic Director, has to be commended for its enthusiasm and commitment in interacting with all the stakeholders in promoting the Decent Work Agenda. However, an area in which we have not yet made much headway is with regard to the effective implementation of the Freedom of Association and Protection of the Right to Organise Convention, 1948 (No. 87), and the Right to Organise and Collective Bargaining Convention, 1949 (No. 98), with successive governments in our county adopting an ambiguous attitude on the need to enforce the relevant Conventions both in law and in practice.

Finally, as a Workers' delegate representing a country that was the first in the South Asian region to liberalize its economy, I have to state that the expected benefits from the transformation have failed to trickle down to the people, and this has led to a strong movement building up in our part of the world against unconditional submission to the conditionalities of international financial institutions. This situation needs to be treated in such a manner as to bring about development with equity.

Mr. LAMBERT *(Employers' delegate, United Kingdom)*

Globalization is a reality. It is all around us and it is unavoidable. The issue is not whether globalization is a good or bad thing in itself but understanding how it can be made to work for all. The Global Report helps us to do this.

The Report takes us forward by refusing to accept the common argument that the advantages of globalization for one group or one part of the world would always be to the detriment of another. Globalization has win-win potential for all. Globalization brings world publicized benefits for business: access to new customers and markets, best practice transfer, and economies of scale, among others. Yet if managed correctly, its benefits extend much wider than this. If it is conducted on a level playing field, trade between different countries and parts of the world facilitates poverty reduction, increases investment and results in economic growth.

Globalization can be good for workers, as firms standardize welfare and working conditions in order to retain staff and preserve the company's image in an increasingly competitive global market; it can also create the essential opportunity for the young to gain employment and to develop into excellent employees for the future.

Globalization can also be good for customers and consumers; they have enhanced power to make economic choices and benefit from the lower prices brought about by global production methods.

The Global Report correctly identifies the potential benefits of globalization. Correctly, it also stresses the necessity of taking steps to ensure that the benefits and opportunities afforded by globalization can be experienced by us all. If one were to identify two fundamental principles on which this Report is built, these would be fairness and effectiveness. The Report stresses the need for fairness and effectiveness in global governance, and also emphasizes the need to ensure that results of international decision-making are fair and effective for all countries concerned. It is because these principles are so important that it is vital we have a structure capable of ensuring they are translated into action. We must be clear about the role of the ILO in achieving this. The ILO must be clear and focused about what it will deliver.

The World Commission report is addressed to a variety of social, economic and governmental actors. The role of the ILO is the promotion of decent employment opportunities and social justice. The World Commission report should not be seen as an opportunity for the ILO to enlarge its mandate to the extent that it interferes with or duplicates the work of other organizations. Its primary focus in helping deliver the goals of the report should be on promoting the creation of employment, looking particularly at SME activities. It will be important to look at existing initiatives, particularly the work of other international agencies. Equally, the ILO must pay close attention to initiatives it has itself instigated, using existing tools where possible rather than inventing new ones.

Universally applicable ideals, discussed in forums such as these, gain substance only when translated into workable ideals at the appropriate level, and the Global Report recognizes this. For this reason there can be no "one-size-fits-all" approach. Different countries have different capacities, and will take varying amounts of time to ratify Conventions. The ILO's role is not to try to direct or control local dialogues, but to work with national or regional organizations to help them communicate with their governments.

In this intervention I have discussed globalization on a global scale, but in my final comments I want to be more specific about what must happen in this Organization if we are going to meet the great challenge that confronts us.

The ILO should be a beacon of best practice; the ILO must lead by example. It employs large numbers of people around the world, people who are at the leading edge of working for a better world. However, this group of employees will only be truly effective if they are themselves empowered; they must be free to contribute ideas that will be listened to and freely debated. Great organizations are distinguished by the quality of their management, and this Organization will become greater if it continues to generate and adopt these types of human resources policies. Only if this happens can the ILO attract the excellent people it needs to be an effective world-class Organization capable of driving change. Next, there must be further internal reform; in particular, reform of the Governing Body, and reform of this Conference itself, will also be crucial to ensuring that the ILO continues to be effective and relevant.

The significant impact of "a fair globalization" should be the hope that it gives to people everywhere, that real change is possible. Consider what this could mean; more and more people achieving employment, a better standard of living for all and, most of all, the great stain of poverty being progressively eliminated. It is up to us all to ensure that the correct framework is in place to achieve these vital objectives.

Mr. LEWIS *(Employers' delegate, Jamaica)*

I consider it an honour to address this Conference. Like others, I too offer my congratulations to the President on his election.

No one can deny that the ILO, through its various efforts, has made a positive difference to the world over the past 85 years, but in the light of global changes it faces tremendous challenges each new day. The question is, can the ILO meet those challenges? The answer is undoubtedly a resounding "yes". With the able leadership and foresight of our Director-General, and the cooperation and commitment of all its Members, I am confident that this Organization will rise to any new challenge. Mankind thrives on challenges. Sometimes inventions and discoveries are the result of passion and the search for perfection; in other cases they are the desire to make the world a safer, more peaceful, more comfortable and a more just place for all peoples to live. It is this search for fairness which has informed the World Commission's report, *A fair globalization: Creating opportunities for all.*

If we are to achieve a fair globalization with any hope of creating opportunities for all, there are certain critical areas which must be addressed with passion.

Every nation must put people at the centre of every plan it makes. No economic plan is worthy of discussion if its ultimate goal is not to achieve meaningful benefits for the people, and chief of the benefits is the provision of decent work. In this respect it must be national governments' responsibility to create the right environment which is conducive to investment, which will grow their economies and create decent jobs. Such environments must include opportunities for education and training as a means of strengthening societies' human capital. Ultimately, this will lead to greater efficiency and increased productivity of goods and services; and when I speak of decent work I also mean that efforts must be made to eliminate child labour, because it cannot be right for children to miss the opportunity of education and training at an early age due to this unreasonable practice of engaging them in child labour.

My second point is that fair globalization must, of necessity, ensure fair rules of trade and fair rules of investment. It is impossible to speak of fair globalization if unfair rules of trade and investment continue to be road blocks to economic opportunities for developing countries.

Fair rules hold benefits not only for developing countries but also positive benefits for developed countries as well. Surely, if there is improved prosperity as a result of market expansion of goods and services of necessity, this also means benefits for poor developing countries. It also means the creation of jobs, the reduction of unemployment, poverty eradication, the reduction of crime and, most importantly, political stability.

The world is now seen as a global village. Space and language no longer separate the world. The vicissitudes of war, poverty and unemployment have resulted in mass international migration. This phenomenon has brought with it concerns in relation to brain drain, which has implications for poor developing countries. We all have an appreciation of what these implications are.

Then, there is the runaway train: I refer to HIV/AIDS. It is estimated that there are over 40 million people living with HIV/AIDS. It is also estimated that nine out of ten are adults at their productive best. The need is now never greater for all three partners – governments, employers and workers – to promote and guide effective action, in the workplace and elsewhere, if we are to contain the spread of this disease.

It is not possible to wish ourselves out of poverty: there is only one way out of poverty, and that is to work ourselves out of it. In order to do this, we have to start at the national level, to work as a team. We must recognize that we have a stake in our nation's well-being. I believe that, collectively, we can make a difference. Divisiveness cannot work. There must be a search for balance so as to ensure peace, harmony, equity and justice in order to create opportunities for our peoples.

Fair globalization, in the final analysis, will only come if there are the following: responsible governance at the national level to influence international governance; ethical business principles and practices which are critical to efficiency and productivity; and social justice.

These same principles are applicable to organizations such as the World Bank and the IMF, and the ILO, as the international standard-setter, must have a role to play in its dialogue with these institutions.

We, the tripartite group of governments, employers and workers, representing countries from all over the world, know what needs to be done. The ILO is doing its part, and we are grateful. We have the capacity to do our part; we seem to lack the will to do it. In the interest of our peoples and a better world, let us do what we know is right, noble and just.

Original Arabic: Mr. MATTAR *(Employers' delegate, United Arab Emirates)*

In the name of God, the Merciful, the Compassionate!

The Federation of UAE Chambers of Commerce and Industry has been participating in the work of the International Labour Conference for many years. We have actively contributed to the debate because we firmly believe in the importance of the activities of the ILO and its various bodies in achieving its objectives of promoting and supporting the efforts of the social partners in member States.

Moreover, the policy of our country is to open up to the international community and to cooperate with all the international organizations and specialized agencies. The best proof of this policy is the fact that the United Arab Emirates has hosted several international meetings, such as the International Bank of Reconstruction and Development and IMF meetings in 2003.

The report of the World Commission on the Social Dimension of Globalization is extremely important, underscoring the importance of work at the national level whilst taking account of international trends. Among the very important realities stressed by the report, we should mention the facts that a successful globalization requires efficient national work, and that a fair globalization comes from within a country, not from outside. Establishing an appropriate climate for investment, trade and the internal labour market is the right way to ensure competition with foreign markets.

Our delegation would fully agree with such an orientation, and I can assure you that our policy is based on a free economy and free trade. Our markets are open to investments from abroad and from within, we do not impose taxes, and we are creating an appropriate environment to ensure security for investors, workers and all those who live in our country.

The international community needs indeed a fair globalization that would give equal opportunities to all, a globalization that would indeed ensure freedom of trade, the free flow of capital and goods, and the free transfer of technology, and which would put an end to protectionist policies imposed by certain large industrialized countries on exports from developing countries.

The report and its recommendations thus require the cooperation of all the international and regional organizations involved in order to analyse and discuss it and to implement its recommendations.

We would agree with the Report of the ILO concerning migrant workers and the need to protect their rights. We are happy to say that migrant and foreign workers in the State of the United Arab Emirates enjoy full legal protection, perfectly in keeping with international labour standards. The situation of foreign workers is considered temporary governed by work contracts between the employer and the worker and ratified by the relevant governmental bodies. They are temporary contracts for a given period of time. Consequently, our experience is not in keeping with the concept of the international migration of workers but rather with the concept of invited workers, a term used by the Director-General to describe the situation of such workers working outside their own countries for given periods of time.

Allow me to express my thanks to the Director-General of the International Labour Office for his constant care and follow up of the situation of employers and workers in Palestine and the other occupied Arab territories. The Report presented by the high-level mission this year has revealed several kinds of suffering to which the employers and the workers in that part of the world are subjected.

From this rostrum and from this session of the Conference, I call upon the Governing Body and the Director-General to take all the necessary steps and measures within their responsibilities and mandate in order to support all the social partners in Palestine and the other occupied Arab territories, and to promote their capacity to face the negative impact of Israeli occupation, settlers' occupation and hostility. It is important for the Organization to continue to help the Palestinian people until occupation ends and their territory is liberated and an independent Palestinian state has been established with Al-Quds as the capital.

We also call upon all the relevant bodies of the ILO to offer help to all the social partners in Iraq because of the very difficult situation they are experiencing.

Original Spanish: Mr. RUGGIERO *(representative, Latin American Union of Municipal Workers)*

First of all, I would like to congratulate the Director-General on his Report to this 92nd Session of the International Labour Conference, from which it is clear that positive results have been achieved through the efforts of the ILO to promote, through tripartism and social dialogue, international labour standards and policies to overcome poverty and unemployment.

This affirmation is corroborated by the documentation of the International Monetary Fund and World Bank. It is apparent that there has been a slight but significant change of tack towards recognition of the importance of social and labour policies and the need to take sustained development policy into account, which is consistent with the ILO's stance on employment and job stability.

This change of tack constitutes a major contribution by the ILO in that the multinational credit organizations are heading for a review of their economic, social and labour policies.

The Latin American Union of Municipal Workers (ULAT-MUN) comprises 20 national trade union organizations of the Latin American and Caribbean region. It was founded in 1994 and since then has participated actively in the International Labour Conference and specific activities on municipal workers convened by the ILO.

Turning to the priorities of this Organization, I would like to highlight the main areas of concern for the Latin American municipal workers' movement.

The information which we received through our intense and constant interchange of information with the Latin American municipal workers' organizations, points to major problems which have a structural impact on the socio-political and economic realities of each of the societies represented and affect the employment situation in each country.

One of these is the problem of the informal economy and the need for the trade union movement to build a genuine strategy to combat informal work, starting with combating the hegemonic model underlying it.

We consider that the trade union movement should be an active participant in promoting the setting of positive standards in public policy and legislation related to work in the informal economy.

My organization would like to express its concern at situations which have been the subject of complaints by the municipal workers in some countries such as Panama, where the national Government is denying municipal governments the right to collect taxes on the installation of public billboards, which is a setback with respect to the policy of decentralization introduced in that country in 1995. Another example is Chile, where municipal governments have begun a new wave of privatization, outsourcing and management of public spaces through the concession of certain spaces to private enterprises, which municipal workers have begun to denounce.

As regards strategy, we consider that the union movement should work to build alliances with organizations in the informal economy instead of pursuing a strategy of incorporating individuals from the informal economy; hence alliance strategies should be adapted to the specific situations in specific sectors and regions. Municipal policies should encourage workers in public life to form associations and cooperatives to improve production and sales.

The ULAT-MUN has geared its activities to the common features of the socio-economic realities of

Latin American countries. The impact in the past decade of neo-liberal and adjustment policies has had direct repercussions in terms of increasingly precarious conditions of employment and unemployment.

Based on this empirical observation, we have been able not only to exchange substantial information on the realities of our countries, but also to build up common positions and formulate a strategy for the defence of individual and collective rights of municipal workers in our region.

Turning now to an assessment of working conditions in the public municipal sector in Latin America, by and large the points raised by representatives to ULAT-MUN in the past still apply; I would like to comment on the following in particular.

In view of the gravity of the situation in regard to trade union activities in Colombia, where there has been an upsurge in violence and murders of union leaders, it is our duty to condemn these events and ask this international organization to adopt drastic measures to ensure the physical safety of union leaders and the unrestricted exercise of their right to organize.

Venezuela too has seen considerable obstructions to union activities through the implementation of mechanisms which make it difficult for workers to join unions and exercise their right to representation.

Municipal workers in Chile are in the midst of a serious struggle against the central Government and have submitted a complaint of violation of labour and trade union rights to this Organization, and this also calls for the explicit public support of ULAT-MUN and all of its affiliates.

In Argentina, the Confederation of Municipal Workers of Argentina (COEMA) is demanding a review of salaries to bring them up to the level of those in the national public service. As a result, unionized workers and their organization have called for industrial action.

We also denounce the violations of union rights which have been committed in most of the municipalities in El Salvador.

In general, privatization and outsourcing of activities in the sector in Latin America have occurred to a lesser extent than in previous years but, in some cases, this is still a major cause of labour disputes, of corruption, of dismissals, of deteriorating working conditions and of a reduction in the quality of public service. The same is true of certain repercussions of neo-liberal policies, which continue to affect the stability of employment in the public sector, since the intention is to reduce or even eliminate it altogether in many countries of the region.

We publicly declare our objection to this policy and advocate the need to apply the principles of protection and the guarantee of rights, in accordance with ILO Conventions Nos. 87, 98 and 151.

Another matter of concern and a source of injustice are the low salaries of municipal workers in Latin America, resulting from the persistence of unfair patterns of wealth distribution which still prevail in the region, and which are among the most backward in the world. Hence the frequent and persistent wage claims by trade union organizations throughout the continent: their income is well below the poverty line in the region.

We need to proceed with the incorporation of the social and labour agenda in economic-integration processes in the region, and this continues to be a matter of concern for my organization, particularly in view of the severe adverse effects of the recent international crisis in the region.

We advocate the incorporation of a social floor as proposed by the ILO, in integration processes with, as a minimum, references to non-discrimination, prohibition of forced labour, freedom of association and the right to collective bargaining, the abolition of child labour – all of which are essential components of a viable integration process.

To conclude, I would like to mention the subject of the foreign debt burden borne by our countries and the heavy pressure brought to bear by groups of creditors, especially what is termed the "vulture funds", and the multilateral credit organizations. All these affects their economic growth and development and the implementation of social justice for a fair and sustainable society. The focus of this Organization should now be on the future.

Mr. DE PURY *(representative, World Organization Against Torture)*

The World Organization Against Torture wants to intervene about the Appendix to the Report of the Director-General on the situation of workers of the occupied Arab territories.

The World Organization Against Torture, also known as the OMCT, is a network of 266 non-governmental organizations, either national or international, which informs the International Secretariat in Geneva of serious human rights violations.

In response to each case, the OMCT launches urgent appeals to the greatest possible number of individuals and organizations, directed towards the authorities involved, demanding that violated rights be respected. These appeals are also important sources of information for the international community.

In November of last year, a mission to Israel and the occupied territories was carried out by the OMCT and the International Federation for Human Rights in the name of the joint programme, the Observatory for the Protection of Human Rights Defenders, together with Forefront, a global network of grass-roots human rights defenders based in New York.

The Report states that among the victims of rights violations is the Democracy and Workers' Rights Centre, as Israeli soldiers broke into the headquarters in Ramallah and the Director-General was prevented from travelling abroad to attend the meeting. Knowing the situation that workers are subjected to, the hostility towards an organization that defends their rights is not surprising, particularly since workers' rights are among the rights in question.

The three organizations thus exposed the serious impact that a purely military approach to security has on human rights and particularly on labour and economic, social and cultural rights. For instance, Israel's construction of its separation fence, more commonly known as the "apartheid wall" in Palestine's West Bank, has led to grave land and housing rights violations. The extension of the wall is annexing land and water wells and will enclave 95,000 Palestinians on the West Bank, in addition to cutting off 200,000 Palestinian residents in East Jerusalem from the West Bank.

Another significant problem is the demolition of houses which has been recognized by the Committee Against Torture as constituting "cruel, inhuman or degrading treatment or punishment", which are the terms defining torture.

On 17th May of this year, the OMCT was informed that 2,197 people were rendered homeless, due to the demolition of 191 homes during the first-15 days of May. The Rafah area was most significantly affected. Furthermore, Israeli forces have destroyed 5,013 houses in Gaza, rendering 38,215 inhabitants homeless from 29 September 2000 to 15 May 2004.

The Israeli Government has also expressed its intention to destroy hundreds more houses in Rafah in spite of the army's statement that it has no future plans to continue demolitions, except in cases of "military necessity".

Furthermore, the situation of workers in the occupied territories is an issue of great concern due to the closures policy. The unemployment rate rose from 10 per cent prior to the intifada in the third quarter of 2000 to 53 per cent in the fourth quarter of 2002 – and is worse today.

In addition, a new aspect of the past system was introduced from May 2002 causing Palestinian residents and, especially workers, to need special Israeli permits to travel within the West Bank and Gaza.

Another issue is the denial of access to medical care. We launched an urgent appeal about two Palestinian detainees with deteriorating health conditions in Israeli prisons. Despite the repeated requests for medical assistance, it was not given to them, which constitutes a clear case of ill-treatment under the convention against torture.

Thus, the Israeli State has clearly violated human rights, international laws and treaties. These include the human rights on property, work, freedom of movement, water and all elements of the right to adequate housing. It has violated such treaties as the International Convention on the Elimination of All Forms of Racial Discrimination, the International Covenant on Civil and Political Rights, the International Covenant on Economic Social and Cultural Rights and several Conventions of the International Labour Organization.

Finally, it has violated the Fourth Geneva Convention and The Hague Regulations of 1907.

Original French: Mr. WALLIMANN *(representative, World Movement of Christian Workers)*

The World Movement of Christian Workers, the WMCW, would like to use this opportunity of being present at the 92nd Session of the International Labour Conference to express its full support for the ILO's highlighting of the theme of decent work for all. In fact, the globalization of our economy continues to make work more insecure, weakening the fabric of society and plunging thousands of workers and their families into poverty and despair. The 21st century is seeing imposed the model of informal work, which, all evidence suggests, has undermined the relationship between people and their work, which, in turn, has dangerous implications for the family and the social environment. There are so many workers who are now being exposed to the risk of being victims of all sorts of physical and mental violence, including murder and imprisonment, unfair dismissal and even unfounded refusal of visas to some WMCW members who wanted to come from southern countries to the north to participate in the international life of our Movement.

It is against this background that the representatives of 70 member organizations of the World Movement of Christian Workers, representing about two and half million workers from 68 countries, met in Quebec in May 2004 for the Movement's international seminar followed by its tenth General Assembly.

Taking to heart the ILO's objectives for "decent work for all", this General Assembly defined three main goals for its initiatives over the next four years.

The first of these is to bring together workers from all spheres, whether they be employed or unemployed, with particular emphasis on those who are socially excluded. The second is to contribute to implementing human rights with particular emphasis on economic, social and cultural rights. The third is to make sure that the voices of workers are heard within the United Nations, through the churches and civil society. These initiatives aim to establish alternatives to existing economic and work patterns in the different continents and also to defend women's rights as a priority.

By the end of this four-year period, the World Movement of Christian Workers intends to publish a White Paper on implementing these goals and we will not fail to deliver it to all relevant institutions.

Original Spanish: Mr. PARRA GAONA *(Workers' adviser, Paraguay)*

May I first be allowed to congratulate the President on his election to preside over the 92nd Session of the International Labour Conference. We emphasize and appreciate the words of the Director-General of the ILO, Dr. Juan Somavia, who, in his Report, highlights the fundamental rights of workers and the dignity of work.

We express our concern about the lack of employment policy in the labour world.

As workers we reiterate our concern about the growing unemployment rates in our Latin American and Caribbean countries.

Once again, we denounce the structural adjustment policies prepared in the inappropriately named "Washington Consensus", aimed at giving priority to macroeconomic policies to control inflation and overlooking employment and investment. The Nobel Peace Prize winner for economy in 2001, Dr Josef Stiglitz, has denounced these policies because they produce economic recession and unemployment.

We reiterate our denunciation of the devastating effects of globalization, as stated by Dr. Josef Stiglitz which is confirmed by the report of the 26 members of the special committee set up by the ILO, which calls for in-depth reforms and a change of direction with respect to globalization so as not to continue destroying the small and medium-sized enterprises, weakening the national state and increasing unemployment, critical poverty and social exclusion.

As workers, we reiterate our objection to any neoliberal model and to the labour reforms that destabilize employment and render labour relations flexible and precarious. If we continue with such policies, there will be no point in the ILO nor the consultative forum and the various MERCOSUR bodies making any efforts.

We demand the establishment of a financial fund of MERCOSUR to promote public, private and social investment to create worthy employment in the subregion.

We are on the alert to avoid precarious employment taking place, as is the case in our countries today.

We request that the agreements established in MERCOSUR be taken up in each of our countries and we support the document signed by our labour ministers in MERCOSUR at the regional conference on employment held in Buenos Aires in April this year which had the support of the ILO. As a major strategy of the States, we have put decent work as a strategy for development. This is very different from what it is claimed is being carried out with the Free Trade Area of the Americas.

However, the practice of our country to date is not in line with these documents, because, in spite of having ratified important ILO Conventions such as ILO Conventions Nos. 87 and 98, these have remained dead letters and companies continue to violate these basic rights with a lack of compliance with social security rights, the right to health and the right to dignity in the lives of workers.

We would like to mention the violations and disregard of the Conventions on freedom of association and collective bargaining, the Indigenous and Tribal Peoples Convention, 1989 (No. 169), the Migration for Employment Convention (Revised), 1949 (No. 97), and the Forced Labour Convention, 1930 (No. 29). The workers in the transport sector continue to work for 14-16 hours a day, violating the legal requirements of eight hours. Workers in the Migone sanitorium are suffering from trade union persecution and dismissals and workers in the communications media, in the case of the Puerto Casado community, are subjugated as regards their rights by pseudo-investors in the Moon Sect, which has reached even this area. We also want to mention the rural communities, which are fighting for the right to land and livelihood, calling for total agrarian reform. We should also mention the public sector workers who are being persecuted in their rights, the workers of the Yacyreta energy company, which is not complying with the collective labour agreement, who are being subject to anti-union persecution and the workers of the Paraguayan Tebycuary sugar refinery and the Iturbe sugar refinery.

The external debt, which channels the savings of our countries towards the payments of interest and commission, leaves nothing available for the necessary public investment.

For quality employment, we must have a structure of distribution of income throughout society, because the logic of the market is accumulation and concentration which aggravates social inequality. We must more clearly propose the role of the State and its relations with the market, avoiding extreme cases where there is either the dictatorship of the State or that of the market. It is also our wish to comply with salary readjustment of 25 per cent for the loss of purchasing power that has accumulated since 1989.

In our country we do not want a speculative economy, we want a productive employment economy.

As a positive aspect, we would like to mention the ratification of the Worst Forms of Child Labour Convention, 1999 (No. 182), and the Minimum Age Convention, 1973 (No. 138).

We would also like to refer, as a positive case, to the payment of the contribution to the ILO, enabling the active participation of our delegates and the right to vote. The Government has raised the question of refinancing of the debt for contributions in arrears.

Finally, we want to express our solidarity with our colleagues from Colombia and Guatemala and other trade union and social organizations which suffer permanent persecution. We demand the liberation of our colleague Rigoberto Dueñas, who has been unfairly jailed in Guatemala for a year now because he fought for the fundamental rights of workers and the freedom of our trade union colleagues in Cuba.

We reaffirm our commitment to the construction of a new society, which should be based on peace and social justice.

Mr. GOODLEIGH *(Workers' delegate, Jamaica)*

We should like to begin by congratulating the President on the occasion of his election to preside over this 92nd Session of the International Labour Conference.

We live in a post-modern age, driven by the forces of globalization, information technology and regionalization. These forces generate a complex range of social, economic and political issues. Many of these issues are not new, but have become critical at this juncture in history.

Primarily among these issues are those of: sustainable economic and social development, which also address questions of equity and social justice; global financial instability; global environmental and climate change; pandemics; international crime and corruption; issues of fair trade; issues of the rise in power of multilateral and transnational companies; and issues of governance.

These surging global issues have arisen at a time when we have not all implemented in a satisfactory manner the fundamental workplace policies advocated by the ILO, over an extended period, during which the ILO has sought to ensure that these policies are established in the world's workplaces.

Despite these efforts by the ILO, many Governments have either failed to ratify, or have ratified and failed to implement, these minimum standards and policies in their planning processes.

The challenge we face is how to ensure that these agreed minimum standards are reflected in the world's workplaces and, at the same time, meet the challenges posed by the post-modern age.

One of the obstacles we face in trying to meet this challenge is the fact that the international multilaterals are not in agreement about ILO standards. They have differing views about workplace governance. We are well aware that, in the past, the Bretton Woods twins, namely the IMF and the World Bank, spoke of structural adjustment programmes and the lowering of workers' standards of living. These prescriptions were advocated whilst the ILO was speaking of the establishment of minimum standards and raising workers' standards of living.

In the current context, the IMF and the World Bank advocate flexible enterprises devoid of labour laws and minimum standards. They consider that laws and standards distort the world's labour markets. On the other hand, the social partners, Governments, unions and Employers in the ILO have accepted the concept of decent work and the establishment of minimum standards in the world's labour markets.

It is precisely this vast disparity in policy approaches between multilaterals that aids and abets many Governments in ignoring the Conventions they have negotiated and agreed to in the ILO.

It is this difference that allows the practice of "situational ethics" by Governments. This is the practice of saying one thing in the ILO and subscribing in the IMF and the World Bank setting to a set of policies that are diametrically opposed to the ILO standards.

It is a problem that the World Commission on the Social Dimension of Globalization has clearly recognized, when it recommended in its report that policy coherence initiatives should be launched by the relevant international organizations, namely the United Nations bodies, the World Bank, the IMF and the WTO. The Commission specifically mentions the issues of global growth, investment, employment creation, gender equality, education and training.

We would expect that in that context, some agreement could be reached in terms of decent work and minimum standards in the world's workplaces. It is our view that, if this is to be accomplished, the world's multilaterals must ignore the World Bank's dated view that the primary objective of a labour market should be efficiency, and they must agree that, in a post-modern age, the multiple objectives of efficiency, productivity, equity and social justice are what the world's labour market should be about.

It is only a reliance on these objectives that can anchor any agreement on policy coherence. It is only a reliance on these objectives that can ensure that trade agreements and WTO rules are fair and socially sensitive. It is only a reliance on these objectives that, in the words of the Commission, will ensure that those countries with greater decision-making power in international bodies will consider all interests and meet their international commitments.

Currently, it is only a commitment to these shared objectives that will ensure that Governments across the spectrum of development honour their obligations in the ILO, because if, in this post-modern age of globalization, we are to succeed politically and socially, we must address questions of equity, social justice, efficiency and productivity in the world's workplaces.

In closing, we in the Jamaican trade union movement would like to thank the ILO Regional Office for its invaluable assistance in the past year.

Original Spanish: Mr. FOSTIK *(Employers' delegate, Uruguay)*

This delegation would like to join other speakers congratulating the President upon his election at this session of the Conference.

We are very aware of the effects of globalization on the relationship between economic and social activities, particularly those based upon new knowledge and technologies.

For many years, our society has been exposed to the influence of outside forces which to a certain degree continue to mark our economy. Globalization requires careful planning so that it involves aspects of world trade and employment, whilst at the same time providing for the well-being of all, thereby creating fair globalization.

It would be opportune for the Office to place proposals before the next Governing Body upon the way in which the Organization can specifically respond to the recommendations of the report of the World Commission.

The follow-up to the report conducted by the Office, through the Governing Body and consultations with its constituents, will certainly determine through a consensus the effective ways whereby a greater number of countries can begin to enjoy the benefits of globalization.

We hope that this process to follow up the report will not affect the resources allocated to further the traditional mandate of the ILO so that the Organization can continue to focus on the promotion of quality employment as the main escape route from poverty.

If we at the ILO were to associate these efforts with an extensive campaign to propagate skills and knowledge, we would be ensuring a move towards offering a better life for all.

The necessary support of the ILO in the development and updating of entrepreneurial spirit will optimize management skills and thus generate better income opportunities and improved sustainability on the world stage. ILO support is also necessary to help employers develop policies which are in keeping with the social responsibilities of the enterprise.

Governments should develop the appropriate environment to stimulate the reinvestment of those companies which still have the capability to do so, to ensure the future of existing business plans and to bring in new investment or genuine national and foreign investors.

There is a most important task that should not be forgotten: giving special and permanent attention to the development of formal SMEs. Decent work begins in the formal sector, whatever the size of the enterprise.

We would like to express our appreciation for the efforts that have been made for migrant workers; workers throughout the world who are seeking means to earn a living.

The Report on the situation of workers of the occupied Arab territories shows that the situation has almost remained unchanged during the reporting period, despite the reinforced programme of technical cooperation specially dedicated to that area.

More than ever it is necessary to obtain the support of donors to maintain the programmes to mitigate the distressing situation in the region.

We must build up a new environment for all of us.

(Mr. Ray Guevara takes the Chair.)

Mr. FINLAY *(Employers' delegate, Canada)*

It is an honour to speak on the Director-General's Report, *A fair globalization: The role of the ILO*.

Canadian business is pleased to see that the debate and discussions surrounding globalization are maturing. There is recognition of the positive socio-economic effects of the evolving world economy. No longer are the world's ills attributed to globalization. Instead we are starting to hear of the potential of globalization as a vehicle for improving opportunities for all.

There are two points in particular that I would like to address today. Further and more detailed examination of the recommendations will take place at the Governing Body meeting in November.

First, I am concerned that policy coherence is not fully understood. We are here because we respect and value the potential of the ILO. Policy coherence means to me that we also respect the expertise and mandates of other institutions. Barely a whisper is made of the tremendous contribution of the United Nations Development Programme (UNDP) report entitled *Unleashing entrepreneurship: Making business work for the poor* and the work the UNDP is doing to generate action from this report. I believe that there is a great potential for synergy here, but it will require greater attention from the ILO to the activities of the UNDP.

I might have considered this an oversight, except for the arguments in the Report made to enter the realm of economic policy. The Report refers to the Declaration of Philadelphia language mandating the ILO to examine and consider all international economic and financial policies and measures, and then concludes from that that this means the ILO must step into the economic policy arena. Such an unfounded interpretation and direction leads me to be concerned that the ILO might conflict with, rather than seek coherence in, international socio-economic policy. The language referred to from the Declaration of Philadelphia suggests consideration of international economic and financial policies; it does not invite the ILO to step into such areas, especially where other agencies have this mandate, or invite the ILO to step out of its own mandate in search of others.

My second concern is that the Report suggests new directions and even new resources for the ILO. The ILO is currently involved in many matters meriting attention, including entrepreneurship, youth employment, small and medium-sized enterprise development, enterprise growth and employment creation. These are just some of the areas that align with the issues and concerns arising in the Report. Thus, the ILO should be cautious about setting out in new directions.

For the most part, the structure for addressing matters arising from the Report falls within the current framework of ILO programmes, to the extent those matters come within the purview of the ILO. We may find we need greater clarity in mandate, greater focus, and possibly the reallocation of existing resources, but the core structure is there, as long as the ILO does not branch out into areas better left to other international, national or local agencies. Thus, I hope that the Governing Body takes the approach of focusing on areas of the ILO's core competencies, and seeks to utilize those resources that the ILO has now, most effectively. This is a basic rule that business knows well. Focus on your core products, and deliver in a cost-efficient and effective way.

We look forward to continuing to be involved in this discussion and look forward especially to the discussion at the meeting of the Governing Body in November.

Ms. WINTOUR *(representative, Public Services International)*

Thank you for the opportunity to speak on behalf of Public Services International (PSI).

PSI welcomes the report of the World Commission on the Social Dimension of Globalization. The report highlights "the important role of the State in managing the process of integration into the global economy, and in ensuring that it meets both economic and social objectives". However, the capacity of the State to fulfil its important role has been severely undermined by the conditionalities laid down by international financial institutions and other forms of bilateral lending.

The Global Report, *Organizing for social justice*, estimates that 15 million public sector jobs were lost in 1999 and 2000 alone. The report recognizes the "policy bias, especially within the international financial community, in favour of private sector solutions". It also recognizes that changes have been introduced through "settlements imposed without discussion or negotiation". These have resulted in public employees becoming "demoralized or radical – or both". Under these conditions, the sense of public service ethos that motivated public employees has been undermined.

These are the same public service employees who are being called upon to meet the targets laid down by the Millennium Development Goals and to provide anti-retroviral drugs to 3 million people with HIV/AIDS by 2005 under the recently launched World Health Organization initiative. If the international community is serious about addressing poverty and saving lives, it must take responsibility for reversing the catastrophic decline of the public service.

One of PSI's main priorities is the global campaign for quality public services. This is a positive and proactive campaign, aimed at strengthening critically important public services. A renewed commitment must be made to the Millenium Development Goals through better and more aid to developing countries, debt relief, fair trade, and investment in quality public services.

Despite the current economic fashion for privatization, there is strong evidence that quality public services are a critical path to building sustainable economies and inclusive societies.

Where access to water and energy is privatized, respect for human rights or for labour rights is undermined, economic growth is reduced and there is increased pressure on women and children and increased risks to the environment. PSI commends the United Nations system for recognizing the right to water and supports the call of the French energy unions for the creation of a United Nations right to energy. PSI calls on all United Nations bodies to support such a rights and to create a global day to draw attention to the right to energy.

Gender equality is central to the PSI programme of action. For a number of years, PSI has voiced concern at the lack of representation of women at this Conference and in the ILO's senior management. PSI has adopted a five-year pay equity campaign. The follow-up action plan to the Global Report on equality at work includes proposals which reflect the needs of public sector unions, including guidelines on gender-neutral job evaluation systems, improved statistical indicators and tripartite meetings to promote pay equity. PSI therefore welcomes the Resolution concerning the promotion of gender equality, pay equity and maternity protection before the Conference this year and its recognition of the positive role of public services in contributing to the achievement of gender equality.

PSI also welcomes the general discussion on migration and the search for a multilateral framework. PSI is particularly concerned about the impact of migration on the delivery of health and education services in developing countries. We call for the adoption of ethical recruitment guidelines, monitoring and sanctions against unscrupulous recruitment agencies. Due consideration should be given to establishing a system to compensate developing countries when their health professionals are recruited to work abroad.

Finally, the Global Report, *Organizing for social justice,* argues for a sea change in the global culture to strengthen respect for freedom of association and collective bargaining. There are too many cases worldwide where public sector trade unions are subjected to discrimination, including arbitrary dismissals and arrests, and on occasion murder. PSI is particularly concerned about the situation in the Republic of Korea and in Tamil Nadu, India, where last year over 200,000 public sector employees were arbitrarily dismissed and 6,000 arrested. In Chile, the Government has prepared draft legislation that would effectively deny municipal employees the right to bargain collectively. These are all cases where the supervisory mechanisms of the ILO have played a vital role. However, in the case of Colombia, and given the continuing and systematic violations of human rights, PSI calls upon the ILO to adopt additional measures to address the situation of impunity in which these crimes are committed.

Original Spanish: The PRESIDENT *(Mr. Ray GUEVARA)*

To conclude our discussion in Plenary of the report of the Chairperson of the Governing Body and of the Report of the Director-General, I now have great pleasure in giving the floor to the spokespersons of the Employers' and the Workers' groups.

Mr. FUNES DE RIOJA *(Employers' adviser and substitute delegate, Argentina, speaking on behalf of the Employers' group)*

It is clear that the recommendations of the World Commission on the Social Dimension of Globalization are relevant to the ILO and its mandate and that they present the ILO with a clear opportunity in terms of its visibility and relevance in the multilateral system. It is also clear that there is absolute unanimity on one crucial point – everybody wants to see the benefits of globalization spread more widely. This perhaps is the most striking message. In that respect, the World Commission has helped to move the debate on globalization away from confrontational polemics. We need to continue this positive process and develop the debate in an appropriate way.

The report is wide-ranging in its recommendations and proposals and evidently only some parts of them are relevant to the ILO. It was evident to me, from listening to many delegates, that the ILO is well placed to give effect to many of the recommendations without changing or weakening its current work or traditional mandate. Increasingly, the ILO is focusing on the promotion of employment as a central route from poverty and this is ostensibly a very positive development.

The goal of decent work as a global goal fits in with the ILO's response to the Millennium Development Goals. This opportunity should be seized. Fostering SMEs and entrepreneurs, which is at the heart of poverty alleviation, is also an objective. Let us see the following kinds of programmes accelerated: SME development, fostering entrepreneurship, helping those in the informal economy formalize their activities, developing innovative social security schemes, developing mechanisms for microfinancing to enable enterprise start-up and development, channelling migrant remittances into microfinancing schemes and, crucially, helping to create the right regulatory environment to see those policies and programmes succeed, in particular those focusing on governance and corruption. These are the essential elements that would enable more developing countries to access the benefits of globalization.

There is also greater recognition by international and national policy-makers that without the role of the private sector we will never successfully combat poverty. The recent report from the UNDP Commission on the Private Sector and Development, *Unleashing entrepreneurship: Making business work for the poor* is another important validation of this trend. The ILO is, however, uniquely placed in the multilateral system to capitalize on this. It has employment creation at the heart of its mandate *and* it has an "institutional" partner in business. The ILO is institutionally connected to the largest network of business in the world. This network represents all the different voices from the business community at the national level. This network needs to be harnessed – it offers enormous potential.

The role of democratic values and good governance and the need to tackle corruption as key enabling tools in accessing the benefits of globalization, were given particular emphasis by a number of delegates. This is an area where Employers would like to see the ILO play more of a role, a fact evidenced by the resolution on governance and democratic values that the Employers tabled in the Resolutions Committee – a resolution that was widely supported.

The calls by many delegates for the Director-General to continue his work in reforming the body of international labour standards is something we also greatly welcome. International labour standards are at the centrepiece of what the ILO does – improving that machinery and making it more suited to the twenty-first century workplace is something Employers strongly support.

The World Commission report places emphasis on responsibility and the fact that globalization starts at home and this is important. Sometimes there is a tendency to look first to the international level for solutions without first examining what can be done at home. Without that as a first step, international responses may not be either sufficient or sustainable.

One recent initiative that aims to try and achieve this coherence and has done so with some success, is the Poverty Reduction Strategy Papers (PRSP) process – a genuine attempt at national policy coherence. This is an area where the ILO is playing a role, but it should deepen its involvement. In this the social partners have a key role and I see this in terms of what the Director-General called for, with the ILO acting as a "collective organization" where the official and the social partners work together. But the social partners will need capacity-building assistance to enable them to play a more effective part in the PRSP process.

Employers are broadly supportive of the calls for policy coherence initiatives. We feel that such initiatives offer an opportunity for the ILO. In such policy coherence initiatives the ILO should bring its very unique tripartite perspective to international policy debates and discussions – it has, we believe, real value to add. All institutions would need to engage in such a process in an even-handed manner, recognizing each other's mandates and responsibilities.

Above all, what needs to be avoided are attempts to try and devise "alternative" policies, policies to compete with, or rival, those of other institutions with specific expertise. Let me emphasize this point – the ILO certainly has very valuable niche in the multilateral system and we do not want to see this niche diluted. The Decent Work Agenda can be a useful tool when engaging in international policy dialogues, but that should be done through the ILO's current strategic objectives.

What nobody wants are more duplicative initiatives – which would, as I said, add confusion. Existing programmes need to be built to have partners found for them where this is possible. There must also be a sense of realism about which of these programmes should be explored. For instance, there are many existing forums that discuss macroeconomic policies and if, for example, a policy coherence initiative were about trying to generate a better set of monetary and fiscal policies, then I think it would be unlikely to succeed.

One of the key areas to which we think that the ILO should really devote its energies and should lead a policy coherence initiative is in the area of the informal economy and how to create the right regulatory environment for informal economy operators to migrate to the formal economy. The Office was given very clear guidance on this issue at the 2002 session of the International Labour Conference, during a discussion which produced excellent conclusions and, may I add, that were agreed and accompanied by a very large consensus on how to proceed. This is the kind of opportunity – and I use that word deliberately – that the ILO needs to seize.

There has been much support for a forum on globalization between international organizations. Certainly, this idea should be explored but again, we need to be mindful of duplication.

The ILO has a unique structure that works well for its needs and aims. However, every organization has its own particular way of structuring itself in line with its own aims. We need to respect such structures and processes. The comparative advantage of this tripartite house needs to be mobilized, built on, developed and fully utilized. We have heard much talk of "coherence" in the last two weeks. Let us try and get greater coherence out of that team.

Sir Roy TROTMAN *(Workers' delegate, Barbados, speaking on behalf of the Workers' group)*

I guess we can say that we have much to be grateful for. For over the last two weeks or so we are convinced that everyone seems to be satisfied that there is need for a fair globalization for all. We do get contradictions from time to time, but at least we start from a position where we all seem to be in agreement.

Some two weeks ago, we suggested that there needed to be some changes in the approach to debt, changes in poverty eradication strategies, in wealth creation approaches, in employment creation efforts, in wealth distribution, and in the development of common respect for our standards governing the world of work, among other things. From the approach of the body that was present, we got the distinct view that most people who were present then, two Mondays ago, were quite happy that these were issues that we wanted to have addressed.

Today, having heard the debate on the Director-General's Report, it is our view that we have to start an initiative: an initiative to incorporate decent work and the respect for labour standards into the policies of the global economy. It is essential to assess the impact which the ILO is having on the core policies of institutions like the IMF, the World Bank, UNCTAD and the WTO. This means, in the words of the World Commission's report, "Making decent work a key goal of the economic policy, by giving priority to employment creation, protecting fundamental rights at work, strengthening social protection, and promoting social dialogue." The report goes on to say that policies should be gender-sensitive and based on a new social contract which reflects the interests of both employers and workers.

We also have to enhance the relevance of the supervisory system of the ILO as a positive global mechanism to promote decent work and social justice. In this regard, measures to be taken to give effect to the recommendation of the World Commission to the effect that the capacity of the ILO to promote respect for core labour standards should be reinforced. All relevant international organizations should assume their responsibility to promote these standards and ensure that their policies and programmes do not impede their realization – I would refer you to paragraph 426 of the World Commission's report.

Further we must seek to follow up the World Commission's report by giving added emphasis and significance to the implementation of the Global Employment Agenda endorsed by the Governing Body way back in the year 2002. There are seven principles or pillars underlying the Global Employment Agenda, which are further elaborated as core elements of the Global Employment Framework. The Agenda promotes both the quantitative object of increasing freely chosen productive employment and the qualitative dimension of employment, and I am pleased to note that we have already had some work in this area in the China Employment Forum. Very shortly, there will be the Ouagadougou Employment Forum in Burkina Faso. There is, or there should be, some discussion with a view to a similar exercise in India, and of course there needs to be one for Central and Eastern Europe. It would seem to us that Latin America should not be forgotten because I do not think that the Chairpersons of the Workers' group and Employers' group would be very happy if that were to happen. It might be desirable for small-island states, possibly the Caribbean and the Pacific working together, to recognize that employment agendas might be able to give us that resurgence of competitiveness which is much to be desired.

Everyone has agreed that we have to promote coherence. In fact, at the last Governing Body meeting, I spoke on the contradiction inherent in the lack of coherence. I refer to this subject again today because some reference to it was made earlier today and might lead those who do not know to the view that the ILO should be boxed in and should not seek to enter into dialogue with other bodies: in short, that the ILO should seek to avoid trying to create change in social conditions across the world.

If we are going to accept the Global Report, we have to accept that the World Commission has to give the ILO the moral high ground and the social responsibility to effect global change. Indeed, we had words to that effect from such a body as the World Bank representatives themselves back in March, when they made a reference to the different voices that individual governments assume at the level of the IMF, at the level of the World Bank, at the level of Ministers of Finance, and then again at the ILO.

We have to guard against killing the baby before it has even been weaned. Recalling the World Commission's recommendation, we would wish to make the point here that there should be stronger action and wider social dialogue to promote decent work in export processing zones and, more generally, in global production systems, and that the ILO should provide advice and assistance to those engaged in such dialogue if and when it is required to do so. Indeed, we would suggest that the ILO should establish a unit to cover work in this area of export processing zones.

Globalization has certainly led to the widening gap between the rich and the poor. Large numbers of poor people in developing countries find themselves working for less than US$1 a day. In fact, it is true to say that the number of people who have moved down to that level has increased by over 30 per cent, especially in the Africa region.

The prospects of achieving the Millennium Development Goals therefore appear to be very slight, and the Workers' group will support measures that are designed to promote the forgiveness of debt and to increase resource flows to developing countries. It is significant for us in this regard that fewer than 50 per cent of the countries involved meet the ODA requirements of 0.7 per cent, and the ILO has got to take a moral stand to address these issues. In summary, the conditions I have referred must be met if we are to address the future of the world with the ILO's assistance. An urgent process is needed, and we have to be able to identify the major issues which must be dealt with: the issues of war, the issues of want, the issues of waste, environmental destruction and dumping, the issue of the weather for, although we cannot control the weather, we can do much to set up rapid response mechanisms – and the issue of migration. We should bear in mind that one is not necessarily exclusive of the other.

The Workers' group and the Employers' group must work and work sometimes together, as well as working with Governments, to ensure that a work programme is put in place which seeks to address these issues as a matter of urgency, and we must be able to give direction to, and support for, the programmes as they are brought together by the house to achieve these objectives. Preliminary work must start, and it must start now. I am obliged to you.

Original Spanish: The PRESIDENT

With these two statements, we now conclude the discussion on the Reports of the Chairperson of the Governing Body and of the Director-General.

(The Conference adjourned at 12.45 p.m.)

Seventeenth sitting

Tuesday 15 June 2004, 3 p.m.

President: Mr Ray Guevara

REPORT OF THE FINANCE COMMITTEE OF GOVERNMENT REPRESENTATIVES: SUBMISSION, DISCUSSION AND APPROVAL

Original Spanish: The PRESIDENT

We shall now proceed to the second item on the agenda, the report of the Finance Committee of Government Representatives, which is published in *Provisional Record* No. 17.

The Officers of the Finance Committee of Government Representatives were as follows: the Chairperson and Reporter was Mr. Jonzon and the Vice-Chairperson was Mr. Kleckner. It is my pleasure now to give the floor to Mr. Jonzon to submit the report of the Finance Committee of Government Representatives.

Mr. JONZON *(Government delegate, Sweden; Chairperson and Reporter of the Finance Committee of Government Representatives)*

I have the honour to submit to the Conference the report of the Finance Committee of Government Representatives. This report is published in *Provisional Record* No. 17 and contains the recommendations of the Committee on the matters it considered. The seven resolutions proposed by the Committee for adoption by the Conference appear at the end of the report, immediately before the appendices.

The main item of business for the Finance Committee was the Financial Report and Audited Financial Statements for 2002-03.

The Committee was pleased to see that the External Auditor had given an unqualified audit opinion and had put forward a number of valuable recommendations concerning the IRIS project, the ILO's Human Resources Strategy, property management and financial matters in his report, all of which were accepted by the Office. The Office is already acting on the recommendations and, in accordance with normal practice, it will be submitting a report to the March 2005 session of the Governing Body on the follow-up action taken. The Committee had no hesitation in proposing that the Financial Report and Audited Financial Statements for 2002-03 be adopted in accordance with article 29 of the Financial Regulations.

The next two items of the report concern requests for the right to vote received from the Governments of Iraq and Paraguay. Satisfied that the non-payment of their past contributions was due to circumstances beyond the control of these two States and that acceptable proposals had been put forward for the settlement of the arrears, the Committee recommends that Iraq and Paraguay be granted the right to vote.

A paper proposing a rate of assessment of the contribution to the ILO regular budget for a new member State, the Democratic Republic of Timor-Leste, was then considered. The proposal, covering contributions for both 2003 and 2004, was accepted.

The Committee looked particularly carefully at the proposal concerning the scale of assessment of contributions to the ILO regular budget for 2005, which had already been the subject of debate three months ago, at the 289th Session of the Governing Body. The Committee noted that, in accordance with normal practice, the 2005 scale of assessment is based on the United Nations scale of assessment. During the discussion, certain member States referred to the difficulties encountered by the sharp increase in the resulting level of contributions. A consensus nevertheless emerged, and the Committee recommends that the Conference adopt the scale of assessment of contributions for 2005.

The Committee considered a paper concerning the composition of the ILO Administrative Tribunal. The Committee unanimously accepted a recommendation from the Governing Body that the Conference express its appreciation to Mr. Jean-Francois Egli for his service to the Tribunal over the last decade and adopt a proposal from the Governing Body concerning two appointments to the ILO Administrative Tribunal. Nominations to the ILO Staff Pension Committee were also examined, and the Committee proposes that the Conference adopt the resolution as set out at the end of the report.

In concluding, I would like to express my thanks to my Vice-Chairperson, Mr. Kleckner of Hungary, to the members of the Committee and also to the members of the secretariat, all of whom helped me greatly in my task as Chairman.

My final word is the deep-felt thanks from the Committee directed to Mr. Juneja and the Employers' and Workers' Vice-Chairpersons the PFAC of the Governing Body join me in this expression of appreciation and thanks.

May I commend our report to you for adoption?

Original Spanish: The PRESIDENT

The general discussion on the report of the Finance Committee of Government Representatives is now open.

Original Arabic: Mr. ALKHULAIFI *(Government delegate, Qatar)*

On behalf of my Government, I would like to thank the Chair and members of the Finance Committee of Government Representatives for the positive results achieved. I should also like to commend Mr. Somavia, the Director-General, and all the Officers of the Conference for their efforts to serve the Members of this Organization and to implement all the programmes.

Qatar is a Member that pays its contributions regularly, but we have noted that our level on the scale of assessment has increased by almost 30 per cent, and while the Government of Qatar approves the scale of assessment, we do share the reservations expressed by some Members as to the method used to compute the new scale, whilst expressing our approval of the programmes adopted and implemented by this Organization.

Original Spanish: THE PRESIDENT

As there are no further speakers, I propose that we proceed with the approval of the report of the Committee, which is contained in paragraphs 1-62 and Appendices I-III. If there are no objections, may I take it that the report is approved?

(The report – paragraphs 1-62 and Appendices I, II and III – is approved.)

RESOLUTION CONCERNING THE FINANCIAL REPORT AND AUDITED FINANCIAL STATEMENTS FOR 2002-03: ADOPTION

Original Spanish: THE PRESIDENT

We shall now proceed with the adoption of the resolutions submitted by the Finance Committee of Government Representatives, starting with the resolution concerning the Financial Report and Audited Financial Statements for 2002-03. If there are no objections, may I take it that the resolution is adopted?

(The resolution is adopted.)

RESOLUTION CONCERNING THE ARREARS OF CONTRIBUTIONS OF IRAQ: ADOPTION

Original Spanish: THE PRESIDENT

We shall now proceed with the adoption of the resolution concerning arrears of contributions of Iraq.

I would like to inform you in this connection that both this resolution and the following one have to do with the arrears of contributions of two member States. In this connection, a record vote will be held in plenary tomorrow morning, in pursuance of article 13, paragraph 4, of the ILO Constitution.

If there are no objections, may I take it that the resolution is adopted?

(The resolution is adopted.)

RESOLUTION CONCERNING THE ARREARS OF CONTRIBUTIONS OF PARAGUAY: ADOPTION

Original Spanish: THE PRESIDENT

We shall now proceed with the adoption of the resolution concerning the arrears of contributions of Paraguay. If there are no objections, may I take it that the resolution is adopted?

(The resolution is adopted.)

RESOLUTION CONCERNING THE ASSESSMENT OF THE CONTRIBUTIONS OF NEW MEMBER STATES: ADOPTION

Original Spanish: THE PRESIDENT

We shall now proceed with the adoption of the resolution concerning the assessment of the contributions of new member States. If there are no objections, may I take it that the resolution is adopted?

(The resolution is adopted.)

RESOLUTION CONCERNING THE SCALE OF ASSESSMENTS OF CONTRIBUTIONS TO THE BUDGET FOR 2005: ADOPTION

Original Spanish: THE PRESIDENT

We shall now proceed with the adoption of the resolution concerning the scale of assessments of contributions to the budget for 2005. If there are no objections, may I take it that the resolution is adopted?

(The resolution is adopted.)

RESOLUTION CONCERNING THE COMPOSITION OF THE ADMINISTRATIVE TRIBUNAL OF THE INTERNATIONAL LABOUR ORGANIZATION: ADOPTION

Original Spanish: THE PRESIDENT

We shall now proceed with the adoption of the resolution concerning the composition of the Administrative Tribunal of the International Labour Organization. If there are no objections, may I take it that the resolution is adopted?

(The resolution is adopted.)

RESOLUTION CONCERNING APPOINTMENTS TO THE ILO STAFF PENSION COMMITTEE (UNITED NATIONS JOINT STAFF PENSION BOARD): ADOPTION

Original Spanish: THE PRESIDENT

We shall now proceed with the adoption of the resolution concerning appointments to the ILO Staff Pension Committee. (United Nations Joint Staff Board). If there are no objections, may I take it that the resolution is adopted?

(The resolution is adopted.)

We have now concluded the consideration of the report submitted by the Finance Committee of Government Representatives. I should like to take this opportunity to thank the Committee, Officers and members, as well as the secretariat and staff, for their good work.

SECOND REPORT OF THE SELECTION COMMITTEE: SUBMISSION, DISCUSSION AND APPROVAL

Original Spanish: THE PRESIDENT

We shall now proceed to the examination of the second report of the Selection Committee, which is published in *Provisional Record* No. 4-2. This refers to the withdrawal of 16 Recommendations, which are considered obsolete. The first report of the Selection Committee, which is published in *Provisional Record* No. 4-1, looked at the generalities pertaining to this. The Officers of the Committee were as follows: the Chairperson and Reporter was Mr. Hasegawa, the Employer Vice-Chairperson was Mr. M'Kaissi and the Worker Vice-Chairperson was Mr. Trotman. I would now like to call upon Mr. Hasegawa to submit the report of the Selection Committee.

Mr. HASEGAWA *(Government delegate, Japan; Chairperson and Reporter of the Selection Committee)*

It is my honour to submit to you the second report of the Selection Committee.

The Committee met on Tuesday 1 and Thursday 3 June 2004.

At its first meeting it decided, in view of the particularly heavy workload before the plenary of this session, to reconvene for a second sitting to determine item VII on the Conference agenda, the withdrawal of 16 Recommendations.

The Conference, and consequently the Committee, had before it two reports concerning the withdrawal of these instruments, Reports VII(1) and VII(2)

The second report of the Selection Committee, which contains a summary of the discussions of the Committee on this item, was published in *Provisional Record* No. 4-2.

The 16 Recommendations in question have been examined firstly by the Working Party on Policy regarding the Revision of Standards of the Committee on Legal Issues and International Labour Standards of the Governing Body, and then by the Governing Body itself, which decided by consensus at its 277th and 279th Sessions that the Recommendations no longer made a useful contribution to attaining the objectives of the ILO and were, consequently, obsolete.

The constituents were also consulted by questionnaire and, as Report VII(1) shows, there was overwhelming support amongst them for the withdrawals.

I am happy to report that the same spirit of consensus prevailed in the Selection Committee which decided, with a view to modernizing the body of international labour standards, to take the 16 instruments together and endorse the Governing Body's proposal to withdraw all 16 en bloc.

In the light of this report, the Conference may wish to take the required preliminary decision referred to in paragraph 3 of article 45bis of the Standing Orders of the Conference for the withdrawal of the 16 Recommendations.

The Officers of the Committee also wholeheartedly recommend that the Conference approve the results of the final vote, which is to be held tomorrow, Wednesday 16 June, in the morning.

In conclusion, I would like to thank both Vice-Presidents, Mr. M'Kaissi and Mr. Trotman, and the secretariat. With these words I submit the second report of the Selection Committee to the Conference for approval.

Original Spanish: Mr. PRESIDENT

The general discussion on the report of the Selection Committee is now open.

Mr. NOAKES *(Employers' delegate, Australia)*

The Employers' group strongly supports the recommendation contained in the second report of the Selection Committee that the Conference should take the preliminary decision concerning the withdrawal of the 16 Recommendations referred to in the report.

Sir Roy TROTMAN *(Workers' delegate, Barbados; Worker Vice-Chairperson of the Selection Committee)*

Out of an abundance of caution, the Workers wish to make it clear that this was a unanimous decision arrived at earlier by consultations with the Governing Body and we support the decision and urge all workers to support the vote.

Original Spanish: Mr. PRESIDENT

As there are no further speakers, I propose that we proceed to adopt the preliminary decision, referred to in article 45bis, paragraph 3, of the Standing Orders of the Conference, for the withdrawal of the 16 Recommendations that are listed in the document. If there are no objections, may I take it that the preliminary decision is adopted?

(The preliminary decision is adopted.)

The record vote to confirm the withdrawal of all 16 Recommendations together will be held in plenary tomorrow morning.

I propose that we now proceed with the approval of the second report of the Committee as a whole. If there are no objections, may I take it that the report is approved?

(The report is approved.)

I would like to express my thanks to the Chairperson and Vice-Chairpersons of the Committee, the members and, of course, the secretariat for the excellent work that they have achieved.

REPORT OF THE STANDING ORDERS COMMITTEE: SUBMISSION AND APPROVAL

Original Spanish: Mr. PRESIDENT

We shall now proceed to the examination of the report of the Standing Orders Committee, which is published in *Provisional Record* No. 16. The Officers of the Committee were as follows: the Chairperson and Reporter was Mr. Oni, the Employer Vice-Chairperson was Ms. Sasso Mazzufferi and the Worker Vice-Chairperson was Ms. Brighi. I would now like to call on Mr. Oni to submit the report of the Standing Orders Committee.

Original French: Mr. ONI *(Government delegate, Benin; Chairperson and Reporter of the Standing Orders Committee)*

It is an honour for me to present to the Conference the report of the Standing Orders Committee which you will find in *Provisional Record* No. 16.

It is proposed that the Conference adopt interim provisions, amending the provisions of the Standing Orders of the Conference regarding the Credentials Committee. These new provisions have been developed at the request of the Credentials Committee itself, so that it may operate more smoothly and efficiently. This matter was dealt with by the Governing Body and the Committee on Legal Issues and International Labour Standards (LILS) during the last three Governing Body sessions and also by the Standing Orders Committee during this session of the Conference.

The main reforms being proposed are the following:

First of all, the mandate of the Credentials Committee is to be broadened. It would, thus, be authorized to examine, not only objections to credentials, but also objections regarding Employers' or Workers' delegates not depositing credentials.

Secondly, the Credentials Committee will, in the future, be able to request that any questions raised in an objection that relate to a breach of freedom of association be referred to the Committee on Freedom of Association.

Finally, if the Conference so decides, the Credentials Committee will be able to ensure the follow-up of its decisions between one session of the Conference and another.

In order to use these last two new powers, a number of procedural guarantees must be fulfilled: the Credentials Committee must be unanimous, and the Conference must make a specific decision.

The interim provisions are also accompanied by a series of practical measures.

As I indicated, these are interim provisions, which would be implemented for a trial period of three years. More specifically, they would come into force at the next session in 2005 and, unless the Conference decides otherwise, they would remain in place until the 96th Session of the ILO Conference in 2007. The Governing Body would then evaluate the system and report back to the Conference in 2008. Nevertheless, the Conference can, of course, modify or cancel measures at any moment, which are not relevant or which turn out to be ineffective.

I am convinced that the proposed reforms will make it possible for the Credentials Committee to operate in a more efficient manner, due to its broadened mandate and strengthened capacity for follow-up and monitoring. May I remind you that the Committee's mandate is mainly to ensure that governments appoint Employers' and Workers' delegations which are as representative as possible of the employers and workers in their countries. The Credentials Committee therefore guarantees true tripartism within our Organization, the tripartism on which the ILO is based and which is its strength.

In conclusion, I would like to thank the two Vice-Chairpersons of the Committee, Ms. Sasso Mazzufferi, and Ms. Brighi, for the spirit of consensus which has characterized our discussions and made it possible for us to discuss calmly the very complex issues we were dealing with. Finally, I would also like to thank the members of the Office of the Legal Adviser for the excellent work they did in preparing this decision.

May I recommend that the Conference adopt this report and the interim provisions which are to be found in the Appendix.

Original Spanish: The PRESIDENT

I propose that we proceed with the approval of the report of the Committee, which is contained in paragraphs 1-30 and the Appendix on interim provisions concerning verification of credentials, effective from the 93rd session (June 2005) to the 96th session (June 2007) of the International Labour Conference.

We shall now proceed with the approval of the report of the Committee, paragraphs 1-30. If there are no objections, may I take it that the report, paragraphs 1-30, is approved?

(The report – paragraphs 1-30 – is approved.)

We shall now proceed with the approval of the Appendix to the report. If there are no objections, may I take it that the Appendix of the report is approved?

(The Appendix of the report is approved.)

If there are no objections, may I take it that the report, paragraphs 1-30 and the Appendix, as a whole, is approved?

(The report, as a whole, is approved.)

The amendments contained in the Appendix will be published separately. This will then be added to the publication containing the Constitution of the International Labour Organization and the Standing Orders of the International Labour Conference.

We have now concluded the consideration of the report submitted by the Standing Orders Committee. I should like to take this opportunity to thank the Committee Officers and members as well as the secretariat and staff for their excellent work.

REPORT OF THE RESOLUTIONS COMMITTEE: SUBMISSION, DISCUSSION AND ADOPTION

Original Spanish: The PRESIDENT

We shall now proceed t the examination of the report of the Resolutions Committee, which is published in *Provisional Record* No. 18. The Officers of the Committee were as follows: the Chairperson and Reporter was Ms. Santestevan, the Employer Vice-Chairperson was Mr. Botha and the Worker Vice-Chairperson was Mr. Blondel. I would now like to call upon Ms. Santestevan to submit the report of the Resolutions Committee.

Original Spanish: Ms. SANTESTEVAN *(Government delegate, Uruguay; Chairperson and Reporter of the Resolutions Committee)*

It is for me a proud moment, as well as a challenge and a great responsibility, to take part in this very prestigious meeting.

First and foremost, I should like, on behalf of my country, Uruguay, and in my own capacity, to express my very sincere thanks to all the delegates who have honoured me with this double appointment as Chairperson and Reporter of the Resolutions Committee of this session of the Conference. It is therefore my responsibility to present at this plenary meeting the results of the work carried out by this Committee. It is not easy to summarize in a few minutes the work of a number of days.

Nevertheless, if I had to sum up in a single sentence the most salient characteristic of the work of the Resolutions Committee, I would simply say that it was a real example of social dialogue. As regards the concrete results of our work, it is with pride that I inform you that, after some very intense work, we completed our session by adopting a draft resolution concerning the promotion of gender equality, pay equity and maternity protection.

It is important to underscore here that the Committee had before it 15 draft resolutions which were submitted in accordance with article 17 of the Standing Orders of the Conference, and which meant that subsequently a number of these had to be merged. Furthermore, we had to prioritize the order in which to examine a total of five resolutions using a secret ballot system in accordance with the Standing Orders.

I am pleased to say in this regard that all the delegates of the Committee made every effort to reach a consensus on a highly technical standard. In this context, I would like to express my special thanks to the Vice-Chairpersons of the Committee, Mr. Blondel and Mr. Botha, for the role they played as spokespersons for the Workers and the Employers, and who demonstrated their vast experience as leaders in the area of negotiation and have shown once again that it is possible to align positions without abandoning the principles which each sector defends.

It is also worth noting that it would have been impossible to carry out any of this work without the constant assistance of the high-level technical team which the ILO made available to the Committee and without the excellent work of the secretariat and the interpreters who made it possible for all the participants to understand each other.

The significance of adopting at this International Labour Conference a resolution concerning the promotion of gender equality, pay equity and maternity protection is unquestionable and I think warrants no further comment.

We know that the increased participation of women in the world of work was perhaps the most significant development of the twentieth century. However, we also know that, even today, in the twenty-first century, women face more difficulties than men when it comes to gaining access to a job, keeping that job and reaching decision-making levels.

Every day we are still packing two days' work into one, because most women shoulder the burden of family responsibilities. We suffer from high levels of unemployment, we are paid lower wages for work of equal value, we are discriminated against because of maternity, and in general we end up in jobs without social security.

Given this reality, we clearly still have a long way to go and the challenge is sizeable. In many cases it entails breaking down cultural barriers, adopting positive action, allocating resources, approving a series of equality plans, in short a change in behaviour encompassing a genuine collective move in favour of equality.

The resolution we are submitting to the Conference today seeks to be a powerful tool for promoting equal treatment and opportunities for women and men and, at the same time, a fundamental instrument for governments, workers and employers when they come to implement action plans to combat discrimination.

Inter alia, the text of the resolution makes it incumbent on all the constituents of the Organization to contribute actively to formulating and putting into practice national policies to foster equality, promoting the setting up of businesses by women, preventing discrimination in recruitment at all levels, eliminating gender-based differences in wages, ensuring a healthy, safe working environment for women and men, promoting measures to reconcile work and family life, developing social security systems which take gender issues into account, mainstreaming gender considerations into labour market regulations and collective agreements and, lastly, promoting opportunities for men and women to participate in work and society on an equal footing.

I therefore invite all delegates to the Conference to adopt the resolution and to commit themselves to returning to their countries with the firm intention of building a society which is more just and fair, because the Committee's work is over, but this just means that a new stage is beginning, that of the actual implementation of the principles contained in this resolution. So this is the challenge before us and we will be able to achieve the goal we have set ourselves only if each and every one of us makes an effort.

Mr. BOTHA *(Employers' delegate, South Africa; and Employer Vice-Chairperson of the Resolutions Committee)*

We concluded the work of our Committee on Saturday morning and present before you here a resolution that has the full support of the Committee.

Let me return at the end of my remarks to the manner in which this was achieved as I think it was noteworthy.

Employers submitted a draft resolution concerning democratic values, good governance and transparency in a global economy and their impact on the world of work, competitiveness and sustainable development which, while well supported, did not come first or second in the list of preferences. However, good governance remains a major issue for employers. We believe that it has now been identified as one of the key enabling tools in accessing the benefits of globalization.

First and foremost, the resolution we did succeed in drafting on "the promotion of gender equality, pay equity and maternity protection", sends an extremely important message of the importance all the constituents attach to this issue. Employers, in particular, feel strongly about the subject, because quite apart from the need for human decency and respect which we all feel, discrimination in any form also undermines enterprise performance.

Employers worked towards achieving a resolution that dealt with gender discrimination in a meaningful way as an issue of substance. Our attitude in this process was to try to work for a focused resolution on gender discrimination, and in particular equal opportunities for, and equal treatment of, men and women. We sought to achieve a text that was workable, that delivers a clear message and, above all, focuses on women in work. In this I think we were successful.

In addition, let me point out that we sought to devise a text that could be used in a variety of national contexts in a practical way. In this also I believe we were successful.

There are clear messages for governments, employers and workers here. One of the central aspects of this issue that we wanted to see given prominence in the text was the area of women's entrepreneurship. The potential of women entrepreneurs in terms of economic development, employment creation and poverty reduction needs to be tapped. This is, in our view, one aspect of the resolution that we feel can now give a real and tangible outcome from our discussions. We have many examples of the kinds of results that can be achieved by developing responses to encourage and support women's entrepreneurship. Let me also state that the ILO has done some really valuable work in this area, indeed working closely with many of our organizations. We would like to see this work given higher priority.

The Employers' group attaches paramount importance to the issue of education and the resolution clearly flags the importance of it, and in particular the fact that so many young girls are being deprived of this essential building block. To our mind, it is equality in education that needs to be the starting point.

Importantly, this resolution was reached through consensus, looking to accommodate everybody's perspectives. The work of the Committee was characterized by listening to and acknowledging all points of view and by seeking compromises. There were no votes. I think it is a very important message of a unified voice emerging from our work on this extremely important issue.

It is time for the ILO to make a powerful statement in favour of gender equality, not least because equal opportunities in the world of work is what will eventually have an impact in all other aspects of life. This resolution we believe does that.

I also believe that it is time for all delegations to this session of the International Labour Conference to make a real effort to achieve equal representation here.

The South African Employers' delegation, of which I am a member, will make this an annual objective.

Finally, let me thank my colleague, Mr. Blondel, and the Workers' group, for the cooperative manner in which we worked. Let me also underline again the point that our Committee achieved its work in a truly tripartite fashion. The Government groupings and many individual Government representatives worked tirelessly throughout the week to arrive at a text that everybody could happily support. We thank them too.

Let me also thank Mr. Jean-Michel Servais and his entire team, who worked enormously hard to facilitate a smooth-running Committee. We do appreciate the hidden work that continues long into the nights.

Let me finally thank our Chairperson, Ms. Ana Santestevan, who led this Committee so expertly to the final resolution and who managed the rush towards the end without a stumble. We thank her for her diligence, efficiency, and particularly for her good humour throughout our work.

Original French: Mr. BLONDEL *(Workers' delegate, France; Worker Vice-Chairperson of the Resolutions Committee)*

Under the chairmanship of Ms. Ana Santestevan, the Government delegate of Uruguay, the Resolutions Committee met regularly and did so relatively effectively.

Once work had been done to combine the 15 draft resolutions that had been approved, eight remained. Through the relevant consultations, they were accorded the following order of priority: the resolution concerning the promotion of gender equality, pay equity and maternity protection; the resolution concerning the ILO's efforts to combat poverty; the resolution concerning the strengthening of the role of the ILO in supporting workers and employers in Palestine and the other occupied Arab territories as a result of continued Israeli occupation and aggressive practices; the resolution concerning democratic values, good governance and transparency in a global economy and their impact on the world of work, competitiveness and sustainable development; and the resolution concerning older workers and employment and social protection. This meant that the responsibility of the Workers was engaged, because the basic structure of the first two draft resolutions emanated from the Workers' group.

Due to lack of time, the Committee only examined the first resolution; the resolution on combating poverty, which came second on the list, was discussed, and I am sure that, given the importance of the issue and the impoverishment, we will return to this matter in future sessions. The enduring nature of this situation, unfortunately, leaves us in no doubt, and – poverty being at the heart of many conflicts – it remains highly relevant. It was with considerable interest and determination that the Committee tackled the first resolution, the title of which, as accepted at the end of the debate, was the Resolution concerning the promotion of gender equality, pay equity and maternity protection.

To tell the truth, our work led us from pay equity to equality generally. It appeared to the participants that although women achieving financial autonomy or even independence was a necessity, it would not be enough to eliminate discrimination between individuals. We also considered the question of property, and the problem of career development to break through the glass ceiling.

Along with the problems inherent with family and maternity, we are aware that in tackling the problem of equality and combating discrimination, we are going against the customs, and the social, the political, cultural and religious practices which stem from a presumption of the superiority of the male sex. It is in this sense that our work is innovative. My colleagues who will also speak about this resolution will talk about the particular points of the resolution submitted for our consideration in terms of where they came from, where they belong, and why they are of interest. I would like to emphasize the responsibilities that are incumbent on the ILO, which are in the preamble to the resolution.

It seems worth recalling the need to promote and give impetus to the ratification of the relevant Conventions in this area, particularly the Equal Remuneration Convention, 1951 (No. 100), the Discrimination (Employment and Occupation) Convention, 1958 (No. 111), as well as the Workers with Family Responsibilities Convention, 1981 (No. 156), and the Maternity Protection Convention, 2000 (No. 183), which has so far been ratified by eight countries but which should be the subject of growing interest.

Our resolution, which fits into the more general context of the Universal Declaration of Human Rights and the Convention on the elimination of discrimination against women and relevant instruments hopes to make the equality of men and women an intersectoral issue, encompassing all the strategic objectives and thus finding a place in the conclusions and recommendations of the report of the World Commission on the Social Dimension of Globalization.

Coherence is needed at the national and international levels.

This will be possible if the statutory measures taken at the initiative of States, and the complementary measures that the social partners are able to negotiate, serve to strengthen the fight against discrimination.

In my country, the press has just commented on a study that shows that women, after leaving school, sometimes spend several years with practically no professional experience, indicating that even in a country where it is felt that there is respect for equality, there are subtle forms of discrimination. There is also a difference of more than 25 per cent in remuneration for the same level of responsibility and competence.

No country can claim to have solved this problem, as illustrated by the statistics and data analysis in our document. I would like to stress the role of the ILO and the energy that it alone can provide to achieve these objectives. Our text should not be static; it should stimulate new desires or at least revive them. We have also pointed out that the financial resources required for this purpose would have to be found. As spokesperson of the Workers' group in the Programme, Financial and Administrative Committee of the Governing Body, I shall not forget this commitment.

I would like all the delegates at the 92nd Session of the International Labour Conference to vote in favour of the text that we are submitting to you. This text is the result of a consensus on a very delicate and complex subject. It, of course, goes counter to societal and conservative practices but it can and must enrich the notion of justice and equality amongst all human beings.

Although the majority of the delegates here today are male, I urge you to vote for this resolution and commit yourselves to its implementation, for, as the French poet Aragon said, "woman is the future of man". Let us work together, that she may be the future of society.

It falls to me, in conclusion, to express my warmest congratulations and my thanks to the Chairperson, Ms. Santestevan, who has presided over this Committee with such efficiency and clarity.

Of course, I would also like to congratulate the representatives of the Employers' group – with whom I am starting to feel a definite affinity – as well as all those who took part in the discussions. I would also like to thank Mr. Servais for his administrative services, which have enabled us to work as speedily and as effectively as possible.

Thank you for listening.

Original Spanish: The PRESIDENT

The general discussion on the report of the Resolutions Committee is now open

Original French: Ms. RAHMANI *(Workers' delegate, Algeria)*

It is a great honour to have the opportunity of speaking here. I would like to express my satisfaction with regard to the symbiosis that marked the tripartite debate preceding the adoption of the resolution concerning the promotion of gender equality, pay equity and maternity protection.

This confirms the convergence of views between the Workers', Employers' and Government groups when it comes to taking a stand on equality and maternity protection. Once again, persuasion has won through, and I would like to thank them for following our train of thought.

Equality between men and women is one of the cornerstones of democracy and underpins the promotion of decent work and social development, in keeping with the 1948 Universal Declaration of Human Rights. Fighting inequality must be at the heart of the trade unions' struggle and the guiding principle of our commitment.

I welcome the consensus we have reached, which will enable us to build together coherent strategies to fight discrimination against women, in particular the obstacles facing women in access to positions of responsibility, in the recruitment process and in equality of remuneration. This is the price we have to pay before we can speak of equality of opportunity between men and women.

The ILO and the social partners have an important role to play in achieving the objectives set forth in this resolution. This is a shared victory; let us all act to ensure that these guidelines are translated into more equality on the ground. What we want is a decent status and genuine promotion of all women in an environment guaranteeing decent work, because defending the right to equality and dignity for working women is the least we can do to ensure respect in terms of human rights.

I therefore urge all of you to vote without reservations for this emancipating document.

Mr. SEN *(Workers' adviser, India)*

To comment on the resolution concerning the promotion of gender equality, pay equity and maternity protection, I would like to note that this resolution attains special relevance in the light of the findings of the report of the World Commission on the Social Dimension of Globalization and the Director-General's Global Report, *Organizing social justice*.

The World Commission's report diagnoses the current model of globalization as unethical and unfair, so far as its impacts on people and society are concerned. The aggravation of the gender gap and discrimination have been one of the major negative reflections of this impact, leading to the aggravation of poverty, pauperization of people, unemployment, job loses. etc. It must also be noted that, in the global context, the gender-based discrimination which had been gradually declining in the pre-globalization period, particularly since the advent of social welfarism after Second World War, has now been put back on an ascending track by the process of neo-liberal globalization, signalling the degeneration and distortion of social values and civilized cultures.

The neo-liberal economic process throughout the world has led to deepening poverty for the masses, widening the economic disparity between and within countries to an unethical level, thereby also widening gender-based disparity in respect of employment opportunities, earnings, job security, and quality of life for the womenfolk in society. We may note that the existing socio-economic structure breeds discrimination against women in respect of their civil, social, economic and political rights, despite all formal arrangements otherwise. In many societies, women are discriminated against in respect of their rights to property and inheritance.

In developing countries, the situation is even more precarious. Downsizing and privatization of public services are affecting women's employment in a big way. In many industries, especially the mining sector, women workers are being targeted through a separate special voluntary separation scheme in a clandestine manner, leading to a sharp reduction of women workers in these sectors.

In many areas, particularly in the informal sector and sectors such as beedi making, brick kilns, garments, small plantations, faming, construction, etc., women workers are being paid lower wages than their male counterparts for the same and equal value of work.

Women workers are also being subjected to inhuman treatment in respect of maternity protection. Maternity benefits are only available in the organized and formal sectors, and in the informal sector with totally insecure and casual working conditions, women workers are losing livelihood in thousands by becoming pregnant. In the export processing zones, married women are compelled by circumstances to conceal their marital status for fear of losing job opportunities. In fact, a social distortion is brought about through the virtual denial of maternity rights to women workers in the vast informal sector, in both the unskilled and high-tech categories. In our society, women who are not able to bear children are not looked upon kindly and workplace conditions in many places are acting as a deterrent for women to become mothers. Along with being discriminated against in terms of employment opportunities, wages and other rights, they are also being denied the right of motherhood.

Under the neo-liberal globalization, with the policy of least governance being followed in practice in matters of economic activities and related areas.

In this context a resolution has been proposed to take concrete steps for the effective detection and elimination of gender discrimination. We feel that the eradication of gender discrimination cannot come automatically. The resolution is an action-oriented document which outlines the tasks for concrete action by all the social partners. I hope everyone will endorse it.

Original Spanish: Ms. ANDERSON *(Workers' delegate, Mexico)*

I would like to say that Latin Americans feel very proud of the President's election.

We women are not unfair competitors competing against men in a world of general rivalry. We are allies and partners in the struggle for fairer societies, for equality in the work place, in education and training, in health and in the legislation in each and everyone of our countries.

Today, the ILO is taking one more step forward in its programme and action in favour of equality for women throughout the world in consolidating at this tripartite forum the resolution concerning the promotion of gender equality, pay equality and maternity protection. This instrument will strengthen gender equality, which is a key element in the programmes and conventions of this Organization which are aimed at generating decent work for both men and women. Therefore, it is necessary for governments, working with employers' and trade union organizations to compile, publish and disseminate, in the most uniform way possible itemized data and gender-based statistics on labour market indicators. They should also promote the spread of good practices in this area. It is necessary to recommend and speed up efforts to achieve genuine equality between men and women, and to offer opportunities at all levels for equality in the world of work, in education, in trade union activities and in professional and business circles.

It is necessary to use genuine social security systems which take account of gender issues, not only in the areas of health and general medicine, but, even more importantly, by paying attention to the maternity needs of working women, to child care, support to working mothers and the right to a fair pension for older women. To promote the mental and physical health of all working women, it is necessary for countries to develop social security systems that take gender issues into account.

Genuine freedom of association cannot exist if there is inequality or discrimination based on race, religion, political opinions or gender, which is, of course, discrimination between men and women.

Therefore, the fundamental rights of the ILO should be implemented in particular the Equal Remuneration Convention, 1951 (No. 100), and the Discrimination (Employment and Occupation) Convention, 1958 (No. 111), which protect working women.

Freedom of association cannot be complete without the participation of women in the workers' struggle.

Since it was founded in 1919, the ILO has viewed men and women to be equal in the world of work. Moreover, there are historic photographs in this Organization which show that the founding group contained a number of women from that time; this is a further reason why women should participate more in all the events of the ILO, in particular the annual sessions of the International Labour Conference.

In the year 2003, during the session on gender equality, it was said that at least 30 per cent of delegates should be women. So, I respectfully ask all those in the tripartite system to take into account this very important question of the participation of women at next year's session of the Conference. Likewise, we consider that the ILO should have the opportunity to review its Constitution and alter the language used so as to take account of gender equality.

Not only men but women, joined together in fraternity, will achieve equality in work and fair pay at the same rate as is paid to men.

Mr. RAMPAK *(Workers' delegate, Malaysia)*

The Workers' group is indeed very happy that this resolution, which constitutes a basis for sustainable development, has received the support of the Resolutions Committee.

The Workers' group has for many years been calling for the full implementation of the ILO's Decent Work Agenda, as this constitutes one of the very foundations of sustainable development as contained in the resolution presented to us this afternoon.

The Workers' group also urges the tripartite dialogue partners to accord due importance to rights-based development, as proposed in this resolution, which refers to the challenges posed by globalization with regard to equality in the world of work.

Maternity protection is provided for in the ILO's Maternity Protection Convention, 2000 (No. 183), as a key component for the empowerment of women workers globally, and particularly in the developing countries where local legislation is inadequate or ineffectively implemented. Women workers in export processing zones, referred to by an earlier speaker, migrant women workers, and those employed in the informal sector in such countries are the most vulnerable and totally lack maternity protection. The Workers' group is urging governments to include in their national strategies measures for protecting workers' lives, the overall quality of life and family life.

To achieve this objective, effective empowerment of women workers, through proactive efforts such as equal remuneration, equal opportunities and maternity protection, is urgently needed. ILO Conventions Nos. 100 and 111 have already laid the foundation for gender and pay equality which should enable working men and women to enjoy the fruits of their labour without discrimination.

In many countries, women workers have been denied their fundamental rights, let alone the right to equality. There are women workers earning only half the wages of male workers for the same type of work, often for longer hours; these women are often exploited physically, mentally and sexually.

Women workers have also been more affected by enterprise downsizing and job-cutting exercises, particularly in the developing countries, where social protection systems are inadequate or totally absent. We call upon governments and employers to recognize women workers as having equal status as partners in progress, and to accord them the recognition and respect that is rightfully theirs for the work they do.

We are pleased that the resolution invites the Governing Body and the ILO, particularly the International Training Centre in Turin, to establish a training programme on gender-neutral job evaluations, intended for governments, and employers' and workers' organizations. This augurs well for the ILO's efforts to establish and reinforce gender-neutral methods of job evaluation and assessment. We believe that the establishment of well-focused training programmes such as this will go far towards promoting gender equality. I can assure the Director of the Centre, Mr. Trémeaud, that we will do everything to ensure that this resolution is implemented at the Turin Centre.

In this context, we also have to consider the funding of the Turin Centre. Less than 10 per cent of its funding comes out of the Regular Budget for Technical Cooperation. Most of its funding is provided by donor countries, in particular, the Italian Government which has given most – not only the premises but much else besides in terms of funding.

That is why we want this programme to be implemented. I urge the Government delegates in this house to support the ILO, and urge the Director-General to allocate more funds so that this resolution can be implemented as the Committee would wish.

Mr. HOWARD *(Workers' delegate, South Africa)*

The resolution that we are presenting to the Conference is a decisive political, economic and industrial intervention. The report of the World Commission on the Social Dimension of globalization recognizes the negative effects of globalization on women.

Therefore, apart from the ever-escalating poverty which has been recognized in the reports – particularly in developing countries – and apart from income inequality between developed and developing countries, and within countries, women bear the brunt of poverty and a lack of access to public services and, therefore, this resolution must be seen as a direct intervention against the exploitation and discrimination of women and the forms of poverty they experience.

In my own country, South Africa, our Government has put in place clear legislation, through the Employment Equity Act, to redress rights and gender imbalances in the workplace; this kind of initiative must be taken up by as many governments and employers as possible to give concrete expression to this resolution. As has been mentioned, this is an action-orientated resolution; it is a campaign-driven resolution, and must be treated as such. Similarly, gender mainstreaming must find expression in all the work of the ILO; the struggle for decent work for good wages, minimum wages and living wages, is an integral part of advancing equality, both in the world of work and in civil life.

I fully commend the adoption of this resolution to the Conference as part of the global struggle for a new world order, based on decent work, the eradication of child labour and forced labour, economic growth – which creates employment for the millions of unemployed – the fundamental right to social dialogue and collective bargaining, so that unions truly have the opportunity, in their own societies, in their own national contexts, to promote and campaign for pro-worker, pro-people, a pro-development, a pro-human rights and pro-trade union agenda at all levels, including multilateral institutions such as the World Bank, the IMF and the WTO, for without this the struggle for gender equality, if not located at all of these levels, will not succeed.

This resolution, therefore, is an important tool – as the Chairperson of the Resolutions Committee pointed out in her address – and must be used to achieve those ends.

Original Spanish: Mr. THULLEN *(Government adviser, Ecuador)*

My delegation would not like to miss this opportunity to express its satisfaction with the results achieved by the Resolutions Committee, under the effective and exemplary leadership of its Chairperson, Ana Santestevan. The resolution concerning the promotion of gender equality, pay equity and maternity protection, which the Committee has adopted, is the outcome of a process of intense tripartite consultations which, I dare say, are a milestone in the history of the International Labour Conference. My delegation supports the adoption of this resolution by the Conference.

Original Spanish: The PRESIDENT

As there are no further speakers, I propose that we proceed with the approval of the report of the Committee, which is contained in paragraphs 1-213. If there are no objections, may I take it that the report is approved?

(The report – paragraphs 1-213 – is approved.)

RESOLUTION CONCERNING THE PROMOTION OF GENDER EQUALITY, PAY EQUITY AND MATERNITY PROTECTION: ADOPTION

Original Spanish: The PRESIDENT

We shall now proceed with the adoption of the resolution concerning the promotion of gender equality, pay equity and maternity protection. If there are no objections, may I take it that the resolution is adopted?

(The resolution is adopted.)

We have now concluded the consideration of the report submitted by the Resolutions Committee. I should like to take this opportunity to thank the Committee, Officers and members, as well as the Secretariat and the staff, for their excellent work.

We have also now concluded our agenda for this afternoon. Once again, I would like to thank all those concerned for the work they have done and their valuable input and contributions to the different discussions and the decisions that we have taken during this sitting.

(The Conference adjourned at 4.40 p.m.)

CONTENTS

Page

Sixteenth sitting

Reports of the Chairperson of the Governing Body and of the Director-General:
Discussion *(concl.)* 1

Speakers: Mr. Arthur Errázuriz, Mr. Ahmed, Mr. Gutiérrez Madueño, Mr. González Gaitán, Mr. Aung, Mr. Cortebeeck, Ms. Muganza, Mr. Barak, Mr. Benydin, Ms. Dejanovic, Mr. Devendra, Mr. Lambert, Mr. Lewis, Mr. Mattar, Mr. Ruggiero, Mr. De Pury, Mr. Wallimann, Mr. Parra Gaona, Mr. Goodleigh, Mr. Fostik, Mr. Finlay, Ms. Wintour, Mr. Funes de Rioja, Sir Roy Trotman.

Seventeenth sitting

Report of the Finance Committee of Government Representatives:
Submission, discussion and approval 20

Speakers: Mr. Jonzon (Chairperson and Reporter of the Committee), Mr. Alkhulaifi

Resolution concerning the Financial Report and Audited Financial Statements for 2002-03:
Adoption 21

Resolution concerning the arrears of contributions of Iraq: Adoption 21

Resolution concerning the arrears of contributions of Paraguay: Adoption 21

Resolution concerning the assessment of the contributions of new member States: Adoption 21

Resolution concerning the scale of assessments of contributions to the budget for 2005:
Adoption 21

Resolution concerning the composition of the Administrative Tribunal of the International
Labour Organization: Adoption 21

Resolution concerning appointments to the ILO Staff Pension Committee
(United Nations Joint Staff Pension Board): Adoption 21

Second report of the Selection Committee: Submission, discussion and approval 21

Speakers: Mr. Hasegawa (Chairperson and Reporter of the Committee), Mr. Noakes, Sir Roy Trotman

Report of the Standing Orders Committee: Submission and approval 22

Speaker: Mr. ONI (Chairperson and Reporter of the Committee)

Report of the Resolutions Committee: Submission, discussion and approval 23

Speakers: Ms. Santestevan (Chairperson and Reporter of the Committee), Mr. Botha, Mr. Blondel, Ms. Rahmani, Mr. Sen, Ms. Anderson, Mr. Rampak, Mr. Howard, Mr. Thullen

Resolution concerning the promotion of gender equality, pay and maternity protection:
Adoption 28

No. 23 – Wednesday, 16 June 2004

International Labour Conference

Provisional Record   **25**

Ninety-second Session, Geneva, 2004

Reply by the Director-General to the discussion of his Report

1. Introduction

The President of this year's session of the International Labour Conference, Minister Ray Guevara of the Dominican Republic, well deserves the many expressions of gratitude he has received over the course of the last two weeks. Let me add my own heartfelt congratulations on behalf of the Office for a job well done, with substance, humour and savvy. My acknowledgment also goes to his hard-working Vice-Presidents, Mr. Maatough of the Libyan Arab Jamahiriya for the Government group, Mr. Wade of Senegal for the Employers' group and Mr. Attigbe of Benin for the Workers' group. The job we have asked them to do is demanding and calls for a dedication to the values of our Organization that is exemplary.

I was talking last week to a young, newly appointed Minister attending her first Conference. She symbolized for me a new generation of leaders who will take the ILO into its second century. So I asked what her first impressions were. She replied, "there is a lot going on and you have a lot of history!" I think that sums up this Conference and our Organization rather well. We have taken a few moments to recall and honour the contribution of our predecessors. But I think they would have been satisfied to see that we spent most of our time positioning the ILO for the future, discussing priorities, strategizing about where we fit into the emerging global governance structures, refreshing our international standards and tackling the central issue of our generation, how to shape a fair globalization.

We were honoured by the presence of five Heads of State and Government. They came because our Organization sponsored the establishment and work of the World Commission on the Social Dimension of Globalization. Presidents Halonen and Mkapa, together with the eminent personalities who constituted the Commission, contributed considerable time, energy and creativity to their report and have given us a remarkable resource. And I have to thank them once again for their unflinching dedication to the task. As both Sir Roy Trotman and Don Daniel Funes de Rioja said at the beginning of our debate, the report creates a tremendous opportunity for our Organization. The subsequent discussions show that we are ready, willing and able to grasp the chance to renew and reinvigorate our global network of tripartism to meet the challenges before us.

In addition to examining the reports on globalization, we also reviewed in the plenary the report on implementation of the 2002-03 programme, the Report on the situation of workers of the occupied Arab territories and *Organizing for social justice*, this year's Global Report under the follow-up to the ILO Declaration on Fundamental Principles and Rights at Work. Together with a full agenda of work in the technical committees, this all amounted to an exceptionally heavy load. I am pleased to say that we completed the business, and I thank you all for your dedication and commitment to our work.

I was particularly pleased that many speakers commented favourably on the implementation report. This is a full record of our performance against the goals set by the Governing Body three years ago. Minister Mdladlana of South Africa commended "the ILO for its report on the road travelled in the period 2002-03 in assisting countries to work their way out of global poverty". Along with many other speakers, particularly those from developing countries, he concurred with the report's description of decent work as "a strategic tool for fighting global poverty and … bringing dignity and prosperity to the poor".

2. A fair globalization

President Tarja Halonen of Finland offered us an insight into the way the Commission approached its work. The Commission was made up of "26 people who came from different backgrounds, have different political views, are from different parts of the world and have their own strong opinions". The "unanimous joint report" was "proof of the power of discussion and dialogue". While stressing the importance of the ILO's mandate to follow up the report, she equally emphasized that "the recommendations in the World Commission's report cover a much wider field than the ILO's direct scope". She explained that she and President Mkapa therefore have as a goal the approval of a resolution by the 59th session of the United Nations General Assembly requesting ECOSOC and other relevant bodies to consider the Commission's report and then report back in 2005. The report was also being taken up by many regional organizations including the European Union and the African Union, as well as being discussed in various national contexts.

President Mkapa of the United Republic of Tanzania explained that in moving the discussion on globalization beyond a stand-off and confrontation to dialogue and cooperation, all the Commission is saying is that "a new thinking is needed to ensure that the good that comes out of globalization reaches more people. Otherwise it will always be politically unbalanced, materially unsustainable, morally indefensible and, from a security standpoint, graphically catastrophic". Highlighting that the theme of globalization begins at home, President Mkapa argued that governments "must emphasize economic development with social protection, decent work and good democratic governance at all levels, including the global level". Welcoming the ILO's collaboration with the African Union for an Extraordinary Summit in Ouagadougou in September 2004, he said that in order for developing countries to link the development and poverty reduction agenda to the building of an inclusive global economy, "the tripartite constituents must work together in a broader alliance to unleash our full potential, which must also include the immense potential of women". Concluding with an appeal to the Conference to accept and support the Commission's efforts to chart the way to a fair globalization, he said, "yes, a better world is possible and is within our collective reach if the leaders of our world summon the courage and the will needed to lead us in that direction".

President Georgi Parvanov of Bulgaria fully supported "the idea that globalization should have a very strong social dimension; it should be based on universal values and should be beneficial for every country, without exception". Calling on governments and business to invest in social policy as a condition for stability, he said, "we have no right to close our eyes to the fact that extremism, notably terrorism, finds fertile ground in the unresolved social problems of the various regions". Countries like Bulgaria needed to find a new balance between the role of the Government and the market. Echoing the report, he stressed an active role for the State "when it comes to creating a stable microeconomic environment or a modern infrastructure, and to reducing unemployment, providing opportunities for decent work, and working to curb poverty".

Prime Minister Helen Clark of New Zealand connected the Commission report's analysis and recommendations to her own country's experience. Economic liberalization had been followed by cuts in social provisions and labour market deregulation. "The changes in New Zealand came without adequate adjustment mechanisms and created a good deal of social distress." Mentioning the World Commission's discussion of the space for national macroeconomic policies, she stressed "that there are policy instruments which can be used. Our Government has been busy creating those instruments to increase the national space for action". Referring to "the lack of coherence and the compartmentalization between the multilateral organizations, with those in trade, finance, health, social affairs, labour and development often working at cross-purposes", she described New Zealand's "whole of government approach" to policy and the desirability of a similar effort at the international level. For Prime Minister Clark, "the central challenge posed by the World Commission is to contemplate reform of global governance in order to ensure that globalization operates according to fair rules and offers opportunities and decent work for all".

The President of the Government of Spain, Mr. José Luis Rodríguez Zapatero, linked the challenges faced by the ILO in its 85-year history to the need for the Organization to play a leading role in building a fair globalization. "It is social rights which provide the necessary balance to economic development, market liberalization, economic cooperation and the constant opening-up of the economies of the world." He expressed his personal commitment to the belief that "decent work must become a major global objective and not just a goal of the International Labour Organization". This however posed the challenge, in Europe and other countries, of meeting the "need to adapt labour legislation, institutions, social dialogue practices and collective bargaining to the demands of an economic competitiveness in which innovation and knowledge reign supreme". He expressed his confidence that dialogue, "the working tool" of the ILO, would be "the great aspiration of a new world order". "Dialogue emanates from reason and reason is always based on ethical principles and values of fellowship. Where reason and dialogue reign, where a forum for dialogue is built, rights will always be improved, and the lot of the most humble will be improved …".

A total of 294 delegates spoke in the plenary debate that followed the presentation of the World Commission report and my own Report on its implications for the role of the ILO. Allow me to thank those many delegates who praised the quality of the Commission's work and my reports. Nearly all addressed the theme of a fair globalization, supporting both the Commission report and my own proposals on how the ILO should respond to the proposals it advances. Some of the most frequently used words to describe the Commission report were "balanced", "thoughtful", "valuable", "rich", providing "an in-depth analysis", and "innovative". A feature of the report particularly appreciated by delegates was that it was both critical of the marginalization of large numbers of people and whole countries from the process, and positive in its view that better governance from the local to the global would lead to coherent policies for a more inclusive globalization.

Many delegates commented favourably on the approach to the Commission's work described by the Co-Chairs. Taking a view of globalization "through the eyes of people" was welcomed, as was the way in which, through a process of dialogue, the diverse views of Commissioners converged on a vision of a fair globalization firmly rooted in values and having decent work for all as a global goal.

My own Report, *A fair globalization: The role of the ILO*, was broadly endorsed as a guideline for a strategic response by the ILO to the Commission report. There were, of course, some qualifications and a number of warnings that we must not take on topics, no matter how relevant and timely, if we do not have the human and financial resources to complete the task effectively. A few speakers were concerned that we might stray into the remits of other organizations. Most, however, agreed that the ILO should have an approach of active partnership, recognizing that where mandates intersect, organizations should collaborate to ensure policy coherence. Many speakers recalled the Constitution of the ILO and its Declaration of Philadelphia that envisaged an Organization whose scope of action was defined by fundamental human values and the pursuit of social justice. I was therefore left with the strong sense of an Organization that has a broad and deep consensus about where it wants to go. Furthermore, I believe we are generating the essential tripartite political energy to play a strong and more prominent role in global debates and in supporting constituents in their national work.

There were many comments on specific chapters of my report, which I address in the following section of my reply. Before doing so, let me assure speakers that we have taken careful note of all the speeches and that senior staff have already been circulated with summaries drawing their attention to contributions of direct relevance to their work. Your interventions are all equally valued and constitute a reference for our assessment of past performance and for our future planning. They are particularly useful as we incorporate your reflections on both the Commission report and the implementation report into the preparation of the Strategic Policy Framework for 2006-09, the Programme and Budget for 2006-07 and a policy development agenda for our Working Party on the Social Dimension of Globalization.

Making decent work a global goal

Many speakers agreed with Mr. Sweeney, Workers' delegate of the United States and a member of the Commission, when he said, "the single most significant conclusion of the report was simply this: that decent work is the cornerstone of creating a fairer globalization". Many argued that although decent work is already an ILO objective, it should also become a global goal integrated into the effort to realize the United Nations Millennium Development Goals. State Secretary Kjørven of Norway reminded us that "if you ask the poor themselves, access to work, or starting a business on their own are the most important avenues out of poverty. Thus, the relevance of the ILO in today's world is clear as day". Opportunities to find decent work were seen by many speakers as central to the search for peace and stability. National policies for decent work were essential but, as Minister Khaleghi of the Islamic Republic of Iran said, "globalization cannot lead to sustainable development, international security and peace unless it promotes more equitable access to commercial and economic opportunities".

The idea of global and national partnerships for decent work was highlighted by Mr. Ola, Minister of Labour of India, who said "in order to achieve the global goal of decent work, we have to ensure the systematic global governance based on democracy, social equity and effective participation of all social partners". In a similar vein, Mr. Andres, Parliamentary Secretary of State, Federal Ministry of Economics and Labour, of Germany, said "we need a global alliance for employment which will combat poverty, will promote sustainability and will ensure that markets are kept open and fair".

The ILO has a mandate to promote decent work as a global goal, and we need the support and collaboration of international agencies in this. Similarly, achieving the United Nations Millennium Development Goals is only feasible if we can mobilize a major drive to create decent work opportunities. It was very clear that the Conference expects us to increase our efforts to ensure that the objective of decent work for all becomes widely used as a means of ensuring a much better alignment of economic and social policies for a fair globalization. As Mr. Wang, Government delegate of China, said, "it is time for us to act immediately in a concerted effort to ensure a decent job for everyone and decent globalization".

National policies

I think all delegates would agree with Mr. Lee, Employers' delegate of the Republic of Korea, who said, "the report aptly emphasized the importance of good governance at the national level". Mr. Pater, Minister of Social Policy of Poland, endorsed the view of the Commission that "good governance, built on democracy, social equity, the rule of law and human rights, ensures the high quality of national and local policies and institutions which must be in place if we want globalization to benefit all of our societies". "The World Commission correctly concluded that efforts to achieve lasting benefits for the world's workers must begin at home, in each sovereign nation", was the view of Ms. Chao, Secretary of Labor of the United States.

Many speakers commented on the employment, social protection, labour rights and dialogue policies needed to maximize the benefits and minimize the costs of participation in the global economy, often expressing appreciation for the ILO's support. Mr. Soriano, Employers' delegate of the Philippines, described how, in a country where 40 per cent of the population lives on $1 a day, "the Decent Work Agenda serves as a unifying concept to underpin our country's democratically based, market-oriented development strategy by aiming to balance growth with equity".

Speakers from a number of countries also identified a regional dimension to decent work strategies. Ms. Gawanas, representing the African Union, talked about collaboration with the ILO to implement a new vision for Africa. Our "development challenges cannot be met unless African countries work in effective partnerships, first and foremost with one another, with the international community, with social partners and civil society organizations, to create productive jobs and effective social protection strategies, to address the negative impact of globalization, poverty and HIV/AIDS on African individuals, families and communities, and to meet the social needs and benefits of the people, especially the poor and the vulnerable".

One of the main messages I take from this year's International Labour Conference is that we must make full use of the integrating power of the concept of decent work to improve and, if possible, increase the technical assistance we are able to offer to the ILO's constituents. We are seen as relevant and effective partners in national development, bringing a practical work-centred approach not available anywhere else. We must extend the coverage of decent work country programmes and connect them to the activities of other agencies in support of national development programmes.

Global production systems

The theme of global production systems embraces a number of topics that attracted comment. Mr. Nordmann, State Secretary of Switzerland, advocated a strong emphasis on promoting decent work in global production systems, particularly through ILO training courses "for the observance of international labour standards at company level", as a response to the constant requests by companies for advice. Mr. Konditi, Employers' delegate of Kenya, appealed to the ILO "to study the use of corporate social responsibility and its impact on business and to formulate some recommendations that would be appropriate for the promotion of corporate social responsibility as a voluntary initiative". Mr. Pond, speaking for the Government of the United Kingdom, welcomed my proposals "for the ILO to build upon its current knowledge base, particularly in the area of multinational enterprises, in order to further [the ILO's] understanding of the functioning of global production systems and the ways in which voluntary initiatives of companies contribute to decent work".

A number of speakers warned, however, that voluntary initiatives should not be thought of as replacing government's responsibilities with regard to international labour standards. Mr. Kearney, representing the International Textile, Garment and Leather Workers' Federation, warned of the dangers of progress in modernizing laws on workers' rights in one country being undercut by lack of enforcement elsewhere. "If governments were doing their job, voluntary initiatives to avoid sweatshop labour would not be needed," he said. The Employers' delegate of Japan, Mr. Okuda, said "that companies are an integral part of society, that the central responsibility of business is to perform well, to be the primary source of prosperity and of well-being, and that, in addition to this, they need to fulfil their social and environmental responsibilities".

I believe we can build on some strong signs of converging views in this area. I concur with Mr. Perigot, who spoke to the Conference on behalf of the International Organisation of Employers but was also a member of the World Commission, when he said "the IOE believes that a major opportunity now exists for employers to intensify their efforts and give more focus to the numerous initiatives companies are taking on corporate social responsibility. The IOE is ready to actively explore areas of collaboration with the ILO in the labour field, including the international forum suggested in the World Commission report". And I also agree very much with Sir Roy Trotman, who proposed on behalf of the Workers' group "that there should be stronger action and wider social dialogue to promote decent work in export processing zones and, more generally, in global production systems, and that the ILO should provide advice and assistance to those engaged in such dialogue".

Policy coherence

A leitmotif of this session of the Conference was policy coherence, on different issues and at different levels. Many speakers commented on the specific proposal of the World Commission on growth, investment and employment. Ms. Bakoko Bakoru, Minister of Gender, Labour and Social Development of Uganda, argued that it was fundamental to working conditions and the corresponding freedoms that developing countries should get their rightful share of world markets. She therefore called upon the ILO "to engage all relevant world institutions and not to rest before inequalities in the world markets are totally removed". Mr. Dimas, European Commissioner for Employment and Social Affairs, said: "The World Commission's report should be a part of the agenda of other international forums which have responsibility for financial, economic and trade issues. Achieving all these objectives will require joined-up global governance."

Minister Berzoini of Brazil also argued that "to combine macroeconomic policies with employment policies, that is, to work towards economic growth in conjunction with social development and environmental protection ... we need to be consistent in our action, both nationally and regionally, to think globally and act locally". Ms. Dejanovic, Workers' delegate of Croatia, said "the message that 'social progress cannot be achieved solely by social policies' is in many aspects a central message of the report and a challenge for the unions." Ms. Filatov, Minister of Labour of Finland, argued that "the market economy accelerates growth and innovation, but to contribute to the fair and sustainable welfare of people at large, it needs responsible governance at the enterprise level as well as at national and international levels. The architecture of this governance has not been up to the task".

Mr. Evans, speaking for the Trade Union Advisory Committee to the OECD, emphasized that "we have to convince the finance, economics and trade ministers that meeting the challenge of achieving fair globalization is crucial to the very survival of both our societies and our economies". Mr. Potter, Employer's delegate of the United States, warned that "a seat at the table where key decisions are taken is earned by being credible". While the ILO had to focus on the priorities of its constituents and maintenance of its entire mandate, there was a need to develop a "world-class macroeconomic research programme that recognizes, among other things, that enterprises are the source of wealth creation and that job creation and a rising standard of living are achievable only if a number of economic, political and legal factors are present". In this regard, a number of employer delegates highlighted the complementarities between the report of the World Commission and that of the United Nations Commission on the Private Sector and Development, *Unleashing entrepreneurship: Making business work for the poor*.

I fully agree with Employer spokesperson Mr. Funes de Rioja's view that "the existing multilateral system needs to be more effective, better resourced and more responsive, and efforts need to be made to avoid duplication and mismanagement". The World Commission makes a powerful political case for a multilateral system that meets the expectations of people all over the world for decent work. The ILO has an obligation under the Declaration of Philadelphia to examine and consider all international economic and financial policies in the light of its fundamental objectives. We must work with all relevant agencies to find the best way to discharge this mandate.

Constructing a socio-economic floor

Ms. Ngindinwa, Deputy Minister of Labour of Namibia, was one of a number of speakers who welcomed the Commission's emphasis on "globalization with solidarity to overcome inequality within and between countries and to contribute to the elimination of poverty". As stated by Ms. Cu, Workers' delegate of Viet Nam, "globalization creates a lot of opportunities but it also poses challenges for the poor and less developed countries". Many delegates found the idea of a socio-economic floor of rights, incomes and basic social services attractive. A significant component would be to assure social protection for all. As Mr. Tilahun, Employers' delegate of Ethiopia, underscored, "the lack of social protection is one of the core problems and affects over 90 per cent of our population" and was hence "unfortunately an integral part of our poverty". Mr. Lublin, Government delegate of the Russian Federation, on the basis of his country's experience of a rapid transition to an open economy and market relations, expressed concern about "the weakening of national systems of social protection, the erosion of social solidarity and the highly unequal distribution of benefits and burdens of globalization between different countries and different social groups within the population".

Ms. Christova, Minister of Labour and Social Policy of Bulgaria, gave a practical example of combating poverty in which tripartite social dialogue had led to reforms which combined a new social security threshold with compulsory registration of employment contracts and had moved about 300,000 people out of the informal economy. Mr. Panayiotopoulos, Minister of Employment and Social Protection of Greece, highlighted "the importance of establishing a global minimum level of social protection … which aims to provide priority coverage of the most vulnerable population groups, such as the elderly" and supported "the action undertaken by the ILO to develop and disseminate the principle of a minimum level of socio-economic security for the world economy".

Supporting socio-economic reforms at the national level can go a long way in eliminating within-country inequality, but does not suffice to close the widening gap between rich and poor countries at the global level. It is time to start the process of examining possibilities and engendering discussion on how we might address the basic issue of global inequality.

Strengthening the international labour standards system

Many speakers stressed that the foundation of a fair globalization is a strong international labour standards system and welcomed the support of the World Commission for the ILO's central role in developing and supervising standards. This was exemplified by the words of Mr. Grönlund, State Secretary of the Ministry of Industry, Employment and Communications of Sweden: "We embrace wholeheartedly the framework which states that the governance of globalization must be based on universally shared values and respect for human rights and core labour standards." Mr. Neffati, Minister of Social Affairs and Solidarity of Tunisia, said that we should develop the "means of making globalization more humane and more just by anchoring it in respect for human rights and human dignity and by ensuring equal opportunities for all peoples without discrimination".

Many speakers recorded how ILO standards had formed the basis for national labour legislation. The Minister of Labour of Nicaragua, Mr. Gurdián Castellón, explained that "the standard-setting function of the ILO has been the cornerstone of our activities and is reflected in ... (our) legislation ... in the social and labour fields and contributes to the improvement of labour standards in all of them". Mr. Van Vuuren, Employers' delegate of South Africa, emphasized that employers there "are keenly aware from their own experience of the fundamental importance of international labour standards and their role in the promotion and maintenance of democracy".

Mr. Gomes Proença, Workers' delegate of Portugal, highlighted that "the role of the ILO in terms of regulation, through Conventions and Recommendations, should be constantly expanded and updated so as to respond to the changes occurring in the economy and in society ...". The Employers' delegate of Thailand, Ms. Romchatthong, argued that it is necessary to mobilize tripartite efforts "to establish a surveillance system in the business world to enforce labour standards at all levels". Mr. Boisson, Employers' delegate of France, envisaged "a standard-setting policy that makes it possible to establish objectives, to offer assistance and cooperation, to measure the progress made and to assess the effectiveness of policies, especially those designed to combat exclusion from the labour market: this, to my mind, is the significant contribution that the ILO should make towards making globalization a real opportunity for all".

As many speakers stressed, the setting, implementation and promotion of standards is the core business of the ILO. The World Commission has encouraged us to further step up and focus our efforts. I believe we should continue to use an integrated approach to standards and identify tools that can capture the essential elements of decent work. We should further enhance the efficiency and relevance of our supervisory machinery, and strive to connect it to assistance for resolving problems. The views put forward at this Conference will certainly help the Governing Body in its further exploration of standards-related questions.

Mobilizing global tripartism

In giving broad endorsement to the report of the World Commission and my own report on its implications for the ILO, many delegates accepted that the ILO and each of its constituents had responsibility to ensure an active follow-up of its recommendations. As Mr. Tou, Minister of Labour, Employment and Youth of Burkina Faso and a member of the World Commission, pointed out, "if social injustice is a danger to humankind, it is high time for us to mobilize against poverty and unemployment, which are its principal manifestations". He and his country are making a major contribution to such a mobilization by hosting the forthcoming Extraordinary Summit of Heads of State and Government of the African Union on Employment and Poverty Alleviation in Africa. Similarly, Ms. Rosas Pérez, Government delegate of Panama, stressed that "to achieve positive change in the globalization process and in order to achieve fairness, equal opportunities and social justice, we need to pool the determination, efforts and commitment of all social actors". Mr. Daer, Workers' delegate of Argentina, said: "We believe in social, tripartite and institutionalized dialogue, not just as a way of preserving and ensuring social peace but also as a key factor in national development and a fundamental driving force for economic and social policies which could end exclusion and poverty."

Mr. Ryder, speaking for the International Confederation of Free Trade Unions, said, "the ICFTU is preparing for its own World Congress dedicated to the task of organizing and strengthening the capacities of our international movement to meet the challenges of globalization, and we will equally mobilize those capacities behind [the ILO's] agenda for justice in the global economy". Mr. Perigot, on behalf of the International Organisation of Employers, also said, "we will strive to involve our members and to promote a debate within our organization on the Report's recommendations and its implications for IOE members at the national, regional and international level". Mr. Thys of the World Confederation of Labour said that his organization would take action to follow up on the recommendations of the Commission report "right away, within and alongside the ILO, and together with other trade union organizations, in order to strengthen a world based on solidarity, a world that is more democratic and more respectful of social justice".

As I said at the beginning of the debate on a fair globalization, the ILO should be judiciously ambitious in meeting the challenges put before us by the World Commission. We will need to balance our objectives and our resources. I believe there is some scope for increasing the extra-budgetary support we can access and, at some point, there has to be a proper assessment of regular budgetary resources against the tasks Members expect us to undertake. As Mr. Meyer, Government delegate of Canada, said, "the Governing Body will need to be clear about the results it wants to achieve and about the selection of a limited set of strategic targets it wants to aim at. It will need to maximize the leverage of the ILO's most strategic assets and make sure it does not deviate from the ILO's most fundamental objectives. Only by being highly focused can our Organization expect to play a leadership role in today's fast-changing world." I believe the ILO's strongest asset is the tripartite network represented by the delegations at this Conference. We have only just begun to realize its potential.

3. Migrant workers in the global economy

One of the main concerns raised by the World Commission was the absence of a multilateral framework for managing the cross-border movement of workers, unlike that which governs the cross-border movement of goods and services. At the same time as the Commission was starting its work in March 2002, the Governing Body placed the issue of how to develop an integrated approach to the problems of migrant workers on this year's Conference agenda.

Many speakers in the plenary debate commented on the complementarities between the ideas of the World Commission and those offered in the ILO report *Towards a fair deal for migrant workers in the global economy*. As Ms. Thienthong, Minister of Labour of

Thailand, said, "trafficking and migration-related issues ... can be best addressed not by a single government, but through engagement and cooperation with other governments". Similarly, as Mr. Lloyd, Government delegate of Australia, pointed out, a "critical issue is the recognition of the fundamental right of each country to determine who should pass its borders. This is particularly so in these times of heightened security concerns". Mr. de Payva, Workers' delegate of Singapore, emphasized that "the challenge confronting the global community is to make migration work for all and direct it in a way that serves the economic well-being and social justice of workers". Ms. Sasso Mazzufferi, Employers' delegate of Italy, said, "there is now a growing need felt in developing and in industrialized countries to have a completely changed framework of reference, one which is inspired by a modern, culturally open approach that is designed to enhance employability and the prospects of high-calibre migrant workers".

Migration is a complex policy field and a sensitive issue in the political debates of many countries. The task we gave to the Committee on Migrant Workers was not an easy one. It is therefore a major achievement to have reached broad consensus on a plan of action to ensure a fair deal for migrant workers in the global economy. Tripartism has proved its worth yet again. When it comes to some very difficult questions, negotiation in good faith, recognizing each party's position, provides a way forward that commands the support of those who will have the responsibility for fulfilling the agreement. The plan of action will engage all of the ILO's constituents in promoting the ratification of ILO Conventions on migrant workers and the wider application of ILO principles regarding the treatment of migrant workers. The plan of action also asks the ILO to develop a non-binding multilateral framework for the rights-based management of labour migration consistent with national sovereignty of States in matters of migration policy, and calls for the establishment of an ILO platform for dialogue on migration in partnership with other international and multilateral organizations.

This tripartite agreement between governments and the social partners on so many important issues relating to the management of migration is truly historic. It envisages a framework drawing on best practices to formulate guidelines on a broad range of issues for policy-makers – such as expanding avenues for regular migration while combating irregular migration, promoting bilateral and multilateral agreements, supervising recruitment and labour contracting, reducing the risks for all migrants, especially women migrant workers, protecting human and labour rights of migrant workers, reducing the cost of remittances and promoting their use for productive investment, facilitating the portability of social security entitlements, promoting the accreditation of skills, promoting ethical recruitment so as to ensure an adequate supply of skills for both sending and host countries, and promoting social integration and inclusion of migrant workers.

The Conference asks the ILO to present the guidelines on this non-binding multilateral framework for managing migration to the Governing Body in its November 2005 session. We will start to implement the plan of action, including the preparation of a draft framework, at once. We will also, as the conclusions specify, enhance our cooperation with other relevant international organizations.

4. Organizing for social justice

The Global Report under the follow-up to the ILO Declaration on Fundamental Principles and Rights at Work, *Organizing for social justice*, was scrutinized during a special interactive session. The report's dynamic picture of the global situation regarding the principles of freedom of association and the right to collective bargaining provoked an informed and varied exchange of views. As Sir Roy Trotman, Workers' spokesperson, reminded us "We need to state unequivocally that freedom of association is a fundamental human right. It is a basic entitlement that should be expected and respected without reference to a country's size or its wealth."

Although many speakers remarked on the positive trend of increased ratifications and wider acceptance of these fundamental rights, this was equally weighted by concern at the evidence of weak implementation, particularly affecting vulnerable groups of workers in many countries. Minister de Geus of the Netherlands put the issue sharply at the beginning of the debate: "There is no doubt that universal ratification of the Conventions concerned remains a priority. This, however, is not enough when universal ratification goes hand in hand with a gross violation of union rights. So the central question is: How can we mobilize the political will to decrease the gap between ratification and implementation?"

Mr. Ahmed, Workers' delegate of Pakistan, drew attention to "a big gap between ratification and implementation both in terms of legislation and in terms of the difficulties encountered by the workers in exercising these rights – victimization, cases of murder and persistent harassment and arrests". The Employers' spokesperson, Mr. Potter, stressed the need for more focus on the "full implementation and achievement of the fundamental principles" themselves rather than ratification. He believed that the report and the promotion of the fundamental principles and rights required more focus on specific issues such as "the right of employers and workers to establish and join organizations of their own choosing, the right to manage internal affairs without interference from public authorities and the right to be free from acts of interference from employer or worker organizations", and on remedying the ILO's lack of "an up-to-date picture of the legislative situation regarding freedom of association and the effective recognition of collective bargaining".

The richness of the discussion might be illustrated by three contributions. Mr. Seguin, Government delegate of France, took up the theme of the relationship between fundamental principles and rights at work and a fair globalization raised by the World Commission. "These rights also enshrine the rights and responsibilities of the various parties involved in the real economy and they also enable us to reconcile the laws of the market and social objectives. We believe, therefore, that it should be a priority for our Organization to ensure that throughout the multilateral system we have proper recognition for the idea that social dialogue is an essential element of, and a determining factor in, good governance." Ms. Hunt, Workers' delegate of the United Kingdom, drew our attention to the particular vulnerability of women, as "freedom of association is most commonly denied in the feminized sectors of the global economy, in export processing zones, in agriculture, in domestic and other informal work and in the public services". Mr. Al Tayer, Minister of Labour and Social Affairs of the United Arab Emirates, speaking on behalf of the Gulf Cooperation Council, described "the reforms and innovative measures adopted by the GCC countries [which] seek mainly to build the capacities of workers and social institutions and to ensure their effective participation in decision-making and the implementation of reforms". "We are thus", he said, "endeavouring to strengthen the role of civil society institutions on the basis of inalienable Islamic principles calling for consultation, peace and equality".

The debate yielded general agreement on four areas of work to be done over the next four years: overcoming obstacles to ratifying and applying Conventions Nos. 87 and 98; supporting organization and bargaining for vulnerable groups of workers; deepening the understanding of how these principles can build a labour market that promotes rights, economic development and poverty reduction; and improving the knowledge base, advisory services, technical cooperation and advocacy activities in this area. This year's discussions on the Global Report represent an important step forward in addressing these fundamental values. In light of these discussions, we will be presenting a draft action plan to the Governing Body in November. In this respect, the President of the Conference, Mr. Ray Guevara, said that "international solidarity, as the necessary framework for attaining social justice, is indispensable and it is for that reason that the wealthiest countries should, in addition to fully respecting their commitments under the Declaration, support those who request their cooperation in order to ensure that rights and experiences can be shared, and make the principles we have been discussing today a reality".

5. Gender equality, pay equity and maternity protection

The resolution concerning the promotion of gender equality, pay equity and maternity protection was selected by the Government, Employer and Worker members of the Resolutions Committee for discussion, out of 15 submitted draft resolutions, later merged into eight resolutions, which were put to the vote. The resolution concerning the ILO's efforts to combat poverty came second in the vote, followed in third place by the resolution concerning the strengthening of the role of the ILO in supporting workers and employers in Palestine and the other occupied Arab territories as a result of continued Israeli occupation and aggressive practices.

An exceptionally constructive and collaborative discussion, in which all changes in the text were agreed by consensus, resulted in a comprehensive resolution. It calls upon governments and the social partners – in their respective fields of competence – to eliminate all forms of gender discrimination in the labour market, promote equality between men and women workers and provide women workers with access to maternity protection. Governments are requested to ratify relevant ILO Conventions and introduce or strengthen all necessary legislative changes. They are also requested to develop gender-sensitive national policies promoting employment and entrepreneurship and to launch measures enabling better reconciliation of work and family life. Employers' and workers' organizations are called upon to promote the negotiation and adoption of employment equity plans and evaluate gender equality policy.

The resolution invites the Director-General, through the Governing Body, to continue and strengthen the efforts to achieve the objective of gender equality and intensify the campaign for the universal ratification and implementation of Conventions Nos. 100 and 111, together with the other fundamental Conventions. It also requests strengthening of training programmes, including those run by the Turin Centre, and continuation of research work on the gender wage gap and the effects of globalization on poverty and pay equity. Finally, the Director-General is asked to ensure that sufficient funding is in place to enable the ILO to promote the objectives of the resolution and to report back to the Governing Body on its implementation.

I welcome the adoption of this vigorous new mandate. It reinforces the gender equality policies I have been implementing since 1999. I must also draw your attention to the lack of real progress in improving the representation of women at the Conference. Last year only 12 per cent of registered delegates were women. This year it has crept up to 14 per cent. If you look at representation on delegations, last year it was 20 per cent and this year 23 per cent. But of a total of 294 speakers in the plenary debates this year only 30 were women. This is less than last year, when the equivalent numbers were 291 speakers of whom 33 were women. We clearly have work to do to implement our own resolution.

As I said in my opening address, we must increase our efforts to meet a target of 30 per cent representation in delegations. The solution is not simply through a reminder in the convocation letter or the Conference Guide. We must start now. Representation at ILO meetings is, of course, symptomatic of gender inequality in society at large and in the institutions of tripartism. But that must not be an excuse for inaction. Rather, we should use the composition of delegations for the Conference as a catalyst for action. And by way of a stimulus, I will ask the Governing Body to consider, as a follow-up measure to the resolution, various possible measures to encourage much stronger efforts towards achieving a target of 30 per cent female participation in delegations.

6. Review of 2002-03 programme implementation

Many speakers acknowledged the overall progress made by the Office in implementing its programme in the 2002-03 biennium and at the same time commented on how performance might be further improved. Mr. De, Minister of Public Services, Labour, Employment and Professional Organizations of Senegal, noted that "the ILO has been able to effectively implement many actions and programmes in the Strategic Policy Framework for 2002-05 as defined by the Governing Body". Vice-Minister Togari of Japan, while appreciating the ILO's activities over the last two years, invited the Office, in view of the massive demand for the ILO's services and the financial constraints, "to implement its activities more efficiently and to make further efforts to reduce personnel costs". Mr. Aloewie, Government delegate of Indonesia, commented that "the actions undertaken have been directed at efficiently addressing the needs and interests of the tripartite constituents. Nevertheless, we would like to reiterate that the ILO should focus on a holistic approach with respect to the assistance it provides to governments and their social partners". Mr. Eremeev, Employers' delegate of the Russian Federation, felt that the social partners' "opinions should be represented in some form, particularly with regard to the implementation of projects, and that this would enhance the objectiveness of the document and the effectiveness of the work of the ILO itself".

Mr. Trabelsi, Workers' delegate of Tunisia, expressed his "appreciation for the activities of the Organization over the period 2002-03 and for its Decent Work Agenda. The results of this work are contained in the Report of the Director-General, who encourages all trade unionists to participate in dialogue in order to strengthen labour standards, respect for workers' rights and respect for their dignity". The Minister of Employment and Civil Service of Guinea, Mr. Keira, said, "a glance at the regions shows the amount spent per region. We see that my continent, Africa, is the region that has most benefited" from the available resources. On the other hand, the Minister of Labour and Administrative Reform of Sudan, Mr. Magaya, said that "the achievements of the ILO in the previous biennium are recognizable, though what remains to be done is enormous to help developing countries in general and African countries in particular to create employment and alleviate poverty".

We will carefully review all the comments made on the implementation report and endeavour to pick up the lessons learnt in the next programme and budget. Our effort to switch to management by results is beginning to pay off, and I am sure that two years from now, when you receive the next report, we will be able to show further progress.

7. The situation of workers of the occupied Arab territories

My Report on the situation of workers of the occupied Arab territories stimulated comments from a large number of delegates, both from countries in the Middle East and from other parts of the world. Ms. Dello, Minister of Social Affairs and Labour of the Syrian Arab Republic, commended "the efforts made by the Director-General of the ILO, the ILO Regional Office for the Arab States in Beirut and the mission which prepared the Report entitled *The situation of workers of the occupied Arab territories*. It is an objective Report, which calls things by their name". Mr. Al-Khatib, Minister of Labour of Palestine, said that "the Report … quite rightly emphasizes the suffering of the Palestinian people in general, and the workers in particular". He added that "we are looking forward to your economic support through your contributions to the Palestinian Fund for Employment and Social Protection, in order to fight unemployment and poverty in our country".

Mr. Al Rabaie, Employers' delegate of Oman, commending the ILO's work, pointed out that "it is essential to continue to help the employers and workers in Palestine through the Palestinian Fund for Employment and Social Protection and to do everything necessary to provide them with technical assistance". Ms. Theodorsen, Workers' delegate of Norway, highlighted the Report's focus on gender: "Palestinian women are facing enormous obstacles and challenges. They have to try to keep their families together in an abnormal life situation. At the same time, they are marginalized on the labour market." A number of delegates echoed her call for the ILO to "continue to present this type of objective information as well as promoting dialogue between Palestinian and Israeli workers".

I am proud that the ILO has maintained a capacity to offer assistance to workers, employers and the Palestinian Authority during these long and difficult years of occupation. That capacity is founded on a professional objectivity which is recognized by all and enables us to continue our dialogue with all parties. As Mr. Basesgioglu, Minister for Labour and Social Security of Turkey, said, the Report "underlines the necessity of the ILO's continued interest and support for this issue". He added that Turkey attaches importance to "the implementation of the Road Map, and to reaching a peaceful solution through negotiations as soon as possible". I must add that during this Conference, Turkey joined others in showing its commitment to our work in the very tangible form of a US$100,000 contribution to the Palestinian Fund for Employment and Social Protection. I hope next year to be able to report that we have many more similarly generous contributions and that we have put them to good use in generating jobs and social and economic recovery.

8. Human resources development and training

Human resources development and, in particular, education and training are critical to the ILO goal of creating greater opportunities for women and men to obtain decent and productive work, in conditions of freedom, equity, security and human dignity. Education and training are therefore a central pillar of the Decent Work Agenda. This year we have adopted a new, dynamic instrument on human resources development with a strong focus on education, training and lifelong learning. This Recommendation is a forward-looking and policy-oriented instrument that addresses the enormous challenges we face in developing the knowledge, skills and employability of all people in the twenty-first century.

It provides, for the first time in an ILO instrument, definitions of contemporary training issues including lifelong learning, competencies and employability. Education and skills facilitate the application of new technologies, increase individuals' employability and enterprises' productivity and competitiveness. Women and men need broad-based skills that can be adapted to rapidly changing economic requirements. Sound education and training policy also provides an important instrument to offset the negative impacts of globalization, while at the same time equipping people with the knowledge and skills to take advantage of the emerging opportunities. They thus make labour markets operate better. But education and training by themselves are insufficient. To be fully effective, they need to form part of integrated policies directed at economic and employment growth.

A number of delegates commented on the analysis of the report by the World Commission on the Social Dimension of Globalization, which highlighted that countries which have benefited from globalization most have invested significantly in their education and training systems. For example, Mr. Fong, Minister of Human Resources of Malaysia, in his address to the Conference, noted that "in the present context of liberalization, globalization and a changed economic scenario, the emphasis needs to be on upgrading the skills of the labour force". Mr. Dowla, Employers' delegate from Bangladesh, while noting that most countries in South Asia had "taken up major economic reforms to reduce poverty", stressed that the basic problem is that the poor are without assets, and unskilled and hence not able to take advantage of the new opportunities.

The new Recommendation deals with many of the challenges posed by globalization, such as the issue of "brain drain", which is causing concern in many developing countries. It calls for international mechanisms that would mitigate the adverse impact on developing countries of the loss of skilled people. It also recognizes that education and training strategies and creating the right enabling conditions – economic growth, investment, creation of decent jobs and human development – will help these countries retain their skilled labour. The new instrument calls for innovative approaches to release additional resources for education, training and lifelong learning to assist these countries. Making the most of the positive links between knowledge and skills on the one hand and productivity improvement, poverty reduction and social inclusion on the other is central to the new human resources development Recommendation.

The Office is preparing a major campaign to promote the new Recommendation. It will include developing the present web site into a digital practical guide to implementing the Recommendation, as called for in the general discussion on human resources development at the 88th Session of the Conference in 2000. We believe that a digital guide is a more innovative and creative way of supporting our constituents. It will link the text of the Recommendation to all international instruments on education and training and to the over 500 examples of national training policy and programme initiatives that we have collected. Your new Recommendation presented in this new digital guide will provide a very useful platform for promoting cooperation between countries on sharing good practices and thus in giving full effect to more than four years' hard work.

9. Conditions of work in the fishing sector

Fishing is a truly globalized sector. Many vessels range far and wide, but even if they work closer to home, the catch is sent around the world to feed us all. Within the context of revising and consolidating existing but outdated standards, the first discussion of a new, comprehensive instrument to protect the world's 35 million fishers has set the framework for the development of a new Convention supplemented by a Recommendation. Although it proved necessary to set aside some provisions, such as accommodation and social security, for further consultations, agreement was reached on the proposed Conclusions with a view to a Convention.

In the light of the hazardous nature of fishing, the Convention contains new provisions on safety and health. It also includes provisions that will enable not only flag States but, for the first time for the fishing industry, port States (ports of other countries which fishing vessels may enter) to monitor compliance with the provisions of the new

Convention. The discussions inevitably took place in the shadow of the new consolidated maritime labour Convention that is still being developed. Nevertheless, good progress was made in finding the delicate balance in protecting the vast majority of small-scale fishers, who work everywhere, not just in developing countries, without diluting the existing protection afforded to fishers on large ocean-going fishing vessels. But more work remains to be done, particularly if the goal of achieving quick and broad implementation and widespread ratification is to be attained.

The Office has been asked to assist during the coming months, particularly with regard to the important issues of accommodation and social security. And we will, but must do it within the confines of an already tight budget. So we will be looking to all of you – Governments, Employers and Workers – for financial assistance as well as counting on your expertise. I am certain that next year when the Committee reconvenes, it will be keen to complete the double-discussion process with a practical Convention that will be quickly and widely ratified and fully implemented to ensure decent and safe work for the world's 35 million fishers.

10. Application of standards

The Committee on the Application of Standards held very interesting and complex discussions on a wide variety of issues. In the general part of its discussion, the Committee continued to examine its own working methods and ways in which its functioning could be improved. This followed a number of earlier discussions going back several years. The principal subject raised was the way in which individual cases are selected for detailed discussion in the Committee. Discussions will have to continue on this in the coming year, as some countries remain unsatisfied that their concerns have yet to be fully met.

The General Survey by the Committee of Experts on the Application of Conventions and Recommendations discussed by the Conference Committee this year was on employment policy, on the contribution of ILO standards on human resources development and on small and medium-sized enterprises (SMEs) achieving full, productive and freely chosen employment. The Committee agreed that employment creation had to remain a central aspect of governments' policies, that the work created had to be decent work, and that human resources and SME development make a real contribution to creating decent jobs.

The Committee again held a special sitting on the application by Myanmar of the Forced Labour Convention, 1930 (No. 29), following up measures taken in the context of article 33 of the Constitution. This was the fourth time such a special sitting has been held, and it discussed not only the comments of the Committee of Experts but also the events which have taken place since that Committee's December 2003 session. It is worth saying that the Committee noted with "deep concern" that the Committee of Experts had pointed out that the three main recommendations of the Commission of Inquiry had yet to be implemented, and that, in spite of the Government's assurances of its good intentions, in actual practice forced labour continues to be exacted in many parts of the country. The Committee also expressed grave concern that three persons had been convicted of high treason, including on grounds of contacts with the ILO, and called for their release. At the same time the Committee welcomed the Government's continuing cooperation with the ILO Liaison Officer in the country, though the practical results had remained slight. We will continue to follow this case attentively.

In addition to this special sitting, the Committee examined 24 other individual cases covering freedom of association, forced labour, discrimination, child labour, employment policy, labour inspection, wages, maternity protection and workers with family responsibilities – the whole range of concerns addressed in ILO standards. While in some cases it found reason to welcome the measures already taken, or being taken, by governments to apply Conventions, it also found it necessary to adopt special paragraphs to express concern over other less positive cases. A special paragraph in the Committee's report expresses its concern with Myanmar over the application of the Freedom of Association and Protection of the Right to Organise Convention, 1948 (No. 87): the Committee found in this case that there was a continued failure to apply the provisions of a ratified Convention. The Committee requested several governments to ask the Office for assistance.

Finally, the Committee had before it the report of the Joint ILO/UNESCO Committee of Experts on the Application of the Recommendations concerning Teaching Personnel.

11. Withdrawal of Recommendations

This year the Conference has, for the third time, withdrawn obsolete ILO instruments. The object of the withdrawal was 16 Recommendations, which had been determined to be obsolete by the Governing Body based on the recommendations of the "Cartier" Working Party on Policy regarding the Revision of Standards (1995-2002). The overwhelming support for these decisions reflects the broad consensus among ILO constituents to pursue efforts to modernize and strengthen the ILO's body of international labour standards.

12. Conclusions

In my opening remarks to the globalization debate I said that I believed the Organization as a whole, the constituents and the Office, must become a truly global team: clear in our strategic choices; efficient in our operations; committed to our values; confident in our message. I think this Conference has shown the qualities of our team: clarity, efficiency, commitment and confidence.

The Chairpersons, the spokespersons of the groups and indeed all the delegates who participated in the work of our committees have shown how global tripartism is able to find agreement on complex issues that call out for international cooperation. I thank you all for the tremendous effort you have made. The plenary debates on the World Commission's report and our response, on organizing for social justice, on the situation of workers of the occupied Arab territories and on the implementation report were full of thoughtful, well-prepared and constructive speeches. None of the reflection that went into your contributions will be wasted.

Our Organization is on the move. We have a broad and deep consensus on the strategies we should follow, which we will now elaborate in a policy framework and a programme and budget for the years ahead. I hope you will go back to your own organizations and ministries and report on what we have achieved, use our reports on globalization to promote a wider dialogue and reach out to form the alliances we need to shape globalization. The potential of tripartism is enormous; let us unleash it fully.

No. 25 – Thursday, 17 June 2004

International Labour Conference

Provisional Record 26

Ninety-second Session, Geneva, 2004

Eighteenth sitting
Wednesday, 16 June 2004, 10.45 a.m.
President: Mr. Ray Guevara

Original Spanish: The PRESIDENT

RATIFICATION OF THE INSTRUMENT OF AMENDMENT OF THE ILO CONSTITUTION BY NIGERIA.

Before we begin our work today, I would like to turn first to the Clerk of the Conference for an important announcement.

Original French: The CLERK OF THE CONFERENCE

I have the pleasure to announce to the Conference that, on 14 June 2004, the Director-General recorded the ratification by Nigeria of the Instrument of Amendment of the ILO Constitution, which was adopted by the Conference in 1997.

REPORT OF THE COMMITTEE ON THE FISHING SECTOR: SUBMISSION, DISCUSSION AND APPROVAL

Original Spanish: The PRESIDENT

We shall now proceed to the examination of the report of the Committee on the Fishing Sector, which is published in *Provisional Record* No. 21. The Officers of the Committee were are follows: the Chairperson was Mr. Ribeiro Lopes, the Employer Vice-Chairperson was Ms. Karikari Anang, the Worker Vice-Chairperson was Mr. Mortensen and the Reporter was Mr. Boumbopoulos. I would now like to call upon Mr. Boumbopoulos to submit the report of the Committee on the Fishing Sector.

Mr. BOUMBOPOULOS *(Government adviser, Greece; Reporter of the Committee on the Fishing Sector)*

I would like, first of, all to express my sincere thanks to the members of the Committee on the Fishing Sector who entrusted me with the duty to introduce the report of our work and provided me with the privilege of addressing accordingly the International Labour Conference. I am deeply honoured and consider that the Committee's decision reflects the recognition of the maritime tradition of my country, Greece.

Taking into account the Report of the Director-General, *A fair globalization: The role of the ILO*, it should be pointed out that the fishing sector is, among others, one of the roots of the maritime industry. The maritime industry is the pioneer and one of the horses to the chariot of globalization from the perspective of development, employment and social cohesion.

Let me say a few words about the background to our work. In March 2002, the 283rd Session of the Governing Body decided to place on the agenda of this session of the Conference an item concerning a comprehensive standard, a Convention supplemented by a Recommendation, on work in the fishing sector.

The new standard, it was agreed, would revise the seven existing ILO instruments on the subject – five Conventions concerning minimum age, medical examination, articles of agreement, accommodation and competency certificates, and two Recommendations concerning vocational training and hours of work. The rationale of this revision would be to reflect the changes in the sector which have occurred over the last 40 years; to achieve more widespread ratification; to reach, where possible, a greater portion of the world's fishers, particularly those working on smaller vessels; and to address other critical issues, such as safety and health. It was agreed that the standard would take into account differences in fishing operations, employment arrangements, methods of remuneration and other aspects.

The work would complement the parallel work being done by the ILO to consolidate its standards for seafarers into a comprehensive new standard. It would also contribute to enhancing and strengthening ILO standards in general to achieve decent work outcomes.

The Committee on the Fishing Sector set up by the Conference had before it two reports prepared by the Office, as well as proposed Conclusions with a view to a Convention and a Recommendation.

The Committee held 20 sittings. It received 210 amendments and many more sub-amendments and sub-sub-amendments. There were quite a few indicative votes. These proved to be an efficient means of finding the feeling of the Committee and moving things along without having to have a formal vote. However, the Committee had two record votes during its 19th sitting. During these sittings, we were able to discuss most, but not all, of the points in the proposed Conclusions with a view to a Convention and a Recommendation.

The Committee adopted provisions on a number of substantive issues.

Firstly, it adopted provisions that would provide broad coverage for all fishers. The existing seven standards for fishing only address a small portion of the world's fishers. The Conclusions adopted by the Committee aim to reach the majority of the world's fishers, including those on small fishing vessels. By doing this, the standard will provide protection to a much greater number of fishers, including the self-employed, such as those paid on a basis of a share of the catch.

Secondly, it provides sufficient flexibility to ensure wide ratification and implementation. Such flexibility is particularly important bearing in mind the complex nature of the fishing sector. The Committee sought to achieve such flexibility without any dilution to the protection provided to fishers working on vessels of different sizes and in various fishing operations.

As the Secretary-General of the Conference said when he addressed our Committee: "It is clearly important that no fisher slips inadvertently through the protective net of the Convention [...] For this to be achieved, the mesh of this net must be just right: not too large that everything is exempt, but not so small that it would stifle ratification and implementation."

This has been done by providing that the competent authority might exclude certain categories of fishers and fishing vessels from the requirements of the Convention, or certain provisions thereof, where the application is considered to be impracticable. However, such exclusions could occur only after consultation with the representative organizations of employers and workers concerned, in particular the representative organizations of fishing vessel owners and fishers. What this effectively does is enhance tripartism in the adoption and implementation of national laws and regulations in the fishing sector.

Thirdly, the instrument will include provisions that will address safety and health in the fishing sector and thus will help to reduce the rate of injuries and fatalities in this sector. This was an important agreement, as the existing ILO standards for fishers did not adequately cover the issue of occupational safety and health. These new provisions would address this issue in a manner that takes into account the specific nature of fishing operations. Equally important, the Committee proposes that the instrument include provisions that would ensure that fishers have protection for work-related sickness, injury or death if such unfortunate events were to occur.

Finally, it is proposed that the instrument include novel provisions on compliance and enforcement. These will not only strengthen the role of the flag State, since they would also promote intervention by port States in relation to conditions on fishing vessels visiting their ports when the conditions on board these vessels are clearly hazardous to the safety and health of the fishers.

This said, much work remains to be done at the next session of the Conference and, of course, all the work done so far continues to be subject to the will of that session of the Conference.

As concerns the work that remains, our Committee decided to refer the provisions concerning accommodation on board fishing vessels to an appropriate mechanism to be put in place between now and the next session of the Conference. This procedure would enable the Committee, when meeting in June 2005, to have before it, as the basis for its discussions, a set of proposals that would seek to achieve the appropriate balance between the mandatory and non-mandatory provisions on accommodation and food.

Owing to limits on the time available, we also were not able to complete our discussion of the issue of fishers' work agreements. Though we made substantial progress on this issue, we did not have time to discuss the annex concerning the specific contents of such agreements. We will return to this issue next year.

We also had only limited discussions on the issue of social security. The Committee thought it would be useful to benefit from the discussion of the issue of social security for seafarers at the Preparatory Technical Maritime Conference to be held in September.

It was agreed that a new Part VII concerning additional requirements for vessels of, a yet unspecified, metres in length or more should be developed by the Office with a view to being examined by the next session of the Conference.

When discussing these proposed Conclusions, our Committee had to deal with a technical, complex and sensitive issue. I strongly believe that during the past two weeks the Committee produced a very good basis and, for some parts, a solid basis for further discussions next year.

The Committee's achievements will set us well on the path for the second, and crucial, discussion this time next year. The spirit of tripartism, the high level of expertise and the commitment to work in our Committee are the guarantees for the achievement of our goal. Our goal is the development and adoption of realistic, modern, cohesive and comprehensive new international standards concerning work in the fishing sector; standards that will benefit all fishers.

The report of our Committee's discussions will be particularly important as we prepare for next year. It is the road map that shows us what we did, how we did it, and why we did it. We will also be taking home the amendments that we did not discuss. Even though they will not appear in the new document, they will guide our deliberations over the coming year.

The report is an excellent reflection of the Committee's work at this session of the Conference. For this, particular thanks for our achievement are due to the Office. We could not have the result we have without a great deal of help and support from the Office. Ms. Cleopatra Doumbia-Henry and all her staff worked tirelessly on our behalf. I would like to thank the Legal Adviser, Mr. Loïc Picard, as well as Ms. Antoinette Juvet-Mir, Mr. Brandt Wagner and Mr. Dani Appave.

I especially want to thank Ms. Ann Herbert and Mr. Norman Jennings, who have skilfully and speedily produced our report. I also wish to thank the interpreters and translators, who facilitated our work and made communication possible. There were of course many other members of the secretariat working hard behind the scenes; I will not name them but they must know of our deep appreciation. They worked tirelessly on our behalf, often late into the night, long after we had gone home.

I request that the International Labour Conference adopt the report of the Committee on the Fishing Sector, the proposed Conclusions with a view to a Convention and Recommendation, and the resolution to place on the agenda of the next session of the Conference an item entitled "Work in the fishing sector".

I am looking forward to seeing you again next year at the Conference and, prior to that, I expect to meet you in Athens for the Olympic Games.

Ms. KARIKARI ANANG *(Employers' delegate, Ghana; Employer Vice-Chairperson of the Committee on the Fishing Sector)*

On behalf of the Employers' group, I have the honour to comment on the Conclusions of the first discussion on the conditions of work in the fishing sector. Before I do so, however, may I extend, on behalf of the Employers' group, our thanks to Mr. Ribeiro Lopes, the Chairperson of our Committee and Minister of Labour and Social Security of Portugal, and also to Mr. Mortensen, the Workers' spokesperson, to the Government members and to Ms. Doumbia-Henry and her efficient staff for all their work.

At its 92nd Session, the International Labour Conference set out to discuss an instrument concerning the conditions of work in the fishing sector, bearing in mind the hazardous nature of many fishing operations in both developing and developed countries and also bearing in mind the fact that there are five existing Conventions, all of which have a very low level of ratification, and two Recommendations. These instruments were adopted as long ago as 1920, 1959 and 1966 and cover medical examinations, fishermen's article of agreement, competency certificates, accommodation and minimum age, which received a maximum of 29 ratifications.

They all therefore require updating, in order to reflect the changes that have occurred in the sector over the last 40 years; to achieve more widespread ratification and to improve the working conditions of a greater percentage of the world's fishers, particularly for those who work on smaller boats.

When considering the revision of these existing standards and the possibility of introducing a new instrument that would cover new issues and that would be applicable to all workers in tandem with the ILO Declaration on Fundamental Principles and Rights at Work, we should take cognizance of the primary goal of the ILO, namely that of promoting opportunities for women and men to obtain decent and productive work in conditions of freedom.

In the Employers' group, we are focusing on the issue of maintaining jobs in order for women and men to obtain decent and productive work. While taking care not to jeopardize the attainment of this goal, we must save enterprises. This all too often becomes a secondary matter in our effort to come up with labour standards. But we must not lose sight of the fact that it is the enterprises that produce these jobs.

The Conference has been given a golden opportunity to come up with a comprehensive and ratifiable instrument that takes into consideration the fact that the fishers on smaller boats who represent over 90 per cent of the world's fishers do not benefit from any protection at all. It is these fishers whose jobs we may want to save. In addition, there are the fishers on larger vessels who have attained some protection and whose protection we would not want to erode. One of our most critical goals therefore is the achievement of the widest ratification possible. Or do we want to see another 40 years go by with a very low level of ratification, as was the case with the previous five Conventions? It is in nobody's interest to come meetings and develop standards that are so prescriptive that they are left on the shelves because they are not just practicable to implement.

Against this background, the new standards to be developed should – as all Committee members agreed at the beginning of our work – be sufficiently broad and flexible to address a number of issues and to be effective for the majority of the world's fishers. They should also be based on principles that take into consideration the diverse economic and social conditions of each country and the differences in fishing fleets.

The statistics on those employed in the fishing sector giving the distribution of fishers as a percentage of the world's total are as follows: 82.7 per cent in Asia; 9.28 per cent in Africa; 2.75 per cent in South America; with Europe, North America and the Russian Federation making up the rest.

Over 90 per cent of fishers live in the developing countries and that is even more reason why, in order to save the jobs of the majority of the world's fishers, we do indeed need to strike a balance by giving minimum protection to such fishers, while not eroding the protection attained by the other 10 per cent. The Conference has the tough job of striking a balance between these two worlds without coming up with an overly prescriptive instrument, which would require over 90 per cent of member States to apply for exclusions if they wish to ratify the Convention.

We would like to thank the Government members and the Workers' group for their contributions. While the Conclusions we have reached at the end of our first discussions are quite broad, we believe we are missing the golden opportunity I have just referred to. There are several critical issues, in particular the categorization of fishing vessels, the formulation of some additional requirements to be applied to some of them and the establishment of exclusions covering those member States which cannot apply such additional requirements. Are we developing two Conventions one for the developing countries or the smaller boats operating in the informal fishing economy, in either the developed or the developing countries, which make up the workplace of the majority of fishers; and one for the large vessels in the formal sector of developed countries?

Is it not the goal of the ILO to gradually draw the informal sector into the formal sector and therefore to gradually and progressively apply ILO standards to it?

We are aware of the central issue of the current discussions on consolidated international maritime labour standards for seafarers. Existing maritime labour standards are primarily designed for seafarers on seagoing ships. This Conference should, however, take cognizance of the fact that fishing is fishing and merchant shipping is merchant shipping, and the two should not be confused. Moreover, the fishers of the world have not been consulted in the current discussion of consolidated maritime labour standards and culturally fishers will not want to be put in the same boat as seafarers.

The President must guide us in our preparations for next year's second round of discussions. I wish to state that there are other pertinent issues, such as accommodation and food on board fishing vessels, and the matter of social security, some of which have been left for examination or consideration by the Conference at its second round of discussions next year. These are critical issues, affecting the living conditions of fishers and we believe the ILO should find the necessary resources to convene a tripartite meeting of experts to enable the Committee to fulfil its mandate of producing a comprehensive standard that is sufficiently broad, flexible and not overly prescriptive, one which will take into account the diversity of the economic and social conditions of countries and differences in fishing fleets within the framework of one, widely ratified Convention.

We therefore invite the Government members and the Workers' group to reconsider the position they have adopted on many of these areas, which are of critical concern to us, so that in 2005 we will finally grasp the golden opportunity and come up with the broad, flexible and ratifiable Convention so dearly needed by the fishers of the world.

Mr. MASEMOLA (Workers' adviser, South Africa)

You know, when I was "instructed to volunteer" – and I hope that this is not a contradiction in terms – I felt very humbled and, therefore, I am honoured and pleased to give the Workers' group's comments on the report and Conclusions of the Committee on the Fishing Sector.

We want to start by thanking all the participants and everybody from the Office, the secretariat of the ILO, for the roles that they played, as well as the spokespersons from various Governments, the Employer spokesperson and, more importantly, the Chairperson of the Committee.

As the Office documents have pointed out, there are 35 million fishers, mostly on small-scale vessels, which lie outside the current ILO fisheries Conventions, and it is essential that they be given protection. The fisheries sector is very diverse, both in terms of the type of vessels, the nature of the fishing operations fishers are engaged in, and the manner and status of their employment or engagement arrangements. Fishing vessels range from very small vessels operating in territorial waters, to large factory vessels operating on the high seas and from foreign ports. This means that some of the larger vessels operate on a global scale, and there is a link to the globalization initiatives of the Organization. It should also be noted that the growth in the international trade in fisheries products means that the ILO's globalization initiative also has implications for the smaller-scale end of the sector. Many fishers are also remunerated through the share system and may not, under some or most of the national laws and practice, be considered employees.

The Workers' group sought the adoption of a balanced Convention that reflected the realities of the industry and was complementary to other international instruments covering the sector. This means that the "one-size-fits-all" approach may not work. We have sought a balanced approach which would be global in scope and reach and provide the flexibility necessary for, and the progressive extension of standards to, the smaller scale sector, as well as ensuring that the protection afforded to the larger vessels by current ILO instruments is retained and not eroded. This will also include covering "share fishers" – in other words the fishers remunerated by a share of the catch. We were also mindful that a number of existing ILO Conventions that cover seafarers contain explicit clauses that provide for their extension to the fisheries sector. These maritime Conventions contain important protections which are currently enjoyed by many fishers. Therefore, there is also a need to ensure that the adoption of the consolidated maritime Convention does not inadvertently result in the worsening of these fishers' conditions of work. The Workers' group also considers that for fishers, the adoption of a consolidated Convention provided an opportunity to bring the standards up to date, and to reflect both developments in the fisheries sector and the dynamic changes, such as technological advances.

The fishing sector has been formally designated as a hazardous industry by the ILO, and the occupational safety and health provisions will need to reflect this. There is also considerable evidence that there is a substantial decent work deficit in the sector, on both small-scale and larger vessels.

The issue of illegal, unreported and unregulated fishing has received a great deal of attention, and many measures have been developed by United Nations' bodies to counter it. The adoption by the ILO of the port State control provisions for the fishing sector may complement the work of other international organizations by providing another tool to counter this illegal unreported and unregulated fishing. It is worth noting that, during the proceedings in a fishing case before the International Tribunal for the Law of the Sea, an agent representing the Government of France mentioned "the deplorable conditions of the crew members on board the ships that had been arrested, with crew members often ill, badly nourished and living in unhygienic conditions close to slavery". That was the submission by an agent representing the Government of France before those proceedings.

There have been many other cases, reported and unreported, worldwide. In fact, during the Committee's first session it was reported that two fishers died on duty, and that gave a sense of urgency to all participants to make sure that they approach these proceedings with a sober mind. Therefore, the Workers' group believes that we have established a firm foundation for the second reading which will reflect the realities of the industry and provide the necessary balance between flexibility and the retention of current standards.

There is a considerable amount of work required to achieve the high expectations which have been placed upon us, and, as a result, a number of key issues have been held over and will be dealt with in the next reading.

Social security protection is fundamental to the ILO mandate and is rightly reflected in the Declaration of Philadelphia. However, Article 77 of the ILO flagship social security instrument, the Social Security (Minimum Standards) Convention, 1952 (No. 102), expressly excludes "sea fishermen", and this needs to be addressed through the fisheries Convention.

Consideration of the provisions addressing accommodation has been deferred. They are very technical in nature and it has been agreed that a mechanism will be developed by the Office to ensure that some progress will be made prior to the next session of the Conference. The adoption of modern accommodation standards is fundamental to securing decent work for those fishers who spend a considerable amount of time at sea.

The report reflects the outcome of a difficult meeting of heated but frank debate of the proceedings of the Committee, and we hope that the Conclusions agreed can be further developed at the next session, so that we will meet the high expectations the international community attaches to this work. The Workers' group would like to see the resulting Convention being widely ratified for it to make a real difference to many fishers in their workplaces and in their daily work across the world.

In other words, we want to achieve meaningful improvements in the working and living conditions of these 35 million fishers on board vessels all over the planet.

With this in mind, the Workers' group will recommend the adoption of the report, its Conclusions and the attached resolutions. We look forward to participating in the next session and hope that the spirit of tripartism that was also present in the Committee proceedings will prevail and that we will have a very successful outcome next session.

Original Portuguese: Mr. RIBEIRO LOPES *(Government delegate, Portugal; Chairperson of the Committee on the Fishing Sector)*

In addressing this sitting of the Conference, first and foremost, I would like to stress that, for my country and for myself, it has been a great privilege to hold the office of Chairman of the Committee on the Fishing Sector.

When, in March 2002, the Governing Body of the ILO decided to place work in the fishing sector on the agenda of the 92nd Session of the Conference, it was indeed recognizing the tremendous economic and social importance of fisheries in many countries throughout the world.

The fishing sector provides employment and a livelihood for a large percentage of the world's population and has a very diverse structure where you have, side by side, large national multinational enterprises with highly sophisticated ships and micro-enterprises of self-employed fishers who practice fishing in small traditional craft.

We know that the living and working conditions of fishers are also very diverse. Many fishers spend long periods at sea and, as far as they are concerned, accommodation and meals on board are real issues. At times, fishers are abandoned in foreign ports because the owner of the vessel has become bankrupt or simply absconded. On other occasions, fishers are detained by the authorities of foreign countries because they have been involved in unlawful fishing, for which the fishers themselves are not at all responsible. Sometimes, fishers are the victims of illegal recruiting methods and they are forced to sign contracts with conditions worse than those they were promised before they embarked. Fishing is an activity which gives rise to a large number of accidents. This is due to the risks involved in seafaring, in the use of fishing gear, and to the fatigue brought about by long working hours. Furthermore, traditional inspection methods have problems in inspecting and achieving compliance as regards working conditions and in particular as regards the security and health of fishers.

These and other aspects mean that it is both important and difficult to regulate work in the fishing sector.

Currently, there are seven standard-setting instruments of the ILO which are applicable specifically to the fishing sector. The mandate of our Committee is to prepare comprehensive standards, namely a Convention supplemented by a Recommendation, which will involve reviewing all the currently existing instruments and also considering other matters that are not catered for therein, in particular recruitment and repatriation of fishers, medical care on board, occupational safety and health and social security.

The Committee has considered these activities and the relevant instruments of other UN bodies, in particular those of the International Maritime Organization (IMO) and the Food and Agriculture Organization (FAO), so as to avoid contradictions or duplication between the standards of the various institutions.

The IMO has various standard-setting instruments which apply to the fisheries, in particular ones for safeguarding human life at sea, insuring of fishing vessels and training fishers, while the FAO adopted a code of Conduct for Responsible Fisheries which calls for all activities in the fishing sector to be carried out in safe, healthy and equitable conditions.

Apart from the Employers' and Workers' groups, 88 Government members took part in the Committee's work. Many of them are organized into regional groupings. The Committee Reporter, Mr. Boumbopoulos, Government member for Greece, submitted a very comprehensive report on the discussions held in the Committee and on the Committee's Conclusions. Furthermore, the Employer Vice-Chairperson, Mrs. Karikari Anang and the Worker Vice-Chairperson, Mr. Sand Morteuseu commented on the work of the Committee from the standpoint of the respective groups. These presentations provide an excellent introduction to the Committee's reports.

The draft Conclusions and the draft resolution, which aim to place the issue of work in the fishing sector on the agenda of the next session of the Conference and which we hope will be approved, will allow us to continue next year the work undertaken with a view to drawing up a new Convention supplemented by a Recommendation on work in the fishing sector.

We are all aware of the fact that the 2005 session of the Conference will have to debate and resolve very complex and controversial matters, in particular, the supplementary provisions relating to longer fishing vessels and accommodation on board. I have every confidence that it will continue to benefit from a spirit of constructive negotiation between the Employers' and Workers' groups and the Government delegates, and that will be possible to adopt a new Convention which will be both adequate and flexible enough to regulate the work of fishers on all vessels involved in commercial operations, and will open to ratification by many Members.

In conclusion, I would like to thank everyone who helped us get though our work in the Committee on the Fishing Sector, including the Employer and Worker Vice-Chairpersons who cooperated with me and gave me timely advice which assisted me greatly in directing the work of the Committee. The Reporter and the Drafting Committee worked in an outstanding fashion in preparing the report and the Conclusions; the Legal Adviser, Mr. Picard, helped the Committee in sorting out the tricky and complex legal problems involved in drafting some of the Conclusions. The Officers and all the secretariat were unstinting in providing information and advice to the Committee, and to me personally, and this assisted us greatly in our work. They also helped us in the preparation and translation of documents, which were always available on time and were of a high quality. Through Mrs. Doumbia-Henry, Head of the Sectoral Activities Department, I would like to thank everyone for their work.

Finally, I would like to thank the members of the Committee, Employer, Worker and Government members, for their efforts, their keenness, their spirit of cooperation and the competence they displayed.

Original Spanish: The PRESIDENT

The general discussion on the report of the Committee of the Fishing Sector is now open.

Mr. PENDER *(Government adviser and substitute delegate, Ireland; speaking on behalf of the European Union)*

Ireland, on behalf of the European Union, would like to thank the Committee for its efforts in advancing the revision of the seven ILO instruments concerning conditions of work in the fishing sector.

In particular, we would like to thank the Chairperson, Mr. Ribeiro Lopes, and the Vice-Chairpersons representing the social partners, namely, Mr. Peter Mortensen representing the Workers and Ms. Rose Karikari Anang representing the Employers, for their work during the two-week sitting of the Committee.

We would also like to thank Ms. Cleopatra Doumbia-Henry and the rest of the ILO personnel who attended and advised the Committee during our deliberations. We also compliment the interpreters for their patience and stamina over the period.

In addition, we would like to thank all of our European Union colleagues, and all our colleagues from attending member States across the world.

We made significant progress during our two-week sitting and agreement was reached on substantial sections of the text. Some issues, such as those included in the proposed Annex II, regarding Accommodation on Fishing Vessels, will not be discussed in detail until next year's session of the Conference.

We note that there was division between the social partners in respect of further consideration of the application of standards to fishing vessels of over a certain size.

We note that the comprehensive standard will be further deliberated at next year's Conference and we hope that a successful conclusion will improve the living and working conditions of fishers worldwide.

Mr. POTTER *(Employers' delegate, United States)*

I am presenting these comments today on behalf of Ms. Tammy French, Vice-President of the American Seafoods Company, who was the United States Employers' adviser on the fishing discussion and who unfortunately was not able to be here because of work and family responsibilities. These are her words.

As I look back on our tripartite discussions and negotiations for standard setting in the fishing sector I have to wonder: Were we all in the same boat?

The Employers' group approached its work with a view to the following general principles.

First, to develop minimum labour standards for the protection of the greatest number of fishers worldwide, taking into account the social and economic realities of fishers in developed and developing countries.

Second, to develop an instrument with the flexibility to motivate widespread ratification and to address, in particular, the vast majority of fishers working on smaller vessels who are at present afforded little, if any, protection with regard to safety and health owing, among other things, to lack of political or economic power or government resources.

Third, to ensure against erosion of such existing higher standards as may be provided under national laws and practice for fishers employed in larger operations and/or in developed countries.

The clear majority of Government representatives voiced agreement with the Employers' approach to the development of the Convention and spoke out against the Worker members, early initiative to, first, introduce the concept of a multi-tiered Convention with separate requirements for fishers working aboard vessels of various lengths; and, second, to link the fishing Convention to an instrument as yet in the development stage geared toward working conditions of seafarers.

With the paradigm agreed upon, Employers worked towards amending the Office text to remove overly prescriptive requirements which likely caused low ratification of earlier fishing Conventions for the last 40 years.

The goal of establishing "minimum standards" seemed to get misplaced at times, as the in the case of requirement for medical certifications. While it is a laudable idea for the protection of fishers and a strategic risk management strategy for employers, it would seem impractical in light of the costs of such examinations and the lack of medical services in many underserved areas of the world.

The inherent risks and hazards of work in the fishing industry cannot be denied and it can seem an indefensible position to argue against medical certifications, work agreements in the languages understandable to all fishers on board, mandatory hours of rest, and so forth. However, the opportunity to dramatically improve conditions for the majority of the world's fishers would be lost if our work towards creating a widely adoptable Convention becomes mired in rigid, dogmatic ideals that forestall implementation and ratification.

The final tripartite meeting of our session concluded with the Worker members' reintroduction of vessel classifications by length. To our surprise, Governments unanimously allowed the amendment to carry into the 2005 session in contradiction to their earlier stated position.

For the next session, I would urge the tripartite participants to take a position early in the Conference with respect to the basic scope of the Convention.

These fundamental principles from the basis of decisions and negotiations that guide our work towards a common purpose.

Original Spanish: The PRESIDENT

As there are no further speakers, I propose that we proceed with the approval of the report of the Committee, which is contained in paragraphs 1-789. If there are no objections, may I take it that the report is approved?

(The report – paragraphs 1-789 – is approved.)

We shall now proceed with the adoption of the proposed Conclusions concerning the fishing sector.

(The Conclusions – paragraphs 1-83 – are adopted.)

If there are no objections, may I take it that the Conclusions concerning the fishing sector are adopted.

(The Conclusions are adopted.)

We shall now proceed to the adoption of the report as a whole. As there are no objections, I take it that the report, as a whole, is adopted.

(The report, as a whole, is adopted.)

RESOLUTION TO PLACE ON THE AGENDA OF THE NEXT ORDINARY SESSION OF THE CONFERENCE AN ITEM ENTITLED "WORK IN THE FISHING SECTOR": ADOPTION

Original Spanish: The PRESIDENT

We shall now proceed with the adoption of the resolution to place on the agenda of the next ordinary session of the Conference an item entitled "Work in the fishing sector". If there are no objections, may I take it that the resolution is adopted?

(The resolution is adopted.)

We have now concluded the consideration of the report of the Committee on the Fishing Sector. I would like to warmly thank the Committee, Officers and members, as well as the secretariat and staff, for their excellent work.

RECORD VOTE ON THE RESOLUTION CONCERNING THE ARREARS OF CONTRIBUTIONS OF IRAQ

Original Spanish: The PRESIDENT

We shall now conduct the record vote on the resolutions concerning the arrears of contributions of Iraq, which is contained in *Provisional Record* No. 17.

With respect to the substance of the vote, may I remind you that, in accordance with article 13, paragraph 4, of the ILO Constitution, the Conference may, by a two-thirds majority of the votes cast by the delegates present, permit such a Member, who is in arrears in the payment of its contributions, to vote if it is satisfied that the failure to pay is due to conditions beyond the control of the Member. Article 19, paragraph 5, of the Standing Orders of the International Labour Conference requires a record vote to be taken in this case.

(A record vote is taken.)

(The detailed results of the vote will be found at the end of this sitting.)

Original Spanish: The PRESIDENT

The result of the vote is as follows: 421 votes in favour, 12 against, with 12 abstentions. As the quorum was 286, and the required two-thirds majority of 297 has been reached, the resolution concerning the arrears of contributions of Iraq is adopted.

(The resolution is adopted.)

RECORD VOTE ON THE RESOLUTION CONCERNING THE ARREARS OF CONTRIBUTION OF PARAGUAY

Original Spanish: The PRESIDENT

We shall now conduct the record vote on the resolution of Paraguay, which is contained in *Provisional Record* No 17.

(A record vote is taken.)

(The detailed results of the vote will be found at the end of the record of this sitting.)

The result of the vote is as follows: 419 votes in favour, 11 against, with 15 abstentions. As the quorum was 286, and the required two-thirds majority of 297 has been reached, the resolution concerning the arrears of contributions of Paraguay is adopted.

(The resolution is adopted.)

FINAL RECORD VOTE ON THE WITHDRAWAL OF 16 RECOMMENDATIONS

Original Spanish: The PRESIDENT

We shall now conduct the record vote on the withdrawal of 16 Recommendations, which is contained in *Provisional Record* No. 4-2A and involves Recommendations Nos. 2, 12, 16, 18, 21, 26, 32, 33, 34, 36, 43, 46, 58, 70, 74 and 96. There will be a single vote, after which delegates will be entitled to make any explanations they wish on their vote.

(A record vote is taken.)

(The detailed results of the vote will be found at the end of the record of this sitting.)

The result of the vote is as follows: 437 votes in favour, one against, with no abstentions. As the quorum was 290, and the required two-thirds majority of 292 has been reached, the withdrawal of 16 Recommendations is adopted.

(The withdrawal of 16 Recommendations is adopted.)

(The Conference adjourned at 12.45 p.m.)

Nineteenth sitting

Wednesday, 16 June 2004, 3 p.m.

President: Mr. Ray Guevara

REPORT OF THE COMMITTEE ON HUMAN RESOURCES:
SUBMISSION, DISCUSSION AND APPROVAL

Original Spanish: The PRESIDENT

We shall now proceed to the examination of the report of the Committee on Human Resources, which is published in *Provisional Record* No. 20.

The Officers of the Committee were as follows: the Chairperson was Mr. Chetwin, the Employer Vice-Chairperson was Mr. Renique, the Worker Vice-Chairperson was Ms. Yacob and the Reporter was Ms. Murty. I would now like to call upon Ms. Murty to submit the report of the Committee on Human Resources.

Ms. MURTY (*Government adviser, India; Reporter of the Committee on Human Resources*)

I am very pleased to be able to present to you today the revised Recommendation concerning human resources development: education, training and lifelong learning and the Report of the second discussion of the Committee on Human Resources which finalized this important ILO instrument. The work of the Committee was steered by its most competent and able Chairperson, Mr Chetwin, Government member of New Zealand. His leadership, grasp of the subject matter and pleasant manner, tinted with a great sense of humour, were instrumental in helping the Committee to complete its tasks in a spirit of respect and dialogue between the social partners.

Equally valuable to the final outcome of the work of the Committee were the efforts to find common ground by the Employer Vice-Chairperson, Mr. Renique of the Netherlands, and the Worker Vice-Chairperson, Ms. Yacob of Singapore.

I would also like to thank our Committee's secretariat, which worked very efficiently under the guidance of Mr. Henriques, the representative of the Secretary-General, for their dedication, commitment and assistance. The advice of the Legal Adviser was indispensable for completing the Committee's work, particularly for overseeing the final drafting of the instrument.

The Committee held 15 sittings. Its report, including the revised Recommendation concerning human resources development: education, training and lifelong learning, was distributed to the plenary sitting this morning.

Economies, society and the world of work have been transformed beyond recognition since 1975 when the International Labour Conference adopted the Human Resources Development Convention, 1975 (No. 142) and its accompanying Human Resources Development Recommendation, 1975 (No. 150). In view of these changes, in 2001 the Governing Body decided to include on the agenda of the 91st Session of the International Labour Conference, that is last year, a first discussion of an item on human resources development and training, with a view to adopting a revised, more dynamic standard in 2004 that would assist member States and the social partners to formulate and implement human resources development and training policies to promote sustainable economic and employment growth and decent work for all.

The Recommendation concerning human resources development: education, training and lifelong learning, 2004, is a broad and comprehensive ILO labour standard. It reflects the social partners' efforts to develop an instrument that is balanced and responsive to present and emerging challenges and that places people at the centre of economic and social development.

The Preamble sets forth the core principles contained in the instrument, namely:

– that education, training and lifelong learning contribute significantly to promoting the interests of people, enterprises, the economy and society as a whole;

– that lifelong learning also contributes to personal development, access to culture and active citizenship;

– that the social partners have roles to play and commitments to fulfil in support of lifelong learning;

– that many developing countries should receive assistance to design, fund and implement education and training policies for economic and employment growth;

– and that the realization of decent work for workers everywhere is a primary objective of the International Labour Organization.

The ILO's values are reflected in these principles. Hence, the Preamble refers to the ILO Declaration on Fundamental Principles and Rights at Work and to essential Conventions and Recommendations concerning human resources development and training.

The instrument defines, for the first time in an ILO instrument, the key concepts of employability and lifelong learning.

The instrument calls on member States to set out ambitious guidelines, based on social dialogue, for the development and implementation of education, training and lifelong learning policies which promote lifelong employability. It emphasizes that education, training and lifelong learning policies must be an integral part of comprehensive economic, social and labour market policies and programmes for economic and employment growth. It urges member States to take up the challenge of transforming, including through education and training, activities in the informal economy and to integrate them into mainstream economic life. The instrument highlights the paramount importance of initial education, literacy and foundation skills, as well as lifelong learning, for the employability of individuals, and the need to recognize skills acquired formally and informally, irrespective of where and how they were acquired.

In this context, member States are called to establish, in consultation with the social partners, transparent mechanisms for skills assessment, certification and recognition that will ensure that skills are portable across enterprises, industries and educational institutions.

Of particular significance is the instrument's recognition that education and training are a right for all people. It recognizes that ensuring access to education, training and lifelong learning for people with special needs will be a powerful tool in their economic and social emancipation. The instrument identifies these groups. They include youth, low-skilled people, people who have disabilities, migrants, older workers, indigenous people, ethnic minority groups and the socially excluded. They also comprise workers in self-employment and in the rural sector. The instrument recognizes that governments have the primary responsibility for the training of these groups. The promotion of equal education and training opportunities for women and men, and overcoming gender bias, is also a firmly supported principle in the instrument.

Tackling the severe problems of the most indebted developing countries was also a major concern for the Committee. The revised instrument calls for innovative approaches to raising additional funds for education, training and lifelong learning to assist these countries.

The instrument also highlights the crucial role of teachers and trainers; the usefulness of information and communication technology; infrastructure and tools; the need to learn from examples of best practices; and the contribution of tripartite dialogue in shaping effective policies and developing relevant programmes on human resources development and training. The instrument introduces a reference to the increasingly significant role that enterprises play in enhancing investment in training and in providing workplace-based learning and training programmes – for example, by using high-performance practices that improve skills. Member States are urged to formally recognize such learning, including formal and non-formal learning, and work experience. The Recommendation makes timely provision for international and technical cooperation on education, training and lifelong learning. The sharing of technical expertise, international best practice models, financial assistance and other forms of cooperation are, indeed, indispensable to building national capacities in support of human resources development and training.

There is also a call to establish international mechanisms that mitigate the adverse impact on developing countries of the loss of skilled people through migration. Such mechanisms would include strategies to strengthen the human resources development systems in the countries of origin.

Putting into practice education, training and lifelong learning policies that reach out to all people will be a formidable undertaking in all countries, both rich and poor. Nevertheless, I am convinced that the Recommendation concerning human resources development and training will be a great asset in this endeavour as member States and the social partners join together in addressing these issues that are crucial to the well-being of our societies.

I take great pride in recommending to the Conference the adoption of the report, including the revised instrument presented by the Committee on Human Resource

Mr. RENIQUE *(Employers' technical adviser and substitute delegate, Netherlands; Employer Vice-Chairperson of the Committee on Human Resources)*

It is a great honour for me to present the Employers' view of the conclusions of the Committee on Human Resources.

This revision of Recommendation No. 150 is timely. The existing Recommendation dating from 1975 only deals with vocational education and vocational guidance. It was strongly based on the idea of good job descriptions, translating these into vocational education and, through guidance, guaranteeing that the right person got the right post.

Now, 30 years later, we still, of course, need good matches between education and the labour market. However, it is clear that vocational qualifications are no longer good for a lifetime. The dynamics of the labour market are accelerating. Core vocational competence related to professional skills is needed but, at the same time, employees need to be prepared for lifelong learning. The revised text captures this new concept well. To begin with, we broadened the scope of the instrument to the whole of lifelong learning, from basic education to further training during a career. We also introduced the concept of employability. The development and portability of competencies and qualifications are as important for employees, since they secure work and enable mobility, as they are for companies since they make it possible to meet the needs of the enterprise.

We also introduced new instruments like assessment of prior learning and the use of a national qualification framework. The whole of lifelong learning is facilitated by the recognition that education and training are a right for all. This is a lofty ambition, but in the present knowledge societies we should not go for less. To work towards access to lifelong learning, we explicitly spell out what the commitments of the three partners are: for governments, to invest and create the conditions to enhance education at all levels; for enterprises to train their employees, and for individuals to develop their competence and careers.

This part of the debate was one of the most important and interesting for several reasons. First of all, it is important to make it quite clear that the implementation of the concept of lifelong learning is a task that really needs the cooperation of the three partners, each of which has its own area of responsibility.

Secondly, and this is a new element that did not exist in the old Recommendation, there is now a clear appeal to the commitment of the individual himself. Let there be no misunderstandings. As I said, Employers feel committed to facilitating agreed learning activities that meet individual needs and the needs of the enterprise, but the employees themselves can take initiatives and put some effort into their own personal development, for example, in the light of current needs in their present job or of ambitions for mobility within the enterprise. So, we Employers deliver, so to speak, bricks and mortar, but the individual of this millennium is becoming the architect and builder, responsible for developing his or her own skills.

Thirdly, this was a very good example of consensus building. We explained our own concern that we should be clear about responsibilities and mainly use existing paragraphs, but that they should be placed in a different order to highlight the fact that the lofty ambitions called for commitment on the part of all three partners. We succeeded in reaching a full consensus. I consider this to be one of the main results of this year's session of the Conference and I am very grateful to the Workers' group and the Government group for achieving this solution.

Besides the introduction of the concept of lifelong learning, the new Recommendation is much too rich for me to be able to mention every substantial improvement, but allow me to mention a selection of some items. What we appreciate very much is the balanced attention paid in the instrument to the economic as well as the social aspects of human resource development. The instrument talks as much about sustainable economic growth, as about social development and social inclusion. We point out that education and training policies should be consistent with, among other things, economic and fiscal policies. We talk about creating economic growth, as well as jobs. We, furthermore, also appreciate the attention given to entrepreneurship. This was completely lacking back in 1975.

We are particularly grateful to the African group of governments, which contributed a great deal to this discussion, and we fully agree that while the development of entrepreneurial skills is important in every country, it plays a particularly important role in the developing countries as a basis for growth and jobs. The fact that developing countries clearly acknowledge the importance of entrepreneurship, is perhaps just another example of the need to monitor both the economic and social aspects of human resources development.

With regard to developing countries themselves, there have been two important improvements, since the first discussion of the item last year. Where we failed last year, we have now managed to include a paragraph that focuses special attention on the problems of indebted developing countries and makes an appeal for innovative approaches to provide additional resources for human resources development. We were also able to agree on a paragraph that addresses the problem of the brain drain in developing countries.

On a more technical note, I should also like to mention that members showed good will to streamline last year's text. Several adjustments were made to make the whole text clearer and easier to read, to reduce redundancies and to make it more logical in structure. We agree with those governments that expressed concern that maybe we could have done even better, but nevertheless major improvements were made and we thank the Governments and the Workers' group for making this possible.

One of our own innocent efforts to streamline the text, however, turned into a real drama. I refer to our amendment merging former clause 5(i) and former Paragraph 7, both of which dealt with the issue of social dialogue from the international to the enterprise levels. After an amendment by the MERCOSUR countries adding the words "and collective bargaining" after the words "social dialogue", however, the meaning of the new text changed completely. Instead of focusing on the promotion of social dialogue on training, we suddenly found ourselves in a debate on collective bargaining on training and the role of governments in promoting this at all levels, in other words from the international to the enterprise levels. This proposal was and remains completely unacceptable for us. Although the procedure was correct, and therefore, in the formal sense, the report could be adopted, it fails by a long way to reflect the spirit that has been shown on many other occasions. In important cases in particular and in cases where there has been a division of opinion, not only between Workers and Employers but also among Governments, there has always been some willingness to find a formulation that was agreeable to all parties. The aforementioned issue of the right to education and training is a very good example of that spirit. With regard to this issue of collective bargaining, such efforts were certainly also made at the bipartite and tripartite levels, up until just before this meeting. We really have appreciated this. Although we did, indeed, make some progress, we could not agree on this crucial issue of levels. I will not go into detail, but will inform you about what was essential and non-negotiable for us, namely that it is not for governments but only for the social partners themselves to decide at which level they wish to engage in collective bargaining on training. There was broad support for this principle, also at the informal tripartite meeting that was held to find a solution. We are amazed and highly disappointed that none of our proposals to refer to this principle explicitly in the new clause 5(f) were accepted. Given this situation, we continue to disagree strongly with the present clause 5(f).

Let me add that, in general, it is very disappointing that a discussion on an issue that could have been raised in the context of a discussion on an ILO instrument on collective bargaining, has now in fact been introduced as a kind of Trojan horse in a discussion on an instrument on human resources development and even seems to have overruled the whole of Troy, as in the famous Greek myth.

But to conclude in a positive way, let me repeat that, except for the paragraph I have just mentioned, we find the new text a huge improvement on the existing Recommendation. Many stand to benefit from this new Recommendation: those in education and pre-employment training, workers, unemployed people, groups with special needs and developing countries. It is also beneficial for enterprises and economic growth, and beneficial in terms of improving employability and promoting secure work.

We thank the Workers' group, lead by Ms. Yacob, and the Governments for the fruitful discussions we had and the many good solutions that we found, in a spirit of consensus. I also thank the Chairperson, who did his utmost to bring the voyage to a good end. He sometimes must have felt like a captain ten seconds before the inevitable collision with an iceberg. I thank the Reporter, Ms. Murty, and the Office team led by Mr. Henriques, and welcome the support of the International Organisation of Employers and the Bureau for Employers Activities. Last, but not least, I thank the members of the Employers' group in the Committee on Human Resources, who shared their rich experiences and views on which my group was able to base its proposals.

Ms. YACOB *(Workers' delegate, Singapore; Worker Vice-Chairperson of the Committee on Human Resources)*

The Workers' group strongly supports the revision of Recommendation No. 150 and its replacement by this Recommendation. Human resources development, education, training and lifelong learning are of immeasurable importance to people all over the world. The right to education and training and to access to lifelong learning is a universal right that has been recognized not only in the ILO but also in other international forums as well. Human resources development is so critical that it cannot be relegated to a secondary status or left to chance without clear leadership from policy-makers and international agencies such as the ILO.

The situation facing us is indeed grave, and there is an urgent need for us to focus on the subject at all levels – a word that has become quite an impossible term in this house, I must say – in our own countries as well as at the international level. If we do not do this, we will never be able to combat social exclusion, poverty or illiteracy. The income gap will continue to widen between rich and poor, both between countries and within countries. All efforts to create a more humane globalization process will remain just a hope, despite the recent adoption by the ILO of the report of the World Commission report on the Social Dimension of Globalization.

We are living in a knowledge society where information can be transmitted just by pushing a button. Despite this, 884 million adults around the world are illiterate, unable to operate effectively even with the tools of the "old economy". UNESCO estimates that, in the least developed countries, while 144 million adults were illiterate in 1985, this figure will rise to 188 million by 2005. In other words, the number of illiterate adults will grow by 30 per cent in the least developed countries. Despite the fact that these countries are very rich in natural resources, with their low education and skill levels, many developing countries are not able to add much value to the products that they export and are therefore not able to optimize the use of their resources.

Indeed, even for highly industrialized economies, the training of their adult workforce is a matter of great urgency and priority. In the year 2000, more than 80 per cent of the economically active adults in the OECD countries were in work and would continue to work for a good number of years after that. The frightening part, though, for the OECD, is that a large part of the workforce of those countries left school with only the minimum school qualifications and the majority do not receive systematic adult education or retraining after that.

This is a serious situation as it will contribute to the increasing problem of structural unemployment in the OECD: that is, even when jobs are available, those who are unemployed cannot perform them because they lack the skills to do so.

In 1999, the G8, a group of eight industrialized countries, adopted the Cologne Charter: Aims and Ambitions for Lifelong Learning. The preamble of the Charter makes this statement.

"The challenge every country faces is how to become a learning society and to ensure its citizens are equipped with the knowledge, skills and qualifications they will need in the next century. Economies and societies are increasingly knowledge based. Education and skills are indispensable to achieving economic success, civic responsibility and social cohesion."

That statement very aptly captures the importance and relevance of this Recommendation on human resources development, education, training and lifelong learning that we are discussing at this plenary session and which we will be voting on tomorrow.

The adoption of this instrument will enable the ILO, as a tripartite international agency, to look proactively into ways to help countries develop policies, strategies and programmes to develop their people. Through this instrument, the ILO could lead international cooperation to build up capacities for social dialogue and partnership-building in training. Hence, this Recommendation on human resources development that is before you is a very important instrument for all countries, regardless of their level of development. It is a dynamic, progressive and balanced instrument that will act as a powerful tool in helping governments to shape their policies on human resources development and will guide the social partners in their involvement.

We recognize that this Recommendation is not a solution in itself. A highly developed human resources development system alone is not the panacea to all ills, and cannot by itself create jobs or ensure higher economic growth. For that to happen, as this Recommendation stresses, there must be policy coherence. Hence, under section "Part I: "Objective, scope and definitions", the Recommendation categorically states that it is important for member States to ensure that they formulate, apply and review national human resources development policies which are consistent with economic, fiscal and social policies.

Since human development is so important, Paragraph 4(a) of this Recommendation boldly reaffirms, as a clear commitment, goal and vision, that education and training are a right for all and governments should, in cooperation with the social partners, work towards ensuring access for all to lifelong learning. We recognize that not all governments have the same level of resources to commit themselves to the same extent, and that is not the intention of this Recommendation. However, the starting point is that governments as a whole need to invest more in education and training and to accord education and training higher priority. Indeed for many individuals and small companies, action by government is the key to enabling them to participate in this process in any way at all, since their immediate perspectives and potential seldom allow them to have longer term or more comprehensive ambitions.

The human resources Recommendation also clearly recognizes the responsibility of enterprises to train their employees and that of individuals to develop their competencies and careers. This clear, specific recognition of and emphasis on the responsibilities of enterprises and the individual is important. Indeed, enterprises have a responsibility to invest in training their employees, for they benefit from a well-trained and skilled workforce. Today, when most companies can no longer provide lifelong employment, they must help to add value to their employees by training them so that they will remain relevant in the face of rapid technological changes and have the skills to look for other jobs when they are retrenched. This is the whole essence of employability, which is for the first time defined in an international instrument, and which is a thread that runs throughout many of the provisions in the instrument.

In this respect the notion of collective bargaining which is included in the text, is a progressive and innovative clause. Many multinational enterprises are already providing training programmes for their employees. A clear case in point is that of Danone, a French food manufacturing company famous for its yoghurt. Some of you may have eaten it every day in Switzerland – it is very widely available! Danone has an agreement on training with the International Union of Food, Agricultural, Hotel, Restaurant, Catering, Tobacco and Allied Workers' Associations (IUF), which applies to its employees worldwide. This global agreement provides for the training of its workers, wherever they may be. Such global agreements have obviously yielded benefits for enterprises such as Danone, as it helps them to develop their staff's competencies, wherever they may be, according to the standards that are required by them, and this also helps them in improving the transferability of their employees from country to country.

Collective bargaining on training is also important for other reasons. Often we hear complaints from workers that the training provided to them is insufficient because the area of training is too narrow, or the methods are ineffective, or that the resources allocated to low-skilled or older workers are not sufficient compared with those allocated to better-skilled or better-educated workers. Through collective bargaining these issues can be addressed. We can ensure that enterprises allocate enough resources for training, that there is greater equity in the utilization and distribution of training resources and that training programmes are relevant to the needs of workers. For this reason, there is a reference to the need for governments to strengthen social dialogue and collective bargaining on training.

Since this is a point that has also been mentioned by the Chairperson of the Employers' group, I would like to assure all governments present here that the government's role on this particular clause is only to support and facilitate collective bargaining on training, not to be a direct party to it. Governments can support collective bargaining on training as they have has done in other areas, through the formulation of policies, for instance, or by providing a proper framework for the resolution of disputes, for instance.

As you can see, we have 22 Paragraphs in the whole Recommendation, and there is only one that talks about collective bargaining on training. One Paragraph. As someone calculated yesterday, that comprises only about maybe 1 per cent, or 1.3 per cent of the whole text of the Recommendation. But, for the reasons that we mentioned, collective bargaining was included, and it is an important instrument for us to ensure proper, effective utilization of training resources and equity down at enterprise level, as well as to ensure that training is not something that is only undertaken by governments – as there are not many governments with a huge amount of resources to be able to provide training – or provided for people who are already in employment.

Another important aspect of this instrument is the fairly extensive references made to the informal sector. The Recommendation acknowledges that there are many countries where the informal sector occupies a much bigger space than the formal sector – in some African countries almost 90 per cent. Hence, the Recommendation recognizes the need to address the concerns of such countries. The Recommendation focuses on the challenge of transforming activities in the informal economy into decent work, fully integrated into mainstream economic life. The Recommendation recognizes the need to develop the skills and capabilities of individuals in the informal sector so that they may move into the formal sector. At the same time, the Recommendation also recognizes that in many developing countries it may be too limited to focus on education and training only as a means to prepare people for salaried employment or jobs in the mainstream economy.

There is also a need to help people acquire entrepreneurial skills so that they can earn an income and support themselves and their families. Hence, the Recommendation calls for support and assistance to be given to individuals through education and training and other policies and programmes, so that they can develop and apply entrepreneurial skills to create decent work for themselves and others.

Creating decent jobs, poverty eradication and sustainable development are key outcomes of education, training and lifelong learning which resonate throughout the whole Recommendation. The Recommendation recognizes that developing countries with massive debt problems need special help in order to develop their human resources and achieve these key outcomes. The Recommendation therefore provides that international and technical cooperation on human resources development, education and training should, taking into account the specific problems of indebted developing countries, explore and apply innovative approaches to provide additional resources for human resources development. In this way, the international community could help to mobilize resources to help developing countries to design, fund and implement modern education and training policies, which are prerequisites for development and economic growth.

This was one of the more difficult clauses that we had to negotiate with all the members of the Committee. If there are members of the Committee on Human Resources seated here, you will understand what I am trying to say. This was one of the more difficult clauses that we had to negotiate. At one stage, we had to call for a short adjournment to discuss the matter with both developed and developing countries. With social dialogue and consensus, although in the beginning when we discussed this particular issue there was no consensus, we asked for an adjournment and we had a discussion with both developed and the developing countries and, as a result of that short adjournment and discussion, we were able to stave off a formal vote on this issue. The Committee could count on consensus and this particular clause which was difficult was actually adopted by consensus without the need for a formal vote. We, in the Workers' group, are extremely happy that we were part of that process of trying to help Governments and Workers and Employers come to a satisfactory consensus on this particularly difficult clause.

Developing countries also face another serious challenge. Whatever limited resources they have, which are used to help their people develop, flow out of the country when people, lured by better jobs and prospects, move elsewhere. Hence, the Recommendation – and this is a new point as well – provides that, through international cooperation on human resources development, mechanisms should be developed to mitigate the adverse impact on developing countries of the loss of skilled people through migration, including strategies to strengthen human resources development systems in the countries of origin. At the same time, it also recognizes that creating enabling conditions for economic growth, investment, creation of decent jobs and human development will have a positive effect on retaining skilled labour.

One of the greatest barriers in workers' efforts to gain access to education and training opportunities is the lack of effective social policies and structures to support them when they undergo training, such as the lack of paid education leave, child-care facilities and the difficulties of balancing work and family demands. We are indeed most happy that, to address this concern, the Recommendation stresses the need for members to promote supportive policies to enable individuals to balance their work, family and lifelong learning interests. This is a truly progressive clause and is a clear recognition of the need to balance work, with the needs of individuals and society.

Another point of great importance to the Workers' group is the strong commitment expressed in the Recommendation to remove all forms of discrimination, whether on the basis of gender, age, ethnic group, special disabilities that people may have, or other factors, so that truly everyone can have access to education, training and lifelong learning.

It would not be complete if I did not say something about the point raised by Mr. Renique, the Employer Vice-Chairperson of the Committee. I must say, at the outset, there was no intent to introduce a Trojan horse. The debate that we have heard today has probably been somewhat influenced by the film "Troy" that is being shown. It is an American film involving very famous actors and actresses. I have not seen it myself but I remember reading about the story of Troy when I was in primary school.

Those of you who are in the Committee on Human Resources know that the matter which Mr. Renique spoke of, concerning the inclusion of collective bargaining under clause 5(f), was voted upon by the Committee at the request of the Employers' group. I have to say that again. A formal vote was requested on this social point for by the Employers. It was not something that was requested by the Workers' group or by the Governments, but we personally felt, at that point in time, that there should have been longer discussions in order for us to be able to forge a more broad-based consensus on the topic. Unfortunately, a vote was called for by the Employers' group on this issue. The result of the formal vote required by the Employers was in favour of including the words "collective bargaining" in that particular clause. We were, of course, shocked when the Employers challenged the decision taken, on the grounds that there was no consensus, despite the fact that they were the ones that had called for the vote. To the Workers, a vote, once taken, must be respected, as otherwise we run the risk of seriously undermining the decision-making process of the ILO. There will be no finality and any decision taken can be reopened ad infinitum. This will create an unhealthy and dangerous precedent and the repercussions go far beyond the Committee on Human Resources. Despite this agonizing dilemma that we were faced with, that is the fundamental importance of upholding the decision-making process of the ILO, and the implications that this will have if we agree to reopen a clause that has been voted on through a formal vote and how this will impact not only on our Committee but on the work of other committees, how will it impact on the future decision-making processes of the ILO. We nevertheless accepted, in good faith and in the spirit of social dialogue, the Employers' invitation for formal consultations to find alternative wordings for that clause. No agreement was reached, and subsequently we accepted the suggestion Mr. John Chetwin, the Chairperson of the Committee, that we involve the Governments to help us. We spent more than three hours last Thursday night with six Government representatives from the various regions to find a form of wording for us to consider. Indeed, a form of wording was agreed on, and the Governments requested both the Workers and Employers to consider them. The Workers' group discussed and supported the wording that was agreed at the tripartite consultations. We were shocked when, for the second time, the Employers rejected even the wording which had been negotiated with the Governments. As a way out of the impasse, the Governments of France and the United Kingdom then submitted an amendment to the Chairperson of the Committee on Human Resources for discussion during the adoption of the report by the Committee on Monday. The amendment was in line with the consensus reached at the tripartite consultation. This form of wording would have greatly clarified the Governments' role in the context of that clause but, unfortunately, the Employers did not join the consensus, and therefore the Chairperson of the Committee on Human Resources could not table it. This resulted in the original text being adopted, which is the one before you. It is most regrettable that we have reached this state of affairs and that the wishes of both the Governments and the Workers have been ignored. Last Monday, when we discussed the adoption of this text, even the Governments, in particular the Government of France, and this is reflected in the provisional record of proceedings of the Committee on Human Resources, agreed that the Workers' group had made great concessions to reach an acceptable text.

Many hours of work have been spent in preparing this Recommendation. In fact, I was told that preparation started five years ago. It is a good instrument – balanced, progressive and dynamic. It is indeed a great pity that this instrument will now be demolished because of one Paragraph out of the entire text of 22 Paragraphs and because of two words, "collective bargaining", which is one of the fundamental rights which the ILO has collectively agreed to uphold and honour. It is also a great pity for us if we allow the status of the formal vote to be reduced to nothing because one group cannot agree and wants to impose its will on others.

In conclusion, I would like to say that we in the Workers' group, throughout the two years that we deliberated on and discussed the text of this Recommendation, have shown tremendous efforts and capacity to try and reach consensus, even on issues where we felt we could asked for a formal vote and win but did not do so. We prefer to find a consensus where we ask for adjournments and discussions, so that everyone can live with the text.

If you ask me what are my feelings right now, I must say that I am tremendously saddened by this development, and I really do hope that these whole proceedings will not be bogged down by this one particular issue alone.

I ask that you go beyond the polemics. I ask that you think of the interests of the millions of men and women whom you represent and to whom we owe an obligation. I ask that you place their welfare as the paramount consideration in your decision tomorrow when you vote. I ask therefore that you support this Recommendation and that you do so not only by of giving us your votes, but also by giving us your overwhelming support.

The ILO is an Organization dedicated to improving the lives of working people. I ask for your support to uphold its dignity and the dignity of all people around the world. I ask also that you support the dignity of the decision-making process of the ILO. We have made every effort to come to an agreement and consensus, but unfortunately we have not been able to do so because the wordings that have been agreed by the Governments and us were not accepted by the Employers.

It would really be remiss of me to end without thanking several people who have worked very hard to put together the work of this Committee.

I would first of all like to thank the Chairperson of the Committee on Human Resources, Mr. John Chetwin, for his stewardship of our Committee. He has shown great skill and tremendous patience throughout the whole period. I want to thank the Office for the great work that it has done in preparing the documents and for the secretariat support it has have provided. My heartfelt thanks also go to all the other members of the Committee, in particular the members of the Workers' group on the Committee, for their tremendous support, encouragement, hard work and dedication. I would also like to thank all members of the Governments. I think we have had some pretty difficult clauses, and difficult periods during the work of the Committee, I think that all of you did your utmost to try and help find a solution and for that I thank you. That was truly in the spirit of ILO social dialogue and tripartism. My gratitude also goes to my team who supported me, Mr. Frank Hoffer and Ms. Len Olsen from the Bureau for Workers' Activities and Ms. Yvonne O'Callaghan from the International Confederation of Free Trade Unions, for their support and commitment.

Mr. CHETWIN *(Government adviser, New Zealand; Chairperson of the Committee on Human Resources)*

I have had the honour and challenge of chairing both discussions of the Committee on Human Resources. I was also Reporter of the committee that held a general discussion on this question at the 88th Session of the International Labour Conference in 2000. If that has given me a biased perspective on the value of this work, I do not apologize.

Human resource development and training have the potential for much good: in equipping people to enter the world of work and participate actively in society; in facilitating lifelong employability in ways that enable people to progress and adapt; in creating decent jobs, improving productivity and contributing to thriving, competitive enterprises; in supporting the achievement of sustainable economic and social development; and in promoting social inclusion and poverty reduction.

The challenge the Committee was given by the Governing Body was to develop a more dynamic instrument that would assist member States and the social partners to formulate human resource development policies for the future. I believe we have done that. Our aim this year was to build on the good work done in 2003 and in the intervening period: to refine and clarify rather than revisit issues that had already been debated extensively. Some would argue that the proposed Recommendation is not as streamlined or succinct as it could have been, and they may have a point. But I believe the Committee did well within the constraints of its process, and certainly the structure of the document is much improved.

I shall not cover the substance of the proposed Recommendation, which has already been summarized so ably by the Reporter of the Committee, Ms. Asha Murty. I shall, however, touch on some points I believe to be of particular significance.

As well as building on the important ideas developed last year – employability, lifelong learning, the roles and responsibilities of the parties, frameworks for the recognition of competencies whenever and wherever acquired, provision of equal opportunities for women and men, and access for people with identified special needs – some new ideas have been introduced. Three of special significance: are the role of training and developing entrepreneurial skills, the impact of the loss of skilled people on developing countries and specific problems facing indebted developing countries.

In tackling its task again this year, the Committee was greatly assisted by two enthusiastic, committed and knowledgeable Vice-Chairpersons, Mr. Chiel Renique for the Employers' group and Ms. Halimah Yacob for the Workers' group. Government members from developing and industrialized countries alike and from all parts of the globe brought to bear a range of perspectives that added greatly to the richness of our discussions. All of us have a natural inclination to view issues through the eyes of our own experience, but I believe members of the Committee on Human Resources showed a great willingness to listen to, learn from and discuss others' viewpoints.

Without an enthusiastic and expert secretariat, our work would have foundered very early on. Those responsible for the preparation, processing and production of our work were a key part of the whole Committee effort. My thanks go to the Representative of the Secretary-General, Mr. Michael Henriques, the Deputy Representative, Mr. Trevor Riordan, and the Coordinator, Mr. Mark Levin, and his team. Their effort was unstinting and, despite some difficulties with computer systems, their good humour almost unfailing. Without a highly professional team of interpreters, who also had technical problems to cope with, we could not have functioned as a Committee. Towards the end of our process, the Drafting Committee ensured that the text of the proposed Recommendation was consistent, intelligible and met ILO standards. The process was led by the Legal Adviser, Mr. Loic Picard, and my thanks go to him, his assistants, the two Vice-Chairpersons, the Reporter of the Committee and the Government representative, Mr. Félix N'zue of Côte d'Ivoire.

As has already been alluded to, the Committee held only one vote during its proceedings. The question decided by that vote has been the subject of much, much discussion, and no doubt will be of more. But, I do not propose to add further to that discussion here. While the subject matter at issue – that of strengthening and supporting collective bargaining on training – is clearly an important one, the clause concerned should be viewed in the context of an instrument comprising 22 substantive paragraphs, five subparagraphs and 71 clauses.

This Recommendation is set in a contemporary context, is forward looking, draws on the latest thinking and is capable of adding value in a dynamic world of ever-changing challenges, needs and priorities. Working people of the world can only gain if their employers, governments, trade unions, educators and training providers draw on it in designing and implementing human resource development policies and systems around the central theme of lifelong learning. The Committee was unanimous in recommending that the proposed new Recommendation should replace the Human Resources Development Recommendation, 1975 (No. 150).

I commend to the Conference the report of the Committee on Human Resources and the proposed Recommendation concerning human resources development, education, training and lifelong learning.

Original Spanish: The PRESIDENT

The general discussion on the report of the Committee on Human Resources is now open.

Original French: Mr. TRICOCHE *(Workers' adviser, France)*

Thank you for giving me the floor to express, on behalf of the workers of the European region, my support for the report on human resources development, education, training and lifelong learning.

The development of workers' skills and competencies is one of the essential keys to sustainable social progress and hence to the creation of decent jobs throughout the world. Investment in education and training is a decisive factor in sustainably promoting the interests of workers, enterprises and society as a whole in order to combat social exclusion, eliminate poverty and transform the activities of the informal economy into decent work.

Our Committee recognized that everyone has the right to education and training. Governments must invest in education and training, and they must define a national strategy with the participation of the social partners and create, through economic, fiscal and social policies, enabling conditions for the development of knowledge and skills. For their part, enterprises must train their workers and the social partners must assume their responsibilities so that workers can benefit from better conditions for training on the job and thus develop and maintain their employability and secure decent work for themselves.

On all of these points, social dialogue and collective bargaining are the best tools for good governance. It is thus natural that the proposed Recommendation should invite governments to strengthen social dialogue and collective bargaining.

On the basis of ILO principles, governments must strengthen tripartite social dialogue and support bipartite collective bargaining at all levels: international, national, sectoral, local and enterprise levels. This provision of the proposed Recommendation refers in fact to Article 4 of Convention No. 98. This Article of one of the eight fundamental Conventions of the ILO specifies that measures appropriate to national conditions shall be taken to encourage and promote the development of the negotiation of collective agreements between employers' and workers' organizations.

Furthermore, the level of collective bargaining is not an obstacle to bipartite dialogue. There are already many examples of this, such as the agreement mentioned by Ms. Yacob, concluded by Danone, an international group that started as a French company, and which opens up possibilities for an agreement on training for the benefit of both the workers and the enterprise. But we, too, in France, at the national level, have some experience of collective bargaining, and a historic national agreement has recently been signed by all the social partners.

Finally, where the prerogatives of the social partners are respected and the framework for intervention takes account of national systems of industrial relations, there is no reason why the social partners should contest the legitimacy of government support for collective bargaining. Collective bargaining is part of the fundamental rights and principles contained in the ILO Declaration of 1998. With freedom of association, it was chosen as the subject of the Global Report before this Conference, *Organizing for social justice*. It is thus quite useful for the ILO's strategy that the draft Recommendation should invite governments to support collective bargaining.

In conclusion, I should also like to thank all the participants in the Committee's work, who have made it possible to draft a Recommendation that can meet the challenges of globalization.

I would like to thank the Chairperson, Mr. Chetwin, the Employer Vice-Chairperson, Mr. Renique, and particularly the governments which, throughout the work of the Committee, have shown themselves most willing to help promote understanding, and I would like most particularly to thank the Governments of France and the United Kingdom which, right up to the last moment, did everything in their power to bring about consensus.

Of course my thanks go also to Ms. Yacob, the Worker Vice-Chairperson, who, thanks to her qualities of conviction, openness and sense of dialogue, made a contribution to the quality and balance of the instrument before you.

I therefore call on all the members of the Conference to adopt the proposed Recommendation concerning human resources development: education, training and lifelong learning, as it is entirely in keeping with the ILO's agenda for the creation of decent work for all and will thus, we all agree, contribute to a more fair globalization.

Ms. LENOIR *(Workers' adviser, United States)*

Our work here is the international expression of tripartism, an idea which, when it became operational 85 years ago, was well ahead of its time. As the President of the Government of Spain, Mr. Zapatero, said in this Assembly Hall last week, the frescos a few metres away from us proclaim "the supreme values of peace, justice, respect for international law and the defence of human dignity".

In the twentieth century, many of us made great strides in human rights. After a struggle, political and civil rights were consolidated and extended to people throughout the world. The twenty-first century, (the African century) must, among other things, consolidate and extend social rights, as social rights form the foundation for balanced economic development. Globalization must take place within a framework of sustainable development, and the most sustainable form of development is that which includes social rights and underpins human dignity. President Zapatero's remarks, informed by his country's struggle, were prescient; so is this Recommendation. Labour, my colleagues, is not a commodity and therefore, as time and technology appear to have shifted into "warp drive", we must establish a new culture of education, training and lifelong learning. This embryonic culture is reflected in our Recommendation. The Recommendation is not merely employment-related, but is also based on human dignity which comes from personal development, achievement and the promotion of equal opportunities, including active citizenship, greater cohesion and family-friendly initiatives which provide greater balance for family life and work to holistically improve our lives and strengthen our society.

In this instrument we advocate a process of globalization which has the social dimension based on shared universal values and respect for human rights and human dignity. Its detractors focus their attention on ensuring that markets and the enterprises that operate therein function efficiently, but in this instrument we have achieved hard-won gains in the true spirit of consensus, to mitigate globalization's impact on individuals, families and their communities. There is no more worthwhile, sustainable and important investment that governments, employers and trade unions can make than thoughtful investment in people. Those investments should provide access to, and support for, education, training and lifelong learning for our collective future.

We must mobilize society in order to act together to maximize our input and change our world for the better. We can begin to do so through this Recommendation. Our constituents and colleagues, the employed, the underemployed, the unemployed, the marginalized and the poor of the world, are waiting to see what decisions we will take on their behalf between now and the vote on this instrument that is due to take place tomorrow. They are convinced that we have the ability to change their collective conditions, including putting them on the ladder of opportunity that will lead to eradication of poverty through decent work. We think that it is within our ability to do so, or we would not have devoted over three years' work to reach this point in our deliberations. We urge you to support this Recommendation; it is the combination of a collaborative consensus between like-minded forward-thinking, innovative and progressive individuals, who work together in the spirit of tripartism to achieve something larger than any one of us for the sake of billions of people around the world.

Mr. RAMAN (Workers' adviser, India)

Coming from the subcontinent India, I feel very proud and honoured to represent the workers from the Asian continent in this Committee and speak in support of the Recommendation.

Under the able chairmanship of Mr. John Chetwin from New Zealand, two years of hard work by the tripartite committee, in an atmosphere of mutual respect and understanding, towards conceptualizing, sharpening, polishing and fine-tuning the text for greater clarity, has resulted in this complete consensus and found expression in the drawing-up of this far-sighted, innovative and progressive proposed Recommendation concerning human resources development, education, training and lifelong learning.

The proposed Recommendation before you, which defines the role and responsibility of Governments, Employers and Workers, is a testament both to the shared commitment of the social partners and to the ability of tripartism to continuously reflect the ever-changing world of work.

The proposed Recommendation encourages all the social partners to understand the key political, social and economic forces and aims to develop knowledge and skills, to help people to understand the world in which they live, and to participate in it as knowledgeable global citizens.

The revised text, which the Committee unanimously resolved should replace the existing Human Resources Development Recommendation, 1975 (No. 150), embodies values. It is practical and focuses on technology, productivity, competencies, employability and investment in education, training and lifelong learning, while emphasizing the importance of social dialogue and collective bargaining in training.

Recognizing the right to education, the proposed text contemplates integrating mechanisms that make it possible to enlarge significantly the group of beneficiaries and to take the needs of the most vulnerable into consideration. While offering specific recommendations and guidelines for the disadvantaged groups in countries in transition and developing countries, the proposed Recommendation addresses every aspect from personal work issues, such as discrimination, and health and safety, to more global ones, like the social and human poverty crisis.

New standards – such as valuation of prior learning and acquired skills; recognition and certification; research on lost traditional skills; creation of decent jobs and maintenance of ethical standards; emigration and settlement; migration of skills and brain drain; social inclusion, etc. – also find a place in this comprehensive document.

Emerging out of the contributions of several governments of developed, transition and developing countries, together with those of the Employers' and Workers' groups across the globe, this beautiful piece of work awaits not only your unanimous adoption as an ILO Recommendation, but also your wholehearted acceptance and prompt implementation.

Original Spanish: Ms. OIZ (Workers' adviser, Uruguay)

For the ILO, the main purpose of the globalized economy should be to promote opportunities for decent work for men and women, productive work in conditions of freedom, equality, security and human dignity. Education and training help individuals to free themselves from poverty, by equipping them with skills and knowledge enabling them to boost their output. But companies also get more out of education and training, because if they invest in workers' training, they improve productivity and can successfully compete on increasingly integrated world markets.

The economic growth and social development of countries are also linked to investment in education and training. In the least developed countries, it is becoming more and more clear that education and training are the basis for sustainable economic and social progress, the promotion of democracy, the mobilization of civil society and efforts to foster economic and social development.

There are many countries which define their targets for human resources development in terms of lifelong education. Many national constitutions underline the right to education and the development of human resources. In Latin America, Argentina, Bolivia, Brazil, Chile, Guatemala and Mexico are some of the countries where this right is recognized. It is also recognized internationally in the Universal Declaration of Human Rights and in the American Declaration of the Duties and Rights of Man and regionally in the MERCOSUR Declaration on Social and Labour Matters.

There is now broad consensus, at both the political and the social level that it is necessary to restructure the supply of education and training to make it sufficiently flexible to meet the demand for diverse and changing skills. Today, nobody can hope to get by all their life with what they first learned when they were young. The rapid pace of change throughout the world calls for the constant updating of knowledge at a time when young people's basic education is tending to last longer. This is essentially a qualitative development. Whereas previously, it was enough to pass on a certain amount of technical know-how and manual skills so that people could take up the job that was waiting for them. Today, it is necessary to offer a whole range of competencies to which insufficient emphasis has been given in the past. Initiative, creativity, entrepreneurship, leadership and team spirit must be accompanied by technical proficiency in less-specific areas than in the past: languages, computer skills, logical reasoning, an analytical mind and an ability to interpret charts, etc.

Priority must therefore go to measures enabling people to manage their own professional and occupational development: to find their first job, to look for a new one, to set up a firm, to obtain new qualifications and to train all the time, no matter whether they are employed or unemployed, at home or at work.

As we know, in Latin America, the interest and involvement of workers' organizations in vocational training is a good deal higher than it was a couple of decades ago, particularly if you look, on the one hand, at the interest in and the commitment to this subject and, on the other, at the ways and means of participating in the educational process.

But it is no different from the employers' point of view. The movement to set up vocational training institutes in the region, which began in Brazil with the National Industrial Apprenticeship Service and the National Commercial Apprenticeship Service, gave firms a starting point for this type of activity. They are continuing to play a leading role in the field of vocational training and, in response to certain demands, they have strengthened vocational training and have managed to get their ideas and vision of training accepted in a variety of forums and in bilateral or tripartite negotiations at sectoral, corporate or national level.

Developing essential qualifications and guaranteeing lifelong education for all is no means undertaking for anyone or any country, even the most wealthy countries. The tasks that lie ahead mean that current educational and training reforms must be continued and speeded up.

The Recommendation, the text of which was approved in the Committee and is before this session of the Conference, covers all the features which we consider to be absolutely necessary to ensure the suitable development of vocational training which will cater for the interests of workers, firms and countries.

Workers, employers and governments, we all have something to say and much to contribute to vocational training. Both by means of social dialogue and through collective bargaining, we can arrive at solutions which will address all these concerns. This Recommendation gives us the wherewithal to attain our goal.

Original Arabic: Mr. ABDULHUSSAIN *(Workers' adviser and substitute delegate, Bahrain)*

The Preamble to the ILO Declaration on Fundamental Principles and Rights at Work states that the ILO should, now more than ever, do everything possible to promote labour standards, employment and training.

This shows the importance of strengthening collaboration amongst all the parties concerned, so as to promote vocational training.

As regards human resources development, all of the discussions we have had and all of the efforts by the Committee are very important, and the Recommendation before us revising the Human Resources Development Recommendation, 1975 (No. 150), emphasizes education, training and lifelong learning. It also stresses the importance of social dialogue because, in the final analysis, there can be no true democracy without collective bargaining and social dialogue at all levels.

The representatives of the Arab countries, and the Gulf States in particular, would like to stress the importance of dialogue for human resources development. For social dialogue and collective bargaining on education, training and lifelong learning is essential, especially since we are now witnessing changes at all levels as a result of globalization.

All parties – Governments, Employers or Workers – must strive to implement this Recommendation, because it comes at a historic moment when the focus is on the need to promote cooperation to think about means of implementing education, training and lifelong learning, reducing unemployment and combating poverty.

On behalf of the Workers of the Arab group who participated in the Committee on Human Resources, we would like to stress the importance of this instrument. It is a key instrument, which will have an important impact on lifelong learning, education and training in Arab countries. This is a concern shared by all Arab countries, and we are in the process of developing projects and programmes for technical apprenticeships, as well as for education and training. All this is the result of the social dialogue we have held among the social partners.

Ms. RIGGS (Workers' adviser, New Zealand)

I am speaking on behalf of the workers of New Zealand, the Pacific region and Australasia.

This Recommendation, as it has been drafted, enables employers and workers alike to agree on education and training provisions and policies that will benefit both social partners and the societies of all our nations.

However, this can only be done in the context of the economic and social realities already existing in the countries concerned. To give life to this Recommendation, all countries need to be mindful of the fact that education and training, access to lifelong learning and human resource development is an investment. It will not happen simply because a Recommendation has been passed here at the ILO; it will not happen simply because people think it is a good idea, and it will not happen unless the resources so sorely needed, in particular in the developing nations, are made available and applied to this area.

The specific problems of indebted developing countries must be addressed, so that innovative approaches to providing additional resources can be explored and applied.

As you have heard, we have had a high degree of consensus in the development of this instrument. We have not always agreed on every aspect of the hows and the whys, but one thing we have all agreed on is that if developing countries are ever going to stop being called "developing", then investment and lifelong learning, education and training will have to be one of the main cornerstones on which this change will be built. That cannot be achieved without resources.

It is incumbent on us all to see to it that this instrument is adopted and that its full intentions and the intentions of the parties are put into effect – not tomorrow, not the day after, but now.

Mr. LAMBERT (Employers' delegate, United Kingdom)

During the three years 2000, 2003 and 2004 in which the Committee on Human Resources has met there has been really excellent work. I have been involved in every one of those discussions. This subject is of enormous importance.

I would like to quote President Bill Clinton, who was an excellent communicator, when he was trying to convince the American population of the message, and he said, "It's the economy, stupid!" I would like to parody that by saying that, for the world's problems, "It's education, stupid!" Or, to parody someone else, it is education, education, education that will change the face of this world.

The debate over these three years has been significant when you consider the prize at the end. Education leads to employment and ultimately, the great goal of the eradication of the stain of poverty.

It is therefore of great sadness to all the Employer team that the clause inserted in the text regarding collective bargaining at all levels for training – not a collective bargaining for pay and conditions, but for training – is clearly at odds with a great proportion of management thinking and practice throughout the world.

The fact that we do not like this clause will not stop enterprises investing in the job-related training of their employees. Employers are the main source of training, following full-time education. They are the people who pay.

It is a well-known fact that a well-trained, flexible team of employees reflects well on the reputation of companies and the employees themselves.

Five years ago – before I ceased my full-time employment – I had the responsibility of closing a major plant in the United Kingdom. Because the market was so irascible – it was so difficult, the market collapsed – we had to close the plant.

What we had been doing for years was to look for flexibility of all the workers in that plant, and not by negotiation, but we discussed with the unions, we consulted, when we talked to them on the fact that we should make sure that every single employee in this plant was flexible over five to ten jobs.

When we closed that plant, within four months, every one of the 2,000 employees who wanted to continue to work had found another job because they had been so flexible and well-trained in the job they did. That was management's decision; they decided that that was the right thing to do.

So there is no debate about the training that needs to be done. The debate is about collective bargaining. Well-based, job-related training can have significant results for enterprises and employees.

Enterprises will always train and educate for the job because it is their responsibility and because the success of the enterprise depends on it. The future of the enterprise depends on the workforce, and its commitment and training to do the job.

This document has many excellent provisions, and I congratulate all those who have worked so hard to achieve a modern document for the future. It is, therefore, with considerable sadness that I reflect, in this brief interjection, the Employers' disappointment regarding this unacceptable clause or, to use Ms. Yacob's words, almost, it is not a satisfactory conclusion.

Mr. WAJDA (Employers' adviser and substitute delegate, Canada)

Thank you for letting me speak on the topic of human resources.

Over the past three years we have been working diligently towards developing a new Recommendation concerning human resources development that would meet the needs of the governments, workers and employers. I believe all parties worked very hard to create a modern, progressive Recommendation that fits well into today's ever-changing global society. The goal was to replace the Human Resources Development Recommendation, 1975 (No. 150), with a short concise document that not only meets today's reality, but also looks forward, taking into account the rapid expansion of information and communication technology and the realization that learning is a lifelong process.

Throughout the discussions we had lively debates with all parties willing to openly discuss the issues. I will only touch on two issues that had substantial debate as my other colleagues will talk about some of the others.

The first one was the recognition that education and training are right for all and that we work towards ensuring access for all to lifelong learning.

From an Employers' point of view, and especially the Canadian Employers, the wording of the text still causes us concern as it may be interpreted that individuals can request training not related to enterprise needs. The Employers tried to clarify the text, indicating that they would commit to train their employees based on individual enterprise needs to reflect the group's understanding of the Employers' commitment. However, we could not come to a consensus on the language. For the sake of building trust and respect between the social partners, the Employers abandoned their position and continued the dialogue.

Over the last two years the tripartite discussions have led to a softening of positions as all agreed that the statement was more of a long-term aspiration or goal. Many countries indicated that in today's environment it would be difficult to implement training at all levels. However, we still believe it is a worthwhile aspiration.

Another important item within the Recommendation was the explicit commitment made by the governments, employers and individuals in recognizing the partners' responsibilities in the realization of lifelong learning. It was agreed that the governments have the responsibility of investing and creating conditions to enhance education and training at all levels. Enterprises need to train their employees to ensure competitiveness and individuals need to develop their competencies and careers. Especially in today's environment, it is extremely important that individuals recognize that they themselves are the architects and builders responsible for developing their skills and careers throughout their lives.

I believe that all parties made many positive movements in the spirit of tripartite dialogue in an effort to reach consensus on all major topics. We believe the Recommendation is modern, progressive and forward-looking and 90-95 per cent of the content is an accurate reflection of the Group's work. However, at the end of the day we were not able to reach agreement on the infamous 5(f) which puts collective bargaining on training at the international/national/regional/local/sectoral and enterprise levels. We all agree that collective bargaining is a component of social dialogue but it is not the only component. I am disappointed that we could not reach a consensus on how to make 5(f) agreeable to all parties. The way 5(f) is currently written will have significant ramifications to Canadian employers and it is for that reason we cannot support the Recommendation, even though 90-95 per cent of the content is a good piece of work as it takes into account the needs of all parties and the unique issues in developing and developed countries.

It is also important to note that we accept the ILO process on how we arrived at the current 5(f).

I would like to thank the Governments and the Workers for contributing to the debates on the topics that are dear to our hearts. It is unfortunate that we could not agree on one item.

I would also like to thank all the Employers who participated in the Employers' debates and I would especially like to thank Mr. Renique, the International Organisation of Employers (IOE) and the ILO Bureau for Employers' Activities (ACT/EMP) representatives in their efforts in trying to reach an agreement on behalf of the Employers.

Original French: Ms. AWASSI ATSIMADJA, *(Employers' delegate, Gabon)*

Allow me, on behalf of the Confederation of Gabonese Employers (CPG), to congratulate and thank the two spokespersons of the Employers and the Workers for the professional and respectful way in which they both conveyed, debated and defended the views of the Employers and Workers during the second discussion of the proposed Recommendation concerning human resources development: Education, training and lifelong learning.

My congratulations also go to the Governments which showed their clear will to achieve the golden mean, and to the Chairperson of the Committee for the expertise, finesse and skill with which he led the work of the tripartite Committee.

I was particularly impressed by the dedication to methods of negotiation and social dialogue which prevailed in the urgent quest for solutions so that a text acceptable to all parties could be produced. However, I cannot help noting that this process of social dialogue did not go all the way.

I think we can safely state that at the very heart of the concerns of this instrument on human resources we find the tripartite concern for decent work, a better well-being for most, if not for all. I would like to state that this well-being can only be achieved if the enterprises creating goods and services are free and satisfied with the legal, economic and other conditions which should encourage private investment. These conditions belong to the field of the State.

Of course, we want education, training and lifelong learning since private enterprises know and are convinced that the human resources which we all are, are at the heart of all human social and economic development and all adequate productivity for as many people as possible, if not for all. The social dialogue which we all advocate in this house must, therefore, prevail.

In the course of the debate on the standard on human resources, reference was made to a series of themes, and I shall only mention a few of them because of time constraints. One of these themes is social dialogue, and I am tempted to add, constructive social dialogue. An example comes to mind: my country, Gabon. We are currently experiencing such constructive social dialogue through the signing of a three-year social truce.

Another theme, and by no means the least important, is the gender approach. With your permission, let me dwell on this theme in a very succinct manner. May I mention in this connection the misunderstanding which persists as to that concept. Indeed, far from being only in favour of women, this concept aims at re-establishing a balance also for men. Side-by-side with the ILC, a round-table discussion was held with the participation of the Director-General of the ILO entitled "The contribution of women to the ILO – future expectations". This meeting, although alongside the ILC, dealt with an issue which, in my opinion, has been addressed satisfactorily by the present instrument. The Employers' representative at that round table gave us a concrete example of the way in which employers are striving to apply the concept of the gender approach. It is a matter of establishing programmes targeted at training and giving responsibility to female human resources, and of progressively, but directly and unequivocally, sharing decision-making posts.

Mr. Henri-Claude Oyima, President of the CPG, and the other Employers' representatives here advocate citizen-based enterprises which respect the free will of our human resources and particularly women so that they can participate effectively and actively in education and lifelong learning.

Finally, I would like to say that last year at the plenary during the first discussion of this instrument, I had pointed out that the CPG was an example of good practices in the field of the gender approach. At the plenary in 2003, I had pointed out as direct proof of this the fact that the representative of the CPG at the ILO, the International Organisation of Employers (IOE) and the Pan African Employers' Confederation (PEC) is a woman. I would like to conclude by stating that the CPG is happy once again to share the fact that it has become enriched by a woman who has joined it as Deputy General-Secretary.

These examples, coming from Gabon and from the Employers' representative who spoke during the round-table discussion and many others from Africa, are interesting examples to cite and share, to serve as inspiration for Africa, where I am from and where my ancestors were born, so that the respective social and cultural aspects can be taken into account.

Ms. GOLDBERG *(Employers' adviser and substitute delegate, United States)*

When the ILO adopted its Human Resources Development Recommendation in 1975, we lived in a different world.

Our political universe was defined by the Cold War. Personal computers, fax machines and cell phones were unknown, as were countless other items that we today regard as indispensable to the conduct of our businesses and our daily lives. The Internet had yet to be invented. The world of work at that time was a largely static place, its horizons determined by physical and geographic boundaries and its potential seemingly defined by ideas of the nature of the labour market that we now regard as outdated.

Today, millions of people around the world are gainfully employed making and using goods and services that were unimagined, indeed unimaginable, 30 years ago, using the technologies that have made globalization possible. These technologies have also transformed the fields of education and training.

It is not only fitting, therefore, but essential, that we revisit the advice on the development of human resources, that we gave to governments, on their responsibility to provide the basic educational foundation that enables individuals to become contributing and productive members of society and to implement the policies that are essential to economic and human development; to enterprises, on the necessity of ensuring the appropriately trained workforce required in order to remain innovative and competitive; and to workers themselves, who have a role to play in managing their own careers, throughout their lives.

For these reasons, United States employers have welcomed the revision and replacement of Recommendation No. 150 with the modern, dynamic and flexible instrument we have before us today. For these same reasons, we deeply regret that the final text includes the infamous clause 5(f) and language that we cannot endorse. However, this is a wide-ranging document that incorporates much of the latest thinking in the field of training and on such concepts as lifelong learning. We hope and trust that the many useful concepts and suggestions contained in this text, on which we were able to achieve widespread consensus, will provide a constructive basis for action by all parties.

Mr. PATIL *(Employers' adviser, India)*

The proposed Recommendation concerning human resources development: Education, training and lifelong learning, is most appropriate and timely in the context of a globalization that is fuelled by communication and information technology. It is also immensely and universally valuable to the least developed, developing and developed countries of the world.

Every society needs to educate its members in order to prepare them for citizenship and also to enable them to pursue gainful and meaningful employment in their own interests and in the interests of society as a whole.

Training for specific employment goes a long way in supporting productivity and competitiveness. Lifelong learning is necessary to boost employability and income protection in a rapidly changing world.

Put together, these are a very powerful means of achieving the goal of decent work for all.

In the Asian context in particular, the proposed Recommendation has the potential to accelerate economic growth with social progress only if the social partners and stakeholders cooperate in initiating and implementing the policies that stem from this instrument.

The document provides above all for a recognition of education and training as a right for all and clearly provides a role for the social partners and stakeholders. It provides for a broad policy framework within which countries would be able to develop their own policies and programmes tailored to their own particular needs and circumstances.

The policy framework relates in a very focused way, but also in broad detail, to the multifarious aspects of education and training, including the development of competencies, the recognition and certification of skills, the certification of training providers, the provision of career guidance and support services, research in human resources development and international and technical cooperation. It also provides for the encouragement of entrepreneurship development. It would, if implemented, help us to move in the direction of attaining our goal of a fairer globalization.

The teeming millions from the least developed and developing countries will find an opportunity to fulfil their fair and just aspirations of leading economically and socially secure lives through gainful employment and meaningful work.

Coming from India, I have seen what a difference investment in education and training can make for a country. It is education, its knowledge of workers in particular and its ability to insource a lot of work from the developed nations, that has given India pride of place in the community of nations. In the process, this has provided jobs for thousands of people and at the same time has provided cost-effective solutions to clients throughout the world. This might potentially create a temporary imbalance in employment in the developed world but it is certainly beneficial in the medium and long term to the outsourcer as well as to the insourcer. This also obviates the need for more migration than necessary on this count.

The greatest potential of the proposed Recommendation is perhaps its capacity to raise global awareness of the need for human resources development, education, training and lifelong learning. I believe that awareness leads to understanding, which is necessary for developing commitment. I firmly believe that once a commitment is achieved, a way can always be found to achieve even the most difficult, seemingly impossible, objective.

Significant efforts have been made to build and refine the text and to produce the document in its present form. I have a fond hope and a strong belief that the social partners will be able to find, even at this stage, a mutually acceptable solution to the difficulties that arose in relation to clause 5(f) during the course of our deliberations on the Recommendation, which in its present form, is not acceptable to the Employers' group. In the unlikely event that this instrument does not find its passage through this august body, I hope that the spirit and the policy framework generated by this instrument will go a long way in achieving the tripartite commitment towards human resources development, education, training and lifelong development.

Mr. ARNOLD (Employers' delegate, New Zealand)

The report of the Committee on Human Resources provides significant scope for ongoing work in the field of education, training and lifelong learning. In the short time I have available I wish to focus on the following areas: entrepreneurship, growth and collective bargaining.

The provisions relating to entrepreneurship are an example of the new Recommendation adapting to the modern world of work. We are encouraged by the support that the developing countries have given to this during the proceedings.

Building educators' understanding of business, enterprise and innovation is a major initiative identified in the Recommendation.

The OECD has noted that improvement in human knowledge is a common factor behind economic growth in recent decades. In the OECD countries, it is estimated that the increase in human knowledge accounted for more than one extra percentage point of growth in the 1990s compared with the previous decades. Investment in education is one of the recognized means of achieving high rates of employment, economic growth and social progress.

Education has two important effects on productivity. First, it generates knowledge, which translates into technological improvements and aggregate productivity gains. Second, education can increase the skills and knowledge of individuals and so enhance their employability and work security. The ability to learn, innovate, adapt and exercise judgement, along with communication, analysis, management and leadership, are fundamental.

The major difference between the tripartite partners has been over the relevance of collective bargaining in one particular clause of the text of the Recommendation. The Employer members in the discussion have been unable to agree with the reference to collective bargaining within the context of clause 5(f) of the section dealing with the development and implementation of education and training policies. However, the Employer members were able to accept a reference to collective bargaining in clause 9(c) of the section dealing with the development of competencies. I would like to briefly digress from my written notes and repeat: there is not just one reference to collective bargaining in the text, as the Worker Vice-Chairperson said, but two, namely in clause 5(f) and clause 9(c). It is unfortunate that this difference stands in the way of improvements to the text made in the Committee when compared with the original text of the Recommendation. Whilst we acknowledge that we, the Employers, have contributed to some procedural problems, we have been consistent in our objection to the inappropriateness of the reference to collective bargaining in clause 5(f), but not in clause 9(c).

As the New Zealand Employers' delegate, I can confirm that we in New Zealand will continue with the voluntary approach to issues of collective bargaining and social dialogue. Business New Zealand is engaged in a number of tripartite or bilateral dialogues involving the New Zealand Council of Trade Unions and the New Zealand Government. These are examples of responsible social partnership at the national level focused on positive agreed areas of work. These engagements include the Skill New Zealand Campaign; bilateral discussions on productivity; and participation in the Government's workplace productivity working group.

The underpinning principle for all of these engagements is that they are voluntary and focus on shared common goals in areas such as skills, productivity, and economic and social development. None of these engagements are related to collective bargaining, either at the enterprise or sector level. In fact, the clear separation between the issues of collective bargaining and action on issues such as skills, productivity and other economic issues has led to progress which would otherwise not have been possible. Business New Zealand and the Council of Trade Unions have been engaged in extremely useful bilateral discussions on the issue of productivity since November 2002. These discussions have identified three broad areas of focus: workplace productivity; infrastructure issues; and skills and training issues. The New Zealand Government has established a working group of public and private sector individuals to consider measures that might be taken by business, employees and Government to improve productivity in the workplace. A key theme for the working group has been a focus on non-regulatory approaches to improving workplace productivity.

In conclusion, the key to the success of engagement between the social partners in the New Zealand context has been a clear demarcation between issues of national importance where there is agreement and common cause between the parties, and issues of industrial relations and collective bargaining, at either an enterprise or sector level. Without this separation, it is likely that very little, if any, progress on critical issues would have been achieved. Without this separation in the Recommendation similar problems can be foreseen.

Mr. LEWIS (Employers' delegate, Jamaica)

I speak not only for Jamaica but the views I shall express are shared by my Caribbean friends on the Employers' side.

Over the past two weeks we have participated with much interest in the discussions on human resources. I am sure that we have all benefited from everyone's participation.

The discussions were positive and frank. There was mutual respect shown on all sides. The Chairperson and Vice-Chairpersons did their jobs professionally. The staff too cannot be faulted for the excellent way in which they went about their jobs and, on behalf of the Caribbean region, I thank them all.

We came out with what can be regarded as an excellent document on education and training, but for one paragraph, which the Employers find unacceptable if the clause relating to collective bargaining is included. After much effort, consensus could not be reached on this paragraph. We find this most disappointing, not only for the Employers' group, but in particular for us in the Caribbean. We, in this part of the world, are a poor developing nation. Unfair trade and unfair investment are already taking their toll on us. In open competitive economies, resources need to be constantly relocated from less to more efficient uses. This in turn requires a constant change in workplace and in the employment structure of the economy. In our enterprises this can mean transferring or laying off workers in the wider economy, which entails structural change, enterprise failures, bankruptcies and dislocations.

Let me hasten to say Employers recognize that enhancing the contribution by working men and women to productivity growth through education and training is an integral part of the whole development process and goes hand in hand with measures to enable workers to express their views in a manner which also provides employers with the mechanism for dialogue on all subjects, including education and training.

To this end, we Employers in the Caribbean support the ILO in setting standards. But the language of such standards should be flexible enough to give poor developing countries a chance.

We recognize that it is essential for poor nations to try to rise to the challenges of a changing world, but standards which are not flexible can be the difference between job creation and job retention, as against job redundancies and the failure of enterprises to expand or even invest in new business.

We in the Caribbean see employment as a principal route out of poverty and to this end all economies must generate opportunities for investment, entrepreneurship, job creation and a sustainable livelihood.

In the 1990s, those in poverty in our region increased from 121 million to 132 million, with a quarter of our population still subsisting on $2 a day or less. It is precisely for these reasons that Caribbean Employers do not support this contentious paragraph which includes collective bargaining. We believe it will be a foot in the door for the introduction of a legislation which will prove burdensome for us and which could ultimately, in today's world, force employers to look at their employment policies and relationships in a different light, and which could have implications for the excellent relationship currently existing between employers and trade unions in our countries.

The position which the discussions have taken on the relevant paragraph makes what could be an excellent document most unfortunate. It is unfortunate because a long time has been spent working towards revision of the current Human Resources Development Recommendation, 1975 (No. 150), and it is fair to say that all Committee members agree that this Recommendation is an improvement over Recommendation No. 150 but for the relevant paragraph.

If there was consensus, this Recommendation would be a useful guide for the development of a skilled and productive workforce but all is not lost. Disappointed we are, yes, but we will all return to our respective countries richer for the depth and richness of the discussions which we have been engaged in. But as we leave, we cannot help but reflect on the fact that if at the centre of the standard-setting body, we all cannot come to a consensus, although we have had the help of experts to reach this difficult decision, then we recognize that as a tripartite group, there is much more work to be done. Bearing in mind that all countries are not at the same level, and all countries are not at the same point of development, we are a responsible group and we ask that when you vote, you take into consideration the plight of the poor developing countries. If we have to deal with education and training through collective bargaining, this is going to be a problem for developing countries.

Ms. ROJVITHEE *(Government adviser, Thailand)*

On behalf of the Thai Government and as one of the members of the Committee on Human Resources, I am pleased to inform you that this proposed Human Resources Development Recommendation, 2004, was carefully drafted by the mutual efforts of member countries, in a spirit of harmony and compromise. Frankly speaking, it is not as perfect as we had expected, because of the differences in the socio-economic politics of each country that form the national policy of that country. But I can assure you that most of the content of this proposed Recommendation will be a vital instrument to empower global human resources to survive through the effects of globalization, as well as being a major tool to alleviate poverty by promoting employment, social inclusion, decent work and protection of the right of people to access to education, training and lifelong learning. The text provides clearly for cooperation between government, employers, workers and the social partners at national and international levels in developing and increasing knowledge, skills and competencies of "global people".

I believe that member countries will reap the benefits of this Recommendation by observing the text and selecting the parts that are compatible with the national environment for implementation. The current national policy of the Thai Government emphasizes that the Thai economy should be a knowledge-based economy with people at the centre of development. They should have the right to develop themselves continuously, in line with the concept of lifelong learning and training not only for employability but also for their quality of life and their happiness. The promotion of entrepreneurial skills to enable our people to run their own businesses as small and medium-sized enterprises also constitutes the main strategy of the Thai Government to promote employment for our people.

As a result, we are pleased to adopt the Human Resources Development Recommendation, 2004, to replace the Human Resources Development Recommendation, 1975.

Lastly, may I express my appreciation for the leadership of the Chairperson and the capacity of both the Employer and Worker Vice-Chairpersons, and also for the dedication of the ILO secretariat and interpreters who bring our work to its conclusion.

Original Spanish: The PRESIDENT

As there are no further speakers, I propose that we proceed with the approval of the report of the Committee, which is contained in paragraphs 1-999.

If there are no objections, may I take it that the report is approved?

(The report – paragraphs 1-999 – is approved.)

PROPOSED RECOMMENDATION CONCERNING HUMAN RESOURCES DEVELOPMENT: EDUCATION, TRAINING AND LIFELONG LEARNING: ADOPTION

Original Spanish: The PRESIDENT

We shall now proceed to the adoption of the proposed Recommendation concerning human resources development: education, training and lifelong learning, Paragraph by Paragraph, beginning with the Preamble.

(The proposed Recommendation – the Preamble and Paragraphs 1-4 – are adopted seriatim.*)*

The Employer Vice-Chairperson of the Committee has the floor to speak about Paragraph 5.

Mr. RENIQUE *(Employers' delegate, Netherlands; Employer Vice-Chairperson of the Committee on Human Resources)*

Many members have made comments on this particular clause 5(f), to which I have been listening carefully. Many members on the Workers' side have also said that we should have a last try to get the instrument adopted unanimously. For that reason, the Employers' group wants to propose an amendment. Before I read the text, I also want to comment on questions raised by Ms. Yacob. A question could be: do the Employers not respect the vote? Yes, we want to respect the vote. We thought the issue was – and you have heard in some contributions that some people have different opinions about that – but the issue is whether or not collective bargaining can be a useful instrument in discussing training issues. We will accept this. Of course, social partners determine their agenda themselves, so in one country more of these issues can be on the agenda in collective bargaining than in another. But in principle we want to accept this.

Second, the other issue is that from the Workers' side, there is a wish to engage this at different levels. We are ready to accept this, so we want to respect completely the essential issues of the voting. Do we want to introduce a new procedure in this house? No, we do not. It is not our intention to have any voting, revoting or repeated discussion in plenary. That would cost us weeks and, of course, that is not our intention.

We wish to make an exceptional request to this audience – and it is exceptional – to accept our proposal in order to make it possible for us to join the overwhelming support for this instrument, and for that reason, I would like now to read the amendment we submit for consideration.

Subparagraph 5(f) would read as follows: "strengthen social dialogue and support voluntary collective bargaining initiatives on training at different levels where they exist, as basic principles for systems development, programme relevance, quality and cost effectiveness, taking the specific national law and practice into account."

Ms. YACOB *(Workers' delegate, Singapore; Worker Vice-Chairperson of the Committee on Human Resources)*

I have listened very carefully to what Mr. Renique said, and he said that the Employers' group respects the vote that has already been taken. There is no intention of reopening the debate, but, by putting in this amendment, the Employers actually are reopening the debate. We had debated exhaustively at the Committee level, where everyone had the chance to give their views, and after we had debated, there was even an attempt to try and seek continuation on the process to reach consensus through the interventions of the Governments. In fact, an amendment was put in by the Governments of the United Kingdom and France. But, unfortunately, that spirit of consensus, social dialogue and tripartism did not prevail over the Employers.

Right now, we are asked once again in this plenary, which is an unusual and exceptional situation. We are asked to reopen the debate. In the history of the ILO we have not done this because it does not show much respect for the Committee. It does not show respect for the fact that a vote was taken at the request of the Employers. It also does not show respect for the fact that we made every effort to try and seek a consensus and, despite the vote being taken, we entered into bilateral consultations. We could not come to an agreement, despite a vote being taken. We entered into tripartite consultations. Suggestions were made for amendments but they did not have the agreement of the Employers.

I would like to ask this question. Is this an institution that respects tripartism, which believes in tripartite dialogue? Or should we have an institution where it must always be the case that the world must be in favour of one group? I think this is a very fundamental and important question.

I would also like to address a point which was raised by one of the speakers from the Employers' group, when he said that I had suggested that there was only one reference to collective bargaining. I would like to correct that. My exact words were, "Do we want to scuttle the whole instrument just because, out of 22 Paragraphs, this one Paragraph talks about collective bargaining?" I did not say that the whole instrument only has one. But I am saying that it is in this particular clause that it is found offensive by the Employers.

So, what is the big problem about collective bargaining? We have heard that there are many countries where collective bargaining also takes place on training, and this is also the case. Do we believe then that there should only be collective bargaining once a country has reached a developed status? The answer is no. The mechanism of collective bargaining is well established. It is an established mechanism accepted under the Declaration on Fundamental Principles and Rights at Work. It was again reinforced by the Global Report. We see that collective bargaining is obviously one process to ensure an inclusive globalization process, to ensure that there is a fair globalization for all.

In view of the amendment which the Employer Vice-Chairperson has tabled, I am obliged on behalf of the Workers' group to table the amendment which has obtained the support of an overwhelming majority of Governments. The Governments of France and the United Kingdom originally tabled this amendment. I will read the text as follows which I am submitting as an amendment. Members should "strengthen social dialogue and support bipartite collective bargaining on training at international, national, regional, local, sectoral and enterprise levels as basic principles for systems development, programme relevance, quality and cost-effectiveness, taking the specific national industrial relations system into account".

Let me conclude, by explaining why we find the Employers' amendment objectionable. The words "voluntary collective bargaining initiatives at different levels where they exist", are completely ambiguous. We are not sure what they refer to in this context. Do the words "different levels where they exist" refer to bargaining and training at the different levels? Does this refer to the basic principles of systems development and so on? What does it really refer to? Secondly, this is in the context of the Government's responsibility, and it says that "members", which means "Governments", should strengthen social dialogue and collective bargaining. If we were to adopt the Employers' amendment, it would amount to saying that Governments should support or strengthen collective bargaining only at the levels where it exists. So, either collective bargaining at the enterprise level is only the level that governments can support, or, only if there is collective bargaining at the sectoral level, then that is only the level that the government can support; if there is an intention to have sectoral bargaining but only enterprise bargaining now exists, then that cannot be done; in fact, if there is no bargaining at all then bargaining is something which governments could not support.

For those reasons, we cannot support the amendment put forward by the Employers.

Original Spanish: The PRESIDENT

The Presidency notes that two amendments have been proposed to Paragraph 5, clause (f), in Part II on development and implementation of education and training policies.

We call upon the Chairpersons of the Employers' group and the Workers' group to approach the secretariat to deliver their proposed amendments.

(The sitting was suspended for a short time.)

Original Spanish: The PRESIDENT

After consultations with the Chairpersons of the Employers' group and Workers' group, Mr. Funes de Riója and Mr. Trotman, respectively, and with the advice of the Legal Adviser of the Organization, and in the presence of the Officers of the Conference and the Vice-Chairpersons, it has been decided that we will not examine the amendments submitted by the Employers and the Workers.

Therefore, the Presidency will submit the original text that the Committee sent to the plenary, and tomorrow there will be a vote on the report of the Committee, at which time each grouping will be able to vote on the report.

Let us, therefore, proceed with the examination of the text of the proposed Recommendation concerning human resources development: Education, training and lifelong learning, Paragraphs 5-22.

(The proposed Recommendation – Paragraphs 5-22 – are adopted seriatim.*)*

If there are no objections, may I take it that the proposed Recommendation, as a whole, is adopted?

(The proposed Recommendation, as a whole, is adopted.)

We have now concluded the consideration of the report of the Committee on Human Resources, as well as the proposed Recommendation submitted to us.

In accordance with paragraph 7 of article 40 of the Standing Orders of the Conference, the provisions of the Recommendation concerning human resources development: Education, training and lifelong learning, will be transmitted to the Conference Drafting Committee for the preparation of the final text.

The record vote on the Recommendation concerning human resources development: Education, training and lifelong learning, will be held in plenary tomorrow morning.

I should like to congratulate the Officers and members of the Committee on Human Resources, and the staff of the secretariat, for the excellent work that they have accomplished.

SECOND AND THIRD REPORTS OF THE CREDENTIALS COMMITTEE: SUBMISSION AND NOTING

Original Spanish: THE PRESIDENT

We shall now proceed to the examination of the second and third reports of the Credentials Committee, which are published in *Provisional Records* Nos. 6C and 6D. The Officers of the Committee were as follows: the Chairperson and Reporter was Mr. Oni, the Employer Vice-Chairperson was Ms. Sasso Mazzuferi and the Worker Vice-Chairperson was Mr. Edström. I would now like to call upon Mr. Oni to submit the second and third reports of the Credentials Committee.

Original French: Mr. ONI *(Government delegate, Benin; Chairperson and Reporter of the Credentials Committee)*

I have the honour to present to the Conference a brief summary of the activities of the Credentials Committee this year, which appears in the second and third reports in *Provisional Record* Nos. 6C and 6D.

During the Conference, the Committee received ten objections concerning the nomination of delegations and six complaints about non-payment or partial payment of the subsistence expenses of delegates of the social partners. We also received one communication. The Committee notes that the number of cases has fallen significantly over recent years. The objections examined by the Committee mostly concern government interference in the appointment of Workers' or Employers' delegates to the Conference.

The Committee notes with concern that a number of situations continue to recur from year to year, and wishes to emphasize the importance of governments abiding by their constitutional obligations and ensuring that employers and workers are able freely to choose the members of their respective delegations.

As regards the complaints, the Committee notes with satisfaction that some governments responded rapidly by paying delegates' expenses so that the complaints have become moot. The Committee hopes that, in future, similar problems can be resolved without delegates having to submit complaints. It notes that the Conference decided yesterday provisionally to change its Standing Orders so as to give the Credentials Committee more effective tools, and welcomes that decision.

I would like to thank the Conference for having renewed its trust in appointing me a member of the Committee. I would like to express my thanks to my two colleagues, Ms. Sasso Mazzuferi and Mr. Edström, for the spirit of consensus which characterized our work, and to the secretariat for its excellent technical support and all the excellent work done.

Original Spanish: THE PRESIDENT

The Credentials Committee adopted these reports unanimously and the Conference is simply called upon to note them.

(The reports are noted.)

I would like to thank the Officers and members of the Credentials Committee, and the staff of the secretariat, for their excellent work.

REPORT OF THE COMMITTEE ON MIGRANT WORKERS: SUBMISSION, DISCUSSION AND APPROVAL

Original Spanish: THE PRESIDENT

We shall now proceed to the examination of the report of the Committee on Migrant Workers, which is published in *Provisional Record* No. 22. The Officers of the Committee were as follows: the Chairperson was Mr. Dé, the Employer Vice-Chairperson was Mr. De Regil, the Worker Vice-Chairperson was Ms. Burrow and the Reporter was Mr. Kebbon. I would now like to call upon Mr. Kebbon to submit the report of the Committee on Migrant Workers.

Mr. KEBBON *(Government adviser, Sweden; Reporter of the Committee on Migrant Workers)*

I am pleased to present to the Conference the report of the Committee on Migrant Workers, as adopted yesterday by that Committee.

The Governing Body decided at its 283rd Session in March 2002 to place on the agenda of the present session of the International Labour Conference a general discussion on migrant workers based on an integrated approach.

Its agenda was to include labour migration in an era of globalization; policies and structures for more orderly migration for employment; and improving migrant worker protection. The task of the Committee on Migrant Workers was to deal with this agenda item on the basis of a report submitted by the Office, *Towards a fair deal for migrant workers in the global economy.*

The Committee initiated its work with a general discussion addressing international labour migration from a more general perspective and, subsequently, more specifically under four points agreed to be the focus of the debate. On the basis of a draft text prepared by a smaller working party, the Committee then reviewed amendments to this draft at some length and in detail, and concluded its work by adopting a set of conclusions by consensus.

The conclusions include a plan of action which, on the one hand, sets in motion a process intended to contribute to the ongoing multilateral exchanges on this subject and, on the other, details how the ILO should contribute to creating a fair deal for migrant workers in a global economy. The plan of action has several components, including: first, a nonbinding multilateral framework including the development of guidelines on a series of relevant issues based on best practices in the field of international labour migration; second, the promotion of ILO standards relevant to migrant workers; third, capacity building and technical assistance; fourth, the development of a global knowledge base; and fifth, support for a sustained social dialogue in this area. In terms of follow-up, a series of different proposals are submitted for consideration by the Governing Body.

Although the issue of migration is complex and controversial, and the discussion in the Committee reflected the diverging perspectives surrounding this issue, it should be noted that the Committee was able to conclude its work on the basis of consensus. Admittedly, the Committee came very close to a vote on one occasion, but a concerted effort by all parties resulted in a compromise which was generally acceptable. Thus, a cooperative spirit prevailed in the end and all parties concerned made genuine efforts to bring the work to a conclusion that would be acceptable to all.

On balance, it seems fair to state that while a consensus is emerging throughout various international forums that migration can be beneficial to all provided it is better and more effectively managed, this consensus is as yet rather fragile, and considerable efforts will have to be deployed in order to enhance the possibilities for an informed debate on this issue, to allay fears, and to strike a balance between different and sometimes diverging interests. The results of the Committee's work will no doubt be an important contribution to that process.

A final comment: Governments are often – and they should often be – pressured to respond to new challenges, by workers and employers or, as is the case in other situations, by NGOs and civil society actors – in short, by those who are directly concerned by the issues and problems under discussion. The ILO's unique tripartite structure gives the social partners considerable power which gives the Organization the weight that makes it a key actor on global social issues. To retain this strength, it is of crucial importance that even where there is a majority view on an issue under discussion, every effort is pursued to reach broad tripartite understandings. In the present context, we can all congratulate ourselves for having made the extra effort to reach an end result which is both progressive and broadly accepted. This should provide a solid basis for the ILO to move forward towards creating a fair deal for migrant workers in a global economy.

Against this background, the International Labour Conference is invited to adopt the draft resolution and conclusions concerning a fair deal for migrant workers in a global economy, including the ILO plan of action for migrant workers contained in the report of the Committee on Migrant Workers, and to invite the Governing Body and the Director-General to give them due consideration in planning future action on migrant workers.

Original Spanish: Mr. DE REGIL *(Employers' adviser and substitute delegate, Mexico; Employer Vice-Chairperson of the Committee on Migrant Workers)*

First of all, as a Latin American, I would like to congratulate the President on his election and also say how happy I am to have such a wise and judicious President at this session of the Conference.

It is a great honour and pleasure for me to be able to present the Employers' views on the report and draft conclusions produced as a result of the intensive work of the Committee on Migrant Workers.

As was apparent during the discussions, the issue of migrant workers and the consequences of migrant labour are extremely important for employers. In a globalized world, with rapid structural change and unprecedented technological progress, jobs can be transferred from one country to another with un-heard-of ease. This means that it is crucial for our companies to have access to the workforce, knowledge and skills that they require in order to increase their productive capacity, efficiency and competitiveness, and is particularly important given the population and employment trends which we see today.

The report reflects current concerns as regards the issue of migration, which is as old as humankind itself. However, the twenty-first century, undoubtedly, will see the greatest migratory movements ever known. Migration levels will continue to increase over the coming years and this century will be marked as the great age of migration.

At present, about 86 million of the 175 million migrants in the world are workers. The figures will rise significantly in the coming years. Therefore, this is an issue that affects all countries, be they countries of destination, origin or transit.

In the case of my country, Mexico, it is clear that all three possibilities apply, because many Mexicans go to destination countries such as the United States and Canada, and many Central Americans come to work in Mexico or pass through it as they travel north.

The case of Mexico clearly illustrates the imperative need to come up with formulas that will help to solve the problems faced by Mexico with regard to migrant workers. In addition to Mexico, many other countries are also affected by this phenomenon. Therefore, the mandate given to the Committee by the Governing Body was to determine how our Organization can face up to these challenges, how it can be equipped to solve these issues and, lastly, how to direct the future work of the ILO in what is such a topical and vitally important area.

There is no doubt that the work carried out by migrants has made a positive contribution to economic growth. The Committee report, which is very good and extremely wide-ranging, shows that labour migration has led to non-inflationary economic growth and to the creation of jobs, has given greater flexibility to qualifications and labour skills and has made populations younger. Of course, it has also led to other trends and has also, unfortunately, given rise to problems.

This full range of issues was analysed and discussed by our Committee and, as our work progressed, a very basic idea started to emerge in the minds of all the members of the Committee, namely how to maximize the benefits of labour migration and how to limit its risks.

The ILO operates on the basis of its standards and, therefore, the Committee deemed that the Conventions concerning migrant labour were of fundamental importance. We therefore discussed the relevance, timeliness and force of Conventions Nos. 97 and 143, which were adopted in 1949 and 1975 respectively. The result was that the Office should investigate the causes of the low level of ratification of these Conventions. Convention No. 97, which was introduced 55 years ago, has been ratified by only 42 countries, in other words by 24 per cent of member States. Convention No. 143 has only had 18 ratifications, which represents 10.2 per cent of the international community.

The debate highlighted many of the reasons for this low level of ratification and rejection by nations. From the outset, the Employers pointed out that these Conventions do not address the present problem of labour migration, do not propose solutions to the current situation of migrant workers and do not take into account the origin and destination of these workers in the twenty-first century. These instruments are obsolete and, although they can be looked at as a source of historic interest, they do not address the root causes of the problems of migrant workers today.

Therefore, our position was that the Office should devote its meagre resources to looking at the obstacles that countries face when considering these instruments. We feel that it is totally inappropriate to launch a campaign to promote the ratification of these Conventions, because this would only be a waste of the Office's resources and would not achieve good results, particularly in destination countries. Instead of this expense, we feel that the Office should focus on providing technical assistance to member States, both origin and destination countries, so that they can formulate appropriate migration policies and policies for receiving migrants and can incorporate into those policies issues relating to national development, family protection, investment of remittances and the promotion of skills and qualifications. In countries of origin, technical assistance poses greater challenges because it has to take into account the causes behind labour migration, identify them and propose solutions to them. We should also consider how workers who return can be given support, and how to negotiate and implement bilateral and regional Conventions. The matters of welfare and social security should also be addressed.

The number of migrant workers has increased considerably over recent years. This is reflected in the greater number of women and young people who are migrating and who, in ever larger numbers, have an irregular status, entering countries of transit and destination illegally. This new and sizeable flow of undocumented workers gives rise to many problems, not only for workers, who can be abused and mistreated, but also for governments which are obliged to safeguard human rights. We must admit that for employers, as well, numerous problems arise, since the hiring of illegal workers always brings with it the threat of administrative sanctions and, in some cases, a prison sentence. Furthermore, for employers who seek to comply with national legislation, unfair competition on the part of those who do not do so constitutes a big obstacle and sometimes puts them at a complete disadvantage. Employers who break the law should be sanctioned but, on the other hand, if employers need workers to meet market demand, then they have no option but to look for that workforce, otherwise they cannot produce and they become less competitive and this in turn affects the company and its workers.

As you can see, this issue involves contradictions and endless problems which affect workers, employers and governments. No one can question governments' natural right to plan, decide and implement their migratory policies, but nor can we deny that the imperatives of the labour market should be borne in mind by governments and the latter should facilitate the hiring of migrants and ensure that their situation is made legal.

In the same way, it would be helpful to have a plan of action and a guide to hiring migrants, because labour rights, taxation, social security and the labour market would be improved immediately.

During the discussion, two subjects that were frequently brought up were the protection of the labour rights of migrants irrespective of their migrant status and the observance of human rights. We, the Employers, agree with the principle, but we must put on record that for this to work national laws and practices must be revised and adjusted accordingly. The matter of social protection is another area of great concern because it is essential that suitable legislation be adopted both at the national level and in bilateral and regional agreements. Europe's rich experience might help us to find ad hoc solutions in other regionalized economies. It is clear that what the Governing Body should do is to find a way of discerning better what migrant workers need in the context of work, to coordinate and work together with other bodies concerned with the subject of migration, for example, the United Nations Global Commission on International Migration and the International Migration Organization, to draw on and select basic principles from other existing instruments relating to migrants to which the report and resolution refer, to do everything necessary to more clearly identify the links which migration forges between countries of origin and countries of destination, to establish better statistics, to more clearly identify needs and lastly to give full backing to technical assistance.

This difficult assignment has taught us some lessons, which are worth mentioning so that we can improve our work. The first lesson is that the Office should focus on very neutral documents of a reasonable length, which do not lead to the discussion of factors which do not relate to the world of work. The second main lesson is that conclusions are just that – conclusions, not a review of the original documents and reports. You cannot finish your work when conclusions go beyond the essential and touch on secondary matters.

The third great lesson is that the spokespersons of the Workers' and Employers' groups should discuss the subject before the Conference, to establish positions and start to look for alternatives. We have done this for the second time and the result is now visible. Furthermore, governments should be supplied with information in advance and an attempt should be made to find an answer to subjects like this one, which have many political implications.

I must point out that the omens for our work were not good. The success of this important Committee required the constant hard work, patience and intelligence of our Chairperson, the Minister of Labour from Senegal, Mr. Dé, the work of Ms. Burrow, spokesperson of the Workers, whose experience, good faith, pragmatism and enormous intelligence made it possible to find solutions, prepare texts, and press on with finding a settlement. My thanks to both of them.

As far as the secretariat is concerned, I would also like to extend my thanks and recognition to the excellent and marvellous team from the Office, especially Monique Zarka-Matres, Manolo Abella, Javier Escobar and Patrick Taran, who, together with their team, and Mr. Assan Diop, always did their utmost to find solutions.

The report you have just heard was prepared by Mr. Kebbon of the Swedish Government, who kept our work in perspective and facilitated the adoption of the report.

For my group, this beautiful mosaic of different national realities, I only have thanks for their support, wisdom and tenacity. To the Government delegates, I would like to express my recognition and gratitude for their ability, intelligence, and patriotism in accepting proposals without having a binding text or proposal so that a solution could be found to a problem which affects us all.

Lastly, a note of gratitude to and admiration for the interpreters and translators, these people who are essential and invisible because we cannot see them from here, but who make it possible for us to communicate.

Ms. BURROW *(Workers' delegate, Australia, Worker Vice-Chairperson of the Committee on Migrant Workers)*

I am very pleased to be able to speak on the conclusions concerning a plan of action for the ILO on the critical topic of migration.

At the outset, I would like to apologize to members of the Committee on Migrant Workers for not being present yesterday for the adoption of our report. Unfortunately, I had accepted an invitation to attend another meeting in Europe when the adoption of our report was originally scheduled for Monday. Nevertheless, my colleagues have briefed me on the developments from yesterday, and I was delighted to hear that the conclusions and the report were adopted with the full endorsement of all members of the Committee.

I wish to particularly thank Mr. Dé, our Chairperson, for the extremely gracious comments he made yesterday at the adoption of the report, and to reiterate the thanks of the Workers' group for the professional and good humoured manner in which our Chairperson managed the work of the Committee over the last two weeks.

My thanks also go to the Government representatives and the Office for the valuable contributions they made to our work.

I also wish to thank Mr. de Regil, my counterpart from the Employers' group, for the extremely constructive collaboration and the genuine friendship that we have developed over the last few weeks. I am confident that we will continue to work closely together on the implementation of these conclusions and the further development of the multilateral framework.

Our collaboration is based on mutual respect and a recognition that both employers' organizations and trade unions have a serious stake in these issues. The needs of the labour market and the need for the protection of workers coincide in a way that provides a powerful and timely concern for both our constituencies.

Unions and employers have a serious stake in the debates taking place on migration at the national and international levels. If our voices are sidelined or ignored, the tensions that already surround migration will be exacerbated.

On the other hand, as the discussions over the last two weeks have demonstrated, we can help reduce fears about the consequences of migration and forge consensus.

The development of a multilateral framework on migration will place the ILO, and thus employers, workers and governments, back at the heart of deliberations on migration.

The ILO has a natural mandate concerning labour migration and we hope that this plan of action will see it realized.

I understand that in his closing comments yesterday, Mr. Dé referred to the strength of tripartism and the way in which the ILO, through its tripartite structure, enables us to consider controversial issues like migration from all perspectives. I fully share his opinion on this issue. Indeed, migration is undoubtedly a complex and, unfortunately, increasingly controversial issue. The debates over the last two weeks were always frank and at times a little heated. Yet we managed, through compromise, on all sides, to reach a full consensus.

The final conclusions fairly reflect the desires of all sides, we believe. In the course of our debate, we considered more than 180 amendments to the draft conclusions.

A large proportion of these amendments was submitted by governments of industrialized market economy countries (IMEC). The majority of these governments have economies dependent on migration, and yet are dealing with significant political and social debate concerning its impact. Through constructive consultations and negotiations, we eventually found compromises and were able to reflect not only the IMEC concerns, but also those of developing country governments, in the final conclusions. It is amazing that, despite the nature of the subject, it was not necessary to have a single vote in the Committee. Our conclusions have been adopted unanimously and this is testament to the balanced nature of the outcome.

I have also received a full report on the comments made by the ILO Director-General at the adoption of our report yesterday. I understand that he described our conclusions as a milestone for the future of coherence in the multilateral system and a concrete response to the report of the World Commission on the Social Dimensions of Globalization. I am told that the Director-General indicated strong support for the plan of action and accepted the request in our conclusions for the ILO to elaborate the multilateral framework for migration. He undertook to report back to the Governing Body in November 2005 as we had asked.

The development of the multilateral framework on migration was the central component of the Workers' group's submissions through the discussion. We adopted this approach because of a fundamental belief that increased and better managed migration has the potential to provide substantial benefits for both receiving and sending countries.

As members of the Committee are aware, I have spoken at great length over the last two weeks about the economic advantages migration contributes to economic growth in receiving countries. There is a need for continuing migration to offset demographic changes and rejuvenate ageing labour forces. In Canada alone, by 2010, all net growth in the labour force will come from migration.

We have focused on the *potential* economic benefits of migration for developing countries. Reduced labour supply in countries with high unemployment, underemployment and massive informal economies can reduce labour market pressure and put up pressure on wages and working conditions, thereby offering greater security and dignity for working families. Remittances, return migration and the potential for migrants to help their home countries, receive the technology investments and increase trade opportunities they require for economic development all add to the positive economic potential represented by migration.

Unfortunately, at present, the economic opportunities presented by migration for both receiving and sending countries are not being maximized. We believe that the multilateral framework can help both industrialized and developing countries to adjust their policies and can assist all countries to achieve the potential benefit that increased migration can provide.

The Workers' group also adopted this stance because we concur with many of the conclusions regarding migration contained in the report of the World Commission on the Social Dimension of Globalization. The World Commission recognized that a major gap exists in the current institutional structure of the global economy. This was the absence of a multilateral framework to govern cross-border movement of peoples. In paragraph 431 of the World Commission's report, it was noted that, "from the perspective of developing countries the absence of a multilateral framework for the cross-border movement of people reflects yet another gap in the rules governing the global economy. Many of them maintain that freer migration to the industrialized world would be a swift and powerful means of increasing the benefit they receive from globalization." In this context, developing countries have increasingly recognized this potential and are now pushing for a significant expansion of temporary migration, or time-bound migration, in the context of the mode four discussions on the General Agreement on Trade in Services (GATS) at the World Trade Organization. We understand that there is still a strong desire amongst developing countries to extend GAT's mode four to cover unskilled workers and dramatically expand the magnitude of workers covered by this agreement.

In fact, despite all the discussions over the last two weeks about the various international forums discussing international migration, it is probably the trade negotiators within the WTO who will exercise the most immediate influence over the magnitude and scope of migration in the near future. However, a major concern for the trade union movement is that the GAT's mode four discussions have so far completely ignored the working conditions that should apply to people moving across borders under this arrangement. There has been no serious discussion of equal treatment, or implementation of relevant ILO standards for these workers within the WTO negotiations. Moreover, the WTO does not have the technical expertise to handle these labour-related issues in isolation from other international organizations.

This is, therefore, another reason why we believe that a multilateral framework is required, to influence and balance all aspects of migration. Again, we concur with the World Commission on the Social Dimension of Globalization, when it says, with regard to this issue: "a multilateral regime for the cross-border movement of people that makes the process more orderly and eliminates the exploitation of migrants could offer considerable gains for all".

In paragraph 433, the World Commission observed that "the lack of an orderly multilateral regime on the cross-border movement of people has, by default, allowed a number of serious collateral problems to emerge". According to the Commission, these problems include brain drain, increasing irregular migration, international trafficking and labour exploitation.

I am pleased to note that the conclusions of our Committee have fully recognized many of these negative consequences of migration. Large sections of our conclusions focus on the extent and the severity of labour abuse associated with migration.

Many, but not all, of the abuses relate to irregular migrant workers. The rapid expansion of irregular forms of migration in recent years is therefore one factor contributing to the increased incidence of abuse. Another explanatory factor is globalization and the increased competition in produce markets which result in the pressure to reduce labour costs. Unfortunately, this has led to the exploitation of irregular migration, of the irregular migrant workers, who are in vulnerable situations and are unable to defend their rights. Industries like agriculture and construction, along with women in domestic labour, are particularly vulnerable to migrant labour abuse and require special attention. The expansion of temporary or time-bound migration, if it takes place without adequate labour protection, could exacerbate these problems.

To mitigate these problems, urgent measures are required to encourage and expand regular migration as a substitute for irregular flows. I am delighted that our conclusions have recognized that the establishment of a more transparent and consistent migration procedure would go some way towards encouraging increased regular and less irregular migration.

During the discussions, the Workers' group argued that amnesties, or rather amnesty programmes, particularly for those migrants making a continuing contribution to both the communities and, indeed, the economies of their destination countries should be considered – programmes that would reduce the existing level of irregular migration through the regularization of such people. We are disappointed that the conclusions do not contain more forthright recommendations on this issue.

During the discussions, the Workers' group also highlighted concerns about the role that private recruitment agencies were playing in the abuse of migrant workers. To reduce the incidence of such problems, we called for the licensing and regular monitoring of migrant recruitment agencies and the introduction of penalties for agencies that infringed the law. Our conclusions reflect and respond to these concerns.

The major potential downside of migration for sending countries is brain drain. While our conclusions recognize the importance of this issue, I am somewhat disappointed that they do not contain more precise commitments to compensate developing countries for the lost investments that they are making in educating highly skilled workers who migrate. Also, I am disappointed that the conclusions did not deal more thoroughly with the inappropriate economic policies being pursued in many developing countries. The continued focus on privatization, labour market flexibility and restrictive macroeconomic policies are important "push" factors behind migration from developing countries.

However, on the positive side, our conclusions did recognize that there are often significant social costs associated with migration when it leads to family dislocation, along with the need for support through the ILO's Global Employment Agenda for the generation of decent work in countries of origin.

Given the economic potential of migration, the recognition that this potential is not being realized, plus the evidence of a series of widespread migrant worker abuses, there is obviously considerable scope to manage migration better and improve outcomes for all parties. We recognize that this is a complex task and will require a careful balance of competing interests. Given the multifaceted nature of the problems and issues that need to be addressed to generate a fair deal for sending countries, receiving countries and the migrants themselves, the Workers' group believes it is highly appropriate that, in paragraph 23 of our conclusions, we decided that: "In order to assist member States to develop more effective labour migration policies, the tripartite constituents have agreed to develop a non-binding multilateral framework for a rights-based approach to labour migration which takes account of national labour market needs."

Paragraph 24 contains 20 bullet points which are examples of the types of issues and policies that we have agreed should be included in the multilateral framework. Many of the issues identified in paragraph 24 respond to the economic, social and labour concerns that I have just elaborated. Paragraph 24 represents an open list of issues that will be addressed by the multilateral framework, and we have agreed that the framework will not be limited to these issues. The 20 issues we have specifically identified fall within the ILO mandate. Many of them concern action designed to more effectively protect the labour and human rights of all migrant workers and the promotion of the economic advantages of migration for both sending and receiving countries.

I have to admit that the term "rights-based" generated much discussion within the Committee. Throughout this discussion, the Workers' group were consistent and clear about the meaning attached to these words. In our opinion, a rights-based approach to migration is one that reflects the relevant international labour standards and principles that have been developed through the ILO. We are pleased that the Committee eventually accepted this approach and reflected this in our conclusions.

The conclusions we have adopted clearly acknowledge that the Migration for Employment Convention (Revised), 1949 (No. 97), and the Migrant Workers (Supplementary Provisions) Convention, 1975 (No. 143), remain relevant today. The Committee has unanimously agreed that the ILO may undertake a campaign to promote ratification of these Conventions and the implementation of the principles within these Conventions that relate to the protection of migrant workers. We call on the Governing Body and the Office to ensure that the resources are available to implement this decision.

We note that some 22 countries have asked for assistance. We believe that this is important foundation work if migrant workers are to be protected and migratory flows efficient and respected. We believe that this is in the interests of all parties – Governments, Workers and Employers – and wards against the unfair competition which the Employers are rightfully concerned about.

Our conclusions also confirm that a number of other ILO instruments are relevant to migrant workers. These include, but are not limited to, the fundamental ILO Conventions and ILO standards concerning private employment agencies, social security, protection of wages, maternity protection, labour inspection and occupational safety and health. Taken together, these instruments provide an appropriate basis for a rights-based approach to migration.

We would also draw attention to paragraph 29 of our conclusions, which states that: "Participants endorsed the conclusions of the 1997 Tripartite

Meeting of Experts." Our conclusions call on the Office to promote the implementation of the guidelines on special protective measures for migrant workers in time-bound activities. These guidelines include provision of equal treatment on wages and other terms of employment for workers in time-bound or temporary activities and nationals performing similar work. In our opinion, these conclusions should help overcome any lacunae that may exist in Conventions Nos. 97 and 143 in respect of what are often referred to as "posted migrant workers".

Paragraph 31 of our conclusions recognizes the importance of capacity building on issues related to migration for governments and employers' and workers' organizations. It is recognized that migration policy, labour rights, legislation and practice, national databases, labour inspection services, campaigns against racism and xenophobia, as well as the generation of decent work, are all areas of critical importance for us all and assistance is vital to achieve such.

The key to ongoing understanding and policy development on migration is social dialogue. In paragraph 34 of the conclusions, the Committee has requested the ILO to support social dialogue at both national and international levels. Let me again thank all concerned and in particular pay an important tribute to my own team: Bob Kyloh, Luc Demaret, Verena Schmidt from the Bureau for Workers' Activities and Ms. Elsa from the International Confederation of Free Trade Unions as the Workers' group secretary. They have been tireless workers; their ability, their capacity to find a way through has been very much respected by me and I think, along with a very competent Bureau and drafting group, we have served the Workers' group well. But I think that we have served the Committee in general and migrant workers well.

In conclusion, this general discussion on migration was one of the first experiments with the new integrated approach to subjects that the ILO has been promoting in recent years. We have decided that there is no need to reopen or revise the existing ILO instruments concerning migration at this time. Rather, we have decided that the existing instruments related to migration should be promoted. We have also decided that the ILO should substantially expand its activities on migration. In fact, we have jointly devised a plan of action for future work of the Office, including the development and implementation of a non-binding multilateral framework on migration.

I would agree with the Director-General that this represents a milestone in ILO work on migration. This moment in time, and these decisions, are comparable to the decisions taken in 1949 and 1975, when the ILO adopted the two existing Conventions on migrant work. We recall that Convention No. 97 set the framework for bilateral agreements that helped govern migration policy in the middle decades of the last century. We are confident that our plan of action and multilateral framework will provide the guidance required to better manage and more appropriately govern labour migration in the twenty-first century. We ask for your support.

Original French: Mr. DE *(Minister of Public Services, Labour, Employment and Professional Organizations, Senegal; Chairperson of the Committee on Migrant Workers)*

Over the past two weeks it has been my honour to chair the Committee on Migrant Workers. Today, I have the great pleasure of informing you that the Committee has reached a broad consensus on a major initiative: a plan of action for the ILO on the issue of migrant workers.

The challenge which we had to meet is reflected in the title of the report, which proved an extremely useful working document for our debates. We had to find ways towards a fair deal for migrant workers in the context of a global economy. Knowing how sensitive migration issues are, it was a truly enormous challenge and I think that we were all a little apprehensive of it as we begun our discussions.

The task was indeed very difficult. Perceptions varied widely on many issues amongst Governments themselves, then between Workers, Employers and Governments. But, thanks to a remarkable spirit of conciliation, the Committee managed to build consensus on issues which, as Mr. Somavia underlined, are some of the most difficult issues that the international community has the responsibility of dealing with.

It is quite clear that one thing really helped us: the fact that all parties involved (Governments, Employers and Workers) share one and the same commitment – to provide better protection for migrant workers and a better system for managing labour migrations. What I think is particularly remarkable is that the Committee undertook to identify a number of very specific questions which are to be included in a multilateral framework for managing migrations. The Committee also managed, in a what I believe to be a truly brilliant manner, to provide the Office with clear guidance on the issues which need to be covered by guidelines for this subject.

It is in the context which I have just described, that we submit to you today the result of our work. You have before you our report: a faithful and objective account of the broad-ranging discussions, and our conclusions on a fair deal for migrant workers in a global economy, including a plan of action for migrant workers. These conclusions are founded on tripartite support, and are backed unanimously by all the members of our Committee. They reflect agreement on paths which we must continue to explore within the context of an ongoing multilateral debate, needed in order to respond to the different concerns expressed, and to help us move towards a fairer deal for migrant workers, it being understood that all this will be done in close cooperation with the relevant United Nations institutions and agencies.

The proposed plan of action contains a number of elements. We have agreed to establish a non-binding multilateral framework to guide us, taking a rights-based approach to the handling of international migration. This framework takes into account labour market needs and respects the sovereign right of all States to determine their own migration policies, including the terms for entry into their territory and under which conditions migrants may remain. It lists a number of issues on which the ILO, in a tripartite context, will have to develop guidelines based on best practices to be considered by the Governing Body in November 2005.

We reiterate the importance of international labour standards on the subject of international migration and also the need to improve knowledge and implementation of these standards. We underline the need for capacity-building in the member States and the need to provide assistance for this, as well as the need to develop our knowledge base when it comes to international migration. Lastly, we reiterate and underline the crucial importance of social dialogue in this context.

I think we all agree that there have been times during the past two weeks when we had our reservations as to whether we would be able to reconcile our different points of view. I am pleased with the efforts made by all members of the Committee to seek and achieve consensus, which enabled us to successfully conclude our work.

It is my honour now to submit, for the consideration of all, the report of the Committee on Migrant Workers to the International Labour Conference in 2004, as well as the conclusions which will allow us to move towards a fairer deal for migrant workers in the global economy.

May I express my hope that this plenary will vote in a positive manner on the results of our deliberations.

May I, before I conclude, address my warm thanks and congratulations to the Employer Vice-Chairperson, Mr. de Regil, and the Worker Vice-Chairperson, Ms. Burrow, for their leadership, perceptiveness, pragmatism, and their awareness of their group's positions, but also their ability to draft and to compromise. In the same way, I would like to thank all the Government, Employer, and Worker members of the Committee.

I would like also to congratulate and thank the entire secretariat, who gave us all the help we required. In particular, I would like to mention Mr. Abella, Ms. Zarka-Martres, Mr. Javier Escobar and Mr. Taran.

Original Spanish: The PRESIDENT

The general discussion on the report of the Committee on Migrant Workers is now open.

Mr. PENDER *(Government adviser and substitute delegate, Ireland; on behalf of the European Union)*

I have the honour to take the floor on behalf of the European Union. I want, at the outset, to thank the Chairperson of the Committee for the way in which he chaired its deliberations. This was done with patience and good humour when required, particularly when delicate or sensitive issues of a political or technical nature were being addressed. I also want to thank the ILO secretariat staff for their work during the sittings of the Committee and behind the scenes in the last two weeks, and the interpreters for their dedication and great patience during some long sessions.

The EU Member States consider that the work undertaken at this Conference makes an important contribution to a future ILO plan of action in the area of improving the position of migrant workers, without duplicating work that is already being undertaken by other international bodies. It was also considered important to ensure that the sovereignty of governments was respected in relation to migration policy.

We welcome the adoption by the Conference of the resolution concerning a fair deal for migrant workers in a global economy. The Governing Body of the ILO has been asked to give due consideration to the conclusions contained in the resolution in planning future action on migrant workers. The Director-General has also been requested to take them into account when preparing the Programme and Budget for the 2006-07 biennium and in allocating such other resources as may be available in the current 2004-05 biennium.

I want to thank my colleagues from the other 24 EU Member States and the European Commission for their assistance. They have demonstrated great friendship towards Ireland during its EU presidency and during the work of the Committee. There is an old Irish proverb which, when translated into English, states "the journey is shorter if there are two of you". In the context of the tripartite system and consensus-building approach of the ILO, I want to acknowledge the contributions from both the Workers' and Employers' representatives; I think that the proverb should perhaps now be changed to read "the journey is shorter if there are three of you". We have all worked very hard on reaching a consensus on this resolution, and on behalf of the European Union, I commend the Committee's report and the resolution to this plenary of the 92nd Session of the International Labour Conference. And finally, I would like to say thank you, or as we say in Irish: go raibh maith agaibh.

Mr. GAMMAMPILA DON *(Government delegate, Sri Lanka)*

We noted with appreciation the rich discussion held in the Committee on Migrant Workers dealing with international migration and the true state of tripartism demonstrated during the proceedings, and the adopting of the Report of the Committee.

Migration is now of global importance and is dealt with in a multitude of forums touching on its various dimensions. The cross-cutting nature of migration has created a need to make effective links between issues and discussions in various international forums. Therefore, Sri Lanka endorses that the ILO should play a central role and hopes that it can work in effective coordination with other relevant organizations.

Sri Lanka is of the view that setting up a permanent committee on migration of the ILO Governing Body is desirable for the purpose of implementing the conclusions and plan of action. In this context, Sri Lanka supports the proposal and urges the member States to seriously consider the setting up of a permanent committee.

Sri Lanka has an estimated 1 million workers overseas which is equivalent to one-seventh of the labour force. It is also the principal source of foreign exchange earnings in the country. Our migratory flow, moreover, is characterized by predominantly unskilled females who are mainly engaged in domestic work and who choose to migrate to improve their living standards.

We therefore place emphasis on the need to protect the rights of migrant workers and endorse the agreement to have a rights-based approach which recognizes labour market needs and the sovereign rights of all nations.

We also agree with the proposed conclusions which underline the complex relationship between migration and development. A comprehensive national approach to improve social welfare and cohesion in the context of a large population of migrant workers is an issue of special interest to Sri Lanka. Accordingly, the situation of the family which faces special problems upon the departure of migrant workers, especially female migrants, is an area to be addressed, and endorses the need to have renewed focus.

Sri Lanka also welcomes all capacity building, awareness raising and technical assistance from the ILO in the field of migration with a view to promoting and protecting human rights and labour rights. We agree with the proposal to develop a framework for international guidelines on best practices and international standards.

Finally, I want to thank the Committee on Migrant Workers and persons involved in its activities for producing an excellent document. I fervently hope that effective implementation of the conclusions will strengthen welfare and protection measures accorded to migrant workers and help both labour-supplying countries and receiving countries to benefit from international migration.

Ms. SAAB (Government delegate, Lebanon)

We highly esteem Report VI, *Towards a fair deal for migrant workers in the global economy*, for its entirety and entire methodology.

We believe that the issue of migrant workers is a complex one. This can be seen when we consider the plan of action for a non-binding multilateral framework which will protect and take into account the particularities of States in dealing with or enacting legislation to address this subject. The International Labour Office has a wide responsibility to disseminate information and provide a database on the global labour market to both receiving and sending countries. The ILO should also provide technical assistance, when required, to thus facilitate the consideration of adequate policies based on the national sovereignty of governments. Lastly, I would like to thank the Committee on Migrant Workers for the value of this work.

Mr. MANLEY (Employers' adviser, United States)

The conclusions and plan of action referred to in the Committee on Migrant Workers' report are significant for international employers in a number of ways; permit me to address just a few of them. First, the conclusion and plan of action are fully supportive of the needs of international businesses for recruiting, training, assigning and allocating human talent around the world. The report clearly acknowledges the benefits to all when individual or enterprises are free to hire and transfer human assets as they judge best for commercial advantage in a competitive global market place. The action plan is explicit in calling for orderly and efficient sovereign migration policies that are coherent, transparent, viable, adaptable and dynamic to facilitate these needs.

Second, the plan of action is significant for the mode of ILO leadership recommended by the tripartite constituents in the complex area of migration. By their consensus to proceed with the non-binding framework of best practice guidelines rather than a more traditional Convention or other such instrument, the parties recognize that progress on such complex topics is likely to be more enduring if partners are led by enlightened example, rather than pushed by inflexible conformity. In this specific regard, the Committee made the correct decision when it retreated from the original suggestion that the ILO undertake a renewed campaign to ratify migration Conventions drafted 50 and 30 years ago.

The nature of global work-based migration has changed drastically in the quarter century to half century that has passed since those instruments were prepared, as the plan of action specifically notes. This has been a chief reason why those instruments have had such a low level of ratification. The Committee report now simply acknowledges that the ILO, of course, may promote those Conventions, but the action plan makes plain that the limited resources of this body are better devoted to other things.

The ILO should not attempt to drive forward on the migration topic by looking in the rear-view mirror at those outdated and inapplicable instruments. To the extent that the Migration for Employment Convention (Revised), 1949 (No. 97), and the Migrant Workers (Supplementary Provisions) Convention, 1975 (No. 143), recite historical principles relevant to modern circumstance, we may, of course learn from them. However, the work of the ILO in the area of work-based migration should focus on a viable and flexible framework of forward-looking best practices; it should not seek further to promote ratification of Conventions Nos. 97 and 143.

Mr. ANDERSON (Employers' adviser and substitute delegate, Australia)

Australian employers support the adoption of the draft report of the Committee on Migrant Workers. This report is the product of the detailed, lively and difficult tripartite social dialogue that has taken place over the past two weeks. The final result is an analysis of the issue of global labour migration, which goes to the heart of its economic and social dimensions.

Many difficulties were encountered in developing a coherent set of conclusions that reflect the tripartite interests within this institution. Given this, it is remarkable that a coherent set of conclusions is now before us. I am particularly pleased that paragraphs 3 and 4 highlight the benefits of labour migration, that paragraph 10 provides an overview of the challenges faced by employers of migrant labour, and that numerous paragraphs juxtapose the recommended "rights-based" approach with a consideration of labour market needs and national sovereignty.

Australian industry, as a significant net employer of labour migrants, is doing its part to offer opportunity, skills development and increased living standards for migrant workers and their families. To be effective and credible, national policy on labour migration needs to be managed to meet the changing needs of industry and the circumstances of migrants themselves. The report accepts this proposition. The end point of the report is a recommendation for a multilateral plan of action at the international level that focuses social dialogue on best practice and on guidelines to influence national law and practice.

The strength of this recommendation is that it does not mandate a policy on member States. It is a non-binding framework. That is the sensible approach, given the obvious problems that member States, and many employers for that matter, have with the content of current instruments and especially with certain aspects of Conventions Nos. 97 and 143, and the supporting Recommendations.

In order to achieve a workable way forward, the Committee resolved early on in its discussions not to debate the rights and wrongs of specific provisions of those instruments; that was sensible. However, from an employer's perspective, the very low ratification rate of these instruments suggests that fundamental problems with them remain. At some point, this institution will need to "bite the bullet" and revise these instruments to render them consistent with the modern world of commerce and industry, and the social reality.

Finally, I join with my colleagues in sincerely thanking all of the Officers of the Committee and the staff from the International Organisation of Employers, the Bureau for Employers' Activities and the ILO. I am especially grateful to our Employer Vice-Chairperson, Mr. Jorge de Regil, whose judgement, patience and humour made many long days and nights worthwhile and fulfilling. I also acknowledge the significant work of the Workers' delegates and Government representatives. I support the adoption of the draft report.

Original Spanish: Mr. TERAN *(Employers' delegate, Ecuador)*

The Committee on Migrant Workers, at this 92nd Session of the International Labour Conference, was faced with an enormous challenge. It has dealt with a matter in which it was difficult to attain a consensus due to the natural complexity of the issue, for this is a matter which can be analysed from different approaches. Furthermore, the practical difficulties which had to be met were derived from studying draft conclusions which were too extensive. Nonetheless, we have achieved satisfactory results. We have drawn up an objective document – which is before this Assembly – which reflects faithfully the opinions expressed by the social partners and governments in the course of our discussions.

What is most important is that the conclusions are fair and also achievable. The document reflects the point of view, from the outset, of the Employers' group, which stated that an attempt to find ways of settling the problems relating to migration should not necessarily be through trying to get more countries to ratify the Migration for Employment Convention (Revised), 1949 (No. 97), and the Migrant Workers (Supplementary Provisions) Convention, 1975 (No. 143). Rather, it should be by identifying policies and structures which were necessary to ensure organized and well-ordered migration within an appropriate legal framework.

The final suggestions in this document are along these lines, and there are several recommendations to member States, to the ILO and to the others involved in this matter, which, if they are applied, will, we are sure, make it possible to find appropriate solutions to this very ambitious and vitally important objective.

In the text of the document, specific reference is made to the importance that migration has for all countries involved, irrespective of whether they are sending countries, receiving countries or transit countries. As was mentioned by our Employer spokesperson in his statement, with regard to Latin America – which is my own region – it is essential to mention the importance of remittances sent by migrant workers to their families remaining at home. These remittances have gradually become a flow which is becoming increasingly important in our very weak economies. If we did not have these flows the problem of poverty would be even greater. This is why it is so important, as the report says, to ensure that migration is appropriately regulated.

As long as the major problems faced by a large proportion of migrant workers are not ignored or hidden, particularly of those workers who are in an irregular situation and are, therefore, easy prey for traffickers who are operating outside the law, the document before us is very proactive and sets out proposals and suggests a series of measures to be adopted, both by governments, the social partners themselves, and the ILO. These proposals seek to ensure that policies are implemented which lessen the negative aspects of migration. The basic premise is that everything should be enshrined in law, and the legal principles contained in international law, while at the same time safeguarding national sovereignty so that countries can develop their domestic standards, thereby developing their own migration policies, which must be in accordance with the needs of their labour markets.

In the light of all these facts, we consider that the draft report which we have before us reflects appropriately the views of the Employers' group on this very delicate issue, and we therefore call upon the members of this Conference to adopt the report, thereby giving an appropriate guide for the work of the ILO in the future.

Original Spanish: Mr. CESTER BEATOBE *(Employers' adviser, Spain)*

It is well known that migratory movements for work purposes are not a new phenomenon, but we need to recognize that in recent years they have increased in intensity, and it is now something which affects nearly all countries in the world, be it as countries of origin, destination or as a place of transit for migrant workers. We can see this from the interesting draft conclusions prepared by the Office for discussion at this 92nd Session of the International Labour Conference, which is very rich in content, but perhaps too long for a discussion which requires a great deal of concentration.

In the European context, our countries have historically been active protagonists in these migratory flows, and today, given the ageing population in many countries of the European Union, and the growing need for labour in certain occupations, the response to the future needs of the labour market can be found in regular migration.

The benefits of regular labour migrations are well known by all. Countries are rejuvenated, their populations are complemented, employers meet their labour requirements, and workers find employment which enables them to develop their future.

For these benefits to occur, and this is the first important point, we need to intensify as far as possible bilateral and multilateral agreements and the exchange of information between countries of origin and destination of migrants, as well as consultations between governments and the social partners of different countries, to ensure that migratory labour flows cover the labour needs of receiving countries and that regular migrant workers find the kind of work they want.

A second important aspect for migration to be effective is the acceleration of administrative procedures so that workers can be regularized and available for work. Entrepreneurs need swift administration to take on workers and workers want to be regularized as soon as possible so that they can work with proper guarantees.

A third important matter for entrepreneurs in the European Union is the necessary distinction that must be made between regular migrants and irregular migrant workers. The regular migrant worker, who has all the administrative permits to reside and work in a country, also enjoys that country's labour rights. Regular immigration is therefore a guarantee of equal treatment with nationals of the receiving country, and is also a guarantee for the employer with respect to the authorities.

Irregular migrants, on the other hand may enjoy fundamental labour rights and decent working conditions, but will never have the same social protection that the regular migrant has. For that reason, it is important that countries should have the proper mechanisms to encourage regular migration and control irregular migration, in order to guarantee the rights of workers and employers as well as instruments to match migration to the need for labour.

In this respect, we need to recognize the right of countries to establish policies to regulate these flows, and entry to a country should not automatically provide the right to regularization of an irregular migrants situation.

Finally, all labour migration policies should be accompanied by measures for social and labour integration of irregular migrants and the possibility to return to their country of origin in due course.

On all these matters, the ILO can and must play an active role, encouraging the exchange of good practice and information between all its members and that is why we think it opportune to support the report which has been drafted by the Committee.

Ms. COKE-LLOYD *(Employers' adviser and substitute delegate, Jamaica)*

The Jamaican and Caribbean employers unhesitatingly endorse the draft conclusions on a fair deal for migrant workers. Many of the issues raised in that document are immediately familiar to us, given our experience in Jamaica and the wider Caribbean.

We note the statement in paragraph 2 that "a very large part of contemporary migration is directly or indirectly related to the world of work". This fact has particular connotations for us in the Caribbean. Initially, migrants to the First World countries were largely workers from the lower end of the labour market who took advantage of opportunities to perform menial tasks that were shunned by citizens in the First World. This offered opportunities for advancement that were beyond the capacity of the developing countries from which these workers came. The impacts of these initial migration outflows were largely positive for both destination and sending countries. The migrants were able to improve their socio-economic status and that of family members left at home.

Since then, most developing countries have moved on and, certainly in the Caribbean, a large body of educated workers is now contributing to development in the region. The rest of the world has also moved on. The intensified globalization of the last few decades has resulted in a marked shift in the quality of migrants leaving the developing countries; instead of the less-skilled workers of the past, highly skilled, educated workers such as nurses, teachers and other professionals, are being aggressively recruited by the developed countries.

This has proven to be a challenge to Caribbean nations. Some of the challenges relate, firstly, to the cost and volume of training and retraining that Caribbean countries have to contend with as they face the well-documented "brain drain"; secondly, to the difficulty of managing the exodus to ensure that the region's productive capacity is not seriously undermined by the loss of essential skills; thirdly, to the need to create relevant and attractively remunerated jobs in the developing world that will compete with overseas markets in attracting and retaining the best skills.

On the other hand, it has been argued that the net economic impact of migration outflows in developing countries has been greater than the contribution of some of the productive sectors in these countries. In this regard, economists estimate that remittances to the Latin American and Caribbean region represent the second largest source of foreign exchange inflows into the region. Remittances from these migrants have been steadily increasing over the last decade.

It has also been shown that, in many instances, migrants have returned to their homelands, bringing enhanced skills and capital with them, and that developing countries, particularly in the Caribbean, are in a position to capitalize on their domestic capacity to produce high-quality workers by marketing their training programmes overseas as relatively low-cost options.

Clearly, then, migration is not a one-way street that works solely against one country to the benefit of another. Indeed, our employers welcome the two-way flow of labour and support the freedom of movement of skills across borders. In this regard, it is a process that needs the collaborative efforts of developed and developing countries, workers and employers, governments and unions. Without this, the negative impacts of migration will be more manifest in the countries from which migrants originate.

To this end, the comprehensive policy framework being developed by the ILO is a substantial springboard which we can use to determine direction and marshal the resources that are necessary to manage this complex and increasingly global process.

In conclusion, we look forward to this effort of helping to ensure that there will be an alleviation for member States in the circumstances that drive migration and in the provision of technical assistance to member States in the development of labour migration policy and administration.

We also take this opportunity of thanking the Chairperson, Vice-Chairpersons, secretariat and members of the Committee on Migrant Workers for a job well done.

Ms. PHILLIPS *(Workers' adviser and substitute delegate, Jamaica)*

My comments speak to the controversial areas of the feminization of migration and its impact on women and their families.

International migration is not new – what is new is that many women are migrating alone, without their families. The typical profile of the migrant worker is no longer than of the male breadwinner: instead, an increasing number of migrant workers, since the 1980s, are women, who may be single or married and are often "better educated than men". Today, women migrate alone since they, too, are breadwinners and are responsible for taking care of their ageing relatives and young children back home. However, the types of employment undertaken by them leave them open to exploitation. Often, their conditions of work do not meet the minimum standards established by the International Labour Organization.

The term feminization is broadly understood to be a positive measure for women, as it allows women to be regarded as actors and contributors to development. Women have always been central to productive and reproductive development. However, women still remain peripheral in policies that address development. Migration therefore is a method of liberation or emancipation used by many women to overcome domination and subservience as required and maintained by the system of patriarchy. Unfortunately, the need for justice and personhood by some women frequently leads to injustices that equate to jumping out of the frying pan and into the fire, as they become victims of unscrupulous persons who recognize their anxiety and exploit their search for a better quality of life.

Women often end up as undocumented, working under appalling conditions and on meagre wages. One reason for this is that there are not many bilateral or multilateral agreements in traditionally female occupations such as nursing and care-giving. Other factors that contribute to women becoming undocumented workers are that domestic work and sex work are often not recognized as work.

In order to improve the situation of female migrants, bilateral and multilateral agreements are needed, like those obtained in the agricultural and construction industries, to allow for the legal migration of women. Regularization procedures have to take into account the special conditions under which female domestic workers and female labour migrants work. These workers often have no formal work contract and no formal contract for housing. Recognition of qualifications would allow women to seek jobs in areas other than the private household sector. Presently, professionals from many sending countries are employed as domestic workers because of non-recognition of their professional qualifications by the receiving countries.

The protection of the rights of migrants and in particular women, who are often at the lowest rung of the migration ladder, cannot be denied by any person who accepts the dignity and right of every person to decent work and a better quality of life. Ratification and implementation of the Migration for Employment Convention (Revised), 1949 (No. 97), and the Migrant Workers (Supplementary Provisions) Convention, 1975 (No. 143), as well as of the 1990 International Convention on the Protection of the Rights of All Migrant Workers and Members of their Families, is fundamental for the improvement of the situation in respect of migrant workers, and in particular women migrant workers. I should point out the ILO Conventions are still valid for us workers, and have never been more important. The ILO Declaration on Fundamental Principles and Rights at Work and its Follow-up is also indispensable for the improvement of the conditions of migrant workers, and in particular women migrant workers.

The Declaration of Philadelphia particularly included women in the following statement: "All human beings, irrespective of race, creed or sex, have the right to pursue both their material well-being and their spiritual development in conditions of freedom and dignity, of economic security and equal opportunity." May I also take this opportunity to remind you of the significance of the ILO's eight core Conventions that encompass freedom of association and the right to bargain collectively in the ILO tradition of tripartism. Let us all cooperate effectively to implement these Conventions and instruments so that the ILO plays a leading role on migrant workers. Indeed, the conclusions adopted by our Committee and tabled to this Conference do provide a sound basis for a renewed impulse by the ILO, and by the social partners, in efforts to protect migrant workers, women and men.

Finally, it is our fervent hope that the spirit of consensus that prevailed in our Committee will ultimately be achieved in all committees.

Original French: Ms. KIPULU KATANI *(Workers' adviser, Democratic Republic of Congo)*

On behalf of Africa, and on behalf of my own country, the Democratic Republic of Congo, faced as we are with the problems of migration, I would like to thank the Committee on Migrant Workers for giving me permission to address this assembly and to put before you an African appeal on behalf of migrant workers.

In Africa, the revival of migratory flows bringing workers towards economically more favourable parts of the continent is giving rise to a series of problems. Linked, in particular, to economic, social or political practices, these difficulties often deprive migrant workers of their fundamental rights. The practices I am referring to are, in part, based on traditional practices which may result in extreme cases of servitude and denial of human dignity. The situation of workers who either choose to go elsewhere, or who are forced to go elsewhere, becomes a problem both with regard to the working conditions and to the displacement, as such, because it entails losing touch with the cultural and social context of the worker's country of origin.

The increase in international mobility and the growth in labour migration is giving rise to problems all over the world. In Africa, in recent years, we have seen a resurgence in violent acts directed against migrant workers and their families, sometimes jeopardizing their fundamental rights and even their physical integrity. In some countries of reception there is xenophobia and forms of racism and exclusion resulting in mass expulsions or in mass denial of the civic rights of long-established migrant workers, thus calling into question the whole process of integration and the process which has made it possible for them to acquire the country of reception's citizenship. This type of behaviour is institutional, and social in origin and is the consequence of the absence of a proper legal framework which would give better treatment to migrants and the absence of a proper legal framework for the rights of migrant workers.

Whereas for a long time, migration in general terms, and involuntary migration, in particular, involved mainly men, at the end of the twentieth century there has been a gradual feminization of migratory flows. Moreover, current migration does not only involve the movement of unskilled workers, increasingly it also involves the brain drain from South to North. Here, too, the phenomenon of feminization of migration is to be seen, especially in the health sector, where a gradual deterioration of living and working conditions linked in particular to reforms in public services is implicated. All over the world, human rights violations are taking on an increasingly female face: poverty, unemployment, discrimination and inequality, physical and psychological violence, insecurity and aggression, and racism and exclusion. Women who migrate do so in the hope of finding their rights more fully respected. To some extent, the structural adjustment programmes in Africa have turned this continent into an exporter of migrant labour because these structural adjustment programmes devastated public services and dismantled decent and stable employment. This is why we say that international financial institutions bear a heavy responsibility for the phenomenon of migration in Africa.

In order to guarantee and promote the rights of migrants, we are making an urgent appeal to all States which have not yet done so to ratify the Migration for Employment Convention (Revised), 1949 (No. 97), and the Migrant Workers (Supplementary Provisions) Convention, 1975 (No. 143), and to do so without further delay. We also ask the tripartite constituents of all countries to support unanimously the principle of establishing multilateral frameworks for migrant workers. With this prospect in mind we expect you to give your unreserved support to the plan of action put to you by the Committee on Migrant Workers.

Ms. AVENDANO-DENIER (Workers' adviser, United States)

I am going to address my comments today to the issues of irregular migration and the struggles of irregular migrant workers, which are critical issues for workers in the United States. As the rich discussion in our Committee showed, these are also issues that are important to trade unions and workers all over the world.

Our Committee's report recognizes that due consideration must be given to the particular problems of irregular migrant workers, and stresses that ILO instruments provide for equal treatment and the respect of basic human rights for all migrant workers, regardless of status. Indeed, we are reminded that ILO instruments apply to all workers, including irregular migrants. Importantly, our Committee unanimously agreed that the ILO will play a crucial role in shaping the future of labour migration, and that ILO instruments are the fundamental building-blocks for a multilateral framework.

I am surprised that several Employer speakers have suggested that the Migration for Employment Convention (Revised), 1949 (No. 97), and the Migrant Workers (Supplementary Provisions) Convention, 1975 (No. 143), are outdated. Arguments in support of this position were not placed before the Committee through the two weeks of our discussions. On the contrary, the Committee unanimously adopted conclusions that reflect the relevance of these Conventions. The specific comments on the Conventions are contained in the following paragraphs of the conclusions and I would like to read them for the record.

In paragraph 11 of our conclusions, all parties unanimously agreed to the following language: "The Migration for Employment Convention (Revised), 1949 (No. 97), and the Migrant Workers (Supplementary Provisions) Convention, 1975 (No. 143), and their accompanying Recommendations Nos. 86 and 151, in particular, call for cooperation among States, and measures to facilitate and control migration movements. They contain the underlying principle of equality of treatment between nationals and regular migrant workers, minimum standards of protection for all migrant workers, and provisions for participation of social partners in national policy formulation."

All the parties also agreed, as reflected in paragraph 21, that our plan of action shall include "identification of relevant action to be taken for a wider application of international labour standards and other relevant instruments", and, importantly, the Committee unanimously agreed to the conclusions reflected in paragraph 27, which drafts ratification of ILO instruments. In that paragraph the parties agreed to the following language: "ILO Convention No. 97 has been ratified by 42 countries and Convention No. 143 has been ratified by 18 countries. The Office shall undertake to identify the impediments to the ratification of these Conventions, taking into account that labour migration has evolved since their inception, and other relevant instruments have been developed at national, regional and international levels."

Furthermore, all parties agreed to the following language: "The ILO may take appropriate steps to better promote the ratification of Conventions Nos. 97 and 143, and the application of the principles they contain pertaining to the protection of migrant workers."

These ILO Conventions are no more outdated than our Declaration of Independence, which remains the cornerstone of the United States' democracy and was ratified many, many, many years before the ILO was even conceived.

Now, I am going to turn quickly to the issue of irregular migrants. By conservative estimates, there are at least 26 million people in the world today without regular migrant status. In the United States alone, we have between 9 and 11 million people without regular migration status.

Irregular migrant workers are the most poorly paid and poorly treated in the workforce, and they work in the most dangerous occupations. For example, a recent investigation by the Associated Press concluded that one Mexican worker dies on the job in the United States every single day.

Lack of formal status, together with cultural and language barriers, often leave irregular migrant workers open to abuse and exploitation, with negative impacts on all segments of society.

Irregular migration is a great concern for all workers because when one class of workers suffers and is vulnerable to abuse, working conditions for all workers suffer. Irregular migrants do not work in isolation. They work side by side with national workers and regular migrants, both male and female, old and young. When an irregular migrant is exploited, so too is her brother and sister.

As the Workers noted, and as is reflected in paragraph 28 of our conclusions, irregular migrants are people who live alongside us in our communities, but without security.

In the United States, 85 per cent of all migrant families with children are "mixed-status" families. That means that at least one household member has irregular status. So, the vulnerability and exploitation experienced by an irregular migrant in the workplace is not isolated to that worker, but is felt by the entire household.

Irregular migration is also a problem for employers, because many unscrupulous employers use irregular workers to gain an unfair competitive advantage through exploitation.

Studies have shown that irregular migrants are significantly less likely to report workplace injuries, and that they have no legal channels by which to complain about unpaid wages and other forms of exploitation. They are too often denied their basic rights to freedom of association.

The exploitation of irregular migrants also strains scarce public resources because it allows unscrupulous employers to privatize all the gains of employing irregular migrants whilst shifting the social cost to the public as a whole.

Despite the major contributions that irregular migrant workers make to the economies of host countries and to our communities, regularization remains a controversial issue in the United States and in the rest of the world. Frankly, we are disappointed that governments could not agree on transparent language on this issue.

Regularization is an issue that is being widely debated in the United States at this very moment, and laws are under debate in our country that would create a programme for "earned legalization" of irregular migrants. That means that men and women who have been working hard, paying their taxes and making contributions to their communities would be able, over time, to regularize their status and thus have a chance for decent work.

The task of fixing our broken immigration system is a daunting one and trade unions in the United States are making this task a key component of our struggle to bring justice to the workplace and ensure decent work for all.

Original French: Mr. JOUBIER *(Workers' adviser, France)*

What a great responsibility it is to be the last speaker.

I welcome the adoption by our tripartite Committee of the conclusions of our general discussion on migrant workers and I have no doubt that the resolution put before this Conference and the report of our work will be adopted by the Government, Employers' and Workers' delegates present.

The role of the ILO is and will continue to be crucial from two points of view. On the one hand, it will have to be able to provide the impetus for the policies and programmes that have a direct impact on the fate of men and women migrants. On the other, the ILO should also be in a position, in the years to come, to influence debates on this issue in other international bodies.

The ILO has to promote the establishment of a multilateral framework and a plan of action for the protection of migrant workers.

Let me now turn to the follow-up to be given to our activities and to the implementation of our resolution.

One of the points underlined in the resolution is the need for the good governance of migrations. In particular, the development of tripartite and bipartite social dialogue should be at the heart of this. There can be no good governance without genuine and constructive social dialogue. In the coming months, Governments should take the initiative to, bring the social partners together in order to consider what sort of follow-up should be given to the resolution before us.

In this respect, I would like to emphasize the importance of the role to be played by ministries of labour, employment or social affairs with regard to issues that increasingly tend to be handled by other administrations with different objectives, in particular, by ministries responsible for security matters. It would be desirable for governments to set up mechanisms and structures, where these do not exist, which allow for an ongoing dialogue on policies dealing with migration.

Apart from the social dialogue at the national level, it would be useful to explore other opportunities for social dialogue on migration, be it at the regional level or in the multilateral forums which until now have not taken into account the key contribution to these issues that can be made by actors with hands-on experience.

Good governance and quality social dialogue based on the representative and independent nature of the partners involved in such dialogue offer the best chance of success in efforts to reach a consensus and to identify common ground for the good management of migratory flows and for the effective protection of men and women migrants.

Freedom of association for all migrant workers also determines the quality and effectiveness of social dialogue at different levels. This is something that is clearly recalled by our Committee.

We should also carefully examine the need to promote the ratification of instruments adopted by the ILO, more specifically Conventions Nos. 97 and 143. I would also like to reiterate that these instruments remain valid and, indeed, some countries are about to ratify them today.

As a Frenchman, may I say that I am most gratified by the pledge given by my own Government to review the question of ratifying Convention No. 143 in the light of the discussions we have had and I hope that other governments will follow suit.

As a worker, may I also highlight the positive role played by the European Union in seeking consensus and a fair compromise in discussions which were sometimes difficult. Tripartite social dialogue is crucial for better cooperation and in finding convergence and synergies between the countries of destination and the countries of origin of migrant workers. It will make it easier to combat poverty and inequality in the countries of origin, which are factors of migration.

Social partnership in the host country will facilitate the integration of migrant workers in firms and must permit the recognition of their rights and, I hope, the development of their skills and qualifications and the recognition of these skills and qualifications. Moreover, I hope that, on this important matter of the recognition of competencies and qualifications, the spirit of consensus which obtained in the Committee on Migrant Workers will also obtain in this august assembly when it comes to adopting other conclusions and instruments.

The implications of migration in Europe and in the European Union are so great that this issue cannot be reduced to a mere economic calculation.

We are talking about the future of millions of people, whether they are migrants or not, whose fate is linked for thousands of social, historic and demographic reasons. The fundamental rights of non-community migrants are and will be of central importance here.

Lastly, I would like to make it clear that the battle to protect the rights of migrant workers is also the battle for democracy. Our Committee mentioned the racism, xenophobia, and prejudice which all too often still constitute the daily lot of these workers. Combating these phenomena also means combating the extreme right-wing groups who have made hatred their political manifesto.

In the future, the ILO will have to be present to fight on all these fronts. In order to spur on the implementation of our resolution, the ILO will have to mobilize resources and beef up its technical assistance in the field of migration. This, in more general terms, raises the question of the ILO's budget. Our responsibilities and the ILO's responsibilities grow with globalization and that is something which also needs to be taken into account.

Original Spanish: The PRESIDENT

As there are no further speakers, I propose that we proceed with the approval of the report of the Committee, which is contained in paragraphs 1-292. If there are no objections, may I take it that the report is approved?

(The report – paragraphs 1-292 – is approved.)

RESOLUTION CONCERNING A FAIR DEAL FOR MIGRANT WORKERS IN A GLOBAL ECONOMY: ADOPTION

Original Spanish: The PRESIDENT

We shall now proceed with the adoption of the resolution concerning a fair deal for migrant workers in a global economy. If there are no objections, may I take it that the resolution is adopted?

(The resolution is adopted.)

CONCLUSIONS ON A FAIR DEAL FOR MIGRANT WORKERS IN A GLOBAL ECONOMY: ADOPTION

Original Spanish: The PRESIDENT

We shall now proceed with the adoption of the proposed conclusions on a fair deal for migrant workers in a global economy. If there are no objections, may I take it that the Conclusions are adopted?

(The Conclusions are adopted.)

We have now concluded the consideration of the report submitted by the Committee on Migrant Workers. I should like to take this opportunity to thank the Committee, Officers and members, as well as the staff of the secretariat, for the very valuable work that they have carried out.

I now declare the nineteenth sitting closed.

(The Conference adjourned at 8 p.m.)

Conférence internationale du Travail - 92e session, Genève, 2004
International Labour Conference - 92nd Session, Geneva 2004
Conferencia Internacional del Trabajo - 92a reunión, Ginebra, 2004

Vote par appel nominal sur la résolution concernant les arriérés de contributions de l'Iraq

Record vote on the Resolution concerning the arrears of contributions of Iraq

Votación nominal relativa a la resolución sobre las contribuciones atrasadas de Iraq

Pour/For/En Pro: 421
Contre/Against/En contra: 12
Abstentions/Abstentions/Abstenciones: 12
Quorum: 286

Pour/For/En Pro: 421

Afrique du Sud/South Africa/Sudáfrica
MDLADLANA, Mr. (G)
KETTLEDAS, Mr. (G)
BOTHA, Mr. (E)
HOWARD, Mr.(T/W)

Albanie/Albania
GOXHI, Mrs. (G)
THANATI, Mr. (G)

Algérie/Algeria/Argelia
RAÏS, M. (G)
MEGREROUCHE, M. (G)
NAÏT-ABDELAZIZ, M. (E)
SIDI SAID, M.(T/W)

Allemagne/Germany/Alemania
SCHLEEGER, Mrs. (G)
KLOTZ, Mr. (G)
GERSTEIN, Mrs. (E)
ADAMY, Mr.(T/W)

Arabie saoudite/Saudi Arabia/Arabia Saudita
ALHADLAQ, Mr. (G)
AL-ZAMIL, Mr. (G)
DAHLAN, Mr. (E)
RADHWAN, Mr.(T/W)

Argentine/Argentina
ROSALES, Sr. (G)
RIAL, Sra. (G)
SPAGHI, Sr. (E)
PETRECCA, Sr.(T/W)

Australie/Australia
SAWERS, Mr. (G)
LLOYD, Mr. (G)
NOAKES, Mr. (E)
BURROW, Ms.(T/W)

Autriche/Austria
DEMBSHER, Mrs. (G)
ZWERENZ, Mr. (G)
TOMEK, Mr. (E)
BOEGNER, Mrs.(T/W)

Bahamas
BROWN, Mr. (G)
SYMONETTE, Mr. (G)
ARNETT, Mr. (E)
HAMILTON, Ms.(T/W)

Bahreïn/Bahrain/Bahrein
AL SHAHABI, Mr. (G)
AMIN MOHAMED, Mr. (G)
AL KHOOR, Mr. (E)
ABDULHUSAIN, Mr.(T/W)

Bangladesh
MD. ZAFRUL, Mr.(T/W)

Barbade/Barbados
LOWE, Mrs. (G)
FARNUM, Ms. (G)
TROTMAN, Mr.(T/W)

Bélarus/Belarus/Belarús
MALEVICH, Mr. (G)

Belgique/Belgium/Bélgica
CLOESEN, M. (G)
D'HONDT, Mme (G)
STORM, Mme (E)
CORTEBEECK, M.(T/W)

Bénin/Benin
ONI, M. (G)
MASSESSI, M. (G)
AHOUDJI, Mme (E)
AZOUA, M.(T/W)

Bosnie-Herzégovine/Bosnia and Herzegovina/Bosnia y Herzegovina
VUKAŠINOVIĆ, Mr. (G)

Botswana
MOJAFI, Mr. (G)
SEEMULE, Ms. (G)
DEWAH, Mr. (E)
BAIPIDI, Mr.(T/W)

Brésil/Brazil/Brasil
BRANCO FREITAS, Mr. (G)
SALDANHA, Mr. (G)
LIMA GODOY, Mr. (E)
VACCARI NETO, Mr.(T/W)

Bulgarie/Bulgaria
MLADENOV, Mr. (G)
APOSTOLOV, Mr. (G)
BEHAR, Mr. (E)
HRISTOV, Mr.(T/W)

Burkina Faso
SEYNOU, M. (G)

Burundi
KANKINDI, Mme (G)
BUDABUDA, M. (E)
HAJAYANDI, M.(T/W)

Cambodge/Cambodia/Camboya
THACH, Mr. (G)
HOU, Mr. (G)

Cameroun/Cameroon/Camerún
NGANTCHA, M. (G)

Canada/Canadá
ROBINSON, Ms. (G)
MACPHEE, Mr. (G)
WAJDA, Mr. (E)
BYERS, Ms.(T/W)

Cap-Vert/Cape Verde/Cabo Verde
SEMEDO, M. (G)
DE CARVALHO, M. (G)
ÉVORA, Mme (E)
SILVA, M.(T/W)

République centrafricaine/Central African Republic/República Centroafricana
ZITONGO-MADENGA, Mme (G)
YANGO-SINDO, M. (G)

Chili/Chile
DEL PICÓ RUBIO, Sr. (G)
MARTABIT SCAFF, Sr. (G)
ULLOA ZAMBRANO, Sr.(T/W)

Chine/China
LIU, Mr. (G)
WANG, Mr. (G)
CHEN, Mr. (E)
FAN, Mrs.(T/W)

Chypre/Cyprus/Chipre
MINA, Ms. (G)
KAPARTIS, Mr. (E)

Colombie/Colombia
ARANGO DE BUITRAGO, Sra. (G)
FORERO UCROS, Sra. (G)
ECHAVARRÍA SALDARRIAGA, Sr. (E)
ALVIS FERNÁNDEZ, Sr.(T/W)

Congo
ITOUA-YOCKA, M. (G)
GALESSAMY-IBOMBOT, M. (E)

République de Corée/Republic of Korea/República de Corea
LEE, Mr. (G)
HONG, Mr. (G)
KIM, Mr. (E)

Costa Rica
CLARAMUNT GARRO, Sra. (G)
GUILLERMET, Sr. (G)
AGUILAR ARCE, Sr.(T/W)

Côte d'Ivoire
BOULLOU BI DJEHIFFE, M. (G)
ADIKO, M.(T/W)

Croatie/Croatia/Croacia
MARKOTIĆ, Mr. (G)
TOTH MUCCIACCIARO, Ms.(T/W)

Cuba
LAU VALDÉS, Sra. (G)
HERNÁNDEZ OLIVA, Sra. (G)
PARRAS ROJAS, Sr. (E)

Danemark/Denmark/Dinamarca
GEDE, Mrs. (G)
PEDERSEN, Mr. (G)
DREESEN, Mr. (E)
SCHMIDT, Mr.(T/W)

République dominicaine/Dominican Republic/República Dominicana
NUÑEZ SALCEDO, Sr. (G)
REYES UREÑA, Sr. (G)

Egypte/Egypt/Egipto
GABR, Mrs. (G)
GHAFFAR, Mr. (G)
EL AZALI, Mr.(T/W)

El Salvador
ESPINAL, Sr. (G)
AVILA DE PEÑA, Sra. (G)
RAMÍREZ URBINA, Sr.(T/W)

Emirats arabes unis/United Arab Emirates/Emiratos Arabes Unidos
HUSSAIN, Mr. (G)
BAMTRAF, Mr. (G)
MATTAR, Mr. (E)
AL MARZOOQI, Mr.(T/W)

Equateur/Ecuador
ESPINOSA SALAS, Sr. (G)
TERÁN, Sr. (E)
YAGUAL, Sr.(T/W)

Espagne/Spain/España
LOPEZ-MONIS DE CAVO, Sr. (G)
BOSCH BESSA, Sr. (G)
FERRER DUFOL, Sr. (E)
JIMENEZ, Sr.(T/W)

Estonie/Estonia
HINDOV, Mrs. (G)
LEHT, Ms. (G)
MERILAI, Ms. (E)
KALDA, Mr.(T/W)

Etats-Unis/United States/Estados Unidos
LEVINE, Mr. (G)
HAGEN, Mr. (G)
POTTER, Mr. (E)
ZELLHOEFER, Mr.(T/W)

Ethiopie/Ethiopia/Etiopía
SIAMREGN, Mr. (G)
MITIKU, Mr. (G)
YIMER, Mr. (E)
ALEMAYEHU, Mr.(T/W)

Ex-Rép. Yougos. de Macédoine/The FYR Macedonia/Ex Rep. Yugoslava de Macedonia
ZAFIROVSKA, Mrs. (G)

Fidji/Fiji
ZINCK, Mr. (G)
KUNATUBA, Mr. (G)
POLITINI, Mr. (E)

Finlande/Finland/Finlandia
VUORINEN, Ms. (G)
SALMENPERÄ, Mr. (G)
HUTTUNEN, Mr. (E)
AHOKAS, Ms.(T/W)

France/Francia
AUER, Mme (G)
SEGUIN, M. (G)
ROILAND, Mme (E)
BRUNEL, Mme(T/W)

Gabon/Gabón
NDONG NANG, M. (G)
MOULOMBA NZIENGUI, M. (G)
AWASSI ATSIMADJA, Mme (E)

Ghana
AMEGEE, Mr. (G)
ADU- AMANKWAH, Mr.(T/W)

Grèce/Greece/Grecia
CHRYSANTHOU, Mme (G)
CAMBITSIS, M. (G)
CHARAKAS, M. (E)
DASSIS, M.(T/W)

Guatemala
MANCILLA GARCÍA, Sr.(T/W)

Guinée/Guinea
DIALLO, M. (G)

Honduras
PONCE, Sr. (G)
CRUZ RAMIREZ, Sra. (G)

Hongrie/Hungary/Hungría
HERCZOG, Mr. (G)
TÓTH, Mr. (G)
CSUPORT, Mr. (E)
TAMÁS, Ms.(T/W)

Inde/India
SHENOY, Mr. (G)
ANAND, Mr. (E)
DAVE, Mr.(T/W)

Indonésie/Indonesia
SULISTYANINGSIH, Ms. (G)
SITUMORANG, Mr. (G)
RACHMAN, Mr. (E)
SILABAN, Mr.(T/W)

République islamique d'Iran/Islamic Republic of Iran/República Islámica del Irán
RAIESI FARD, Mr. (E)
SALIMIAN, Mr.(T/W)

Irlande/Ireland/Irlanda
PENDER, Mr. (G)
MCDONNELL, Mr. (G)
MAGUIRE, Ms. (E)
LYNCH, Ms.(T/W)

Islande/Iceland/Islandia
DAVIDSDOTTIR, Ms. (G)
KRISTINSSON, Mr. (G)
MAGNUSSON, Mr. (E)

Israël/Israel
WAXMAN, Mr. (G)
FURMAN, Ms. (G)
BARAK, Mr. (E)
KARA, Mr.(T/W)

Italie/Italy/Italia
SIMONETTI, M. (G)
COLOMBO, M. (G)
SASSO MAZZUFFERI, Mme (E)
TARTAGLIA, M.(T/W)

Jamaïque/Jamaica
SMITH, Mr. (G)
LEWIS, Mr. (E)
GOODLEIGH, Mr.(T/W)

Japon/Japan/Japón
OSHIMA, Mr. (G)
HASEGAWA, Mr. (G)
SUZUKI, Mr. (E)
NAKAJIMA, Mr.(T/W)

Jordanie/Jordan/Jordania
AL-RUSAN, Mr. (G)

Kenya
KAVULUDI, Mr. (G)
MOHAMED, Mrs. (G)
KONDITI, Mr. (E)
ATWOLI, Mr.(T/W)

Kiribati
AWIRA, Mr. (G)
AATA, Ms.(T/W)

Koweït/Kuwait
AL-MUDADI, Mr. (G)
RAZZOOQI, Mr. (G)
AL-RABAH, Mr. (E)

Lesotho
MANDORO, Mr. (G)
MATSOSO, Ms. (G)
MAKEKA, Mr. (E)
TYHALI, Mr.(T/W)

Lettonie/Latvia/Letonia
KARKLINS, Mr. (G)
KALNINS, Mr. (G)

Liban/Lebanon/Líbano
GHORAYEB, M. (G)
SAAB, Mme (G)
BALBOUL, M. (E)

Libéria/Liberia
WAHYEE, Mr. (G)

Jamahiriya arabe libyenne/Libyan Arab Jamahiriya/Jamahiriya Arabe Libia
ALZWAM, Mr. (G)
DERBI, Mr. (G)

Lituanie/Lithuania/Lituania
JAKUCIONYTE, Ms. (G)
RIMKUNAS, Mr. (G)
VASILEVSKIS, Mr. (E)
BALSIENE, Ms.(T/W)

Luxembourg/Luxemburgo
FABER, M. (G)
SCHOLTUS, Mme (G)
BERTRAND-SCHAUL, Mme (E)
PIZZAFERRI, M.(T/W)

Madagascar
RASOLOFONIAINARISON, M. (G)
RANDRIAMAHOLISON, M.(T/W)

Malaisie/Malaysia/Malasia
SOH, Mr. (G)
ISMAIL, Mr. (G)
SHAMSUDIN, Mr. (E)
RAMPAK, Mr.(T/W)

Malawi
MONONGA, Mr. (G)
KAMBUTO, Mr. (G)
SINJANI, Mr. (E)
KALIMANJIRA, Mr.(T/W)

Mali/Malí
DIAKITE, M. (G)
MAHAMANE, M. (G)
TRAORE, M. (E)
DIAKITE, M.(T/W)

Malte/Malta
PULLICINO, Mr. (G)
AZZOPARDI, Mr. (G)
FARRUGIA, Mr. (E)

Maroc/Morocco/Marruecos
HILALE, M. (G)
CHATER, M. (G)

Maurice/Mauritius/Mauricio
ARNACHELLUM, Mr. (G)
BENYDIN, Mr.(T/W)

Mauritanie/Mauritania
OULD MOHAMED LEMINE, M. (G)
OULD CHEIKHNA, M. (G)
OULD MOHAMED, M.(T/W)

Mexique/Mexico/México
ROVIROSA, Sra. (G)
SILVA, Sr. (G)
DE REGIL, Sr. (E)
ANDERSON, Sra.(T/W)

Mongolie/Mongolia
SUKHBAATAR, Mr.(T/W)

Mozambique
CAIFAZ, Mr. (G)
SITOE, Mr.(T/W)

Namibie/Namibia
HIVELUAH, Ms. (G)
SHINGUADJA, Mr. (G)
SHIPENA, Mr. (E)
KAPENDA, Mr.(T/W)

Népal/Nepal
ACHARYA, Mr. (G)

Nicaragua
MARTÍNEZ FLORES, Srta. (G)
CRUZ TORUÑO, Sr. (G)

Niger/Níger
MAÏNA, M. (G)
HAMADOU, M. (G)
SANDA, M.(T/W)

Nigéria/Nigeria
ADEYEYE-OLUKOYA, Mrs. (G)
SULAI, Mrs. (G)
OSHIOMHOLE, Mr.(T/W)

Norvège/Norway/Noruega
BRUAAS, Mr. (G)
VIDNES, Mr. (G)
LINDEFJELD, Mr. (E)
THEODORSEN, Ms.(T/W)

Nouvelle-Zélande/New Zealand/Nueva Zelandia
BUWALDA, Mr. (G)
STEFFENS, Ms. (G)
ARNOLD, Mr. (E)
BEAUMONT, Ms.(T/W)

Oman/Omán
AL-ABDUWANI, Mr. (G)
AL-AMRI, Mr. (G)
AL RABAIE, Mr. (E)

Ouganda/Uganda
NAGGAGA, Mr. (G)
OGARAM, Mr. (G)
PAJOBO, Mr.(T/W)

Pakistan/Pakistán
FARSHORI, Mr. (G)
TABANI, Mr. (E)
AHMED, Mr.(T/W)

Panama/Panamá
ORTIZ BARBER, Sra. (G)
ROSAS PÉREZ, Sra. (G)
AIZPURÚA, Sr. (E)
PUGA RODRÍGUEZ, Sr.(T/W)

Papouasie-Nouvelle-Guinée/Papua New Guinea/Papua Nueva Guinea
JEFFERY, Mr. (E)

Pays-Bas/Netherlands/Países Bajos
NOTEBOOM, Ms. (G)
BEETS, Mr. (G)
RENIQUE, Mr. (E)
ETTY, Mr.(T/W)

Pérou/Peru/Perú
BERAUN, Sra. (G)
VILLAVICENCIO RIOS, Sr. (G)
GUTIÉRREZ MADUEÑO, Sr.(T/W)

Philippines/Filipinas
BALDOZ, Mrs. (G)
VALERIO, Mr.(T/W)

Pologne/Poland/Polonia
LEMIESZEWSKA, Mrs. (G)
JAKUBOWSKI, Mr. (G)
BOBROWSKI, Mr. (E)
WOJCIK, Mr.(T/W)

Portugal
RIBEIRO LOPES, M. (G)
BARCIA, M. (G)
FERNANDES SALGUEIRO, M. (E)
GOMES PROENÇA, M.(T/W)

Qatar
HAIDAR, Mr. (G)
AL SHAWI, Mr. (G)
AL SAIARI, Mr.(T/W)

République dém. du Congo/Democratic Republic of the Congo/República Democrática del Congo
MUTOMB MUJING, M. (G)
SAMBASSI, M. (G)
MUTABUNGA RUGINA, M. (E)
MUKALAYI HANGA, M.(T/W)

Roumanie/Romania/Rumania
NEMES, M. (G)
CONSTANTINESCU, Mme (G)
COSTACHE, M. (E)
PETCU, M.(T/W)

Royaume-Uni/United Kingdom/Reino Unido
BRATTAN, Ms. (G)
NELLTHORP, Ms. (G)
LAMBERT, Mr. (E)
STEYNE, Mr.(T/W)

Fédération de Russie/Russian Federation/Federación de Rusia
BAVYKIN, Mr. (G)
LUBLIN, Mr. (G)

Rwanda
KAVARUGANDA, M. (G)
UKUYEMUYE, M. (G)
BITWAYIKI, M. (E)
KAYUMBA, M.(T/W)

Saint-Marin/San Marino
BIGI, Mme (G)
GASPERONI, M. (G)
GIORGINI, Mme (E)
PIERMATTEI, M.(T/W)

Sénégal/Senegal
DIALLO, Mme (G)
DIOP, M. (E)
GUIRO, M.(T/W)

Serbie et Monténégro/Serbia and Montenegro/Serbia y Montenegro
BEGOVIĆ, Mr. (G)
ŠAHOVIĆ, Mr. (G)
ZAGORAC, Mr. (E)
ČANAK, Mr.(T/W)

Seychelles
MERITON, Mr. (G)
BAKER, Mr. (G)
SULTAN-BEAUDOUIN, Mr. (E)
ROBINSON, Mr.(T/W)

Singapour/Singapore/Singapur
NG, Mr. (G)
YONG, Ms. (G)

Slovaquie/Slovakia/Eslovaquia
PETÖCZ, Mr. (G)
SEPTÁKOVÁ, Ms. (G)
BORGULA, Mr. (E)
MESTANOVÁ, Mrs.(T/W)

Slovénie/Slovenia/Eslovenia
ZIDAR, Mr. (G)
RIHAR BAJUK, Ms. (G)
JEREB, Ms. (E)
KRZIŠNIK, Mr.(T/W)

Soudan/Sudan/Sudán
SHENTOUR, Mr. (G)
ELHASSAN, Mr. (G)
ELGURASHI, Mr. (E)
GHANDOUR, Mr.(T/W)

Sri Lanka
GAMMAMPILA DON, Mr. (G)
MADIHAHEWA, Mr. (G)
DASANAYAKE, Mr. (E)
DEVENDRA, Mr.(T/W)

Suède/Sweden/Suecia
WIKLUND, Ms. (G)
JONZON, Mr. (G)
LAURENT, Ms. (E)
BENGTSSON, Mr.(T/W)

Suisse/Switzerland/Suiza
ALVESALO-ROESCH, Mme (G)
ELMIGER, M. (G)
PLASSARD, M. (E)
VIGNE, M.(T/W)

Suriname
PIROE, Mr. (G)
VAN OMMEREN, Mr. (E)

République arabe syrienne/Syrian Arab Republic/República Arabe Siria
IBRAHIM, M. (G)
AKASHE, M. (G)
MOHAMMAD NASSER, M. (E)
AZOZ, M.(T/W)

République-Unie de Tanzanie/United Republic of Tanzania/República Unida de Tanzanía
RWEYEMAMU, Mrs. (G)
SITTA, Mrs.(T/W)

Tchad/Chad
ABDERAHIM, M. (G)
DJEGUEDEM, M. (G)
DJIBRINE, M.(T/W)

République tchèque/Czech Republic/República Checa
SAJDA, Mr. (G)
SLABÝ, Mr. (G)
DRBALOVÁ, Mrs. (E)
BAUEROVÁ, Mrs.(T/W)

Thaïlande/Thailand/Tailandia
RUANGSUWAN, Mr. (G)
SATJIPANON, Mr. (G)
ROMCHATTHONG, Mrs. (E)
TECHATEERAVAT, Mr.(T/W)

Trinité-et-Tobago/Trinidad and Tobago/Trinidad y Tabago
RAMNARINE, Mr. (G)
SINGH, Ms. (G)
HILTON CLARKE, Mr. (E)

Tunisie/Tunisia/Túnez
MANSOUR, M. (G)
CHOUBA, Mme (G)
M'KAISSI, M. (E)
TRABELSI, M.(T/W)

Turquie/Turkey/Turquía
GENC, Mr. (G)
OYMAN, Mr. (G)
CENTEL, Mr. (E)

Ukraine/Ucrania
YAMPOLSKYI, Mr. (G)
BELASHOV, Mr. (G)
ZHADAN, Mr. (E)

Uruguay
LAGARMILLA, Sra. (G)
DONO, Sra. (G)
FOSTIK, Sr. (E)

Venezuela
DE ARBELOA, Sr. (E)

Viet Nam
PHAM, Mr. (G)
VU, Mr. (G)
VI, Mrs. (E)
VO, Mr.(T/W)

Yémen/Yemen
AL-FAYSALI, Mr. (G)

Zimbabwe
MUSEKA, Mr. (G)

Contre/Against/En contra: 12

Angola
TIAGO GOMES, M. (E)
PEDRO GARCIA, Mme(T/W)

Burkina Faso
NAMA, M.(T/W)

Cuba
GONZÁLEZ GONZÁLEZ, Sr.(T/W)

Kiribati
KABUBUKE, Mr. (E)

Myanmar
THAN, Mr. (G)
NYUNT, Mr. (G)

République-Unie de Tanzanie/United Republic of Tanzania/República Unida de Tanzanía
KABYEMERA, Mr. (E)

Venezuela
DORADO CANO, Sr. (G)
MOLINA, Sr. (G)
INFANTE, Sr.(T/W)

Zambie/Zambia
HIKAUMBA, Mr.(T/W)

Abstentions/Abstentions/ Abstenciones: 12

Angola
BONGA, M. (G)
N'GOVE LUSSOKE, M. (G)

Bolivie/Bolivia
RODRÍGUEZ SAN MARTÍN, Sr. (G)

Guatemala
CHAVEZ BIETTI, Sra. (G)
GORDILLO GALINDO, Sr. (G)

Guinée équatoriale/Equatorial Guinea/Guinea Ecuatorial
ESUÁ NKÓ, Sr. (G)
ASAMA NTUGU, Sr. (G)
MATZEN MAKOSO, Sr. (E)

Nicaragua
GONZÁLEZ GAITÁN, Sr.(T/W)

Swaziland/Swazilandia
NKHAMBULE, Mr. (G)
MAPHANGA, Mrs. (E)

Uruguay
FERNÁNDEZ, Sr.(T/W)

Conférence internationale du Travail - 92e session, Genève, 2004
International Labour Conference - 92nd Session, Geneva 2004
Conferencia Internacional del Trabajo - 92a reunión, Ginebra, 2004

Vote par appel nominal sur la résolution concernant les arriérés de contributions du Paraguay
Record vote on the Resolution concerning the arrears of contributions of Paraguay
Votación nominal relativa a la resolución sobre las contribuciones atrasadas de Paraguay

Pour/For/En Pro: 419
Contre/Against/En contra: 11
Abstentions/Abstentions/Abstenciones: 15
Quorum: 286

Pour/For/En Pro: 419

Afrique du Sud/South Africa/Sudáfrica
MDLADLANA, Mr. (G)
KETTLEDAS, Mr. (G)
BOTHA, Mr. (E)
HOWARD, Mr.(T/W)

Albanie/Albania
GOXHI, Mrs. (G)
THANATI, Mr. (G)

Algérie/Algeria/Argelia
RAÏS, M. (G)
MEGREROUCHE, M. (G)
NAÏT-ABDELAZIZ, M. (E)
SIDI SAID, M.(T/W)

Allemagne/Germany/Alemania
SCHLEEGER, Mrs. (G)
KLOTZ, Mr. (G)
GERSTEIN, Mrs. (E)
ADAMY, Mr.(T/W)

Arabie saoudite/Saudi Arabia/Arabia Saudita
ALHADLAQ, Mr. (G)
AL-ZAMIL, Mr. (G)
DAHLAN, Mr. (E)
RADHWAN, Mr.(T/W)

Argentine/Argentina
ROSALES, Sr. (G)
RIAL, Sra. (G)
SPAGHI, Sr. (E)
PETRECCA, Sr.(T/W)

Australie/Australia
SAWERS, Mr. (G)
LLOYD, Mr. (G)
NOAKES, Mr. (E)
BURROW, Ms.(T/W)

Autriche/Austria
DEMBSHER, Mrs. (G)
ZWERENZ, Mr. (G)
TOMEK, Mr. (E)
BOEGNER, Mrs.(T/W)

Bahamas
BROWN, Mr. (G)
SYMONETTE, Mr. (G)
ARNETT, Mr. (E)
HAMILTON, Ms.(T/W)

Bahreïn/Bahrain/Bahrein
AL SHAHABI, Mr. (G)
AMIN MOHAMED, Mr. (G)
AL KHOOR, Mr. (E)
ABDULHUSAIN, Mr.(T/W)

Bangladesh
MD. ZAFRUL, Mr.(T/W)

Barbade/Barbados
LOWE, Mrs. (G)
FARNUM, Ms. (G)
TROTMAN, Mr.(T/W)

Bélarus/Belarus/Belarús
MALEVICH, Mr. (G)

Belgique/Belgium/Bélgica
CLOESEN, M. (G)
D'HONDT, Mme (G)
STORM, Mme (E)
CORTEBEECK, M.(T/W)

Bénin/Benin
ONI, M. (G)
MASSESSI, M. (G)
AHOUDJI, Mme (E)
AZOUA, M.(T/W)

Bolivie/Bolivia
RODRÍGUEZ SAN MARTÍN, Sr. (G)

Bosnie-Herzégovine/Bosnia and Herzegovina/Bosnia y Herzegovina
VUKAŠINOVIĆ, Mr. (G)

Botswana
DEWAH, Mr. (E)
BAIPIDI, Mr.(T/W)

Brésil/Brazil/Brasil
BRANCO FREITAS, Mr. (G)
SALDANHA, Mr. (G)
LIMA GODOY, Mr. (E)
VACCARI NETO, Mr.(T/W)

Bulgarie/Bulgaria
MLADENOV, Mr. (G)
APOSTOLOV, Mr. (G)
BEHAR, Mr. (E)
HRISTOV, Mr.(T/W)

Burkina Faso
SEYNOU, M. (G)

Burundi
KANKINDI, Mme (G)
BUDABUDA, M. (E)
HAJAYANDI, M.(T/W)

Cambodge/Cambodia/Camboya
THACH, Mr. (G)
HOU, Mr. (G)

Cameroun/Cameroon/Camerún
NGANTCHA, M. (G)

Canada/Canadá
ROBINSON, Ms. (G)
MACPHEE, Mr. (G)
WAJDA, Mr. (E)
BYERS, Ms.(T/W)

Cap-Vert/Cape Verde/Cabo Verde
SEMEDO, M. (G)
DE CARVALHO, M. (G)
ÉVORA, Mme (E)
SILVA, M.(T/W)

République centrafricaine/Central African Republic/República Centroafricana
YANGO-SINDO, M. (G)

Chili/Chile
DEL PICÓ RUBIO, Sr. (G)
MARTABIT SCAFF, Sr. (G)
ULLOA ZAMBRANO, Sr.(T/W)

Chine/China
LIU, Mr. (G)
WANG, Mr. (G)
CHEN, Mr. (E)
FAN, Mrs.(T/W)

Chypre/Cyprus/Chipre
MINA, Ms. (G)
KAPARTIS, Mr. (E)

Colombie/Colombia
ARANGO DE BUITRAGO, Sra. (G)
FORERO UCROS, Sra. (G)
ECHAVARRÍA SALDARRIAGA, Sr. (E)
ALVIS FERNÁNDEZ, Sr.(T/W)

Congo
ITOUA-YOCKA, M. (G)
GALESSAMY-IBOMBOT, M. (E)

République de Corée/Republic of Korea/República de Corea
LEE, Mr. (G)
HONG, Mr. (G)
KIM, Mr. (E)

Costa Rica
CLARAMUNT GARRO, Sra. (G)
GUILLERMET, Sr. (G)
AGUILAR ARCE, Sr.(T/W)

Côte d'Ivoire
BOULLOU BI DJEHIFFE, M. (G)
ADIKO, M.(T/W)

Croatie/Croatia/Croacia
MARKOTIĆ, Mr. (G)
TOTH MUCCIACCIARO, Ms.(T/W)

Cuba
LAU VALDÉS, Sra. (G)
HERNÁNDEZ OLIVA, Sra. (G)
PARRAS ROJAS, Sr. (E)
GONZÁLEZ GONZÁLEZ, Sr.(T/W)

Danemark/Denmark/Dinamarca
GEDE, Mrs. (G)
PEDERSEN, Mr. (G)
DREESEN, Mr. (E)
SCHMIDT, Mr.(T/W)

République dominicaine/Dominican Republic/República Dominicana
NUÑEZ SALCEDO, Sr. (G)
REYES UREÑA, Sr. (G)

Egypte/Egypt/Egipto
GABR, Mrs. (G)
GHAFFAR, Mr. (G)
EL AZALI, Mr.(T/W)

El Salvador
ESPINAL, Sr. (G)
AVILA DE PEÑA, Sra. (G)
RAMÍREZ URBINA, Sr.(T/W)

Emirats arabes unis/United Arab Emirates/Emiratos Arabes Unidos
HUSSAIN, Mr. (G)
BAMTRAF, Mr. (G)
MATTAR, Mr. (E)
AL MARZOOQI, Mr.(T/W)

Equateur/Ecuador
ESPINOSA SALAS, Sr. (G)
TERÁN, Sr. (E)
YAGUAL, Sr.(T/W)

Espagne/Spain/España
LOPEZ-MONIS DE CAVO, Sr. (G)
BOSCH BESSA, Sr. (G)
FERRER DUFOL, Sr. (E)
JIMENEZ, Sr.(T/W)

Estonie/Estonia
HINDOV, Mrs. (G)
LEHT, Ms. (G)
MERILAI, Ms. (E)
KALDA, Mr.(T/W)

Etats-Unis/United States/Estados Unidos
LEVINE, Mr. (G)
HAGEN, Mr. (G)
POTTER, Mr. (E)
ZELLHOEFER, Mr.(T/W)

Ethiopie/Ethiopia/Etiopía
SIAMREGN, Mr. (G)
MITIKU, Mr. (G)
YIMER, Mr. (E)
ALEMAYEHU, Mr.(T/W)

Ex-Rép. Yougos. de Macédoine/The FYR Macedonia/Ex Rep. Yugoslava de Macedonia
ZAFIROVSKA, Mrs. (G)

Fidji/Fiji
ZINCK, Mr. (G)
KUNATUBA, Mr. (G)
POLITINI, Mr. (E)

Finlande/Finland/Finlandia
VUORINEN, Ms. (G)
SALMENPERÄ, Mr. (G)
HUTTUNEN, Mr. (E)
AHOKAS, Ms.(T/W)

France/Francia
AUER, Mme (G)
SEGUIN, M. (G)
ROILAND, Mme (E)
BRUNEL, Mme(T/W)

Gabon/Gabón
NDONG NANG, M. (G)
MOULOMBA NZIENGUI, M. (G)
AWASSI ATSIMADJA, Mme (E)

Ghana
AMEGEE, Mr. (G)
ADU- AMANKWAH, Mr.(T/W)

Grèce/Greece/Grecia
CHRYSANTHOU, Mme (G)
CAMBITSIS, M. (G)
CHARAKAS, M. (E)
DASSIS, M.(T/W)

Guatemala
CHAVEZ BIETTI, Sra. (G)
GORDILLO GALINDO, Sr. (G)
MANCILLA GARCÍA, Sr.(T/W)

Guinée/Guinea
DIALLO, M. (G)

Honduras
PONCE, Sr. (G)
CRUZ RAMIREZ, Sra. (G)

Hongrie/Hungary/Hungría
HERCZOG, Mr. (G)
TÓTH, Mr. (G)
CSUPORT, Mr. (E)
TAMÁS, Ms.(T/W)

Inde/India
SHENOY, Mr. (G)
ANAND, Mr. (E)
DAVE, Mr.(T/W)

Indonésie/Indonesia
SILABAN, Mr.(T/W)

République islamique d'Iran/Islamic Republic of Iran/República Islámica del Irán
RAIESI FARD, Mr. (E)
SALIMIAN, Mr.(T/W)

Irlande/Ireland/Irlanda
PENDER, Mr. (G)
MCDONNELL, Mr. (G)
MAGUIRE, Ms. (E)
LYNCH, Ms.(T/W)

Islande/Iceland/Islandia
DAVIDSDOTTIR, Ms. (G)
KRISTINSSON, Mr. (G)
MAGNUSSON, Mr. (E)

Israël/Israel
WAXMAN, Mr. (G)
FURMAN, Ms. (G)
BARAK, Mr. (E)
KARA, Mr.(T/W)

Italie/Italy/Italia
SIMONETTI, M. (G)
COLOMBO, M. (G)
SASSO MAZZUFFERI, Mme (E)
TARTAGLIA, M.(T/W)

Japon/Japan/Japón
OSHIMA, Mr. (G)
HASEGAWA, Mr. (G)
SUZUKI, Mr. (E)
NAKAJIMA, Mr.(T/W)

Jordanie/Jordan/Jordania
AL-RUSAN, Mr. (G)

Kenya
KAVULUDI, Mr. (G)
MOHAMED, Mrs. (G)
KONDITI, Mr. (E)
ATWOLI, Mr.(T/W)

Kiribati
AWIRA, Mr. (G)
AATA, Ms.(T/W)

Koweït/Kuwait
AL-MUDADI, Mr. (G)
RAZZOOQI, Mr. (G)
AL-RABAH, Mr. (E)

Lesotho
MANDORO, Mr. (G)
MATSOSO, Ms. (G)
MAKEKA, Mr. (E)
TYHALI, Mr.(T/W)

Lettonie/Latvia/Letonia
KARKLINS, Mr. (G)
KALNINS, Mr. (G)

Liban/Lebanon/Líbano
GHORAYEB, M. (G)
SAAB, Mme (G)
BALBOUL, M. (E)

Libéria/Liberia
WAHYEE, Mr. (G)

Jamahiriya arabe libyenne/Libyan Arab Jamahiriya/Jamahiriya Arabe Libia
ALZWAM, Mr. (G)
DERBI, Mr. (G)

Lituanie/Lithuania/Lituania
JAKUCIONYTE, Ms. (G)
RIMKUNAS, Mr. (G)
VASILEVSKIS, Mr. (E)
BALSIENE, Ms.(T/W)

Luxembourg/Luxemburgo
FABER, M. (G)
SCHOLTUS, Mme (G)
BERTRAND-SCHAUL, Mme (E)
PIZZAFERRI, M.(T/W)

Madagascar
RASOLOFONIAINARISON, M. (G)
RANDRIAMAHOLISON, M.(T/W)

Malaisie/Malaysia/Malasia
SOH, Mr. (G)
ISMAIL, Mr. (G)
SHAMSUDIN, Mr. (E)
RAMPAK, Mr.(T/W)

Malawi
MONONGA, Mr. (G)
KAMBUTO, Mr. (G)
SINJANI, Mr. (E)
KALIMANJIRA, Mr.(T/W)

Mali/Malí
DIAKITE, M. (G)
MAHAMANE, M. (G)
TRAORE, M. (E)
DIAKITE, M.(T/W)

Malte/Malta
PULLICINO, Mr. (G)
AZZOPARDI, Mr. (G)
FARRUGIA, Mr. (E)

Maroc/Morocco/Marruecos
HILALE, M. (G)
CHATER, M. (G)

Maurice/Mauritius/Mauricio
ARNACHELLUM, Mr. (G)
BENYDIN, Mr.(T/W)

Mauritanie/Mauritania
OULD MOHAMED LEMINE, M. (G)
OULD CHEIKHNA, M. (G)
OULD MOHAMED, M.(T/W)

Mexique/Mexico/México
ROVIROSA, Sra. (G)
SILVA, Sr. (G)
DE REGIL, Sr. (E)
ANDERSON, Sra.(T/W)

Mongolie/Mongolia
SUKHBAATAR, Mr.(T/W)

Mozambique
CAIFAZ, Mr. (G)
SITOE, Mr.(T/W)

Namibie/Namibia
HIVELUAH, Ms. (G)
SHINGUADJA, Mr. (G)
KAPENDA, Mr.(T/W)

Népal/Nepal
ACHARYA, Mr. (G)

Nicaragua
MARTÍNEZ FLORES, Srta. (G)
CRUZ TORUÑO, Sr. (G)

Niger/Níger
MAÏNA, M. (G)
HAMADOU, M. (G)
SANDA, M.(T/W)

Nigéria/Nigeria
ADEYEYE-OLUKOYA, Mrs. (G)
SULAI, Mrs. (G)
OSHIOMHOLE, Mr.(T/W)

Norvège/Norway/Noruega
BRUAAS, Mr. (G)
VIDNES, Mr. (G)
LINDEFJELD, Mr. (E)
THEODORSEN, Ms.(T/W)

Nouvelle-Zélande/New Zealand/Nueva Zelandia
BUWALDA, Mr. (G)
STEFFENS, Ms. (G)
BEAUMONT, Ms.(T/W)

Oman/Omán
AL-ABDUWANI, Mr. (G)
AL-AMRI, Mr. (G)
AL RABAIE, Mr. (E)

Ouganda/Uganda
NAGGAGA, Mr. (G)
OGARAM, Mr. (G)
PAJOBO, Mr.(T/W)

Pakistan/Pakistán
FARSHORI, Mr. (G)
TABANI, Mr. (E)
AHMED, Mr.(T/W)

Panama/Panamá
ORTIZ BARBER, Sra. (G)
ROSAS PÉREZ, Sra. (G)
AIZPURÚA, Sr. (E)
PUGA RODRÍGUEZ, Sr.(T/W)

Pays-Bas/Netherlands/Países Bajos
NOTEBOOM, Ms. (G)
BEETS, Mr. (G)
RENIQUE, Mr. (E)
ETTY, Mr.(T/W)

Pérou/Peru/Perú
BERAUN, Sra. (G)
VILLAVICENCIO RIOS, Sr. (G)
GUTIÉRREZ MADUEÑO, Sr.(T/W)

Philippines/Filipinas
BALDOZ, Mrs. (G)
VALERIO, Mr.(T/W)

Pologne/Poland/Polonia
LEMIESZEWSKA, Mrs. (G)
JAKUBOWSKI, Mr. (G)
BOBROWSKI, Mr. (E)
WOJCIK, Mr.(T/W)

Portugal
RIBEIRO LOPES, M. (G)
BARCIA, M. (G)
FERNANDES SALGUEIRO, M. (E)
GOMES PROENÇA, M.(T/W)

Qatar
HAIDAR, Mr. (G)
AL SHAWI, Mr. (G)
AL SAIARI, Mr.(T/W)

République dém. du Congo/Democratic Republic of the Congo/República Democrática del Congo
MUTOMB MUJING, M. (G)
SAMBASSI, M. (G)
MUTABUNGA RUGINA, M. (E)
MUKALAYI HANGA, M.(T/W)

Roumanie/Romania/Rumania
NEMES, M. (G)
CONSTANTINESCU, Mme (G)
COSTACHE, M. (E)
PETCU, M.(T/W)

Royaume-Uni/United Kingdom/Reino Unido
BRATTAN, Ms. (G)
NELLTHORP, Ms. (G)
LAMBERT, Mr. (E)
STEYNE, Mr.(T/W)

Fédération de Russie/Russian Federation/Federación de Rusia
BAVYKIN, Mr. (G)
LUBLIN, Mr. (G)

Rwanda
KAVARUGANDA, M. (G)
UKUYEMUYE, M. (G)
BITWAYIKI, M. (E)
KAYUMBA, M.(T/W)

Saint-Marin/San Marino
BIGI, Mme (G)
GASPERONI, M. (G)
GIORGINI, Mme (E)
PIERMATTEI, M.(T/W)

Sénégal/Senegal
DIALLO, Mme (G)
DIOP, M. (E)
GUIRO, M.(T/W)

Serbie et Monténégro/Serbia and Montenegro/Serbia y Montenegro
BEGOVIĆ, Mr. (G)
ŠAHOVIĆ, Mr. (G)
ZAGORAC, Mr. (E)
ČANAK, Mr.(T/W)

Seychelles
MERITON, Mr. (G)
BAKER, Mr. (G)
SULTAN-BEAUDOUIN, Mr. (E)
ROBINSON, Mr.(T/W)

Singapour/Singapore/Singapur
NG, Mr. (G)
YONG, Ms. (G)

Slovaquie/Slovakia/Eslovaquia
PETÖCZ, Mr. (G)
SEPTÁKOVÁ, Ms. (G)
BORGULA, Mr. (E)
MESTANOVÁ, Mrs.(T/W)

Slovénie/Slovenia/Eslovenia
ZIDAR, Mr. (G)
RIHAR BAJUK, Ms. (G)
JEREB, Ms. (E)
KRZIŠNIK, Mr.(T/W)

Soudan/Sudan/Sudán
SHENTOUR, Mr. (G)
ELHASSAN, Mr. (G)
ELGURASHI, Mr. (E)
GHANDOUR, Mr.(T/W)

Sri Lanka
GAMMAMPILA DON, Mr. (G)
MADIHAHEWA, Mr. (G)
DASANAYAKE, Mr. (E)
DEVENDRA, Mr.(T/W)

Suède/Sweden/Suecia
WIKLUND, Ms. (G)
JONZON, Mr. (G)
LAURENT, Ms. (E)
BENGTSSON, Mr.(T/W)

Suisse/Switzerland/Suiza
ALVESALO-ROESCH, Mme (G)
ELMIGER, M. (E)
PLASSARD, M. (E)
VIGNE, M.(T/W)

Suriname
PIROE, Mr. (G)
VAN OMMEREN, Mr. (E)

République arabe syrienne/Syrian Arab Republic/República Arabe Siria
IBRAHIM, M. (G)
AKASHE, M. (G)
MOHAMMAD NASSER, M. (E)
AZOZ, M.(T/W)

République-Unie de Tanzanie/United Republic of Tanzania/República Unida de Tanzanía
RWEYEMAMU, Mrs. (G)
KABYEMERA, Mr. (E)
SITTA, Mrs.(T/W)

Tchad/Chad
ABDERAHIM, M. (G)
DJEGUEDEM, M. (G)
DJIBRINE, M.(T/W)

République tchèque/Czech Republic/República Checa
SAJDA, Mr. (G)
SLABÝ, Mr. (G)
DRBALOVÁ, Mrs. (E)
BAUEROVÁ, Mrs.(T/W)

Thaïlande/Thailand/Tailandia
RUANGSUWAN, Mr. (G)
SATJIPANON, Mr. (G)
ROMCHATTHONG, Mrs. (E)
TECHATEERAVAT, Mr.(T/W)

Trinité-et-Tobago/Trinidad and Tobago/Trinidad y Tabago
RAMNARINE, Mr. (G)
SINGH, Ms. (G)
HILTON CLARKE, Mr. (E)

Tunisie/Tunisia/Túnez
MANSOUR, M. (G)
CHOUBA, Mme (G)
M'KAISSI, M. (E)
TRABELSI, M.(T/W)

Turquie/Turkey/Turquía
GENC, Mr. (G)
OYMAN, Mr. (G)
CENTEL, Mr. (E)

Ukraine/Ucrania
YAMPOLSKYI, Mr. (G)
BELASHOV, Mr. (G)
ZHADAN, Mr. (E)

Uruguay
LAGARMILLA, Sra. (G)
DONO, Sra. (G)
FOSTIK, Sr. (E)
FERNÁNDEZ, Sr.(T/W)

Venezuela
DORADO CANO, Sr. (G)
MOLINA, Sr. (G)
DE ARBELOA, Sr. (E)
INFANTE, Sr.(T/W)

Viet Nam
PHAM, Mr. (G)
VU, Mr. (G)
VI, Mrs. (E)
VO, Mr.(T/W)

Yémen/Yemen
AL-FAYSALI, Mr. (G)

Zambie/Zambia
HIKAUMBA, Mr.(T/W)

Zimbabwe
MUSEKA, Mr. (G)

Contre/Against/En contra: 11

Angola
TIAGO GOMES, M. (E)
PEDRO GARCIA, Mme(T/W)

Burkina Faso
NAMA, M.(T/W)

Jamaïque/Jamaica
SMITH, Mr. (G)
LEWIS, Mr. (E)
GOODLEIGH, Mr.(T/W)

Kiribati
KABUBUKE, Mr. (E)

Myanmar
THAN, Mr. (G)
NYUNT, Mr. (G)

Namibie/Namibia
SHIPENA, Mr. (E)

Nouvelle-Zélande/New Zealand/Nueva Zelandia
ARNOLD, Mr. (E)

Abstentions/Abstentions/ Abstenciones: 15

Angola
BONGA, M. (G)
N'GOVE LUSSOKE, M. (G)

Botswana
MOJAFI, Mr. (G)
SEEMULE, Ms. (G)

République centrafricaine/Central African Republic/República Centroafricana
ZITONGO-MADENGA, Mme (G)

Guinée équatoriale/Equatorial Guinea/Guinea Ecuatorial
ESUÁ NKÓ, Sr. (G)
ASAMA NTUGU, Sr. (G)
MATZEN MAKOSO, Sr. (E)

Indonésie/Indonesia
SULISTYANINGSIH, Ms. (G)
SITUMORANG, Mr. (G)
RACHMAN, Mr. (E)

Nicaragua
GONZÁLEZ GAITÁN, Sr.(T/W)

Papouasie-Nouvelle-Guinée/Papua New Guinea/Papua Nueva Guinea
JEFFERY, Mr. (E)

Swaziland/Swazilandia
NKHAMBULE, Mr. (G)
MAPHANGA, Mrs. (E)

Conférence internationale du Travail - 92e session, Genève, 2004
International Labour Conference - 92nd Session, Geneva 2004
Conferencia Internacional del Trabajo - 92a reunión, Ginebra, 2004

Vote final par appel nominal sur le retrait des recommandations nos. 2, 12, 16, 18, 21, 26, 32, 33, 34, 36, 43, 46, 58, 70, 74, 96.

Final record vote relating to the withdrawal of Recommendations Nos. 2, 12, 16, 18, 21, 26, 32, 33, 34, 36, 43, 46, 58, 70, 74, 96.

Votación final nominal sobre el retiro de las recommendaciones núms. 2, 12, 16, 18, 21, 26, 32, 33, 34, 36, 43, 46, 58, 70, 74, 96.

Pour/For/En Pro: 437
Contre/Against/En contra: 1
Quorum: 290

Pour/For/En Pro: 437

Afrique du Sud/South Africa/Sudáfrica
MDLADLANA, Mr. (G)
KETTLEDAS, Mr. (G)
BOTHA, Mr. (E)
HOWARD, Mr.(T/W)

Albanie/Albania
GOXHI, Mrs. (G)
THANATI, Mr. (G)

Algérie/Algeria/Argelia
RAÏS, M. (G)
MEGREROUCHE, M. (G)
NAÏT-ABDELAZIZ, M. (E)
SIDI SAID, M.(T/W)

Allemagne/Germany/Alemania
SCHLEEGER, Mrs. (G)
KLOTZ, Mr. (G)
GERSTEIN, Mrs. (E)
ADAMY, Mr.(T/W)

Angola
BONGA, M. (G)
N'GOVE LUSSOKE, M. (G)
TIAGO GOMES, M. (E)
PEDRO GARCIA, Mme(T/W)

Arabie saoudite/Saudi Arabia/Arabia Saudita
ALHADLAQ, Mr. (G)
AL-ZAMIL, Mr. (G)
DAHLAN, Mr. (E)
RADHWAN, Mr.(T/W)

Argentine/Argentina
ROSALES, Sr. (G)
RIAL, Sra. (G)
SPAGHI, Sr. (E)
PETRECCA, Sr.(T/W)

Australie/Australia
SAWERS, Mr. (G)
LLOYD, Mr. (G)
NOAKES, Mr. (E)
BURROW, Ms.(T/W)

Autriche/Austria
DEMBSHER, Mrs. (G)
ZWERENZ, Mr. (G)
TOMEK, Mr. (E)
BOEGNER, Mrs.(T/W)

Bahamas
BROWN, Mr. (G)
ARNETT, Mr. (E)

Bahreïn/Bahrain/Bahrein
AL SHAHABI, Mr. (G)
AL-FAIHANI, Mr. (G)
AL KHOOR, Mr. (E)
ABDULHUSAIN, Mr.(T/W)

Bangladesh
MD. ZAFRUL, Mr.(T/W)

Barbade/Barbados
LOWE, Mrs. (G)
FARNUM, Ms. (G)
TROTMAN, Mr.(T/W)

Bélarus/Belarus/Belarús
MALEVICH, Mr. (G)

Belgique/Belgium/Bélgica
CLOESEN, M. (G)
D'HONDT, Mme (G)
STORM, Mme (E)
CORTEBEECK, M.(T/W)

Bénin/Benin
ONI, M. (G)
MASSESSI, M. (G)
AHOUDJI, Mme (E)
AZOUA, M.(T/W)

Bolivie/Bolivia
RODRÍGUEZ SAN MARTÍN, Sr. (G)

Bosnie-Herzégovine/Bosnia and Herzegovina/Bosnia y Herzegovina
VUKAŠINOVIĆ, Mr. (G)

Brésil/Brazil/Brasil
BRANCO FREITAS, Mr. (G)
SALDANHA, Mr. (G)
LIMA GODOY, Mr. (E)
VACCARI NETO, Mr.(T/W)

Bulgarie/Bulgaria
MLADENOV, Mr. (G)
APOSTOLOV, Mr. (G)
BEHAR, Mr. (E)
HRISTOV, Mr.(T/W)

Burkina Faso
SEYNOU, M. (G)
NAMA, M.(T/W)

Burundi
KANKINDI, Mme (G)
BUDABUDA, M. (E)
HAJAYANDI, M.(T/W)

Cambodge/Cambodia/Camboya
THACH, Mr. (G)
HOU, Mr. (G)

Cameroun/Cameroon/Camerún
NGANTCHA, M. (G)

Canada/Canadá
ROBINSON, Ms. (G)
MACPHEE, Mr. (G)
WAJDA, Mr. (E)
BYERS, Ms.(T/W)

Cap-Vert/Cape Verde/Cabo Verde
SEMEDO, M. (G)
DE CARVALHO, M. (G)
ÉVORA, Mme (E)
SILVA, M.(T/W)

République centrafricaine/Central African Republic/República Centroafricana
ZITONGO-MADENGA, Mme (G)
YANGO-SINDO, M. (G)

Chili/Chile
DEL PICÓ RUBIO, Sr. (G)
MARTABIT SCAFF, Sr. (G)

Chine/China
LIU, Mr. (G)
WANG, Mr. (G)
CHEN, Mr. (E)
FAN, Mrs.(T/W)

Chypre/Cyprus/Chipre
MINA, Ms. (G)
KAPARTIS, Mr. (E)

Colombie/Colombia
ARANGO DE BUITRAGO, Sra. (G)
FORERO UCROS, Sra. (G)
ECHAVARRÍA SALDARRIAGA, Sr. (E)
ALVIS FERNÁNDEZ, Sr.(T/W)

Congo
ITOUA-YOCKA, M. (G)
GALESSAMY-IBOMBOT, M. (E)

République de Corée/Republic of Korea/República de Corea
LEE, Mr. (G)
HONG, Mr. (G)
KIM, Mr. (E)

Costa Rica
CLARAMUNT GARRO, Sra. (G)
GUILLERMET, Sr. (G)
AGUILAR ARCE, Sr.(T/W)

Côte d'Ivoire
BOULLOU BI DJEHIFFE, M. (G)
ADIKO, M.(T/W)

Croatie/Croatia/Croacia
MARKOTIĆ, Mr. (G)
TOTH MUCCIACCIARO, Ms.(T/W)

Cuba
LAU VALDÉS, Sra. (G)
HERNÁNDEZ OLIVA, Sra. (G)
PARRAS ROJAS, Sr. (E)

Danemark/Denmark/Dinamarca
GEDE, Mrs. (G)
PEDERSEN, Mr. (G)
DREESEN, Mr. (E)
SCHMIDT, Mr.(T/W)

République dominicaine/Dominican Republic/República Dominicana
NUÑEZ SALCEDO, Sr. (G)
REYES UREÑA, Sr. (G)

Egypte/Egypt/Egipto
GABR, Mrs. (G)
GHAFFAR, Mr. (G)
EL AZALI, Mr.(T/W)

El Salvador
ESPINAL, Sr. (G)
AVILA DE PEÑA, Sra. (G)
RAMÍREZ URBINA, Sr.(T/W)

Emirats arabes unis/United Arab Emirates/Emiratos Arabes Unidos
HUSSAIN, Mr. (G)
BAMTRAF, Mr. (G)
AL GAIZI, Mr. (E)
AL MARZOOQI, Mr.(T/W)

Equateur/Ecuador
ESPINOSA SALAS, Sr. (G)
TERÁN, Sr. (E)
YAGUAL, Sr.(T/W)

Espagne/Spain/España
LOPEZ-MONIS DE CAVO, Sr. (G)
BOSCH BESSA, Sr. (G)
FERRER DUFOL, Sr. (E)
JIMENEZ, Sr.(T/W)

Estonie/Estonia
HINDOV, Mrs. (G)
LEHT, Ms. (G)
MERILAI, Ms. (E)
KALDA, Mr.(T/W)

Etats-Unis/United States/Estados Unidos
LEVINE, Mr. (G)
HAGEN, Mr. (G)
POTTER, Mr. (E)
ZELLHOEFER, Mr.(T/W)

Ethiopie/Ethiopia/Etiopía
SIAMREGN, Mr. (G)
MITIKU, Mr. (G)
YIMER, Mr. (E)
ABREHA, Mr.(T/W)

Ex-Rép. Yougos. de Macédoine/The FYR Macedonia/Ex Rep. Yugoslava de Macedonia
ZAFIROVSKA, Mrs. (G)

Fidji/Fiji
ZINCK, Mr. (G)
KUNATUBA, Mr. (G)
POLITINI, Mr. (E)

Finlande/Finland/Finlandia
VUORINEN, Ms. (G)
SALMENPERÄ, Mr. (G)
HUTTUNEN, Mr. (E)
AHOKAS, Ms.(T/W)

France/Francia
GAUCI, M. (G)
SEGUIN, M. (G)
ROILAND, Mme (E)
BRUNEL, Mme(T/W)

Gabon/Gabón
NDONG NANG, M. (G)
MOULOMBA NZIENGUI, M. (G)
AWASSI ATSIMADJA, Mme (E)

Ghana
AMEGEE, Mr. (G)
ADU- AMANKWAH, Mr.(T/W)

Grèce/Greece/Grecia
CHRYSANTHOU, Mme (G)
CAMBITSIS, M. (G)
CHARAKAS, M. (E)
DASSIS, M.(T/W)

Guatemala
CHAVEZ BIETTI, Sra. (G)
GORDILLO GALINDO, Sr. (G)
MANCILLA GARCÍA, Sr.(T/W)

Guinée/Guinea
DIALLO, M. (G)
DOUMBOUYA, M. (G)

Guinée équatoriale/Equatorial Guinea/Guinea Ecuatorial
ESUÁ NKÓ, Sr. (G)
ASAMA NTUGU, Sr. (G)
MATZEN MAKOSO, Sr. (E)

Honduras
PONCE, Sr. (G)
CRUZ RAMIREZ, Sra. (G)

Hongrie/Hungary/Hungría
HERCZOG, Mr. (G)
TÓTH, Mr. (G)
CSUPORT, Mr. (E)
TAMÁS, Ms.(T/W)

Inde/India
SHENOY, Mr. (G)
ANAND, Mr. (E)
DAVE, Mr.(T/W)

Indonésie/Indonesia
SULISTYANINGSIH, Ms. (G)
SITUMORANG, Mr. (G)
RACHMAN, Mr. (E)
DAVID, Mr.(T/W)

République islamique d'Iran/Islamic Republic of Iran/República Islámica del Irán
RAIESI FARD, Mr. (E)
SALIMIAN, Mr.(T/W)

Iraq
KHODIR, Mr. (G)

Irlande/Ireland/Irlanda
PENDER, Mr. (G)
MCDONNELL, Mr. (G)
MAGUIRE, Ms. (E)
LYNCH, Ms.(T/W)

Islande/Iceland/Islandia
DAVIDSDOTTIR, Ms. (G)
KRISTINSSON, Mr. (G)
MAGNUSSON, Mr. (E)

Israël/Israel
WAXMAN, Mr. (G)
FURMAN, Ms. (G)
BARAK, Mr. (E)
KARA, Mr.(T/W)

Italie/Italy/Italia
SIMONETTI, M. (G)
COLOMBO, M. (G)
SASSO MAZZUFFERI, Mme (E)
TARTAGLIA, M.(T/W)

Jamaïque/Jamaica
SMITH, Mr. (G)
LEWIS, Mr. (E)
GOODLEIGH, Mr.(T/W)

Japon/Japan/Japón
OSHIMA, Mr. (G)
HASEGAWA, Mr. (G)
SUZUKI, Mr. (E)
NAKAJIMA, Mr.(T/W)

Jordanie/Jordan/Jordania
AL-RUSAN, Mr. (G)

Kenya
KAVULUDI, Mr. (G)
MOHAMED, Mrs. (G)
KONDITI, Mr. (E)
ATWOLI, Mr.(T/W)

Kiribati
AWIRA, Mr. (G)
KABUBUKE, Mr. (E)
AATA, Ms.(T/W)

Koweït/Kuwait
AL-MUDADI, Mr. (G)
RAZZOOQI, Mr. (G)
AL-RABAH, Mr. (E)

Lesotho
MATSOSO, Ms. (G)
MAKEKA, Mr. (E)
TYHALI, Mr.(T/W)

Lettonie/Latvia/Letonia
KARKLINS, Mr. (G)
KALNINS, Mr. (G)

Liban/Lebanon/Líbano
GHORAYEB, M. (G)
SAAB, Mme (G)
BALBOUL, M. (E)

Libéria/Liberia
WAHYEE, Mr. (G)

Jamahiriya arabe libyenne/Libyan Arab Jamahiriya/Jamahiriya Arabe Libia
ALZWAM, Mr. (G)
DERBI, Mr. (G)

Lituanie/Lithuania/Lituania
JAKUCIONYTE, Ms. (G)
RIMKUNAS, Mr. (G)
VASILEVSKIS, Mr. (E)
BALSIENE, Ms.(T/W)

Luxembourg/Luxemburgo
FABER, M. (G)
SCHOLTUS, Mme (G)
BERTRAND-SCHAUL, Mme (E)
PIZZAFERRI, M.(T/W)

Madagascar
RASOLOFONIAINARISON, M. (G)
RANDRIAMAHOLISON, M.(T/W)

Malaisie/Malaysia/Malasia
SOH, Mr. (G)
ISMAIL, Mr. (G)
SHAMSUDIN, Mr. (E)
RAMPAK, Mr.(T/W)

Malawi
MONONGA, Mr. (G)
KAMBUTO, Mr. (G)
SINJANI, Mr. (E)
KALIMANJIRA, Mr.(T/W)

Mali/Malí
DIAKITE, M. (G)
MAHAMANE, M. (G)
TRAORE, M. (E)
DIAKITE, M.(T/W)

Malte/Malta
PULLICINO, Mr. (G)
AZZOPARDI, Mr. (G)
FARRUGIA, Mr. (E)

Maroc/Morocco/Marruecos
HILALE, M. (G)
CHATER, M. (G)

Maurice/Mauritius/Mauricio
ARNACHELLUM, Mr. (G)
BENYDIN, Mr.(T/W)

Mauritanie/Mauritania
OULD MOHAMED LEMINE, M. (G)
OULD CHEIKHNA, M. (G)

Mexique/Mexico/México
ROVIROSA, Sra. (G)
SILVA, Sr. (G)
DE REGIL, Sr. (E)
ANDERSON, Sra.(T/W)

Mongolie/Mongolia
SUKHBAATAR, Mr.(T/W)

Mozambique
CAIFAZ, Mr. (G)
SITOE, Mr.(T/W)

Myanmar
THAN, Mr. (G)
NYUNT, Mr. (G)

Namibie/Namibia
HIVELUAH, Ms. (G)
SHINGUADJA, Mr. (G)
SHIPENA, Mr. (E)
KAPENDA, Mr.(T/W)

Népal/Nepal
ACHARYA, Mr. (G)

Nicaragua
MARTÍNEZ FLORES, Srta. (G)
CRUZ TORUÑO, Sr. (G)
GONZÁLEZ GAITÁN, Sr.(T/W)

Niger/Níger
HAMADOU, M. (G)
MAÏNA, M. (G)
SANDA, M.(T/W)

Nigéria/Nigeria
ADEYEYE-OLUKOYA, Mrs. (G)
SULAI, Mrs. (G)
OSHIOMHOLE, Mr.(T/W)

Norvège/Norway/Noruega
BRUAAS, Mr. (G)
VIDNES, Mr. (G)
RIDDERVOLD, Ms. (E)
THEODORSEN, Ms.(T/W)

Nouvelle-Zélande/New Zealand/Nueva Zelandia
BUWALDA, Mr. (G)
STEFFENS, Ms. (G)
ARNOLD, Mr. (E)
BEAUMONT, Ms.(T/W)

Oman/Omán
AL-ABDUWANI, Mr. (G)
AL-AMRI, Mr. (G)
AL RABAIE, Mr. (E)

Ouganda/Uganda
NAGGAGA, Mr. (G)
OGARAM, Mr. (G)
PAJOBO, Mr.(T/W)

Pakistan/Pakistán
FARSHORI, Mr. (G)
UMER, Mr. (G)
TABANI, Mr. (E)

Panama/Panamá
ORTIZ BARBER, Sra. (G)
ROSAS PÉREZ, Sra. (G)
AIZPURÚA, Sr. (E)
PUGA RODRÍGUEZ, Sr.(T/W)

Paraguay
RAMÍREZ LEZCANO, Sr. (G)
BARREIRO PERROTTA, Sr. (G)
BOGARIN, Sr. (E)
PARRA GAONA, Sr.(T/W)

Pays-Bas/Netherlands/Países Bajos
NOTEBOOM, Ms. (G)
BEETS, Mr. (G)
RENIQUE, Mr. (E)
ETTY, Mr.(T/W)

Pérou/Peru/Perú
BERAUN, Sra. (G)
VILLAVICENCIO RIOS, Sr. (G)
GUTIÉRREZ MADUEÑO, Sr.(T/W)

Philippines/Filipinas
BALDOZ, Mrs. (G)
VALERIO, Mr.(T/W)

Pologne/Poland/Polonia
LEMIESZEWSKA, Mrs. (G)
JAKUBOWSKI, Mr. (G)
BOBROWSKI, Mr. (E)
WOJCIK, Mr.(T/W)

Portugal
RIBEIRO LOPES, M. (G)
BARCIA, M. (G)
FERNANDES SALGUEIRO, M. (E)
GOMES PROENÇA, M.(T/W)

Qatar
ALKAWARI, Mr. (G)
AL MAL, Ms. (G)
AL SAIARI, Mr.(T/W)

République dém. du Congo/Democratic Republic of the Congo/República Democrática del Congo
MUTOMB MUJING, M. (G)
SAMBASSI, M. (G)
MUTABUNGA RUGINA, M. (E)
MUKALAYI HANGA, M.(T/W)

Royaume-Uni/United Kingdom/Reino Unido
RICHARDS, Mr. (G)
NELLTHORP, Ms. (G)
LAMBERT, Mr. (E)

Fédération de Russie/Russian Federation/Federación de Rusia
BAVYKIN, Mr. (G)
LUBLIN, Mr. (G)

Rwanda
KAVARUGANDA, M. (G)
UKUYEMUYE, M. (G)
BITWAYIKI, M. (E)
KAYUMBA, M.(T/W)

Saint-Marin/San Marino
BIGI, Mme (G)
GASPERONI, M. (G)
GIORGINI, Mme (E)
PIERMATTEI, M.(T/W)

Sénégal/Senegal
DIALLO, Mme (G)
THIAM, M. (G)
DIOP, M. (E)
GUIRO, M.(T/W)

Serbie et Monténégro/Serbia and Montenegro/Serbia y Montenegro
BEGOVIĆ, Mr. (G)
ŠAHOVIĆ, Mr. (G)
ZAGORAC, Mr. (E)
ČANAK, Mr.(T/W)

Seychelles
MERITON, Mr. (G)
BAKER, Mr. (G)
SULTAN-BEAUDOUIN, Mr. (E)
ROBINSON, Mr.(T/W)

Singapour/Singapore/Singapur
NG, Mr. (G)
YONG, Ms. (G)

Slovaquie/Slovakia/Eslovaquia
PETÖCZ, Mr. (G)
SEPTÁKOVÁ, Ms. (G)
BORGULA, Mr. (E)
MESTANOVÁ, Mrs.(T/W)

Slovénie/Slovenia/Eslovenia
ZIDAR, Mr. (G)
RIHAR BAJUK, Ms. (G)
JEREB, Ms. (E)
KRZIŠNIK, Mr.(T/W)

Soudan/Sudan/Sudán
SHENTOUR, Mr. (G)
ELHASSAN, Mr. (G)
ELGURASHI, Mr. (E)
GHANDOUR, Mr.(T/W)

Sri Lanka
GAMMAMPILA DON, Mr. (G)
MADIHAHEWA, Mr. (G)
DASANAYAKE, Mr. (E)
DEVENDRA, Mr.(T/W)

Suède/Sweden/Suecia
WIKLUND, Ms. (G)
JONZON, Mr. (G)
LAURENT, Ms. (E)
BENGTSSON, Mr.(T/W)

Suisse/Switzerland/Suiza
ALVESALO-ROESCH, Mme (G)
ELMIGER, M. (G)
PLASSARD, M. (E)
VIGNE, M.(T/W)

Suriname
PIROE, Mr. (G)
VAN OMMEREN, Mr. (E)

Swaziland/Swazilandia
NKHAMBULE, Mr. (G)
MAPHANGA, Mrs. (E)

République arabe syrienne/Syrian Arab Republic/República Arabe Siria
IBRAHIM, M. (G)
AKASHE, M. (G)
MOHAMMAD NASSER, M. (E)
AZOZ, M.(T/W)

République-Unie de Tanzanie/United Republic of Tanzania/República Unida de Tanzanía
RWEYEMAMU, Mrs. (G)
KABYEMERA, Mr. (E)
SITTA, Mrs.(T/W)

Tchad/Chad
ABDERAHIM, M. (G)
DJEGUEDEM, M. (G)
DJIBRINE, M.(T/W)

République tchèque/Czech Republic/República Checa
SAJDA, Mr. (G)
SLABÝ, Mr. (G)
DRBALOVÁ, Mrs. (E)
BAUEROVÁ, Mrs.(T/W)

Thaïlande/Thailand/Tailandia
RUANGSUWAN, Mr. (G)
SATJIPANON, Mr. (G)
ROMCHATTHONG, Mrs. (E)
TECHATEERAVAT, Mr.(T/W)

Trinité-et-Tobago/Trinidad and Tobago/Trinidad y Tabago
RAMNARINE, Mr. (G)
SINGH, Ms. (G)
HILTON CLARKE, Mr. (E)
GUISEPPI, Mr.(T/W)

Tunisie/Tunisia/Túnez
MANSOUR, M. (G)
CHOUBA, Mme (G)
M'KAISSI, M. (E)
TRABELSI, M.(T/W)

Turquie/Turkey/Turquía
GENC, Mr. (G)
OYMAN, Mr. (G)
CENTEL, Mr. (E)

Ukraine/Ucrania
YAMPOLSKYI, Mr. (G)
BELASHOV, Mr. (G)
ZHADAN, Mr. (E)

Uruguay
LAGARMILLA, Sra. (G)
DONO, Sra. (G)
FOSTIK, Sr. (E)
FERNÁNDEZ, Sr.(T/W)

Venezuela
DORADO CANO, Sr. (G)
MOLINA, Sr. (G)
DE ARBELOA, Sr. (E)
INFANTE, Sr.(T/W)

Viet Nam
PHAM, Mr. (G)
VU, Mr. (G)
VI, Mrs. (E)
VO, Mr.(T/W)

Yémen/Yemen
AL-FAYSALI, Mr. (G)

Zambie/Zambia
HIKAUMBA, Mr.(T/W)

Zimbabwe
MUSEKA, Mr. (G)

———

Contre/Against/En contra: 1

Mauritanie/Mauritania
OULD MOHAMED, M.(T/W)

———

CONTENTS

Page

Eighteenth sitting

Ratification of the Instrument of Amendment of the ILO Constitution by Nigeria. 1

Report of the Committee on the Fishing Sector: Submission, discussion and approval 1

    Speakers: Mr. Boumbopoulos *(Reporter)*, Ms. Karikari Anang, Mr. Masemola, Mr. Ribeiro Lopes, Mr. Pender, Mr. Potter

Resolution to place on the agenda of the next ordinary session of the Conference an item entitled "Work in the Fishing Sector": Adoption 7

Record vote on the resolution concerning the arrears of contributions of Iraq 7

Record vote on the resolution concerning the arrears of contribution of Paraguay 7

Final record vote on the withdrawal of 16 Recommendations 7

Nineteenth sitting

Report of the Committee on Human Resources: Submission, discussion and approval 8

    Speakers: Ms. Murty *(Reporter)*, Mr. Renique, Ms. Yacob, Mr. Chetwin, Mr. Tricoche, Ms. Lenoir, Mr. Raman, Ms. Oiz, Mr. Abdulhussain, Ms. Riggs, Mr. Lambert, Mr. Wajda, Ms. Awassi Atsimadja, Ms. Goldberg, Mr. Patil, Mr. Arnold, Mr. Lewis, Mr. Rojvithee

Proposed Recommendation concerning human resources development: Education, training and lifelong learning: Adoption 23

    Speakers: Mr. Renique, Ms. Yacob

Second and third reports of the Credentials Committee: Submission and noting 24

    Speaker: Mr. Oni *(Chairperson and Reporter)*

Report of the Committee on Migrant Workers: Submission, discussion and approval 25

    Speakers: Mr.Kebbon *(Reporter)*, Mr. de Regil, Ms. Burrow, Mr. Dé, Mr. Pender, Mr. Gammampila Don, Ms. Saab, Mr. Manley, Mr. Anderson, Mr. Terán, Mr. Cester Beatobe, Ms. Coke-Lloyd, Ms. Phillips, Ms. Kipulu Katani, Ms. Avendano Denier, Mr. Joubier

Resolution concerning a fair deal for migrant workers in a global economy: Adoption 38

Conclusions on a fair deal for migrant workers in a global economy: Adoption 38

Record vote on the resolution concerning the arrears of contributions of Iraq: Results 39

Record vote on the resolution concerning the arrears of contributions of Paraguay: Results 44

Final record vote on the withdrawal of 16 Recommendations: Results 49

No. 26 – Thursday, 17 June 2004

International Labour Conference

Provisional Record

Ninety-second Session, Geneva, 2004

27

Twentieth sitting

Thursday, 17 June 2004, 10.15 a.m.

President: Mr. Ray Guevara

FINAL RECORD VOTE ON THE RECOMMENDATION CONCERNING HUMAN RESOURCES DEVELOPMENT: EDUCATION, TRAINING AND LIFELONG LEARNING

Original Spanish: The PRESIDENT

We shall now conduct the record vote on the proposed Recommendation concerning human resources development: Education, training and lifelong learning, which is contained in *Provisional Record* No. 20A.

(A record vote is taken.)

(The detailed results of the vote will be found at the end of the record of this sitting.)

The result of the vote is as follows: 338 votes in favour, 93 against, with 14 abstentions. As the quorum was 290, and the required two-thirds majority of 297 has been reached, the Recommendation is adopted.

(The Recommendation is adopted.)

The floor is now open to delegates who might wish to explain their vote.

Original Spanish: Mr. FUNES DE RIOJA *(Employers' adviser and substitute delegate, Argentina; Chairperson of the Employers' group)*

On behalf of the Employers' group I would like to explain why we cast the vote we did. We are very much in favour of this tripartite Organization and committed to its objectives; We feel that it is important that discussion be conducted and instruments applied in full. We believe in social dialogue and in consensus. We uphold the Constitution and the regulations of the Organization, and have done so throughout this debate, right up to the adoption of this instrument which has just been voted, an achievement on which I would like to congratulate the Conference and the Office.

We wanted to explain our difficulties with the Recommendation. We sought improvement through the amendments mechanism. This is not by any manner of means anti-constitutional. It is a mechanism provided for under the Standing Orders for reaching consensus. Unfortunately this was not possible. We did make some mistakes during the discussions. We should not have had a vote in the Committee. I also believe that there were those who were not attentive enough to the central issue we raised regarding one of the paragraphs – not the Recommendation, just one paragraph of it. But it is not an insignificant paragraph, and the Recommendation is not insignificant. It has above all to do with the development of human resources, something that is very close to our heart. From now on – and we will be saying this in the Governing Body – we will be encouraging the Office to continue and increase its efforts in this area, so as to find the necessary subjects and the right agreements.

This general discussion on human resources development began in 2000 and yet recently, just a few days ago, at this particular session of Conference, in a paragraph referring to social dialogue, international collective bargaining made an appearance as something to be included in the Recommendation, in the context of training. It recommended that governments should support initiatives in this particular area.

What was not properly considered is that international collective bargaining is a phenomenon that we are examining, something that is emerging, but not thus far something on which our Organization should take up an explicit position, because there are only 20 such cases, and it goes beyond the scope of Conventions Nos. 98 and 154 in that collective bargaining, which States should provide at the national level is a matter of collective autonomy, not a matter for States, who cannot specify any given model for collective bargaining.

This matter has not been discussed since 2000; our opposition to it now has to do with the fact that we believe that it is legally unacceptable and technically unfeasible in an instrument of this kind. You may say that we are dealing with a Recommendation, not a Convention; it is not binding, it is a political instrument. But we believe that Recommendations do have considerable authority. We believe in them for their own sake, not as a "catch all" for all the non-implementable clauses that we cannot include in a Convention. We see them as autonomous instruments that express the views and decisions of the tripartite constituents regarding policy in particular areas therefore we do rank them high among instruments.

From the legal point of view, there are three points that need to be recognized and which justify our negative vote. Supporting international collective bargaining goes beyond the terms of any international standard. It goes beyond existing national standards. It could clearly have an impact on the social and economic life of countries, not only those countries where such international collective bargaining might take place, but also in those developing countries which may suffer the effects of any such negotiations, even in terms of their potential competitive advantages.

Vocational training, as far as we are concerned, is as important as human resources development. It is as important as the standard-setting system. These unwanted consequences lead to a practical problem, not an ideological one. They do not destroy our belief in a tripartite approach or in social dialogue.

We have not looked for procedural means of impeding the adoption of this Recommendation, which as we know has been supported by both Workers and Governments. We have just spelt out our position in a very loyal way. because we believe in tripartism. We spell out the things upon which we can concur and those upon which we cannot agree; not by seeking to create substantial divergences, but affirming our willingness to take part in dialogue.

We would urge the delegates and the Office, in the light of the adoption of this Recommendation, and in view of the fact that collective bargaining in any area is a reflection of the collective will and requires the participation of Employers, to carry on working together so as to find ways and means of implementing all the principles contained in this Recommendation which we endorse. We would also hope respectfully that, just as we bow to the consensus of those who carried the day here, you will also respect those whose voice on this occasion did not prevail and we would ask you to think more about this in the future. Consensus and social dialogue are not merely a matter of arithmetic, they are a shared responsibility to act together.

This is why we voted against the adoption of the Recommendation. Once again I would like to highlight the very respectful way in which the Worker Vice-Chairperson listened to my arguments as we sought a solution that eluded us. I would also like to express my appreciation, not only for Sir Roy Trotman, but also for the efforts by the Office and by the President of the Conference. We regret these differences of opinion between us, which are of a substantive nature. International collective bargaining did not come within the scope of this discussion, and cannot do so in this forum. Nevertheless, we will carry on with our dialogue because that is indeed our mission.

Mr. PENDER *(Government adviser and substitute delegate, Ireland; speaking on behalf of the European Union)*

On behalf of the European Union, I would like to explain the reasons why the European Union Member States have voted in favour of the Recommendation. The Governments of Bulgaria, Turkey and Romania also wish to associate themselves with this statement.

On behalf of the European Union, I welcome the adoption of the new Recommendation concerning human resources development: Education, training and lifelong learning. Many elements of the new Recommendation have resonances in current policy developments in the field of lifelong learning within the European Union.

The European Union is engaged in ongoing discussions on the changes that are needed in education and training policies and systems in Europe to adapt them to meet the challenges of the knowledge-based society and economy. The European Union has given political priority to the need to reform career guidance services, to support lifelong learning, and to improve the quality and transparency of vocational education and training within a lifelong learning framework, and has recently adopted a new resolution in that field. Furthermore, work is about to begin on building stronger links between vocational education and training and higher education.

In the field of employment policy, the current European Employment Guidelines place particular emphasis on increasing workforce and enterprise adaptability, investing more, and more effectively, in human capital and lifelong learning, and attracting more people to enter and remain in the labour market. Education, training and employment policies in the European Union are interlinked, as is necessary in order to achieve its social and economic goals. Better educated and more skilled individuals are more likely to secure employment and thereby contribute to the economy and to society as a whole, and thus help to create a more cohesive and inclusive society and to eradicate poverty. I believe that the new Recommendation being adopted here today will also contribute to fulfilling these objectives.

Original French: Ms.ALVESALO-ROESCH (Government adviser and substitute delegate, Switzerland)

Switzerland abstained during the vote, not because of the content of the Recommendation but for the following reasons.

What is clearly understood can be clearly expressed. This is the principle that has guided Switzerland's unchanging policy in the last few years with regard to the ILO. Switzerland has, indeed, worked hard to encourage the ILO to draw up simple instruments which are easy to understand and access so that they can actually be applied and implemented in the daily lives of employers and workers. Now, the Recommendation we had to adopt today is not at all in keeping with this policy. The text is exceedingly complicated and repetitive; the same idea is expressed in many different ways in several paragraphs; there are redundancies and it is so difficult to access this Recommendation that we wonder whether it is going to really be used outside of this institution. We are disappointed with this result. If it were to be the precursor of a trend, we would be very worried. We agree with the substance of the instrument and thus, Switzerland will not refuse it, but we are forced to abstain in order to be in consistency with our policy that standards should be accessible.

Mr. SHEPARD *(Government adviser and substitute delegate, United States)*

The United States strongly supports most of the elements of the Recommendation, which brings the old Recommendation No. 150 into the 21st century by providing important and appropriate guidance on training issues relevant to today's knowledge and skills-based labour market.

We regret however, that we were unable to vote "yes" to this Recommendation. We are concerned by the use of vague and imprecise language in some instances. In Part II, clause 5(f), for example, seems to advocate a government role in collective bargaining, in violation of a fundamental principle. In addition, while the United States fully recognizes the importance of training and adapting labour forces to new challenges and conditions and to increasing productivity, prosperity and development, we do not support the view that training has the status of a right; we are opposed to labelling goals, however laudable, as rights. To do so could dilute the rights and freedoms enshrined in the Universal Declaration of Human Rights.

We commend the Committee for its work and hope that the ILO will continue to assist in the development of modern training systems that can enable workers and enterprises to reap the benefits of new technology and new work arrangements.

Original Spanish: Ms. ARANGO DE BUITRAGO *(Government adviser and substitute delegate, Colombia)*

I am the delegate of the Government of Colombia. Colombia voted against the Recommendation, not because it disapproves of the Recommendation as a whole – we do recognize the progress that has been made in this Conference in terms of education, training and learning for the world's workers – but because it believes that collective bargaining on certain issues should be circumscribed to the terms laid down in national legislation. The Government of Colombia believes it appropriate that human resources and other issues of interest should be discussed within the national labour consultation committee, which has a constitutional origin, with a view to reaching national, regional and local agreements and agreements at the sectoral or company level. Colombia is of the view that developing countries such as our own that are trying to find their place in global trade are not yet ready to adjust to decisions on this matter.

REPORT OF THE COMMITTEE ON THE APPLICATION OF STANDARDS: SUBMISSION, DISCUSSION AND APPROVAL

Original Spanish: The PRESIDENT

We shall now proceed to the examination of the report of the Committee on the Application of Standards, which is published in *Provisional Record* No. 24, of which there are three parts. The Officers of the Committee were as follows: the chairperson was Ms. Rial, the Employer Vice-Chairperson was Mr. Wisskirchen, the Worker Vice-Chairperson was Mr. Cortebeeck, and the Reporter was Ms. Robert Lopez. I would now like to call upon Ms. Robert Lopes to submit the report of the Committee on the Application of Standards.

Original Portuguese: Ms. ROBERT LOPES *(Government adviser, Portugal; Reporter of the Committee on the Application of Standards)*

It is an honour for me to submit to this plenary sitting of the Conference the report of the Committee on the Application of Standards. This is a Committee whose work has always elicited a keen interest and everybody, we believe, backs up its outcomes and the impact of its work. When it comes to the application of standards of the ILO, this is one of the main ways in which we must act.

I would like to remind you that the Committee on the Application of Standards is one of the Conference bodies whose functions are laid down in article 7 of the Standing Orders under which the Committee shall consider the measures taken by Members to give effect to the provisions of Conventions to which they are parties and the information furnished by Members concerning the results of inspections, as well as the information and reports concerning Conventions and Recommendations communicated by Members in accordance with article 19 of the Constitution, except for information requested under paragraph 5(e) of that article. The Committee on the Application of Standards is, therefore, a core element in the machinery for inspecting the implementation of the standards adopted by this Organization; it bases its work on reports from the Committee of Experts on the Application of Conventions and Recommendations, which draw on written reports from Governments who are answering questions put to them by the experts. These two bodies were set up by the Conference in 1926 and are complementary.

The report I am submitting for the consideration of this Conference falls into three parts: the first part is a general report from the Committee; the second part contains observations on certain countries, namely the automatic cases concerning failure to submit reports, and mentions debates have a bearing on the application of the standards; the third has to do with the special sitting to examine developments concerning the question of observance by the Government of Myanmar of the Forced Labour Convention, 1930 (No. 29), in pursuance of the resolution of the session of the Conference held in 2000.

The first part contains a tribute to Sir William Douglas, and to Mr. Nicolas Valticos, who passed away respectively in August and September 2003. We regret their loss and we have underlined the very important role they played in the cause of the application of the standards of this Organization.

The Committee reviewed its working methods; most members came out in favour of the current working methods, without ruling out possible adjustments which might further improve its efficacy. However, a consensus was not reached on this; there were a number of members of the Committee who made different views known, particularly as regards the choice of cases to be debated. The dialogue will proceed with the consultations the ILO will undertake in this area.

The Committee began its work with a debate on general matters having to do with international labour standards, and the way in which member States comply with their obligations. In the general debate, a lot of detailed information was provided, in particular as regards national situations, and we listened to many interventions. Emphasis was placed on the need to have effective labour inspection systems whose role is essential in order for labour standards to be properly implemented. Deficiencies were pointed out with regard to material and human resources, and also importance of technical assistance from the ILO was underscored. Furthermore, technical assistance from the ILO was requested in other contexts, all connected with standards, to enable States to properly fulfil their obligations in that regard.

The second part of the discussion looked at the General Survey of the Committee of Experts on the application of the Employment Policy Convention, 1964 (No. 122), and the Employment Policy (Supplementary Provisions) Recommendation, 1984 (No. 169), and the aspects of the Human Resources Development Convention, 1975 (No. 142), and of the Job Creation in Small and Medium-Sized Enterprises Recommendation, 1998 (No. 189), relating to the promotion of full, productive and freely chosen employment. The value of this study was underscored, given the current global situation. The discussions stressed the need for education and training on a lifelong basis, the need to invest in knowledge, and the importance of social dialogue in promoting employment. Out of this debate there emerged the need for social dialogue in generating employment, and what an important role the ILO plays in this connection.

We also spent time in the general discussion on the report of the Eighth Session of the Joint ILO/UNESCO Committee of Experts on the Application of Recommendations concerning Teaching Personnel. In this connection the very important role of teachers was discussed, as was the need for training to acquire specialized skills and knowledge and the need for social dialogue, with a view to implementing the two Recommendations.

Most of the work of the Committee and indeed its main task, involved looking at individual cases. The idea here is to encourage governments, through tripartite dialogue, to fulfil the obligations arising from the ILO Constitution. The debate began with what we call the automatic cases which have to do with the ratification of standards. One of the important obligations placed on governments is to inform its legislative authorities of all the Conventions and Recommendations or Protocols adopted by the Conference, irrespective of whether they are going to ratify them immediately or not. This is a fundamental obligation placed upon governments for the application and implementation of the ILO standard-setting instruments. Also essential to this implementation is the obligation to submit reports on the Conventions and Recommendations which have not been ratified which, furthermore, is intended as a means of testing the validity of the standards in question. With regard to the other automatic cases and the failure to comply with obligations, which means that governments are approached for reports, failure to submit reports, including in particular the first report and, failure to respond to observations made by the Experts all mean that the control and monitoring mechanism, based on dialogue, cannot operate. In most instances, the Committee was informed of difficulties arising out of the lack of human and material resources to implement this machinery, and there were many requests made to the ILO for technical assistance.

The Committee then held a special sitting to examine developments concerning the observance by the Government of Myanmar of the Forced Labour Convention, 1930 (No. 29). This is reported in *Provisional Record* No. 24, *Part Three*. This special sitting was due to the ILO's tremendous concerns about persistent forced labour in Myanmar.

After having looked at the automatic cases, the Committee then looked at 24 individual cases pertaining to the implementation of Conventions, in respect of which the Committee of Experts had pointed out difficulties of implementation. We considered cases concerning both core Conventions and also so-called technical Conventions and their proper implementation, which is vital for improving working conditions.

Arising from the dialogue which took place when we addressed these cases, there were real commitments on the part of the Governments to implement the Conventions, de jure and de facto, and to consult the social partners in order to achieve this.

The Committee felt it was necessary to devote a special paragraph to Myanmar's total disregard for the Freedom of Association and Protection of the Right to Organise Convention, 1948 (No. 87).

I would like to stress that the Committee did not only look at cases of non-compliance. We also showed great interest in cases where progress has been made in implementing Conventions and this is mentioned at length in the Committee of Experts' report.

Finally, I would like, on behalf of all the members of the Committee, to thank the Governments who took part in the tripartite discussion on the problems their respective countries were having in implementing the various Conventions, and for trying to seek possible solutions. Their participation was essential and very valuable indeed. I should also like to thank the Chairperson of the Committee, Ms. Rial, and the Employer and Worker Vice-Chairpersons, Mr. Wisskirchen and Ms. Cortebeeck, for their knowledge and efficiency which enabled us to complete our work successfully. I should also like to thank Mr. Javillier and his team for the support they have given us, as did the secretariat – their help was valuable. I should also like to thank the interpreters.

I would like to recommend to the Conference the adoption of this report.

Original German: Mr. WISSKIRCHEN *(Employers' adviser and substitute delegate, Germany; Employer Vice-Chairperson of the Committee on the Application of Standards)*

As we have done in the last few years, we are submitting a three-part report of over 200 pages to the Conference. This year's report of the Committee of Experts, which constituted an important basis for discussions within the Committee on the Application of Standards, albeit not the only basis, differs significantly from many of its predecessors over the last 25 years. It is, however, only the substantive differences which deserve our attention. In the past, there was deep criticism of the fact that the report of the Committee of Experts dealt with themes which did not fall within the mandate of that Committee. This applied above all to questions of standards policies, such as standard setting, to the ratification and denunciation of Conventions and to many other activities of the Office. Nor is it appropriate that the Committee of Experts' report should contain recommendations concerning the ratification or the denunciation of Conventions, particularly when these are not in line with the discussions and decisions taken by the Governing Body which is responsible for these matters. Many of the comments made by the Committee of Experts in its report were often associated with value judgements consisting of agreement or criticism. This gave the impression that the Committee of Experts was the judge and jury of the whole International Labour Organization. Of course, this prompts suspicions that the Committee of Experts is somehow being used as an instrument by other parts of the Organization.

We, therefore, welcome the changes which have now been effected that is to say, the inclusion of many extremely interesting and important items of information in a separate report of the Office, which used to contain only the list of ratifications. In this way, we avoid a muddling of the duties of the Committee of Experts and those of other ILO bodies. The competence and responsibilities of each body, as determined by their mandate, are now correctly apportioned.

But in this respect further steps are necessary. These are described in more detail in the general part of our report, in paragraphs 49-50. They concern the common title and symbol used for both brochures. They do not belong together and this could therefore give rise to some misunderstandings.

Furthermore, the chapter on collaboration with other international organizations and functions relating to other international instruments does not belong in the report of the Committee of Experts. This section in paragraphs 101-112 mentions the exchange of various documents and instruments with other international organizations. The experts are acting completely *ultra vires*. The experts' activities rest on an administrative agreement between the International Labour Organization and the Council of Europe. Moreover, since most of the delegates here do not come from Europe, they probably have little interest in knowing who has signed the European Social Charter or the Additional Protocol thereto.

We also have some doubts as regards the long chapter which is to be found in paragraphs 12 to 43. The so-called "Highlights and major trends in the application of international labour standards in certain areas" described there are an attempt to produce mini general surveys, although the prerequisites of article 19 of the Constitution of the Organization, which provides for such General Surveys, are not met. In the report before our Committee, the Experts must assess the reports member States submit in pursuance of articles 22 and 35 of the Constitution. It is not incumbent upon the Committee of Experts to make general comments or lay down general rules of interpretation which go beyond individual cases.

This year, what is said in the abovementioned section on the three separate Conventions is mostly of a very general nature and therefore does not call for any comment.

The demand that a particular kind of penalty be imposed for the violation of Labour Inspection Convention, 1947 (No. 81), contradicts the text of the Convention and earlier statements made by the Committee of Experts itself. I therefore recommend, that you look at paragraphs 79 to 80 of our report.

This year's General Survey of several employment policy standards focuses more than ever before on the relationship between the economy and labour standards. Since the adoption of Employment Policy Convention, 1964 (No. 122), the world economy has developed very fast in a new direction. Unfortunately, not everyone has digested the fact that labour standards established in periods when there appears to be never-ending economic growth can have negative repercussions on the creation of new jobs and on the standard of living. The General Survey, quite correctly, notes that strategies for more growth and employment must be accompanied by greater flexibility of the labour markets, which implies flexible labour legislation and flexible working hours. Small and medium-sized enterprises have a special role to play here. All in all, it is absolutely essential that the International Labour Organization scrutinize its standards to see whether they are still pertinent to jobs in the twenty-first century. The ratification of any standard which does not satisfy this prerequisite means a spectacular competitive disadvantage for the ratifying state. The conclusion we draw from the General Survey is that, the impression must not be given that the International Labour Organization concentrates its efforts only on those who already have jobs, but rather, the Organization must ensure, through the standards it establishes, that entrepreneurs can create new jobs within the framework of flexible basic conditions.

The last part of the general discussion in the Committee concerned the report of a special body convened by the International Labour Organization and UNESCO to monitor the implementation of two UNESCO Recommendations on the status of teachers. It is a great privilege if two specialized agencies of the United Nations which are active worldwide, that is to say, the International Labour Organization and UNESCO, deal with instruments concerning just one profession. This can be justified only on the grounds that the importance of education and training for the future of mankind cannot be overestimated. We support the call for social dialogue between the teachers and the education authorities. But in this connection, we should not forget parents, who are not referred to, yet it is they who have the right to decide on the education to be given to their children, or employers who know exactly what qualifications will be needed later in jobs. The demand for more thorough, up-to-date basic and further training for teachers deserves our full support, as does the demand for reasonable working conditions. As in other professions, this cannot and will not lead to a uniform world standard. But in keeping with the possibilities of each country, teachers should not find themselves at the lower end of the social scale.

The Committee on the Application of Standards, like any committee, constantly scrutinizes its own working methods. In recent years the frequently voiced criticism of our working methods has focused on the list of individual cases to be dealt with. It is obvious, but not surprising, that most criticism comes from the states which must often be placed in the list because the Committee of Experts and the Committee on the Application of Standards believe that major discrepancies exist in relation to the ratified Conventions. The critics have repeatedly complained about the lack of transparency or generally a lack of justice. But no practical suggestions for feasible improvements are ever made. The majority of committee members therefore feel that the decisive criteria, which have been known for years, are the right ones. However, since there are no mechanical criteria offering scientific accuracy, the actual result of the selection process does not always satisfy everyone. We consider that the selection this year was not a complete success. We, Employers, are not convinced about this year's cluster of four Central American States which are on our list. In addition, in two case trade union complaints are reported lock stock and barrel and the Experts did not have any opportunity to comment on their substance, so of course the Committee on the Application of Standards did not express any criticism in these cases.

It is to be expected that today some governments will take up the subject of the list and some have already announced their intention to do so. If the substantive comments seem to be pertinent, next year the Committee on the Application of Standards will no doubt come back to them, for the Committee alone decides on its working methods. For this reason they are not and should not be discussed in detail in a plenary sitting. When it begins to look at individual cases, the Committee considers divers reporting duties, the "automatic cases". This year, once again, unfortunately, it noted huge omissions. In addition, we discovered that not even half of the states concerned felt that it was necessary to appear when their case was discussed.

This is alarming and absolutely unacceptable. The generally highly commended monitoring system of the ILO cannot function unless the divers reporting duties are fulfilled.

The actual substance of the individual cases we dealt with each day last week is accurately recorded in the second part or our report. Each case has its own particular characteristics. We will not do justice to these 24 specific cases, or to the work of the Committee, if we lump them together and try to describe them in just a few words. It should not, however, be forgotten that there has been a considerable increase in the number of cases dealt with by the Experts where progress has been made over the previous year. It is, therefore, worth looking at the cases in detail in order to see what position the Committee on the Application of Standards has adopted in each cases. It is always a question of whether and to what extent member States fulfil the obligations they have freely accepted as a result of their ratification of Conventions. Criticisms must frequently, but not always voiced and it must be subtly differentiated. All of this can be found in the extensive second part of our Committee's report.

A special paragraph of the general first part of the report only lists Myanmar on account of Convention No. 87. There is no sign whatsoever of even rudimentary conditions for freedom of association. The Government does not deny the facts and, as it has done on previous occasions, only talks about possible future developments.

Unfortunately, this year it was impossible to agree on a separate paragraph for Venezuela, where violations of the freedom of association undoubtedly occur. The de facto and de jure situation has not improved at all compared with previous years. The Employers will therefore file a complaint under article 26 of the Constitution of the ILO. A letter on that subject is probably already in the post.

For the fourth time, our Committee, in accordance with the decision taken by the Conference in the year 2000, had to organize a special session because of Myanmar's violation of the Forced Labour Convention 1930 (No.29). The numerous demands made over the years that the widespread practice of forced labour should be abolished have still not been heeded. Various discussions between the liaison officer, the informal facilitator and the authorities have not produced any positive results. The courts have even imposed death sentences mainly on the grounds that people had been in contact and cooperating with the ILO.

Generally speaking, the Conference Committee feels that the prerequisites for the implementation of the action plan signed last year just do not exist. It is especially important for the Conference Committee that the work done in the Committee between the Workers' and the Employers' groups, should be satisfactory. Once again, this has been achieved this year. For this, we would like to express our thanks to the Worker Vice-Chairperson, Mr. Cortebeeck, and Ms. Rial, the Deputy Minister of Labour of Argentina, who led us in a magnificent manner through our work and ensured that we worked rapidly. The Reporter, Ms. Maria Robert Robert Lopes is someone who is a very experienced and much-appreciated member of the Committee and, of course, we also know that without the intensive work and preparation by the Office in the department of Mr. Javillier, head of the department and his team, our Committee would be unable to work. Therefore, to Mr. Javillier and his team, a special word of thanks, and a concluding word of thanks, as always, to the members of the Employers' group. This is the 22nd year I have been the spokesperson for this group and I would like to express a special word of thanks to my friend, Ed Potter and our young colleague, Andrès Yuren of the International Organisation of Employers. We recommend our report to all of you.

Original French: Mr. CORTEBEECK *(Workers' delegate, Belgium; Worker Vice-Chairperson of the Committee on the Application of Standards)*

It was a great pleasure for me to have taken the role of Vice-Chairperson and spokesperson of the Workers' group in this Committee. Today, I have the honour of submitting to you the report of the Committee on the Application of Standards.

I should like to thank: our Chairperson, Ms. Noemi Rial, for the way in which she led our work; our Reporter, Ms. Maria Robert Lopes; Mr. Javillier and the International Labour Standards Department; the Experts, for the excellent work they have done; our Officers is of the Conference and the members of the Workers' group; Monique Cloutier and Claude Akpokavie from ACTRAV; Mr. Wisskirchen and our colleagues from the Employers' group; and the Government delegates.

I would like to share with you a few final comments about our work. With regard to the report of the Committee of Experts on the Application of Conventions and Recommendations, of the three areas that were given close consideration by the Experts this year, the Conventions on Labour inspections were the most important, for us. Although the Experts have noted improvements in the field, there is still much to be done. Moreover, we noted that inspection is particularly important in the export processing zones – as has been shown by the case of Bangladesh – or for child labour – as we have seen in the case of Bolivia.

In this connection, we would like to reiterate the request that we made to the Experts last year for them to study in depth the trafficking and exploitation of children, particularly in West Africa. We are not talking about just a few isolated cases, but about very serious, closely interconnected problems.

Lastly, still on the subject of labour inspection, the ILO could address the question of corporate social responsibility by developing a strategy to ensure that the responsibility of business does not remain just a form of self-verification and self-advertisement.

However, Conventions concerning maternity are also of great interest to us: we are very concerned at the low rate of ratification of these Conventions.

Now I would like to talk about the General Survey (Employment). The second part of our work was devoted to the General Survey, which this year was devoted to the Employment Policy Convention, 1964 (No. 122). Given the market deterioration in employment virtually everywhere in the world, this study was very topical. That is why we included the case of Slovakia on our list of cases for discussion this year.

I would like to highlight the following key points: the emphasis that the Experts placed on full employment; that to achieve this, the ILO should develop a two-fold approach, namely to put pressure on member States and to embark on a process of dialogue with them, and to put pressure on the other international organizations.

But we also have a number of concerns: how do we define full employment? The concept of full employment cannot be separated from the concept of decent work; the objective of full employment should be central to macroeconomic policy – that is to say, the budgetary, fiscal, monetary and economic policies of governments; one must not lose sight of the link between the concept of full employment and the right to work; the role of the public sector as regards employment; the policy of small and medium-sized enterprises (SMEs) should not be separated from global, economic and social policy; and we need to find a solution to ensure participation of workers in SMEs. Full employment should therefore not be left out of tripartite dialogue in the member States, as the ILO reports clearly show.

And now I come to the next topic, which was education. This year we discussed the conclusions and recommendations of the eighth Joint ILO/UNESCO Committee of Experts on Application of Recommendations concerning Teaching Personnel.

Three fundamental issues attracted our attention and call for urgent action: one – financing of teaching in order to offset the shortage of teachers and to provide teachers with good living and working conditions; two – the urgent need for ensuring real and effective social dialogue, which is a cornerstone for a just and lasting solution to the problems in teaching; three – the importance of promoting instruments, and particularly the UNESCO Recommendation concerning the status of Higher Education Teaching Personnel, 1997. These are three basic conditions for being able to achieve the aims of education for all.

Now I would like to tell you about our work concerning the application of standards. First, I would like to talk about the selection of cases. This year, the Experts put before us 643 observations and 1,406 direct requests. Altogether, that is more than 2,000 comments on the application of Conventions. The list of cases selected is a sample of these which should help us to think about the letter and the spirit of the Conventions.

In our list, we selected 11 cases relating to problems with the application of Conventions on freedom of association. Thus, we discussed the cases concerning the difficulties in meeting the requirements of the Conventions on freedom of association as a result of a climate of insecurity, violence or even threats or oppression, which exist in certain countries. This applies to Colombia and we were sorry that a special paragraph was not possible given the seriousness of the case. It also applies to Zimbabwe and to some extent, to Venezuela. With regard to the specific case of Guatemala, we were forced to note that trade union leaders and activists are currently being held in prison, despite the fact that the ILO called for their immediate release.

We were also forced to note many problems with the application because of conditions set on, or interference in, the internal affairs of trade union organizations or social dialogue, either through legislation or in practice. Apart from the cases I have mentioned, and the blatant case of Myanmar, which we placed in a special paragraph on account of its continued non-compliance, there were the cases of Costa Rica, Bangladesh, Iceland, Serbia and Montenegro.

In addition to the cases on the list and discussed in the Committee, there were other observations that attracted the attention of the Workers' group in which, despite the observations and conclusions of last year, neither the geo-political situation nor the specific circumstances described can explain why trade union leaders are still being held in prison or do not have the right to organize themselves in a union of their choice, which is recognized, and has the right to negotiate freely.

This applies particularly in the cases of Cuba, Denmark and Argentina. The Workers' group was surprised and upset by the tone and content of the report of the Government of Germany on the situation as regards freedom of association in the public services. The cases of Cameroon, Ecuador and Burundi continue to be a source of concern to us.

Although freedom of association is a very important part of the work of our Committee, we were also concerned by the continuing difficulties as regards forced labour, discrimination and child labour. On these subjects, we held discussions with Australia, Indonesia, Niger and Sudan. Like last year, we devoted a special sitting to Myanmar, with a clear conclusion which gives the Government a last chance to improve the situation. Nevertheless, the Workers' group recalls the comments of the Experts to the effect that questions are still unanswered as regards Mauritania, Japan and Swaziland.

On our list, we took up three observations concerning equal opportunity and treatment, for El Salvador, the Dominican Republic and Japan. We venture to hope that in the case of the Libyan Arab Jamahiriya, concerning Equality of Treatment (Social Security) Convention, 1962 (No. 118), which was taken up in a special paragraph last year, the experts will have available to them next year the information requested from the Government. As regards observations concerning the fundamental Conventions, we selected two important cases namely Bolivia and Ukraine.

Of course, although the problems of the application of fundamental Conventions, by their very nature and extremely serious character, are the most important in the list, observations concerning the Conventions which we refer to as technical Convention, also hold all the attention of the Workers' group. Thus, we held dialogue about the application of four Conventions: Maternity Protection Convention (Revised), 1952 (No. 103) – this was for the Netherlands; Protection of Wages Convention, 1949 (No. 95) – this was for Poland; Labour Inspection Convention, 1947 (No. 81), for the Republic of Korea; and Employment Policy Convention, 1964 (No. 122), for Slovakia.

Although we only discussed 25 cases, and although we expressed our concern only for a few other cases, this does not detract from the importance of observations made on other cases by the experts. Dialogue is necessary in the various countries for each and every case We must undertake urgent action for each and every observation. This is an appeal to all partners involved.

After two weeks of intensive work in our Committee and after the assessment carried out within the Workers' group, I must tell you that our group is satisfied overall with the work which has been done but we are rather disappointed with the results. We, the Workers' group, remain convinced that the work of our Committee is very important and does have a direct and indirect influence on the lives of workers throughout the world but on this point the Committee has not fully achieved its goal this year.

Probably this assessment is linked to the comments which I would like to make on the work of our Committee.

Already last year, and again this year, we witnessed, and I am sure we will witness again today, opposition by certain governments to our methods and procedures of work. This opposition is something which we felt to be an attack against the standard-setting system of the ILO itself, and above all against the universality of the standards themselves.

Let us not forget that we are talking here only about a minority of member States. Also, let us remember that most of the member States are fully in compliance with the rules and methods of work of the Committee and the ILO and deserve our appreciation.

But, some countries clearly oppose the way in which the list of the countries is drawn up and once the list has been adopted, I could not help feeling that I also could see opposition which was less explicit and more diplomatic, but was not less organized.

A short study of the list of individual cases of this year, and all the more so, the lists of the previous years overall, shows that the balance which has been sought has been achieved and it can be considered to be just and fair. However, it is very clear that it is not possible to fix criteria which will virtually automatically lead to identification of individual cases for discussion. There is a need to achieve a balance between the various categories of Conventions and also a geographical or geopolitical balance where the rates of industrialization or development have to be taken into account, together with the urgent and serious nature of individual cases. Therefore, even though the establishment of a mathematically perfect balance is not possible, the need to have an overall balance which is adequate is borne in mind throughout the process, because we wish this process to be seen to be transparent, fair and just.

Some governments have pinpointed the fact that there are too many countries from the same continent or subcontinent on the list. I cannot help feeling that they have put forward the pretext of a political operation in order to better dissimulate or reduce the scope of violations or infringements noted by experts or experienced by Workers.

Other governments have stated that this Committee is not a court of law, but it should be helping the countries concerned to improve their situation. This is absolutely fair and true, but our Committee is not just a place for good intentions. Countries have to work harder to bring their legislation and practice in line with the Conventions.

Some governments have gone even further and they have called into question the work and objectivity of the Committee of Experts.

Methods are not the only points to consider. We also have to think about the rules of the game in our Committee and the practices. I am putting the word "practices" in the plural, because people may well think of several different types of trends which, should they coincide, may develop into a major risk.

First of all, there is a trend which has been growing this year, and that is that several governments have launched into long statements and presentations which did not really correspond to what the experts were commenting on, but really described developments plans and intentions and initiatives and committee systems for the future.

Now, these statements and presentations were full of good news and were very well prepared, but they were virtually never given in a "D" document for prior information to our Committee as provided for in our rules and in our practice.

We are worried about this trend for two other reasons as well.

First of all there is growing discrepancy between the speaking time for the Governments and the speaking time for the Employers and Workers of the country. This disproportion struck us all the more so because we, the Workers' group, tried to organize, structure and limit our own statements so as to keep within the time allotted to us.

Secondly, this trend seems to be justified by the fact that in most of these cases the Conclusions refer explicitly to oral explanations from the Government. We appeal to the Office to maintain an objective attitude in this very sensitive process of dialogue between Governments, Employers and Workers. The Conclusions have to focus on initiatives to be taken to improve compliance with commitments undertaken. This is the first challenge.

The second challenge comes from the Employers' side. Our field of discussion seems to be narrowing down. It seems to be confining itself to a very legal approach which is confined only to the letter of the text, or to the text of the Experts' report without taking account of the complaints described in all the texts or even the text of the provisions of the Convention under consideration.

This year, this confining of our discussions to a very legal scope was even more marked. For instance, as soon as the word strike was pronounced, the discussion collapsed.

I can say it in legal terms – an understanding of law which is confined to the letter, and only to the letter of the law, cannot work and is not functional at all. Of course every state functions on the basis of a legal corpus involving law and order, but also there is the case law of the Supreme Court, or the Court of Justice, for example, for the European Union. This case law also includes doctrine. This means that the Committee of Experts and the Committee on Freedom of Association are also a full part of the legal entity of the ILO.

The questioning of standards, the challenge of our methods and the lack of compliance with our practices and this very strict legal focus are a worry to us, the Workers' group. We feel that all these trends together will bring us to a stalemate, or at least to weaken the structure of our work and our conclusions. Therefore I clearly want to say that the work of the ILO must not lose its value. The Workers' group will continue to defend the role of the ILO, and in particular the crucial role of our Committee.

Our report was unanimously approved by our Committee and I request that this session of the Conference to likewise approve it unanimously. Thank you.

Original Spanish: Ms. RIAL *(Government delegate, Argentina; Chairperson of the Committee on the Application of Standards)*

As was clearly stated by our Reporter, the Committee on the Application of Standards began its deliberations with a general discussion on the application of Conventions and Recommendations. Previous speakers have spoken at length about the work of the Committee, but I would just like to draw your attention to a number of points.

As last year, the working methods of the Committee were carefully reviewed by delegates. The debate was very interesting and the majority came out in favour of the current system for selecting cases, which they felt was fair and just, while they recognized that, as in any procedure, there was room for improvement. Even those countries who disagreed with a number of the selection criteria made their proposals while fully respecting all the other positions – thus there is no doubt that, while there is room for improvement in some aspects of the procedure, this has to be done through tripartism and dialogue.

We must not lose sight of the essential purpose of the Committee, which is to ensure full compliance with ratified Conventions.

The full exercise of the rights laid down in the fundamental Conventions is an essential tool in strengthening democracy. It emerged from the deliberations that the best way of achieving genuine progress in member countries is for ILO technical cooperation to help Governments bring their law and practice into conformity with the Conventions.

With this constructive purpose in mind, the selected cases were reviewed and the countries involved, and delegates, were free to express their points of view. In particular, the Committee focused on labour inspection. The delegates emphasized the fundamental role of labour inspection in ensuring the application of labour standards while pointing out that many countries lacked the necessary technical and financial resources to strengthen it.

Concerning the Conventions on indigenous and tribal peoples, Members agreed on the need to improve the living conditions of these peoples. The Committee also focused on the Maternity Protection Convention (Revised), 1952 (No. 103), and the Maternity Protection Convention, 2000 (No. 183). A substantive issue that elicited active participation by delegates was the report of the joint ILO/UNESCO Committee of Experts on the Application of the Recommendations concerning Teaching Personnel. The Committee agreed that there was a need to preserve ongoing training for such personnel to improve the quality of education through social dialogue.

The Committee also devoted a large portion of its debates to the General Survey carried out by the Committee of Experts on employment policy. Delegates agreed that employment should be at the heart of the social policies of all countries as a fundamental strategy to fight poverty, especially in developing countries. It should be recalled that freely chosen and productive employment is one of the ILO's major objectives and should also be a policy goal of member States.

The Committee worked hard and with dedication, giving pride of place to freedom of expression and dialogue. This was made possible thanks to the excellent management by the Director of the International Labour Standards Department and his team, whose professional attitude and dedication facilitated the task of the Committee.

We would also like to acknowledge the work done by the interpreters and translators, who assisted us in completing our work.

Finally, I cannot fail to mention the work done by the Employer and Worker Vice-Chairpersons who, in a very balanced, serious and responsible way contributed to the results contained in the report that the Committee is submitting to the Conference. I should also like to thank the Reporter, Ms. Robert Lopes, for her good work.

Lastly, my special thanks go to all the delegates who worked in the Committee and contributed to the quality of the exchange of views and of the outcomes achieved.

Original Spanish: The PRESIDENT

The general discussion on the report of the Committee on the Application of Standards is now open.

Mr. NKHAMBULE *(Government delegate, Swaziland)*

I appreciate the fact that you have given me the floor and I will try my level best to stick to the five minutes that you have given me.

First of all, I ask your indulgence to make a brief statement on the report of the Committee on the Application of Standards. The report quite largely represents the deliberations and conclusions of the Committee as I understand them. This is the Committee where issues concerning the application of standards are discussed. The International Labour Organization has established sound procedures for dealing with complaints against any member State, and we expect those procedures to be observed, even if Swaziland is the subject.

Normally, the matters referred to are first discussed elaborately by the Committee on the Application of Standards and only come to the house for adoption. Such a system allows concerned member States an opportunity to respond to any allegations made against them. However, my Government delegation would like to call your attention to a matter of procedure that arose here on 14 June 2004 which concerns the statement that was made by Mr. Sithole, the Workers' delegate of Swaziland. My delegation would like to register its profound objection to this kind of reference being able to bring matters to this assembly through what we may perceive to be unprocedural means.

We all know that the session was only meant to discuss the Reports of the Director-General and of the Chairperson of the Governing Body, in particular the thematic issues arising therefrom. Our understanding of the practice informs us that the discussion was only to be centred on these Reports. It is my delegation's view that the statement made here seriously missed the target in this respect, in that it did not discuss the contents of these valuable Reports at all. We do not remember these Reports' discussions, or, for that matter, warranting the discussion of Swaziland. A detailed report will be filed with the Office of the Director-General. It is my humble submission that the statement under reference be removed from the *Provisional Record* on account of being out of procedure, and my objection should be recorded accordingly.

Finally, I submit that past conflicts, whether perceived or real, should not be used against the country as a member State. I think Swaziland needs to be encouraged in its efforts as we may have mentioned, and will be mentioning to the Director-General, instead of being discouraged.

Mr. MANGWANA *(Minister of Public Service, Labour and Social Welfare, Zimbabwe)*

Zimbabwe is calling for a review of the working methods of the Conference Committee on the Application of Standards.

With particular reference to the listing of countries, my country has appeared on the list for three successive years, including at this session. On all these occasions, Zimbabwe has not been warned before the Conference that it would be appearing on the list. Instead, the list is clandestinely prepared by the Workers' group and circulated nicodemously to the Employers' group, skirting the Governments concerned.

Governments have to discover for themselves that they are on the list. It seems to be a game of hide and seek.

May it be noted that the report of the Committee of Experts does not indicate which countries will be appearing.

Governments cannot prepare replies in the dark.

The listing is not transparent at all.

The current procedure has an element of surprise and it leads to inadequate preparation by Governments. Hence, the quality of the proceedings is highly compromised.

It would appear that the countries are chosen by casting dice or by lottery.

The ILO Rules of Procedure are not cast in stone. They should be amended if they have become obsolete or if they can be abused.

Recommendation: Zimbabwe strongly recommends that Governments be alerted of a pending appearance at least three months before the Conference or when the report of the Committee of Experts becomes available.

The current practice apparently makes it mandatory that at least 25 countries have to appear before the Committee.

At the end of the day, the Committee rushes pellmell through the proceedings in order to beat the target.

Also the fixing of cases at 25 leads to countries with effectively non-serious infringements being dragged into the hearing for the Committee to meet its "quota".

Recommendation: A lesser number of countries should be listed so that ample attention is given to individual countries appearing before the Committee.

There is a practice where the Conference Committee proceeds to determine the competence of legislation as raised in the report of the Committee of Experts. This practice tends to usurp and distort the functions of the Committee of Experts.

By way of example, in 2003, Zimbabwe intimated this observation to the Conference Committee, but the Conference Committee, nonetheless, proceeded to determine the competence of our legislative amendments and made adverse findings. Based on those findings, it went on to impose a direct contacts mission and mentioned Zimbabwe in a special paragraph.

However, when the Committee of Experts subsequently met in late 2003, it found that most of our amendments were satisfactorily addressing the issues it had raised.

It should have been an embarrassing contradiction.

All it means is that Zimbabwe was wrongly mentioned in a special paragraph in 2003. Had our legislation been competently considered, we would not have been liable to those severe penalties or sanctions which were inappropriately imposed by the Conference Committee.

Those penalties should be reserved for proven worst cases.

Recommendation: Zimbabwe is of the view that the Conference Committee should refrain from approving the listing of countries whose listing requires determination of the competence of national legislation. It is the Committee of Experts which has the technical capacity to assess the competence of national laws. In any case, it is the experts who would have raised the issue.

The Conference Committee patently simply rubber stamps the list initiated and provided by the workers, some of whom may be pursuing political agenda.

Recommendation: The Committee should independently assess the grounds for listing and, in appropriate cases, it should delist a country where, on the basis of responses supplied, there is no issue for further discussion.

By way of example, despite positive observations by the Committee of Experts in respect of Zimbabwe's legislative amendments and despite Zimbabwe's timely submission of its considerate and positive reply on document D.9 after the listing, Zimbabwe was, nonetheless, hauled before the Committee on 12 June 2004.

Zimbabwe's case was a proper one for delisting by the Committee. We understand that the rules provide for such procedure, or they should.

As a passing observation, confidence in the work of the Committee may be eroded, where, after handing down its conclusions, the Committee engages in further unrecorded debate with the parties to the extent that it alters its own findings. It reviews its own work, casting doubt on whether it would have properly come to a decision in the first place. This appears to have been the case with Serbia and Montenegro.

Recommendation: Proceedings should be held in open forum and on record, with the full participation of the whole Committee. This ensures transparency.

There is a current practice of consulting the complainants before the judgement is delivered, in the absence of the accused Government member. This leads to loss of confidence in the decision to be delivered.

It appears that one's accusers play an active role in the decision-making process by the Committee.

Recommendation: The Committee should recognize in practice the time-honoured adage, viz, justice should not only be done but be seen to be done.

The other current practice in the Committee is that certain delegates bring up extraneous matters which have nothing to do with the issues raised and they are not ruled out of order by the Chair *mero motu* or at the instigation of other delegates. These extraneous issues find their way into the conclusions of the Committee.

It also appears that the Committee does not make rulings on points of law raised *in limine* during the proceedings or on matters of a technical nature, which can be independently decided upon outside the merits of the matter.

Recommendation: The Committee or Chairperson should not merely assume the role of umpire but should be actively involved in the proceedings and give directions.

With these specific observations, this may be an appropriate time for the Committee to seriously consider reviewing its working methods. A lot of members could have been prejudiced by current practices.

Original Spanish: Mr. SÁNCHEZ OLIVIA *(Government adviser and substitute delegate, Cuba)*

My delegation has sought the floor to speak to a number of statements made in the general part of the report of the Committee on the Application of Standards. Above all, we wish to recall the ideas proposed by a group of countries, and already supported by the movement of non-aligned countries, which were submitted in a fine spirit of cooperation as a contribution to improving the working methods of the Committee.

My country is not included on the list of cases where countries are required to provide explanations. Yet, there were comments in the report regretting the fact that this has not been the case, and we totally reject the arguments adduced for this purpose.

There are no imprisoned trade unionists in Cuba. The 19 national trade unions, and the Confederation of Workers to which they all historically and voluntarily belong, perform their trade union activities in complete independence in all workplaces throughout the country, where their leaders are elected by the workers themselves. No such trade union leader is imprisoned or hindered in his or her trade union activities.

We would like the record to show that we are thoroughly dissatisfied with the comments in paragraph 15 of the general report.

Mr. CAHALANE *(Government adviser and substitute delegate, Ireland, speaking on behalf of the European Union and IMEC)*

I have the honour to speak on behalf of the European Union and on behalf of the members of IMEC. The European Union candidate countries Bulgaria and Romania also align themselves with this statement.

We wish to congratulate Ms. Rial, the Chairperson of the Committee, and the other Officers for their work in ensuring the successful discharging by the Committee of its role. We would also wish to thank all the other participants involved in the Committee's activities.

We wish to take this opportunity to comment on the proposals made by 18 member States concerning the mechanisms of the Committee and the procedures for choosing the individual cases.

We support the reinforcement of the effectiveness of the ILO supervisory mechanisms, including better publicity, more effective follow-up and more widespread use of the findings of the ILO supervisory mechanisms throughout the international system. Furthermore, we are committed to looking for ways to strengthen these mechanisms and to promote respect for labour standards at country level. However, we cannot support proposals for changes to the fundamental structure of the Committee. This established and agreed structure has been carefully weighted and balanced to reflect the unique tripartite nature of the ILO. We are, of course, prepared to consider any reasonable proposals for a forum which would contribute to greater overall efficiency.

Mr. ETTY *(Workers' delegate, Netherlands)*

There is one thing I would like to add to the statement by the Workers' Vice-Chairperson of the Conference Committee on the Application of Standards which relates in particular to his concerns about the dangers facing the supervisory system.

It is not only the attack on the working methods of the Conference Committee by the group of so-called "like-minded states" that worries us. We are equally concerned at the attitude adopted by the Australian Government this year, namely its rejection of the judgement of the Committee of Experts concerning the legislation and practices relating to prison labour, particularly in privatized prisons. The Experts say that the Australian Government's policy is not in line with the ILO Forced Labour Convention, 1930 (No. 29). The Australian Government thinks that the Experts are wrong and is supported in this view by other members of the group of Industrialized Market-Economy Countries (the IMEC group) and by employers.

The differences manifested themselves some five years ago. Since then, the situation has reached a stalemate. The Government of Australia is ignoring the recommendations of the Experts and the Conference Committee can only accept the stalemate and repeat its earlier conclusion on the case – at best. We did not even get that best this year.

The situation is not good for the Conference Committee, or for the Committee of Experts. Neither is it good for the ILO. It sets a very bad example, which, if followed by other countries (and why would they not follow?), would seriously weaken and damage our work.

During this year's debate, we made a few suggestions to the Australian Government with regard to resuming a constructive dialogue, and we hope that those suggestions will be taken on board. We also suggested that the Government, if it really is convinced that the critique of the Committee of Experts is wrong and misguided, should take the case to the International Court of Justice in The Hague. The Government did not react to that proposal, and I would be very surprised indeed if it gave any consideration to the matter. I am pretty sure that it fears that the odds are against it. But even if that were not the case and even if it had a good chance of winning the appeal, we the Workers would prefer that some clarity be brought to the present state of affairs.

In these circumstances I would recommend that the ILO request an advisory opinion of the International Court of Justice on this case. The ILO is entitled to seek such an opinion on the basis of the 1946 agreement between the ILO and the United Nations. The request should be discussed with the Committee of Experts later this year.

It has been observed that it would be useful to take this step in cases where Governments do not admit the existence of discrepancies between their legislation and practices on the one hand, and a Convention on the other, and in cases where they disagree with the interpretations the ILO's supervisory bodies.

This is one such case, and the Convention in question is one of the fundamental human rights Conventions. In the interest of our Committee and of the ILO, I kindly request the Office to give serious consideration to this, what I would call a modest proposal.

Mr. STEYNE *(Workers' adviser and substitute delegate, United Kingdom)*

The Trade Unions Congress (TUC), too, has grave concerns about the attacks on the workings of our Committee. We believe that the list of cases should be decided on its merits, without fear or favour. We should continue also to examine good practice, but we concentrate, rightly, on cases of real suffering of working people. Regarding favour, we have sought to balance regions, industrialized and developing countries, technical and fundamental Conventions. And regarding fear, the Burmese and the Zimbabwean Governments' threats against Worker members violate Conference rules.

The TUC supports the supervisory bodies, including the Committee of Experts. We are dismayed by the constant challenge to the Experts' authority and competence by the Employers and certain Governments, including Governing Body members. This is most noticeable where their interests coincide – in their attempts to undermine the fundamental right to strike (which they will not defend even in Colombia) to extend the definition of essential services and their determination to drive forward the privatization of prisons.

We fear our Committee is being politicized in a manner which has debilitated other agencies of the United Nations. A bizarre alliance of governments has emerged, though describing themselves as likeminded, some have little in common other than a desire to avoid scrutiny of their own obligations. In this session, many of them defended the indefensible – questioning the examination of cases of the grossest abuse of fundamental rights – including anti-union violence and slavery. They were led by one country, whose sovereignty has been strongly defended by many in the international trade union movement. But I am not sure that that Government appreciates how much it has damaged its reputation by its behaviour here. This unholy alliance was supported in some cases – in particular that of Zimbabwe – by some who claim to represent workers, yet defended a regime which has attacked and beaten trade unionists and killed farm workers in pursuit of its dictatorial cronyism. The TUC disassociates itself from such comments, which are inimical to free trade unionism.

These members are not alone in undermining the objectivity of our work. In the Conference plenary, the TUC's delegate this year expressed our dismay at the crass failure of the Committee on Standards to agree appropriate measures on Colombia – for us, a key priority. That neo-liberal, anti-democratic regime is defended, not only by some of the "likeminded" group, but also by the Employers and by other Governments, including, unfortunately, my own. They claim, misguidedly, that the regime is defending a democracy against terrorism, rather than waging a war on democracy and free trade unionism with the backing of paramilitary terrorists. Colombia remains the gravest case of violations of trade union rights in any ratifying member State. More trade unionists are murdered there still than in the rest of the world put together.

Many Governments and Employers have joined the Workers' group this year to demand, quite rightly, strong measures in the cases of Belarus, Myanmar, Venezuela and Zimbabwe. But when those same Governments and Employers deny that the continuing gross violations in Colombia merit similar measures, we have to question their economic and foreign policy motives. Inevitably, however, they are undermining the authority of the ILO and the reputation for objectivity and impartiality of the Committee on Standards. It appears to us increasingly that only governments which reject the current model of globalization are subject to stronger measures but that not those which pursue neo-liberalism. The Employers miss the point when they say in the Committee that the violations in Zimbabwe are inimical to a market economy. Fundamental rights must apply even if there is no immediate business case. It is incomprehensible to trade unionists in the United Kingdom, who believed that only a Commission of Inquiry could shed light on the shadowy relations which perpetuate impunity in Colombia, that not even a special paragraph has been agreed in that case, this year or last.

I have concentrated on Colombia because it is a priority for the TUC and because it highlights, more than any other case, the damaging double standards which are now undermining our Committee. All ratifying member States should be subject to impartial judgement, regardless of whether they pursue neo-liberalism or command economics. If our Committee allows a hideous mutated recreation of former Cold War blocs overlaid with the scars of a newly weakened multilateralism, I fear it will degenerate into a shadow of its former self, as sounding brass, a mere clashing of cymbals.

International law should unite us all. But it is a seamless tissue. If you pick at the threads, it will soon fall apart. We call on all constituents, regardless of their political perspectives, to pause for breath and consider whether the weakening of the ILO's supervisory bodies is truly in their interests. For we can be sure that it will not be in the interests of the working people of the world whom this house was established to protect.

Original Spanish: Mr. FERNANDEZ *(Workers' delegate, Uruguay)*

Without a doubt, the Committee on the Application of Standards is the centrepiece of each session of the Conference. Its task is to analyse, discuss and contribute to improving labour relations where they are not being respected.

Every year the Committee has to select a group of countries, since time does not permit us to deal with all of them. This selection is always very controversial, since it is no easy matter to determine at the outset which violations are the most serious.

A choice has to be made between violations of fundamental and technical Conventions, striking a balance between countries on all the continents. There is always room for improvement with regard to the mechanisms applied. But there can be no doubt that year after year, despite the progress made in ratifications, violations are increasing.

It has been reiterated on a number of occasions that since the 1990s, with the advent of neo-liberal policies, the world has suffered a marked deterioration in terms of the distribution of wealth. Millions of men and women sink into poverty daily. New forms of employment relationships have in some cases played havoc with more democratic and humane relations. Hundreds of thousands of working men and women are dismissed merely for attempting to organize in trade unions, while still others have been threatened and many have been killed. Every year, there are many cases in which governments fail to provide their labour ministries with the necessary resources to carry out their tasks properly, even preventing the labour inspectorates from doing their work for lack of resources.

Based on the report of the Committee of Experts on the Application of Conventions and Recommendations, the Committee on the Application of Standards tries to remain as objective as possible in the face of so many atrocities. We cannot accept those who contend that there are other intentions behind our handling of the cases other than the desire to make social justice a real right for working men and women and a duty of governments and employers. Now more than ever before, in an increasingly integrating world, we have to see that all trade agreements concluded are accompanied by social and labour agreements to help improve the lot of the most vulnerable. Hence this Committee must remain vigilant in regard to the application of Conventions and Recommendations, so that governments will understand that there can be no fair globalization without giving effect to social agreements and declarations.

I hope that all of us will contribute to strengthening the way the ILO works and seek the necessary changes, but always in respect for tripartism, which the European Union has held up as an example of international democracy. Therefore I endorse the report presented by consensus.

Mr. SANKAR SAHA *(Workers' adviser, India)*

While recording the support of the Indian Workers for the report adopted by my Committee, I would like to place before this august house some relevant points that have been agitating my mind during my 17 days' work in the Committee.

During the 85 years of the ILO's existence, many Conventions and Recommendations have been adopted, but many of them – including the fundamental Recommendations – are not ratified by many countries. Again, ratified Conventions are more often violated than implemented; the total number of violations cannot even be assessed because of the absence of reports resulting from intimidation, which comes from a desire to achieve economic benefits from trade and business and from international institutions as well. Many countries do appear to behave that way.

Most of the developing countries, including the more developed amongst them, plead that their economic situations do not permit them to ratify, although ratification of a fundamental Convention does not depend on capacity as such, but more on the political will of the Government and its approach to the working class movement. It is a basic right to human life and a matter of human freedom, and no justice can be given without this. It is also alarming that the superpowers and their allies, the champions of democracy, refuse to ratify Conventions, even the basic Conventions like the Freedom of Association and Protection of the Right to Organise Convention, 1948 (No. 87), and the Right to Organise and Collective Bargaining Convention, 1949 (No. 98).

A question that very often haunts the mind of global workers is that of whose democracy we are existing in. Where millions of workers – according to the ILO, 50 per cent of working people – are denied their fundamental right to collective bargaining and forming associations, 4 billion people live a subhuman life, with only US$1,500 a year, when the fact remains that total accumulated wealth created by them, coupled with advanced technology so far achieved, could be sufficient to satisfy the needs of the people of all countries.

In this era of neo-liberal globalization, and the unrestricted freedom of exploitative finance capital and goods, the noble standards of the ILO are the first victim. Informalization of the formal sector is going on rapidly, and, as a result, workers who once used to enjoy the benefits of standards are now deprived of them. Throughout the world, informal sector workers are now in the majority.

Every day there is downsizing, retrenchment, layoff, lockout and closure, putting millions of workers out of employment everywhere in the world. Loss of employment and employment opportunity is a common factor in all countries. Contractualization, outsourcing, casualization, part-time and temporary jobs are the order of the day for globalization. Permanent jobs are a matter of ancient history. Social security systems, so long built up, are being dismantled. I am saying this because these things have an adverse impact on standards. If the globalization is allowed to go on, a day will soon come when the ILO standards will stand irrelevant.

The matter of migrant workers and forced labour are of prime importance. Migrant workers everywhere are tortured and discriminated against, compared with workers of the country. They do not enjoy any rights whatsoever, let alone those of association and collective bargaining, equal wages for equal work, social security benefits, etc. etc; the standard is still being violated thus.

According to Indian Apex Court, anybody made to work on wages below the established minimum wage is in forced or compulsory labour. I understand my worker friends in all countries will appreciate this observation of our Supreme Court, as the situation in all countries is almost equal. In advanced countries, even prison workers are made to work for private companies; again the standard is violated.

Lastly, I shall draw the attention of this house to the urging by the multinational companies for union-free industry. This process has been started with export processing zones and will spread in all industries. Thus, a process of dehumanization started long ago will be completed very soon. There may be little time left for the ILO to protect its standards. We in the ILO should be alarmed and act and react more actively.

Mr. SITHOLE *(Workers' delegate, Swaziland)*

I will start by supporting all of the comments made by the Worker spokesperson and all Workers who spoke after him. Indeed, we do not believe that there is anything wrong with the working methods of the Committee on the Application of Standards. We also believe that there is no scientific way to select individual countries; it has to be by merit, and it has to be by those affected by the violations and injustices that are being reported in the report itself.

On the issue raised by my Government, I have this to say: the Report of the Director-General addressed the World Commission on the Social Dimension of Globalization, which goes beyond the concept of globalizing social justice, which, indeed, is a broad subject that unfortunately only exists within an enabling environment; this remains a scarce commodity in my country, Swaziland.

A country that voluntarily ratifies Conventions or joins the ILO, voluntarily surrenders its sovereignty in terms of criticism on this floor. Therefore, when countries do violate those Conventions, we should not be apologetic about offering such criticism.

Apartheid in South Africa would not have been abolished at the pace that it was, and we would not have celebrated the tenth anniversary of its abolition, if this house was selective of issues that are affecting people and the suffering masses in countries where democracy and social justice are not respected. Therefore, it is out of order to say that mentioning such issues at this forum is out of order.

My advice to all governments concerned about being mentioned at this forum or criticized is that there is a solution; the solution is one and one alone: if and when you ratify a Convention, if you then apply it in law, in spirit and in practice, your name will not be mentioned.

Original Spanish: Mr. DORADO CANO *(Government delegate, Venezuela)*

My Government has been referred to regarding the approval of the report of the Committee on the Application of Standards. I would like to state that, although the conclusions do not fully reflect the constructive spirit of dialogue and frank exchange of views and the balanced nature of the debate, nor the support for the policies of my Government in favour of the workers, we nevertheless feel that the conclusions are to be welcomed, apart from the reservations made. It is also important to point out, however, that it is necessary to improve and perfect our working methods. They need to be more transparent, more objective and more impartial.

The Government of my country has, down the years, shown that it is seeking to make progress and advance on the basis of the recommendations made by the Committee of Experts, and we feel that it is essential that these efforts be recognized, since they were made in an atmosphere of democratic destabilization, with essential public services being affected, and chaos and an acute national crisis being caused, precisely for having faced up to neo-liberal policies.

Therefore, the request to improve our working methods, to which my Government is committed, has not been implemented exclusively by the few countries who, for political motives, are sometimes included on the list. They are supported by countries from five continents. I must point out that, some years back, GRULAC, before the Conference and the Governing Body underscored the need to review working methods and make the necessary efforts to ensure that the conclusions reflect the tripartite debate transparently and impartially in every case.

The Non-Aligned Movement have expressed the same need, and we believe that, committed to fair globalization, no kind of debate should be censored, and we should have the will to hold discussions so that we can improve the situation and so that democratic participation can be applied to these cases, so that we can increase transparency and improve the application of Conventions and Recommendations.

Original Russian: Mr. MALEVICH *(Government adviser and substitute delegate, Belarus)*

Responding to the comments that have been made by the distinguished representative of the Employers, by the EU and by others in attendance here, I would like very briefly to clarify why our delegation considers that the methods of the work of the Committee on the Application of Standards require some improvement.

In this august body, each and every year we hear about the harassment that is suffered by hundreds of trade unions throughout the world and even the killing of many trade unionists. We all know that there are still many countries where the right of freedom of association is a right that has not yet been achieved by even half of the workers. Many categories of workers, including in developed countries, are, in fact, also deprived of this right, because it is claimed that the work they do is somehow of particular importance to the government of the State in question.

We all know just how difficult things are in the world today in terms of employment. We know that, in some countries, in fact, between 20-50 per cent of workers do not have the possibility of having a job; they are therefore unable to implement or exercise their fundamental right, their right to work.

We all also know that there are many other burning issues in the world today that require urgent consideration and resolution. At the same time, for some strange reason, it would seem that the ILO monitoring mechanisms focus on just a few countries, countries like Belarus, countries in which the social and economic position is, in fact, more than acceptable.

I will give you just a few examples of what I am talking about. More than 90 per cent, I would like to stress this, more than 90 per cent of the workers in Belarus are members of different trade unions, that is to say, the right to freedom of association is fully exercised, and only around 2.5 per cent of people working in Belarus are not actually able to exercise that right at present, so you are talking about a very small number of people. Furthermore, we are, in fact, 56th in the index of the world's developed countries and that shows that, in fact, the development of our economy is more than successful; we are doing pretty well.

That being so, in the light of all that I have said, you cannot fail to come to the conclusion that something is not right in the way in which this Committee, the Committee on the Application of Standards, is working. Something therefore needs to be corrected. For that reason, our delegation would like to support the proposal that has been put forward to move forward with dialogue along these lines, and we would like this to be appropriately reflected in the report and in the minutes of this meeting.

Mr. AHMED *(Workers' delegate, Pakistan)*

I intend to speak on a point of order in the first instance. The distinguished representative of Swaziland spoke on the intervention by his country's Workers' delegate and referred to the discussion of the Report of the Director-General. He is entitled to request the right of reply, but it was not possible to grant his request because we are discussing the report of the Committee on the Application of Standards. I would ask you, as we are coming to the end of the Conference, and since we in the Workers' group fully observe this discipline, to discuss this with our colleagues. I have consulted the spokesperson of our group and also my other Worker colleagues. The report which has been presented before this Committee should be adopted. We fully support it, because it relates to the fundamental rights which are at the heart of this Conference.

This great Organization, which has been called the world parliament of labour, is rightly expected to assist member States in fulfilling their obligations in relation to ratified Conventions.

The report of the Committee on the Application of Standards is produced by people of independent and international reputation from all parts of the world. Conventions which are ratified are universal in nature, and applicable both to north and south, east and west. They embody basic rights.

The Committee wants to open a dialogue with member States. Its observations are intended to assist member States in bringing their legislation into conformity, and also to provide the necessary technical assistance.

We note that there are many countries, like Colombia and Myanmar, where flagrant violations are taking place. In countries like Australia and Japan, issues include the forced labour and the Workers with Family Responsibilities Convention, 1981 (No. 156).

It is therefore useful to assist member States in bringing their legislation into conformity. There are those who are raising their voices as if it is a sort of a judgement – it is not, it is simply a question of assisting member States to fulfil the obligations they have voluntarily accepted.

We are coming to the end of this session of the Conference. We hope that the positive work which has been done by this Committee will be fully supported. We hope that all those member States that have ratified Conventions will take note of what is said in the report, for the sake of the working class and for social justice and progress and prosperity all over the world.

Original Spanish: THE PRESIDENT

As there are no further speakers, I propose that we proceed with the approval of the report of the Committee on the Application of Standards. If there are no objections, may I take it that the report is approved as a whole, i.e. its first, second and third parts.

(The report, as a whole, is approved.)

We have now concluded the consideration of the report submitted by the Committee on the Application of Standards. I should like to take this opportunity to thank the Committee, Officers and members, as well as the staff of the secretariat, for their excellent work.

CLOSING SPEECHES

Original Spanish: THE PRESIDENT

We shall now proceed to the closing speeches of the 92nd Session of the International Labour Conference.

Original Arabic: Mr. MAATOUGH *(Secretary, General People's Committee of Labour Force, Training and Employment, Libyan Arab Jamahiriya; Government Vice-President of the Conference)*

We are now coming to the end of this session of the International Labour Conference and, on my own behalf, on behalf of my country, and, indeed, on behalf of all of those who did me the honour of electing me as a Vice-President of this Conference, it is a great pleasure for me to convey our congratulations to the President of the Conference and to thank him for the success we have achieved. My thanks also go to all of his colleagues who assisted him in presiding over this session of the Conference, which has been crowned with success.

I would also like to express my thanks to the Director-General of the ILO, who is constantly committed to attaining the objectives and principles of this Organization in the field of social dialogue among the social partners – principles that are of paramount importance in today's world of work.

I would also like to express my thanks to the World Commission on the Social Dimension of Globalization and all its members for their work, which is reflected in their report, a report that meets the expectations and aspirations of all three social partners.

Speaking on behalf of all the Governments, I would like to convey my thanks to the President of the Government of Spain, Mr. José Luis Rodríguez Zapatero, who participated with us and shared his ideas with us at this important session. There can be no doubt that his ideas will be a guiding light for all of us as we move forward.

I would also like to thank the African group, which selected my country to serve as Government Vice-President, and the Employers' and Workers' groups for their support, as well as all those who supported my candidacy. I hope that I was able to do my job well and to meet the expectations of those who supported me.

There can be no doubt that we are all working here together for human progress and to ensure that all the workers in the world can enjoy the same conditions. We also seek to ensure that workers have access to freedom of movement, to put an end to violence in our world and to eliminate the causes of conflict and war.

Our discussion here within the ILO, and at this session of the Conference in particular, will undoubtedly have reflected some divergence in our views and in our ideas. Nonetheless, we must join forces to serve the common good.

We came here to discuss issues and to reach agreement as to how best to move forward in the interests of all three social partners.

There can be no doubt that the use of force or abuse, particularly against migrant workers and the most vulnerable groups in our society, will provoke a reaction by the workers concerned, and in the long run, will undermine the stability of the countries of the world.

The only way we can achieve progress is through social dialogue and understanding, and that means eradicating discrimination and separation from our political thinking.

I would like to thank all those who worked in the committees at this Conference: the Committee on the Application of Standards, the Resolutions Committee, the Committee on the Fishing Sector, the Committee on Human Resources, and all the other Committees, especially the Finance Committee.

All of those who have worked for this Conference have done an excellent job. We have achieved as much as could be done on all the issues that we have discussed, in particular in our discussion on the report of the World Commission on the Social Dimension of Globalization, which reflected a general willingness to make this world a fairer place and to allow everyone to develop their full potential. I would like to thank all of those who contributed to making this session of the Conference a success, and especially all the members of the Committees and of the secretariat, who worked behind the scenes: translators, interpreters, and other secretariat staff. They all did an excellent job.

And, if I myself have failed to live up to your expectations, I apologize; I did my very best. I now wish you all a safe journey home and until the next session of the Conference, I wish our colleagues in Geneva every success.

Original French: Mr. WADE (*Employers' adviser and substitute delegate, Senegal; Employer Vice-President of the Conference*)

It is a great honour for me to be here today. It is also a very pleasant duty and a real pleasure for me to be taking the floor, here in this august body, at the closing ceremony of this session of our Conference.

Allow me to begin, most sincerely, by expressing my thanks to the International Organisation of Employers (IOE). The IOE showed great confidence in me by selecting me as the Employers' Vice-President for the 92nd Session of the International Labour Conference, that is coming to an end here this morning.

I would also like to take this opportunity to thank those Governments and the Workers who supported my candidacy.

I would also like to take advantage of this opportunity to express congratulations to the President of this session of our Conference, Mr. Ray Guevara. His skill, his authority and his sound knowledge of the way in which our Organization operates meant that we were able to perform our work here successfully. And, I would like to extend those congratulations to cover the secretariat also, because the secretariat was able, indeed, to provide quality support which we truly appreciate and I am sure that this has resulted in the extremely successful results of this session of the Conference.

The short amount of experience that I have had as Chair of this session of the Conference, in fact, has convinced me still more than before that we really need to rethink our methods of work and our agenda to improve the content and format of the Conference. In fact, frequently people take the floor in plenary here and address a room that is almost empty and I am sure that you all know what I mean and that you will give thought to what I am saying.

We noted that very wide-ranging contributions have been made at this session of the Conference on extremely topical issues and we must recognize that there can be no alternative to that approach than to have a discussion on all aspects of globalization, including the social dimension of globalization and the Secretary-General of this session of our Conference, Ambassador Juan Somavia, the Director-General of the ILO, reported on that particular aspect to us. Allow me once again to congratulate him most wholeheartedly on his political lucidity and his spirit of pragmatism.

Looking at the conclusions of that report, Africa certainly recognizes its role and the Summit of African Union Heads of State to be held in Ougadougou in Burkina Faso in September this year will be an important milestone for us in the relationship that exists between the ILO and the African Union. Indeed, the special theme of that Summit will be employment and efforts to combat poverty, but we will also be discussing globalization and we have the Director-General's Report that sets out a whole programme.

You will understand why I wish to then, in my concluding comments, focus on that issue which is really a red-hot issue for Africa today.

I would like to conclude once again by congratulating the President on his successful stewardship of this 92nd Session of the International Labour Conference and I would also like, lastly, to share with you an idea that is very dear to my heart: everything that is good for enterprise we represent, is good for the world of work and is also good for governments, so by working together we can build our common future. Let us do that through social dialogue, freely accepted and regularly monitored by all.

Original French: Mr. ATTIGBE (*Workers' delegate, Benin; Worker Vice-President of the Conference*)

I have attended the International Labour Conference as the Workers' delegate for Benin for several years, but this year, for the first time, I felt that there was something different in the air: a leap forward, fresh impetus, a breath of inspiration, specific goals, a new vision of the role and the potential of the ILO. All of this has been inspired by Mr. Juan Somavia, our Director-General, during the work of this first Conference of his second term of office.

In the course of the plenary debate, all the speakers who came up to the podium, one after another, expressed their confidence in the ILO, in its raison d'être and in its ability to play a lead role in the management of globalization, in order to make globalization fairer, more just and more human. The spirit of the Declaration of Philadelphia which runs through our Organization requires the ILO to intervene in the global management of business in order to put an end to social exclusion, poverty and unemployment throughout our world in order to ensure that social justice and decent work prevail.

This answer came in the many statements made in support of the Director-General's proposals, contained in his Report on the World Commission on the Social Dimension of Globalization. The massive support expressed by ILO constituents should now make it possible for the Director-General to initiate the process of implementing those measures in order to reset the sights of economic globalization.

Furthermore, discussions about the Global Report relating to freedom of association and the right to collective bargaining confirmed the fundamental and human nature of that right for all workers. It is beyond our understanding that we are still fighting to ensure respect for that right, when it is a right that is as natural as the right to live. Even animals have the right to come together in groups, so why should human beings require permission to do so and to form organizations of their choice? Sadly this right is flouted and denied to workers by several governments. We would urgently appeal to those governments that have not yet ratified the Freedom of Association and Protection of the Right to Organise Convention, 1948, (No. 87), and the Right to Organise and Collective Bargaining Convention, 1949 (No. 98), to do so immediately so that we can attain the objective of universal ratification of those instruments as soon as possible.

Turning now to the standard-setting activities of this Conference, which undoubtedly remain the ILO's major comparative advantage, the Conclusions that we have adopted on working conditions in the fishing industry lay the basis for a new global standard. The balanced approach that was adopted will make it possible to take into account the considerable differences that exist between the various subsectors, the various categories of fishers, and also the various types of fishing vessels. We are encouraged by the statements made by Governments and Employers to the effect that they have no intention of watering down or whittling away the protection that is provided for in existing instruments. Nonetheless, we note that a number of difficult issues remain in abeyance and we hope that these issues will be resolved to everybody's satisfaction. It is clear that the question of accommodation and the question of social security, as well as issues relating to health and safety, are vital if we are to make decent work a reality in the fishing industry. We hope that good sense and tripartism will win out over ideology and dogmatism.

Turning now to the Recommendation concerning human resources development, education, training and lifelong learning, we regret that the Employers decided to throw the baby out with the bath water. We have been working on this Recommendation for two years, and there was a general discussion just a few years ago on this very topic. Losing a vote – a vote that they themselves had asked for on a clause within the Recommendation – is no reason to decide that all that work could be thrown away. We also regret that despite our efforts and those of Governments to provide a revised text in order to take the Employers' concerns into account were not successful. We do not dare to think that the Employers might be opposed to social dialogue and collective bargaining at the international level. But, in the globalized economy, it is a fact of life. Several international trade union federations have signed around 20 framework agreements with multinationals such as Danone, Ikea, Volkswagen, Daimler, Chrysler, and so on, and collective agreements exist at the national level in the maritime sector. The world is changing, and we hope that our friends, the Employers, will not cling to an outdated ideology. Fortunately, most of the Governments once again saved this instrument and thus confirmed the important role that they play as a referee or an umpire. We believe that this Recommendation will allow Governments to develop, with the participation of social partners, national strategies for education and training in order to achieve the goals of full employment, the eradication of poverty, social inclusion, and sustainable economic growth within a globalized economy.

The Committee on the Application of Standards continued its important work during this session of the Conference. This year it looked at 24 individual cases and also held a special sitting concerning respect by Burma of Forced Labour Convention, 1930 (No. 29). In the course of the consideration of individual cases, the Committee decided to include a special paragraph in its report containing its conclusions regarding the case of freedom of association in Burma, due to that country's continuing failure to apply Convention No. 87. The list of individual cases, included the names of a number of industrialized countries as well as developing countries, so it was a balanced list in that respect as well as with respect to the mixture of fundamental Conventions and the so-called technical Conventions that were considered. The Workers' group protests against one Government that levelled personal criticism against a Workers' delegate and an African delegate in the Committee – delegates who were expressing their support for trade unions that are being severely oppressed in Zimbabwe. We utterly deplore the attitude of the Government in question.

We are happy to note that the International Labour Conference has clearly defined the mandate of our Organization with regard to international migration.

The general discussion that we had did, indeed, allow us to establish a clear link between decent work and the fair lot that all of the 85 million workers who are migrants in our world today have a right to. The contribution of the ILO to this discussion and to policy formulation in the area of migration is not just important, it is essential, it is central, and we would hope that all of the issues involved in this could be addressed. First and foremost, the question of the right to equal treatment for all migrant workers, women and men, and the question of their fundamental human rights, regardless of their status. Another question is the key role that should be played in this discussion by ILO constituents, labour ministers and social partners, who are grappling with the real situation on the ground. Who is better placed than the tripartite partners to develop rights-based migration policies that are both coherent and effective? The non-binding multilateral framework that should be established in the wake of our work here will, I have no doubt, show us the way forward along a path that integrates the human and social dimension of migration which can only increase in the future.

No issue, no matter how sensitive, escaped our attention: exploitation and the abuse suffered by many migrants, the trafficking of workers, consideration of the situation of illegal or undocumented workers, or the question of the brain drain. The plan of work adopted by this session of the Conference offers a specific range of policies and actions, including the promotion of standards and technical assistance; these are areas in which the ILO, which is the sole tripartite agency within the United Nations system, can make a difference.

The protection of female workers and migrant workers must be at the heart of all that we do. We now have an outline for our programme, we are now responsible for ensuring that it is followed up.

Discussions within the Resolutions Committee, reflected the enormous changes that have occurred as regards the role played by women in economic and social life. Hence, the Workers' group welcomes the adoption of our resolution concerning the promotion of gender equality, pay equity and maternity protection. This resolution is a plan of action in itself. We very much hope that the Office will shoulder its responsibilities in moving towards attainment of the objectives established by that resolution when it comes to gender equality, including pay equity and application of the principle "equal pay for work of equal value", as well as maternity protection.

In conclusion, allow me to express my appreciation to the Chairperson for his remarkable skills which have allowed us to achieve what we have achieved. I would also like to thank all of those who serviced the Conference for their skills and dedication, including the interpreters and all those who worked behind the scenes.

Also, I would like to express my thanks to Mr. Ray Guevara, the President of the Conference, and to my colleagues, the other Vice-Presidents, Mr. Wade and Mr. Maatough, for their cooperation in completing our difficult task.

Lastly, a big "thank you" to the Workers' group for giving me such an opportunity.

Original Spanish: The SECRETARY-GENERAL

Mr. President, I would like to extend to you my special thanks for the remarkable manner in which you have guided this Conference with humour, with style, but also with substance and considerable know-how in your management of the Conference's affairs. I would also like to thank my friends, the Officers; thank you all for your work and for your very kind words during this session.

I would also like to thank the Chairpersons of the committees and all of the officers of the committees, some of whom I have had the opportunity to speak to personally.

(Speaker continues in English.)

As in other years, I am presenting a formal written reply to the many issues that were raised in the Conference. But I do want to take the opportunity to say a couple of words before we all leave.

I think that we have done an extraordinary job, whether in the resolution concerning the promotion of gender equality, pay equity and maternity protection or on gender equality or in the discussions on the fishing sector and on migrant workers: this is the first time that an international organization says that we need a multilateral framework for migration non-binding and rights-based, but multilateral.

Even the difficulties that we observed in the discussion on human resources show that we are dealing with real issues, but we do have a decision and we do have an instrument. And having just listened to the discussion this morning on the report of the Committee on the Application of Standards, whatever the ways in which we move forward and take account of all of the different dimensions of the problem, we cannot but have the feeling that this unique role that the old ILO has played in the past, it is still playing today, and will have to continue playing in the future if we want to retain the identity of this institution. It does have to worry about the application of standards: we are the only ones to do this job, and we have to do it well.

Today, what I would like to do is to reflect a little with you on what I saw coming out of the Conference discussion on globalization. I have a feeling that this is not just another Conference. It is very much, I feel, a defining moment, but you have defined it for us by what you have said in relation to the two reports on globalization. I have a feeling that we came into this Conference with a report and a challenge, and that we are leaving this Conference with a mandate and a message.

The message, I think, is right for our times. A message that is balanced and fair. A message that people are asking for – and it is a message of hope.

We said, during this week here, that there are ways of making globalization work better for more people, and that it is not a hopeless cause; that we do not need to continue to have purely ideological debates on globalization; that there is an institution that is thinking for the world, and that it is thinking for the world in terms of its own experience, and that it says, "here is an opportunity"; we are not telling anybody in the world that this is the way to do it, we are saying that this is an approach, this is a manner, this is a style, this is utilizing the strength of dialogue that is the strength of the ILO, to try to get a process going. And I think that it is very important that, as we all leave for the next stage of our responsibilities, we remember what happened here. From my point of view, the mandate that your deliberations on the World Commission and on my Report have bestowed on the Office and the Governing Body for the months and the years to come is obviously more than a challenging one. It is truly historical. I am confident that, with the support you have expressed for my Report, and the imaginative use of all the institutional and practical tools that the ILO has at its disposal, we can address this task.

I thank you for what you have done, and my special thanks go to the support staff, the countless invisible hands that keep the operation running smoothly. In one of the committees, I joked that this was definitely not the invisible hand of the market! It was truly the very visible hands that are there every day making things happen, so that at 10 o'clock in the morning or 9 o'clock in the morning, whatever the time is, you receive the documents here. I visited some of the staff simply to let them know how much I appreciate the incredible work that they do. We have become accustomed at the Conference to everything running smoothly but, let me tell you, success is measured by the fact that we do not see it. It just works. But it does not just happen. There is an enormous amount of work behind the scenes and I feel a responsibility for highlighting that with you today on behalf of all of them.

To all the delegates and participants, thank you for your energies and ideas. This Conference, by its very composition, underscores our special place in the international system.

Of course, after 85 years, it is something that we take for granted. This gathering has been going on for 85 years. It does not happen anywhere else. No institution has this knowledge base on society and the productive system, not to mention the real actors of the economy present here.

Governments, workers, employers: this is an assembly representing an important part of the real world, and no other organization has the range of expertise and experience that is sitting in this room. And this is not just a sort of feel-good talk at the end of the Conference when we are all a little tired and maybe need a bit of uplifting! Not at all. You are a source of real power. You are a source; when you work together, when you dialogue, when tripartism functions, you are a source of change, of making things happen.

Since we have such big challenges in front of us, I do not want you to leave without saying how much I believe that we need to unleash the power of tripartism to help address the problems of today. And that does not mean that we are not going to have problems; we may not like a resolution here or an instrument there. That is not the issue. The issue is that this instrumentality is needed in the world today; this places an incredible responsibility on us in choosing how we want to use it, because we have seen, in practical terms, what its use can imply for solving the problems arising out of globalization.

We cannot have a successful globalization without successful localization, and we cannot have successful localization without you, for all of the reasons I have mentioned. So what I feel today is that harnessing all this power has to begin at home, as the Commission report tells us. You will have to see how you take this report and put it into the mill in your own organizations: what does it mean for your own organizations, in the governments, in tripartite dialogue, with other sources, with other partners, etc? The way you develop and promote the report of the Commission, plus the areas that we can deal with at home, is going to play a very important role in how we move forward.

You may start at home tomorrow, and we will start at the Governing Body tomorrow. We will have to look at this, and at your discussions, and then decide how to move forward reasonably within our means, with clarity, with prioritization, but moving forward on the basis of the energy that you have given me, and I would like to end on that note.

I think we have given ourselves collectively an enormous amount of strength and energy. We have all listened to each other, and we know what is going on, and the possibilities and the potentials that have emerged out of this discussion. I did not want to leave without saying so, and without thanking you for the very profound way in which you took up this issue. I think the key to understanding the potential that we have in front of us came through, speech after speech after speech, here in the plenary.

I cannot conclude without thanking all of you for this extraordinary collective work that we have done together. Thank you so much.

Original Spanish: The PRESIDENT

I should like to thank Dr. Juan Somavia, Director-General of the ILO, Secretary-General of the Conference and dear friend for his words.

In a few moments, the 92nd Session of the International Labour Conference will become part of the collective memory of our Organization and also of my own memory.

As the comments of the Secretary-General – which, as in previous years, will be reflected in the record of the Conference – provide more than just a summary of the discussions and the results of this Conference, there is very little need to add anything further. But I should like to share with you, very briefly, some of the thoughts that have inspired me during these more than two weeks of intensive work.

My first reflection is that there has been a common thought or idea in the minds of all delegates who have taken part in the discussions of this Conference. This thought, this idea, is that globalization, as it operates today, is lacking a social message. More than a social message, I would say that it lacks a moral message. One way or another, the 294 individuals who registered to speak before this assembly during the plenary discussion shared this concern. They also shared the conviction that a discussion on globalization that is limited to the problems of the world economy and global trade, does not live up to the expectations of those who feel that, in today's world, social problems have both a national and an international and world dimension. Therefore, the task of giving globalization a human face and a social and moral message, is unfinished business. It is a challenge that the world has a duty to take up.

Let me quote our Dominican poet, Héctor Incháustegui Cabral – "For as long as men and women have to cope with disease and hunger and their children are scattered across the world like harmful insects, and they wander across mountains and plains, aliens in their homelands, there will be no rest, no peace, no sacred leisure – and excess will not be tolerated."

My second reflection is on the ILO proposals concerning the social aspects of globalization. The Director-General has given us a magnificent report which reflects the long months of hard work of the World Commission on the Social Dimension of Globalization. We should welcome this initiative of the Director-General, as well as his inspired leadership. The discussion arising from his Report has been extremely stimulating. When the time comes in the future to review the way in which our ideas have developed in respect of the social problems of globalization, I am sure that it will be recognized that we have reached a milestone here. We shall be talking about a "before" and an "after" the document *A fair globalization*, which this Conference had the enormous privilege of discussing. A document that already deserves a place of honour on the bookshelves of all of those who are interested in the positive social impact of globalization.

My third reflection, which is a sort of appeal to all of you, is that it seems to me to be essential that this extremely important document *A fair globalization: The role of the ILO* should also have pride of place on the work desks of all of those who have some responsibility in the design and implementation of social and economic policies in their countries, in their regions and also across the whole world.

In short, the discussion also highlighted the relevance of the Decent Work Agenda and the privileged place occupied by international labour standards within the daily work of our Organization. It is clear that the ILO, without its standards, is not the ILO. Therefore, it seems essential to me that our Organization should continue to reflect on the best way of strengthening and giving greater credibility to its standard-setting message.

A couple of words now about my experience as President. I must confess to you that, at the outset of the session, I had serious doubts about the way in which the current problems of world politics – which we all know are very serious – might affect the Conference, and I was afraid that I might have been forced to intervene to keep the level of discussion within the confines of what is known as "diplomatic" or "parliamentary" style. The truth of the matter is that all of you have conspired to ensure that my fears were unfounded.

I would like to express to you not only my thanks but also my admiration for the dignified and moderate style of your statements, which made it unnecessary for me to have to react from the podium. The truth is that my experience as President has been supremely pleasant and it is somewhat regrettable that I have to conclude my work today. I would like to say that, thanks to you all, I will only have very fond memories of this experience. Obviously, I would not have been able to say this if, over and above your qualities, I had not been able to count on the support of a magnificent team.

First and foremost, I should like to recognize the efficient way in which my Vice-Presidents worked together with me. Mr. Maatough, Mr. Wade and Mr. Attigbe – sharing the podium with individuals of your calibre was indeed a pleasure for me. I would like to thank you warmly for your cooperation and I would also like to say that I count you amongst my friends.

Secondly, I should like to underscore the effective way in which the delegation of my own country, the

Dominican Republic, worked together with me, enabling me to leave aside my concerns as head of delegation of my country so that I could deal solely with questions relating to the running of the Conference. My thanks go to the whole delegation, and also to Ambassador Claudia Hernández Bona and Ysset Román Maldonado from the Dominican Mission here in Geneva. Many thanks also to my colleagues, the Ministers of Labour in the Central American and Caribbean group.

Last, but by no means least, what can I say about the secretariat? The word "professionalism" defines just one of their qualities, which is perhaps the most important in terms of ensuring that the Conference overcomes any difficulties. But this is not enough to explain why I shall have enduring memories of this Conference. To the word "professionalism," I should like to add three other words. The first is "motivation," the second is "unselfishness" and the third is "friendship". If this were not enough, I would also like to add "good humour". The list of all the professionals on the secretariat team is very long and on it there are many people who are invisible. Although we cannot see them, we do hear them and without their voices, we could not carry out our work. I refer to the interpreters, and I would ask you to give them a big round of applause.

I would also like to give special recognition to the Clerk of the Conference, Mr. Damen, and his assistant Ms. Raquel Ponce de Léon, who used their expertise and experience to craft the very full notes which the secretariat gave me and the Vice-Presidents in our work, both before and after each of our meetings.

My eternal thanks also go to Arturo Bronstein, a great legal authority, a great friend of Dominicans, an excellent human being and an ILO Officer through and through.

Now what would have happened to me if I had not been able to count on Mila Cueni who, together with my assistant Elga Batista, took charge of the logistics of the Conference Presidency. I sincerely wish that the future Presidents of the Conference are able to count on the support of secretaries with the calibre and efficiency of Mila and Elga.

To sum up, I would say that our secretariat has worked like a finely-tuned Swiss watch and in a country like Switzerland this, of course, is to be expected. But, it has also shown the warmth, spontaneity and light-heartedness of a Caribbean country and, believe you me, as a Caribbean I have indeed appreciated this, and enjoyed it as well.

One last word, I should like to pay tribute to Barbados, Belize, Croatia, Slovakia, Slovenia, Estonia, Macedonia, Finland, Italy, Kyrgyzstan, Latvia, Nicaragua, Norway, the United Kingdom, Rwanda, San Marino, Sweden, Tajikistan and Uruguay, whose delegations were made up of at least 40 per cent women. I hope that next year, my successor will be able to read out an even longer list of delegations, that had a female participation of 40 per cent or more, and that in the years to come it will not even be necessary to name them. I am absolutely convinced that better governance at the national and global levels requires a greater presence of women at the highest executive levels.

With these words, I come to the end of my work as President of the 92nd Session of the International Labour Conference. I declare the work of the session closed and I wish you all a safe return to your countries. God bless you.

Original Spanish: THE SECRETARY-GENERAL

As you know, it is customary for the Director-General to hand over this gavel to the President of the Conference as a token of his authority. I am honoured to present him with this keepsake in appreciation of the skill that he has shown in conducting our work.

Original Spanish: The PRESIDENT

Thank you very much indeed Director-General. I now declare the work of the 92nd Session of the International Labour Conference closed and wish you all a very safe and happy journey home. May God bless you all. You have all done a good job.

(The Conference adjourned sine die *at 1.45 p.m.)*

Conférence internationale du Travail - 92e session, Genève, 2004
International Labour Conference - 92nd Session, Geneva 2004
Conferencia Internacional del Trabajo - 92a reunión, Ginebra, 2004

Vote final par appel nominal sur l'adoption de la Recommandation sur la mise en valeur des ressources humaines, 2004

Final record vote on the Adoption of the Human Resources Development Recommendation, 2004

Votación nominal final sobre la adopción de la Recomendación sobre el desarrollo de los recursos humanos, 2004

Pour/For/En Pro: 338
Contre/Against/En contra: 93
Abstentions/Abstentions/Abstenciones: 14
Quorum: 290

Pour/For/En Pro: 338

Afrique du Sud/South Africa/Sudáfrica
MDLADLANA, Mr. (G)
KETTLEDAS, Mr. (G)
HOWARD, Mr.(T/W)

Albanie/Albania
GOXHI, Mrs. (G)
THANATI, Mr. (G)

Algérie/Algeria/Argelia
RAÏS, M. (G)
MEGREROUCHE, M. (G)
SIDI SAID, M.(T/W)

Allemagne/Germany/Alemania
SCHLEEGER, Mrs. (G)
KLOTZ, Mr. (G)
ADAMY, Mr.(T/W)

Angola
N'GOVE LUSSOKE, M. (G)
PEDRO GARCIA, Mme(T/W)

Arabie saoudite/Saudi Arabia/Arabia Saudita
ALHADLAQ, Mr. (G)
AL-ZAMIL, Mr. (G)
RADHWAN, Mr.(T/W)

Argentine/Argentina
ROSALES, Sr. (G)
RIAL, Sra. (G)
PETRECCA, Sr.(T/W)

Australie/Australia
BURROW, Ms.(T/W)

Autriche/Austria
DEMBSHER, Mrs. (G)
ZWERENZ, Mr. (G)
BOEGNER, Mrs.(T/W)

Bahamas
BROWN, Mr. (G)
SYMONETTE, Mr. (G)
ARNETT, Mr. (E)

Bahreïn/Bahrain/Bahrein
AL SHAHABI, Mr. (G)
AL-FAIHANI, Mr. (G)
AL KHOOR, Mr. (E)
ABDULHUSAIN, Mr.(T/W)

Barbade/Barbados
LOWE, Mrs. (G)
FARNUM, Ms. (G)
TROTMAN, Mr.(T/W)

Bélarus/Belarus/Belarús
MALEVICH, Mr. (G)

Belgique/Belgium/Bélgica
CLOESEN, M. (G)
D'HONDT, Mme (G)
CORTEBEECK, M.(T/W)

Bénin/Benin
ONI, M. (G)
MASSESSI, M. (G)
ATTIGBE, M.(T/W)

Bolivie/Bolivia
RODRÍGUEZ SAN MARTÍN, Sr. (G)

Bosnie-Herzégovine/Bosnia and Herzegovina/Bosnia y Herzegovina
VUKAŠINOVIĆ, Mr. (G)

Botswana
BAIPIDI, Mr.(T/W)

Brésil/Brazil/Brasil
BRANCO FREITAS, Mr. (G)
SALDANHA, Mr. (G)
VACCARI NETO, Mr.(T/W)

Bulgarie/Bulgaria
TCHOLASHKA, Mrs. (G)
MLADENOV, Mr. (G)
BEHAR, Mr. (E)
HRISTOV, Mr.(T/W)

Burundi
HAJAYANDI, M.(T/W)

Cambodge/Cambodia/Camboya
THACH, Mr. (G)
HOU, Mr. (G)

Cameroun/Cameroon/Camerún
NGANTCHA, M. (G)

Canada/Canadá
ROBINSON, Ms. (G)
MACPHEE, Mr. (G)
BYERS, Ms.(T/W)

Cap-Vert/Cape Verde/Cabo Verde
SILVA, M.(T/W)

Chili/Chile
DEL PICÓ RUBIO, Sr. (G)
MARTABIT SCAFF, Sr. (G)

Chine/China
LIU, Mr. (G)
WANG, Mr. (G)
FAN, Mrs.(T/W)

Chypre/Cyprus/Chipre
DROUSIOTIS, Mr. (G)

Colombie/Colombia
ALVIS FERNÁNDEZ, Sr.(T/W)

République de Corée/Republic of Korea/República de Corea
LEE, Mr. (G)
HONG, Mr. (G)

Costa Rica
CLARAMUNT GARRO, Sra. (G)
GUILLERMET, Sr. (G)
AGUILAR ARCE, Sr.(T/W)

Côte d'Ivoire
BOULLOU BI DJEHIFFE, M. (G)
ADIKO, M.(T/W)

Croatie/Croatia/Croacia
SOČANAC, Mr. (G)
KULUSIĆ, Ms. (E)
TOTH MUCCIACCIARO, Ms.(T/W)

Cuba
LAU VALDÉS, Sra. (G)
HERNÁNDEZ OLIVA, Sra. (G)
GONZÁLEZ GONZÁLEZ, Sr.(T/W)

Danemark/Denmark/Dinamarca
GEDE, Mrs. (G)
PEDERSEN, Mr. (G)
SCHMIDT, Mr.(T/W)

République dominicaine/Dominican Republic/República Dominicana
NUÑEZ SALCEDO, Sr. (G)
REYES UREÑA, Sr. (G)

Egypte/Egypt/Egipto
GABR, Mrs. (G)
GHAFFAR, Mr. (G)
EL AZALI, Mr.(T/W)

Emirats arabes unis/United Arab Emirates/Emiratos Arabes Unidos
HUSSAIN, Mr. (G)
AL MUHAIRI, Mr. (G)

Espagne/Spain/España
LOPEZ-MONIS DE CAVO, Sr. (G)
BOSCH BESSA, Sr. (G)
JIMENEZ, Sr.(T/W)

Estonie/Estonia
HINDOV, Mrs. (G)
LEHT, Ms. (G)
KALDA, Mr.(T/W)

Etats-Unis/United States/Estados Unidos
ZELLHOEFER, Mr.(T/W)

Ethiopie/Ethiopia/Etiopía
SIAMREGN, Mr. (G)
MITIKU, Mr. (G)
ALEMAYEHU, Mr.(T/W)

Finlande/Finland/Finlandia
VUORINEN, Ms. (G)
SALMENPERÄ, Mr. (G)
AHOKAS, Ms.(T/W)

France/Francia
AUER, Mme (G)
SEGUIN, M. (G)
BRUNEL, Mme(T/W)

Gabon/Gabón
NDONG NANG, M. (G)
MOULOMBA NZIENGUI, M. (G)

Ghana
AMEGEE, Mr. (G)
PARKER-ALLOTEY, Mr. (G)
ADU- AMANKWAH, Mr.(T/W)

Grèce/Greece/Grecia
LAIOU-SPANOPOULOU, Mme (G)
CHRYSANTHOU, Mme (G)
DASSIS, M.(T/W)

Guatemala
PIRA, Sr. (G)
ARGUETA, Sr. (G)
MANCILLA GARCÍA, Sr.(T/W)

Guinée/Guinea
DIALLO, M. (G)

Guinée équatoriale/Equatorial Guinea/Guinea Ecuatorial
ESUÁ NKÓ, Sr. (G)
ASAMA NTUGU, Sr. (G)
MATZEN MAKOSO, Sr. (E)

Hongrie/Hungary/Hungría
HERCZOG, Mr. (G)
TÓTH, Mr. (G)
TAMÁS, Ms.(T/W)

Inde/India
SHENOY, Mr. (G)
DAVE, Mr.(T/W)

Indonésie/Indonesia
SULISTYANINGSIH, Ms. (G)
SITUMORANG, Mr. (G)
DAVID, Mr.(T/W)

République islamique d'Iran/Islamic Republic of Iran/República Islámica del Irán
SHEIKH, Mr. (G)
HEFDAHTAN, Mr. (G)
RAIESI FARD, Mr. (E)
SALIMIAN, Mr.(T/W)

Iraq
KHODIR, Mr. (G)

Irlande/Ireland/Irlanda
PENDER, Mr. (G)
MCDONNELL, Mr. (G)
LYNCH, Ms.(T/W)

Islande/Iceland/Islandia
DAVIDSDOTTIR, Ms. (G)
KRISTINSSON, Mr. (G)
FINNBOGASON, Mr.(T/W)

Israël/Israel
WAXMAN, Mr. (G)
FURMAN, Ms. (G)
KARA, Mr.(T/W)

Italie/Italy/Italia
COLOMBO, M. (G)
TRIA, M. (G)
TARTAGLIA, M.(T/W)

Japon/Japan/Japón
OSHIMA, Mr. (G)
HASEGAWA, Mr. (G)
NAKAJIMA, Mr.(T/W)

Kenya
KAVULUDI, Mr. (G)
MOHAMED, Mrs. (G)
ATWOLI, Mr.(T/W)

Koweït/Kuwait
AL-MUDADI, Mr. (G)
RAZZOOQI, Mr. (G)

Lesotho
MANDORO, Mr. (G)
MATSOSO, Ms. (G)
TYHALI, Mr.(T/W)

Lettonie/Latvia/Letonia
KARKLINS, Mr. (G)
KALNINS, Mr. (G)

Jamahiriya arabe libyenne/Libyan Arab Jamahiriya/Jamahiriya Arabe Libia
ALZWAM, Mr. (G)
DERBI, Mr. (G)
AL TALHI, Mr.(T/W)

Lituanie/Lithuania/Lituania
JAKUCIONYTE, Ms. (G)
RIMKUNAS, Mr. (G)
BALSIENE, Ms.(T/W)

Luxembourg/Luxemburgo
FABER, M. (G)
SCHOLTUS, Mme (G)
PIZZAFERRI, M.(T/W)

Madagascar
RASOLOFONIAINARISON, M. (G)
RANDRIAMAHOLISON, M.(T/W)

Malaisie/Malaysia/Malasia
NORDIN, Mr.(T/W)

Malawi
MONONGA, Mr. (G)
KAMBUTO, Mr. (G)
KALIMANJIRA, Mr.(T/W)

Mali/Malí
DIAKITE, M. (G)
MAHAMANE, M. (G)
DIAKITE, M.(T/W)

Malte/Malta
PULLICINO, Mr. (G)
AZZOPARDI, Mr. (G)
MICALLEF, Mr.(T/W)

Maroc/Morocco/Marruecos
HILALE, M. (G)
CHATER, M. (G)

Maurice/Mauritius/Mauricio
ARNACHELLUM, Mr. (G)
BENYDIN, Mr.(T/W)

Mexique/Mexico/México
ROVIROSA, Sra. (G)
SILVA, Sr. (G)
ANDERSON, Sra.(T/W)

Mozambique
DENGO, Mr. (G)
SITOE, Mr.(T/W)

Myanmar
THAN, Mr. (G)
NYUNT, Mr. (G)

Namibie/Namibia
HIVELUAH, Ms. (G)
SHINGUADJA, Mr. (G)
SHIPENA, Mr. (E)
KAPENDA, Mr.(T/W)

Népal/Nepal
ACHARYA, Mr. (G)

Nicaragua
MARTÍNEZ FLORES, Srta. (G)
CRUZ TORUÑO, Sr. (G)
GONZÁLEZ GAITÁN, Sr.(T/W)

Niger/Níger
MAÏNA, M. (G)
SANDA, M.(T/W)

Nigéria/Nigeria
ADEYEYE-OLUKOYA, Mrs. (G)
SULAI, Mrs. (G)
OSHIOMHOLE, Mr.(T/W)

Norvège/Norway/Noruega
BRUAAS, Mr. (G)
VIDNES, Mr. (G)
THEODORSEN, Ms.(T/W)

Nouvelle-Zélande/New Zealand/Nueva Zelandia
BUWALDA, Mr. (G)
STEFFENS, Ms. (G)
BEAUMONT, Ms.(T/W)

Oman/Omán
AL-ABDUWANI, Mr. (G)
AL-AMRI, Mr. (G)
AL RABAIE, Mr. (E)
AL-NAHARI, Mr.(T/W)

Ouganda/Uganda
NAGGAGA, Mr. (G)
OGARAM, Mr. (G)

Pakistan/Pakistán
FARSHORI, Mr. (G)
UMER, Mr. (G)
AHMED, Mr.(T/W)

Panama/Panamá
ORTIZ BARBER, Sra. (G)
ROSAS PÉREZ, Sra. (G)
PUGA RODRÍGUEZ, Sr.(T/W)

Papouasie-Nouvelle-Guinée/Papua New Guinea/Papua Nueva Guinea
ARUA, Mr. (G)
LOVAGA, Mrs. (G)
JEFFERY, Mr. (E)
MELAN, Mr.(T/W)

Paraguay
RAMÍREZ LEZCANO, Sr. (G)
BARREIRO PERROTTA, Sr. (G)
BOGARIN, Sr. (E)
PARRA GAONA, Sr.(T/W)

Pays-Bas/Netherlands/Países Bajos
NOTEBOOM, Ms. (G)
BEETS, Mr. (G)
ETTY, Mr.(T/W)

Pérou/Peru/Perú
VEGAS, Sr. (G)
BERAUN, Sra. (G)
GUTIÉRREZ MADUEÑO, Sr.(T/W)

Philippines/Filipinas
BALDOZ, Mrs. (G)
SORIANO, Mr. (E)
VALERIO, Mr.(T/W)

Pologne/Poland/Polonia
LEMIESZEWSKA, Mrs. (G)
JAKUBOWSKI, Mr. (G)
WOJCIK, Mr.(T/W)

Portugal
RIBEIRO LOPES, M. (G)
BARCIA, M. (G)
GOMES PROENÇA, M.(T/W)

Qatar
ALKAWARI, Mr. (G)
AL MAL, Ms. (G)
AL SAIARI, Mr.(T/W)

République dém. du Congo/Democratic Republic of the Congo/República Democrática del Congo
MUTOMB MUJING, M. (G)
SAMBASSI, M. (G)
MUKALAYI HANGA, M.(T/W)

Roumanie/Romania/Rumania
NEMES, M. (G)
CONSTANTINESCU, Mme (G)
COSTACHE, M. (E)

Royaume-Uni/United Kingdom/Reino Unido
BRATTAN, Ms. (G)
RICHARDS, Mr. (G)
STEYNE, Mr.(T/W)

Fédération de Russie/Russian Federation/Federación de Rusia
BAVYKIN, Mr. (G)
LUBLIN, Mr. (G)
SIDOROV, Mr.(T/W)

Rwanda
KAVARUGANDA, M. (G)
UKUYEMUYE, M. (G)
BITWAYIKI, M. (E)
KAYUMBA, M.(T/W)

Saint-Marin/San Marino
BIGI, Mme (G)
GASPERONI, M. (G)
PIERMATTEI, M.(T/W)

Sénégal/Senegal
DIALLO, Mme (G)
THIAM, M. (G)
GUIRO, M.(T/W)

Serbie et Monténégro/Serbia and Montenegro/Serbia y Montenegro
BEGOVIĆ, Mr. (G)
ŠAHOVIĆ, Mr. (G)
ZAGORAC, Mr. (E)

Seychelles
MERITON, Mr. (G)
BAKER, Mr. (G)
SULTAN-BEAUDOUIN, Mr. (E)

Singapour/Singapore/Singapur
NG, Mr. (G)
YONG, Ms. (G)
YACOB, Mrs.(T/W)

Slovaquie/Slovakia/Eslovaquia
PETÖCZ, Mr. (G)
SEPTÁKOVÁ, Ms. (G)
MESTANOVÁ, Mrs.(T/W)

Slovénie/Slovenia/Eslovenia
ZIDAR, Mr. (G)
RIHAR BAJUK, Ms. (G)
KRZIŠNIK, Mr.(T/W)

Soudan/Sudan/Sudán
SHENTOUR, Mr. (G)
ELHASSAN, Mr. (G)
GHANDOUR, Mr.(T/W)

Sri Lanka
DEVENDRA, Mr.(T/W)

Suède/Sweden/Suecia
WIKLUND, Ms. (G)
JONZON, Mr. (G)
BENGTSSON, Mr.(T/W)

Suisse/Switzerland/Suiza
VIGNE, M.(T/W)

Suriname
PIROE, Mr. (G)
SEMMOH, Ms. (G)
SOUPRAYEN, Ms.(T/W)

Swaziland/Swazilandia
NKHAMBULE, Mr. (G)
SITHOLE, Mr.(T/W)

République arabe syrienne/Syrian Arab Republic/República Arabe Siria
IBRAHIM, M. (G)
AKASHE, M. (G)
MOHAMMAD NASSER, M. (E)
AZOZ, M.(T/W)

République-Unie de Tanzanie/United Republic of Tanzania/República Unida de Tanzanía
RWEYEMAMU, Mrs. (G)
MAPURI, Mr. (G)
SITTA, Mrs.(T/W)

Tchad/Chad
ABDERAHIM, M. (G)
DJEGUEDEM, M. (G)
DJIBRINE, M.(T/W)

République tchèque/Czech Republic/República Checa
SAJDA, Mr. (G)
SLABÝ, Mr. (G)
BAUEROVÁ, Mrs.(T/W)

Thaïlande/Thailand/Tailandia
ROJVITHEE, Ms. (G)
NAKCHUEN, Mr. (G)
TECHATEERAVAT, Mr.(T/W)

Trinité-et-Tobago/Trinidad and Tobago/Trinidad y Tabago
RAMNARINE, Mr. (G)
SINGH, Ms. (G)

Tunisie/Tunisia/Túnez
CHATTI, M. (G)
MANSOUR, M. (G)
TRABELSI, M.(T/W)

Turquie/Turkey/Turquía
GENC, Mr. (G)
ERCAN, Mr. (G)

Ukraine/Ucrania
YAMPOLSKYI, Mr. (G)
BELASHOV, Mr. (G)
SHYLOV, Mr.(T/W)

Uruguay
LAGARMILLA, Sra. (G)
DONO, Sra. (G)
FERNÁNDEZ, Sr.(T/W)

Venezuela
DORADO CANO, Sr. (G)
MOLINA, Sr. (G)
INFANTE, Sr.(T/W)

Viet Nam
PHAM, Mr. (G)
VU, Mr. (G)
VI, Mrs. (E)
VO, Mr.(T/W)

Yémen/Yemen
AL-FAYSALI, Mr. (G)

Zambie/Zambia
SINJELA, Mrs. (G)
HIKAUMBA, Mr.(T/W)

Zimbabwe
DZVITI, Mr. (G)
MUSEKA, Mr. (G)
MATOMBO, Mr.(T/W)

Contre/Against/En contra: 93

Afrique du Sud/South Africa/Sudáfrica
BOTHA, Mr. (E)

Algérie/Algeria/Argelia
MEGATELI, M. (E)

Allemagne/Germany/Alemania
GERSTEIN, Mrs. (E)

Angola
TIAGO GOMES, M. (E)

Arabie saoudite/Saudi Arabia/Arabia Saudita
DAHLAN, Mr. (E)

Argentine/Argentina
SPAGHI, Sr. (E)

Australie/Australia
SAWERS, Mr. (G)
LLOYD, Mr. (G)
NOAKES, Mr. (E)

Autriche/Austria
TOMEK, Mr. (E)

Bahamas
HAMILTON, Ms.(T/W)

Belgique/Belgium/Bélgica
DA COSTA, M. (E)

Bénin/Benin
AHOUDJI, Mme (E)

Botswana
DEWAH, Mr. (E)

Brésil/Brazil/Brasil
LIMA GODOY, Mr. (E)

Burkina Faso
NACOULMA, M. (E)

Burundi
BUDABUDA, M. (E)

Canada/Canadá
WAJDA, Mr. (E)

Cap-Vert/Cape Verde/Cabo Verde
ÉVORA, Mme (E)

Chili/Chile
ARTHUR ERRÁZURIZ, Sr. (E)

Chine/China
CHEN, Mr. (E)

Chypre/Cyprus/Chipre
KAPARTIS, Mr. (E)

Colombie/Colombia
ARANGO DE BUITRAGO, Sra. (G)
ECHAVARRÍA SALDARRIAGA, Sr. (E)

République de Corée/Republic of Korea/República de Corea
SUH, Mr. (E)

Cuba
PARRAS ROJAS, Sr. (E)

Danemark/Denmark/Dinamarca
DREESEN, Mr. (E)

El Salvador
ESPINAL, Sr. (G)
AVILA DE PEÑA, Sra. (G)
TOMASINO, Sr. (E)
SARAHI MOLINA, Sra.(T/W)

Emirats arabes unis/United Arab Emirates/Emiratos Arabes Unidos
MATTAR, Mr. (E)
AL MARZOOQI, Mr.(T/W)

Equateur/Ecuador
TERÁN, Sr. (E)

Espagne/Spain/España
FERRER DUFOL, Sr. (E)

Estonie/Estonia
MERILAI, Ms. (E)

Etats-Unis/United States/Estados Unidos
GOLDBERG, Ms. (E)

Ethiopie/Ethiopia/Etiopía
YIMER, Mr. (E)

Fidji/Fiji
ZINCK, Mr. (G)
KUNATUBA, Mr. (G)
POLITINI, Mr. (E)

Finlande/Finland/Finlandia
HUTTUNEN, Mr. (E)

France/Francia
BOISSON, M. (E)

Gabon/Gabón
AWASSI ATSIMADJA, Mme (E)

Ghana
AMPIAH, Mr. (E)

Grèce/Greece/Grecia
CHARAKAS, M. (E)

Honduras
URTECHO LOPEZ, Sr. (E)

Inde/India
ANAND, Mr. (E)

Indonésie/Indonesia
RACHMAN, Mr. (E)

Irlande/Ireland/Irlanda
MAGUIRE, Ms. (E)

Islande/Iceland/Islandia
MAGNUSSON, Mr. (E)

Israël/Israel
BARAK, Mr. (E)

Italie/Italy/Italia
SASSO MAZZUFFERI, Mme (E)

Jamaïque/Jamaica
LEWIS, Mr. (E)

Japon/Japan/Japón
SUZUKI, Mr. (E)

Kenya
KONDITI, Mr. (E)

Koweït/Kuwait
AL-RABAH, Mr. (E)

Lesotho
MAKEKA, Mr. (E)

Lituanie/Lithuania/Lituania
VASILEVSKIS, Mr. (E)

Luxembourg/Luxemburgo
BERTRAND-SCHAUL, Mme (E)

Malaisie/Malaysia/Malasia
SHAMSUDIN, Mr. (E)

Malawi
SINJANI, Mr. (E)

Mali/Malí
TRAORE, M. (E)

Malte/Malta
FARRUGIA, Mr. (E)

Maurice/Mauritius/Mauricio
JEETUN, Mr. (E)

Norvège/Norway/Noruega
RIDDERVOLD, Ms. (E)

Nouvelle-Zélande/New Zealand/Nueva Zelandia
ARNOLD, Mr. (E)

Pakistan/Pakistán
TABANI, Mr. (E)

Panama/Panamá
AIZPURÚA, Sr. (E)

Pays-Bas/Netherlands/Países Bajos
RENIQUE, Mr. (E)

Pologne/Poland/Polonia
BOBROWSKI, Mr. (E)

Portugal
FERNANDES SALGUEIRO, M. (E)

Royaume-Uni/United Kingdom/Reino Unido
LAMBERT, Mr. (E)

Fédération de Russie/Russian Federation/Federación de Rusia
POLUEKTOV, Mr. (E)

Saint-Marin/San Marino
GIORGINI, Mme (E)

Sénégal/Senegal
DIOP, M. (E)

Slovaquie/Slovakia/Eslovaquia
BORGULA, Mr. (E)

Slovénie/Slovenia/Eslovenia
JEREB, Ms. (E)

Soudan/Sudan/Sudán
ELGURASHI, Mr. (E)

Sri Lanka
DASANAYAKE, Mr. (E)

Suède/Sweden/Suecia
LAURENT, Ms. (E)

Suisse/Switzerland/Suiza
PLASSARD, M. (E)

Suriname
VAN OMMEREN, Mr. (E)

Swaziland/Swazilandia
MAPHANGA, Mrs. (E)

République-Unie de Tanzanie/United Republic of Tanzania/República Unida de Tanzanía
KABYEMERA, Mr. (E)

République tchèque/Czech Republic/República Checa
DRBALOVÁ, Mrs. (E)

Thaïlande/Thailand/Tailandia
ROMCHATTHONG, Mrs. (E)

Trinité-et-Tobago/Trinidad and Tobago/Trinidad y Tabago
HILTON CLARKE, Mr. (E)

Tunisie/Tunisia/Túnez
M'KAISSI, M. (E)

Turquie/Turkey/Turquía
CENTEL, Mr. (E)

Uruguay
FOSTIK, Sr. (E)

Venezuela
DE ARBELOA, Sr. (E)

Zambie/Zambia
NONDE, Ms. (E)

Abstentions/Abstentions/ Abstenciones: 14

Belize/Belice
HUNT, Ms. (G)

Botswana
MOJAFI, Mr. (G)
SEEMULE, Ms. (G)

Equateur/Ecuador
ESPINOSA SALAS, Sr. (G)
THULLEN, Sr. (G)

Etats-Unis/United States/Estados Unidos
LEVINE, Mr. (G)
HAGEN, Mr. (G)

Liban/Lebanon/Líbano
GHORAYEB, M. (G)
SAAB, Mme (G)
BALBOUL, M. (E)

Malaisie/Malaysia/Malasia
SOH, Mr. (G)
ISMAIL, Mr. (G)

Suisse/Switzerland/Suiza
ALVESALO-ROESCH, Mme (G)
ELMIGER, M. (G)

CONTENTS

Page

Twentieth sitting

Final record vote on the Recommendation concerning human resources development: Education, training and lifelong learning 1

    Speakers: Mr. Funes de Rioja, Mr. Pender, Ms. Alvesalo-Roesch, Mr. Shepard, Ms. Arango de Buitrago.

Report of the Committee on the Application of Standards: Submission, discussion and approval .. 3

    Speakers: Ms. Robert Lopes *(Reporter)*, Mr. Wisskirchen, Mr. Cortebeeck, Ms. Rial, Mr. Nkhambule, Mr. Mangwana, Mr. Sánchez Oliva, Mr. Cahalane, Mr. Etty, Mr. Steyne, Mr. Fernández, Mr. Sankar Saha, Mr. Sithole, Mr. Dorado Cano, Mr. Malevich, Mr. Ahmed.

Closing speeches 15

    Speakers: Mr. Maatough, Mr. Wade, Mr. Attigbe, the Secretary-General, the President.

Final record vote on the adoption of the Human Resources Development Recommendation, 2004: Results 21

DELEGATIONS

Supplément au Compte rendu provisoire (16 juin 2004)

LISTE FINALE DES DÉLÉGATIONS

Conférence internationale du Travail

Quatre-vingt-douzième session, Genève

Supplement to the Provisional Record (16 June 2004)

FINAL LIST OF DELEGATIONS

International Labour Conference

Ninety-second Session, Geneva

Suplemento de Actas Provisionales (16 de junio de 2004)

LISTA FINAL DE DELEGACIONES

Conferencia Internacional del Trabajo

Nonagésima segunda reunión, Ginebra

2004

DÉLÉGATIONS – DELEGATIONS – DELEGACIONES

La liste des délégations est présentée sous une forme trilingue. Elle contient d'abord les délégations des Etats membres de l'Organisation représentés à la Conférence dans l'ordre alphabétique selon le nom en français des Etats. Figurent ensuite les représentants des observateurs, des organisations intergouvernementales et des organisations internationales non gouvernementales invitées à la Conférence.

Toutes les informations concernant les noms des pays ou des organisations sont données en français, en anglais et en espagnol. Toute autre information (titres et fonctions des participants) est indiquée dans une seule de ces langues: celle que doit utiliser le Bureau international du Travail dans la correspondance officielle avec le pays dont relève la personne intéressée.

Les noms, titres et qualités figurant dans la liste finale des délégations correspondent aux indications fournies dans les pouvoirs officiels reçus au lundi 14 juin 2004, 16 heures.

The list of delegations is presented in trilingual form. It contains the delegations of the member States represented at the Conference in the French alphabetical order, followed by the representatives of the observers, intergovernmental organizations and international non-governmental organizations invited to the Conference.

The names of the countries and organizations are given in French, English and Spanish. Any other information (title and functions of participants) is given in the language used for official correspondence between the ILO and the country in question.

The names and designations appearing in the final list of delegations are those given in the official credentials received up to Monday 14 June 2004 at 4.00 p.m.

La lista de delegaciones se presenta en forma trilingüe. En primer lugar figuran los Estados miembros de la Organización en orden alfabético francés. Seguidamente aparecen las delegaciones de los observadores, organizaciones intergubernamentales y organizaciones internacionales no gubernamentales invitados a la Conferencia.

Figuran en francés, inglés y español los nombres de los Estados y organizaciones asistentes a la Conferencia. Los demás datos (títulos y cargos de los participantes) aparecen sólo en la lengua utilizada por la Oficina Internacional del Trabajo para sus comunicaciones oficiales con el correspondiente Estado.

Los nombres, títulos y cargos que figuran en la lista final de delegaciones son los que constan en los poderes oficiales recibidos hasta el lunes 14 de junio de 2004 a las 16 horas.

Afghanistan   Afghanistan   Afganistán

Délégués gouvernementaux

QARQEIN, Noor Mohammad, M., Ministre du Travail et des Affaires sociales.
BASHIRI, Mohammad Ghaus, M., Vice-ministre du Travail et des Affaires sociales.

Conseillers techniques et délégués suppléants

MEHRZAD, Ghulam Fariiq, M., Ministère du Travail et des Affaires sociales.
HAKIM, Soyaya abdullah, Mme, Ministère du Travail et des Affaires sociales.

Conseillers techniques

OMER, Assad, M., Ambassadeur, Représentant permanent, Mission permanente, Genève.
ANWARZAI, Mohammad Anwar, M., Ministre Conseiller, Mission permanente, Genève.
NASRI, Ahmad Khalil, M., Premier Secrétaire, Mission permanente, Genève.
RASULI, Ghulam Sediq, M., Deuxième Secrétaire, Mission permanente, Genève.

Délégué des employeurs

DADMANISH, Sayed Mahmood, M., Président, Qoyas Construction Association Ltd.

Délégué des travailleurs

EHSAS, Mohammad Qasem, M., Président, Conseil central, Union nationale des Travailleurs afghans.

Afrique du Sud   South Africa   Sudáfrica

Minister attending the Conference

MDLADLANA, M.M.S., Mr., Minister of Labour.

Person accompanying the Minister

MOTHEOHANE, T., Ms., Personal Assistant to the Minister.

Government Delegates

KETTLEDAS, L., Mr., Deputy Director-General, Labour Policy and Labour Market Programmes.
NDEBELE, S.J., Mr., Executive Manager, International Relations, Department of Labour.

Advisers and substitute delegates

LUSENGA, F.L.N.W., Ms., Counsellor (Labour), Permanent Mission, Geneva.
LENYAI, N.T., Ms., Assistant Manager, International Relations, Department of Labour.

Advisers

GUMBI, L., Mr., Deputy Permanent Representative, Permanent Mission, Geneva.
MACUN, I., Mr., Executive Manager, Labour Market Information Statistics, Department of Labour.
BIRD, A., Ms., Deputy Director-General, Skills Development, Department of Labour.
SEAFIELD, V., Mr., Manager, Employment Standards, Department of Labour.
NDEMA, R., Mr., Regional Manager, Immigration, Department of Home Affairs.
CAMPBELL, N.T., Mr., Head, Fishing Vessel Safety Unit, South African Maritime Authority (SAMSA).
PILLAY, D., Ms., Assistant Manager, Legal Services, Department of Labour.

Representatives of a State or Province

MANIE, S.M., Mr., MP.
RASMENI, S.M., Mr., MP.
LOWE, C.M., Mr., MP.

Other person attending the Conference

SOLER, J., Ms., Secretary, Permanent Mission, Geneva.

Employers' Delegate

BOTHA, B., Mr., Advisor on International Affairs, Business Unity South Africa (BUSA).

Adviser and substitute delegate

VAN VUUREN, V., Mr., Chief Operations Officer, BUSA.

Advisers

DE BEER, H., Mr., Executive Manager, I&J and BUSA.
DOWIE, F., Ms., Chief Officer Strategic Services, BUSA.
ESSELAAR, V., Mr., Migration Advisor, Chamber of Mines and BUSA.
LAMPRECHT, A., Mr., Council Member, BUSA.
NDONI, A., Ms., Black Lawyers'Association and BUSA.
VAN NIEKERK, A., Mr., Legal Advisor, BUSA.
ZAMISA, S., Mr., Human Resources Executive, Continental, BUSA.

Workers' Delegate

HOWARD, R., Mr., Secretary General, SATAWU.

Advisers and substitute delegates

MILANI, C., Mr., General Secretary, FEDUSA.

MAQHEKENI, Joseph, Mr., President, NACTU.

Advisers

BHENGU, H., Ms., Education Officer, COSATU.
MASEMOLA, K., Mr., Deputy General Secretary, FAWU.

Albanie   Albania   Albania

Government Delegates

BEJTAJ, Engjell, Mr., Minister of Labour and Social Affairs.
THANATI, Vladimir, Mr., Ambassador, Permanent Representative, Permanent Mission, Geneva.

Advisers and substitute delegates

MULITA, Reis, Mr., Minister's Chief of Cabinet.
MUÇA, Gjergj, Mr., Director, Labour Relations Directorate, Ministry of Labour and Social Affairs.
MERSINI, Spartak, Mr., Director, External Relations and Cooperation.
XHANGOLLI, Gramoz, Mr., Labour Relations Directorate.
ZOTO, Naim, Mr.
GOXHI, Pranvera, Mrs., First Secretary, Permanent Mission, Geneva.

Employers' Delegate

VAROSHI, Ismail, Mr., General Secretary, Council of Employers' Organizations.

Advisers and substitute delegates

KOKEDHIMA, Koco, Mr., Chairman, Business Organisations Union.
NOCKA, Ivis, Mrs., Organisations Council of the Employer.
KOKA, Vladimir, Mr., Organisations Council of the Employer.

Workers' Delegate

MUÇO, Kastriot, Mr., Chairman, Albanian Confederation Trade Union.

Adviser and substitute delegate

KALAJA, Gezim, Mr., Chairman, Independent Trade Union.

Algérie   Algeria   Argelia

Ministre assistant à la Conférence

LOUH, Tayeb, M., Ministre du Travail et de la Sécurité sociale.

Personne accompagnant le Ministre

DEMBRI, Mohamed-Salah, M., Ambassadeur, Représentant permanent, Mission permanente, Genève.

Délégués gouvernementaux

RAÏS, El Hadi, M., Chef de Cabinet, Ministère du Travail et de la Sécurité sociale.
MEGREROUCHE, Mouloud, M., Directeur des Etudes juridiques et de la Coopération.

Conseillers techniques

KHENCHOUL, Ahmed, M., Directeur général, CACOBATPH.
KACI ABDALLAH, Ahmed, M., Director, Administration des Moyens, Ministère de la Pêche et des Ressources halieutiques.
SEDKI, Boualem, M., Ministre Plénipotentiaire, Mission permanente, Genève.
TOBAL, Mohamed, M., Conseiller diplomatique, Ministère des Affaires étrangères.
FERDIOU, Malika, Mlle, Attachée diplomatique, Ministère des Affaires étrangères.
GUERIRA, Djamel, M., Chargé du Protocole du Ministre.
FERHAT CHIKH, Ali, M., Inspecteur général, Ministère de la Formation et de l'Enseignement professionnels.

Délégué des employeurs

NAÏT-ABDELAZIZ, Mohamed Saïd, M., Président, Confédération nationale du Patronat algérien (CNPA).

Conseillers techniques

MERAKECHE, Boualem, M., Président, Confédération algérienne du Patronat (CAP).
MEGATELI, El Mahfoudh, M., Représentant, Confédération générale des Opérateurs économiques algériens (CGOEA).
YOUSFI, Habib, M., Président, CGOEA.
AIT AHCENE, Hocine, M., CNPA.
BENDRIS, Brahim, M., CAP.
SAHARI, Djelloul, M., CNPA.
AMOUR, Riadh, M., CAP.
HAMOUTENE, Rachid, M., CNPA.
BAHLOULI, Lyazid, M., CAP.
LARDJANE, Mohamed Rachid, M., CNPA.

Personnes désignées en conformité avec l'article 2, alinéa 3 i)

RAISSEMCH, Abderrahmane, M., CAP.

SIACI, Ali, M., CNPA.
DJAADI, Mohamed, M., CNPA.
CHERFAOUI, Tayeb, M., CAP.
BEN GAOUD, Ahmed, M., CNPA.

Autre personne assistant à la Conférence

AIT ANCEUR, Hamid, M., CNPA.

Délégué des travailleurs

SIDI SAID, Abdelmadjid, M., Secrétaire général, Union générale des Travailleurs algériens (UGTA).

Conseillers techniques

RAHMA, Boudjemâ, M., Secrétaire national, UGTA.
MEZIANI, Abdelali, M., Secrétaire national, UGTA.
BOUZIDI, Boualem, M., Secrétaire national chargé des Conflits, UGTA.
MERABET, Ali, M., Secrétaire national chargé de la Fonction publique, UGTA.
BENMOUHOUB, El Hachemi, M., Secrétaire national chargé de l'Education et de la Formation Syndicale, UGTA.
KERROUM, Lakhdar, M., Secrétaire national chargé de la Solidarité et de l'Action sociale, UGTA.
DJENOUHAT, Salah, M., Secrétaire national chargé de l'Organique, UGTA.
MALKI, Abdelkader, M., Secrétaire national chargé des Relations générales, UGTA.
ADJABI, Salah, M., Secrétaire national chargé de l'Emploi et de la Formation professionnelle, UGTA.
BADREDDINE, Mohamed Lakhdar, M., Secrétaire national chargé des Affaires économiques et Etudes, UGTA.

Personnes désignées en conformité avec l'article 2, alinéa 3 i)

SALHI, Soumia, Mme, UGTA.
RAHMANI, Messaouda, Mme, UGTA.

Allemagne   Germany   Alemania

Minister attending the Conference

ANDRES, Gerd, Mr., Parliamentary Secretary of State, Federal Ministry of Economics and Labour.

Government Delegates

STEINER, Michael, Mr., Ambassador, Permanent Representative, Permanent Mission, Geneva.
KOBERSKI, Wolfgang, Mr., Director-General, European Policy and International Employment and Social Policy Department, Federal Ministry of Economics and Labour; Representative, Governing Body of the ILO.

Advisers and substitute delegates

HELLER, Wolfgang, Mr., Director, International Employment and Social Policy, Federal Ministry of Economics and Labour; Substitute Representative, Governing Body of the ILO.
METSCHER, Klaus, Mr., Minister, Permanent Mission, Geneva.
SCHLEEGER, Magdalena, Mrs., Head of Division for ILO and UN Affairs, Federal Ministry of Economics and Labour; Substitute Representative, Governing Body of the ILO.
KLOTZ, Valentin, Mr., Permanent Mission, Geneva.

Advisers

HÖFER-WISSING, Neithart, Mr., First Counsellor, Permanent Mission, Geneva.
STILGENBAUER, Günther, Mr., Counsellor, Permanent Mission, Geneva.
PENSKY, Angela, Mrs., Federal Institute for Occupational Safety and Health.
VON OPPEN, Hella, Mrs., Federal Ministry of Economics and Labour.
ZEITZ, Birgit, Mrs., Federal Ministry of Economics and Labour.
PUHLMANN, Angelika, Mrs., Federal Institute for Vocational Training.
ANTON, Heinz, Mr., Federal Ministry of Consumer Protection, Food and Agriculture, Division for General and Market Policy Affairs and Fisheries.
MÖLLER, Tanya, Ms.

Employers' Delegate

GERSTEIN, Antje, Mrs., Deputy Director, European Union and International Social Policy, Confederation of German Employers' Associations, BDA.

Adviser and substitute delegate

WISSKIRCHEN, Alfred, Mr., Former Head, Labour Law Department, BDA.

Advisers

HORNUNG-DRAUS, Renate, Mrs., Head, European Union and International Social Policy Department, BDA.
ABEL, Klaus, Mr., Former Member, Educational Policy Department, BDA.
PRINZ, Thomas, Mr., Deputy Head, Labour Law Department, BDA.
GUNDEL, Elke, Mrs., Labour Market Department, BDA.
LINDEMANN, Dierk, Mr., Managing Director, Association of German Shipyards (VDR).

Other person attending the Conference

CLEVER, Peter, Mr., Member, Executive Board, Confederation of German Employers' Associations.

Workers' Delegate

ENGELEN-KEFER, Ursula, Mrs., Vice-President, German Confederation of Trade Unions, DGB; Member, Governing Body of the ILO.

Adviser and substitute delegate

ADAMY, Wilhelm, Mr., Labour Market and International Social Policy Department, Federal Executive Board, DGB.

Advisers

ECKL, Jürgen, Mr., European and International Trade Union Policy Department, Federal Executive Board, DGB.
VON SEGGERN, Burkhard, Mr., Labour Market and International Social Policy Department, Federal Executive Board, DGB.
KOLF, Ingo, Mr., Labour Market and International Social Policy Department, Federal Executive Board, DGB.
GIESSLER, Thomas, Mr., DGB-Regional Area.
TEICHERT, Werner, Mr., United Service Union (Ver.di), Federal Executive Board.
GRAF, Sabine, Mrs., Construction, Agriculture and Environment Union.
PAPE, Karin, Mrs., Trade Union of Food, Beverages, Tobacco, Hotel and Catering.

Other persons attending the Conference

KERBUSCH, Ernst-J., Mr., Friedrich-Ebert-Foundation.
FEICHT, Roland, Mr., Friedrich-Ebert-Foundation.
SCHWEISSHELM, Erwin, Mr., Friedrich-Ebert-Foundation.
MUND, Horst, Mr., Friedrich-Ebert-Foundation.
LANZ, Hajo, Mr., Friedrich-Ebert-Foundation.
ANONUEVO, Tos, Mr., Friedrich-Ebert-Foundation.
MAY, Helga, Mrs., Friedrich-Ebert-Foundation.
ADAM, Erfried, Mr., Friedrich-Ebert-Foundation.
BLANKE, Svenja, Mrs., Friedrich-Ebert-Foundation.
SINHA, Pravin, Mr., Friedrich-Ebert-Foundation.
SCHILLINGER, Hubert, Mr., Friedrich-Ebert-Foundation.
TRAUB-MERZ, Rudolf, Mr., Friedrich-Ebert-Foundation.

Angola   Angola   Angola

Ministre assistant à la Conférence

LUQUINDA, Sebastião Constantino, M., Vice-Ministre de l'Administration publique, de l'Emploi et de la Sécurité sociale.

Délégués gouvernementaux

N'GOVE LUSSOKE, David, M., Directeur des Relations et de Coopération internationales, Ministère de l'Administration publique, de l'Emploi et de la Sécurité sociale.
FERRO, Albino, M., Directeur provincial, Ministère de l'Administration publique, de l'Emploi et de la Sécurité sociale de la Province de Huila.

Conseillers techniques

EVARISTO, Manuel, M., Juriste, Assistant de Migration, Service de la Migration et des Étrangers de l'Angola.
CARDOSO PINTO, Eduardo, M., Juriste, Chef, Département des Organisations internationales, Ministère des Pêches.
MARTINS, João Filipe, M., Ambassadeur, Représentant permanent, Mission permanente, Genève.
PEGADO DA SILVA, Sofia, Mme, Ministre conseillère, Ministère des Relations extérieures.
BONGA, Mendes, M., Premier Secrétaire, Mission permanente, Genève.
MACHADO LUIS, António Luis, M., Directeur du Travail et des Salaires, MAPESS.

Délégué des employeurs

TIAGO GOMES, António, M., Secrétaire général, Chambre du Commerce et de l'Industrie de l'Angola (CCIA).

Conseillers techniques

PAULINA MÁRIO, Herminia de Asunção, Mme, Juriste, Sonangol; Membre de la CCIA.
ANDRÉ, Victor Manuel, M., Juriste, Sonangol; Membre de la CCIA.
LOPES, Armenio Alexandre, M., Secrétaire-général, Armateurs industriels privés de la Pêche.

Délégué des travailleurs

PEDRO GARCIA, Ana da Conceição, Mme, Secrétaire générale, Centrale générale des Syndicats indépendants et libres de l'Angola (CGSILA).

Conseiller technique et délégué suppléant

RODRIGUES DA COSTA, Mario de Jesus, M., Secrétaire, Relations internationales, Union nationales des Travailleurs angolais (UNTA-CS).

Conseillers techniques

RAUL, João, M., Chef, Département Juridique et d'Analyse économique, UNTA-CS.
JACINTO PEDRO GASPAR, Francisco, M., Secrétaire national exécutif, CGSILA.
OLINDO, José Augusto, M., Secrétaire national exécutif, CGSILA.
SOUSA GARCIA, M., Membre, Comité national, CGSILA.

Arabie saoudite   Saudi Arabia
Arabia Saudita

Government Delegates

ATTAR, Abdulwahab, Mr., Ambassador, Permanent Representative, Permanent Mission, Geneva.
AL-ZAMIL, Ahmad A. Al-Mansour, Mr., Deputy Minister for Labour, Ministry of Labour.

Advisers and substitute delegates

ALHADLAQ, Abdulaziz I.S., Mr., Director-General, International Organizations, Ministry of Labour.
ALANGARI, Khaled Hamad S., Mr., Vice Governor, General Organization for Technical Education and Vocational Training.
AL-TOOYMI, Suliman A.S., Mr., Director-General, Manpower Directorate, Ministry of Labour.
AL-AGAIL, Mohammed, Mr., First Secretary, Permanent Mission, Geneva.
ALYAHYA, Abdulaziz Abdullah M., Mr., Director-General, Marine Fisheries Department, Ministry of Agriculture.
ALYAHYA, Yahya N., Mr., Assistant Director-General, International Organizations, Ministry of Labour.
ALOMARI, Ahmed Mohammad, Mr., Specialist, International Organizations Directorate, Ministry of Labour.
ALNAHIT, Khalid M. Othman, Mr., Legal Adviser, International Organizations, Ministry of Labour.

Employers' Delegate

DAHLAN, Abdullah Sadiq, Mr., Businessman; Member, Governing Body of the ILO.

Adviser and substitute delegate

ALHUMAIDAN, Saleh A., Mr., Director-General, Dar Alyaum Press and Publication; Member, Chamber of Commerce, Eastern Region.

Workers' Delegate

ALGABGAB, Fahad Ismail S., Mr., Chairman, Workers' Committee, Saudi Aramco.

Adviser and substitute delegate

RADHWAN, Nedhal M. Rashied, Mr., Chairman, Workers' Committee, Saudi Telecom.

Advisers

ALRAMMAH, Kussay A., Mr., Chief, Employee Relations Services Department, Saudi Aramco.
AL-ROWAITIE, Abdullah S., Mr., General Manager, Personnel, Saudi Telecom.

Argentine   Argentina   Argentina

Ministro asistente a la Conferencia

TOMADA, Carlos Alfonso, Sr., Ministro de Trabajo, Empleo y Seguridad Social.

Delegados gubernamentales

RIAL, Noemí, Sra., Secretaria de Trabajo.
CHIARADIA, Alfredo Vicente, Sr., Embajador, Representante Permanente, Misión Permanente, Ginebra.

Consejeros técnicos y delegados suplentes

VERON, Héctor Oscar, Sr., Asesor, Ministerio de Trabajo, Empleo y Seguridad Social.
NOVICK, Marta, Sra., Asesora, Ministerio de Trabajo, Empleo y Seguridad Social.
ROSALES, Julio Guillermo, Sr., Asesor, Ministerio de Trabajo, Empleo y Seguridad Social.
CORRES, Gerardo Alfredo, Sr., Asesor, Ministerio de Trabajo, Empleo y Seguridad Social.
VARELA, Eduardo, Sr., Consejero, Misión Permanente, Ginebra.
CAMPORA, Pedro Daniel, Sr., Asesor, Ministerio de Trabajo, Empleo y Seguridad Social.
TITIRO, Jorge Pablo, Sr., Asesor, Ministerio de Trabajo, Empleo y Seguridad Social.

Otras personas que asisten a la Conferencia

UBALDINI, Saúl, Sr.
PRADES, Carlos Alfonso, Sr.
ROJAS, Héctor Américo, Sr.
VISCHI, Eduardo Alejandro, Sr.
VARELA, Sandra Elsa, Sra.
SEGUEL, José Ernesto, Sr.
MERCADO, Rogelio Andrés, Sr.
NIEVA, Alejandro, Sr., Diputado Nacional.
CAMAÑO, Graciela, Sra., Diputado Nacional.
FERRO, Horacio, Sr.
LATORRE, Norberto, Sr.

Delegado de los empleadores

ALVAREZ GAIANI, Alberto, Sr., Presidente, Unión Industrial Argentina (UIA).

Consejero técnico y delegado suplente

FUNES DE RIOJA, Daniel, Sr., UIA; Vice-Presidente Empleador, Consejo de Administracion de la OIT.

Consejeros técnicos

ETALA, Juan José, Sr., UIA.
HERMIDA MARTINEZ, Dario, Sr., UIA.
ALDAO-ZAPIOLA, Carlos, Sr., UIA.
MANTILLA, Enrique, Sr., UIA.

SPAGHI, Patricio, Sr., UIA.
SCHAER, Juan José, Sr., UIA.
BARBER SOLER, Patricio, Sr., UIA.
MELIAN, Carlos, Sr., Asociación de Bancos de Capital Argentino (ADEBA).

Personas designadas de conformidad con el artículo 2, párrafo 3, i)

CACCIABUE, Santiago, Sr., Cámara Argentina de Comercio.
CARREGA, Enrique, Sr., Unión de Empresas de Servicios.
AGUDO, Daniel, Sr., Asociación de Bancos Argentinos.
RODRIGUEZ MARENGO, Ricardo, Sr., Unión de Aseguradoras de Riesgos del Trabajo.
MATILLA, Francisco, Sr.

Delegado de los trabajadores

DAER, Rodolfo A., Sr., Secretario General, Confederación General del Trabajo (CGT).

Consejero técnico y delegado suplente

CAVALLIERI, Armando, Sr., Secretario de Relaciones Internacionales, CGT.

Consejeros técnicos

VENTURINI, Enrique, Sr., CGT, Movimiento de Trabajadores Argentinos (MTA).
BASTERIO, Ariel, Sr., Central de Trabajadores Argentinos (CTA).
PETRECCA, Domingo, Sr., CGT.
WEST OCAMPO, Carlos, Sr., CGT.
RODRIGUEZ, Andrés, Sr., CGT.
MEGUIRA, Horacio, Sr., CTA.
PIUMATO, Julio, Sr., CGT-MTA.
LESCANO, Oscar, Sr., CGT.
MARTINEZ, Gerardo, Sr., CGT.

Personas designadas de conformidad con el artículo 2, párrafo 3, i)

SUAREZ, Omar, Sr., CGT.
TOMASSONE, Alberto, Sra., CGT.
DÍAZ,, José Aníbal, Sr., CGT-MTA.
OLAVIAGA, Miguel Angel, Sr., CTA.
WEST OCAMPO, Federico, Sr., CGT.

Otras personas que asisten a la Conferencia

PUJADAS, Marta, Sra., CGT.
MASTROCOLA, Vicente, Sr., CGT.
ANGRIMAN, Horacio, Sr., CGT-MTA.
RINALDI, Juan Antonio, Sr., CGT.
BARRIONUEVO, Luis, Sr., CGT.
AMSLER, Alfredo, Sr.
DOMINGUEZ, Hugo, Sr.
PERES, Edgardo, Sr.

Arménie   Armenia   Armenia

Government Delegates

VARDANYAN, Aghvan, Mr., Minister of Labour and Social Affairs.
MNATSAKANIAN, Zohrab, Mr., Permanent Representative, Permanent Mission, Geneva.

Advisers

AYVAZYAN, Marta, Ms., First Secretary, Permanent Mission, Geneva.
PAPIKYAN, Armen, Mr., Second Secretary, Permanent Mission, Geneva.
MINASYAN, Levon, Mr., Third Secretary, Permanent Mission, Geneva.

Employers' Delegate

BARSEGHYAN, Vanoush, Mr., Representative, Union of Manufacturers and Businessmen of Armenia.

Workers' Delegate

HARUTYUNYAN, Martin, Mr., President, Confederation of Trade Unions.

Australie   Australia   Australia

Government Delegates

LLOYD, John, Mr., Deputy Secretary, Department of Employment and Workplace Relations.
LIPP, Linda, Ms., Assistant Secretary, Safety, Compensation and International Branch, Department of Employment and Workplace Relations.

Adviser and substitute delegate

SAWERS, Mark, Mr., First Secretary, Permanent Mission, Geneva.

Advisers

SMITH, Michael, Mr., Ambassador, Permanent Representative, Permanent Mission, Geneva.
GORELY, Amanda, Ms., Counsellor, Deputy Permanent Representative, Permanent Mission, Geneva.
PARKER, Vicki, Ms., Counsellor (Immigration), Permanent Mission, Geneva.
MATHESON, Scott, Mr., Assistant Secretary, Economic and Labour Market Analysis Branch, Department of Employment and Workplace Relations.
HART, Denis, Mr., Director, Occupatonal and Skills Analysis, Department of Employment and Workplace Relations.

Employers' Delegate

NOAKES, Bryan, Mr., Adviser, International Labour Affairs, Australian Chamber of Commerce and Industry (ACCI).

Adviser and substitute delegate

ANDERSON, Peter, Mr., Director, Workplace Policy, ACCI.

Other persons attending the Conference

BALZARY, Steve, Mr., Director, Employment and Training, ACCI.
GLYNN, Peter, Mr., Chief Executive, National Electrical and Communications Association.

Workers' Delegate

BURROW, Sharan, Ms., President, Australian Council of Trade Unions (ACTU).

Adviser

MATHESON, Alan, Mr., International Officer, ACTU.

Autriche Austria Austria

Minister attending the Conference

BARTENSTEIN, Martin, Mr., Federal Minister of Economic Affairs and Labour.

Persons accompanying the Minister

PETRITSCH, Wolfgang, Mr., Ambassador, Permanent Representative, Permanent Mission, Geneva.
ATZLER, Elke, Mrs., Deputy Permanent Representative for UN-Affairs, Permanent Mission, Geneva.
REICH-ROHRWIG, Maria, Mrs., Deputy Permanent Representative for WTO-Affairs, Permanent Mission, Geneva.
STEYRER, Christian, Mr., Federal Minister's Secretary.

Government Delegates

DEMBSHER, Iris, Mrs., Head, International Social Policy Unit, Federal Ministry of Economic Affairs and Labour.
ZWERENZ, Georg, Mr., International Social Policy Unit, Federal Ministry of Economic Affairs and Labour.

Advisers and substitute delegates

MARSCHANG, Elisabeth, Mrs., Counsellor, Permanent Mission, Geneva.
RADOSZTICS, Matthias, Mr., Social and Health Policy, Division VI.3, Federal Ministry of Foreign Affairs.

Advisers

KUTROWATZ, Heinz, Mr., International Labour Market Law Division, Federal Ministry of Economic Affairs and Labour.
LEIDWEIN, Alois, Mr., Attaché for Agricultural and Environmental Affairs, Permanent Mission, Geneva.

Employers' Delegate

TOMEK, Peter, Mr., Manager, Legal and Staff Division, Boehringer-Ingelheim Austria.

Advisers and substitute delegates

BRAUNER, Heinrich, Mr., Chief, Social Insurance and Worker's Protection Division, Federation of the Austrian Industry.
AUBAUER, Helwig, Mr., Social Policy and Health Division, Economic Chamber Austria.

Workers' Delegate

VERZETNITSCH, Friedrich, Mr., President, Austrian Confederation of Trade Unions.

Advisers and substitute delegates

NEUGEBAUER, Fritz, Mr., Vice-President, Austrian Confederation of Trade Unions.
BOEGNER, Johanna, Mrs., President of Work Council, Boehringer-Ingelheim Austria.

Advisers

DJALINOUS, Dinah, Mrs., Social Policy, Austrian Confederation of Trade Unions.
SAUER, Walter, Mr., International Unit, Austrian Confederation of Trade Unions.
VOITL, Harald, Mr., International Unit, Trade Union of Railroad Workers.
BEI, Neda, Mrs., Social Affairs Management, Chamber of Labour, Vienna.

Azerbaïdjan Azerbaijan Azerbaiyán

Minister attending the Conference

NAGHIYEV, Ali, Mr., Minister of Labour and Social Protection of Population.

Government Delegates

NAJAFOV, Murad, Mr., First Secretary, Permanent Mission, Geneva.
MARDALIYEV, Seymur, Mr., Attaché, Permanent Mission, Geneva.

Employers' Delegate

MAMMADOV, Alakbar, Mr., President, National Confederation of Entrepreneurs (Employers) Organizations.

Advisers

RZAYEVA, Gulshan, Mrs., Deputy Secretary-General, National Confederation of Entrepreneurs (Employers) Organizations.
TOSAYEV, Murteza, Mr., President, M. Tosun Ltd.
MUSTAFEYEV, Tajaddin, Mr., President, Saloghlu Company.
MAMMADOV, Nazim, Mr., President, Khatai Tajhizat Open Joint Stock Company.
MAMMADLI, Rovshan, Mr., President, Azeri Construction Company.

Workers' Delegate

MEHBALIYEV, Sattar, Mr., Chairman, Azerbaijan Trade Unions Confederation.

Adviser

ALKHASOV, Djavanshir, Mr., Deputy Chairman, Azerbaijan Trade Unions Confederation.

Person appointed in accordance with Article 2, paragraph 3(i)

MEHBALIYEVA, Boyukkhanim, Mrs., Senior Consultant, Azerbaijan Trade Unions Confederation.

Other person attending the Conference

MEHBALIYEVA, Lala, Ms., Secretary-Interpreter.

Bahamas

Minister attending the Conference

PEET, Vincent A., Mr., Minister of Labour and Immigration.

Government Delegates

BROWN, Harcourt, Mr., Director of Labour, Ministry of Labour and Immigration.
SYMONETTE, Donald, Mr., Under Secretary, Ministry of Labour and Immigration.

Employers' Delegate

ARNETT, T.V., Mr., Executive Director, Bahamas Employers Confederation.

Workers' Delegate

HAMILTON, Cleola, Ms., Trade Union Congress.

Adviser and substitute delegate

BAIN, Patrick, Mr., President, National Congress of Trade Unions.

Bahreïn   Bahrain   Bahrein

Minister attending the Conference

AL ALAWI, Majeed Bin Muhsen, Mr., Minister of Labour and Social Affairs.

Person accompanying the Minister

AL DOSERI, Subah Salem, Mr., Director, Office of the Minister, Ministry of Labour and Social Affairs.

Government Delegates

AL-FAIHANI, Saeed Mohamed, Mr., Ambassador, Permanent Representative, Permanent Mission, Geneva.
AL-KHALIFA, Abdulrahman Bin Abdulla, Mr., Undersecretary, Ministry of Labour and Social Affairs.

Advisers and substitute delegates

AL SHAHABI, Sadiq, Mr., Assistant Undersecretary for Labour, Ministry of Labour and Social Affairs.
AL BANNA, Ahmed, Mr., Director, Human Resources Development, Ministry of Labour and Social Affairs.
HUBAIL, Redha, Mr., Director, Administration and Financial Affairs, Ministry of Labour and Social Affairs.
AMIN MOHAMED, Farooq, Mr., Head, International Relations Section, Ministry of Labour and Social Affairs.
AL ARADI, Ali Abdulla, Mr., Third Secretary, Permanent Mission, Geneva.

Employers' Delegate

AL SALEH, Yousif Saleh, Mr., Vice President, Bahrain Chamber of Commerce and Industry.

Advisers and substitute delegates

SHRIF, Othman Mohamed, Mr., Member, Bahrain Chamber of Commerce and Industry.
AL KHOOR, Mondher, Mr., Researcher, Bahrain Chamber of Commerce and Industry.

Workers' Delegate

ABDULHUSAIN, Abdulghaffar, Mr., General Federation for Bahrain Workers' Trade Unions.

Advisers and substitute delegates

HUSSAIN, Abdulla, Mr., General Federation for Bahrain Workers' Trade Unions.
ABDULHUSSAIN, Ahmed, Mr., General Federation for Bahrain Workers' Trade Unions.

Bangladesh

Minister attending the Conference

AMAN, Amanullah, Mr., Minister of Labour and Employment.

Government Delegates

ALI, Toufiq, Mr., Ambassador, Permanent Representative, Permanent Mission, Geneva.
HOSSAIN, Kazi Imtiez, Mr., Counsellor, Permanent Mission, Geneva.

Advisers and substitute delegates

FATIMA, Rabab, Ms., Counsellor, Permanent Mission, Geneva.
AHMED, Saleh, Mr., Private Secretary to the Minister.
RAHMAN, Taufiqur, Mr., Second Secretary, Permanent Mission, Geneva.
ISLAM, Daniul, Mr., Second Secretary, Permanent Mission, Geneva.

Employers' Delegate

DOWLA, M. Anis Ud., Mr., President, Bangladesh Employers' Federation.

Adviser and substitute delegate

HYDER, C.K., Mr., Secretary-General, Bangladesh Employers' Federation.

Workers' Delegate

MD. ZAFRUL, HASSAN, Mr., General Secretary, Bangladesh Jatiotabadi Sramik Dal.

Barbade   Barbados   Barbados

Minister attending the Conference

EASTMOND, Rawle, Mr., Minister of Labour and Social Security.

Government Delegates

FARNUM, Shirley, Ms., Permanent Secretary, Ministry of Labour and Social Security.
CLARKE, C. Trevor, Mr., Ambassador, Permanent Representative, Permanent Mission, Geneva.

Advisers

LOWE, Edla, Mrs., Chief Labour Officer.
RUDDER, Simone, Ms., Deputy Permanent Representative, Permanent Mission, Geneva.
WILSON, Matthew, Mr., First Secretary, Permanent Mission, Geneva.

Employers' Delegate

HUSBANDS, Harcourt, Mr., Barbados Employers' Confederation.

Workers' Delegate

TROTMAN, Roy, Mr., Barbados Workers' Union; Worker Vice-Chairperson, Governing Body of the ILO.

Adviser

BRAITHWAITE, Gillian, Ms.

Belarus

Government Delegates

MORAVA, Antanina, Mrs., Minister of Labour and Social Protection.
STAROVOYTOV, Igor, Mr., Director, External Relations and Partnership Policy Department, Ministry of Labour and Social Protection.

Advisers and substitute delegates

MALEVICH, Vladimir, Mr., Deputy Permanent Representative, Permanent Mission, Geneva.
VASILEUSKAYA, Ina, Ms., First Secretary, Permanent Mission, Geneva.

Advisers

RUMAK, Alexander, Mr., Deputy Director, Financial Relations Branch, Principle Economic Department, Prime Minister's Office.
MOLCHAN, Andrey, Mr., Adviser, Permanent Mission, Geneva.

Employers' Delegate

CHACHKOV, Valeri, Mr., First Deputy Chairman - Director-General, Belarusian Confederation of Industrialists and Entrepreneurs.

Adviser and substitute delegate

KISEL, Edvard, Mr., Deputy Director-General - Deputy Director on Social and Labour Issues, Executive Board,

Belarusian Confederation of Industrialists and Entrepreneurs.

Adviser

TARASEVICH, Zhanna, Mrs., Executive Director, Belarusian Union of Entrepreneurs and Employers named after Professor Kunyavsky.

Workers' Delegate

KOZIK, Leonid, Mr., Chairman, Trade Unions Federation of Belarus.

Adviser and substitute delegate

MATULIS, Edvard, Mr., Deputy Chairman, Trade Unions Federation of Belarus.

Adviser

SEDINA, Elena, Mrs., Director, International Cooperation Section, Trade Unions Federation of Belarus.

Belgique   Belgium   Bélgica

Ministre assistant à la Conférence

VANDENBROUCKE, Frank, M., Ministre de l'Emploi.

Personnes accompagnant le Ministre

JADOT, Michel, M., Président, Comité de direction, Service public fédéral Emploi, Travail et Concertation sociale; Représentant, Conseil d'administration du BIT.
VANHERCKE, Bart, M., Conseiller "international", Cellule Stratégique du Ministre de l'Emploi.

Délégués gouvernementaux

D'HONDT, Greta, Mme, Membre, Chambre des Répresentants.
VANDAMME, François, M., Conseiller général, Chef, Division des Affaires internationales, Service public fédéral Emploi, Travail et Concertation sociale.

Conseiller technique et délégué suppléant

ADAM, Michel, M., Ambassadeur, Représentant permanent, Mission permanente, Genève.

Conseillers techniques

ZIKMUNDOVA, Jana, Mme, Conseillère, Mission permanente, Genève.
CROMPHOUT, Pieter, M., Conciliateur social adjoint, Direction générale Relations collectives de Travail, Service public fédéral Emploi, Travail et Concertation sociale.

CLOESEN, Joseph, M., Conseiller, Division des Affaires internationales, Service public fédéral Emploi, Travail et Concertation sociale.
BUYSSE, Bart, M., Conseiller adjoint, Direction générale Relations individuelles du Travail, Service public fédéral Emploi, Travail et Concertation sociale.
WINDEY, Pol, M., Président, Conseil national du Travail.
VAN PEER, Ria, Mme, Chargée de mission, Sociaal Economische Raad van Vlaanderen.
MAENAUT, David, M., Délégué du Gouvernement de la Flandre, Mission permanente, Genève.
VAN WIELE, Isabel, Mme, Adjointe du Directeur, Administration de l'Emploi de la Communauté flamande.
NAYER, Philippe, M., Délégué de la Communauté française de Belgique et de la Région wallonne, Mission permanente, Genève.
LOOP, Robert, M., Directeur, Formation, FOREM.
ROLAND, Dominik, M., Conseiller adjoint, Direction générale Emploi et Marché du Travail, Service public fédéral Emploi, Travail et Concertation sociale.
HAUTOT, Stephanie, Mme, Conseillère adjoint, Service des Relations multilatérales, Service public fédéral Emploi, Travail et Concertation sociale.
EVEN, Laure, Mme, Conseillère adjointe, Service des Relations multilatérales, Service public fédéral Emploi, Travail et Concertation sociale.
BUELENS, Theo, M., Expert administratif, Service des Relations multilatérales, Service public fédéral Emploi, Travail et Concertation sociale.

Délégué des employeurs

STORM, Marie-Louise, Mme, Conseillère sociale internationale, Agoria.

Conseiller technique et délégué suppléant

DA COSTA, Jacques, M., Directeur honoraire, Fédération pétrolière belge.

Conseillers techniques

DE KOSTER, Arnout, M., Directeur, Département social, Fédération des entreprises de Belgique.
VAN DAMME, Ivo, M., Directeur adjoint, Département social, Fédération des entreprises de Belgique.
CLAUS, Michèle, Mme, Conseiller, Département social, Fédération des entreprises de Belgique.
HELSMOORTEL, Frank, M., Human Resources Director, NV Philips.

Délégué des travailleurs

CORTEBEECK, Luc, M., Président, Confédération des Syndicats chrétiens.

Conseiller technique et délégué suppléant

MORDANT, André, M., Président a.i., Fédération générale du Travail de Belgique.

Conseillers techniques

HAAZE, Guy, M., Président, Centrale générale des Syndicats libéraux de Belgique.
DE LEEUW, Rudy, M., Secrétaire fédéral, Fédération générale du Travail de Belgique.
DEMOOR, Ann, Mme, Conseillère, Service d'Etude, Confédération des Syndicats chrétiens.
DEMUELENAERE, Donald, M., Conseiller général, Centrale générale des Syndicats libéraux de Belgique.
GEYBELS, René, M., Conseiller, Fédération générale du Travail de Belgique.
DESWERT, Gilbert, M., Chef, Service d'Etude, Confédération des Syndicats chrétiens.
DELCROIX, Jean-Paul, M., Directeur, Service d'Etudes, Fédération générale du Travail de Belgique.

Personnes désignées en conformité avec l'article 2, alinéa 3 i)

SERROYEN, Chris, M., Conseiller, Service d'Etude, Confédération des Syndicats chrétiens.
DEREYMAEKER, Jan, M., Chef, Service des Relations internationales, Confédération des Syndicats chrétiens.
CLAES, Michel, M., Responsable, Transport Maritime et Pêche, Confédération des Syndicats chrétiens-Transcom.
DUROI, Hilde, Mme, Attachée, Service d'Etudes, Fédération générale du Travail de Belgique.
MACOURS, Jean-François, M., Attaché, Service d'Etudes, Fédération générale du Travail de Belgique.

Autres personnes assistant à la Conférence

GRUSELIN, Paul, M., Coordinateur, Service des Relations internationales, Fédération générale du Travail de Belgique.
VICTOR, Ivan, M., Président, Union belge des Ouvriers du Transport, Fédération générale du Travail de Belgique.
VANMOERKERKE, Celien, Mme, Attachée, Service d'Etudes, Fédération générale du Travail de Belgique.
PALSTERMAN, Paul, M., Conseiller, Service d'étude, Confédération des Syndicats chrétiens.

Belize   Belize   Belice

Government Delegates

HUNT, Alicia, Ms., Chargée d'Affaires.
TAMASKO, Maté, Mr.

Benin

Ministre assistant à la Conférence

AROUNA, Boubacar, M., Ministre de la Fonction publique, du Travail et de la Réforme administrative.

Personnes accompagnant le Ministre

AMEHOU, Samuel, M., Ambassadeur, Représentant permanent, Mission permanente, Genève.
ADJANONHOUN, Rosemonde, Mme, Mission permanente, Genève.

Délégués gouvernementaux

ONI, Jules, M., M., Directeur général du Travail.
MASSESSI, Adrien, M., Directeur des Normes du Travail.

Conseiller technique et délégué suppléant

ADJINDA, Prosper, M., Secrétariat général du Gouvernement.

Conseillers techniques

AKIBOU, Naïm, M., Premier Conseiller, Mission permanente, Genève.
LAOUROU, Eloi, M., Mission permanente, Genève.
AGUESSY, Colette, Mme, Conseiller technique au Travail, Ministère de la Fonction publique, du Travail et de la Réforme administrative.
HOUESSOU, René, M., Directeur général adjoint, Caisse nationale de Sécurité sociale.
KEMOKO, Alassane, M., Directeur technique, Caisse nationale de Sécurité sociale.

Délégué des employeurs

GLELE, Lucien, M., Président, Conseil national du Patronat du Bénin.

Conseiller technique et délégué suppléant

AHOUDJI, Alexandra, Mme, Trésorière générale adjointe, Conseil national du Patronat du Bénin.

Délégué des travailleurs

ATTIGBE, Guillaume, M., Secrétaire général, Confédération des Syndicats autonomes du Bénin (CSA-Bénin).

Conseiller technique et délégué suppléant

AZOUA, K. Gaston, M., Secrétaire général, Confédération des Syndicats des Travailleurs du Bénin (CSTB).

Conseillers techniques

AGOSSOU, Sourou Jean, M., Secrétaire général, Centrale des Syndicats unis du Bénin.
ASSOGBA, Nicodème, M., Secrétaire général, Union nationale des Syndicats de Travailleurs du Bénin.
GLELE, Kakaï Georges, M., Secrétaire général, Confédération des Organisations Syndicales indépendantes.
HOUNSINOU, Gratien, M., Secrétaire général, Centrale des Syndicats des Secteurs privé et informel du Bénin.

TODJINOU, D. Pascal, M., Secrétaire général, Confédération générale des Travailleurs du Bénin.
ASSOGBA, Innocent, M., CSTB.
OGBONI, Antoinette, Mme, Représentante des Femmes travailleuses, Confédération générale des Travailleurs du Bénin.

Bolivie   Bolivia   Bolivia

Ministro asistente a la Conferencia

FERNÁNDEZ FAJALDE, Luis, Sr., Ministro de Trabajo.

Delegados gubernamentales

MOSCOSO BLANCO, Alvaro, Sr., Embajador, Representante Permanente, Misión Permanente, Ginebra.
RODRÍGUEZ SAN MARTÍN, Gualberto, Sr., Ministro Consejero, Misión Permanente, Ginebra.

Consejeros técnicos

POGGI BORDA, Gino, Sr., Consejero.
BAPTISTA, Rosario, Sra., Asesora responsable de Relaciones Internacionales, Ministerio de Trabajo.
NAVARRO, Angélica, Sra., Segundo Secretario, Misión Permanente, Ginebra.

Delegado de los empleadores

ESPAÑA-SMITH, Raúl, Sr., Presidente, Comisión de Asuntos Jurídicos y Sociales, Confederación de Empresarios Privados de Bolivia.

Delegado de los trabajadores

SOLARES, Jaime, Sr., Secretario General, Central Obrera Boliviana.

Bosnie-Herzégovine
Bosnia and Herzegovina
Bosnia y Herzegovina

Minister attending the Conference

HALILOVIC, Safet, Mr., Minister of Civil Affairs.

Government Delegates

VUKAŠINOVIC, Milos, Mr., Ambassador, Permanent Representative, Permanent Mission, Geneva.
GAGULIC, Drazen, Mr., Counsellor, Permanent Mission, Geneva.

Adviser and substitute delegate

KREMENOVIC-KUSMUK, Dragana, Mrs., First Secretary, Permanent Mission, Geneva.

Employers' Delegate

MILJEVIC, Damir, Mr., Employers Union of the Republika Srpska.

Workers' Delegate

BIBER, Edhem, Mr., Confederation of Independent Trade Unions from Bosnia and Herzegovina (Federation of Bosnia and Herzegovina).

Botswana

Minister attending the Conference

MOGAMI, Thebe D., Mr., Minister of Labour and Home Affairs.

Government Delegates

MOJAFI, Claude A., Mr., Commissioner of Labour, Department of Labour and Social Security.
SEEMULE, Sissy V., Ms., Principal Industrial Relations Office.

Advisers and substitute delegates

NTWAAGAE, C.T., Mr., Ambassador, Permanent Representative, Permanent Mission, Geneva.
LEKUNI, T.M., Mr., Minister Counsellor, Permanent Mission, Geneva.

Advisers

DE VILLIERS, David J., Mr., Judge, Industrial Court.
TEBOGO-MARUPING, Goemekgabo L., Mr., Registrar, Industrial Court.
MMOPELWA, Trevor, Mr., Principal Scientific Officer.
MODUNGWA, Abel, Mr., Chief Executive Officer, Botswana Training Authority.
PITSO, Gobe, Mr., First Secretary (Political), Permanent Mission, Geneva.
MOGOTSI, Tshepo, Mr., Second Secretary, Permanent Mission, Geneva.

Employers' Delegate

DEWAH, Elias M., Mr., Executive Director, Botswana Confederation of Commerce, Industry and Manpower (BOCCIM).

Workers' Delegate

BAIPIDI, Ronald D., Mr., President, Botswana Federation of Trade Unions.

Brésil   Brazil   Brasil

Minister attending the Conference

BERZOINI, Ricardo, Mr., Ministry of Labour and Employment.

Persons accompanying the Minister

DE SEIXAS CORRÊA, Luiz Felipe, Mr., Ambassador, Permanent Representative, Permanent Mission, Geneva.

DA ROCHA PARANHOS, Carlos Antonio, Mr., Ambassador, Deputy Permanent Representative, Permanent Mission, Geneva.

Government Delegates

BRANCO FREITAS, Nilton Benedito, Mr., Special Adviser to the Minister of Labour and Employment.

SALDANHA, Pedro, Mr., Second Secretary, Permanent Mission, Geneva.

Advisers and substitute delegates

BIONDI LIMA, Antonio Almerico, Mr., Director, Professional Qualification Department, Public Employment Policies Secretary, Ministry of Labour and Employment.

TEIXEIRA ROMANO PEREIRA, Hebe, Ms., General Coordinator for Migrations, Ministry of Labour and Employment.

NOVAES MONIZ DE ARAGAO, Jose Roberto, Mr., Deputy Coordinator, Unidade Especial de Fiscalização do Trabalho Portuario e Aquaviario, Ministry of Labour and Employment.

PAIXAO PARDO, Sergio, Mr., Chief, International Organizations Division, International Relations, Ministry of Labour and Employment.

MARTINES BARGAS, Oswaldo, Mr., Secretary, Labour Relations, Ministry of Labour and Employment.

DO NASCIMENTO PEDRO, Antonio Carlos, Mr., Minister Counsellor, Permanent Mission, Geneva.

DE CARVALHO NETO, Paulino Franco, Mr., First Secretary, Permanent Mission, Geneva.

DE BORBA MACIEL, Cláudia, Ms., Second Secretary, Permanent Mission, Geneva.

BARBOSA, Cláudia, Ms., Second Secretary, Permanent Mission, Geneva.

GONÇALVES DE MELO, Regiane, Ms., Third Secretary, Permanent Mission, Geneva.

Other persons attending the Conference

ABDALA, Vantuil, Mr., Minister, President, High Labour Court.

FONTES DE FARIA FERNANDES, Jose Simpliciano, Mr.

PEREIRA, Emmanoel, Mr.

SIMON, Sandra Lia, Ms., General Attorney for Labour.

ALVES PEREIRA FILHO, Jose, Mr., Deputy General Attorney for Labour.

CURADO FLEURY, Ronaldo, Mr., Regional Labour Attorney.

CORDÃO, Francisco Aparecido, Mr., Counsellor, Camara de Educação Básica, National Education Council, Ministry of Education.

MARQUES FERREIRA, Getúlio, Mr., Director, Technological and Professional Training, Ministry of Labour and Employment.

ZIMMERMANN, Tarcisio, Mr., Member of Parliament.

BRAGA, Lúcia, Ms., Member of Parliament.

LERÉIA, Carlos Alberto, Mr., Member of Parliament.

CARDIAS, Milton, Mr., Member of Parliament.

PONTES, Ann, Ms., Member of Parliament.

ALMEIDA, Daniel, Mr., Member of Parliament.

CORRÊA, Pedro, Mr., Member of Parliament.

RIQUE, Ricardo, Mr., Member of Parliament.

MASIERO, Juraci, Mr., Director of Human Resources, Banco do Brasil.

Employers' Delegate

FATTORI COSTA, Thiers, Mr., Honorary President, Confederação Nacional do Transporte (CNT).

Advisers and substitute delegates

SFOGGIA, Ubajara, Mr., Legal Adviser, CNT.

LIMA GODOY, Dagoberto, Mr., Vice-President, Confederação Nacional da Industria (CNI); President, Labour Relations and Social Development Council, CNI.

BITTENCOURT DA SILVA, Luiz Gastão, Mr., First Secretary, Confederação Nacional do Comércio (CNC).

SABBADINI, Flávio Roberto, Mr., Director, Vice-President, CNC.

MEDALHA TRIGUEIROS, Márcio, Mr., Special Secretary, SENAC.

ASSIS BENEVIDES GADELHA, Francisco, Mr., Vice-President, CNI.

Advisers

CERQUEIRA COIMBRA DUQUE, Patricia, Ms., Adviser, Trade Unions Matters, CNC.

RONDON LINHARES, Lucia Maria, Ms., CNI.

OLIVEIRA SANTOS, Antônio, Mr., President, CNC.

OLIVEIRA RODRIQUES, Renato, Mr., Consultant, Trade Union Matters, CNC.

Persons appointed in accordance with Article 2, paragraph 3(i)

SIUFFO PEREIRA, Luis Gil, Mr., Director, Treasurer, CNC.

OLIVEIRA SCHMIDT, Lenoura, Ms., Chief, President's Cabinet, CNC.

Workers' Delegate

VACCARI NETO, João, Mr., Secretary, International Relations, Central Unica de Trabalhadores (CUT).

Advisers and substitute delegates

CRIVELLI, Ericson, Mr., Legal Adviser, CUT.
FERREIRA DO PRADO, Lourenço, Mr., Secretary, International Relations, Confederação Geral dos Trabalhadores (CGT).
RODRIGUES LEITE PENTEADO, Luis, Mr., Director, Confederação Nacional dos Trabalhadores em Transportes Aquaviário e Aereo na Pesca e nos Portos (CONTTMAF).
TRINDADE, Valclécia de Jesus, Ms., Director, Força Sindical (FS).
SOUZA, Wagner Jose, Mr., Director, International Relations, Social Democracia Sindical (SDS).
SOUZA BENEDETTI, Arnaldo, Mr., Central Autonoma dos Trabalhadores (CAT).
PIMENTEL, Maria Lúcia, Ms., Director, International Relations, Central Geral dos Trabalhadores do Brasil (CGTB).

Persons appointed in accordance with Article 2, paragraph 3(i)

CORTIZO, Antônio Thaumaturgo, Mr., Vice-President, CGT.
DE BARROS, Valdir Vicente, Mr., Secretary for Finance, CGT.
OLIVEIRA ROCHA SOUZA, Leonice, Ms., Director, Informal Work, Self-Employment and Micro Enterprises, SDS.

Bulgarie   Bulgaria   Bulgaria

Minister attending the Conference

CHRISTOVA, Christina, Mrs., Minister of Labour and Social Policy.

Government Delegates

APOSTOLOV, Valery, Mr., Deputy Minister of Labour and Social Policy.
TZANTCHEV, Dimiter, Mr., Ambassador, Permanent Representative, Permanent Mission, Geneva.

Advisers and substitute delegates

EVTIMOV, Alexander, Mr., Director, European Integration and International Relations, Ministry of Labour and Social Policy.
ANDREEV, Konstantin, Mr., Director, Human Rights and International Humanitarian Organizations, Ministry of Foreign Affairs.

Advisers

TCHOLASHKA, Assia, Mrs., Head of Unit, International Relations, Ministry of Labour and Social Policy.
MEHANDJIYSKA, Deana, Mrs., Attaché, Permanent Mission, Geneva.

NAYDENOV, Nikolay, Mr., Head of Section, International Organizations, Ministry of Labour and Social Policy.
MLADENOV, Branimir, Mr., Head, International Humanitarian Organizations Department, Ministry of Foreign Affairs.
GARKOV, Philipe, Mr., Expert, International Humanitarian Organizations Department, Ministry of Foreign Affairs.

Employers' Delegate

DECHEV, Teodor, Mr., Vice-President, Union for Private Economic Enterprises.

Advisers and substitute delegates

SIMEONOV, Tzvetan, Mr., Vice-President, Bulgarian Chamber of Commerce and Industry.
SEMOV, Atanas, Mr., Vice-Chairman, Consultative Council of Union for Private Economic Enterprises.
BEHAR, Nansen, Mr., Chairman, Consultative Council of Union for Private Enterprises.
BOYADJIEV, Vasko, Mr., Vice-President, Bulgarian Union for Private Entrepreneurs.

Advisers

DANEV, Bojidar, Mr., President, Bulgarian Industrial Association.
GEORGIEVA, Magdalena, Mrs., Lawyer, Bulgarian Chamber of Commerce and Industry.
VASSILEV, Vassil, Mr., President, Employers' Union.

Workers' Delegate

HRISTOV, Jeliazko, Mr., President, Confederation of Independent Trade Unions in Bulgaria.

Adviser and substitute delegate

MANOLOV, Dimitar, Mr., Vice-President, Confederation of Labour - Podkrepa.

Advisers

NANKOV, Plamen, Mr., Executive Secretary, Confederation of Independent Trade Unions in Bulgaria.
MIHAILOV, Daniel, Mr., Confederation of Labour - Podkrepa.

Burkina Faso

Ministre assistant à la Conférence

TOU, Alain Ludovic, M., Ministre du Travail, de l'Emploi et de la Jeunesse.

Délégués gouvernementaux

OUATTARA, Alimata, Mme, Directrice générale du Travail et de la Sécurité Sociale.
SEYNOU, Saïdou, M., Directeur de la Sécurité sociale et des Mutualités.

Conseillers techniques

LEFEBVRE, Colette, Mme, Chef, Service des Normes et des Relations Internationales.
ZAMPALEGRE, Idrissa, M., Directeur général, Caisse nationale de Sécurité sociale.
TRAORE, Adama, M., Directeur général, Office national de la Promotion de l'Emploi.
SAWADOGO, Salifou, M., Directeur, Fonds d'Appui au Secteur informel.
ZAIDA, Dieudonné, M., Directeur, Fonds d'Appui au Secteur informel.
ZEBA, Maurice, M., Caisse nationale de la Sécurité sociale.
ZOMBRE, Léontine, Mme, Présidente, Tribunal du Travail.
SOUROU, Awa, Mme, Directrice, Fonds d'Appui à la Formation Professionnelle.
NITIEMA, Jean-Paul, M., Coordonnateur, Programme national d'Appui à la Réinsertion des Travailleur déflatés.
KABORE, Claire Marie, Mme, Direction des Organisations internationales, Ministère des Affaires étrangères et de la Coopération régionale.
KARFO, Kapouné, M., Directeur général, Office de Santé des Travailleurs.

Délégué des employeurs

NACOULMA, Birahima, M., 1er Vice-Président, Conseil national du Patronat Burkinabè.

Conseillers techniques

DIAWARA, Lassiné, M., 4ème Vice-président, Conseil national du Patronat Burkinabè.
KABORE, Belko Pierre, M., Secrétaire Exécutif, Conseil national du Patronat Burkinabè.

Délégué des travailleurs

NAMA, Mamadou, M., Secrétaire général, Union syndicale des Travailleurs du Burkina.

Conseillers techniques

SAGNON, Tolé, M., Secrétaire général, Confédération générale des Travailleurs du Burkina.
OUEDRAOGO, Laurent, M., Secrétaire général, Confédération nationale des Travailleurs du Burkina.

Burundi

Ministre assistant à la Conférence

NDITABIRIYE, Dismas, M., Ministre du Travail et de la Sécurité sociale.

Délégués gouvernementaux

KANKINDI, Régine, Mme, Conseillère du Ministre.
NKUNDWANABAKE, Nestor, M., Premier Conseiller, Mission permanente, Genève.

Délégué des employeurs

BUDABUDA, Isaac, M., Président, Centrale syndicale des Employeurs du Burundi (CESEBU).

Conseiller technique

NZISABIRA, Gaspard, M., Secrétaire exécutif, Association des Employeurs du Burundi.

Délégué des travailleurs

HAJAYANDI, Pierre Claver, M., Président, Confédération des syndicats du Burundi (COSYBU).

Conseiller technique

RUVARI, Mathias, M., Secrétaire général, Confédération des Syndicats libres du Burundi (CSB).

Cambodge   Cambodia
Camboya

Minister attending the Conference

SAY, Siphonn, Mr., Under Secretary of State, Ministry of Social Affairs, Labour, Vocational Training and Youth Rehabilitation.

Government Delegates

THACH, Sem, Mr., Advisor, Ministry of Social Affairs, Labour, Vocational Training and Youth Rehabilitation.
HOU, Vudthy, Mr., Deputy Director-General for Labour and Vocational Training.

Adviser

PHAN, Peuv, Mr., Second Secretary, Permanent Mission, Geneva.

Employers' Delegate

VAN, Sou Ieng, Mr., Chairman, Garment Manufacturers Association in Cambodia (GMAC); Chairman,

Cambodia Federation of Employers and Business Association (CAMFEBA).

Workers' Delegate

CHUON, Mom Thol, Mr., President, Cambodia Confederation of Trade Unions (CCTU).

Advisers

SOM, Aun, Mr., President, Cambodia Labour Union Federation (CLUF).
NAY, Sok Veasna, Mr., President, Federal Union of Solidarity (FUS).
HENG, Bun Chhun, Mr., President, Cambodia Industrial Food Union Federation (CIFUF).
KONG, Ouk, Mr., Adviser, CLUF.
THOUK, Sok Thach, Ms., Adviser, CLUF.

Cameroun   Cameroon   Camerún

Ministre assistant à la Conférence

NKILI, Robert, M., Ministre de l'Emploi, du Travail et de la Prevoyance sociale.

Personne accompagnant le Ministre

NDJEMBA ENDEZOUMOU, Jean Simplice, M., Ambassadeur, Représentant permanent, Mission permanente, Genève.

Délégués gouvernementaux

BODOU, Pierre, M., Conseiller technique, Service du Premier Ministre.
NGANTCHA, Francis, M., Ministre Conseiller, DELECAM, Genève.

Conseillers techniques

NOAH MANGA, Léon, M., Directeur du Travail.
MOUTE A BIDIAS, Camille, M., Directeur général, Fonds national de l'Emploi.
MVENG EVINA, Etienne, M., Sous-directeur de la Main-d'oeuvre.
BELL, Louis Mathias, M., Sous-directeur, Réglementation et de la Coopération internationale.
NJIKI, Jeanine, Mme, Chef de Service, Santé et Sécurité du Travail.
KALATI LOBE, Marie Cathérine, Mme, Assistant, Chargé d'Etudes.

Délégué des employeurs

AYANGMA, Protais, M., Vice-Président, GICAM.

Conseiller technique

ABEGA, Martin, M., Secrétaire-général, GICAM.

Délégué des travailleurs

NTONE DIBOTI, Maximilien, M., Président, CSTC.

Conseillers techniques

MOUSSOLE, Flaubert, M., Président, USLC.
NDZANA OLONGO, Gilbert, M., Secrétaire-général, CSIC.

Canada

Government Delegates
Délégués gouvernementaux

ROBINSON, Debra, Ms., Director, International Labour Affairs, Labour Program, Human Resources Development Canada.
MACPHEE, Donald, Mr., Counsellor and Consul, Permanent Mission, Geneva.

Advisers and substitute delegates
Conseillers techniques et délégués suppléants

MEYER, Paul, Mr., Alternate Permanent Representative, Permanent Representative for Disarmament, Permanent Mission, Geneva.
MCKENNIREY, John, Mr., Assistant Deputy Minister of Labour; Head, Federal Mediation and Conciliation Service, Human Resources and Skills Development Canada.

Advisers
Conseillers techniques

EWART-JOHNSON, Shelley, Ms., Deputy Minister, Human Resources and Employment, Government of Alberta.
O'NEILL, Joseph, Mr., Deputy Minister of Labour, Government of Newfoundland and Labrador.
FERGUSON, Ian, Mr., Minister, Deputy Permanent Representative, Permanent Mission, Geneva.
BANKS, Kevin, Mr., Director, Inter-American Labour Cooperation, Human Resources and Skills Development Canada.
NASSIF, Saïd, Mr., Manager, Personnel Safety, Marine Occupational Health and Safety, Transport Canada.
L'HEUREUX, Linda, Ms., Deputy Director, International Labour Affairs, Human Resources and Skills Development Canada.
DUPONT, Denis, Mr., Analyste principal en matières des politiques, Affaires Internationales du Travail, Ressources humaines et Développement des compétences Canada.
HEYDER, Ella, Ms., Senior Policy Analyst, International Labour Affairs, Human Resources and Skills Development Canada.
HOANG, Lan, Mrs., Conseillère, Agences spécialisées de l'ONU, Ministère des Affaires étrangères et du Commerce international.

PIERRE-JÉROME, Frantz, Mr., Analyste principal en matières des politiques, Coopération inter-Américaine dans le domaine du Travail, Ressources humaines et Développement des compétences Canada.

TUDAKOVIC, Emina, Ms., Senior Policy Adviser, International Policy Coordination, Citizenship and Immigration Canada.

FETZ, Thomas, Mr., Second Secretary, Permanent Mission, Geneva.

Representative of a State or Province
Représentant d'un Etat ou province

BACHAND, Patrice, Mr., Conseiller, Affaires internationales, Ministère des Relations internationales du Québec.

Employers' Delegate
Délégué des employeurs

FINLAY, Andrew J., Mr., Vice-President and Assistant General Counsel, Employee Relations and Employment Law Group, Scotiabank; Chairperson, Canadian Employers' Council.

Adviser and substitute delegate
Conseiller technique et délégué suppléant

WAJDA, Paul, Mr., Director, Learning and Development, Canadian Pacific Railways.

Advisers
Conseillers techniques

COON, Kevin, Mr., International Partner, Baker and McKenzie, Barristers and Solicitors.

REGENBOGEN, Sonia, Mrs., Heenan Blaikie, Barristers and Solicitors.

KELLY, Dan, Mr., Vice-President, Western Canada, Canadian Federation of Independent Business (CFIB).

Workers' Delegate
Délégué des travailleurs

BYERS, Barbara, Ms., Vice-President, Canadian Labour Congress.

Adviser and substitute delegate
Conseiller technique et délégué suppléant

BENEDICT, Stephen, Mr., Director, International Department, Canadian Labour Congress.

Advisers
Conseillers techniques

GEORGETTI, Kenneth, Mr., President, Canadian Labour Congress.

ANSTEY, Reg, Mr., President, Newfoundland and Labrador Federation of Labour.

ONYALO, David, Mr., Director, Anti-Racism and Human Rights, Canadian Labour Congress.

LE BRASSEUR, Lola, Mrs., Conseillère, Fédération des travailleurs et travailleuses du Québec.

ROY, Josée, Mrs., Adjoint, Comité exécutive, Confédération des syndicats nationaux.

Other person attending the Conference
Autre personne assistant à la Conférence

CARON, Laurier, Mr., Centrale des syndicats du Québec, CSQ.

Cap-Vert
Cape Verde   Cabo Verde

Ministre assistant à la Conférence

MONTEIRO, Sidonio Fontes Lima, M., Ministre du Travail et de la Solidarité.

Personnes accompagnant le Ministre

ALVES LOPES, António Pedro, M., Chargé d'affaires a.i., Mission permanente, Genève.

NEVES, António Pereira, M., Président, Institut national de Prévoyance sociale.

ALVES, Joanilda Lúcia Silva, Mme, Directrice, Cabinet du Ministre.

Délégués gouvernementaux

SEMEDO, Horácio Moreira, M., Directeur général du Travail, Ministère du Travail et de la Solidarité.

DE CARVALHO, Mafaldo de Jesus Varela, M., Technicien supérieur, Direction générale du Travail, Ministère du Travail et de la Solidarité.

Délégué des employeurs

ÉVORA, Ronise Carla Pires, Mme, Membre, Association commerciale, industrielle et agricole de Barlavento.

Délégué des travailleurs

SILVA, Julio Ascenção, M., Secrétaire général, Union nationale des Travailleurs du Cap Vert-Centrale syndicale (UNTC-CS).

République centrafricaine
Central African Republic
República Centroafricana

Ministre assistant à la Conférence

BOTI, Jacques, M., Ministre de la Fonction publique, du Travail, de la Sécurité sociale et de l'Insertion professionnelle.

Délégués gouvernementaux

ZITONGO-MADENGA, Odile, Mme, Chargée de mission en matière de Travail.
YANGO-SINDO, Alexandre-Désiré, M., Directeur général du Travail.

Conseillers techniques et délégués suppléants

NGREBADA, Firmin, M., Chargé de mission en matière du Travail et de l'Emploi à la Primature.
TOMONKOUA, François, M., Directeur-général, Agence centrafricaine pour la Formation professionnelle et l'Emploi (ACFPE).
DJINDOT, Jean, M., Chargé de mission en matière de Prévoyance sociale.
MATENDAKAMA-ONDOMA, Nicole, Mme, Directrice générale par intérim, Office centrafricain de Sécurité sociale (OCSS).
MBATOUBÉ, Luther, M., Inspecteur principal de Sécurité, Membre de l'Inspection centrale, OCSS.

Délégué des employeurs

ZAGUI, Faustin, M., Président de l'Union nationale du Patronat centrafricain (UNPC).

Délégué des travailleurs

SONNY-COLÉ, Thèophile, M., Secrétaire général, Union syndicale des Travailleurs de Centrafrique (USTC).

Chili   Chile   Chile

Ministro asistente a la Conferencia

SOLARI SAAVEDRA, Ricardo, Sr., Ministro del Trabajo y Previsión Social.

Delegados gubernamentales

MARTABIT SCAFF, Juan Antonio, Sr., Embajador, Representante permanente, Misión Permanente, Ginebra.
LJUBETIC GODOY, Yerko, Sr., Subsecretario del Trabajo.

Consejeros técnicos y delegados suplentes

SAEZ CARLIER, Luis Felipe, Sr., Jefe de Gabinete, Subsecretario de Trabajo.
VELOZO ALCAIDE, Pablo, Sr., Jefe, Departamento de Relaciones Internacionales, Ministerio del Trabajo.
DONAIRE GAETE, Claudia, Sra., Asesora, Subsecretario del Trabajo.
DEL PICÓ RUBIO, Bernardo, Sr., Segundo Secretario, Misión Permanente, Ginebra.
BARRERA, Manuel, Sr., Agregado Laboral, Misión Permanente, Ginebra.

Otras personas que asisten a la Conferencia

VIDAL LÁZARO, Ximena, Sra., Diputada, Presidente, Comisión de Trabajo y Seguridad Social, Cámara de Diputados de Chile.
REBOLLEDO CODDOU, Mario, Sr., Abogado, Ayudante, Comisión de Trabajo y Seguridad Social, Cámara de Diputados de Chile.
LOYOLA OSORIO, Eduardo, Sr., Gerente General, Consejo Minero.
ÁLVAREZ FAÚNDEZ, Jorge, Sr., Subgerente Corporativo de Relaciones Laborales.
MORALES PUELMA, Roberto, Sr., Asesor Jurídico Laboral, Gerencia Corporativa de Relaciones Laborales y Calidad de Vida.

Delegado de los empleadores

ARTHUR ERRÁZURIZ, Guillermo, Sr., Abogado, Confederación de la Producción y del Comercio.

Consejeros técnicos

BRUNA VARGAS, Augusto, Sr., Abogado, Confederación de la Producción y del Comercio.
PIZARRO MAASS, Alvaro, Sr., Abogado, Confederación de la Producción y del Comercio.
HUMERES NOGUER, Héctor, Sr., Abogado, Confederación de la Producción y del Comercio.
LETURIA INFANTE, Francisco Javier, Sr., Abogado, Confederación de la Producción y del Comercio.

Delegado de los trabajadores

MARTÍNEZ MOLINA, Arturo, Sr., Central Unitaria de Trabajadores (CUT).

Consejeros técnicos

ORTIZ ARCOS, José, Sr., CUT.
GONZÁLEZ CASTILLO, Jorge, Sr., CUT.
ULLOA ZAMBRANO, Víctor, Sr., CUT.
CONSALES CARVAJAL, Jorge, Sr., CUT.
MUÑOZ CÁCERES, Ana, Sra., CUT.
MOLLO VARGAS, Jorge, Sr., CUT.
FERNÁNDEZ VALDÉS, Héctor, Sr., CUT.
ROBLES SAAVEDRA, Pedro, Sr., Central Autónoma de Trabajadores (CAT).

Personas designadas de conformidad con el artículo 2, párrafo 3, i)

LEMAITRE SALINAS, Guillermo, Sr., CUT.
ESPINOZA CONCHA, Raimundo, Sr., CUT.
ALLAN DÍAZ, Hugo, Sr., CUT.
BRICKLE ROESTAL, Patricio, Sr., CUT.
FRITZ CHACÓN, Freddy, Sr., CUT.

Otras personas que asisten a la Conferencia

BRAVO MUÑOZ, Manuel, Sr., CUT.
LABBÉ ARANEDA, Mario, Sr., Secretario, Abogado, Comisión Trabajo y Previsión Social, Senado.

Chine   China   China

Government Delegates

WANG, Dongjin, Mr., Vice Minister, Ministry of Labour and Social Security.
SHA, Zukang, Mr., Permanent Representative, Permanent Mission, Geneva.

Advisers and substitute delegates

LIU, Xu, Mr., Director-General, Department of International Cooperation, Ministry of Labour and Social Security.
ZHANG, Guoqing, Mr., Counsellor, Permanent Mission, Geneva.

Advisers

ZHANG, Yali, Mrs., Deputy Director-General, Department of International Cooperation, Ministry of Labour and Social Security.
WANG, Yadong, Mr., Deputy Director-General, Department of Training and Employment, Ministry of Labour and Social Security.
GUANG, Jinghe, Mrs., Director, Department of International Cooperation, Ministry of Labour and Social Security.
RUI, Lixin, Mr., Director, Department of Legal Affairs, Ministry of Labour and Social Security.
ZHANG, Lu, Mr., Director, Department of International Cooperation, Ministry of Labour and Social Security.
LIU, Yutong, Mr., Deputy Director, Department of International Cooperation, Ministry of Labour and Social Security.
CHEN, Feng, Mr., Official, Office of General Affairs, Ministry of Labour and Social Security.
HAN, Jixiu, Ms., Official, International Department, Ministry of Foreign Affairs.
LIU, Yang, Mr., Official, Department of Social Security, Ministry of Finance.
HUANG, Dongxian, Mr., Deputy Director, Department of Fishery, Ministry of Agriculture.
DUAN, Dongwen, Mr., First Secretary, Permanent Mission, Geneva.
DO PANG, Wai Yee, Mrs., Assistant Commissioner for Labour, Labour Department Hong Kong Special Administrative Region.
NG, Kwok Keung Byron, Mr., Senior Labour Officer, Labour Department, Hong Kong Special Administrative Region.
CHENG CHAN, Oi Lin Mary, Ms., Labour Officer, Labour Department, Hong Kong Special Administrative Region.
LOU, Soi Peng, Ms., Chief, Research and Organization Department, Labour and Employment Affaire Bureau, Macao Special Administrative Region.
HUNG, Ling Biu, Mr., Chief, Vocational Training Center, Labour and Employment Affairs Bureau, Macao Special Administrative Region.

Employers' Delegate

CHEN, Lantong, Mr., Vice President, China Enterprise Confederation.

Adviser and substitute delegate

CHENG, Ying, Mrs., Deputy Head of the Board, China Enterprise Confederation.

Advisers

LIU, Peng, Mr., Director General, Department of Employer Affairs, China Enterprise Confederation.
LIU, Hansong, Ms., Director, Department of Employer Affairs, China Enterprise Confederation.
HO, Sai Chu, Mr., Employer Representative, Labour Advisory Board, Hong Kong Special Administrative Region.
YIN, Tek Shing, Paul, Mr., Employer Representative, Labour Advisory Board, Hong Kong Special Administrative Region.
VONG, Kok Seng, Mr., Employer Representative, Permanent Council of Macao Social Coordination.

Workers' Delegate

XU, Zhenhuan, Mr., Vice President, All-China Federation of Trade Unions.

Adviser and substitute delegate

FAN, Jiying, Mrs., Director General, International Department, All-China Federation of Trade Unions.

Advisers

ZHANG, Guoxian, Mr., Deputy Director-General, International Department, All-China Federation of Trade Unions.
WANG, Liming, Mr., Deputy Director-General, International Department, All-China Federation of Trade Unions.
LIU, Jiyong, Mr., Director, International Department, All-China Federation of Trade Unions.
ZHAO, Changjiu, Ms., Deputy Director, International Department, All-China Federation of Trade Unions.
LI, Jingfang, Ms., Deputy Director and Interpreter, International Department, All-China Federation of Trade Unions.
CHEUNG, Pak Chi, Mr., Employee Representative, Labour Advisory Board, Hong Kong Special Administrative Region.
WONG, Kwok Kin, Mr., Employee Representative, Labour Advisory Board, Hong Kong Special Administrative Region.
FONG, Koc Hon, Mr., Employee Representative, Permanent Council of Macao Social Coordination.

Chypre   Cyprus   Chipre

Minister attending the Conference

TALIADOROS, Christos, Mr., Minister of Labour and Social Insurance.

Government Delegates

SAMUEL, Lenia, Mrs., Permanent Secretary, Ministry of Labour and Social Insurance.
DROUSIOTIS, James, Mr., Ambassador, Permanent Representative, Permanent Mission, Geneva.

Adviser and substitute delegate

MINA, Helena, Ms., Second Secretary, Permanent Mission, Geneva.

Advisers

DAMIANOU, Elena, Ms., Administrative Officer, Ministry of Labour and Social Insurance.
LASETAS, Panicos, Mr., Senior Human Resource Officer, Training Directorate, Human Resource Authority.

Employers' Delegate

PILIKOS, Michael, Mr., Director-General, Cyprus Employers and Industrialists Federation.

Adviser and substitute delegate

KAPARTIS, Costas Chr., Mr., Adviser, Cyprus Employers and Industrialists Federation.

Advisers

ROLOGIS, Vasilis, Mr., President, Cyprus Chamber of Commerce and Industry.
LOIZIDES, Panayiotis, Mr., General Secretary, Cyprus Chamber of Commerce and Industry.
MICHAEL, Emilios, Mr., Director, Industrial Relations Department, Cyprus Chamber of Commerce and Industry.
KARIDIS, Lefteris, Mr., Industrial Relations Officer, Cyprus Chamber of Commerce and Industry.
ANTONIOU, Michael, Mr., Head, Industrial Relations and Labour Legislation, Cyprus Employers and Industrialists Federation.
VASILA, Christina, Mrs., Industrial Relations and Labour Legislation Officer, Cyprus Employers and Industrialists Federation.
KRANIDIOTIS, Byron, Mr., President, Cyprus Employers and Industrialists Federation.
STYLIANOU, Michael, Mr., Assistant Director-General, Cyprus Broadcasting Corporation.

Workers' Delegate

KITTENIS, Demetris, Mr., General Secretary, Cyprus Workers Confederation.

Adviser and substitute delegate

MOYSEOS, Nicos, Mr., Deputy General Secretary, Cyprus Workers Confederation.

Advisers

KYRITSIS, Pambis, Mr., General Secretary, Pancyprian Federation of Labour.
TSOUTSOUKI, Chrystalla, Mrs., Secretary of International Relations Department, Pancyprian Federation of Labour.
DIOMEDOUS, Diomedes, Mr., General Secretary, Democratic Labour Federation.
PILAVAKI, Anna, Mrs., Deputy General Secretary, Democratic Labour Federation.
CONSTANTINOU, Constantinos, Mr., International Relations Secretary, Democratic Labour Federation.

Colombie   Colombia   Colombia

Ministro asistente a la Conferencia

SANTOS CALDERÓN, Francisco, Sr., Vicepresidente de la República.

Delegados gubernamentales

PALACIO BETANCOURT, Diego, Sr., Ministro de la Protección Social.
FORERO UCROS, Clemencia, Sra., Embajadora, Jefe, Misión Permanente, Ginebra.

Consejero técnico y delegado suplente

ARANGO DE BUITRAGO, Luz Stella, Sra., Viceministra de Relaciones Laborales, Ministerio de la Protección Social.

Consejeros técnicos

OSORIO ISAZA, Luis Camilo, Sr., Fiscal General.
MAYA VILLAZÓN, Edgardo José, Sr., Procurador General.
GRILLO RUBIANO, Fernando Antonio, Sr., Director, Departamento Administrativo de la Función Pública.
VARGAS DÍAZ, Isaura, Sra., Presidenta, Sala de Casación Laboral, Corte Suprema de Justicia.
TAFUR GALVIS, Álvaro, Sr., Magistrado, Corte Constitucional.
MONROY CABRA, Marco Gerardo, Sr., Magistrado, Corte Constitucional.
LEMOS BUSTAMANTE, Jesús María, Sr., Magistrado, Sección Segunda, Consejo de Estado.

GONZÁLEZ ARIZA, Victoria, Sra., Ministra Consejera, Misión Permanente, Ginebra.
MONTOYA MEJÍA, Darío, Sr., Director General, Servicio Nacional de Aprendizaje (SENA).
MESA CÁRDENAS, José Gabriel, Sr., Jefe, Oficina de Cooperación y Relaciones Internacionales, Ministerio de Protección Social.
SÁNCHEZ ACOSTA, Ana María, Srta., Coordinadora, Oficina de Derechos Humanos, Ministerio de Protección Social.
PRIETO, Ana María, Sra., Ministra Plenipotenciaria, Misión Permanente, Ginebra.
GUZMÁN, Luis Gerardo, Sr., Ministro Plenipotenciario, Misión Permanente, Ginebra.
VÉLEZ, Ricardo, Sr., Ministro Consejero, Misión Permanente, Ginebra.
QUINTERO, Rafael, Sr., Segundo Secretario, Misión Permanente, Ginebra.

Delegado de los empleadores

VILLEGAS ECHÉVERRI, Luis Carlos, Sr., Presidente, Asociación Nacional de Industriales (ANDI).

Consejero técnico y delegado suplente

ECHAVARRÍA SALDARRIAGA, Alberto, Sr., Vicepresidente de Asuntos Jurídicos y Sociales, ANDI.

Consejeros técnicos

MEJÍA GIRALDO, Gustavo, Sr., Director, Relaciones Industriales, Grupo Empresarial Bavaria.
GÓMEZ MORALES, Gerardo, Sr., Gerente Corporativo de Gestión Integral, Organización Corona.
FRANCO AGUDELO, Pedro Luis, Sr., Comité de Laboralistas, ANDI.
OJALVO PRIETO, Fernando, Sr., Comité de Laboralistas, ANDI.
DEL RÍO MAYA, Octavio, Sr., Comité de Laboralistas, ANDI.
JARAMILLO VALLEJO, Humberto Jairo, Sr., Comité de Laboralistas, ANDI.
MONSALVE CUÉLLAR, Martha Elisa, Sra., Convenio ANDI-ACRIP.
BURGOS DE LA ESPRIELLA, Jairo Miguel, Sr., Comité de Laboralistas, ANDI.
MOLINA MONSALVE, Carlos Ernesto, Sr., Comité de Laboralistas, ANDI.

Delegado de los trabajadores

ALVIS FERNÁNDEZ, Apecides, Sr., Presidente, Confederación de Trabajadores de Colombia (CTC).

Consejeros técnicos

RODRÍGUEZ DÍAZ, Carlos Arturo, Sr., Presidente, Central Unitaria de Trabajadores (CUT).
GÓMEZ ESGUERRA, Julio Roberto, Sr., Secretario General, Confederación General de Trabajadores Democráticos (CGTD).
MONTES DE OCA ANAYA, Boris, Sr., Secretario General, CUT.
MORANTES ALFONSO, Luis Miguel, Sr., Secretario General, CTC.
BEDOYA TABARES, Carlos Antonio, Sr., Vicepresidente, CGTD.

Otras personas que asisten a la Conferencia

RAMÍREZ RÍOS, Gloria Inés, Sra.
ALVIS ULLOQUE, Gabriel, Sr.
SCHMALBACH CRUZ, Luis Roberto, Sr., Unión Sindical Obrera (USO).
GÓMEZ ZULUAGA, Alberto León, Sr.
RODRÍGUEZ MEJÍA, Carlos, Sr.
MALAGÓN, Lina Paola, Sra.
RÍOS NAVARRO, Luis Norberto, Sr.
MARADIAGO, Ever, Sr.
PEDRAZA, Juan José, Sr.
CORTÉS, Blanca Marina, Sra.
MEDINA DUEÑAS, Luis Ernesto, Sr.
TRIANA, Miriam Luz, Sra., Presidenta, Sindicato de Trabajadores de la Cruz Roja Nacional (SINTRACRONAL).
ARMEL ARENAS, Ariel, Sr., Presidente, Confederación Colombiana de Consumidores (CCC).

Congo

Ministre assistant à la Conférence

OKOMBI SALISSA, André, M., Ministre du Travail, de l'Emploi et de la Sécurité sociale.

Personne accompagnant le Ministre

MENGA, Roger Julien, M., Ambassadeur, Représentant permanent, Mission permanente, Genève.

Délégués gouvernementaux

ONDONGO, Evariste, M., Directeur général du Travail et de la Sécurité sociale.
ITOUA-YOCKA, Josias, M., Conseiller au Travail et à la Sécurité sociale.

Conseillers techniques

NYANGA ELENGA, André, M., Directeur général, Office national de l'Emploi et de la Main-d'Œuvre.
IBARA, Félix, M., Directeur général, Caisse nationale de Sécurité sociale.
OTINA, Albert, M., Directeur général, Caisse de Retraite des Fonctionnaires.
OKOMBI, Auxence Léonard, M., Directeur des Etudes et la Planification, ONEMO.
MACKET PEMBA, Brigitte, Mme, Directrice de l'Administration et de l'Equipement, CRF.
IWANDZA WAMMENET, M., Directeur de la Liquidation et de la Vérification, CRF.

MINDOU, Aimé Charles, M., Directeur de l'Administration, des Finances et des Gens de Mer, Direction générale de la Marine Marchande.
KOSSALOBA, Nicolas, M., Attaché à l'Emploi.
BIKOUTA, Delphine, Mme, Premier Conseiller, Mission permanente, Genève.
NGUENGUE-MONTSE, Gabriel, M., Deuxième Conseiller, Mission permanente, Genève.
MEGOT, Jean-Marcellin, M., Troisième Conseiller, Mission permanente, Genève.
BORET BOKWANGO, Serge, M., Chargé du Protocole, Mission permanente, Genève.
OVOUROU, Lucien, M., Inspecteur général, Caisse nationale de Sécurité sociale.
EVOUNDOU, Léonie, Mme, Chef de service, Action sanitaire et sociale.
OKUYA, Benjamin, M., Attaché financier.
ONDZAMBE-NGOYI, Eugène, M., Attaché de direction, CNSS.

Délégué des employeurs

GALESSAMY-IBOMBOT, Jean, M., Président, Confédération générale du Patronat congolais.

Conseiller technique

SAMBA, Jean-Jacques, M., Secrétaire général, Union patronale et interprofessionnelle du Congo.

Délégué des travailleurs

SOUZA, Michel, M., Président, Confédération syndicale des Travailleurs du Congo.

Conseillers techniques

MONGO, Daniel, M., Secrétaire général, Confédération syndicale congolaise.
AKOUELAKOU, Emmanuel, M.
BONGO, Nicole, Mme
LOEMBA, Guy, M.
YALINGUI, Jean-Claude, M.
NGUIE, Zéphyrin, M.
EKANGA, Marcel, M.
ANDZOUANA, Gilbert Sédar, M.

République de Corée
Republic of Korea
República de Corea

Government Delegates

KIM, Dae-Hwan, Mr., Minister of Labour.
CHOI, Hyuck, Mr., Ambassador, Permanent Representative, Permanent Mission, Geneva.

Advisers and substitute delegates

JUNG, Chul-Gyun, Mr., Director-General, International Cooperation Bureau, Ministry of Labour (MOL).
HONG, Jong-Ki, Mr., Deputy Permanent Representative, Permanent Mission, Geneva.

Advisers

KWON, Jae-Chul, Mr., Labour Secretary, Office of the President.
PAIK, Ji-Ah, Ms., Counsellor, Permanent Mission, Geneva.
LEE, Soo-Young, Mr., Director, International Cooperation Division, MOL.
PARK, Hyung-Jung, Mr., Secretary to the Minister, MOL.
YI, Sung-Ki, Mr., Advisor, MOL.
JUNG, Ji-won, Mr., Advisor, Office of the President.
KWON, Hyeuk-Tae, Mr., First Secretary, Permanent Mission, Geneva.
LEE, Chul, Mr., Deputy Director, Human Rights and Social Affairs Division, Ministry of Foreign Affairs and Trade.
LEE, Dae-Joong, Mr., Deputy Director, International Cooperation Division, MOL.
CHO, Jeong-Sook, Ms., Deputy Director, International Cooperation Division, MOL.
CHOI, Sang-Un, Mr., Deputy Director, Human Resource Development Division, MOL.
HONG, Jung-Woo, Mr., Deputy Director, Foreign Workers' Division, MOL.
HONG, Jong-Hae, Mr., Deputy Director, Seafarers and Labour Policy Division, Ministry of Maritime Affairs and Fisheries.
PARK, Moon-Kab, Mr., Professor, Korea Institute of Maritime and Fisheries Technology.
PARK, Dong-Hoon, Mr., Director, Planning Team Secretariat, 6th Global Forum on Reinventing Government.
PARK, Min-sig, Mr., Deputy Director, Planning Team Secretariat, 6th Global Forum on Reinventing Government.
AN, Jung-tae, Mr., Deputy Director, Conference Support Team Secretariat, 6th Global Forum on Reinventing Government.

Employers' Delegate

LEE, Soo-Young, Mr., Chairman, Korea Employers' Federation (KEF).

Adviser and substitute delegate

KIM, Young-Vae, Mr., Vice-Chairman and CEO, KEF.

Advisers

LEE, Dong-Eung, Mr., Managing Director, KEF.
LEE, Ho-Sung, Mr., Chief, Economic Research Bureau, KEF.
RHU, Kee-Jung, Mr., Director, Planning and PR Bureau, KEF.

KIM, Hwan-Il, Mr., Research Fellow, Labour Economics Institute.
SUH, Young-Jin, Mr., Researcher, International Affairs Team, KEF.
SON, Seok-Ho, Mr., Researcher, International Affairs Team, KEF.
CHO, Nam-Hong, Mr., Advisor, KEF.

Workers' Delegate

LEE, Soo-Ho, Mr., President, Korean Confederation of Trade Unions (KCTU).

Adviser and substitute delegate

YU, Jae-Sub, Mr., Vice-President, Federation of Korean Trade Unions (FKTU).

Advisers

WOON, Won-Geun, Mr., Advisor, FKTU.
YEOM, Jin-Doo, Mr., Advisor, FKTU.
LIM, Woon-Taek, Mr., Research Fellow, Research Centre, FKTU.
KANG, Choong-Ho, Mr., International Secretary, FKTU.
SHIN, Hye-soo, Ms., Adviser, FKTU.
KIM, Ji-Ye, Ms., Vice-President, KCTU.
KIM, Hyuk, Mr., Specialist, Irregular Sector, KCTU.
LEE, Chang-Keun, Mr., International Secretary, KCTU.
YOON, Mi-Hyang, Ms., Advisor, KCTU.

Person appointed in accordance with Article 2, paragraph 3(i)

BAE, Jun-Bum, Mr., Advisor, KCTU.

Costa Rica

Ministro asistente a la Conferencia

PACHECO SALAZAR, Ovidio, Sr., Ministro, Ministerio de Trabajo y Seguridad Social.

Persona que acompaña al Ministro

GONZÁLEZ SANZ, Manuel Antonio, Sr., Embajador, Representante Permanente, Misión Permanente, Ginebra.

Delegados gubernamentales

CLARAMUNT GARRO, Carmen, Sra., Embajadora, Representante Permanente Alterna, Misión Permanente, Ginebra.
GUILLERMET, Christian, Sr., Ministro Consejero, Misión Permanente, Ginebra.

Consejeros técnicos

SOLANO, Alejandro, Sr., Ministro Consejero, Misión Permanente, Ginebra.
BLANCO MORA, Wilfrido, Sr., Viceministro, Ministerio de Educación Pública.
GAMBOA ACUÑA, Grace, Sra., Jefe Departamento de Asuntos Internacionales, Ministerio de Trabajo y Seguridad Social.
ARROYO YANNARELLA, Ricardo, Sr., Asesor Legal, Instituto Nacional de Aprendizaje.
CASCANTE ZÚÑIGA, Edgar, Sr., Departamento de Asesoría en Asuntos Internacionales, Ministerio de Trabajo y Seguridad Social.

Delegado de los empleadores

PIGNATARO PACHECO, Eugenio, Sr., Director de Desarrollo Social, Unión Costarricense de Cámaras y Asociaciones de la Empresa Privada.

Delegado de los trabajadores

AGUILAR ARCE, Rodrigo, Sr., Presidente, Confederación de Trabajadores Rerum Novarum.

Côte d'Ivoire

Ministre assistant à la Conférence

OULAYE, Hubert, M., Ministre de la Fonction publique et de l'Emploi.

Délégués gouvernementaux

BEKE DASSYS, Claude, M., Ambassadeur, Représentant permanent, Mission permanente, Genève.
BOULLOU BI DJEHIFFE, Désiré, M., Directeur général du Travail, Ministère de la Fonction publique et de l'Emploi.

Conseillers techniques

ZEHIA KOUADIO, Maurice, M., Directeur général, Agence d'Etudes et de la Promotion de l'Emploi (AGEPE).
N'ZUE, Félix Fofana, M., Directeur général de l'Emploi, Ministère de la Fonction publique et de l'Emploi.
GUEU, Etienne, M., Directeur, Inspection du Travail, Ministère de la Fonction publique et de l'Emploi.
GNANGBO, Célestin, M., Directeur, Réglementation du Travail, Ministère de la Fonction publique et de l'Emploi.
LOBA KIESSEY, Barthélemy, M., Directeur régional du Travail, Ministère de la Fonction publique et de l'Emploi d'Gdienné.
N'GUESSAN COFFIE, Francis José, M., Directeur, Promotion de l'Emploi, AGEPE.
DAMONOKO BIAGNE, Lucien, M., Conseiller technique du Directeur général, AGEPE.

WEYA, Jérôme Klôh, M., Premier Conseiller, Mission permanente, Genève.
N'GUESSAN N'GUESSAN, Bernard, M., Conseiller, Mission permanente, Genève.
BAMBA, Joël Lanciné, M., Attaché, Chargé du Protocole, Mission permanente, Genève.
ABOKE, Damase, M., Directeur de la Promotion humaine.
LAGO, Bodo Daniel, M., Chef, Service juridique.
KOUTOUAN, Benjamin, M., Chargé de mission du Ministre.
TANO, Koffi Bertin, M., Directeur de la Navigation maritime et des Gens de mer.
AYRA, Koko Pierre, M., Sous-directeur des Auxiliaires des Transports maritimes.
KONAN, Kouadio Alphonse, M., Sous-Directeur de l'Administration et de la Formation des Gens de mer.

Délégué des employeurs

DIACK, Diawar, M., Président, Conseil national du Patronat ivoirien (CNPI).

Conseiller technique

N'DOUMI, Bernard, M., Président, Commission sociale du Conseil national, CNPI.

Délégué des travailleurs

ADIKO, Niamkey, M., Secrétaire général, Union générale des Travailleurs de Côte d'Ivoire (UGTCI).

Conseillers techniques

MAHAN GAHÉ, Basile, M., Secrétaire général, Centrale Dignité.
NIAMIEN MESSOU, N'Guessan, M., Premier Secrétaire général adjoint, Fédération des Syndicats autonomes de Côte d'Ivoire (FESACI).
ADE MENSAH, François, M., Premier Secrétaire adjoint, UGTCI.
KOSSA, Bernard, M., Secrétaire national chargé du Secteur privé, UGTCI.
GUEHOA COULIBALY, Maliatou, Mme, Deuxième Secrétaire adjointe, UGTCI.
TRAORE DOHIA, Mamadou, M., Deuxième Secrétaire générale adjoint, FESACI.
KOUAME KOFFI KRA, Félix, M., Premier Secrétaire national, FESACI.

Croatie   Croatia   Croacia

Minister attending the Conference

KOSOR, Jadranka, Ms., Deputy Premier, Government of Croatia; Minister of Family, War Veterans and Intergeneration Solidarity.

Person accompanying the Minister

BABIC, Vera, Ms., State Secretary, Ministry of Economy, Labour and Entrepreneurship.

Government Delegates

MARKOTIC, Gordan, Mr., Ambassador, Permanent Representative, Permanent Mission, Geneva.
MAROVIC, Franjo, Mr., Head, Department for Health and Safety at Work, Ministry of Economy, Labour and Entrepreneurship.

Advisers and substitute delegates

SOCANAC, Branko, Mr., Minister Counsellor, Permanent Mission, Geneva.
ZIC, Inga, Ms., Head, Department for European Integration and International Cooperation, Ministry of Economy, Labour and Entrepreneurship.

Employers' Delegate

HORVATIC, Lidija, Ms., Head, Department for International Cooperation, Croatian Employers Association.

Adviser and substitute delegate

KULUSIC, Jasna, Ms., Head, Regional Office in Rijeka, Croatian Employers Association.

Workers' Delegate

TOTH MUCCIACCIARO, Evelin, Ms., Head, Department for International Cooperation, Union of Autonomous Trade Unions of Croatia.

Advisers and substitute delegates

HANZEVACKI, Marija, Ms., First Secretary, Independent Croatian Unions.
IVAS-BURA, Kristina, Ms., Member, Presidency, Worker's Trade Union Association of Croatia.
DEJANOVIC, Vesna, Ms., President, Union of Autonomous Trade Unions of Croatia.

Cuba

Ministro asistente a la Conferencia

MORALES CARTAYA, Alfredo, Sr., Ministro de Trabajo y Seguridad Social.

Delegados gubernamentales

MORENO FERNÁNDEZ, Abelardo, Sr., Viceministro de Relaciones Exteriores.

MORA GODOY, Jorge Iván, Sr., Embajador, Representante Permanente, Misión Permanente, Ginebra.

Consejeros técnicos y delegados suplentes

LAU VALDÉS, Miriam, Sra., Directora, Relaciones Internacionales, Ministerio de Trabajo y Seguridad Social.
HERRERA CASEIRO, María del Carmen, Sra., Consejera, Misión Permanente, Ginebra.
HURTADO LABRADOR, Carlos, Sr., Consejero, Misión Permanente, Ginebra.
FANEGO SEA, Pedro Antonio, Sr., Funcionario, Ministerio de Relaciones Exteriores.
HERNÁNDEZ OLIVA, Gretel, Sra., Dirección Relaciones Exteriores, Ministerio de Trabajo y Seguridad Social.
LEÓN SANTANA, Oscar, Sr., Segundo Secretario, Misión Permanente, Ginebra.
SÁNCHEZ OLIVA, Manuel, Sr., Tercer Secretario, Misión Permanente, Ginebra.
RODRÍGUEZ RODRÍGUEZ, Marta, Sra., Agregada Diplomática, Misión Permanente, Ginebra.

Delegado de los empleadores

PARRAS ROJAS, Rodolfo Antonio, Sr., Presidente, Grupo Nacional de Empleadores; Director General, General Nickel Co.

Consejero técnico y delegado suplente

MESA GARCÍA, Fermín, Sr., Vicepresidente, Grupo Nacional de Empleadores; Asesor Jurídico, Empresa de Seguros Nacionales.

Delegado de los trabajadores

GONZÁLEZ GONZÁLEZ, Leonel, Sr., Secretario de Relaciones Internacionales, Central de Trabajadores de Cuba.

Consejeros técnicos y delegados suplentes

ROSS LEAL, Pedro, Sr., Secretario General, Central de Trabajadores de Cuba.
BERNAL CAMERO, Joaquín, Sr., Miembro, Comité Nacional, Central de Trabajadores de Cuba.
LÓPEZ GÓMEZ, Agustín, Sr., Departamento de Relaciones, Central de Trabajadores de Cuba.
LAZA CÁRDENAS, Florentina, Sra., Departamento de Relaciones Internacionales, Central de Trabajadores de Cuba.
MONTERO BISTILLEIRO, Manuel, Sr., Departamento de Relaciones Internacionales, Central de Trabajadores de Cuba.
OVIEDO DE LA TORRE, Osiris, Sra., Departamento de Relaciones Internacionales, Central de Trabajadores de Cuba.
ALONSO DÍAZ, Pablo Lino, Sr., Miembro, Secretariado Nacional, CTC.

Danemark   Denmark
Dinamarca

Minister attending the Conference

HJORT FREDERIKSEN, Claus, Mr., Minister for Employment.

Persons accompanying the Minister

SMITH, Bo, Mr., Permanent Secretary to the Minister.
JEPSEN, Charlotte Boline, Mrs., Head of Press and Communication, Ministry of Employment.
JUUL JØRGENSEN, Annemette, Mrs., Private Secretary to the Minister, Ministry of Employment.
HANSEN NOERGAARD, Stig, Mr., Func. Head of Division, International and Legal Department, Ministry of Employment.

Government Delegates

IVERSEN, Henrik Rée, Mr., Ambassador, Permanent Representative, Permanent Mission, Geneva.
PEDERSEN, Klaus, Mr., Legal Adviser, International and Legal Department, Ministry of Employment.

Advisers and substitute delegates

GEDE, Charlotte, Mrs., Legal Adviser, International and Legal Department, Ministry of Employment.
KRISTENSEN, Lene Wang, Mrs., Attachée, Permanent Mission, Geneva.
LYNGE OTTOSEN, Halfdan, Mr., Stagiaire Attaché, Permanent Mission, Geneva.

Advisers

BAUCHY, Philippe, Mr., Special Adviser, Centre for Seafarers and Fishermen, Education and Register of Shipping, Maritime Authority.
KARSTENSEN, Svend, Mr., Ship Surveyor, Maritime Authority.
POBLADOR, Christina, Mrs., Head of Office; Adviser, Ministry of Refugees, Immigration and Integration.

Other persons attending the Conference

MELDGAARD, Anne-Marie, Mrs., Member of Danish Parliament (Folketinget).
VIBJERG, Jens, Mr., Member of Danish Parliament (Folketinget).

Employers' Delegate

DREESEN, Flemming, Mr., Senior Labour Law Counsellor, Confederation of Danish Employers.

Advisers

GADE, Henning, Mr., Senior Counsellor, Confederation of Danish Employers.
SCHILDER, Henrik, Mr., Senior Political Adviser, National Association of Local Authorities.
SKANTING, Lise, Mrs., Advisor, Confederation of Danish Employers.

Other persons attending the Conference

VORSHOLT, Joergen, Mr., Chairman, Confederation of Danish Employers.
NEERGAARD LARSEN, Joern, Mr., Director-General, Confederation of Danish Employers.
ROENNEST, Joergen, Mr., Director, International Affairs, Confederation of Danish Employers.

Workers' Delegate

SVENNINGSEN, John, Mr., International Adviser, Danish Confederation of Trade Unions.

Adviser and substitute delegate

KNUPPERT, Marie-Louise, Mrs., Confederal Secretary, Danish Confederation of Trade Unions.

Advisers

JAKOBSEN, Michael, Mr., Consultant, Danish Confederation of Trade Unions.
SCHMIDT, Erik, Mr., Adviser, Salaried Employees' and Civil Servants Confederation.
SAND MORTENSEN, Peter, Mr., Local Chairman, Fishery Division, General Workers Unions.
GULMANN, Lars D., Mr., Lawyer, Danish Confederation of Trade Unions.
SMIDT, Flemming, Mr., Counsellor, Transport Division, General Workers Union.

Other persons attending the Conference

SORGENFREY, Bente, Mrs., President, Salaried Employees' and Civil Servants Confederation.
WIENE, Jens, Mr., Confederal Secretary, Salaried Employees' and Civil Servants Confederation.
KRAGH, Jens, Mr., Director, Salaried Employees' and Civil Servants Confederation.

Djibouti

Délégués gouvernementaux

BARKAT ABDILLAHI, Mohamed, M., Ministre, Ministère de l'Emploi et de la Solidarité nationale.
YACOUB MAHAMOUD, Ali, M., Secrétaire général, Ministère de l'Emploi et de la Solidarité nationale.

Conseillers techniques et délégués suppléants

AHMED GOD, Moumina, Mme, Chef de Service, Service juridique et Relations internationales.
EUSMAN HOUFFANEH, Djibril, M., Chef de Service, Service national de l'Emploi.

Délégué des employeurs

DAOUD YOUSSOUF, Hikmat, Mme, 2ème Vice-Présidente, Association des Employeurs.

Délégué des travailleurs

SIKIEH DIRRIEH, Abdo, M., Secrétaire général, UGTD.

Conseiller technique et délégué suppléant

KARRIEH BOULALEH, Mohamed, M., 1er Secrétaire général adjoint, UGTD.

République dominicaine
Dominican Republic
República Dominicana

Ministro asistente a la Conferencia

RAY GUEVARA, Milton, Sr., Secretario de Estado de Trabajo.

Delegados gubernamentales

NUÑEZ SALCEDO, Zoilo, Sr., Subsecretario de Estado de Trabajo, Secretaría de Estado de Trabajo.
REYES UREÑA, Nelson, Sr., Director, Relaciones Internacionales, Secretaría de Estado de Trabajo.

Consejeros técnicos

HERNANDEZ BONA, Claudia, Sra., Embajadora, Representante Permanente Alterna, Misión Permanente, Ginebra.
BATISTA, Elga, Sra., Asistente del Secretario, Secretaría de Estado de Trabajo.
JANA, William, Sr., Director General, Instituto Dominicano de Seguros Sociales.
VARGAS SAILLANT, Agustín, Sr., Asesor Laboral, Poder Ejecutivo, Presidencia de la República.
ROMAN MALDONADO, Ysset, Sra., Ministra Consejera, Misión Permanente, Ginebra.
BELLO DE KEMPER, Magaly, Sra., Consejera, Misión Permanente, Ginebra.
PADILLA ROMÁN, Isabel, Sra., Consejera, Misión Permanente, Ginebra.
AQUINO, Gladys Josefina, Sra., Consejera, Misión Permanente, Ginebra.
POLANCO, Rafael, Sr., Prensa, Secretaría de Estado de Trabajo.

Delegado de los empleadores

ORTEGA NADAL, Virgilio, Sr., Presidente, Confederación Patronal de la República Dominicana (COPARDOM).

Consejero técnico y delegado suplente

CASTILLO CAMINERO, Francisco, Sr., Vice-Presidente Ejecutivo, Consejo Nacional de la Empresa Privada (CONEP).

Consejeros técnicos

LEON DE FERNANDEZ, Stella, Sra., Vice-Presidenta, COPARDOM.
GONZALEZ, Jaime, Sr., Miembro, Comisión Técnica, COPARDOM.
CAPELLAN, Fernando, Sr., Miembro, Junta Directiva, Asociación de Industrias de Zonas Francas de Santiago.
CASTILLO, Yudith, Sra., Vice-Secretaria, Junta Directiva, COPARDOM.
ESPINAL, Salvador, Sr., Presidente, Asociación Dominicana de Administración de la Gestión Humana.
HERRERA ROA, Fabio, Sr., Asesor, COPARDOM.
PEREZ MONTAS, Hernando, Sr., Actuario, COPARDOM.

Delegado de los trabajadores

NEGRON TEJADA, Mariano, Sr., Secretario General, Confederación Nacional de Trabajadores Dominicanos (CNTD).

Consejero técnico y delegado suplente

DEL RIO, Gabriel, Sr., Secretario General, Confederación Autónoma Sindical Clasista (CASC).

Consejeros técnicos

ABREU, Rafael, Sr., Presidente, Consejo Nacional de Unidad Sindical (CNUS); Secretario General, Central General de Trabajadores (CGT).
ALVAREZ, Víctor Rufino, Sr., Secretario General, Confederación de Trabajadores Unitaria (CTU).
FRIAS, María, Sra., Vice-Presidenta, CNUS.
MESA FURCAL, Jesús, Sr., Secretario General, Asociación de Hoteles, Bares y Restaurantes, CNTD.

Egypte   Egypt   Egipto

Minister attending the Conference

EL AMAWY, Ahmed Ahmed, Mr., Minister of Manpower and Emigration.

Government Delegates

GABR, Naéla, Mrs., Permanent Representative, Permanent Mission, Geneva.
GHAFFAR, Amgad Abdel, Mr., Deputy Permanent Representative, Permanent Mission, Geneva.

Advisers

ABD EL MONSEF, Mostafa Mohamed, Mr., Director, Emigration and Egyptians Abroad Sector, Ministry of Manpower and Emigration.
KHATER, Azza, Mrs., Under Secretary for Foreign Affairs, Ministry of Manpower and Emigration.
EL GAZZAR, Nadia, Mrs., Labour Attaché, Permanent Mission, Geneva.
EL ERRIAN, Soheir, Mrs., Director General, Conference and Organizations Department, Ministry of Manpower and Emigration.
SELIM LABIB, Hany, Mr., Counsellor, Permanent Mission, Geneva.
ROUSHDY, Alaa, Mr., First Secretary, Permanent Mission, Geneva.
SHALABY, Omar, Mr., Second Secretary, Permanent Mission, Geneva.

Employers' Delegate

ALLAM, Samir, Mr., Member of the Board, Egyptian Federation for Industries.

Advisers

REFAAT, Essam, Mr., Member of the Board, Egyptian Federation for Industries.
ABDO, Mohamed Ibrahim, Mr., Member of the Labour Committee, Egyptian Federation for Industries.
BEKHIET, Abd El Moneim, Mr., Director, Egyptian Federation for Industries.
EL MASRY, Mohamed, Mr., First Deputy, Egyptian Chamber of Commerce.

Workers' Delegate

EL AZALI, Abd El Moneim, Mr., Deputy Chairman for Economic Affairs, Federation of Egyptian Trade Unions.

Adviser and substitute delegate

ABD EL HADY, Aisha, Mrs., Secretary-General for Working Women and Children, Federation of Egyptian Trade Unions.

Advisers

EL SAID MORSY, Mohamed, Mr., Secretary-General, Federation of Egyptian Trade Unions.
EL SOBEHY, Adel, Mr., Chairman, General Union for Maritime Transport.
TAHA, Hamdy Mohamed, Mr., Advisor for International Relations, Federation of Egyptian Trade Unions.

AHMED, Mohamed, Mr., Chairman, General Union of Agriculture.
ROSTOM, Mostafa, Mr., Federation of Egyptian Trade Unions.
EL SHEIKH, Rehab Abd Elhalim, Mrs., General Union for Agriculture.
EL BASOSY, Mohamed, Mr., Secretary-General, General Union for Agriculture.
MORAD, Mohamed Salem, Mr., Director, General Union for Agriculture Fund.

El Salvador

Delegados gubernamentales

ESPINAL, Roberto, Sr., Ministro de Trabajo y Previsión Social.
AVILA DE PEÑA, Elia Estela, Sra., Directora, Relaciones Internacionales del Trabajo, Ministerio de Trabajo y Previsión Social.

Consejeros técnicos

CASTRO GRANDE, Mario, Sr., Encargado de Negocios a.i., Misión Permanente, Ginebra.
ORELLANA S., Carlos Antonio, Sr., Secretario, Consejo Superior del Trabajo.

Delegado de los empleadores

TOMASINO, José Eduardo, Sr., Asociación Nacional de la Empresa Privada (ANEP).

Consejero técnico

KRAVETZ, Alexander A., Sr., ANEP.

Delegado de los trabajadores

RAMÍREZ URBINA, Miguel Angel, Sr., Secretario General, FESTRAES.

Consejero técnico y delegado suplente

SARAHI MOLINA, Vilma, Sra., Secretario de Organización y Estadística, Federación Nacional Sindical de Trabajadores Salvadoreños (FENASTRAS).

Consejero técnico

BLANCO, Félix, Sr., Comisión Intersindical (CATS-CGT-CTD-CTS-CUTS-CSTS)

Emirats arabes unis
United Arab Emirates
Emiratos Arabes Unidos

Minister attending the Conference

AL TAYER, Matar Humaid, Mr., Minister of Labour and Social Affairs.

Person accompanying the Minister

AL SHAALI, Mohammed Bin Hussain, Mr., Ambassador, Permanent Representative, Permanent Mission, Geneva.

Government Delegates

AL KHAZRAJI, Khaled Mohammed, Mr., Under-Secretary for Labour Affairs, Ministry of Labour and Social Affairs.
AL MUHAIRI, Salem Ali, Mr., Director, International Relations Department, Ministry of Labour and Social Affairs.

Advisers and substitute delegates

HUSSAIN, Abdul Riddah Askar, Mr., Counsellor, Ministry of Foreign Affairs.
AL DALEI, Fadhle Ahmed, Mr., Director, Office of the Minister.
BAMTRAF, Omar Mohammed, Mr., Director, Establishments Affairs Unit, Ministry of Labour and Social Affairs.
EL NOUR, Yousif Jafar Sirag, Mr., Labour Expert, Ministry of Labour and Social Affairs.
AL ABDOOLI, Mohammed Rashed, Mr., Director, Man Power Planning Department, Ministry of Labour and Social Affairs.
BIN DEEMAS, Tareq Abdallah, Mr., Director, Labour Licence Department, Ministry of Labour and Social Affairs.
AL KATHEERI, Ali Suhail, Mr., International Relations Department, Ministry of Labour and Social Affairs.

Employers' Delegate

MATTAR, Khalifah Khamis Al Kaabi, Mr., Member, Federal Chambers of Commerce and Industry.

Adviser and substitute delegate

AL GAIZI, Ahmed Jama, Mr., Director, Economics Department, Federal Chambers of Commerce and Industry.

Workers' Delegate

AL MARZOOQI, Saleh Abdul Rahman, Mr., Chairman, Board of Directors, Coordinating Committee of the Professional Associations.

Adviser and substitute delegate

ALHAMMADI, Hasa Ahmed, Mr., Deputy Chairman, Board of Directors, Coordinating Committee of the Professional Associations.

Equateur   Ecuador   Ecuador

Ministro asistente a la Conferencia

IZURIETA MORA BOWEN, Raúl, Sr., Ministro del Trabajo y Recursos Humanos.

Delegados gubernamentales

ESCUDERO, Hernán, Sr., Embajador, Representante Permanente, Misión Permanente, Ginebra.
PAREDES, Rafael, Sr., Ministro del Servicio Exterior, Misión Permanente, Ginebra.

Consejeros técnicos y delegados suplentes

ESPINOSA SALAS, Luis, Sr., Segundo Secretario, Misión Permanente, Ginebra.
MAYORGA, Danny, Sr., Primer Secretario, Misión Permanente, Ginebra.

Consejeros técnicos

THULLEN, Jorge, Sr., Asesor, Ministro del Trabajo.
PÁEZ, Andrés, Sr., Presidente, Comisión de lo Laboral, Congreso Nacional.
CABRERA, Arturo, Sr., Consejero, Misión Permanente, Ginebra.

Delegado de los empleadores

TERÁN, Manuel, Sr., Representante, Camára de Comercio.

Delegado de los trabajadores

YAGUAL, Santiago, Sr., Presidente, Central de Trabajadores del Ecuador (CTE).

Erythrée   Eritrea   Eritrea

Minister attending the Conference

MENKERIOS, Askalu, Ms., Minister of Labour and Human Welfare.

Government Delegates

ELISA, Woldeyesus, Mr., Director-General, Department of Labour, Ministry of Labour and Human Welfare.
WOLDEYOHANNES, Bereket, Mr., Chargé d'Affaires, a.i., Permanent Mission, Geneva.

Workers' Delegate

BAYRE, Tekeste, Mr., Secretary-General, National Confederation of Eritrean Workers.

Advisers

NEGASI, Ammanuel, Mr., Head, Foreign Relations Department, National Confederation of Eritrean Workers.
YIGZAW, Tecle, Mr., Advisor, National Confederation of Eritrean Workers.

Espagne   Spain   España

Ministro asistente a la Conferencia

CALDERA SANCHEZ-CAPITAN, Jesús, Sr., Ministro de Trabajo y Asuntos Sociales.

Personas que acompañan al Ministro

PÉREZ SANZ, Julio, Sr., Director, Gabinete del Ministro de Trabajo y Asuntos Sociales.
DE PASCUAL-TERESA FERNÁNDEZ, Gloria, Sra., Asesora para Asuntos Internacionales del Ministro, Ministerio de Trabajo y Asuntos Sociales.
GONZÁLEZ DE LENA ALVAREZ, Francisco José, Sr., Secretario General Técnico, Ministerio de Trabajo y Asuntos Sociales.

Delegados gubernamentales

BOSCH BESSA, Josep María, Sr., Representante Permanente Adjunto, Misión Permanente, Ginebra.
DOMINGUEZ GONZALEZ, Aurora, Sra., Subsecretaria, Ministerio de Trabajo y Asuntos Sociales.

Consejeros técnicos y delegados suplentes

LOPEZ MAC LELLAN, Guillermo, Sr., Consejero, Misión Permanente, Ginebra.
LOPEZ-MONIS DE CAVO, Carlos, Sr., Consejero de Trabajo y Asuntos Sociales, Misión Permanente, Ginebra.

Consejeros técnicos

BRES GARCIA, Juan Ramón, Sr., Inspector de Trabajo y Seguridad Social, Cádiz, Ministerio de Trabajo y Asuntos Sociales.
MONTES MEANA, Manuel, Sr., Consejero Técnico, Subdirección General de Regulación de Imigración y Migraciones Interiores, Ministerio de Trabajo y Asuntos Sociales.
MORALA DEL CAMPO, Aranzazu, Sra., Subdirección General de Gestión de los Fondos Estructurales y Acuicultura, Secretaría General de Pesca Marítima, Ministerio de Agricultura, Pesca y Alimentación.

ORIZAOLA GURRIA, Santos, Sr., Asesor Técnico Laboral Marítimo, Instituto Social de la Marina, Ministerio de Trabajo y Asuntos Sociales.
ALONSO BECERRA, Luis, Sr., Técnico Laboral, Institutito de Empleo, Servicio Público de Empleo Estatal, Ministerio de Trabajo y Asuntos Sociales.
MARTINEZ BENITO, Aurelio, Sr., Jefe de Servicio, Area de Internacional del IMSERSO, Ministerio de Trabajo y Asuntos Sociales.
GARCIA-CONDE DEL LLANO, Rodrigo, Sr., Adjunto al Consejero de Trabajo y Asuntos Sociales, Misión Permanente, Ginebra.
DE LA SERNA ARENILLAS, Carlos, Sr., Director, Gabinete Técnico, Secretario General de Empleo, Ministerio de Trabajo y Asuntos Sociales.
SEARA SOTO, Delmira Paz, Sra., Consejera Técnica, Gabinete Técnico, Secretaría General de Empleo, Ministerio de Trabajo y Asuntos Sociales.
ARELLANO CATALÁN, Juan Cruz, Sr., Consejero Técnico, Subdirección General de Relaciones Sociales Internacionales, Ministerio de Trabajo y Asuntos Sociales.
ALBERTOS CARRION, D. Felix, Sr., Asesor de Comunicaciones del Ministro de Trabajo y Asuntos Sociales.

Delegado de los empleadores

FERRER DUFOL, Javier, Sr., Presidente, Confederación de Empresarios de Zaragoza; Miembro, Junta Directiva, Confederación Española de Organizaciones Empresariales (CEOE).

Consejero técnico y delegado suplente

LACASA ASO, José María, Sr., Director de Relaciones Internacionales, CEOE.

Consejeros técnicos

JIMÉNEZ AGUILAR, Juan, Sr., Secretario General, CEOE.
MORENO PIÑERO, Fernando, Sr., Director de Relaciones Laborales, CEOE.
SUÁREZ GARCÍA, Roberto, Sr., Secretario General, Federación Española Leonesa de Empresarios, (FELE).
GÓMEZ ALBO, Pablo, Sr., Director de Relaciones Laborales, CEIM.
MARÍN ANDRÉS, Luis Francisco, Sr., Organización de Productores de Pesca de Altura de Ondarroa, Vizcaya.
CESTER BEATOBE, José María, Sr., Secretario General Técnico, Confederación de Empresarios de Zaragoza.
SUÁREZ SANTOS, Roberto, Sr., Departamento de Relaciones Laborales, CEOE.
MENÉNDEZ VALDÉS, Juan, Sr., Departamento de Relaciones Laborales, CEOE.
DEL PUEYO PÉREZ, Eduardo, Sr., Departamento de Relaciones Internacionales, CEOE.

Delegado de los trabajadores

DOZ, Javier, Sr., Secretario Confederal de Política Internacional, Comisiones Obreras (CCOO).

Consejero técnico y delegado suplente

JIMENEZ, Juan Carlos, Sr., Coordinador, Secretaria Confederal de Política Internacional, CCOO.

Consejeros técnicos

TORRES, Gema, Sra., Miembro, Secretaría Confederal de Formación, CCOO.
JIMÉNEZ, José Antonio, Sr., Secretario de Acción Social, Comisión Obrera Nacional de Andalucía.
BONMATI, Manuel, Sr., Secretario de Relaciones Internacionales, Unión General de Trabajadores (UGT).
FRADES, Jaime, Sr., Miembro del Gabinete Técnico Confederal, UGT.
RODRIGUEZ ALVARIÑO, José Mario, Sr., Coordinador, Secretaría Confederal de Formación, UGT.
CORRAL JUAN, Ana María, Sra., Responsable, Departamento Confederal de Migraciones, UGT.
ALBERDI ARELLANO, Olatz, Sra., Miembro, Departamento Internacional, ELA/STV.
GONZÁLEZ BOAN, Xesús Ramón, Sr., Secretario de Relaciones Internacionales, CIG.

Estonie   Estonia   Estonia

Minister attending the Conference

POMERANTS, Marko, Mr., Minister of Social Affairs.

Government Delegates

HINDOV, Eike, Mrs., Chief Specialist, Working Life Development Department, Ministry of Social Affairs.
LEHT, Hene, Ms., Third Secretary, Permanent Mission, Geneva.

Adviser and substitute delegate

KULL, Clyde, Mr., Ambassador, Permanent Representative, Permanent Mission, Geneva.

Advisers

LUGNA, Alice, Mrs., Head of Department, International and Personel Department, Labour Market Board.
RAIK, Ivar, Mr., Head of Work Environment, Working Life Development Department, Ministry of Social Affairs.

Employers' Delegate

MERILAI, Marika, Ms., Managing Director, Estonian Traders Association.

Adviser and substitute delegate

PÄÄRENDSON, Eve, Ms., Advisor on International Relations, Estonian Confederation of Employers.

Workers' Delegate

KALDA, Kalle, Mr., Member of the Council, Confederation of Estonian Trade Unions.

Adviser and substitute delegate

KAUGURS, Ruth, Ms., Lawyer, Estonian Communication Workers' Trade Union.

Etats-Unis   United States
Estados Unidos

Minister attending the Conference

CHAO, Elaine L., Ms., Secretary of Labor.

Persons accompanying the Minister

REDMOND, Sean, Mr., Staff Assistant to the Secretary, Office of the Secretary, Department of Labor.
ATHEY, Robert, Mr., Regional Representative, Office of the Secretary, Department of Labor.

Government Delegates

LEVINE, Arnold, Mr., Deputy Under Secretary, International Affairs, Department of Labor.
HAGEN, Robert, Mr., Director, Office of International Labor Affairs, Bureau of Democracy, Human Rights and Labor, Department of State.

Advisers and substitute delegates

MOLEY, Kevin E., Mr., Ambassador, Permanent Representative, Permanent Mission, Geneva.
CASSEL, Lynn L., Ms., Deputy Chief, Permanent Mission, Geneva.
SHEPARD, Robert B., Mr., Director, Office of International Organizations, Bureau of International Labor Affairs, Department of Labor.

Advisers

CHAMBERLIN, John, Mr., Labor Attache, Permanent Mission, Geneva.
DELAURENTIS, Jeffrey, Mr., Chief, Political and Specialized Agencies Section, Permanent Mission, Geneva.
DRISCOLL, Richard J., Mr., Deputy Director, Office of Technical Specialized Agencies, Bureau of International Organization Affairs, Department of State.
GORMLY, Sarah, Ms., Labor Economist, Division of Foreign Economic Research, Bureau of International Labor Affairs, Department of Labor.
KARESH, Lewis, Mr., Acting Director, US National Administrative Office, Bureau of International Labor Affairs, Department of Labor.
KRAMER, Roger G., Mr., Director, Division of Immigration Policy and Research, Bureau of International Labor Affairs, Department of Labor.
LESSER, William C., Mr., Deputy Associate Solicitor for Fair Labor Standards, Solicitor's Office, Department of Labor.
LEVIN, Matthew, Mr., Attorney Adviser, Division of Labor-Management Laws, Solicitor's Office, Department of Labor.
MISNER, Julia E., Ms., Assistant Director, Office of International Organizations, Bureau of International Labor Affairs, Department of Labor.
OWEN, Donald Robert, Mr., Counselor to the Deputy Secretary, Office of the Secretary, Department of Labor.
RAMGOOLIE, Monique, Ms., Migration Policy Officer, Bureau of Population, Refugees and Migration, Department of State.
RASA, Tanya, Ms., Labor Rights Officer, Office of Foreign Relations, Bureau of International Labor Affairs, Department of Labor.
STONECIPHER, Charles A., Mr., First Secretary, Permanent Mission, Geneva.

Employers' Delegate

POTTER, Edward E., Mr., Attorney-at-Law, International Labor Counsel, US Council for International Business.

Adviser and substitute delegate

GOLDBERG, Ronnie L., Ms., Senior Vice President, Policy and Program, US Council for International Business.

Advisers

BRUS, Helena, Ms., Director, Economic and Helath Care Policy, Merck & Co., Inc.
COWMAN, Jordan, Mr., Partner, Baker & McKenzie.
FRENCH, Tammy, Ms., Vice President, Human Resources, American Seafoods Company.
MANLEY, Thomas J., Mr., Partner, Hunton & Williams.

Workers' Delegate

ZELLHOEFER, Jerald A., Mr., AFL-CIO European Representative.

Adviser and substitute delegate

SWEENEY, John J., Mr., President, AFL-CIO.

Advisers

AVENDANO-DENIER, Ana, Ms., Associate General Counsel, Legal Department, AFL-CIO.
GACEK, Stanley A., Mr., Assistant Director, International Affairs Department, AFL-CIO.
HERRNSTADT, Owen, Mr., Director, International Affairs Department, International Association of Machinists and Aerospace Workers.

LENOIR, Juliette D., Ms., Assistant Director, International Affairs Department, AFL-CIO.
SCHANTZ, Penny, Ms., AFL-CIO European Office.
SHAILOR, Barbara, Ms., Director, International Affairs Department, AFL-CIO.
FISHMAN, Phillip A., Mr., Assistant Director, International Affairs Department, AFL-CIO.

Other persons attending the Conference

BADER, Shawna, Ms., Program Officer for the Middle East, Solidarity Center, AFL-CIO.
BAYARD, Marc, Mr., Regional Director for Africa, Solidarity Center, AFL-CIO.
BOUSLAH, Khereddine, Mr., Senior Program Officer for the Middle East Office, Solidarity Center, AFL-CIO.
CASERTANO, Teresa, Ms., Regional Director for the Americas, Solidarity Center, AFL-CIO.
HASSING, Anca, Ms., Regional Director for Eastern Europe and Eurasia, Solidarity Center, AFL-CIO.
KAMBERIS, Harry G., Mr., Executive Director, Solidarity Center, AFL-CIO.
MACDONALD, Lynn, Ms., Acting Regional Director for the Middle East, Solidarity Center, AFL-CIO.
SWEENEY, Maureen, Ms., AFL-CIO.
WALSH, Louise D., Ms., Global Programs Director, Solidarity Center, AFL-CIO.

Ethiopie   Ethiopia   Etiopía

Minister attending the Conference

ABDELLA, Hassen, Mr., Minister, Ministry of Labour and Social Affairs.

Government Delegates

YIMER, Fisseha, Mr., Ambassador, Permanent Representative, Permanent Mission, Geneva.
MITIKU, Getaneh, Mr., Head, Labour Affairs Department, Ministry of Labour and Social Affairs.

Advisers and substitute delegates

SIAMREGN, Bekele, Mr., Head, International Relations Team, Ministry of Labour and Social Affairs.
MENGESHA, Seleshi, Mr., Counsellor, Permanent Mission, Geneva.
GOTTA, Esayas, Mr., First Secretary, Permanent Mission, Geneva.

Employers' Delegate

TILAHUN, Tadesse, Mr., President, Ethiopian Employers' Federation.

Adviser and substitute delegate

YIMER, Tadele, Mr., Secretary-General, Ethiopian Employers' Federation.

Workers' Delegate

ALEMAYEHU, Amare, Mr., President, Confederation of Ethiopian Trade Unions.

Adviser and substitute delegate

ABREHA, Haileselassie, Mr., Head, International Relations, Confederation of Ethiopian Trade Unions.

Ex-Rép. Yougos. de Macédoine
The FYR Macedonia
Ex Rep. Yugoslava de Macedonia

Minister attending the Conference

MANASIEVSKI, Jovan, Mr., Minister of Labour and Social Policy.

Government Delegates

ZAFIROVSKA, Dragica, Mrs., Chargé d'Affaires, Permanent Mission, Geneva.
DZAFERI, Nazif, Mr., Second Secretary, Permanent Mission, Geneva.

Advisers

AVRAMOSKA, Biljana, Ms., Head, Department for Labour and Social Policy.
ATANASOV, Gabriel, Mr., Third Secretary, Permanent Mission, Geneva.

Employers' Delegate

KUZMANOVSKA, Slobandanka, Mrs., Chairman, Board of Employers.

Workers' Delegate

MURATOVSKI, Vanco, Mr., Chairman, Federation of Trade Union.

Fidji   Fiji   Fiji

Government Delegates

ZINCK, Kenneth Vincent, Mr., Minister for Labour, Industrial Relations and Productivity.
KUNATUBA, Tevita, Mr., Divisional Labour Officer.

Employers' Delegate

POLITINI, Howard, Mr., Member, Fiji Employers' Federation.

Other person attending the Conference

WARADI, Taito, Mr., President, Fiji Chamber of Commerce and Industry.

Workers' Delegate

URAI MANUFOLAU, Daniel, Mr., President, Fiji Trade Union Congress.

Finlande   Finland   Finlandia

Minister attending the Conference

FILATOV, Tarja, Ms., Minister of Labour.

Persons accompanying the Minister

HIMANEN, Vesa, Mr., Ambassador, Permanent Representative, Permanent Mission, Geneva.
FELDT-RANTA, Maarit, Ms., Ministerial Adviser, Ministry of Labour.

Government Delegates

SALMENPERÄ, Matti, Mr., Director, Working Environment Policy Department, Ministry of Labour.
POTILA, Sirkka, Ms., Ministerial Adviser, Ministry of Labour.

Advisers and substitute delegates

VUORINEN, Anneli, Ms., Minister Counsellor, Permanent Mission, Geneva.
KYRÖLÄINEN, Hannu, Mr., Director General, Ministry for Foreign Affairs.

Advisers

AARNIO, Kirsti, Ms., Director, Unit for UN Development Issues, Ministry for Foreign Affairs.
SAASTAMOINEN, Liisa, Ms., Senior Officer, Legal Affairs, Ministry of Labour.
SIHTO, Matti, Mr., Labour Market Counsellor, Ministry of Labour.
KRÖGER, Tarja, Ms., Senior Adviser, Legislative Affairs, Ministry of Labour.
ESKOLA, Meri-Sisko, Ms., Senior Adviser, Ministry of Labour.
HÄIKIÖ, Kristiina, Ms., Counsellor, Permanent Mission, Geneva.
SANTANEN, Anton, Mr., Permanent Mission, Geneva.

Other persons attending the Conference

GUSTAFSSON, Jukka, Mr., Chairman, Employment and Equality Committee, Parliament.
KAIKKONEN, Antti, Mr., Member, Employment and Equality Committee, Parliament.
KILJUNEN, Anneli, Ms., Member, Employment and Equality Committee, Parliament.
RAUHALA, Leena, Ms., Member, Employment and Equality Committee, Parliament.
YLÄ-MONONEN, Jaana, Ms., Member, Employment and Equality Committee, Parliament.
BÄCKSTRÖM, Ritva, Ms., Committee Counsellor, Parliament.

Employers' Delegate

RISKI, Seppo, Mr., Director, Confederation of Finnish Industry and Employers.

Adviser and substitute delegate

HUTTUNEN, Martti, Mr., Head, International Affairs, Employers' Confederation of Service Industries.

Advisers

LEPPÄNEN, Katja, Ms., Legal Adviser, Confederation of Finnish Industry and Employers.
VEHVILÄINEN, Tuija, Ms., Adviser, Technology Industries of Finland.
WÄRN, Riitta, Ms., Legal Adviser, Employers' Confederation of Service Industries.

Workers' Delegate

VALKONEN, Marjaana, Ms., Director, International Affairs, Central Organization of Finnish Trade Unions.

Adviser and substitute delegate

AHOKAS, Heli, Ms., Head, Collective Bargaining, Finnish Confederation of Salaried Employees.

Advisers

HEINÄNEN, Salla, Ms., International Secretary, Confederation of Unions for Academic Professionals in Finland.
LEHTO-KOMULAINEN, Katja, Ms., Legal Adviser, Central Organization of Finnish Trade Unions.
RÄISÄNEN, Kalle, Mr., Legal Adviser, Central Organization of Finnish Trade Unions.
SUOKAS, Kyösti, Mr., Second Chairman, Construction Trade Union.

France   France   Francia

Ministre assistant à la Conférence

LARCHER, Gérard, M., Ministre Délégué aux Relations du Travail auprès du Ministre de l'Emploi, du Travail et de la Cohésion sociale.

Personne accompagnant le Ministre

KESSEDJIAN, Bernard, M., Ambassadeur, Représentant permanent, Mission permanente, Genève.

Délégués gouvernementaux

SEGUIN, Philippe, M., Représentant au Conseil d'administration du BIT.
THIERRY, Michel, M., Inspecteur général, Affaires sociales; Représentant suppléant au Conseil d'administration du BIT.

Conseillers techniques et délégués suppléants

GIACOMINI, Marc, M., Représentant permanent adjoint, Mission permanente, Genève.
AUER, France, Mme, Conseiller, Mission permanente, Genève.

Conseillers techniques

TEIXEIRA, Pacal, M., Directeur adjoint des Nations Unies et des Organisations internationales, Ministère des Affaires étrangères.
COLLET, Brigitte, Mme, Conseillère, Affaires étrangères, Sous-directrice des Droits de l'Homme, des Affaires humanitaires et sociales, Ministère des Affaires étrangères.
POINSOT, François, M., Conseiller, Affaires étrangères, Direction des Nations Unies, Ministère des Affaires étrangères.
COENT, Marie-Christine, Mme, Chef, Bureau des Affaires multilatérales, Délégation aux Affaires européennes et internationales, Ministère de l'Emploi, du Travail et de la Cohésion sociale.
PARRA, Carine, Mme, Chargée de mission, Délégation aux Affaires européennes et internationales, Ministère de l'Emploi, du Travail et de la Cohésion sociale.
GAUCI, Pascal, M., Mission permanente, Genève.
PETITGUYOT, Marie-Christine, Mme, Chargée de Mission à la Division Synthèse, Délégation générale à l'Emploi et à la Formation professionnelle, Ministère de l'Emploi, du Travail et de la Cohésion sociale.
ILLIONNET, Philippe, M., Sous-directeur, Gens de mer, Direction des Affaires maritimes et des Gens de mer, Ministère de l'Equipement, des Transports, de l'Aménagement du Territoire, du Tourisme et de la Mer.
MOUSSAT, Alain, M., Chef, Bureau de l'Inspection du Travail maritime, Direction des Affaires maritimes et des Gens de mer, Ministère de l'Equipement, des Transports, de l'Aménagement du Territoire, du Tourisme et de la Mer.
PERON, Michel, M., Bureau de l'Inspection du Travail maritime, Direction des Affaires maritimes et des Gens de mer, Ministère de l'Equipement, des Transports, de l'Aménagement du Territoire, du Tourisme et de la Mer.
BOUVIER, Jean, M., Chef, Bureau des Etudes juridiques et des Conventions internationales, Etablissement national des Invalides de la Marine.
SAN MARTIN, Aînhoa, Mme, Adjointe au Chef, Bureau des Etudes juridiques et des Conventions internationales, Etablissement national des Invalides de la Marine.
BIGOT, Jacques, M., Membre du Comité national des Pêches maritimes et des Elevages marins.
RIPAMONTI, Jean-Pierre, M., Direction des Affaires économiques, sociales et culturelles de l'Outre-mer, Ministère de l'Outre-mer.
FRENAIS-CHAMAILLARD, Brigitte, Mme, Sous-directrice, Direction de la Population et des Migrations, Ministère de l'Emploi, du Travail et de la Cohésion sociale.
MAROT, Nadia, Mme, Chef de Bureau, Direction de la Population et des Migrations, Ministère de la l'Emploi, du Travail et de la Cohésion sociale.
GUICHAOUA, Hervé, M., Conseiller technique, Direction de la Population et des Migrations, Ministère de l'Emploi, du Travail et de la Cohésion sociale.
LEFEUVRE, Christian, M., Direction de la Population et des Migrations, Ministère de l'Emploi, du Travail et de la Cohésion sociale.

Personnes désignées en conformité avec l'article 2, alinéa 3 i)

GUERRE, Michel, M., Conseiller technique, Direction des Relations du Travail, Ministère de l'Emploi, du Travail et de la Cohésion sociale.
LECLERC, Agnès, Mme, Conseiller chargée des Affaires européennes et internationales, Cabinet du Ministre Délégué.
CAUJOLLE, Marie, Mme, Conseiller technique chargée de la Presse, Cabinet du Ministre Délégué.
FITOU, Jean-François, M., Délégué aux Affaires européennes et internationales, Ministère de l'Emploi, du Travail et de la Cohésion sociale.
RAMOND, Maurice, M., Inspecteur général honoraire des Affaires sociales.
MAZEL, Maurice, M., Chargé de Mission, DAEI, Ministère de l'Emploi, du Travail et de la Cohésion sociale.

Délégué des employeurs

BOISSON, Bernard, M., Conseiller, Mouvement des Entreprises de France (MEDEF).

Conseiller technique et délégué suppléant

ROILAND, Marie-Paule, Mme, Directeur, Affaires européennes et internationales, Union des Industries métallurgiques et minières (UIMM).

Conseillers techniques

ANDRIEU, Françoise, Mme, Membre, Commission sociale de la CGPME.
BENHAMOU, Annie, Mme, Conseiller, Service international, UIMM.
FAUCHOIS, Marie-Christine, Mme, Directeur, Sécurité sociale, UIMM.
HERVOUET-DION, Marie-Christine, Mme, Chargée de Mission, Affaires sociales, Union des Armateurs de la Pêche (UAPF).

PATINET, Didier, M., Directeur, Emploi, UIMM.
SENECHAL, Eric, M., Secrétaire général, Groupement des Producteurs et Conditionneurs de Boissons.
SAIDI, Siham, Mme, MEDEF.

Personne désignée en conformité avec l'article 2, alinéa 3 i)

GUY, Monique, Mme, MEDEF.

Délégué des travailleurs

BRUNEL, Huguette, Mme, Responsable, Service international et Europe, CFDT.

Conseiller technique et délégué suppléant

TROGRLIC, Jean-François, M., Secrétaire national en charge des questions internationales, CFDT.

Conseillers techniques

GERARD, Thomas, M., Secrétaire permanent, Service international, CFDT.
JOUBIER, Jean-Michel, M., Conseiller confédéral, CGT.
RETUREAU, Daniel, M., Conseiller confédéral, CGT.
BLONDEL, Marc, M., Ex-secrétaire général de la CGT-FO; Membre adjoint, Conseil d'administration du BIT.
VEYRIER, Yves, M., Secrétaire confédéral, Secteur international-Europe, CGT-FO.
JULIA, Christian, M., Président, FNEMA CFE-CGC, Fédération nationale des Métiers de l'Aérien.
TRICOCHE, Jean-Claude, M., Délégué général, UNSA.
PICANDET, Patrick, M., Correspondant Europe, CFTC.
ROCHE, Paul, M., Correspondant Europe, CFTC.

Personnes désignées en conformité avec l'article 2, alinéa 3 i)

GARRIDO, Raquel, Mme, CGT-FO.
MARTINET, Luc, M., CFDT.
PINGLIN, Phillippe, M., CFDT.
JUQUEL, Guy, M., CGT.
NAILLOD, Marie-Chrisitine, Mme, CGT.

Autres personnes assistant à la Conférence

BOUNEAUD, Hélène, Mme, CGT.
GOIRAND, Pierre, M., CGT.
GUIGON, Jean-Jacques, M., CGT.
THIBAULT, Bernard, M., CGT.
MARITIUS, Bruno, M., CGT
COURBE, Jean-François, M., CGT.
THOUVENEL, Joseph, M., Responsable politique, Service Europe-International, CFTC.

Gabon

Ministre assistant à la Conférence

IVALA, Clotaire Christian, M., Ministre du Travail et de l'Emploi.

Personnes accompagnant le Ministre

BIKE, Yolande, Mme, Ambassadeur, Représentant permanent, Mission permanente, Genève.
LINDZODZO MAMBANYA, Christophe, M., Conseiller du Premier Ministre.
NDEMBY, Josué, M., Attaché, Cabinet du Ministre du Travail et de l'Emploi.

Délégués gouvernementaux

NDONG NANG, Daniel, M., Secrétaire général, Ministère du Travail et de l'Emploi.
MOULOMBA NZIENGUI, M., Conseiller technique du Ministre du Travail et de l'Emploi.

Conseillers techniques et délégués suppléants

BIVEGHE NDOUTOUME, Jean-François, M., Directeur général du Travail.
MOURENDE TSIOBA, Jacques, M., Directeur général des Ressources Humaines.
OYONO NGOMO, Henri Jacob, M., Directeur général, Office national de l'Emploi.

Conseillers techniques

ANGONE ABENA, Mme, Conseiller technique, Mission permanente, Genève.
ZENG MEGNER, Edouard, M., Inspecteur général adjoint, Hygiène et de la Médecine du Travail.
PAMBO, Joseph, M., Directeur, Relations internationales, Ministère du Travail et de l'Emploi.

Délégué des employeurs

AWASSI ATSIMADJA, Félicité, Mme, Confédération patronale gabonaise (CPG).

Conseillers techniques

TCHOUA, Jean Pierre, M., Président, Confédération nationale du Patronat gabonais (CNPG).
AKOULOU EYELEKO, Claude, M., Vice-Président, CNPG.

Délégué des travailleurs

ALLINI, Martin, M., Secrétaire général, Confédération syndicale du Gabon (COSYGA).

Conseillers techniques

MAYOMBO, Etienne Francis, M., Secrétaire général, Confédération gabonaise Syndicats libres (CGSL).
MBOKO APANGHA, Fidèle, M., Membre confédéral, CGSL.
MOMBO MOUELET, Camille, M., Secrétaire général, FLEEMA; Conseiller, CGSL.
MEBIAME EVOUNG, Léon, M., Président, Congrès syndical du Gabon, CSG.
BOUASSA, Valentin, M., Vice-Président chargé des Normes internationales du Travail, CSG.
MINTSA MI-ESSONO, Marcel, M., Membre confédéral, COSYGA.
ENGONGA ONDO, François, M., Membre confédéral, COSYGA.
WETI ANAM YAWA, Mme, Membre, COSYGA.
MOUSSAVOU MOUSSAVOU, M., Secrétaire général, Union des Travailleurs du Gabon (UTG).
ISSOGUI, Jean Marie, M., Secrétaire exécutif chargé des Normes internationales du Travail, UTG.

Personnes désignées en conformité avec l'article 2, alinéa 3 i)

MBOU MBINE, Aloïse, M., Président, Confédération des Syndicats autonomes (CDSA).
IBESSA, Martin, M., Membre confédéral, CGSL.
IGNANGA, Germaine, M., Secrétaire confédéral, Conseiller, CGSL.
MOZOGO, Albert, M., Membre confédéral chargé de l'Education ouvrière, UTG.
NSA BENGONE, Carine, Mme, Secrétaire national à la Promotion de la Femme, CSG.

Gambie   Gambia   Gambia

Government Delegates

NDOYE, Ebou, Mr., Commissioner of Labour, Department of State for Trade, Industry and Employment.
BOJANG, Famara, Mr., Senior Human Resources Economist, Department of State for Trade, Industry and Employment.

Géorgie   Georgia   Georgia

Government Delegates

CHIKVAIDZE, Alexander, Mr., Ambassador, Permanent Representative, Permanent Mission, Geneva.
EDILASHVILI, Kartlos, Mr., First Secretary, Permanent Mission, Geneva.

Employers' Delegate

MELADZE, Elguja, Mr., President, Georgian Employers Association.

Advisers

AGLADZE, Zurab, Mr., Georgian Employers Association.
MIKELASHVILI, Nana, Ms., Georgian Employers Association.
MELADZE, Dea, Ms., Georgian Employers Association.
ENUKIDZE, Gocha, Mr., Georgian Employers Association.
KOIAVA, George, Mr., Georgian Employers Association.
GOLUKE, Rudiger, Mr., Georgian Employers Association.
KHUKHASHVILI, Nodar, Mr., Georgian Employers Association.

Workers' Delegate

TUGUSHI, Irakli, Mr., Chairman, Georgian Trade Unions Amalgamation.

Advisers

ABASHIDZE, Tamar, Mrs., Georgian Trade Unions Amalgamation.
JAFARIDZE, Tamaz, Mr., Georgian Trade Unions Amalgamation.
CHICHINADZE, Lasha, Mr., Georgian Trade Unions Amalgamation.

Ghana

Minister attending the Conference

BARIMAH, Yaw, Mr., Minister of Manpower Development and Employment.

Government Delegates

POKU, Fritz K., Mr., Ambassador, Permanent Representative, Permanent Mission, Geneva.
PARKER-ALLOTEY, S.J.K., Mr., Deputy Permanent Representative, Permanent Mission, Geneva.

Adviser and substitute delegate

AMEGEE, Paul Kofi, Mr., Assistant Chief Labour Officer, Regional Head, Labour Department.

Advisers

NYARKO, Ebenezer Asiedu, Mr., Assistant Chief Labour Officer, Head, Legal and International Affairs, Labour Department.
MANU, Kwaku Baladu, Mr., Chairman, Parliamentary Select Committee on Employment, Social Welfare and State Enterprises.

BENYIWA-DOE, Ama, Ms., Ranking Member, Select Committee on Employment, Social Welfare and State Enterprises.
TETTEGAH, Victoria, Ms., First Secretary, Permanent Mission, Geneva.

Employers' Delegate

AMPIAH, Ato, Mr., President, Ghana Employers' Association; Chief Executive, Crystal Auto Ltd.

Adviser and substitute delegate

MENSA, Charles, Mr., Vice-President, Ghana Employers' Association; Resident Director, Valco Mobilehouse.

Advisers

KARIKARI ANANG, Rose, Mrs., Executive Director, Ghana Employers' Association.
QUIST-ADDO, Evelyn, Mrs., Director for Administration and Human Relations, Ghana Chamber of Mines.
OSEI-NUMO, Eva, Mrs., Director of Administration, GNPA Ltd.
ANTO-BOATENG, George, Mr., Senior Human Resource Manager, Ghana Cocoa Board.
ADANSI BONNA, Kwadwo, Mr., General Manager, Administration, Ghana Ports and Harbours Authority.
MMAAME HAJAR, Victoria, Mrs., Managing Director, Managing Director, Atlantic Port Services Ltd.
YAO DEGBOR, Kenneth Desmond, Mr., Ag. Administration and Human Resources Manager, Atlantic Port Services Ltd.
ANTWI-BOASIAKO, Kwaku Addae, Mr., Executive Director, Corporate Division, Ashanti Goldfields Co. Ltd.
HAGAN, Ellen, Mrs., Resident Director, Human Resource Consultant, L'AINE SERVICES LTD.

Persons appointed in accordance with Article 2, paragraph 3(i)

OWUSU-ANSAH, Michael, Mr., Finance and Administration Manager, Ghana Employers' Association.
MAASODONG, Peter, Mr., Chief Manager and Industrial Relations and Recruitment, Ghana Telecom.
APPIAH-NKANSAH, Irene Stella, Mrs., Senior General Manager and Human Resource Manager, Ghana Telecom.
SARPONG, Samuel, Mr., Chief Executive Officer, OXIA.

Workers' Delegate

ADU-AMANKWAH, Kwasi, Mr., Secretary General, TUC.

Adviser and substitute delegate

DORKENOO KWABLA, David, Mr., Head of International Affairs Department, TUC.

Advisers

ASAMOAH, Kofi, Mr., Deputy Secretary-General (OPS), TUC.
DANSO-ACHEAMPONG, Kwasi, Mr., Legal and Industrial Relations Officer, TUC.
ANKRAH, Prince William, Mr., Deputy General Secretary, GMWU, TUC.
KOOMSON, Kenneth, Mr., Deputy General Secretary, FAWU, G.F.L.
AGBESINYALE, Patrick, Mr., International APADEP Co-ordinator.

Grèce   Greece   Grecia

Ministres assistant à la Conférence

PANAYIOTOPOULOS, Panos, M., Ministre de l'Emploi et la Protection sociale.
GIAKOUMATOS, Gerassimos, M., Secrétaire d'Etat de l'Emploi et de la Protection sociale.
AGGELOPOULOS, Nicolaos, M., Secrétaire d'Etat de l'Emploi et de la Protection sociale.

Personnes accompagnant le Ministre

KRIEKOUKIS, Tassos, M., Ambassadeur, Représentant permanent, Mission permanente, Genève.
KARAYIANNIS, Eleftherios, M., Ambassadeur, Conseiller special, Cabinet du Ministre.

Délégués gouvernementaux

KONTOS, Dimitrios, M., Secrétaire général, Ministère de l'Emploi et de la Protection sociale.
CAMBITSIS, Andreas, M., Expert, Ministre conseiller, Mission permanente, Genève.

Conseillers techniques et délégués suppléants

LAIOU-SPANOPOULOU, Maria, Mme, Directrice, Direction des Relations internationales, Ministère de l'Emploi et de la Protection sociale.
CHRYSANTHOU, Eudokia, Mme, Chef, Section relation avec OIT, Direction des Relations internationales, Ministère de l'Emploi et de la Protection sociale.

Conseillers techniques

TSOUMANI, Eygenia, Mme, Secrétaire générale, Secrétariat général de l'Egalité des Sexes.
DANELLIS, Charalambos, M., Vice-président, Organisme de l'Emploi et de la Main-d'œuvre.
PAPANDREOU, Chrysoula, Mme, Directrice générale, Ministère de l'Emploi et de la Protection sociale.
PISSIMISSI, Stamatina, Mme, Chef de Section, Direction des Conditions de Travail, Ministère de l'Emploi et de la Protection sociale.
BIRI, Antonia, Mme, Chef de section, Direction des Conditions de Travail, Ministère de l'Emploi et de la Protection sociale.

BAGGE, Evangelia, Mme, Chef de section, Direction de la Sécurité sociale transnationale, Secrétariat général de la Sécurité sociale.
SOTIRIADOU, Anastasia, Mme, Chef de Section, Education-Formation, Secrétariat général de l'Egalité de Sexes.
BOUMBOPOULOS, Georgios, M., Commandant, Direction de Relations du Travail maritime, Ministère de la Marine marchande.
MAKRIDOU, Eleni, Mme, Chef de Section, Orientation professionnelle scolaire, Ministère de l'Education nationale et de Religion.
KOLIOPOULOS, Ilias, M., Chef de Section, Organisme de l'Emploi et de la Main-d'œuvre.
STAMATOPOULOS, Nicos, M., Chef de Section, Organisme de l'Emploi et de la Main-d'œuvre.
GEORMAS, Konstantinos, M., Fonctionnaire, Direction de Relations internationales, Ministère de l'Emploi et de la Protection sociale.
ASSIMAKIS, Georgios, M., Avocat, Collaborateur special, Ministère de l'Emploi et de la Protection sociale.
NERATZIS, Georgios, M., Direction de l'Emploi, Ministère de l'Emploi et de la Protection sociale.
BISKINIS, Ioannis, M., Inspecteur spécial, Ministère de l'Emploi et de la Protection sociale.
TSAOUSSOGLOU, Bassilia, Mme, Secrétariat général, Sécurité sociale.

Personnes désignées en conformité avec l'article 2, alinéa 3 i)

VOURTSIS, Charalambos, M.
LIASKOS, Georgios, M.
MAGAS, Konstantinos, M.
KOSTAKI, Chrysoula, Mme
BOUKOUVALAS, Charalambos, M.
MANOLIS, Nikos, M.
MYROYANNI, Myriam, Mme
DIMOPOULOU, Barbara, Mme
KATZOURAKI, Ekaterini, Mme
TSIVERIOTIS, George, M.

Autres personnes assistant à la Conférence

FYTRAKIS, Ioannis, M.
FYTRAKIS, George, M.
TSELEPI, Anna, Mme
RAPTI, Paraskevi, M.
ZAKYNTHINAKI, Marina, Mme
ZARANI, Nectaria, Mme, Fonctionnaire, Ministère de l'Interieur, de l'Administration publique et de la Décentralisation.

Délégué des employeurs

ANALYTIS, Nicolaos, M., Vice-Président, Fédération des Industries grecques (FIG).

Conseiller technique et délégué suppléant

CHARAKAS, Charilaos, M., Conseiller juridique, FIG.

Conseillers techniques

ARMENAKIS, Dimitrios, M., Président, Confédération nationale du Commerce.
DRAPANIOTIS, Yiannis, M., Directeur général, FIG.
PAPAIOANNOU, Lambros, M., Avocat, Fédération des Industries grecques.
VAYAS, Antonios, M., Conseiller du Travail, FIG.
CHATZARIDIS, Constantinos, M., Membre, Conseil d'administration, Confédération nationale du Commerce.
IOANNIDOU, Efthimia, Mme, Conseillère, Confédération nationale du Commerce.
BAXEVANIS, Michalis, M., Membre, Conseil d'administration, Confédération nationale du Commerce.
DRIKOS, Georgios, M., Confédération des petits et moyens entrepreneurs, artisans et commerçants.
KALOCHRISTIANAKIS, Georgios, M., Confédération des petits et moyens entrepreneurs, artisans et commerçants.

Délégué des travailleurs

POUPAKIS, Constantinos, M., Secrétaire général, Confédération générale des Travailleurs grecs.

Conseillers techniques et délégués suppléants

DELIYANNAKIS, Theodoros, M., Conseiller juridique, Confédération générale des Travailleurs grecs.
DASSIS, Georgios, M., Secrétaire, Relations internationales, Institut du Travail, Confédération générale des Travailleurs grecs.

Conseillers techniques

AGADAKOS, Fotis, M., Secrétaire adjoint, Confédération générale des Travailleurs grecs.
LANARA-TZOTZE, Zoi, Mme, Secrétaire des Relations internationales, Confédération générale des Travailleurs grecs.
ZOGANAS, Sotiris, M., Membre de Direction, Confédération générale des Travailleurs grecs.
PANAGOPOULOS, Yiannis, M., Secrétaire d'organisation, Confédération générale des Travailleurs grecs.
THOMAS, Philippos, M., Trésorier, Confédération générale des Travailleurs grecs.
MOUTAFIS, Vagelis, M., Secrétaire général adjoint, Confédération générale des Travailleurs grecs.
KATSOTIS, Christos, M., Membre, Comité exécutif, Confédération générale des Travailleurs grecs.
FOTAKIDIS, Fotis, M., Syndicat des Travailleurs (AGNO).

Personnes désignées en conformité avec l'article 2, alinéa 3 i)

KRATIMENOU, Vassiliki, Mme, Relations internationales, Confédération générale des Travailleurs grecs.

PECHLIVANIDOU, Evangelia, Mme, Relations internationales, Confédération générale des Travailleurs grecs.
PSAROYIANNI, Kyriaki, Mme, Relations internationales, Confédération générale des Travailleurs grecs.
PETROPOULOU, Ioulia, Mme, Relations internationales, Confédération générale des Travailleurs grecs.

Guatemala

Delegados gubernamentales

GALLARDO FLORES, Jorge Francisco, Sr., Ministro de Trabajo y Previsión Social.
GORDILLO GALINDO, Mario Estuardo, Sr., Segundo Viceministro de Trabajo y Previsión Social.

Consejeros técnicos y delegados suplentes

PIRA, Lars, Sr., Embajador, Representante Permanente, Misión Permanente, Ginebra.
ARGUETA, Alejandro, Sr., Asesor juridico, Ministerio Trabajo.
CHAVEZ BIETTI, Angela María, Sra., Ministro Consejero, Misión Permanente, Ginebra.
HOCHSTETTER SKINNER KLEE, Stephanie, Sra., Consejero, Misión Permanente, Ginebra.
MARTINEZ GALINDO, Ingrid, Sra., Primera Secretaria, Misión Permanente, Ginebra.
ARROYAVE PRERA, Carlos, Sr., Primer Secretario, Misión Permanente, Ginebra.

Otras personas que asisten a la Conferencia

SOLÓRZANO RIVERA, Carlos Alberto, Sr., Presidente, Comisión de Trabajo, Congreso de la República.
MIRALDA ROCA, Carlos Hipólito, Sr., Vicepresidente, Comisión de Trabajo, Congreso de la República.
BARRIOS FALLA, Jorge Mario, Sr., Secretario, Comisión de Trabajo, Congreso de la República.
VELASQUEZ CERDAS, Luis Alberto, Sr., Comisión de Trabajo, Congreso de la República.

Delegado de los empleadores

RICCI MUADI, Guido Domenico, Sr., Comité Coordinador de Asociaciones Agrícolas, Comerciales, Industriales y Financieras (CACIF).

Delegado de los trabajadores

MANCILLA GARCÍA, Carlos Enrique, Sr., Unión Guatemalteca de Trabajadores (UGT).

Guinée   Guinea   Guinea

Ministre assistant à la Conférence

KEIRA, Alpha Ibrahima, M., Ministre de l'Emploi et de la Fonction publique.

Délégués gouvernementaux

DIALLO, Nounkouman, M., Directeur national de l'Emploi et de la Réglementation du Travail.
DOUMBOUYA, Mamady, M., Inspecteur général du Travail.

Conseillers techniques

TOURE, Mame Penda, Mme, Directeur général, Agence guinéenne pour la Promotion de l'Emploi.
DIALLO, Saïdou, M., Directeur général, Caisse nationale de la Sécurité sociale.
SOUMAH, Mamadi Sam, M., Directeur général, Office national de Formation et de Perfectionnement professionnels.
DIALLO, Kadiatou Barry, Mme, Chef, Service des Accidents de Travail (CNSS).
TOURE, Réza, M., Médecin Conseil adjoint, CNSS.
KOUROUMA, Aminata, Mme, Chargé d'Affaires a.i., Mission permanente, Genève.
CAMARA, Balla Mousa, M., Représentant permanent adjoint, Mission permanente, Genève.
YOULA, Ibrahima, M., Premier Secrétaire, Mission permanente, Genève.

Délégué des employeurs

SYLLA, Mamadou, M., Président, Conseil du Patronat guinéen (CPG).

Conseillers techniques

DIALLO, Youssouf, M., Membre, Bureau exécutif, CPG; Président du CA, CNSS.
BANGOURA, Abdoul Karim, M., Membre, Bureau exécutif, CPG.
DABO, Abdoulaye Dima, M., Secrétaire exécutif, CPG.

Délégué des travailleurs

DIALLO, Rabiatou Serah, Mme, Secrétaire général, Confédération nationale des Travailleurs de Guinée (CNTG).

Conseillers techniques

FOFANA, Ibrahima, M., Secrétaire général, Union syndicale des Travailleurs de Guinée (USTG).
TOURE, Yamoudou, M., Secrétaire général, Organisation nationale des Syndicats libres de Guinée (ONSLG).
BANGOURA, Magbé, Mme, Secrétaire général, Confédération générale des Syndicats libres (CGSL).
DIALLO, Mariama Penda, Mme, USTG.

Guinée-Bissau   Guinea-Bissau
Guinea-Bissau

Délégués gouvernementaux

MUSSA BALDÉ, Carlos, M., Secrétaire d'Etat à la Fonction publique et au Travail.
MANÉ, Mussa, M., Conseiller, secteur de la gestion de la pêche.

Délégué des employeurs

BARBOSA, António, M., Directeur, Secrétariat de la Chambre du Commerce, de l'Industrie et de l'Agriculture.

Délégué des travailleurs

LIMA DA COSTA, Sebastião Desejado, M., Secrétaire général, Union nationale des Travailleurs de Guinée-Bissau (UNTG).

Conseiller technique

MENDES, Vença, M., Président, Confédération générale des Syndicats indépendants de Guinée-Bissau (CGSI-GB).

Guinée équatoriale
Equatorial Guinea
Guinea Ecuatorial

Ministro asistente a la Conferencia

IYANGA DJOBA MALANGO, Miguel, Sr., Ministro Asistente, Ministerio de Trabajo y Seguridad Social.

Delegados gubernamentales

ESUÁ NKÓ, Santiago, Sr., Director General, Trabajo y Fomento de Empleo.
ASAMA NTUGU, Honorato, Sr., Director General, Seguridad Social.

Consejeros técnicos

ALOGO MBA, Mariano, Sr., Jefe de Gabinete, Técnico-Asesor.
NSE MAYÉ, Amadeo, Sr., Jefe, Servicio Nacional de Empleo.

Delegado de los empleadores

MATZEN MAKOSO, Mariano, Sr.

Delegado de los trabajadores

SIMA MEA, Juan, Sr.

Guyana

Government Delegates

BISNAUTH, Ramnauth D.A., Mr., Minister of Labour, Human Services and Social Security.
OGLE, Charles, Mr., Senior Labour Officer.

Employers' Delegate

YANKANA, David, Mr.

Workers' Delegate

CULBARD, Grantley, Mr.

Haiti

Ministre assistant à la Conférence

CALIXTE, Pierre Claude, M., Ministre des Affaires Sociales.

Personne accompagnant le Ministre

GEORGES, Jean Yves, M., Directeur général, Ministère des Affaires sociales.

Délégués gouvernementaux

PIERRE, Jean Wilner, M., Directeur du Travail, Ministère des Affaires sociales.
JOSEPH, Jean Ronald, M., Directeur général, Office National Assurance Vieillesse.

Conseillers techniques

HILAIRE, Jeannot, M., Chargé d'Affaires a.i., Mission permanente, Genève.
JOSEPH, Eucher-Luc, M., Ministre conseiller, Mission permanente, Genève.

Délégué des employeurs

VICTOR, Guilaine, Mme, Secrétaire exécutive, Association des Industries d'Haïti (ADIH).

Conseiller technique

LIAUTAUD DIAZ, Nathalie, Mlle, Consultante, ADIH.

Délégué des travailleurs

NUMAS, Patrick, M., Secrétaire général, Organisation générale indépendante des Travailleurs haïtiens (OGITH).

Conseillers techniques et délégués suppléants

JOSEPH, Montès, M., Secrétaire général, Confédération des Ouvriers haïtiens (COH).
CHARLES, Fritz, M., Secrétaire général, Coordination syndicale haïtienne (CSH).

Honduras

Ministro asistente a la Conferencia

LEITZELAR VIDARRUETA, Germán Edgardo, Sr., Secretario de Estado de Trabajo y Seguridad Social.

Delegados gubernamentales

PONCE, Jorge, Sr., Asesor, Despacho Ministerial.
CRUZ RAMIREZ, Jacqueline, Sra., Asistente, Secretario de Estado.

Consejeros técnicos

ZAPATA, José Benjamín, Sr., Embajador, Representante Permanente, Misión Permanente, Ginebra.
BU FIGUEROA, Gracibel, Sra., Consejero, Misión Permanente, Ginebra.
PEREZ ZEPEDA, Mauricio Alfredo, Sr., Segundo Secretario, Misión Permanente, Ginebra.
LEITZELAR HERNANDEZ, Germán, Sr., Asesor, Secretaría de Estado, Despacho del Trabajo y Previsión Social.

Delegado de los empleadores

URTECHO LOPEZ, Armando, Sr., Asesor Legal, Consejo Hondureño de la Empresa Privada (COHEP).

Consejero técnico y delegado suplente

SIERRA, Vilma, Sra., Presidente Ejecutiva, Fundación para la Investigación y Desarrollo de Exportaciones (FIDE).

Consejero técnico

AGURCIA, José María, Sr., Presidente, COHEP.

Delegado de los trabajadores

IBARRA, Deysi Felipa, Sra., Confederación General de Trabajadores.

Hongrie   Hungary   Hungría

Government Delegates

HERCZOG, László, Mr., Deputy Secretary of State, Ministry of Employment and Labour.
TÓTH, Tibor, Mr., Ambassador, Permanent Representative, Permanent Mission, Geneva.

Advisers and substitute delegates

BÉKÉS, András, Mr., President, National Labour Inspectorate.
FÁRI, László, Mr., Deputy Head of Department, Ministry of Employment and Labour.

Advisers

BIHARY, Pál, Mr., Expert, Ministry of Employment and Labour.
BLAZSEK, Dóra, Ms., Third Secretary, Permanent Mission, Geneva.
FEHÉR, Zoltán, Mr., Attaché, Ministry of Foreign Affairs.
HORVÁTH, István, Mr., Head of Department, Ministry of Employment and Labour.
HORVÁTH, László, Mr., Chargé d'Affaires, Permanent Mission, Geneva.
KLEKNER, Péter, Mr., Chief Adviser, Prime Minister's Office.
SZALÓKINÉ-CSIMA, Katalin, Mrs., First Secretary, Permanent Mission, Geneva.
SZÉCSÉNYI, Rozália, Ms., Expert, Ministry of Employment and Labour.
THÁR, Orsolya, Ms., Expert, Ministry of Employment and Labour.
TÓTH, Judit, Ms., Senior Legal Adviser, Prime Minister's Office.
SZIGETI, Borbála, Ms.

Employers' Delegate

SZIRMAI, Péter, Mr., Co-president, National Association of Entrepreneurs and Employers.

Adviser and substitute delegate

CSUPORT, Antal, Mr., Managing Director, National Confederation of Companies for Strategic Services and Public Utilities.

Advisers

BOROSNÉ-BARTHA, Terézia, Mrs., International Director, Confederation of Hungarian Employers and Industrialists.
TÓTH, Károly, Mr., Consultant, National Confederation of Companies for Strategic Services and Public Utilities.
OLAY, Péterné, Mrs., Chief Counsellor, Hungarian Industrial Association.
SZABADKAI, Antal, Mr., Head of Secretariat, Union of Agrarian Employers.

SZEREMI, Lászlóné, Mrs., Chief Counsellor, National Federation of Agricultural Co-operators and Producers.
SZÜCS, György, Mr., President, National Association of the Industrial Corporation.

Workers' Delegate

GASKÓ, István, Mr., President, Democratic League of Independent Trade Unions.

Adviser and substitute delegate

TAMÁS, Erika, Ms., Expert, Democratic League of Independent Trade Unions.

Advisers

AGG, Géza, Mr., Expert, Cooperative Forum of Trade Unions.
CZUGLERNÉ-IVÁNY, Judit, Mrs., Director, Human Rights and Labour Standards, National Federation of Workers' Councils.
GERGELY, Pál, Mr., Senior Expert, National Federation of Autonomous Trade Unions.
GYÖRGY, Károly, Mr., Member, Executive Board, National Confederation of the Hungarian Trade Unions.
HUSZTA, Krisztián, Mr., Expert, Democratic League of Independent Trade Unions.
WITTICH, Tamás, Mr., President, National Confederation of the Hungarian Trade Unions.
TÓTH, Atilla, Mr., Adviser, Trade Union Group of Professionals.

Inde   India   India

Minister attending the Conference

OLA, Sis Ram, Mr., Minister of Labour.

Government Delegates

SHENOY, P.D., Mr., Secretary (Labour).
RAI, Baleshwar, Mr., Additional Secretary, Ministry of Labour.

Adviser and substitute delegate

PURI, H.S., Mr., Ambassador, Permanent Representative, Permanent Mission, Geneva.

Advisers

MURTY, Asha, Mrs., Joint Secretary and Director-General of Employment and Training, Ministry of Labour.
CHANDRAMOULI, K., Mr., Joint Secretary, Ministry of Labour.
SAHA, Debabrata, Mr., Deputy Permanent Representative, Permanent Mission, Geneva.
POONIA, D.S., Mr., Joint Secretary, Ministry of Labour.

PATTANAIK, P.K., Mr., Joint Secretary, Department of Animal Husbandry, Ministry of Agriculture.
SINGH, A.V., Mr., Director, Ministry of Labour.
MANN, J.S., Mr., Private Secretary to the Minister of Labour.
CHATTERJEE, Arun Kumar, Mr., First Secretary, Permanent Mission, Geneva.

Representatives of a State or Province

CHATURVEDI, Satish, Mr., Minister of Labour, Government of Maharshtra.
SINGH, Ch. Jagjit, Mr., Minister of Labour, Government of Punjab.
SEKHRI, Ashwani, Mr., Minister of State, Labour & Employment, Government of Punjab.
SINGH, Jaspal, Mr., Labour Commissioner, Government of Punjab.
BEHL, Ramesh, Mr., Additional Labour Commissioner, Governement of Punjab.
AMIN, Mohd., Mr., Minister of Labour, Government of West Bengal.

Employers' Delegate

PODDAR, S.K., Mr., President, Council of Indian Employers (CIE).

Advisers

ANAND, I.P., Mr., Member, Governing Body of the ILO.
JAIN, C.P., Mr., Chairman and Managing Director, National Thermal Power Corporation; Chairman, Standing Conference of Public Enterprises (SCOPE).
DEWAN, S.M., Mr., Director General, SCOPE.
PANT, B.P., Mr., Secretary, CIE.
PATIL, Sharad, Mr., Secretary-General, Employers' Federation of India (EFI).
SOMANY, R.K., Mr., President, EFI.
TARNEJA, Ram, Mr., Chairman, M/s Jolly Board Limited.
TODI, Babulal, Mr., President, All India Manufacturers' Organisation (AIMO).
KALANTRI, Vijay G., Mr., President, All India Association of Industries (AIAI).
WIG, Ravi, Mr., President, PHD Chamber of Commerce and Industry (PHDCCI).

Person appointed in accordance with Article 2, paragraph 3(i)

DHAKA, B.P., Mr., Secretary-General, PHDCCI.

Workers' Delegate

DAVE, Hasumukhlal G., Mr., President, Bhartiya Mazdoor Sangh (BMS).

Advisers

RAMAN, Ravi, Mr., Member, BMS.

GHATOWAR, P.S., Mr., Vice-President, Indian National Trade Union Congress (INTUC).
KALAN, G., Mr., Organizing Secretary, INTUC.
SEN, Tapan, Mr., Secretary, Centre of Indian Trade Unions (CITU).
THOMAS, Thampan, Mr., President, Hind Mazdoor Sabha (HMS).
MAHADEVAN, H., Mr., Deputy General Secretary, All India Trade Union Congress (AITUC).
SANKAR SAHA, P., Mr., Secretary, United Trade Union Centre (LS).

Indonésie   Indonesia   Indonesia

Government Delegates

SITUMORANG, Edison, Mr., Expert Adviser to the Minister of Manpower and Transmigration, Department of Manpower and Transmigration.
ALOEWIE, Tjepy F., Mr., Secretary General, Department of Manpower and Transmigration.

Advisers and substitute delegates

HARIYADHI, Eddi, Mr., Chargé d'Affaires/Ambassador, Deputy Permanent Representative, Permanent Mission, Geneva.
SULISTYANINGSIH, Endang, Ms., Head, Administration Centre of Foreign Cooperation, Department of Manpower and Transmigration.

Advisers

TAMBUSAI, Muzni, Mr., Director-General for Industrial Relations, Department of Manpower and Transmigration.
MUDJIMAN, Mochamad, Mr., Head, Education and Training, and Productivity, Department of Manpower and Transmigration.
BAHARUDDIN, Amrinal, Mr., Inspector General, Department of Manpower and Transmigration.
MUFIDZ, Ali, Mr., Vice Governor, Jawa Tengah.
HANARTANI, Myra M., Mrs., Head, Bureau for Laws, Department of Manpower and Transmigration.
HENDARTI, Tati, Mrs., Director, Standardization and Certification, Department of Manpower and Transmigration.
NAPITUPULU, Togarisman, Mr., Director, Employment Learning, Department of Manpower and Transmigration.
DHARMA, Adji, Mr., Director, Promotion and Placement of Indonesian Migrant Workers, Department of Manpower and Transmigration.
PANCADEWA, Fifi Arianti, Ms., Director, Dissemination and Information of Migration, Department of Manpower and Transmigration.
SINAGA, Tianggur, Mrs., Director, Wages, Social Security and Welfare, Department of Manpower and Transmigration.
SUGANDHI, Gandhi, Mr., Director, Settlement and Dispute of Industrial Relations, Department of Manpower and Transmigration.
SOETRISNO, Noer, Mr., Deputy, Resources Analysis for SMEs and Cooperatives, Office of the State Minister for Cooperatives and SMEs.
PUJA, I. Gusti Agung Wesaka, Mr., Director, Human Rights, Humanitarian, Social and Culture, Department of Foreign Affairs.
MULYONO, Mr., Secretary, Directorate General of Labour Supervision, Department of Manpower and Transmigration.
WARSITO, Indro, Mr., Director, Placement Institutional, Department of Manpower and Transmigration.
SUGIYANTO, Agus, Mr., Director, Employment Productivity, Department of Manpower and Transmigration.
SOEMARNO, Sunu Mahadi, Mr., Counsellor, Permanent Mission, Geneva.
SARWONO, Ade Padmo, Mr., First Secretary, Permanent Mission, Geneva.

Persons appointed in accordance with Article 2, paragraph 3(i)

DARADJAT, Adjat, Mr., Acting Director, Labour Norms Supervision, Department of Manpower and Transmigration.
SUROBIYANTO, Mr., Head, Provincial Labour Dispute Settlements, Provincial Government of Jawa Tengah.
SINAGA, Pariaman, Mr., Official, Office of the State Minister for Cooperatives and SMEs.
YUWANTI, Sri, Ms., Official, Provincial Government of Jawa Tengah.
RUMONDANG, Haiyani, Ms., Official, Department of Manpower and Transmigration
WICAKSONO, Guntur, Mr., Official, Department of Manpower and Transmigration
AGAH, Hariyadi, Mr., Official, Department of Manpower and Transmigration
ANGGRAENI, Diah, Ms., Head, Manpower and Transmigration Agency, Provincial Government of Jawa Tengah.
SINAGA, Godang, Mr., Official, Department of Manpower and Transmigration.
SUMIRAT, Agung C., Mr., Third Secretary, Permanent Mission, Geneva.

Other persons attending the Conference

DJAELANI, M., Mr., Head, Manpower and Transmigration Agency, Provincial Government of Jawa Timur.
HENDRARSO, Win, Mr., Regent of Sidoardjo.
WIDAGDO, Bambang S., Mr., Head, Manpower and Transmigration Agency, Regency of Sidoardjo.
LESTARI, Sri, Ms., Official, Department of Manpower and Transmigration.
RITONGA, Orina, Ms., Head of Section, Directorate of Human Rights, Ministry of Foreign Affairs.

Employers' Delegate

RACHMAN, Hasanuddin, Mr., Chairperson, Employers' Association of Indonesia.

Advisers

WANANDI, Sofyan, Mr., General Chairman, Employers' Association of Indonesia.
SETIONO, Gatut Djoko, Mr., Deputy Secretar-General, Employers' Association of Indonesia.
WIBISONO, Bambang, Mr., Coordinator for International Relations and Cooperation, Employers' Association of Indonesia.
MASRANA, Mr., Coordinator, Organizational Development on Regions, Employers' Association of Indonesia.
NAE SOI, Joseph A., Mr., Head Coordinator, Education and Training, Employers' Association of Indonesia.
ZAINI, Muchlison, Mr., Philips Seafood.
ALAYDRUS, Husein A., Mr., General Chairman, APJATI.
UMAR, H. Said, Mr., Vice-General Chairman, APJATI.
MARGONO, Heri, Mr., BP Migas.
DJUNAIDI, A., Mr., Chief Director, PT Jamsostek.

Persons appointed in accordance with Article 2, paragraph 3(i)

HERMANSYAFM, Harry, Mr., BP Migas.
KESWARA, Iwa, Mr., BP Migas.
WELEM, Liem, Mr., Chairman, BO-APJATI "HOKINDO".
HARYADI, Indra, Mr., Director, Operation and Services, PT Jamsostek.
SUPARWANTO, Mr., Member of Commissioner, PT Jamsostek.

Other persons attending the Conference

WANADI, Riantini Sofyan, Mrs., Commissioner of PT Gemala.
ROOZANTY, Amalia Mungzy, Ms., Tripartite Magazine.
BAHASUAN, Rusydi, Mr., Chairman, Paramitra Foundation.
DJAJANEGARA, Afiat, Mr., PT. Conoco Phillips.

Workers' Delegate

DAVID, M.Ch., Mr., Confederation of Indonesian Workers Union (KSPSI).

Advisers and substitute delegates

SARTO, Syukur, Mr., Confederation of Indonesian Labour Union (KSBSI).
SIRAIT, Martin, Mr., SBMI.
SILABAN, Rekson, Mr., General Chairman, KSBSI.
ZAIDY, Achfin, Mr., Group 17.

Advisers

ROSIDIN, Idin, Mr., Confederation of Indonesian Labour Union (KSBSI).
AKSAN, Rustam, Mr., KSPSI.
MUNASWAR, Indra, Mr., SPSI Reformasi.
SUTARNADI, Hidayat, Mr., F. PBI/Others Groups.
SUDIONO, Achmad, Mr., SPSI - Jawa Tengah.
PALAR, Idris, Mr., Association of Informal Economy.

Other persons attending the Conference

AMIR, Yenny, Ms., Chairperson, Farkes KSPSI.
LATIEF, Lina, Ms., Chairperson, Women Institution, KSPSI.
SYUKUR, Bambang S., Mr., General Chairman, FSP BUMN.
SYAFRIE, Nazir, Mr., General Secretary, FSP BUMN.
SALIM, Helmy, Mr., Deputy Secretary-General, KSPSI.
AHMAD, Hanief, Mr., Deputy Secretary-General, KSPSI.
ACHMAD, Arsyad, Mr., General Secretary, KEP.
SIMAMORA, John D.P., Mr., Chairman, SPBPU KSPSI.

République islamique d'Iran
Islamic Republic of Iran
República Islámica del Irán

Minister attending the Conference

KHALEGHI, Naser, Mr., Minister of Labour and Social Affairs.

Persons accompanying the Minister

ALBORZI, Mohammad-Reza, Mr., Ambassador, Permanent Representative, Permanent Mission, Geneva.
MOJTAHED SHABESTARI, Ali A., Mr., Ambassador, Permanent Mission, Geneva.
MEHRPOUR, Hussein, Mr., Presidential Adviser.

Government Delegates

SALAMATI, Mohammad, Mr., Deputy Labour Minister, Ministry of Labour and Social Affairs (MOLSA).
HEFDAHTAN, S. Hassan, Mr., Director-General, International Relations Department, MOLSA.

Advisers and substitute delegates

SEPEHRI, Mohammad-Reza, Mr., Head, Labour and Social Security Institute.
SHEIKH, Behzad, Mr., Deputy Director-General, International Relations Department, MOLSA.

Advisers

TASDIGHI, Shohreh, Ms., Senior Expert, ILO's Affairs, MOLSA.

RAJABI, Morteza, Mr., Director-General, Labour Relations Department, MOLSA.
ALAFAR, Elahe, Ms., Director-General, Women's Employment Office, MOLSA.
ASLI, Ebrahim, Mr., Expert, Financial and Administrative Affairs, MOLSA.
GHORBANI, Hekmatollah, Mr., Third Secretary, Permanent Mission, Geneva.
GHASEMI, Ali, Mr., Director-General, Iran's Fisheries Company.
TAJJEDIN, Abdelrahman, Mr., Senior Expert, Deputy Ministers Council, MOLSA.
ZIARAN, Bozorgmehr, Mr., Director-General, Office for UN Specialized Agencies, Ministry of Foreign Affairs.
RAES SHAGHAGHI, Abdolreza, Mr., Expert, Ministry of Foreign Affairs.

Persons appointed in accordance with Article 2, paragraph 3(i)

GHARAIE, Gholam-Ali, Mr., Secretariat's Head, Iranian Auto Parts Manufacturers Association, NGO.
MARA'SHI, Amir Hossain, Mr., NGO.

Employers' Delegate

NAJAFIMANESH, Mohammad Reza, Mr., Member, Iran's Confederation of Employers' Associations (ICEA).

Adviser and substitute delegate

RAIESI FARD, Nasser, Mr., Member, ICEA.

Advisers

SHA'BANI, Fatemeh, Ms., Member, ICEA.
SHOGHI, Ali, Mr., Member, ICEA.
HAGH-BAYAN, Mohammadi Hussein, Mr., Member, ICEA.
AHMADI-ZADEH, Hossein, Mr., Member, ICEA.

Workers' Delegate

SALIMIAN, Jabbar Ali, Mr., Representative of Iranian Workers; Chairman, Islamic Labour Coordination Council, Yazd Province.

Adviser and substitute delegate

HAMZEH, Mohammad, Mr., Director, International Relations Department, Workers' House.

Advisers

MAHJOOB, Alireza, Mr., Secretary General, Workers' House.
JELODARZADEH, Sohaila, Ms., Head of Women's Branch, Workers' House.
SAVAEDI, Ghadir, Mr., Chairman, Islamic Labour Council, Khuzestan Pipe Manufacturing Company.

SADEGHI, Hassan, Mr., President, Confederation of Islamic Labour Councils (CILC); Member, Executive Board, Workers' House.
DEHGHAN DEHNAVI, Sedigheh, Mrs., Head of Women's Branch, Workers' House, Yazd Province.
GHILANPOOR, Maryam, Mrs.

Iraq

Minister attending the Conference

AL-MA'JUN, Sami Azara, Mr., Minister of Labour.

Government Delegates

LATIF, Nouri Marza Jaafar, Mr., Ministry of Labour.
KHODIR, Mondir Abdeljabar, Mr., Director, Arab and International Relations.

Advisers

SALMAN, Mukdad Hadi, Mr., Chargé d'Affaires, Permanent Mission, Geneva.
YAS, Miada Abdelhadi, Ms., First Secretary, Ministry of Foreign Affairs.
MAJID, Mohammed S., Mr., Second Secretary, Permanent Mission, Geneva.
ALDIN, Omar Naji Zain, Mr., Second Secretary, Permanent Mission, Geneva.
MANDAN, Hussein Ali, Mr., Director, Legal Affairs, Labour and Social Security Service.
ELIA, Jackeline Selio, Ms., Adviser, National Recruitment Centre.

Employers' Delegate

AL-KHAFAJI, Kais Khadim, Mr., President, Iraki Industrial Union.

Advisers

ZANKANA, Hussein Ali Ahmed, Mr., Member, Council.
JAMIL, Khadim Turqui, Mr., Member, Council.

Workers' Delegate

AL-AWADI, Rassim Hussein, Mr., President, General Union of Trade Unions.

Advisers

ADLIMI, Mahal Hardan, Mr., Vice-President, General Union of Trade Unions.
MUSHIN, Abdullah, Mr., Employee.
ALI, Kamel Aziz, Mr., Member, Executive Bureau.

Irlande   Ireland   Irlanda

Minister attending the Conference

FAHEY, Frank, Mr., Minister for Labour Affairs.

Person accompanying the Minister

NI SHUILLEABHAIN, Aoibheann, Ms., Private Secretary to the Minister.

Government Delegates

WHELAN, Mary,, Ms., Ambassador, Permanent Representative, Permanent Mission, Geneva.
BENNETT, Paul, Mr., Deputy Permanent Representative, Permanent Mission, Geneva.

Advisers and substitute delegates

WALSH, John, Mr., Assistant Secretary, Department of Enterprise, Trade and Employment.
CUNNIFFE, Michael, Mr., Principal, Department of Enterprise, Trade and Employment.
O'CALLAGHAN, Tom, Mr., Nautical Surveyor, Maritime Safety Directorate, Department of Communications, Marine and Natural Resources.
KEATINGE, Michael, Mr., Seafisheries Development Manager, Irish Fisheries Board (B.I.M.).
PENDER, Michael, Mr., Assistant Principal, Department of Enterprise, Trade and Employment.
COLFER, Denis, Mr., Assistant Principal, Department of Enterprise, Trade and Employment.
MCDONNELL, John, Mr., Higher Executive Officer, Department of Enterprise, Trade and Employment.
DALY, Evelyn, Ms., Higher Executive Officer, Department of Enterprise, Trade and Employment.
ROSS, Anne-Marie, Ms., Administrative Officer, Department of Enterprise, Trade and Employment.
O'DONNELL, Mary, Ms., Executive Officer, Department of Enterprise, Trade and Employment.
CARPENTER, Breffini, Mr., Assistant Principal, Permanent Mission, Geneva.
CAHALANE, Brian, Mr., First Secretary, Permanent Mission, Geneva.
MANGAN, Sarah, Ms., First Secretary, Permanent Mission, Geneva.
O'RAGHALLAIGH, Michael, Mr., Third Secretary, Permanent Mission, Geneva.
MAHER, Orla, Ms., Third Secretary, Permanent Mission, Geneva.
MOLLAGHAN, Patricia, Ms., Permanent Mission, Geneva.
MOORE, Olive, Ms., Permanent Mission, Geneva.
RYAN, Elaine, Ms., Permanent Mission, Geneva.
NI MHUIRCHEARTAIGH, Nuala, Ms., Permanent Mission, Geneva.

Other persons attending the Conference

MANGIN, Kate, Ms., Permanent Mission, Geneva.
VALENTE, Ana, Ms., Permanent Mission, Geneva.

Employers' Delegate

FLOOD, Peter, Mr., Assistant Director of Social Affairs - Equality, Irish Business and Employers Confederation (IBEC).

Adviser and substitute delegate

MAGUIRE, Catherine, Ms., Social Policy Executive, IBEC.

Workers' Delegate

LYNCH, Esther, Ms., Legislative Officer, Irish Congress of Trade Unions (ITCU).

Adviser and substitute delegate

MACKIN, Brendan, Mr., President, ICTU.

Islande   Iceland   Islandia

Government Delegates

HAUKUR JOHANNESSON, Stefan, Mr., Ambassador, Permanent Representative, Permanent Mission, Geneva.
KRISTINSSON, Gylfi, Mr., Director, Ministry of Social Affairs.

Advisers and substitute delegates

DAVIDSDOTTIR, Ingibjorg, Ms., First Secretary, Permanent Mission, Geneva.
SIGRIDUR GUNNSTEINSDOTTIR, Hanna, Ms., Legal Adviser, Ministry of Social Affairs.

Advisers

SKULI AUDUNSSON, Hlynur, Mr., Legal Adviser, Icelandic Maritime Administration.
EGILSSON, Vilhjálmur, Mr., Permanent Secretary, Ministry of Fisheries.

Employers' Delegate

STEFANSDOTTIR, Hrafnhildur, Ms., Chief Attorney at Law, Confederation of Icelandic Employers.

Adviser and substitute delegate

MAGNUSSON, Jon H., Mr., Attorney at Law, Confederation of Icelandic Employers.

Workers' Delegate

NORDDAHL, Magnus, Mr., Chief Lawyer, Icelandic Confederation of Labour.

Adviser and substitute delegate

FINNBOGASON, Palmi, Mr., Office Manager, Federation of Skilled Construction and Industrial Workers, Icelandic Confederation of Labour.

Advisers

GUNNARSSON, Saevar, Mr., President, Seamen's Federation, Icelandic Confederation of Labour.
GUDMUNDSDOTTIR, Erna, Ms., Lawyer, Federation of State and Municipal Employees.
STEFANSDOTTIR, Ólöf Lilja, Ms., Icelandic Confederation of Labour.

Israel

Government Delegates

DINUR, Raanan, Mr., Director-General, Ministry of Industry, Trade and Labour.
LEVY, Yaakov, Mr., Ambassador, Permanent Representative, Permanent Mission, Geneva.

Advisers and substitute delegates

PAZ, Eli, Mr., Senior Deputy Director-General, Ministry of Labour.
ITZHAKI, Shlomo, Mr., Chief Labour Relations Officer, Ministry of Labour.
SHTRAUS, Shoshana, Ms., Legal Adviser, Ministry of Labour.
WASSERMAN, Judith, Ms., Legal Adviser, The Knesset.
BEN-TURA, Eli, Mr., Deputy Director, Ministry of Foreign Affairs.
WAXMAN, Haim, Mr., Counsellor, Permanent Mission, Geneva.
AKERMAN, Joseph, Mr., First Secretary, Permanent Mission, Geneva.
FURMAN, Noa, Ms., Counsellor, Ministry of Foreign Affairs.

Advisers

AVRAHAM HERLIN, Sigal, Mrs., Adviser, Permanent Mission, Geneva.
GULUMA, Teizu, Ms., Adviser, Permanent Mission, Geneva.
GOULDMAN-ZARKA, Esther, Ms., Adviser, Permanent Mission, Geneva.
WURCEL, Gabriela, Ms., Adviser, Permanent Mission, Geneva.

Employers' Delegate

GATTEGNO, Joseph, Mr., Head, Labour and Human Resources Division, Manufacturers' Association of Israel.

Adviser and substitute delegate

BARAK, Yitzhak, Mr., Labour Lawyer.

Workers' Delegate

KARA, Youssef, Mr., Member, Executive Bureau, Histadrut.

Advisers and substitute delegates

MASSALHA, Nawaff, Mr., Chairman, New Histadrut.
GELMAN, Gershon, Mr., Chairman, Labour Council.
BENYAISH, Samy, Mr., Chief Operations Officer, Histadrut.
FROHLICH, Michael, Mr., Programming Director, International Institute of the Histadrut.

Italie   Italy   Italia

Ministre assistant à la Conférence

MARONI, Roberto, M., Ministre du Travail.

Personnes accompagnant le Ministre

BRUNI, Paolo, M., Ambassadeur, Représentant permanent, Mission permanente, Genève.
VILLANI, Marco, M., Conseiller diplomatique du Ministre du Travail.

Délégués gouvernementaux

TRIA, Giovanni, M., Ministère des Affaires étrangères.
PRIA, Angela, Mme, Chef, Cabinet du Ministre du Travail.

Conseillers techniques

NEGROTTO CAMBIASO, Andrea, M., Ambassadeur.
SIMONETTI, Valentino, M., Représentant permanent adjoint, Mission permanente, Genève.
COLOMBO, Filippo, M., Premier Secrétaire, Mission permanente, Genève.
TRENTO, Luigi, M., Protection des Conditions de Travail, Ministère du Travail.
POLSELLI, Massimo, M., Direction de l'Emploi, Ministère du Travail.
NICOLETTI, Paola, Mme, ISFOL.
RICCI, Daniela, Mme, ISFOL.
DESSI, Giorgia, Mme, Protection des Conditions de Travail, Ministère du Travail.

TRIPODI, Attillio, M., Direction générale Pêche et Aquaculture, Ministère des Politiques agricoles et forestières.
MOLTONI, Stefania, Mme, Transport maritime et Interne, Ministère des Infrastructures et des Transports.
MONTERISI, Sara, Mme, Direction générale de l'Immigration, Ministère du Travail.
HENRY, Giulia, Mme, Direction générale pour l'Immigration, Ministère du Travail.
FRANCESCHELLI, Renato, M., Direction centrale pour les Politiques de l'Immigration et de l'Asile, Ministère de l'Intérieur.
FERRAIOLO, Carmen, Mme, Protection des Conditions de Travail, Ministère du Travail.
ZAMBRANO, Anna, Mme, Expert, Ministère des Affaires étrangères.
VIGLIETTA, Germana, Mme, Ministère du Travail et des Politiques sociales.

Personne désignée en conformité avec l'article 2, alinéa 3 i)

DE CICCO, Giuseppe, M., Protection des Conditions de Travail, Ministère du Travail.

Délégué des employeurs

SASSO MAZZUFFERI, Lucia, Mme, Dirigeant, Bureau Affaires industrielles, Confindustria; membre adjoint, Conseil d'administration du BIT.

Conseillers techniques

FERRARA, Giancarlo, M., Travail et Relations industrielles, Association bancaire italienne.
CATAPANO, Claudio, M., Travail et Relations syndicales, ConfCommercio.
MINERVINI, Domenico, M., Marché du Travail, Confederazione Nazionale dell'Artigianato e della Piccola e Media Impresa (CNA).
ROSSI, Stefania, Mme, Travail et Relations Industrielles, Confindustria.

Délégué des travailleurs

TARTAGLIA, Leopoldo, M., Departement international, CGIL.

Conseiller technique et délégué suppléant

BRIGHI, Cecilia, Mme, Confederazione Italiana Sindacato Lavoratori (CISL).

Conseillers techniques

TIMI, Mietta, Mme, UIL.
DEL RIO, Cinzia, Mme, UIL.
SOLDINI, Piero, M., CGIL.
OCMIN ALVAREZ, Liliana, Mme, CISL.
COROSSAZ, Anna, Mme, CGIL.
BENZI, Gianfranco, M., CGIL.
ITALIA, Gianni, M., ISCOS-CISL.

Personnes désignées en conformité avec l'article 2, alinéa 3 i)

BARBIERI, Giacomo, M., CGIL.
CAL, Luigi, M., CISL.
CEDRONE, Carmelo, M., UIL.
IULIANO, Giuseppe, M., CISL.
DI SALVO, Titti, Mme, CGIL.

Jamaïque   Jamaica   Jamaica

Minister attending the Conference

DALLEY, Horace, Mr., Minister of Labour and Social Security.

Government Delegates

SMITH, Ransford, Mr., Ambassador, Permanent Representative, Permanent Mission, Geneva.
SMITH, Gresford, Mr., Chief Technical Director, Ministry of Labour and Social Security.

Advisers and substitute delegates

DAVIES, Philippa, Ms., First Secretary, Permanent Mission, Geneva.
YING, Neville, Mr., Director of Business Studies, Mona School of Business, University of the West Indies.
GREGORY, Robert, Mr., Executive Director, HEART Trust.
DACOSTA, Barbara, Ms., Chief Liaison Officer in Washington.
BETTON, Symone, Ms., First Secretary, Permanent Mission, Geneva

Employers' Delegate

LEWIS, Herbert, Mr., President, Jamaica Employers Federation.

Adviser and substitute delegate

COKE-LLOYD, Jacqueline, Ms., Executive Director, Jamaica Employers' Federation.

Workers' Delegate

GOODLEIGH, Lloyd, Mr., General Secretary, Jamaica Confederation of Trade Unions.

Advisers and substitute delegates

NELSON, Dwight, Mr., Vice President, Jamaica Confederation of Trade Unions.
DAVIS-WHYTE, Helene, Mrs., Vice-President, Jamaica Confederation of Trade Unions.
DOBSON, Clive, Mr., Council Member, Jamaica Confederation of Trade Unions.

BROWN, Lambert, Mr., First Vice-President, University and Allied Workers Union.
PHILLIPS, Marva, Ms., Council Member, Jamaica Confederation of Trade Unions.

Japon   Japan   Japón

Minister attending the Conference

TOGARI, Toshikazu, Mr., Vice-Minister for Policy Coordination, Ministry of Health, Labour and Welfare.

Persons accompanying the Minister

HORIE, Masakazu, Mr., Ministry of Health, Labour and Welfare.
NOCHI, Yuji, Mr., Director, International Information Office, International Affairs Division, Minister's Secretariat, Ministry of Health, Labour and Welfare.

Government Delegates

OSHIMA, Shotaro, Mr., Ambassador, Permanent Representative, Permanent Mission, Geneva.
HASEGAWA, Shinichi, Mr., Assistant Minister, Minister's Secretariat, Ministry of Health, Labour and Welfare.

Advisers and substitute delegates

ENDO, Shigeru, Mr., Ambassador, Permanent Mission, Geneva.
TSUNEKAWA, Kenji, Mr., Director-General, Industrial Safety and Health Department, Labour Standards Bureau, Ministry of Health, Labour and Welfare.
SOBASHIMA, Hidenobu, Mr., Minister, Permanent Mission, Geneva.
HAYASHI, Masahiko, Mr., Counsellor, Permanent Mission, Geneva.
HORIE, Hiroyuki, Mr., Counsellor, Permanent Mission, Geneva.

Advisers

UEDA, Hiroshi, Mr., Director, Local Public Service Personnel Division, Local Administration Bureau, Ministry of Public Management, Home Affairs, Posts and Telecommunications.
KOUDA, Masaharu, Mr., Director, Fire Defence Division, Fire and Disaster Management Agency, Ministry of Public Management, Home Affairs, Posts and Telecommunications.
KUSANO, Takahiko, Mr., Director for Labour Policies, Ministry of Health, Labour and Welfare.
OGAWA, Makoto, Mr., Director, Foreign Worker's Affairs Division, Employment Security Bureau, Ministry of Health, Labour and Welfare.
YOSHIMOTO, Akiko, Ms., Director, Social Infrastructure Office, General Affairs Division, Human Resources Development Bureau, Ministry of Health, Labour and Welfare.

TAKAKUWA, Mitsuaki, Mr., Vice-Counsellor for Industrial Relations, Ministry of Health, Labour and Welfare.
SHIMADA, Hiroko, Ms., Director, Public Relations and Information Office, General Affairs Division, Secretariat of National Personnel Authority.
TAKAHASHI, Ichiro, Mr., Counsellor, Permanent Mission, Geneva.
MATSUURA, Junya, Mr., First Secretary, Permanent Mission, Geneva.
TAKEBA, Yuki, Mr., Deputy Director, Policy Planning Division, Fisheries Agency, Ministry of Agriculture, Forestry and Fisheries.
KAMITANI, Masashi, Mr., Deputy Counsellor, Reform Promotion Division for Civil Service System, Administrative Reform Promotion Bureau, Cabinet Secretariat.
TAKAHASHI, Hidenori, Mr., First Secretary, Embassy of Japan in the Federal Republic of Germany.
TOMITA, Nozomi, Mr., First Secretary, Delegation of Japan to the Organization of Economic Cooperation and Development.
KINOSHITA, Kazuhiro, Mr., Deputy Counsellor, Personnel and Pension Bureau, Ministry of Public Management, Home Affairs, Posts and Telecommunications.
HIRATSUKA, Yoichi, Mr., Deputy Director, International Affairs Division, Minister's Secretariat, Ministry of Health, Labour and Welfare.

Other persons attending the Conference

ARAI, Yusuke, Mr., First Secretary, Permanent Mission, Geneva.
YAMAGUCHI, Tadahiko, Mr., First Secretary, Permanent Mission, Geneva.
TERAKADO, Shigechika, Mr., First Secretary, Permanent Mission, Geneva.
KATAFUCHI, Hirofumi, Mr., Deputy Director, Office of Counsellor for Labour Relations, Ministry of Health, Labour and Welfare.
MIYAHARA, Shintaro, Mr., Deputy Director, International Affairs Division, Minister's Secretariat, Ministry of Health, Labour and Welfare.
KOYAMA, Shigeki, Mr., First Secretary, Permanent Mission, Geneva.
UCHIDA, Hiroyuki, Mr., Deputy Counsellor, Personnel and Pension Bureau, Ministry of Public Management, Home Affairs, Posts and Telecommunications.
ISHIKAWA, Satoshi, Mr., Section Chief, General Affairs Division, Equal Employment, Children and Families Bureau, Ministry of Health, Labour and Welfare.
SASAKI, Kouki, Mr., Section Chief, Fire and Disaster Management Agency, Ministry of Public Management, Home Affairs, Posts and Telecommunications.
MAEDA, Nahoko, Ms., Official, Specialized Agencies' Administration Division, Multilateral Cooperation Department, Foreign Policy Bureau, Ministry of Foreign Affairs.
EGUCHI, Tetsuro, Mr., Senior Official, Local Public Service Personnel Division, Local Administration Bureau, Ministry of Public Management, Home Affairs, Posts and Telecommunications.

YOSHIDA, Makoto, Mr., Section Chief, Foreign Workers' Affairs Division, Employment Security Bureau, Ministry of Health, Labour and Welfare.
ARAI, Junko, Ms., Official, International Affairs Division, Minister's Secretariat, Ministry of Health, Labour and Welfare.
KAWAI, Natsumi, Ms., Official, International Affairs Division, Minister's Secretariat, Ministry of Health, Labour and Welfare.

Employers' Delegate

OKUDA, Hiroshi, Mr., Chairman, Japan Business Federation (JBF).

Advisers and substitute delegates

SUZUKI, Toshio, Mr., Executive Advisor, Nippon-Keidanren International Cooperation Center; Member of the ILO Governing Body.
YANO, Hironori, Mr., Senior Managing Director, JBF.

Advisers

SAGAE, Ryoichi, Mr., General Manager, Japan Deep Sea Trawlers Association.
SANUI, Nobuko, Ms., Director, International Labor Policy Bureau, JBF.
TAKAZAWA, Takio, Mr., Manager, International Relations Group, International Labor Policy Bureau, JBF.
ABE, Hiroshi, Mr., Employment and Personnel Management Group, Labor Policy Bureau, JBF.

Other persons attending the Conference

FUJII, Tsunehiko, Mr., General Manager, Government and Industrial Affairs Division, Toyota Motor Corporation.
HIGUCHI, Kenichiro, Mr., Assistant Manager, Planning Department, Government and Industrial Affairs Division, Toyota Motor Corporation.
YOSHIMURA, Kazutaka, Mr., Project General Manager, Secretarial Division, Toyota Motor Corporation.
GOTO, Shigefumi, Mr., Directeur général, Bureau de Paris, Toyota Motor Europe.

Workers' Delegate

KUSANO, Tadayoshi, Mr., General Secretary, Japanese Trade Union Confederation (JTUC-RENGO).

Adviser and substitute delegate

NAKAJIMA, Shigeru, Mr., Executive Director, International Affairs Department, JTUC-RENGO; Member of the ILO Governing Body.

Advisers

SUGA, Yasutaka, Mr., Executive Director, Department of Working Conditions, JTUC-RENGO.

INOKUCHI, Noboru, Mr., Director, International Department, All Japan Prefectural and Municipal Workers Union (JICHIRO).
AIHARA, Kumiko, Ms., Deputy Director, Organisational Management Department (JICHIRO).
YOSHIHARA, Kikue, Ms., Vice President, Japan Teachers' Union, JTU.
KOBORI, Hiroyuki, Mr., Secretary, Bureau of Fisheries, Member of Central Executive Board Committee, All Japan Seamen's Union (JSU).
KON, Hideo, Mr., Representative, Indonesia Representative Office, JSU.
INABA, Michiko, Ms., Assistant Director, Gender Equality Division, JTUC-RENGO.
OKUBO, Akiko, Ms., Section Chief, International Division, JTUC-RENGO.
SUZUKI, Hitoshi, Mr., Social Policy Division, JTUC-RENGO.

Other persons attending the Conference

IIJIMA, Yuji, Mr., Chief, European Office, JSU.
URUSHIHARA, Hajime, Mr., Staff Member, Employment Legislation Division, JTUC-RENGO.
BANNAI, Mitsuo, Mr., Secretay-General, National Confederation of Trade Unions (ZENROREN).
IWATA, Yukio, Mr., Deputy Secretary-General, Head, International Bureau, ZENROREN.
WATANABE, Masamichi, Mr., Head, Planning Bureau, ZENROREN.
SHIBATA, Masako, Ms., Member, Executive Committee, ZENROREN.
FUSE, Keisuke, Mr., Organization Bureau, ZENROREN.

Jordanie   Jordan   Jordania

Minister attending the Conference

MAJALI, Amjad, Mr., Minister of Labour.

Person accompanying the Minister

AL-HABASHNEH, Majed, Mr., Secretary-General, Ministry of Labour.

Government Delegates

MADI, Shehab A., Mr., Ambassador, Permanent Representative, Permanent Mission, Geneva.
AL-RUSAN, Ghandi, Mr., Permanent Mission, Geneva.

Advisers

AL-SHEIKH, Jafar, Mr., Labour Inspector, Inspection Directorate.
DAJANI, Shukri, Mr., Conseiller spécial (BIT), Permanent Mission, Geneva.
OBEIDAT, Walid, Mr., First Secretary, Permanent Mission, Geneva.
MAJALI, Abdel-Rahman, Mr.

DAOUD, Mona, Mrs.
ODEH, Mazen, Mr., Director, Information and
International Cooperation Directorate.

Other person attending the Conference

AL-KHALAYLEH, Moussa, Mr., Member of Parliament.

Employers' Delegate

AYOUBI, Zaki M., Mr., Jordan Chamber of Industry.

Workers' Delegate

HAYASAT, Khalil, Mr., Member, Executive Office.

Advisers

ISMA'IL, Jameel, Mr., Member, Executive Office.
AL-FANATSEH, Khalid, Mr., President, Mining Workers Union.

Kazakhstan   Kazakhstan
Kazajstán

Government Delegates

KARAGOUSOVA, Gulzhana, Mrs., Minister of Labour and Social Protection of Population.
DANENOV, Nurlan, Mr., Ambassador, Permanent Representative, Permanent Mission, Geneva.

Advisers and substitute delegates

TASHIBAYEV, Murat, Mr., Counsellor, Permanent Mission, Geneva.
BUBEYEV, Mukhtar, Mr., Third Secretary, Permanent Mission, Geneva.

Employers' Delegate

BAIKENOV, Kadyr, Mr., President, Confederation of Employers.

Adviser and substitute delegate

RADOSTOVETS, Nikolai, Mr., Chairman, Eurasian Industrial Association.

Workers' Delegate

MUKASHEV, Siyazbek, Mr., Chairman, Federation of Trade Unions.

Adviser and substitute delegate

BELKIN, Sergey, Mr.

Kenya

Minister attending the Conference

MWAKWERE, Chirau Ali, Mr., Minister for Labour and Human Resource Development.

Government Delegates

ONGEWE, Deborah A., Mrs., Permanent Secretary, Ministry of Labour and Human Resource Development.
MOHAMED, Amina Chawahir, Mrs., Ambassador, Permanent Representative, Permanent Mission, Geneva.

Advisers and substitute delegates

OWADE, Philip R.O., Mr., Deputy Permanent Representative, Permanent Mission, Geneva.
KAVULUDI, Johnstone M., Mr., Labour Commissioner.
OTIENO, Grace A., Mrs., Director of Human Resource Development and Employment.
NGARE, Ephraim Waweru, Mr., Counsellor, Permanent Mission, Geneva.

Advisers

YIDAH, Joseph Ajanga, Mr., Assistant, Labour Commissioner (ILO duties).
KARANJA, Peter M., Mr., L.O. (ILO duties).
MUENDO, C., Mr., Senior Immigration Officer, Office of the Vice-President and Ministry of Home Affairs.
KITONGA, Winfred, Mrs., Public Relations Officer, Ministry of Labour and Human Resource Development.
NZOMO, Lydia, Mrs., Deputy Secretary, Teachers Service Commission.
TABU, Irina, Ms., First Secretary, Permanent Mission, Geneva.
NYAMBU, Lenah, Mrs., First Secretary, Permanent Mission, Geneva.

Employers' Delegate

KONDITI, Gershon N., Mr., Deputy Executive Director, Federation of Kenya Employers.

Advisers and substitute delegates

MBUI, Aram, Mr., Chairman, Federation of Kenya Employers.
MOGERE, Naftali, Mr., Managing Trustee, National Social Security Fund.

Advisers

KAZUNGU, Grace K., Mr., Compliance Manager, National Social Security Fund.
TUM, Esther C., Mrs., Human Resource Manager, National Social Security Fund.

WAKAYANDA, Vincent, Mr., Human Resource Director, Kenya Ports Authority.
OKUNGU, Grace, Ms., Human Resource Manager, Kenya Sugar Board.
MARITIM, Epimach, Mr., Human Resource Director, Bamburi Cement Limited.

Workers' Delegate

ATWOLI, Francis, Mr., General Secretary, Central Organization of Trade Union.

Advisers and substitute delegates

MUCHAI, George, Mr., Deputy Secretary General, Central Organization of Trade Unions.
KUBAI, Isaiah, Mr., General Secetary, Kenya Banking, Insurance and Finance Union.

Advisers

AKUMU, Dennis, Mr., COTU.
MUTUNGI, John M., Mr., Legal Officer, Central Organization of Trade Unions.
GITHINJI, Anthony, Mr., Economist, Central Organization of Trade Unions.
MOSETI, Joyce, Mrs., Women Leader, Central Organization of Trade Unions.

Kirghizistan   Kyrgyzstan   Kirguistán

Government Delegates

SHAIMERGENOVA, Zeinep, Mrs., Ambassador, Permanent Representative, Permanent Mission, Geneva.
ERKIN, Aidit, Mr., First Secretary, Permanent Mission, Geneva.

Kiribati   Kiribati   Kiribati

Minister attending the Conference

TONGAAI, Bauro, Mr., Minister of Labour and Human Resource Management, MLHRD.

Government Delegates

NGALU, Francis, Mr., Permanent Secretary, MLHRD.
AWIRA, Ngutu, Mr., Director of Labour, MLHRD.

Employers' Delegate

KABUBUKE, Teroutaki, Mr., Executive Member, Kiribati Chamber of Commerce.

Workers' Delegate

AATA, Ramanibina, Ms., Member, Executive Committee, Kiribati Trade Union Congress.

Koweït   Kuwait   Kuwait

Minister attending the Conference

AL-HAJJI, Faisal Mohammad, Mr., Minister of Social Affairs and Labour.

Persons accompanying the Minister

MOHAMMED, Hassan K., Mr., Director, Minister's Office.
AL-AJMI, Abdullah H., Mr., Director, Minister's Cabinet of Boards and Committees.

Government Delegates

RAZZOOQI, Dharar A.R., Mr., Ambassador, Permanent Representative, Permanent Mission, Geneva.
AL-SABAH, Duaij K., Mr., Under-Secretary, Ministry of Social Affairs and Labour.

Advisers and substitute delegates

AL-MUDADI, Hamad, Mr., Assistant Under-Secretary, Labour Affairs.
AL-OMAR, Adnan A., Mr., Director, Foreign Relations Department.

Advisers

AL-SUMAIT, Mubarak M., Mr., Director, Labour Coordination Department.
AL-AWADI, Nader A., Mr., Director, Capital Governorate Labour Department.
AL-SHAMARI, Kazem, Mr., Director, Al-Ahmadi Governorate Labour Department.
ALI, Khaled A., Mr., Director, Under-Secretary's Office.
AL-BISHR, Abdullah M., Mr., Assistant Director, Informatics Department, Al-Ferawnia Governorate.
AL-SAHLAWI, Abdallah, Mr., Assistant Director, Human Resources Development.
AL-ALI, Jaber A., Mr., International Relations Researcher, Foreign Relations Department.
AL-BADER, Najeeb, Mr., First Secretary, Permanent Mission, Geneva.
ALI MANDANI, Samera, Mrs., Assistant Director, Work Coordination Department.
AL-SONI, Adel, Mr., Ministry of Labour.
BASHA, Nabeel M., Mr., Controller Marine Registration.
ABDULLAH, Hishem Issa, Mr., Head, Marine's Affairs Department.

Employers' Delegate

AL-RABAH, Rabah A. K., Mr., Assistant Director-General, Kuwait Chamber of Commerce and Industry.

Adviser and substitute delegate

BUDAI, Nujud K., Mrs., Researcher, Industry and Labour Department.

Adviser

AL-FALIJI, Abdulaziz F., Mr., Researcher, Labour and Industry Department.

Workers' Delegate

AL-AZMI, Naqa R., Mr., Vice-Chairman, Kuwait Trade Union Federation.

Adviser and substitute delegate

AL-AZMI, Khaled M., Mr., Member of the Executive Council, Kuwait Trade Union Federation.

Advisers

AL-MUDAETH, Mohamed M., Mr., Member of the Executive Council, Kuwait Trade Union Confederation.
AL-AJMI, Menaa F., Mr., Member of the Executive Council, Kuwait Trade Union Confederation.
AL-AZMI, Fahd A., Mr., Member of the Executive Council, Kuwait General Trade Union.

République dém. populaire lao
Lao People's Dem. Republic
República Dem. Pop. Lao

Ministre assistant à la Conférence

PHENGKHAMMY, Somphanh, M., Ministre du Travail et des Affaires sociales.

Délégués gouvernementaux

TANDAVONG, Sisouvan, M., Directeur général, Département du Travail, Ministère du Travail et des Affaires sociales.
VISISOMBAT, Khamphan, M., Expert de loi.

Délégué des employeurs

BOUTSIVONGSAKD, Onesy, M., Comité exécutif, Chambre du Commerce et de l'Industrie.

Délégué des travailleurs

VONGDARA, Bosaykham, M., Président, Organisation de la Fédération des Syndicats.

Lesotho

Minister attending the Conference

PHORORO, D.R., Mr., Minister of Agriculture and Food Security, Acting Minister of Employment and Labour.

Government Delegates

MANDORO, L., Mr., Principal Secretary, Ministry of Employment and Labour.
MATSOSO, M., Ms., Labour Commissioner, Ministry of Employment and Labour.

Advisers and substitute delegates

MASUPHA, M., Ms., Migrant Labour Liaison Officer, Ministry of Employment and Labour.
MATLANYANE, M.A., Mrs., Ambassador, Permanent Representative, Permanent Mission, Geneva.
MOSISILI, R., Mr., Counsellor, Permanent Mission, Geneva.

Employers' Delegate

MAKEKA, T., Mr., Excutive Director, Association of Lesotho Employers and Business.

Adviser and substitute delegate

MONAHENG, G.T., Mr., President, Association of Lesotho Employers and Business.

Workers' Delegate

TYHALI, V., Mr., Secretary-General, Congress of Lesotho Trade Unions.

Lettonie   Latvia   Letonia

Minister attending the Conference

STAKE, Dagnija, Ms., Minister of Welfare.

Government Delegates

KARKLINS, Janis, Mr., Ambassador, Permanent Representative, Permanent Mission, Geneva.
KALNINS, Edgars, Mr., Third Secretary, Permanent Mission, Geneva.

Employers' Delegate

GAVRILOVS, Vitalijs, Mr., President, Latvian Employers Confederation.

Workers' Delegate

MARCINKEVICA, Livija, Mrs., Vice President, Latvian Free Trade Union Federation.

Liban   Lebanon   Líbano

Délégués gouvernementaux

AOUN, Samir, M., Représentant du Ministre du Travail; Président du Comité technique à la Sécurité sociale.
SAAB, May, Mme, Chef, Section des Relations étrangères.

Conseiller technique et délégué suppléant

GHORAYEB, William, M., Conseiller du Ministre du Travail.

Conseillers techniques

SALIBA, Ratib, M., Directeur général, Ministère du Travail.
RAZZOUK, Abdallah, M., Chef, Section du Travail et des Relations du Travail.
FAYYAD, Ali, M., Chef du Bureau (Diwan).
CHALITA, Nazha, Mme, Expert, Education et Affaires sociales.
KANAAN, Fouad, M., Consultant.
TOUMA, Wadi'a, Mme, Consultant.

Délégué des employeurs

HAMADEH, Sa'id, M., Membre du Conseil, Association libanaise des Industriels; Coordinateur auprès du Minisitère de l'Industrie.

Conseillers techniques et délégués suppléants

BSAT, Mounir, M., Association libanaise des Industriels; Membre, Chambre de Commerce de Sidon.
BALBOUL, Fouad, M., Association libanaise des Industriels; Membre du Conseil d'administration du BIT.

Conseillers techniques

SADER, Joseph, M., Membre du Conseil, Chambre de Commerce de Beyrouth.
BAYDOUN, Rachid, M., Association libanaise des Industriels.
NASR, Arij, Mme, Comité des femmes, Association libanaise des Industriels; Comité arabe des femmes au Travail.
AL-BARBIR, Ghina, Mme, Comité des femmes, Association libanaise des Industriels.
CHEHAB, Iman, Mme, Comité des femmes, Association libanaise des Industriels.
KHATER, Mohammad, M., Membre, Chambre de Commerce de Beyrouth.

Délégué des travailleurs

GHOSN, Ghassan, M., Président, Confédération générale des Travailleurs.

Conseillers techniques

ISSA, Ibrahim, M.
SAKR, Saadeddine Homeidi, M., Secrétaire général, Confédération générale des Travailleurs.
ABD ASSAMAD, Ismat, M., CGTL.
CHREIF, Fadllalah, M., CGTL.
SAADE, Boutros, M., Secrétaire, Affaires du Travail, CGTL.
ALAM, Georges, M., Membre du Conseil exécutif, CGTL.

Liberia

Government Delegates

SUPUWOOD, J. Laveli, Mr., Minister of Labour.
MEHNPAINE, S. Reginald Z., Mr., Director-General, International Labour Affairs, Ministry of Labour.

Advisers

WAHYEE, Matthew K., Mr., Deputy Minister, Planning, Ministry of Labour.
MULBAH, George S., Mr., Assistant Minister, Trade Union Affairs, Ministry of Labour.
KORTIMAI, J. Lavela, Mr., Special Assistant to the Minister, Ministry of Labour.
CUMMINGS, Christine M., Mrs., Executive Secretary to the Minister, Ministry of Labour.
KAINE, Roland C., Mr., Chairman, NTLA Committee on Labour.

Workers' Delegate

FREEMAN, Joyce M., Ms., President-General, United Seaman, Ports & General Workers' Union of Liberia; Vice-President Liberia Federationa of Labour Unions of Liberia.

Adviser

GUEH, Freeman, Mr., President, Fisheries Section, United Seamen Ports and General Workers' Union of Liberia.

Jamahiriya arabe libyenne
Libyan Arab Jamahiriya
Jamahiriya Arabe Libia

Minister attending the Conference

MAATOUGH, Maatough Mohamed, Mr., Secretary, General's People's Committee of Labour Force Training and Employment.

Government Delegates

AL HAJJAJI, Najat Al-Mahdi, Mrs., Ambassador, Permanent Representative, Permanent Mission, Geneva.
DERBI, Abdelhafid Mohamed, Mr., General People's Committee for Labour Force, Training and Employment.

Advisers and substitute delegates

ALZWAM, Adreess, Mr., General People's Committee for Labour Force, Training and Employment.
ALI, Hammad, Mr., General People's Committee for Labour Force, Training and Employment.
DUKALI, Mohamed Rida, Mr., Counsellor, General's People's Committee for Foreign Liaison.

Advisers

GARABLI, Tarik Ali, Mr., General's People's Committee.
BEN OMRANE, Abdurrahman, Mr., Permanent Mission, Geneva.

Employers' Delegate

ALMABROUK, Mohamed Abou Ajila, Mr., President, General Steel Company.

Adviser and substitute delegate

ABULLAH, Hassan Hamed, Mr., President, Libyan Cement Company.

Adviser

AL FELLAH, Abdullah Mohamed, Mr., Chamber of Trade and Industry.

Workers' Delegate

AL ZLITNI, Mahmoud Mustapha, Mr., Secretary General, Libyan Trade Union.

Adviser and substitute delegate

AL TALHI, Ahmed Mussa, Mr., Assistant Secretary General, Libyan Trade Union.

Advisers

ALHGAIBI MEJBERI, Mohamed Al Snoussi, Mr., Secretary for Media, Culture and Training Affairs, Libyan Trade Union.
ALNAEELI, Salem Mokhtar, Mr., Secretary, Libyan Trade Union.
ALI JLASSI, Khairia, Mrs., Member, Women Committee, Secretariat Libyan Trade Union

Lituanie   Lithuania   Lituania

Government Delegates

KAIRELIS, Rimantas, Mr., State Secretary, Ministry of Social Security and Labour.
RIMKUNAS, Algimantas, Mr., Ambassador, Permanent Representative, Permanent Mission, Geneva.

Advisers and substitute delegates

PETRIKAS, Erikas, Mr., Consul General, Consultate General, Geneva.
JAKUCIONYTE, Rede, Ms., Attaché for Social Security and Labour, Permanent Mission, Geneva.

Adviser

MISKINYTE, Vilmanté, Ms., Chief Specialist, European Integration and International Relations Department, Ministry of Social Security and Labour.

Employers' Delegate

ARLAUSKAS, Danukas, Mr., Director General, Lithuanian Business Employers' Confederation.

Adviser and substitute delegate

GUZAVICIUS, Jonas, Mr., Presidium Member, Confederation of Lithuanian Industrialists.

Adviser

VASILEVSKIS, Tomas, Mr., Director, Foreign Relations Department, Confederation of Lithuanian Industrialists.

Workers' Delegate

BALSIENE, Aldona, Ms., President, Lithuanian Trade Union "Solidarumas".

Adviser and substitute delegate

PUSKEPALIS, Vydas, Mr., Chairman, Lithuanian Labour Federation.

Luxembourg   Luxembourg   Luxemburgo

Ministre assistant à la Conférence
BILTGEN, François, M., Ministre du Travail et de l'Emploi.

Personne accompagnant le Ministre
BERNS, Alphonse, M., Ambassadeur, Représentant permanent, Mission permanente, Genève.

Délégués gouvernementaux
ZAHLEN, Jean, M., Premier Conseiller de Gouvernement, Ministère du Travail et de l'Emploi.
SCHOLTUS, Mariette, Mme, Directeur, Administration de l'Emploi.

Conseillers techniques et délégués suppléants
WEBER, Paul, M., Directeur, Inspection du Travail et des Mines.
FABER, Joseph, M., Conseiller de Direction première classe, Ministère du Travail et de l'Emploi.

Conseillers techniques
TUNSCH, Gary, M., Inspecteur Principal premier en rang, Ministère du Travail et de l'Emploi.
FURLANI, Patrice, Mme, Attaché de Gouvernement, Ministère du Travail et de l'Emploi.
GODEFROID, Marc, M., Premier Secrétaire, Mission permanente, Genève.
RIPPERT, Jacqueline, Mme, Attachée, Mission permanente, Genève.
FISCH, Maryse, Mme, Conseillère de Gouvernement, Ministère du Travail et de l'Emploi.
WELTER, Nadine, Mme, Attaché de Gouvernement premier en rang, Ministère du Travail et de l'Emploi.

Délégué des employeurs
BERTRAND-SCHAUL, Christiane, Mme, Conseiller, Fédération des Industriels luxembourgeois (FEDIL).

Conseiller technique et délégué suppléant
SCHMIT, Romain, M., Directeur, Fédération des Artisans.

Conseillers techniques
KIEFFER, Marc, M., Conseiller juridique, FEDIL.
ENGELS, François, M., Conseiller économique, Fédération des Artisans.

Délégué des travailleurs
PIZZAFERRI, René, M., Membre, Comité national, Confédération générale du Travail.

Conseiller technique et délégué suppléant
GOERGEN, Viviane, Mme, Secrétaire générale adjointe, Confédération luxembourgeoise des Syndicats chrétiens.

Conseillers techniques
BAUSCH, Eugène, M., Membre, Comité national, Confédération générale du Travail.
DALEIDEN, Joseph, M., Secrétaire général, Confédération générale de la Fonction publique.
NIELES, Danièle, Mme, Membre, Comité national, Confédération générale du Travail.
SANNIPOLI, Marie-Thérèse, Mme, Membre, Comité national, Confédération générale du Travail.
SPIER, Joé, M., Responsable des Relations publiques, Confédération luxembourgeoise des Syndicats chrétiens.
TRAUSCH, Pierre, M., Premier Vice-président, Confédération générale de la Fonction publique.
WOLFF, Romain, M., Vice-président, Confédération générale de la Fonction publique.
SPAUTZ, Marc, M., Secrétaire général, Confédération luxembourgeoise des Syndicats chrétiens.

Madagascar

Ministre assistant à la Conférence
RANJIVASON, Jean Théodore, M., Ministre de la Fonction publique, du Travail et des Lois sociales.

Délégués gouvernementaux
RAMBELOSON, Alfred, M., Ambassadeur, Représentant permanent, Mission permanente, Genève.
RASOLOFONIAINARISON, Lauréat, M., Directeur, Travail et des Relations professionnelles, Ministère du Travail, de la Fonction publique et des Lois sociales.

Conseillers techniques
RASOLONJATOVO, Jean-Michel, M., Premier Conseiller, Mission permanente, Genève.
RAKOTONARIVO, Rochel, M., Conseiller, Mission permanente, Genève.
ANDRIANJAKA, Clarah, Mme, Conseillère, Mission permanente, Genève.

Délégué des employeurs
ANDRIANTSITOHAINA, Charles, M., Vice-Président d'honneur, Groupement des Entreprises de Madagascar (GEM).

Conseiller technique et délégué suppléant

RABEMANANTSOA, Emile, M., Vice-Président, Fivondronan'ny Mpandraharaha Malagasy (FIVMPAMA).

Délégué des travailleurs

RANDRIAMAHOLISON, Jules Henri, M., Secrétaire général, Fédération nationale des Agents de l'Etat; Membre Dirigeant-Fondateur, Conférence des Travailleurs de Madagascar.

Conseiller technique et délégué suppléant

RABENANDRIANINA, Louis, M., Membre, Bureau Central du Syndicat FISEMA.

Malaisie   Malaysia   Malasia

Minister attending the Conference

FONG, Chan Onn, Mr., Minister of Human Resources.

Persons accompanying the Minister

CHEN, Mong Hee, Mr., Press Secretary to the Minister.
HAI SAN, Tiew, Mr., Private Secretary to the Minister.

Government Delegates

MANOGRAN, P., Mr., Secretary-General, Ministry of Human Resources.
ISMAIL, Abd. Rahim, Mr., Director-General of Labour, Ministry of Human Resources.

Advisers and substitute delegates

YAU, De Piyau, Mr., Chief Executive, HRDB, Ministry of Human Resources.
TECK, Ng, Mr., Executive Director, SOCSO.
PAGUMAN, Singh, Mr., Director, SOCSO.

Advisers

RAJMAH, Hussain, Mrs., Ambassador, Permanent Representative, Permanent Mission, Geneva.
SOH, Chee Seng, Mr., Under Secretary, Ministry of Human Resources.
ZAINOL, Rahim Zainuddin, Mr., Deputy Permanent Representative, Permanent Mission, Geneva.
HAZIM, Jamaluddin, Mr., Principal Assistant Secretary, Ministry of Human Resources.
BALA CHANDRAN, Tharman, Mr., Counsellor, Permanent Mission, Geneva.
ROSLEE, Sabaruddin Abu, Mr., Assistant Secretary, Ministry of Human Resources.
RUSLIN, Josoh, Mr., First Secretary, Permanent Mission, Geneva.
WAN ZULKFLI, Wan Setapa, Mr., Labour Attaché, Permanent Mission, Geneva.
WAN A. YUSRI, Wan Abdul Rashid, Mr., Second Secretary, Permanent Mission, Geneva.

Employers' Delegate

SHAMSUDIN, Bardan, Mr., Executive Director, Malaysian Employers Federation.

Adviser and substitute delegate

NATHAN, V. T., Mr., Vice-President, Malaysian Employers Federation.

Workers' Delegate

RAMPAK, Zainal, Mr., President, Malaysian Trade Unions Congress.

Advisers

NORDIN, Abdul Hamid, Mr., President, Congress of Unions of Employees in the Public and Civil Services.
ANDREW, Lo Kian Nyan, Mr., Secretary, Malaysian Trade Union Congress, Sarawak Branch.
OTHMAN, Ismail, Mr., Malaysian Trade Union Congress.
JAMIL, Mordipi, Mr., Malaysian Trade Union Congress.
SUHAIMY, Zaman, Mr., Malaysian Trade Union Congress.
BALASUBRAMANIAM, Karuppiah, Mr., Malaysian Trade Union Congress.
SUHAIMI, Othman, Mr., Malaysian Trade Union Congress.
RAJENTHARAN, K., Mr., Malaysian Trade Union Congress.
JAPELUS, Zainal, Mr., Malaysian Trade Union Congress.
RUSDI TAHIR, Ahmad, Mr., Malaysian Trade Union Congress.

Persons appointed in accordance with Article 2, paragraph 3(i)

MOHD SAID, Sadali, Mr., Malaysian Trade Union Congress.
MOHAMED MYDIN, Abdul Rahman, Mr., Malaysian Trade Union Congress.
RAVINDRAN AL, Siridaran Pillai, Mr., Malaysian Trade Union Congress.
TAIB, Sitam, Mr., Malaysian Trade Union Congress.
MOHD AKHIR, Manshor, Mr., Malaysian Trade Union Congress.

Other persons attending the Conference

MOHD YUNUS, Mr., Malaysian Trade Union Congress.
MOHD MALEK, Said, Mr., Malaysian Trade Union Congress.
MUNION AL, Appoo, Mr., Malaysian Trade Union Congress.
ANDREW, Loh, Mrs., MTUC.
MD. NOH, Bin Hamid, Mr., MTUC.

MOHD RASHIDAN, Ahmad, Mr., President, Officers' Union, SOCSO.
ABDUL, Mohd Shukri, Mr., MTUC.
MOHD NOOR, Abdullah, Mr., President, Workers' Union, SOCSO.
SAMSUDIN, Samudi, Mr., MTUC.
PAZAL, Yunos, Mr., MTUC.
BAHARUDIN, Jaafar, Mr., MTUC.

Malawi

Government Delegates

MONONGA, M.M., Mr., Principal Secretary, Ministry of Labour and Vocational Training.
KAMBUTO, Z.M.K., Mr., Labour Commissioner, Ministry of Labour and Vocational Training.

Advisers and substitute delegates

BANDA, A.P.A., Mr., Director, Technical and Vocational Training, Ministry of Labour and Vocational Training.
NYANGULU, H.K.K., Mr., Director, Occupational Safety and Health, Ministry of Labour and Vocational Training.

Advisers

CHIRWA, B.M., Mr., Chief Labour Officer.
KAWAMBA, L., Mrs., Principal Labour Officer.
CHAFA, J., Mr., Executive Director, TEVETA.

Employers' Delegate

SINJANI, Mr., Executive Director, Employers' Consultative Association of Malawi (ECAM).

Workers' Delegate

KALIMANJIRA, A., Mr., Secretary-General, MCTU.

Adviser and substitute delegate

BANDA, T.I., Mr., President, COMATU.

Mali

Ministre assistant à la Conférence

BADI OULD GANFOUD, M., Ministre de la Fonction publique, de la Réforme de l'Etat et des Relations avec les Institutions.

Personne accompagnant le Ministre

BASTIDE, Louis Marie Joseph, M., Ambassadeur, Représentant permanent, Mission permanente, Genève.

Délégués gouvernementaux

DIAKITE, Mahamadou, M., Conseiller technique, Ministère de la Fonction publique, de la Réforme de l'Etat et des Relations avec les Institutions.
MAHAMANE, Baba Samba, M., Directeur national du Travail.

Conseillers techniques

DICKO, Fatoumata, Mme, Chef de Division chargé des Relations internationales, Direction nationale du Travail.
KASSÉ, Sekou, M., Premier Conseiller, Mission permanente, Genève.
SIDIBE, El Hadji Brahima, M., Directeur général adjoint, Agence nationale pour l'Emploi (ANPE).
SIDIBE, Nouhoum, M., Conseiller technique, Ministère du Développement social, de la Solidarité et des Personnes agés.
BOUARE, Lassiné, M., Directeur général, Institut national de la Prévoyance sociale.

Autre personne assistant à la Conférence

N'DIAYE, Astou, Mme, Conseiller technique chargé des Questions de Travail, Assemblée nationale du Mali.

Délégué des employeurs

TOURE, Mahamane M'Bodji, M., Vice-Président chargé des Relations extérieures, Conseil national du Patronat du Mali (CNPM).

Conseiller technique et délégué suppléant

TRAORE, Lassina, M., Secrétaire général, CNPM.

Délégué des travailleurs

DIAKITE, Siaka, M., Secrétaire général, Union nationale des Travailleurs du Mali (UNTM).

Conseiller technique et délégué suppléant

GUINDO, Hammadoun Amion, M., Secrétaire général, Confédération syndicale des Travailleurs du Mali (CSTM).

Conseiller technique

DOUMBIA, Mama Koïté, Mme, Secrétaire, Relations extérieures, UNTM.

Malte   Malta   Malta

Minister attending the Conference

GALEA, Louis, Mr., Minister of Education, Youth and Employment.

Person accompanying the Minister

BONNICI, Charlo, Mr., Head of the Minister's Secretariat.

Government Delegates

PULLICINO, Frank, Mr., Director of Industrial and Employment Relations.
AZZOPARDI, Anthony, Mr., Assistant Director, Department of Industrial and Employment Relations.

Advisers and substitute delegates

BORG, Saviour F., Mr., Ambassador, Permanent Representative, Permanent Mission, Geneva.
SARSERO, Ray, Mr., Counsellor, Permanent Mission, Geneva.
BUSUTTIL, John, Mr., First Secretary, Permanent Mission, Geneva.
BONNICI, Tony, Mr., Second Secretary, Permanent Mission, Geneva.
VELLA, Noel, Mr., Consultant, Department of Industrial and Employment Relations.
GRIXTI, Mario, Mr., Assistant principal, Department of Industrial and Employment Relations.

Employers' Delegate

FARRUGIA, Joseph, Mr., Director General, Malta Employers' Association.

Adviser and substitute delegate

MUSCAT, Arthur, Mr., President, Malta Employers' Association.

Advisers

ZAMMIT, Philip, Mr., Member, Human Resources and Social Affairs Committee, Federation of Industry.
SCICLUNA, John, Mr., Administration Manager, Malta Federation of Industry.

Workers' Delegate

MICALLEF, Emmanuel, Mr., Deputy Secretary General, General Workers' Union.

Advisers and substitute delegates

SAMMUT, Saviour, Mr., President, General Workers' Union.
ZARB, Tony, Mr., Secretary General, General Workers' Union.

Advisers

BUHAGIAR, Alfred, Mr., President, Confederation of Malta Trade Unions.
GRILLO, Joseph, Mr., Council Member, Confederation of Malta Trade Unions.
PORTELLI, William, Mr., Council Member, Confederation of Malta Trade Unions.
VELLA, Gaetano, Mr., Council Member, Confederation of Malta Trade Unions.

Maroc   Morocco   Marruecos

Ministre assistant à la Conférence

MANSOURI, Mustapha, M., Ministre de l'Emploi, des Affaires sociales et de la Solidarité.

Délégués gouvernementaux

HILALE, Omar, M., Ambassadeur, Représentant permanent, Mission permanente, Genève.
CHATER, ElHadi, M., Chef, Division de la Réglementation et des Organismes internationaux du Travail, Ministère de l'Emploi, des Affaires sociales et de la Solidarité.

Conseillers techniques

FAHEM, Saadia, Mme, Chef, Service des Organismes internationaux du Travail, Ministère de l'Emploi, des Affaires sociales et de la Solidarité.
BOUASSA, Siham, Mme, Conseiller, Mission permanente, Genève.
MESBAHI, Mohamed, M., Chef, Service de la Formation et du Perfectionnement, Ministère de la Pêche Maritime.
RHOUNI BELLOUTI, Ouafae, Mme, Directrice de la Recherche et du Développement.
EZZOUMI, Khadija, Mme, Directrice, Affaires administratives et financières, Agence nationale de la Promotion de l'Emploi et des Compétences.
BOUAYACHE, Amina, Mme, Chargée de mission auprès du Premier Ministre.

Délégué des employeurs

KOULLOU, Larbi, M., Confédération générale des Entreprises du Maroc (CGEM).

Conseillers techniques

OUSSLIM, El Hassane, M., Féderation des Chambres marocaines de Commerce, d'Industrie et des Services (FCCISM).
BOUDHAIM, Mohamed, M., FCCISM.
AYOUCHE, Mohcine, M., CGEM.
JALAL, Mohamed, M., CGEM.

Délégué des travailleurs

EL MOKHARIK, Miloudi, M., Union marocaine du Travail (UMT).

Conseillers techniques

AMAOUI, Noubir, M., Secrétaire général, Confédération démocratique du Travail (CDT).

AFILAL, Abderrazak, M., Secrétaire général, Union générale des Travailleurs du Maroc (UGTM).
CHAHIR, Farouk, M., UMT.
KAFI CHERAT, Mohamed, M., UGTM.
BOUZIA, Mohamed, M., CDT.
KAFOUNI, Lhoucine, M., Fédération démocratique du Travail (FDT).
IOUY, Abdelaziz, M., FDT.

Autres personnes assistant à la Conférence

ZAHI, Habiba, Mme, CDT.
BRAHMA, Mustapha, M., CDT.
KABBAJ, Mohamed Larbi, M., UGTM.
ZBIRI, Mahjouba, Mme, UGTM.
EL GHALI, Kenza, Mme, UGTM.
ZIDOUH, Brahim, M., UGTM.
KHALIL, Mustapha, M., UGTM.
EFFINIA, Driss, M., FDT.
BENSHILI, Saadia, Mme, FDT.

Maurice   Mauritius   Mauricio

Minister attending the Conference

SOODHUN, Showkutally, Mr., Minister of Labour, Industrial Relations and Employment.

Person accompanying the Minister

MEETOO, Jaynarain, Mr., Ambassador, Permanent Representative, Permanent Mission, Geneva.

Government Delegates

NABABSING, Nirmala Devi, Mrs., Permanent Secretary, Ministry of Labour, Industrial Relations and Employment.
MERCURE, Roberston, Mr., Commissioner for Social Security, Labour and Industrial Relations.

Adviser and substitute delegate

ARNACHELLUM, Krishnen Vijayen, Mr., Director, Labour and Industrial Relations.

Advisers

RUDHEE, Bipin Kumar, Mr., Minister Counsellor, Permanent Mission, Geneva.
MUNGUR, Vishwakarmah, Mr., First Secretary, Permanent Mission, Geneva.
PERTAUB, Nundini, Ms., Second Secretary, Permanent Mission, Geneva.

Employers' Delegate

JEETUN, Azad, Mr., Director, Mauritius Employers' Federation.

Advisers

GARRIOCH, Gerard, Mr., President, Mauritius Employers' Federation.
ESSOO, Vedna, Mrs., Assistant Director, Mauritius Employers' Federation.

Workers' Delegate

BENYDIN, Toolsyraj, Mr.

Mauritanie   Mauritania   Mauritania

Ministre assistant à la Conférence

MINT BILAL OULD YAMAR, Salka, Mme, Ministre de la Fonction publique et de l'Emploi.

Délégués gouvernementaux

OULD MOHAMED LEMINE, Mohamed Saleck, M., Ambassadeur, Représentant permanent, Mission permanente, Genève.
OULD CHEIKHNA, Khaled, M., Directeur du Travail et de la Prévoyance sociale, Ministère de la Fonction publique et de l'Emploi.

Conseillers techniques et délégués suppléants

OULD CHEIKH AHMED, Lemrabott Sidi Mahmoud, M., Directeur général, Caisse nationale de Sécurité sociale.
OULD MAGHA, Mahfoudh, M., Premier Conseiller, Mission permanente, Genève.

Conseiller technique

SIDI, Cissé, M., Chef, Division de la Coopération internationale, Ministère de la Fonction publique et de l'Emploi.

Délégué des employeurs

OULD ABDALLAHI, Seyid, M., Secrétaire général, Conseil national du Patronat mauritanien.

Délégué des travailleurs

OULD BOUBOU, Abderrahmane, M., Secrétaire général, Union des Travailleurs de Mauritanie.

Conseillers techniques et délégués suppléants

OULD MOHAMED, Abdallahi, M., Secrétaire général, Confédération générale des Travailleurs de Mauritanie.
OULD BEYE, Samory, M., Secrétaire général, Confederation libre des Travailleurs de Mauritanie.
KANE, Moktar, M., Secrétaire général, Union des Syndicats libres de Mauritanie.

Mexique   Mexico   México

Ministro asistente a la Conferencia

ABASCAL, Carlos, Sr., Secretario del Trabajo y Prevision Social.

Personas que acompañan al Ministro

VAZQUEZ, Raúl, Sr., Secretario Particular del Secretario del Trabajo y Previsión Social.
REBOLLO, Herminio, Sr., Director General, Comunicación Social, Secretaría del Trabajo y Previsión Social.

Delegados gubernamentales

DE ALBA, Luis Alfonso, Sr., Embajador, Representante Permanente, Misión Permanente, Ginebra.
MACEDO, Pablo, Sr., Embajador, Representante Permanente Alterno, Misión Permanente, Ginebra.

Consejeros técnicos y delegados suplentes

FRANCO, Claudia, Sra., Jefa, Unidad de Asuntos Internacionales, Secretaría del Trabajo y Previsión Social.
ROVIROSA, Socorro, Sra., Ministro, Misión Permanente, Ginebra.
MARTINEZ, Erasmo, Sr., Ministro, Misión Permanente, Ginebra.
MORONES, Guadalupe, Sra., Subcoordinadora de Política Laboral, Secretaría del Trabajo y Previsión Social.
HERRERA, Raúl, Sr., Director General de Capacitación, Secretaría del Trabajo y Previsión Social.
FRAILE, Heliodoro, Sr., Director General de Productividad, Secretaría del Trabajo y Previsión Social.
VALLE, Dulce María, Sra., Consejero, Misión Permanente, Ginebra.
SILVA, Enrique, Sr., Director para la OIT, Secretaría del Trabajo y Previsión Social.
SIMON, David, Sr., Segundo Secretario, Misión Permanente, Ginebra.
PIZANO, Eva, Srta., Tercer Secretario, Misión Permanente, Ginebra.

Otras personas que asisten a la Conferencia

ORNELAS, Karla, Sra., Tercer Secretario, Misión Permanente, Ginebra.
CERVANTES, Mónica, Sra., Profesional Ejecutiva de Servicios Especializados de la Dirección para la OIT, Secretaría del Trabajo y Previsión Social.

Delegado de los empleadores

HALKIN, León, Sr., Presidente, Confederación de Cámaras Industriales de los Estados Unidos Mexicanos (CONCAMIN).

Consejero técnico y delegado suplente

DE REGIL, Jorge, Sr., Miembro Titular, Consejo de Administración de la OIT.

Consejeros técnicos

REGUERA, Manuel, Sr., Presidente, Comisión Jurídica, CONCAMIN.
DIAZ, Amado, Sr., Comisión Laboral, CAINTRA, Nuevo León.
YLLANEZ, Fernando, Sr., Vicepresidente, Comisión Jurídica, CONCAMIN.
ITALO, Hugo, Sr., Presidente, Comisión Laboral, CANACINTRA.
GONZALEZ, Yesica, Sra., Directora de Enlace Internacional, COPARMEX.
GARZA, María Fernanda, Sra., Miembro, Comisión Ejecutiva, COPARMEX.
BARONA, Adela, Sra., Presidenta, Comisión de Seguridad, Salud en el Trabajo y Protección Civil, COPARMEX.
SANTOS, Enrique, Sr., Miembro, Comisión Laboral, COPARMEX.
MENA, Virgilio, Sr., Director, Relaciones Laborales y Sociales, FEMSA, S.A. de C.V.

Otras personas que asisten a la Conferencia

GUTIERREZ, Reynold, Sr., Director, Relaciones Laborales, Grupo CYDSA.
CAMPUZANO, Guillermo, Sr., Vicepresidente, Asuntos del Trabajo, COPARMEX.
NATIVIDAD, Tomas, Sr., Presidente, Comisión Laboral, COPARMEX.
LOMBERA, Rosario, Sra., CONCAMIN.
SANCHEZ MEJORADA, Regina, Sra., COPARMEX.

Delegado de los trabajadores

ANDERSON, Hilda, Sra., Secretaria de Acción Femenil, Comité Nacional, CTM.

Consejeros técnicos

PEREZ, Eduardo, Sr., Secretario del Exterior, Comité Ejecutivo Nacional, Sindicato de Trabajadores del Seguro Social de UNT.
OJEDA, Ramón, Sr., Presidente, Comisión de Relaciones Nacionales e Internacionales, Congreso del Trabajo.
LARIOS, Graciela, Sra., Diputada, Secretaría de Relaciones, Comité Nacional, CTM.
DE LA VEGA, Netzahualcoyotl, Sr., Secretario General Substituto 1, CTM.
ACEVES, Carlos, Sr., Secretario de Acción Política, CTM.
MEDINA, Salvador, Sr., Subsecretario de Relaciones, CTM.
SOSA, Juan José, Sr., Secretario General, Sindicato Nacional de Trabajadores de la Compañía "FORD MOTOR COMPANY", S.A.

DEL VALLE, José, Sr., Secretario de Relaciones Exteriores, Coordinador General, Comité de Políticas Internacionales, CROC.
SANCHEZ, Rene, Sr., Representante, CROC.
VEGA, Roberto, Sr., Secretario General, Comité Ejecutivo Nacional, Sindicato de Trabajadores del Seguro Social de UNT.

Otras personas que asisten a la Conferencia

MIRELES, Carlos, Sr., Secretario General, CROC, Estado de Nuevo León.
RENDON, Hugo, Sr., Secretario de Agenda Internacional, CROC.
GUTIERREZ, José Luis, Sr., Secretario de Organización Administrativa, STUNAM.
SANTOS, Ismael, Sr., Secretario, Comisión de Asuntos Políticos, CT.

République de Moldova
Republic of Moldova
República de Moldova

Délégués gouvernementaux

REVENCO, Valerian, M., Ministre du Travail et de la Protection sociale.
CROITOR, Dumitru, M., Ambassador, Représentant permanent, Mission permanente, Genève.

Conseiller technique

REVENCO, Eugeniu, M., Conseiller, Mission permanante, Genève.

Délégué des employeurs

CERESCU, Leonid, M., Président, Confédération nationale du Patronat.

Conseiller technique

AXENTII, Adrian, M., Directeur général exécutif, Confédération nationale du Patronat.

Délégué des travailleurs

CHIRIAC, Petru, M., Président, Confédération des Syndicats.

Conseiller technique

MANEA, Leonid, M., Président, Confédération des Syndicats libres "Solidarité".

Mongolie   Mongolia   Mongolia

Government Delegates

BATBAYAR, Shiileg, Mr., Minister of Social Welfare and Labour.
BEKHBAT, Khasbazaryn, Mr., Ambassador, Permanent Representative, Permanent Mission, Geneva.

Advisers

TUMENBAYAR, Nyamaa, Ms., Head, Foreign Relations Division, Ministry of Social Welfare and Labour.
TUVSHINSANAA, Jadamba, Mr., First Secretary, Permanent Mission, Geneva.

Employers' Delegate

GANBAATAR, Khuyag, Mr., Executive Director, Mongolian Employers Federation.

Adviser

NERGUI, Shagdarsuren, Mr., Mongolian Employers' Federation.

Workers' Delegate

SUKHBAATAR, Zalmaa, Mr., Head, Foreign Relations, Confederation of Mongolian Trade Unions.

Adviser

ADIYA, Gorchinsuren, Mr., President, Confederation of Mongolian Trade Unions.

Mozambique

Minister attending the Conference

SEVENE, Mário Lampião, Mr., Minister of Labour.

Person accompanying the Minister

ZANDAMELA, Alexandre Conceição, Mr., Ambassador, Permanent Representative, Permanent Mission, Geneva.

Government Delegates

CAIFAZ, Ilídio Fernando Vicente, Mr., Director, Ministry of Labour.
GOMES, Elína Mafuiane, Mrs., Director, National Institute for Social Security.

Adviser and substitute delegate

TAIMO, Pedro, Mr., Delegate to South Africa, Ministry of Labour.

Advisers

DENGO, Juvenal Arcanjo, Mr., Technician, Ministry of Labour.
FRANCISCO, Atanásio, Mr., Director, SAFMAR, Ministry of Transport and Communications.
PALE, Maria de Lurdes, Mrs., Second Secretary, Permanent Mission, Geneva.
CARLOS, Manuel, Mr., Second Secretary, Permanent Mission, Geneva.

Employers' Delegate

MUSSANHANE, Egas, Mr., President, Confederation of Economic Associations (CTA).

Adviser

UINGE, Nuno Sidonio, Mr., Vice-President, AEPRIMO.

Workers' Delegate

SITOE, Mário Raimundo, Mr., Secretary, International Relations, Organisation of Workers of Mozambique (OTM).

Myanmar

Minister attending the Conference

WINN, Tin, Mr., Minister, Ministry of Labour.

Persons accompanying the Minister

SHIN, Tun, Mr., Deputy Attorney-General, Attorney General's Office.
AUNG, Yu Lwin, Mr., Director-General, Ministry of Labour.

Government Delegates

THAN, Mya, Mr., Ambassador, Permanent Representative, Permanent Mission, Geneva.
NYUNT, Soe, Mr., Director-General, Department of Labour.

Advisers

MRA, Win, Mr., Director-General, Ministry of Foreign Affairs.
MU, Aye Aye, Mrs., Counsellor, Permanent Mission, Geneva.
NYUN, Tha Aung, Mr., Counsellor, Permanent Mission, Geneva.

MYINT, Win, Mr., Assistant Director, Department of Labour.
THU, Myint, Mr., First Secretary, Permanent Mission, Geneva.
NYEIN, Kyaw Thu, Mr., Second Secretary, Permanent Mission, Geneva.
SAITO, Daw Flora, Ms., Attachée, Permanent Mission, Geneva.
AUNG, U Soe, Mr., Attaché, Permanent Mission, Geneva.

Employers' Delegate

AUNG, Win, Mr., Vice Chairman, Union of Myanmar Federation of Chambers of Commerce and Industry.

Namibie   Namibia   Namibia

Minister attending the Conference

NGINDINWA, Rosalia, Ms., Deputy Minister of Labour.

Government Delegates

HIVELUAH, Ulitala, Ms., Permanent Secretary, Ministry of Labour.
SHINGUADJA, Bro-Matthew, Mr., Labour Commissioner, Ministry of Labour.

Adviser and substitute delegate

USIKU, Vilbard Thomas, Mr., Employment Equity Commission, Ministry of Labour.

Advisers

HORN, Christiaan, Johannes, Mr., Acting Deputy Director, International Relations and Advice Division, Ministry of Labour.
MWIYA, Albius Shamu, Mr., Deputy Director, Labour Market Division, Ministry of Labour.
MBANGO, Christophinah, Ms., Chief, Labour Relations Officer, International Relations and Advice Division, Ministry of Labour.

Employers' Delegate

SHIPENA, Gebson, Mr., Human Resources Manager, Namibia Employers Federation.

Adviser and substitute delegate

VAN ROOYEN, Johann, Mr., Consultant, Namibia Employers Federation.

Adviser

MUSUKUBILI, Felix, Mr., Industrial Relations Manager, Namibia Employers Federation.

Workers' Delegate

KAPENDA, Risto, Mr., President, National Union of Namibian Workers.

Advisers

HAMUTENYA, Miriam, Ms., National Union of Namibian Workers.
NAMALENGA, David, Mr., National Union of Namibian Workers.

Nepal

Government Delegates

ACHARYA, Gyan Chandra, Mr., Ambassador, Permanent Representative, Permanent Mission, Geneva.
SILWAL, Narayan Prasad, Mr., Secretary, Ministry of Labour and Transport Management.

Adviser and substitute delegate

ACHARYA, Binod Prasad, Mr., Deputy Permanent Representative (Commerce), Permanent Mission, Geneva.

Advisers

KHANAL, Sanjaya Kumar, Mr., Under-Secretary, Ministry of Labour and Transport Management.
THAPA, Gopal Bahadur, Mr., Minister Counsellor, Permanent Mission, Geneva.

Employers' Delegate

THAPALIYA, Rohini, Mr., President, Employer's Council, Federation of Nepalese Chamber of Commerce and Industries.

Workers' Delegate

BASNET, Laxman Bahadur, Mr., President, Nepal Trade Union Congress.

Adviser

RIMAL, Bishnu, Mr., Vice-Chairman, General Federation of Nepalese Trade Unions.

Nicaragua

Ministro asistente a la Conferencia

GURDIÁN CASTELLÓN, Virgilio, Sr., Ministro del Trabajo.

Persona que acompaña al Ministro

CASTILLO PEREIRA, Eduardo, Sr., Embajador, Representante Permanente Adjunto, Misión Permanente, Ginebra.

Delegados gubernamentales

MARTÍNEZ FLORES, Yadira, Srta., Directora, Asuntos Internacionales del Trabajo, Ministerio del Trabajo.
CRUZ TORUÑO, Néstor, Sr., Primer Secretario, Misión Permanente, Ginebra.

Consejeros técnicos y delegados suplentes

MARTINICA LÓPEZ, Paulino, Sr., Viceministro del Trabajo.
PALACIOS, Addie Mairena, Sra., Directora General de Empleo y Salarios, Ministerio del Trabajo.

Consejeros técnicos

URBINA GUERRERO, Santiago, Sr., Primer Secretario, Misión Permanente, Ginebra.
HERNÁNDEZ, María Pía, Srta., Primer Secretario, Misión Permanente, Ginebra.
CAMPBELL GONZALEZ, Patricia, Srta., Primer Secretario, Misión Permanente, Ginebra.
RODRÍGUEZ, Ligia, Srta., Asesora Legal y de Recursos Humanos, Instituto Nacional Tecnológico.
DÁVILA, Mario Benito, Sr., Responsable, Departamento de Desarrollo, Instituto Nacional Tecnológico.

Otra persona que asiste a la Conferencia

CHAMORRO MARÍN, Edgar, Sr., Coordinador General, Programas Laborales, USAID-SIECA, Guatemala.

Delegado de los empleadores

CUADRA GARCÍA, Alfredo, Sr., Presidente, Consejo Superior de la Empresa (COSEP).

Consejero técnico y delegado suplente

SEGURA, Armando, Sr., Asesor, COSEP.

Delegado de los trabajadores

GONZÁLEZ GAITÁN, Roberto, Sr., Secretario General, Central Sandinista de Trabajadores.

Consejero técnico y delegado suplente

CÁRDENAS, Martha Lorena, Sra., Central Autónoma de Trabajadores.

Consejeros técnicos

MEZA SOZA, Adrián, Sr., Asesor.
DURIEZ GONZÁLEZ, Susy, Sra., Asesora.
PÉREZ, Domingo, Sr., Asesor.

Niger

Ministre assistant à la Conférence

KASSEY, Seybou Moussa, M., Ministre de la Fonction publique et du Travail.

Délégués gouvernementaux

MAÏNA, Chégou Kochi, M., Conseiller technique en matière de Travail et Sécurité sociale.
HAMADOU, Siddo, M., Directeur général, Administration du Travail.

Conseillers techniques

KABO MAYAKI, Mariama, Mme, Directrice, Travail et Sécurité sociale.
SAKO, Zeïnabou, Mme, Directrice générale, Caisse nationale de la Sécurité sociale (CNSS).
BARINGAYE, Akilou Ahmed, M., Conseiller, CNSS.
IDRISSA, Amadou, M., Directeur, Agence nationale pour la Promotion de l'Emploi, (ANPE).

Délégué des employeurs

OUSMANE, Amadou, M., Conseil national du Patronat nigérien (CNPN).

Conseillers techniques

SALEY, Seybou, M., CNPN.
LAOUEL, Kader Assane, M., Président, Conseil d'administration, Agence nationale pour la promotion de l'Emploi (ANPE).

Délégué des travailleurs

SANDA, Seydou, M., Confédération nigérienne du Travail (CNT).

Conseillers techniques

MAIGANDI, Abdou, M., Union des Syndicats des Travailleurs du Niger (USTN).
MALLAM SOFFO, Salifou, M., Union générale des Travailleurs du Niger (UGTN).
SIDIBÉ, Issoufou, M., Confédération démocratique des Travailleurs du Niger (CDTN).
DEYABOU, Mahamadou, M., UGTN.

Nigeria

Minister attending the Conference

LAWAL, Hassan M., Mr., Minister of Labour.

Person accompanying the Minister

TUKURA, Victor M., Mr., Special Assistant to the Minister.

Government Delegates

KORIPAMO-AGARY, Timiebi A., Mr., Permanent Secretary.
AYALOGU, J. U., Mr., Ambassador, Permanent Representative, Permanent Mission, Geneva.

Advisers and substitute delegates

ADEYEYE-OLUKOYA, M. I., Mrs., Director, Planning, Research and Statistics, FMLP..
SULAI, Rhoda, Mrs., Director, Finance and Supplies.

Advisers

HENSHAW, Ewa, Mr., Senator, Chairman, Senate Committee on Labour.
MBATA, J. A., Mr., Senator, Chairman, Senate Appropriations Committee.
HANGA, Rufai, Mr., Senator, Senate Committe on Labour.
UMAR, U. K., Mr., Senator, Senate Committee on Labour.
MOMOH, A., Mr., Member, House of Representatives.
EDEM, B. E., Mrs., Director, Personnel Management, FMLP.
EGHOBAMIEN, V. A., Mrs., Director, Trade Union Services and Industrial Relations.
AHMAD, A. S., Mr., Deputy Director, E & W.
OKPARA, R. U., Mr., Deputy Director, Delta State Office.
AIMIUWU, O., Ms., Assistant Chief Labour Officer, INTER.
JEMIDE, V. E., Mrs., Principal Labour Officer.
ADELODUN, S. O., Mr., Director-General, National Directorate of Employment (NDE).
MOHAMMED, Ahmed Rufai, Mr., Managing Director, Nigeria Social Insurance Trust Fund (NSITF).
EBURAJOLO, Victor O., Mr., Executive Director (Operations), NSITF.
RHAMALLAN, T., Mr., Executive Director, Joint Maritime Labour Industrial Council (JOMALIC).
ILLOM, C., Mr., Assistant Director, JOMALIC.
EZEASOR, Chiedozie Bartholomew, Mr., Legal Adviser, Joint Maritime Labour Industrial Council.

Persons appointed in accordance with Article 2, paragraph 3(i)

BOLAJI, Kehinde, Mrs., Joint Maritime Labour Industrial Council.
DIPEOLU, Yemi, Mr., Minister (Economic), Permanent Mission, Geneva.
SERKI, U., Mr., Minister-Counsellor, Permanent Mission, Geneva.

Employers' Delegate

OSHINOWO, O. A., Mr., Director-General, NECA.

Advisers

ATTOH, Uche, Mr., Chairman, Committee on Human Resources Experts, NECA.
ONATU, Ray, Mr., General Manager, Human Resources, Elf Petroleum Nigeria Ltd.
OWEI, Daru, Mr., General Manager, Human Resources, Nigeria Agip Oil Company Ltd.
YARO, Alhaji W., Mr., Executive Director, Nigerian Ports Authority.
JATAU, Mallam R. S., Mr., Ag. General Manager (ADMIN), Nigerian Ports Authority.
EFIOM, Laura, Ms., Assistant General Manager (IR/WS), Nigerian Ports Authority.
ADAMU, Babayo, Mr., Personal Assistant to Executive Director (CS), Nigerian Ports Authority.
OLADI-MEJI, C. A., Mr., Head, Training and Conference Planning, Chartered Institute of Personnel Management of Nigeria.

Workers' Delegate

OSHIOMHOLE, Adams Aliyu, Mr., President, Nigeria Labour Congress (NLC).

Advisers

OMAR, Abdul Waheed, Mr., Deputy President, NLC.
EDEH, Fidelis, Mr., Vice-President, NLC.
IRABOR, Onikolease, Mr., Vice-President, NLC.
OYERINDE, Olaitan, Mr., Head of International Department, NLC.
ONYENEMERE, John, Mr., President, National Union of Food Beverage and Tobacco Employees.
TAKOR, Ivor M., Mr., Treasurer, NLC.
MANTU, Ahura, Mr., General Secretary, National Association of Nigeria Nurses and Midwives.
ANTHONY, Emmanuel Nted, Mr., Maritime Workers Union.
OGBONNA, Edwin, Mr., Maritime Workers Union.
OGUNLEYE, Oladipo, Mr., Maritime Workers Union.

Person appointed in accordance with Article 2, paragraph 3(i)

DURU, Chinyere, Ms., Assistant Secretary, NLC.

Norvège   Norway   Noruega

Ministers attending the Conference

KJØRVEN, Olav, Mr., State Secretary, Ministry of Foreign Affairs.
TORSØE, Eldbjørg, Ms., State Secretary, Ministry of Labour and Government Administration.

Persons accompanying the ministers

KVAM, Gundla, Mrs., Director-General, Ministry of Labour and Government Administration.
HANSEN, Thorfrid, Mrs., Deputy Director-General, Ministry of Labour and Government Administration.

Persons accompanying the Minister

BREVIK, Olav, Mr., Deputy Director-General, Ministry of Foreign Affairs.
PAULSEN, Kjetil, Mr., Minister, Permanent Mission, Geneva.
GASSER, Kari, Ms., Secretary, Permanent Mission, Geneva.

Government Delegates

JOHANSEN, Sverre Bergh, Mr., Ambassador, Permanent Representative, Permanent Mission, Geneva.
VIDNES, Øyvind, Mr., Counsellor, Permanent Mission, Geneva.

Advisers and substitute delegates

BRUAAS, Odd, Mr., Adviser, Ministry of Labour and Government Administration.
STENVOLD, Thoralf, Mr., Adviser, Ministry of Foreign Affairs.

Advisers

STORHAUG, Haakon, Mr., Principal Engineer, Norwegian Maritime Directorate.
LUNDE, Wenche, Ms., Higher Executive Officer, Norwegian Maritime Directorate.
GRØNLIE, Atle, Mr., Senior Principle Surveyor, Norwegian Maritime Directorate.
EVENSEN, Kristin, Ms., Adviser, Ministry of Education and Research.
HOLTER, Magne, Mr., Assistant Director General, Ministry of Local Government and Regional Development.

Other person attending the Conference

BAKKE, Cecilie Figenschou, Ms., Project Coordinator, Norwegian Centre for Human Rights.

Employers' Delegate

LINDEFJELD, Vidar, Mr., Director, Confederation of Norwegian Business and Industry.

Adviser and substitute delegate

RIDDERVOLD, Toril, Ms., Consultant, Confederation of Norwegian Business and Industry.

Advisers

LUNDSGAARD, Inger Beate, Ms., Department Manager, Federation of Norwegian Manufacturing Industries.
MEYER, Inger Elisabeth, Ms., Lawyer, Federation of Norwegian Commercial and Service Enterprises.
NORDLIE, Kim, Mr., Director, Federation of Norwegian Commercial and Service Enterprises.

BARSTAD, Webjørn, Mr., Head of Department, Norwegian Fishing Vessels Owners' Association.

Workers' Delegate

LEKANG, Rita, Ms., Confederal Secretary/Elected Official, Norwegian Confederation of Trade Unions (LO-Norway).

Adviser and substitute delegate

THEODORSEN, Karin Beate, Ms., Deputy International Secretary, LO-Norway.

Advisers

HANSEN, Kristine, Ms., Deputy Head, Norwegian Union of School Employees.
HANSEN, Johnny, Mr., Union Officer, Norwegian Seamen's Union.
GJERDING, Stein, Mr., Head of Division, Confederation of Vocational Unions.

Persons appointed in accordance with Article 2, paragraph 3(i)

SMITH, Jacqueline, Ms., National Secretary, Norwegian Seamen's Union.
MJØBERG, Nina, Ms., Adviser, LO-Norway.
SIKAZWE, Robinson, Mr., Consultant, LO-Norway.
PARKER, Christine, Ms., Adviser, LO-Norway.
JERIES, Moussa El, Mr., Adviser, LO-Norway.

Other persons attending the Conference

SLÅTTEN, Bente, Ms., Vice-President, Confederation of Higher Education Unions.
BLYVERKET, Inger Lise, Ms., Negotiator, Confederation of Higher Education Unions.
NIELSEN, Victor-Bjørn, Mr., Negotiator, Confederation of Higher Education Unions.
EGGEN, Gjertrud, Ms., Senior Adviser, Confederation of Higher Education Unions.
BERNTSEN, Hasse, Mr., Counsellor, United Nations Association in Norway.

Nouvelle-Zélande   New Zealand
Nueva Zelandia

Minister attending the Conference

SWAIN, Paul, Mr., Minister of Labour.

Person accompanying the Minister

FOX, Phillippa, Ms., Private Secretary, Office of the Minister of Labour.

Government Delegates

BUWALDA, James, Mr., Secretary of Labour, Department of Labour.
STEFFENS, Rebecca, Ms., Manager (International), Department of Labour.

Adviser and substitute delegate

LOCKHART, Andrew, Mr., General Manager, Immigration Service, Department of Labour.

Advisers

CHETWIN, John, Mr., Department of Labour.
CAUGHLEY, Tim, Mr., Ambassador, Permanent Representative, Permanent Mission, Geneva.
DEMPSTER, Jillian, Ms., First Secretary, Permanent Mission, Geneva.

Employers' Delegate

ARNOLD, Terry, Mr., President, Business New Zealand.

Adviser

CLEARY, Tim, Mr., Principal Adviser, Business New Zealand.

Workers' Delegate

BEAUMONT, Carol, Ms., Secretary, New Zealand Council of Trade Unions, NZCTU.

Adviser

RIGGS, Sharn, Ms., National Secretary, Association of Staff in Tertiary Education; Member, NZCTU National Affiliates Council.

Oman

Minister attending the Conference

JUMA, Juma Ali, Mr., Minister of Manpower.

Government Delegates

AL-BUSAIDI, Hamad Hilal, Mr., Undersecretary of Labour, Ministry of Manpower.
AL-RIYAMI, Ahmed Mohamed Masoud, Mr., Ambassador, Permanent Representative, Permanent Mission, Geneva.

Advisers and substitute delegates

AL-RAHBI, Abdulla Mussalam, Mr., Director of the Office of the Minister of Manpower.
AL-ABDUWANI, Ali Hassan Ali, Mr., Adviser to the Minister of Manpower.

AL-AMRI, Hamad Khamis, Mr., Director-General of Manpower Planning, Ministry of Manpower.

Advisers

AL-SHIBLI, Rashid Saeed, Mr., Director, Under-Secretary Office, Ministry of Manpower.
AL-KHANJARI, Idris Abdulrahman, Mr., First Secretary, Permanent Mission, Geneva.
AL-QASSIMI, Ali Ahmed, Mr., First Secretary, Permanent Mission, Geneva.
AL-SA'ADI, Zakariya Hamad, Mr., First Secretary, Permanent Mission, Geneva.
AL-MAQBALI, Nadia, Ms., Ministry of Manpower.

Employers' Delegate

AL RABAIE, Hamdan Seif, Mr., Chamber of Commerce and Industry.

Advisers

AL-ZUBAIR, Rashad Mohammed, Mr., Board of Employers.
AL-KHUNJI, Khalil Abdulla, Mr., Board of Employers.
BAHWAN, Hind Suheil, Mrs., Bahwan Cyber-Tech. Company.
AL-HARTHY, Assela Zahir, Mrs., Oman Oil Company, Member of the Board, Chamber of Commerce and Industry.
AL-HINAI, Rashid Bin Ahmed Bin Mohamed, Mr., Chamber of Commerce and Industry.

Workers' Delegate

ASSADALLAH, Abdulazim Abbas, Mr., Head, Workers Committee, Omantel (Oman Telecommunications company).

Advisers

AL-NAHARI, Saud Ahmed, Mr., Head, Workers Committee, Port Services Establishment.
AL-RIZAIQI, Mohammed Ahmed, Mr., Head, Workers Committee, Group of Galfar Companies.

Ouganda   Uganda   Uganda

Minister attending the Conference

BAKOKO BAKORU, Zoé, Ms., Minister of Gender, Labour and Social Development.

Government Delegates

NAGGAGA, William G., Mr., Ambassador, Permanent Mission, Geneva.
OGARAM, David, Mr., Commissioner for Labour.

Advisers

KWERONDA-RUHEMBA, Mr., Ambassador, Permanent Representative, Permanent Mission, Geneva.
GAKWANDI, Arthur, Mr., Ambassador, Permanent Mission, Geneva.
IRUMBA, Nathan, Mr., Ambassador, Permanent Mission, Geneva.
MANANA, Denis, Mr., First Secretary, Permanent Mission, Geneva.
NDOBOLI, Nathan, Mr., First Secretary, Permanent Mission, Geneva.
BANYA, Jackie A., Ms., Labour Officer, International Relations.
ONEGI OBEL, Geoffrey, Mr., Senior Presidential Adviser, AGOA.

Employers' Delegate

SSENABULYA, Rosemary, Ms., Executive Director, Federation Uganda Employers.

Advisers

KASEKENDE, Martin, Mr., General Manager, National Housing and Construction Corporation.
MPUUMA, Leonard, Mr., Managing Director, National Social Security Fund.
GIDONGO, Rose, Mrs., Director, Personnel and Administration, Civil Aviation Authority.
THENGE, Moses, Mr., Human Resource Manager, Kakira Sugar Works.
SSEMANDA, Aloysius, Mr., Chairman, Federation of Uganda Employers.

Workers' Delegate

PAJOBO, Joram B., Mr., General Secretary, NUPAW and Workers; Member of Parliament.

Adviser

NKOJJO, David, Mr., Chairman, National Organisation of Trade Unions (NOTU).

Ouzbékistan   Uzbekistan   Uzbekistán

Government Delegates

OBIDOV, Badriddin, Mr., First Secretary, Chargé d'affaires a.i., Permanent Mission, Geneva.
GANIYEV, Nodir, Mr., Third Secretary, Permanent Misison, Geneva.

Pakistan

Government Delegates

FARSHORI, Muhammad Humayun, Mr., Secretary, Ministry of Labour, Manpower and Overseas Pakistanis.
UMER, Shaukat, Mr., Ambassador, Permanent Representative, Permanent Mission, Geneva.

Advisers

HASSAN FAIZ, Raja Faizul, Mr., Central Labour Advisor, Ministry of Labour, Manpower and Overseas Pakistanis.
KHAN, Mansoor A., Mr., First Secretary, Permanent Mission, Geneva.
TIRMIZI, Faisal Niaz, Mr., First Secretary, Permanent Mission, Geneva.

Employers' Delegate

TABANI, Ashraf W., Mr., President, Employers' Federation of Pakistan; Member of the ILO Governing Body.

Workers' Delegate

AHMED, Khursheed, Mr., General Secretary, All Pakistan Federation of Trade Unions; Member, ILO Governing Body.

Panama

Delegados gubernamentales

ROSAS PÉREZ, Isaura, Sra., Viceministra de Trabajo y Desarrollo Laboral.
BELIZ, Anel E., Sr., Embajador, Representante Permanente, Misión Permanente, Ginebra.

Consejero técnico y delegado suplente

ORTIZ BARBER, Xenia, Sra., Asesora Legal, Ministerio de Trabajo y Desarrollo Laboral.

Consejeros técnicos

MADURO, Nelly, Sr., Asesora, Despacho Superior, Ministerio de Trabajo y Desarrollo Laboral.
DOMÍNGUEZ, Arsenio, Sr., Jefe, Centro Regional, Autoridad Marítima de Panamá en Europa.
MANZUR BARREDA, Beatriz, Sra., Jefa, Departamento de Colaboración con la OIT, Asesoría de Asuntos Internacionales, Ministerio de Trabajo y Desarrollo Laboral.

Delegado de los empleadores

AIZPURÚA, Manuel Virgilio, Sr., Presidente, Comisión Laboral; Asesor, Consejo Nacional de la Empresa Privada (CONEP).

Consejeros técnicos

RIVERA, José Javier, Sr., Ex-Presidente, Miembro, Cámara de Comercio, Industrias y Agricultura.
FOSSATTI, Mónica, Sra., Asistente Técnica, Dirección Jurídica, Cámara Panameña de la Construcción (CAPAC).

Delegado de los trabajadores

PUGA RODRÍGUEZ, Guillermo, Sr., Secretario General, Confederación de Trabajadores de la República de Panamá (CTRP); Miembro, Consejo Nacional de Trabajadoes Organizados (CONATO).

Consejeros técnicos

PEDROZA RODRÍGUEZ, José Angel, Sr., Secretario de Defensa, Confederación Gremial de Trabajadores (CGT); Miembro, CONATO.
HURTADO JAÉN, Pedro Antonio, Sr., Secretario, Asuntos Internacionales, Federación Sindical de Trabajadores República (FSTRP); Miembro, CONATO.

Papouasie-Nouvelle-Guinée
Papua New Guinea
Papua Nueva Guinea

Minister attending the Conference

BIYAMA, Roy, Mr., Minister for Labour and Industrial Relations.

Person accompanying the Minister

GRANT, Warren, Mr., First Secretary to the Minister.

Government Delegates

ARUA, George, Mr., Director, National Training Council, Ministry for Labour and Industrial Relations.
LOVAGA, Maria, Mrs., First Assistant Secretary, Labour Standards, Department of Labour and Industrial Relations.

Advisers and substitute delegates

WANGISAUSE, Thomas, Mr., Regional Industrial Relations Officer, Department of Labour.
PASMALENG, Dessie E., Ms., Director, International Labour Affairs, Department of Labour and Industrial Relations.

Other person attending the Conference

DIALA, Arthur, Mr., Director, National Tripartite Consultative Council, Ministry for Labour and Industrial Relations.

Employers' Delegate

JEFFERY, John, Mr., President, Employers' Federation of Papua New Guinea.

Workers' Delegate

MELAN, Ayang, Mr., Vice President, Papua New Guinea Trade Union Congress.

Paraguay

Ministro asistente a la Conferencia

MONGES ESPÍNOLA, Juan, Sr., Ministro de Justicia y Trabajo.

Persona que acompaña al Ministro

CANDIA AMARILLA, Rubén, Sr., Viceministro de Trabajo y Seguridad Social.

Delegados gubernamentales

GAUTO, Rigoberto, Sr., Embajador, Representante Permanente, Misión Permanente, Ginebra.
BARREIRO PERROTTA, Francisco, Sr., Primer Secretario, Misión Permanente, Ginebra.

Consejeros técnicos y delegados suplentes

RAMÍREZ LEZCANO, Rubén, Sr., Misión Permanente, Ginebra.
PATIÑO, Lorena, Sra., Segunda Secretaria, Misión Permanente, Ginebra.
LATERZA, Estefanía, Sra., Primera Secretaria, Misión Permanente, Ginebra.

Consejero técnico

LÓPEZ, Verónica, Sra., Sección de Normas Internacionales, Ministerio de Justicia y Trabajo.

Delegado de los empleadores

BOGARIN, Walter Manuel, Sr., Federación Paraguaya de la Industria y el Comercio (FEPRINCO).

Delegado de los trabajadores

INSFRÁN, Víctor, Sr., Central Unitaria de Trabajadores.

Consejeros técnicos

PARRA GAONA, Pedro, Sr., Central Nacional de Trabajadores.
ALONSO, Sixto, Sr., Confederación Paraguaya de Trabajadores.

Pays-Bas   Netherlands
Países Bajos

Ministers attending the Conference

DE GEUS, Aart Jan, Mr., Minister for Social Affairs and Employment.
POULO, Domingo H., Mr., Junior Minister of Labour Affairs, Netherlands Antilles.

Persons accompanying the ministers

VERSTEEG, Bea, Ms., Information Officer, Communication Directorate, Ministry of Social Affairs and Employment.
SLUIS, Ronald, Mr., Advisor to the Junior Minister, Netherlands Antilles.

Government Delegates

BEETS, Lauris C., Mr., Director, International Affairs, Ministry of Social Affairs and Employment.
DE JONG, Ian, Mr., Ambassador, Permanent Representative, Permanent Mission, Geneva.

Advisers and substitute delegates

KOOPMAN, Alieke, Ms., Deputy Head of Department, Ministry of Social Affairs and Employment.
NOTEBOOM, Mariana J., Ms., First Secretary, Permanent Mission, Geneva.

Advisers

ALDERS, Peter, Mr., Policy Advisor, Ministry of Social Affairs and Employment.
BASTIAANSEN, Lian, Ms., Policy Advisor, Ministry of Social Affairs and Employment.
BLOM, Anita, Ms., Policy Advisor, Ministry of Social Affairs and Employment.
BRINKMAN, Onno, Mr., Policy Advisor, Ministry of Social Affairs and Employment.
DONK, Joan, Ms., Policy Advisor, Ministry of Social Affairs and Employment.
VAN DER LOUW, Cynthia, Ms., Policy Advisor, Ministry of Social Affairs and Employment.
VAN RENSELAAR, Jan, Mr., Policy Advisor, Ministry of Foreign Affairs.
TEN NAPEL, Henk, Mr., Director, Directorate of Labour, Government of the Netherlands Antilles.
ELS, Virlene, Ms., Policy Adviser, Directorate of Labour, Government of the Netherlands Antilles.

Other persons attending the Conference

VAN ARKEL, Grace, Ms., Advisor, Erasmus University Rotterdam.
DOUMA, Kris, Mr., Member of Parliament.
GRILK, Marianne, Ms., Policy Advisor, Ministry of Social Affairs and Employment.
LANGEJAN, Theo, Mr., Director-General, Ministry of Social Affairs and Employment.
VAN OERLE, Niny, Ms., Member of Parliament.
WEEKERS, Frans, Mr., Member of Parliament.

Employers' Delegate

HUNTJENS, Ton M., Mr., Director, International Social Affairs, Confederation of Netherlands Industry and Employers (VNO-NCW); Deputy Member, Governing Body of the ILO.

Adviser and substitute delegate

RENIQUE, Chiel J.E.G., Mr., Head, Education and Training Department, VNO-NCW.

Advisers

NIEUWSMA, Sip J.L., Mr., Head, Labour Market Department, VNO-NCW.
BLONK, Cor, Mr., Adviser, Labour Relations, Pelagic Freezer Trawler Association.
VAN DER ZWAN, Ment, Mr., Adviser, Employment and Social Affairs, Pelagic Freezer Trawler Association.
PICHARDO, Andrey, Mr., Vice-President, Association for Business Curaçao, Manager Human Resources, Netherlands Antilles.

Other persons attending the Conference

VAN DEN BRAAK, Jan Willem, Mr., Director, Social Affairs, VNO-NCW.
TEUNISSEN, Petra F.M., Ms., Adviser, VNO-NCW.
BOR, Anneke, Ms., Adviser, VNO-NCW.

Workers' Delegate

ETTY, Tom, Mr., Policy Adviser, International Affairs, Netherlands Trade Union Confederation (FNV).

Adviser and substitute delegate

PRUIM, Gerrit, Mr., Secretary for International Affairs, National Federation of Christian Trade Unions.

Advisers

VAN KRUINING, Paul F., Mr., Trade Union Confederation for Middle and Higher Level Employees.
GARCIA SOTO, Daniel, Mr., Policy Adviser, Ethnic Minorities, FNV.
VRIELING, Margreet, Ms., Policy Adviser, National Federation of Christian Trade Unions.

ALCIDES COVA, Pablo, Mr., President, Union Sentral Sindikal di Korsou (SSK), Netherlands Antilles.

Other person attending the Conference

ROEPER, Corrie, Ms., Policy Adviser, FNV.

Pérou   Peru   Perú

Ministro asistente a la Conferencia

NEVES MÚJICA, Javier, Sr., Ministro de Trabajo y Promoción del Empleo.

Delegados gubernamentales

VILLAVICENCIO RIOS, Alfredo, Sr., Viceministro de Trabajo, Ministerio de Trabajo y Promoción del Empleo.
SALINAS, José Luis, Sr., Ministro, Representante Permanente Adjunto, Misión Permanente, Ginebra.

Consejeros técnicos y delegados suplentes

VEGAS, Juan Pablo, Sr., Consejero, Misión Permanente, Ginebra.
BERAUN, Eliana, Sra., Segunda Secretaria, Misión Permanente, Ginebra.
NEYRA, Alejandro, Sr., Segundo Secretario, Misión Permanente, Ginebra.

Delegado de los empleadores

BARRENECHEA CALDERÓN, Julio César, Sr., Presidente, Comité de Asuntos Laborales, Confederación Nacional de Instituciones Empresariales Privadas.

Consejero técnico

PEDRAZA AZURIN, Néstor, Sr., CONFIEP.

Delegado de los trabajadores

GUTIÉRREZ MADUEÑO, Joaquín, Sr., Confederación General de Trabajadores del Perú (CGTP).

Consejeros técnicos y delegados suplentes

BAZÁN FIGUEROA, Julio César, Sr., Presidente, Central Unitaria de Trabajadores (CUT).
FIGUEROA SILVA, Douglas, Sr., Presidente, Confederación de Trabajadores del Perú.
CORTEZ BENITES, Betty, Sra., CUT.

Philippines   Philippines   Filipinas

Minister attending the Conference

STO. TOMAS, Patricia A, Mrs., Secretary, Department of Labor and Employment.

Government Delegates

MANALO, Enrique A, Mr., Ambassador, Permanent Representative, Permanent Mission, Geneva.
BALDOZ, Rosalinda D., Mrs., Administrator, Philippine Overseas Employment Administration.

Advisers

BRILLANTES, Jose, Mr., Undersecretary, Department of Foreign Affairs.
JURIDICO, Elmor D., Mr., Executive Director, Employees Compensation Commission.
EASTWOOD, Veronica A., Mrs., Labor Attaché, Permanent Mission, Geneva.
MENDOZA, Marianita, Mrs., Commissioner, Social Security System.
OSMENA, John H., Mr., Senator.

Other persons attending the Conference

CUENCO, Antonio, Mr.
CARINO, Noel M., Mr.

Employers' Delegate

SORIANO, Rene Y., Mr., President, Employers' Confederation of the Philippines.

Advisers

VARELA, Miguel B., Mr., Chairman of the Board, Employers Confederation of the Philippines.
TAN, Ancheta K., Mr., President Emeritus, Employers Confederation of the Philippines.
BAGABALDO, Aniano G., Mr., Vice-President, Employers Confederation of the Philippines.

Workers' Delegate

VALERIO, Avelino V., Mr., Vice-President, Trade Union Congress of the Philippines (TUCP).

Advisers

MENDOZA, Democrito T., Mr., President, TUCP.
DELA CRUZ JR., Zoilo V., Mr., President, National Congress of the Unions of Sugar Industry of the Philippines.
BALAIS, Victorino F., Mr., President, Philippine Transport and General Workers Organization - Dinglasan.

Pologne   Poland   Polonia

Government Delegates

PATER, Krzysztof, Mr., Minister of Social Policy.
JAKUBOWSKI, Krzysztof, Mr., Ambassador, Permanent Representative, Permanent Mission, Geneva.

Advisers and substitute delegates

PRZYGODZKI, Stanislaw, Mr., Ambassador, Deputy Permanent Representative, Permanent Mission, Geneva.
LEMIESZEWSKA, Renata, Mrs., First Secretary, Permanent Mission, Geneva.
MACIEJEWSKA, Joanna, Mrs., Deputy Director, Coordination of Social Security Schemes Department, Ministry of Economy and Labour.

Advisers

DUSZCZYK, Maciej, Mr., Head of Division, Economic and Social Analyses Department, Office of the Committee for European Integration.
KASSANGANA, Margareta, Mrs., Second Secretary, Department of the United Nations' System and Global Affairs, Ministry of Foreign Affairs.
NOJSZEWSKA - DOCHEV, Magdalena, Mrs., Chief Expert, Labour Market Department, Ministry of Economy and Labour.
SWIATKOWSKI, Andrzej, Mr., Professor, Jagiellonian University.
WYSOCKA, Magdalena, Mrs., Expert, Coordination of Social Security Schemes Department, Ministry of Economy and Labour.
BARANSKA, Magdalena, Mrs., Expert, Labour Market Department, Ministry of Economy and Labour.

Employers' Delegate

BOBROWSKI, Boguslaw, Mr., Deputy President, Confederation of Polish Employers.

Adviser and substitute delegate

KACZURBA, Janusz, Mr., Advisor to the Executive Board, Polish Confederation of Private Employers.

Advisers

SKOLIMOWSKA, Agnieszka, Ms., Expert, Confederation of Polish Employers.
PRUSZANOWSKI, Norbert, Mr., Expert, Polish Craft Association.
JANKOWSKI, Andrzej, Mr., Expert, Confederation of Polish Employers.
MECINA, Jacek, Mr., Expert, Polish Confederation of Private Employers.
KLIS, Tadeusz, Mr., Deputy President, Polish Craft Association.

Other person attending the Conference

MALINOWSKI, Andrzej, Mr., President, Confederation of Polish Employers.

Workers' Delegate

WOJCIK, Tomasz, Mr., Member of the National Commission, Independent Self-Governing Trade Union "Solidarnosc".

Adviser and substitute delegate

LEPIK, Ryszard, Mr., Deputy President, All-Poland Alliance of Trade Unions.

Advisers

GORSKA, Zuzanna, Mrs., Expert, "Solidarnosc".
KOTOWSKI, Zbigniew, Mr., Expert, "Solidarnosc".
KULESZA, Czeslaw, Mr., Expert, All-Poland Alliance of Trade Unions.
MIERZEJEWSKI, Zygmunt, Mr., Deputy President, Trade Unions' Forum.

Portugal

Ministres assistant à la Conférence

PAIS ANTUNES, Luís Miguel, M., Secrétaire d'Etat du Travail.
BRAZÃO DE CASTRO, Eduardo António, M., Secrétaire régional, Ressources humaines, Région autonome de Madère.

Personnes accompagnant les ministres

DA COSTA PEREIRA, José Caetano, M., Ambassadeur, Représentant permanent, Mission permanente, Genève.
PEREIRA MARQUES, Carlos, M., Représentant permanent adjoint, Mission permanente, Genève.
DE SOUSA FIALHO, José António, M., Conseiller, Cabinet du Ministre de la Sécurité sociale et du Travail.
GONÇALVES DA SILVA, Luís, M., Adjoint du Secrétaire d'Etat du Travail.

Délégués gouvernementaux

RIBEIRO LOPES, Fernando, M., Directeur général de l'Emploi et des Relations du Travail, Ministère de la Sécurité sociale et du Travail.
BARCIA, Paulo, M., Conseiller pour les Affaires du Travail et de l'Emploi, Mission permanente, Genève.

Conseillers techniques

CHARANA, António, M., Directeur, Département de l'Emploi, Institut de l'Emploi et de la Formation professionnelle.
MAIA MACHADO, Carlos, M., Secrétaire général, Conseil Régional de Concertation stratégique, Région autonome des Açores.
DE MELO MEDEIROS, João, M., Directeur, Services du Travail, Région autonome des Açores.
HENRIQUES, João Pedro, M., Expert, Institut de l'Emploi et de la Formation professionnelle.
DE MATOS, Manuel, M., Conseiller social, Direction générale des Affaires consulaires et Communautés portugaises.
SOARES, Maria Cândida, Mme, Directeur général, Département d'Etudes, Statistiques et Planification, Ministère de la Sécurité sociale et du Travail.
ROBERT LOPES, Maria Helena, Mme, Chef de Division, Cabinet pour les Affaires de l'Organisation internationale du Travail, Ministère de la Sécurité sociale et du Travail.
PACCETTI DOS SANTOS LOBO CORRE, Maria Teresa, Mme, Assesseur principal, Direction générale de l'Emploi et des Relations de Travail.
GONÇALVES DA SILVA, Rui, M., Directeur régional du Travail, Région autonome de Madère.

Autres personnes assistant à la Conférence

LEITE BETTENCOURT, Rui, M., Directeur régional de la Jeunesse, Emploi et Formation professionnelle, Région autonome des Açores.
FIGUEIRA, Lucília, Mme, Directeur général, Département de la Coopération, Ministère de la Sécurité sociale et du Travail.
REIS RODRIGUES, Felicidade, Mme, Assesseur principal, Département de la Coopération, Ministère de la Sécurité sociale et du Travail.
PENEDOS, Artur, M., Député.
SANTOS, Arménio, M., Député.
DE PORTUGAL, Luísa, Mme, Député.
VEIGA, Paulo, M., Député.
SANTOS, Maria Teresa, Mme
VEIGA, Tânia, Mme

Délégué des employeurs

DE MEIRELES V. DE CASTRO, Rui, M., Membre de la Direction, Confédération de l'Industrie portugaise.

Conseillers techniques

GUERREIRO, Clara, Mme, Expert, Confédération des Agriculteurs du Portugal.
LEOPOLDO, Florbela, Mme, Expert, Confédération des Agriculteurs du Portugal.
FERNANDES SALGUEIRO, Heitor, M., Directeur général adjoint, Confédération de l'Industrie Portugaise.
DE CARVALHO, Luzia, Mme, Expert, Confédération du Commerce et Services du Portugal.
CORREIA CUSTÓDIO, Mário Jorge, M., Secrétaire général, Chambre du Commerce et de l'Industrie, Région autonome des Açores.
BERNARDO, Nuno, M., Expert, Confédération du Tourisme Portugais.
SIBORRO, Rita, Mme, Expert, Confédération du Commerce et Services du Portugal.

DOS SANTOS CRUZ, Sandra Isabel, Mme, Expert, Association commerciale et industrielle du Funchal.

Délégué des travailleurs

GOMES PROENÇA, João António, M., Secrétaire général, Union générale des Travailleurs (UGT).

Conseillers techniques

DOS SANTOS CARDOSO MACEDO, António José, M., Membre, Conseil national, Confédération générale des Travailleurs portugais (CGTP-IN).
DE CARVALHO, Carlos António, M., Membre, Conseil national, CGTP-IN.
ALVES TRINDADE, Carlos Manuel, M., Membre, Commission exécutive, Conseil national, CGTP-IN.
MEIRINHO DE JESUS, José Manuel, M., Membre, UGT.
CORTEZ DOS SANTOS, Maria Leonor, Mme, Membre, UGT.
CARVALHO DA SILVA, Manuel, M., Secrétaire général, CGTP-IN.
LANÇA, Florival, M., Secrétaire des Relations Internationales, CGTP-IN.

Qatar

Minister attending the Conference

AL-THANI, Falah Bin Jassim Bin Jabr, Mr., Minister of Civil Service Affairs and Housing.

Government Delegates

AL SULAITI, Khaled Salman, Mr., Director, Labour Department.
ALKHULAIFI, Ali Ahmad, Mr., Head, International Relations Section, Labour Department.

Advisers and substitute delegates

AL-THANI, Fahad Awaida, Mr., Ambassador, Permanent Representative, Permanent Mission, Geneva.
AL KHAYAREEN, Zayed Saeed, Mr., Director, Department of Public Relations and Information.
HAIDAR, Khaled Ahmad, Mr., Head, Employment Section, Labour Department.
AL SHAWI, Saleh Saeed, Mr., Head, Labour Inspection Section, Labour Department.
ALKAWARI, Abdel Aziz Ahmad, Mr., Accountant.
AL MAL, Noor Abdulla, Ms., International Relations Researcher, Minister's Office.
AL KUBAISI, Yasmin Mohammad, Ms., Researcher, International Relations Section, Labour Department.

Employers' Delegate

AL ANSARI, Mohammad Khazim, Mr., Member of the Board, Qatar Chamber of Commerce and Industry.

Workers' Delegate

AL SAIARI, Abu Bakr Amer, Mr., Human Resources Requirements Coordinator, Qatar Workers' General Committee.

République dém. du Congo
Democratic Republic of the Congo
República Democrática del Congo

Ministre assistant à la Conférence

BUNDA BITENDWA, Jeanne, Mme, Vice-ministre du Travail et de la Prévoyance sociale.

Personne accompagnant le Ministre

BAMBA, Irène, Mme, Secrétaire particulière de la Ministre.

Délégués gouvernementaux

BOLA BOLAILOKO, Boniface, M., Secrétaire général au Travail.
MWAMBA MVIDIMUKULU, M., Secrétaire général à la Prévoyance sociale.

Conseillers techniques

IYELEZA, M., Conseiller, Présidence de la République.
ELEMBO, Jean Christophe, M., Conseiller chargé du Travail, Vice-Présidence de la République, Commission Socio-culturelle.
LUKOO, Ruffin, M., Conseiller juridique.
SHABANI, Crispin, M., Conseiller chargé de la Formation.
BAKARI KABWE, Léopold, M., Directeur du Travail.
MINCHIABO MUTOMBO, Henriette, Mme, Directrice, Direction d'Etudes et Planification, Secrétariat général au Travail.
KOFFI MULUMBA, M., Chef, Division Contrôle et Surveillance, Direction des Pêches.
KAWAYA SEFU, Papa, M., Directeur, MIDA.
MATONDO KUA NZAMBI, David Abraham, M., Directeur général, ONEM.
SAMBASSI, Fidèle, M., Ministre Conseiller, Mission permanente, Genève.
MUTOMB MUJING, SéBASTIEN, M., Deuxième Conseiller, Mission permanente, Genève.

Délégué des employeurs

NTAMBWE KITENGE, Maurice, M., Secrétaire général, Fédération des Entreprises du Congo (FEC).

Conseillers techniques

NGUB'USIM MPEY-NKA, Richard, M., Administrateur secrétaire exécutif, Association nationale des Entreprises du Portefeuille (ANEP).

BUKASA TSHIENDA, Georges, M., Président, Conseil d'Administration, Confédération des Petites et Moyennes Entreprises.
MBUKU MBUMBA, Jean-Pierre, M., Président, Fédération nationale des petites et moyennes Entreprises congolaises, (FENAPEC).
BADIBAKE KAPENDA, Bob Robert, M., Administrateur délégué général, Institut national de Sécurité sociale, (INSS).
ATIBU SALEH MWEKEE, Marc, M., Directeur, Département social, FEC.
MUTABUNGA RUGINA, Placide, M., Directeur administratif, RVA.
MUSSIMBI KILANGI, Marie-José, Mme, Chef, Service Circulation aérienne, RVA.
MIGUMBU KAHOZI, François, M., Directeur administratif et financier, Association nationale des Entreprises portefeuille (ANEP).
HEMEDI BAYOLO, Christian, M., Directeur de l'Administration du Personnel, (SNEP), ANEP.
NTUMBA KABESA, Jean-Pierre, M., Directeur général adjoint (MIDEMA-FEC).

Délégué des travailleurs

KATALAY MULELI SANGOL, Henri, M., Président, UNTC.

Conseillers techniques

BWENSA DI MALOSA, M., Président, OTUC.
DUNIA MUTIMANWA LUBULA, Symphorien, M., Président, CSC.
MULAMBA MBUMBA, Justin, M., Président, CDT.
MUKALAYI HANGA, Jean-Marie, M., Président, CTP.
LUIZI BAILU, M., Président, Syndicat des Travailleurs libres (STL).
MIBIKAYI, Steve, M., Président, Solidarité.
NGAMBO MOLOMBO, Alexis, M., Conseiller technique, STL.
KASONGO MUKADI, Paul Henri, M., Conseiller technique, STL.
KIPULU KATANI, Angélique, Mme, Vice-présidente, CSC.
CHOUCOU MUTEKIE LUBUIKA, Sylvie, Mme, Chargée du Département des Femmes, CDT.

Personnes désignées en conformité avec l'article 2, alinéa 3 i)

NYANGUILE-TSHIAMALA KATAKU, Placide-Thomas, M., Président national, FGTK.
AMUZO MULEBINGE, Mme, Déléguée syndicale, SATOCC.
AKONDA EKONGOLO, Jean-Claude, M., Délégué syndical, SATOCC.

Roumanie   Romania   Rumania

Ministre assistant à la Conférence

SARBU, Marian, M., Ministre, Relations avec les Partenaires sociaux.

Personnes accompagnant le Ministre

CIRICA, Razvan Ionut, M., Secrétaire d'Etat, Ministère du Travail, de la Solidarité sociale et de la Famille.
COSTEA, Doru, M., Ambassadeur, Représentant permanent, Mission permanente, Genève.

Délégués gouvernementaux

NEMES, Bogdan, M., Inspecteur supérieur, Direction des Relations internationales, Ministère du Travail, de la Solidarité sociale et de la Famille.
CONSTANTINESCU, Gabriela, Mme, Premier Secrétaire, Mission permanente, Genève.

Conseiller technique et délégué suppléant

ANDREESCU, Daniela Nicoleta, Mme, Directeur exécutif, Office pour la Migration de la Main-d'œuvre.

Conseillers techniques

ROSCA, Cristian, M., Conseiller, Ministère du Travail, de la Solidarité sociale et de la Famille.
BADESCU, Cristian, M., 2ème Secrétaire, Mission permanente, Genève.

Délégué des employeurs

COSTACHE, Florian, M., Président, Patronat national roumain.

Conseiller technique et délégué suppléant

NICOLESCU, Ovidiu, M., Président, Conseil national des Petites et Moyennes Entreprises privées.

Conseillers techniques

CONSTANTINESCU, Mihaela, Mme, Directeur, Union générale des Industriels de Roumanie-1903.
MIHALACHE, Dragos, M., Vice-président, Union générale des Industriels de Roumanie.
CEACALOPOL, Gabriel, M., Directeur, Conseil national du Patronat roumain.
SANCIULESCU, Constantin Nicolae, M., Premier Vice-président, Patronat roumain.
KOVACS, Lorant, M., Directeur, CONPIROM.
FLORESCU, Marcel, M., Président, ARACO.
MUNTEANU, Marian, M., Vice-président, Confédération nationale du Patronat roumain.
GEORGESCU, Sorin, M., Directeur-général, Union national du Patronat roumain.

BUTNARU, Iulian, M., Directeur, Patronat national roumain.

Autre personne assistant à la Conférence

PLATONA, Pavel, M., Adviser, UGIR-1903.

Délégué des travailleurs

PETCU, Marius, M., Président, CNSLR-Fratia.

Conseiller technique et délégué suppléant

RUSU, Sabin, M., Secrétaire-général, CSDR.

Conseillers techniques

BACIU, Iacob, M., Président, Confédération des Syndicats démocrates de Roumanie (CSDR).
JURCA, Ovidiu, M., Vice-président, Bloc national syndical.
KNIESNER, Mariana, Mme, Vice-président, Bloc national syndical.
HOSSU, Bogdan Iuliu, M., Président, Confédération national syndicale "Cartel ALFA".
ALBU, Ion, M., Secrétaire-général, Confédération syndicale "Meridian".
POPA, Ionut Cosmin, M., Conseiller, Confédération syndicale "Meridian".
LUCA, Liviu, M., Premier Vice-président, CNSLR-Fratia.
STAN, Sorin, M., Secrétaire-général, CNSLR-Fratia.
POPESCU, Ovidiu, M., Premier Vice-président, FSLCP.

Personne désignée en conformité avec l'article 2, alinéa 3 i)

SORA, Gheorghe, M., Président, FNS "Solidaritatea '90".

Royaume-Uni   United Kingdom
Reino Unido

Minister attending the Conference

POND, Chris, Mr., Parliamentary Undersecretary, Department for Work and Pensions.

Person accompanying the Minister

GORDON-FARLEIGH, Robin, Mr., Private Secretary.

Government Delegates

RICHARDS, Stephen, Mr., Head, ILO and UN Team, Department for Work and Pensions, Department for Education and Skills.
NELLTHORP, Helen, Ms., First Secretary, Permanent Mission, Geneva.

Advisers and substitute delegates

THORNE, Nick, Mr., Ambassador, Permanent Representative, Permanent Mission, Geneva.
BRATTAN, Sara, Ms., Senior Policy Adviser, Department for Work and Pensions, Department for Education and Skills.

Advisers

TUCKER, Clive, Mr., Director, Joint International Unit, Department for Work and Pensions, Department for Education and Skills.
NIVEN, Marie, Ms., Head, International Relations Division, Department for Work and Pensions, Department for Education and Skills.
PENNEY, Stefan, Mr., Policy Adviser, Department for Work and Pensions, Department for Education and Skills.
JOHNSON, Anne, Ms., Policy Adviser, Department for Work and Pensions, Department for Education and Skills.
COLE, Emma, Ms., Policy Adviser, Immigration and Nationality Directorate, Home Office.
MARTYN, Mary, Ms., Head, Seafarer Health and Safety Branch, Maritime and Coastguard Agency.
DOWNIE, John, Mr., Deputy-Head, EU and International Relations Branch, International Liaison Branch, Maritime and Coastguard Agency.
COLLIGAN, Jan, Ms., Food and Hygiene Inspector, Maritime and Coastguard Agency.
MILROY, David, Mr., Head, EU and International Relations, Shipping Policy Sector, Department for Transport.
DEVINE, Tim, Mr., Head, Employment Rights, Employment Rights Division, Department for Employment and Learning Devolved Administration, Northern Ireland.
RUSHTON, Jane, Ms., Team Leader, National Economy and International Issues, Economy and Labour Market Division, Department for Works and Pensions.
DRUMMOND, Peter, Mr., Global Economic Issues Team, Foreign and Commonwealth Office.
HAUGHEY, Patrick, Mr., Global Economic Issues Team, Foreign and Commonwealth Office.
GUTHRIE, Anna, Ms., Policy Adviser.
DUNNERY, Michael, Mr., Policy Adviser.

Other persons attending the Conference

ONI, Ade, Mr., Policy Advisor, Department for Work and Pensions, Department for Education and Skills.
DEWITT, Dan, Mr., Policy Advisor, Department for Work and Pensions, Department for Education and Skills.
TARIF, Pam, Ms., Second Secretary, Permanent Mission, Geneva.
ROBINSON, Julia, Ms., Attachée, Permanent Mission, Geneva.
DEJENE, Tasew, Mr.
HORTON, Randolph, Mr., Minister, Home Affairs and Public Safety, Bermuda.
HORTON, Robert K., Mr., Permanent Secretary, Ministry of Labour, Home Affairs and Public Safety, Bermuda.

FUBLER, Glen, Mr., Acting Director, Labour and Training, Bermuda.
GRAY, Kieran, Mr., Policy Adviser, Department for Work and Pensions, Department for Education and Skills.
SAADEH, Hanan, Ms., Desk Officer, Foreign and Commonwealth Office.
DEJENE, Tasew, Mr.

Employers' Delegate

LAMBERT, Mel, Mr., Confederation of British Industry (CBI); Member, Governing Body of the ILO.

Advisers and substitute delegates

WARMAN, Bruce, Mr., CBI.
OWENS, Emmeline, Ms., Senior Policy Adviser, CBI.

Advisers

JONES, Mark, Mr., Coningsbys Solicitors.
PIGGOTT, Allan, Mr., Safety and Training Officer, National Federation of Fishermen's Organisations.
SYDER, Chris, Mr., Associate, Clark's Solicitors.

Other persons attending the Conference

GOYDER, Martha, Ms., Senior Policy Adviser, Human Resources Directorate, CBI.
MOWBRAY, Andrea, Ms., Executive Director, Bermuda Employers' Association, Bermuda.
SAINTS, Edward, Mr., President, Bermuda Employers' Council, Bermuda.

Workers' Delegate

HUNT, Sally, Ms., General-Secretary AUT, Trades Union Congress General Council.

Adviser and substitute delegate

STEYNE, Simon, Mr., International Officer, Trades Union Congress; Member, Governing Body of the ILO.

Advisers

SMITH, Caroline, Ms., Policy Officer (Learning and Skills), Organisation and Services Department, Trades Union Congress.
TAYLOR, Sofi, Ms., Member, Executive Council Union; Member, Trades Union Congress General Council.
PENDRED, Mike, Mr., Disability Representative, Docks, Waterways and Fishing Trades Group Committee, Region 1, TGWU; Member, SERTUC Executive Committee.
MURPHY, Rory, Mr., Joint General Secretary, UNIFI.

Other persons attending the Conference

JONES, Catherine, Ms.
STEVENS, James, Mr.

DILL, Maynard, Mr., President, Bermuda Trades Union Congress.
BURGESS, Derrick V., Mr., President, Bermuda Industrial Union, Bermuda.
BARBER, Brendan, Mr., General Secretary, Trades Union Congress.
KHOTALAWALA, Bandula, Mr., International Officer, Trades Union Congress.

Fédération de Russie
Russian Federation
Federación de Rusia

Government Delegates

LUBLIN, Yuri, Mr., Acting Minister of Labour and Social Development; Member, Governing Body of the ILO.
SKOTNIKOV, Leonid, Mr., Ambassador, Permanent Representative, Permanent Mission, Geneva.

Advisers and substitute delegates

BAVYKIN, Alexander, Mr., Deputy Permanent Representative, Permanent Mission, Geneva.
LUKYANENKO, Svyatoslav, Mr., Head, Division of International Cooperation, Ministry of Labour and Social Development.

Advisers

STUKALO, Alexei, Mr., Deputy Director, Department of Economic Cooperation, Ministry of Foreign Affairs.
VLASOVA, Natalia, Ms., Deputy Head, Department of Employment, Ministry of Labour and Social Development.
PROSHIN, Vladimir, Mr., Head of Section, Department of Economic Cooperation, Ministry of Foreign Affairs.
STEPANOV, Viktor, Mr., Head of Section, Division of International Cooperation, Ministry of Labour and Social Development.
LOZINSKIY, Nikolay, Mr., Senior Counsellor, Permanent Mission, Geneva.
ZAGAYNOV, Evgeny, Mr., Counsellor, Permanent Mission, Geneva.
STEPANETS, Valeriy, Mr., Senior Expert, Division of International Cooperation, Ministry of Labour and Social Development.
GRIBKOV, Ilya, Mr., Attaché, Permanent Mission, Geneva.
KOCHETKOV, Maxim, Mr., Attaché, Permanent Mission, Geneva.
BOGATYRENKO, Zahariy, Mr., Chief Editor, Magazine "Bulletin of the Ministry of Labour and Social Development".

Employers' Delegate

EREMEEV, Oleg, Mr., Director-General, Coordinating Council of Employers Union of Russia (KSORR).

Adviser and substitute delegate

POLUEKTOV, Alexander, Mr., Director for International Cooperation, KSORR.

Advisers

LUKONIN, Sergey, Mr., Deputy Director-General, KSORR.
GOLODETS, Olga, Ms., Deputy Director-General, Mining and Metallurgical Company Norilsk Nikel.
ELTSOVA, Lyubov, Ms., Head, Labour Relations and Social Partnership Division, Mining and Metallurgical Company Norilsk Nikel.
TSURSIN, Gennady, Mr., Executive Director, All-Russia Association of Fisheries Enterprises, Entrepreneurs and Exporters (VARPE).

Workers' Delegate

SHMAKOV, Mikhail, Mr., Chairman, Federation of Independent Trade Unions of Russia (FNPR).

Adviser and substitute delegate

SIDOROV, Evgeny, Mr., Secretary, FNPR; Member, ILO Governing Body.

Advisers

EFREMENKO, Andrey, Mr., Chairman, Council of the All-Russia Confederation of Labour (VKT).
SURIN, Anatoly, Mr., Head, Section for International Cooperation, FNPR.
STRELA, Galina, Ms., Secretary, FNPR.
GLADKOV, Nikolay, Mr., Secretary, FNPR.
SOSHEPKO, Boris, Mr., Chairman, Trade Union of Construction and Industrial Materials Workers of Russia.
SHALONIN, Yuri, Mr., Chairman, Trade Union of Fishery Workers (KTR).
SHEPEL, Alexander, Mr., President, Confederation of Labour of Russia (KTR).
NAGAITSEV, Mikhail, Mr., Chairman, Moscow Trade Union Federation.

Rwanda

Délégués gouvernementaux

MUGANZA, Angelina, Mme, Secrétaire d'Etat chargée de la Formation professionnelle, des Métiers et du Travail, Ministère de la Fonction publique, de la Formation professionnelle, des Métiers et du Travail.
UKUYEMUYE, François, M., Directeur du Travail a.i., Ministère de la Fonction publique, de la Formation professionnelle, des Métiers et du Travail.

Conseiller technique et délégué suppléant

RUGWABIZA, Valentine, Mme, Ambassadeur, Représentant permanent, Mission permanente, Genève.

Conseillers techniques

KARIBATA, Anaclet, M., Directeur général de l'Immigration et de l'Emigration, Service national de sécurité.
MUTETERI, Bernadette, Mme, Secrétaire particulière du Secrétaire d'Etat.
KAVARUGANDA, Guillaume, M., Conseiller, Mission permanente, Genève.

Délégué des employeurs

BITWAYIKI, Eugène, M., Directeur des Programmes multisectoriels, Fédération rwandaise du Secteur privé (FRSP).

Conseillers techniques

RUSENGAMIHIGO, Cécile, Mme, Vice-présidente, Association des Femmes entrepreneurs.
UKOBIZABA, François, M., Directeur des Ressources humaines, Banque continentale africaine au Rwanda (BACAR).

Délégué des travailleurs

KAYUMBA, Jean-Baptiste, M., Président, Conseil national des Organisations syndicales libres du Rwanda (COSYLI).

Conseillers techniques

MUKANDAMUTSA, Florida, Mme, Présidente, Centrale des Syndicats des Travailleurs du Rwanda (CESTRAR).
MUKARUZIMANA, Dativa, Mme, Membre du Bureau exécutif chargée de la Promotion feminine et Genre, CESTRAR.
MUGANYINKA, Olive, Mme, Membre du Bureau exécutif chargée des jeunes Travailleurs, CESTRAR.
MANZI MWEZI, Eric, M., Secrétaire général, CESTRAR.
NKIRAMACUMU, Dominique, M., Président, Association des Syndicats chrétiens UMURIMO (ASC-UMURIMO).
BICAMUMPAKA, Dominique, M., Coordinateur permanent, Congrès du Travail et de la Fraternité (COTRAF).

Saint-Marin   San Marino
San Marino

Ministre assistant à la Conférence

ANDREOLI, Paride, M., Ministre du Travail et de la Coopération, du Tourisme, du Sport et de la Poste.

Personnes accompagnant le Ministre

BRONZETTI, Denise, Mme, Fonctionnaire, Ministère du Travail et de la Coopération.
CRESCENTINI, Paolo, M., Secrétaire privé du Ministre.

Délégués gouvernementaux

BIGI, Federica, Mme, Ambassadeur, Représentant permanent, Mission permanente, Genève.
GASPERONI, Eros, M., Secrétaire d'Ambassade, Ministère des Affaires étrangères et Politiques.

Conseiller technique et délégué suppléant

RONDELLI, Maria Luisa, Mme, Directeur, Centre de Formation professionnelle.

Délégué des employeurs

UGOLINI, Pio, M., Secrétaire général, Union nationale des Artisans (UNAS).

Conseillers techniques et délégués suppléants

MENICUCCI, Romina, Mme, Fonctionnaire, Association nationale de l'Industrie (ANIS).
GIORGINI, Cinzia, Mme, Fonctionnaire, Organisation des Travailleurs autonomes (OSLA).

Conseiller technique

DELLA BALDA, Silvia, Mme, Fonctionnaire, Union saint-marinaise des Commerçants (USC).

Délégué des travailleurs

PIERMATTEI, Gilberto, M., Secrétaire confédéral, Confédération du Travail (CSDL).

Conseiller technique et délégué suppléant

TONI, Ivan, M., Membre, Conseil confédéral, CSDL.

Conseiller technique

BECCARI, Marco, M., Secrétaire général, Confédération démocratique des Travailleurs (CDLS).

Sao Tomé-et-Principe
Sao Tome and Principe
Santo Tomé y Príncipe

Délégués gouvernementaux

VAZ DE ALMEIDA, Damião, M., Ministre du Travail, de l'Emploi et de la Solidarité.
ASSUNÇÃO RAMOS, Manuel da C., M., Directeur, Cabinet d'Etudes, Coopération et Solidarité.

Délégué des employeurs

AFONSO RITA, Cosme Bonfim, M., Secrétaire général, Chambre de Commerce, d'Industrie, Agriculture et Services.

Délégué des travailleurs

DA COSTA CARLOS, Manuel, M., Secrétaire général, Union générale des Travailleurs.

Senegal

Ministre assistant à la Conférence

DE, Yéro, M., Ministre de la Fonction publique, du Travail, de l'Emploi et des Organisations professionnelles.

Personne accompagnant le Ministre

CAMARA, Ousmane, M., Ambassadeur, Représentant permanent, Mission permanente, Genève.

Délégués gouvernementaux

DIALLO, Ndèye Bâ, Mme, Directeur par intérim, Travail et de la Sécurité sociale.
THIAM, Babacar, M., Chef, Division des Relations internationales, Ministère de la Fonction publique, du Travail, de l'Emploi et des Organisations professionnelles (MFPTEOP).

Conseillers techniques

BASSE, André, M., Mission permanente, Genève.
WADE, Aboubacar, M., Conseiller technique, MFPTEOP.

Délégué des employeurs

DIOP, Hamidou, M., Secrétaire général, Conseil national du Patronat (CNP).

Conseiller technique et délégué suppléant

WADE, Youssoufa, M., Président d'honneur, CNP.

Conseiller technique

THIAO, Gora, M., Conseiller aux Affaires sociales, Confédération nationale des Employeurs du Sénégal (CNES).

Délégué des travailleurs

GUIRO, Mody, M., Secrétaire général, Confédération nationale des Travailleurs du Sénégal (CNTS).

Conseillers techniques

SOCK, Mademba, M., Secrétaire général, Union nationale des Syndicats autonomes du Sénégale (UNSAS).
TALL, Oumar, M., Secrétaire général, Fédération générale des Travailleurs du Sénégal (FGTS, Tendance A).
NDIAYE, Sidya, M., Secrétaire général, Fédération générale des Travailleurs du Sénégal (FGTS, Tendance B).
NDIAYE, Malamine, M., Secrétaire général adjoint, Union démocratique des Travailleurs du Sénégal (UDTS).
NDIAYE, Saliou, M., Secrétaire général adjoint, Confédération démocratique des Syndicats autonomes (CDSA).
DIOP, Cheikh, M., Secrétaire général, Confédération nationale des Travailleurs du Sénégal/Forces de Changement (CNTS/FC).
DIAO, Meïssa, M., Secrétaire permanent, Confédération générale des Syndicats de Cadres et du Personnel d'encadrement (COGES).
FALL, Mamadou, M., Membre, Bureau confédéral des Syndicats autonomes (CSA).
SYLLA, Ibrahima, M., Secrétaire général, Union des Travailleurs du Sénégal (UTS).
DIAKHATE, Cheikh Tidiane, M., Secrétaire général, Confédération générale des Travailleurs démocratiques du Sénégal (CGTDS).

Personnes désignées en conformité avec l'article 2, alinéa 3 i)

SOW, Alioune, M., Secrétaire général, UDTS.
DIOP, Ndiassé, M., Secrétaire général adjoint, UNSAS.
SAMBA, Mame Coumba, Mme, Secrétaire confédérale chargée de l'Alphabétisation CNTS.
NDIAYE, Ibrahima, M., Secrétaire à la Jeunesse, UTLS, Tendance B.
DIENE, Elimane, M., Secrétaire chargé de la Trésorerie, UTLS, Tendance A.

Autres personnes assistant à la Conférence

SAMB, Makhary, M., Secrétaire général adjoint, CNTS.
MBAYE, Sidy, M., Département Gens de Mer, CNTS.
SARR, Ibrahima, M., 1er Secrétaire général adjoint, CNTS/FC.
NDONGO, Hamidou, M., Département Gens de Mer, CNTS.
LEYE, Dieynaba, Mme, Chargée, Secteur Parapublic, CNTS.
BA NDIAYE, Fatou, Mme, Chargée, Question Genre, CNTS/FC.
FALL NIANG, Doudou, M., Chargé, Projets de Développement, CNTS/FC.
MANE, Joseph, M., Membre, Bureau, CSA.
DIAGNE, Adama Aïta, Mme, Présidente, Mouvement des Femmes, UDTS.
BA, Aliou, M., 3ème Secrétaire général adjoint, UNSAS.
DIALLO, Abdou Aziz, M., Secretaire chargé des Relations extérieures, CSA.
DIOUF, Bakhao Diongue, Mme, 2ème Secrétaire générale adjointe, CNTS/FC.
SOW, Baïla, M., Secrétaire confédéral chargé des Relations extérieures, CNTS/FC.
DIOP, Sokhna Bèye, Mme, Présidente, Mouvement des Femmes, Fédération générale des Travailleurs du Sénégal (FGTS, Tendance A).
GUEYE, Mbaye, M., Secrétaire général, Confédération démocratique des Syndicats autonomes (CDSA).
TOURE, Youssou, M., Trésorier, Fédération générale des Travailleurs du Sénégal (FGTS, Tendance B).

Serbie et Monténégro
Serbia and Montenegro
Serbia y Montenegro

Minister attending the Conference

STIJEPOVIC, Slavoljub, Mr., Minister of Labour and Social Welfare, Republic of Montenegro.

Government Delegates

ŠAHOVIC, Dejan, Mr., Ambassador, Permanent Representative, Permanent Mission, Geneva.
ŠCEKIC, Vukoica, Mr., Deputy Minister of Labour, Employment and Social Policy, Republic of Serbia.

Advisers and substitute delegates

VUKOVIC, Zeljko, Mr., Assistant Minister of Labour and Social Welfare, Republic of Montenegro.
BEGOVIC, Milan, Mr., Deputy Permanent Representative, Permanent Mission, Geneva.
BURZAN, Zdenka, Ms., Head, Employment Unit, Ministry of Labour and Social Welfare, Republic of Montenegro.

Advisers

LUBARDA, Branko, Mr., Professor, Faculty of Law, University of Belgrade.
RADOVANOVIC, Aleksandar, Mr., Counsellor, Permanent Mission, Geneva.
IVANOVIC, Marina, Ms., Second Secretary, Permanent Mission, Geneva.
STAJIC, Marija, Ms., Attaché, Permanent Mission, Geneva.

Employers' Delegate

ZAGORAC, Dragutin, Mr., President, Employers' Union.

Adviser and substitute delegate

MITROVIC, Ivan, Mr., President, Employers' Union, Montenegro.

Advisers

MITROVIC, Predrag, Mr., Vice-President, Employers' Union, Montenegro.

NINKOVIC, Rato, Mr., President, Employers' Union, Serbia.

Workers' Delegate

DRAŠKOVIC, Dragoljub, Mr., Member of Presidency, Association of Independent Trade Unions of Energy, Montenegro.

Advisers and substitute delegates

CANAK, Branislav, Mr., President, United Branch Trade Unions "Nezavisnost".
JOVOVIC, Đurdjica, Mrs., President, Trade Union of Scientific Research Field, Serbia.
SAVIC, Ranka, Mrs., President, Association of Free and Independent Trade Unions of Serbia (ASNS).

Seychelles

Government Delegates

MERITON, Vincent Angelin Emmanuel, Mr., Minister for Social Affairs and Employment.
BAKER, Jules Georges, Mr., Director, Cooperation Unit, Ministry of Social Affairs and Employment.

Employers' Delegate

SULTAN-BEAUDOUIN, Gilbert Rency, Mr., Executive Secretary, Association of Seychelles Employers.

Adviser

CEDRAS, Michelle, Ms., Assistant Executive Secretary, Association of Seychelles Employers.

Workers' Delegate

ROBINSON, Antoine Roland, Mr., General Secretary, Seychelles Federation of Workers' Unions.

Sierra Leone   Sierra Leone   Sierra Leona

Minister attending the Conference

TIMBO, Alpha O., Mr., Minister of Labour, Social Security and Industrial Relations.

Person accompanying the Minister

GENDA, J.P., Mr., Commissioner of Labour, Ministry of Labour, Social Security and Industrial Relations.

Government Delegates

KOROMA, M.A., Mr., Acting Chief Inspector of Factories, Ministry of Labour, Social Security and Industrial Relations.
STEPHEN, James, Mr., Desk Officer, ILO, Ministry of Labour, Social Security and Industrial Relations.

Adviser

MUSTAPHA, A.M., Mr., Administrative Officer, Ministry of Labour, Social Security and Industrial Relations.

Employers' Delegate

JOHNSON, L.E., Mr., Executive Secretary, Sierra Leone Employers' Federation.

Adviser and substitute delegate

STEPHEN, Nusu, Ms., Administrative Assistant, Sierra Leone Employers' Federation.

Workers' Delegate

YILLA, Kandeh, Mr., Secretary-General, Sierra Leone Labour Congress.

Adviser and substitute delegate

JALLOH, Fatmata, Ms., Secretary, Women's Wing, Sierra Leone Labour Congress.

Adviser

BRANCHE, Gladys, Ms., Desk Officer, Women's Wing, Sierra Leone Labour Congress.

Singapour   Singapore   Singapur

Government Delegates

NG, Eng Hen, Mr., Acting Minister for Manpower.
YONG, Ying-I, Ms., Permanent Secretary, Ministry of Manpower.

Advisers

ONG, Yen Her, Mr., Divisional Director, Labour Relations and Welfare Division, Ministry of Manpower.
NG, Hwei Min, Ms., Deputy Director, Income Security Department, Ministry of Manpower.
TOH, Swee Chien, Mr., International Relations and Policy Officer, Labour Relations and Welfare Division, Ministry of Manpower.
MENON, Vanu Gopala, Mr., Ambassador, Permanent Representative, Permanent Mission, Geneva.
MANIAR, Sudesh, Mr., Deputy Permanent Representative, Permanent Mission, Geneva.

LIM, Kevin, Mr., First Secretary, Permanent Mission, Geneva.
ONG, Soo Chuan, Mr., First Secretary, Permanent Mission, Geneva.
BASHA, Munwar, Mr., First Secretary, Permanent Mission, Geneva.

Employers' Delegate

KOH, Juan Kiat, Mr., Executive Director, Singapore National Employers' Federation.

Adviser

TAN, Bob, Mr., Vice President, Singapore National Employers' Federation.

Workers' Delegate

YACOB, Halimah, Mrs., Assistant Secretary-General, Singapore National Trades Union Congress.

Adviser and substitute delegate

DE PAYVA, John, Mr., President, Singapore National Trades Union Congress.

Advisers

YAO, Matthias, Mr., Deputy Secretary-General, Singapore National Trades Union Congress.
YEO, Guat Kwang, Mr., Director, Quality Lifestyle Department, Singapore National Trades Union Congress.
HASSAN, Attyah, Ms., General Secretary, Keppel FELS Employees' Union.
CHEW, How Yang Eddie, Mr., President, Singapore Airlines Staff Union.
SIM, Boh Kwang, Mr., President, Amalgamated Union of Statutory Board Employees.
NEO, Gim Kian, Mr., Director, Membership and Corporate Communications Department, Singapore National Trades Union Congress.
SREEDHARAN, Rema, Ms., Assistant Director, Legal Services Department, Singapore National Trades Union Congress.

Slovaquie   Slovakia   Eslovaquia

Minister attending the Conference

KANÍK, L'udovit, Mr., Minister of Labour, Social Affairs and Family.

Person accompanying the Minister

ROZHOLDOVÁ, Nadezda, Mrs., Interpreter.

Government Delegates

PETÖCZ, Kálmán, Mr., Ambassador, Permanent Representative, Permanent Mission, Geneva.
SEPTÁKOVÁ, Nora, Ms., First Secretary, Permanent Mission, Geneva.

Advisers and substitute delegates

MACHALÍKOVÁ, Anna, Mrs., Director, Personal Office, Ministry of Labour, Social Affairs and Family.
HUSÁRIKOVÁ, Vlasta, Mrs., Director-General, Legislative Section, Ministry of Labour, Social Affairs and Family.
MICHALDOVÁ, Elena, Mrs., Director-General, Strategy and Co-ordination Section, Ministry of Labour, Social Affairs and Family.
KULICH, Dusan, Mr., Director, Department for Further Education, Ministry of Education.

Advisers

ILLKOVÁ, Barbara, Ms., Deputy Permanent Representative, Permanent Mission, Geneva.
CIGÁNIK, Milan, Mr., First Secretary, Permanent Mission, Geneva.
SOTNIK, Stanislav, Mr., Ministry of Labour, Social Affairs and Family.
BAROCHOVÁ, Zora, Ms., Ministry of Labour, Social Affairs and Family.

Employers' Delegate

BORGULA, Juraj, Mr., Expert for International Affairs, Republic Union of Employers.

Advisers

HRDINA, Daniel, Mr., Director, Department of International Relations and Training, Federation of Employers' Unions and Associations.
KROMEROVÁ, Viola, Ms., Secretary-General, Slovak Trade Union.

Workers' Delegate

MESTANOVÁ, Eva, Mrs., Chief, International Relations Department, Confederation of Trade Unions.

Advisers

ANCICOVÁ, Margita, Mrs., Expert, International Relations Department, Confederation of Trade Unions.
BUSO, Milan, Mr., Expert, International Relations Department, Confederation of Trade Unions.

Slovénie   Slovenia   Eslovenia

Minister attending the Conference

DIMOVSKI, Vlado, Mr., Minister of Labour, Family and Social Affairs.

Person accompanying the Minister

BALOH PLAHUTNIK, Staša, Ms., State Secretary, Labour Market, Employment and Education Department, Ministry of Labour, Family and Social Affairs.

Government Delegates

GOSNAR, Aljaz, Mr., Ambassador, Permanent Representative, Permanent Mission, Geneva.
BELOPAVLOVIC, Nataša, Ms., State Secretary, Labour Relations and Labour Rights Department, Ministry of Labour, Family and Social Affairs

Advisers and substitute delegates

ZIDAR, Andraz, Mr., Second Secretary, Permanent Mission, Geneva.
RIHAR BAJUK, Katja, Ms., Adviser, International Relations and European Affairs Department, Ministry of Labour, Family and Social Affairs.

Advisers

CVELBAR BEK, Renata, Ms., Secretary, International Relations and European Affairs Department, Ministry of Labour, Family and Social Affairs.
JENKO, Gorazd, Mr., Secretary, Labour Market, Employment and Education Department, Ministry of Labour, Family and Social Affairs.
RADAK, Radivoj, Mr., Under-secretary, Labour Market, Employment and Education Department, Ministry of Labour, Family and Social Affairs.
RIJAVEC, Maja, Ms., Adviser, Labour Relations and Labour Rights Department, Ministry of Labour, Family and Social Affairs.
ŠARCEVIC, Damjana, Ms., Adviser, Labour Market, Employment and Education Department, Ministry of Labour, Family and Social Affairs.

Employers' Delegate

HRIBAR MILIC, Samo, Mr., Secretary General, Association of Employers of Slovenia.

Adviser and substitute delegate

JEREB, Urška, Ms., Legal Adviser, Association of Employers of Craft Activities of Slovenia.

Workers' Delegate

MAZALIN, Boris, Mr., President, Trade Union Confederation '90 of Slovenia.

Adviser and substitute delegate

KRZIŠNIK, Edvard, Mr., Member of Presidency, Neodvisnost (Independence), Confederation of New Trade Unions.

Somalie   Somalia   Somalia

Government Delegates

DUBAD, Mohamed Omar, Mr., Chargé d'Affaires, Permanent Mission, Geneva.
ISSE, Ahmed Abdi, Mr., Permanent Mission, Geneva.

Soudan   Sudan   Sudán

Minister attending the Conference

MAGAYA, Allison Manani, Mr., Minister of Labour and Administrative Reform.

Person accompanying the Minister

EL HAJ, Mohamed El Hassan, Mr., Ambassador, Permanent Representative, Permanent Mission, Geneva.

Government Delegates

SHENTOUR, Ahmed M., Mr., Under-Secretary, Ministry of Labour and Administrative Reform.
ELHASSAN, Alsabaty M., Mr., Director, International Relations, Ministry of Labour and Administrative Reform.

Advisers and substitute delegates

JADA, Christopher Leonardo, Mr., Second Secretary, Permanent Mission, Geneva.
HAMID, Elsham Mohamed, Mrs.
HUSSEIN, Abdel Moniem, Mr., Government Council.

Employers' Delegate

ELGURASHI, Elfatih Abbas, Mr., Sudanese Employers Federation.

Adviser and substitute delegate

MUSTAFA, Elsheikh Osman, Mr., Sudanese Employers Federation.

Workers' Delegate

GHANDOUR, Ibrahim Ahmed Abdelaziz, Mr., President, Sudan Workers Trade Unions Federation.

Adviser and substitute delegate

ABDELKARIM, Yousif Ali, Mr., Sudan Workers Trade Unions Federation.

Advisers

ELSIDDIG, Abu Bakr, Mr., Sudan Workers Trade Unions Federation.
OSMAN, Abdellatif Alahmar, Mr., Sudan Workers Trade Unions Federation.

Sri Lanka

Minister attending the Conference

ATHAUDA, Seneviratne, Mr., Minister of Labour Relations and Foreign Employment.

Persons accompanying the Minister

FERNANDO, Sarala, Mrs., Ambassador, Permanent Representative, Permanent Mission, Geneva.
ATHAUDA, P.S., Mrs., President, Seva Vanitha Unit, Ministry of Labour Relations and Foreign Employment.

Government Delegates

GAMMAMPILA DON, Mahinda, Mr., Secretary, Ministry of Labour Relations and Foreign Employment.
MADIHAHEWA, Mahinda, Mr., Commissioner General of Labour, Department of Labour.

Advisers and substitute delegates

ATHUKORALA, U.S., Mr., Acting Senior Assistant Secretary, Ministry of Labour Relations and Foreign Employment.
WIJAYAWEERA, W.J.L.U., Mr., Commissioner of Labour, Department of Labour.

Adviser

PATHIRANA, S.P.W., Mr., Second Secretary, Permanent Mission, Geneva.

Employers' Delegate

DASANAYAKE, G.K.B., Mr., Director-General, Employers Federation of Ceylon.

Workers' Delegate

DEVENDRA, Leslie Shelton, Mr., General Secretary, Sri Lanka Nidahas Sevaka Sangamaya.

Advisers

SANDRASEKERA, Harindranath, Mr., Senior Vice-President (I& IR), Ceylon Workers Congress.
SENEVIRATNE, A.W.D.D. Rajah, Mr., President, Lanka Jathika Estate Workers Union.
SIRIWARDANE, S.A.S., Mr., General Secretary, Ceylon Federation of Labour.
SUBASINGHE, D.W., Mr., General Secretary, Ceylon Federation of Trade Unions.

Persons appointed in accordance with Article 2, paragraph 3(i)

HETTIARACHCHI, Ranjith, Mr., Assistant Secretary, Sri Lanka Nidahas Sevaka Sangamamya.
ADIKARI, A.A.J., Mr., Deputy Secretary, Inter Company Employees Union.

Suède   Sweden   Suecia

Minister attending the Conference

GRÖNLUND, Jan, Mr., State Secretary, Ministry of Industry, Employment and Communications.

Person accompanying the Minister

HULT, Stefan, Mr., Director, Ministry of Industry, Employment and Communications.

Government Delegates

JONZON, Björn, Mr., Director, Ministry of Industry, Employment and Communications.
BORSIIN BONNIER, Elisabet, Ms., Ambassador, Permanent Representative, Permanent Mission, Geneva.

Advisers and substitute delegates

WIKLUND, Kerstin, Ms., Counsellor, Ministry of Industry, Employment and Communications.
SUNDQUIST, Ingemar, Mr., Counsellor, Ministry for Foreign Affairs.

Advisers

ALSTERDAL, Lotte, Ms., National Institute for Working Life.
ANDERSSON, Magnus, Mr., First Secretary, Permanent Mission, Geneva.
BOMAN-LINDBERG, Emma, Ms., Desk Officer, Ministry of Industry, Employment and Communications.

GOTARE, Rolf, Mr., Principal Administrative Officer, Swedish Maritime Administration.
KEBBON, Niklas, Mr., Counsellor, Permanent Mission, Geneva.
STAVÅS, Pia, Ms., Counsellor, Permanent Mission, Geneva.

Employers' Delegate

LAURENT, Birgitta, Ms., Legal Adviser, Confederation of Swedish Enterprise.

Adviser and substitute delegate

TROGEN, Göran, Mr., Director-General, Almega IT-Employers' Association.

Advisers

RUDEBERG, Sverker, Mr., Director, Confederation of Swedish Enterprise.
TROGEN, Anita, Ms., Senior Adviser, Confederation of Swedish Enterprise.

Workers' Delegate

EDSTRÖM, Ulf, Mr., Head, International Department, Swedish Trade Union Confederation.

Adviser and substitute delegate

BENGTSSON, Lars, Mr., International Secretary, Swedish Confederation of Professional Employees.

Advisers

ELFVING, Anna-Stina, Ms., Senior Research Officer, Swedish Confederation of Professional Employees.
REINHOLD, Kenny, Mr., Chairman, Seafarers' Branch, Union for Service and Comunication Employees.
JOHANSSON, Christin, Ms., President, Swedish Association of Graduates in Social Science, Personnel and Public Administration, Economics and Social Work.
THAPPER, Keth, Ms., International Secretary, Swedish Trade Union Confederation.

Suisse   Switzerland   Suiza

Ministre assistant à la Conférence

NORDMANN, Jean-Luc, M., Secrétaire d'Etat, Directeur, Direction du Travail (DA), Secrétariat d'Etat à l'Economie (SECO), Département fédéral de l'Economie (DFE).

Délégués gouvernementaux

ELMIGER, Jean-Jacques, M., Ambassadeur, Chef, Affaires internationales du Travail, DA, SECO.
FÄSSLER, Christian, M., Ambassadeur, Chef, Division multilatérale, Mission permanente, Genève.

Conseiller technique et délégué suppléant

ALVESALO-ROESCH, Tanja, Mme, Suppléante du Chef, Affaires internationales du Travail, DA, SECO.

Conseillers techniques

CLERC, Bertrand, M., Suppléant du Chef, Secteur Questions fondamentales et Services généraux, Marché du Travail et Assurance-chômage, DA, SECO.
GRATWOHL, Stephanie, Mme, Collaboratrice diplomatique, Section Organisations internationales et Politique d'accueil, Division politique III, Département fédéral des Affaires étrangères (DFAE).
KOCHERHANS, Nathalie, Mme, Adjointe scientifique, Service juridique, Conditions de Travail, DA, SECO.
MULLER, Elisabeth, Mme, Collaboratrice spécialisée, Affaires internationales du Travail, DA, SECO.
REISLE, Markus, M., Chargé des Questions de Migration, Section Prévention des Conflits, Direction du Développement et de la Coopération (DDC), DFAE.
ROHNER, Kurt, M., Chef, Section Main-d'oeuvre et Immigration, Office fédéral de l'Immigration, de l'Intégration et de l'Emigration (IMES), Département fédéral de Justice et Police (DFJP).
SCHAER BOURBEAU, Béatrice, Mme, Deuxième secrétaire, Mission permanente, Genève.
TINGUELY MATTLI, Florence, Mme, Collaboratrice scientifique, Cheffe suppléante, Section Organisations internationales et Politique d'accueil, Division politique III, DFAE.
MÜNGER, Tamara, Mme, Collaboratrice diplomatique, Section politique humanitaire et migration, Division politique IV, DFAE.

Délégué des employeurs

BARDE, Michel, M., Directeur général, Fédération des Entreprises romandes Genève (FER Genève).

Conseiller technique et délégué suppléant

PLASSARD, Alexandre, M., Membre de la Direction, Union patronale suisse (UPS).

Conseillers techniques

HEFTI, Daniel, M., Conseiller économique, UPS.
TELEKI, Géza, M., Directeur, Union économique de Bâle.

Délégué des travailleurs

PRINCE, Jean-Claude, M., Secrétaire central, Union syndicale suisse (USS).

Conseiller technique et délégué suppléant

VIGNE, Jacques, M., Avocat, Communauté genevoise d'Action syndicale (CGAS).

Conseillers techniques

ALLEVA, Vania, Mme, Présidente, Commission des migrations de l'USS, Syndicat Industrie & Bâtiment (SIB).
BARONE, Charly, M., Membre du comité, CGAS.
BEJA, Manuel, M., SIB.
GIARRANA, Giovanni, M., Syndicat de l'Industrie, de la Construction et des Services (FTMH).
LEPORI, Rolando, M., Secrétaire régional, FTMH.
MITROVIC, Vica, M., SIB.
MOLO, Romolo, M., Secrétaire central, USS.
RIAZI, Nourzaman, M., Commission des migrations, USS, Comedia.
REBRINA, Nino, M., Commission des Migrations, USS, FTMH.

Personne désignée en conformité avec l'article 2, alinéa 3 i)

TORCHE, Denis, M., Secrétaire, Travail Suisse.

Suriname

Minister attending the Conference

MARICA, Clifford P., Mr., Minister of Labour, Technological Development and Environment.

Government Delegates

PIROE, Mohamed, Mr., Head, International Affairs.
SEMMOH, Nadischa, Ms., Labour Market Official.

Employers' Delegate

VAN OMMEREN, Tim, Mr., Suriname Trade and Industry Association (VSB).

Adviser

WELZIJN, Ferdinand, Mr., VSB.

Workers' Delegate

SOUPRAYEN, Charlotte Y., Ms., De Vakcentrale C.47.

Swaziland   Swaziland   Swazilandia

Minister attending the Conference

DLAMINI, Lutfo, Mr., Minister.

Government Delegates

VILAKAZI, M.E., Mr.

NKHAMBULE, Jinno, Mr.

Adviser

MAMBA, Thembinkosi, Mr.

Other person attending the Conference

MTETHWA, Mathokoza, Mr.

Employers' Delegate

MAPHANGA, Treasure, Mrs.

Advisers

DLAMINI, Thulisile, Mrs.
NKOSI, Zakes, Mr.

Workers' Delegate

SITHOLE, Jan, Mr.

Adviser

KHUMALO, Mduduzi P., Mr.

République arabe syrienne
Syrian Arab Republic
República Arabe Siria

Ministre assistant à la Conférence

DELLO, Siham, Mme, Ministre des Affaires sociales et du Travail.

Délégués gouvernementaux

WEHBE, Mikhail, M., Ambassadeur, Représentant permanent, Mission permanente, Genève.
AKASHE, Tarik, M., Directeur, Relations internationales, Ministère des Affaires sociales et du Travail.

Conseillers techniques et délégués suppléants

IBRAHIM, Rakan, M., Directeur, Département du Travail, Ministère des Affaires sociales et du Travail.
AL-ABDULLA, Khalaf, M., Directeur général, Institution générale des Assurances sociales.
AL-KOWATLI, Reem, Mme, Chef, Section de la Traduction, Ministère des Affaires sociales et du Travail.
AUKLA, Walid, M., Responsable, Relations générales, Ministère des Affaires sociales et du Travail.
IBRAHIM, Ghiath, M., Attaché, Mission permanente, Genève.

Délégué des employeurs

AL DEBS, Samer, M., Président, Chambre d'Industrie.

Conseillers techniques et délégués suppléants

MOHAMMAD NASSER, Shaheen, M., Directeur, Audit interne, Ministère de l'Industrie.
AWAD, Ali, M., Président, Fédération générale des Associations d'Artisans.
EL-YAFI, Haitham, M., Membre, Conseil d'administration, Chambre de Commerce.
AL DIEN, Mohammad Riad Jamal, M., Membre, Bureau exécutif; Président, Bureau administratif et juridique, Fédération générale des Associations d'Artisans.
MALAS, Hanan, Mme, Membre, Bureau exécutif; Présidente, Bureau des Finances, Fédération générale des Associations d'Artisans.

Délégué des travailleurs

AZOZ, Mohammad Shaaban, M., Président, Confédération générale des Syndicats des Travailleurs.

Conseillers techniques et délégués suppléants

DARWISH, Adnan, M., Secrétaire général, Confédération générale des Syndicats des Travailleurs.
HABAB, Ahmad, M., Secrétaire, Relations arabes et internationales, Confédération générale des Syndicats des Travailleurs.
AL-BARSHA, Faiez, M., Secrétaire, Affaires législatives et juridiques, Confédération générale des Syndicats des Travailleurs.

Tadjikistan   Tajikistan
Tayikistán

Government Delegate

ILOLOV, Mamadsho, Mr., Minister of Labour and Social Protection.

Employers' Delegate

ALIMKULOV, Alisher, Mr., Chairman, Human Resources, Aluminium Factory.

Workers' Delegate

SALIKHOV, Murodali, Mr., Chairman, Tajik Federation of Trade Unions.

République-Unie de Tanzanie
United Republic of Tanzania
República Unida de Tanzanía

Ministers attending the Conference

KAPUYA, Juma A., Mr., Minister for Labour, Youth Development and Sports.
HASSAN, Samia S., Mr., Minister of Youth, Employment, Women and Children Development, Zanzibar.

Persons accompanying the Minister

RAJABU, Abubakar R.M.S., Mr., Permanent Secretary, Ministry of Labour, Youth Development and Sports.
MUTALEMWA, Charles A.K., Mr., Ambassador, Permanent Representative, Permanent Mission, Geneva.

Government Delegates

RWEYEMAMU, Regina, Mrs., Labour Commissioner, Ministry of Labour, Youth Development and Sports.
MAPURI, Iddi R., Mr., Commissioner for Labour, Ministry of Youth, Employment, Women and Children Development, Zanzibar.

Advisers

KITUMBO, Hamisi I., Mr., Executive Director, Occupational Safety and Health Agency.
NDIMBO, Ernest K., Mr., Director, Employment Department, Ministry of Labour, Youth Development and Sports.
MMARI, N.T., Mrs., Director of Administration and Personnel.
KADEGE, Nyasugara A., Mrs., Minister Plenipotentiary, Permanent Mission, Geneva.
KASYANJU, Irene F., Mrs., Minister Counsellor, Permanent Mission, Geneva.
MMANGA, Hawa M., Mrs., Director General, Public Services Pension Fund (PSPF).
DAU, Ramadhani K., Mr., Director General, National Social Security Fund (NSSF).
LIGALAMA, Epimack, Mr., Principal Immigration Officer.
NYAMBO, S.J., Mr., Acting Director General, Vocational Education and Training Authority (VETA).
BURA, A.J., Mr., Director General, Local Authorities Provident Fund.
NGAMBO, Ibrahim P., Mr., Lawyer, Public Service Pension Fund (PSPF).
HUMBA, Emmanuel B.D., Mr., Director General, National Health Insurance Fund.
HAFIDH, Abdulwakil Haji, Mr., Managing Director, Zanzibar Social Security Fund (ZSSF).
KAMARA, Mary, Mrs., Labour Officer, Ministry of Labour, Youth Development and Sports.
MWANJALI, Saimon F.E., Mr., Private Secretary to the Minister, Ministry of Labour, Youth Development and Sports.

Employers' Delegate

KABYEMERA, Dominico M., Mr., Chairman, Association of Tanzania Employers.

Advisers

MAENDA, Africanus T., Mr., Executive Director, Association of Tanzania Employers.
NSEMWA, Naftal, Mr., Director General, Parastatal Pension Fund (PPF).
SAID NASSER, Salim, Mr., Chairman, Zanzibar Employers Association (ZANEMA).

Workers' Delegate

SITTA, Margareth, Mrs., Chairperson, Trade Union Congress of Tanzania.

Advisers

MAKAME, Makame L., Mr., Secretary General, Zanzibar Trade Union (ZATUC).
SWAI, Reatha, Mrs., Director, Disaster Unit, Prime Minister's Office.

Tchad   Chad   Chad

Ministre assistant à la Conférence

ALHADJI ABAKAKA, Mustapha Lopa, M., Ministre de la Fonction Publique, du Travail et de l'Emploi.

Délégués gouvernementaux

ABDERAHIM, Nguekidaïna, M., Secrétaire général, Ministère de la Fonction publique, du Travail et de l'Emploi.
DJEGUEDEM, Mbaïbardoum, M., Directeur du Travail et de la Sécurité Sociale.

Conseillers techniques

KADE NDILGUEM, Elisabeth, Mme, Conseillère technique du Ministre.
MANSOUNGARAL, Nassingar, M., Directeur, Caisse nationale de la Prévoyance sociale (CNPS).
MAHAMAT, Zalba Abdoulaye, M., Directeur, Office national pour la Promotion de l'Emploi (ONAPE).
MAHAMAT, Adam, M., Chef, Service de la Prévention, CNPS.
TONDIBAYE, Toïna, M., Inspecteur général adjoint, Ministère de la Fonction publique, du Travail et de l'Emploi.

Délégué des employeurs

ALI ABBAS, Seitchy, M., Membre du Bureau, Conseil national du Patronat tchadien (CNPT).

Conseiller technique

BEREMADJI, Madengar, M., Secrétaire général, CNPT.

Délégué des travailleurs

DJIBRINE, Assali Hamdallah, M., Secrétaire général, Union des Syndicats du Tchad (UST).

Conseiller technique

BRAHIM, Ben Seid, M., Président, Confédération libre des Travailleurs du Tchad (CLTT).

République tchèque
Czech Republic
República Checa

Minister attending the Conference

SKROMACH, Zdenek, Mr., Minister of Labour and Social Affairs.

Persons accompanying the Minister

FERBAROVÁ, Alena, Mrs., Personal Assistant to the Minister.
PREJDOVÁ, Katarina, Mrs., Spokesperson, Ministry of Labour and Social Affairs.
SADILOVÁ, Jana, Mrs., Interpretor.

Government Delegates

SAJDA, Cestmír, Mr., Deputy Minister, Ministry of Labour and Social Affairs.
SLABÝ, Alexander, Mr., Ambassador, Permanent Representative, Permanent Mission, Geneva.

Advisers and substitute delegates

TOMKOVÁ, Dagmar, Mrs., Director, Department for European Integration and International Relations, Ministry of Labour and Social Affairs.
PINTÉR, Ivan, Mr., Counsellor, Permanent Mission, Geneva.

Advisers

HRDÁ, Edita, Mrs., Director, Department of Multilateral Economic Relations, Ministry of Foreign Affairs.
KOSTKA, Miroslav, Mr., Director of Department, Ministry of Labour and Social Affairs.
MARESOVÁ, Jarmila, Mrs., Office of the Government.
IVANOVICOVÁ, Vera, Mrs., Ministry of Labour and Social Affairs.
POKORNÝ, Pavel, Mr., Ministry of Labour and Social Affairs.
TOIFL, Jirí, Mr., Ministry of Foreign Affairs.

Employers' Delegate

PRIOR, Pavel, Mr., Vice-President, Union of Industry and Transport.

Adviser and substitute delegate

DRBALOVÁ, Vladimíra, Mrs., Head of Section, Union of Industry and Transport.

Advisers

ERNST, Pavel, Mr., Chairman, Confederation of Employers and Entrepreneurs Unions; President, Union of Employers Organizations.
STURMOVÁ, Ivana, Mrs., Union of Industry and Transport of the Czech Republic.
ZVOLSKÁ, Marie, Mrs., Union of Czech and Moravian Production Cooperatives.

Workers' Delegate

STECH, Milan, Mr., Chairman, Czech-Moravian Confederation of Trade Unions.

Adviser and substitute delegate

BAUEROVÁ, Jaroslava, Mrs., Advisor, Czech-Moravian Confederation of Trade Unions.

Advisers

KUBÍNKOVÁ, Marcela, Mrs., Head of Unit, Czech-Moravian Confederation of Trade Unions.
MARTINEK, Dusan, Mr., Head of Unit, Czech-Moravian Confederation of Trade Unions.
JANÍCKO, Pavel, Mr., Advisor, Czech-Moravian Confederation of Trade Unions.
SAMEK, Vít, Mr., Expert, Czech-Moravian Confederation of Trade Unions.
SUCHEL, Josef, Mr., Advisor, Czech-Moravian Confederation of Trade Unions.

Thaïlande   Thailand   Tailandia

Minister attending the Conference

THIENTHONG, Uraiwan, Mrs., Minister of Labour.

Persons accompanying the Minister

PRAMMANEE, Sawai, Mr., Chairman, Standing Committee on Labour and Social Welfare of the Senate.
PEARYURA, Premsak, Mr., Chairman, Committee on Labour; Member of Parliament, Khon Kaen Province.
BUTTANADAMRONGCHIT, Chakarin, Mr., Secretary to the Minister of Labour.

Government Delegates

RUANGSUWAN, Charupong, Mr., Permanent Secretary, Ministry of Labour.
SATJIPANON, Chaiyong, Mr., Ambassador, Permanent Representative, Permanent Mission, Geneva.

Advisers

JAMASEVI, Thapabutr, Mr., Deputy Permanent Secretary, Ministry of Labour.
PONGPANGAN, Orawan, Mrs., Deputy Director-General, Department of Employment.
CHAVALITNITIKUL, Chaiyuth, Mr., Deputy Director-General, Department of Labour Protection and Welfare.
ROJVITHEE, Areeya, Ms., Senior Expert in Skill Development, Department of Skill Development, Ministry of Labour.
NAKCHUEN, Kamjorn, Mr., Director, Bureau of International Coordination, Office of the Permanent Secretary, Ministry of Labour.
AMORNCHEWIN, Pakorn, Mr., Minister Counsellor (Labour), Permanent Mission, Geneva.
THONGTIP, Chuleerat, Ms., Senior Labour Officer, Bureau of International Coordination, Office of the Permanent Secretary, Ministry of Labour.
CHANDRAPRABHA, Krisana, Mrs., Minister, Permanent Mission, Geneva.
PRONGTHURA, Supark, Mr., First Secretary, Permanent Mission, Geneva.
BALANKURA, Nikorndej, Mr., First Secretary, Permanent Mission, Geneva.

Employers' Delegate

ROMCHATTHONG, Siriwan, Mrs., Executive Director, Employers' Confederation of Thailand.

Advisers

CHANASIT, Samreong, Mr., Advisory Committee, Employers' Confederation of Thai Business.
BUTSAMONGKHAL, Watcharapol, Mr., Secretary-General, Employers' Confederation of Thai Business.
LEEYAVANIJA, Atthayuth, Mr., Legal Advisor, Employers' Confederation of Thai Business.
MEYANYIEAM, Jade, Mr., Advisory Committee, Employers' Confederation of Thai Business.
BUTSAMONGKHOL, Nuanjan, Mrs., Advisor, Employers' Confederation of Thai Business.
CHAIEAR, Weerapong, Mr., Advisor, Employers' Confederation of Thai Business.
CHOONHAVEJSAKUL, Piyachart, Mr., Advisor, Employers' Confederation of Thai Business.

Other person attending the Conference

SRIWONG, Paweena, Mrs., Employers' Confederation of Thai Business.

Workers' Delegate

TECHATEERAVAT, Thavee, Mr., General Secretary, Thai Trade Union Congress.

Advisers

THAILUAN, Suchart, Mr., Advisor, Labour Congress of Thailand.
KOSAISOOK, Somsak, Mr., General Secretary, State Enterprises Workers' Relations Confederation.
THAILUAN, Panus, Mr., President, National Congress of Thai Labour.
CHAROENSILP, Khachit, Mr., General Secretary, National Free Labour Union Congress.
SIRIVORAPA, Sorayuth, Mr., General Secretary, National Free Labour Union Congress.

République dém. du Timor-Leste
Democratic Rep. of Timor-Leste
Rep. Democrática de Timor-Leste

Government Delegates

AMORIM, José Dias, Mr., Ambassador, Embassy, Brussels.
DA COSTA, Augusto dos Santos, Mr., Assistant Director, Labour Inspection, Secretariat for Labour and Solidarity.

Togo

Ministre assistant à la Conférence

OSSEYI, Rodolphe Kossivi, M., Ministre de la Fonction publique, du Travail et de l'Emploi.

Délégués gouvernementaux

AKOUETE, Tékpoh, M., Directeur Général du Travail et des Lois sociales.
TCHAO, Padumhèkou, M., Directeur de l'Emploi et des Lois sociales, SAZOF.

Conseiller technique

AMOUSSOU-KOUETETE, Ekoué, M., Chef, Division des Normes, Direction générale du Travail et des Lois sociales.

Délégué des employeurs

NAKU, Kossivi Démanya, M., Président, Conseil National du Patronat.

Conseiller technique

LASSEY, Séwa, M., Conseiller Principal du Patronat.

Délégué des travailleurs

TSIKPLONOU, Mokli Agbélégbé, M., Secrétaire Général, CGCT.

Conseillers techniques

HLOMADOR, Kokou Dodzi, M., Secrétaire général adjoint, UGSL.
PALANGA, Agui Yves, M., Secrétaire général, CNTT.
ZOUNNADJALA, Agbogbé Koffi, M., Secrétaire général adjoint, CSTT.
AKOLLY, Anani, M., Secrétaire général, GSA.
MONDEDJI, Abla Déla, Mme, Secrétaire, Comité des Femmes, CGCT.

Trinité-et-Tobago
Trinidad and Tobago
Trinidad y Tabago

Minister attending the Conference

ROBERTS, Anthony, Mr., Minister of Labour and Small and Micro-Enterprise Development.

Government Delegates

GEORGE, Emmanuel, Mr., Permanent Secretary, Ministry of Labour and Small and Micro-Enterprise Development.
SINGH, Shanmatee, Ms., Director, Research and Planning, Ministry of Labour and Small and Micro-Enterprise Development.

Advisers

KHAN, Addison, Mr., President, Industrial Court.
INNISS, Noel, Mr., Registrar, Industrial Court.
RAMNARINE, Christandyal, Mr., Senior Human Resource Adviser, Personnel Department.
WESTON, Bernard, Mr., Ambassador, Permanent Representative, Permanent Mission, Geneva.
TOUSSAINT, Reita G., Ms., Deputy Permanent Representative, Permanent Mission, Geneva.
CLARKE-HINDS, Shelly-Ann, Ms., First Secretary, Permanent Mission, Geneva.

Employers' Delegate

HILTON CLARKE, W.A., Mr., Vice Chairman, Employers' Consultative Association.

Advisers

RAMBHARAT, Clarence, Mr., Chairman Designate, Employers' Consultative Association.

MCSWEEN, Ruben, Mr., Director of the Board, Employers' Consultative Association.
BESSON, Linda, Ms., Executive Director, Employers' Consultative Association.

Workers' Delegate

GUISEPPI, Robert, Mr., President, National Trade Union Centre.

Adviser

CABRERA, Vincent, Mr., General Secretary, National Trade Union Centre.

Tunisie   Tunisia   Túnez

Ministre assistant à la Conférence

NEFFATI, Chedly, M., Ministre des Affaires sociales et de la Solidarité.

Personne accompagnant le Ministre

TITECH, Chakib, M., Chef de Cabinet du Ministre des Affaires sociales et de la Solidarité.

Délégués gouvernementaux

MANSOUR, Habib, M., Ambassadeur, Représentant permanent, Mission permanente, Genève.
CHOUBA, Samia, Mme, Directrice, Coopération internationale et Relations extérieures, Ministère des Affaires sociales et de la Solidarité.

Conseillers techniques et délégués suppléants

CHATTI, Mohamed Salah, M., Directeur général du Travail, Ministère des Affaires sociales et de la Solidarité.
LANDOULSI, Hatem, M., Conseiller, Mission permanente, Genève.

Conseillers techniques

MEGDICHE, Rabah, M., Directeur des Négociations collectives, Direction générale du Travail, Ministère des Affaires sociales et de la Solidarité.
JAOUANI, Ali, M., Attaché, Cabinet du Ministre des Affaires sociales et de la Solidarité.
LAAJILI, Abdelmajid, M., Attaché, Cabinet du Ministre des Affaires sociales et de la Solidarité.

Délégué des employeurs

DJILANI, Hédi, M., Président, Union tunisienne de l'Industrie, du Commerce et de l'Artisanat.

Conseiller technique et délégué suppléant

M'KAISSI, Ali, M., Conseiller, Directeur central pour les Affaires sociales, Union tunisienne de l'Industrie, du Commerce et de l'Artisanat; Membre titulaire, Conseil d'administration du BIT.

Conseillers techniques

BEN SEDRINE, Mohamed, M., Membre, Bureau exécutif, Union tunisienne de l'Industrie, du Commerce et de l'Artisanat.
SELLINI, Sami, M., Directeur des Affaires sociales, Union tunisienne de l'Industrie, du Commerce et de l'Artisanat.

Délégué des travailleurs

JRAD, Abdessalam, M., Secrétaire général, Union générale tunisienne du Travail.

Conseiller technique et délégué suppléant

TRABELSI, Mohamed, M., Secrétaire général adjoint chargé des Relations extérieures arabes et de l'Emigration, Union générale tunisienne du Travail.

Conseillers techniques

ROMDHANE, Ali, M., Secrétaire général adjoint chargé des Législations et des Conflits, Union générale tunisienne du Travail.
SHIMI, Mohamed, M., Secrétaire général adjoint chargé des Etudes, Union générale tunisienne du Travail.
BOUZRIBA, Ridha, M., Secrétaire général adjoint chargé de la Protection sociale, de la Santé et de la Sécurité au Travail, Union générale tunisienne du Travail.
MEDDAHI, Abdennour, M., Secrétaire général adjoint chargé du Secteur privé, Union générale tunisienne du Travail.
BRIKI, Abid, M., Secrétaire général adjoint chargé de la Formation syndicale, Union générale tunisienne du Travail.
GHODHBANI, Hédi, M., Secrétaire général adjoint chargé du Règlement intérieur, Union générale tunisienne du Travail.
MAJDI, Slimane, M., Secrétaire général adjoint chargé des Offices et des Entreprises publics, Union générale tunisienne du Travail.
NEJI, Messaoud, M., Secrétaire général adjoint chargé de la Fonction publique, Union générale tunisienne du Travail.
CHENDOUL, Mohamed, M., Secrétaire général adjoint chargé de la Communication et de l'Edition, Union générale tunisienne du Travail.

Personne désignée en conformité avec l'article 2, alinéa 3 i)

SAAD, Mohamed, M., Secrétaire général adjoint chargé des Finances et de l'Administration, Union générale tunisienne du Travail.

Turquie   Turkey   Turquía

Minister attending the Conference

BASESGIOGLU, Murat, Mr., Minister for Labour and Social Security.

Government Delegates

KURTTEKIN, Türkekul, Mr., Ambassador, Permanent Representative, Permanent Mission, Geneva.
YETER, Enis, Mr., Under-Secretary, Ministry of Labour and Social Security (MLSS).

Advisers and substitute delegates

GENC, Levent, Mr., Deputy General Director, MLSS.
BASA, Riza, Mr., Counsellor, Labour and Social Security, Embassy, Bern.
OYMAN, Halit, Mr., Counsellor, Labour and Social Security, Permanent Mission, Geneva.
ERCAN, Halidun, Mr., Head of Department, MLSS.

Advisers

BASARAN, Güngor, Mr., General Director, External Relations and Services for Workers Abroad, MLSS.
DELIBAS, Cengiz, Mr., General Director, General Labour, MLSS.
UNAL, Kayhan, Mr., Press Adviser.
DERELI, Toker, Mr., Dean, Faculty of Economics, University of Istanbul.
ARICI, Kadir, Mr., Academic Gazi University.
YALCIN, Ugur, Mr., Chef de Cabinet.
DEMIRCAN, Ebru, Ms., Counsellor, Permanent Mission, Geneva.
UNAL, Nihat, Mr., Attaché, Labour and Social Security, General Consulate, Strasbourg.
ERGANI, Hüseyin, Mr., Second Secretary, Permanent Mission, Geneva.
ERDIN, Birsen, Mrs., Labour Inspector.
KORKMAZ, Talat, Mr., Expert.
ONAKIN, Goksu, Mrs., Expert.

Persons appointed in accordance with Article 2, paragraph 3(i)

GULER, Mahfuz, Mr., Member of the Parliament; President, Health, Family, Labour and Social Affairs' Commission.
TANRIVERDI, Hüseyin, Mr., Member of Parliament.
SAHIN, Feramuz, Mr., Member of Parliament.

Employers' Delegate

PIRLER, Bülent, Mr., Secretary-General, Turkish Confederation of Employer Association (TISK).

Advisers

AKSU, Mehmet Azmi, Mr., Chairman, Executive Board, Sugar Industry Employers' Association.
EMIROGLU, Metin, Mr., Secretary-General, Textile Industry Employers' Association.
CENTEL, Tankut, Mr., Dean, Faculty of Law, University of Istanbul.
BAYAZIT, Sancar, Mr., Secretary-General, Cement Producers Employers' Association.
BÜYÜKUSLU, Ali Riza, Mr., Secretary-General, Chemistry, Patrol, Rubber and Plastic Employers' Association.
ERSOY, Necati, Mr., Secretary-General, Construction Installation Contractors Employers' Association.
KOC, Akansel, Mr., Deputy Secretary-General, Leather Industry Employers' Association.
BÖLÜKBASI, Ahmet Nedim, Mr., Deputy Secretary-General, Employers' Association of Metal Industries.
ARSLAN, Türker, Mr., Deputy Secretary-General, Textile Industry Employers' Association.
KIZILOGLU, Hakki, Mr., Lawyer, TISK.

Workers' Delegate

KILIC, Salih, Mr., President, Confederation of Turkish Trade Unions (TURK-IS).

Advisers

USLU, Salim, Mr., President, Confederation of Real Trade Unions (HAK-IS).
CELEBI, Süleyman, Mr., President, Confederation of Progressive Trade Unions (DISK).
YÜCEL, Nevres, Mr., External Expert, TURK-IS.
SUKUN, Hakan, Mr., External Expert, TURK-IS.
ERDOGDU, Seyhan, Mrs., Academic, Faculty of Policital Sciences, Ankara University, TURK-IS.
UZUNER, Hülya, Mrs., Expert, TURK-IS.
GÖK, Ugras, Mr., External Expert, TURK-IS.
SENOL, Adnan, Mr., Finance Secretary-General, MEMUR-SEN.
AKTAY, Nizamettin, Mr., Academic, Faculty of Economics, Gazi University, KAMU-SEN.

Persons appointed in accordance with Article 2, paragraph 3(i)

POLAT, Zeki, Mr., President, Textile and Garment Workers' Union (TEKSIF).
YILMAZ, Turgut, Mr., President BASS.
ARSLAN, Mahmut, Mr., Vice-President, HAK-IS.
AKYILDIZ, Bircan, Mr., President, KAMU-SEN.
KARACAN, Abdullah, Mr., President, Rubber Workers' Union (DISK).

Other persons attending the Conference

BAKINDI, Cemail, Mr., President, TOLEYIS.
BARIN, Fikret, Mr., President, YOL-IS.
TURKEL, Mustafa, Mr., Training Secretary, TURK-IS.
ALEMDAR, Eyüp, Mr., President, KOOP-IS.
SONAY, Ziya, Mr., Adviser to the Presidency, TGS.

ENGIN, Yusuf, Mr., Vice-President, HAK-IS.
AKYIGIT, Irfan, Mr., Finance Secretary-General, GENEL MADEN-IS.
KAYKAC, Bedrettin, Mr., President TARIM-IS.
DENIZER, Ramazan, Mr., Training Secretary-General, GENEL MADEN-IS.
DEMIR, Mustafa, Mr., Secretary-General, TARIM-IS.
SEREN, Mahmut, Mr., President, GENEL-IS.
YILMAZ, Kemal, Mr., President, TUMKA-IS.
CARDAKCI, Mustafa, Mr., Training Secretary-General, TARIM-IS.
TÜYSÜZ, Sinasi, Mr., YOL-IS.
CELIK, Omer, Mr., President, SEKER-IS.
KAYABASI, Hüseyin, Mr., President, MADEN-IS.
COLAK, Mesuthan, Mr., Training Secretary-General, TEK GIDA-IS.
AYBER, Turhan, Mr., Organization Secretary-General, TEK GIDA-IS.
SESEN, Zeki, Mr., Finance Secretary-General, TEK GIDA-IS.
OZBEK, Mustafa, Mr., President, TURK METAL-SEN.
TIRYAKIOGLU, Metin, Mr., President, BASISEN.
KOCAOGLU, Emre, Mr., Adviser to the Presidency, BASISEN.
DEMIR, Hüseyin, Mr., Secretary-General, DEMIRYOL-IS.
YILDIZ, Osman, Mr., Adviser for External Relations, HAK-IS.
KAHVECI, Önder, Mr., President, SAGLIK-SEN.
OZCAN, Suayip, Mr., President, EGITIM-SEN.
ISIK, Firdes, Mr., Secretary-General, EGITIM-SEN.
BILGIN, Yüksel, Mr., Secretary-General, TARIM ORMAN-SEN.
CIMEN, Osman, Mr., President, HAK-IS.
ALSAN, Ergin, Mr., President, SELÜLOZ-IS.
AYHAN, Ruhi, Mr., Training Secretary, CELIK-IS.
YAVUZ, Rahmi, Mr., Secretary General, HIZMET-IS.
AKSU, Ahmet, Mr., President, MEMUR-SEN.
YILMAZ, Cemal, Mr., Adviser, MEMUR-SEN.
SAMASTI, Mustafa, Mr., Adviser, MEMUR-SEN.
DEMIRCI, Ahmet, Mr., President, TARIM ORMAN-SEN.
SANLIER, Ibrahim Ethem, Mr., Adviser, MEMUR-SEN.
AKYILDIZ, Ömür, Mr., Adviser, MEMUR-SEN.
YILMAZ, Gülay, Mrs., Adviser, MEMUR-SEN.
YILMAZ, Mustafa, Mr., Adviser to Presidency, SGLIK-SEN.
DÖGÜCÜ, Semsettin, Mr., Adviser, MEMUR-SEN.
KESKIN, Sabri, Mr., Secretary-General, TARIM-IS.
BENLI, Hasan, Mr., Press-Adviser, TURK-IS.
ÖZKAN, Kemal, Mr., Coordinator, Rubber Workers' Union, DISK.
PARSIN, Fatma, Ms., Adviser, MEMUR-SEN.
TUNC, Metin, Mr., Adviser, MEMUR-SEN.
ATALAY, Ergün, Mr., Finance Secretary, TURK-IS.
KOMURCU, Zeynep, Mrs., Adviser to the Presidency, TEKSIF.

Ukraine   Ukraine   Ucrania

Government Delegates

PAPIEV, Mykhailo, Mr., Minister of Labour and Social Policy.
BELASHOV, Volodymyr, Mr., Permanent Representative, Permanent Mission, Geneva.

Advisers and substitute delegates

KRASYLSCHYKOV, Anatolii, Mr., Head, Department of Social Relations Reforming, Cabinet of Ministers.
YAMPOLSKYI, Serhii, Mr., Counsellor, Permanent Mission, Geneva.

Advisers

GALYTS, Georgiy, Mr., Deputy Minister of Labour and Social Policy.
MALYI, Oleh, Mr., Attaché, Department for Economic Cooperation, Ministry of Foreign Affairs.
KOVALEVSKYI, Vadim, Mr., Chief Consultant, Administration of the President.

Employers' Delegate

GRYSHCHENKO, Volodymyr, Mr., First Deputy Head, Federation of Employers of Ukraine.

Advisers

BYKOVETS, Vyacheslav, Mr., First Vice President, Ukrainian Association of Employers.
KHMIL'OVSKYI, Viktor, Mr., President, Union of Leaseholders and Entrepreneurs.
ZHADAN, Serhii, Mr., Director, Department of Relations with Compulsory State Insurance Funds, Federation of Employers.

Workers' Delegate

STOYAN, Oleksander, Mr., Head, Federation of Trade Unions of Ukraine.

Advisers

SHYLOV, Vassyl, Mr., Chief, International Cooperation Department, Federation of Trade Unions of Ukraine.
VOLYNETS, Mykhailo, Mr., Head, Confederation of Free Trade Unions of Ukraine.

Uruguay

Ministro asistente a la Conferencia

PÉREZ DEL CASTILLO, Santiago, Sr., Ministro de Trabajo y Seguridad Social.

Persona que acompaña al Ministro

VALLES GALMÉS, Guillermo, Sr., Embajador, Representante Permanente, Mision Permanente, Ginebra.

Delegados gubernamentales

LAGARMILLA, Rosario, Sra., Directora General, Secretaría, Ministerio de Trabajo y Seguridad Social.
DONO, Liliana, Sra., Dirección Jurídica, Inspección General del Trabajo y la Seguridad Social, Ministerio de Trabajo y Seguridad Social.

Consejeros técnicos

SANTESTEVAN, Ana, Sra., Asesoría de Relaciones Internacionales, Ministerio de Trabajo y Seguridad Social.
GONZALEZ ARENAS, Ricardo, Sr., Ministro, Misión Permanente, Ginebra.
LUGRIS, Fernando, Sr., Primer Secretario, Misión Permanente, Ginebra.
ROCANOVA, Ana Inés, Sra., Segunda Secretaria, Misión Permanente, Ginebra.
PEREIRA, Carlos, Sr., Misión Permanente, Ginebra.

Delegado de los empleadores

FOSTIK, Andrés, Sr., Asesor Técnico, Cámara de Industrias.

Consejero técnico

MAILHOS, Juan, Sr., Asesor Jurídico, Cámara Nacional de Comercio y Servicios.

Delegado de los trabajadores

FERNÁNDEZ, Eduardo, Sr., Secretario de Relaciones Internacionales, Plenario Intersindical de Trabajadores - Convención Nacional de Trabajadores (PIT-CNT).

Consejero técnico

OIZ, Rosario, Sra., Sala de Abogados, Plenario Intersindical de Trabajadores, PIT-CNT.

Venezuela

Ministro asistente a la Conferencia

IGLESIAS, María Cristina, Sra., Ministra de Trabajo.

Persona que acompaña al Ministro

PORTOCARRERO, Blancanieve, Sra., Embajadora, Representante Permanente, Misión Permanente, Ginebra.

Delegados gubernamentales

DORADO CANO, Manuel Ricardo, Sr., Viceministro de Trabajo.
MOLINA, Rubén Darío, Sr., Director, Oficina de Relaciones Internacionales y Enlace con la OIT, Ministerio del Trabajo.

Consejeros técnicos y delegados suplentes

LOPEZ, Francisco, Sr., Consultor Jurídico, Ministerio del Trabajo.
HANDS, Rafael, Sr., Consejero, Misión Permanente, Ginebra.

Consejeros técnicos

HERNÁNDEZ, Madai, Sra., Ministro Consejero, Misión Permanente, Ginebra.
PICONE, Jhony, Sr., Director de Inspección y Condiciones de Trabajo, Ministerio del Trabajo.
SERRANO, Liliana, Srta., Directora de Migraciones, Ministerio del Trabajo.
ARIAS, Juan, Sr., Asesor Político, Misión Permanente, Ginebra.
MANZOUL CAMPOS, Dellis, Sr., Diputado, Vicepresidente, Comisión de Desarrollo Social Integral, Asamblea Nacional.
FRANCESCHI, Luis Eduardo, Sr., Diputado, Presidente, Subcomisión de Asuntos Gremiales y Sindicales, Comisión de Desarrollo Social Integral, Asamblea Nacional.
KHAN FERNANDEZ, José Salamat, Sr., Diputado, Comisión de Desarrollo Social Integral, Asamblea Nacional.

Delegado de los empleadores

DE ARBELOA, Bingen, Sr., Federación de Cámaras y Asociaciones de Comercio y Producción de Venezuela (FEDECAMARAS); Presidente, Comisión OIT/OIE.

Consejeros técnicos

MUÑOZ, Albis, Sra., Presidenta, FEDECAMARAS.
SÁNCHEZ, Alexis, Sr., Vicepresidente, FEDECAMARAS.
CONCHESO, Aurelio, Sr., FEDECAMARAS.
GARRIDO SOTO, Alexis, Sr., FEDECAMARAS.
REQUENA, Ricardo, Sr., FEDECAMARAS.
SANTORO, José Luis, Sr., Federación de Artesanos, Micros, Pequeños y Medianos Industriales (FEDEINDUSTRIA).
VALDERRAMA, Miguel, Sr., FEDEINDUSTRIA.
RANGHI, Espartaco, Sr., FEDEINDUSTRIA.
DE LA ROSA MARTÍNEZ, Keyla Margarita, Sra., Empresarios por Venezuela (EMPREVEN).
MEDINA, Héctor, Sr., Confederación Nacional de Agricultores y Ganaderos (CONFAGAN).

Delegado de los trabajadores

INFANTE, Carlos, Sr., Presidente, Confederación de Sindicatos Autónomos de Venezuela (CODESA).

Consejeros técnicos

DÍAZ, Jesús Asdrúbal, Sr., Secretario, Relaciones Internacionales, Comité Ejecutivo, Confederación General de Trabajadores (CGT).
MÁSPERO, Marcela, Sra., Coordinación General, Unión Nacional de Trabajadores (UNT); Presidenta, Federación Nacional de Trabajadores de Medicina, Cosméticos y Farmacéuticos (FETRAMECO).
RAMOS, Alfredo, Sr., Confederación de Trabajadores de Venezuela (CTV).
RODÓN, Caridad, Sra., Directora de Formación, CODESA.
NUÑEZ, Nelson, Sr., Presidente, Sindicato Nacional Único de Trabajadores Petroleros (SINUTRAPETROL).
COVA, Manuel, Sr., CTV.
CHIRENO, Juana María, Sra., Secretaria General, CGT.
CHIRINO, Orlando, Sr., Coordinación General, UNT.
CASTELLANOS, Rosa, Sra., CTV.
IBARRA, José Gregorio, Sr., Secretario de Relaciones Internacionales, Comité Ejecutivo, CUTV.

Viet Nam

Minister attending the Conference

LE, Duy Dong, Mr., Deputy Minister of Labour, Invalids and Social Affairs.

Government Delegates

NGO, Quang Xuan, Mr., Ambassador, Permanent Mission, Geneva.
NGUYEN, Manh Cuong, Mr., Deputy Director, Department of International Relations, Ministry of Labour, Invalids and Social Affairs.

Advisers and substitute delegates

TRUONG, Trieu Duong, Mr., Deputy Permanent Representative, Permanent Mission, Geneva.
PHAM, Hong Nga, Mr., Counsellor, Permanent Mission, Geneva.
VU, Huy Tan, Mr., Counsellor, Permanent Mission, Geneva.
PHUNG, Thi Lan Huong, Ms., Officer, Department of the International Organizations, Ministry of Foreign Affairs.
NGUYEN, Thanh Hai, Mr., International Cooperation Officer, Department of International Relations, Ministry of Labour, Invalids and Social Affairs.

Employers' Delegate

HOANG, Van Dung, Mr., Vice Permanent President, Chamber of Commerce and Industry of Viet Nam (VCCI).

Advisers and substitute delegates

BUI, Viet Cuong, Mr., Permanent Representative, Vietnam Cooperative Alliances to the CAC, Geneva.
VI, Thi Hong Minh, Mrs., Officer, International Relations Unit, VCCI.

Workers' Delegate

CU, Thi Hau, Mrs., Chairman, Vietnam General Confederation of Labour (VGCL).

Advisers and substitute delegates

NGUYEN, Thi Kim Hai, Mrs., Member of Presidium, VGCL.
VO, Van Nhat, Mr., Deputy Director, Department of International Relations, VGCL.
TRAN, Van Ly, Mr., Deputy Director, International Relations Department, VGCL.

Yemen

Minister attending the Conference

AL-ARHABI, Abdulkarim Ismaïl, Mr., Minister of Social Affairs and Labour.

Government Delegates

AL-FAYSALI, Mohammad Ahmad Mukil, Mr., Under-Secretary, Human Resources.
HAJAR, Zaid Mohammad, Mr., Minister Plenipotentiary, Permanent Mission, Geneva.

Advisers

OBAD, Ali Saleh, Mr., Adviser for Foreign Relations.
AL-BAKILI, A'del, Mr., Adviser.
AL-SHAHARI, Yahya Hashem, Mr., Third Secretary, Permanent Mission, Geneva.

Employers' Delegate

TABET, Ahmed, Mr., Yemeni General Union of Chambers of Commerce and Trade.

Workers' Delegate

AL-KUHLANI, Yahya Mohammad, Mr., President, General Federation of Trade Unions (GFTU).

Advisers

AL-A'QEL, Fadl Abdulla, Mr., Chairman, Culture and Information, GFTU.
QARHASH, Reda Ahmad, Ms., Chairman, Yemeni Women's Unit, GFTU.

Zambie   Zambia   Zambia

Government Delegates

SIASIMUNA, Noah S., Mr., Labour Commissioner.
SICHINSAMBWE, John, Mr., Director, Occupational Health and Safety.

Advisers and substitute delegates

MTESA, Love, Mr., Ambassador, Permanent Representative, Permanent Mission, Geneva.
SINJELA, Encyla. T., Mrs., Counsellor, Permanent Mission, Geneva.

Employers' Delegate

NONDE, Joan, Ms., Executive Director, Zambia Federation of Employers.

Advisers

MUSENGE, Danny K., Mr., Director-General, National Pensions Scheme Authority.
KAPEZA, Shadreck, Mr., Commissioner, Workers' Compensation Fund Control Board.
HAMUKOMA, P.P., Mr., Vice President, Human Resources, Konkola Copper Mines.

Workers' Delegate

HIKAUMBA, Leonard, Mr., President, Zambia Congress of Trade Unions.

Adviser

NONDE, Joyce, Ms., President, Federation of Free Trade Unions of Zambia.

Zimbabwe

Minister attending the Conference

MANGWANA, M. P., Mr., Minister of Public Service, Labour and Social Welfare.

Government Delegates

CHIPAZIWA, Chitsaka, Mr., Ambassador, Permanent Representative, Permanent Mission, Geneva.
MUSEKA, L. C., Mr., Secretary for Public Service, Labour and Social Welfare.

Advisers

DZVITI, P. Z., Mr., Director, Labour Administration.
NYAMWANZA, K., Mr., Legal Advisor, Legal Division.
MUDYAWABIKWA, P., Mr., Deputy Director, International Relations Division, Labour Administration.
NGORIMA, L., Mr., Labour Officer, International Relations Division, Labour Administration.
TAKAWIRA, A.M., Mr., Acting General Manager, National Social Security Authority (NSSA).
MTUBUKI, N., Mr., Acting Assitant General Manager, Occupational Health and Safety, NSSA.
MHANGO, S. C., Mr., Minister Counsellor, Permanent Mission, Geneva.
MUKANDURI, S. T., Mr., Minister Counsellor, Permanent Mission, Geneva.
MAONERA, F., Mr., Minister Counsellor, Permanent Mission, Geneva.
KATSAMBA, C., Mr.

Employers' Delegate

BIMHA, Michael Chakanaka, Mr., President, Employers Confederation of Zimbabwe (EMCOZ).

Advisers

MUFUKARE, J. W., Mr., Executive Director, EMCOZ.
MANIKAI, E., Mr., Chairman, National Social Security Board (NSSA).

Workers' Delegate

MATOMBO, L., Mr., President, Zimbabwe Congress of Trade Unions (ZCTU).

Advisers

CHIBEBE, W., Mr., Secretary-General, ZCTU.
TSVARINGE, E., Mr., Secretary-General, Zimbabwe Federation of Trade Unions (ZFTU).
MANYENGA, L., Ms., Chairperson, Women's Wing, ZCTU.

OBSERVATEURS

OBSERVERS

OBSERVADORES

Saint-Siège   The Holy See
Santa Sede

Représentants

TOMASI, Silvano M., Mgr., Nonce Apostolique, Mission permanente, Genève.
NWACHUKWU, Fortunatus, Mgr., Conseiller, Mission permanente, Genève.
DE GREGORI, Massimo, Mgr., Attaché de nonciature.
GHANEM, Abi, M., Expert.
SALINA, Giorgio, M., Expert.
GUTIÉRREZ, Plácido, M., Expert.
BATTISTELLA, Graziano, M., Expert.
MERICO COLOMBO, Francesca, Mme, Expert.

MOUVEMENT DE LIBERATION

LIBERATION MOVEMENT

MOVIMIENTO DE LIBERACION

Palestine   Palestine   Palestina

Palestinian Authority Representatives

AL-KHATIB, Ghassan Abdelwahab, Mr., Minister of Labour.
AL-SABBAH, Mhamed Mahmoud Ibrahim, Mr., Deputy General Assistant.
AS'AD, Acef Sa'id Mhamed, Mr., Director-General, International Arab Cooperation.
A'MARNEH, Racha Tawfiq Sa'id, Mr., Legal Assistant.
AL-GHENEIMI, Zeineb Abdelfattah, Mrs., Deputy Director-General, Employment.
AL-ADJOURI, Taissir, Mr., Counsellor.

Employers' Representatives

HEJJAWI, Hussam Abderrahman Abdelfattah, Mr.
AL-YAZGI, Mahmoud Tawfiq Hosni, Mr.

Workers' Representatives

SAED, Shaher, Mr., General Sercretary, Palestine General Federation of Trade Union (PGFTU).
EL-BEYYARI, Rassem Mahomoud, Mr., Public Union of Palestinian Workers' Trade Unions.
KHREISHEH, Khaled, Mr., Public Union of Palestine Workers.
ABUALLAIL, Mohammed M. A., Mr., Public Union of Palestine Workers.

REPRÉSENTANTS DES NATIONS UNIES, DES INSTITUTIONS SPÉCIALISÉES ET D'AUTRES ORGANISATIONS INTERNATIONALES OFFICIELLES

REPRESENTATIVES OF THE UNITED NATIONS, SPECIALIZED AGENCIES AND OTHER OFFICIAL INTERNATIONAL ORGANIZATIONS

REPRESENTANTES DE LAS NACIONES UNIDAS, DE LOS ORGANISMOS ESPECIALIZADOS Y DE OTRAS ORGANIZACIONES OFICIALES

Programme alimentaire mondial
World Food Programme
Programa Mundial de Alimentos

BELGASMY, Daly, Mr., Director, Geneva Office.

Programme commun des Nations Unies sur le VIH/SIDA
Joint United Nations Programme on HIV/AIDS

FAHLEN, Marika, Ms., Director, Social Mobilization and Information.
PLUMLEY, Benedict, Mr., Chief, Executive Office.
CHAHIL-GRAF, Renu, Ms., Associate Director, Programme Development Coordination and UN System Relations.
BAGASAO, Bai, Ms., Chief, Partnerships.
VELA, Edward, Mr., Senior Adviser, Partnerships.
TYSZKO, Jacek, Mr., External Relations Officer, GUR.
JAUNY, François, Mr., Adviser, GUR.

Programme des Nations Unies pour les établissements humains
United Nations Programme for Human Settlements
Programa de las Naciones Unidas para los Asentamientos Humanos

LACROUX, Sylvie, Ms., Director, Geneva Office.

Institut de recherche des Nations Unies pour le développement social
United Nations Research Institute for Social Development
Instituto de Investigaciones de las Naciones Unidas para el Desarrollo Social

PIPER, Nicola, Ms.

Organisation des Nations Unies pour l'alimentation et l'agriculture
Food and Agriculture Organization of the United Nations
Organización da las Naciones Unidas para la Agricultura y la Alimentación

MASUKU, Themba N., Mr., Director, Liaison Office, Geneva.
SMITH, Andrew, Mr., Fishery Industry Officer, Fishery Technology Service, Fishery Industries Division, Fisheries Department.

Organisation des Nations Unies pour l'éducation, la science et la culture
United Nations Educational, Scientific and Cultural Organization
Organización de las Naciones Unidas para la Educación, la Ciencia y la Cultura

BREINES, Ingeborg, Ms., Representative, Liaison Office, Geneva.
HOLST, Kerstin, Ms., Liaison Officer.

Banque internationale pour la reconstruction et le développement
International Bank for Reconstruction and Development
Banco Internacional de Reconstrucción y Fomento

INGRAM, Joseph, Mr., Representative to the UN and the WTO.
HOLZMANN, Robert, Mr., Social Protection Department.
ZARCONE, Fabrizio, Mr., Economist.

Organisation mondiale de la propriété intellectuelle
World Intellectual Property Organization
Organización Mundial de la Propiedad Intelectual

PETIT, Philippe, Mr., Deputy Director-General.
KHLESTOV, Nikolay, Mr., Head, Sector of External Relations and Cooperation with Certain Countries & Asia.
WENDLAND, Wend, Mr., Head, Traditional Creativity and Cultural Expressions Section.

Organisation mondiale du Commerce
World Trade Organization
Organización Mundial del Comercio

LIU, Vivien, Ms., Trade and Environment Division.
PARDO DE LEÓN, Josefina, Ms., External Relations Officer, External Relations Division.

Organisation internationale pour les migrations
International Organization for Migration
Organización Internacional para las Migraciones

MCKINLEY, Brunson, Mr., Director-General.
APPAVE, Gervais, Mr., Director, Migration Policy and Research Department.
PAIVA, Robert G., Mr., Director, Department for External Relations.
HELKE, Jill, Ms., Special Assistant to the Director-General.
KLEIN SOLOMON, Michele, Ms., Deputy Director, Migration Policy and Research Department.
BARUAH, Nilim, Mr., Head, Labour Migration Service, Migration Management Services.
USHER, Erica, Ms., Senior Policy Adviser, Migration Policy and Research Department.
NONNENMACHER, Sophie, Ms., Programme Officer, Labour Migration Service.
WIRTH, Christiane, Ms., Associate Migration Policy Officer, Migration Policy and Research Department.
CHOI, Ka Dae, Ms., Intern, Migration Policy and Research Department.
BUSCHMAN-PETIT, Anne-marie, Ms., Special Adviser to the Director-General.
SETHI, Meera, Ms., Regional Adviser for Sub-Saharan Africa.
ZHAO, Jian, Mr., Regional Adviser for East and South-East Asia and Oceania, a.i.
ABDEL MONEIM MOSTAFA, Hassan, Mr., Senior Regional Adviser for the Middle East/South West, Egypt/Sudan and Special Envoy to the Gulf States.
OROPEZA, Jose Angel, Mr., Regional Adviser for the Americas.

Organisation internationale de la francophonie

CASSAN, Hervé, M., Représentant permanent, Genève.
COULIBALY LEROY, Sandra, Mme, Adjointe au Représentant permanent, Genève.

Union interparlementaire
Inter-Parliamentary Union
Unión Interparlamentaria

JOHNSON, Anders B., M., Secrétaire général.
TCHELNOKOV, Serguei, M., Chargé des questions économiques et sociales.

Union africaine
African Union   Unión Africana

GAWANAS, Bience, Ms., Commissioner, Social Affairs.
KALINDE, Sophie Asimenye, Ms., Ambassador, Permanent Observer, Geneva.
KALIMUGOGO, Grace, Ms., Director a.i., Social Affairs.
TAYEB, Khaldi Mohamed, Mr.
RAHIM, Sadéqua, Ms.
WEGE-NZOMWITA, Venant, Mr., Counsellor.
MBAYE, Alassane Kaolack, Mr.

Centre régional africain d'administration du travail
African Regional Labour Administration Centre
Centro Regional Africano de Administración de Trabajo

YOELE, Pierrot, M., Directeur.
DAO, Moumounou, M., Chef, Service financier.

Union économique et monétaire ouest-africaine
West African Economic and Monetary Union

BARROS, Rui Duarte, M., Commissaire, Département du Développement social.
NIANGO, Agustin, M., Directeur, Enseignement supérieur et Formation professionnelle.
KPOTA, Eugène, M., Conseiller juridique.

Organisation des Etats américains
Organization of American States
Organización de Estados Americanos

GUTIÉRREZ TREJO, Freddy, Sr., Relator Especial de Trabajadores Migratorios, Comisión Interamericana de Derechos Humanos (CIDH).

Organisation arabe du travail
Arab Labour Organization
Organización Arabe del Trabajo

GUIDER, Ibrahim, Mr., Director-General.
HUMSI, Adib, Mr., Head, Permanent Delegation, Geneva.
KCHAOU, Mohamed, Mr., Director, ACLAE.
HILAL, Amira, Ms., Permanent Delegation, Geneva.
KASBAOUI, Zahira, Ms., Permanent Delegation, Geneva.

Ligue des Etats arabes
League of Arab States
Liga de Estados Arabes

HACHED, Noureddine, Mr., Deputy General Secretary.
ALFARARGI, Saad, Mr., Ambassador, Permanent Observer, Geneva.
MOUAKI BENANI, Mohamed Lamine, Mr., Counsellor, Permanent Delegation, Geneva.
EL-HAEJJE, Osman, Mr., Permanent Delegation, Geneva.

Organisation de la Conférence islamique
Organization of the Islamic Conference
Organización de la Conferencia Islámica

BA, Babacar, Mr., Ambassador, Permanent Observer, Geneva.
MOJTABA, Amiri Vahid, Mr., Deputy Permanent Observer, Geneva.

Groupe d'Etats d'Afrique, des Caraïbes et du Pacifique
African, Caribbean and Pacific Group of States

KISIRI, Marwa Joel, Mr., Ambassador, Head of ACP Geneva Office.
BASSILEKIN, Achille, Mr., Assistant to Head of ACP Geneva Office.
PUCHOOA, Prakash, Mr., Intern.
DE CARLI, Luca, Mr., Intern.

Conseil des ministres du Travail et des Affaires sociales des Etats du Conseil de coopération du Golfe
Council of Ministers of Labour and Social Affairs in Gulf Cooperation Council States

AL-TEWAIGRY, Othman Abdulla, Mr., General Director, Executive Bureau.
HUMAIDAN, Jameel M. Ali, Mr., Labour Affairs Director.
AL-SALMAN, Jamal Hassan, Mr., Labour Researcher.

Union européenne
European Union   Unión Europea

DIMAS, Stavros, Mr., European Commissioner for Employment and Social Affairs.
TROJAN, Carlo, Mr., Ambassador, Head of Delegation, Permanent Delegation, Geneva.
GIOTAKOS, Dimitrios, Mr., Member of Cabinet, Employment and Social Affairs.
PAVAN-WOOLFE, Luisella, Ms., Director, Directorate General for Employment.
TRICART, Jean-Paul, Mr., Head of Unit, Directorate General for Employment.
CONINSX, Marie-Anne, Ms., Minister Counsellor, Permanent Delegation, Geneva.

ALVAREZ HIDALGO, Francisco Jesus, Mr., Administrator, Directorate General for Employment.
DE KONING, Astrid, Ms., Administrator, Directorate General for Employment.
DELARUE, Rudie, Mr., Administrator, Directorate General for Employment.
FUENTE MARTIN, Angel, Mr., Administrator, Directorate General for Employment.
HEUZE, Thibault, Mr., Administrator, Directorate General for Employment.
RYCHENER, Frédérique, Ms., Administrator, Directorate General for Employment.
MCCARTHY, John, Mr., Administrator, Directorate General for Education and Culture.
MOCHEL, France, Ms., Directorate General for Justice and Home Affairs.
PASQUETTI, Stefania, Ms., Directorate General for Justice and Home Affairs.
DUFOUR, Christian, Mr., Attaché, Permanent Delegation, Geneva.
BARRAGAN, Laure-Anne, Ms., Advisor, Permanent Delegation, Geneva.

* * *

BRODIN, Jacques, Mr., Ambassador, Head, Liaison Office, Geneva, Council.
HOUTTUIN, Guus, Mr., Deputy Head, Liaison Office, Geneva, Council.
ALLEN, Oliver, Mr., First Secretary, Liaison Office, Geneva, Council.
HARMS, Uwe, Mr., Administrator, DG Social Affairs, Council.
VAN VUURE, Rogier Paul, Mr., Advisor, Liaison Office, Geneva, Council.

Comité économique et social européen
European Economic and Social Committee
Comité Económico y Social Europeo

BRIESCH, Roger, M., Président.
HUNTJES, Ton, M., Membre, Groupe I.
RETUREAU, Daniel, M., Membre, Groupe II.
PARIZA CASTAÑO, Luis Miguel, M., Membre représentant, Section SOC.

Conseil de l'Europe   Council of Europe
Consejo de Europa

VLADYCHENKO, Alexander, M., Directeur général a.i., Cohésion sociale (DGIII).
OCHOA LLIDO, Maria, Ms., Chef, Service des Migrations et des Roms/Tsiganes.

Regional Organization for the Protection of the Marine Environment

BACCOUCHE, Habib Ben Ali, M., Conseiller.

REPRÉSENTANTS D'ORGANISATIONS INTERNATIONALES NON GOUVERNEMENTALES

REPRESENTATIVES OF NON-GOVERNMENTAL ORGANIZATIONS

REPRESENTANTES DE ORGANIZACIONES NO GUBERNAMENTALES

Alliance coopérative internationale
International Co-operative Alliance
Alianza Cooperativa Internacional

BARBERINI, Ivano, Mr., President.
MACDONALD, Iain, Mr., Director-General.
CHAVEZ, Maria Elena, Ms., Deputy Director-General.
IMBSEN, Jan-Eirik, Mr., Director of Development.
SOZANSKI, Gabriella, Ms., Director, Member and Sectorial Services; Regional Director for Europe.
CRONAN, Garry, Mr., Communication Manager.

Confédération internationale des syndicats libres
International Confederation of Free Trade Unions
Confederación Internacional de Organizaciones Sindicales Libres

RYDER, Guy, Mr., General Secretary.
CISSÉ, Mamounata, Ms., Assistant General Secretary.
OLIVEIRA, José Olivio, Mr., Assistant General Secretary.
BAEZ MOSQUEIRA, Victor, Mr., General Secretary, ICFTU Inter-American Regional Organization.
SUZUKI, Noriyuki, Mr., General Secretary, ICFTU Asian and Pacific Regional Organization.
KAILEMBO, Andrew, Mr., General Secretary, ICFTU African Regional Organization.
CUNNIAH, Dan, Mr., Director, Geneva Office.
BIONDI, Anna, Ms., Assistant Director, Geneva Office.
DE BLONAY, Victoria, Ms., Geneva Office.
BLUMER, Eva, Ms., Geneva Office.
BUSSER, Esther, Ms., Geneva Office.
GHANBARI, Atiyeh, Ms., Geneva Office.
HOWARD, James, Mr., Director, Employment and International Labour Standards Department.
RAMOS, Elsa, Ms., Director, Equality and Youth Department.
KUCZKIEWICZ, Janek, Mr., Director, Human and Trade Union Rights Department.
O'CALLAGHAN, Yvonne, Ms., Secretariat.
SHAMENDA, Fackson, Mr., President.
ROYER, Lucien, Mr., Secretariat, ICFTU-TUAC.
JUSTICE, Dwight, Mr., Informal Economy.
NOONAN, Tim, Mr., Director, Campaigns and Communications.
CAMBIER, Hubert, Mr., Head, Central and Eastern Europe.
DIALLO, Mamadou, Mr., Director, Development, Cooperation and Education.
KAMALAN, Ms., Asian Desk.
OULATAR, Jean, Mr., Development, Cooperation and Education.
MAUNG, Maung, Mr., General Secretary, Federation of Trade Unions, Myanmar.
MAUNG THAN LWIN, Ronnie, M., Administrative Executive, Federation of Trade Unions, Myanmar.
DONGFANG, Han, Mr., Director, China Labour Bulletin, Hong Kong.
MUNROE, Robin, Mr., China Labour Bulletin, Hong Kong.
CHONGGUO, Cai, Mr., European Representative, China Labour Bulletin, Hong Kong.
MEDINA, Horacio, Mr., President, UNAPETROL.
EVREN, Sami, Mr., President, Confederation of Public Servants Trade Unions (KESK).
VOLNEYTS, Mr., Confederation of Free Trade Unions of Ukraine (KVPU).
BOZGUNBAEV, Sagyn B., Mr., President, Trade Unions of Kyrgyzstan,
BORISOV, Vadim, Mr., Moscow Office.
YAROSHUK, Alexander, Mr., Congrès démocratique des Syndicats de Belarus (BKDP).
PODOLINSKI, Oleg, Mr., Congrès démocratique des Syndicats de Belarus (BKDP).
L. DEWI, Mrs., Hong Kong Confederation of Trade Unions (HKCTU).
RAMOS, Alfredo, Mr., Confederación de Trabajadores de Venezuela (CTV).
COVA, Manuel, Mr., General Secretary, Confederación de Trabajadores de Venezuela (CTV).
BUKHVOSTAU, Aliaxandr, Mr., Ex-President, Agricultural Machinery Workers' Union, Belarus.
FEDYNITCH, Gennnadi, Mr., Chairperson, Radio and Electronics Workers' Union (REWU), Belarus.
EGULU, Lawrence, Mr., Director, Economic and Social Policy, AFRO.
TUCH, Margarita, Ms., ICFTU Secretariat.
KWATENG, Barbara, Mrs., Campaigns and Communications.
BELLAMY, Marie-Thérèse, Ms., Secretariat.

Confédération mondiale du travail
World Confederation of Labour
Confederación Mundial del Trabajo

THYS, Willy, M., Secrétaire général.
ESTEVEZ, Eduardo, M., Secrétaire générale adjoint.
WIENEN, Jaap, M., Secrétaire général adjoint.
SEA, Hervé, M., Représentant permanent à Genève.
VIVANCO, Ramón, M., Représentant permanent à Genève.
BOSSE, Claire, Mme, Conseillère.
AARTS, Eric, M., Capacity Building.
DEGROOF, Wim, M., Economie informelle.
PAREDES, Kattia, Mme, Directrice, Département Femmes et Travail.

DEBROUX, Mathieu, M., Directeur, Département information.
CICERON, Gaston, M., Conseiller.
FAUCHERE, Béatrice, Mme, Conseillère.
PRAVATA, Pierre, M., Conseiller.
PINZON, José Escolástico, M., Secrétaire général, CGTG.
LAWSON, Kouglo B., M., Conseiller.
DEBATTY, Jacques, M., Conseiller.
ROBEL, Blaise, M., Conseiller.
DE HARASCIVC, Petre, M., Conseiller.
IBARRA, Felipu Deysi, M., Conseiller.
MORENO, Juan, Mr., Conseiller, CES.
RIVERO, José Ramon, Mr., Conseiller.
STEYNEN, Maria, Ms.
VAN APEREN, Faustina, Mme

Fédération syndicale mondiale
World Federation of Trade Unions
Federación Sindical Mundial

ZHARIKOV, Alexander, Mr., General Secretary.
CARDONA, Ramón, Mr., Deputy General Secretary, Permanent Representative, Geneva.
MIRO, Adib, Mr., Deputy General Secretary.
PACHO, Valentín, Mr., Deputy General Secretary.
AVELLA, Aida, Ms., Additional Permanent Representative, Geneva.
PAGE, Jean-Pierre, Mr., Additional Permanent Representative, Geneva.
SAUVIN, Philippe, Mr., Additional Permanent Representative, Geneva.
DIAZ MARTINEZ, Jaime Antonio, Mr.
ALFONSO ACOSTA, Edgar Luis, Mr.
SUAREZ ORJUELA, Rafael Ernesto, Mr.
RODRIGUEZ PEÑA, José Antonio, Mr.
SAUVIN, Philippe, Mr.
GUTIERREZ, Mercedes, Ms.
RIVERO, Juan A., Mr.
NARVAEZ, Luis, Mr.
BARRETO GUEVARA, José Joaquín, Sr.
GAMLUCH, Rada, Mr.
QUISPE, Jaime, Mr.
SABÓIA, Paulo, Mr.
MORA, Victor, Sr.
VARGAS, Julio, Sr.

Organisation internationale des employeurs
International Organization of Employers
Organización Internacional de Empleadores

PERIGOT, François, Mr., President.
FUNES DE RIOJA, Daniel, Mr., Executive Vice-President.
PEÑALOSA, Antonio, Mr., Secretary-General.
WILTON, Brent, Mr., Deputy Secretary-General.
DEJARDIN, Jean, Mr., Adviser.
JAMES, George, Mr., Adviser.
MUIA, Frederick, Mr., Adviser.
OECHSLIN, Eric, Mr., Adviser.
RYNHART, Gary, Mr., Adviser.
GROS-LOUIS, Sandy, Ms., Adviser.
YURÉN, Andrés, Mr., Adviser.
PERKINS, Barbara, Ms., Assistant to Secretary-General.

Organisation de l'unité syndicale africaine
Organization of African Trade Union Unity
Organización para la Unidad Sindical Africana

SUNMONU, Hassan A., Mr., Secretary-General.
DIOP, Demba, Mr., Assistant Secretary-General.
BESHA, Michel P., Mr., Assistant Secretary-General.
ABUZEID, Mohamed M., Mr., Treasurer-General.
GBOLU, Emmanuel K., Mr., Head, International Cooperation.
DIALLO, Lelouma, Mr., Deputy Permanent Representative, Geneva.
AMOAH, Ann, Ms., Coordinator for Women Workers.
OFOSU, Hannah, Ms., Senior Secretary.
BUSATA, Mohamad, Mr., Secretary General, Pan-African Federation of Petroleum and Allied Workers, Trade Secretariat, OATUU.

Confédération panafricaine des employeurs
Pan-African Employers' Confederation
Confederación Panafricana de Empleadores

JEETUN, Azad, Mr., Secretary General.

Alliance internationale du spectacle
International Entertainment Alliance

LUQUER, Dominick, M., Secrétaire général, Fédération internationale des Acteurs.
MACHUEL, Benoit, M., Secrétaire général, Fédération internationale des Musiciens.
WILSON, Jim, M., Directeur, Media and Entertainment International.

Amnistie Internationale
Amnesty International
Amnistía Internacional

BALDWIN-PASK, Tania, Ms., Adviser on International Organisations.
SCANELLA, Patrizia, Ms., Assistant Adviser on International Organisations.
SPLINTER, Peter, Mr., Representative, United Nations Office, Geneva.
CHING, Melinda, Ms., Adviser, United Nations Office, Geneva.
LESTER, Eve, Ms., Refugee Coordinator, International Secretariat.

Association internationale des Conseils économiques et sociaux et Institutions similaires
International Association of Economic and Social Councils and similar Institutions
Asociación Internacional de Consejos Económicos y Sociales e Instituciones Similares

WIJFFELS, Herman H.F., M., Président, Conseil écomonique et social des Pays-Bas, Membre du Conseil d'administration, Association internationale des Conseils économiques et sociaux et Institutions similaires, ancien Président, AICESIS.
DURUFLÉ, Bertrand, M., Secrétaire exécutif, AICESIS.
VAN NIEKERK, Niko, M., Conseiller du Président.

Association internationale d'orientation scolaire et professionnelle
International Association for Educational and Vocational Guidance
Asociación Internacional para la Internacional Orientación Educativa y Profesional

FLUBACHER, Verena, Mme

Association internationale de la sécurité sociale
International Social Security Association
Asociación Internacional de la Seguridad Social

HOSKINS, Dalmer D., Mr., Secretary General.
MCGILLIVRAY, Warren, Mr., Chief of Studies and Operations Branch.
D'HAENE, Yannick, Mr., Chief of Development, Communications and Research Branch.
MUSENGE, Dan, Mr., Vice-President.

Association internationale des universités du troisième âge
International Association of Universities of the Third Age
Asociación Internacional de Universidades para la Tercera Edad

IBRAHIM, Ibrahim-A., M., Représentant, AIUTA.

Association mondiale des petites et moyennes entreprises
World Association for Small and Medium Enterprises
Asociación Mundial de Empresas Pequeñas y Medianas

AGRAWAL, Arun, M., Secretary General.
PRASAD, V. N., Mr., Senior Economic Adviser.

URANGA, Raul, Mr., Permanent Representative, WASME, Geneva.

Association de Volontaires pour le Service international
Association of Volunteers for International Service
Asociación de Voluntarios para el Servicio Internacional

PIATTI, Alberto, Mr., Managing Director.
CASTELLI, Ezio, Mr., Vice-President, and AVSI Representative, USA.
GATTI, Maria Teresa, Mme
SILVESTRI, Giampaolo, M.
REPOSSI, Alberto, M.

Caritas Internationalis

PAZ, Roxana, Mme

Centrale latinoaméricaine des travailleurs
Latin American Central of Workers
Central Latinoamericana de Trabajadores

MARIUS, Luis Enrique, Sr., Secretario General Adjunto, Director, Departamento Internacional.
NAVARRO, Carlos, Sr., Secretario General Adjunto, Director del Departamento Internaciónal.
MUÑOZ, Manuel, Sr., Dirigente, Federación de Trabajadores de la Construcción de Venezuela.

Centre d'échanges et coopération pour l'Amérique latine
Exchange and Cooperation Centre for Latin America
Centro de Intercambios y Cooperación para América Latina

CELI VEGAS, Michel, M., Président.
CERTEJAN, Tiberius, M.
TOMONARI, Kei, M.
TAPIA, Ricardo, M.
JANZ EGLI, Rosy, Mme

Centre international pour les droits syndicaux
International Centre for Trade Union Rights
Centro Internacional para los Derechos Sindicales

BLACKBURN, Daniel, Mr.
PUERTO, Miguel, Mr.
GIBBONS, Steve, Mr.
HENDY, John, Mr.
EWING, Keith, Mr.

Collectif international d'appui aux travailleurs de la pêche
International Collective in Support of Fishworkers
Colectivo Internacional de Apoyo a los Trabajadores de la Pesca

MATHEW, Sebastian, Mr., Programme Adviser.
DEBNATH, Harekrishna, Mr.

Comité consultatif mondial des amis
Friends World Committee for Consultation

WATSON, Martin, Mr., Representative, Global Economic Issues.
BRETT, Rachel, Ms., Representative, Human Rights and Refugees.
GRACE, Brewster, Mr., Consultant, Trade and Development.
TAYLOR, Rachel, Ms., Programme Assistant, Human Rights and Refugees.
PEREZ-BUSTILLO, Camilo, Mr., Director, Migration and Mobility Goal Division, Philadelphia.

Commission des églises auprès des migrants en Europe
Churches' Commission for Migrants in Europe
Comisión de Iglesias para los Migrantes en Europa

BURGER, Christina, Mrs.

Commission internationale catholique pour les migrations
International Catholic Migration Commission
Comisión Católica Internacional de Migración

CANNY, William, M., Secrétaire général.
GRANGE, Mariette, Mme, Chargée du Programme de Promotion et de défense des droits des migrants et des réfugiés.
SLINCKX, Isabelle, Mlle

Commission syndicale consultative auprès de l'Organisation de coopération et de développement économiques
Trade Union Advisory Committee to the Organisation for Economic Cooperation and Development
Comisión Sindical Consultativa ante la OCDE

EVANS, John, Mr., General Secretary.
JONES, Roy, Mr., Senior Policy Adviser.
SCHNEIDER, Roland, Mr., Senior Policy Adviser.
ROYER, Lucien, Mr., Senior Policy Adviser.
NILSSON, Veronica, Ms.

Confédération européenne des syndicats
European Trade Union Confederation
Confederación Europea de Sindicatos

PASSCHIER, Catelene, Ms., ETUC Confederal Secretary.

Confédération européenne des syndicats indépendants
European Confederation of Independent Trade Unions
Confederación Europea de Sindicatos Independientes

FREDERIKSEN, Arne, M., Président, Firma Funktionaererne (FF).
HANSEN, John, M., Secrétaire général, Firma Funktionaererne (FF).
WOLFF, Romain, M., Vice-président, Confédération générale de la Fonction publique (CGFP).
EYSCHEN, Irène, Mme, Confédération générale de la Fonction publique (CGFP).

Confédération générale des syndicats
General Confederation of Trade Unions

SCHERBAKOV, Vladimir, Mr., General Secretary.
POTAPOV, Albert, Mr., Deputy General Secretary.
KRAVTSOV, Valery, Mr., Head, GCTU International Department.
BULGAKOV, Alexander, Mr., Adviser.

Confédération internationale des fonctionnaires
International Confederation of Public Service Officers
Confederacion Internacional de Funcionarios

TRAUSCH, Pierre, M., Président.
EYSCHEN, Irène, Mme

Confédération internationale des syndicats arabes
International Confederation of Arab Trade Unions
Confederación Internacional de Sindicatos Arabes

DJEMAM, Hacene, Mr., General Secretary.

MAATOUK, RAJAB, Mr., Deputy General Secretary, Head, International Relations.
BEN AOUF SAAD, Farouk, Mr., Director, International Relations Department.
ZINEDDIN, Naïm, Mr., Adviser.
EL HASSAN, Musa Mohamed, Mr., Vice-President, Arab Trade Union of Health.

Confédération syndicale mondiale de l'enseignement
World Confederation of Teachers
Confederación Sindical Mundial de la Enseñanza

CORRIES, Claudio, M., Président.
VAN DONGEN, Gust, M., Premier Vice-Président.
DE LA HAYE, Gaston, M., Secrétaire général.
VAN OVERBEEK, Cees, M., Trésorier.

Congrès permanent de l'unité syndicale des travailleurs d'Amérique latine
Permanent Congress of Trade Union Unity of Latin American Workers
Congreso Permanente de la Unidad Sindical de los Trabajadores de América Latina

BERNAL CAMERO, Joaquín, Sr., Coordinador General.
FLORES FLORES, Rosendo, Sr., Secretario General del Sindicato Mexicano de Electricistas.
ESPARZA FLORES, Martín, Sr., Secretario del Exterior del Sindicato Mexicano de Electricistas.
ALMAGUER COSSÍO, Sergio, Sr., Secretario General del Comité Nacional de la Central Unitaria de Trabajadores México (CUT).
VARGAS SILVA, Luis Alfonso, Sr., Miembro del Consejo Nacional de la Central Unitaria de Trabajadores, México (CUT).

Conseil de coordination des syndicats d'Afrique australe
Southern African Trade Union Coordination Council
Consejo de Coordinación Sindical de Africa Austral

KACHIMA, Moses Tito, Mr., Executive Secretary.

Conseil international des femmes
International Council of Women
Consejo Internacional de Mujeres

DE BOCCARD, Jeanne-Marie, Mme
POLONOVSKI VAUCLAIR, Brigitte, Mme
PASCHOUD VAN DE KERCHOVE, Francine, Mme
PERRET, Sylvie, Mme
FONYUY, Nyang Carren, Mme

Conseil international des infirmières
International Council of Nurses
Consejo Internacional de Enfermeras

OULTON, Judith A., Mrs., Chief Executive Officer.
KINGMA, Mireille, Mrs., ICN Consultant, Nursing and Health Policy.
WILBURN, Susan, Ms., ICN Project Coordinator.

Conseil syndical du Commonwealth
Commonwealth Trade Union Council
Consejo Sindical de la Commonwealth

WATSON, Annie, Ms., Director.
ISSAJI, Umi, Ms., Administrator.

Coopération internationale pour le Développement et la Solidarité
International Cooperation for Development and Solidarity
Cooperación Internacional para el Desarrollo y la Solidaridad

GRIMOUD, Nathalie, Ms.

Coordination de la recherche pour l'action sur le SIDA et la mobilité-Asie
Coordination of Action Research on Aids and Mobility-Asia
Coordenadora de Investigaciones para acción sobre el SIDA y Mobilidad-Asia

SOYSA, David, Mr., Representative.

Fédération arabe des employés des banques, des assurances et des affaires financières
Arab Federation of Employees in Banking, Insurance and Finance Employees
Federación Arabe de Empleados de la Banca, Seguros y Negocios Financieros

GLIYA, Salah, M., Secrétaire général.
CHAHATA, Farouk, M., Conseiller.

Fédération arabe des ouvriers du pétrole, des mines et industries chimiques
Arab Federation of Petroleum, Mines and Chemical Workers

ADBEL-BARI HUSSEIN, Fawzi, Mr., General Secretary, President, General Trade Union of Petroleum Workers (Egypt).

Fédération arabe des travailleurs des transports
Arab Federation of Transport Workers
Federación Arabe de los Trabajadores del Transporte

AWIDAT, Khalaf Allah, M., Président général.

Fédération internationale des associations pour l'éducation des travailleurs
International Federation of Workers' Education Associations
Federación Internacional de Asociaciones para la Educación de los Trabajadores

SPOONER, Dave, Mr., General Secretary.
PROENÇA, João, Mr., President.
CHUNGU, Mike, Mr.
GALLIN, Dan, Mr.
PIPER, Nicola, Ms.

Fédération internationale des femmes de carrières libérales et commerciales
International Federation of Business and Professional Women
Federación Internacional de Mujeres de Negocios y Profesionales

KAUSCH, Karin, Ms.

Fédération internationale des femmes diplômées des universités
International Federation of University Women
Federación Internacional de Mujeres Universitarias

PONCINI, Conchita, Ms., Coordinator, UN-ILO.
HAGEN, Katherine, Ms.
HANSEN, Eva, Ms.
BROWN, Susan, Ms.

Fédération internationale des journalistes
International Federation of Journalists
Federación Internacional de periodistas

WHITE, Aidan, Mr., General Secretary.

Fédération internationale des organisations de formation et de développement
International Federation of Training and Development Organizations

TWIGGER, Anthony, Mr., Executive Director.
WAUGH, David, Mr., Representative, Bretton Woods Organisations.
HARTENSTEIN, Annette, Ms., Research Officer.

Fédération Internationale des Organisations Syndicales du Personnel des Transports
International Federation of Trade Unions of Transport Workers
Federación Internacional de sindicatos del personal de Transporte

LANCIOT, Christian, M., Vice-Président.

Fédération internationale des organisations de travailleurs de la métallurgie
International Metalworkers' Federation
Federación Internacional de Trabajadores de las Industrias Metalúrgicas

MALENTACCHI, Marcello, Mr.
FREDRICKS, Brian, Mr.
KAMADA, Hiroshi, Mr.
COLETTI, Carla, Ms.
BLUM, Ronald, Mr.

Fédération internationale des ouvriers du transport
International Transport Workers' Federation
Federación Internacional de los Trabajadores del Transporte

COCKROFT, David, Mr., General Secretary.
WHITLOW, Jon, Mr., Seafarers' Section Secretary.
KARAVACHEV, Rossen, Mr.
CASTRO, Marcos, Sr.
ROBINSON MARIN, Carlos, Sr.

Fédération internationale syndicale de l'enseignement
World Federation of Teachers' Unions
Federación Internacional Sindical de la Enseñanza

MONTEUX, Daniel, M., Secrétaire.

Fédération internationale des syndicats de travailleurs de la chimie, de l'énergie, des mines et des industries diverses
International Federation of Chemical, Energy, Mine and General Workers' Unions
Federación Internacional de Sindicatos de Trabajadores de la Química, de la Energía, Minas e Industrias Diversas

HIGGS, Fred, Mr., General Secretary.
CATTERSON, Jim, Mr., Director of Organization.
GREEN, Reg, Mr., Health, Safety and Environment Officer.

Fédération internationale Terre des Hommes
International Federation Terre des Hommes
Federación Internacional Terre des Hommes

KADJAR-HAMOUDA, Eylah, Mme, Coordinatrice.

LIENGME, Corinne, Mlle, Stagiaire.

Fédération internationale des travailleurs du bâtiment et du bois
International Federation of Building and Woodworkers
Federación Internacional de Trabajadores de la Construcción y la Madera

NORMARK, Anita, Mrs., General Secretary.
HELLMANN-THEURER, Marion, Mr., Assistant General Secretary.
MURIE, Fiona, Mrs., Director, Global Programme on Occupational Safety and Health.
STREET, Bill, Mr., Director, Global Wood and Forestry Programme.
MAST, Toni, Mr., Information Technology Project Coordinator.

Fédération internationale des travailleurs du textile, de l'habillement et du cuir
International Textile, Garment & Leather Workers' Federation
Federación Internacional de Trabajadores del Textil, Vestuario y Cuero

KEARNEY, Neil, Mr., General Secretary.
CAPPUCCIO, Silvana, Ms., Health and Safety Assistant.

Fondation Scalabrini
The Scalabrini Foundation for a Culture of Integration and Solidarity in the Field of Human Mobility
Fundación Scalabrini

ZILIO, Renato, Mr., Member, Scientific Advisory Committee.

Forum civique Européen
European Civic Forum
Foro Civico Europeo

REISER, Hannes, M.
GETAZ, Raymond, M.
MEIJERS BRAUN, Caroline, Mme
BELL, Nicholas, M.
MENDEZ DE ANDES, Lourdes, Mme

Forum pour les migrants en Asie
Migrant Forum in Asia
Foro para los Migrantes en Asia

GOIS, Ashley William Bonaventure, Mr.
YOUNG, Soon Choe, Ms.
KRISHNA, Shekhar Lal Das, Mr.
SAJIDA, Zareen Ally, Ms.

Fraternité des syndicalistes d'Asie
Brotherhood of Asian Trade Unionists
Fraternidad de Sindicalistas de Asia

LUCERO, Nicetas M., Ms., Secretary General.
ALI, Shouket, Mr., Executive Board Member; Secretary General, APTUC.
ZAIN, Ahmad Shah Bin Mohammad, Mr., Secretary General, MKTR.
SILABAN, Rekson, Mr., Chairman, SBSI.
BHATTACHARJEE, Ashoke, Mr., President, ICL.

Institut international de la construction
International Construction Institute
Instituto Internacional de la Construcción

JOYCE, John T., Mr.
LOFBLAD, John, Mr.
LA FERLA, Francis, Ms.
O'LEARY, James, Mr.

International Council of Societies of Industrial Design

BREITENBERG, Mark, Mr., Member of the ICSID Board.

TEODORESCU, George, Mr., Member of the ICSID Board.

Internationale des droits des migrants
Migrants Rights International
Internacional para los Derechos de Migrantes

GENCIANOS, Geneviève J., Ms.
HAQUE, Syed Saiful, Mr.
AL-TA'AMNEH, Firas, Mr.
SANA, Ellene A., Ms.
QOIRIAH, Nurul, Mr.

Internationale de l'éducation
Education International
Internacional de la Educación

VAN LEEUWEN, Fred, Mr., General Secretary.
JOUEN, Elie, Mr., Deputy General Secretary.
ASPER, Linda, Mrs., Deputy General Secretary.
FOUILHOUX, Monique, Mrs., Advocacy Coordinator.
HARRIS, Bob, Mr., Special Consultant.

Internationale des services publics
Public Services International
Internacional de Servicios Públicos

BOYS, David, Mr., Sectoral Activities Officer.
CAIRD, Wendy, Mrs., Quality Public Services Campaign Coordinator.
ENGELBERTS, Hans, Mr., General Secretary.
GERMANOTTA, Paul, Mr., PSI resource person.
WINTOUR, Nora, Mrs., Equality and Rights Office.

Jeunesse ouvrière chrétienne internationale
International Young Christian Workers
Juventud Obrera Cristiana Internacional

DESROSIERS, Josée, Mrs., President.
CIROCCO, Anna, Mrs., General Secretary.

Mouvement international ATD Quart Monde
International Movement ATD Fourth World
Movimiento Internacional ATD Cuarto Mundo

VIARD, Thierry, M.
VERZAT, Xavier, M.

Mouvement mondial des travailleurs chrétiens
World Movement of Christian Workers
Movimiento Mundial de Trabajadores Cristianos

NDONG, Brigitte, Mme, Secrétaire générale.
SINAPAN, Samydorai, M., Coordinateur de la Région de l'Asie du Sud-Ouest.
BALISWAMY, Anthony, M., Aumônier.
WALLIMANN, Thomas, M.
DURAND BALLIVET, Hélène, Mme

Organisation africaine des syndicats des mines, métaux, énergie, chimie et assimilés
African Organisation of Mines, Metal, Energy, Chemical and Allied Trade Unions
Organización Africana de Sindicatos Mineros, del Metal, de la Energía, la Química y Afines

ZITOUNI, Lemtai, M., Secrétaire général.
EL BRECHT, Derick, M., Vice-Président.
EL MAGHERBI, Saad Sadek, M., Membre du Conseil.
AISSAOUI, Hassen, M., Secrétaire général adjoint.

Organisation démocratique syndicale des travailleurs africains
Democratic Organization of African Workers' Trade Union
Organización Democrática Sindical de los Trabajadores Africanos

BENYDIN, Toolsyraj, M., Président.
AKOUETE, Adrien Beleki, M., Secrétaire général.

Organisation internationale de l'énergie et des mines
International Energy and Mines' Organisation
Organización Internacional de Energía y Minas

SIMON, Alain, M.
TERRIER, Serge, M.
CARLIER, Jean-François, M.
RIEU, Bernard, M.
NUSTAD, Terje, M.

Organisation internationale de perspective mondiale
World Vision International
Visión Mundial Internacional

GETMAN, Thomas, Mr., Director.
GOW, Melanie, Ms.
PHILPOT-NISSEN, Jennifer, Ms.

Organisation mondiale contre la torture
World Organization Against Torture
Organización Mundial contra la Tortura

SOTTAS, Eric, M., Directeur.
LACROIX, Anne-Laurence, Mme, Directrice adjointe.
MÜTZENBERG, Patrick, Mr., Responsable de programme.
DE PURY, Sylvain, M.
O'NEILL, Caroline, Mme

Social Alert

RUIZ, Marta, Mme, Coordinatrice.
HOUNGAN AYEMONNA, Claire, Mme, Conseiller.

Soroptimist International

NORDBACK, Inger, Ms.
GALLEY-SCHROPP, Jacqueline, Ms.

StreetNet International

HORN, Patricia, Mrs., International Co-ordinator.
HEE-CHUL, Shin, Mr., Technical Advisor.
MUSONDA, Mishack, Mr., Technical Advisor.

Union générale des chambres de commerce, industrie et agriculture des pays arabes
General Union of Chambers of Commerce, Industry and Agriculture for Arab Countries
Unión General de Cámaras de Comercio, Industria y Agricultura de los Países Arabes

GHANTOUS, Elias, Mr., Secretary General.

Union internationale chrétienne des dirigeants d'entreprise
International Christian Union of Business Executives
Unión Internacional Cristiana de Dirigentes de Empresa

LEDOUBLE, Philippe, M., Administrateur.
BONAMY, Benoît, M., Secrétaire général.
KLEIN, Jean-Pierre, M., Représentant.

Union internationale des syndicats des travailleurs de l'agriculture, l'alimentation, du commerce, de l'industrie textile et similaires
Trade Unions International of Workers in Agriculture, Food, Commerce, Textiles and Allied Industries

HUCK, Freddy, M., Président.

Union internationale des syndicats des travailleurs du bâtiment, du bois et des matériaux de construction
Trade Unions International of Workers of the Building, Wood and Building Materials Industries
Unión Internacional de Sindicatos de Trabajadores de la Construcción, Madera y Materiales de Construcción

SUTTON, John, Mr., National Secretary, CFMEU Construction and General Workers' Union, Australia

Union internationale des syndicats des travailleurs de l'énergie, des métaux, de la chimie, du pétrole et des industries similaires
Trade Unions International of Workers of Energy, Metal, Chemical, Oil and Allied Industries
Unión Internacional de Sindicatos de Trabajadores de la Energía, el Metal, la Química, el Petróleo e Industrias Afines

FLORES FLORES, C. Rosendo, Sr., Secretario General.
ESPARZA FLORES, Martín, Sr., Secretario del Exterior.
PAZ LAMIGUEIRO, Fermín, Sr.
PONCE ITURRIAGA, Edgar, Sr.
PACHO, Valentín, Sr.

Union internationale des syndicats des travailleurs de la fonction publique et assimilés
Trade Unions International of Public and Allied Employees
Unión Internacional de Sindicatos de Trabajadores de Servicios Públicos y Similares

SUKOMAL SEN, Mr., General Secretary.

Union internationale des travailleurs de l'alimentation, de l'agriculture, de l'hôtellerie-restauration, du tabac et des branches connexes
International Union of Food, Agricultural, Hotel, Restaurant, Catering, Tobacco and Allied Workers' Associations
Unión Internacional de Trabajadores de la Alimentación, Agrícolas, Hoteles, Restaurantes, Tabaco y Afines

AMUKO, Omara, Mr.
BARONCINI, Jacqueline, Ms.
BUDIN, Barbro, Ms.
DALBAN MOREYNAS, Patrick, Mr.
GARVER, Paul, Mr.

Union latino-américaine des travailleurs municipaux
Latin American Union of Municipal Workers
Unión Latinoamericana de Trabajadores Municipales

ATANASOF, Alfredo Nestor, Sr.
GENTA, Amadeo Nolasco, Sr.
PEREYRA CASTRO, Osvaldo Pablo, Sr.
RUGGIERO, Oscar Tomas, Sr.
DULKE, Alfredo, Sr.

Union mondiale des organisations féminines catholiques
World Union of Catholic Women's Organizations
Unión Mundial de las Organizaciones Femeninas Católicas

BARTER-HEMMERICH, Ursula, Mme

Union Network International

JENNINGS, Philip J., Mr., General Secretary.
BOWYER, Philip, Mr., Deputy General Secretary.
PEDERSEN, John, Mr., Assistant General Secretary.

REQUENA, Raul, Mr., Assistant General Secretary.

Union syndicale des Travailleurs du Maghreb arabe
Union of Workers of the Arab Maghreb
Unión Sindical de Trabajadores del Maghreb Arabe

JRAD, Abdessalem, M., Sécretaire général.
SAHRAOUI, Abdelmajid, M., Sécretaire général adjoint.
DORSI, Baubaker Moussa, M., Sécretaire général adjoint.
ACHOUR, Amdelhamid, M., Conseiller.

Zonta International

SÉGURET, Marie-Claire, Mme, Representative, Member United Nations Committee, Zonta International.

BUREAUX DE LA CONFERENCE, DES COMMISSIONS ET DES GROUPES

OFFICERS OF THE CONFERENCE, THE COMMITTEES AND THE GROUPS

MESAS DE LA CONFERENCIA, DE LAS COMISIONES Y DE LOS GRUPOS

Bureau de la Conférence

Président

RAY GUEVARA, Milton, M., Secrétaire d'Etat au Travail (République dominicaine)

Vice-présidents

MAATOUGH, M., M., Ministre du Travail (Jamahiriya arabe libyenne)
WADE, Y., M. (Employeur, Sénégal)
ATTIGBE, G., M. (Travailleur, Bénin)

Secrétaire général

SOMAVIA, Juan, M., Directeur général du Bureau international du Travail

Bureaux des Commissions

Commission de proposition

Président

HASEGAWA, S., M. (Japon)

Vice-présidents

M'KAISSI, A., M. (Employeur, Tunisie)
TROTMAN, L., M. (Travailleur, Barbade)

Commission de vérification des pouvoirs

Président

ONI, J.M., M. (Bénin)

Vice-présidents

SASSO-MAZZUFFERI, L., Mme (Employeur, Italie)
EDSTRÖM, U., M. (Travailleur, Suède)

Commission des finances

Président

JONZON, B., M. (Suède)

Vice-président

KLEKNER, P., M. (Hongrie)

Commission de l'application des normes

Président

RIAL, N., Ms., (Argentine)

Vice-présidents

WISSKIRCHEN, A., M. (Employeur, Allemagne)
CORTEBEECK, L., M., (Travailleur, Belgique)

Commission des Ressources humaines

Président

CHETWIN, J., M. (Nouvelle-Zélande)

Vice-présidents

RENIQUE, C. (Employeur, Pays-Bas)
YACOB, H., Mme (Travailleur, Singapour)

Commission du Secteur de la pêche

Président

RIBEIRO LOPES, F., M. (Portugal)

Vice-présidents

KARIKARI ANANG, R., Mme, (Employeur, Ghana)
SAND MORTENSEN, P., M. (Travailleur, Danemark)

Commission des Travailleurs Migrants

Président

DÉ, Y., M. (Sénégal)

Vice-présidents

DE REGIL, J., M. (Employeur, Mexique)
BURROW, S., Mme (Travailleurs, Australie)

Commission des Résolutions

Président

SANTESTEVAN, A., Mme (Uruguay)

Vice-présidents

BOTHA, P., M., (Employeur, Afrique du Sud)
BLONDEL, M., M. (Travailleur, France)

Commission du Règlement

Président

ONI, J. M., M. (Bénin)

Vice-présidents

SASSO-MAZZUFFERI, L., Mme, (Employeur, Italie)
BRIGHI, C., Mme (Travailleur, Italie)

Bureaux des groupes

Groupe gouvernemental

Président

LLOYD, J., M. (Australie)

Groupe des employeurs

Président

FUNES DE RIOJA, D., M. (Argentine)

Vice-présidents

SUZUKI, T., M. (Japon)
BOTHA, P., M. (Afrique du Sud)
LIMA GODOY, D., M. (Brésil)
POTTER, E., M. (Etats-Unis)
BARDE, M., M. (Suisse)

Secrétaire

PEÑALOSA, A., M. (Organisation internationale des Employeurs)

Groupe des travailleurs

Président

TROTMAN, L., M. (Barbade)

Vice-présidents

AHMED, K., M. (Pakistan)
ANDERSON, H, Mme (Mexique)
DIALLO, R., M. (Guinée)
SIDOROV, E., M. (Fédération de Russie)

Secrétaire

CUNNIAH, D., M. (Confédération internationale des Syndicats libres)

Membres du bureau

ATTIGBE, B., M. (Bénin)
ATWOLI, F., M. (Kenya)
BEAUMONT, C., Mme (Nouvelle Zélande)
BYERS, B, Mme (Canada)
ENGELEN KEFER, U., Mme (Allemagne)
NAKAJIMA, S., M. (Japon)
SAÏD, S., M. (Algérie)
VALKONEN, M., Mme (Finlande)
ZELHOEFER, J., M. (Etats Unis)

Président du Conseil d'administration du Bureau international du Travail

CHUNG, Eui-Yong, M. (République de Corée)

Secrétariat général de la Conférence

Secrétaire Général

SOMAVIA, Juan, M.

Conseiller Juridique

PICARD, L., M.

Directeurs exécutifs

DIOP, A. M.
HÜLTIN, G., M.
JUNEJA, M., M.
PAXTON, S., Mme
SKERRETT, D., M.
TAPIOLA, K., M.
TREMEAUD, F., M.

Directeurs régionaux

AMADI-NJOKU, R., Mme.
BUTTLER, F., M.
MUÑOZ, A., M.
LIM, L. Mme
RIFAI, T., M.